GU01034309

HANDBOOK OF STATISTICS
VOLUME 11

Handbook of Statistics

VOLUME 11

General Editor

C. R. Rao

NORTH-HOLLAND
AMSTERDAM · LONDON · NEW YORK · TOKYO

Econometrics

Edited by

G. S. Maddala

Department of Economics
Arps Hall, Ohio State University
Columbus, OH, USA

C. R. Rao

Center for Multivariate Analysis
Department of Statistics, The Pennsylvania State University
University Park, PA, USA

H. D. Vinod

Department of Economics
Fordham University
Bronx, NY, USA

1993

NORTH-HOLLAND
AMSTERDAM · LONDON · NEW YORK · TOKYO

ELSEVIER SCIENCE PUBLISHERS B.V.
Sara Burgerhartstraat 25
P.O. Box 211, 1000 AE Amsterdam, The Netherlands

Library of Congress Cataloging-in-Publication Data

Econometrics / edited by G.S. Maddala, C.R. Rao, H.D. Vinod.
    p. cm. -- (Handbook of statistics ; 11)
   Includes bibliographical references and index.
   ISBN 0-444-89577-9
   1. Econometrics. 2. Economics--Statistical methods. I. Maddala,
G.S. II. Rao, C. Radhakrishna (Calyampudi Radhakrishna), 1920– .
III. Vinod, Hrishikesh D., 1939– . IV. Series.
HB139.E288 1993
330'.01'5195--dc20   93-12857
                                                         CIP

ISBN: 0-444-89577-9

This book is printed on acid-free paper.

Printed in The Netherlands.

Preface

As with the earlier volumes in this series, the main purpose of this volume of the *Handbook of Statistics* is to serve as a source, reference, and teaching supplement in econometrics, the branch of economics concerned with statistical methods applied to the empirical study of economic relationships. The papers in this volume provide reasonably comprehensive and up-to-date surveys of recent developments in various aspects of econometrics. They are written at a level intended for use by professional econometricians and statisticians, as well as advanced graduate students in econometrics. The present volume complements the 3-volume series: *Handbook of Econometrics* by Z. Griliches and M. D. Intrilligator, eds., also published by North-Holland in the mid 1980s. This volume presents surveys of some developments in the last decade on semi-parametric and non-parametric estimation, limited dependent variable models, time series analysis, alternatives to likelihood methods, and computer-intensive methods in econometrics.

The first part of the volume covers endogenous stratification, semi-parametric methods and non-parametric methods. The samples used in econometrics are not always drawn randomly from the population of interest. Often stratified sampling schemes are adopted, but the stratification is endogenous rather than exogenous as in most of the statistical literature. The paper by Cosslett reviews the various estimation methods proposed, the types of models and sampling schemes for which they are suited, and the large-sample properties of the estimators. The paper also discusses some semi-parametric estimators of discrete choice models. The paper by Horowitz reviews the different semi-parametric and non-parametric estimation methods that have been suggested for quantal response models. The paper by Manski deals with the problem created by selective observation of random sample data. It outlines the different approaches (parametric, semi-parametric and non-parametric) to the selection problem analyzed by econometricians and statisticians. The paper by Ullah and Vinod presents a survey of non-parametric regression methods and outlines several areas of empirical applications in economics. One other paper in this volume that deals with the topic of semi-parametric and non-parametric estimation is the paper by Newey in Part V. It discusses non-parametric estimations of optimal instrumental variables.

Part II of this volume covers several recent developments in limited dependent variable models. Blundell and Smith discuss several estimation procedures for simultaneous equation models with censored and qualitative dependent variables. The paper by Lee reviews the area of multivariate tobit models. These models should be of interest to statisticians working in multivariate analysis. The paper by Maddala discusses the estimation of limited dependent variable models under rational expectations, an area with important empirical applications of practical interest in economic policy. In addition to these papers, there are other papers in this volume that deal with some problems involving limited dependent and qualitative variables. These are: the papers by Cosslett, Horowitz and Manski in Part I, Hajivassiliou in Part V, Mariano and Brown in Part V, and Donald and Maddala in Part VI.

Part III covers some recent developments in time series econometrics. During the past decade, this has been an extremely active area of research in econometrics. Due to space limitations, and in view of other surveys available, two areas, ARCH models and unit roots and cointegration, have been omitted from this volume. The other areas covered, non-linear time series models reviewed by Brock and Potter, Markov switching regression (MSR) models for time series, discussed in the paper by Hamilton, and structural time series models discussed in the paper by Harvey and Shepherd, are all active areas of research in econometrics. The paper by Harvey and Shepherd also covers recent developments in the application of Kalman filtering in econometrics. The paper by Pagan in Part IV comments on different brands of ARCH models (the ARCHES of econometrics). Another paper that deals with time series problems is the paper by Sawyer in Part VI.

Part IV of the volume covers likelihood methods and Bayesian inference. The paper by Florens and Mouchart surveys Bayesian procedures of testing. Two main avenues are discussed. The first is the usual procedure of deriving posterior probabilities of models or hypotheses. The second one, developed recently, is a Bayesian extension of the encompassing principle. Maximum likelihood methods are among the most important tools used by statisticians and econometricians. But their optimality properties depend on the assumption that the true probability distribution is the one assumed in deriving the likelihood function. It is important to consider the properties of ML estimators when this assumption is not made. In this case, the likelihood function is called pseudo (or quasi) likelihood function. The paper by Gourieroux and Monfort presents a review of the different variants of pseudo-likelihood methods and simulated pseudo-likelihood methods and their use in econometric work. What they call pseudo-likelihood methods are quasi-likelihood methods but they give reasons why they use the term 'pseudo-likelihood'. Rao's score test is one of the most often used tests in econometric work – both for hypothesis testing and for specification testing (though it is often called the Lagrangian multiplier test, or LM test). The paper by Mukerjee reviews recent work on score tests. This review should be useful to statisticians and econometricians alike.

Part V of the volume covers alternatives to likelihood methods, (such as M-estimators and GMM-estimators). The properties of M-estimators in the linear model have been studied by several authors for some particular choices of the discrepancy function. The paper by Bai, Liu and Rao considers a very general discrepancy function and establishes strong consistency of the M-estimators. The unifying results in this paper should be useful to econometricians working in the area of robust methods. The papers by Hall and Ogaki discuss the generalized methods of moments (GMM) estimators. The GMM method is a very popular alternative to the ML method among econometricians. The paper by Newey (also related to GMM) discusses efficient estimation of models with conditional moment restrictions. These estimators, which are typically referred to as instrumental variable (IV) estimators, are based on much weaker assumptions than the ML estimates. The paper derives the form of the optimal instruments and describes parametric and non-parametric estimations of the optimal instruments. The paper by Pagan reviews work done on testing for heteroskedasticity. The basic approach taken is that all tests can be regarded as 'conditional moment tests'. The paper outlines tests for heteroskedasticity in non-linear models – in particular, discrete choice models, censored data models, and count data models. It also presents specification tests for different variants of the ARCH models.

Part VI is on computer-intensive methods. Due to the advances in computer technology, many estimation problems that were intractable earlier have been within reach of applied statisticians and econometricians. The papers by Hajivassiliou and Keane discuss methods of estimation of limited dependent variable models from panel data. Problems involving multiple integrals in several dimensions can now be tackled using simulation methods. The paper by Mariano and Brown presents a review of stochastic simulation methods for non-linear errors in variables models (including the probit and tobit models with errors in variables). Another area that uses computer-intensive techniques is that of bootstrap, which is useful for studying small-sample distributions in several econometric problems. The papers by Jeong and Maddala, and Vinod, survey several applications of the bootstrap methods in econometrics.

The final part of the volume contains reviews of miscellaneous problems of practical interest. There is an extensive statistical literature on identifying outliers and influential observations. The paper by Donald and Maddala presents a review of this area with reference to econometric applications and suggests some extensions of these methods to non-linear models, in particular to logit, probit and tobit models, based on the method of generalized residuals and artificial regressions. The paper by Gregory and Smith reviews some statistical aspects of the calibration method used very widely during recent years in macro-econometrics. The paper by Lahiri reviews the literature on efficient estimation and testing strategies in the context of panel data models with rational expectation and testing strategies in the context of panel data models with rational expectations, discusses efficient estimation of such models in a generalized method of moments (GMM) framework, and extends the analysis to simultaneous equations. The paper also presents an empirical illustration of the methodology. Finally, the paper by Sawyer surveys statistical applications of stochastic processes in finance. The one major characteristic of recent research in the area of finance is the increased use of continuous time stochastic processes.

In summary, the volume covers a wide variety of applications of statistical methodology to econometric problems that should be of interest to econometricians as well as statisticians. The open problems in the papers might lead to further work on these subjects.

We are thankful to all the authors for their cooperation and patience during the preparation of this volume. Stephen Cosslett and Joel Horowitz provided valuable comments on many of the papers. Elizabeth Ann Crisafulli, In-Moo Kim and Hongyi Li provided efficient assistance in the preparation of the volume.

G. S. Maddala
C. R. Rao
H. D. Vinod

Table of Contents

PART III. TIME-SERIES

PART IV. LIKELIHOOD METHODS AND BAYESIAN INFERENCE

PART V. ALTERNATIVES TO LIKELIHOOD METHODS

PART VII. OTHER PROBLEMS

Ch. 24. Identifying Outliers and Influential Observations in Econometric Models   663
S. G. Donald and G. S. Maddala

Ch. 25. Statistical Aspects of Calibration in Macroeconomics   703
A. W. Gregory and G. W. Smith

Contributors

Z. D. Bai, *Department of Statistics, Temple University, Speakman Hall, Philadelphia, PA 19122, USA* (Ch. 14)

R. W. Blundell, *Department of Economics, University College London, Gower Street, London WC1E 6BT, UK* (Ch. 5)

W. A. Brock, *Department of Economics, University of Wisconsin, 1180 Observatory Drive, Madison, WI 53706, USA* (Ch. 8)

B. W. Brown, *Department of Economics, Rice University, Houston, TX 77251, USA* (Ch. 22)

S. R. Cosslett, *Department of Economics, Arps Hall, Ohio State University, Columbus, OH 43210-1172, USA* (Ch. 1)

S. G. Donald, *Department of Economics, University of Florida, Gainesville, FL 32611, USA* (Ch. 24)

J.-P. Florens, *GREMAQ, Université des Sciences Sociales, Place Anatole France, F-31042 Toulouse, France* (Ch. 11)

C. Gourieroux, *INSEE (CREST-ENSAE), 18, Boulevard Adolphe Pinard, F-75675 Paris Cedex 14, France* (Ch. 12)

A. W. Gregory, *Department of Economics, Queens University, Kingston, Ont. K7L 3N6, Canada* (Ch. 25)

V. A. Hajivassiliou, *Cowles Foundation for Research in Economics, Dept. of Economics, Yale University, Yale Station, New Haven, CT 06520-2125, USA* (Ch. 19)

A. Hall, *Department of Economics, North Carolina State University, Raleigh, NC 27695-7506, USA* (Ch. 15)

J. D. Hamilton, *Department of Economics, 0508, University of California at San Diego, La Jolla, CA 92093-0508, USA* (Ch. 9)

A. C. Harvey, *Department of Mathematical and Statistical Sciences, London School of Economics, Houghton Street, London WC2A 2AE, UK* (Ch. 10)

J. L. Horowitz, *Department of Economics, College of Business Administration, The University of Iowa, Iowa City, IA 52242, USA* (Ch. 2)

J. Jeong, *Department of Economics, Emory University, Atlanta, GA 30322, USA* (Ch. 21)

M. P. Keane, *Research Department, Federal Reserve Bank of Minneapolis, 250 Marquette Avenue, Minneapolis, MN 55401-0291, USA* and *Industrial Relations Center and Department of Economics, 537 Management and*

Economics Building, University of Minnesota, Minneapolis, MN 55455, USA (Ch. 20)

K. Lahiri, *Department of Economics, State University of New York, Albany, NY 12222, USA* (Ch. 26)

L.-F. Lee, *Department of Economics, University of Michigan, Ann Arbor, MI 48109, USA* (Ch. 6)

Z. J. Liu, *Department of Mathematics and Statistics, Mississippi State University, Mississippi, MS 39762, USA* (Ch. 14)

G. S. Maddala, *Department of Economics, Arps Hall, Ohio State University, Columbus, OH 43210-1172, USA* (Ch. 7, Ch. 21, Ch. 24)

C. F. Manski, *Department of Economics, University of Wisconsin, 1180, Observatory Drive, Madison, WI 53706, USA* (Ch. 3)

R. S. Mariano, *Department of Economics, University of Pennsylvania, School of Arts and Sciences, 3718 Locust Walk, Philadelphia, PA 19104-6297, USA* (Ch. 22)

A. Monfort, *Département de la Recherche, INSEE, 18, Boulevard Adolphe Pinard, F-75675 Paris Cedex 14, France* (Ch. 12)

M. Mouchart, *CORE, Université Catholique de Louvain, 34, Voie du Roman Pays, B-1348 Louvain-la-Neuve, Belgium* (Ch. 11)

R. Mukerjee, *Indian Institute of Management, Joke, Diamond Harbour Road, Calcutta 700 027, India* (Ch. 13)

W. K. Newey, *Department of Economics, Massachusetts Institute of Technology, Cambridge, MA 02139, USA* (Ch. 16)

M. Ogaki, *Department of Economics, University of Rochester, Rochester, NY 14627, USA* (Ch. 17)

A. R. Pagan, *Department of Economics, R.S.S.S., Australian National University, Canberra, ACT 2601, Australia* (Ch. 18)

Y. Pak, *Department of Economics, University of Rochester, Rochester, NY 14627, USA* (Ch. 18)

S. M. Potter, *Department of Economics, University of California, Los Angeles, CA 90024, USA* (Ch. 8)

C. R. Rao, *Center for Multivariate Analysis, Department of Statistics, 326 Classroom Building, The Pennsylvania State University, University Park, PA 16802, USA* (Ch. 14)

K. R. Sawyer, *Department of Economics and Finance, Royal Melbourne Institute of Technology, Melbourne, Vic. 3001, Australia* (Ch. 27)

N. Shephard, *Nuffield College, Oxford OX1 1NF, UK* (Ch. 10)

G. W. Smith, *Department of Economics, Queens University, Kingston, Ont. K7L 3N6, Canada* (Ch. 25)

R. J. Smith, *Department of Applied Economics, University of Cambridge, Cambridge CB3 9DE, UK* (Ch. 5)

A. Ullah, *Department of Economics, University of California, Riverside, CA 92521, USA* (Ch. 4)

H. D. Vinod, *Department of Economics, Fordham University, Bronx, NY 10458-5158, USA* (Ch. 4, Ch. 23).

G. S. Maddala, C. R. Rao and H. D. Vinod, eds., *Handbook of Statistics, Vol. 11*

Estimation from Endogenously Stratified Samples

Stephen R. Cosslett

1. Introduction

The samples used in econometric estimation are not always drawn randomly from the populations of interest. Often a stratified sampling scheme is adopted. The population is divided into subpopulations, called *strata*, based on the value of an observed vector x (for example, geographic location). Then a random sample of pre-assigned size is drawn from each stratum, or, in some cases, from each of a randomly selected subset of the strata. This might be just for operational convenience in collecting the data. On the other hand, there may be deliberate oversampling of a small subpopulation that is of particular interest in the subsequent analysis (for example, families below the poverty level).

The objective is to estimate the structural econometric model $p(y \mid z, \theta)$, which gives the density of the endogenous variables y, conditional on the exogenous variables z in terms of an unknown parameter vector θ. (In semiparametric models, p also depends on the unknown distribution of a stochastic 'error' term.) In random sampling, the likelihood is $p(y \mid z, \theta) h(z)$, where h is the density of z. Because of this factorization, h plays no role in estimation, as long as h does not depend on θ. Exogenous stratification (where the stratifying variables x are exogenous in the model) is innocuous: in effect, it just replaces one density h by another. The extreme case is a controlled experiment, where the values of z are selected by the experimenter. Estimators for these cases just use the conditional likelihood $p(y \mid z, \theta)$.

In endogenous stratification, the strata are defined in terms y (and possibly other variables). Now the distribution of z in each stratum does depend on θ. The simplest case is where y is discrete and its values define the strata – this is called choice-based sampling. In an exogenously stratified sample, the informative part of the likelihood is the density of y conditional on z. In a choice-based sample, by contrast, it is the density of z conditional on y. That density is easily found by Bayes' rule: it is a nontrivial function of both θ and h.

The first issue, therefore, is estimation: if the sample is treated as random, the wrong likelihood is being used and the estimators are generally inconsistent. Once the problem of consistent estimation has been recognized and solved, however, endogenous stratification can be a useful tool. It can substantially improve the precision of estimates from a sample of given size or cost, usually by oversampling rare but informative outcomes.

The first econometric work on endogenous stratification was in the context of discrete choice models.[1] Data had been collected on individuals' choices of transportation mode (automobile or bus), using choice-based sampling. Manski and Lerman (1977) recognized the problem, and proposed a consistent estimator. Another classic example, using the normal linear regression model, is the estimation of a wage equation from strata consisting of families in different income brackets (Hausman and Wise, 1977, 1981). Numerous other applications followed, but the focus of this review is methodological: an account of various estimators that have been proposed, the types of models and sampling schemes for which they are suited, and their large-sample statistical properties. Areas not covered here are the epidemiological literature on endogenous stratification (where it is called case-control or retrospective sampling), and applications of endogenous stratification to longitudinal studies and failure-time models.

After a discussion of sampling schemes, we start with the estimation of parametric models, which have attracted the most research. A general formulation is given, covering both discrete and continuous dependent variables. Section 4 discusses estimators that are consistent but generally not efficient. Section 5 is about a class of estimators that deal with the unknown density $h(z)$ by nonparametric maximum likelihood. These estimators achieve the semiparametric efficiency bounds (semiparametric because of the presence of h). Various special cases follow. Finally, we consider some semiparametric models: regression models in Section 8, and semiparametric discrete choice models in Section 9.

2. Notation and definitions

The spaces of exogenous and endogenous variables z and y are $\mathbb{Z}$ and $\mathbb{Y}$ respectively. Since these variables may have discrete and continuous components, we define measures μ and ν (on $\mathbb{Z}$ and $\mathbb{Y}$) which in general may be products of Lebesgue measure and counting measure. Then $p(y \mid z, \theta_0) h_0(z)$ is the population density of (z, y) with respect to $\mu \times \nu$. In most cases, the conditional density function p is supposed to be a known parametric function of $\theta \in \Theta$, so the task is to estimate the unknown finite-dimensional parameter vector θ_0. We shall also consider some cases where the underlying model is semiparametric, i.e., p also depends on an unknown distribution function F. In all cases, the density function $h_0(z)$ is unknown.

---

[1] Choice-based sampling was proposed by Warner (1963). Warner's subsequent analysis was based on discriminant analysis for normally distributed explanatory variables, rather than on a structural model.

Here are three simple but typical examples of models for the conditional density $p(y \mid z, \theta)$.

(i) Logit model of discrete choice. In a discrete choice model, there is no loss in identifying y with a discrete index, $i = 1, \ldots, M$. The probabilities can be specified as

$$p(i \mid z, \theta) = \frac{\exp(z_i' \theta)}{\sum_{j=1}^{M} \exp(z_j' \theta)}, \tag{2.1}$$

where z_i is a subvector of z associated with alternative i, and the normalization is $z_M = 0$.

(ii) Normal linear regression model:

$$p(y \mid z, \theta) = \frac{1}{\sigma} \phi\left(\frac{y - z'\beta}{\sigma}\right),$$

where $\theta' = (\beta', \sigma)$.

(iii) Nonlinear regression with unknown error distribution:

$$p(y \mid z, \theta) = f(y - g(z, \theta)).$$

Here g is a known parametric regression function, while f is an unknown density function.

Sample stratum s $(s = 1, \ldots, S)$ is the subpopulation $\{(z, y) \mid z \in \mathbb{Z}, y \in \mathcal{Y}(s)\}$ defined by a specified subset $\mathcal{Y}(s) \subseteq \mathbb{Y}$. This is *endogenous* stratification, because the strata are defined in terms of the endogenous variable y. More generally, endogenous strata could be defined by selection of both z and y; that case will be considered briefly in Section 6.4.

In order to deal with complicated sample designs that may have overlapping strata, we first define a finite collection of substrata (or 'response categories') $\mathcal{Y}_i \subset \mathbb{Y}$, $i = 1, \ldots, M$, that are mutually exclusive and cover the whole space $\mathbb{Y}$. If y is a discrete variable with a finite range, one would normally choose the response categories to be the values of y, i.e., $\mathcal{Y}_i = \{i\}$. In general, the response categories are defined so that each sample stratum $\mathcal{Y}(s)$ is a union of one or more of them. The indicator function

$$\eta_{is} = I[\mathcal{Y}_i \subseteq \mathcal{Y}(s)] \tag{2.2}$$

shows which response categories make up stratum s. Here are two standard examples, both involving a discrete choice model with M alternatives:

(i) A 'simple' choice-based sample, with one stratum corresponding to each choice alternative. In this case, the strata and the response categories coincide, so we have $S = M$ and $\mathcal{Y}(i) = \mathcal{Y}_i = \{i\}$, $i = 1, \ldots, M$.

(ii) A random sample that has been 'enriched' or 'augmented' by combining it with a choice-based sample on one alternative (say, $i = 1$) that is of particular interest in the analysis but which is rarely chosen in the population. In this case there are two strata ($S = 2$) with $\mathcal{Y}(1) = \mathcal{Y}_1 = \{1\}$ and $\mathcal{Y}(2) = \mathbb{Y} = \{1, \ldots, M\}$.

Sample observations are denoted (z_n, y_n), $n = 1, \ldots, N$, where N is the sample size. We say that observation n belongs to response category i (or substratum i) if $y_n \in \mathcal{Y}_i$. We use the following notation for the response categories:

$i(y)$ is the response category that contains the random variable y;
$i(n)$ is the response category to which observation n belongs;
$\mathcal{N}_i$ is the subset of observations belonging to response category i;
N_i is the number of observations in $\mathcal{N}_i$;

and for the sample strata:

s_n is the stratum from which observation n was drawn;
$\mathcal{N}(s)$ is the subset of observations drawn from stratum s;
$N(s)$ the number of observations in $\mathcal{N}(s)$.

Sample proportions for strata and for response categories are defined by

$$H(s) = N(s)/N , \qquad H_i = N_i/N . \tag{2.3}$$

For any subset $\mathcal{Y} \in \mathbb{Y}$, define

$$p(\mathcal{Y} \mid z, \theta) = \int d\nu(y) \, I[y \in \mathcal{Y}] p(y \mid z, \theta) , \tag{2.4}$$

$$Q(\mathcal{Y} \mid \theta, h) = \int d\mu(z) \, h(z) p(\mathcal{Y} \mid z, \theta) . \tag{2.5}$$

Special cases of the marginal probabilities Q (also called 'aggregate shares' or 'population shares') are

$$Q_i = Q(\mathcal{Y}_i \mid \theta, h) , \tag{2.6}$$

$$Q(s) = Q(\mathcal{I}(s) \mid \theta, h) = \sum_{i=1}^{M} \eta_{is} Q_i . \tag{2.7}$$

Sometimes prior information is available about Q. If so, we assume that it refers to $\{Q_i\}$, the marginal probabilities of the response categories $\mathcal{Y}_i$. The case where some information is available, but not enough to recover all the Q_i, is more involved but can be analyzed by the same methods.

The operator E_0 denotes expectation under the population density $p(y \mid z, \theta_0) \, h_0(z)$, while $E[\cdot \mid \mathcal{Y}]$ denotes expectation over a response category or stratum defined by $\mathcal{Y} \in \mathbb{Y}$; the relevant conditional density functions are

$$\frac{p(y \mid z, \theta_0) h_0(z)}{Q(\mathcal{Y} \mid \theta_0, h_0)} I[y \in \mathcal{Y}] . \tag{2.8}$$

The operator E by itself is used for the expectation of sample statistics under whatever sampling scheme is currently in use.

3. Sampling schemes and likelihood functions

Three different endogenous sampling schemes have appeared in the literature, as described in the following three subsections.

Unknown sample design parameters, if present, are treated here simply as additional unknown parameters of the likelihood function. Typically, these are sampling probabilities that were chosen by the person responsible for data collection, but which are not known to the econometrician who is analyzing the data. If we knew the decision rule for the sample design (for sample, in terms of preliminary estimates of Q) then the likelihood would be more complicated.

3.1. Standard stratified sampling

In this scheme, which seems to correspond most closely to the original idea of stratified sampling, a separate random sample of size $N(s)$ is drawn from each stratum. The subsample sizes $N(s)$ are fixed, as part of the experimental design, but it is not difficult to extend the analysis to the case where attrition of the sample causes $N(s)$ to be random. This type of sampling would be appropriate when members of each stratum are readily identifiable, such as people who use a particular type of transportation to get to work, or people who are undergoing medical treatment for some specific condition. The results given by Cosslett (1981a,b) and by Hsieh, Manski and McFadden (1985) apply to this sampling scheme. The name 'standard stratified sample' is used by Jewell (1985) and by Imbens and Lancaster (1991); Gourieroux (1991) uses 'plan stratifié'.

An important consideration is the availability of additional information about the marginal probabilities Q. Three cases have been addressed in the literature: (i) Q is unknown, (ii) Q is known exactly, and (iii) there is additional sample data from which Q can be estimated. For some choice probability models and sample designs, θ is not identified when Q is unknown, so one might expect that knowledge of Q can sometimes greatly improve the efficiency of estimation.[2] The use of additional sample data to estimate Q is discussed separately in Section 6.1.

(a) If Q is unknown, the log likelihood can be written as

$$\log L(\theta, h) = \sum_{s=1}^{S} \sum_{n \in \mathcal{N}(s)} \log \frac{p(y_n \mid z_n, \theta) h(z_n)}{Q(\mathcal{I}(s) \mid \theta, h)}. \tag{3.1}$$

Two points to note: the stratum s to which observation n belongs is not a random variable, because it is fixed by the sample design; and the observations are not identically distributed, because the density is different in each stratum. The essential problem with likelihood-based estimation from endogenously

---

[2] Use of information on aggregate shares for identification from choice-based samples was proposed by Warner (1963).

stratified samples can be seen in (3.1): the unknown density of the exogenous variables $h(z)$ cannot be factorized out of the likelihood. In *random* samples, by contrast, the log likelihood

$$\log L(\theta, h) = \sum_{n=1}^{N} (\log p(y_n \mid z_n, \theta) + \log h(z_n)) \tag{3.2}$$

is the sum of separate functions of θ and of h; when the log likelihood is maximized with respect to θ, the term in h is a constant and can be ignored.

(b) If Q is known, the factor $Q(s)^{-1}$ in the likelihood function is a constant and can be ignored in maximum likelihood estimation. On the other hand, we have to take into account the constraints $Q(\mathcal{Y}_i \mid \theta, h) = Q_i$, $i = 1, \ldots, M$ (one is redundant). Again, h cannot be dropped, this time because it appears in the constraint equation.

3.2. Variable probability sampling

This scheme starts with a random sample of observations on y. If y is in response category $\mathcal{Y}_i$, then that observation is retained in the sample with probability $\pi_i \geq 0$. These probabilities are chosen by the experimenter. For each retained observation, the rest of the data is then collected, including z. The other observations are discarded. The strata in this scheme must be mutually exclusive, so there is no distinction between the strata $\mathcal{S}(s)$ and the substrata $\mathcal{Y}_i$; for convenience they are called $\mathcal{Y}_i$ here.

The term 'variable probability sampling' is used by Jewell (1985); it is referred to as 'Bernoulli sampling' by Kalbfleisch and Lawless (1988) and Imbens and Lancaster (1991), while Gourieroux (1991) uses 'plan à probabilités inégales'. It is the type of sample used by Hausman and Wise (1981), where the strata are income brackets. It is appropriate when data on y can be collected relatively cheaply compared with the cost of the rest of the information set; this would be true particularly if individuals were being selected for a longitudinal study.

Let N_0 be the initial sample size (which may or may not be known), and let N be the number of retained observations. The numbers of retained and rejected observations in stratum i are N_i and N_i^* respectively. The form of the likelihood depends on whether the numbers N_i^* are known.

(a) If there is no information about the discarded observations (in which case we condition on N, the size of the retained sample), the log likelihood is

$$\log L(\theta, h) = \sum_{n=1}^{N} \log \frac{\pi_{i(n)} p(y_n \mid z_n, \theta) h(z_n)}{\bar{\pi}(\theta, h)}, \tag{3.3}$$

where $i(n)$ is the stratum to which observation n belongs, and $\bar{\pi}$ is the marginal probability of keeping an initial observation,

$$\bar{\pi}(\theta, h) = \sum_{i=1}^{M} \pi_i Q(\mathcal{Y}_i | \theta, h) . \tag{3.4}$$

In contrast with standard stratified sampling, note that $i(n)$ is a random variable, and that all observations are identically distributed. This applies when π is known but Q is unknown; otherwise, see Section 3.4.

(b) If the number of discarded observations in each category is known, and if the initial sample size N_0 is taken as fixed, then the log likelihood is

$$\log L(\theta, h) = \sum_{n=1}^{N} \log\{p(y_n | z_n, \theta)h(z_n)\}$$

$$+ \sum_{i=1}^{M} (N_i \log \pi_i + N_i^* \log(1 - \pi_i) + N_i^* \log Q(\mathcal{Y}_i | \theta, h)) . \tag{3.5}$$

The terms in π have now separated from the terms in θ, and can be dropped; it no longer matters whether π is known. If Q is known, see Section 3.4. The log likelihood (3.5), applied to the normal linear regression model, is given by Hausman and Wise (1981). It does not appear to have been investigated further, and estimation of θ from (3.5) will not be discussed in detail (although the same general methods can be applied).

Unlike the other two schemes, variable probability sampling can be extended to a continuum of strata. The sampling probability $\pi(y)$ can be defined as a function of the continuous random variable y. The probability $\pi_{i(n)}$ in the log likelihood (3.3) becomes $\pi(y_n)$, and the marginal probability $\bar{\pi}(\theta, h)$ becomes

$$\bar{\pi}(\theta, h) = \int d\mu(z) \int d\nu(y) \, \pi(y)p(y | z, \theta)h(z) . \tag{3.6}$$

3.3. Multinomial sampling

In this scheme, each observation is generated in two steps. First, a stratum is selected randomly, with probabilities $P(s)$, $s = 1, \ldots, S$; then an observation is drawn randomly from that stratum. The probabilities P are chosen by the experimenter. This scheme differs from standard stratified sampling in that the numbers of observations in each stratum, $N(s)$, are random variables with a multinomial distribution instead of being fixed. Although it does not seem to correspond to any sampling method that one would use in practice, it has the feature that all observations are identically distributed, which makes it somewhat easier to find the asymptotic distributions of estimators and other sample statistics.[3]

---

[3] This type of sampling is used by Manski and Lerman (1977) and Manski and McFadden (1981).

The log likelihood for multinomial sampling is

$$\log L(\theta, h) = \sum_{n=1}^{N} \log \frac{P_{i(n)}p(y_n \mid z_n, \theta)h(z_n)}{Q(\mathcal{Y}_i \mid \theta, h)} . \tag{3.7}$$

This is isomorphic with the log likelihood for variable probability sampling, under the substitution

$$P_i = Q_i \pi_i / \bar{\pi} . \tag{3.8}$$

But in practice they are different because the sample design parameters are usually assumed to be known: π in the case of variable probability sampling, and P in the case of multinomial sampling.

An explained in the next subsection, there is in fact no need to use the likelihood (3.7): we can proceed, without loss, as if the stratum sizes $N(s)$ were fixed.

3.4. Conditioning on subsample sizes

Suppose the likelihood for a vector of random variables x has the form $L(x \mid \theta) = L_1(x \mid \tau, \theta)L_2(\tau)$, where $\tau = \tau(x)$ is a statistic and θ is a parameter to be estimated. Then τ is said to be an 'ancillary' statistic with respect to θ: its distribution does not depend on θ, and so knowledge of the realized value of τ conveys no information about θ. In that case, the 'principle of conditionality' says that inference about θ should be based on $L_1(x \mid \tau, \theta)$, the likelihood conditional on the ancillary statistic τ. Lancaster (1990) has emphasized the importance of conditioning on ancillary statistics when dealing with endogenously stratified samples. Examples of paradoxes that can arise when the principle of conditionality is ignored are given by Cox and Hinkley (1974) and by Lancaster.

In an endogenously stratified sample, the stratum sizes $N(s)$ or N_i may be ancillary statistics, depending on our knowledge of the population shares Q and, when relevant, the sample design parameters π or P. By conditioning on ancillary statistics, we can drastically reduce the number of different cases that have to be investigated. The three main sampling schemes are considered separately.

(a) *Standard stratified sample.* Suppose Q is known and the strata overlap, i.e., for some i and s, $\mathcal{Y}_i$ is a proper subset of $\mathcal{J}(s)$. Let N_{is} be the number of observations in stratum s that have $y \in \mathcal{Y}_i$. The random variables N_{is} have a multinomial distribution with sample size $N(s)$ and probabilities $\eta_{is}Q_i/Q(s)$. Because this does not depend on θ or h, the N_{is} are ancillary statistics, and therefore we should use the likelihood conditional on $\{N_{is}\}$. That conditional likelihood is the same as the likelihood for a sample stratified on $\mathcal{Y}_i, i =$

$1, \ldots, M$, with fixed subsample sizes N_i:

$$\log L(\theta, h) = \sum_{i=1}^{M} \sum_{n \in \mathcal{N}_i} \log \frac{p(y_n \mid z_n, \theta) h(z_n)}{Q(\mathcal{Y}_i \mid \theta, h)} \ . \tag{3.9}$$

In other words, we should proceed as if the sample had been stratified on the response categories $\mathcal{Y}_i$ rather than on the original strata $\mathcal{J}(s)$, and with subsample sizes given by the *sample* values of $N_i = \sum_s N_{is}$.

(b) *Variable probability sample*. First, suppose there is no information on the discarded observations. The subsample sizes N_i have a multinomial distribution with sample size N and probabilities P_i given by (3.8). If π and Q are both known, then P is known. If π is unknown, (3.8) imposes no restrictions on P, apart from $\sum_i P_i = 1$, and the log likelihood (3.3) can be rewritten in terms of the unknown parameters (θ, P) instead of (θ, π). In either case, P known or P unrestricted, the distribution of $\{N_i\}$ does not involve θ or h. The N_i are therefore ancillary statistics, and we should condition on $\{N_i\}$.

A similar argument holds in the case where we know the number of discarded observations in each stratum: if Q is known, we should condition on $\{N_i\}$.

(c) *Multinomial sampling*. This is the case considered by Lancaster (1990). The stratum sizes $N(s)$ are ancillary, because the probabilities P do not involve θ or h. A sample of this type can therefore always be treated as if it were a standard stratified sample. However, some of the original work on choice-based sampling presented estimators and asymptotic variances based on the likelihood (3.7), as discussed in Section 4.

To summarize the results of conditioning on ancillary statistics: in most cases, the sample can be treated as a standard stratified sample. If Q is unknown, the log likelihood is (3.1), with strata $\mathcal{J}(s)$ and fixed subsample sizes $N(s)$; if Q is known, then use (3.9), with strata $\mathcal{Y}_i$ and fixed N_i. Of the cases considered above, the only exceptions are variable probability samples with: (i) π known, Q unknown, and no information on discarded observations; and (ii) Q unknown, with information on discarded observations. The log likelihoods for these cases are (3.3) and (3.5).

3.5. Identification

The model $p(y \mid z, \theta)$ is assumed to allow θ to be identified from a random sample, but further conditions are needed when the sample is endogenously stratified. For example, if the data is obtained by simple choice-based sampling (i.e., each stratum corresponds to a single value of the discrete variable y) with Q unknown, and the model is multinomial logit with alternative-specific dummy variables, then the coefficients of those dummy variables are not identified (Manski and McFadden, 1981). Some identification criteria are given by Cosslett (1981b) (see also Gill, Vardi and Wellner, 1988).

The problem arises if a discrete choice model includes 'multiplicative intercept' terms (Manski and McFadden, 1981), i.e., if the parameterization is such that

$$p(i \mid z, \theta_0) = \frac{c_i p(i \mid z, \theta^*)}{\sum_{j=1}^{M} c_j p(j \mid z, \theta^*)} \qquad (3.10)$$

for some $\theta^* \in \Theta$ and some set of constants $c_1, \ldots, c_M$ (not all equal). This holds for the multinomial logit model (2.1) if there are constant terms in the exponents, i.e., if $z_i'\theta = \alpha_i + \tilde{z}_i'\beta$. (The constant α_i can also be viewed as the coefficient of a dummy variable for alternative i.) Let

$$h^*(z) = \frac{c_0 h(z)}{\sum_{j=1}^{M} c_j p(j \mid z, \theta^*)}, \qquad (3.11)$$

where the constant c_0 normalizes h^* to a probability density. Then, if c_i is constant for all alternatives in a stratum, the likelihoods in (3.1) (standard stratified sampling) and (3.7) (multinomial sampling) satisfy $L(\theta, h) = L(\theta^*, h^*)$, i.e., θ and h are not identified. The population shares Q_i are not invariant under this transformation, however, so the problem arises only if Q is unknown.

This happens also in variable probability sampling if both the sampling probabilities π and the population shares Q are unknown: the likelihood in (3.3) is invariant under $\theta \to \theta^*$, $h \to h^*$, and $\pi_i \to \pi_i^* = c_i \pi_i$.

There are two ways to go: to restrict the classes of sample designs or of models. A key step in the argument above was finding constants c_i that were equal within each stratum but not equal for all alternatives. One criterion for identification, therefore, is to exclude sample designs which let that happen. The conditions are:

 (i) All alternatives are included, i.e., $\bigcup_s \mathcal{J}(s) = \mathbb{Y}$.

 (ii) The strata cannot be grouped into two nonoverlapping sets of alternatives, i.e., if $\mathcal{S}$ is a proper subset of $\{1, \ldots, S\}$ and $\mathcal{S}'$ is its complement, then

$$\left(\bigcup_{s \in \mathcal{S}} \mathcal{J}(s) \right) \cap \left(\bigcup_{s \in \mathcal{S}'} \mathcal{J}(s) \right) \neq \emptyset. \qquad (3.12)$$

In particular, this rules out the simple choice-based sample design mentioned above. This identification condition obviously can never apply to variable probability sampling, where the strata must be mutually exclusive.

Another approach is to leave the class of sample designs unrestricted, but to exclude models that satisfy (3.10). In particular, this rules out the multinomial logit model with alternative-specific dummy variables (i.e., with 'intercept' terms). This is somewhat unsatisfactory, because then identification depends on the particular functional form assumed for $p(i \mid z, \theta)$, which is not really fundamental; it is likely that in other, similar discrete choice models, such as multinomial probit, the intercept terms will be poorly determined even though they are formally identified.

In fact, it may be better to take advantage of the transformation (3.10). If (3.12) fails, the basic problem is lack of information in the sample about relative probabilities, which cannot really be overcome by a clever parameterization. If our model *does* satisfy (3.10), then at least the lack of identification is confined to the intercept terms, and the remaining parameters can be consistently estimated.

4. Estimators based on maximum likelihood

This heading covers estimators based on the maximum likelihood (ML) method, but where the function to be maximized is not necessarily the likelihood function itself. The conditional density $p(y|z, \theta)$ must be a known parametric function. There are two main approaches (with some overlap): (i) look at the score function for the likelihood under random sampling, and see what changes are needed for it to have zero expectation under endogenous sampling; and (ii) estimate the unknown density $h(z)$ by nonparametric maximum likelihood (NPML), concentrate the likelihood function with respect to h, and then maximize the concentrated likelihood by conventional methods. The NPML approach is covered in Section 5.

The likelihood-based estimators all have the same general form: maximize a function $\mathcal{L}(\theta) = \Sigma_n \ell(y_n, z_n, s_n, \theta)$ over θ. Consistency and asymptotic normality, under suitable regularity conditions, then follow from general results on M-estimators: see, for example, Chapter 4 of Amemiya (1985).[4] Asymptotic variances are discussed in Section 4.5. In general, apart from the need to check identification (see Section 3.5), conditions that suffice for consistency and asymptotic normality of maximum likelihood estimators from random samples will suffice here too. If, however, the strata are incomplete, i.e., if $\bigcup_s \mathcal{J}(s) \neq \mathbb{Y}$, then the conditions are those for maximum likelihood estimation from truncated samples.

4.1. Modified score

Suppose Q is known. According to Section 3.4, the sample should be treated as a *standard stratified sample* with strata $\mathcal{Y}_i$ (the most disaggregate strata for which marginal probabilities Q_i are known). We can call the $\mathcal{Y}_i$ 'response categories' to distinguish them from the sampling strata $\mathcal{J}(s)$, which may be different.

Let $\Psi(\theta) = \Sigma_n \psi(y_n, z_n, \theta)$ be a statistic such that $E_0[\Psi(\theta_0)] = 0$. Then the solution of the moment equation $\Psi(\theta) = 0$ is a consistent estimator of θ from

---

[4] Proofs for discrete y, with varying degrees of generality, are given by Manski and Lerman (1977), Manski and McFadden (1981), and Hsieh, Manski and McFadden (1985).

random samples (under conventional regularity and identification conditions). In a standard endogenously stratified sample, with log likelihood (3.9),

$$E[\Psi(\theta_0)] = \sum_{i=1}^{M} N_i E[\psi(y, z, \theta_0) \mid \mathcal{Y}_i] = N E_0\left(\frac{H_{i(y)}}{Q_{i(y)}} \psi(y, z, \theta_0)\right), \quad (4.1)$$

which is generally not zero. The operator E_0 denotes expectation under the population density.

In particular, this applies to the score vector for θ under random sampling: let $\psi(y, z, \theta) = \partial \log p(y \mid z, \theta)/\partial\theta$. Then $E_0[\Psi(\theta_0)] = 0$, but according to (4.1), $E[\Psi(\theta_0)]$ is generally nonzero under endogenously stratified sampling (except in the special case where $H_i = Q_i$). This means that ML estimators are generally inconsistent if we fail to take account of endogenous stratification. One solution is to find a modified version of Ψ, say Ψ^*, such that $E[\Psi^*(\theta_0)]$ is again zero. Here are two methods.

(a) Weight the observations: if $\psi(y_n, z_n, \theta)$ is replaced by $\psi^*(y_n, z_n, \theta) = (Q_{i(n)}/H_{i(n)})\psi(y_n, z_n, \theta)$, then the unwanted factors in (4.1) cancel and we get $E[\Psi^*(\theta_0)] = 0$.

(b) An additive correction: replace $\psi(y, z, \theta)$ by $\psi^*(y, z, \theta) = \psi(y, z, \theta) - \bar{\psi}(z, \theta)$. For any sample statistic of the form $T = N^{-1} \Sigma_n \tau(z_n)$, the expected value under standard stratified sampling is $E[T] = E_0[\bar{p}(z, \theta)\tau(z)]$, where

$$\bar{p}(z, \theta) = \sum_{i=1}^{M} \frac{H_i}{Q_i} p(\mathcal{Y}_i \mid z, \theta) . \quad (4.2)$$

A suitable correction term is therefore

$$\bar{\psi}(z, \theta) = \frac{1}{\bar{p}(z, \theta)} E_0\left(\frac{H_{i(y)}}{Q_{i(y)}} \psi(y, z, \theta)|z\right) . \quad (4.3)$$

Similar arguments apply to a *variable probability sample* with known sampling weights π. The weight factor in (a) is $1/\pi_{i(n)}$, while the correction term in (b) is given by substituting π_i for H_i/Q_i in (4.2)–(4.3). Note, however, that if π and Q are *both* known, then we should condition on N_i (as explained in Section 3.4); in that case we should continue to use H_i/Q_i, not π_i.

4.2. Weighted exogenous sample maximum likelihood

The first consistent estimator for endogenously stratified sampling was the *weighted exogenous sample maximum likelihood* (WESML) estimator (Manski and Lerman, 1977). It was originally proposed for estimation of discrete-choice models from choice-based samples, but it extends to continuous dependent variables and general endogenously stratified sampling schemes (see McFadden, 1979). Although generally not optimal, it is computationally straightforward and can be run on many existing statistical software packages.

Apply the multiplicative weighting scheme in Section 4.1 to the score for θ

under random sampling. The modified score is $(Q_{i(n)}/H_{i(n)}) \, \partial \log p(y_n \,|\, z_n, \theta)/\partial\theta$, which corresponds to the weighted log likelihood function

$$\log L_{\mathrm{W}}(\theta) = \sum_{n=1}^{N} \frac{Q_{i(n)}}{H_{i(n)}} \log p(y_n \,|\, z_n, \theta) \,. \tag{4.4}$$

In each response category, the weight factor is the ratio of the population share to the sample share. Oversampled categories are given a low weight, and vice-versa. If each observation is counted according to its weight, the sample shares and population shares are now the same. Maximization of (4.4) over θ gives the WESML estimator. It is consistent but not asymptotically efficient.

The WESML estimator is also applicable to variable probability sampling with known sampling probabilities π and unknown Q. The weights $Q_{i(n)}/H_{i(n)}$ are replaced by $1/\pi_{i(n)}$. (If Q and π are both known, use the version (4.4) as given.)

The original version of the WESML estimator[5] is slightly different: it was introduced in the context of multinomial sampling, and uses the stratum sampling probabilities P_i instead of the observed sample shares H_i in the weighted likelihood. More generally, one could use $E[H_i]$ instead of H_i. However, the estimator based on (4.4), using H_i, is asymptotically more efficient (except, of course, when the sample shares H_i are fixed by the sample design, in which case there is no difference). At first sight this seems surprising: we lose efficiency when a sample statistic H_i is replaced by its 'true' value $E[H_i]$. An explanation in terms of conditioning on N_i is given by Lancaster (1990).

Although the WESML estimator can sometimes be close to optimal, there are cases where its efficiency is low in comparison with other available estimators. The example given by Cosslett (1981a) involves a binary choice model in which one alternative is rarely chosen. Heuristically, the problem is this: endogenous stratification is used to oversample the rare alternative, but the WESML estimator then dilutes the information by assigning low weights to the extra observations.

4.3. Weighted moment equations

The WESML estimator for variable probability sampling remains consistent if the weights are $w^*(z_n)/\pi_{i(n)}$, where $w^*(z)$ is any function of z. This idea is generalized by Gourieroux (1991), who considers a set of weighted moment equations. In the present case, these come from the likelihood equations for random sampling:

$$\sum_{n=1}^{N} \frac{1}{\pi_{i(n)}} W(z_n) \frac{1}{p_n} \frac{\partial p_n}{\partial \theta} = 0 \,, \tag{4.5}$$

[5] Manski and Lerman (1977) and Manski and McFadden (1981).

where W is a $(K \times K)$ matrix of weight factors. If W is scalar, then (4.5) corresponds to a weighted maximum likelihood estimator, but in general it does not. Gourieroux (1991) derives the optimal W for variable probability sampling. It depends on θ, so a preliminary consistent estimator $\tilde{\theta}$ is needed. An obvious choice for $\tilde{\theta}$ is the WESML estimator. If the model is of 'single-index' form, i.e., $p(y|z,\theta) = F(y, g(z,\theta))$ for some functions F and g, then W is scalar.

Define the $(K \times K)$ matrices

$$a(z) = \mathrm{E}_0\left[\frac{1}{p^2}\frac{\partial p}{\partial \theta}\frac{\partial p}{\partial \theta'}\bigg|z\right], \qquad b(z) = \mathrm{E}_0\left[\frac{1}{\pi_{i(y)}}\frac{1}{p^2}\frac{\partial p}{\partial \theta}\frac{\partial p}{\partial \theta'}\bigg|z\right]. \quad (4.6)$$

Since p is a known function, these expressions can be evaluated analytically in terms of z and $\tilde{\theta}$. Then the optimal weight matrix is $W = ab^+$, and the asymptotic variance of $\hat{\theta}$ is $V(\hat{\theta}) = \mathrm{E}_0[ab^+a]$, where the superscript $+$ denotes a generalized inverse.

If Q is known, on the other hand, we should condition on N_i and treat the sample as a standard stratified sample. The optimal W can be found for this case also, although it is somewhat more complicated. Replace $1/\pi_{i(y)}$ by $Q_{i(y)}/H_{i(y)}$ in (4.5)–(4.6), and define the $(K \times M)$ matrix

$$c_{.j}(z) = \mathrm{E}_0\left[I(y \in \mathcal{Y}_j)\frac{1}{p}\frac{\partial p}{\partial \theta}\bigg|z\right]. \qquad (4.7)$$

Then we find that the optimal W is

$$W = \{a + \mathrm{E}_0[ab^+c](H - \mathrm{E}_0[c'b^+c])^{-1}c'\}b^+ \qquad (4.8)$$

and the asymptotic variance of $\hat{\theta}$ is

$$V(\hat{\theta}) = \{\mathrm{E}_0[ab^+a] + \mathrm{E}_0[ab^+c](H - \mathrm{E}_0[c'b^+c])^{-1}\mathrm{E}_0[c'b^+a]\}^{-1}, \quad (4.9)$$

where H is an $(M \times M)$ diagonal matrix with elements H_i. The expected values E_0 in (4.8) and (4.9) can be consistently estimated by sample means of observations weighted by $\bar{p}(z_n, \hat{\theta})^{-1}$ (see Section 4.5).

Although better than WESML, this estimator is still not asymptotically efficient, and it is no longer clear that the computational cost is less than that of alternative estimators (which come next). We shall return to (4.8) when we come to the regression model with unknown error distribution, where full-scale semiparametric MLE is much more difficult.

4.4. Conditional maximum likelihood, Q known

This time, the additive correction scheme of Section 4.1 is applied to the score vector for random sampling. The correction term (4.3) is $\bar{\psi} = \bar{p}^{-1}\partial\bar{p}/\partial\theta$, where $\bar{p}$ is defined by (4.2), and the modified score is $\psi^* = \psi - \bar{\psi} = \partial \log(p/\bar{p})/\partial\theta$.

The new function to be maximized is (with some additional constant factors)

$$\log L_C(\theta) = \sum_{n=1}^{N} \log \frac{(H_{i(n)}/Q_{i(n)})p(y_n \mid z_n, \theta)}{\sum_{j=1}^{M} (H_j/Q_j)p(\mathcal{Y}_j \mid z_n, \theta)}. \tag{4.10}$$

This gives the *conditional maximum likelihood* (CML) estimator. It was introduced by Manski and McFadden (1981) for discrete-choice models under choice-based sampling, but can be extended to general endogenous sampling problems (McFadden, 1979). The name arises because under variable probability sampling or multinomial sampling (4.10) is, in fact, the log likelihood of y conditional on z. It can also be interpreted as a conditional likelihood under standard stratified sampling (which we are using here) if we first randomize the observations from the different strata. The CML estimator is particularly useful when $p(y \mid z, \theta)$ is given by the multinomial logit model (2.1): it reduces to a trivial modification of the MLE for random sampling and becomes asymptotically efficient. The special case of the multinomial logit model is discussed in Section 5.6. In general, however, the CML estimator is not asymptotically efficient when there is prior information on Q.

As with the WESML estimator, there is an alternative version of the CML estimator that uses the expected values $E[H_i]$ instead of the sample proportions H_i in the conditional likelihood and in (4.2), the definition of $\bar{p}$. It is, however, asymptotically less efficient than the estimator based on (4.10). (See the discussion of this point in Section 4.2.)

The case of unknown Q is postponed to Section 5, because in that case the CML estimator turns out to be the full-information MLE.

Amemiya and Vuong (1987) compare the asymptotic variances of the WESML and CML estimators, and show that CML is more efficient. One can show, by the same method, that the optimal weighted moment estimator given by Gourieroux (1991) lies between WESML and CML in efficiency. These comparisons are valid for variable probability sampling with unknown Q. However, when Q is known (in any of the sampling schemes), they are generally valid only if we use the less efficient versions of the estimators, substituting $E[H_i]$ for H_i. If we use the standard versions of the estimators for known Q, the optimal weighted moment estimator is necessarily more efficient than WESML, but it is no longer possible to compare their asymptotic efficiencies with that of CML. For some sample designs, WESML can in fact be more efficient than CML (Cosslett, 1981a). In any event, more efficient estimators are available, provided Q is known: see Section 5.

4.5. Estimation of asymptotic variances

The asymptotic variance of $\hat{\theta}$ has the form $V(\hat{\theta}) = J^{-1}MJ$, where, as usual, $J = \lim E[-N^{-1} \partial^2 \log \bar{L}/\partial\theta \, \partial\theta']$ and M is the limiting variance of

$N^{-1/2} \partial \log \tilde{L}/\partial\theta$. Write the objective function of a generic estimator as

$$\log \tilde{L}(\theta) = \sum_{n=1}^{N} \ell(y_n, z_n, s_n) . \tag{4.11}$$

(The dependence on s_n occurs only when the stratum sizes are fixed.) For standard stratified sampling,

$$J = -\sum_{s=1}^{S} H(s) E\left[\frac{\partial^2 \ell}{\partial\theta \, \partial\theta'} \middle| \mathcal{I}(s) \right], \tag{4.12}$$

$$M = \sum_{s=1}^{S} H(s) E\left[\frac{\partial \ell}{\partial\theta} \frac{\partial \ell}{\partial\theta'} \middle| \mathcal{I}(s) \right] - \sum_{s=1}^{S} H(s) E\left[\frac{\partial \ell}{\partial\theta} \middle| \mathcal{I}(s) \right] E\left[\frac{\partial \ell}{\partial\theta'} \middle| \mathcal{I}(s) \right], \tag{4.13}$$

where the expectations over strata use the density (2.8). For variable probability sampling (without conditioning on N_i), the second term on the right of (4.13) is dropped.

Explicit expressions for the asymptotic variances of the WESML, CML, and full-information ML estimators have been given by several authors for the case where y is discrete. Under standard stratified sampling, asymptotic variances for WESML, CML with known and with unknown Q, and full-information ML with known Q are given by Cosslett (1981a) (where the CML estimator is called the Manski–McFadden estimator). Hsieh, Manski and McFadden (1985) present results for WESML, CML and full-information ML when Q is estimated from an auxiliary sample (see Section 6.1), again under standard stratified sampling; the case of known Q can be recovered in the limit where the auxiliary sample becomes infinitely large relative to the main sample. For WESML and CML under variable probability sampling with known π and unknown Q, substitute π_i for H_i/Q_i in the asymptotic variance expressions given by Manski and McFadden (1981) for multinomial sampling with known Q.

These expressions can be consistently estimated from sample data, after substituting $\hat{\theta}$ for θ_0. If the model is not too complicated, the expectation over y conditional on z can be evaluated analytically. (If y is discrete, it is just a sum of terms over responses i.) This leaves expressions of the form $E_0[\tau(z)]$ to be estimated as weighted sample means. Two convenient weighting schemes are

$$\frac{1}{N} \sum_{n=1}^{N} \frac{Q_{i(n)}}{H_{i(n)}} \tau(z_n) \xrightarrow{P} E_0[\tau(z)], \tag{4.14}$$

$$\sum_{n=1}^{N} \frac{\tau(z_n)}{\bar{p}(z_n, \hat{\theta})} \left(\sum_{n=1}^{N} \frac{1}{\bar{p}(z_n, \hat{\theta})} \right)^{-1} \xrightarrow{P} E_0[\tau(z)]. \tag{4.15}$$

If unknown, Q is replaced by a consistent estimate. The sum in the denominator of (4.15) is optional and can be replaced by N, its probability limit. Although there is no experimental evidence to favor either one, (4.15) might be recommended on the grounds that its weight factor is the NPMLE of the density h.

For variable probability sampling (with unknown Q), $1/\pi_i$ is substituted for Q_i/H_i in (4.14) and the sum in the denominator of (4.15) is dropped. This puts an additional factor $1/\bar{\pi}$ on the right-hand sides of (4.14)–(4.15). The unknown constant $\bar{\pi}$ then disappears from the estimated asymptotic variances, but if needed it can be estimated from

$$\hat{\bar{\pi}}^{-1} = \sum_{n=1}^{N} \bar{p}(z_n, \hat{\theta})^{-1}. \tag{4.16}$$

This allows Q to be estimated as $\hat{Q}_i = H_i \hat{\bar{\pi}}/\pi_i$.

If the conditional expected value is not computationally tractable, then an expected value of the form $E[\tau(y, z) \mid \mathcal{Y}] = E_0[I(y \in \mathcal{Y})\tau(y, z)/Q(\mathcal{Y})]$ has to be estimated from a weighted sample mean of $I(y_n \in \mathcal{Y})\tau(y_n, z_n)$. The NPMLE of the joint density of y and z is difficult to compute (see Jewell, 1985), so we would fall back on the weights $Q_{i(n)}/H_{i(n)}$, as in (4.14).

5. Efficient estimation of parametric models

The estimators in this section replace the unknown density $h(z)$ by its nonparametric maximum likelihood estimator (NPMLE) (Cosslett, 1981a,b). Asymptotic efficiency bounds have been derived for most of the cases considered here, generally based on the method of Begun et al. (1983): see Cosslett (1985), Imbens and Lancaster (1991), and Cosslett (1991). Bickel et al. (1993) give characterizations of these bounds, but in most cases without presenting explicit expressions. Where bounds are known, estimators based on the NPMLE of h are asymptotically efficient.

5.1. Variable probability sampling, Q unknown

We start with the simplest case. The sampling weights π are known. The NPMLE of h from the log likelihood (3.3) is the discrete density with weight[6]

$$\omega_n = \frac{1}{\displaystyle\sum_{j=1}^{M} \pi_j p(\mathcal{Y}_j \mid z_n, \theta)} \left(\sum_{m=1}^{N} \frac{1}{\displaystyle\sum_{j=1}^{M} \pi_j p(\mathcal{Y}_j \mid z_m, \theta)} \right)^{-1} \tag{5.1}$$

at each data point $z = z_n$. Substituting this back into (3.3), and dropping

---

[6] This is given by Jewell (1985) for linear regression under variable probability sampling.

constant terms, gives the concentrated log likelihood

$$\log L_0(\theta) = \sum_{n=1}^{N} \log \frac{\pi_{i(n)} p(y_n \mid z_n, \theta)}{\sum_{j=1}^{M} \pi_j p(\mathcal{Y}_j \mid z_n, \theta)}. \tag{5.2}$$

Maximization over θ then gives $\hat{\theta}$, the MLE. The concentrated likelihood (5.2) is obviously the same as the conditional likelihood of y given z (Section 4.4). Consistency and asymptotic normality follow from standard results on maximum likelihood estimation.[7] If the sampling probability varies continuously with y, the term $\pi_{i(n)}$ is replaced by $\pi(y_n)$ and the sum in the denominator is replaced by the corresponding integral over y.

5.2. Standard stratified sampling, Q unknown

In this case, the NPMLE of h from the log likelihood (3.1) is the discrete density with weight

$$\omega_n = \frac{1}{N \sum_{s=1}^{S} [H(s)/\hat{Q}(s,\theta)] p(\mathcal{J}(s) \mid z_n, \theta)} \tag{5.3}$$

at $z = z_n$, where the estimated shares $\hat{Q}(s,\theta)$ are determined by substituting (5.3) into the equations

$$\hat{Q}(s,\theta) = Q(\mathcal{J}(s) \mid \theta, \hat{h}) = \sum_{n=1}^{N} \omega_n p(\mathcal{J}(s) \mid z_n, \theta) \tag{5.4}$$

$(s = 1, \ldots, S-1)$, and

$$\sum_{n=1}^{N} \omega_n = 1. \tag{5.5}$$

The resulting concentrated likelihood is

$$\log L_0(\theta) = \sum_{n=1}^{N} \log \frac{[H(s_n)/\hat{Q}(s_n,\theta)] p(y_n \mid z_n, \theta)}{\sum_{t=1}^{S} [H(t)/\hat{Q}(t,\theta)] p(\mathcal{Y}_j \mid z_n, \theta)}. \tag{5.6}$$

This can be expressed in a more convenient form: after substituting for ω_n, the equations (5.4) are the same as the first-order conditions for maximization of

---

[7] Hausman and Wise (1981) apply this estimator to the normal linear regression model.

the log *pseudo-likelihood*

$$\log \bar{L}(\theta, Q) = \sum_{n=1}^{N} \log \frac{[H(s_n)/Q(s_n)]p(y_n \mid z_n, \theta)}{\sum_{t=1}^{S} [H(t)/Q(t)]p(\mathcal{Y}_j \mid z_n, \theta)} \tag{5.7}$$

over Q. Maximization of (5.7) over both θ and Q then gives consistent estimators $\hat{\theta}$ and $\hat{Q}$. In order to estimate Q, we also need an inhomogeneous restriction on $\hat{Q}$: it comes from (5.5), substituting (5.3) for ω. If there is an identity of the form $\Sigma_s c_s \eta_{is} = 1$ $(i = 1, \ldots, M)$ (which is true for most conventional sample designs), then (5.5) simplifies to $\Sigma_k c_s \hat{Q}(s) = 1$.

The term *pseudo-likelihood* is used here in the following sense: a function of θ that, when maximized, gives an estimator with the same properties as the MLE (Cosslett, 1981a). In general, no θ and no h make the log pseudo-likelihood (5.7) equal to the true log likelihood (3.1); it does not satisfy the 'information matrix' equality, i.e., $\text{var}[\partial \log \bar{L}/\partial \theta] \neq -\text{E}[\partial^2 \log \bar{L}/\partial \theta \, \partial \theta']$; and the estimator is inconsistent if p is misspecified. That is to be distinguished from *quasi* maximum likelihood estimation (Koopmans and Hood, 1953; see also McCullagh and Nelder, 1989, for a more general definition): in that case the objective function is the log likelihood under a particular distributional assumption (normality, in many cases), but gives a consistent estimator regardless of the true distribution.[8]

The objective function (5.7) is again the same as the conditional log likelihood proposed by Manski and McFadden (1981) (see Section 4.5). But in general the CML estimator is not the same as the full-information MLE, so we prefer to use the term *pseudo-likelihood* rather than *conditional likelihood* here. Note that $\bar{L}(\theta, Q)$ is *not* the same as the concentrated log likelihood $L_0(\theta, Q)$, which would be obtained by maximizing $L(\theta, h)$ over h at fixed θ and Q subject to the restriction $Q_i = \int d\mu(z)h(z)p(\mathcal{Y}_i \mid z, \theta)$. Both functions are maximized at $(\hat{\theta}, \hat{Q})$, but the concentrated likelihood is less useful because there is no analytic expression for it.

Variable probability sampling with both π and Q unknown can be treated as standard stratified sampling (by conditioning on N_i), and so the present estimator can be used also in that case. If the parameterization of $p(y \mid z, \theta)$ allows θ to be identified from nonoverlapping endogenous strata, then π can be estimated up to a scale factor by $\hat{\pi}_i = \bar{\pi}H_i/\hat{Q}_i$. ($\bar{\pi}$ is not identifiable.) This equivalence provides another interpretation of the estimator: maximize the concentrated log likelihood (5.2) over π.[9]

---

[8] Gourieroux, Monfort and Trognon (1984) use the term 'pseudo maximum likelihood estimation' for what we would call (following Koopmans and Hood, 1953) 'quasi maximum likelihood estimation'.

[9] Hausman and Wise (1981) also consider this estimator in the case of normal linear regression.

The maximum pseudo-likelihood estimator based on (5.7) (i.e., the CML estimator for unknown Q) achieves the asymptotic efficiency bound.[10]

5.3. Standard stratified sampling, Q known

When Q is known, h is estimated by NPML from the likelihood (3.1) subject to the restrictions $Q(\mathcal{Y}_i | \theta, h) = Q_{0i}$, where Q_{0i} denotes the 'true' value $Q(\mathcal{Y}_i | \theta_0, h_0)$. The resulting pseudo-likelihood function is

$$\log \bar{L}(\theta, \lambda | Q_0) = \sum_{n=1}^{N} \log \frac{p(y_n | z_n, \theta)}{\sum_{j=1}^{M} \lambda_j p(\mathcal{Y}_j | z_n, \theta)} . \tag{5.8}$$

The new parameters λ_i are the Lagrange multipliers for the constrained maximization over h. They satisfy the restriction

$$\sum_{i=1}^{M} \lambda_i Q_{0i} = 1 . \tag{5.9}$$

This time the optimization problem is more complicated. First, minimize $\bar{L}(\theta, \lambda | Q_0)$ over λ at fixed θ, subject to (5.9), to get $\hat{\lambda}(\theta)$. If there is no minimum, set $\bar{L}(\theta, \hat{\lambda}(\theta)) = -\infty$. (This would happen if the known aggregate shares cannot be reproduced from the sample data by any density $\hat{h}$.) Then maximize $\bar{L}(\theta, \hat{\lambda}(\theta))$ over θ to get $\hat{\theta}$ and $\hat{\lambda} = \hat{\lambda}(\hat{\theta})$.

Under standard regularity conditions, both $\hat{\theta}$ and $\hat{\lambda}$ are consistent and asymptotically normal. The probability limit of $\hat{\lambda}_i$ is $\lambda_{0i} = H_i / Q_{0i}$. The asymptotic variance of $\hat{\theta}$ achieves the efficiency bound for known Q (Imbens and Lancaster, 1991; Cosslett, 1991).

This estimator is somewhat more complicated than usual: there are M additional parameters, which have known probability limits and so provide no useful information; the solution of the likelihood equations corresponds to a saddle point rather than a maximum; and the algorithm has to allow for the possibility that the minimum over λ might not exist. (If this happens for all θ, which is possible in small samples, then the estimator does not exist.) One method is just to solve the first-order conditions as a set of nonlinear simultaneous equations, using the WESML or CML estimator $\hat{\theta}$ and the known shares Q_0 as the starting point. That approach is used by Hsieh, Manski and McFadden (1985) to estimate θ in a slightly more complicated sampling scheme, where Q is estimated from an auxiliary sample. Another method is to iteratively apply the CML estimator, starting with $Q = Q_0$ and subsequently updating Q as

---

[10] See Cosslett (1991). The efficiency bound was also given by Cosslett (1981b), but that paper used a different definition of asymptotic efficiency: the bound was derived as the asymptotic limit of the semiparametric Cramér–Rao lower bound on the variance of an unbiased estimator, instead of as a lower bound on the asymptotic variance of a regular consistent estimator.

$$Q_i = \frac{1}{N} \sum_{n=1}^{N} p(\mathcal{Y}_i \mid z_n, \theta) / \bar{p}(z_n, \hat{\theta}),$$ (5.10)

where $\bar{p}(z_n, \hat{\theta})$ is defined by (4.2) in terms of the previous values of $\hat{\theta}$ and Q.

Although the maximum pseudo-likelihood estimator for known Q appears computationally tractable, there has been some effort to find alternative estimators that are simpler yet still efficient. Two recent results are as follows.

5.4. Penalized maximum likelihood estimator

The auxiliary parameters $\hat{\lambda}$ in the pseudo-likelihood (5.8) converge to known limits, and so appear to convey no useful information. But replacing them by their probability limits λ_0 just gets us back to the conditional likelihood (4.10). Again, we have a somewhat counterintuitive result: the 'true' weights λ_0 give a less efficient estimator of θ than do the estimated weights $\hat{\lambda}$.

One way of eliminating λ without loss of efficiency is to apply a first-order Taylor series expansion at $\lambda = \lambda_0$ to the likelihood equations for λ (Cosslett, 1991). This is like the linearized maximum likelihood estimator used by Rothenberg and Leenders (1964), but applied only to the auxiliary parameters λ. The solution for λ is

$$\lambda^* = \lambda_0 - \left(\frac{\partial^2 \log \tilde{L}(\theta, \lambda_0 \mid Q_0)}{\partial \lambda \, \partial \lambda'} \right)^{-1} \frac{\partial \log \tilde{L}(\theta, \lambda_0 \mid Q_0)}{\partial \lambda}.$$ (5.11)

One component of λ is eliminated via (5.9). Substituting λ^* into (5.8), and keeping terms up to second order in $(\lambda - \lambda_0)$, gives the concentrated pseudo-likelihood

$$\log L^*(\theta \mid Q_0) = \log \tilde{L}(\theta, \lambda_0 \mid Q_0)$$
$$- \frac{1}{2} \frac{\partial \log \tilde{L}(\theta, \lambda_0 \mid Q_0)}{\partial \lambda} \left(\frac{\partial^2 \log \tilde{L}(\theta, \lambda_0 \mid Q_0)}{\partial \lambda \, \partial \lambda'} \right)^{-1} \frac{\partial \log \tilde{L}(\theta, \lambda_0 \mid Q_0)}{\partial \lambda}.$$ (5.12)

Maximization of $\log L^*(\theta \mid Q_0)$ over θ gives an estimator asymptotically equivalent to the original maximum pseudo-likelihood estimator.

The first term on the right in (5.12) is just the conditional log likelihood (4.10). The second term can be written as

$$\frac{N}{2} (\hat{Q}^* - Q_0)' \Pi' (\Pi \hat{C} \Pi')^{-1} \Pi (\hat{Q}^* - Q_0),$$ (5.13)

with

$$\hat{Q}_i^* = \frac{1}{N} \sum_{n=1}^{N} p(\mathcal{Y}_i \mid z_n, \theta) / \bar{p}(z_n, \theta),$$ (5.14)

$$\hat{C}_{ij} = \frac{1}{N} \sum_{n=1}^{N} p(\mathcal{Y}_i \mid z_n, \theta) p(\mathcal{Y}_j \mid z_n, \theta) / \bar{p}(z_n, \theta)^2 , \tag{5.15}$$

where $\bar{p}(z, \theta)$ is defined by (4.2) in terms of Q_0, and Π is a $(M-1) \times M$ projection matrix that accounts for the constraint (5.9), such as $\Pi_{ij} = \delta_{ij} - (Q_{0i}/Q_{0M})\delta_{jM}$. The term $(\hat{Q}^* - Q_0)$ can be viewed as the difference between the predicted and actual values of Q at the parameter point θ. The matrix $\hat{C}$ is positive semi-definite, and under suitable regularity and identifiability conditions it is nonsingular with probability approaching one (Cosslett, 1991). The term (5.13) then has an obvious interpretation as the penalty function of a penalized maximum likelihood estimator.

Since the constraint $\hat{Q}^* = Q_0$ does not have to hold exactly, this estimator avoids any potential problem of incompatibility between the sample data and the aggregate shares. The maximization problem can be simplified by evaluating $\hat{C}$ at an initial consistent estimator of θ and then holding it fixed; this does not affect the asymptotic properties of $\hat{\theta}$.

5.5. Generalized method of moments estimators

Imbens (1992) proposes a generalized method of moments (GMM) estimator, using moments that are closely related to the first-order equations of the pseudo-maximum likelihood estimator (see also Imbens and Lancaster, 1991). An attractive feature is that the moment equations have the same form when Q is known as when Q is unknown.

The moments have the following form for multinomial sampling (which is the primary scheme considered by Imbens):

$$\Psi_{1s}(H, \theta, Q) = H(s) - N(s)/N , \tag{5.16}$$

$$\Psi_{2i}(H, \theta, Q) = Q_i - \frac{1}{N} \sum_{n=1}^{N} p(\mathcal{Y}_i \mid z_n, \theta) / \bar{p}_*(z_n, \theta) , \tag{5.17}$$

$$\Psi_3(H, \theta, Q) = \frac{1}{N} \sum_{n=1}^{N} \left(\frac{1}{p(y_n \mid z_n, \theta)} \frac{\partial p(y_n \mid z_n, \theta)}{\partial \theta} \right.$$
$$\left. - \frac{1}{\bar{p}_*(z_n, \theta)} \frac{\partial \bar{p}_*(z_n, \theta)}{\partial \theta} \right) , \tag{5.18}$$

where

$$\bar{p}_*(z, \theta) = \sum_{s=1}^{S} \frac{H(s)}{Q(s)} p(\mathcal{J}(s) \mid z, \theta) \tag{5.19}$$

and $Q(s)$ is expressed in terms of Q_i by (2.7). The parameters are H, θ, and Q, with dimensions $S - 1$, K, and $M - 1$. Note that there has been a (temporary) change of notation: in this system, $H(s)$ is a parameter rather than the observed stratum share, and its true value is the sampling probability $P(s)$. Define the combined moment vector, of dimension $(K + S + M - 2)$, as $\Psi = (\Psi_1', \Psi_2', \Psi_3')'$, and the corresponding parameter vector $\gamma = (H', \theta', Q')'$. At the true parameter values, $E[\Psi] = 0$, so these moments can be used in GMM estimation.

The GMM estimator is obtained by minimizing $\Psi'\Omega\Psi$, with some suitable weight matrix Ω. When Q is unknown, there are as many parameters as moments, so GMM is the same as solving $\Psi = 0$. The first equation is then trivial; the solution of the other moment equations, from (5.17)–(5.18), is the same as the maximum pseudo-likelihood (or CML) estimator from (5.7). (The presence of additional parameters Q_i does not affect the estimators $\hat{\theta}$ or $\hat{Q}(s)$.) The asymptotic variance of γ is $\Gamma^{-1}\Delta\Gamma'^{-1}$, where $\Gamma = E[\partial\Psi/\partial\gamma]$ and $\Delta = E[\Psi\Psi']$.

If the aggregate shares are known, then the parameter Q is fixed at Q_0. But the corresponding moment equation, (5.17), is retained in the GMM system; it is similar to (5.13) in that it attempts to equalize the predicted and actual values of Q. This clearly improves on the CML estimator, which drops the score equation for Q when Q is known. The optimal Ω is any consistent estimator of Δ^{-1}; one could use CML for preliminary consistent estimates of the parameters. Imbens shows that the asymptotic variance of the remaining parameters (H, θ) is then $(\Gamma_1'\Delta\Gamma_1)^{-1}$, where Γ_1 is the submatrix of Γ corresponding to (H, θ).

Imbens and Lancaster (1991) derive an asymptotic efficiency bound which is achieved by the GMM estimator. It is therefore asymptotically equivalent to the maximum pseudo-likelihood estimator and the penalized maximum likelihood estimator in Sections 5.3–5.4.

5.6. The logit model

In the special case where $p(y \mid z, \theta)$ is given by the multinomial logit model (2.1) with a full set of intercept terms (or, more generally, any model of 'multiplicative intercept' form), we have

$$\frac{c_i p(i \mid z, \theta)}{\sum_{j=1}^{M} c_j p(j \mid z, \theta)} = p(i \mid z, \theta^*), \tag{5.20}$$

where θ^* differs from θ only in the intercept terms, $\alpha_i^* = \alpha_i + \log(c_i/c_M)$ (with the normalization $\alpha_M = 0$), for any set of constants $c_1, \ldots, c_M$. The conditional likelihood (4.10) has just this form: it is therefore the same as the likelihood for random sampling, except for a shift in the intercept terms (Manski and McFadden, 1981). The logit model can therefore be estimated as if the sample were random; all parameters are consistently estimated, provided that the estimated intercepts are corrected by

$$\hat{\alpha}_i = \hat{\alpha}_i^* - \log\{(H_i/Q_i)/(H_M/Q_M)\}\ . \tag{5.21}$$

Applying the transformation (5.20) to the pseudo-likelihood (5.8) leads to a drastic simplification: it reduces to the conditional likelihood (4.10). The CML estimator with known Q is therefore asymptotically efficient for the logit model.

The same applies to variable probability sampling with known π and unknown Q: the correction term is $-\log(\pi_i/\pi_M)$. If π is unknown, the intercepts obviously cannot be identified.

If Q is unknown in a standard stratified sample, then not all intercept terms are identified unless the 'overlap' condition (3.12) holds. (The other parameters are still consistently estimated by the maximum likelihood estimator for random sampling.) If identified, the correction terms can easily be computed, see Cosslett (1981a).

6. Other sample designs

In this section, we discuss some miscellaneous topics related to endogenous sampling strategies: additional sample information on the aggregate shares Q; additional sample information on the density of the exogenous variables $h(z)$; estimating a transition rate from simultaneous observations on stocks and flows, which can be considered as a special case of endogenous stratification; and stratification on both endogenous and exogenous variables, including a brief discussion of the case of 'matched' response-based samples.

6.1. Sample information on aggregate shares

Knowledge of the aggregate shares Q can often greatly improve the variance of estimators from an endogenously stratified sample; as we have seen, it is actually necessary for identification in some cases. If the population shares are unknown, they can be estimated from a separate random survey which just determines each individual's response category (but not the exogenous variables z). This strategy was proposed by Lerman and Manski (1975): if the additional data can be collected relatively cheaply, for example, by a telephone survey, then it may be more cost-effective than an increase in the size of the main sample. Lerman and Manski (1975) use the term 'supplementary survey', while Cosslett (1981a) refers to the additional data as an 'auxiliary' sample. Let N and N_0 be the sizes of the main and auxiliary samples; the asymptotic limit is taken with $H_0 = N_0/N$ fixed.

The simplest approach is to estimate Q from the auxiliary sample frequencies, and to substitute this estimator $\tilde{Q}$ for Q in either the WESML or the

CML estimators of Section 4. Hsieh, Manski and McFadden (1985) present the asymptotic variances of $\hat{\theta}$ in these cases.[11]

An efficient estimator can be obtained by concentrating the likelihood with respect to h, as in Section 5. The resulting log pseudo-likelihood (Cosslett, 1981a; see also Hsieh, Manski and McFadden, 1985) can be written in the form

$$
\begin{aligned}
\log \bar{L}(\theta, Q \mid \tilde{Q}) \\
= \sum_{n=1}^{N} \log \frac{p(y_n \mid z_n, \theta)}{1 + \dfrac{1}{H_0} \sum_{s=1}^{S} \dfrac{H(s)}{Q(s)} p(\mathcal{J}(s) \mid z_n, \theta) - \sum_{i=1}^{M} \dfrac{\tilde{Q}_i}{Q_i} p(\mathcal{Y}_i \mid z_n, \theta)} \\
- N \sum_{s=1}^{S} H(s) \log Q(s) + N H_0 \sum_{i=1}^{M} \tilde{Q}_i \log Q_i
\end{aligned} \tag{6.1}
$$

with $Q(s)$ given by (2.7). The parameters are θ and $(Q_1, \ldots, Q_{M-1})$. Let $\hat{Q}(\theta)$ be the solution of the first-order conditions $\partial \log \bar{L}(\theta, Q \mid \tilde{Q})/\partial Q = 0$. (If not unique, it may be best to pick the solution closest to the consistent initial estimator $\tilde{Q}$.) In general, the matrix $\partial^2 \log \bar{L}(\theta, \hat{Q}(\theta) \mid \tilde{Q})/\partial Q \, \partial Q'$ has both positive and negative eigenvalues, so this step cannot be expressed in terms of a maximum or minimum. Then θ is estimated by maximizing the concentrated log likelihood $\log \bar{L}(\theta, \hat{Q}(\theta) \mid \tilde{Q})$, which gives consistent estimators $\hat{\theta}$ and $\hat{Q} = \hat{Q}(\hat{\theta})$. Asymptotic variances are given by Cosslett (1981a) for $\hat{\theta}$ and by Hsieh, Manski and McFadden (1985) for $(\hat{\theta}, \hat{Q})$; the estimator is asymptotically efficient (Cosslett, 1991).

Hsieh, Manski and McFadden call this the 'full information concentrated likelihood estimator' (FICLE). Note that the pseudo-likelihood in (6.1) is not, in fact, the concentrated likelihood (it does not satisfy the 'information matrix' equality). It becomes a concentrated likelihood only after solving for $\hat{Q}(\theta)$.

A simpler (but still efficient) estimator is given by Cosslett (1991), based on the method described in section 5.4. The objective function, to be maximized over θ, is

$$
\begin{aligned}
\log L^*(\theta \mid \tilde{Q}) = \log \bar{L}(\theta, \tilde{Q} \mid \tilde{Q}) \\
- \tfrac{1}{2} N (\hat{Q}^* - \tilde{Q})' \{ \hat{\Gamma} - \hat{\Gamma}(\hat{C}^{-1} + \hat{\Gamma})^{-1} \hat{\Gamma} \} (\hat{Q}^* - \tilde{Q}),
\end{aligned} \tag{6.2}
$$

where $\hat{Q}^*$ and $\hat{C}$ are given by (5.14)–(5.15), and

$$
\hat{\Gamma}_{ij} = \delta_{ij} H_0 / \hat{Q}_i^* - \sum_{s=1}^{S} \eta_{is} \eta_{js} H(s) / [\hat{Q}^*(s)]^2. \tag{6.3}
$$

The first term on the right in (6.2) is just the conditional log likelihood (4.10)

---

[11] In Hsieh, Manski and McFadden (1985), the space $\mathbb{Z}$ is discrete and there are many observations for each value of z. Their estimators of asymptotic variances cannot easily be translated to the case where some components of z are continuous. For another way of estimating from this kind of data, see Section 7.

evaluated at $Q = \tilde{Q}$. If H_0 is not too small, so that the auxiliary sample is more informative about Q than the main sample (see Cosslett, 1991), then the second term is negative definite with probability approaching one, and so (6.2) can be interpreted as a penalized maximum likelihood estimator. (This is just a question of interpretation – the estimator does not depend on the 'penalty' being positive.) The efficient estimator of Q is then

$$\hat{Q} = \tilde{Q} + [I - (\hat{C}^{-1} + \hat{\Gamma})^{-1}\hat{\Gamma}](\hat{Q} - \tilde{Q}), \tag{6.4}$$

with the right-hand side evaluated at $\hat{\theta}$.

6.2. Sample information on the distribution of independent variables

Since the underlying problem with endogenous stratification is the unknown density $h(z)$, additional information on h is clearly useful. While it is unrealistic to suppose that h is known (except when z is discrete), a random sample of observations on z provides an empirical density $\bar{h}$. Cosslett (1981a) refers to this as a 'supplementary sample': an example is the public use sample of the U.S. census. It must contain all the independent variables of the model $p(y \mid z, \theta)$.

A supplementary sample generally allows estimation from sample designs where θ would not otherwise be identified. This applies even to an incomplete endogenously stratified sample: for example, a survey of consumers who bought some specified product. Normally, we could not estimate a choice model unless we also had data on people who did not buy the product. Instead, however, we can use census data on the individual-specific explanatory variables of the model: we do not need to know whether an individual in the census sample actually bought the product or not. In effect, the estimator compares the distribution of z for purchasers with the distribution of z in the population.

The additional data on z can be incorporated directly into the likelihood; there is no need for, say, a kernel estimate of the density h. The pseudo-likelihood is given by Cosslett (1981a) for the case of unknown Q. It is essentially the same as the usual pseudo-likelihood (5.7): the supplementary sample is treated as one more stratum (say, $s = 0$), except that $p(y_n \mid z_n, \theta)$ is replaced by $p(\mathcal{Y}(0) \mid z_n, \theta) \equiv 1$ for observations in the supplementary sample. The asymptotic variance matrix generally remains nonsingular even if a response category is omitted.

Obviously many other cases are possible, combining different kinds of prior information on Q and h: the general principle of replacing h by its NPMLE is probably more useful than a list of pseudo-likelihood functions or penalty functions.

The weighted likelihood approach can be applied also to the case of an incomplete stratified sample plus a random sample on z (Cardell and Steinberg, 1991). Consider estimation of a discrete choice model from a simple stratified sample (i.e., $\mathscr{I}(i) = \mathscr{Y}_i$) with stratum 1 missing; let stratum 0 be the supplementary sample. The original WESML approach, with weights Q_i/H_i, obviously fails because $H_1 = 0$. Cardell and Steinberg propose weighting the nonmissing strata by Q_i/H_i (with $Q_0 = 1$), and artificially assigning the likelihood $p(1|z_n, \theta)$ to observations in the supplementary sample. The expected value of the score is then $E_0[\Sigma_{i=2}^M \partial \log p(1|z, \theta)/\partial\theta]$, which can be corrected by assigning an additional factor $1/p(1|z_n, \theta)$ to the likelihood of every other observation. The weighted log likelihood is then

$$\log \tilde{L}(\theta) = \sum_{n \in \mathscr{N}(0)} \frac{1}{H_0} \log p(1|z_n, \theta) + \sum_{i=2}^M \sum_{n \in \mathscr{N}(i)} \frac{Q_i}{H_i} \log \frac{p(i|z_n, \theta)}{p(1|z_n, \theta)}.$$

$$(6.5)$$

Cardell and Steinberg give the asymptotic variance for $\hat{\theta}$ under multinomial sampling. While not efficient, this estimator can easily be implemented as a WESML estimator (with an appropriate correction of the asymptotic variance): duplicate each of the strata $2, \ldots, M$; then assign weight $-Q_i/H_i$ to the second copy and change its response variable from i to 1.

6.3. Estimating a transition rate from data on stocks and flows

When estimating a transition rate from one state to another (say, from unemployment into employment), we may have to work with a special kind of endogenously stratified sample, consisting of 'stock and flow' data. The stock data would consist of a sample of currently unemployed people, while the flow data would consist of a sample of people who had found work during a specified time period. Econometric work on this type of sample, covering both estimation and sample design, includes Chesher and Lancaster (1983), Lancaster and Imbens (1991), and other papers cited by those authors. Rather than summarize this literature, we give two simple examples to show how stock and flow data can fit into the standard scheme for endogenous stratification. (The examples are simplified in that they refer to a single time period.)

Suppose $\pi_i(z, \theta)$ is the transition rate per unit time from state i to the other state $(i = 1, 2)$, let $h_i(z)$ be the density of z in state i, and let P_i be the proportion of the population in state i, so that $h(z) = P_1 h_1(z) + P_2 h_2(z)$. Usually π_1 and π_2 will contain different parameters.

In the first example, we do not assume stochastic equilibrium, so there is no loss in estimating the rates separately. Let stratum 1 consist of a random sample of individuals in state 1, during some period $\mathscr{T}$ short enough to suppose h_1 does not change. Each observation is a 'snapshot': the data for that individual was gathered in a time short enough to ignore the probability of transition. Let stratum 2 consist of a random sample of individuals who changed from state 1 to state 2 at some time during period $\mathscr{T}$. The underlying 'population' in this case is the population of state 1. Then the likelihoods for observations in the two strata (apart from constants) are $h_1(z_n)$ and

$\pi_1(z_n, \theta)h_1(z_n)/Q_1(\theta)$ respectively, where $Q_1(\theta) = \int d\mu(z)h_1(z)\pi_1(z)$. This has exactly the same form as the likelihood in Section 6.2: a 'supplementary' random sample on the exogenous variables, plus an endogenously stratified sample on stratum 1.

Now suppose we also assume stochastic equilibrium between the two states. In that case the stock data contains more information, because now the composition of each state $h_i(z)$ depends on θ. Let the three strata be: (1) a random sample drawn from state 1 in period $\mathcal{T}$, (2) a similar random sample from state 2, and (3) a random sample of people who changed state in period $\mathcal{T}$ (it does not matter which way they went, because the two transition rates are the same in equilibrium). Then

$$h_1(z, \theta) = \frac{1}{P_1(\theta)} \frac{\pi_2(z, \theta)}{\pi_1(z, \theta) + \pi_2(z, \theta)} h(z) \, ,$$

$$P_1(\theta) = \int d\mu(z) \frac{\pi_2(z, \theta)}{\pi_1(z, \theta) + \pi_2(z, \theta)} h(z) \, , \tag{6.6}$$

$$Q_1(\theta) = \int d\mu(z) \, \pi_1(z, \theta)h_1(z)$$

and similarly for the corresponding quantities in state 2. It follows that the likelihood is the same as that of a discrete-choice model, with 'probabilities'

$$p(1 \mid z, \theta) = \frac{\pi_2(z, \theta)}{\pi_1(z, \theta) + \pi_2(z, \theta)} \, ,$$

$$p(2 \mid z, \theta) = \frac{\pi_1(z, \theta)}{\pi_1(z, \theta) + \pi_2(z, \theta)} \, , \tag{6.7}$$

$$p(3 \mid z, \theta) = \frac{\pi_1(z, \theta)\pi_2(z, \theta)}{\pi_1(z, \theta) + \pi_2(z, \theta)} \, ,$$

exogenous density h, and strata based on the three alternatives. (Note that the 'probabilities' do not sum to 1, so the WESML estimator cannot be used.)

6.4. Stratification on both endogenous and exogenous variables

If a sample is stratified on T exogenous strata, then the stratification can be ignored when estimating a structural model. But if each of those strata is then split into S endogenous strata, we have to work with a total of $T \times S$ endogenous strata: the exogenous stratification can no longer be ignored. The problem is that each exogenous stratum has its own density $h_t(z)$, and in general there is no a priori relationship between them. To deal with the endogenous stratification, each $h_t(z)$ has to be estimated, so the exogenous strata have to be handled separately. Equivalently, the aggregate shares $Q(s)$ are different for each t.

This is closely related to 'matched' stratified sampling. Suppose y is a binary variable. Divide the exogenous variables into two subvectors, z_1 and z_2. Draw a random sample from the stratum with $y = 1$; then, for each observation n, draw one observation from the stratum with $y = 0$ and $z_2 = z_{2n}$. For example, the two endogenous strata could be firms that did or did not go out of business last year, while z_2 is a classification based on size. Or $y = 1$ could be the incidence of some disease, while z_2 classifies individuals by age, gender, and ethnic group. The basic rationale for this approach, assuming that z_1 is the variable of interest, seems to be that the investigator does not trust the model $p(y \mid z, \theta)$ to control adequately for z_2. However, it makes the analysis more complicated. The estimation techniques described above can still be used, but Q_i is replaced by $Q_i(z_2)$.

If z_2 can be considered as a continuous variable, or if it has a very large number of categories, then existing techniques break down. (For a continuous variable, there would have to be a 'near' rather than exact match.) In a logit model, for example, the correction to the intercept would be $\log[Q_1(z_2)/Q_2(z_2)]$, which is generally an unknown *function*. In practice, one could attempt to parameterize this function (on the grounds that the parametric function in the exponent of the logit model is an approximation anyway). But it should be estimated nonparametrically, for example via the method of kernel density estimation. No results are currently available on that approach.

7. Logistic regression

For discrete choice models, logistic regression (Berkson, 1955) is an alternative to maximum likelihood estimation when there are (numerous) repeated observations on each choice setting. This happens if the explanatory variables z are discrete, or if the values of z have been selected in a controlled experiment. Gourieroux and Montfort (1989) have extended Berkson's method to (standard) endogenously stratified samples.

Let $z = z_j$, $j \in \{1, \ldots, J\}$ and, as before, $y = i \in \{1, \ldots, M\}$. Let $p(i \mid j)$ denote $\Pr\{y = i \mid z = z_j\}$. The number of observations with $z = z_j$ and $y = i$ is n_{ji}, and the total number with $z = z_j$ is n_j. The choice probability model can be written as

$$\log \frac{p(i \mid j)}{p(M \mid j)} = g_{ji}(\theta), \quad i = 1, \ldots, M - 1, \tag{7.1}$$

where the $g_{ji}(\theta)$ are parametric functions of θ. The multinomial logit model is the special case $g_{ij}(\theta) = (z_{ij} - z_{Mj})'\theta$, where z_{ij} is a subvector of z_j that characterizes the choice i. However, since there is no restriction on the specification of g (apart from regularity conditions), there is no loss of generality in the logistic representation (7.1). Berkson's method is to estimate the nonlinear regression equation

$$\log \frac{n_{ji}}{n_{jM}} = g_{ji}(\theta) + \varepsilon_{ji}, \quad i = 1, \ldots, M - 1 \tag{7.2}$$

by generalized least squares, using the following consistent estimator of the inverse of the error covariance matrix Ω:

$$\hat{\Omega}^{-1}_{jl,ik} = \delta_{jl}\left(n_{ji}\delta_{ik} - \frac{n_{ji}n_{jk}}{n_j}\right). \tag{7.3}$$

In this notation, the inverse is defined by $\Sigma_{sr}\,\Omega_{js,ir}\Omega^{-1}_{sl,rk} = \delta_{ji}\delta_{ik}$, i.e., each pair of indices behaves like the indices of a matrix. This estimator is consistent and asymptotically efficient under random sampling (or any kind of exogenous stratification).

Under endogenous stratification, Berkson's estimator is not consistent, but, if the population shares Q_i are known, the inconsistency is easily remedied by changing the dependent variable to

$$\log \frac{n_{ji}}{n_{jM}} - \log \frac{H_i Q_M}{Q_i H_M}. \tag{7.4}$$

If Q is unknown, the method does not work unless the regression function g has an 'intercept' term, i.e.,

$$g_{ji}(\theta) = \alpha_i + \tilde{g}_{ji}(\beta), \tag{7.5}$$

where $\theta = (\alpha', \beta')'$ (as in the multinomial logit model with alternative-specific dummy variables). Then, as with the MLE, $\hat{\beta}$ is consistent. The intercept $\hat{\alpha}_i$ has asymptotic bias $\log(H_i Q_M / Q_i H_M)$, and evidently cannot be estimated unless Q is known.

However, (7.3) is no longer correct. The original version of the Berkson estimator is not efficient, and the asymptotic variance of $\hat{\theta}$ is not consistently estimated. Gourieroux and Montfort (1989) derive the error covariance matrix under endogenous stratification, and propose GLS estimation with the matrix. In fact, an explicit expression can be derived for the inverse of the new covariance matrix Ω^*. A consistent estimator of $(\Omega^*)^{-1}$ is

$$(\hat{\Omega}^*)^{-1} = \hat{\Omega}^{-1} + \hat{\Omega}^{-1}\mathscr{I}[\Omega_0^{-1} - \mathscr{I}'\hat{\Omega}^{-1}\mathscr{I}]^{-1}\mathscr{I}'\hat{\Omega}^{-1}, \tag{7.6}$$

where $\hat{\Omega}^{-1}$ is given by (7.3), and

$$\Omega_{0,ik}^{-1} = H_i\delta_{ik} - H_i H_k,$$
$$\mathscr{I}_{j,ik} = \delta_{ik}.$$

(Ω_0^{-1} has dimensions $(1 \times 1) \times (M \times M)$ and $\mathscr{I}$ has dimensions $(J \times 1) \times (M \times M)$.)

The asymptotic variance of $\hat{\theta}$ is $\text{plim}(N^{-1}(\partial g'/\partial\theta)(\Omega^*)^{-1}(\partial g/\partial\theta'))^{-1}$, which turns out to be the same as the asymptotic efficiency bound for the case of known Q (see Imbens and Lancaster, 1991, and Cosslett, 1991). Note that the only place where Q is used is in (7.4), where it is used to weight the cell counts n_{ji} to correct the sampling bias.

This must still work if we specialize to random sampling. If Q is known, the asymptotic efficiency of the original Berkson estimator can be improved (to the bound for known Q) by using (7.4) as the dependent variable.

8. Regression models with unknown error distribution

A semiparametric model for $p(y \mid z, \theta)$ contains an unknown distribution function (typically, the distribution of an 'error' term) as well as the finite-dimensional parameter vector θ, and so the endogenous stratification problem will now involve two unknown distributions. This section and the next discuss two important examples: regression models and semiparametric discrete-choice models. While most previous work takes the regression function to be linear, there is no essential problem in generalizing to nonlinear regression.[12]

Let $g(z, \theta) = \mathrm{E}(y \mid z, \theta)$ and $u = y - g(z, \theta)$. Suppose $g(z, \theta)$ is a parametric regression function of known form, but u may have an unknown probability density function f. Several authors have investigated the problem of con-sistently estimating θ from endogenously stratified samples. Holt, Smith and Winter (1980) and Nathan and Holt (1980) discuss the case of a linear model where the sampling probability depends on z, a vector of stratifying variables correlated with y. Much of that work is about a maximum likelihood estimator, based on work by Anderson (1957) and DeMets and Halperin (1977); it requires x, y, and z to be jointly normally distributed, which limits its usefulness in econometric applications. However, they also investigate the probability weighted least squares estimator, which does not depend on normality and is discussed next. Improved weighted least squares estimators using an iterative method, are presented by Jewell (1985). Hausman and Wise (1981) estimate a linear model from a variable probability sample with strata defined by intervals of y. They assume normality for the error term u (only) and proceed by maximum likelihood: their estimator is the CML method applied to the normal linear model.

8.1. Weighted least squares

Suppose each observation (y, z) in a variable probability sample is assigned

---

[12] For conditions under which nonlinear least squares estimation is consistent, see Burguette, Gallant and Souza (1982) or Gallant (1987).

weight $w(i, z)$, where $y \in \mathcal{Y}_i$. Then the conditional expectation of wu is

$$E[wu \,|\, z] = \sum_{i=1}^{M} \pi_i w(i, z) \frac{1}{\bar{p}(z, \theta)} \int du \, uf(u)I[u + g(z, \theta) \in \mathcal{Y}_i], \quad (8.1)$$

where

$$\bar{p}(z, \theta) = \sum_{i=1}^{M} \pi_i p(\mathcal{Y}_i \,|\, z, \theta) = \sum_{i=1}^{M} \pi_i \int du \, f(u)I[u + g(z, \theta) \in \mathcal{Y}_i]. \quad (8.2)$$

If the weights have the form

$$w(i, z) = w^*(z)/\pi_i, \quad (8.3)$$

then $E[wu \,|\, z] = 0$, so the weighted least squares estimator of θ is consistent (under conventional regularity conditions). The variance of $\hat{\theta}_{\text{WLS}}$ can be consistently estimated from the residuals $\hat{u}_n$ in the usual way:

$$\hat{V}(\hat{\theta}) = \left(\sum_{n=1}^{N} w_n \frac{\partial g_n}{\partial \theta} \frac{\partial g_n}{\partial \theta'} \right)^{-1} \sum_{n=1}^{N} \hat{u}_n^2 w_n^2 \frac{\partial g_n}{\partial \theta} \frac{\partial g_n}{\partial \theta'} \left(\sum_{n=1}^{N} w_n \frac{\partial g_n}{\partial \theta} \frac{\partial g_n}{\partial \theta'} \right)^{-1}, \quad (8.4)$$

where $w_n = w(i_n, z_n)$ and $g_n = g(z_n, \theta)$. Any heteroskedasticity or serial correlation of the errors u can be taken into account at the same time by standard techniques.

A similar result holds for *standard stratified sampling*, with known population shares $Q_i, i = 1, \ldots, M$. Because we condition on the observed sample shares H_i, the weights have the form $w(i, z) = w^*(z)Q_i/H_i$. The middle term on the right-hand side of (8.4) becomes the sum of the variations of $\hat{u}_n w_n \cdot \partial g_n/\partial \theta$ in each substratum instead of the sum of squares.

The WLS method cannot be used for a standard stratified sample with unknown population shares Q.

The basic estimator uses the 'probability weights' $1/\pi_i$ or Q_i/H_i, which do not depend on z, i.e., $w^*(z) = 1$. Consistency of this form of the WLS estimator is shown by Nathan and Holt (1980) under fairly weak conditions. These weights have been used extensively in least squares estimation from stratified samples, whether endogenously or exogenously stratified. In applications where the regression coefficients are viewed as descriptive statistics of the population, rather than as parameters of a structural model, this is the best thing to do. But if the regression model is correctly specified, the use of these weights with *exogenously* stratified samples is a mistake: unweighted least squares is, of course, more efficient.

8.2. Estimation of the error distribution

More efficient WLS estimation requires initial consistent estimators of θ and F. The basic probability-weighted regression provides the estimator $\tilde{\theta}$. The NPMLE of F is complicated, however, and appears to be computationally intractable for large samples: it involves solving a set of nonlinear equations in which the number of equations is of the same order as the sample size (see Vardi, 1985). Jewell (1985) suggests another estimator of F, based on the NPMLE of the joint density of y and z but without taking into account the underlying structure $p(y, z) = f(y - g(z, \theta))h(z)$. Let $\hat{f}$ be the resulting marginal density of $\tilde{u}$, where $\tilde{u} = y - g(z, \hat{\theta})$. It has the form

$$\hat{f}(u) = \sum_{n=1}^{N} \delta(u - \tilde{u}_n)v_n ,$$ (8.5)

where $\tilde{u}_n = y_n - g(z_n, \hat{\theta})$. For random sampling, $v_n = 1/N$. For a variable probability sample,

$$v_n = \sum_{i=1}^{M} I(y_n \in \mathcal{Y}_i) \frac{1}{\pi_i} \left(\sum_{i=1}^{M} \frac{N_i}{\pi_i} \right)^{-1}.$$ (8.6)

This also holds for a standard stratified sample, but with $1/\pi_i$ replaced by Q_i/H_i; the sum in the denominator then disappears (because it is unity).

8.3. Improved WLS

Jewell (1985) proposes WLS estimation with $w^*(z) = \bar{p}(z, \theta)$, defined by (8.2). This is intuitively appealing because then $g(z, \theta)$ is the regression function of the weighted dependent variable wy (although, as we shall see next, this is not the optimal choice of w^*). Of course $\bar{p}$ is unknown, but it can be estimated consistently by

$$\hat{\bar{p}}(z, \hat{\theta}) = \sum_{i=1}^{M} \pi_i \sum_{n=1}^{N} v_n I[\tilde{u}_n + g(z, \hat{\theta}) \in \mathcal{Y}_i].$$ (8.7)

Jewell (1985) iterates this procedure, at each step using the WLS estimate of θ from the previous step. An accompanying Monte Carlo study, using a model with normal errors and variable probability sampling, finds that (i) this estimator is very nearly as efficient as the maximum likelihood estimator of Hausman and Wise (1981), and (ii) using the NPMLE of F to construct the weights, instead of the simpler estimator given by (8.5)–(8.6), yielded little or no improvement in the WLS estimator.

Under suitable regularity conditions, $\hat{\bar{p}}(z, \theta)$ converges in probability to $\bar{p}(z, \theta)$ uniformly in z and θ. In that case, as in conventional two-step generalized least-squares estimation, the asymptotic distribution of $\hat{\theta}$ would be the same as if $\bar{p}(z, \theta_0)$ had been used in the weights. In particular, there would be no gain in asymptotic efficiency from iteration, nor from a more efficient estimator of F.

8.4. Instrumental variables

The first-order conditions for consistent WLS estimation suggest the following moment condition for $\hat{\theta}$:

$$\sum_{n=1}^{N} W(z_n, \bar{\theta}) \sum_{i=1}^{M} \frac{1}{\pi_i} I(y_n \in \mathcal{Y}_i)(y_n - g(z_n, \hat{\theta})) = 0 , \tag{8.8}$$

where W is a k-dimensional vector of instruments and $\bar{\theta}$ is a preliminary consistent estimator of θ. We can then look for the optimal W. In the case of variable probability sampling, it is

$$W(z, \theta) = \frac{1}{\bar{\sigma}^2(z, \theta)} \frac{\partial g(z, \theta)}{\partial \theta} , \tag{8.9}$$

where

$$\bar{\sigma}^2(z, \theta) = \sum_{i=1}^{M} \frac{1}{\pi_i} \int du \, u^2 f(u) I[u + g(z, \theta) \in \mathcal{Y}_i] . \tag{8.10}$$

The asymptotic variance matrix of $\hat{\theta}$ is the inverse of $E_0[(\partial g/\partial\theta)(\partial g/\partial\theta')\bar{\sigma}^{-2}]$. The term $\bar{\sigma}^2$ is consistently estimated by substituting $\theta = \bar{\theta}$ and $f = \hat{f}$, as given by (8.5)–(8.6).

Apart from the fact that $\partial g/\partial\theta$ is evaluated at $\bar{\theta}$ instead of at $\hat{\theta}$, which makes no difference asymptotically, (8.9) corresponds to a WLS estimator with $w^*(z) = 1/\bar{\sigma}^2(z, \theta)$. This is the result of Gourieroux (1991) for weighted M-estimation from a variable-probability sample. It also shows that the WLS estimator with $w^*(z) = \bar{p}(z, \theta)$, discussed in the previous subsection, is not optimal.

An analogous result can be found for standard stratified sampling: the optimal choice of W is

$$W(z, \theta) = \frac{1}{\bar{\sigma}^2(z, \theta)} \left\{ \frac{\partial g(z, \theta)}{\partial \theta} + E_0\left[\frac{1}{\bar{\sigma}^2(Z, \theta)} \frac{\partial g(Z, \theta)}{\partial \theta} \mu'(Z, \theta) \right] \right.$$
$$\left. \cdot \left(H - E_0\left[\frac{\mu(Z, \theta)\mu'(Z, \theta)}{\bar{\sigma}^2(Z, \theta)} \right] \right)^{-1} \mu(z, \theta) \right\} , \tag{8.12}$$

where H is the diagonal matrix with elements H_i and $\mu(z, \theta)$ is an M-dimensional vector with components

$$\mu_i(z, \theta) = \int du \, u f(u) I[u + g(z, \theta) \in \mathcal{Y}_i] , \tag{8.13}$$

which can be consistently estimated by substituting $\bar{\theta}$ and $\hat{f}$ (with $1/\pi_i$ again replaced by Q_i/H_i). The asymptotic variance matrix of $\hat{\theta}$ is now the inverse of

$$\mathrm{E}_0\!\left[\frac{\partial g}{\partial \theta}\frac{\partial g}{\partial \theta'}\,\bar{\sigma}^{-2}\right]$$

$$+\,\mathrm{E}_0\!\left[\frac{\partial g}{\partial \theta}\,\mu'\bar{\sigma}^{-2}\right]\!(\boldsymbol{H}-\mathrm{E}_0[\mu\mu'\bar{\sigma}^{-2}])^{-1}\mathrm{E}_0\!\left[\mu\,\frac{\partial g}{\partial \theta'}\,\bar{\sigma}^{-2}\right].$$

In this case, the estimator is not a WLS estimator because W is not proportional to $\partial g/\partial \theta$.

8.5. Bias-corrected regression function

The preceding estimators are based on the strategy used by WESML: re-weight inconsistent moment equations. An alternative strategy is suggested by the CML estimator: make the moment equations for random sampling consistent by subtracting the conditional means. This corresponds to adding the correction term $\bar{p}^{-1}\Sigma_i\,\pi_i\mu_i$ to the regression function (or $\bar{p}^{-1}\Sigma_i\,(Q_i/H_i)\mu_i$, in the case of standard stratified sampling), where $\bar{p}$ and μ are defined by (8.2) and (8.13). As yet, there has been no attempt to apply this method.

8.6. Asymptotic variance bounds

Asymptotic variance bounds for the linear regression model with i.i.d. errors and unknown error distribution are given by Cosslett (1985) (see also Bickel et al., 1993). The extension to nonlinear regression is straightforward. The bounds apply to standard endogenous stratification with two strata, and are given for Q unknown and for Q known.

These bounds are different from the corresponding lower bounds that apply when the error distribution is known (and which are attained by the likelihood-based estimators of Section 5), except for the special case of proportional sampling ($H_i = Q_i$). This means that adaptive estimation is not possible from this kind of stratified sample: unlike the case of random sampling (see Bickel, 1982, and Manski, 1984), lack of knowledge of the error distribution F necessarily leads to a less efficient estimator of θ.

It is intuitively clear that none of the estimators discussed above can achieve the efficiency bound: in the case of proportional sampling they are all equivalent to ordinary least squares, which is not asymptotically efficient except in the special case of normally distributed errors. The most promising approach to efficiency is that developed for adaptive estimation by Bickel (1982): first, construct a differentiable estimator of the density f by replacing the δ-functions in (8.5) with differentiable kernels; substitute this $\hat{f}$ into the appropriate log pseudo-likelihood from Section 5; and then estimate θ by carrying out one Newton–Raphson iteration starting from the initial consistent estimator $\tilde{\theta}$.

9. Semiparametric models of discrete choice

Econometric models of discrete response, where $y \equiv i \in \{1, \ldots, M\}$, are often based on an underlying model of optimization over a set of latent random variables (see, for example, McFadden, 1984). Let

$$U_j = g_j(z, \theta) + \varepsilon_j , \quad j = 1, \ldots, M ,$$

where g is a specified parametric function, θ is the parameter vector to be estimated, z is a vector of exogenous variables, and the random variables ε have a joint probability density function f (which may depend on additional unknown parameters and on z). According to the model, i is the index of the largest of these latent variables, i.e., $U_i = \max_j \{U_j\}$. Then

$$p(i \mid z, \theta) = \Pr\{U_i > U_j \text{ for all } j = 1, \ldots, M, \ j \neq i\} ,$$

is a parametric function determined by g and f.

In a semiparametric discrete-choice model, a functional form is specified for g but not for f. The only assumption about f is that it satisfies some set of regularity conditions. Estimation from endogenously stratified samples is then a semiparametric problem involving two unknown density functions: the density f of the underlying random variables ε, and the density h of the independent variables z. A general strategy is to take one of the techniques in Section 4 and 5 for eliminating h, and apply it to an existing semiparametric estimation method that works for random samples.

Most of the research on semiparametric discrete-choice models has been focussed on binary choice models $(M = 2)$. In that case,

$$p(1 \mid z, \theta, F) = 1 - F[-g(z, \theta)] , \tag{9.1}$$

where $g = g_1 - g_2$ is a known parametric function and F is the unknown cumulative distribution function of $\varepsilon_1 - \varepsilon_2$. This is a special case of the 'single-index' model, where F can be a more general transformation of g.

A number of semiparametric estimators have been proposed for models of this kind.[13] We discuss three estimators, which were developed specifically for binary choice: the maximum score estimator (Manski, 1975, 1985), which was extended to response-based sampling in Manski (1986); and two likelihood-based methods, one using nonparametric maximum likelihood to estimate F (Cosslett, 1983), and the other using a kernel density estimation method (Klein and Spady, 1993). The general conclusion, at least for binary choice, is that semiparametric estimators are affected very little by endogenous stratification.

---

[13] Other semiparametric estimators that could be used include the index-model estimators of Ichimura (1986) and Powell, Stock and Stoker (1989), and the maximum rank correlation estimator of Han (1987).

9.1. Maximum score estimator

This is consistent under very weak conditions: $F(0)$ is fixed at some value $\alpha \in (0, 1)$, but otherwise F can depend quite generally on z. For example, any form of heteroskedasticity is allowed. (See Manski, 1985, for some additional, more technical, regularity conditions.) The trade-off is a slower rate of convergence, $N^{-1/3}$ instead of $N^{-1/2}$. We temporarily adopt the conventional notation for the maximum score estimator: $y = \text{sgn}(y^*)$, where y^* is an underlying latent variable, so the range of y is now $\{-1, 1\}$ instead of $\{1, 2\}$. The index function is assumed to be linear, $g(z, \theta) = z'\theta$, with normalization $\|\theta\| = 1$. The condition on $F(0)$ can then be restated: the α-quantile of y^* is $z'\theta$.

Under random sampling, maximization of the score function

$$S_\alpha(\theta) = \frac{1}{N} \sum_{n=1}^{N} [y_n - (1 - 2\alpha)] \, \text{sgn}(z_n'\theta) , \tag{9.2}$$

with respect to θ gives a consistent estimator. The usual case is $\alpha = \frac{1}{2}$, so that the median of F is zero.

Now suppose we have a standard stratified sample, with $\mathcal{Y}_1 = \{1\}$, $\mathcal{Y}_2 = \{-1\}$, and known Q. Manski (1986) investigates two methods: (i) a weighting scheme analogous to WESML estimation (Section 4.2), and (ii) a modified score function based on the distribution of y conditional on z, which is analogous to the CML estimator (Section 4.5). In the first estimator, each observation in stratum i is assigned the weight factor Q_i/H_i, i.e., the ratio of the population share to the sample share for that stratum. This gives the weighted score function

$$W_\alpha(\theta) = \frac{1}{N} \sum_{n=1}^{N} \left(I(y_n = 1) \frac{Q_1}{H_1} + I(y_n = -1) \frac{Q_2}{H_2} \right)$$
$$\times [y_n - (1 - 2\alpha)] \, \text{sgn}(z_n'\theta) . \tag{9.3}$$

As before, $\hat{\theta}$ is obtained by maximization over θ; the proof of consistency follows along the same lines as for random sampling.

If the two subsamples are combined, and an observation is randomly drawn from the pooled sample, then the distribution of y conditional on z is

$$\Pr\{y = 1 \mid z\} = \frac{H_1}{Q_1} [1 - F(-z'\theta)] \left(\frac{H_1}{Q_1} [1 - F(-z'\theta)] + \frac{H_2}{Q_2} F(-z'\theta) \right)^{-1}$$
$$\equiv 1 - F^*(-z'\theta) . \tag{9.4}$$

In effect, this is a new binary choice model with F replaced by F^*. From (9.4), $F^*(0) = \gamma$, where

$$\gamma = \alpha \frac{Q_1}{H_1} \left(\alpha \frac{Q_1}{H_1} + (1 - \alpha) \frac{Q_2}{H_2} \right)^{-1} , \tag{9.5}$$

which does not depend on z. This suggests another estimator: maximize $S_\gamma(\theta)$ over θ. However, as pointed out by Manski (1986), the functions $W(\theta)$ and $S_\gamma(\theta)$ differ only by a constant factor. Thus the analogues of the WESML and CML methods turn out to be the same when applied to Manski's score.

If Q is unknown, then θ cannot be estimated without further assumptions. Suppose that (i) the distribution F is independent of z, and (ii) the regression function contains a constant term, i.e., $z'\theta = \beta_0 + \bar{z}'\beta$. The model is then invariant under the following transformation: increase the constant term by c and replace F by $\bar{F}$ where $\bar{F}(\varepsilon) = F(\varepsilon + c)$. The new α is then $\bar{\alpha} = F(c)$. This shows that, under the additional assumptions, the maximum score estimator with misspecified α is still consistent for the slope parameters β (but not, of course, for the constant term β_0). The same argument holds when the sample is response-based: maximization of $S_\gamma(\theta)$ with misspecified γ is still consistent for β, and therefore we do not need to know Q. The actual choice of γ to be used in estimation is arbitrary; Manski suggests $\gamma = H_1$.

Under the independence assumption, knowledge of Q does not help in estimating the slope parameters, but it allows consistent estimation of the intercept term. Note, however, that once independence has been assumed, only a little strengthening of the regularity conditions on F (including differentiability of its density f) would permit estimators with a better rate of convergence.

9.2. Semiparametric maximum likelihood estimation

For likelihood-based estimation methods, we must assume that the distribution F is independent of z. We also need conditions to ensure that F and g are separately identified: the usual convention is to let F be unrestricted, but to restrict the parameters θ so that there is no monotonic transformation that leaves the functional form g invariant (see, for example, Cosslett, 1983). If g is linear, this means normalizing the constant term and a scale parameter. This is different from the parametric case, where the convention is to standardize F.

The log likelihood for the binary choice model under random sampling is

$$\log L(\theta, F) = \sum_{n=1}^{N} \{I(y_n = 1) \log[1 - F(-g_n)] + I(y_n = 2) \log F(-g_n)\}\,,$$

$$(9.6)$$

where $g_n \equiv g(z_n, \theta)$. For fixed θ, let $\hat{F}(v \mid \theta)$ be a consistent estimator of $1 - \Pr\{y = 1 \mid -g(z, \theta) = v\}$. Maximizing $\log L(\theta, \hat{F}(\cdot \mid \theta))$ over θ then gives estimators $\hat{\theta}$ and $\hat{F} = \hat{F}(\cdot \mid \hat{\theta})$. If $\hat{F}(\cdot \mid \theta)$ converges fast enough (see Severini and Wong, 1987), and if suitable regularity conditions hold, then $\hat{\theta}$ and $\hat{F}$ are consistent semiparametric estimators. (The consistency of $\hat{F}$ is pointwise.)

Endogenous stratification just requires duplication of the first step, in principle: first h (the density of z) is estimated by a nonparametric method and eliminated from the objective function; then the same is done for F.

Consider a weighted probability sample with $\mathcal{Y}_i = \{i\}$ and sampling weights π_i $(i = 1, 2)$. The NPMLE of h is the same for any likelihood-based estimator, F known or not, so the concentrated log likelihood is still given by (5.1) as

$$\log L_0(\theta, F) = \sum_{n=1}^{N} \{I(y_n = 1) \log[1 - F^*(-g_n)]$$
$$+ I(y_n = 2) \log F^*(-g_n)\} , \qquad (9.7)$$

where

$$F^*(v) = \pi_2 F(v)(\pi_1[1 - F(v)] + \pi_2 F(v))^{-1} . \qquad (9.8)$$

This implies that F^* is a distribution function, provided that the sampling weights π are strictly positive, but, as long as F is unknown, imposes no further restrictions. Evidently (9.6) and (9.7) are indistinguishable: one unknown distribution function (F) has been replaced by another (F^*). Consequently, under our convention for the normalization of g, a likelihood-based semiparametric estimator that works for random sampling can be used without modification when the sample is choice-based.

For standard stratified sampling on strata $\{1\}$ and $\{2\}$, the result (9.7)–(9.8) still holds, with π_i replaced by H_i/Q_i. In this case, however, the NPMLE of h has to satisfy $Q(s) = \int d\mu(z) h(z) p(\mathcal{I}(s) | z, \theta)$ (if Q is unknown) or $Q_i = \int d\mu(z) h(z) p(\mathcal{Y}_i | z, \theta)$ (if Q is known), which imposes a restriction on F^*:

$$\frac{1}{N} \sum_{n=1}^{N} [1 - F^*(-g_n)] = H_1 . \qquad (9.9)$$

Although a consistent estimator of F^* satisfies (9.9) in the probability limit, the restriction may not hold exactly, in which case $\hat{F}^*$ has to be adjusted.

Knowledge of the sampling weights π (in variable probability sampling) or the population shares Q (in standard stratified sampling) has no effect on estimation of θ. If π (or Q) is unknown, it cannot be estimated, which is not surprising because there is a simple parametric example (the logit model with an intercept term) in which π (or Q) is not identified. If π is known, a consistent estimator of F can be recovered by inverting (9.8),

$$\hat{F}(v) = \pi_2^{-1} \hat{F}^*(v)(\pi_1^{-1}[1 - \hat{F}^*(v)] + \pi_2^{-1} \hat{F}^*(v))^{-1} . \qquad (9.10)$$

A similar equation, with π_i replaced by H_i/Q_i, holds for standard stratified sampling with known Q. Although the parameter estimate $\hat{\theta}$ is unchanged, we recall that our normalization converted a location parameter of g (the intercept term, if there was one) into a corresponding location statistic of F (for example, the median); evidently this can be estimated from (9.10), but only if π or Q is known.

One method of estimating the unknown distribution function F from a random sample is NPML. A description of the algorithm, together with additional references, is given by Cosslett (1983). The resulting estimator

$\hat{F}(\cdot \mid \theta)$ is a step function. The discussion above shows that the estimator is still consistent when applied to choice-based samples. Condition (9.9), which should hold in standard stratified sampling, is not exact in finite samples when F^* is estimated by NPML; if the adjustment is small, however, a correction term $\delta \cdot \hat{F}^*(1 - \hat{F}^*)$ can be added to the unrestricted NPMLE of F^*, where δ is a constant that makes the adjusted estimate satisfy (9.9).

Although the maximum likelihood principle is attractive, the asymptotic properties of the semiparametric maximum likelihood estimator are difficult to analyze. Because of this, alternative estimators of F have been proposed, which are 'smoother' than the NPMLE.

9.3. Klein–Spady estimator

This is also based on the log likelihood (9.6), but uses a different estimator $\hat{F}(\cdot \mid \theta)$, based on the kernel method of density estimation. Let $p(\cdot, \cdot)$ be the joint density of y and $-g(z, \theta)$. For random sampling,

$$1 - F(v) = \Pr(y = 1 \mid -g(z, \theta) = v) = \frac{p(1, v)}{p(1, v) + p(2, v)} . \tag{9.11}$$

The density $p(i, v)$ is estimated from the subsample with $y = i$:

$$\hat{p}(i, v) = \frac{1}{N} \sum_{n=1}^{N} I(y_n = i) \frac{1}{b_N} K\left(\frac{v - v_n}{b_N}\right), \tag{9.12}$$

where $v_n = -g(z_n, \theta)$. (See Klein and Spady, 1993, for regularity conditions and for the rate of convergence of the bandwidth b_N.) The symmetric kernel K satisfies $\int du\, K(u) = 1$, $\int du\, u^i K(u) = 0$, $i = 1, 2, 3$ and $\int du\, u^4 K(u) < \infty$. A nonpositive kernel of this type allows the bias of $\hat{p}$ to converge at the rate $O(b_N^{-4})$, which is fast enough for asymptotic normality and efficiency of $\hat{\theta}$, but it introduces complications in the need to suppress any negative density estimates: a lower bound $c_N > 0$ has to be imposed on (9.11).

As noted by Klein and Spady (1993), this approach can be extended to multiple-choice models. The index function g and the kernel K are then $(M - 1)$-dimensional (see also Lee, 1989).

What we just found for likelihood-based semiparametric estimation must apply here too: the estimator can be applied to binary choice-based samples without modification. It may be useful, however, to see how it works in a more general setting. For a general discrete-choice model and a variable probability sample with $\mathcal{Y}_i = \{i\}$, the concentrated likelihood (with respect to h) is (5.2). That is the same as the likelihood for y conditional on $g(z, \theta)$. We can use (9.12) (with the dimension of the kernel increased to $M - 1$, if necessary) to estimate the joint density of y and $g(z, \theta)$ in the sample:

$$\hat{p}(i, v_n) \rightarrow \frac{H_i}{Q_i} p(i \mid z_n, \theta) h^*(v_n), \tag{9.13}$$

where h^* is the marginal density of $-g(z, \theta)$. (Lower bounds on the estimated densities are not shown explicitly.) The concentrated likelihood for observation n, which is the density of y_n conditional on $g(z_n, \theta)$, can therefore be estimated by $\hat{p}(i_n, v_n)/\Sigma_i \hat{p}(i, v_n)$. Viewed in this way, the Klein–Spady estimator is intrinsically choice-based; it works also for random sampling because a random sample can be split into choice-based subsamples.

For standard choice-based sampling, there are also constraints of the form (9.9). These can be handled as they were for parametric choice probabilities: assign weights $\xi(s)$ to the strata, and maximize

$$\bar{L}(\theta, \xi) = \sum_{n=1}^{N} \log \frac{\xi(s_n)\hat{p}(i_n, v_n)}{\sum_{s=1}^{S} \xi(s) \sum_{i=1}^{M} \eta_{is}\hat{p}(i, v_n)} \tag{9.14}$$

over θ and ξ, subject to some normalization of ξ (for example, $\xi(1) = 1$). In terms of the parameters Q in (5.7), the new stratum weights are $\xi(s) = Q_0(s)/Q(s)$. Under conditions sufficient for consistency of the Klein–Spady estimator of θ, it follows that plim $\hat{\xi}(s) = 1$. This suggests eliminating ξ by the method of Section 5.4.

9.4. Asymptotic variance bounds

An asymptotic variance bound for the semiparametric binary choice model under standard endogenous stratification is given by Cosslett (1985) (see also Bickel et al., 1993). If $\hat{\theta}$ is a regular consistent estimator of θ, then a lower bound on its asymptotic variance is the inverse of the matrix

$$I^* = \frac{H_1 H_2}{Q_1 Q_2} \int dv \, h^*(v) \frac{[f(v)]^2}{\bar{F}(v)F(v)[1 - F(v)]} \, \text{var}\left[\left. \frac{\partial g}{\partial \theta} \right| - g(z, \theta) = v \right], \tag{9.15}$$

where $\bar{F}$ is defined by

$$\bar{F}(u) = \frac{H_1}{Q_1} [1 - F(u)] + \frac{H_2}{Q_2} F(u) . \tag{9.16}$$

The bound is the same whether Q is known or not, so knowledge of Q contains no information about θ (assuming that the bound is attainable). The bound also has the same form for variable probability sampling, with H_i/Q_i replaced by π_i. At present, the only estimator known to attain the bound is the Klein–Spady estimator for random sampling.

References

Amemiya, T. (1985). *Advanced Econometrics*. Harvard Univ. Press, Cambridge, MA.
Amemiya, T. and Q. Vuong (1987). A comparison of two consistent estimators in the choice based sampling qualitative response model. *Econometrica* **55**, 699–702.

Anderson, T. W. (1957). Maximum likelihood estimates for a multivariate normal distribution when some observations are missing. *J. Amer. Statist. Assoc.* **52**, 200–203.

Begun, J. M., W. J. Hall, W.-M. Huang and J. A. Wellner (1983). Information and asymptotic efficiency in parametric–nonparametric models. *Ann. Statist.* **11**, 432–452.

Berkson, J. (1955). Maximum likelihood and minimum χ^2 estimates of the logistic functions. *J. Amer. Statist. Assoc.* **50**, 930–962.

Bickel, P. (1982). On adaptive estimation. *Ann. Statist.* **10**, 647–671.

Bickel, P., C. A. J. Klaasen, Y. Ritov and J. A. Wellner (1993). *Efficient and Adaptive Inference in Semiparametric Models.* To appear.

Burguette, J. F., A. R. Gallant and G. Souza (1982). On the unification of the asymptotic theory of nonlinear models. *Econometric Rev.* **1**, 151–190.

Cardell, N. S. and D. Steinberg (1991). Estimating quantal choice models from pooled choice-based and supplementary random samples. Working Paper, Department of Economics, San Diego State University, San Diego, CA.

Chesher, A. D. and T. Lancaster (1983). The estimation of models of labour market behaviour. *Rev. Econ. Stud.* **50**, 609–624.

Cosslett, S. R. (1981a). Efficient estimation of discrete-choice models: In C. F. Manski and D. McFadden, eds., *Structural Analysis of Discrete Data with Econometric Applications.* MIT Press, Cambridge, MA.

Cosslett, S. R. (1981b). Maximum likelihood estimators for choice-based samples. *Econometrica* **49**, 1289–1316.

Cosslett, S. R. (1983). Distribution-free maximum likelihood estimator of the binary choice model. *Econometrica* **51**, 765–782.

Cosslett, S. R. (1985). Efficiency bounds for distribution-free estimators from endogenously stratified samples: Summary of results. Working Paper, Department of Economics, University of Florida, Gainesville, FL.

Cosslett, S. R. (1991). Efficient estimation from endogenously stratified samples with prior information on marginal probabilities. Working Paper, Department of Economics, Ohio State University, Columbus, OH.

Cox, D. R. and D. V. Hinkley (1974). *Theoretical Statistics.* Chapman and Hall, London.

DeMets, D. and M. Halperin (1977). Estimation of a simple regression coefficient in samples arising from a sub-sampling procedure. *Biometrika* **33**, 47–56.

Gallant, A. R. (1987). *Nonlinear Statistical Models.* Wiley, New York.

Gill, R. D., Y. Vardi and J. A. Wellner (1988). Large sample theory of empirical distributions in biased sampling models. *Ann. Statist.* **16**, 1069–1112.

Gourieroux, C. (1991). M-estimateurs pondérés ou comment corriger des biais de sondage. Working Paper 9111, Centre de Recherche en Economie et Statistique, Institut National de la Statistique et des Etudes Economiques, Paris.

Gourieroux, C. and A. Monfort (1989). Econometrics based on endogenous samples. Working Paper 8903, Ecole Nationale de la Statistique et de l'Administration Economique, Institute National de la Statistique et des Etudes Economiques, Paris.

Gourieroux, C., A. Monfort and A. Trognon (1984). Pseudo maximum likelihood methods: Theory. *Econometrica* **52**, 681–700.

Han, A. (1987). Nonparametric analysis of a generalized regression model: The maximum rank correlation estimator. *J. Econometrics* **35**, 303–316.

Hausman, J. A. and D. A. Wise (1977). Social experimentation, truncated distributions, and efficient estimation. *Econometrica* **45**, 919–938.

Hausman, J. A. and D. A. Wise (1981). Stratification on endogenous variables and estimation: The Gary income maintenance experiment. In: C. F. Manski and D. McFadden, eds., *Structural Analysis of Discrete Data with Econometric Applications.* MIT Press, Cambridge, MA.

Holt, D., T. M. F. Smith and P. D. Winter (1980). Regression analysis of data from complex surveys. *J. Roy. Statist. Soc. Ser. A* **143**, 474–487.

Hsieh, D., C. Manski and D. McFadden (1985). Estimation of response probabilities from augmented retrospective observations. *J. Amer. Statist. Assoc.* **80**, 651–662.

Ichimura, H. (1986). Consistent estimation of index coefficient models. Working Paper, Department of Economics, Massachusetts Institute of Technology, Cambridge, MA.

Imbens, G. (1992). An efficient method of moments estimator for discrete choice models with choice-based sampling. *Econometrica* **60**, 1187–1214.

Imbens, G. and T. Lancaster (1991). Efficient estimation and stratified sampling. Discussion Paper 1545, Harvard Institute of Economic Research, Harvard University, Cambridge, MA.

Jewell, N. P. (1985). Least squares regression with data arising from stratified samples of the dependent variable. *Biometrika* **72**, 11–21.

Kalbfleisch, J. D. and J. F. Lawless (1988). Estimation of reliability in field performance studies. *Technometrics* **30**, 365–388.

Klein, R. W. and R. H. Spady (1993). An efficient semiparametric estimator for binary response models. *Econometrica* **61**, 387–421.

Koopmans, T. C., and W. C. Hood (1953). The estimation of simultaneous linear economic relationships. In: W. C. Hood and T. C. Koopmans, eds., *Studies in Econometric Method*, Yale Univ. Press, New Haven, CT.

Lancaster, T. (1990). A paradox in choice-based sampling. Working Paper 90-17, Department of Economics, Brown University, Providence, RI.

Lancaster, T. and G. Imbens (1991). Optimal stock/flow panels. Working Paper 91-27, Department of Economics, Brown University, Providence, RI.

Lee, L. F. (1989). Semiparametric maximum profile likelihood estimation of polytomous and sequential choice models. Discussion Paper 253, Center for Economic Research, Department of Economics, University of Minnesota, Minneapolis, MN.

Lerman, S. and C. Manski (1975). Alternative sampling procedures for disaggregate choice model estimators. *Transportation Res. Record* **592**, 24–28.

Manski, C. (1975). Maximum score estimation of the stochastic utility model of choice. *J. Econometrics* **3**, 205–228.

Manski, C. F. (1984). Adaptive estimation of nonlinear regression models. *Econometric Rev.* **3**, 145–194.

Manski, C. (1985). Semiparametric analysis of discrete response: Asymptotic properties of the maximum score estimator. *J. Econometrics* **27**, 313–333.

Manski, C. (1986). Semiparametric analysis of binary response from response-based samples. *J. Econometrics* **31**, 31–40.

Manski, C. and S. Lerman (1977). The estimation of choice probabilities from choice-based samples. *Econometrica* **45**, 1977–1988.

Manski, C. and D. McFadden (1981). Alternative estimators and sample designs for discrete choice analysis. In: C. F. Manski and D. McFadden, eds., *Structural Analysis of Discrete Data with Econometric Applications*. MIT Press, Cambridge, MA.

McCullagh, P., and J. A. Nelder (1989). *Generalized Linear Models*. Chapman and Hall, London.

McFadden, D. (1979). Econometric analysis of discrete data. Fisher–Schultz Lecture, Econometric Society, Athens, Greece.

McFadden, D. L. (1984). Econometric analysis of qualitative response models. In: Z. Griliches and M. D. Intriligator, eds., *Handbook of Econometrics*, Vol. II. North-Holland, New York.

Nathan, G. and D. Holt (1980). The effect of survey design on regression analysis. *J. Roy. Statist. Soc. Ser. B* **42**, 377–386.

Powell, J. L., J. H. Stock and T. M. Stocker (1989). Semiparametric estimation of index coefficients. *Econometrica* **57**, 1403–1430.

Rothenberg, T. J. and C. T. Leenders (1964). Efficient estimation of simultaneous equation systems. *Econometrica* **32**, 57–76.

Severini, T. and W. H. Wong (1987). Profile likelihood and semiparametric methods. Working Paper, Department of Statistics, University of Chicago, Chicago, IL.

Vardi, Y. (1985). Empirical distributions in selection bias models. *Ann. Statist.* **13**, 178–203.

Warner, S. L. (1963). Multivariate regression of dummy variables under normality assumptions. *J. Amer. Statist. Assoc.* **58**, 1054–1063

G. S. Maddala, C. R. Rao and H. D. Vinod, eds., *Handbook of Statistics, Vol. 11*

2

Semiparametric and Nonparametric Estimation of Quantal Response Models

Joel L. Horowitz *

1. Introduction

Many problems in economics and related disciplines involve modeling the relation between a set of explanatory variables and a qualitative dependent variable. Examples include modeling a commuter's choice of travel mode (e.g., automobile, transit, bicycle), a migrant's choice of destination, and an individual's employment status (employed or unemployed). The objectives of such 'quantal response' modeling may include:

(1) Testing whether a particular variable influences the dependent variable. For example, does the cost of parking influence mode choice? Does the level of an individual's education influence the likelihood of being unemployed?

(2) Estimating important behavioral parameters, such as the value of time in mode choice or the reservation wage in a model of an individual's employment status.

(3) Predicting the effects of changes in the values of one or more explanatory variables. For example, what is the change in transit ridership that would result from a $0.25 increase in the fare?

In the best-known method for developing an empirical quantal response model, the probability of each state of the dependent variable conditional on the explanatory variables is specified a priori up to a finite set of parameters. This specification is called a 'parametric model'. The numerical values of the parameters are estimated by fitting the model to data, usually by using the method of maximum likelihood. Often, a parametric model is based on principles of economic theory, such as utility maximization, in which case some or all of the estimated parameters may have important behavioral interpretations that are of interest in their own right.

An important drawback of parametric modeling is that economic theory provides only partial guidance on how a parametric model should be specified. Consequently, there can be no assurance that the chosen specification is

* Preparation of this paper was supported in part by NSF grant no. SES-8922460.

correct, even in the unlikely event that the theory on which it is based is beyond question. Misspecification of the model causes maximum likelihood estimators of behavioral parameters to be inconsistent, and predictions obtained from a misspecified model can be highly erroneous. This has motivated the development of methods that enable one to estimate the behavioral parameters of a quantal response model and the probability distribution of the dependent variable conditional on the explanatory variables without having to make a full parametric specification of the model. Such methods are called 'semiparametric' or 'nonparametric', depending on the extent to which they relax the assumptions of parametric models.

This paper presents some of the results of recent research on semi- and nonparametric estimation of quantal response models. The paper does not provide a complete treatment of the subject, which is not possible in the available space. It concentrates on methods for binary response models – that is, models in which the dependent variable has only two states, such as employed or unemployed. Semi- and nonparametric methods for binary response models are more highly developed than are such methods for models with multiple responses, and to date binary response is the only setting in which semi- or nonparametric methods have been applied. Even within the area of binary response, the presentation here is selective, reflecting my own judgments and experience regarding the topics and methods that are most likely to be useful in applications.

Section 2 reviews parametric models, identifies the assumptions of these models that semi- and nonparametric methods relax, and explains the distinction between semiparametric and nonparametric methods. Section 3 discusses the consequences of adopting a misspecified parametric model. This is an important topic because semi- and nonparametric methods are not needed if the errors resulting from use of a misspecified parametric model are small. Section 4 discusses the problem of identifying behavioral parameters when parametric assumptions are relaxed. Section 5 deals with rates of convergence and asymptotic efficiency in semiparametric models. Section 6 presents methods for semi- and nonparametric estimation of binary response models. Section 7 discusses estimation from choice-based samples. The few applications of semiparametric estimators for binary response models that have been carried out to date are reviewed in Section 8. Models for multinomial responses are discussed briefly in Section 9.

2. Parametric models

The general binary response model has the form

$$Y = \begin{cases} 1 & \text{if } g(X) - U \geq 0 , \\ 0 & \text{otherwise} , \end{cases} \tag{2.1}$$

where Y is the dependent variable, X is a $\kappa \times 1$ vector of explanatory variables, U is an unobserved scalar random variable, and g is a real-valued function. In most applications it is assumed that $g(x) = \beta'x$, where β is a $\kappa \times 1$ vector of parameters whose values must be estimated from observations of (Y, X). This assumption will be made here except as otherwise noted. Thus,

$$Y = \begin{cases} 1 & \text{if } \beta'X - U \geq 0, \\ 0 & \text{otherwise}. \end{cases} \tag{2.2}$$

Let $F(u \mid x, \theta)$ denote the cumulative distribution function of U conditional on the event $X = x$, where θ is a vector of parameters on which the distribution of U depends. It follows from (2.2) that

$$P(Y = 1 \mid x, \beta, \theta) = F(\beta'x \mid x, \theta). \tag{2.3}$$

Once the specification of F is given, (2.3) constitutes a parametric binary response model. In many applications, it is assumed that F is either the cumulative normal or cumulative logistic distribution function. Equation (2.3) is the binary probit model if F is the cumulative normal distribution function and the binary logit model if F is the cumulative logistic distribution function. Let $\{Y_i, X_i : i = 1, \ldots, n\}$ denote a random sample of size n on (Y, X). The log-likelihood of the model (2.3) is

$$\log L(\beta, \theta) = \sum_{i=1}^{n} \{Y_i \log F(\beta'X_i \mid X_i, \theta)$$
$$+ (1 - Y_i) \log[1 - F(\beta'X_i \mid X_i, \theta)]\}. \tag{2.4}$$

Let $\hat{\beta}_n$ and $\hat{\theta}_n$ denote the maximum likelihood estimators of β and θ. Define $\hat{\tau}_n = (\hat{\beta}_n', \hat{\theta}_n')$. Subject to regularity conditions, $\hat{\tau}_n$ converges almost surely to a limit $\tau^* \equiv (\beta^*, \theta^*)$, and $n^{1/2}(\hat{\tau}_n - \tau^*)$ is asymptotically normally distributed (see, e.g., White, 1982). Moreover, if (2.3) is a correctly specified model, $1 - F(\beta^{*\prime}x \mid x, \theta^*)$ is the true conditional probability that $Y = 1$. Amemiya (1985), Maddala (1983), and McFadden (1974) provide detailed discussions of maximum likelihood estimation of parametric quantal response models.

It can be seen from (2.1)–(2.3) that a parametric binary response model entails a priori specification of g and the distribution of U conditional on X up to finite-dimensional parameters β and θ. In general, incorrect specification of either g or the distribution of U causes maximum likelihood parameter estimators to be inconsistent for any behavioral parameters of the data generation process, and it causes predictions to be erroneous. Exceptions can occur in special cases (Ruud 1983). Semi- and nonparametric methods avoid the need for specifying parametric forms for either or both of g and the conditional distribution of U, thereby reducing (though not eliminating) the possibility of specification error. Most semiparametric methods use a parametric specification for g but not for the conditional distribution of U. Such models contain an unknown finite-dimensional parameter β that is associated with g and an unknown function (or infinite-dimensional parameter), which is the conditional distribution of U. Some semiparametric models specify the distribution of U parametrically but not the function g (Matzkin 1991, 1990). In these models, there is an unknown finite-dimensional parameter associated with the distribution of U and an unknown function g. Nonparametric methods avoid parametric assumptions about either g or the distribution of U. Thus, nonparametric models contain only unknown functions.

3. Effects of misspecifying the distribution of U

Semiparametric methods that eliminate the need for parametrically specifying the distribution of U conditional on X are better developed and more ready for use in applications than are other semi- and nonparametric estimation methods for binary response models. Their usefulness depends on the severity of the errors that result from misspecifying the conditional distribution of U. If the errors are small, there is little to be gained from the use of methods that avoid the need for specifying the distribution parametrically. This section presents the results of a numerical investigation of some of the consequences of misspecifying the distribution of U. Related results are given by Arabmazar and Schmidt (1982), Domencich and McFadden (1975), Horowitz (1992), and Manski and Thompson (1986).

Suppose that in estimating a binary response model, the distribution of Y conditional on X is assumed to be given by a binary logit model:

$$P(Y = 1 \mid x, \beta) = 1/[1 + \exp(-\beta'x)] . \tag{3.1}$$

According to this model, which is widely used in applications, $g(x) = \beta'x$, and U is logistically distributed independently of X. Let $Q(x)$ denote the true probability that $Y = 1$ conditional on $X = x$. Model (3.1) is misspecified if there is no β such that $Q(x) = P(Y = 1 \mid x, \beta)$ for all x except, possibly, a set of x values whose probability is zero.

Let β^* denote the almost sure limit of the maximum likelihood estimator of β in (3.1). One way to characterize the consequences of estimating a misspecified model is to compare β^* with the true value of β and $P(Y = 1 \mid x, \beta^*)$ with $Q(x)$. The almost sure limit of the maximum likelihood estimator of β can be obtained by observing that as a consequence of (2.4)

$$\beta^* = \arg \max_{\beta \in B} E_X \{ Q(X) \log P(Y = 1 \mid X, \beta)$$

$$+ [1 - Q(X)] \log[1 - P(Y = 1 \mid X, \beta]\} , \tag{3.2}$$

where B is the parameter set containing β and E_X denotes the expectation relative to the distribution of X. Therefore, the asymptotic errors in parameter estimates and predicted probabilities that $Y = 1$ can be investigated by solving (3.2) for various specifications of Q and using the result to compute $P(Y = 1 \mid x, \beta^*)$.

I have computed β^* for a variety of specifications of Q with $\kappa = 2$. The two components of X, X_1 and X_2, are independent. X_1 is distributed as N(0, 1), X_2 is distributed as χ^2 with 1 degree of freedom, and $(\beta_1, \beta_2) \equiv \beta_0' = (1, 1)$. Q is obtained from (2.3) with $\beta = \beta_0$ and each of the following distributions of U:

(1) Logistic independent of X.

(2) Standard normal independent of X.

(3) Student-t with 3 degrees of freedom independent of X.

(4) Uniform on $[-1, 1]$ independent of X.

(5) Laplace independent of X.

(6) A 50–50 mixture of the normal distributions N(3, 1) and N(−3, 1) independent of X.

(7) $U = h(X)V$, where V has the logistic distribution independent of X and $h(X) = 1 + |\beta_0'X|$.

(8) $U = h(X)V$, where V has the logistic distribution independent of X and $h(X) = 0.25[1 + 2(\beta_0'X)^2 + (\beta_0'X)^4]$.

(9) Normal distribution with mean 0 and variance $1 + 0.2(X_1^2 + X_2^2)$.

The parametric model (3.1) is correctly specified in case (1) and misspecified in all of the other cases. In cases (2)–(5), the distribution of U is unimodal and independent of X. In case (6), the distribution of U is bimodal. In cases (7)–(9), U is heteroskedastic. In case (8), $Q(X)$ is a nonmonotonic function of $\beta_0'X$. It has a global minimum at $\beta_0'X = -1/\sqrt{3}$, a global maximum at $\beta_0'X = 1/\sqrt{3}$, and converges to 0.5 as $\beta_0'X \to \pm\infty$. In case (9), Q is a random-coefficients probit model.

Table 1 shows β_2^*/β_1^*, $E_X|P(Y = 1 \mid X, \beta^*) - Q(X)|$ and $\max_X|P(Y = 1 \mid x, \beta^*) - Q(x)|$ for each of the 9 cases. For a correctly specified model, $\beta_2^*/\beta_1^* = 1$, and $E_X|P(Y = 1 \mid X, \beta^*) - Q(X)| = \max_X|P(Y = 1 \mid x, \beta^*) - Q(x)| = 0$. β_2^*/β_1^* is used as a measure of the asymptotic bias (or inconsistency) of the parameter estimator, rather than β_1^* and β_2^* individually, because (2.2) continues to hold if $\beta'X - U$ is multiplied by any positive constant. Therefore, β is identified only up to an arbitrary scale, and only the ratio β_2^*/β_1^* has behavioral significance. $E_X|P(Y = 1 \mid X, \beta^*) - Q(X)|$ and $\max_X|P(Y = 1 \mid x, \beta^*)$

Table 1
Asymptotic results of estimating a misspecified binary logit model

Case[1]	Distr. of U	β_2^*/β_1^*	$E_X\|Q(X)$ $- P(Y = 1 \mid X, \beta^*)\|$	$\max_X\|Q(x)$ $- P(Y = 1 \mid X, \beta^*)\|$
(1)	Logistic	1.00	0.0	0.0
(2)	Normal	1.00	0.01	0.02
(3)	Student $t(3)$	0.97	0.01	0.04
(4)	Uniform	1.01	0.03	0.07
(5)	Laplace	0.98	0.01	0.04
(6)	Bimodal	0.87	0.05	0.20
(7)	Hetero. logistic	0.75	0.04	0.14
(8)	Hetero. logistic	0.45	0.11	0.37
(9)	Hetero. normal	0.91	0.02	0.15

[1] The complete definitions of the cases are given in the text.

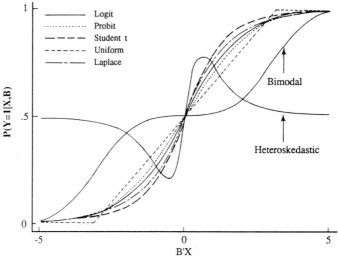

Fig. 1. Models with various distributions of U.

$- Q(x)|$ characterize the errors caused by using a misspecified model to predict the probability that $Y = 1$ conditional on X.

The message of Table 1 is clear. The errors caused by incorrectly assuming that U is logistically distributed independent of X are small when the true distribution of U is both unimodal and independent of X. The errors are relatively large when U has a bimodal distribution or the distribution of U is heteroskedastic. Similar results have been reported by Horowitz (1992) and Manski and Thompson (1986).

To understand these results, consider cases (1)–(8), where $Q(x)$ depends only on $\beta_0'x$. When the distribution of U is unimodal, a graph of $Q(x)$ against $\beta_0'x$ yields an ogival curve whose shape is not much affected by details of the distribution of U. In contrast, bimodality of the distribution of U and heteroskedasticity cause substantial departures from an ogival shape. These statements are illustrated in Figure 1, which shows graphs of $Q(x)$ for cases (1)–(6) and (8). To facilitate comparison of the various models, the unimodal distributions of U have been scaled to have variances equal to that of the logistic distribution. The functions $Q(x)$ arising from unimodal distributions of U are all similar in shape, so these functions all yield similar estimation results. Large estimation errors arise only under bimodality and heteroskedasticity, which cause large deviations from the ogival shape associated with the binary logit model.

4. Identification

Weakening the assumptions of parametric modeling has the effect of reducing the amount of information that is available for estimating β or g and the distribution of U conditional on X. It is possible to weaken the assumptions so much that g and the conditional distribution of U are not identified. That is, they cannot be recovered, regardless of the size of the data set. Clearly, there is no point in trying to estimate β, g, or the distribution of U if this happens. To illustrate, let $I(\cdot) = 1$ if the event in parentheses occurs and 0 otherwise, and let $F(\cdot \mid x)$ denote the cumulative distribution of U conditional on the event $X = x$. Consider the following two models:

$$Y = I(\beta'X - U \geq 0) , \tag{4.1a}$$

$$F(u \mid x) = \Phi[u/(1 + |\beta'x|)] \tag{4.1b}$$

and

$$Y = I[\beta'x/(1 + |\beta'x|) - U \geq 0] , \tag{4.2a}$$

$$F(u \mid x) = \Phi(u) , \tag{4.2b}$$

where Φ denotes the cumulative normal distribution function. It is easy to see that although these models have different functions g and different conditional distributions of U, they are observationally equivalent; that is, they both yield the same expression for $P(Y = 1 \mid x)$ and, therefore, the same data generation process. Consequently, it is not possible to identify g and $F(\cdot \mid x)$ or to discriminate empirically between models (4.1) and (4.2) without a priori information that rules one of the models out. A parametric specification is one form of a priori information that can identify g and $F(\cdot \mid x)$. For example, if (4.1) is assumed to be correct, (4.2) is ruled out except in the trivial case that $\beta = 0$. This section discusses conditions for identification under assumptions that are weaker than those made by parametric models.

Let F_X denote the probability distribution of X. Assume that the data generation process consists of independent random sampling from the joint distribution of (Y, X). In general, this data generation process identifies $P(Y = 1 \mid x)$ for each x in the support of X except, possibly, for a set whose probability according to F_X is 0. That is, $P(Y = 1 \mid x)$ is identified almost everywhere (F_X). For example, $P(Y = 1 \mid x)$ can be estimated consistently almost everywhere (F_X) by nonparametric regression (Stone, 1977). The problem of identification, therefore, consists of finding conditions under which $P(Y = 1 \mid x)$ uniquely determines β or g and the conditional distribution of U.

Before turning to conditions under which identification is possible, it is worth asking why identification matters. That is, if $P(Y = 1 \mid x)$ is known, why is it important to know β or g and $F(\cdot \mid x)$? There are several answers to this question. First, β and/or g may contain important behavioral information. This happens, for example, if Y is determined by utility maximization. Second, knowledge of β or g and $F(\cdot \mid x)$ can make it possible to predict Y at x values that are not in the support of X. See Manski (1988) for further discussion of this point. Finally, the information required for identification, possibly combined with other information, often can be used to improve estimation efficiency. In particular, the 'curse of dimensionality' associated with non-parametric estimation of $P(Y = 1 \mid x)$ (Stone, 1980) often can be avoided.

4.1. Identification with $g(x) = \beta'x$ and an unknown distribution of U

Consider, first, the problem of identifying β and, possibly, $F(\cdot \mid x)$ in the semiparametric model (2.2). According to this model

$$P(Y = 1 \mid x) = F(\beta'x \mid x) . \tag{4.3}$$

To define identification of β and $F(\cdot \mid x)$ formally, let Ψ^X denote the set of all conditional probability distributions $F(u \mid x)$ where u is on the real line and x is in the domain of X. Let $\mathbb{R}^\kappa$ denote κ-dimensional Euclidean space, and let Ξ denote a subset of $\mathbb{R}^\kappa \times \Psi^X$ that is known to contain $(\beta, F_{U \mid X})$, where $F_{U \mid X} = F(\cdot \mid X = \cdot)$. The following definition formalizes the idea that β and $F(\cdot \mid x)$ are identified if they are uniquely determined by $P(Y = 1 \mid x)$.

DEFINITION 4.1. $(\beta, F_{U \mid X})$ is identified if for each $(b, G_{U \mid X}) \in \Xi$ such that $(b, G_{U \mid X}) \neq (\beta, F_{U \mid X})$,

$$F_X\{x: G(b'x \mid x) \neq P(Y = 1 \mid x)\} > 0 , \tag{4.4}$$

where $F_X\{\cdot\}$ denotes the probability of the set $\{\cdot\}$ under F_X.

There are circumstances in which it is useful to consider whether β is identified independently of the identifiability of $F(\cdot \mid x)$. The following definition accommodates this case.

DEFINITION 4.2. Let B denote the parameter set that contains β. β is identified if (4.4) holds for every $G \in \Psi^X$ and each $b \in B$ such that $b \neq \beta$.

Equation (2.2) continues to hold if β is divided by any real $c > 0$ and U is replaced by a random variable that is distributed as U/c. Therefore, β can be identified only up to scale, and it is necessary to impose a scale normalization to proceed further. It will be assumed here that the components of X are ordered so that $\beta_1 \neq 0$. Scale normalization will be achieved by setting $|\beta_1| = 1$. An alternative normalization is $\|\beta\| = 1$. This normalization may seem more general than $|\beta_1| = 1$ since it does not assume a priori knowledge of a nonzero component of β. However, as will be seen below, other assumptions needed for identification require a priori knowledge of a nonzero component of β, so it is only a matter of convenience which normalization is adopted.

Mean independence. In the linear regression model $Y = \beta'X + U$, β is identified if $E(U \mid x) = 0$ almost surely and the support of X is not a proper linear subspace of $\mathbb{R}^\kappa$. However, this condition is not sufficient to identify β in the binary response model (Manski, 1988). To demonstrate this, suppose that $P(Y = 1 \mid x) = 1/[1 + \exp(-\beta'x)]$. Let $b \neq \beta$ be any other parameter value that satisfies the scale normalization. Given any x in the support of X, it is possible to construct a random variable V_X with cumulative distribution function $F_{V|X}$ such that $E(V_X | x) = 0$ and

$$F_{V|X}(b'x) = 1/[1 + \exp(-\beta'x)] . \tag{4.5}$$

Therefore, β is not identified according to definition (4.2). To see how the construction proceeds, let x be given and consider the random variable W whose cumulative distribution function conditional on $X = x$ is

$$F_W(w | x) = 1/\{1 + \exp[-w + (b - \beta)'x]\} . \tag{4.6}$$

Then $F_W(b'x | x) = P(Y = 1 | x)$ and $E(W | x) = (b - \beta)'x \equiv \delta_x$. If $\delta_x > 0$, form $F_{V|X}$ from the distribution of W by taking part of the probability mass of W that is to the left of $b'x$ and moving it enough further to the left to make the resulting distribution have mean zero conditional on $X = x$. Conversely, if $\delta_x < 0$, form $F_{V|X}$ by moving probability mass rightward from the part of the distribution of W that is to the right of $b'x$. Since no probability mass crosses the point $W = b'x$ in these movements, the resulting distribution satisfies (4.5) with $E(V | x) = 0$. Therefore, β is not identified.

I now present several sets of conditions under which identification of β and, in some cases $F(\cdot | x)$, is possible.

(a) *U and X are independent.* Suppose that U and X are independent, and let $F(\cdot)$ denote the cumulative distribution function of U. Cosslett (1983) and Manski (1988) have shown that β and $F(\cdot)$ are identified under the conditions given in Proposition 4.3.

PROPOSITION 4.3. *Let U and X be independent and let $F(\cdot)$ denote the cumulative distribution function of U. β and F are identified if*:

(i) *X does not include a constant (intercept) term.*

(ii) *The support of the distribution of X is not contained in any proper linear subspace of $\mathbb{R}^\kappa$.*

(iii) *For almost every $\tilde{X} = (X_2, \ldots, X_\kappa)'$, the distribution of X_1 conditional on $\tilde{X}$ has everywhere positive density with respect to Lebesgue measure. (Recall that $|\beta_1| = 1$ by scale normalization.)*

Condition (i) is a location normalization. It is needed because there is no assumption that centers the distribution of U (e.g., $E(U) = 0$). Therefore, the coefficient of an intercept term is not identified and must be set by normalization. The normalization used here sets the coefficient of the intercept term equal to 0. Condition (ii) rules out multicollinearity, which is a well-known source of nonidentification. Condition (iii) is needed because β and $F(\cdot)$ may not be identified if the support of X is too small. For example, suppose that F and G are two distribution functions such that for some $c > 0$ $F(u) = G(u)$ if $|u| \leq c$ but not if $|u| > c$. Then $F(\cdot)$ is not identified if the support of $\beta'X$ is completely contained in $[-c, c]$. An example of nonidentification of β when the support of X is too small is discussed below in connection with single-index models.

The assumption that U and X are independent is highly restrictive since it excludes the possibility of heteroskedasticity of U. The next two sets of conditions permit U to be heteroskedastic.

(b) *Single-index models.* In a single-index model, $P(Y = 1 | x)$ depends on x only through an 'index' function $h(x, \beta)$ that is known up to a finite-dimensional parameter β. Thus, $P(Y = 1 | x) = G[h(x, \beta)]$ for some function G (not necessarily a distribution function). In this discussion, it is assumed that $h(x, \beta) = \beta'x$, so $P(Y = 1 | x) = G(\beta'x)$.

Identification of β in single-index models has been investigated by Ichimura (1987), Klein and Spady (1993) and Manski (1988). Ichimura (1987) provides the most general set of identification conditions. Note that in a single index model the sign of β is not identified because $P(Y = 1 | x) = G(\beta'x)$ for some G implies $P(Y = 1 | x) = G^*(-\beta'x)$, where for any real ξ, $G^*(\xi) = G(-\xi)$. A slightly modified form of the identification conditions of Ichimura (1987) is as follows.

PROPOSITION 4.4. *Suppose that* $P(Y = 1 | x) = G(\beta'x)$ *for some G. β is identified up to sign if*

   (i) *X does not include a constant (intercept) term.*

   (ii) *The support of the distribution of X is not contained in any proper linear subspace of $\mathbb{R}^\kappa$.*

   (iii) *For almost every $\tilde{X} = (X_2, \ldots, X_\kappa)'$, the distribution of X_1 conditional on $\tilde{X}$ is absolutely continuous with respect to Lebesgue measure. As before, $|\beta_1| = 1$ by scale normalization.*

   (iv) *If there is a discrete component of X, say X_i, for each $b \in B$ and each t in the support of $b'X$, there are at least two distinct elements in the support of X_i such that $b'x = t$.*

   (v) *G is differentiable.*

   (vi) *Let μ_b be the probability distribution of $b'X$. For each $b \in B$ and all c_1 and c_2 satisfying $c_1 c_2 \neq 0$, there is a set T contained in the support of $b'X$ such that $\mu_b(T) \neq 0$ and for all $t \in T$, $G(c_1 t + c_2) \neq G(t)$.*

As when U and X are independent, condition (i) is needed because the distribution of U is uncentered, and condition (ii) rules out multicollinearity. To understand condition (iii), observe that in a single-index model, $P(Y = 1 | x)$ is constant whenever $\beta'x$ is constant. Therefore, β is not identified if $P(Y = 1 | x)$ is constant along more than one set of parallel hyperplanes in the support of X. If X is discrete, it may be possible to find infinitely many sets of parallel hyperplanes each containing a single point in the support of X, in which case β is not identified. Condition (v) makes possible the identification up to sign of components of β associated with continuous components of X. This is because if X_i is continuous, then under the single-index assumption and condition (iii)

$$[\partial P(Y = 1 | x) / \partial x_i] / [\partial P(Y = 1 | x) / \partial x_1] = \beta_i / \beta_1 = \beta_i \, \text{sgn}(\beta_1) . \qquad (4.7)$$

Condition (vi) insures that the derivatives in (4.7) are not everywhere 0. It is also used to identify components of β corresponding to discrete components of X.

Unlike models in which U and X are independent, single-index models permit U to be heteroskedastic. However, the assumption that $P(Y = 1|x)$ depends only on $\beta'x$ greatly limits the forms of heteroskedasticity that can be accommodated by single-index models. For example, models with random coefficients have been found to be important in several applications (Fischer and Nagin, 1981; Hausman and Wise, 1978; Horowitz, 1991) but are not compatible with the single-index specification. The following setup permits virtually arbitrary heteroskedasticity of unknown form, although at the cost of a centering assumption.

(c) *Quantile independence*. In quantile independence, it is assumed that there is an α between 0 and 1 such that the α quantile of U is independent of X. X is assumed to include a constant (intercept) component, so the α quantile of U can be set equal to 0 without loss of generality. Thus, $P(U < 0|x) = \alpha$ for all x in the support of X. Quantile independence permits arbitrary heteroskedasticity of unknown form provided that the centering assumption $P(U < 0|x) = \alpha$ is satisfied. Random-coefficients models can be accommodated within the quantile-independence framework. However, it would be incorrect to conclude that the quantile-independence setup is more general than the single-index one. Rather, they are nonnested. It is possible to construct models that fit within the single-index framework but not the quantile independence one and vice versa.

Identification of β in binary response models with quantile independence has been investigated by Manski (1985, 1988). Manski's (1985) identification conditions are given in the following proposition.

PROPOSITION 4.5. *Let $P(U < 0|x) = \alpha$ for some α ($0 < \alpha < 1$) and for all x in the support of X. β is identified if*:

(i) *The support of the distribution of X is not contained in any proper linear subspace of $\mathbb{R}^\kappa$.*

(ii) *For almost every $\tilde{X} = (X_2, \ldots, X_\kappa)'$, the distribution of X_1 conditional on $\tilde{X}$ has everywhere positive density with respect to Lebesgue measure. As before, $|\beta_1| = 1$ by scale normalization.*

Manski (1988) provides a slightly weaker version of condition (ii). As before, condition (i) prevents multicollinearity, and condition (ii) excludes the possibility that the support of $\beta'X$ is too small to enable β to be identified.

4.2. Identification with unknown g and distribution of U

Suppose that (2.1) holds and that neither g nor the distribution of U is known parametrically. Then

$$P(Y = 1|X) = F[g(x)|X]. \tag{4.8}$$

Let Γ be a known set of functions that contains g. The definition of identification in this nonparametric setting is analogous to definition (4.1) for a semiparametric model.

DEFINITION 4.6. $(g, F_{U|X})$ is identified if for each $(g^*, F_{U|X}^*) \in (\Gamma \times \Psi^X)$ such that $(g^*, F_{U|X}^*) \neq (g, F_{U|X})$,

$$F_X\{x: F_{U|X}^*[g^*(x)|x] \neq P(Y = 1 | x)\} > 0 . \tag{4.9}$$

Identification in nonparametric binary response models has been investigated by Matzkin (1992), who shows that g and the distribution of U are identified under the conditions given in the following proposition.

PROPOSITION 4.7. *In the nonparametric binary response model, $g(\cdot)$ and the distribution of U are identified if*:
   (i) *U and X are independent.*
   (ii) *Γ is a set of real-valued, continuous functions with domain T that is contained in the support of F_X.*
   (iii) *$g(x)$ is a strictly increasing function of x_1.*
   (iv) *There is a subset T^* of T such that*
   (a) *For all g, $g^* \in \Gamma$ and all $x \in T^*$, $g(x) = g^*(x)$, and*
   (b) *For all $g^* \in \Gamma$ and all t in the range of g, there is an $x \in T^*$ such that $g^*(x) = t$.*
   (v) *$F(\cdot)$, the distribution of U, is strictly increasing on the range of g.*
   (vi) *For almost every $\bar{X} = (X_2, \ldots, X_\kappa)'$, the distribution of X_1 conditional on $\bar{X}$ has a density with respect to Lebesgue measure.*

Conditions (i) and (iv) make it possible to separate F from g. Under these conditions, $P(Y = 1 | x) = F(t)$ for some $x \in T^*$, so F can be recovered over the entire range of g from knowledge of $P(Y = 1 | x)$ for $x \in T^*$. Condition (v) makes possible the recovery of g, which would not necessarily be possible if F were constant over part of the range of g.

As has already been discussed, heteroskedasticity of U has been found in several applications of binary response models. Condition (i) does not permit heteroskedasticity. It is an open question whether identification of g and/or F is possible in nonparametric settings that do not assume independence of U and X.

The following example, which is a modified version of one given by Matzkin (1992), illustrates how conditions (iii) and (iv) might be satisfied in applications.

EXAMPLE 4.8. In most applications it is assumed that $g(x) = \beta'x$. A considerably more general specification is $g(x) = \alpha x_1 + \tilde{g}(\tilde{x})$, where $\alpha > 0$, $\tilde{g}$ is a function that satisfies a normalization condition given below but is otherwise unspecified, and $\tilde{x} = (x_2, \ldots, x_\kappa)'$. Let $\tilde{x}_0$ be any point in the support of $\bar{X}$. By suitably normalizing the location and scale of the distribution of U, it can be assumed without loss of generality that $\alpha = 1$ and $\tilde{g}(\tilde{x}_0) = 0$. Accordingly, let Γ be the set of all functions h of the form

$$g(x) = x_1 + \tilde{g}(\tilde{x}) , \qquad \tilde{g}(\tilde{x}_0) = 0 . \tag{4.10}$$

Assume that the support of X_1 conditional on $\tilde{X} = \tilde{x}$ is $(-\infty, \infty)$ for all $\tilde{x}$ in the support of $\tilde{X}$. Set $T^* = \{x : x = (x_1, \tilde{x}_0')', \ -\infty < x_1 < \infty\}$. Then conditions (iii) and (iv) are satisfied.

5. Rates of convergence and asymptotic efficiency bounds

In parametric estimation, the inverse of the information matrix (the Cramér–Rao bound) gives a lower bound on the variance of the asymptotic distribution (hereinafter called the asymptotic variance) of any estimator that satisfies certain mild regularity conditions. The maximum likelihood estimator achieves this bound so, subject to the regularity conditions, no estimator for a parametric model can have greater asymptotic efficiency than the maximum likelihood estimator. Moreover, no regular estimator can converge in probability at a rate that is faster than $n^{-1/2}$, which is the rate of convergence of the maximum likelihood estimator. That is, if $\hat{\beta}_n$ is a regular estimator of a parameter whose true value is β_0 and if $\hat{\beta}_n$ converges in probability to β_0 at the fastest possible rate, $n^{1/2}(\hat{\beta}_n - \beta_0) = O_p(1)$.

Since semi- and nonparametric estimation use weaker assumptions than does parametric estimation, it cannot be expected that semi- and nonparametric estimators will be as efficient asymptotically as parametric ones except, possibly, in special cases. Rates of convergence of semi- and nonparametric estimators and asymptotic efficiency bounds for these estimators often can be investigated by reducing the problem of semi- and nonparametric estimation to consideration of appropriate parametric families of models. A semi- or nonparametric estimator cannot be more efficient than a parametric estimator that satisfies the same regularity conditions. Therefore, a bound on the asymptotic efficiency of a semi- or nonparametric estimator can be obtained by finding the supremum of the Cramér–Rao bounds over all parametric models that satisfy the regularity conditions. This approach was proposed originally by Stein (1956). It has been developed for situations in which $n^{1/2}$-consistent estimators exist by Koshevnik and Levit (1976), Pfanzagl (1982) and Begun et al. (1983). Newey (1989) provides a review. In such situations, an asymptotic efficiency bound can be obtained as the supremum of the Cramér–Rao bounds for all parametric models satisfying the regularity conditions of the semi- or nonparametric model.

As will be discussed below, there are situations in which $n^{1/2}$-consistent estimators do not exist. In these situations, the approach of finding the supremum of Cramér–Rao bounds is not useful since the supremum is infinite.

However, it is often possible to obtain results on the fastest achievable rate of convergence by using the asymptotic minimax approach developed by Le Cam (1953), Hajek (1972), Stone (1980), and Ibragimov and Has'minskii (1981). In this approach, one considers *sequences* of parametric models that satisfy the regularity conditions of the semi- or nonparametric estimator and whose information matrices converge to 0. The rate of convergence of a semi- or nonparametric estimator is the minimum of the rate over all sequences of parametric models that satisfy the regularity conditions.

At present, results on rates of convergence and efficiency bounds for semiparametric estimation of binary response models are available for the cases of independence of U and X and quantile independence of U. No results have yet been developed for nonparametric estimation of binary response models.

5.1. Models with $g(x) = \beta'x$ and U and X independent

Let $H(\cdot)$ denote the cumulative distribution function of the random variable $\beta_0'X$, where β_0 is the unknown true value of β. Let $F(\cdot)$ denote the cumulative distribution function of U, which is assumed to be independent of X, and $f(\cdot)$ denote the probability density function of U. Let $X = (X_1, \tilde{X}')'$, where $\tilde{X} = (X_2, \ldots, X_\kappa)'$, and let $\tilde{\beta} = (\beta_2, \ldots, \beta_\kappa)'$. Assume that $|\beta_1| = 1$. Let $\tilde{\beta}_n$ denote a semiparametric estimator of $\tilde{\beta}$ based on a random sample of size n on (Y, X). By applying the methods of Begun et al. (1983), Cosslett (1987) has shown that subject to regularity conditions, the asymptotic covariance matrix of $n^{1/2}(\tilde{\beta}_n - \tilde{\beta}_0)$ is bounded from below by the inverse of the matrix I^*, where

$$I^* = \int_{-\infty}^{\infty} \frac{[f(v)]^2}{F(v)[1 - F(v)]} \operatorname{var}(\tilde{X} \mid \beta_0'X = v) \, dH(v) . \tag{5.1}$$

A similar result has been obtained by Chamberlain (1986). A semiparametric estimator that achieves this asymptotic efficiency bound is described in Section 6. Cosslett (1987) also shows that $(I^*)^{-1}$ exceeds the parametric (Cramér–Rao) asymptotic efficiency bound by a positive semidefinite matrix that is zero only if

$$E(\tilde{X} \mid \beta_0'X = v) = C_1 + C_2 v \tag{5.2}$$

for some vector-valued constants C_1 and C_2. One case in which (5.2) holds is when X is multivariate normally distributed. Cosslett (1987) gives the generalization of (5.1) to parametric specifications of g that are nonlinear in parameters.

5.2. Quantile independence of U and X

Chamberlain (1986) has shown that under the assumptions of Proposition 4.5 it is possible to construct sequences of parametric models whose information matrices for β converge to 0. Therefore, the supremum over parametric models of the inverse of the information matrix for β is infinite, and under regularity conditions that rule out the pathology of superefficiency, there is no $n^{1/2}$-consistent estimator of β. The following example, which is based on one given by Chamberlain (1986), illustrates the construction of a sequence of parametric models whose information for β converges to 0.

EXAMPLE 5.1. Let (2.2) hold with $\kappa = 2$, so that under scale normalization $\beta'x = x_1 + \beta_2 x_2$. Let β_{02} denote the unknown true value of β_2. Given any $\varepsilon > 0$, let $Q_\varepsilon(x)$ be a function with bounded support in $\mathbb{R}^2$ such that

$$\int \left[\frac{\phi(x_1 + \beta_{02} x_2)}{\Phi(x_1 + \beta_{02} x_2)} x_2 - Q_\varepsilon(x) \right]^2 \mathrm{d}F_X(x) < \varepsilon , \tag{5.3}$$

where ϕ and Φ, respectively, are the normal density and cumulative normal distribution functions. In addition, given $\eta > 0$ let $C_\eta(u)$ be a continuously differentiable function on $\mathbb{R}$ such that $0 \leq C_\eta(u) \leq 1$ for all u,

$$C_\eta(u) = 0 \quad \text{if } |u| < \eta/2 \text{ or } |u| > 2\rho \tag{5.4}$$

and

$$C_\eta(u) = 1 \quad \text{if } \eta < |u| \leq \rho , \tag{5.5}$$

where ρ is sufficiently large that $|x_1 + \beta_{02} x_2| < \rho$ if x is in the support of Q. Let the conditional distribution of U be

$$F(u \,|\, x, \delta) = \Phi(u)[1 + \delta Q_\varepsilon(x) C_\eta(u)] , \tag{5.6}$$

where δ is a parameter on which F depends. Then

$$\begin{aligned} &P(Y = 1 \,|\, x, \beta_2, \delta) \\ &\quad = \Phi(x_1 + \beta_{02} x_2)[1 + \delta Q_\varepsilon(x) C_\eta(x_1 + \beta_{02} x_2)] . \end{aligned} \tag{5.7}$$

This model has two parameters that must be estimated, β_2 and δ.

Suppose the unknown true value of δ is 0, and let $I_{\beta\delta}$ denote the information matrix for (β_2, δ) under model (5.7). $I_{\beta\delta}$ is a 2×2 matrix. Let J_β denote the element of $I_{\beta\delta}^{-1}$ that gives the asymptotic variance of $n^{1/2}(\hat{\beta}_{2n} - \beta_{02})$, where $\hat{\beta}_{2n}$ is the maximum likelihood estimator of β_2. Then J_β^{-1} is the (partial) information for β_2. It is not difficult to show that J_β^{-1} can be made arbitrarily small by making ε and η sufficiently small. Therefore, it is possible to construct a sequence of models of the form (5.7) whose information for β_2 converges to 0.

If $n^{1/2}$-consistency is not possible under quantile independence, how fast a rate of convergence can be achieved? The answer to this question depends on how smooth the cumulative distribution function of U conditional on X and the cumulative distribution function of $\beta_0'X$ conditional on $\bar{X} = (X_2, \ldots, X_\kappa)'$ are. Horowitz (1993) uses the asymptotic minimax approach to show that the rate of convergence of an estimator of β under quantile independence depends on the number of derivatives that these functions have. The rate of convergence is faster when higher-order derivatives exist than when they do not. Specifically, let $p_\beta(\cdot \mid \tilde{x})$ denote the probability density of $\beta'x$ conditional on $\tilde{X} = \tilde{x}$. Let $z = \beta'x$, and write $F(u \mid x)$ in the form $F_\beta(u \mid z, \tilde{x})$. For $i, j = 0, 1, 2, \ldots$, define

$$F_{\beta ij}(u \mid z, \tilde{x}) = \partial^{i+j} F_\beta(u \mid z, \tilde{x}) / \partial u^i \, \partial z^j$$

and

$$p_{\beta i}(z \mid \tilde{x}) = \partial^i p_\beta(z \mid \tilde{x}) / \partial z^i$$

if the derivatives exist. Horowitz (1993) shows that under quantile independence with $\alpha = 0.50$ and subject to regularity conditions, the fastest possible minimax rate of convergence in probability of an estimator of $\tilde{\beta}$ is $n^{-h/(2h+1)}$, where $h \geq 2$ is the largest integer such that for all β sufficiently close to β_0:

(1) For almost every $\tilde{x}$ and for all (u, z) in a neighborhood of $(0, 0)$, $F_{\beta ij}(u \mid z, \tilde{x})$ is uniformly bounded and is a continuous function of (u, z) if $0 \leq i + j \leq h$.

(2) For almost every $\tilde{x}$ and for all z in a neighborhood of 0, $p_{\beta i}(z \mid \tilde{x})$ is uniformly bounded and is a continuous function of z if $0 \leq i \leq h - 1$.

An estimator that achieves the rate of convergence $n^{-h/(2h+1)}$ is described in Section 6. It follows that under quantile independence and given sufficient smoothness (that is, large enough h), it is possible to estimate $\tilde{\beta}$ with a rate of convergence in probability that is arbitrarily close but never quite equal to $n^{-1/2}$.

6. Estimators

This section describes methods for estimating β or $g(x)$ in semi- and nonparametric binary response models. It is assumed that the estimation data set is a simple random sample of size n from the joint distribution of (Y, X). Ideally, an estimator should require minimal assumptions beyond those needed for identification. Therefore, it is natural to classify estimators according to the assumptions required for identification of semi- and nonparametric models.

6.1. Models with $g(x) = \beta'x$ and an unknown distribution of U

(a) *U and X are independent.* This class of models is nested within the classes of single-index models and models with quantile independence. Therefore, any estimator that applies to single-index models or models with quantile independence also applies to models in which U and X are independent. This subsection deals only with estimators that require U and X to be independent as a condition for consistency. Estimators that apply to single-index and quantile-independence models are discussed below.

Let F denote the cumulative distribution function of U, which is unknown in the setting considered here. Write $P(Y = 1 | x, \beta)$ in the form

$$P(Y = 1 | x, \beta) = \int I(u \leq \beta'x)\, dF(u)\,. \tag{6.1}$$

Equation (6.1) belongs to a class of mixture models in which the cumulative distribution function of a random variable Z has the form

$$P(z | \gamma) = \int P(z | u, \gamma)\, dF(u)\,, \tag{6.2}$$

where γ is a parameter, U is a random variable with cumulative distribution function F, and $P(\cdot | u, \gamma)$ is the cumulative distribution function of Z conditional on the event $U = u$ and the parameter γ. Kiefer and Wolfowitz (1956) give conditions under which both γ and F in (6.2) can be estimated consistently by maximum likelihood. This entails maximizing the likelihood function with respect to the unknown distribution function F as well as the unknown parameter γ. Cosslett (1983) shows that under regularity conditions the result of Kiefer and Wolfowitz (1956) can be applied to (6.1), thereby making possible consistent maximum likelihood estimation of β (up to scale) and F in (6.1). Cosslett (1983) also gives an algorithm for maximizing the likelihood function.

Neither the asymptotic distributions of the semiparametric maximum likelihood estimators of β and F nor their rates of convergence in probability are known. In this nonclassical setting, there is no reason to expect that the maximum likelihood estimator is $n^{1/2}$-consistent, asymptotically normal or asymptotically efficient.

Han (1987) observed that Y and $\beta'X$ are positively correlated when U and X are independent. Based on this observation he proposed estimating β by maximizing an indicator of the correlation of Y and $\beta'X$. The resulting 'maximum rank correlation' estimator selects β to maximize

$$S_{\mathrm{RC}}(\beta) = \binom{n}{2}^{-1} \sum_{i,j \in R} [I(Y_i > Y_j)I(\beta'X_i > \beta'X_j)$$
$$+ I(Y_i < Y_j)I(\beta'X_i < \beta'X_j)] \tag{6.3}$$

subject to scale normalization, where R is the set of distinct combinations of (i, j) pairs such that $i, j = 1, \ldots, n$. Han (1987) established the consistency of the maximum rank correlation estimator. Its asymptotic distribution and rate of convergence in probability are unknown. Deriving the asymptotic distribution of the estimator is quite difficult because the objective function it maximizes is a discontinuous function of β. As a result, the usual Taylor series methods of asymptotic distribution theory cannot be applied.[1]

(b) *Single-index models.* In these models, $P(Y = 1 | x, \beta) = G(\beta'x)$, where G is a function (not necessarily a distribution function) whose range is $[0, 1]$. If all

---

[1] In a paper that appeared recently, Sherman (1993) shows that the maximum rank correlation estimator converges in probability at the rate $n^{-1/2}$ and is asymptotically normally distributed.

of the components of X are continuous, β can be estimated up to sign and scale by forming a sample analog of $\partial G(\beta'x)/\partial x$, which is proportional to β. This idea was first exploited by Stoker (1986). However, Stoker's estimator has the undesirable property of requiring the analyst to know the distribution of X up to a finite-dimensional parameter.

Powell et al. (1989) developed a modification of Stoker's (1986) estimator that avoids this problem. Their idea is to estimate the density-weighted average derivative

$$D = \int [f_X(x)]^2 [\partial G(\beta'X)/\partial x]\, dx , \qquad (6.4)$$

where f_X is the probability density function of X and it is assumed that G is differentiable. Under the single-index specification, D is proportional to β. Assuming that $f_X = 0$ on the boundary of its support, integration by parts in (6.4) yields

$$D = -2 \int G(\beta'x) f_X(x)[\partial f_X(x)/\partial x]\, dx . \qquad (6.5)$$

Therefore,

$$D = -2E[Y\, \partial f_X(X)/\partial x] . \qquad (6.6)$$

If f_X were known, D could be estimated consistently by the sample analog

$$D_n^* = -2n^{-1} \sum_{i=1}^{n} Y_i\, \partial f_X(X_i)/\partial x . \qquad (6.7)$$

Powell et al. (1989) replace the unknown density $f_X(X_i)$ with a kernel estimator:

$$\hat{f}_{Xn}(X_i) = (n-1)^{-1} s_n^{-\kappa} \sum_{\substack{j=1 \\ j \neq i}}^{n} K\left(\frac{X_i - X_j}{s_n}\right) , \qquad (6.8)$$

where K is a kernel function on $\mathbb{R}^\kappa$, κ is the dimension of X, and $\{s_n\}$ is a sequence of bandwidths that converges to 0 as $n \to \infty$. See Prakasa Rao (1983) for a discussion of kernel density estimation.

Let $\hat{D}_n$ be the estimator of D that is obtained by replacing $f_X(X_i)$ with $\hat{f}_{Xn}(X_i)$ in (6.7). Powell et al. (1989) show that if K is a kernel of order l, $ns_n^{2l} \to 0$ and $ns_n^{\kappa+2} \to \infty$ as $n \to \infty$, and certain regularity conditions are satisfied, then $n^{1/2}(\hat{D}_n - D)$ is asymptotically normally distributed with mean 0 and a covariance matrix that can be estimated consistently. This is equivalent to estimating β up to sign and scale. The estimator of the covariance matrix is

$$\hat{V}_D = 4n^{-1} \sum_{i=1}^{n} r_n(z_i) r_n(z_i)' - 4\hat{D}_n \hat{D}_n' , \qquad (6.9)$$

where

$$r_n(z_i) = -(n-1)^{-1} \sum_{\substack{j=1 \\ j \neq i}}^{n} s_n^{-(k+1)} K' \left(\frac{X_i - X_j}{s_n} \right) (Y_i - Y_j) , \tag{6.10}$$

and K' is the gradient of K.

The need for continuously distributed explanatory variables X is removed by an estimator developed by Ichimura (1987). Ichimura's estimator is based on the observation that if G were known, β could be estimated by nonlinear least squares. The estimator $\hat{\beta}_n$ would minimize the objective function

$$S_{LS}(\beta) = n^{-1} \sum_{i=1}^{n} [Y_i - G(\beta'X_i)]^2 . \tag{6.11}$$

Since G is unknown, Ichimura (1987) replaces it with the consistent estimator obtained from a kernel nonparametric regression of Y on X. That is, $G(\beta'X_i)$ is replaced by

$$G_n(\beta'X_i) = A_{ni}/B_{ni} , \tag{6.12}$$

where

$$A_{ni} = \sum_{\substack{j=1 \\ j \neq i}}^{n} Y_j K \left(\frac{\beta'X_i - \beta'X_j}{s_n} \right) , \tag{6.13}$$

$$B_{ni} = \sum_{\substack{j=1 \\ j \neq i}}^{n} K \left(\frac{\beta'X_i - \beta'X_j}{s_n} \right) , \tag{6.14}$$

K is a kernel function on the real line, and $\{s_n\}$ is the bandwidth sequence. Ichimura's estimator minimizes

$$S_{LS}^* = n^{-1} \sum_{i=1}^{n} [Y_i - G_n(\beta'X_i)]^2 \tag{6.15}$$

subject to the scale and sign normalization $\beta_1 = 1$. Ichimura (1987) shows that under regularity conditions, if $ns_n^8 \to 0$ and $ns_n^7/\log n \to \infty$ as $n \to \infty$, then $n^{1/2}(\tilde{\beta}_n - \tilde{\beta}_0)$ is asymptotically normally distributed with mean 0, where $\tilde{\beta} = (\beta_2, \ldots, \beta_\kappa)'$ and $\tilde{\beta}_n$ is the estimator of $\tilde{\beta}$. The covariance matrix is estimated consistently by $\hat{V}^{-1} \hat{\Omega} \hat{V}^{-1}$, where

$$\hat{V} = n^{-1} \sum_{i=1}^{n} \tilde{X}_i \tilde{X}_i' G_n'(\hat{\beta}_n' X_i)^2 , \tag{6.16}$$

$$\hat{\Omega} = n^{-1} \sum_{i=1}^{n} \tilde{X}_i \tilde{X}_i' G_n'(\hat{\beta}_n' X_i)^2 [Y_i - G_n(\hat{\beta}_n' X_i)]^2 , \tag{6.17}$$

G_n' is the derivative of G_n, and $\hat{\beta}_n = (1, \tilde{\beta}_n')'$.

The same idea has been used by Klein and Spady (1993) to carry out quasi-maximum-likelihood estimation of β. If G were known, β could be estimated by maximizing the log-likelihood function

$$\log L(\beta) = n^{-1} \sum_{i=1}^{n} \{ Y_i \log G(\beta'X_i)$$
$$+ (1 - Y_i) \log[1 - G(\beta'X_i)] \} . \tag{6.18}$$

Klein and Spady (1993) replace the unknown G with a nonparametric estimate $\tilde{G}_n$ that is given below in equations (6.20)–(6.22). They then estimate B by maximizing the quasi-log-likelihood function

$$\log L_{KS}(\beta) = n^{-1} \sum_{i=1}^{n} \tau_i \{ Y_i \log \tilde{G}_n(\beta'X_i)$$
$$+ (1 - Y_i) \log[1 - \tilde{G}_n(\beta'X_i)] \} \tag{6.19}$$

subject to scale and sign normalization, where τ_i is a trimming function that downweights observations near the boundary of the support of $\beta_0'X$, and β_0 is the unknown true value of β. Trimming is important in establishing the asymptotic distributional properties of the quasi-maximum-likelihood estimator but appears to have little effect on the numerical results obtained in applications.

$\tilde{G}_n$ is obtained as follows. Define $P_n = n^{-1} \sum_{i=1}^{N} Y_i$. P_n is the sample proportion of Y values that equal 1. Then for any real v

$$\tilde{G}_n(v) = \frac{P_n q_n(v \mid Y = 1)}{P_n q_n(v \mid Y = 1) + (1 - P_n) q_n(v \mid Y = 0)}, \tag{6.20}$$

where $q_n(\cdot \mid Y = y)$ is a kernel estimate of $q(\cdot \mid Y = y)$, the conditional density of $\beta'x$. This estimate is given by

$$q_n(v \mid Y = 1) = (n P_n s_n)^{-1} \sum_{i=1}^{n} Y_i K[(v - \beta'x_i)/s_n], \tag{6.21}$$

and

$$q_n(v \mid Y = 0) = [n(1 - P_n)s_n]^{-1} \sum_{i=1}^{n} (1 - Y_i) K[(v - \beta'x_i)/s_n], \tag{6.22}$$

where K is a kernel function on the real line, and $\{s_n\}$ is a sequence of bandwidths satisfying $Ns_n^6 \to \infty$ and $Ns_n^8 \to 0$ as $N \to \infty$. If K is a higher-order kernel, any sequence of bandwidths satisfying these convergence conditions can be used. If K is a second order kernel, it is necessary to use a local smoothing procedure in which s_n varies according to the observation. See Klein and Spady (1993) for details. Klein and Spady (1993) show that under regularity conditions and with the scale/sign normalization $\beta_1 = 1$, the quasi-maximum-likelihood estimator of $\tilde{\beta}$ satisfies $n^{1/2}(\tilde{\beta}_n - \tilde{\beta}_0) \sim N(0, V)$, where V is estimated consistently by the Hessian and outer-product gradient matrices of the quasi-log-likelihood function. V coincides with the asymptotic efficiency bound of Cosslett (1987) if U and X are independent. Thus, the quasi-maximum-likelihood estimator is asymptotically efficient if U and X are independent.

(c) *Quantile independence.* Manski (1975, 1985) shows that under the assumptions of Proposition 4.5 with $\alpha = 0.5$ and with the additional assumption that $0 < P(Y = 1 | x) < 1$ almost everywhere (F_X), β can be estimated consistently by maximizing the following 'score' function subject to scale normalization:

$$S_M(\beta) = n^{-1} \sum_{i=1}^{n} [2I(Y_i = 1) - 1]I(\beta'X_i \geq 0) . \tag{6.23}$$

This estimation procedure amounts to predicting that $Y_i = 1$ if $\beta'X_i \geq 0$, $Y_i = 0$ if $\beta'X_i < 0$, and choosing β to maximize the number of correct predictions.

Cavanagh (1987) and Kim and Pollard (1990) show that the maximum score estimator converges in distribution at the rate $n^{-1/3}$ and that the centered, normalized estimator has a complicated nonnormal limiting distribution. The slow rate of convergence of the maximum score estimator is not surprising. As was discussed in Section 5, $n^{1/2}$-consistent estimation is not possible under the assumptions of quantile-independence, and Manski (1975, 1985) does not make the smoothness assumptions necessary to achieve a convergence rate of $n^{-h/(2h+1)}$ for $h \geq 2$.

The properties of the asymptotic distribution of the maximum score estimator are largely unknown, and this distribution appears not to be useful for making inferences in applications. Manski and Thompson (1986) suggest using the bootstrap to make inferences in applications. The suggested bootstrap procedure is a Monte Carlo simulation of the distribution of the maximum score estimator. The simulation is carried out by sampling n (Y, X) pairs randomly and with replacement from the estimation data set. This bootstrap sample is used to estimate β by maximizing S_M. An estimate of the probability distribution of $\hat{\beta}_n$ is constructed by repeating these sampling and estimation steps many times. Manski and Thompson (1986) give Monte Carlo evidence indicating that the accuracy of the bootstrap estimate of the distribution of the maximum score estimator depends on the details of $P(Y = 1 | x)$ but is satisfactory in many cases of interest.

Maximizing S_M requires the use of a nonstandard optimization procedure since S_M is a step function. An algorithm due to Manski and Thompson (1986) is available in the software package LIMDEP. This algorithm uses the scale normalization $\|\beta\| = 1$, where $\|\cdot\|$ denotes the Euclidean norm. It searches for maxima of S_M along great circles on the unit sphere in $\mathbb{R}^\kappa$. The search is efficient computationally because S_M has only finitely many values along any great circle, and these can be evaluated rapidly.

The maximum score estimator has a slow rate of convergence and a complicated asymptotic distribution because it maximizes a discontinuous objective function. Horowitz (1992) proposes smoothing S_M to make it continuous and differentiable. The resulting smoothed maximum score estimator maximizes

$$S_{\mathrm{H}}(\beta) = n^{-1} \sum_{i=1}^{n} [2I(Y_i = 1) - 1]J(\beta'X_i/s_n) \tag{6.24}$$

subject to the scale normalization $|\beta_1| = 1$, where s_n is a sequence of bandwidths that converges to 0 as $n \to \infty$, and J is a twice differentiable function of the real line into itself that satisfies

$$|J(v)| < M \quad \text{for some finite } M \text{ and all } v \text{ in } (-\infty, \infty),$$
$$\lim_{v \to -\infty} J(v) = 0 \quad \text{and} \quad \lim_{v \to \infty} J(v) = 1.$$

J is analogous to the *integral* of a kernel function for nonparametric density estimation. Typically, dJ/dv has the properties of a kernel. Assume that smoothness conditions 1 and 2 of Section 5.2 are satisfied, J is the integral of an h-th order kernel on $\mathbb{R}$, and $s_n = \lambda n^{-1/(2h+1)}$ for some $\lambda > 0$. Then under regularity conditions, the estimator of $\bar{\beta}$ obtained by maximizing (6.24) satisfies $n^{h/(2h+1)}(\bar{\beta}_n - \bar{\beta}_0) \sim N(-\lambda^{1/2}Q^{-1}A, Q^{-1}DQ^{-1})$ asymptotically, where A, D, and Q are estimated consistently as follows:

$$\hat{A}_n = n^{-1}(s_n^*)^{-h} \sum_{i=1}^{n} [2I(Y_i = 1) - 1](\tilde{X}_i/s_n^*)J'(\hat{\beta}_n X_i/s_n^*), \tag{6.25}$$

where $\hat{\beta}_n$ is the estimate of β (not of $\bar{\beta}$), $s_n^* = s_n^{\delta}$ for some δ satisfying $0 < \delta < 1$, and J' is the derivative of J;

$$\hat{D}_n = (ns_n)^{-1} \sum_{i=1}^{n} \tilde{X}_i \tilde{X}_i' J'(\hat{\beta}_n' X_i/s_n)^2; \tag{6.26}$$

and

$$\hat{Q}_n = \partial^2 S_{\mathrm{H}}(\hat{\beta}_n)/\partial\beta\,\partial\beta'. \tag{6.27}$$

An asymptotically unbiased estimator of $\bar{\beta}$ can be obtained by replacing $\bar{\beta}_n$ with

$$\bar{b}_n = \bar{\beta}_n + (\lambda/n)^{h/(2h+1)}\hat{Q}_n\hat{A}_n. \tag{6.28}$$

The rate of convergence in probability of $\bar{b}_n$ and $\bar{\beta}_n$, $n^{h/(2h+1)}$, is the fastest possible under smoothness conditions 1 and 2 of Section 5.2.

Monte Carlo experiments with the smoothed maximum score estimator have shown that samples much larger than those typically encountered in applications are needed to make the approximations of asymptotic theory accurate (Horowitz, 1992). In particular, the finite-sample sizes of t tests of hypotheses about $\bar{\beta}$ tend to be much larger than their nominal sizes based on asymptotic theory. This problem can be greatly reduced by using the bootstrap to estimate critical values for the t statistic. The bootstrap procedure for testing the hypothesis H_0: $\bar{\beta}_i = \bar{\beta}_{0i}$, where $\bar{\beta}_i$ is the i-th component of $\bar{\beta}$ is:
(1) Generate a sample of (Y, X) of size n by sampling the estimation data

set randomly with replacement. Use this sample to compute the t statistic for testing the hypothesis $\tilde{\beta}_i = \bar{b}_{ni}$, where $\bar{b}_{ni}$ is the bias-corrected smoothed maximum score estimator of $\tilde{\beta}_i$ obtained from the original estimation sample.

(2) Estimate the critical value of the t statistic from the empirical distribution of this statistic that is obtained by repeating step 1 many times. Horowitz (1992) reports that in Monte Carlo experiments with $n = 250$, the empirical size of the nominal 0.05-level t test was in the range 0.041–0.066 when bootstrap-based critical values were used, whereas the empirical size was in the range 0.116–0.208 when asymptotic critical values were used. See Beran (1988) and Hall (1986) for discussions of the theory underlying the use of the bootstrap to obtain critical values for test statistics.

The objective function $S_{\mathrm{H}}(\cdot)$ can have many local extrema, so it is necessary to use a global optimization method to compute $\hat{\beta}_n$. Examples of such methods are tunneling (Levy and Montalvo, 1985) and simulated annealing (Bohachevsky et al., 1986; Szu and Hartley, 1987).

6.2. Estimation with unknown g and distribution of U

Matzkin (1992) has proposed estimating g and F under the assumptions of Proposition 4.7 by maximizing the following nonparametric log-likelihood function over g and F:

$$\log L_{\mathrm{NP}}(g, F) = \sum_{i=1}^{n} \{Y_i \log F[g(X_i)]$$
$$+ (1 - Y_i) \log[1 - F[g(X_i)]]\} . \tag{6.29}$$

To establish consistency of the resulting nonparametric maximum likelihood estimator of (g, F), it is necessary to define metrics on the spaces Γ and Ψ that contain the functions g and F. Define the metrics ρ_g and ρ_F on Γ and Ψ, respectively, by

$$\rho_g(g_1, g_2) = \int |g_1(x) - g_2(x)| \, \mathrm{e}^{-\|x\|} \, \mathrm{d}F_X \tag{6.30}$$

and

$$\rho_F(F_1, F_2) = \int |F_1(u) - F_2(u)| \, \mathrm{e}^{-|u|} \, \mathrm{d}u \tag{6.31}$$

Matzkin (1992) shows that the nonparametric maximum likelihood estimators of g and F are consistent relative to these metrics if the assumptions of Proposition 4.7 hold, Γ is a set of monotone increasing functions, and several technical regularity conditions are satisfied. Matzkin (1992) also shows that maximization of (6.29) can be carried out by solving an equivalent nonlinear programming problem and discusses algorithms for solving this problem. The rate of convergence and asymptotic distribution of the nonparametric maximum likelihood estimator are not known.

7. Estimation from choice-based samples

A choice-based sample is one that is stratified on the dependent variable Y. The fraction of observations with $Y = 1$ is selected by design, and X is sampled conditional on Y. For example, a data set for analyzing travel mode choice might be obtained by interviewing randomly selected automobile travelers at the roadside and randomly selected transit travelers on their vehicles. The numbers of automobile and transit travelers interviewed are selected by design.

Except in special cases, estimators that work with random samples are inconsistent when the sample is choice based. Parametric estimation from choice-based samples has been investigated by Cosslett (1981), Hsieh et al. (1985), Manski and Lerman (1977), and Manski and McFadden (1981). This section treats semiparametric estimation from choice-based samples under the assumption that $g(x) = \beta'x$ and the distribution of U is unknown. It is also assumed that the population values of the aggregate shares, $P_1 = P(Y \geqslant 0)$ and $P_0 = 1 - P_1$, are known. It is not unusual in applications for aggregate shares to be known quite accurately. For example, in work trip mode choice analysis aggregate shares often are available in data from the U.S. Census, although Census data typically do not include information on all of the variables needed to develop a useful mode choice model.

Suppose that the assumptions of Proposition 4.5 hold with $\alpha = 0.5$. Manski (1986) has shown that under these conditions, β can be estimated consistently from a choice-based sample by maximizing the modified score function

$$S_{\text{CB}}(\beta) = (P_1/n_1) \sum_{\substack{i=1 \\ Y_i=1}}^{n} I(\beta'X_i \geqslant 0) - (P_0/n_0) \sum_{\substack{i=1 \\ Y_i=0}}^{n} I(\beta'X_i \geqslant 0) \qquad (6.32)$$

subject to scale normalization, where n_i $(i = 0, 1)$ is the number of observations for which $Y_i = i$, and $n = n_0 + n_1$. The asymptotic distribution of this estimator is not known, although it likely can be found by using the methods of Kim and Pollard (1990).

Like the objective function $S_{\text{M}}(\cdot)$ for maximum score estimation from a random sample, $S_{\text{CB}}(\cdot)$ can be smoothed by replacing the indicator function with the integral of a kernel function. The resulting estimator maximizes the smoothed modified score function

$$S_{\text{HCB}}(\beta) = (P_1/n_1) \sum_{\substack{i=1 \\ Y_i=1}}^{n} J(\beta'X_i/s_n) - (P_0/n_0) \sum_{\substack{i=1 \\ Y_i=0}}^{n} J(\beta'X_i/s_n), \qquad (6.33)$$

where J and s_n are defined as in (6.24). Suppose that conditions 1 and 2 of Section 5.2 hold and that $s_n = \lambda n^{-1/(2h+1)}$. Then using methods similar to those in Horowitz (1992), it may be shown that the smoothed choice-based estimator of $\tilde{\beta}$ satisfies $n^{h/(2h+1)}(\tilde{\beta}_n - \tilde{\beta}_0) \sim N(-\lambda^{1/2}Q_{\text{C}}^{-1}A_{\text{C}}, Q_{\text{C}}^{-1}D_{\text{C}}Q_{\text{C}}^{-1})$ asymptotically, where A_C, D_C and Q_C are estimated consistently by

$$\hat{A}_{Cn} = (s_n^*)^{-h}\Bigg[(P_1/n_1)\sum_{\substack{i=1\\Y_i=1}}^{n}(\tilde{X}_i/s_n^*)J'(\hat{\beta}_n X_i/s_n^*)$$

$$- (P_0/n_0)\sum_{\substack{i=1\\Y_i=0}}^{n}(\tilde{X}_i/s_n^*)J'(\hat{\beta}_n'X_i/s_n^*)\Bigg]$$

$$s_n^* = (s_n)^\delta, \; 0 < \delta < 1, \tag{6.34}$$

$$\hat{D}_{Cn} = (P_1/n_1 s_n)\sum_{\substack{i=1\\Y_i=1}}^{n}\tilde{X}_i\tilde{X}_i'J'(\hat{\beta}_n'X_i/s_n)^2$$

$$+ (P_0/n_0 s_n)\sum_{\substack{i=1\\Y_i=1}}^{n}\tilde{X}_i\tilde{X}_i'J'(\hat{\beta}_n'X_i/s_n)^2, \tag{6.35}$$

and

$$\hat{Q}_{Cn} = \partial^2 S_{HCB}(\hat{\beta}_n)/\partial\beta\,\partial\beta'. \tag{6.37}$$

Let $W_1 = \lim_{n\to\infty}(n_1/n)$ and $W_0 = 1 - W_1$. Then it may also be shown that the asymptotic variance of the smoothed choice-based estimator is minimized by designing the sample to minimize $(P_0/W_0 + P_1/W_1)$.

The single-index estimator of Klein and Spady (1993) can be applied to a choice-based sample by replacing P_n with P_1 in (6.20).

8. Applications

There have been few applications of semiparametric methods for binary response models and no applications of nonparametric methods. As a result, it is difficult to judge to what extent these methods yield results in practice that are substantially different from those of familiar parametric methods such as logit and probit modeling.

Newey et al. (1990) estimated parametric probit and semiparametric single-index models of labor-force participation by married women. They report that there is little difference between the parametric and semiparametric parameter estimates. Das (1991) estimated a model of the decision whether to idle a cement kiln. She used a parametric logit estimator and Manski's (1975, 1985) maximum score estimator. An informal examination of the estimation results suggested that the logit model may have been misspecified, but no formal tests were carried out.

Horowitz (1991) estimated a model of the choice between automobile and transit for the work trip. He used a parametric probit model with fixed coefficients, a parametric probit model with random coefficients, a single-index model that was estimated by the method of Klein and Spady (1993), and a quantile-independence model that was estimated both by Manski's (1975, 1985) maximum score estimator and the smoothed maximum score estimator. Specification tests resulted in rejection of the fixed-coefficients probit model and the semiparametric single-index model but not of the random-coefficients probit model or the model based on quantile independence. These results show that distributional assumptions can be important in applied binary response modeling. In particular specifications that make overly restrictive assumptions about heteroskedasticity can be rejected in specification tests.

9. Models for multinomial choice

This paper has concentrated on semi- and nonparametric estimation of binary response models. There also has been some work on semiparametric estimation of models for multinomial response. In a multinomial response model with M possible responses, latent dependent variables Y_m^* ($m = 1, \ldots, M$) satisfy

$$Y_m^* = g_m(X) + U_m ,\tag{7.1}$$

where g_m is a parametric or nonparametric function to be estimated and U_m is a random variable. One observes $(Y_1, \ldots, Y_M, X)$, where $Y_m = 1$ if $Y_m^* > Y_l^*$ for all $l \neq m$ and $Y_m = 0$ otherwise.

Manski (1975) considers a model in which $g_m(x) = \beta' x_{(m)}$, where for each m, $x_{(m)}$ is a subvector of x that is conformable with the parameter β. He gives conditions under which β can be estimated consistently by a version of the maximum score technique of equation (6.23). Matzkin (1991, 1990) has developed consistent estimators for multinomial response models in which the g_m are nonparametric but the joint distribution of the U_m belongs to a known parametric family. To date, semiparametric estimators for multinomial response models have not been used in applications.

References

Arabmazar, A. and P. Schmidt (1982). An investigation of the robustness of the tobit estimator to non-normality. *Econometrica* **50**, 1055–1063.

Amemiya, T. (1985). *Advanced Econometrics*. Harvard Univ. Press, Cambridge, MA.

Begun, J. M., W. J. Hall, W.-M. Huang and J. A. Wellner (1983). Information and asymptotic efficiency in parametric–nonparametric models. *Ann. Statist.* **11**, 432–452.

Beran, R. (1988). Prepivoting test statistics: A bootstrap view of asymptotic refinements. *J. Amer. Statist. Assoc.* **83**, 687–697.

Bohachevsky, I. O., M. E. Johnson and M. L. Stein (1986). Generalized simulated annealing for function optimization. *Technometrics* **28**, 209–217.

Cavanagh, C. L. (1987). Limiting behavior of estimators defined by optimization. Unpublished manuscript, Department of Economics, Harvard University.

Chamberlain, G. (1986). Asymptotic efficiency in semi-parametric models with censoring. *J. Econometrics* **32**, 189–218.

Cosslett, S. R. (1981). Efficient estimation of discrete-choice models. In: C. F. Manski and D.

McFadden, eds., *Structural Analysis of Discrete Data with Econometric Applications*. MIT Press, Cambridge, MA, 51–111.

Cosslett, S. R. (1983). Distribution-free maximum likelihood estimator of the binary choice model. *Econometrica* **51**, 765–782.

Cosslett, S. R. (1987). Efficiency bounds for distribution-free estimators of the binary choice and the censored regression models. *Econometrica* **55**, 559–585.

Das, S. (1991). A semiparametric structural analysis of the idling of cement kilns. *J. Econometrics* **50**, 235–256.

Domenich, T. A. and D. McFadden (1975). *Urban Travel Demand: A Behavioral Analysis*. North-Holland, Amsterdam.

Fischer, G. W. and D. Nagin (1981). Random versus fixed coefficient quantal choice models. In: C. F. Manski and D. McFadden, eds., *Structural Analysis of Discrete Data with Econometric Applications*. MIT Press, Cambridge, MA, 273–304.

Hajek, J. (1972). Local asymptotic minimax and admissibility in estimation. In: L. Le Cam and J. Neyman, eds., *Proc. 6th Berkeley Sympos. on Mathematical Statistics and Probability*. Univ. of California Press, Berkeley, CA, 175–194.

Han, A. K. (1987). Non-parametric analysis of a generalized regression model. *J. Econometrics* **35**, 303–316.

Hall, P. (1986). On the bootstrap and confidence intervals. *Ann. Statist.* **14**, 1431–1452.

Hausman, J. A. and D. A. Wise (1987). A conditional probit model for qualitative choice: Discrete decisions recognizing interdependence and heterogeneous preferences. *Econometrica* **46**, 403–426.

Horowitz, J. L. (1991). Semiparametric estimation of a work-trip mode choice model. To appear in *J. Econometrics*.

Horowitz, J. L. (1992). A smoothed maximum score estimator for the binary response model. *Econometrica* **60**, 505–531.

Horowitz, J. L. (1993). Optimal rates of convergence of parameter estimators in the binary response model with weak distributional assumptions. *Econometric Theory* **9**, 1–18.

Hsieh, D., C. F. Manski and D. McFadden (1985). Estimation of response probabilities from augmented retrospective observations. *J. Amer. Statist. Assoc.* **80**, 651–662.

Ibragimov, I. A. and R. Z. Has'minskii (1981). *Statistical Estimation: Asymptotic Theory*. Springer, New York.

Ichimura, H. (1987). Estimation of single index models. Ph.D. Dissertation, Department of Economics, Massachusetts Institute of Technology, Cambridge, MA.

Kiefer, J. and J. Wolfowitz (1956). Consistency of the maximum likelihood estimator in the presence of presence of infinitely many incidental parameters. *Ann. Math. Statist.* **27**, 887–906.

Kim, J. and D. Pollard (1990). Cube root asymptotics. *Ann. Statist.* **18**, 191–219.

Klein, R. L. and R. H. Spady (1993). An efficient semiparametric estimator for discrete choice models. *Econometrica* **61**, 387–422.

Koshevnik, Yu. A. and B. Ya. Levit (1976). On a nonparametric analogue of the information matrix. *Theory Probab. Appl.* **21**, 738–753.

Le Cam, L. (1953). On some asymptotic properties of maximum likelihood estimates and related Bayes estimates. *Univ. California Publ. Statist.* **1**, 277–330.

Levy, A. V. and A. Montalvo (1985). The tunneling algorithm for the global minimization of functions. *SIAM J. Sci. Statist. Comput.* **6**, 15–29.

Maddala, G. S. (1983). *Limited-Dependent and Qualitative Variables in Econometrics*. Cambridge Univ. Press, Cambridge.

Manski, C. F. (1975). Maximum score estimation of the stochastic utility model of choice. *J. Econometrics* **3**, 205–228.

Manski, C. F. (1985). Semiparametric analysis of discrete response: Asymptotic properties of the maximum score estimator. *J. Econometrics* **27**, 313–334.

Manski, C. F. (1986). Semiparametric analysis of binary response from response-based samples. *J. Econometrics* **31**, 31–40.

Manski, C. F. (1988). Identification of binary response models. *J. Amer. Statist. Assoc.* **83**, 729–738.

Manski, C. F. and S. R. Lerman (1977). The estimation of choice probabilities from choice-based samples. *Econometrica* **45**, 1977–1988.

Manski, C. F. and D. McFadden (1981). Alternative estimators and sample designs for discrete choice analysis. In: C. F. Manski and D. McFadden, eds., *Structural Analysis of Discrete Data with Econometric Applications*, MIT Press, Cambridge, MA, 2–50.

Manski, C. F. and T. S. Thompson (1986). Operational characteristics of maximum score estimation. *J. Econometrics* **32**, 65–108.

Matzkin, R. L. (1990). Estimation of multinomial models using weak monotonicity assumptions. Discussion paper no. 957, Cowles Foundation for Research in Economics, Yale University, New Haven, CT.

Matzkin, R. L. (1991). Semiparametric estimation of monotone and concave utility functions for polychotomous choice models. *Econometrica* **59**, 1315–1327.

Matzkin, R. L. (1992). Nonparametric and distribution-free estimation of the binary threshold crossing and the binary choice models. *Econometrica* **60**, 239–270.

McFadden, D. (1974). Conditional logit analysis of qualitative choice behavior. In: P. Zarembka, ed., *Frontiers in Econometrics*. Academic Press, New York, 105–142.

Newey, W. K. (1989). An introduction to semiparametric efficiency bounds. *Ann. Econ. Statist.* **13**, 1–47.

Newey, W. K., J. L. Powell and J. R. Walker (1990). Semiparametric estimation of selection models: Some empirical results. *Amer. Econ. Rev. Papers Proc.* **80**, 324–328.

Pfanzagl, J. (1982). *Contributions to a General Asymptotic Statistical Theory*. Springer, New York.

Powell, J. L., J. H. Stock and T. M. Stoker (1989). Semiparametric estimation of index coefficients. *Econometrica* **57**, 1403–1430.

Prakasa Rao, B. L. S. (1983). *Nonparametric Functional Estimation*. Academic Press, New York.

Ruud, P. A. (1983). Sufficient conditions for the consistency of maximum likelihood estimation despite misspecification of distribution. *Econometrica* **51**, 225–228.

Sherman, R. P. (1993). The limiting distribution of the maximum rank correlation estimator. *Econometrica* **61**, 123–138.

Stein, C. (1956). Efficient nonparametric testing and estimation. In: *Proc. 3rd Berkeley Sympos. on Mathematical Statistics and Probability*, Vol. 1. Univ. of California Press, Berkeley, 187–195.

Stoker, T. M. (1986). Consistent estimation of scaled coefficients. *Econometrica* **54**, 1461–1481.

Stone, C. J. (1977). Consistent nonparametric regression. *Ann. Statist.* **5**, 595–645.

Stone, C. J. (1980). Optimal rates of convergence of nonparametric estimators. *Ann. Statist.* **8**, 1348–1360.

Szu, H. and R. Hartley (1987). Fast simulated annealing. *Phys. Lett. A* **122**, 157–162.

White, H. (1982). Maximum likelihood estimation of misspecified models. *Econometrica* **50**, 1–25.

G. S. Maddala, C. R. Rao and H. D. Vinod, eds., *Handbook of Statistics*, Vol. 11
© 1993 Elsevier Science Publishers B.V. All rights reserved.

3

The Selection Problem in Econometrics and Statistics

Charles F. Manski

1. Introduction

Some respondents to a household survey decline to report their incomes. Some youth enrolled in high school opt not to take the scholastic aptitude test. Some welfare recipients drop out of a vocational training program. These very different situations share the common feature that an outcome is *censored*; survey respondents' incomes, youths' SAT scores, or welfare recipients' employment status after completion of vocational training.

Because censored data are so common, econometricians and statisticians have denoted much effort to their analysis. In particular, the following *selection problem* has drawn substantial attention: Each member of a population is characterized by a triple (y, z, x), where y lies in a finite dimensional real space Y, $z = 0$ or 1, and x lies in a finite dimensional real space X. A researcher draws a random sample, observes all the realizations of (z, x), but observes realizations of y only when $z = 1$. The researcher wants to learn a feature of the probability measure of y conditional on x,

$$P(y \mid x) = P(y \mid x, z = 1)P(z = 1 \mid x) + P(y \mid x, z = 0)P(z = 0 \mid x) . \qquad (1)$$

The selection problem is the failure of the censored-sampling process to identify $P(y \mid x)$. The sampling process does identify the selection probability $P(z = 1 \mid x)$, the censoring probability $P(z = 0 \mid x)$, and the measure of y conditional on selection, $P(y \mid x, z = 1)$. It is uninformative regarding the measure of y conditional on censoring, $P(y \mid x, z = 0)$. Hence the censored-sampling process reveals only that

$$P(y \mid x) \in [P(y \mid x, z = 1)P(z = 1 \mid x) + \gamma P(z = 0 \mid x), \gamma \in \Gamma] , \qquad (2)$$

where Γ denotes the space of all probability measures on Y.

Econometric analysis. Although the selection problem arises in very many settings, formal analysis in economics is a relatively recent development. Until the early 1970s, empirical researchers either explicitly or implicitly assumed that, conditional on x, y and z are statistically independent. That is,

$$P(y \mid x) = P(y \mid x, z = 0) = P(y \mid x, z = 1) . \tag{3}$$

Given that $P(y \mid x, z = 1)$ is identified by the sampling process, hypothesis (3) identifies $P(y \mid x)$. Moreover, in the absence of prior information, this hypothesis is not rejectable. The reason is that $P(y \mid x, z = 1)$ belongs to the set of feasible values for $P(y \mid x)$; just let $\gamma = P(y \mid x, z = 1)$ in (2).

The empirical plausibility of (3) was eventually questioned sharply, especially when researchers observed that, in many economic settings, the process by which observations on y become censored is related to the value of y (see, for example, Gronau, 1974). It also became clear that (3) is not necessary to identify $P(y \mid x)$. An alternative is to specify a latent variable model jointly explaining (y, z) conditional on x (see, for example, Heckman, 1976; or Maddala, 1983).

Statistical analysis. Statisticians analyzing censoring data often assume that (3) holds. This is sometimes referred to as the assumption of 'ignorable nonresponse'. The term 'nonignorable nonresponse' is used to cover all situations in which y and z are dependent conditional on x (see, for example, Rubin, 1987).

Whereas the latent-variable model framework has dominated econometric thinking about dependence between y and z, no similarly pervasive idea appears in the statistics literature. Some statisticians, particularly Rubin (1987), directly impose assumptions on the censored distribution $P(y \mid x, z = 0)$. Researchers analyzing failure times often use the competing-risks model, which is a type of latent-variable model (see, for example, Kalbfleisch and Prentice, 1980).

Organization of this chapter. Although the econometrics and statistics literatures on the selection problem differ in important respects, they both focus primarily on situations in which one has strong prior information on the distribution of (y, z) conditional on x. As I see it, the logical starting point for an investigation of the selection problem is to characterize the problem in the absence of prior information; Section 2 summarizes my recent work on this subject. Then Section 3 describes the main ideas of the econometrics and statistics literature. Section 4 makes concluding comments.

2. The selection problem in the absence of prior information

It is well known that, in the absence of prior information on the distribution of (y, z, x), the selection problem is fatal for inference on the mean regression of y on x,

$$E(y \mid x) = E(y \mid x, z = 1)P(z = 1 \mid x) + E(y \mid x, z = 0)P(z = 0 \mid x) . \tag{4}$$

The censored-sampling process identifies $E(y \mid x, z = 1)$ and $P(z \mid x)$ but provides no information on $E(y|x, z = 0)$, which can take any value in Y. Hence, whenever the censoring probability $P(z = 0|x)$ is positive, the sampling process imposes no restrictions on $E(y|x)$.

One must, however, be careful not to extrapolate from the mean to other distributional features. Identification of the mean from censored data is a particularly difficult problem. In the absence of prior information, censored data imply informative, easily interpretable bounds on other important features, including quantiles, distribution functions, and the means of bounded functions of y. This section presents some of the findings of Manski (1989, 1993).

2.1. Population bounds

Mean regressions of bounded functions of y. The central finding, from which others may be derived, concerns the mean of a bounded function of y. Let $g(\cdot)$ be a function mapping Y into a bounded interval $[K_{0g}, K_{1g}]$ on the real line. Observe that

$$E[g(y)|x] = E[g(y)|x, z = 1]P(z = 1|x)$$
$$+ E[g(y)|x, z = 0]P(z = 0|x) . \qquad (5)$$

The sampling process identifies $E[g(y)|x, z = 1]$ and $P(z|x)$ but provides no information on $E[g(y)|x, z = 0)$. The last quantity, however, necessarily lies in the interval $[K_{0g}, K_{1g}]$. This simple fact yields the following powerful result:

$$E[g(y)|x, z = 1]P(z = 1|x) + K_{0g}P(z = 0|x)$$
$$\leqslant E[g(y)|x] \leqslant E[g(y)|x, z = 1]P(z = 1|x) + K_{1g}P(z = 0|x) . \qquad (6)$$

Thus, a censored-sampling process bounds the mean regression of any bounded function of y. The lower bound is the value $E[g(y)|x]$ takes if, in the censored subpopulation, $g(y)$ always equals K_{0g}; the upper bound is the value of $E[g(y)|x]$ if all the censored y equal K_{1g}. The bound is a proper subset of $[K_{0g}, K_{1g}]$, hence informative, whenever censoring is less than total. At each $x_0 \in X$, the bound width $(K_{1g} - K_{0g})P(z = 0|x = x_0)$ is proportional to the censoring probability $P(z = 0|x)$. It is therefore meaningful to say that the degree of underidentification of $E[g(y)|x = x_0]$ is proportional to the censoring probability at x_0.

The conditional probability measure and distribution function. The bound (6) has numerous applications. Perhaps the most farreaching is the bound it implies on the probability that y lies in any measurable set $A \subset Y$. Let $g_A(\cdot)$ be the indicator function $g_A(y) \equiv 1[y \in A]$. Observe that $E[g_A(y)|x] = P(y \in A|x)$. Hence (6) implies that

$$P(y \in A|x, z = 1)P(z = 1|x) \leqslant P(y \in A|x)$$
$$\leqslant P(y \in A|x, z = 1)P(z = 1|x) + P(z = 0|x) . \qquad (7)$$

It is often convenient to characterize a probability measure on a real space by its distribution function $P(y \leq t \mid x)$, $t \in Y$. It follows from (7) that

$$P(y \leq t \mid x, z = 1)P(z = 1 \mid x) \leq P(y \leq t \mid x)$$
$$\leq P(y \leq t \mid x, z = 1)P(z = 1 \mid x) + P(z = 0 \mid x), \quad \forall t \in Y. \tag{8}$$

It may seem surprising that one should be able to bound the distribution function of a random variable but not its mean. The explanation is a fact that is widely appreciated by researchers in the field of robust statistics: the mean of a random variable is not a continuous function of its distribution function. Hence small perturbations in a distribution function can generate large movements in the mean. See Huber (1981).

To obtain some intuition for this fact, consider the following thought experiment. Let w be a random variable with $1 - \varepsilon$ of its probability mass in the interval $(-\infty, T]$ and ε mass at some point $S > T$. Suppose w is perturbed by moving the mass at S to some $S_1 > S$. Then $P(w \leq \tau)$ remains unchanged for $\tau < S$ and falls by at most ε for $\tau \geq S$. But $E(w)$ increases by the amount $\varepsilon(S_1 - S)$. Now let $S_1 \to \infty$. The perturbed distribution function remains within an ε-bound of the original one but the mean of the perturbed random variable converges to infinity.

Quantile regressions. Let $Y = R^1$ and $\alpha \in (0, 1)$. The α-quantile of $P(y \mid x)$ is defined by

$$q(\alpha, x) \equiv \min t: P(y \leq t \mid x) \geq \alpha. \tag{9}$$

The bound (8) on $P(y \leq \cdot \mid x)$ can be inverted to show that $q(\alpha, x)$ must lie between two quantiles of the identified distribution $P(y \mid x, z = 1)$. Define

$$r(\alpha, x) \equiv \begin{cases} [1 - (1 - \alpha)/P(z = 1 \mid x)]\text{-quantile of } P(y \mid x, z = 1) \\ \qquad \text{if } P(z = 1 \mid x) > 1 - \alpha, \\ -\infty \quad \text{otherwise}. \end{cases} \tag{10}$$

$$s(\alpha, X) \equiv \begin{cases} [\alpha/P(z = 1 \mid x)]\text{-quantile of } P(y \mid x, z = 1) \\ \qquad \text{if } P(z = 1 \mid x) \geq \alpha, \\ \infty \quad \text{otherwise}. \end{cases}$$

It is proved in Manski (1993) that

$$r(\alpha, x) \leq q(\alpha, x) \leq s(\alpha, x). \tag{11}$$

Moreover, in the absence of prior information, this bound on $q(\alpha, x)$ cannot be improved upon.

The lower and upper bounds $r(\alpha, x)$ and $s(\alpha, x)$ are increasing functions of α; hence the bound shifts to the right as α increases. The lower bound is informative if $P(z = 1 \mid x) > 1 - \alpha$; the upper bound if $P(z = 1 \mid x) \geq \alpha$. So the bound (11) restricts $q(\alpha, x)$ to an interval of finite length if $P(z = 1 \mid x) > \max(\alpha, 1 - \alpha)$ and is uninformative if $P(z = 1 \mid x) < \min(\alpha, 1 - \alpha)$.

2.2. Sample inference

The selection problem is, first and foremost, a failure of identification. It is only secondarily a difficulty in sample inference. To keep attention focussed on the central identification question, it is simplest to suppose that the conditional distributions identified by the sampling process, $P(y \mid x, z = 1)$ and $P(z \mid x)$, are known. But it is also important to recognize that the population bounds reported in Section 2.1 are easily estimable.

Estimation of the bound (6) on the mean of a bounded function of y is a conventional problem in nonparametric regression analysis (see, for example, Bierens, 1987; or Hardle, 1990). Rewrite (6) in the equivalent form

$$E[g(y)z + K_{0g}(1 - z) \mid x] \leq E[g(y) \mid x] \leq E[g(y)z + K_{1g}(1 - z) \mid x]. \quad (6')$$

The censored-sampling process enables consistent nonparametric estimation of $E[g(y)z + K_{0g}(1 - z) \mid x]$ and $E[g(y)z + K_{1g}(1 - z) \mid x]$ at almost all values of x. Consistent estimation of the bound at a given x_0 in the support of x is possible if $P(x = x_0) > 0$ or if $E[g(y)z + K_{0g}(1 - z) \mid x]$ and $E[g(y)z + K_{1g}(1 - z) \mid x]$ are continuous at x_0. Given regularity conditions, asymptotically valid sampling confidence intervals can be placed around estimates of the bounds. Empirical applications are presented in Manski (1989) and in Manski, Sandefur, McLanahan and Powers (1992).

It is proved in Manski (1993) that the bound (11) on a quantile regression can be estimated consistently if $r(\cdot, x)$ and $s(\cdot, x)$ are continuous at α. Given a random sample of size N, let $P_N(y \leq \cdot \mid x, z = 1)$ and $P_N(z \mid x)$ be appropriate nonparametric estimates of $P(y \leq \cdot \mid x, z = 1)$ and $P(z \mid x)$. Let

$$r_N(\alpha, x) \equiv \begin{cases} [1 - (1 - \alpha)/P_N(z = 1 \mid x)]\text{-quantile of } P_N(y \mid x, z = 1) \\ \qquad \text{if } P_N(z = 1 \mid x) > 1 - \alpha, \\ -\infty \quad \text{otherwise}. \end{cases} \quad (12)$$

$$s_N(\alpha, X) \equiv \begin{cases} [\alpha/P_N(z = 1 \mid x)]\text{-quantile of } P_N(y \mid x, z = 1) \\ \qquad \text{if } P_N(z = 1 \mid x) \geq \alpha, \\ \infty \quad \text{otherwise}. \end{cases}$$

Then, as $N \to \infty$, $[r_N(\alpha, x), s_N(\alpha, x)]$ converges with probability one to $[r(\alpha, x), s(\alpha, x)]$ at almost all values of x.

3. The selection problem with prior information

The bounds reported in Section 2 can be improved if suitable prior information on $P(y, z \mid x)$ is available. A restriction has identifying power if it implies that $P(y \mid x)$ belongs to a set of distributions smaller than that given in (2). Restrictions on $P(y \mid x)$, $P(y \mid x, z = 0)$, and $P(z \mid x, y)$ may have identifying power. Restrictions on $P(y \mid x, z = 1)$ and $P(z \mid x)$ are superfluous as these quantities are identified by the censored-sampling process. (The fact that the latter restrictions have no identifying power does not imply that they are useless in practice; they may enable one to improve the precision of sample estimates of $P(y|x, z = 1)$ and $P(z|x)$.)

Functional-form restrictions. Information directly constraining $P(y|x)$ is often referred to as a functional-form restriction. A functional-form restriction may constrain $P(y|\cdot)$ as a function on X; one might, for example, know that y is statistically independent of some component of x or that $E(y|x)$ is a linear function of x. Or it may constrain the shape of $P(y|x = x_0)$ at a specified $x_0 \in X$; one might know that $P(y|x = x_0)$ is a symmetric distribution or a normal distribution.

Censored-distribution restrictions. A second type of information is a restriction on the censored-distribution $P(y|x, z = 0)$. A simple example is the statistical independence assumption (3). More generally, let $P(y|x, z = 0)$ be known to be a member of a class Γ_{0x} of probability measures. Then (2) can be improved to

$$P(y|x) \in [P(y|x, z = 1)P(z = 1|x) + \gamma P(z = 0|x), \gamma \in \Gamma_{0x}] . \qquad (13)$$

Selection restrictions. Information constraining $P(z|x, y)$ is sometimes referred to as a selection restriction. One example is the conditional independence assumption (3), which can be rewritten as

$$P(z|x, y) = P(z|x) . \qquad (3')$$

A different conditional independence assumption, studied in Manski (1993), is

$$P(z|x, y) = P(z|y) . \qquad (14)$$

To see why a selection restriction may have identifying power, observe that, for any measurable set $A \subset Y$,

$$P(y \in A|x) = P(y \in A|x, z = 1)P(z = 1|x)/P(z = 1|x, y \in A) . \qquad (15)$$

The quantities $P(y \in A|x, z = 1)$ and $P(z = 1|x)$ are identified by the sampling process, so a restriction on $P(z = 1|x, y \in A)$ implies a restriction on $P(y \in A|x)$.

Identification strategies. Ideally, we would like to learn the identifying power of all types of prior information, so as to characterize the entire frontier of inferential possibilities. Then the empirical researcher would be able to make the inferences that are possible given whatever restrictions he or she believes to hold. But there does not appear to be any effective way to conduct a complete identification analysis. So researchers have investigated the power of specific bundles of restrictions thought to have application to empirical problems of interest. Section 3.1 describes the dominant strategy of the econometrics literature. Section 3.2 describes the practices of statisticians.

3.1. Econometric latent variable models

For twenty years, econometric thinking on the selection problem has been expressed through latent-variable models of the form

$$y = f_1(x) + u_1 , \tag{16a}$$

$$z = 1[f_2(x) + u_2 > 0] . \tag{16b}$$

Here $Y = R^1$, $[f_1(\cdot), f_2(\cdot)]$ are real functions of x, and (u_1, u_2) are random variables whose realizations are unobserved by the researcher. The threshold-crossing form of the selection function (16b) is well-motivated in empirical analyses where the observability of y is determined by the binary choice behavior of a rational decision maker. In such cases $f_2(x) + u_2$ is the difference between the values of the two alternatives and (16b) states that the more highly-valued alternative is chosen. Many examples are given in Maddala (1983).

Equations (16) alone do not restrict the distribution of (y, z) conditional on x. A model takes on content when restrictions are imposed on $[f_1(\cdot), f_2(\cdot)]$ and on the distribution of (u_1, u_2) conditional on x. The overriding concern of the literature has been to find plausible restrictions that identify the mean regression of y on x, although most of the restrictions studied actually identify the conditional measure $P(y|x)$ fully. In what follows, I describe three types of restrictions that have received considerable attention. These restrictions are neither nested nor mutually exclusive. A latent variable model may impose any combination of them.

Model with conditionally independent disturbances. The early literature assumed that u_1 and u_2 are statistically independent conditional on x. It follows that

$$
\begin{aligned}
P(y|x, z = 1) &= P[f_1(x) + u_1 | x, f_2(x) + u_2 \geq 0] \\
&= P[f_1(x) + u_1 | x] = P(y|x) .
\end{aligned} \tag{17}
$$

Thus, independence of u_1 and u_2 conditional on x implies independence of y and z conditional on x, the restriction stated in (3). Given this, $P(y|x)$ is identified even if no restrictions are imposed on $[f_1(\cdot), f_2(\cdot)]$. In practice, researchers have typically imposed restrictions on $f_1(\cdot)$; most applications make $f_1(\cdot)$ linear in x.

Parametric models. A second type of restriction became prominent in the middle 1970s. Suppose that $f_1(\cdot)$ is known up to a finite dimensional parameter β_1, $f_2(\cdot)$ up to a finite dimensional parameter β_2, and the distribution of (u_1, u_2) conditional on x up to a finite dimensional parameter γ. Then

$$P(y, z = 1 | x) = P[f_1(x, \beta_1) + u_1, f_2(x, \beta_2) + u_2 \geq 0 | x, \gamma] . \tag{18}$$

The left-hand side of (18) is identified by the censored sampling process. The right-hand side is a function of the parameters $(\beta_1, \beta_2, \gamma)$. If there exists only one parameter value solving (18), then $P(y|x)$ is identified.

Parametric latent variable models have usually been studied through analysis of the mean of y conditional on $(x, z = 1)$. Following the practice in the literature, assume that $E(u_1, u_2|x) = 0$. Then

$$E(y|x) = f_1(x, \beta_1),\tag{19a}$$

$$E(y|x, z = 1) = f_1(x, \beta_1) + E[u_1|x, f_2(x, \beta_2) + u_2 \geq 0, \gamma]$$
$$\equiv f_1(x, \beta_1) + g(x, \beta_2, \gamma).\tag{19b}$$

The left-hand side of (19b) is identified by the sampling process. The parameter β_1 is identified, hence $E(y|x)$, if there exists only one value of $(\beta_1, \beta_2, \gamma)$ solving (19b).

The most widely applied model makes $f_1(\cdot)$ and $f_2(\cdot)$ linear functions, (u_1, u_2) statistically independent of x, and the distribution of (u_1, u_2) normal with mean zero and unrestricted correlation; the variance of u_1 is unrestricted but that of u_2 is set equal to one as a normalization. In this case,

$$E(y|x) = x'\beta_1,\tag{20a}$$

$$E(y|x, z = 1) = x'\beta_1 + \gamma\phi(x'\beta_2)/\Phi(x'\beta_2),\tag{20b}$$

where $\phi(\cdot)$ and $\Phi(\cdot)$ are the standard normal density and distribution functions and where $\gamma = E(u_1 u_2)$. Identification of β_1 hinges on the fact that the linear function $x'\beta_1$ and the nonlinear function $\gamma\phi(x'\beta_2)/\Phi(x'\beta_2)$ affect $E(y|x, z = 1)$ in different ways. See Heckman (1976) or Maddala (1983).

There is a common perception that the normal-linear model generalizes the model with conditionally independent disturbances. In fact, the two models are not nested. The normal-linear model permits u_1 and u_2 to be dependent but assumes linearity of $[f_1(\cdot), f_2(\cdot)]$, normality of (u_1, u_2), and independence of (u_1, u_2) from x. The model with conditionally independent disturbances assumes u_1 and u_2 to be independent conditional on x but does not restrict the distributions of u_1 and u_2. Nor does it restrict the form of $[f_1(\cdot), f_2(\cdot)]$.

Index models. By the early 1980s, parametric models were increasingly criticized. Several articles reported that estimates of $E(y|x)$ obtained under the normal-linear model are sensitive to misspecification of the distribution of (u_1, u_2) conditional on x. Hurd (1979) showed the consequences of heteroskedasticity; Arabmazar and Schmidt (1982) and Goldberger (1983) described the effect of nonnormality. Concern with this led to the development of a third type of latent-variable model.

Let $h(x)$ be a known index; that is, a many-to-one function of x. Assume that

$f_2(x)$ and the distribution of (u_1, u_2) vary with x only through $h(x)$. Then

$$E(y \mid x) = f_1(x), \tag{21a}$$

$$E(y \mid x, z = 1) = f_1(x) + E\{u_1 \mid x, f_2[h(x)] + u_2 \geq 0\}$$
$$\equiv f_1(x) + g[h(x)]. \tag{21b}$$

Let (ξ, ρ) denote a pair of points in the support of x such that $h(\xi) = h(\rho)$. For each such pair, (21) implies that

$$E(y \mid x = \xi, z = 1) - E(y \mid x = \rho, z = 1) = E(y \mid x = \xi) - E(y \mid x = \rho). \tag{22}$$

The left-hand side of (22) is identified by the sampling process; hence the difference $E(y \mid x = \xi) - E(y \mid x = \rho)$ is identified.

The usefulness of this result depends on the size of the sets $[(\xi, \rho): h(\xi) = h(\rho)]$. The index assumption with the greatest identifying power is that in which $h(\cdot)$ is constant on X; then (22) identifies $E(y \mid x)$ up to an additive constant. At the other extreme is the trivial case in which $h(\cdot)$ is one-to-one; then $h(\xi) = h(\rho) \Rightarrow \xi = \rho$ and (22) is uninformative.

The recent practice has been to impose an index assumption in combination with other restrictions. Robinson (1988) combines an index assumption with the functional-form assumption that $f_1(\cdot)$ is linear. In Ahn and Powell (1993), Powell (1987), Heckman and Honore (1990), and Cosslett (1991), the index $h(\cdot)$ is not a priori known but assumptions are imposed that make $h(\cdot)$ nonparametrically estimable from data on (z, x).

3.2. Statistical practices

The competing-risks model applied in medical and quality-control research supposes that y and s are the random failure times for two components of a system and assumes that the system breaks down when the first component fails. In latent-variable notation, the model can be written

$$y = f_y(x) + u_y, \tag{23a}$$

$$s = f_s(x) + u_s, \tag{23b}$$

$$z = 1[y < s] = 1[f_y(x) + u_y < f_s(x) + u_s]. \tag{23c}$$

This model has the same structure as the short-side model of markets in disequilibrium in econometrics (see Maddala, 1983).

Whereas competing-risks models and econometric latent-variable models embody substantive theories of censoring processes, some statisticians approach censored-sampling from a very different perspective: as a mixture problem, wherein $P(y \mid x, z = 1)$ and $P(y \mid x, z = 0)$ characterize two primitive populations and $P(z \mid x)$ is the mixing distribution. In particular, Rubin (1987,

Section 6.2) supposes that one has prior information restricting the censored distribution $P(y|x, z = 0)$ to a class Γ_{0x} of probability measures on y; thus (13) holds. He also suggests that one place a subjective probability distribution on the elements of Γ_{0x}. This then induces a subjective distribution on the set

$$[P(y|x, z = 1)P(z = 1|x) + \gamma P(z = 0|x), \gamma \in \Gamma_{0x}]$$

of possible values of $P(y|x)$.

Such Bayesian 'sensitivity analysis' is feasible only if the set Γ_{0x} is sufficiently small; otherwise a subjective distribution cannot be placed on Γ_{0x}. The practice has been to make Γ_{0x} finite or at most a finite dimensional set of distributions. The case of no prior information, in which Γ_{0x} is the set of all distributions on y, has not received attention in the statistics literature.

Two world views. Econometric latent-variable models and statistical mixture models express different ideas about the nature of the selection problem and imply different conclusions about the appropriate way to assert prior information. From the latent-variable-model perspective, the censored distribution is a derived quantity, not a primitive concept; hence, a researcher who thinks in latent-variable terms finds it difficult to judge the plausibility of restrictions imposed on $P(y|x, z = 0)$. From the mixture model perspective, $P(y|x, z = 0)$ is a primitive so it is natural to assert prior information through restrictions on this distribution; mixture modellers find it difficult to interpret prior information stated as restrictions on latent variable models. The different world views expressed in latent-variable and mixture models have been aired recently in Wainer (1986, 1989).

The conflicting econometric and statistical perspectives on the selection problem recalls a closely related conflict regarding the analysis of discrete data. Econometricians have typically asserted prior information through latent variable models of discrete choice. Many statisticians have imposed restrictions through the mixture model, referred to as discriminant analysis in that context. See Manski and McFadden (1981, pp. 4–6) for a discussion and references.

4. Conclusion

Twenty years ago few economists paid attention to the fact that selective observation of random sample data has implications for empirical analysis. Then the profession became sensitized to the selection problem. The heretofore maintained assumption, conditional independence of y and z, became a standard object of attack. For a while the normal-linear latent variable model became the standard 'solution' to the selection problem. But researchers soon became aware that this model does not solve the selection problem; it trades one set of assumptions for another. So econometricians sought to widen the menu of latent variable models. Recent work weakens the parametric assumptions of the normal-linear model at the cost of imposing an index assumption.

During the same period, statisticians were struggling to deal with nonignorable nonresponse. Those with failure-time applications developed competing risk models. Other statisticians came to think in mixture-model terms.

The current diversity of approaches to the selection problem is unsurprising. Moreover, it will almost certainly persist. Censoring creates an identification problem. Identification depends on the prior knowledge a researcher is willing to assert in the application of interest. As researchers are heterogeneous in their applications and in their prior beliefs, so must be their perspectives on the selection problem.

Econometricians and statisticians can assist empirical researchers by clarifying the nature of the selection problem and by widening the set of cases for which the inferential possibilities are understood. My own view is that both the econometrics and statistics literatures have overemphasized situations in which one has strong prior information. Empirical analysis should begin by determining what one can learn from the data alone, in the absence of prior information. This done, then prior information may be brought to bear, in whatever form and strength as one believes appropriate in the application of interest.

References

Ahn, H. and J. Powell (1993). Semiparametric estimation of censored selection models with a nonparametric selection mechanism. *J. Econometrics* **58**.

Arabmazar, A. and P. Schmidt (1982). An investigation of the robustness of the tobit estimator to non-normality. *Econometrica* **50**, 1055–1063.

Bierens, H. (1987). Kernel estimators of regression functions. In: T. Bewley, ed., *Advances in Econometrics*, Vol. 1, Cambridge Univ. Press, New York, 99–144.

Cosslett, S. (1991). Semiparametric estimation of a regression model with sample selectivity. In: W. Barnett, J. Powell and G. Tauchen, eds., *Nonparametric and Semiparametric Methods in Econometrics and Statistics*, Cambridge Univ. Press, New York, 175–197.

Goldberger, A. (1983). Abnormal selection bias. In: S. Karlin, T. Amemiya and L. Goodman, eds., *Studies in Econometrics, Time Series, and Multivariate Statistics*, Academic Press, Orlando, FL, 67–84.

Gronau, R. (1974). Wage comparisons – A selectivity bias. *J. Politic. Econ.* **82**, 1119–1143.

Hardle, W. (1990). *Applied Nonparametric Regression*. Cambridge Univ. Press, New York.

Heckman, J. (1976). The common structure of statistical models of truncation, sample selection, and limited dependent variables and a simple estimator for such models. *Ann. Econ. Social Measurement* **5**, 479–492.

Heckman, J. and B. Honore (1990). The empirical content of the Roy model. *Econometrica* **58**, 1121–1149.

Huber, P. (1981). *Robust Statistics*. Wiley, New York.

Hurd, M. (1979). Estimation in truncated samples when there is heteroskedasticity. *J. Econometrics* **11**, 247–258.

Kalbfleisch, J. and R. Prentice (1980). *The Statistical Analysis of Failure Time Data*. Wiley, New York.

Maddala, G. S. (1983). *Limited-Dependent and Qualitative Variables in Econometrics*. Cambridge Univ. Press, Cambridge, UK.

Manski, C. (1989). Anatomy of the selection problem. *J. Human Resources* **24**, 343–360.

Manski, C. (1993). The selection problem. In: C. Sims, ed., *Advances in Econometrics*. Cambridge Univ. Press, New York. To appear.

Manski, C. and D. McFadden (1981). Alternative estimators and sample designs for discrete choice analysis. In: C. Manski and D. McFadden, eds., *Structural Analysis of Discrete Data with Econometric Applications*, MIT Press, Cambridge, MA, 2–50.

Manski, C., G. Sandefur, S. McLanahan and D. Powers (1992). Alternative estimates of the effects of family structure during childhood on high school graduation. *J. Amer. Statist. Assoc.* **87**, 25–37.

Powell, J. (1987). Semiparametric estimation of bivariate latent variable models. Social Systems Research Institute Working Paper 8704, University of Wisconsin–Madison.

Robinson, P. (1988). Root-*N*-consistent semiparametric regression. *Econometrica* **56**, 931–954.

Rubin, D. (1987). *Multiple Imputation for Nonresponse in Surveys*. Wiley, New York.

Wainer, H., ed. (1986). *Drawing Inferences from Self-Selected Samples*. Springer, New York.

Wainer, H., ed. (1989). *J. Ed. Statist.* **14**(2).

G. S. Maddala, C. R. Rao and H. D. Vinod, eds., *Handbook of Statistics, Vol. 11*
4

General Nonparametric Regression Estimation and Testing in Econometrics

A. Ullah and H. D. Vinod

1. Introduction

Generalization of the familiar histogram called kernel and 'nearest neighbor' density estimation was pioneered by Rosenblatt (1956), and its applications to regression by Nadaraya (1964), Watson (1964), Stone (1977) and others. Major books on the subject include: Prakasa Rao (1983), Silverman (1986), Eubank (1988), Hasti and Tibshirani (1990) and Hardle (1990). Window widths, bandwidths or smoothing parameters denoted here by h, are a generalization of the widths of bars appearing in a histogram. The basic computer algorithm in nonparametric density estimation replaces an estimate of a density $f(x)$ by a *weighted sum*, where weights can be complicated functions $w(x, h)$ defined in Section 2 below. We use these weighted sums to unify the vast literature dealing with nonparametric estimation and inference. Our focus is beyond kernel based regressions and their derivatives, since these are covered in other surveys. We include discussions of testing and asymptotic properties in terms of a general class of estimators. Our unification keeps the discussion closely tied to a practical computation of weighted sums and hopes to attract computationally talented researchers. Computational pointers are included at the end of most sections to focus attention on practical results.

We shall show that these methods have numerous applications in many areas including regressions, as shown by Gasser and Muller (1979a,b, 1984) and Ullah (1988a). Description of economic data often requires estimation of higher order moments and quantiles, which can be made richer with the help of nonparametric methods described in Section 3. We show in Section 4 that nonparametric weighted sums can offer truly flexible functional forms. For example, Vinod and Ullah (1988) consider what they call an 'amorphous regression' of y on x, with errors ε. We consider the standard nonparametric regression model:

$$y = m(x) + \varepsilon . \tag{1.1}$$

Typical assumptions on $m(x)$ are that it has an adequate number of derivatives. The regression function $m(x)$ is completely amorphous, having no functional form. It is defined simply as the expectation $E(y|x)$, and may be viewed in terms of the ratio of densities $f(y, x)/f(x)$. Hence, an estimate of $m(x)$ is feasible in terms of a ratio of weighted sums. Thus, nonparametric methods involving weighted sums are feasible in the estimation of the regression function $m(x)$ and with a bit more work, in the computation of the partial derivatives of $m(x)$ with respect to the regressors.

Econometrics is concerned with computation of marginal productivities, elasticities, etc. which are related to partial derivatives of $m(x)$. The initial appeal of these nonparametric estimators is that one need not specify the functional forms of $m(x)$ to estimate the partials of $E(y|x)$ with respect to x. One can compute analytical expressions of the derivatives of the ratios of weighted sums mentioned above, or numerical approximations, Gasser and Muller (1979b). When this possibility was presented at the Rutgers productivity conference in 1985 by one of us, the questions asked were: How can one estimate a relationships without specifying functional forms? Can empirical econometrics be really free from a need to specify functional forms and testing for specification errors? Independent of our work in Vinod and Ullah (1988), Powell, Stock and Stoker (1986), among others, proposed estimating a weighted average of derivatives. Recently, an application to household Engel curve estimation is reviewed with comments in Bierens and Pott-Buter (1990). We will mention many more applications later. When one starts with a known arbitrary functional form and a small data sample and compares several kernel type estimators, there are no clear winners, and the performance of non-parametric derivative estimators can be erratic. By now, we are aware of many informal comparisons, including some by our students. We shall indicate the current state of knowledge as well as challenging problems in this area, including the so-called curse of dimensionality. Our tentative conclusion is that empirical econometrics cannot be free from parametric forms, especially for small sample sizes with dependent observations and several regressors. A fruitful role for nonparametrics appears to be to piggyback on the parametric methods and see whether further progress can be made toward capturing any missing features.

We note that the performance of nonparametric methods in the estimation $m(x)$ itself, if not its derivatives, is now well established. To illustrate estimation of $m(x)$, let us consider Canadian data on earnings versus age. For data sources see Ullah (1985) and Ullah and Vinod (1988). Figure 1 plots the natural log of earnings (y_i) against age (x_i) for the 205 observations as dotted line. We have joined the scatter of points so that they are not missed visually. One can see that there is a reduction in earnings associated with an increase in age beyond 50, which may be called drooping. The linear regression estimator shown by a line interspersed with squares does not capture the drooping of earnings at high (or low) values of the age. The line with triangles depicts a kernel estimator, which does show some drooping. Toward the end of Section 2 we mention a compromise estimator from Ullah and Vinod (1991), which hopes to combine the advantages of parametric and nonparametric methods,

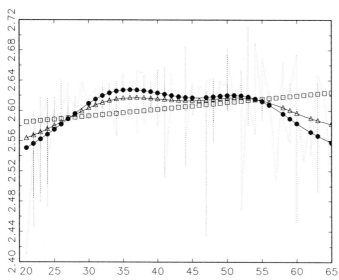

Fig. 1. Canadian cross section, log of earnings (dotted line), OLS forecasts (dotted line with squares), nonparametric and compromise forecasts (solid lines with triangles and bullets, respectively).

and includes a quadratica and a cubic. A line with circles which droops even further than the kernel estimator illustrates the compromise estimator. More work is needed to attempt boundary correction methods from Rice (1984) or Hall and Wehrly (1991).

Nonparametric estimation of variance of residuals from any parametric model can help recover what is missed by the parametric model, and possibly refine statistical inference. As is well known, the Box–Cox transformation is a generalization of the commonly used logarithmic transformation. These have been further generalized to achieve normality of the sampling distribution and homoscedasticity of errors, at the cost of further computational burden. We review these and additive models along with a systematic summary of finite sample properties of nonparametric estimators and misspecification tests.

In summary, we ask: Why study nonparametric smoothing methods? Because they offer versatility and flexibility in estimation and forecasting – one does not need to specify functional forms. These methods include powerful tools for exploratory analysis, improving the parametric fit and for locating the outliers and missing observations. Why do they work? Because they use local smoothing and because the theory reviewed here demonstrates so. What does not work? They fail when there are too many regressors and/or too few observations. What is the main context of this study? We are concerned with econometric applications where the design is random since the data are passively observed.

2. Nonparametric model and estimators

Let us consider $q = p + 1$ economic variables (Y, X') where Y is the dependent variable and X is a $p \times 1$ vector of regressors. These p variables are completely determined by their unknown joint density $f(y, x_1, \ldots, x_p) = f(y, x)$ at the points y, x. Then the nonparametric regression model can be expressed as

$$Y = m(x) + U , \tag{2.1}$$

where $m(x) = E(Y | X = x)$ provided $E|Y| < \infty$ and U represents errors. The term nonparametric is used because we are not necessarily writing $m(x)$ as $\beta_0 + \Sigma_{j=1}^{p} \beta_j x_j$ with parameters β_j, or some other parametric functional form. The function $m(x)$ can be highly nonlinear and is not assumed to be expressible in some parametric form. However, we require $m(x)$ to have p continuous derivatives (i.e., it is smooth) compared to the errors U.

Now suppose that we have data (y_i, x_i') $(i = 1, \ldots, n)$ upon $(1 \times q)$ vector (Y, X'), where x_i is a $p \times 1$ vector of variables and y_i is a scalar. Then from (2.1)

$$y_i = m(x_i) + u_i , \tag{2.2}$$

where the error term u_i has the properties $E(u_i | x_i) = 0$ and $E(u_i^2 | x_i) = \sigma^2(x_i)$. Throughout this paper capital letters Y, X etc. will be population random variables, lower case letters y_i, x_i will be sample (data) random variables, and y, x without a subscript will be certain fixed points whose ranges of values are the same as those of Y and X, respectively. We also assume throughout, that y_i, x_i, u_i are either iid (independent and identically distributed) or stationary for dependent data.

The aim of nonparametric estimation of $m(x)$ in (2.1) is to approximate $m(x)$ arbitrarily closely, given a large enough sample. This can be accomplished by a simple observation that the estimation of $m(x)$ implies the estimation of the population mean of Y when $X = x$. This is given by a general class of linear nonparametric estimators, essentially the weighted mean of y_i, as

$$\hat{m}(x) = \sum_{i=1}^{n} w_{ni}(x) y_i , \tag{2.3}$$

where $w_{ni}(x) = w_n(x_i, x)$ represents the weight assigned to the i-th observation y_i, and it depends on the distance of x_i from the point x. Usually, the weight is high if the distance is small and low if the distance is large. If the weights are such that $w_{ni}(x) \geq 0$ and $\Sigma w_{ni}(x) = 1$ then they may be called 'probability weights'. The conditions on weights w_{ni} which ensure consistency and asymptotic normality are given in Section 7.4.

For fixed x, let $m(x)$ be regarded as a single unknown parameter m. Now the estimator $\hat{m}(x)$ in (2.3) can be seen to be the minimizer of the weighted sum of squares $\Sigma_{i=1}^{n} w_{ni}(x)(y_i - m)^2$, where $\Sigma w_{ni}(x) = 1$. Hence, the estimator $\hat{m}$ is a weighted least squares estimator.

2.1. *Special cases of* $\hat{m}$

A large class of nonparametric estimators are special cases of (2.3). They differ mainly with respect to choice of w_{ni}. Some are developed for the case of nonstochastic (fixed) design X, even though econometric applications usually have random X's. For example, for a fixed design $x_i = i/n$ or $x_i = (i - 0.5)/n$, $(i = 1, \ldots, n)$, x_i are evenly distributed over an interval, which may be taken to be $[0, 1]$, without loss of generality. It is important for asymptotic results that $|x_i - x_{i-1}| = O(1/n)$.

(i) *Nadaraya–Watson (NW) kernel estimator.* The kernel is a continuous, bounded function which integrates to one, $\int K(u) \, du = 1$. For Nadaraya (1964) and Watson (1964) estimator the choice of w_{ni} in $\hat{m}$ is

$$w_{ni}(x) = K\left(\frac{x_i - x}{h}\right) \Big/ \sum_{i=1}^{n} K\left(\frac{x_i - x}{h}\right), \tag{2.4}$$

where $K(\cdot)$ is a kernel function with a scale factor $h = h_n \to 0$ as $n \to \infty$ is the window width. This is one of the most well-known estimators and it was developed by estimating $m(x) = \int yf(y \mid x) \, dy$ by using a nonparametric density estimator for $f(y \mid x)$. Its properties for the fixed design case have been explored in Gasser and Muller (1979a), Gasser and Engel (1990) and Chu (1989). Usually the kernel is chosen as a density function which integrates to one, e.g., normal. Higher order kernels are often useful in providing estimates with less bias. Let p denote the number of regressors comprising x. The choice of h which minimizes the approximate mean squared error (MSE) of $\hat{m}$ is $\propto n^{-1/(p+4)}$. Useful choices of h are obtained by using the leave-one-out or cross validation procedure of Wahba (1975, 1981) and iterative plug-in methods recently mentioned in Gasser et al. (1991).

If $h = h_i$ in (2.4) is a sequence of positive numbers, then (2.4) leads to recursive kernel estimators studied by Devroye and Wagner (1980) and Singh and Ullah (1986). Further if $K(\cdot)$ in (2.4) is replaced by $h_i^{-q} K[(x_i - x)/h_i]$ we get the recursive estimators due to Ahmand and Lin (1976). For details on the properties of NW and recursive estimators, see the review by Ullah (1988b) and the books by Eubank (1988) and Hardle (1990).

(ii) *Mack and Muller (MM) estimator.* Mack and Muller (1989) noted that the denominator of NW weight depends on x. This leads to complicated higher order derivatives of $\hat{m}(x)$ with respect to x. More importantly, it can lead to unstable and poorer estimates. Thus they developed the estimator of $m(x) = \int y^* f(y^*, x) \, dy^*$, where $y^* = y/f(x)$, by using nonparametric density estimator of $f(y^*, x)$. This gives the weights as

$$w_{ni}(x) = \frac{1}{nh^p} \frac{1}{f(x_i)} K\left(\frac{x_i - x}{h}\right), \tag{2.5}$$

where the denominator does not have $f(x)$, evaluated at the fixed point x. In practice, the $f(x_i)$ evaluated at the sample value is replaced by its kernel estimate:

$$\hat{f}(x_i) = (1/nh^p) \sum_{j=1}^{n} K(h^{-1}[x_j - x_i]) .$$ (2.6)

This is just the NW estimator evaluated at $\hat{f}(x_i)$ rather than at $\hat{f}(x)$ and would have to be estimated for each sample value. Obtaining the derivatives of $\hat{m}(x)$ with the weight (2.5) would need the explicit derivatives of $K(h^{-1}[x_i - x])$ only. This is because $f(x_i)$ or its estimate is evaluated at x_i not x. This is an advantage compared to (2.4) for the NW estimator, where the denominator is evaluated at x.

(iii) *k-nearest neighbor (NN) estimator.* The general NN estimator of m was proposed by Royall (1966), Stone (1977), Mack (1981) for the random design case. The w_{ni} for this estimator is

$$w_{ni}(x) = K\left(\frac{x_i - x}{k_n}\right) \bigg/ \sum_{i=1}^{n} K\left(\frac{x_i - x}{k_n}\right) ,$$ (2.7)

where $K(\cdot)$ is a bounded, nonnegative kernel functions with compact support, satisfying $K(\psi) = 0$, for $\|\psi\| > 1$. The notation k_n is the Euclidian distance between x and its k-th nearest neighbor among the x_i and $k = k_n$ satisfies $k_n \to \infty$ as $n \to \infty$. Here k is the smoothing parameter similar to h in the NW estimator.

Stone (1977) considers the estimator $\hat{m}$ in (2.3) where the w_{ni} are uniform, quadratic and triangular. Uniform weights lead to one among the well-known NN estimators. For the choice of k and the properties of NN estimator, see Mack (1981), Stone (1977) among others.

(iv) *Ahmad–Lin estimator.* The Ahmad and Lin (1984) estimator of m was proposed in the context of fixed design x_i, and it is given by

$$w_{ni}(x) = K\left(\frac{x_i - x}{h}\right) \frac{\Delta(A_i)}{h^p} ,$$ (2.8)

where $A_1, \ldots, A_n$ are partitions of the space defined by closed intervals $A = [0, 1]^p$ into n regions such that the volume $\Delta(A_i)$ is of order n^{-1}, $K(\cdot)$ is a p-dimensional bounded density, $h = h_n$ is a sequence of real numbers converging to zero as $n \to \infty$, and $x_i \in A_i$. If $p = 1$ and we select $A_i = (x_{i-1}, x_i)$, $i = 1, \ldots, n$ where $0 = x_0 < x_1 < \cdots < x_n = 1$, (2.8) reduces to the weight proposed earlier by Priestley and Chao (1972). For the properties of this estimator, see Ahmad and Lin (1984).

(v) *Gasser–Muller (GM) estimator.* This estimator was also developed for the fixed design case, and is closely related to the Priestley–Chao estimator mentioned above. It is applicable to random designs subject to regularity conditions. The weights for this estimator are

$$w_{ni}(x) = \frac{1}{h^p} \int_{A_i} K\left(\frac{u - x}{h}\right) du ,$$ (2.9)

where $A_i, K(\cdot)$ and $h = h_n$ are as defined in (2.6). For $p = 1$ we let $A_i = (S_{i-1}, S_i)$, where $S_i = (x_i + x_{i+1})/2$ is the mid point. For properties and details about this estimator, see Gasser and Muller (1979a,b, 1984), Ahmad and Lin (1984) and Georgiev (1984). For the applications, see Gasser and Muller (1984).

(vi) *Weights for other estimators*. There is a large class of weights $w_{ni}(x)$ and hence $\hat{m}(x)$ available in the literature. For example, Yang (1981) considered the symmetrized NN estimator where w_{ni} is the same as in NW or NN estimator except that x_i and x in their definitions are replaced by the empirical distributions $F_n(x_i)$ and $F_n(x)$, respectively. Silverman (1984) shows that the smoothing spline estimators due to Reinsch (1967) are approximately the $\hat{m}(x)$, (2.4) with $w_{ni}(x) = (nh(x_i))^{-1}K(x_i - x)/h(x_i)$, where $h(x_i)\alpha(f(x_i))^{-1/4}$. Rice (1984) and more recently Ryu (1990) use the variable kernels $K(x, x_i)$

$$w_{ni}(x) = K(x, x_i) \Big/ \sum_{i=1}^{n} K(x, x_i), \quad \text{where } K(x, x_i) = \sum_{m=0}^{M(n)} P_m(x)P_m(x_i),$$

(2.10)

where $P_m(x)$ are orthogonal polynomials and the upper limit $M(n)$ depends on n. For details on some of these estimators, see Hardle (1990) and Pagan and Ullah (1990).

(vii) *Other estimators of $m(x)$ (parametric and semi-parametric)*. In econometrics, there is an extensive literature on the approximation of $m(x)$ by a suitable parametric form; see Lau (1985) for a detailed survey. In recent years, the method of sieves, see German and Hwang (1982), has become an important tool for approximating unknown functions like $m(x)$. According to this method, which is similar to (2.10), the object of interest lies in a general (non necessarily finite) space, and $m(x)$ is approximated by using a sequence of parametric models in which the dimensionality of the parameter space grows along with the sample size n. To succeed, the approximating parametric models must be capable of providing an arbitrarily accurate approximation to the elements of general space as the underlying parameter space grows. Among useful practical procedures used in this context are Fourier series, see Gallant and Nychka (1987). Ryu (1990) provides a maximum entropy interpretation of the Fourier series approximation. Another method with universal approximation properties is that of multi-layer feed-forward network functions considered in White (1990).

In many econometric models, the problem of nonparametric estimation arises in the models of the form

$$y_i = m(z_i) + u_i, \quad \text{where } z_i = x_i'\beta. \tag{2.11}$$

Note that z_i is known as a single index variable. The models of this type are called semi-nonparametric or semi-parametric because z_i depends on the parameter vector β. Some initial value of β is needed in order to estimate these models with the help of nonparametric estimator $\hat{m}$ in (2.2). The examples of models which can be of the form (2.11) are macro models with expectation variables, discrete choice models and sample selectivity models, among others. For details on semiparametric models, see the survey by Robinson (1987).

Other types of semi-parametric estimators arise in the models where $m(x) = x'\beta$, or $y_i = x_i'\beta + u_i$, but the form of heteroscedasticity and/or autocorrelation structure of u_i is unknown. The autocorrelation structures have been estimated nonparametrically by using the estimators given in Section 3. Usually, an estimator of β has $\sqrt{n}$ convergence in these models. For details regarding the heteroscedasticity case see Carroll (1982), and for the autocorrelation case see Altman (1990).

A semi-parametric estimator of $m(x)$ can be developed on the lines of Olkin and Spiegelman (1987) semiparametric density estimation. Essentially, one forms the estimator of $m(x)$ as a convex combination of the parametric ordinary least squares estimator $x'\hat{\beta}$, (where $\hat{\beta} = (\bar{X}'\bar{X})^{-1}\bar{X}'y$, where $\bar{X}$ is the matrix of regressors) and the nonparametric estimator $\hat{m}(x) = \Sigma\, w_{ni}(x)y_i$ of (2.4). This gives an estimator detailed in Ullah and Vinod (1991) and illustrated in Figure 1. We have

$$\bar{m}(x, \lambda) = (1 - \lambda)x'\hat{\beta} + \lambda\hat{m}(x) = \sum_{i=1}^{n} w_{ni}(x, \lambda)y_i \,, \qquad (2.12)$$

where $w_{ni}(x, \lambda) = (1 - \lambda)a_i(x) + \lambda w_{ni}(x)$, where $a_i(x)$ is the i-th element of the $p \times 1$ vector $x(\bar{X}'\bar{X})^{-1}\bar{X}'$. Observe that $w_{ni}(x, \lambda)$ and hence $\bar{m}(x, \lambda)$ is a special form of the general nonparametric estimators studied here. However, we can call it semi-parametric because λ is an unknown parameter. The parameter λ can be chosen so as to minimize the error sum of squares:

$$\sum_{i=1}^{n} [y_i - \bar{m}(x, \lambda)]^2 = \sum_{i=1}^{n} [y_i - (1 - \lambda)x'\hat{\beta} - \lambda\hat{m}(x)]^2 \,. \qquad (2.13)$$

The solution to the minimization is obtained simply by least squares regression:

$$(y_i - x_i'\hat{\beta}) = \lambda(\hat{m}(x_i) - x_i'\hat{\beta}) + u_i \qquad (2.14)$$

which is

$$\hat{\lambda} = \frac{\sum (y_i - x_i'\hat{\beta})(\hat{m}(x_i) - x_i'\hat{\beta})}{\sum (\hat{m}(x_i) - x_i'\hat{\beta})^2}\,, \qquad (2.15)$$

where the summation ranges from $i = 1$ to n, and where we assume that $\hat{m}(x_i) \neq x_i'\hat{\beta}$ with probability 1. Indeed substitution of $\hat{\lambda}$ in (2.12) gives a data dependent $\hat{m}(x) = \Sigma\, w_{ni}(x, \hat{\lambda})y_i$. Stainswalis and Severini (1991) discuss further techniques for detection of global and local lack of fit in the regression content. Computer programming for the section involves simple weighted sums as in (2.3) with weights from equations similar to (2.6). One can use a standard regression package to estimate the parameter λ of (2.15) after computing the variables defined in (2.14).

3. Estimation of higher order moments and quantiles

Let $g(Y)$ be a smooth function such that $E|g(Y)| < \infty$. Let $M(x) = E(g(Y)|X = x)$ be the conditional mean of $g(Y)$ given $X = x$. Then a general linear (nonparametric) estimator of $M(x)$ can be written in the same way as $\hat{m}(x)$ in (2.3) and it is given by

$$\hat{M}(x) = \sum_{i=1}^{n} w_{ni}(x)g(y_i) , \qquad (3.1)$$

where the weights $w_{ni}(x)$ are as discussed above.

When $g(Y) = Y^2$, $\hat{M}(x)$ in (3.1) gives the nonparametric estimate of the second conditional moment around the origin. The estimator of the second central moment of Y, $\hat{V}(Y|X)$, can then be obtained as $\hat{V}(Y|X = x) = \hat{M}(x) - \hat{m}^2(x)$, where $\hat{m}(x)$ is as in (2.3). This estimator is useful in analyzing conditional heteroscedasticity. Nonparametric estimators of higher order moments and conditional covariances can be similarly obtained.

Often, in practice, one is interested in estimating the median (50-th percentile) of the conditional distribution, instead of its mean $m(x)$. Let the α-quantile of the conditional distribution of Y given $X = x$ be $q_\alpha(x)$, which is the solution of

$$F(q_\alpha(x)|x) = P(Y \leq q_\alpha(x)|x) = \int_{-\infty}^{q_\alpha} f(y|x)\,dy .$$

The nonparametric estimator of $q_\alpha(x)$ is $\hat{q}_\alpha(x)$ which solves

$$\hat{F}(\hat{q}_\alpha(x)|x) = \alpha , \quad \text{where } \hat{F} = \int_{-\infty}^{y} \hat{f}(y|x)\,dy . \qquad (3.2)$$

Note that $\hat{F}$ is the estimator of $F(y|x)$ and $\hat{f}(y|x)$ can be obtained by kernel or NN density estimators, see Stone (1977). Samanta (1989) suggests the use of a kernel estimator and has studied the consistency and asymptotic normality of the estimator. Bhattacharya and Gangopadhyay (1990) have obtained the estimator using both kernel and NN estimators of the conditional density. They have studied the asymptotic properties and the choices of smoothing parameters. The numerical computation of variances etc. requires expressions containing weighted sums. For econometric applications and a workable computer algorithm for quantiles see Magee et al. (1991).

4. Estimation of derivatives

Let us write the s-th order derivative of $m(x)$ with respect to the j-th x variable as

$$\beta_j^{(s)}(x) = \frac{\partial^s m(x)}{\partial x_j^s}, \quad s = 0, 1, 2, \ldots, \tag{4.1}$$

where $\beta_j^{(0)}(x) = m(x) = m(x_1, \ldots, x_p)$, and for $s = 1$, $\beta_j^{(1)}(x) = \partial m(x)/\partial x_j$ is the j-th response coefficient.

The s-th order average derivative is given by

$$\beta_j^{(s)} = \mathrm{E}(\beta_j^{(s)}(x)) = \int \beta_j^{(s)}(x) f(x) \, dx. \tag{4.2}$$

In practice, the first order partial derivative provides information regarding the regression coefficients. Second order partial derivatives provide information regarding curvature properties, cross elasticities, etc. For example, if $m(x)$ is the production function with p-inputs, one can study convexity, interdependence and cross elasticities of inputs. Finally the average derivatives may be useful for estimation of single index models, see Hardle and Stoker (1989).

The nonparametric estimates of $\beta_j^{(s)}(x)$ can be obtained by simply replacing $m(x)$ by $\hat{m}(x) = \Sigma \, w_n(x) y_i$. Thus

$$\hat{\beta}_j^{(s)}(x) = \sum_{i=1}^{n} w_{ni}^{(s)}(x) y_i, \tag{4.3}$$

where $w_{ni}^{(s)}$ is the s-th order derivative of $w_{ni}(x)$ with respect to x_j. (4.3) can be written easily for the special cases of w_{ni} given in (2.1). Details for the NW weights are given by Ullah (1988a, 1988b). For $s = 1$ see Vinod and Ullah (1988) and an application to $s = 2$ case is in McMillan et al. (1989).

The average derivative $\beta_j^{(s)} = \mathrm{E} \, \beta_j^{(s)}(x)$ can be estimated by

$$\hat{\beta}_j^{(s)} = \frac{1}{n} \sum_{i=1}^{n} \hat{\beta}_j^{(s)}(x_i). \tag{4.4}$$

The asymptotic properties of this are given in Rilstone (1991). Fan (1990a) considers the estimator of average derivative based on Mack–Muller weight in (2.5). Her estimator is

$$\hat{\beta}_F^{(s)} = \frac{1}{n} \sum_{i=1}^{N} \hat{B}_{MM}^{(s)}(X_i). \tag{4.5}$$

It has been shown by Fan (1990a) that for $s = 1$ her average derivative estimator is identical with the average derivative estimator of Hardle and Stoker (1989), which is

$$\hat{\beta}_{HS}^{(1)}(x) = -\frac{1}{n} \sum_{i=1}^{n} \frac{\hat{f}^{(1)}(x_i)}{\hat{f}(x_i)} y_i, \tag{4.6}$$

where $\hat{f}(x)$ is the kernel density estimator. Note that, under the boundary assumption, $f(x)$ vanishes on its boundary of support. Hardle and Stoker (1989) first show that $E\beta^{(1)}(x)f(x)\,dx = -E(f^{(1)}(x)y/f(x))$ and then estimate it by (4.6). In contrast, Fan's (1990a) derivation is straightforward and does not need the boundary condition. A comparison of $\hat{\beta}_{NW}^{(s)}$ and $\hat{\beta}_{MM}^{(s)}$ would be useful in the present context. Typical computer programming for this section involves equations (4.3) and (4.4).

5. Estimation of error variance

Let us consider the nonparametric model $y_i = m(x_i) + u_i$ from (2.2), where $Eu_i = 0$ and $Eu_i^2 = \sigma^2$. Then the question is: what is an optimal estimate of σ^2? For this purpose let us rewrite the model in vector notation as

$$y = m + u , \tag{5.1}$$

where y, u and $m = [m_1, \ldots, m_n]'$ are each $n \times 1$ vectors. Further, using

$$\hat{m}(x_i) = \sum_{j=1}^{n} w_{nj}(x_i)y_j$$

yields

$$\hat{u} = y - \hat{m} = y - Wy = (I - W)y ,$$

where W is an $n \times n$ matrix of smoothing elements $w_{nj}(x_i) = w_j(x_i), i, j = 1, \ldots, n$. An obvious estimator of σ^2 is

$$\hat{\sigma}^2 = \frac{\hat{u}'\hat{u}}{\text{tr}(M)} = \frac{y'My}{\text{tr}(M)} , \quad \text{where } M = (I - W)^2 . \tag{5.2}$$

Note that the M in (5.2) is a stochastic matrix of weights. However, if the x_i are fixed design variables, or if we consider conditioning on random x_i then M will be nonstochastic. Buckley et al. (1988), under the assumption of normality of errors u, provide the optimal M which minimizes the MSE of $\hat{\sigma}^2$. The expressions for the optimal M are, however, quite involved and they depend on the moments of u. Ullah and Zinde-Walsh (1992) have extended the Buckley et al. results for the non-normal errors u.

Recently Hall and Marron (1990) considered the estimation $\hat{\sigma}^2$ in (5.2) in a special case where the weights $w_j(x_i)$ are NW weights as given in (2.4). For this case they derived the approximate bias and variance of $\hat{\sigma}^2$ and showed that the optimal window width h which minimizes MSE is proportional to $n^{-2/9}$ instead of usual $h \propto n^{-1/5}$ if m has two derivatives and $p = 1$. For the kernels with $r - 1$ moments zero, the optimal $h \propto n^{-2/(4r+1)}$.

Another point is that the MSE of $\hat{\sigma}^2$ is of the usual $O(n^{-1})$. This is despite the fact that the MSE of $\hat{m}_{NW}$ is known to have a slow speed of convergence. The intuitive reason for $\hat{\sigma}^2$ to be of $O(n^{-1})$ is that it is an average over n values and hence it further smooths out the $\hat{m}_{NW}$. Computer programming for this section would involve equation (5.2).

6. Nonparametric regression with a generalized Box–Cox transformation

The Box and Cox (1964) family of power transformation, familiar in econometrics, has been recently generalized by introducing certain computer intensive methods. For further discussion of econometric applications see Maddala (1977, pp. 316–317). The purpose of the Box–Cox transformation in the regression context is to achieve a close approximation to normality, linearity and homoscedasticity. The Box–Cox transformation is defined as

$$f_z = z_t^* = \begin{cases} \lambda_1^{-1}[(z_t + \lambda_2)^{\lambda_1} - 1] & \text{if } \lambda_1 > 0, \\ g \ln(z_t + \lambda_2) & \text{if } \lambda_1 = 0, \end{cases} \tag{6.1}$$

where λ_2 is a number added to the data before the transformation (usually $\lambda_2 = 0$), g is the sample geometric mean of $(z_t + \lambda_2)$, λ_1 governs the strength (power) of the transformation such that when $\lambda_1 = 1$ we simply use the original data without any transformation. When $\lambda_1 = 0$, this is the usual logarithmic transformation. The Box–Cox transformation is well defined for $z_t > 0$. Econometrics texts usually consider the special case $z^* = f_z = (z^\lambda - 1)/\lambda$. In typical applications when y is regressed on $x_1, x_2, \ldots, x_p$ one computes y^* and x_i^* for all i with an additive model

$$y^* = X^* \beta + u = \sum_{i=1}^{p} f_i(x_i)\beta_i + u, \qquad u \sim N(0, \sigma^2 I) \tag{6.2}$$

in an obvious notation where an aim of the transformation f_i is to achieve normality and homoscedasticity. In econometrics it is common to use $y^* = \tilde{X}\beta + u$, where only the dependent variable is transformed. If a common λ is used in defining all variables bearing the superscript *, only one additional parameter λ needs to be estimated by a version of the maximum likelihood methods.

Friedman and Struetzle (1981) introduced a generalization of the linear regression model called the projection pursuit (PP)

$$E(Y) = \sum_{i=1}^{p} \beta_i(x_i, a_i), \tag{6.3}$$

where we have β_i as the functions f_i, which are not necessarily linear but unspecified, and where the a_i are unit vectors representing the so-called directions. It is the presence of these directions a_i which require us to use a notation different from f_i. The computer intensive PP algorithm is difficult to describe intuitively, except to say that it searches over all possible unit directions and chooses the functions $\hat{\beta}$ and estimated directions $\hat{a}_i$ that minimize the error sum of squares. From the first round residuals the algorithm selects the next best direction and functions. It stops when further improvement in the fit defined in terms of residual sum of squares is negligible. Note that OLS is a special case because least squares algorithm finds the best direction and the best linear function of that direction. Hence the proponents of PP argue that adding another linear term will not improve matters. Hastie and Tibshirani (1987) apply bootstrap methods to show that in one example, the second direction found by the PP algorithm is quite unstable.

Instead of using (6.1) one can use arbitrary smooth transformations $f_i(x_i)$ based on the scatterplot of the data. Cleveland (1979) and Cleveland and Devlin (1988) devised a powerful scatterplot smoothing algorithm and Cleveland et al. (1988) illustrate it with social science applications. This may be interpreted as a kernel estimator, Muller (1987), and provides an attractive alternative, because its sampling theory is very close to that of ordinary regression.

Breiman and Friedman (1985) proposed a generalization of Box–Cox model called the alternating conditional expectation (ACE) algorithm. Given two random variables X and Y the ACE algorithm finds the best transformations f_x and f_y that maximize the ordinary correlation between f_x and f_y such that homoscedasticity is achieved in the sense that the variance $f_y = 1$. An equivalent formulation of ACE is to minimize $E(f_y - f_x)^2$ subject to $var(f_y) = 1$. Unlike Box–Cox, ACE is obviously symmetric in X and Y and hence more suitable for a correlation rather than regression framework. Recently additivity is emphasized and the normality requirement is dropped by Tibshirani's (1988) additive variance stabilization (AVAS) algorithm. The AVAS algorithm exploits the power of modern computers for numerical implementation of the following well-known asymptotic variance stabilization formula from elementary statistics, Kendall and Stuart (1977, Ex. 16.18). Let the variance of a statistic t based on n observations be a function of the unknown parameter θ, $var(t) = f(\theta)/n + o(n^{-1})$. We seek a transformation $g(t)$ such that $var(g(t)) = 1/n + o(n^{-1})$ replacing $f(\theta)$ by unity. The solution is

$$g(t) = \int^t d\theta / \sqrt{f(\theta)} . \tag{6.4}$$

The AVAS algorithm starts by standardizing all variables to make mean zero and variance unity. When there is only one regressor, AVAS iteratively standardizes the Y conditional on X, stabilizes its variance and standardizes again until R^2 does not change very much. When more regressors are present, one needs to loop over them by an inner loop similar to the backfitting algorithm used in ACE. Although additivity implies the absence of interaction terms, it is shown by Hastie and Tibshirani (1986, p. 315) that simple interactions involving cross products $x_i x_j$ or $\hat{f}_i(x_i)\hat{f}_j(x_j)$ can be incorporated as additional additive terms.

For potential econometric applications Andrews and Whang (1991) study interactive spline models in the literature, Wahba (1986), after renaming them as additive interactive regression (AIR) models. Unlike the interactive spline, the AIR models can be computed using standard statistical software. Both models appear to resolve the 'curse of dimensionality' which plagues almost all nonparametric regression methods. Additive regression models discussed by Stone (1985) do not permit interactions. Assuming that the regression function is twice differentiable, Stone (1985) shows that the fastest possible rate of convergence in L^q norm with $0 < q < \infty$ is $n^{-2/(4+p)}$ where p is the number of regressors. The idea behind additive regression and AIR models is to estimate several lower dimensional surfaces instead of one large dimensional surface. Stone (1985) proved that a convergence rate for $p > 1$ can be improved to the rate for $p = 1$, if the additive regression model is valid. Chen (1988) proved that even after allowing for certain types of interactions among the regressors, the convergence rate for $p > 1$ is no worse than that for $p = 1$. Chen's proof requires that assumption of independent and identically distributed (iid) errors and a tensor product design for regressors. The AIR model is of the form (2.2) with

$$m(x_i) = \sum_{a=1}^{A} \sum_{b=1}^{B(a)} m_{ab}(x_i), \qquad (6.5)$$

where $m_{ab}(x_i)$ is an unknown function of the observable elements $x_i = (x_{i1}, x_{i2}, \ldots, x_{ip})'$. The first subscript a ranges over $1, 2, \ldots, A$ counts the number of elements of x_i included in the function, with both A and $B(a) \leq p$. For example, $m_{1b}(x_{i3})$ has $a = 1$, and is a function of x_{i3} only. Similarly, $m_{3b}(x_{i2}, x_{i3}, x_{i4})$ is a function of $a = 3$ components of x_i. The range of the second subscript $b = 1, \ldots, B(a)$ can be different for each a by an appropriate choice of $B(a)$. When all possible combinations are considered, $B(a) = p!/[a!(p-a)!]$. Usually $B(a) \leq p!/[a!(p-a)!]$. Andrews (1991) suggests a series estimator which approximates m_{ab} by a finite series expansion containing k_{ab} terms in a weighted sum having weights as parameters to be estimated.

$$m_{ab}(x_i^*) = \sum_{c=1}^{k_{ab}} \theta_{abc} z_{abc}(x_i^*), \qquad (6.6)$$

where x_i^* represents the same subset of x_i containing the same number a of elements and where z_{abc} belongs to a known 'series'. For example, it may be a polynomial, trigonometric or Fourier flexible form (FFF) of Gallant (see Gallant and Souza, 1991, for references). An AIR model of order 2 with $p = 3$

is illustrated by

$$m(x_{i1}, x_{i2}, m_{i3}) = m_1(x_{i1}) + m_2(x_{i2}) + m_3(x_{i3})$$
$$+ m_{12}(x_{i1}x_{i2}) + m_{13}(x_{i1}x_{i3}) + m_{23}(x_{i2}x_{i3}) .$$

Partially linear regression (PLR) model considered by Chamberlain (1986), Wahba (1986), Rice (1986), Speckman (1988) and Robinson (1988), among others, can also mitigate the cure of dimensionality. This is a special case of (6.5) and it can be written as

$$m(x_i) = x'_{ai}\beta + m_b(x_{bi}) , \qquad (6.7)$$

where $m_b(x_{bi})$ is an unknown function of x_{bi}. Chamberlain (1986) and Robinson (1988) are concerned with $\sqrt{n}$ consistent estimation of β.

Semiparametric index regression (SIR) models have been suggested by Ruud (1986) and Stoker (1986) as in (2.11). Unfortunately a comparative study of the various proposals, in conjunction with the various scatterplot smoothers by Cleveland (1979), Cleveland and Devlin (1988) and others mentioned before, is missing from the literature. This may be because it will involve a massive simulation and computer programming effort. Asymptotic and finite sample properties provide a useful guidance, pending such a study. Computer programs for PP, ACE, AVAS, and scatterplot smoothers are readily available in the S computer language from the Bell Laboratories.

7. Finite sample properties

We shall consider the finite sample properties of the estimator $\hat{m}$ when x is nonstochastic and when it is stochastic. These results are useful in determining window width and weight functions. It is easy to verify that when x is fixed and u_i is iid $(0, \sigma^2)$ then the exact bias and variance of $\hat{m}$ are

$$\text{Bias}(\hat{m}) = \text{E}\hat{m} - m = \sum_{i=1}^{n} w_{ni}(m_i - m) + m \left(\sum_{i=1}^{n} w_{ni} - 1 \right) \qquad (7.1)$$

and

$$\text{V}(\hat{m}) = \sigma^2 \sum_{i=1}^{n} w_{ni}^2 = \sigma^2 / n(x) , \qquad (7.2)$$

where $n(x) = (\sum_{i=1}^{n} w_{ni}^2)^{-1}$. For a fixed sample, $n(x)$ can be used to compare the precision of various estimators. The bias and variance of the s-th derivative estimator $\hat{\beta}^{(s)}$ can be similarly written by replacing w_{ni} with $w_{ni}^{(s)}$.

When u_i is a stationary time series process with $\gamma_j = \text{cov}(u_i, u_{i-j})$, then

$$V(\hat{m}) = \sigma^2/n(x) + 2 \sum_{j=1}^{n-1} \sum_{i=j+1}^{n} w_{ni} w_{nj} \gamma_{i-j} . \tag{7.3}$$

This implies that if we use positive w, then $V(\hat{m})$ for dependent observations is greater than that for the independent observations case when the γ_j is positive, and smaller when the γ_j is negative. Further the $V(\hat{m})$ and hence the MSE $(\hat{m})$ increases with the increase in the serial correlation of observations.

In a recent work Ullah (1992), for fixed x, has obtained the exact as well as approximate density of

$$z_n(x) = \frac{\hat{m}(x) - E\hat{m}(x)}{[V(\hat{m}(x))]^{1/2}} \tag{7.4}$$

under the assumption that u_i in (2.2) follows an Edgeworth or Gram–Charlier density. This result also provides correction terms for the well-known asymptotic normality of z_n. When X is random the exact density is difficult to obtain. However, under the assumption of normal or spherical density of u, Ullah (1989) has shown that the exact distribution of z_n is $N(0, 1)$ and $S(0, 1)$, respectively. Results based on the assumption that u is a mixture of normals have also been obtained. Although these results are based on the parametric assumptions of u, they would provide benchmarks for any Monte Carlo study in this area.

The exact results above, especially for the bias term, are not of much help in determining the optimal w. Approximation of these results are useful and have been studied by Jennen-Steinmetz and Gasser (1988), Chu (1989) and Gasser and Engel (1990). No result exists for $\hat{m}$ in (2.3) with general w_{ni}. Jennen-Steinmetz and Gasser (1988) and Chu (1989) have considered $\hat{m}$ with w given by kernel weights, spline smoothing weights and NN weights. Under the assumptions that (i) m is twice continuously differentiable, (ii) weights are symmetric with finite second moment, (iii) weights and m are Holder-continuous (iv) $h = h_n \to 0$ and $nh \to \infty$ as $n \to \infty$, they show that for the fixed X and $p = 1$ case

$$\text{Bias}(\hat{m}) = \frac{h^2}{2} \frac{\mu_2(w) m^{(2)}(x)}{(f(x))^{2\alpha}} = O(h^2)$$

$$V(\hat{m}) = \frac{\sigma^2}{nh} \frac{g(w)}{(f(x))^{1-\alpha}} = O\left(\frac{1}{nh}\right) , \tag{7.5}$$

where $\mu_2(w) = \int t^2 w(t)\, dt$, $g(w) = \int w^2(t)\, dt$, and $\alpha = 0, \frac{1}{4}, 1$ for kernel, spline smoothing and NN weights. Recently, many authors, e.g., Staniswalis and Severini (1991), use an approximation to the integrated mean squared error $(\text{IMSE}) = \int [(\text{Bias})^2 + \text{variance}]\, dx$ instead of considering the bias and variance separately.

When X is stochastic, an additional assumption $nh/(\log n) \to \infty$ as $n \to \infty$ is needed. In this case there is no unified formula for the bias and variance of kernel, NN and spline smoothing as in (7.5). Among kernel weights the results for the NW and GM are quite different. These are, from Jennen-Steinmetz and Gasser (1988),

$$\text{Bias}(\hat{m})_{\text{GM}} = \frac{h^2}{2} \frac{m^{(2)}(x)}{\mu_2(w)} ,$$

$$\text{V}(\hat{m})_{\text{GM}} = C \frac{\sigma^2 g(w)}{nhf(x)} , \tag{7.6}$$

where the factor C equals 1 for the fixed and 1.5 for a random design. For $s_i = x_i$ instead of $s_i = (x_i + x_{i+1})/2$, the C in the variance formula is 2. For the NW estimator, Gasser and Engel (1990) show that

$$\text{Bias}(\hat{m})_{\text{NW}} = \frac{h^2}{2} \mu_2(w)[\tfrac{1}{2}m^{(2)}(x) + m^{(1)}(x)f^{(1)}(x)/f(x)] ,$$

$$\text{V}(\hat{m})_{\text{NW}} = \sigma^2 g(w)/nhf(x) , \tag{7.7}$$

also see Collomb (1981) and Singh et al. (1987).

Traditionally, the NN estimator has been studied with weights similar to those of the Nadaraya–Watson estimator. This gives bias and variance of the estimator similar to those of NW estimation in (7.7); see Mack (1981). Similar results can be developed for the s-th derivative estimator $\hat{\beta}^{(s)}$ and the average derivative estimator. Some results on them can be found in Pagan and Ullah (1990). Computer programming for this section typically involves equations (7.6) or (7.7).

7.1. Bandwidth selection

An important issue in implementation of the estimator $\hat{m}$ in practice is the choice of the bandwidth in various weights. Two major approaches are: an automatic method (cross-validation) and a 'plug-in' method (minimum integrated MSE, or IMSE). For a survey of these approaches in the density estimation case, see Marron (1988). Staniswalis (1989b) suggests a novel local bandwidth selection method and compares it favorably in a simulation with global methods. Goldstein and Messer (1990) derive conditions for a plug-in estimator to achieve optimal convergence rate.

According to the plug-in method, the optimal window width is chosen as the value which minimizes the IMSE or MSE of $\hat{m}$. Usually the optimal value depends on the unknown regression, density and their derivatives. To implement this in practice, preliminary estimates of these unknowns are plugged in. Certain results in this context for the kernel, NN and spline estimator are given by Jenner-Steinmetz and Gasser (1988). For fixed X, based on the results in (7.5) they obtain the IMSE and choose h for which this is minimum. The solution is

$$h_{opt} = \left[\frac{\sigma^2 g(w) \int f(x)^{\alpha-1} \, dx}{n\mu_2^2(w) \int m^{(2)}(x)^2 (f(x))^{-4\alpha} \, dx}\right]^{1/5} \propto n^{-1/5}, \tag{7.8}$$

with $\alpha = 0$ (kernel estimator), $\alpha = \frac{1}{4}$ (spline) and $\alpha = 1$ (NN). The plug-in estimator of h is the $\hat{h}_{opt}$ which is obtained by substituting σ^2, f and $m^{(2)}$ by their sample estimators. Note that if the true m is linear h_{opt} is ∞. Another point to note is that for kernel, NN and spline weights the optimal h is (proportional to) $\propto n^{-1/5}$ as indicated in the formula above.

When X is stochastic, one can obtain the optimal h for kernel and NN estimators by minimizing IMSE based on (7.6) and (7.7). The h_{opt} will be again $\propto n^{-1/5}$, though the proportionality form will be different compared to the fixed X case. Also, the proportionality form of two kernel estimators, NW and GM, will be different from each other. In the GM case it will be the same as in the fixed X case given in (7.8) with $\alpha = 0$ and σ^2 replaced by $\sigma^2 C$. The h_{opt} for NW is also the same as h_{opt} in (7.8) with $\alpha = 0$ and $m^{(2)}$ replaced by $[1/2 m^{(2)} + m^{(1)} f^{(1)}/f]$. Tsybakov (1982) provides h_{opt} in this case where he minimizes the MSE instead of the IMSE. These can be obtained from the above formulas for the IMSE based on (7.7) by simply dropping the integrals appearing in the numerator and the denominator. In the MSE minimizing solution, however, $h_{opt}(x)$ will depend on x.

When the functions m and f are unknown, Tsybakov (1986) suggests an estimated $\hat{h}_{opt}(x)$, which is asymptotically equal to $h_{opt}(x)$ in the sense that $\hat{h}_{opt}(x)/h_{opt}(x) \to 1$ in probability, as $n \to \infty$. He also shows that $\hat{m}$ based on $\hat{h}_{opt}$ is asymptotically equivalent to $\hat{m}$ based on h_{opt}. For these results to go through one needs the kernel to be bounded with compact support, f and $m^{(s)}$, $s = 1, 2$, to be continuously differentiable, $E(|y|^{2+\delta}|x) < \infty$ for same $\delta > 0$, $\sigma^2 < \infty$ and $\int [k(qx) - k(x)]^2 \, dx \leq L|q - 1|^\delta$, and $|q - 1| < \varepsilon_0$ for some number $L > 0$, and $\delta \in (1, 2)$ and $\varepsilon_0 \in (0, 1)$. The h_{opt} of Tsybakov simply replaces the unknowns in (7.8) by their consistent estimators. That is, let $\sigma^2 = \hat{\sigma}^2$,

$$\hat{m}^{(2)}(x) = \left(\frac{1}{nh^3} \sum_{i=1}^{n} y_i K_2\left(\frac{x_i - x}{h}\right) - \hat{m}^{(0)}(x)\hat{f}^{(2)}(x)\right.$$
$$\left. - 2\hat{m}^{(1)}(x)\hat{f}^{(1)}(x)\right) \Big/ \hat{f}^{(0)}(x) \tag{7.9}$$

and

$$\hat{m}^{(1)}(x) = \left(\frac{1}{nh^2} \sum_{i=1}^{n} y_i K_1\left(\frac{x_i - x}{h}\right) - \hat{f}^{(1)}\hat{m}^{(0)}(x)\right) \Big/ \hat{f}^{(0)}(x), \tag{7.10}$$

where $\hat{f}^{(j)}(x) = (nh^{j+1})^{-1} \Sigma K_j(x_i - x)/h)$, $j = 0, 1, 2$ and K_j is the higher order bounded kernel with compact support, whose first $j - 1$ moments are zero. Such kernels are $K_0(u) = \frac{1}{2}$, if $|u| \leq 1$, and $= 0$ if $|u| > 1$; $K_1(u) = 2 \operatorname{sgn} u K_0(u)$

and $K_2(u) = -4$, if $|u| \leq \frac{1}{2}$, $=4$, if $\frac{1}{2} \leq |u| \leq 1$, and 0, if $|u| > 1$. Alternative, one can use $\hat{m}^{(1)}(x) = \hat{\beta}^{(0)}(x)$ and $\hat{m}^{(2)} = \hat{\beta}^{(1)}(x)$ as given in (4.3).

Cross-validation (CV) is regarded as an automatic method of choosing h. The basic algorithm involves removing a single value, say x_i, from the sample, computing $\hat{m}$ at the x_i from the remaining sample values.

$$\hat{m}(x_i) = \sum_{j \neq i} y_i w_{nj}(x_i)$$

and then choosing $h = h_{cv}$ such that $\Sigma (y_i - \hat{m}(x_i))^2 = \Sigma u_i^2$ is at the minimum. This is called least squares cross-validation, LSCV. Hall (1984) and Hardle and Marron (1985) have shown, in the kernel context, that h_{cv} is asymptotically equivalent to h_{opt} based on minimizing IMSE. However, Tsybakov (1986) has pointed out that h_{cv} is worse than $h_{opt}(x)$ as well as the $\hat{h}_{opt}(x)$ proposed by him in the sense that

$$\int \min_{c>0} (MSE(x)) f(x) \, dx \leq \min_{c>0} \int MSE(x) f(x) \, dx , \tag{7.11}$$

where $c(x)$ is the proportionality constant in $h_{opt}(x) = c(x) n^{-1/5}$. Gasser et al. (1991) report simulations showing that an iterative plug-in estimator of bandwidth (proportional to the ratio: variance/squared bias) is superior to cross-validation, and works even for small (15–25) sample sizes. Typical computer programs first tabulate for a grid of h values: (i) MSE-type criterion from (7.6) or a similar expression, or (ii) the residual sum of squares (RSS) of the leave-one-out CV model, or (iii) generalized CV (GCV) which penalizes RSS for bias, choosing the h minimizing the criterion.

7.2. Curse of dimensionality

From the results on optimal $h \propto n^{-1/5}$ along with the expressions for bias and variance of $\hat{m}$ in (7.5), it is clear that the asymptotic rate of MSE convergence of $\hat{m}$ to m is $O(n^{-4/5})$. For the case when X is a vector of p variables, the rate will be $O(n^{-4/(4+p)})$. This implies that the higher the p, the slower is the speed of convergence, and one may need a large data set to get nonparametric estimates. This is the well-known curse of dimensionality. One way to handle this problem is to use a very large data set. An alternative is to use additive techniques described in Section 6 which increases the convergence rate of the p-dimensional problem to that of a one-dimensional problem. Projection pursuit, ACE, etc. are successfully used for this problem.

7.3. High order kernels and optimal weight w

High order kernels are simply densities whose first $(r - 1)$ moments are zero; see Singh (1981), Muller (1984), Ullah and Singh (1989) and Vinod (1987) for the construction of such kernels. Vinod (1987) proves a recursive relation for any $r > 1$. For example, the first nine moments of the following are shown to be zero.

$$g(x) = \tfrac{1}{384}(945 - 1260x^2 + 378x^4 - 36x^6 + x^8)g_1 , \qquad (7.12)$$

where g_1 is the unit normal density: $g_1(x) = (1/\sqrt{2\pi}) \exp(-x^2/2)$.

Such kernels can take negative values, reduce the bias to $O(h^r)$ and lead to the rate of convergence of MSE to $O(n^{-2r/2r+p})$. Thus by choosing r to be large, the speed of convergence can be made close to $O(n^{-1/2})$, the usual parametric rate. However, practical difficulties in using large r were encountered in the example used in Vinod (1989) if one permits negative values. Important theoretical results in this area are found in Muller (1984, 1987, 1988) and Stone (1982).

In applied as well as theoretical work a natural question of great interest is the choice of w in the multitude of nonparametric estimators given in (2.3), see Stone (1982), Muller (1984). Unfortunately, the asymptotic properties of $\hat{m}$ provide no precise guide to the choice of the weight function for a limited data set. For example, the asymptotic variance of $\hat{m}$ may be the same for iid and dependent observations. Thus, these methods fail to discriminate between these two types of observational assumptions. Even within the iid context the asymptotic theory fails to provide an optimal w, especially for the fixed design case, where Silverman (1984) indicated that various w can approximately be represented by kernel estimators.

Some idea about the optimal choice of w can, however, be obtained by looking into finite sample approximate results on the bias and variance of $\hat{m}$. This has been attempted in Jennen-Steinmetz and Gasser (1988) where they have considered a wide class of estimators which include kernel estimators, smoothing splines and nearest-neighbor estimators as special cases, also see the recent work of Chu (1989) and Gasser and Engel (1990). The findings of these authors indicate that there is no w which is uniformly best in terms of having smallest IMSE. But, they show that the kernel estimator is minimal optimal in the sense of having smallest IMSE.

Within the family of kernel weights two enjoy particular popularity; the Nadaraya–Watson type and the convolution type of Gasser and Muller. Traditionally, the Nadaraya–Watson method is used for the random X case and the convolution method for the fixed X case. The results of Gasser and Engel (1990) suggest that between these two weights, the convolution weight based estimator of m is minimax for both kinds of X. They also point out, see (7.6) and (7.7), that the bias of convolution weights is simple and depends on $m^{(2)}$ only whereas the bias on NW weight depends on $m^{(1)}$ and $m^{(2)}$, f, and $f^{(1)}$. Further, while the bias of the convolution weight is zero if the true regression is linear, this is not the case with the NW bias. Also the pattern of the NW bias will be difficult to understand, and may be severely affected by certain methods of bandwidth choice. Further, the variance of both weights is the same for the fixed X case, but the variance of NW weight is smaller than that of convolution weights for the random X case. However, the IMSE is smaller for convolution weights which makes it a preferred weight compared to the NW weight.

7.4. Asymptotic properties

The asymptotic properties of $\hat{m}$ have been studied for the kernel, NN and some other special cases of $\hat{m}$ quite extensively in the literature, see Ullah (1988b) for a review. For fixed X a systematic study of the properties of $\hat{m}$ for general weights w has been done by Georgiev (1988) for the independent observations case and in Muller (1987) for the iid case. In an excellent study, Fan (1990b) generalizes Georgiev (1988) and Muller (1987) results for dependent and heterogeneous processes. For the stochastic X case, the results for $\hat{m}$ with general w are given by Stone (1977) and Owen (1987). Here we present the assumptions and indicate the asymptotic results.

For fixed X we first state the following assumptions on w:

(A1) (a) u_i are independent random variables with $Eu_i = 0$.

    (b) $\sup_i E|u_i|^{2+\delta} < \infty$, for some δ.

    (c) The function m is bounded on a compact set $A \subseteq \mathbb{R}^p$.

(A2) The weight functions $w_{ni}(x)$ satisfy the following assumptions:

    (a) $\sum_{i=1}^{n} w_{ni}(x) \to 1$ as $n \to \infty$.

    (b) $\sum_{i=1}^{n} |w_{ni}(x)| \leq B$ for all n for an arbitrary constant B.

    (c) $\sum_{i=1}^{n} |w_{ni}(x)| I_{(\|x_i - x\| > a)} \to 0$ as $n \to \infty$ for all $a > 0$.

(A3) (a) $\sup_{i \leq n} |w_{ni}(x)| \to 0$ as $n \to \infty$.

    (b) $\sum_{i=1}^{n} w_{ni}^2(x) \to 0$ as $n \to \infty$.

    (c) $\sup_i w_{ni}^2(x) n \log \log n \to 0$ as $n \to \infty$.

It can be verified that many special cases of w_{ni} in Section 2 satisfy the conditions (A2) and (A3). Georgiev has shown that under conditions (A1,a,c) and (A2) the estimator $\hat{m}$ is asymptotically unbiased. Furthermore, if (A3,a) also holds, $\hat{m}$ is weakly consistent. The MSE and strong consistency, respectively, follow if in addition to asymptotic unbiasedness, (A1,b) for $\delta = 0$ and (A3,b) hold and if (A1,b) for $\delta > 0$ and (A3,c) hold. Regarding asymptotic normality we have the following result. Under (A1,a), and (A1,b) for some $\delta > 0$, and the further assumption that

(A4) $$\frac{\sum_{i=1}^{n} |w_{ni}(x)|^{2+\delta}}{\left(\sum_{i=1}^{n} w_{ni}^2\right)^{1+\delta/2}} \to 0 \quad \text{as } n \to \infty,$$

$z_n = [\hat{m} - E\hat{m}]/[\sqrt{V(\hat{m})}] \to N(0, 1)$ as $n \to \infty$.

For the s-th order derivative of $\hat{m}$, that is for $\hat{\beta}^{(s)}$, given in (4.3) above, one can show asymptotic unbiasedness, consistency, and normality under the following conditions on w_{ni} as $n \to \infty$.

(A5) $\sum_{i=1}^{n} w_{ni}^{(s)}(x)(x_i - x)^j \to 0$ for $0 < j \leq s$, and $\to s!$ for $j = s$.

(A6) $\Sigma_{i=1}^{n}|w_{ni}(x)(x_i - x)^s| \leqslant L < \infty$, where $x_i = x_{ki}$, $x = x_k$; $k = 1, \ldots, p$.
The additional conditions are the same as (A3) and (A4) with w_{ni} replaced by $w_{ni}^{(s)}$. For details see Muller (1987).

Fan (1990c) proved consistency and asymptotic normality results for dependent observations when u_i are near-epoch dependent with respect to certain (α and $\bar{\phi}$) mixing sequences. The conditions on w_{ni} needed for $z_n = [\hat{m} - E\hat{m}]/\sqrt{V(\hat{m})}] \to N(0, 1)$ as $n \to \infty$ are (A1,c), (A2,b), (A3,a) and

(A7) (a) $\sup_n n_x \sup_{i \leqslant n}|w_{ni}(x)| < \infty$.
   (b) $\sqrt{(n_x)} \sup_{i \leqslant n}|w_{ni}(x)| = O(n^{-\delta/2})$ for some $1 > \delta > \frac{2}{3}$.
   (c) $\Sigma_{i=1}^{n} w_{ni}^2(x)E|\varepsilon_i|^2 = \sigma^2/n_x + o(1/n_x)$ where n_x is defined in (7.2) above.

For forming the confidence intervals it is useful to consider a variable defined by $z_n^* = [\hat{m} - m]/[\sqrt{V(\hat{m})}]$. Fan (1990c) gives similar conditions for proving that $z_n^* \to N(0, 1)$.

For stochastic X, Stone's (1977) sufficient conditions for consistency of $\hat{m}$ for general w_{ni} assume (A2,a,c) and (A3,a) in probability, (A2,b) with probability 1 and

(A8) $E \Sigma_{i=1}^{n}|w_{ni}(x)|f(x_i) \leqslant CEf(x)$ for $C \geqslant 1$ and $n \geqslant 1$.
When the weights satisfy $w_{ni}(x) \geqslant 0$ and $\Sigma_{i=1}^{n} w_{ni}(x) = 1$, the above conditions are both necessary and sufficient. For the NW weights (A8) is not satisfied. Stone (1977, Theorem 2) suggests construction of w for which $\hat{m}$ is consistent without any regularity conditions on $f(x)$. This includes the uniform, triangular or NN estimators.

The asymptotic normality is neatly proved by Owen (1987). It is shown that if (i) $n_x = [\Sigma_{i=1}^{n} w_{ni}^2(x)]^{-1} \to \infty$ in probability, (ii) $\sup_{i \leqslant n} \sqrt{(n_x)}|w_{ni}(x)| \to 0$ in probability, (iii) $\sqrt{(n_x)} [1 - \Sigma_{i=1}^{n} w_{ni}(x)] \to 0$ in probability. Then, if (A4) also holds in probability,

$$z_n = [\hat{m}(x) - E_X\hat{m}(x)]/\sqrt{[V(\hat{m})]} \to N(0, 1) \quad \text{as } n \to \infty.$$

where $E_X\hat{m}(x)$ is the conditional mean of $\hat{m}$ defined by $\Sigma w_{ni}(x)\hat{m}(x_i)$. Now we wish to prove that $z_n^* = \sqrt{n_x}[\hat{m} - m]/[\sqrt{V(\hat{m})}] \to N(0, 1)$ as $n \to \infty$. Note that $z_n^* = \sqrt{n_x}(\hat{m} - E_X\hat{m}) + \sqrt{n_x}(E_X\hat{m} - m)$ and we need to prove that the asymptotic bias $\sqrt{n_x}(E_X\hat{m} - m) = \sqrt{n_x}(\Sigma w_{ni}\hat{m} - m) \to 0$ as $n \to \infty$. Owen (1987) indicates that this bias disappears when x_i is close to x. This implies that $m(x_i)$ be close to $m(x)$, that is, $m(x_i)$ be such that $\|m(x_i) - m(x)\| \leqslant C_x\|x_i - x\|$ for a constant C_x.

The asymptotic results for the s-th derivative of $\hat{m}(x)$, that is $\hat{\beta}^{(s)}$ have not been studied in the literature. Similar asymptotic results for the average derivative based on general $\hat{m}(x)$ are also not reported in the literature. This section has few computer programming implications.

8. Misspecification tests

As in the case of parametric regression, several misspecification tests or diagnostic tests are also useful in the context of nonparametric regression (2.2).

Earlier references to the theory of hypothesis testing for the nonparametric models may be found in Staniswalis (1989a). The following recent attempts open avenues for future research in this area. The tests of interest in econometrics are:

(i) Tests of restrictions on the derivatives $\beta^{(s)}$ evaluated at individual points and average derivatives in Section 4. For those evaluated at individual points, $H_0: R\beta^{(1)}(x) = r$ against $H_1: R\beta^{(1)}(x) \neq r$, where R is a $1 \times p$ matrix of constants and r is a constant. Tests of more general types of restrictions can also be developed as in Ullah (1988b) where only the NW estimator is considered, also see Rilstone (1991).

(ii) Diagnostic tests for conditional heteroscedasticity, serial correlation and normality of errors u in (2.2). Large sample tests for these problems can be carried out in the same way as the corresponding diagnostic tests in the parametric regression developed in Pagan and Hall (1983) and Pagan (1984). This is because, for large samples, the nonparametric residual is $\hat{u}_i = u_i + o_p(1)$; and thus it behaves in the same way as the least squares residuals in parametric regressions. The basic idea from Pagan (1984) and Pagan and Hall (1983) is to augment the model (2.2) as

$$y_i = m(x_i) + z_i\delta + u_i \tag{8.1}$$

and then test for $\delta = 0$. This is the partial regression model described in Section 6. Whang and Andrews (1990) give a more general and systematic treatment of the distribution of misspecification tests in semiparametric models; also see Robinson (1989) who considers the case of dependent observations for time series data.

(iii) Test for omitted variables on the number of regressors can be carried out by regarding the z_i in (ii) above as a vector of omitted variables and then testing for $\delta = 0$ in (8.1). An alternative method would be to compare the residual variance from the null model $y_i = m(x_i) + u_i$ with the residual variance from the alternative model $y_i = m(x_i, z_i) + u_i$. This can be done by splitting the sample into $n_1 = n_2$ observations and considering the test statistic

$$S = n_1^{-1/2}\left\{\sum_{i=1}^{n_1} \hat{u}_i^2 - \sum_{j=1}^{n_2} \hat{u}_j^2\right\},$$

where $\bar{u}$ is the nonparametric residual from the alternative model. The sampling distribution of S is not known, but it can be determined by using the approach of Whang and Andrews (1990).

A related issue of interest is the determination of the number of included regressor variables p and/or lag length in cases where x_i in $m(x_i)$ is a vector of lagged values of y_i. Auestad and Tjostheim (1990) have recently looked into this problem and extended the Akaike information criterion (AIC) for this purpose. The AIC formula turns out to be the residual variance multiplied by a factor depending on n, the NW kernel weight and the p number of regressors.

(iv) The test for linearity or, in general, for any parameter specification

$m(x_i, \theta)$ against a nonparametric alternative $m(x_i)$ has received much attention in recent years. Ullah (1985) suggested using the test statistic $S = n^{-1} \Sigma \, \tilde{u}_i^2 - n^{-1} \Sigma \, \hat{u}_i^2$ which compares the parametric residual variance $n^{-1} \Sigma \, \tilde{u}_i^2$ with the nonparametric residual variance. However, the distribution of this statistic was not established. A related pseudo likelihood ratio approach was developed by Azzalini et al. (1989). Their test statistic is

$$\sum_{i=1}^{n} \{\log f(y_i, \hat{m}(x_i)) - \log f(y_i, \hat{m}(x_i, \hat{\theta}))\} \,, \tag{8.2}$$

where $\hat{\theta}$ is a consistent estimator of θ. They also provide estimates of significance points by simulating the sampling distribution of the test statistic under the null model.

Yatchew (1992), and Whang and Andrew (1990) consider an Ullah (1985) type test statistic

$$S = n_1^{-1} \sum_{i=1}^{n_1} \tilde{u}_i^2 - n_1^{-1} \sum_{j=1}^{n_2} \hat{u}_j^2$$

by splitting the sample into the parts of equal sizes $n_1 = n_2$ and show that

$$n_1^{1/2} S / (2\eta)^{1/2} \sim \mathrm{N}(0, 1) \quad \text{as } n \to \infty,$$
$$\text{where } \eta = n_1^{-1} \sum \tilde{u}_i^4 - \left(n_1^{-1} \sum \tilde{u}_i^2\right)^2 .$$

Newey's (1985) conditional moment restriction test provides an alternative test for the functional form in a nonlinear regression setting with $m(x_i, \theta)$. Bierens (1990) argued that Newey's approach uses only a finite number of restrictions and thus the resultant test cannot be consistent under all possible alternatives. He uses an infinite set of moment conditions and provides a test statistic which is consistent under all alternatives. However, the power of the test depends crucially on the type of the moment condition used. For a related test statistic, also see Su and Wei (1991).

An alternative way to develop the test statistic for functional form is to consider a combined estimator of $m(x_i)$ as $\bar{m}(x_i, \lambda) = (1 - \lambda) m(x_i, \hat{\theta}) + \lambda \hat{m}(x_i)$ and write

$$y_i - m(x_i, \hat{\theta}) = \lambda(\hat{m}(x_i) - m(x_i, \hat{\theta})) + u_i \tag{8.3}$$

as in (2.14) where $m(x_i, \hat{\theta}) = x_i \hat{\beta}$ is taken as a linear model. The test statistic for $\lambda = 0$ is then $t = \hat{\lambda} / (V(\hat{\lambda}))^{1/2}$ where $\hat{\lambda}$ is the least squares estimator. It is conjectured that, under certain regularity conditions, t will be asymptotically standard normal. In a recent paper Eubank and Spiegelman (1990) considered, instead, $y_i = m(x_i, \theta) + m(x_i) + u_i$, where $m(x_i \theta) = x_i \theta$ is linear in scalar x_i and suggested a test for $m = 0$ based on orthogonal polynomials and smooth spline functions. They found out that, under regularity conditions, their test is consistent against all smooth alternatives. A generalization of their procedure to the vector x_i case, however, appears to be difficult.

We have presented the alternative approaches to testing functional form. Some other fruitful approaches are developed in Hardle and Marron (1990) and Abramson and Goldstein (1991). A detailed comparative analysis of these approaches would be a useful future study.

(v) Nonnested hypothesis testing for $H_0: m(x_i, z_i) = m(x_i)$ against $H_1: m(x_i, z_i) = m(z_i)$ has been considered extensively in parametric econometrics, see Davidson and Mackinnon (1982). Ullah and Singh (1989) suggested testing this hypothesis by using a distance measure. Alternatively, one can write the combined model $y_i = m(x_i, z_i) + u_i = (1 - \lambda)m(x_i) + \lambda m(z_i) + u_i$ and testing for $\lambda = 0$ in the last squares regression of $y_i - \hat{m}(x_i) = \lambda[\hat{m}(z_i) - \hat{m}(x_i)] + u_i$ as in (2.14). The distribution of this and other statistics have been analyzed in Delgado and Stengos (1990).

Hall and Jeffrey (1990) have considered the problem of testing $H_0: y_i = m(x_i) + u_i$ against $H_1: z_i = g(x_i) + u_i$ and provide examples where such testing problems would be of interest. They propose a bootstrap test statistic for the scaled version of $n^{-1} \sum_{i=1}^{n} [\hat{m}(x_i) - \hat{g}(x_i)]^2$, where $\hat{m}$ and $\hat{g}$ are nonparametric estimators. They show that the test has a high level of accuracy compared to an exact test. Further the proposed test can be generalized for testing for differences between several regression means.

(vi) The nonparametric test of independence of x with u, that is $H_0: f(x, u) = f(x)f(u)$ against $H_1: f(x, u) \neq f(x)f(u)$ has been suggested in Ullah and Singh (1989) using distance (entropy) measures, e.g., Kulback–Leibler. Robinson (1990) also provides entropy based test statistics and systematically develops the distribution theory for dependent observations. An alternative distance measure is used in Ahmad and Cerrito (1989) who also study the asymptotic distribution under iid assumption. Also see Abramson and Goldstein (1991) for a different approach. Computer programming for this section involves test statistics similar to (8.2) or parameters similar to λ.

9. Applications

In the last three decades of the nonparametric estimation of regression and other functions, the statistical literature has been dominated by the asymptotic theory results on consistency, unbiasedness and normality with some recent results on the small sample theory. This is also evident in the nonparametric econometrics literature developed so far. However, very little has been done on exploring these results in applied settings, though with the advances in computer technology etc., it is hoped that applications of data based nonparametric approaches to inference will soon become a common phenomenon. We merely provide here some of the references which use the nonparametric approach in applied statistics and econometrics. For more examples and other references, see Hardle (1990), Ullah (1988) and Rilstone (1991).

In labor econometrics, the nonparametric analysis of earning/age and consumption functions have been analyzed by Ullah (1985), Basu and Ullah (1992), Chu and Marron (1991), and Magee et al. (1991). For production function estimation, see Vinod and Ullah (1988), and Gallant (1981). For demand and consumption functions, see Moschini (1989), Bierens and Pott-Buter (1990), McMillan et al. (1989), and Hardle et al. (1991). For income distribution studies, see Hildebrand and Hildebrand (1986), Deaton (1989), and Hardle and Jerison (1988). Most recent work has, however, developed in the area of financial time series econometrics where generally large data sets are available. These include Diebold and Nason (1989) for exchange rate forecasts, and Tengesdel (1991) and Frank and Stengos (1989) for nonparametric forecasts in diamond and gold markets, respectively. Pagan and Hong (1991), Gallant and Tauchen (1989), Zhou (1990) and Santana and Wadhwani (1989) for stock market returns; Wulwick and Mack (1990) and Samiullah (1991) for the macroeconomic Phillips curve estimation; and Racine and Smith (1991) in resource economics. Vinod (1988, 1989) report applications to estimation of a random walk in consumption and for disequilibrium models respectively. Stock (1990) reports an application to estimating the benefits of hazardous waste.

Most of the results in the above mentioned applied papers are encouraging for future applications of the nonparametric procedures. In particular, they point out important facts of the data which are otherwise not detectable through the raw plots or parametric regressions. Also, since many data sets tend to behave in a nonlinear way, the nonparametric procedures are found to perform better than the ad hoc parametric models. However, efficiency and computational problems in higher dimensions, problems of nonstationarity in time series, misspecification and finite sample issues still remain the challenges for future applied work. Although it is clear form our survey that the major computations involve weighted averaging and brute force minimization of MSE-type quantities, professionally written general purpose software remains unavailable.

Acknowledgment

We are grateful to K. Messer of California State University at Fullerton and J. Racine of York University, Canada and referees for detailed helpful comments. The responsibility for any remaining errors however is ours.

References

Abramson, J. and L. Goldstein (1991). Efficient testing by nonparametric functional estimation. *J. Theor. Probab.* **4**, 137–159.

Ahmad, I. and P. B. Cerrito (1989). Hypothesis testing using density estimation: Testing for independence. Unpublished manuscript. Northern Illinois University, Dekalb, USA.

Ahmad, I. and P. Lin (1976). Nonparametric sequential estimation of a multiple regression function. *Bull. Math. Statist.* **17**, 63–75.

Ahmad, I. and P. Lin (1984). Fitting a multiple regression. *J. Statist. Plann. Inference* **2**, 163–176.

Altman, N. S. (1990). Kernel smoothing of data with correlated error. *J. Amer. Statist. Assoc.* **85**, 749–777.

Andrews, D. W. K. (1991). Asymptotic normality of series estimators for nonparametric and semiparametric regression models. *Econometrica* **59**, 307–345.

Andrews, D. W. K. and Y. J. Whang (1991). Additive interactive regression models: Circumvention of the curse of dimensionality. *Econometric Theory* **6**, 466–479.

Auestad, B. and D. Tjostheim (1990). Identification of nonlinear time series: First order characterization and order determination. *Biometrika* **77**, 669–687.

Azzaline, A., A. W. Bowman and W. Hardle (1989). On the use of nonparametric regression for model checking. *Biometrika* **76**, 1–11.

Basu, R. and A. Ullah (1992). Chinese earnings – age profile: A nonparametric analysis. *J. Internat. Trade and Econ. Development* **1**, 151–165.

Bhattacharya, P. K. and A. K. Gangopodhyay (1990). Kernel and nearest-neighbor estimation of a conditional quantile. *Ann. Statist.* **18**, 1400.

Bierens, H. (1990). A consistent conditional moment test of functional form. *Econometrica* **58**, 1443–1458.

Bierens, H. and M. A. Pott-Buter (1990). Specification of household Engel curves by nonparametric regression. *Econometric Rev.* **9**, 123.

Box, G. E. P. and D. Cox (1964). An analysis of transformations. *J. Roy. Statist. Soc. Ser. B* **26**, 211–264.

Breiman, L. and J. Friedman (1985). Estimating optimal transformations for multiple regression and correlation. *J. Amer. Statist. Assoc.* **80**, 580–619.

Buckley, M. J., A. R. Eagleson and B. W. Silverman (1988). The estimation of residual variance in nonparametric regression. *Biometrika* **75**(2), 189–199.

Carroll, R. J. (1982). Adapting for heteroskedasticity in linear models. *Ann. Statist.* **10**, 1224–1233.

Chamberlain, G. (1986). Note on semiparametric regression. Unpublished manuscript, Department of Economics, Harvard University.

Chen, H. (1988). Convergence rates for parametric components in a partly linear model. *Ann. Statist.* **16**(1), 136–146.

Chu, C. K. (1989). Some results in nonparametric regression, Ph.D. Thesis, University of North Carolina.

Chu, C. K. and J. S. Marron (1991). Choosing a kernel regression estimator. *Statist. Sci.* **6**, 404–433.

Cleveland, W. S. (1979). Robust locally weighted regression and smoothing scatter plots. *J. Amer. Statist. Assoc.* **74**, 829–836.

Cleveland, W. S. and S. J. Devlin (1988). Locally weighted regression: An approach to regression analysis by local fitting. *J. Amer. Statist. Assoc.* **83**, 590–610.

Cleveland, W. S., S. J. Devlin and E. Grosse (1988). Regression by local fitting: Methods, properties and computational algorithms. *J. Econometrics* **37**, 87–114.

Collomb, G. (1981). Estimation nonparametrique de la regression: Revue bibliographique. *Internat. Statist. Rev.* **49**, 75–93.

Davidson, R. and J. G. Mackinnon (1982). Some non-nested hypothesis tests and the relations among them. *Rev. Econ. Stud.* **49**, 781–793.

Deaton, A. (1989). Rice prices and income distribution in Thailand: A nonparametric analysis. *Econometric J.* **99**, 1–37.

Delgado, M. A. and T. Stengos (1990). Semiparametric specification testing of non-nested econometrics. Manuscript, Economics Department, Indiana University.

Devroye L. P. and T. J. Wagner (1980). Distribution free consistency results in nonparametric discrimination and regression function estimates. *Ann. Statist.* **8**, 231–239.

Diebold, F. and J. M. Nason (1989). Nonparametric exchange rate prediction. Manuscript, Board of Governors, Federal Reserve System, Division of Research and Statistics, Washington, DC.

Eubank, R. L. (1988). *Smoothing Splines and Nonparametric Regression.* Marcel Dekker, New York.

Eubank, R. L. and C. H. Spiegelman (1990). Testing the goodness of fit of a linear model via nonparametric regression techniques. *J. Amer. Statist. Assoc.* **85**, 387–392.

Fan, Y. (1990a). A direct way to formulate indirect estimators of average derivatives. Manuscript, Economics Department, University of Windsor, Windsor, Canada.

Fan, Y. (1990b). Consistent nonparametric multiple regression for dependent heterogeneous processes: The fixed design case. *J. Multivariate Anal.* **33**, 72–88.

Fan, Y. (1990c). Seemingly unrelated essays in econometrics. Ph.D. Thesis, University of Western Ontario.

Frank, M. Z. and T. Stengos (1989). Measuring the strangeness of gold and silver rates of return. *Rev. Econ. Stud.* **56**, 375–385.

Friedman, J. and Struetzle W. (1981). Projection pursuit regression. *J. Amer. Statist. Assoc.* **76**, 817–823.

Gallant, A. R. (1981). On the bias in flexible functional forms and an essentially unbiased form: The Fourier flexible form. *J. Econometrics* **15**, 211–245.

Gallant, A. R. and D. W. Nychka (1987). Semi-nonparametric maximum likelihood estimation. *Econometrica* **55**, 363–390.

Gallant, A. R. and G. Tauchen (1989). Semi-nonparametric estimation of conditionally constrained heterogeneous process: Asset pricing applications. *Econometrica* **157**, 1091.

Gallant, A. R. and G. Souza (1991). On the asymptotic normality of Fourier flexible form estimates. *J. Econometrics* **50**, 329–353.

Gasser, T. and J. Engel (1990). The choice of weights in kernel regression estimation. *Biometrika* **77**, 377.

Gasser, T., A Kneip and W. Kohler (1991). A flexible and fast method for automatic smoothing. *J. Amer. Statist. Assoc.* **86**, 643–652.

Gasser, T. and H. G. Muller (1979a). Kernel estimates of regression functions. In: T. Gasser and M. Rosenblatt, eds., *Smoothing Techniques for Curve Estimation.* Springer, New York, 23–68.

Gasser, T. and H. G. Muller (1979b). Nonparametric estimation of regression functions and their derivatives. Reprint 38 (Sonderforschungsbereich, 123), University of Heidelberg, West Germany, Dept. of Biostatistics.

Gasser. T. and H. G. Muller (1984). Estimating regression functions and their derivatives by the kernel method. *Scand. J. Statist.* **11**, 171–185.

German, S. and C. Hwang (1982). Nonparametric maximum likelihood estimation by the method of sieves. *Ann. Statist.* **10**, 401–414.

Georgiev, A. A. (1984). Speed of convergence in nonparametric kernel estimation of a regression function and its derivatives. *Ann. Inst. Statist. Math.* **36**, 455–462.

Georgiev, A. A. (1988). Consistent nonparametric multiple regression: The fixed design case. *J. Multivariate Anal.* **31**, 100–110.

Goldstein, L. and K. Messer (1990). Optimal plug-un estimators for nonparametric estimation of functionals. Technical Report No. 277, Stanford University, Dept. of Statistics.

Hall, P. (1984). Asymptotic properties of integrated square error and cross-validation for kernel estimation of regression function. *Z. Wahrsch. Verw, Geb.* **67**, 175–196.

Hall, P. and D. Jeffrey (1990). Bootstrap test for difference between means in nonparametric regression. *J. Amer. Statist. Assoc.* **85**, 1039–1049.

Hall, P. and J. S. Marron (1990). On variance estimation in nonparametric regression. *Biometrika* **77**, 4–5.

Hall, P. and E. Wehrly (1991). A geometrical method for removing edge effects from kernel-type nonparametric regression estimators. *J. Amer. Statist. Assoc.* **86**, 665–672.

Hardle, W. (1990). *Applied nonparametric regression.* Cambridge Univ. Press, New York.

Hardle, W., W. Hildenbrand and M. Jerison (1991). Empirical evidence on the law of demand. *Econometrica* **59**, 1525–1549.

Hardle, W. and M. Jerison (1988). Evolution of Engel curves over time. Discussion Paper A-178, SFB 303 University of Bonn, West Germany.

Hardle, W. and J. S. Marron (1985). Optimal bandwidth selection in nonparametric regression function estimation. *Ann. Statist.* **13**, 1465–1481.

Hardle, W. and J. S. Marron (1990). Semi-parametric comparison of regression curves. *Ann. Statist.* **18**, 63–89.

Hardle, W. and T. M. Stoker (1989). Investigating smooth multiple regression by the method of average derivatives. *J. Amer. Statist. Assoc.* **84**, 986–995.

Hastie, T. and R. Tibshirani (1986). Generalized additive models. *Statist. Sci.* **1**, 295–318.

Hastie, T. and R. Tibshirani (1987). Generalized additive models: Some applications. *J. Amer. Statist. Assoc.* **82**, 371–386.

Hastie, T. J. and R. Tibshirani (1990). *Generalized Additive Models*. Chapman and Hall, London.

Hildebrand, K. and W. Hildebrand (1986). On the mean demand effect: A data analysis of the U.K. family expenditure survey. In: W. Hildebrand and A. Mas-Colell, eds., *Contributions to Mathematical Economics*. North-Holland, Amsterdam, 267–268.

Jennen-Steinmetz, C. and T. Gasser (1988). A unifying approach to nonparametric regression estimation. *J. Amer. Statist. Assoc.* **83**, 1084–1089.

Kendall, M. and A. Stuart (1977). *The Advanced theory of Statistics*, Vol. 1. 4th ed., McMillan, New York.

Lau, L. (1985). Functional forms in econometric model building. In: Z. Grilliches and M. D. Intriligator eds., *Handbook Of Econometrics*, Vol. 3. North-Holland, Amsterdam, Chapter 13.

Mack, Y. P. (1981). Local properties of R-NN regression estimates. *SIAM J. Algebraic Discrete Methods* **2**, 311–323.

Mack, Y. P. and H. Muller (1989). Derivative estimation in nonparametric regression with random predictor variable. *Sankhyā Ser. A* **51**, 59–72.

Maddala, G. S. (1977). *Econometrics*. McGraw Hill, New York.

Magee, L., J. B. Burbidge and A. L. Robb (1991). Kernel smoothed consumption-age quantiles. *J. Amer. Statist. Assoc.* **86**, 673–677.

Marron, J. S. (1988). Automatic smoothing parameter selection: A survey. *Empirical Econ.* **13**, 187–208.

McMillan, J. A., A. Ullah and H. D. Vinod (1989). Estimation of the shape of the demand curve by nonparametric kernel methods. Mimeo in B. Raj, ed., *Advances in Econometrics and Modelling*. Kluwer, New York, 85–92.

Moschini, G. (1989). Preferences changes bias in consumer demand: An indirectly separate semiparametric model. Manuscript, Economics Department, Iowa State University.

Muller, H. G. (1984). Smooth optimum kernel estimators of densities, Regression curves and models. *Ann. Statist.* **12**, 766–774.

Muller, H. G. (1987). Weighted local regression and kernel methods for nonparametric curve fitting. *J. Amer. Statist. Assoc.* **82**, 231–238.

Muller, H. G. (1988). *Nonparametric Regression Analysis of Longitudinal Data*. Lecture Notes in Math., Vol 46. Springer, New York.

Nadaraya, E. A. (1964). On estimating regression. *Theory Probab. Appl.* **9**, 141–142.

Newey, W. K. (1985). Maximum likelihood specification testing and conditional moment tests. *Econometrica* **53**, 1047–1070.

Olkin, I. and C. M. Spiegelman (1987). A semiparametric approach to density estimation. *J. Amer. Statist. Assoc.* **82**, 858–865.

Owen, A. B. (1987). Nonparametric conditional estimation. Ph.D. Thesis, Stanford University.

Pagan, A. R. and A. D. Hall (1983). Diagnostic tests as residual analysis. *Econometric Rev.* **2**, 159–218.

Pagan, A. R. (1984). Model evaluation by variable addition. In: D. F. Hendry and K. F. Wallis, eds., *Econometric and Quantitative Economics*. Basil Blackwell, Oxford, UK.

Pagan, A. R. and A. Ullah (1990). Nonparametric econometric methods. Manuscript, Economics Department, University of California, Riverside, USA.

Pagan, A. R. and Y. S. Hong (1991). Nonparametric estimation and the risk premium. In: W. Barnett, J. Powell and G. Tauchen, eds., *Nonparametric and Semiparametric methods in Econometrics*, by Cambridge Univ. Press, Cambridge, UK.

Powell, J. L., J. H. Stock and T. M. Stoker (1986). Semiparametric estimation of weighted average derivatives, WP 1793-86, MIT, MA, USA.

Prakasa Rao, B. L. S. (1983). *Nonparametric Functional Estimation*. Academic Press, New York.

Priestley, M. B. and M. T. Chao (1972). Nonparametric function fitting. *J. Rov. Statist. Soc. Ser. B* **34**, 385–392.

Racine, J. S. and J. B. Smith (1991). Nonparametric estimation of growth in replenishable resource stocks. Manuscript, Economics Department, York University, Canada.

Reinsch, H. (1967). Smoothing by spline functions. *Numer. Math.* **10**, 177–183.

Rice, J. (1984). Boundary modification for kernel regression. *Comm. Statist. Theory Methods* **13**, 893–900.

Rice, J. (1986). Convergence rates for partially splined models. *Statist. Probab. Lett.* **4**, 203–208.

Rilstone, P. (1991). Nonparametric hypothesis testing with parametric rates of convergence. *Internat. Econ. Rev.* **12**, 209–227.

Robinson, P. M. (1987). Semiparametric econometrics: A survey. *J. Appl. Econometrics*.

Robinson, P. M. (1988). Root-N-consistent semiparametric regression. *Econometrica* **56**, 931–954.

Robinson, P. M. (1989). Hypothesis testing in semiparametric and nonparametric models for econometric time series. *Rev. Econ. Stud.* **56**, 511–534.

Robinson, P. M. (1990). Consistent nonparametric entropy-based testing. Manuscript, London School of Economics.

Rosenblatt, M. (1956). Remarks on some nonparametric estimates of a density function. *Ann. Math. Stat.* **27**, 642–669.

Royall, R. M. (1966). A class of nonparametric estimators of a smooth regression function. Ph.D. Thesis, Stanford University.

Ruud, P. A. (1986). Consistent estimation of limited dependent variable models despite misspecification of distribution. *J. Econometrics* **32**, 157–187.

Ryu, H. K. (1990). Orthonomial basis and maximum entropy estimation of probability density and regression function. Ph.D. Thesis, University of Chicago.

Samanta, M. (1989). Nonparametric estimation of conditional quantiles. *Statist. Probab. Lett.* **7**, 407–412.

Samiullah, S. (1991). Phillips curve revisited via nonparametric way. Manuscript, Economics Department, University of California, Riverside, CA.

Sentana, E. and S. Wadhwani (1989). Semiparametric estimation and the predictability of stock market returns: Some lessons from Japan. Manuscript, April, London School of Economics.

Silverman, B. W. (1984). Spline smoothing: The equivalent variable Kernel method. *Ann. Statist.* **12**, 898–916.

Silverman, B. W. (1986). *Density Estimation for Statistics and Data Analysis*. Chapman and Hall, New York.

Singh, R. S. (1981). Speed of convergence in nonparametric estimation of a multivariate mu-density and its mixed partial derivatives. *J. Statist. Plann. Inference* **5**, 287–298.

Singh, R. S. and A. Ullah (1986). Nonparametric recursive estimation of a multivariate, marginal and conditional DGP with an application to specification of econometric models. *Comm. Statist. Theory Methods* **15**, 3489–3513.

Singh, R. S., A. Ullah and R. A. L. Carter (1987). Nonparametric inference in econometrics: new applications. In: I. MacNeill and G. Umphrey, eds., *Time series and econometric modelling*. Reidel, Dordrecht.

Speckman, P. (1988). Kernel smoothing in partial linear models. *J. Roy. Statist. Soc. Ser. B* **50**, 413–436.

Staniswalis, J. G. (1989a). On the kernel estimate of a regression function in likelihood based models. *J. Amer. Statist. Assoc.* **84**(405), 276–283.

Staniswalis, J. G. (1989b). Local bandwidth selection for kernel estimates. *J. Amer. Statist. Assoc.* **84**(405), 284–288.

Staniswalis, J. G. and T. A. Severini (1991). Diagnostics for assessing regression models. *J. Amer. Statist. Assoc.* **86**, 684–692.

Stock, J. H. (1990). Nonparametric policy analysis: An application to estimating hazardous waste cleanup benefits. In: W. Barnett, J. Powell and G. Tauchen, eds., *Nonparametric and Semiparametric methods in Econometrics*. Cambridge Univ. Press, Cambridge, UK.

Stoker, T. M. (1986). Consistent estimation of scaled coefficients. *Econometrica* **54**, 1461–1481.

Stone, C. J. (1977). Consistent nonparametric regression. *Ann. Statist.* **5**, 595–645.

Stone, C. J. (1982). Optimal global rates of convergence for nonparametric regression. *Ann. Statist.* **10**, 1040–1053.

Stone, C. J. (1985). Additive regression and other nonparametric models. *Ann. Statist.* **13**, 689–705.

Su, J. Q. and L. J. Wei (1991). A lack of fit test for the mean function in a generalized linear model. *J. Amer. Statist. Assoc.* **85**, 1039–1049.

Tauchen, G. (1985). Diagnostic testing and evaluation of maximum likelihood models. *J. Econometrics* **30**, 415–443.

Tibshirani, R. (1988). Estimating transformations for regression via additivity and variance stabilization. *J. Amer. Statist. Assoc.* **83**, 394–405.

Tsybakov, A. B. (1982). Robust estimates of a function (in Russian). English translation in: *Problems Inform. Translation* **18**, 190–201.

Tsybakov, A. B. (1986). Robust reconstruction of functions by the local approximation method (in Russian). English translation in: *Problems Inform. Translation* **22**, 133–146.

Tengesdel, M. O. (1991). Testing diamond market rates of return. Manuscript, Economics Department, University of California, Riverside, CA.

Ullah, A. (1985). Specification analysis of econometric models. *J. Quant. Econ.* **1**, 187–210.

Ullah, A. (1988a). Nonparametric estimation of econometric functionals. *Canad. J. Econ.* **21** (3), 625–658.

Ullah, A. (1988b). Nonparametric estimation and hypothesis testing. *Empirical Econ.* **13**, 101–127.

Ullah, A. (1989). The exact density nonparametric regression estimators: Random design case, Manuscript, University of California, Riverside, CA.

Ullah, A. (1992). The exact density of nonparametric regression estimators: Fixed design case. *Commun. Stat.* **21**, 1251–1254.

Ullah, A. and R. S. Singh (1989). The estimation of probability density functions with applications to nonparametric inference econometrics. In: B. Raj, ed., *Advances in Econometrics and Modelling*, Kluwer Academic Press, Dordrecht.

Ullah, A. and H. D. Vinod (1988). Nonparametric kernel estimation of parameters. *J. Quant. Econ.* **4**, 81–87.

Ullah, A. and H. D. Vinod (1991). Semiparametric compromise kernel regression for applications in econometrics. Manuscript, Dept. of Economics, Fordham University, Bronx, NY.

Ullah, A. and V. Zinde-Walsh (1992). On the estimation of residual variance in nonparametric regression. *J. Nonparametric Stat.* **1**, 263–265.

Vinod, H. D. (1987). Simple new densities with zero low order moments. Discussion paper No. ES188, Dept. of Econometrics, University of Manchester, Manchester M13-9PL, UK.

Vinod, H. D. (1988). Random walk in consumption: Maximum likelihood and nonparametrics. In: G. F. Rhodes Jr. and T. M. Fomby, ed., *Advances in Econometrics*, Vol. 7. JAI Press, Greenwich, CT, 291–309.

Vinod, H. D. (1989). Kernel estimation for disequilibrium models for floorspace efficiency in retailing. *J. Product. Anal.* **1**, 79–84.

Vinod, H. D. and A. Ullah (1988). Nonparametric kernel estimation of Econometric parameters. In: G. F. Rhodes Jr. and T. M. Fomby, eds., *Advances in econometrics*, Vol. 7, JAI Press, Greenwich, CT, 139–160.

Wahba, G. (1975). Periodic splines for spectral density estimation: The use of cross validation for determining the degree of smoothing. *Comm. Statist. A* **4**, 125.

Wahba, G. (1981). Data based optimal smoothing of orthogonal series density estimates. *Ann. Statist.* **9**, 146–156.

Wahba, G. (1986). Partial and interaction spline models for the semiparametric estimation of functions of several variables. In: T. J. Boardman, ed., *Computer Science and Statistics: Proc. 18th Sympos on the Interface*, American Statistical Association, Washington, DC.

Whang, Y. J. and D. W. K. Andrews (1990). Tests of specification for parametric and semiparametric models. WP 943, Yale University.

Watson, G. S. (1964). Smooth regression analysis. *Sankhyā Ser. A* **26**, 359–372.

White, H. (1990). Connectionist nonparametric regression: Multilayer feedforward networks can learn arbitrary mappings. WP 90-S, University of California, San Diego, CA.

Wulwick, N. J. and Y. P. Mack (1990). A kernel regression of Phillips's data. WD 40, Jerone Levy Economics Institute, Bard College, Annandale-on-Hudson, New York.

Yang, S. S. (1981). Linear function of concomitants of order statistics with application to nonparametric estimation of a regression function. *J. Amer. Statist. Assoc.* **76**, 658–662.

Yatchew, A. J. (1992). Nonparametric regression model tests based on least squares. *Econometric Theory* **8**, 435–451.

Zhou, Z. (1990). Economic variables and the stock market; A nonparametric analysis. Manuscript, Economics Department, University of California, Riverside, CA.

G. S. Maddala, C. R. Rao and H. D. Vinod, eds., *Handbook of Statistics, Vol. 11*
5

Simultaneous Microeconometric Models with Censored or Qualitative Dependent Variables

Richard W. Blundell and Richard J. Smith

1. Introduction

Many applications of microeconomic theory to individual data face the joint problems of censoring and simultaneity. In particular, the dependent variable under investigation may not be continuously observed and some of the conditioning variables representing the outcome of other decisions by the individual may be simultaneously determined. In this paper we define two classes of simultaneous limited dependent variable regression models. The distinction between these two classes depends on whether the structural economic model is simultaneous in the *latent* or *observed* dependent variables. This distinction corresponds closely to whether or not the censoring mechanism itself acts as a constraint on individual agents' behaviour.

Type I models, which form the first class, are defined to be simultaneous in the underlying latent dependent variables. As a result, there exists an *explicit* and *unique reduced form* in the latent dependent variables under the usual identification conditions. Simultaneous Probit (Amemiya, 1978; Rivers and Vuong, 1988; Blundell and Smith, 1989) and Tobit (Amemiya, 1979; Nelson and Olsen, 1978; Smith and Blundell, 1986; Blundell and Smith, 1989) models among others are special cases of this class. In Type I models, individual behaviour is completely described by the latent variable model and the censoring process simply acts as a constraint on the information available to the econometrician. For example, in a model describing household labour supply and consumption behaviour, hours of work may only be available to the econometrician in grouped form – part-time and full-time – even though individual agents themselves have complete flexibility in their hours' choices. In this case, optimal consumption behaviour is a function of *latent* rather than *observed* labour supply behaviour. As a result, the underlying reduced form can be derived uniquely in terms of the latent dependent variables.

Type II models form a general class in which the nonlinearity implicit in the censoring or discrete grouping process prevents an explicit solution for the reduced form. This occurs in the structural shift models of Heckman (1978), the switching models described in Gourieroux, Laffont and Monfort (1980), as well as many applications of joint decision making models on discrete data. In Type II models, the observability rule also constrains the agent's choice set. For example, if the two discrete hours packages (part-time, full time) are all that is available, then household labour supply decisions will reflect this and will depend on the *actual* discrete labour market outcomes. Similar models arise where there are corner solutions or points of rationing. For this second class of discrete or censored models a further *coherency condition* is required, this condition imposes restrictions that guarantee the existence of a *unique but implicit reduced form* for the observable endogenous variables.

The coherency condition is naturally related to the conditions for a unique solution for the agent's optimal decision rule. As such the coherency condition is necessary (but not always sufficient) for the specification to correspond to that of an economic optimising model. Moreover, if conditions for economic optimisation are imposed on the model, coherency is satisfied. A discussion of coherency conditions in switching and disequilibrium econometric models is provided by Gourieroux, Laffont and Monfort (1980). For models with discrete dependent variables, a comprehensive discussion is found in Heckman (1978), who refers to this condition as the *principal assumption*. An excellent review of coherency and its relationship to plausible economic behaviour is contained in Maddala (1983).

The paper is organised as follows. Section 2 outlines the models. Section 3 focuses on Type I models and derives marginal and conditional maximum likelihood estimators analogous to those of Nelson and Olsen (1978), Amemiya (1978, 1979), Heckman (1978) and Smith and Blundell (1986). The minimum chi-squared approach of Ferguson (1958), Malinvaud (1970) and Rothenberg (1973) is used to compare the asymptotic relative efficiency of the various estimators considered. A simple efficient two-step algorithm based on the conditional maximum likelihood estimator is given. The joint maximum likelihood estimator is obtained by iteration of this algorithm until convergence. Section 4 considers Type II models. The absence of an explicit (linear) reduced form has a nontrivial impact on the form of the maximum likelihood estimator. Nevertheless, a simple consistent estimator may be obtained mirroring the conditional maximum likelihood estimator for Type I models. In addition, this estimator reveals directly how both identification and consistent estimation of structural form parameters depend critically on the satisfaction of appropriate coherency restrictions. The models considered include simultaneous Probit and Tobit models as well as simultaneous extensions of selectivity and double-hurdle models. In each case, the appropriate coherency conditions and identification are discussed briefly. As Type I and II models form nonnested alternatives, a simple method is suggested for discrimination between them. Section 5 presents an empirical application to labour supply and savings behaviour. The relationship between statistical coherency and the logical consistency of the economic model for Type II specifications is emphasised. Finally, Section 6 concludes.

2. Models

The latent dependent variable of interest is denoted by y_{1i}^* with observed value y_{1i}, $i = 1, \ldots, N$. The observation rule linking y_{1i} to y_{1i}^* is given by

$$y_{1i} \equiv g_1(y_{1i}^*, y_{3i}^*), \tag{1}$$

where $g_1(\cdot, \cdot)$ is a known function independent of parameters and y_{3i}^* is another latent variable described below which allows consideration of selectivity or double-hurdle observability rules on y_{1i}^*; in simple cases such as those of Tobit or Probit, y_{3i}^* does not enter (1), thus $y_{1i} \equiv g_1(y_{1i}^*)$, $i = 1, \ldots, N$. The general structural model for y_{1i}^* is defined by

$$y_{1i}^* = \alpha_1 h(y_{1i}^*, y_{3i}^*) + \beta_1 y_{2i} + \gamma_1' x_{1i} + u_{1i}, \tag{2}$$

where $h(\cdot, \cdot)$ is a known function independent of parameters and x_{1i} denotes a K_1-vector of exogenous variables, $i = 1, \ldots, N$.

In (2), $y_{2i} \equiv y_{2i}^*$ is a simultaneously determined variable, which is assumed to be continuously observed, and also implicitly depends on the latent variables y_{1i}^* and y_{3i}^* [1]

$$y_{2i} = \alpha_2 h(y_{1i}^*, y_{3i}^*) + \gamma_2' x_{2i} + u_{2i}, \tag{3}$$

where x_{2i} is a K_2-vector of exogenous variables, $i = 1, \ldots, N$.

The function $h(y_{1i}^*, y_{3i}^*)$ is included to complete the class of models that permit coherency and allows us to distinguish the two types of model which are the subject of this paper:

Type I: $\quad h(y_{1i}^*, y_{3i}^*) \equiv y_{1i}^*$,
Type II: $\quad h(y_{1i}^*, y_{3i}^*) \equiv y_{1i}[=g_1(y_{1i}^*, y_{3i}^*)]$.

In the Type I specification, (3) may be replaced by the reduced from (RF)

$$y_{2i} = x_i' \pi_2 + v_{2i}, \tag{3'}$$

together with the identification condition $\alpha_1 = 0$ in (2).

We introduce a further reduced form model to allow for possible selectivity:

$$y_{3i}^* = x_i' \pi_3 + v_{3i}, \tag{4}$$

where the K-vector of exogenous variables x_i comprises the nonoverlapping variables of x_{1i} and x_{2i}, $i = 1, \ldots, N$. The observation rule linking the observed value y_{3i} to the latent variable y_{3i}^* is denoted by

---

[1] If y_{2i}^* is not continuously observed, that is, $y_{2i} \equiv g_2(y_{2i}^*)$, where $g_2(\cdot)$ is a known function independent of parameters, then recourse must be made to the joint estimation of (2)–(4) subject to (1) and (5).

$$y_{3i} \equiv g_3(y_{3i}^*),\tag{5}$$

where $g_3(\cdot)$ is a known function independent of parameters.

Finally, we assume the disturbance terms $(u_{1i}, u_{2i}, v_{3i}) \mid x_i \sim \mathrm{NI}(0, \Sigma)$, where $\Sigma = [(\sigma_{jk})]$ is positive definite, and the observations y_{ji}, $j = 1, 2, 3$ and x_i, $i = 1, \ldots, N$, constitute a random sample.

For the later discussion, model Type I consists of (1), (2) (with $\alpha_1 = 0$), (3′) [with $h(y_{1i}^*, y_{3i}^*) \equiv y_{1i}^*$ in (2) and (3)], (4) and (5) whereas model Type II consists of (1)–(5) [with $h(y_{1i}^*, y_{3i}^*) \equiv y_{1i}$ in (2) and (3)]. As will be detailed below, these two specifications are nonnested.

To illustrate particular instances of the application of the framework described above, we present the following examples for the observability rules (1) and (5). Define the *indicator function* $\mathbf{1}\,(z > 0) \equiv 1$ if $z > 0$ and 0 otherwise.

EXAMPLE 1 (*Simultaneous Tobit model*, Amemiya, 1979; Nelson and Olsen, 1978; Smith and Blundell, 1986). The observability rule (1) is

$$y_{1i} \equiv \mathbf{1}(y_{1i}^* > 0)y_{1i}^*.\tag{O1}$$

EXAMPLE 2 (*Simultaneous Probit model*, Amemiya, 1978; Rivers and Vuong, 1988). The observability rule (1) is

$$y_{1i} \equiv \mathbf{1}(y_{1i}^* > 0).\tag{O2}$$

EXAMPLE 3 (*Simultaneous Selectivity model*, Heckman, 1979; Cogan, 1981). The observability rule (1) is

$$y_{1i} \equiv \mathbf{1}(y_{3i}^* > 0)y_{1i}^*,\tag{O3}$$

where the dependent variable y_{3i}^* is only observed up to sign, that is $y_{3i} \equiv \mathbf{1}(y_{3i}^* > 0)$ for (5).

EXAMPLE 4 (*Simultaneous Double-hurdle*, Cragg, 1971; Blundell, Ham and Meghir, 1987). The observability rule (1) is

$$y_{1i} \equiv \mathbf{1}(y_{1i}^* > 0,\ y_{3i}^* > 0)y_{1i}^*,\tag{O4}$$

with a similar rule (5) to that of Example 3 for y_{3i}.

Other examples of microeconometric models subsumed by the observability rule (1) include grouped (Stewart, 1983) and grouped and censored (Chesher, 1985b) models.

3. The type I simultaneous equation model and some consistent estimation procedures

From (2) (with $\alpha_1 = 0$), (3') and (4), consider the following RF model:

$$y_{1i}^* = x_i' \pi_1 + v_{1i} , \tag{6a}$$

$$y_{2i} = x_i' \pi_2 + v_{2i} , \tag{6b}$$

$$y_{3i}^* = x_i' \pi_3 + v_{3i} , \tag{6c}$$

where $v_i | x_i \sim \text{NID}(0, \Omega)$, $v_i \equiv (v_{1i}, v_{2i}, v_{3i})'$, $i = 1, \ldots, N$, $\Omega \equiv [(\omega_{jk})]$ and π_1, π_2 and π_3 are conformable vectors of parameters.

Write v_{1i} conditional on v_{2i},

$$v_{1i} = v_{2i} \tau_1 + \varepsilon_{1i} ,$$

where $\tau_1 \equiv \omega_{12} / \omega_{22}$, $i = 1, \ldots, N$. Therefore, $\varepsilon_{1i} | x_i \sim \text{NI}(0, \omega_{11.2})$, where $\omega_{11.2} \equiv \omega_{11} - \omega_{12}^2 / \omega_{22}$, and ε_{1i} is independent of v_{2i} conditional on x_i, $i = 1, \ldots, N$. Thus, the conditional model for y_{1i}^* given y_{2i} is

$$y_{1i}^* = x_i' \pi_1 + v_{2i} \tau_1 + \varepsilon_{1i} . \tag{7}$$

Similarly, defining $\tau_3 \equiv \omega_{32} / \omega_{33}$ and $\omega_{33.2} \equiv \omega_{33} - \omega_{32}^2 / \omega_{22}$, the conditional model for y_{3i}^* given y_{2i} is

$$y_{3i}^* = x_i' \pi_3 + v_{2i} \tau_3 + \varepsilon_{3i} , \tag{8}$$

where $\varepsilon_{3i} | x_i \sim \text{NI}(0, \omega_{33.2})$ is independent of v_{2i} conditional on x_i, $i = 1, \ldots, N$.

From (2) (with $\alpha_1 = 0$), the parameter vectors π_1 and π_2 in (6a), (6b) are subject to the (over-)identifying restrictions:

$$\pi_1 = \pi_2 \beta_1 + J_1 \gamma_1 , \tag{9}$$

where $J_1 = (I_{K_1}, 0_{(K_1, K - K_1)})'$ is a (K, K_1) selection matrix, which after substitution in (6a) yields the (limited information) simultaneous equation model (2) (with $\alpha_1 = 0$),

$$y_{1i}^* = y_{2i} \beta_1 + x_{1i} \gamma_1 + u_{1i} , \tag{10}$$

where $u_{1i} = v_{1i} - v_{2i} \beta_1$, or conditional on y_{2i},

$$y_{1i}^* = y_{2i} \beta_1 + x_{1i} \gamma_1 + \rho_1 v_{2i} + \varepsilon_{1i} , \tag{11}$$

where $\rho_1 \equiv \tau_1 - \beta_1$, $i = 1, \ldots, N$.

Several consistent estimation procedures for (6b), (6c) or (8) and (10) or (11) subject to the censoring schemes (1) and (5) may be developed given the availability of a maximum likelihood (ML) estimation procedure for (6a) or (7) and (6c) or (8) subject to (1) and (5).

3.1. Consistent estimation procedures

We briefly review some simple estimation procedures that have been suggested in the literature.

3.1.1. The Nelson–Olsen procedure

For the Tobit model, Nelson and Olsen (1978) suggested replacing y_{2i}, $i = 1, \ldots, N$, in (10) by its OLS predictor from (6b) and estimating the revised (10) subject to (O1) by Tobit ML.

3.1.2. The Amemiya GLS procedure

Following Amemiya (1978, 1979), consider restrictions (9) directly after substitution of the ML estimator for π_1 from (6a) under observation rules (O1) or (O2) and the OLS estimator for π_2 from (6b). By applying either an OLS or GLS procedure to the revised (9), consistent estimators for β_1 and γ_1 may be obtained.

3.1.3. The Heckman procedure

Heckman (1978) rewrites the restrictions (9) as

$$\pi_2 = (\pi_1 - J_1 \gamma_1)/\beta_1 \, ,$$

which after substitution into (6b) gives

$$y_{2i} = x_1' \pi_i / \beta_1 - x_{1i}' \gamma_1 / \beta_1 + v_{2i} \, , \tag{12}$$

$i = 1, \ldots, N$. Replacing π_1 in (12) by the marginal ML estimator for π_1 from (6a) subject to (O1), OLS estimation of the revised (12) yields consistent estimators for $1/\beta_1$ and $-\gamma_1/\beta_1$ and thus (β_1, γ_1). [2]

3.1.4. The Smith–Blundell procedure

This method estimates the conditional model (11) by ML subject to observation rules of the type $y_{1i} = g(y_{1i}^*)$, for example (O1) (Smith and Blundell, 1986) and (O2) (Rivers and Vuong, 1988), by substitution of the OLS residuals for v_{2i} obtained from (6b), $i = 1, \ldots, N$; see Blundell and Smith (1989). An advantage of this procedure is that the t-statistic associated with ρ_1 in (11) provides an asymptotically optimal test of the simultaneity of y_{2i}, $i = 1, \ldots, N$. [3]

---

[2] The Nelson–Olsen, Amemiya OLS and the Heckman procedures are robust to nonnormality in v_{2i} requiring only that $(v_{1i}, v_{3i}) \mid x_i$ is independently normally distributed, $i = 1, \ldots, N$.

[3] The Smith–Blundell estimator requires that $(v_{1i}, v_{3i}) \mid v_{2i}, x_i \sim \text{NI}(v_{2i}\tau, \Omega_{.2})$, where $\tau \equiv (\tau_1, \tau_3)'$ and $\Omega_{.2} \equiv [(\omega_{jk.2})]$; in this sense, this estimator is robust to nonnormality in v_i, $i = 1, \ldots, N$.

3.2. Efficiency comparisons of alternative estimators

To examine the relative efficiency of the estimators described in Section 3.1, we exploit the relationship between restricted ML estimation and the minimum chi-squared (MC) estimation procedure (Ferguson, 1958).

3.2.1. The minimum chi-squared procedure (Ferguson, 1958; Malinvaud, 1970; Rothenberg, 1973)

Let the likelihood function be known up to the parameter vector $\delta \equiv (\theta', \psi')'$ which is to be estimated subject to the freedom equation restrictions $\theta = \theta(\phi)$ where $\dim(\theta) > \dim(\phi)$ and the function $\theta(\cdot)$ is first-order continuously differentiable with the derivative matrix $\Theta = \partial\theta/\partial\phi'$ of full column rank at least in a neighbourhood of the true parameter value. The restricted ML estimator is asymptotically equivalent to the MC estimator obtained from

$$\min_{\phi,\psi}[\hat{\delta} - \delta(\phi, \psi)]'\mathcal{I}[\hat{\delta} - \delta(\phi, \psi)], \tag{13}$$

where $\delta(\phi, \psi) \equiv [\theta(\phi)', \psi']'$ (Ferguson, 1958, p. 1048; Rothenberg, 1973, p. 34), $\hat{\delta}$ denotes the unrestricted ML estimator for δ and $\mathcal{I}$ the asymptotic information matrix, that is, $\text{avar}[N^{1/2}(\hat{\delta} - \delta)] = \mathcal{I}^{-1}$. [4] Thus, importantly for the results below, the restricted ML method implicitly places the metric $\mathcal{I}$ in the equivalent MC procedure.

Concentrating out the nuisance parameters ψ from (13) gives the equivalent MC criterion in θ,

$$[\hat{\theta} - \theta(\phi)]'[\mathcal{I}^{\theta\theta}]^{-1}[\hat{\theta} - \theta(\phi)], \tag{14}$$

where $\text{avar}[N^{1/2}(\hat{\theta} - \theta)] = \mathcal{I}^{\theta\theta}$ is that block of $\mathcal{I}^{-1}$ corresponding to θ. The resultant MC estimator for ϕ, $\check{\phi}$, has asymptotic variance matrix $\text{avar}[N^{1/2}(\check{\phi} - \phi)] = \{\Theta'[\mathcal{I}^{\theta\theta}]^{-1}\Theta\}^{-1}$ which is also that of the restricted ML estimator for ϕ. Moreover, N times the minimised value of (14) provides a test statistic for the restrictions $\theta = \theta(\phi)$ which has a limiting chi-squared distribution with $\dim(\theta) - \dim(\phi)$ degrees of freedom when the restrictions hold.

Restrictions (9) may be expressed in the above freedom equation form by defining $\theta \equiv (\pi_1', \pi_2')'$ and $\phi \equiv (\beta_1, \gamma_1', \pi_2')'$. Partitioning θ and ϕ as $\theta_1 \equiv \pi_1$, $\theta_2 \equiv \pi_2$ and $\phi_1 \equiv (\beta_1, \gamma_1')'$ and $\phi_2 \equiv \pi_2$ respectively, (9) may be re-expressed as $\theta_1 = \theta_1(\phi)$ and $\theta_2 = \phi_2$. Note that π_2 appears both in θ and ϕ. However, all the estimation methods discussed in Section 3.1 neglect this fact and substitute a CAN estimator for π_2 (θ_2 and ϕ_2) into the criterion (14). Although this estimator for π_2 may be efficient relative to the ML estimator in the unrestricted model, it is no longer efficient in the restricted model. Therefore, in general, the resultant estimator for ϕ_1 obtained from (14) will also be inefficient relative to the restricted ML estimator for ϕ_1. If, however, the

---

[4] Estimation of $\mathcal{I}$ and the metrics used later is ignored as only a consistent estimator of $\mathcal{I}$ is required.

substituted estimator for π_2 in (14) is efficient relative to the restricted ML estimator for π_2, then, of course, the resultant estimator for ϕ_1 will also be efficient.

A further contribution to the inefficiency of the derived estimator for ϕ_1 from (14) is the use of an inappropriate positive-definite metric S, either implicitly or explicitly imposed by the estimation procedure of Section 3.1. The corresponding inefficient MC criterion function is given by

$$[\hat{\theta}_1 - \theta_1(\phi_1, \phi_2)]'S[\hat{\theta}_1 - \theta_1(\phi_1, \phi_2)] , \tag{15}$$

where a CAN estimator for ϕ_2 (π_2) is substituted. The ML procedures of Nelson–Olsen and Smith–Blundell (and similarly Heckman) both implicitly assume that ϕ_2 (π_2) does not enter the restrictions $\theta_1 = \theta_1(\phi)$ and impose a metric S appropriate to the ML procedure adopted which is inefficient relative to the criterion (15). These two factors destroy the optimality of these procedures whereas it is the inefficiency of the ϕ_2 (π_2) estimator which prevents Amemiya's (1978, 1979) GLS estimators achieving optimality relative to the restricted ML estimator for ϕ_1. Moreover, the methods of Amemiya, Nelson–Olsen and Heckman also use an inefficient estimator for θ_1 (π_1).

Defining $V \equiv \text{avar}[N^{1/2}(\hat{\theta}_1 - \theta_1(\phi))]$, after substitution of the CAN estimator for ϕ_2, the resultant estimator for ϕ_1 has asymptotic variance,

$$[\Theta_1'S\Theta_1]^{-1}\Theta_1'SVS\Theta_1[\Theta_1'S\Theta_1]^{-1} , \tag{16}$$

where $\Theta_1 \equiv \partial\theta_1/\partial\phi'$. This expression is minimized by choosing $S = V^{-1}$ rendering (16) as $[\Theta_1'S\Theta_1]^{-1}$ (Ferguson, 1958, Theorem 2, p. 1056; Malinvaud, 1970, p. 336).

We partition the likelihood for (1), (5) and (6) into the *conditional* likelihood for (y_{1i}, y_{3i}) given y_{2i} and the *marginal* likelihood for y_{2i}, $i = 1, \ldots, N$. This corresponds to a partition of the parameters into $(\pi_1, \pi_3, \tau_1, \tau_3, \omega_{11.2}, \omega_{33.2}, \omega_{13.2})$, where $\omega_{13.2} \equiv \omega_{13} - \omega_{12}\omega_{32}/\omega_{22}$, and (π_2, ω_{22}). Throughout the remainder of this section, we shall denote the asymptotic information matrix corresponding to the conditional likelihood as $\mathcal{B}$ given by (A4) of Appendix A. Similarly $\mathcal{I}_{13}$ and $\mathcal{I}_2$ respectively represent the asymptotic information matrices of the marginal likelihoods for (y_{1i}, y_{3i}) with parameters $(\pi, \pi_3, \omega_{11}, \omega_{33}, \omega_{13})$ and y_{2i}, $i = 1, \ldots, N$, from (6a), (6c) subject to (1), (5) and (6b) respectively and are presented in (A2) and (A5) of Appendix A.

3.2.2. The Nelson–Olsen procedure

The generalisation of the Nelson–Olsen procedure described in Section 3.1.1 for observability rules (1), (5) is equivalent to estimating (6a), (6c) subject to (1), (5) by ML after substitution of the restrictions (9) replacing π_2 with the OLS estimator obtained from (6b); (this is identical to replacing y_{2i}, $i = 1, \ldots, N$, in (10) by its OLS predictor from (6b) and estimating the revised (6c), (10) subject to (1), (5) by ML).

In terms of (15), this estimator implicitly minimises

$$[\dot{\pi}_1 - \dot{\pi}_2\beta_1 - J_1\gamma_1]'S[\dot{\pi}_1 - \dot{\pi}_2\beta_1 - J_1\gamma_1], \tag{17}$$

where $\dot{\pi}_1$ and $\dot{\pi}_2$ are the respective marginal ML estimators for π_1 from (6a), (6c) subject to (1), (5) and π_2 from (6b). The implicit metric S in (17) is that derived from the marginal likelihood for (6a), (6c) subject to (1), (5); thus, $S = [\mathscr{I}_{13}^{11}]^{-1}$, where the superscript indicates the appropriate block of the inverse of $\mathscr{I}_{13}$ corresponding to π_1. However, because $\mathrm{avar}[N^{1/2}(\dot{\pi}_1 - \dot{\pi}_2\beta_1 - J_1\gamma_1)] \neq \mathscr{I}_{13}^{11}$, the resultant Nelson–Olsen estimator is not optimal. Setting $V^0 \equiv \mathrm{avar}[N^{1/2}(\dot{\pi}_1 - \dot{\pi}_2\beta_1 - J_1\gamma_1)]$, the Nelson–Olsen estimator for (β_1, γ_1) has asymptotic variance matrix given by (16) with $S^{-1} = \mathscr{I}_{13}^{11}$, $V = V^0$ and $\Theta_1 = (\pi_2, J_1)$. In computing this matrix product, V^0 may be easily calculated as $(I_K, -\beta_1 I_K)[\mathrm{avar}[N^{1/2}(\dot{\pi}_1 - \pi_1, \dot{\pi}_2 - \pi_2)]](I_K, -\beta_1 I_K)'$ and may be deduced from (A6) of Appendix A.

3.2.3. *The Amemiya GLS procedure*
Substitute the marginal ML estimator for π_1 from (6a), (6c) subject to (1), (5) and the OLS estimator for π_2 from (6b) into the restrictions (9) (cf. Amemiya, 1978, 1979). For an arbitrary choice of S, the asymptotic variance matrix for the resultant estimator of (β_1, γ_1) is given by (16) with $V = V^0$ and $\Theta_1 = (\pi_2, J_1)$. Setting $S = I_K$ yields the analogy of Amemiya's marginal LS (MLS) estimator, whereas choosing $S^{-1} = V^0$ gives that of Amemiya's marginal GLS (MGLS) estimator. The advantage of the MGLS procedure is that the asymptotic variance matrix of the (β_1, γ_1) estimator derived from criterion (15) is minimised.

3.2.4. *The Heckman procedure*
The marginal ML estimator for π_1 from (6a), (6c) subject to (1), (5) is substituted into (12); the revised (12) is then estimated by OLS. This estimator implicitly minimises;

$$[\dot{\pi}_2 - \dot{\pi}_1/\beta_1 + J_1\gamma_1/\beta_1]'S[\dot{\pi}_2 - \dot{\pi}_1/\beta_1 + J_1\gamma_1/\beta_1]$$

with respect to (β_1, γ_1) with $S^{-1} = \mathscr{I}_2^{22}$ which is derived from the marginal likelihood for (6b) where the superscripts refer to that block of $\mathscr{I}_2^{-1}$ corresponding to π_2. Because these restrictions are a nonsingular transformation of (9), the resultant estimator has asymptotic variance matrix (16) with $V = V^0$ and $\Theta_1 = (\pi_2, J_1)$; see also Amemiya (1979, equation (4.28), p. 179), but, contrary to Amemiya's assertion, the efficient MGLS estimator is identical to that discussed in Section 3.2.3 with $S^{-1} = V^0$.

3.2.5. *The Smith–Blundell procedure*
All of the methods discussed above are marginal ML procedures being based on the marginal likelihoods for (y_{1i}, y_{3i}) and y_{2i}, $i = 1, \ldots, N$. The procedure due to Smith and Blundell (1986) and Blundell and Smith (1989) uses the

conditional RF (7), (8) rather than the marginal RF (6a), (6c). This method estimates (7), (8) subject to (1), (5) after substitution of the restrictions (9), the OLS estimator obtained from (6b) replacing π_2 in (9) and in $v_{2i} = y_{2i} - x_i'\pi_2$, $i = 1, \ldots, N$, which is identical to estimating (8), (11) subject to (1), (5) by ML after replacing v_{2i} by the corresponding least squares residual from (6b), $i = 1, \ldots, N$. Hence, This approach is a conditional ML procedure.

The Smith–Blundell estimator implicitly minimises from (15),

$$[\hat{\pi}_1 - \hat{\pi}_2\beta_1 - J_1\gamma_1]'S[\hat{\pi}_1 - \hat{\pi}_2\beta_1 - J_1\gamma_1], \tag{18}$$

where $(\hat{\pi}_1, \hat{\pi}_2)$, $(\hat{\pi}_2 \equiv \tilde{\pi}_2)$, are the joint unrestricted ML estimators for (π_1, π_2) obtained from (7), (8) subject to (1), (5) and (6b) (Chesher, 1985a) and the metric $S^{-1} = \mathcal{B}^{22}$, where the superscripts indicate that block of $\mathcal{B}^{-1}$ corresponding to π_1. Denoting the asymptotic variance matrix of $[\hat{\pi}_1 - \hat{\pi}_2\beta_1 - J_1\gamma_1]$ by V^*, the asymptotic variance of the Smith–Blundell estimator is given by $[\Theta_1'S\Theta_1]^{-1}\Theta_1'SV^*S\Theta_1[\Theta_1'S\Theta_1]^{-1}$; $V^* = (I_K, -\beta_1 I_K)[\text{avar}[N^{1/2}[(\hat{\pi}_1 - \pi), (\hat{\pi}_2 - \pi_2)]](I_K, -\beta_1 I_K)'$ and may be deduced from (A7) of Appendix A.

An alternative conditional approach is based on the Heckman (1978) approach given in Section 3.2.3 employing $\hat{\pi}_1$ in place of $\tilde{\pi}_1$. The corresponding MC criterion is thus given by

$$[\hat{\pi}_2 - \hat{\pi}_1/\beta_1 + J_1\gamma_1/\beta_1]'S[\hat{\pi}_2 - \hat{\pi}_1/\beta_1 + J_1\gamma_1/\beta_1], \tag{19}$$

where, as in Section 3.2.4, $S^{-1} = \mathcal{I}_2^{22}$. The resultant estimator for (β_1, γ_1) has asymptotic variance matrix $[\Theta_1'S\Theta_1]^{-1}\Theta_1'SV^*S\Theta_1[\Theta_1'S\Theta_1]^{-1}$.

3.2.6. The conditional GLS procedure

The optimal conditional GLS (CGLS) estimator for (β_1, γ_1) in the sense of having minimal asymptotic variance matrix with respect to criterion (18), is obtained by setting $S^{-1} = V^*$ and has asymptotic variance matrix $[\Theta_1'V^{*-1}\Theta_1]^{-1}$; cf. Amemiya's (1978, 1979) MGLS procedure in Section 3.2.3. An identical CGLS estimator is given by applying the Heckman (1978) criterion (19) with $S^{-1} = V^*$. See also Newey (1987).

3.2.7. Some relative efficiency comparisons

Because $(\hat{\pi}_1, \hat{\pi}_2)$ is the joint unrestricted ML estimator for (π_1, π_2) we have $V^0 - V^* \geqslant 0$ and thus the CGLS of Section 3.2.6 is relatively more efficient than the MGLS of Section 3.2.3 as $[\Theta_1'V^{0-1}\Theta_1]^{-1} - [\Theta_1'V^{*-1}\Theta_1]^{-1} \geqslant 0$. Moreover, therefore, CGLS is relatively more efficient than Nelson–Olsen, Smith–Blundell and both marginal and conditional Heckman estimators of Sections 3.2.4 and 3.2.5. Using a similar argument, the conditional Heckman estimator is relatively more efficient than the marginal Heckman estimator as the implicit metric in both procedures is the same.

Although $V^0 - V^* \geqslant 0$, as $\mathcal{I}_{13}^{11} - \mathcal{B}^{11} \geqslant 0$ and thus $(\mathcal{B}^{11})^{-1} - (\mathcal{I}_{13}^{11})^{-1} \geqslant 0$, in general we are unable to rank the marginal Nelson–Olsen and conditional Smith–Blundell estimators. Similar comments apply to other pairwise comparisons of marginal and conditional estimators which use different metrics. However, for methods which use the same metric, by an equivalent argument to that above for the Heckman procedure, the conditional estimator will dominate the corresponding marginal estimator. For example, when $S = I_K$, the conditional LS estimator is relatively more efficient than Amemiya's marginal LS estimator of Section 3.2.3.

If the restrictions (9) are just-identifying, that is θ and ϕ are one-to-one, and therefore Θ_1 is nonsingular, the Nelson–Olsen and MGLS estimators are asymptotically equivalent. Moreover, the Smith–Blundell and CGLS estimators are both asymptotically equivalent to the restricted ML estimator and therefore Smith–Blundell dominates Nelson–Olsen and MGLS unequivocally.

If, however, $\tau = 0$ then $(\hat{\pi}_1, \hat{\pi}_2)$ are joint unrestricted ML estimators for (π_1, π_2) and thus, as the conditional procedures do not incorporate this restriction, the CGLS and MGLS ranking is reversed with a similar result for the conditional and marginal Heckman and LS estimators. In particular, if the restrictions (9) are just identifying, the Nelson–Olsen estimator will be asymptotically equivalent to the restricted ML estimator.

3.2.8. The limited information MC procedure
From Section 3.2.1, the efficient MC procedure minimises

$$[(\hat{\pi}_1 - \pi_2\beta_1 - J_1\gamma_1)', (\hat{\pi}_2 - \pi_2)']S[(\hat{\pi}_1 - \pi_2\beta_1 - J_1\gamma_1)', (\hat{\pi}_2 - \pi_2)']'$$

with respect to $(\beta_1, \gamma_1, \pi_2)$ where $S^{-1} = \text{avar}[N^{1/2}[(\hat{\pi}_1 - \pi_1), (\hat{\pi}_2 - \pi_2)]]$. This produces estimation equations of the form

$$\phi_1 = [\Theta_1'S_{11}\Theta_1]^{-1}\Theta_1'[S_{11}\hat{\pi}_1 + S_{12}(\hat{\pi}_2 - \pi_2)],$$
$$\pi_2 = \hat{\pi}_2 + [S_{22} + \beta_1S_{12}]^{-1}[S_{21} + \beta_1S_{11}](\hat{\pi}_1 - \pi_1),$$
$$\pi_1 = \Theta_1\phi_1,$$

where S is partitioned conformably with π_1 and π_2 and $\phi_1 = (\beta_1, \gamma_1')'$. These equations may then be iterated in a step-wise fashion until convergence. The use of initial consistent estimators for ϕ_1 and π_2 such as the Smith–Blundell estimator and the OLS estimator $\hat{\pi}_2$ should assist convergence and also avoid the need to recalculate the inverse of $S_{22} + \beta_1S_{12}$ at each iteration.

3.3. Efficient estimation

By exploiting the partitioning of the joint likelihood into the conditional and marginal likelihoods of (y_{1i}, y_{3i}) and y_{2i} respectively, a striking feature is that the score vector evaluated at the Smith–Blundell estimator for $(\beta_1, \gamma_1, \rho_1, \omega_{11.2})$, $\hat{\pi}_2$ and $(\hat{\pi}_3, \hat{\rho}_3, \hat{\omega}_{33.2})$ has null elements except for $\partial \ln \mathcal{L}/\partial \pi_2$. Denoting evaluation at these estimators by $\hat{}$, a simple *linearised* ML

(LML) estimator based on the method of scoring is from (B3) of Appendix B,

$$\tilde{\pi}_2 = \hat{\pi}_2 - \left(\sum_{i=1}^{N} x_i [1/\hat{\omega}_{22} + \hat{\tau}' \hat{\Omega}_{.2}^{-1} \operatorname{v\hat{a}r}[\varepsilon_{13i}^{(1)}] \hat{\Omega}_{.2}^{-1} \hat{\tau}] x_i' \right.$$
$$- \sum_{i=1}^{N} x_i [\hat{\tau}' \hat{\Omega}_{.2}^{-1} \operatorname{c\hat{o}v}[\varepsilon_{13i}^{(1)}, \zeta_{.2i}]] \hat{w}_i' \left[\sum_{i=1}^{N} \hat{w}_i \operatorname{v\hat{a}r}[\zeta_{.2i}] \hat{w}_i' \right]^{-1}$$
$$\left. \times \sum_{i=1}^{N} \hat{w}_i [\operatorname{c\hat{o}v}[\zeta_{.2i}, \varepsilon_{13i}^{(1)}] \hat{\Omega}_{.2}^{-1} \hat{\tau}] x_i' \right)^{-1} \sum_{i=1}^{N} x_i [\hat{\tau}' \hat{\Omega}_{.2}^{-1} \hat{\varepsilon}_{13i}^{(1)}] .$$

The suggested LML estimator for $[\beta_1, \gamma_1, \tau_1, \pi_3^*, v(\Omega_2)]$ is: (i) calculate $\hat{\pi}_2$ from above, and (ii) substitute $\tilde{\pi}_2$ into (8), (11) via $\hat{v}_{2i} = y_{2i} - x_i'\tilde{\pi}_2$, $i = 1, \ldots, N$, and estimate the revised (8), (11) subject to (1), (5) by ML.

The above algorithm may be iterated in a step-wise fashion to compute the exact ML estimator. However, for step (i) above, the last term should be revised to

$$\sum_{i=1}^{N} x_i [\hat{\tau}' \hat{\Omega}_{.2}^{-1} \hat{\varepsilon}_{13i}^{(1)} - \hat{v}_{2i}/\hat{\omega}_{22}] ,$$

where $\hat{}$ now indicates evaluation at the previous iterate from steps (i) and (ii); step (ii) remains unaltered. It is also necessary to check that at each stage steps (i) and (ii) increase the value of the joint log-likelihood $\ln \mathcal{L}$ to ensure global convergence of the algorithm.

4. Type II simultaneous equation models and some consistent estimation procedures

This general class of model nests the specifications considered in Heckman (1978) and Gourieroux, Laffont and Monfort (1980). Unlike the Type I models, no explicit reduced form (3') exists for the Type II specification. This class of models puts $h(y_{1i}^*, y_{3i}^*) = y_{1i}$, $i = 1, \ldots, N$, in (2), (3).

For a well specified econometric model a unique (implicit) reduced form must exist. Indeed, this is a necessary requirement of any model based on economic optimisation (see Ransom, 1987 and Van Soest et al., 1990). As a result knowledge of the parameter space under which coherency and therefore the logical consistency of the economic model is satisfied, becomes crucial. As Madalla (1983) points out, if the parameter space can be restricted to areas in which economic models 'make sense' then the coherency condition is often automatically satisfied.

4.1. The coherency problem and identification

To aid our discussion, substitute (1) and (3) into (2),

$$y_{1i}^* = (\alpha_1 + \alpha_2 \beta_1) g_1(y_{1i}^*, y_{3i}^*) + x_{2i}' \gamma_2 \beta_1 + x_{1i}' \gamma_1 + v_{1i'} \tag{19}$$

where $v_{1i} \equiv u_{1i} + \beta_1 u_{2i}$, $i = 1, \ldots, N$. As above the binary indicator function is denoted by $\mathbf{1}(\cdot)$.

EXAMPLE 1 (*Tobit model*). The observability rule is as in (O1). Consider (19) when $y_{1i}^* > 0$,

$$(1 - \alpha_1 - \alpha_2 \beta_1) y_{1i}^* = x_{1i}' \gamma_1 + x_{2i}' \gamma_2 \beta_1 + v_{1i} , \tag{20}$$

from which we see that the coherency condition $(1 - \alpha_1 - \alpha_2 \beta_1) > 0$ is sufficient to guarantee a unique reduced form; see Maddala (1983) and Gourieroux, Laffont and Monfort (1980). Rewriting (20) using (3) as

$$y_{1i}^* = \beta_1^* \bar{y}_{2i} + x_{1i}' \gamma_1^* + u_{1i}^* , \tag{21}$$

when $y_{1i}^* > 0$, where $\bar{y}_{2i} \equiv y_{2i} - \alpha_2 y_{1i}^*$ and $\beta_1^* \equiv \beta_1 / (1 - \alpha_1 - \alpha_2 \beta_1)$, $\gamma_1^* \equiv \gamma_1 / (1 - \alpha_1 - \alpha_2 \beta_1)$, $u_{1i}^* \equiv u_{1i} / (1 - \alpha_1 - \alpha_2 \beta_1)$. Given α_2, although β_1^* and γ_1^* are identified, it is easily seen that neither α_1 nor β_1 are. A suitable normalisation is thus required; for example, $\alpha_1 = 0$ or $\alpha_1 + \alpha_2 \beta_1 = 0$.

EXAMPLE 2 (*Probit model*). The observability rule (1) is as in (O2). Again examining (19), it can be seen that the coherency condition $\alpha_1 + \alpha_2 \beta_1 = 0$ is required for the existence of a unique reduced form: see Heckman (1978). Moreover, following the discussion of Example 1, this condition is sufficient to identify α_1 and β_1, given α_2.

EXAMPLE 3 (*Selectivity model*, Heckman, 1979; Cogan, 1981). The observability rules (1), (5) are as in (O3). When $y_{3i}^* > 0$, (2) reduces to (20) as in the Tobit model. Thus, both coherency and identification conditions for Example 1 hold here also.

EXAMPLE 4 (*Double-Hurdle*, Cragg, 1971; Blundell, Ham and Meghir, 1987). The observability rules (1), (5) are as in (O4). Again, coherency and identification conditions are as in Example 1, because (20) holds when $y_{1i}^* > 0$, $y_{3i}^* > 0$.

4.2. Consistent estimation and inference in type II models

Following the conditional maximum likelihood approach of Smith and Blundell (1986), we rewrite (2) conditionally on u_{2i} as

$$y_{1i}^* = \alpha_1 y_{1i} + \beta_1 y_{2i} + x_{1i}' \gamma_1 + \rho_1 u_{2i} + \varepsilon_{1i} , \tag{22}$$

where $\rho_1 \equiv \sigma_{21} / \sigma_{22}$ and, due to the joint normality of u_{1i} and u_{2i}, $\varepsilon_{1i} \equiv u_{1i} - \rho_1 u_{2i}$ is independent of u_{2i}, $i = 1, \ldots, N$. However, in contrast to the standard simultaneous model, it is the constructed variable $\bar{y}_{2i} \equiv y_{2i} - \alpha_2 y_{1i}$ *not* y_{2i} which is independent of ε_{1i} in this problem. Thus, we rewrite (20) as

$$y_{1i}^* = (\alpha_1 + \alpha_2 \beta_1) y_{1i} + \beta_1 \bar{y}_{2i} + x_{1i}' \gamma_1 + \rho_1 u_{2i} + \varepsilon_{1i} , \tag{23}$$

which forms the basis of the suggested estimation procedure for the structural parameters of (2).

To implement (23), it is necessary to obtain suitable estimators of $\bar{y}_{2i}$ and u_{2i} (or α_2 and γ_2). Consider instrumental variable (IV) estimation of (3). Given sufficient exclusion restrictions on x_i to form x_{2i} $(K > K_2)$, α_2 and γ_2 will be identified by the standard conditions. Although $y_{1i} \equiv g_1(y_{1i}^*, y_{3i}^*)$ is a nonlinear function of the latent variables, it is easily shown that α_2 and γ_2 are consistently estimated by IV using x_i as instruments. Denote these estimators by $\hat{\alpha}_2$ and $\hat{\gamma}_2$ respectively and the corresponding estimated constructed variable and IV residual by $\hat{\bar{y}}_{2i}$ and $\hat{u}_{2i}$ respectively. Thus, the relevant estimating equation becomes from (23)

$$y_{1i}^* = (\alpha_1 + \alpha_2\beta_1)y_{1i} + \beta_1\hat{\bar{y}}_{2i} + x_{1i}'\gamma_1 + \rho_1\hat{u}_{2i} + \hat{\varepsilon}_{1i} , \tag{24}$$

where

$$\hat{\varepsilon}_{1i} \equiv \varepsilon_{1i} + \beta_1(\bar{y}_{2i} + \hat{\bar{y}}_{2i}) + \rho_1(u_{2i} + \hat{u}_{2i}) ,$$

$i = 1, \ldots, N$. The appropriate standard ML methods of estimation may now be applied to (24) to provide consistent estimators of the structural parameters, if necessary in conjunction with

$$y_{3i}^* = x_1'\pi_3 + \rho_3 u_{2i} + \varepsilon_{3i} , \tag{25}$$

subject to (1), (5), where $\rho_3 \equiv \sigma_{32}/\sigma_{22}$ and $\varepsilon_i \equiv (\varepsilon_{1i}, \varepsilon_{3i}) \mid x_i \sim \mathrm{NI}(0, \Sigma_{.2})$, $\Sigma_{.2} = [(\sigma_{jk.2})]$, $\sigma_{jk.2} \equiv \sigma_{jk} - \sigma_{j2}\sigma_{2k}/\sigma_{22}$, $j, k = 1, 3$, and ε_i is independent of u_{2i} conditional on x_i, $i = 1, \ldots, N$; see Blundell and Smith (1990).

Note that the Type I models discussed in Section 3 are *not* generally equivalent to setting $\alpha_2 = 0$ in equation (3). Although both classes of models are formulated conditionally on the same set of exogenous variables x_i, in Type II models it is necessary to provide some exclusion restrictions on x_i to identify the parameters α_2 and γ_2. That is, Type I and II simultaneous models are *nonnested*. The following simple method discriminating between them is available.

Under the null hypothesis that the Type I simultaneous model is correct, one can test the Type I specification by estimating

$$y_{2i} = x_i'\pi_2 + \hat{y}_{1i}\delta_1 + \xi_{1i} , \tag{26}$$

by least squares and testing $\delta_1 = 0$, where $\hat{y}_{1i}$ is the estimated prediction for y_{1i} from the Type II specification (19). [5] Alternatively, under the Type II null, the

---

[5] For example, the Tobit specification (7) gives $y_{1i}^* = x_{1i}'\gamma_1^* + x_{2i}'\gamma_2\beta_1^* + v_{1i}^*$, where $v_{1i}^* \equiv u_{1i}^* + \beta_1^* u_{2i}$, for $y_{1i}^* > 0$. Thus, $E[y_{1i} \mid x_i] = \Phi[(x_{1i}'\gamma_1^* + x_{2i}'\gamma_2\beta_1^*)/\omega^*](x_{1i}'\gamma_1^* + x_{2i}'\gamma_2\beta_1^*) + \omega^*\phi[(x_{1i}'\gamma_1^* + x_{2i}'\gamma_2\beta_1^*)/\omega^*]$, where $\omega^{*2} \equiv \mathrm{var}(v_{1i}^*)$, $\phi(\cdot)$ and $\Phi(\cdot)$ denote the standard normal density and distribution functions respectively.

Type II specification may be tested by estimating

$$y_{2i} = y_{1i}\alpha_2 + x'_{2i}\gamma_2 + \hat{y}_{2i}\delta_2 + \xi_{2i} , \tag{27}$$

by instrumental variables using x_i as instruments and testing $\delta_2 = 0$, where $\hat{y}_{2i}$ is the estimated prediction of y_{2i} under the Type I explicit linear reduced form for y_{2i} in (3'). See Davidson and MacKinnon (1981) and Godfrey (1983).

We now turn to implement the above estimation procedure for the various examples discussed in Section 4.1.

EXAMPLE 1 (*continued*). Consider (24) for $y_{1i}^* > 0$. After re-arrangement, we obtain

$$(1 - \alpha_1 - \alpha_2\beta_1)y_{1i} = \beta_1\hat{\tilde{y}}_{2i} + x'_{1i}\gamma_1 + \rho_1\hat{u}_{2i} + \hat{\varepsilon}_{1i} ,$$

or

$$y_{1i} = \beta_1^* \hat{\tilde{y}}_{2i} + x'_{1i}\gamma_1 + \rho_1^*\hat{u}_{2i} + \hat{\varepsilon}_{1i}^* , \tag{28}$$

where β_1^*, γ_1^* are defined below (21), $\rho_1^* \equiv \rho_1/(1 - \alpha_1 - \alpha_2\beta_1)$ and $\hat{\varepsilon}_{1i}^* \equiv \hat{\varepsilon}_{1i}/(1 - \alpha_1 - \alpha_2\beta_1)$. Standard Tobit ML on (28) provides consistent estimators $\hat{\beta}_1^*$, $\hat{\gamma}_1^*$ and $\hat{\rho}_1^*$.

EXAMPLE 2 (*continued*). Imposing the coherency condition $\alpha_1 + \alpha_2\beta_1 = 0$ on (28) gives

$$y_{1i}^* = \beta_1\hat{\tilde{y}}_{2i} + x'_{1i}\gamma_1 + \rho_1\hat{u}_{2i} + \hat{\varepsilon}_{1i} , \tag{29}$$

which may be estimated by standard Probit ML to yield the consistent estimators $\hat{\beta}_1$, $\hat{\gamma}_1$ and $\hat{\rho}_1$ of the structural parameters.

EXAMPLE 3 (*continued*). When $y_{3i}^* > 0$, (28) is reproduced. It is necessary in this case also to consider the conditional reduced form equation (25). Proceeding as for the Tobit case of Example 1 above by replacing u_{2i} by the IV residual $\hat{u}_{2i}$ gives

$$y_{3i}^* = x'_i\pi_3 + \rho_3\hat{u}_{2i} + \hat{\varepsilon}_{3i} , \tag{30}$$

where $\hat{\varepsilon}_{3i} \equiv \varepsilon_{3i} + \rho_2(u_{2i} - \hat{u}_{2i})$, $i = 1, \ldots, N$. Hence, a ML estimation procedure for selectivity models applied to (28) and (30) is appropriate to obtain consistent estimators $\hat{\beta}_1^*$, $\hat{\gamma}_1^*$ and $\hat{\rho}_1^*$ for β_1^*, γ_1^* and ρ_1^*. Alternatively, the Heckman (1979) procedure applied to (28) would also yield consistent estimators for β_1^*, γ_1^* and ρ_1^*.

EXAMPLE 4 (*continued*). The approach discussed in Example 3 above applies except that a ML estimation procedure appropriate for the double-hurdle model is used.

Define $\hat{\theta}^* \equiv (\hat{\beta}_1^*, \hat{\gamma}_1^*, \hat{\rho}_1^*, \hat{\pi}_3, \hat{\rho}_3, \hat{\Sigma}_{.2}^*)$ as the ML estimator for the parameters of (28) and (30), where $\Sigma_{.2}^*$ ($\equiv \mathrm{var}(\varepsilon_{1i}^*, \varepsilon_{3i})) = S_* \Sigma_{.2} S_*$, $S_* \equiv \mathrm{diag}[1/(1 - \alpha_1 - \alpha_2\beta_1), 1]$. Letting $\ln \mathcal{L}_2$ denote the log-likelihood of the conditional model for (y_{1i}, y_{3i}) given u_{2i}, $i = 1, \ldots, N$, $\phi = (\alpha_2, \gamma_2')'$ and defining $\mathcal{I} \equiv -N^{-1}\mathrm{E}[\partial^2 \ln \mathcal{L}_2/\partial\theta^* \partial\theta^{*'}]$, $\mathcal{K} \equiv \mathcal{I}^{-1}\{-N^{-1}\mathrm{E}[\partial^2 \ln \mathcal{L}_2/\partial\theta^* \partial\phi']\}$, which are presented in Appendix C ($\mathrm{E}[\cdot]$ denotes expectation taken conditional on x_i and u_{2i}, $i = 1, \ldots, N$), we have

$$N^{1/2}(\hat{\theta}^* - \theta^*) \overset{L}{\to} \mathrm{N}[0, V(\hat{\theta}^*)],$$

where

$$V(\hat{\theta}^*) \equiv \mathcal{I}^{-1} + \mathcal{K}V(\hat{\phi})\mathcal{K}',$$

with $\hat{\phi} = (\hat{\alpha}_2, \hat{\gamma}_2')'$, the IV estimator for ϕ; thus

$$V(\hat{\phi}) \; (\equiv \mathrm{avar}[N^{1/2}(\hat{\phi} - \phi)]) = \sigma_{22}(M_{Z_*X}M_{XX}^{-1}M_{XZ_*})^{-1},$$

where $M_{Z_*X} \equiv \lim_{T\to\infty} N^{-1} \sum_{i=1}^{N} z_{*i}x_i'$ etc. and $z_{*i} \equiv (y_{1i}, x_{2i}')'$, $i = 1, \ldots, N$. See Blundell and Smith (1990). Note that the above limiting distribution result is all that is required to undertake inference for exclusion restrictions on $\theta_1 \equiv (\beta_1, \gamma_1', \rho_1)'$ in Examples 1–4, given the just identifying assumption $\alpha_1 = 0$ or, trivially, $\alpha_1 + \alpha_2\beta_1 = 0$.

In Examples 1, 3 and 4, having obtained $\hat{\theta}^*$, it is still necessary to derive a suitable estimator for θ_1. Given conditions that just identify θ_1 from $\theta_1^* \equiv (\beta_1^*, \gamma_1^{*'}, \rho_1^*)'$ such as discussed in those Examples, this matter is relatively straightforward. Consider the following set of constraints linking θ^*, θ and ϕ:

$$q(\theta^*, \theta, \phi) = 0,$$

where the number of restrictions equals the number of elements comprising *both* θ^* and θ; furthermore, as above, assume that θ is just identified from θ^* for given ϕ through these constraints. Hence, the required estimator $\hat{\theta}$ for θ is determined uniquely by

$$q(\hat{\theta}^*, \hat{\theta}, \hat{\phi}) = 0.$$

As both Q_θ ($\equiv \partial q/\partial\theta'$) and Q_{θ^*} ($\equiv \partial q/\partial\theta^{*'}$) are nonsingular, we have, following Szroeter (1983),

$$N^{1/2}(\hat{\theta} - \theta) \overset{L}{\to} \mathrm{N}(0, QVQ'),$$

where $Q \equiv Q_\theta^{-1}[Q_{\theta^*}, Q_\phi]$, $Q_\phi \equiv \partial q/\partial\phi'$ and

$$V \equiv \begin{pmatrix} I_{\mathrm{dim}(\theta)} & -\mathcal{K} \\ 0 & I_{\mathrm{dim}(\phi)} \end{pmatrix} \begin{pmatrix} \mathcal{I}^{-1} & 0 \\ 0 & V(\hat{\phi}) \end{pmatrix} \begin{pmatrix} I_{\mathrm{dim}(\theta)} & 0 \\ -\mathcal{K}' & I_{\mathrm{dim}(\phi)} \end{pmatrix},$$

where $\mathcal{I}$ and $\mathcal{K}$ are defined above; this latter expression for V

($\equiv$avar$[N^{1/2}(\hat{\theta}^* - \theta^*)$, $N^{1/2}(\hat{\phi} - \phi)]$) is obtained from noting that $N^{-1/2} \partial \ln \mathcal{L}_2/\partial\theta^*$ and $N^{1/2}(\hat{\phi} - \phi)$ are uncorrelated, cf. Smith and Blundell (1986, Appendix).

For Examples 1, 3, 4, the above analysis produces particularly convenient results. Firstly under the assumption that $\alpha_1 = 0$,

$$\hat{\beta}_1 = \hat{\beta}_1^*/(1 + \hat{\alpha}_2 \hat{\beta}_1^*),$$

$$\hat{\gamma}_1 = \hat{\gamma}_1^*/(1 - \hat{\alpha}_2 \hat{\beta}_1^*),$$

$$\hat{\rho}_1 = \hat{\rho}_1^*/(1 + \hat{\alpha}_2 \hat{\beta}_1^*),$$

and, secondly,

$$N^{1/2}(\hat{\theta}_1 - \theta_1) \xrightarrow{L} N(0, \mathbf{Q}_1 \mathbf{V} \mathbf{Q}_1'),$$

where $\mathbf{Q}_1 \equiv [(1 - \alpha_2\beta_1)\mathbf{Q}_{\theta\theta}^{11}, \mathbf{0}_{(K_1+2, K+4)}, \beta_1\theta_1, \mathbf{0}_{(K_1+2, K_2)}]$ with

$$\mathbf{Q}_{\theta\theta}^{11} \equiv - \begin{pmatrix} 1 - \alpha_2\beta_1 & \mathbf{0}' & 0 \\ -\alpha_2\gamma_1 & \mathbf{I}_{k_1} & \mathbf{0} \\ -\alpha_2\rho_1 & \mathbf{0}' & 1 \end{pmatrix}$$

5. An empirical application

In this application we consider the case of a joint decision making model for married women's hours of work and other household income (including savings). This serves as a useful application since other household income is continuously observed whereas female hours of work may sensibly be subject to any of the four observability rules (O1)–(O4) described earlier. For example, the standard classical model of hours of work and participation is described by the Tobit observability rule (O1). This is often extended to the selectivity model (O3) if either wages are not observed for nonworkers (Heckman, 1979) or fixed costs of work break the relation between hours of work and participation (Cogan, 1981). If hours of work are not observed then a simple participation Probit (O2) may be adopted. Finally, if some nonworkers would like to work but cannot obtain employment, the double-hurdle model (O4) results (Blundell, Ham and Meghir, 1987).

The other income variable will contain the labour supply decisions of other household members as well as any household savings decisions. If these decisions are *jointly determined* with female hours of work then they will depend on the *actual* hours of work not the underlying latent desired hours variable. Thus, the model will fit into the Type II simultaneous framework rather than the standard Type I model. In this situation no explicit reduced form for other household income will be derivable and a coherency condition will be required for the logical consistency of the economic model in this joint decision-making framework.

Therefore, notationally, y_{1i} in (2) relates to hours of work while y_{2i} refers to the other income variable.[6] The data, brief details of which are provided in the Data appendix, are drawn from the UK family expenditure survey for 1981. The hours of work variable refers to the normal hours of work for a sample of married women of working age for whom the sample participation rate is 56%. The exogenous factors x_{1i} that determine hours of work relate to the age and household composition variables (a_f, D_1) and the married women's education level (e_f). The exogenous variables in the other income equation in x_{2i} include demographic variables (a_f, n_i) plus tenure dummies (T_i), husband's skill characteristics (MO_i) and the local unemployment rate. The exclusion restrictions on the education, skill variables etc. provide the identification conditions on the model.

Table 1
The other income model

Variable	Parameter estimate	Standard error	Variable mean
y_1	−0.4659	0.1803	15.161
a_f	4.9003	1.3108	−0.401
n_1	3.8115	3.7197	0.391
n_2	6.9561	1.8189	0.467
T_1	−7.2911	1.9492	0.285
T_2	−5.2239	3.8164	0.046
MO_1	−12.2799	3.0812	0.080
MO_2	−10.8431	1.9086	0.392
MO_3	−14.5201	2.4212	0.175
UN	−0.5017	0.2722	13.482
Const	77.7339	7.2661	1.00

Exact definitions of variables in Data appendix. All calculations were performed using GAUSS-386.

Table 2
The hours of work equation

Variable	Parameter estimate	Standard error	Variable mean
$\bar{y}_2$	−0.0929	0.0222	50.525
a_f	−2.0437	0.3257	−0.401
a_f^2	0.5391	0.2506	1.282
e_f	0.6762	0.1182	2.928
e_f^2	0.0164	0.0114	14.825
D_1	−24.0999	1.5226	0.295
$\hat{u}_2$	0.2104	0.0509	0.00
Const	25.1666	2.1531	1.00

Exact definitions of variables in Data appendix. All calculations were performed using GAUSS-386.

[6] This we define in the life-cycle consistent manner (Blundell and Walker, 1986).

Table 1 presents the Type II instrumental variable estimates of the other income equation corresponding to (3). Notice that α_2 is negative and significant. Following the procedure for Type II model estimation outlined in Section 4, we estimate the structural parameters of the censored hours equation conditional on $\hat{\alpha}_2$ and $\hat{u}_{2i}$ using the standard Tobit estimator in (28). These results are represented in Table 2 where we have recovered the underlying structural parameters β_1, γ_1 and ρ_1 from the β_1^*, γ_1^* and ρ_1^* estimates, using the identification condition $\alpha_1 = 0$. The coherency condition then simply reduces to $\alpha_2\beta_1 < 1$ which, given our estimate for β_1 in Table 2, is seen to be satisfied.

Although the argument for including actual hours y_{1i} rather than y_{1i}^* as an explanatory factor for other income y_{2i} is convincing when y_{1i} and y_{2i} are jointly determined, it is quite possible that other income y_{2i} is not the result of such a joint decision making model. This does not mean that y_{2i} is statistically exogenous for the parameters in the structural model for y_{1i} but it does result in an explicit reduced form for y_{2i}. In particular, the model is Type I and has a recursive structure. The conditional model simply involves the inclusion of the reduced form residual, $\hat{v}_{2i} = y_{2i} - x_1'\hat{\pi}_2$, in the structural equation for y_{1i}. From our earlier discussion, the two classes of models are strictly nonnested and may be compared using the statistics from (26) and (27); these are given after presenting a comparison of the estimation results for each model.

To provide a reference point in the comparison, the first column in Table 3 contains the standard Tobit estimates for the model of Table 2. A comparison with the estimates in Table 2 indicates the degree of bias involved in assuming y_{2i} to be exogenous in the determination of y_{1i}. The second column in Table 3

Table 3
Alternative models for hours or work

Variable	Tobit	Type I
y_2	−0.1211	−0.0477
	(0.0109)	(0.0291)
a_f	−3.8571	−5.4313
	(0.4407)	(0.6379)
a_f^2	−0.9234	0.8332
	(0.4166)	(0.4252)
e_f	0.7082	0.6545
	(0.1769)	(0.1834)
e_f^2	−0.0089	−0.0258
	(0.0171)	(0.0179)
D_1	−24.7218	−28.7210
	(1.2545)	(2.2119)
$\hat{v}_2$	–	−0.1251
		(0.0491)
Const	29.0583	25.2148
	(1.1996)	(1.8434)

Standard errors in parentheses.

presents the estimation results from the conditional model assuming y_{1i}^* enters the determination of y_{2i}, $\hat{v}_{2i}$ is then the reduced form error term where all x_i are used as instruments.

A comparison of Table 2 with Table 3 suggests that incorrectly assuming the standard simultaneous model could lead to an overadjustment for simultaneous equation bias. However, that conclusion rests on the assumption that the Type II structure is the correct specification. To assess this we consider the tests developed in equations (26) and (27) above, the t-value for $\delta_1 = 0$ is 4.031 whereas that for $\delta_2 = 0$ has the value 1.712. This provides reasonably strong evidence in favour of the Type II model.

6. Summary and conclusions

A number of estimators are proposed for two nonnested classes (Types I and II) of simultaneous microeconometric models in which censoring or grouping of the dependent variable is present. In Type I models, the simultaneity is in terms of the *latent* dependent variables and an explicit reduced form solution exists. In the second class (Type II), simultaneity is in the *observed* dependent variables. Thus, in this later class the censoring or grouping mechanism implies the lack of an explicit reduced form and a coherency condition is consequently required to ensure a unique (implicit) reduced form solution. Our main focus is on conditional maximum likelihood estimation. We show that such estimation procedures may be applied across a wide variety of popular models and provide a useful basis for comparison and inference in such models.

This methodology is applied to a model for the joint determination of hours of work and other household income for a sample of married couples in the UK family expenditure survey. This illustration serves to highlight the potential for simultaneity bias in microeconometric models and also documents the importance of our distinction between Type I and Type II models, suggesting quite different results may occur depending on the specification adopted.

Appendix A

To obtain $\mathcal{I}_1$, consider the system (6a), (6c).

$$y_{1i}^* = x_i' \pi_1 + v_{1i}, \qquad y_{3i}^* = x_i' \pi_3 + v_{3i}, \tag{A1}$$

subject to (1), (5), $i = 1, \ldots, N$. Define $\pi \equiv (\pi_1', \pi_3')$, $\Omega_{13} \equiv [(\omega_{jk})]$, $j, k = 1, 3$, and denote the corresponding marginal log-likelihood by $\ln \mathcal{L}_{13}$. Then the score vector for system (A1) is given by

$$\partial \ln \mathcal{L}_{13} / \partial [\pi, v(\Omega_{13})] = \sum_{i=1}^{N} w_{13i} \zeta_{13i},$$

where $\zeta_{13} \equiv [v_{13}^{(1)\prime}, (v_{13} \otimes v_{13})^{(2)\prime}]'$, $v_{13} \equiv (v_1, v_3)'$,

$$w_{13} \equiv S_{13} \begin{pmatrix} \Omega_{13}^{-1} \otimes x & 0 \\ 0 & \frac{1}{2}(\Omega_{13}^{-1} \otimes \Omega_{13}^{-1}) \end{pmatrix},$$

$S_{13} \equiv \text{diag}(I_K, I_K, D)$; D obeys $D'v(\Omega_{13}) = \text{vec}(\Omega_{13})$ with $v(\cdot)$ selecting out the distinct elements of a symmetric matrix (Magnus and Neudecker, 1980). The term ζ_{13} above is defined by the *generalised error products* discussed in Gourieroux et al. (1987) and Smith (1987); thus

$$v_{13}^{(1)} \equiv E[v_{13} | y_{13}],$$
$$(v_{13} \otimes v_{13})^{(2)} \equiv E[(v_{13} \otimes v_{13}) | y_{13}] - \text{vec}(\Omega_{13}),$$

where $E[\cdot | y_{13}]$ denotes conditional expectation given the observability rules (1), (5) and $y_{13} \equiv (y_1, y_3)'$. By the familiar information matrix equality and the assumption of the independence of observations $i = 1, \ldots, N$, we have that conditional on x,

$$\mathcal{I}_{13} = N^{-1} \sum_{i=1}^{N} w_{13i} \text{var}[\zeta_{13i}] w_{13i}'. \tag{A2}$$

In a similar fashion, to derive $\mathcal{B}$, consider the system (7), (8),

$$y_{1i}^* = x_i'\pi_1 + v_{2i}\tau_1 + \varepsilon_{1i},$$
$$y_{3i}^* = x_i'\pi_3 + v_{2i}\tau_3 + \varepsilon_{3i}, \tag{A3}$$

subject to (1), (5), $i = 1, \ldots, N$. Define $\pi^* \equiv (\pi_1^{*\prime}, \pi_3^{*\prime})'$, $\pi_1^* \equiv (\pi_1', \tau_1)'$, $\pi_3^* \equiv (\pi_3', \tau_3)'$, $\Omega_{.2} \equiv [(\omega_{jk.2})]$, $j, k = 1, 3$, and denote the corresponding conditional log-likelihood by $\ln \mathcal{L}_2$. Then the score vector for system (A3) is given by

$$\partial \ln \mathcal{L}_2 / \partial[\pi^*, v(\Omega_{.2})] = \sum_{i=1}^{N} w_{.2i} \zeta_{.2i},$$

where $\zeta_{.2} \equiv [\varepsilon_{13}^{(1)\prime}, (\varepsilon_{13} \otimes \varepsilon_{13})^{(2)\prime}]'$, $\varepsilon_{13} \equiv (\varepsilon_1, \varepsilon_3)'$,

$$w_{.2} \equiv S_{.2} \begin{pmatrix} \Omega_{.2}^{-1} \otimes x^* & 0 \\ 0 & \frac{1}{2}(\Omega_{.2}^{-1} \otimes \Omega_{.2}^{-1}) \end{pmatrix},$$

$S_{.2} \equiv \text{diag}(I_{K+1}, I_{K+1}, D)$ and $x^* \equiv (x', v_2)'$; the term $\zeta_{.2}$ above is defined by

$$\varepsilon_{13}^{(1)} \equiv E[\varepsilon_{13} | y_{13}],$$
$$(\varepsilon_{13} \otimes \varepsilon_{13})^{(2)} \equiv E[(\varepsilon_{13} \otimes \varepsilon_{13}) | y_{13}] - \text{vec}(\Omega_{.2}).$$

Thus, conditional on x^*, we have

$$\mathcal{B} = N^{-1} \sum_{i=1}^{N} w_{.2i} \, \mathrm{var}[\zeta_{.2i}] w'_{.2i} \, . \tag{A4}$$

Finally,

$$\mathscr{I}_2 = \begin{pmatrix} N^{-1} \sum_{i=1}^{N} x_i x'_i / \omega_{22} & \mathbf{0} \\ \mathbf{0}' & 1/2\omega_{22}^2 \end{pmatrix} . \tag{A5}$$

To derive the matrices V^0 and V^*, note that

$$N^{1/2}(\dot{\lambda}_{13} - \lambda_{13}) = \mathscr{I}_{13}^{-1} N^{-1/2} \sum_{i=1}^{N} w_{13i} \zeta_{13i} + o_P(1) \, ,$$

$$N^{1/2}(\dot{\pi}_2 - \pi_2) = \mathscr{I}_2^{22} N^{-1/2} \sum_{i=1}^{N} x_i v_{2i} / \omega_{22} + o_P(1) \, ,$$

where $\lambda_{13} \equiv [\pi', v(\Omega_{13})']'$ and $\dot{}$ denotes the marginal ML estimator. Thus,

$$\mathrm{avar}[N^{1/2}(\dot{\lambda}_{13} - \lambda_{13}), N^{1/2}(\dot{\pi}_2 - \pi_2)]$$

$$= \begin{pmatrix} \mathscr{I}_{13}^{-1} & \mathbf{0} \\ \mathbf{0} & \mathscr{I}_2^{22} \end{pmatrix}$$

$$\times N^{-1} \begin{pmatrix} \sum_{i=1}^{N} w_{13i} \, \mathrm{var}[\zeta_{13i}] w'_{13i} & \sum_{i=1}^{N} w_{13i} \, \mathrm{cov}[\zeta_{13i}, v_{2i}] x'_i / \omega_{22} \\ \sum_{i=1}^{N} x_i \, \mathrm{cov}[v_{2i}, \zeta_{13i}] w'_{13i} / \omega_{22} & \sum_{i=1}^{N} x_i x'_i / \omega_{22} \end{pmatrix}$$

$$\times \begin{pmatrix} \mathscr{I}_{13}^{-1} & \mathbf{0} \\ \mathbf{0} & \mathscr{I}_2^{22} \end{pmatrix} . \tag{A6}$$

The variances and covariances required for (A6) are obtained by noting that $v_{2i} = v'_{13i} \Omega_{13}^{-1} \tau \omega_{22} + \varepsilon_{2i}$, where $\varepsilon_{2i} \sim \mathrm{NI}[0, (\omega_{22} - \omega_{22}^2 \tau' \Omega_{13}^{-1} \tau)]$ independent of v_{13i}, $i = 1, \ldots, N$. Thus,

$$\mathrm{cov}[\zeta_{13i}, v_{2i}] = \begin{pmatrix} \mathrm{var}[v_{13i}^{(1)}] \\ \mathrm{cov}[(v_{13i} \otimes v_{13i})^{(2)}, v_{13i}^{(1)}] \end{pmatrix} \Omega_{13}^{-1} \tau \omega_{22} \, .$$

Similarly, noting $\hat{\pi}_2 = \dot{\pi}_2$, as

$$N^{1/2}(\hat{\lambda}_{.2} - \lambda_{.2}) = \mathcal{B}^{-1} \left(N^{-1/2} \sum_{i=1}^{N} w_{.2i} \zeta_{.2i} - \mathscr{I}_{.2} N^{1/2}(\hat{\pi}_2 - \pi_2) \right) + o_P(1) \, ,$$

where $\lambda_{.2} \equiv [\pi^{*\prime}, v(\Omega_2)^\prime]^\prime$, $\hat{}$ denotes the conditional ML estimator and

$$\mathscr{I}_{.2} = -N^{-1} \sum_{i=1}^{N} w_{.2i} \begin{pmatrix} \mathrm{var}[\varepsilon_{13i}^{(1)}] \\ \mathrm{cov}[(\varepsilon_{13i} \otimes \varepsilon_{13i})^{(2)}, \varepsilon_{13i}^{(1)}] \end{pmatrix} \Omega_{.2}^{-1} \tau x_i^\prime .$$

Hence

$$\mathrm{avar}[N^{1-2}(\hat{\lambda}_{.2} - \lambda_{.2}), N^{1/2}(\hat{\pi}_2 - \pi_2)]$$

$$= \begin{pmatrix} \mathscr{B}^{-1} + \mathscr{B}^{-1} \mathscr{I}_{.2} \mathscr{I}_2^{22} \mathscr{I}_{.2}^\prime \mathscr{B}^{-1} & -\mathscr{B}^{-1} \mathscr{I}_{.2} \mathscr{I}_2^{22} \\ -\mathscr{I}_2^{22} \mathscr{I}_{.2}^\prime \mathscr{B}^{-1} & \mathscr{I}_2^{22} \end{pmatrix}, \qquad (A7)$$

cf. Smith and Blundell (1986) and Blundell and Smith (1989).

Appendix B

To derive the information matrix for the full system (6) subject to the restrictions (9) and the observability rules (1), (5), define $z \equiv (y_2, x^{*\prime})^\prime$ and the selection matrices S_1 and S_3 which select out those elements of z appropriate for (11) and (8) respectively. Thus, the score vector corresponding to the conditional model [(8), (11) subject to (1), (5)] parameters is given by

$$\partial \ln \mathscr{L} / \partial [\beta_1, \gamma_1^\prime, \rho_1, \pi_3^{*\prime}, v(\Omega_2)] = \sum_{i=1}^{N} w_i \zeta_{.2i} , \qquad (B1)$$

where

$$w \equiv \begin{pmatrix} S_1 & 0 & 0 \\ 0 & S_3 & 0 \\ 0 & 0 & D \end{pmatrix} \begin{pmatrix} \Omega_{.2}^{-1} \otimes z & 0 \\ 0 & \frac{1}{2}(\Omega_{.2}^{-1} \otimes \Omega_{.2}^{-1}) \end{pmatrix} ,$$

and $\zeta_{.2}$ is defined in Appendix A. The score vector for the marginal model [(6b)] parameters is

$$\partial \ln \mathscr{L} / \partial \pi_2 = \sum_{i=1}^{N} x_i [(v_{2i}/\omega_{22}) - \tau^\prime \Omega_{.2}^{-1} \varepsilon_{13i}^{(1)}] . \qquad (B2)$$

Hence, the information matrix is given by

$$\mathscr{I} = N^{-1} \begin{pmatrix} \sum_{i=1}^{N} w_i \, \mathrm{var}[\zeta_{.2i}] w_i^\prime & -\sum_{i=1}^{N} w_i [\mathrm{cov}[\zeta_{.2i}, \varepsilon_{13i}^{(1)}] \Omega_{.2}^{-1} \tau] x_i^\prime \\ -\sum_{i=1}^{N} x_i [\tau^\prime \Omega_{.2}^{-1} \, \mathrm{cov}[\varepsilon_{13i}^{(1)}, \zeta_{.2i}]] w_i^\prime & \sum_{i=1}^{N} x_i [1/\omega_{22} + \tau^\prime \Omega_{.2}^{-1} \, \mathrm{var}[\varepsilon_{13i}^{(1)}] \Omega_{.2}^{-1} \tau] x_i^\prime \end{pmatrix} .$$

$$(B3)$$

Appendix C

Consider the system

$$y_{1i}^* = \beta_1^* \bar{y}_{2i} + x_{1i}' \gamma_1^* + \rho_1^* u_{2i} + \varepsilon_{1i}^* , \tag{C1}$$

$$y_{3i}^* = x_i' \pi_3 + \rho_3 u_{2i} + \varepsilon_{3i} , \quad i = 1, \ldots, N . \tag{C2}$$

Following Smith (1987, Appendix B, pp. 120–121) and noting that $\theta^* \equiv (\beta_1^*, \gamma_1^{*'}, \rho_1^*, \pi_3', \rho_3, v(\Sigma_{.2}^*))'$, the score vector for system (C1), (C2), assuming that $\bar{y}_{2i}$ and u_{2i} are observed, $i = 1, \ldots, N$, is given by

$$\partial \ln \mathscr{L}_2 / \partial \theta^* = \sum_{i=1}^{N} w_i \zeta_i ,$$

where $\ln \mathscr{L}_2$ denotes the log-likelihood for system (C1) and (C2) under the assumption that ε_i^* $(\equiv (\varepsilon_{1i}^*, \varepsilon_{3i})) \sim \mathrm{NI}(0, \Sigma_{.2}^*)$, $i = 1, \ldots, N$, $\zeta \equiv [\varepsilon^{*(1)'}, (\varepsilon^* \otimes \varepsilon^*)^{(2)'}]'$,

$$w \equiv S \begin{pmatrix} \Sigma_{.2}^{*-1} \otimes z & 0 \\ 0 & \frac{1}{2}(\Sigma_{.2}^{*-1} \otimes \Sigma_{.2}^{*-1}) \end{pmatrix} ,$$

$z \equiv (\bar{y}_2, x', u_2)'$ and $S \equiv \mathrm{diag}(S_1, S_3, D)$; S_1 and S_3 select out the appropriate elements of z included in (C1) and (C2) respectively whereas D obeys $D'v(\Sigma) = \mathrm{vec}(\Sigma)$ with $v(\cdot)$ selecting out the distinct elements of a symmetric matrix (Magnus and Neudecker, 1980). The term ζ above is defined by the generalized error products discussed in Gourieroux et al. (1987) and Smith (1987); thus

$$\varepsilon^{*(1)} \equiv \mathrm{E}[\varepsilon^* \mid y], \quad (\varepsilon^* \otimes \varepsilon^*)^{(2)} \equiv \mathrm{E}[\varepsilon^* \otimes \varepsilon^* \mid y] - \mathrm{vec}(\Sigma_{.2}^*) ,$$

where $\mathrm{E}[\cdot \mid y]$ denotes conditional expectation given the observability rule linking $y^* = (y_1^*, y_3^*)'$ to $y = (y_1, y_3)'$ and z. By the familiar information matrix equality and the assumption of the independence of observations $i = 1, \ldots, N$, we have that conditional on z,

$$-N^{-1} \mathrm{E}[\partial^2 \ln \mathscr{L}_2 / \partial \theta^* \, \partial \theta^{*'}] = N^{-1} \sum_{i=1}^{N} w_i \, \mathrm{var}[\zeta_1] w_i' .$$

The score vector of $\ln \mathscr{L}_2$ with respect to $\phi = (\alpha_2, \gamma_2')'$ is

$$\partial \ln \mathscr{L}_2 / \partial \phi = -\sum_{i=1}^{N} w_{2i} \varepsilon_i^{*(1)} ,$$

where $w_2 \equiv S_2(\Sigma_{.2}^{*-1} \otimes z_2)$, $z_2 \equiv (y_1, x_2')'$ and

$$S_2 \equiv \begin{pmatrix} (\beta_1 + \rho_1) & \mathbf{0}' & \rho_3 & \mathbf{0}' \\ \mathbf{0} & \rho_1 I_{K_2} & \mathbf{0} & \rho_3 I_{K_2} \end{pmatrix} .$$

Thus, again by independence and the information matrix equality

$$-N^{-1}E[\partial^2 \ln \mathscr{L}_{.2} / \partial \theta^* \partial \phi'] = -N^{-1} \sum_{i=1}^{N} w_i \, \mathrm{cov}[\zeta_i, \varepsilon_i^{*(1)}] w_{2i}' ;$$

cf. Smith and Blundell (1986).

Data appendix

The data are a sample of 2539 married women from the 1981 family expenditure survey for the UK. All women are of working age and are not self employed.

Variables		Mean	Standard deviation
Female hours	y_1	15.1611	15.7452
Other Income	y_2	50.5254	41.7982
(Age -40)/10	a_f	-0.4008	1.0593
(Age $-40)^2$/100	a_f^2	1.2823	1.1580
(Education -8)	e_f	2.9283	2.5005
(Education $-8)^2$	e_f^2	14.8251	25.3807
Youngest kid age $(-, 5]$	D_1	0.2954	0.4563
Youngest kid age $[5, 10]$	D_2	0.2209	0.4149
Youngest kid age $[11, -]$	D_3	0.1394	0.3463
Number of kids $[-, 5]$	N_1	0.3911	0.6680
Number of kids $[5, 10]$	N_2	0.4667	0.7400
Number of kids $[11, -]$	N_3	0.4124	0.7499
Owner occupier	T_1	0.2847	0.4514
Local authority	T_2	0.0456	0.2088
Husband : skilled	MO_1	0.0803	0.2718
Husband : semiskilled	MO_2	0.3919	0.4882
Husband : unskilled	MO_3	0.1748	0.3798
Local unemployment	UN	13.4821	2.9086

Notes: y_1 – normal weekly hours of work for married women; y_2 – normal weekly earnings minus expenditures.

References

Amemiya, T. (1978). The estimation of a simultaneous equation generalised Probit model. *Econometrica* **46**, 1193–1205.

Amemiya, T. (1979). The estimation of a simultaneous equation Tobit model. *Internat. Econ. Rev.* **20**, 169–181.

Blundell, R. W. and I. Walker (1986). A life-cycle consistent model of family labour supply using cross section data. *Rev. Econ. Stud.* **53**, 539–558.

Blundell, R. W., J. Ham and C. Meghir (1987). Unemployment and female labour supply. *Econ. J.* **97**, 44–64.

Blundell, R. W. and R. J. Smith (1989). Estimation in a class of limited dependent variable models, *Rev. Econ. Stud.* **56**, 37–58.

Blundell, R. W. and R. J. Smith (1990). Coherency and estimation in simultaneous models with censored or qualitative dependent variables. *J. Econometrics*, to appear.

Chesher, A. (1985a), Improving the efficiency of Probit estimators. *Rev. Econ. Statist.* **66**, 523–527.

Chesher, A. (1985b). Score tests for zero covariances in recursive linear models for grouped or censored data. *J. Econometrics* **28**, 291–306.

Cogan, J. F. (1981). Fixed costs and labour supply. *Econometrica* **49**, 945–964.

Cragg, J. G. (1971). Some statistical models for limited dependent variables with applications to the demand for durable goods. *Econometrica* **39**, 829–844.

Davidson, R. and J. G. MacKinnon (1981). Several tests for model specification in the presence of alternative hypotheses. *Econometrica* **49**, 781–793.

Ferguson, T. (1958). A method of generating best asymptotically normal estimates with application to the estimation of bacterial densities. *Ann. Math. Statist.* **29**, 1046–1061.

Godfrey, L. G. (1983). Testing non-nested models after estimation by instrumental variables or least squares. *Econometrica* **51**, 355–366.

Gourieroux, C., J. J. Laffont and A. Monfort (1980). Coherency conditions in simultaneous linear equation models with endogenous switching regimes. *Econometrica* **48**, 675–695.

Gourieroux, C., A. Monfort, E. Renault and A. Trognon (1987). Generalised residuals. *J. Econometrics* **34**, 5–32.

Heckman, J. J. (1978). Dummy endogenous variables in a simultaneous equation system. *Econometrica* **46**, 931–959.

Heckman, J. J. (1979). Sample selection bias as specification error. *Econometrica* **47**, 153–162.

Maddala, G. S. (1983). *Limited-Dependent and Qualitative Variables in Econometrics*. Cambridge University Press, Cambridge.

Malinvaud, E. (1970). *Statistical Methods of Econometrics*. North-Holland, Amsterdam.

Magnus, J. R. and H. Neudecker (1980). The elimination matrix: Some theorems and applications. *SIAM J. Algebraic Discrete Methods* **1**, 422–449.

Nelson, F. and L. Olsen (1978). Specification and estimation of a simultaneous equation model with limited dependent variables. *Internat. Econ. Rev.* **19**, 695–705.

Newey, W. K. (1987). Efficient estimation of limited dependent variable models with endogenous explanatory variables. *J. Econometrics* **36**, 231–250.

Ransom, M. R. (1987). A comment on consumer demand systems with binding non-negativity constraints. *J. Econometrics* **34**, 355–60.

Rivers, D. and Q. H. Vuong (1988). Limited information estimators and exogeneity tests for simultaneous probit models. *J. Econometrics* **39**, 347–366.

Rothenberg, T. J. (1973). Efficient estimation with a priori information. Yale University Press, New Haven, CT.

Smith, R. J. (1987). Testing the normality assumption in multivariate simultaneous limited dependent variable models. *J. Econometrics* **34**, 105–123.

Smith, R. J. and R. W. Blundell (1986). An exogeneity test for a simultaneous equation Tobit model with an application to labor supply. *Econometrica* **54**, 679–685.

Stewart, M. (1983). On least squares estimation when the dependent variable is grouped. *Rev. Econ. Stud.* **50**, 737–753.

Szroeter, J. (1983). Generalised Wald methods for testing nonlinear implicit and overidentifying restrictions. *Econometrica* **51**, 335–353.

Van Soest, A., P. Kooreman and A. Kapteyn (1990). Coherency specification of demand systems with corner solutions and endogenous regimes. Research Memorandum FEW 336, Department of Economics, Tilburg University.

G. S. Maddala, C. R. Rao and H. D. Vinod, eds., *Handbook of Statistics, Vol. 11*

6

Multivariate Tobit Models in Econometrics

Lung-Fei Lee

1. Introduction

The use of household or firm microeconomic data offers important advantages for the empirical analysis of consumer demand and labor supply of consumers, and production and input demand of producers. Demographic variables and heterogeneity of individuals can be easily incorporated in the estimable equations, but these effects are not easily measured with aggregated data. Microeconomic data, however, contain certain attributes which complicate the econometric modelling and estimation. For example, household budget data, which contain detailed information on the consumption of certain disaggregated commodities, often contain a significant proportion of observations with zero expenditures. The consumer demand functions contain limited dependent variables. Pioneering works on limited dependent variables in microeconometric models (for example, Tobin, 1958; Amemiya, 1973; and Heckman, 1974) have emphasized an univariate limited dependent variable. A survey on the econometric developments of model specification and estimation of limited dependent variables by Amemiya (1984) (see also, Maddala, 1983) has focused mainly on univariate limited dependent variable models. Much developments on multivariate limited dependent variables models have taken place recently. In this article, we provide a brief survey on multivariate tobit models. The term 'tobit models' in this survey refers solely to models with either censored or truncated dependent variables. Qualitative variables or sample selection models are not covered in this survey. This survey will emphasize models formulated with neoclassical microeconomic theories. Consumer demand models are important members.

This survey is organized as follows. Section 2 provides some familiar multivariate and simultaneous equation models with multivariate tobit variables, which are generalizations of the classical multivariate regression model and the classical linear simultaneous equation model. Section 3 discusses the formulation of consumer demand systems and production systems, which are compatible with microeconomic theories and incorporate features of microeconomic data with zero expenditures or kink points. The derived equation systems are essentially nonlinear simultaneous equations with complicated cross-equation constraints. Some of the simultaneous equation tobit models are nonlinear in variables. Such models may not be well-defined stochastic models without appropriate restrictions on some of the structural parameters. This is an issue on model coherency. Section 4 surveys such an issue. For consumer demand or production systems, the model coherent conditions are essentially the familiar concavity conditions. Structural models with sound theoretical foundations are coherent. The estimation of multivariate tobit models by the classical maximum likelihood method is known to be computationally ineffici-ent, since the computation of multivariate normal probabilities of high dimensions is difficult. Section 5 surveys some recent developments on estimation methods that are computationally tractable, and model specification strategies that provide computationally tractable and reasonably flexible structures. Instrumental variable estimation methods and simulated methods of moments are two of such methods. Lagrange multiplier tests are computation-ally simple diagnostic tests for such models. Section 6 points out some of such tests.

2. Some multivariate tobit models

Multivariate tobit models in this article are models which generalize univariate tobit models to systems of equations. In the econometric literature, there are several popular generalizations. Each of them designed to capture certain special features of empirical issues is unique on its own. The following several models are the familiar ones in the literature. Some other models will be introduced in the subsequent sections.

2.1. Amemiya's multivariate regression and simultaneous equation models

Amemiya (1974) extends Tobin's model (Tobin, 1958) to some multivariate regression and simultaneous equation models. He considered the models with all the dependent variables being censored or truncated. The simultaneous equations system is specified as follows:

$$By_t \geq \Gamma x_t + u_t, \quad y_t \geq 0, \tag{2.1.1}$$

and

$$(By_t)_i = (\Gamma x_t + u_t)_i, \quad \text{whenever } y_{it} > 0,$$

where i stands for the ith component of the relevant vector, x_t is a vector of exogenous variables, and $u_t \sim N(0, \Omega)$. The sample observations for the dependent variable y take only nonnegative values. If all the components of y are positive, y is an interior solution of the system. Observations of y with some components zero are corner solutions. Depending on the pattern of solutions, different reduced form equations may appear in different regimes.

For example, conditional on an interior solution, the reduced form equations for the interior regime form a truncated multivariate regression model,

$$y_t = \Pi x_t + v_t ,$$ (2.1.2)

where $\Pi = B^{-1}\Gamma$ and $v = B^{-1}u$. These reduced form structures, which are switching across different regimes, raise model coherency issues. The model coherency issue is a problem for structural models to be well-defined probability models. For the classical linear simultaneous equation model, there is no model coherency issue (when B is nonsingular). The presence of switching regimes for the simultaneous tobit models creates changes in the stochastic structures, from which the model coherency problem has arisen. This issue will be picked up in a subsequent discussion. An empirical application of this model to the study of time allocation of youths can be found in Waldman (1981).

2.2. Multivariate regression and simultaneous equation models with some dependent variables truncated

Sickles and Schmidt (1978) and Lee (1977) extended the Amemiya model to the cases where only some of the dependent variables are censored or truncated. Applications of such a model are in Sickles, Schmidt and Witte (1979), and Amemiya, Saito and Shimono (1987). Let $y_t = (y_t^{(1)\prime}, y_t^{(2)\prime})'$ and $u_t = (u_t^{(1)\prime}, u_t^{(2)\prime})'$. The simultaneous equation system is

$$B_{11}y_t^{(1)} + B_{12}y_t^{(2)} = \Gamma_1 x_t + u_t^{(1)} ,$$
$$B_{21}y_t^{(1)} + B_{22}y_t^{(2)} \geqslant \Gamma_2 x_t + u_t^{(2)} , \quad y_t^{(2)} \geqslant 0 ,$$ (2.2.1)

and

$$(B_{21}y_t^{(1)} + B_{22}y_t^{(2)})_i = (\Gamma_2 x_t + u_t^{(2)})_i , \quad \text{whenever } y_{it}^{(2)} > 0 .$$

An observation y with all its components of $y^{(2)}$ being positive corresponds to an interior solution of the system. Conditional on the interior solutions, the reduced form equation system of the interior regime is a multivariate regression model with truncated distributions.

2.3. The Nelson and Olsen simultaneous equation model

Nelson and Olsen (1978) introduced a simultaneous equation model with latent endogenous variables:

$$By^* + \Gamma x = u ,$$ (2.3.1)

where y^* is a vector of latent variables. The sample observation y is related to y^* as $y = \max\{y^*, 0\}$. This model has much simpler structures than the Amemiya simultaneous equation model. There is a unique reduced form equation system of latent variables. Each equation in the reduced form equation system is a univariate censored regression equation. In terms of the latent variables, this model has all of the familiar structure of a classical linear simultaneous equation model. The model is coherent when B is nonsingular. The structural parameters are identified under the classical rank identification condition. This equation system can obviously be generalized to cases where only some of the endogenous variables are latent variables and the remaining variables are observables. Other simultaneous equation models with more complicated structures, which contain both qualitative and limited dependent variables, have been formulated in Heckman (1978).

2.4. Some disequilibrium market models

It is interesting to point out that some of the disequilibrium market models in the econometric literature can be regarded as special cases of the above simultaneous equation tobit models. The relations among these models are not apparent in their original formulations. But with some proper transformations of variables, the relations can be revealed. Studies on econometric disequilibrium models can be found in Quandt (1988).

The disequilibrium model of the watermelon market in Suits (1955) and Goldfeld and Quandt (1975) is a simultaneous equation model with some censored dependent variables. The basic equations of the model are

$$
\begin{aligned}
q_t &= \beta_1 x_{1t} + \beta_2 + u_{1t}, \\
z_t &= \beta_3 p_t + \beta_4 q_t + \beta_5 x_{2t} + \beta_6 + u_{2t}, \\
y_t &= \min(q_t, z_t), \\
p_t &= \beta_7 x_{3t} + \beta_8 y_t + \beta_9 + u_{3t},
\end{aligned}
\tag{2.4.1}
$$

where x_{jt}, $j = 1, 2, 3$ are vectors of predetermined variables, and u_{jt}, q_t, p_t and y_t are observables but z_t is not. The first equation describes the determination of the size of the crop q_t at the period t. The second equation is a harvest equation, which states that the intended amount of harvest is a function of current price p_t, the size of the crop itself, and other factors. The third equation says that the harvest is the minimum quantity of intended harvest and the size of the crop. Under certain circumstances, it may not be worthwhile to harvest the entire crop. On the other hand, it may be possible that the intended harvest exceeds the crop, and in this case the actual harvest will equal the crop. The last equation is a standard demand equation. Define $y_{1t} = q_t$, $y_{2t} = p_t$, and $y_{3t} = \max\{q_t - z_t, 0\}$. The model can be rewritten as

$$
\begin{aligned}
y_{1t} &= \beta_1 x_{1t} + \beta_2 + u_{1t}, \\
y_{2t} &= \beta_7 x_{3t} - \beta_8 y_{3t} + \beta_8 y_{1t} + \beta_9 + u_{3t}, \\
y_{3t} &\geq -\beta_3 y_{2t} + (1 - \beta_4) y_{1t} - \beta_5 x_{2t} - \beta_6 - u_{2t}, \\
y_{3t} &\geq 0,
\end{aligned}
$$

and

$$y_{3t} = -\beta_3 y_{2t} + (1 - \beta_4)y_{1t} - \beta_5 x_{2t} - \beta_6 - u_{2t}, \quad \text{when } y_{3t} > 0.$$

This is a three equations model with only one censored endogenous variable.

The following disequilibrium marked model with fixed supply is a Nelson and Olsen simultaneous equation model:

$$\begin{aligned}
d_t &= \alpha_1 p_t + x_t \alpha_2 + u_{1t}, \\
s_t &= \bar{s}_t, \\
p_t - p_{t-1} &= \gamma_1(d_t - s_t) + x_t \gamma_1 + u_{2t}, \\
q_t &= \min(d_t, s_t),
\end{aligned} \tag{2.4.2}$$

where the first equation is a demand equation, the second equation is a (fixed) supply equation with $\bar{s}_t$ predetermined, and the third equation is a price adjustment equation. The demand d is a latent variable, and the transacted quantity is determined by the short side condition. Define $y_{1t}^* = \bar{s}_t - d_t$, $y_{2t} = p_t - p_{t-1}$, and $y_{1t} = \max\{\bar{s}_t - q_t, 0\}$. The equations (2.4.2) can then be rewritten as

$$\begin{aligned}
y_{1t}^* &= \bar{s}_t - \alpha_1 p_t - x_t \alpha_2 - u_{1t}, \\
y_{2t} &= -\gamma_1 y_{1t}^* + x_{2t} \gamma_2 + u_{2t}.
\end{aligned}$$

y_{1t} is the observed censored variable of y_{1t}^*. Indeed, one can check that $y_{1t} = \max\{y_{1t}^*, 0\}$.

3. Some convex programming models

The development of the econometric literature of limited dependent variables was motivated by a consumer demand problem in a two commodities model in Tobin (1958). It is natural for later developments to extend the approach to models with any finite number of commodities. The following paragraphs point out several generalizations, which are compatible with the neoclassical microeconomic theory.

3.1. Econometric models of consumer demand on convex budget sets

Convex budget sets result naturally from labor supply problems (see, e.g., Heckman, 1974; Burtless and Hausman, 1978; Moffitt, 1982; and Hausman and Ruud, 1984). It arises also from consumer demand problems with binding nonnegativity constraints, quantity rationing, and increasing block pricing (see, e.g., Hausman, 1985; Wales and Woodland, 1983; and Lee and Pitt, 1987). Consumer demand systems derived from utility maximization over convex budget sets with kink points are, in general, nonlinear simultaneous equation systems with multivariate limited dependent variables. The demand quantities are limited dependent variables because there are positive probabilities for the demand quantities to occur at the kink or boundary points. Those points of the demand equations are atoms in the corresponding probability spaces.

Consider a general multi-commodity model, every commodity in the model may be subject to increasing block pricing. For commodity j, assume that there are I_j different block prices p_{jk}, $k = 1, \ldots, I_j$, with $p_{j1} < p_{j2} < \cdots < p_{jI_j}$, corresponding to the kink points $y_j(1), \ldots, y_j(I_j - 1)$, where $y_j(i) < y_j(i + 1)$ for $i = 1, \ldots, I_j - 2$. The case $I_j = 1$ is the standard single price situation. If $y_j(I_j - 1)$ is the upper limit for commodity j in rationing, $p_{jI_j} = \infty$. As a convention, $y_j(0) = 0$, and $y_j(I_j) = \infty$. Let $U(y_1^*, \ldots, y_m^*)$ be a utility function which is continuously differentiable, increasing, and strictly quasi-concave. The utility maximization problem is

$$\max_{y_1^*, \ldots, y_m^*} U(y_1^*, \ldots, y_m^*)$$

subject to

$$\sum_{j=1}^{m} \sum_{i \in K_j} p_{ji} y_{ji}^* \leq M \,,$$

$$0 \leq y_{ji}^* \leq y_j(i) - y_j(i - 1) \equiv \bar{y}_j(i) \,, \quad i \in K_j \,, \quad j = 1, \ldots, m \,, \qquad (3.1.1)$$

$$y_j^* = \sum_{i \in K_j} y_{ji}^* \,,$$

where $K_j = \{1, \ldots, I_j\}$ is the set of integers describing the pink points for product j, and y_{ji}^* is defined as the purchase of product j in block i. The optimal solution y is characterized by Kuhn–Tucker conditions:

$$\frac{\partial L}{\partial y_{ji}} = \frac{\partial U(y)}{\partial y_j} - \mu p_{ji} - \lambda_{ji} \leq 0 \leq y_{ji} \,, \qquad \frac{\partial L}{\partial y_{ji}} y_{ji} = 0 \,,$$

$$\frac{\partial L}{\partial \mu} = M - \sum_j \sum_i p_{ji} y_{ji} \geq 0 \leq \mu \,, \qquad \frac{\partial L}{\partial \mu} \mu = 0 \,, \qquad (3.1.2)$$

$$\frac{\partial L}{\partial \lambda_{ji}} = \bar{y}_j(i) - y_{ji} \geq 0 \leq \lambda_{ji} \,, \qquad \frac{\partial L}{\partial \lambda_{ji}} \lambda_{ji} = 0 \,,$$

where L is the Lagrange function, and μ and λ are Lagrange multipliers. Because of the block pricing structure, purchases will always be made in lower price blocks before higher price blocks. Hence, if $y_{ji} > 0$, $y_{jl} = y_j(l)$ for all $l < i$, and if $y_{ji} = 0$, $y_{jl} = 0$ for all $l > i$. Thus the demand for good j is $y_j = \sum_{l=1}^{i_j} y_{jl}$, where i_j is the highest integer for which $y_{ji_j} > 0$. The optimal quantities can also be characterized by virtual prices. For an illustration, consider the demand vector y:

$$y_j = 0 \,, \quad j \in J_1 \,,$$

$$y_j = y_j(i_j) \,, \quad j \in J_2 \,, \qquad (3.1.3)$$

$$y_j(i_j - 1) < y_j < y_j(i_j) \,, \quad j \in J_3 \,,$$

for some i_j, $j \in J_2 \cup J_3$, where J_1, J_2 and J_3 are some partition of the set $\{1, 2, \ldots, m\}$. The virtual price vector at y is $\xi(y) = (\xi_1(y), \ldots, \xi_m(y))'$, where $\xi_j(y) = (1/\mu) \partial U(y)/\partial y_j$. The virtual prices are strictly positive because $\mu > 0$ follows from the assumed strictly increasing property of the utility function. The Kuhn–Tucker conditions for y can be rewritten as

$$\xi_j(y) \leqslant p_{j1}, \quad j \in J_1,$$
$$p_{ji_j} \leqslant \xi_j(y) \leqslant p_{ji_j+1}, \quad j \in J_2, \tag{3.1.4}$$
$$\xi_j(y) = p_{ji_j}, \quad j \in J_3.$$

The kink point $y_j(i_j)$ is the quantity demanded for good j, $j \in J_2$. Because the block price p_{ji_j} for good j, $j \in J_2$, is less than the virtual price $\xi_j(y^*)$, the consumer buys as much of the good as permitted under p_{ji_j}, but the second block price p_{ji_j+1} is sufficiently high so that the consumer does not wish to purchase any more. If $y_j(i_j)$ is purely an upper limited rationed amount, optimality at the rationed limit will be characterized by $p_{ji_j} \leqslant \xi_j(y)$. The goods y_j, $j \in J_3$, are purchased at the quantities y_j such that their virtual prices equal market prices. With the specification of a stochastic parametric utility function U, a likelihood function can be derived through either the Kuhn–Tucker conditions or the virtual price characterization.

Instead of the specification of a direct stochastic utility function, Lee and Pitt (1986a) have pointed out that the dual approach, which specifies an indirect utility function or a system of demand equations, is also feasible with the virtual price characterization. Suppose that $D_i(p, M; \varepsilon)$, $i = 1, \ldots, m$, are the specified stochastic demand functions, which are solutions to the utility maximization problem $\max\{U(y^*) \mid p'y^* = M\}$. Consider the demand vector y in (3.1.3), where $J_1 = \{1, 2, \ldots, l_1 - 1\}$, $J_2 = \{l_1, \ldots, l_2 - 1\}$, and $J_3 = \{l_2, l_2 + 1, \ldots, m\}$. The virtual prices ξ and the virtual income c, which support y, are characterized by the inequalities (3.1.4) and the demand relations,

$$0 = D_j(\xi_1, \ldots, \xi_{l_2-1}, p_{l_2 i_{l_2}}, \ldots, p_{mi_m}, c; \varepsilon), \quad j = 1, \ldots, l_1 - 1,$$
$$y_j(i_j) = D_j(\xi_1, \ldots, \xi_{l_2-1}, p_{l_2 i_{l_2}}, \ldots, p_{mi_m}, c; \varepsilon), \quad j = l_1, \ldots, l_2 - 1,$$
$$y_j = D_j(\xi_1, \ldots, \xi_{l_2-1}, p_{l_2 i_{l_2}}, \ldots, p_{mi_m}, c; \varepsilon), \quad j = l_2, \ldots, m, \tag{3.1.5}$$

where

$$c = M + \sum_{j=l_1}^{m} \sum_{l=1}^{i_j-1} (p_{jl+1} - p_{jl}) y_j(l) + \sum_{j=l_1}^{l_2-1} (\xi_j - p_{ji_j}) y_j(i_j).$$

These equations imply an implicit function from the disturbance ε to $(\xi_1, \ldots, \xi_{l_2-1}, y_{l_2}, \ldots, y_m)$. The likelihood function of y can be derived from these equations. Since the demand vector y lies on a budget plane, the equation y_m is functionally dependent on the other equations and is redundant.

Given a joint density function for ε, these equations imply a joint density function for $(\xi_1, \ldots, \xi_{l_2-1}, y_{l_2}, \ldots, y_{m-1})$. Let $g(\xi_1, \ldots, \xi_{l_2-1}, y_{l_2}, \ldots, y_{m-1})$ be the implied joint density function. The likelihood function for this observation is

$$\left(\prod_{j=l_1}^{l_2-1} \int_{p_{ji_j}}^{p_{j(i_j+1)}} \right) \left(\prod_{j=1}^{l_1-1} \int_0^{p_{j1}} \right)$$
$$\times g(\xi_1, \ldots, \xi_{l_2-1}, y_{l_2}, \ldots, y_{m-1}) \, d\xi_1 \cdots d\xi_{l_2-1} \,,$$

where $(\Pi \int)$ denotes multiple integrals. Given that the utility function is strictly concave, the demand vector is uniquely determined. As long as the utility function does not exclude any zero consumption for the zero expenditure case or the domain of the utility function covers the sampling space of demand quantities, the model is a well-specified stochastic model. However, for models with utility functions which do not satisfy the global concavity property, model coherency problem may occur. This issue will be considered in a subsequent section.

3.2. Production analysis

Kink points in the production analysis may occur because of binding non-negativity constraints on inputs or outputs. Production quotas or quantity rationing of inputs will also create kink points. Increasing block pricing in inputs or decreasing block pricing of outputs are similar to quantity rationing. Consider a profit maximization problem subject to quantity constraints

$$\max_{y^*, q^*} p'q^* - r'y^*$$

subject to

$$F(q^*, y^*) = 0 \,, \quad \bar{q} \geq q^* \geq 0, \quad \bar{y} \geq y^* \geq 0 \,,$$

where y^* and q^* are $k \times 1$ and $m \times 1$ vectors of inputs and outputs, respectively, and $\bar{y}$ and $\bar{q}$ are the quantity quotas. The production function F is an increasing function of q^* and a decreasing function of y^*. The optimal solutions for this problem can also be characterized by virtual price inequalities. To illustrate the construction of virtual prices, consider, for example, $y = (0, y_2, \ldots, y_k)'$ and $q = (\bar{q}_1, q_2, \ldots, q_m)'$, where the first input is not utilized and the first output is produced at the quota level. The virtual price ξ_{d1} for input 1 and the virtual price ξ_{s1} for output 1 at y are $\xi_{d1} = -\lambda \, \partial F(q, y)/\partial y_1$ and $\xi_{s1} = \lambda \, \partial F(q, y)/\partial q_1$. The optimality of y is then characterized by

$$r_1 \geq \xi_{d1} \,, \quad 0 < y_i < \bar{y}_i \,, \quad i = 2, \ldots, k \,,$$
$$p_1 \geq \xi_{s1} \,, \quad 0 < q_j < \bar{q}_j \,, \quad j = 2, \ldots, m \,.$$

Input 1 is not used because the market price for this input is too high, and output 1 is produced up to the quota limit because the market price for this output is high enough. The case of increasing block prices in inputs and/or decreasing block prices in outputs can also be formulated in this framework (Lee and Pitt, 1987).

The formulation and analysis of the above models rely on the concavity of the objective function and the convexity of the constraints. The Kuhn–Tucker conditions characterize the optimal solution because of the convexity properties. Some optimization models, such as a consumer demand model with decreasing block pricing, may not possess all the convexity structures. For such models, the occurrence of regimes will be determined by maximized utility comparisons, and the stochastic models are, in general, endogenous switching regression models. Kinked points in such models will, in general, occur with probability zero (see, e.g., Hausman, 1985). Such models are not multivariate tobit models. For consumer demand data with zero expenditures, some authors argue that zero expenditures occur solely due to the possibility that the survey period was too short to have many commodities purchased. The zero expenditure problem was then regarded as a measurement issue but was not due to price responses of consumers. Such models (see, e.g., Pudney, 1987) are not multivariate tobit models.

4. Model coherency in simultaneous equation models

4.1. Coherency conditions in linear simultaneous equation models

For the classical linear simultaneous equation system $By_t = \Gamma x_t + u_t$, given the predetermined variable vector x_t, the disturbance vector u_t, and the nonsingularity of B, y_t will be uniquely determined by the system. However, the simultaneous equation tobit system (2.1.1) does not necessarily define the random vector y_t when B is nonsingular. For given values of u_t and x_t, there might be no values of y_t that would satisfy (2.1.1), or there might be more than one value of y_t that would satisfy (2.1.1). These contradict the classical linear simultaneous equation model, because the present model is a system of nonlinear equations – nonlinear in variables. Further properties or restrictions on B are required for the model to be a well-defined stochastic model.

The equations in (2.1.1) have the general form

$$By \geqslant w, \quad y \geqslant 0,$$
$$y'(By - w) = 0. \tag{4.1.1}$$

The problem of the existence of a unique solution of (4.1.1) is known as the complementarity problem in the mathematical programming literature (e.g., see Samelson, Thrall and Wesler, 1958). The system has a unique solution if and only if every principal minor of B is positive. Thus for the model to be a well-defined statistical model, Amemiya (1974) assumes that every principal minor of B is positive. Amemiya has pointed out that a sufficient condition is that $B + B'$ is positive definite. Also if B has positive dominant diagonals, it has the required properties (Gale and Nikaido, 1965). Waldman (1981) provided an interpretation of the coherency condition in a time allocation model.

For the model with only some dependent variables truncated (2.2.1), the coherency condition can be easily derived with an extension of the above coherency condition. Since B_{11} is nonsingular, it follows from the first set of equations in (2.2.1) that

$$y_t^{(1)} = -B_{11}^{-1}B_{12}y_t^{(2)} + B_{11}^{-1}\Gamma_1 x_t + B_{11}^{-1}u_t^{(1)} \, ,$$

which in turn implies that

$$(B_{22} - B_{21}B_{11}^{-1}B_{12})y_t^{(2)} \geq -B_{21}B_{11}^{-1}\Gamma_1 x_t + \Gamma_2 x_t + u_t^{(2)} - B_{21}B_{11}^{-1}u_t^{(1)} \, .$$

A necessary and sufficient condition for model coherency is that every principal minor of $B_{22} - B_{21}B_{11}^{-1}B_{12}$ is positive. An equivalent condition on B has been derived in Sickles and Schmidt (1978) and Schmidt (1981). The coherency condition is equivalent to the condition that all principal minors of B that involve at least the rows and columns containing B_{11} have the same sign. In many other simultaneous linear equation models with limited or qualitative endogenous variables, model coherency problems exist. A general analysis on coherency conditions, which cover many simultaneous equation qualitative variable models, simultaneous equation limited dependent variables models, and simultaneous disequilibrium market models, can be found in Gourieroux, Laffont and Monfort (1980). Even though the coherency conditions in Gourieroux et al. cover many important simultaneous equation models, their analysis has been limited to models with certain linear structures. Their results do not cover models with complicated nonlinear structures as in some of the consumer demand models.

4.2. Coherency conditions in consumer demand or production systems

The consumer demand or production systems with kink points (3.1.5) are essentially simultaneous nonlinear equation models with multivariate limited dependent variables. The model coherency problem is more complicated than the ones in the previous section. The practice of simply appending additive error terms to demand equations, derived from deterministic direct or indirect utility functions, may result in stochastic models which are not compatible with the utility maximization hypothesis. Stochastic demand systems consistent with the utility maximization hypothesis are likely to result if random terms are introduced into the underlying direct or indirect utility functions (see, e.g., McFadden, 1973, Burtless and Hausman, 1978, and Wales and Woodland, 1983, among others). The model is coherent if for every possible value of the disturbance vector ε, a unique vector of endogenous variables y is generated; and for every vector of endogenous variables in the sample space, there exists an ε vector that can generate the sample observation from the structural equations. For the consumer demand problem, the monotonicity and strict quasi-concavity properties of the utility function $U(y; \varepsilon)$ of y guarantees the existence of a unique demand vector for each ε vector. Satisfaction of the second coherency condition will depend on the functional form of the structural equations and the way that the stochastic elements are introduced in the utility maximization problem.

Models derived from flexible indirect utility functions might not satisfy the model coherency conditions without restrictions on parameter spaces of interest, because some of the flexible indirect utility functions did not satisfy globally concavity conditions. An example is the translog indirect utility function

$$H(v) = \sum_{j=1}^{m} \alpha_j \ln v_j + \tfrac{1}{2} \sum_{l=1}^{m} \sum_{j=1}^{m} \beta_{jl} \ln v_j \ln v_l \,, \tag{4.2.1}$$

where $v_j = p_j/M$, $j = 1, \ldots, m$, are income normalized prices, $\sum_{j=1}^{m} \alpha_j = -1$, and $\beta_{jl} = \beta_{lj}$ for symmetry. The Roy identity yields the notational budget share equations:

$$s_j^* = -\alpha_j - \sum_{l=1}^{m} \beta_{jl} \ln v_l \,, \quad j = 1, \ldots, m \,. \tag{4.2.2}$$

Consider a fixed vector v. Denote $z_j^*(v) = -\alpha_j - \sum_{l=1}^{m} \beta_{jl} \ln v_l$ and $D^*(v) = 1 - \sum_{j=1}^{m} \sum_{l=1}^{m} \beta_{jl} \ln v_l$. Let $s = (s_1, \ldots, s_m)$ be a vector of observable shares. With the specification that, for each j, α_j includes a random component ε_j with an unrestricted support, the share equations (4.2.2) will have additive errors. It is easy to see that, for each given vector (s, v), there exists a vector ε which will generate s given v as the optimal solution of the demand system. For the model with binding nonnegativity constraints, Soest and Kooreman (1990) derived sufficient conditions for this model to satisfy the remaining coherency condition – the uniqueness of solution condition. In terms of virtual price inequalities, the optimality of s is characterized by the following relations:

$$s_j = \frac{z_j^* + \sum_{l=1}^{m} \beta_{jl}(\ln v_l - \ln v_l^*)}{D^*(v) + \sum_{l=1}^{m} \sum_{k=1}^{m} \beta_{lk}(\ln v_l - \ln v_l^*)} \,, \quad j = 1, \ldots, m \,, \tag{4.2.3}$$

and

$$s \geq 0 \,, \quad v^* \leq v \,, \quad s'(v - v^*) = 0 \,, \tag{4.2.4}$$

where $v^* = (v_1^*, \ldots, v_m^*)$ is a vector of virtual prices at s. With $y_j = \ln v_j - \ln v_j^*$, $j = 1, \ldots, m$; $y = (y_1, \ldots, y_m)'$; and $e = (1, \ldots, 1)'$. Soest and Kooreman recognized that the coherency issue for (4.2.3) and (4.2.4) is the uniqueness of solution y satisfying the problem

$$y \geq 0 ,$$
$$(z^* + By)/(D^*(v) + y'Be) \geq 0 ,$$
$$y'(z^* + By) = 0 .$$
(4.2.5)

Since the indirect utility function H must be an increasing function of M, a necessary condition for the monotonicity property is that $D^*(v) > 0$ for each sample v. Under the additional restrictions that $Be \geq 0$, (4.2.5) simplifies to

$$z^* + By \geq 0 , \quad y \geq 0 ,$$
$$y'(z^* + By) = 0 .$$
(4.2.6)

The problem (4.2.6) is the complementarity problem. Hence the sufficient conditions for model coherency for this model are that B is a positive definite matrix, $Be \geq 0$, and $D^*(v) > 0$ for all v. Soest and Kooreman pointed out that these sufficient conditions imply also concavity of the (implicit) direct utility function on the feasible region $S = \{s: s \geq 0 \text{ and } s'e \leq 1\}$. The concave direct utility function attains a unique maximum on S, and hence the model is coherent.

One can see from the above analysis that the model coherency conditions are specific for each functional specification of the utility function. For utility functions that do not possess the globally concavity property, one has to restrict the relevant parameter space so that the concavity property can be satisfied on the restricted parameter space. For the model with a quadratic utility function, model coherency conditions have been derived in Ransom (1987). The quadratic utility function is not monotonically increasing everywhere on the commodity space, but it is globally concave. By restricting the demand quantities to satisfy budget constraints, the Kuhn–Tuckner conditions are necessary but not sufficient to characterize the maximum solution. However, the likelihood function derived from the Kuhn–Tuckner conditions is a well-defined function, because there is a well-defined mapping from the stochastic element in the utility function to the solution vector of quantities. The model is a coherent stochastic model. The only unsatisfactory problem with this utility function is the possibility that, for some sample observations, the property of nonsatiated preference would not be satisfied, and the utility maximization hypothesis might be violated at those points. The quadratic utility function model has been used in empirical studies in Wales and Woodland (1983) on the consumption of foods for Australian households, and in Amemiya, Saito and Shimono (1987) for household investment patterns in Japan.

5. Estimation methods

With parametric distributional assumptions on stochastic elements in a model, an asymptotically efficient estimation method is the classical maximum likelihood method. For the univariate tobit model with normal disturbances, Amemiya (1973) has proved under mild regularity conditions that the tobit maximum likelihood estimator is consistent and asymptotically normal. Since there are no irregularities for the multivariate generalizations, Amemiya's analysis can be generalized to establish the consistency and asymptotic normality properties of the maximum likelihood estimators for the various multivariate tobit models. The difficulty of the maximum likelihood approach is the computational complexity of the multivariate normal probability functions. Gaussian quadrature formulas (see Stroud and Secrest, 1966) become computationally inefficient for multivariate normal probability functions with dimensions larger than three or four. This difficulty is well-known in both the econometrics and statistics literatures. In this section, we will survey some other estimation methods that are computationally tractable, even though they may be less efficient.

5.1. Truncated moments and recursive formulas

The truncated moments of the dependent variables can be used for estimation and specification testing of the models. Consider an m-dimensional multivariate regression model with a normal disturbance,

$$y^* = \alpha x + \varepsilon^*, \qquad (5.1.1)$$

where x is a $k \times 1$ exogenous variable vector; y^* is an $m \times 1$ vector of unobservable dependent variables; α is an $m \times k$ matrix of unknown coefficients; and ε^* is $N(0, \Sigma)$ where Σ is a positive definite matrix. The sample y is observed with $y = y^*$ if and only if $y_j^* > 0$, $j = 1, \ldots, m$. The first two moments and the moment generating function of the truncated multivariate normal distribution have been derived in Tallis (1961). Amemiya (1974) has found an interesting relationship between these two moments and has suggested an instrumental variable estimation method without computing multivariate normal probabilities. Specifically, conditional on $y^* > 0$,

$$\sigma^{i'} E(y_i y) = 1 + \sigma^{i'} \alpha x E(y_i), \quad i = 1, \ldots, m. \qquad (5.1.2)$$

This relation forms the moment equations for Amemiya's instrumental variable estimation of the model. Similar relations are also available for some of the more complicated multivariate tobit models. For the models with only some of the dependent variables truncated, relations between the first two moments of the truncated multivariate normal distribution have been derived in Sickles and Schmidt (1978) and Lee (1979). Further generalization to multivariate models with doubly truncated normal distributions is in Lee (1983). The derivations of the relations between the first two moments in Amemiya (1974) and the subsequent generalizations in Sickles and Schmidt (1978) and Lee (1979) are rather complicated and tedious. Explicit expressions for the first two truncated moments are first derived, and the relationship between these two moments are then discovered. A much simpler and systematic approach is based on a differential equation characterization of the multivariate normal distribution in Lee (1983). This approach is motivated by the pioneer work of Cohen (1951) for the univariate Pearson family of truncated distributions.

Consider the generalization of the multivariate regression model in (5.1.1) to the case that the sample y can be observed if and only if it satisfies the following conditions (i) and (ii):

(i) $0 \leq y^*_{G+j} \leq k_{G+j}$, $j = 1, \ldots, J$,

(ii) $0 \leq y^*_{G+J+l} \leq \infty$, $l = 1, \ldots, m - G - J$,

where $y^* = (y^*_1, \ldots, y^*_G, y^*_{G+1}, \ldots, y^*_{G+J}, y^*_{G+J+1}, \ldots, y^*_m)'$, $0 \leq G \leq m$, and $0 \leq G + J \leq m$. Depending on the values of G, J, and k_{G+j}, this model contains many special cases. For this general model, many relations among the moments in addition to the first two can be derived from the differential equation approach:

(1) For the equations $i \in \{1, \ldots, G\}$,

$$\sigma^{i'} E(y) = \sigma^{i'} \alpha x, \quad l = 0, \tag{5.1.3}$$

and

$$\sigma^{i'} E(y^l_i y) = \sigma^{i'} \alpha x E(y^l_i) + l E(y^{l-1}_i), \quad l = 1, 2, \ldots. \tag{5.1.4}$$

(2) $i \in \{G + J + 1, \ldots, m\}$. For these equations,

$$\sigma^{i'} E(y^l_i y) = \sigma^{i'} \alpha x E(y^l_i) + l E(y^{l-1}_i), \quad l = 1, 2, \ldots. \tag{5.1.5}$$

(3) $i \in \{G + 1, \ldots, G + J\}$. In this case,

$$\sigma^{i'} E(y^l_i y) = k_i \sigma^{i'} E(y^{l-1}_i y) + \sigma^{i'} \alpha x [E(y^l_i) - k_i E(y^{l-1}_i)] \\ + l E(y^{l-1}_i) - k_i (l - 1) E(y^{l-2}_i), \quad l = 2, 3, \ldots. \tag{5.1.6}$$

These recursive formulas are ready to be generalized to models with distributions which can be characterized by differential equations in the form $\partial \ln f(u)/\partial u = Q_1(u)/Q_2(u)$, where $Q_1(u)$ and $Q_2(u)$ are finite order polynomials. Apparently, this will include the family of multivariate distributions of Van Uven (see, e.g., Elderton and Johnson, 1969) which generalizes the univariate Pearson family of distributions to the multivariate case. The multivariate normal distribution is an important member of the Van Uven family. Many popular multivariate distributions belong to this family.

5.2. Truncated moments on a simplex

In the previous sections, the moments are derived for truncated distributions defined on rectangles. For consumer demand models with share equations, the truncated distribution of all positive shares will be defined on a simplex. Recursive relations for the truncated moments on a simplex can be derived. Consider a multivariate normal variable y^* of dimension m with mean μ and covariance matrix Ω, such that $\Sigma_{j=1}^{m} y_j^* = 1$, and the truncated distribution of y, where $y = y^*$ with $y_j^* > 0$, $j = 1, \ldots, m$. Since the sum of the components of y^* is unity, y_m^* is a linear function of $y_1^*, \ldots, y_{m-1}^*$. Let $\bar{\mu} = (\mu_1, \ldots, \mu_{m-1})$, and let Σ be the covariance matrix of $(y_1^*, \ldots, y_{m-1}^*)$, which is the submatrix of Ω with the last row and column deleted. The truncated density of $\bar{y}$, where $\bar{y} = (y_1, \ldots, y_{m-1})$, is

$$f(\bar{y}) = \frac{g(\bar{y})}{P}, \tag{5.2.1}$$

where

$$g(\bar{y}) = (2\pi)^{-(m-1)/2} |\Sigma|^{-1/2} \exp\{-\tfrac{1}{2}(\bar{y} - \bar{u})'\Sigma^{-1}(\bar{y} - \bar{\mu})\},$$

and

$$P = \int_0^1 \int_0^{1-y_1} \cdots \int_0^{1-\Sigma_{i=1}^{m-2} y_i} g(\bar{y}) \, dy_{m-1} \cdots dy_1.$$

The density function in (5.2.1) satisfies the differential equation

$$\frac{\partial f(\bar{y})}{\partial y_{m-1}} = -\sigma^{(m-1)'}(\bar{y} - \bar{\mu})f(\bar{y}),$$

where $\sigma^{(m-1)}$ is the $(m-1)$-th column of Σ. It follows that

$$y_j^r y_{m-1}^s \left(1 - \sum_{i=1}^{m-1} y_i\right)^l \frac{\partial f(\bar{y})}{\partial y_{m-1}}$$

$$= -\sigma^{(m-1)'}(\bar{y} - \bar{\mu})y_j^r y_{m-1}^s \left(-\sum_{i=1}^{m-1} y_i\right)^l f(\bar{y}),$$

for $r \geq 0$, $s \geq 1$, $l \geq 1$, and $j \neq m - 1$. By the integration by parts,

$$\int_0^{1-\Sigma_{i=1}^{m-2} y_i} y_{m-1}^s \left(1 - \sum_{i=1}^{m-1} y_i\right)^l \frac{\partial f(\bar{y})}{\partial y_{m-1}} \, dy_{m-1}$$

$$= -s \int_0^{1-\Sigma_{i=1}^{m-2} y_i} y_{m-1}^{s-1} \left(1 - \sum_{i=1}^{m-1} y_i\right)^l f(\bar{y}) \, dy_{m-1}$$

$$+ l \int_0^{1-\Sigma_{i=1}^{m-2} y_i} y_{m-1}^s \left(1 - \sum_{i=1}^{m-1} y_i\right)^{l-1} f(\bar{y}) \, dy_{m-1}.$$

Therefore,

$$lE(y_j^r y_{m-1}^s y_m^{l-1}) - sE(y_j^r y_{m-1}^{s-1} y_m^l)$$
$$= E(y_j^r y_{m-1}^s y_m^l)\sigma^{(m-1)\prime} \bar{\mu} - E(y_j^r y_{m-1}^s y_m^l \bar{y}')\sigma^{(m-1)}, \qquad (5.2.2)$$

where $y_m = 1 - \Sigma_{j=1}^{m-1} y_j$ and the expectations are taken with respect to the truncated density $f(\bar{y})$ in (5.2.1). As every variable can be treated as the $(m-1)$-th variable, (5.2.2) can be generalized to

$$lE(y_j^r y_i^s y_m^{l-1}) - sE(y_j^r y_i^{s-1} y_m^l)$$
$$= E(y_j^r y_i^s y_m^l)(\sigma^i)' \bar{\mu} - E(y_j^r y_i^s y_m^l \bar{y}')\sigma^i, \qquad (5.2.3)$$

for $j \neq i$ for $i, j = 1, \ldots, m-1$, $r \geq 0$, $s \geq 1$, and $l \geq 1$.

5.3. Instrumental variable estimation

The recursive relations among the moments of the multivariate normal distribution and the Van Uven family of multivariate distributions can be used for the estimation of the regression coefficients of the multivariable tobit models. An instrumental variable estimation (IV) procedure has been introduced in Amemiya (1974) for the estimation of a multivariate regression model with all its dependent variables being truncated normal. The Amemiya IV procedure has utilized only the relation between the first two moments of the truncated multivariate normal distribution. With the recursive formulas in the previous sections, his procedure can be generalized to the estimation of more complicated models and the consumer demand models with nonnegativity constraints. The efficiency of IV estimators may also be improved by using more moments equations. For an example, (5.1.8) implies

$$\sigma^{i'} y_{it}^l y_t = \sigma^{i'} \alpha x y_{it}^l + l y_{it}^{l-1} + \eta_{it}^{(l)}, \quad l = 1, 2, \ldots, \ i = 1, \ldots, G, \quad (5.3.1)$$

where $E(\eta_{it}^{(l)} | x) = 0$. (5.3.1) can be rearranged into

$$y_{it}^{l+1} = \frac{1}{\sigma^{ii}} l y_{it}^{l-1} + \frac{1}{\sigma^{ii}} \sigma^{i'} \alpha x y_{it}^l - \frac{1}{\sigma^{ii}} \sum_{j \neq i}^m \sigma^{ij} y_{it}^l y_{jt} + \frac{1}{\sigma^{ii}} \eta_{it}^{(l)},$$

for $l = 1, 2, \ldots$, and $i = 1, \ldots, G$. These moment equations provide the structural equations for estimation by the instrumental variable method. Instrumental variables can be constructed as functions of x in the model. These equations can also be estimated by the generalized method of moments (GMM) in Hansen (1982). Some of the moment equations can be used for estimation, and some of the remaining equations can be used for model specification tests (Newey, 1985). The instrumental variable method is computationally simple in that the computation of truncated multivariate probabilities can be completely avoided. However, with samples of moderate or small sizes, this procedure may be rather inefficient as evidences provided by a Monte

Carlo study in Warner (1976) show for the univariate tobit model. An empirical application of the instrumental variable method to a household labor supplies and commodity demands model is in Blundell and Walker (1982).

5.4. Amemiya's least squares estimation of linear simultaneous equation models

Amemiya (1978, 1979) introduced a general method for the estimation of structural parameters from reduced form parameters in linear simultaneous equation systems. The method is a two-stage method. The reduced form parameters of the model are estimated by some consistent methods. The structural parameters are then estimated by the least squares or generalized least squares methods. The Amemiya method is applicable to the estimation of the tobit simultaneous equation models in (2.1.1) and (2.3.1).

As an illustration, consider the model (2.3.1),

$$y^* = y^*B + x\Gamma + \varepsilon , \qquad (5.4.1)$$

where y^* is a $1 \times m$ row vector of (latent) endogenous variables and x is a $1 \times K$ vector of exogenous variables. The reduced form equations are

$$y^* = x\Pi + u , \qquad (5.4.2)$$

where $\Pi = \Gamma(I - B)^{-1}$ and $x = \varepsilon(I - B)^{-1}$. For this model, each equation in the reduced form system can be estimated by some conventional methods, such as the tobit likelihood method, depending on the distribution of the disturbances. Without any parametric distributional assumption, various semiparametric methods are also available (e.g., Powell, 1984). Consider the first structural equation

$$y_1^* = y_{(1)}^* \beta_1 + x_1 \gamma + \varepsilon_1 , \qquad (5.4.3)$$

where $y_{(1)}^*$ is an m_1-dimensional subvector consisting of endogenous variables other than y_1^* in y^*, and x_1 is a k_1-dimensional subvector of x. Let J_1 and J_2 be selection matrices such that $y_{(1)}^* = y^* J_1$ and $x_1 = x J_2$. It follows that

$$\begin{aligned} y_1^* &= y^* J_1 \beta_1 + x J_2 \gamma_1 + \varepsilon_1 \\ &= x(\Pi J_1 + J_2 \gamma_1) + u_1 , \end{aligned} \qquad (5.4.4)$$

where $u_1 = u J_1 \beta_1 + \varepsilon_1$. Let π_1 denote the first column of Π. Comparing (5.4.2) with (5.4.4),

$$\pi_1 = \Pi J_1 \beta_1 + J_2 \gamma_1 . \qquad (5.4.5)$$

Let $\hat{\Pi}$ be the first stage estimate of Π. Amemiya's method is to apply either a least squares procedure or a generalized least squares (AGLS) procedure to estimate the following equation:

$$\hat{\pi}_1 = \hat{\pi}J_1\beta_1 + J_2\gamma_1 + \xi_1 , \tag{5.4.6}$$

where

$$\xi_1 = \hat{\pi}_1 - \pi_1 - (\hat{\Pi} - \Pi)J_1\beta_1 .$$

Suppose that $\sqrt{n}\xi_1 \xrightarrow{D} N(0, \Omega_1)$. Let $\hat{\Omega}_1$ be a consistent estimate of Ω_1. The AGLS estimator $\hat{\theta}$ of $\theta = (\beta_1', \gamma_1')'$ is derived from

$$\min_{\beta_1, \gamma_1} (\hat{\pi}_1 - \hat{\Pi}J_1\beta_1 - J_2\gamma_1)' \hat{\Omega}_1^{-1} (\hat{\pi}_1 - \hat{\Pi}J_1\beta_1 - J_2\gamma_1) . \tag{5.4.7}$$

The Amemiya least squares estimation is

$$\min_{\beta_1, \gamma_1} (\hat{\pi}_1 - \hat{\Pi}J_1\beta_1 - J_2\gamma_1)'(\hat{\pi}_1 - \hat{\Pi}J_1\beta_1 - J_2\gamma_1) , \tag{5.4.8}$$

without weighting. Under some general regularity conditions, Amemiya (1979) has shown that the estimators are consistent and asymptotically normal. The generalized least squares estimator is more efficient relative to the least squares estimator. The asymptotic distributions will depend on the asymptotic distributions of the reduced form estimates.

The generalized least squares estimators are asymptotically efficient relative to many conventional two-stage estimators. For the estimation of the model (5.4.1), a two-stage estimator $\hat{\theta}_1$ of $\theta_1 = (\beta_1, \gamma_1)$ has been proposed by Nelson and Olsen (1978). Let $\hat{\Pi}$ be a tobit estimator of Π in (5.4.2), i.e., each reduced form equation is estimated by a tobit maximum likelihood method. Let $\hat{\Pi}_1 = \hat{\Pi}J_1$. With an independent sample of size n, the two-stage estimator $\hat{\theta}_1$ is derived by maximizing the function $\ln L_1$, where

$$\ln L_1 = \sum_{i=1}^{n} \left\{ -\tfrac{1}{2}I_i \ln(2\pi\sigma^2) - \frac{1}{2\sigma^2} I_i[y_{1i} - (x_i\hat{\Pi}_1)\beta_1 - x_{1i}\gamma_1]^2 \right.$$
$$\left. + (1 - I_i) \ln[1 - \Phi(\{(x_i\hat{\Pi}_1)\beta_1 + x_{1i}\gamma_1\}/\sigma)] \right\} ,$$

where I is a dichotomous indicator with $I = 1$ if $y^* > 0$, and Φ is the standard normal distribution. The asymptotic distribution of $\hat{\theta}_1$ has been derived in Nelson and Olsen (1978). Amemiya (1979) showed that the AGLS estimator is asymptotically efficient relative to the Nelson and Olsen two-stage estimator. For many simultaneous equation models with qualitative and limited dependent variables, the AGLS method provides relatively more efficient estimators than several two-stage estimators (Amemiya, 1978, 1983; Lee, 1981; and Newey, 1987). In addition to efficient estimation of structural parameters, the AGLS method is also valuable for providing a goodness-of-fit test statistic. Lee (1992) has shown that the AGLS method is a minimum chi-square estimation method. The multiplication of the minimized objective function by the sample size n, i.e.,

$$n(\hat{\pi}_1 - \hat{\Pi}J_1\hat{\beta}_1 - J_2\hat{\gamma}_1)'\hat{\Omega}_1^{-1}(\hat{\pi}_1 - \hat{\Pi}J_1\hat{\beta}_1 - J_2\hat{\gamma}_1)$$

is asymptotically chi-square distributed with $k - m_1 - k_1$ degrees of freedom. This statistic provides a test statistic for the test of overidentification. $k - m_1 - k_1$ is the degree of overidentification of the structural equation (5.4.3). Amemiya's method described above is a limited information estimation method. For the estimation of the classical linear simultaneous equation model, the AGLS estimator is exactly the familiar Theil two-stage least squares estimator (Amemiya, 1978). Amemiya's method can be easily generalized to estimate the full system of structural equations. An empirical application of the Amemiya procedure to estimate a simultaneous equation model on health and wage is in Lee (1982).

5.5. Estimation of consumer demand models

Consumer demand model with kink points are nonlinear simultaneous equation models. Estimation of such models becomes more complicated. Multivariate normal probabilities do not have closed form expressions and are known to be too complicated to be evaluated effectively by numerical integration methods unless the dimension is small (see, e.g., Dutt, 1976). Wales and Woodland (1983) and Lee and Pitt (1987) have estimated only three goods models, because with more than three goods their models involve multiple numerical integrals. To overcome such difficulty, a possible approach is to consider stochastic specifications which are relatively restrictive but capture reasonable correlations due to individual specific error components. When the errors are either independent or their dependence has the one- or two-factor analytic structure, the probabilities can be effectively evaluated by some numerical approximation or numerical integration methods. For the one-factor analytic structure, the multivariate probabilities can be written as a univariate integral of a product of univariate normal probabilities, which can be evaluated effectively by Gaussian quadrature methods (see, e.g., Butler and Moffit, 1982). In the microeconometric literature, such strategy is used quite often for model specifications. The conditional logit model in McFadden (1973) is specified by assuming that the disturbances in the discrete choice models are iid with a Gumbel type distribution. Such a strategy will also be useful for the specification and estimation of consumer demand or production models with kink points. Examples are in Lee and Pitt (1986b).

Consider the problem of consumer demand with binding nonnegativity constraints. Let $V(y)$ be a deterministic utility function which satisfies the classical monotonicity and strict concavity properties. A possible way of introducing stochastic components into the model is to introduce additive random components in the utility function, similarly, to the approach in Wales and Woodland (1983). A random utility specification consistent with monotonicity and strict concavity is $U(y^*; \varepsilon) = V(y^*) + \Sigma_{i=1}^{m} e^{\varepsilon_i} W_i(y_i^*)$, where $W_i(y_i^*)$, $i = 1, \ldots, m$, are also strictly increasing and strictly concave functions. Computational tractability can be achieved by assuming that either e_i, $i = 1, \ldots, m$, are mutually independent or conditional on ε_m, ε_i, $i = 1, \ldots, m - 1$, are conditionally independent. The latter case covers the popular error component specification in panel data models. Consider the general demand pattern with demand vector $y = (0, \ldots, 0, y_{l+1}, \ldots, y_m)$, where the first l goods are zero and the remaining goods are positive. The virtual prices at y are

$$\xi_j = \frac{v_m \left[\dfrac{\partial V(y)}{\partial y_j} + e^{\varepsilon_j} \dfrac{\partial W_j(y)}{\partial y_j} \right]}{\dfrac{\partial V(y)}{\partial y_m} + e^{\varepsilon_m} \dfrac{\partial W_m(y)}{\partial y_m}}, \quad j = 1, \ldots, m - 1.$$

The virtual price conditions that characterize the optimality of y are

$$e^{\varepsilon_j} \leq \frac{\left\{ \dfrac{v_j}{v_m} \left[\dfrac{\partial V(y)}{\partial y_m} + e^{\varepsilon_m} \dfrac{\partial W_m(y)}{\partial y_m} \right] - \dfrac{\partial V(y)}{\partial y_j} \right\}}{\dfrac{\partial W_j(y)}{\partial y_j}}, \quad j = 1, \ldots, l,$$

$$(5.5.1)$$

and

$$e^{\varepsilon_k} = \frac{\left\{ \dfrac{v_k}{v_m} \left[\dfrac{\partial V(y)}{\partial y_m} + e^{\varepsilon_m} \dfrac{\partial W_m(y)}{\partial y_m} \right] - \dfrac{\partial V(y)}{\partial y_k} \right\}}{\dfrac{\partial W_k(y)}{\partial y_k}},$$

$$k = l + 1, \ldots, m - 1.$$
$$(5.5.2)$$

Since it is necessary that

$$\frac{v_j}{v_m} \left[\frac{\partial V(y)}{\partial y_m} + e^{\varepsilon_m} \frac{\partial W_m(y)}{\partial y_m} \right] - \frac{\partial V(y)}{\partial y_j} > 0 \quad \text{for all } j = 1, \ldots, m - 1,$$

feasible values of ε_m are determined by $\varepsilon_m > R(y)$, where

$$R(y) = \ln \left\{ \max \left[0, \max_{j=1,\ldots,m-1} \frac{\left(\dfrac{v_m}{v_j} \dfrac{\partial V(y)}{\partial y_j} - \dfrac{\partial V(y)}{\partial y_m} \right)}{\dfrac{\partial W_m(y)}{\partial y_m}} \right] \right\},$$

and $\ln 0 = -\infty$ as a conventional rule. As $y_m = (1 - v_{l+1} y_{l+1} - \cdots - v_{m-1} y_{m-1}) / v_m$, given a conditional distribution of $\varepsilon_{l+1}, \ldots, \varepsilon_{m-1}$, conditional on ε_m, (5.5.2) implies a conditional distribution for $y_{l+1}, \ldots, y_{m-1}$. Let f_j and F_j be, respectively, the density function and the distribution function of ε_j conditional on ε_m. Denote

$$\varepsilon_j(y, \varepsilon_m) = \ln\left\{\frac{v_j}{v_m}\left[\frac{\partial V(y)}{\partial y_m} + e^{\varepsilon_m}\frac{\partial W_m(y)}{\partial y_m}\right] - \frac{\partial V(y)}{\partial y_j}\right\} - \ln\frac{\partial W_j(y)}{\partial y_j},$$

$$j = 1, \ldots, m - 1.$$

Conditional on ε_m, the joint density function of $y_{l+1}, \ldots, y_{m-1}$ is $\Pi_{j=l+1}^{m-1} f_j(\varepsilon_j(y, \varepsilon_m))|J(y, \varepsilon_m)|$, where $J(y, \varepsilon_m)$ is the Jacobian of the transformation from $\varepsilon_{l+1}^*, \ldots, \varepsilon_{m-1}^*$ to $y_{l+1}, \ldots, y_{m-1}$. Conditional on ε_m, the probability that (5.5.1) holds is $\Pi_{j=1}^{l} F_j(\varepsilon_j(y, \varepsilon_m))$. Hence the likelihood function for y is

$$L(y) = \int_{R(y)}^{\infty} \sum_{j=1}^{l} F_j(\varepsilon_j(y, \varepsilon_m)) \prod_{j=l+1}^{m-1} f_j(\varepsilon_j(y, \varepsilon_m))|J(y, \varepsilon_m)|f_m(\varepsilon_m)\,d\varepsilon_m.$$

With an independent sample of size n, the log likelihood function for the whole sample is $L(y_1, \ldots, y_n) = \Pi_{i=1}^{n} L(y_i)$. The likelihood function is computationally tractable as it involves effectively a single integral for each sample observation. The integral can be evaluated effectively by a Gaussian quadrature formula (Stroud and Secrest, 1966).

The above approach is applicable to models with the specification of a direct utility function, but cannot be easily extended to the dual approach, which specifies an indirect utility or a cost function. A specification, which may be useful for both direct or indirect approaches, is based on a scaling method. The scaling method is a familiar method for introducing consumer's characteristics into demand systems, and it is also used to introduce a consumer's subjective evaluation of quality of goods into the utility function. The scaling procedure appends multiplicatively random terms to the consumption vector y in the utility function. Let W be a strictly increasing and concave function. A random utility function can be specified as $U(y; \varepsilon) = W(e^{\varepsilon_1}y_1, \ldots, e^{\varepsilon_m}y_m)$, where, conditional on ε_m, ε_j, $j = 1, \ldots, m - 1$, are mutually independent. Corresponding to this utility function, the indirect utility function $V(v; \varepsilon)$ has the form $V(v; \varepsilon) = H(v_1 e^{-\varepsilon_1}, \ldots, v_m e^{-\varepsilon_m})$, where $H(p) = \max\{W(y^*) \mid p'y^* = 1\}$. The notional demand system corresponding to $V(v; \varepsilon)$ is $y_j = D_j(v_1 e^{-\varepsilon_1}, \ldots, v_m e^{-\varepsilon_m})e^{-\varepsilon_j}$, $j = 1, \ldots, m$. Consider $y = (0, \ldots, 0, y_{l+1}, \ldots, y_m)$. The virtual prices ξ_j, $j = 1, \ldots, l$, for the first l goods at y are characterized by the relations

$$0 = D_j(\xi_1 e^{-\varepsilon_1}, \ldots, \xi_l e^{-\varepsilon_l}, v_{l+1} e^{-\varepsilon_{l+1}}, \ldots, v_m e^{-\varepsilon_m})e^{-\varepsilon_j},$$

$$j = 1, \ldots, l, \tag{5.5.3}$$

$$y_k = D_k(\xi_1 e^{-\varepsilon_1}, \ldots, \xi_l e^{-\varepsilon_l}, v_{l+1} e^{-\varepsilon_{l+1}}, \ldots, v_m e^{-\varepsilon_m})e^{-\varepsilon_k},$$

$$k = l + 1, \ldots, m.$$

Suppose that the factors $\xi_j e^{-\varepsilon_j}$, $j = 1, \ldots, l$, can be solved from the first set of equations in (5.5.3) as functions of $(v_{l+1}e^{-\varepsilon_{l+1}}, \ldots, v_m e^{-\varepsilon_m})$,

$$\xi_j e^{-\varepsilon_j} = h_j(v_{l+1}e^{-\varepsilon_{l+1}}, \ldots, v_m e^{-\varepsilon_m}), \quad j = 1, \ldots, l. \tag{5.5.4}$$

Substituting (5.5.4) into the second set of equations in (5.5.3),

$$y_j = D_j(h_1, \ldots, h_l, v_{l+1}e^{-\varepsilon_{l+1}}, \ldots, v_m e^{-\varepsilon_m})e^{-\varepsilon_j},$$
$$j = l+1, \ldots, m-1, \tag{5.5.5}$$

which involves only the random variables $\varepsilon_{l+1}, \ldots, \varepsilon_m$. The virtual price inequalities $\xi_j \leq v_j$, $j = 1, \ldots, l$, become $\varepsilon_j \leq \ln v_j - \ln h_j(v_{l+1}e^{-\varepsilon_{l+1}}, \ldots, v_m e^{-\varepsilon_m})$, $j = 1, \ldots, l$. Suppose that $\varepsilon_{l+1}, \ldots, \varepsilon_{m-1}$ can be solved from (5.5.5) as functions of $y_1, \ldots, y_{m-1}$ and ε_m, denote these functions as $\varepsilon_j(y, \varepsilon_m)$, $j = l+1, \ldots, m-1$. Denote also $\varepsilon_j(y, \varepsilon_m) = \ln v_j - \ln h_j(v_{l+1}e^{-\varepsilon_{l+1}}, \ldots, v_m e^{-\varepsilon_m})$ for $j = 1, \ldots, l$. Let $S(y)$ be the range of possible values of ε_m for the given y. The likelihood function for y is

$$L(y) = \int_{S(y)} \prod_{j=1}^{l} F_j(\varepsilon_j(y, \varepsilon_m)) \prod_{j=l+1}^{m-1} f_j(\varepsilon_j(y, \varepsilon_m))|J(y, \varepsilon_m)|f_m(\varepsilon_m) \, d\varepsilon_m.$$

The likelihood function involves a single integral and is computationally tractable. The limitation of this approach relies on the tractability of solving the functions h_j in (5.5.4) and ε_j, $j = l+1, \ldots, m-1$, from (5.5.5). For some functional specifications, these might not be an easy task. Several other stochastic specifications, which provide computationally tractable likelihood functions, can be found in Lee and Pitt (1986b). Some of these methods have been used in an empirical study of a seven-goods model in Lee and Pitt (1986b).

5.6. Estimation with simulation

In a recent development in McFadden (1989), methods of simulated moments (MSM) are introduced. With methods of simulated moments, the need for numerical integration can be avoided.

To illustrate the method of simulated moments for the estimation of multivariate tobit models, consider the latent regression model

$$y_i^* = x_i\beta + u_i, \quad i = 1, \ldots, n, \tag{5.6.1}$$

where u is an m-multivariate $N(0, \Omega)$ variable and is independent of x. The observed dependent variables are y_i, $i = 1, \ldots, n$, where $y_i = (y_{1i}, \ldots, y_{mi})$ with $y_{ji} = \max(0, y_{ji}^*)$. Let $f(u; \Omega)$ denote the multivariate normal density of u. Define $I_i = \{j \mid y_{ji} = 0, j = 1, \ldots, m\}$ and $J_i = \{j \mid y_{ji} > 0, j = 1, \ldots, m\}$. With conformably conditional distributions and partitioned matrices,

$$f(y^* - x\beta; \Omega) = f(y_I^* - \mu_I; \bar{\Omega}_{II}) \cdot f(y_J^* - x_J\beta; \Omega_{JJ}), \tag{5.6.2}$$

where $\mu_I = x_I\beta + \Omega_{IJ}\Omega_{JJ}^{-1}(y_J^* - x_J\beta)$ and $\tilde{\Omega}_{II} = \Omega_{II} - \Omega_{IJ}\Omega_{JJ}^{-1}\Omega_{JI}$. The first component on the right-hand side of (5.6.2) is the conditional normal density of the subvector y_I^* of y^* conditional on the subvector $y_J{}^*$, and the second component is the marginal normal density of y_J^*. Let $\delta(K, I)$ be a dichotomous indicator such that $\delta(K, I) = 1$ if and only if $K = I$. For any subset $K \subseteq I$, define $A(K, I) = \{y_I^* \mid y_K^* \leq 0, \ y_{I-K}^* \geq 0\}$, and let $I_{A(K,I)}$ be the indicator function of $A(K, I)$. The score of an observation is

$$
\frac{\partial \ln l(\theta; y_i)}{\partial \theta}
$$

$$
= \frac{\partial \ln f(y_{J_i} - x_J\beta; \Omega_{J_iJ_i})}{\partial \theta} + \mathrm{E}_\theta\left[\frac{\partial \ln f(y_I^* - \mu_I; \tilde{\Omega}_{II})}{\partial \theta} \ \middle| \ A(I_i, I_i) \right]
$$

$$
= \frac{\partial \ln f(y_{J_i} - x_J\beta; \Omega_{J_iJ_i})}{\partial \theta} + \sum_{K \subseteq I_i} [\delta(K, I_i) - \mathrm{E}_\theta(I_{A(K,I_i)})]
$$

$$
\cdot \mathrm{E}_\theta\left[\frac{\partial \ln f(y_I^* - \mu_I; \tilde{\Omega}_{II})}{\partial \theta} \ \middle| \ A(K, I_i) \right].
$$

The MSM estimation of Hajivassiliou and McFadden (1988) and McFadden (1989) replaces hard-to-compute terms in the above expressions with unbiased simulators. For the above score, as pointed out in Hajivassiliou and McFadden (1988), there are at least two ways to estimate the model. The first approach is to construct unbiased simulators of the conditional expectation

$$
\mathrm{E}_\theta\left[\frac{\partial \ln f(y_I^* - \mu_I; \tilde{\Omega}_{II})}{\partial \theta} \ \middle| \ A(I_i, I_i) \right] \quad \text{for each } i \, .
$$

The second method is to generate an unbiased simulator of $\mathrm{E}_\theta(I_{A(K,I)})$ and use any independent, not necessarily unbiased, simulator for

$$
\mathrm{E}_\theta\left[\frac{\partial \ln f(y_I^* - \mu_I; \tilde{\Omega}_{II})}{\partial \theta} \ \middle| \ A(K, I_i) \right].
$$

Several simulation procedures, which include the simple frequency method, the acceptance–rejection method, and importance sampling methods (see McFadden, 1989; and Hajivassiliou and McFadden, 1988), can be used to construct unbiased simulators. In general, the second method has the disadvantage of requiring evaluation at all K for which the simulator for $\mathrm{E}_\theta(I_{A(K, I)})$ is nonzero, but unbiased simulation of $\mathrm{E}_\theta(I_{A(K,I)})$ is much easier computationally than unbiased simulation of the conditional expectation of the first method.

The methods of simulated moments, which replace the hard-to-estimate components by some unbiased simulators, create additional errors in the score equations. The estimators of θ are in general inefficient relative to the classical maximum likelihood estimator. Asymptotically efficient simulators can be attained only at the expense of a large number of simulations such that the moment simulators become consistent estimators of the corresponding moments. The asymptotic distributions of the estimators have been derived in McFadden (1989) and McFadden and Hajivassiliou (1988). The asymptotic distributions of the estimators depend on constructed simulators. The details can be found in Hajivassiliou and McFadden (1988). An empirical application of these methods to the study of an external debt problems is in Hajivassiliou and McFadden (1988). The McFadden methods of simulated moments provide a new direction, which may render the estimation of complicated multivariate tobit models tractable.

6. Specification error tests

The classical maximum likelihood test, the Wald test, and the Lagrange multiplier test (LM or the efficient score test) are well-known testing procedures, which are useful for testing various model specification errors, such as heteroskedasticity, serial correlation, omitted variables, and exogeneity. Since the limited dependent variable models have rather complicated structures, the Lagrange multiplier test procedure has received the most attention as it requires only estimation of a model under the null hypothesis, which is, in many cases, simpler than the model under the alternative hypothesis. In the univariate limited dependent variable model, score tests for omitted variables, heteroskedasticity, and serially correlation have been derived in Lee and Maddala (1985), Robinson, Bera and Jarque (1985), Gourieroux, Monfort, Renault and Trognon (1987a), and Chesher and Irish (1987); and score tests for normality can be found in Bera, Jarque and Lee (1984). Some of the tests statistics have been generalized to the testing of multivariate models. In a bivariate context, Lee (1984) derives a test for normality, and Smith (1985) derives score tests for heteroskedasticity, nonnormality, and exogeneity. An exogeneity test has also been derived in Smith and Blundell (1986). Subsequently, Smith (1987) provides a generalization of the normality test to the general multivariate model. Since the principle and the derivation of Lagrange multiplier test statistics are rather simple and straightforward, most of these test statistics can be generalized as long as the null hypothesis can be nested in a model, which contains both the null and alternative hypotheses. The Lagrange multiplier test statistics are, in general, computationally simpler than the maximum likelihood test or the Wald test for such complicated models. The Lagrange multiplier test statistics can have simple interpretations for some cases.

As an illustration of the methodology, consider the testing of normality in an m-multivariate truncated regression model

$$y_j^* = x\beta_j - \sigma_j\varepsilon_j , \quad j = 1, \ldots, m ,$$

where ε_j, $j = 1, \ldots, m$, are normal with zero means, unit variances, and a correlation coefficient matrix R. The sample $y = (y_1, \ldots, y_m)$ is observed and equal to $y^* = (y_1^*, \ldots, y_m^*)$ if and only if $y_j^* > 0$ for all $j = 1, \ldots, m$. A normality test can be derived by expressing the multivariate normal distribution as a special case in a multivariate Edgeworth series expansion (Lee, 1984 and Smith, 1987). Let $f(\varepsilon_1, \ldots, \varepsilon_m)$ be the density function of $(\varepsilon_1, \ldots, \varepsilon_m)$, and let $b(\varepsilon_1, \ldots, \varepsilon_m)$ be the standardized multivariate normal distribution. The Edgeworth series expansion of f is

$$
f(\varepsilon_1, \ldots, \varepsilon_m) = b(\varepsilon_1, \ldots, \varepsilon_m)
$$

$$
+ \sum_{r_1 + \cdots + r_m \geq 3} A_{r_1 \cdots r_m} \frac{1}{r_1! \cdots r_m!} H_{r_1, \ldots, r_m}
$$

$$
\times (\varepsilon_1, \ldots, \varepsilon_m) b(\varepsilon_1, \ldots, \varepsilon_m) , \tag{6.1}
$$

where $H_{r_1, \ldots, r_m}(\varepsilon_1, \ldots, \varepsilon_m)$ are Hermite polynomials. The corresponding distribution F has the expansion

$$
F(a_1, \ldots, a_m) = B(a_1, \ldots, a_m) + \sum_{r_1 + \cdots + r_m \geq 3} A_{r_1 \cdots r_m} \frac{1}{r_1! \cdots r_m!}
$$

$$
\times \int_{-\infty}^{a_m} \cdots \int_{-\infty}^{a_1} H_{r_1, \ldots, r_m}(\varepsilon_1, \ldots, \varepsilon_m)
$$

$$
\times b(\varepsilon_1, \ldots, \varepsilon_m) \, d\varepsilon_1 \cdots d\varepsilon_m ,
$$

where B is the standard multivariate normal distribution function. The coefficients $A_{r_1, \ldots, r_m}$ are functions of the cumulants of $\varepsilon_1, \ldots, \varepsilon_m$. For practical purposes, the series expansion will be truncated to include only a finite number of terms. In Lee (1984) and Smith (1987), terms of order higher than four are truncated. When $A_{r_1, \ldots, r_m}$ are all zero, the distribution corresponds to the normal distribution. The log likelihood function for a random sample of size n for this truncated regression model is

$$
\ln L = \sum_{i=1}^{n} \left\{ -\frac{1}{2} \sum_{j=1}^{m} \ln \sigma_j^2 + \ln f\left(-\frac{y_1 - x\beta_1}{\sigma_1}, \ldots, -\frac{y_m - x\beta_m}{\sigma_m} \right) \right.
$$

$$
\left. - \ln F\left(\frac{x\beta_1}{\sigma_1}, \ldots, \frac{x\beta_m}{\sigma_m} \right) \right\} . \tag{6.2}
$$

The scores $\partial \ln L / \partial A_{r_1 \cdots r_m}$ with $A_{r_1 \cdots r_m}$ can be easily derived from (6.2). At the null hypothesis H_0 that the distribution is normally distributed, it is simplified to

$$
\frac{\partial \ln L}{\partial A_{r_1 \cdots r_m}} \bigg|_{H_0}
$$

$$
= \frac{1}{r_1! \cdots r_m!} \sum_{i=1}^{n} \left\{ H_{r_1, \ldots, r_m}\left(-\frac{y_{1i} - x_i\beta_1}{\sigma_1}, \ldots, -\frac{y_{mi} - x_i\beta_m}{\sigma_m} \right) \right.
$$

$$-\int_{-\infty}^{x_i\beta_m/\sigma_m} \cdots \int_{-\infty}^{x_i\beta_1/\sigma_1} \frac{H_{r_1,\ldots,r_m}(\varepsilon_1,\ldots,\varepsilon_m)b(\varepsilon_1,\ldots,\varepsilon_m)\,\mathrm{d}\varepsilon_1\cdots\mathrm{d}\varepsilon_m}{B(x_i\beta_1/\sigma_1,\ldots,x_i\beta_m/\sigma_m)}\Bigg\}.$$

(6.3)

The LM test (or $C(\alpha)$ test) is based on the testing of the difference between the (estimated) sample Hermit polynomials and the theoretically expected Hermit polynomials evaluated under the null.

The same approaches can be generalized to the censored tobit models. The article by Gourieroux et al. (1987a) provides a general discussion on the interpretation of LM test statistics in terms of estimated residuals. For graphical presentations of the residuals for diagnostics, see Chesher and Irish (1987) and Gourieroux et al. (1987b).

Acknowledgment

I appreciate having financial support from the National Science Foundation under grant SES-9010516 for my research. I am grateful to Professors C. R. Rao, S. Cosslett, and G. S. Maddala for their suggestions to improve the presentation of this article. Any remaining errors are solely of my own.

References

Amemiya, T. (1973). Regression analysis when the dependent variable is truncated normal. *Econometrica* **41**, 997–1016.
Amemiya, T. (1974). Multivariate regression and simultaneous equation models when the dependent variables are truncated normal. *Econometrica* **42**, 999–1012.
Amemiya, T. (1978). The estimation of a simultaneous equation generalized probit model. *Econometrica* **46**, 1193–1205.
Amemiya, T. (1979). The estimation of a simultaneous equation tobit model. *Internat. Econ. Rev.* 20, 169–181.
Amemiya, T. (1983). A comparison of the Amemiya GLS and the Lee–Maddala–Trost G2SLS in a simultaneous-equations tobit model. *J. Econometrics* **23**, 295–300.
Amemiya, T. (1984). Tobit models: A survey. *J. Econometrics* **24**, 3–61.
Amemiya, T., M. Saito and K. Shimono (1987). A study of household investment patterns in Japan: An Application of generalized tobit models. Technical report no. 29, Econometric Workshop, Stanford University, Stanford, CA.
Bera, A. K., C. M. Jarque and L.-F. Lee (1984). Testing the normality assumptions in limited dependent variable models. *Internat. Econ. Rev.* **25**, 563–578.
Blundell, R. W. and I. Walker (1982). Modelling the joint determination of household labour supplies and commodity demands. *Econ. J.* **92**, 351–364.
Burtless, G. and J. A. Hausman (1978). The effect of taxation on labor supply: Evaluating the Gary negative income-tax experiment. *J. Politic. Econ.* **86**, 1103–1130.

Butler, J. S. and R. Moffitt (1982). A computationally efficient quadrature procedure for the one-factor multinomial probit model. *Econometrica* **50**, 761–764.

Chesher, A. and M. Irish (1987). Residual analysis in the grouped and censored normal linear model. *Econometrics* **34**, 33–62.

Cohen, A. C. Jr. (1951). Estimation of parameters in truncated Pearson frequency distributions. *Ann. Math. Statist.* **22**, 256–265.

Dutt, J. E. (1976). Numerical aspects of multivariate normal probabilities in econometric models. *Ann. Econ. Social Measurement* **5**, 547–561.

Elderton, W. P. and N. J. Johnson (1969). *Systems of Frequency Curves*. Cambridge Univ. Press, New York.

Gale, D. and H. Nikaido (1965). The Jacobian matrix and global univalence of mappings. *Math. Ann.* **159**, 81–93.

Goldfeld, S. M. and R. Quandt (1975). Estimation in disequilibrium model and the value of information. *J Econometrics* **3**, 325–348.

Gourieroux, C., J. J. Laffont and A. Monfort (1980). Coherency conditions in simultaneous linear equation models with endogenous switching regimes. *Econometrica* **48**, 675–695.

Gourieroux, C., A. Monfort, E. Renault and A. Trognon (1987a). Generalised residuals. *J. Econometrics* **34**, 5–32.

Gourieroux, C., A. Monfort, E. Renault and A. Trognon (1987b). Simulated residuals. *J. Econometrics* **34**, 201–252.

Hajivassiliou, V. A. and D. McFadden (1988). External debt crises: Estimation by the method of simulated moments. Manuscript, Department of Economics, M.I.T., Cambridge, MA.

Hansen, L. P. (1982). Large sample properties of generalized method on moments estimators. *Econometrica* **50**, 1029–1954.

Hausman, J. A. (1985). The econometrics of nonlinear budget sets. *Econometrica* **53**, 1255–1282.

Hausman, J. A. and P. Ruud (1984). Family labour supply with taxes. *Amer. Econ. Rev.* **74**, 242–523.

Heckman, J. J. (1974). Shadow prices, market wages, and labor supply. *Econometrica* **42**, 679–694.

Heckman, J. J. (1978). Dummy endogenous variables in a simultaneous equation system. *Econometrica* **46**, 931–960.

Lee, L.-F. (1977). Multivariate regression and simultaneous equation models with some dependent variables truncated. Discussion Paper no. 79, Center for Economics Research, Department of Economics, University of Minnesota, Minneapolis, MN.

Lee, L.-F. (1979). On the first and second moments of the truncated multi-normal distribution and a simple estimator. *Econ. Lett.* **3**, 165–169.

Lee, L.-F. (1981). Simultaneous equations models with discrete and censored variables. In: C. F. Manski and D. McFadden, eds., *Structural Analysis of Discrete Data with Econometric Applications*. MIT Press, Cambridge, MA.

Lee, L.-F. (1982). Health and wages: A simultaneous equations model with multiple discrete indicators. *Internat. Econ. Rev.* **23**, 199–221.

Lee, L.-F. (1983). The determination of moments of the doubly truncated multivariate normal tobit model. *Econ. Lett.* **11**, 245–250.

Lee, L.-F. (1984). Tests for the bivariate normal distribution in econometric models with selectivity. *Econometrica* **52**, 843–863.

Lee, L.-F. (1992). Amemiya's generalized least squares and tests of overidentification in simultaneous equation models with qualitative or limited dependent variables. *Econ. Rev.* **11**, 319–328.

Lee, L.-F. and G. S. Maddala (1985). The common structure of tests for selectivity bias, serial correlation, heteroskedasticity and nonnormality in the tobit model. *Internat. Econ. Rev.* **26**, 1–20.

Lee, L.-F. and M. M. Pitt (1986a). Microeconometric demand systems with binding non-negativity constraints: The dual approach. *Econometrica* **54**, 1237–1242.

Lee, L.-F. and M. M. Pitt (1986b). Specification and estimation of consumer demand systems with many binding non-negativity constraints. Discussion Paper no. 236, Center for Economic Research, University of Minnesota, Minneapolis, MN.

Lee, L.-F. and M. M. Pitt (1987). Microeconometric models of rationing, imperfect markets, and nonnegativity constraints. *J. Econometrics* **36**, 89–110.

Maddala, G. S. (1983). *Limited-Dependent and Qualitative Variables in Econometrics*. Cambridge Univ. Press, Cambridge, MA.

McFadden, D. (1973). Conditional logit analysis of qualitative choice behavior. In: P. Zarembka, ed., *Frontier in Econometrics*, Academic Press, New York.

McFadden, D. (1989). A method of simulated moments for estimation of discrete response models without numerical integration. *Econometrica* **57**, 997–1026.

Moffitt, R. (1982). The tobit model, hours of work and institutional constraints. *Rev. Econ. Statist.* **64**, 510–515.

Nelson, F. and L. Olsen (1978). Specification and estimation of a simultaneous-equation model with limited dependent variables. *Internat. Econ. Rev.* **19**, 695–709.

Newey, W. K. (1985). Maximum likelihood specification testing and conditional moment tests. *Econometrica* **53**, 1047–1069.

Newey, W. K. (1987). Efficient estimation of limited dependent variable models with endogenous explanatory variables. *J. Econometrics* **36**, 231–250.

Powell, J. L. (1984). Least absolute deviations estimation for the censored regression model. *J. Econometrics* **25**, 303–325.

Pudney, S. E. (1987). Estimating engle curves: A generalization of the *P*-tobit model. *Finnish Econ. Papers* **1**.

Quandt, R. E. (1988). *The Econometrics of Disequilibrium*. Basil Blackwell, New York.

Ransom, M. R. (1987). A comment on consumer demand systems with binding non-negativity constraints. *J. Econometrics* **34**, 355–360.

Robinson, P. M., A. K. Bera and C. M. Jarque (1985). Tests for serial dependence in limited dependent variable models. *Internat. Econ. Rev.* **26**, 629–638.

Samuelson, H., R. M. Thrall and O. Wesler (1958). A partition theorem for euclidean *n*-space. *Proc. Amer. Math. Soc.* **9**, 805–807.

Schmidt, P. (1981). Constraints on the parameters of simultaneous tobit and probit models. In: C. Manski and D. McFadden, eds., *Structural Analysis of Discrete Data with Econometric Applications*, MIT Press, Cambridge, MA.

Sickles, R. C. and P. Schmidt (1978). Simultaneous equations models with truncated dependent variables: A simultaneous tobit model. *J. Econ. Business* **31**, 11–21.

Sickles, R. C., P. Schmidt and A. D. Witte (1979). An application of the simultaneous tobit model: A study of the determinants of criminal racidivism. *J. Econ. Business* **31**, 166–171.

Smith, R. J. (1985). Some tests of misspecification in bivariate limited dependent variable models. *Ann. INSEE* **59/60**, 97–123.

Smith, R. J. (1987). Testing the normality assumption in multivariate simultaneous limited dependent variable models. *J. Econometrics* **34**, 105–123.

Smith, R. J. and R. W. Blundell (1986). An exogeneity test for a simultaneous equation tobit model with an application to labour supply. *Econometrica* **54**, 679–685.

Soest, A. and P. Kooreman (1990). Coherency of the indirect translog demand system with binding nonnegativity constraints. *J. Econometrics* **44**, 391–400.

Stroud, A. H. and D. Secrest (1966). *Gaussian Quadrature Formulas*. Prentice-Hall, Englewood Cliffs, NJ.

Suits, D. (1955). An econometric model of the watermelon market. *J. Farm Econ.* **37**, 237–251.

Tallis, G. M. (1961). The moment generating function of the truncated multi-normal distributions. *J. Roy. Statist. Soc. Ser. B* **23**, 223–229.

Tobin, J. (1958). Estimation of relationships for limited dependent variables. *Econometrica* **26**, 24–26.

Wales, T. J. and A. D. Woodland (1983). Estimation of consumer demand systems with binding non-negativity constraints. *J. Econometrics* **21**, 263–285.

Waldman, D. M. (1981). An economic interpretation of parameter constraints in a simultaneous-equations model with limited dependent variables. *Internat. Econ. Rev.* **22**, 731–739.

Warner, D. (1976). A monte-carlo study of limited dependent variable estimation. In: S. M. Goldfeld and R. E. Quandt, eds., *Studies in Nonlinear Estimation*, Ballinger, Cambridge, MA, Chapter 10.

G. S. Maddala, C. R. Rao and H. D. Vinod, eds., *Handbook of Statistics, Vol. 11*
7

Estimation of Limited Dependent Variable Models under Rational Expectations

G. S. Maddala

1. Introduction

There is an enormous literature on the estimation of rational expectations models. In these models the underlying variables are all observed. There is, however, a large class of models where the variables under consideration are censored or truncated either because of governmental intervention or because of institutional constraints. The issue of how rational economic agents form their expectations in the presence of interventions in prices and quantities (price supports, quotas, target zones for exchange rates, and so on) is an important one for policy purposes. The present paper reviews the methodology of estimation for limited dependent variable models under rational expectations. The paper discusses rational expectations in the context of the different models outlined in Maddala (1983a): the tobit model, the friction model, the disequilibrium model, and the self-selection model.

2. The tobit model

The tobit model is the simplest limited dependent variable model. Its basic version is given by

$$
y_t^* = \beta'X_t + u_t, \quad u_t \sim \mathrm{IN}(0, \sigma^2),
$$
$$
y_t = \begin{cases} y_t^* & \text{if } y_t^* > 0, \\ 0 & \text{otherwise}. \end{cases} \tag{2.1}
$$

In this model the expected value of y_t is given by

$$
\mathrm{E}(y_t \mid X_t) = \Phi_t \beta'X_t + \sigma\phi_t, \tag{2.2}
$$

where Φ_t and ϕ_t are the distribution function and density function of the standard normal evaluated at $(\beta'X_t/\sigma)$. See Maddala (1983a, p. 159).

Expression (2.2) gives the rational expectation of y_t in this simple model. There are essentially two types of situations where the tobit model can occur.

The first is where y_t is a censored variable as depicted in equation (2.1) and the expectation of y_t occurs as an explanatory variable in some other equation. For instance, suppose y_t denotes dividends and we have another equation depicting stock valuation V_t which can be written as

$$V_t = f \text{ (expected dividends and other variables)} .$$

In this case expected dividends are generated by equation (2.2), and estimation of the rational expectation model with a censored variable involves the use of nonlinear estimation methods. Studies incorporating such valuation equations have traditionally used aggregate data so that the problem of censoring dividends does not occur. See, for instance, Litzenberger and Ramaswamy (1982) and Morgan (1982). Other studies that have used the valuation equations based on individual firm data have used only firms that pay dividends on a continuous basis so that again the censoring problem does not occur. Thus, the censoring problem has been largely ignored in the literature.

There is also an additional problem. If, as Marsh and Merton (1987) argue, dividends depend on permanent earnings changes (rather than changes in accounting earnings) and we use changes in stock prices to measure permanent earnings changes, then we have a simultaneity problem, and the reduced form for dividends would not be as simple as (2.1). In fact, it will be similar to the one we shall discuss in Section 4 later for the disequilibrium model.

The other set of tobit models where we have to consider rational expectations is those where the tobit model is considered in its reduced form, either as a prelude to the estimation of the structural system, or as an end by itself. In this case the tobit model would have a more complicated structure and would be given by the following equation:

$$
\begin{aligned}
y_t^* &= \gamma y_t^e + \beta' X_t + u_t , \\
y_t &= \begin{cases} y_t^* & \text{if } y_t^* > 0 , \\ 0 & \text{otherwise} , \end{cases}
\end{aligned}
\tag{2.3}
$$

where y_t^e is the rational expectation of y_t. The reduced form for the Marsh and Merton model if simultaneity is taken into consideration would be of this form. Since this is also the reduced form for the disequilibrium model considered later in Section 4, we shall discuss the estimation problems there.

In summary, in the case of rational expectations in tobit models, we are usually faced with models of the form (2.1) where the expected value of y_t occurs as an explanatory variable in another equation in which case the rational expectation is given by (2.2) and we have a standard nonlinear estimation problem, or we are faced with the estimation of the tobit model given by (2.3), which is obtained as a reduced form from a more elaborate simultaneous equations system, in which case we have to derive an expression for the rational expectation y_t^e before we can discuss any estimation procedures.

The two-limit tobit model. The extension of the previous methods to the case of the two-limit tobit model is straightforward. The two-limit tobit model

(Maddala, 1983a, p. 161) is given by[1]

$$y_t^* = \beta'X_t + u_t, \quad u_t \sim \text{IN}(0, \sigma^2),$$

$$y_t = \begin{cases} L_{1t} & \text{if } y_t^* \leq L_{1t}, \\ y_t^* & \text{if } L_{1t} < y_t^* < L_{2t}, \\ L_{2t} & \text{if } y_t^* \geq L_{2t}. \end{cases} \tag{2.4}$$

Here L_{1t} and L_{2t} are, respectively, the lower and upper limits for y_t. In this case the rational expectation for y_t is given by

$$\text{E}(y_t) = \Phi_{1t}L_{1t} + (\Phi_{2t} - \Phi_{1t})\beta'X_t + (1 - \Phi_{2t})L_{2t} + \sigma(\phi_{1t} - \phi_{2t}), \tag{2.5}$$

where Φ_{1t} and ϕ_{1t} are the distribution function and the density function for the standard normal evaluated at $(L_{1t} - \beta'X_t)/\sigma$ and Φ_{2t} and ϕ_{2t} are the corresponding functions evaluated at $(L_{2t} - \beta'X_t)/\sigma$. Equation (2.5) corresponds to equation (2.2).

Again, if we consider simultaneity we end up with a model similar to that given by (2.3), that is, the first equation in (2.4) has to be changed to the first equation in (2.3). The estimation problems for such models are discussed in Section 6.

3. The friction model

The friction model (Maddala, 1983a, p. 162) arises in situations where the observed change in the response variable to changes in the exogenous variables is zero unless the potential change in the response variable is above or below certain limits. Examples of this are changes in dividends (in response to changes in earnings) and changes in asset holdings (in response to changes in yield). In the case of asset holdings, because of transactions costs, small changes in yield will have no effect on the changes in asset holdings.

Let y_t^* be the desired change in asset holdings, y_t the observed change, and X_t the set of variables determining y_t^*. Then the model we have is

$$y_t^* = \beta'X_t + u_t, \quad u_t \sim \text{IN}(0, \sigma^2),$$

$$y_t = \begin{cases} y_t^* - \alpha_1 & \text{if } y_t^* < \alpha_1, \\ 0 & \text{if } \alpha_1 \leq y_t^* \leq \alpha_2, \\ y_t^* - \alpha_2 & \text{if } y_t^* > \alpha_2, \end{cases} \tag{3.1}$$

where $\alpha_1 < 0$ and $\alpha_2 > 0$. Actual holdings do not change for small negative or positive changes in desired holdings. In this case the rational expectation of y_t

---

[1] In equation (6.38) of Maddala (1983a) $y_i \leq L_{1i}$ should read $y_i^* \leq L_{1i}$ and $y_i^* \leq L_{2i}$ should read $y_i^* \geq L_{2i}$.

is given by

$$E(y_t) = \Phi_{1t}(\beta'X_t - \alpha_1) + (1 - \Phi_{2t})(\beta'X_t - \alpha_2) + \sigma(\phi_{2t} - \phi_{1t}), \qquad (3.2)$$

where Φ and ϕ refer as before to the distribution function and density function of the standard normal, and the subscript $1t$ refers to these functions evaluated at $(\alpha_1 - \beta'X_t)/\sigma$, and the subscript $2t$ refers to these functions evaluated at $(\alpha_2 - \beta'X_t)/\sigma$.

In the case of dividends, it is well known that dividends are sticky. But there is a question of whether the friction model given by (3.1) is directly applicable in the case of dividends because the transaction costs in this case are negligible. Though the transaction costs are negligible, one can argue that the signalling costs (costs of sending the wrong signals to the market) are not. As Cragg (1986) argues, dividend changes are made only if they are not likely to be changed by subsequent events. It can be shown that Cragg's model is essentially the friction model given by (3.1).

If one is interested in studying the relationship of the effect on stock prices of dividend changes (see Wooldridge, 1983), then one can get the rational expectation of dividend change using equation (3.2). In the case of dividends, there are two problems: the censoring problem discussed in Section 2 (studied by Anderson, 1986, and Kim and Maddala, 1992) and the stickiness problem (studied by Cragg, 1986). Ideally, we need to combine both these aspects. In addition, there may be the simultaneity problem that was mentioned in Section 2 when we consider the relationship between dividends, expected earnings, and stock prices. These problems need further investigation.

4. The disequilibrium model

The estimation of disequilibrium models has been an active area of research during the last two decades. See Quandt (1988). The methods of estimation depend on the source of the disequilibrium – whether it is due to imperfect adjustment of prices or because of controlled prices (or controlled quantities as in quota systems). In Maddala (1983b) methods have been suggested for the estimation of disequilibrium models when there are limits on the movement of prices.

These models, however, do not take account of the mechanism of the formation of price expectations in the presence of controls on the movement of prices. This analysis was first developed in Chanda and Maddala (1983) and applied to the price support program in the case of the U.S. corn market by Shonkwiler and Maddala (1985). Since then other papers have refined this analysis.

The disequilibrium model that is considered here is one that is described in Maddala (1983a, pp. 326–334) where, because of some controls in prices, the market is sometimes in disequilibrium (if the controls are operative) and sometimes in equilibrium (if the controls are not operative). When the market is in equilibrium, or when it is in disequilibrium, is determined endogenously because of the control on price, which is an endogenous variable. This accounts for the endogenous switching simultaneous system. Initially, we shall discuss the model with price supports. We shall then present the extension to both lower and upper limits. The model with rational expectations discussed in Chanda and Maddala (1983), Shonkwiler and Maddala (1985), and Holt and Johnson (1989) is the following.

$$S_t = a_1 P_t^* + a_2' W_t + e_{1t}, \quad a_1 > 0, \tag{4.1}$$

$$D_t = b_1 P_t + b_2' X_t + e_{2t}, \quad b_1 < 0, \tag{4.2}$$

$$D_t = S_t \quad \text{if } P_t \geq \underline{P}_t, \tag{4.3}$$

$$D_t < S_t \quad \text{if } P_t < \underline{P}_t, \tag{4.4}$$

where S_t is quantity supplied, D_t is quantity demanded, P_t is the market-clearing price, $\underline{P}_t$ is the exogenously set lower limit on price, P_t^* is the rational expectation of price formed at the time production decisions are made, W_t and X_t are, respectively, the supply and demand shifters, and e_{1t} and e_{2t} are errors that are jointly normal with mean zero and covariance matrix Σ.

The equilibrium case. Consider first the case of an equilibrium model. Equating D_t to S_t we get the reduced form for P_t as

$$P_t = \lambda P_t^* + Z_t + e_t, \tag{4.5}$$

where

$$\lambda = a_1/b_1, \quad e_t = (e_{1t} - e_{2t})/b_1 \quad \text{and} \quad Z_t = (a_2' W_t - b_2' X_t)/b_1.$$

If the supply and demand shifters W_t and X_t are not known at time t and their rational expectations are W_t^* and X_t^*, respectively, we can write

$$W_t = W_t^* + u_{1t},$$

$$X_t = X_t^* + u_{2t}$$

and we get

$$Z_t = Z_t^* + v_t,$$

where

$$v_t = (a_2' u_{1t} - b_1' u_{2t})/b_1.$$

Equation (4.5) now becomes

$$P_t = \lambda P_t^* + Z_t^* + u_t, \tag{4.6}$$

where $u_t = e_t + v_t$. Under rational expectations

$$P_t^* = \text{E}(P_t/\text{Information at } t-1),$$

and, hence, we get

$$P_t^* = \frac{1}{1-\lambda} Z_t^* . \tag{4.7}$$

For estimation purposes we have to specify the prediction equations for W_t and X_t. Usually these equations are specified as autoregressive equations so that

$$\binom{W_t^*}{X_t^*} = D\binom{W_{t-1}}{X_{t-1}}. \tag{4.8}$$

For the estimation of the model in this equilibrium case, we substitute P_t^* from (4.7) into equations (4.1) and (4.2) and estimate these equations along with equations (4.8) by FIML. See Wallis (1980).

The case of price supports. Under the price support program, we have the observed price $P_t \geq \underline{P}_t$. Whether the model is an equilibrium model or a disequilibrium model depends on whether the market equilibrating price given by (4.6) is $\geq \underline{P}_t$ or $< \underline{P}_t$.

Let $\pi_t = \text{Prob}(P_t \geq \underline{P}_t)$. Then, using (4.6) we get

$$\pi_t = 1 - \Phi(C_t), \tag{4.9}$$

where $C_t = \sigma^{-1}(\underline{P}_t - \lambda P_t^* - Z_t^*)$ and $\sigma^2 = \text{Var}(u_t)$. We will use $\phi(\cdot)$ and $\Phi(\cdot)$ to denote the density function and the distribution function of the standard normal.

The rational expectation of P_t is given by

$$P_t^* = \pi_t P_{1t}^* + (1 - \pi_t)\underline{P}_t \tag{4.10}$$

where P_{1t}^* is the rational expectation of P_t if $P_t \geq \underline{P}_t$. We shall consider the derivation of the rational expectations solution under two assumptions. The first is the 'perfect foresight' assumption under which the economic agents are assumed to know what regime they will be in, in the next period. It is not necessary that they know this. What is needed is that economic agents *think* they have this information, and form their expectations accordingly. In this case the sample separation is assumed to be known *ex ante*. Note that the sample separation is always known *ex post*. This implies that if $P_t \geq \underline{P}_t$, then in forming their expectations, agents assume $\pi_t = 1$, and equation (4.10) gives $P_t^* = P_{1t}^*$. Hence, taking expectations of both sides of (4.6) conditional on

$P_t \geqslant \underline{P}_t$, we get

$$P_{1t}^* = \lambda P_{1t}^* + Z_t^* + \sigma \frac{\phi(C_t)}{1 - \Phi(C_t)} \quad \text{or}$$

$$P_{1t}^* = (1 - \lambda)^{-1} \left[Z_t^* + \sigma \frac{\phi(C_t)}{1 - \Phi(C_t)} \right]. \tag{4.11}$$

One can perhaps argue that this is not the appropriate expression for rational expectations since the sample separation is not known at the time expectations are formed. If we drop this assumption, then to obtain the expression for P_{1t}^* we take expectations of both sides of (4.6) conditional on $P_t \geqslant \underline{P}_t$. Since $E(P_t^* | \text{information at time } t - 1) = P_t^*$, we get

$$P_{1t}^* = \lambda P_t^* + Z_t^* + \sigma \frac{\phi(C_t)}{1 - \Phi(C_t)}. \tag{4.12}$$

Equations (4.9)–(4.11) together determine the P_t^* in the case of perfect foresight (sample separation known ex ante) and equations (4.9), (4.10), and (4.12) determine the P_t^* when sample separation is unknown ex ante, which is the correct expression for rational expectations in this model. It is the one derived in Shonkwiler and Maddala (1985) and Holt and Johnson (1989). The expression (4.11) was introduced in Maddala (1990) without stating the perfect foresight assumption. In both cases, of course, the sample separation is known ex post. Thus, the estimation methods are essentially the same except for the expression for P_t^* that one uses. In the next section, it is demonstrated that the uniqueness of the value for P_t^* holds for both these cases.

The case of upper and lower limits. The extension of these results to the case of upper and lower limits on prices is pretty straightforward. For the case with no rational expectation, they are given in Maddala (1983a).

Let $\underline{P}_t$ be the lower limit and $\bar{P}_t$ the upper limit on prices. Analogous to equation (4.9), we define

$$\bar{\pi}_t = \text{Prob}(P_t \geqslant \bar{P}_t) \quad \text{and} \quad \underline{\pi}_t = \text{Prob}(P_t \leqslant \bar{P}_t).$$

Define

$$\bar{C}_t = \frac{1}{\sigma}(\bar{P}_t - \lambda P_t^* - Z_t^*) \quad \text{and} \quad \underline{C}_t = \frac{1}{\sigma}(\underline{P}_t - \lambda P_t^* - Z_t^*) \tag{4.13}$$

Then

$$\bar{\pi}_t = 1 - \Phi(\bar{C}_t) \quad \text{and} \quad \underline{\pi}_t = \Phi(\underline{C}_t).$$

Hence,

$$\text{Prob}[\underline{P}_t < P_t < \bar{P}_t] = \Phi(\bar{C}_t) - \Phi(\underline{C}_t).$$

Corresponding to equation (4.10), we have

$$P_t^* = \underline{\pi}_t \underline{P}_t + \bar{\pi}_t \bar{P}_t + (1 - \underline{\pi}_t - \bar{\pi}_t) P_{1t}^* , \qquad (4.14)$$

where

$$P_{1t}^* = E(P_t \mid \underline{P}_t \leqslant P_t \leqslant \bar{P}_t, I_{t-1}) .$$

P_{1t}^* is, as before, obtained by taking expectation of (4.6) conditional on $\underline{P}_t \leqslant P_t \leqslant \bar{P}_t$ and I_{t-1}.

Using the well-known expectation of a doubly truncated normal variable, see Maddala (1983a, pp. 329–332), we get the expression analogous to (4.11) (under perfect foresight)

$$P_{1t}^* = (1 - \lambda)^{-1} \left[Z_t^* + \frac{\sigma(\phi(\bar{C}_t) - \phi(\underline{C}_t))}{\Phi(\bar{C}_t) - \Phi(\underline{C}_t)} \right] . \qquad (4.15)$$

The rational expectation solution corresponding to (4.12) is

$$P_{1t}^* = \lambda P_t^* + Z_t^* + \frac{\sigma[\phi(\bar{C}_t) - \phi(\underline{C}_t)]}{\Phi(\bar{C}_t) - \Phi(\underline{C}_t)} . \qquad (4.16)$$

Pesaran and Samei (1992) use (unknowingly) the perfect foresight assumption. The expression for P_{1t}^* they use is the one given by equation (4.15) which is a straightforward extension of (4.11) which was given in Maddala (1990). Thus, their formulation does not use the rational expectation version in equations (4.12) and (4.16).

It is important to keep in mind the distinction between the three expressions for rational expectations:

(i) Equation (4.7), which depends on the assumption that economic agents ignore the price limits while forming their expectations, that is, the price limits are not credible,

(ii) P_t^* given by equations (4.13) to (4.15) where economic agents take into account the price limits but behave *as if* they know what regime they will be in, in the next period, and

(iii) P_t^* given by equations (4.13), (4.14), and (4.16) where economic agents take into account the price limits and are uncertain about what regime they will be in, in the next period.

The last case is the appropriate one for the analysis of rational expectations under disequilibrium though one can make an argument for the other two cases as well as a mixture of the three (some traders not believing that the price limits will be effective and use case (i) and some traders thinking that they are smarter than others and, hence, forming their expectations as in case (ii)).

Before we discuss the appropriate estimation procedures, we shall consider the issue of uniqueness of the rational expectations solution.[2]

5. Uniqueness of the rational expectations solution

The uniqueness of the rational expectations solution for the 'perfect foresight' case given by equations (4.13) to (4.15) has been discussed in Pesaran and Samei (1992). Since $\underline{C}_t$ and $\bar{C}_t$ are both functions of P_t^*, we can write equation (4.13) as

$$P_t^* = F(P_t^*) .$$

Pesaran and Samei show that as long as $\lambda < 1$, this equation has a unique solution, thus, establishing the uniqueness of the rational expectation in the 'perfect foresight' case. As discussed earlier, this is not the rational expectations solution.

It is shown in Donald and Maddala (1992) that there is a unique solution in the case of rational expectations, given by equations (4.13), (4.14), and (4.16). Observe that these equations give after simplification

$$P_t^* = \frac{1}{1 - \lambda} [Z_t^* + \sigma \Phi(\underline{C}_t) \cdot \underline{C} + \sigma(1 - \Phi(\bar{C}_t))\bar{C}_t - \sigma(\phi(\bar{C}_t) - \phi(\underline{C}_t))]$$
$$= F(P_t^*) .$$

The proof of the existence of a unique solution to this equation follows from the following factors about the function $F(\cdot)$:
  (i) $0 \leq F'(P) < 1$ when $\lambda \leq 0$ and $F'(P) < 0$ for $0 < \lambda < 1$,
  (ii) $F(\underline{P}_t) \geq \underline{P}_t$ and $F(\bar{P}_t) \leq \bar{P}_t$.
The first condition (i) implies that the function F crosses the 45 degree line (where the fixed point must occur) at exactly one place establishing the existence of a unique solution. Result (ii), which is based on the inequality for the normal distribution:

$$\frac{\phi(x)}{1 - \Phi(x)} \geq x \quad \text{for all } x$$

guarantees that the solution (or fixed point) is in the interval $(\underline{P}_t, \bar{P}_t)$. Details of the proof of these propositions can be found in Donald and Maddala (1992).

The interesting result is that there is a unique solution for P_t^* in all the three cases of expectation formation mentioned earlier. However, the actual value of P_t^* differs under the different assumptions.

---

[2] Holt and Johnston (1989) claim that they checked the uniqueness of P_t^* by numerical experiments. Pesaran and Samei claim to have proved this, but they proved it for a different model. The proof for the Holt–Johnson numerical results is in Donald and Maddala (1992).

6. Estimation methods

The estimation methods for the models discussed in the previous section can be discussed under the following categories:
   (i) Structural vs. reduced form methods.
   (ii) Maximum likelihood (ML) vs. two-step methods.
   The ML procedure follows by noting that the model is like a switching simultaneous regression model with endogenous switching and sample separation known. We first partition the data into three sets.

$$\Psi_1: D_t = S_t , \qquad \Psi_2: D_t < S_t , \quad \text{and} \quad \Psi_3: D_t > S_t .$$

In Ψ_1 we have an equilibrium model with P_t and Q_t as endogenous variables. In Ψ_2 and Ψ_3 we have disequilibrium models with D_t and S_t as the endogenous variables and $\underline{P}_t$ and $\bar{P}_t$ substituted in equation (4.2), respectively. As for P_t^* we substitute the same expression in all the three regimes.
   The models differ in the expression for P_t^* that is used.
   Case (i). Price limits not credible, we use P_t^* given by (4.7).
   Case (ii). Price limits credible but traders think they are smart and know what regime they will be in. P_t^* is given by (4.13) to (4.15).
   Case (iii). Price limits credible and expectations are formed rationally: P_t^* is given by (4.13), (4.14), and (4.16).
   In addition we treat W_t and X_t as endogenous variables if they are not part of the information set I_{t-1}. See Wallis (1980). If $f_1(Q_t, P_t, W_t, X_t)$, $f_2(D_t, S_t, W_t, X_t)$ and $f_3(D_t, S_t, W_t, X_t)$ are the joint densities of the endogenous variables in the three regimes, then the ML estimates are obtained by maximizing

$$L = \prod_{\Psi_1} Jf_1 \prod_{\Psi_2} f_2 \prod_{\Psi_3} f_3 , \tag{6.1}$$

where J is the jacobian $|b_1|$. The jacobians of the transformations in the three regimes are $|b_1|$, 1, 1, respectively. The probabilities of the three regimes do not appear in the likelihood function because it is an endogenous switching model. See Maddala and Nelson (1974).
   In Case (i) obtaining the ML estimates is easy. In Cases (ii) and (iii) P_t^* has to be obtained iteratively. That the ML estimation is feasible is demonstrated by Holt and Johnson (1989) for Case (iii) and Maddala, Shonkwiler and Jeong (1991) where both the Cases (ii) and (iii) have been considered. The appropriate methods to use in such models are discussed in Fair and Taylor (1983, 1990).
   Since the procedures in Cases (ii) and (iii) are similar, we shall discuss only Case (iii). One can think of solving equation (4.17) by the method suggested by Pesaran in his comment on Maddala (1990) starting with some initial values of the parameters. But obtaining P_t^* is not our sole objective. What we are interested in is estimation of the parameters in the structural system (4.1) and

(4.2). Thus, iterating on both the parameters in the structural system and P_t^* is much faster. The iteration procedure would be as follows:

(1) Start with some initial values of P_t^*, say P_t^* is the actual value of P_t in regime 1, $\underline{P}_t$ in regime 2 and $\bar{P}_t$ in regime 3. Call this starting value $P_t^*(0)$.

(2) Using these values maximize the likelihood function (6.1). Using these parameter values and $P_t^*(0)$, compute $\bar{C}_t$ and $\underline{C}_t$ in equation (4.13).

(3) Use equation (4.16) to compute P_{1t}^* and equation (4.13) to compute the probabilities of the three regimes.

(4) Now use (4.14) to get a new value of P_t^*. Call this $P_t^*(1)$.

(5) Continue with steps (1) through (4) and iterate until convergence. This method has been found to converge and involve as much computational effort as a single solution for P_t^* by the method of successive substitution applied to equation (4.17), as suggested by Pesaran. Since our objective is to find the ML estimates and not just P_t^*, the iteration method suggested above is to be preferred. This iteration method was found to work well. See Maddala, Shonkwiler and Jeong (1991).

The ML estimation method described here considers the estimation of the structural parameters and the parameters determining the variables X_t and W_t simultaneously. One can think of a two-step procedure where the equations for W_t and X_t are estimated separately and then the fitted values $\hat{W}_t$ and $\hat{X}_t$ are substituted in the likelihood function (6.1). In the case with no limits on prices, this eliminates the cross-equation constraints arising from the joint estimation of the structural equations and the equations for W_t and X_t and, thus, simplifies the estimation. However, in the case of limits on prices, since P_t^* is a nonlinear function and we need to use iterative methods anyway, there is not much saving in computational effort by using the two-step procedures.

Estimation of the reduced form. In cases where data on quantities are not available, the structural estimation method is not feasible, and we can estimate only the reduced form. In the case of upper and lower limits on prices, the reduced form equation (4.6) can be written as a two-limit tobit model,

$$
P_t = \begin{cases} \lambda P_t^* + Z_t^* + e_t & \text{if } \underline{P}_t < P_t < \bar{P}_t , \\ \underline{P}_t & \text{if } P_t \leq \underline{P}_t , \\ \bar{P}_t & \text{if } P_t \geq \bar{P}_t . \end{cases} \tag{6.2}
$$

The iterative estimation discussed earlier in the case of the ML estimation can also be used with this reduced form estimation, and this results in significant saving in computational effort compared to the procedure of first obtaining P_t^* for each set of parameter values and then estimating again equation (6.2) iteratively.

Pesaran and Samei conduct some Monte Carlo studies to compare the ML estimation with two-step procedures where the equations for X_t and W_t are estimated separately. However, the Monte Carlo study is not very informative because of the way it was designed. The Monte Carlo study referred to the model with a lower price limit (price support). But more importantly, the main defect of their Monte Carlo study is that in each experiment, π_t is a fixed constant. If π_t is a fixed constant, by equation (4.9) C_t is a fixed constant. This implies that $\underline{P}_t - \lambda P_t^* - Z_t^*$ is a constant for all observations. That is, there is a linear relationship between P_t^* and $\underline{P}_t$. This is contrary to the structure of the disequilibrium model with rational expectations where all the complications in estimation arise from the highly nonlinear relationships between $\underline{P}_t$, P_t^*, and Z_t^*. Thus, the Monte Carlo study throws no light on the problems of estimation for the model under consideration. The only conclusion that emerges from it is that ignoring the limits produces misleading results which is not at all surprising for any tobit type model.

There are many interesting issues that one can study by a properly designed Monte Carlo study; some of which are:

(i) The loss of information due to the estimation of the reduced form equation rather than the structural model.

(ii) The effect of misspecification of the exogenous variables X_t and Z_t on the estimates of the structural parameters and so on.

But to analyze all these problems the Monte Carlo study needs to be designed in such a way that the data generated capture the essentials of the model under consideration.

7. Extensions of the disequilibrium model

In many practical applications, the model presented in Section 4 needs to be extended in several directions. Here we shall consider the issues of endogenous price supports and quotas or quantity constraints. Expectations of future endogenous variables, which are very important in macroeconomic applications – such as the demand for money and models of exchange rates (target zones), are discussed in the next section.

Endogenous price supports. In the case of the price support program discussed in Section 4, we assumed that the price support $\underline{P}_t$ was exogenously determined. It would be reasonable to assume that the price support would be changed depending on the previous period's surplus. Thus, we can write,

$$\underline{P}_t = \underline{P}_{t-1} + \delta(S_{t-1} - D_{t-1}) + e_{3t}. \tag{7.1}$$

This would imply that equation (4.9) be changed to

$$\pi_t = \text{Prob}(P_t^* \geq \underline{P}_t)$$
$$= \text{Prob}(\lambda P_t^* + Z_t^* + u_t \geq \underline{P}_{t-1} + \delta(S_{t-1} - D_{t-1}) + e_{3t})$$
$$= 1 - \Phi(C_t),$$

where

$$C_t = \sigma^{-1}[\underline{P}_{t-1} + \delta(S_{t-1} - D_{t-1}) - \lambda P_t^* - Z_t^*]$$

and

$$\sigma^2 = \text{Var}(u_t - e_{3t}) \,.$$

Everything else is the same as discussed in Sections 4–6, except that we now have an additional equation to the model: equation (7.1).

Disequilibrium model with risk. Holt (1989) considers an extension of the model for price supports discussed in Section 4. Here we shall present a simplified exposition of this model. Holt considers third moments as well, but we shall omit these. The supply equation (4.1) is changed to

$$S_t = a_1 P_t^* + a_2' W_t + a_3 V_t^* + e_{1t} \,, \tag{7.2}$$

where V_t^* is expected variance of price. The expected signs for the coefficients of P_t^* and V_t^* are $a_1 > 0$, $a_3 < 0$.

Equation (4.6) now becomes

$$P_t = \lambda_1 P_t^* + \lambda_2 V_t^* + Z_t^* + u_t \,, \tag{7.3}$$

where

$$\lambda_1 = a_1/b_1 \quad \text{and} \quad \lambda_2 = a_3/b_1 \,.$$

The other changes are

(i) In equation (4.9) in the definition of C_t we replace λP_t^* by $\lambda_1 P_t^* + \lambda_2 V_t^*$.

(ii) To equation (4.10) we add

$$V_t^* = \pi_t V_{1t}^* + (1 - \pi_t) \cdot 0 = \pi_t V_{1t}^*$$

since the expected variance is zero if price supports are effective. Also,

$$V_{1t}^* = \sigma^2 \left[1 - \frac{P_{1t}^*}{\sigma} \left(\frac{P_{1t}^*}{\sigma} - C_t \right) \right]$$

(see Maddala, 1983a, p. 365). With these changes, the estimation proceeds as discussed in the previous section. We start our iterations with starting values for both P_t^* and V_t^*, and we compute λ_1 and λ_2 instead of just one λ.

Quotas. The problem of price expectations under quantity constraints (quotas) is an interesting one. Oczkowski (1988, 1991) considers disequilibrium and bargaining theories in the determination of quotas and discusses econometric methods for markets with quotas. The model does not incorporate price expectations. Here we shall assume that there is an exogenously determined quota $\bar{Q}_t$ (which the government maintains by imposing a tax). Consider the demand and supply model given by equations (4.1) and (4.2). The imposition of the quota implies that $S_t \leq \bar{Q}_t$. If the quota is not binding we have an equilibrium model. Let π_t be the probability that the quota is not binding.

Then from equation (4.1) we have

$$\pi_t = \text{Prob}[a_1 P_t^* + a_2' W_t + e_{1t} \le \bar{Q}_t]$$
$$= \Phi(C_t),$$

where

$$C_t = \sigma^{-1}[\bar{Q}_t - a_1 P_t^* - a_2' W_t] \quad \text{and} \quad \sigma^2 = \text{Var}(e_{1t}).$$

As before, if we assume that W_t is not known at time t, we redefine C_t as

$$C_t = \sigma_1^{-1}[\bar{Q}_t - a_1 P_t^* - a_2' W_t^*], \tag{7.4}$$

where $\sigma_1^2 = \text{Var}(e_{1t} + a_2' u_{1t})$ and $W_t = W_t^* + u_{1t}$. Let P_{1t}^* be the rational expectation of P_t, conditional on the quota being not binding and P_{2t}^*, the corresponding expectation when the quota is binding. Then, we have

$$P_t^* = \pi_t P_{1t}^* + (1 - \pi_t) P_{2t}^*. \tag{7.5}$$

We have to determine P_{1t}^* and P_{2t}^*. In the case of the equilibrium model, as before, we consider the reduced form equation (4.6) and take expectations conditional on the quota being nonbinding. We then get

$$P_{1t}^* = \lambda P_t^* + Z_t^* + \text{E}(u_t \,|\, e_{1t} + a_2' u_{1t} < \bar{Q}_t - a_1 P_t^* - a_2' W_t^*)$$
$$= \lambda P_t^* + Z_t^* - \theta \cdot \frac{\phi(C_t)}{\Phi(C_t)} \tag{7.6}$$

(see p. 367 of Maddala, 1983a) where

$$\theta = \text{Cov}\left(u_t, \frac{e_{1t} + a_2' u_{1t}}{\sigma_1}\right)$$

and C_t and σ_1 are as defined in (7.4).

As for P_{2t}^*, note that when the quota is effective, we have a disequilibrium model, and hence, the reduced form equation (4.6) does not apply. What we are concerned with is the price suppliers expect to get. This is clearly given by

$$P_{2t}^* = \frac{1}{a_1}[\bar{Q}_t - a_2' W_t^*].$$

We now substitute the expressions for P_{1t}^* and P_{2t}^* in equation (7.5) to get P_t^*. As discussed earlier in the case of price supports in Section 4, we again have a nonlinear expression for P_t^*.

As for estimation, we again partition the data into two groups:

Ψ_1: Observations for which the quota is not effective.

Ψ_2: Observations for which the quota is effective.

The likelihood function to be maximized is again

$$L = \prod_{\psi_1} |b_1| f_1(P_t, Q_t) \cdot \prod_{\psi_2} f_2(S_t, D_t),$$

where we substitute $S_t = D_t = \bar{Q}_t$ for the observation in Ψ_2. The iterative method of estimation described in Section 5 can also be applied here, and hence, it will not be discussed in detail.

The issue of credibility. In the previous sections we derived the rational expectation P_t^* of P_t under the assumption that the limits on prices (or quantities) imposed by the governments are credible. In practice this need not be the case. In fact, in the case of target zone models, there is a considerable discussion on the credibility issue. For instance, Flood, Rose and Mathieson (1990) argue that expected future exchange rates often fall outside the EMS bands. There is, however, the question of how to generate expected exchange rates when the data are generated by target zones.

In the case of the disequilibrium model we discussed in Section 4, if the limits are not credible, the expression for P_t^* is the one given by the equilibrium model, that is (4.7). If we assume that there is a probability θ that the economic agents assume the limits not to be credible, then the expected price P_t^* would be given by

$$P_t^* = \theta P_t^*(e) + (1 - \theta) P_t^*(de),\qquad (7.7)$$

where $P_t^*(e)$ is the value of P_t^* under the equilibrium model and $P_t^*(de)$ is the value of P_t^* under the disequilibrium model. Since we established the uniqueness of the rational expectation in both cases it follows that P_t^* given by (7.7) would be unique.

The implicit assumption in the case of target zones is that the central bank intervenes whenever the exchange rate is at the end of one of the currency bands, so as to prevent it from crossing the band. Empirically, this was not the case. In the case of the European Monetary System (EMS) it was observed that the central banks intervened intra-marginally to keep the exchange rate well within the target zone, and not at the edges of the zone to keep rates from crossing them. In 1987 they changed this strategy to one of intervention at the edges of the zone. Dominguez and Kenen (1991) argue that the effect of this change in policy shows up in the behavior of some exchanges rates (in the EMS) before and after 1987. It appears from this that exchange rate expectations might be affected not merely by the presence of the target zone but also by the nature of intervention – intra-marginal or at the edges of the zone.

8. Applications to exchange rates

There have been several attempts to apply the disequilibrium model under rational expectations discussed in Section 4, to models of exchange rates.

However, there are many deficiencies in these papers, the major one being that the exchange rate model (as well as the Cagan hyperinflation model) depend on expectations of a future endogenous variable, as opposed to the supply equation in agricultural markets, given by equation (4.1), that depends on expectation of a current endogenous variable. The reduced form from the monetary model of the exchange rate can be written as

$$e_t = \alpha e_{t+1}^* + f(x_t) + u_t \,,$$

where e_t is the logarithm of the exchange rate, e_{t+1}^* is the expected value of e_{t+1} formed at time t, and x_t is the set of variables describing the fundamentals (money supplies and incomes, both domestic and foreign).

The reduced form equation in (4.6) from which we derived the rational expectation P_t^* is no longer applicable in these models. The reduced forms for rational expectations models involving future expectations have been discussed in Hoffman and Schlagenhauf (1983), Woo (1985) and Broze, Gourieroux and Szafarz (1990). However, the expressions for the rational expectations in models with future expectations cannot be simply derived by using these reduced forms, as done in Section 4.

Pesaran and Samei (1991) apply the disequilibrium model discussed in Section 4 to the case of Deutsche Mark/French Franc exchange rate (within a target zone model). Their analysis suffers from many deficiencies. First, the model estimated explains P_t, the log of current exchange rate, with P_t^*, the log of the expected exchange rate for the *current* period. This is *not* a valid model of exchange rate because the crucial equation in exchange rate models is the dependence of P_t on $(P_{t+1}^* - P_t)$. It is not clear what the expectation formation used by Pesaran and Samei really means. Second, the expectation for P_t^* used by them is not the rational expectation (4.16), but the perfect foresight expectation (4.15). It is not clear how appropriate this assumption is. In view of these limitations, it is hard to give any reasonable interpretation to the empirical results. The major conclusion that emerges from this study is that taking account of the limits makes a difference to the empirical results (even though the model is not correct).

Another study of target zones using limited dependent variable models is the paper by Edin and Vredin (1991). The paper does not, however, analyze the problem of the effect of target zones on exchange rate expectations. What it does is to formulate a policy rule for central bank authorities which treats the central parity as as censored variable, which is changed only if the shadow floating rate deviates too much from the prevailing central parity. The shadow floating rate is determined from a monetary model of the exchange rate. This model gives, as its reduced form, the current exchange rate as a function of expected future exchange rate and some fundamental factors. Edin and Vredin use the 'bubble-free' solution to this reduced form.

A study that considers rational expectations in switching regression models is that by Hsieh (1992). He considers the usual monetary model of exchange rates and considers an intervention rule where the central bank intervenes only if the rate of depreciation of the exchange rate would exceed a constant A if no intervention takes place. In the target zone model and in typical two-sided intervention rules of 'managed float', intervention takes place whenever the rate of depreciation or appreciation is large. Hsieh obtains a rational expectation solution under some restrictive assumptions. There is no explicit solution in the general case.

9. Prediction problems and policy issues

In the preceding section we described the methods of estimation in limited dependent variable models with rational expectations. The models estimated could be used to study the effects of different policies of eliminating or changing the limits imposed. For instance, in the case of the price support program in agriculture, one might be interested in the effect of the elimination or reduction of the price support on production, prices received by farmers and on price variability (which affects production risk). It is not appropriate to obtain these predictions from an equilibrium model consisting of just equations (4.1) and (4.2) ignoring the constraints on prices which underlie the data generated. Once the model has been estimated as a disequilibrium model, the estimated parameters can be used to simulate the effects of different policies regarding price supports.

In the case of the target zone models, the issues are different. Some of the empirical issues are the following.

(i) Did the adoption of target zones reduce the overall volatility of exchange rates? To answer this question, one needs an estimate of what the variance of the exchange rate would have been if the target zone did not exist. This estimate can be obtained (as in the case of the farm price support program) by stimulating the behavior of the exchange rate (using the estimated parameter values from the disequilibrium model) under the equilibrium assumptions. However, since we do not have the correct disequilibrium model yet, it is hard to answer this question. Some others have argued that the volatility of exchange rates is down after the institution of the target zones, but that it is due to better control over exchange rate 'fundamentals' (see Bodnar and Leahy, 1990). Another study that tries to estimate the effect of governmental interventions on exchange-rate volatility is the paper by Mundaca (1990). She studies the effect of government intervention on estimates of conditional variances within the GARCH framework.

(ii) Are there nonlinear relationships between exchange rates and measures of fundamentals that are attributable to target zones? The answer to this is unclear. The nonlinearities exist, but they are present in floating exchange rate regimes as well. Further, Flood, Rose, and Mathieson (1990) argue that these nonlinearities do not improve out of sample predictions.

(iii) How does one reconcile the within-zone behavior of exchange rates, which tend to spend more time in the center of the zone and exhibit higher volatility at the edge of the target zone, with any of the existing target zone models? This is an important econometric issue in the analysis of target zone models. As mentioned earlier, Dominguez and Kenen (1991), argue that before 1987, the European central banks often intervened in the middle of the target zone rather than the ends, which is what the models we have discussed, as well as other target zone models, suggest.

(iv) Are re-alignment probabilities and reserve levels important in the empirical analysis of target zone models? Some have investigated re-alignment probabilities with mixed results. (Flood, et al., 1990, and Bodnar and Leahy, 1990). There is no investigation of reserve levels.

The above mentioned issues suggest that the disequilibrium model with expectations of current endogenous variables discussed in Section 4 needs several modifications before it can be fruitfully used to analyze data on exchange rate. First, there is the issue of expectations of future endogenous variables. Second, there is the issue of credibility of the currency bands and expectations about future alignments.

10. Concluding remarks

We have presented a review of the methods of estimation for limited dependent variable models with rational expectations. We considered tobit models and disequilibrium models at length and outlined some applications in finance as well. Models with self-selection have not been discussed because they do not seem to have been used empirically as yet. Their structure is similar to that of disequilibrium models discussed here (both are switching regression models with endogenous switching).

There is a fair amount of work on models with expectations of current endogenous variables. These models are applicable to farm markets, where there are empirical illustrations (Shonkwiler and Maddala, 1985 and Holt and Johnson, 1989) and to financial markets where applications have yet to come. They have also been (mis)applied to exchange rate models, which fall in the category of models with future expectations. Models with expectations of future endogenous variables is an area that needs to be worked out.

Acknowledgment

I would like to thank Stephen Cosslett and Pok-Sang Lam for comments on an earlier version of this paper. Thanks are also due to Stephen Donald for comments on this version and to Christino Arroyo for discussions on the target zone models. None of them, however, is responsible for any possible errors.

References

Anderson, G. J. (1986). An application of the tobit model to panel data: Modelling dividend behavior in Canada. Economics Discussion Paper, McMaster University.

Bodnar, G. and J. Leahy (1990). Are target zone models relevant? Working Paper, University of Rochester.

Broze, L., C. Gourieroux, and A. Szafarz (1990). *Reduced Forms of Rational Expectations Models*. Harwood Academic Publishers, Chur, Switzerland.

Chanda, A. K. and G. S. Maddala (1983). Methods of estimation for models of markets with bounded price variation under rational expectations. *Econ. Lett.* **47**, 181–184. Erratum in *Econ. Lett.* **15**, 195–196 (1984).

Cragg, J. G. (1986). The relationship of dividend payments to the characteristics of the earnings streams of corporation. In: M. H. Preston and R. E. Quandt, eds., *Prices, Competition and Equilibrium*. Barnes and Noble, New York.

Dominguez, K. M. and P. B. Kenen (1991). On the need to allow for the possibility that governments mean what they say: Interpreting the target-zone model of exchange-rate behavior in the light of EMS experience. Princeton University Discussion Paper.

Donald, S. and G. S. Maddala (1992). A note on the estimation of limited dependent variables under rational expectations. *Econ. Lett.* **38**, 17–23.

Edin, P. A. and A. Vredin (1991). Devaluation risk in target zones: Evidence from the nordic countries. Discussion paper, Trade Union Institute for Economic Research, Stockholm, Sweden.

Fair, R. C. and J. B. Taylor (1983). Solution and maximum likelihood estimation of dynamic nonlinear rational expectations models. *Econometrica* **51**, 1169–1185.

Fair, R. C. and J. B. Taylor (1990). Full information estimation and stochastic simulation of models with rational expectations. *J. Appl. Econ.* **4**, 381–392.

Flood, R. P., A. K. Rose and D. J. Mathieson (1990). An empirical exploration of exchange-rate target zones. Working Paper, IMF, Washington, DC.

Hoffman, D. L. and D. E. Schlagenhauf (1983). Rotational expectations and monetary models of exchange rate determination. *J. Mon. Econ.* **11**, 247–260.

Holt, M. T. (1989). Bounded price variation models with rational expectations and price risk. *Econ. Lett.* **31**, 313–317.

Holt, M. T. and S. R. Johnson (1989). Bounded price variation and rational expectations in an endogenous switching model of the U.S. corn market. *Rev. Econ. Statist.* **71**, 605–613.

Hsieh, D. A. (1992). A nonlinear stochastic rational expectations model of exchange rates. Manuscript, Graduate School of Business, University of Chicago. *J. Internat. Money Finance* **11**, 235–250.

Kim, B. S. and G. S. Maddala (1992). Estimation and specification analysis of models of dividend behavior based and censored panel data. *Empirical Econ.* **17**, 111–124.

Litzenberger, R. H. and K. Ramaswamy (1982). The effect of dividends on common stock prices: Tax effects or information effects. *J. Finance* **37**, 429–443.

Maddala, G. S. (1983a). *Limited Dependent Variables in Econometrics*. Cambridge Univ. Press, Cambridge.

Maddala, G. S. (1983b). Methods of estimation for models of markets with bounded price variation. *Internat. Econ. Rev.* **24**, 361–378.

Maddala, G. S. (1990). Estimation of dynamic disequilibrium models with rational expectations: The case of commodity markets. In: L. A. Winters and D. Sapsford, eds., *Primary Commodity Prices: Economic Models and Policy*. Cambridge Univ. Press, Cambridge.

Maddala, G. S. and F. D. Nelson (1974). Maximum likelihood methods for models of markets in disequilibrium. *Econometrica* **42**, 1013–1030.

Maddala, G. S., J. S. Shonkwiler and J. Jeong (1991). On the value of sample separation information in a disequilibrium model under rational expectations. Discussion Paper, University of Florida.

Marsh, T. A. and R. C. Merton (1987). Dividend behavior for the aggregate stock market. *J. Business* **60**, 1–40.

Morgan, I. G. (1982). Dividends and capital asset prices. *J. Finance* **37**, 1071–1086.

Mundaca, B. G. (1990). The effect of official sterilized interventions on the Norwegian currency basket: A GARCH-switching regression model. Working Paper, Research Department, Norges Bank.

Oczkowski, E. (1988). A theory of market quantity controls: The use of disequilibrium and bargaining theories. *Austral. Econ. Papers* **27**, 285–297.

Oczkowski, E. (1991). The econometrics of markets with quantity controls. *Appl. Econ.* **23**, 497–504.

Pesaran, M. H. and H. Samei (1992). Estimating limited-dependent rational expectations models: With an application to exchange-rate determination in a target zone. *J. Econometrics* **53**, 141–163.

Quandt, R. E. (1988). *The Econometrics of Disequilibrium*. Blackwell, New York.

Shonkwiler, J. S. and G. S. Maddala (1985). Modelling expectations of bounded prices: An application to the market for corn. *Rev. Econ. Statist.* **67**, 634–641.

Wallis, K. F. (1980). Econometric implications of the rational expectations hypothesis. *Econometrica* **48**, 49–73.

Woo, W. T. (1985). The monetary approach to exchange rate determination under rational expectations. *J. Internat. Econ.* **18**, 1–16.

Wooldridge, J. R. (1983). Dividend changes and security prices. *J. Finance* **38**, 1607–1616.

G. S. Maddala, C. R. Rao and H. D. Vinod, eds., *Handbook of Statistics, Vol. 11*

8

Nonlinear Time Series and Macroeconometrics

William A. Brock and Simon M. Potter

1. Introduction

> If you hit a wooden rocking horse with a club, the movement of
> the horse will be very different to the movement of the club.

Frisch (1933, p. 198) quoting Wicksell.

This quote from Frisch's seminal Cassel paper captures succinctly the
standard way economists view time series: There are impulses (club movements) and a propagation mechanism (rocking horse) which together produce
the fluctuations or cycles of economic time series around their upward
movements. Frisch's article culminated a line of criticism started in the classic
articles of Yule (1927) and Slutzky (1927) of earlier econometric work which
had modeled business cycles by assuming that the economy was driven by a
process with the same time series properties as the economy itself. Jevons'
(1884) sunspot theory of the business cycle is the standard example.

In criticizing the work all three (Yule, Slutzky, and Frisch) had made use of
the properties of linear difference equations driven by random disturbances.
They found that such statistical models were very capable of producing
simulated time series that mimicked the behavior of the actual business cycle.
After the Second World War the linear time series techniques they promoted
came to dominate the study of economic time series. The dominance was not
achieved because economic theories imply that economic time series should be
linear or because statistical tests were performed supporting the assumption of
linearity. But rather because given the state of statistical knowledge and
computational resources linear time series were easy to apply and appeared to
give superior results to earlier approaches.

However, if we return to the physical analogy introduced by the rocking
horse example it is not clear that the behavior of the rocking horse is accurately
described by a linear difference equation for movements far away from its
resting point (see Ozaki, 1985 for a similar example involving a ship).
Furthermore, there are examples of physical phenomena where the requirement of clubbing or external force is not necessary for fluctuations to continue
indefinitely.

   In our review we discuss recent advances in econometric techniques that have allowed economists to assess both the validity of the assumption of linear stochastic dynamics and the requirement of exogenous driving forces.

   We examine two potential types of nonlinear economic time series. The first type are time series generated by a nonlinear map with chaotic ('chaotic' will be defined below) properties. The output of the nonlinear map may be observed through an 'observer' function which is, perhaps, buffeted with measurement noise. The map itself may be perturbed by exogenous noise. There are examples of such series which appear random to the eye and to traditional linear statistical techniques because the spectrum is flat (i.e., the autocorrelation function (ACF) is zero at all leads and lags. It is important to realize that not all chaoses display white noise autocorrelation functions. For example consider an ARMA(p, q) driven by a chaotic innovation process.

   The second type is time series generated by a nonlinear difference equation propagated by additive noise that satisfies a martingale difference property. Our emphasis is on testing for nonlinear structure of both types.

   We concentrate on a testing methodology with its origins in the deterministic chaos concept of correlation integrals. We exploit a connection between correlation integrals and classical U- and V-statistics derived by Brock, Dechert and Scheinkman (1987), 'BDS' hereafter, to produce a test for both types of nonlinearity in time series data.[1]

2. Chaos and stochastic nonlinearity

Let us state notation at the outset. Denote vector valued random variables by bold capitals, A, X, Y, M, N, scalar valued random variables by capitals, and their sample values by lower case. In order to keep the exposition clear we shall concentrate on scalar valued processes. For the most part, we shall keep a convention that X signifies a chaotic time series and Y a stochastic time series.

   Following Eckmann and Ruelle (1985), and Brock (1986), we start with some definitions and background for chaotic time series. Next we provide some definitions of stochastic linearity.

2.1. Chaotic time series

DEFINITION. We shall say the observed data process $\{A(t)\}$ is *generated by a*

---

[1] We assume throughout that the data under examination has been transformed to stationarity and ignore any questions of estimation error in this transformation.

noisy deterministically chaotic explanation, 'noisy chaotic' for short, if

$$A_t = h(X_t, M_t),\qquad\qquad\qquad (2.1.1a)$$

$$X_t = G(X_{t-1}, V_t),\qquad V_t = f(X_{t-1}, N_t)\quad\text{and}\quad E[f(X_{t-1}, N_t) \mid X_{t-1}] = 0,$$
$$\qquad\qquad\qquad (2.1.1b)$$

where $\{X_t\}$ (when $V_t = 0$) is generated by the deterministic dynamics,

$$x_t = G(x_{t-1}, 0),\qquad\qquad\qquad (2.1.1c)$$

which is *chaotic*, that is to say the largest Lyapunov exponent (defined below) exists, is constant almost surely with respect to the assumed unique natural (cf. Eckmann and Ruelle, 1985) invariant measure of $G(\cdot)$, and is positive.

Here $\{M_t\}$, $\{N_t\}$ are mutually independent mean zero, finite variance, independent and identically distributed (IID) processes. The function $f(x, n)$ may be constructed, for example, to ensure that the noise $\{V_t = f(X_{t-1}, N_t)\}$ does not move $\{X_t\}$ out of its basin of attraction. We interpret our setup thus: $\{M_t\}$ represents measurement error, $h(x, m)$ is a noisy observer function of the state X_t, and $\{V_t\}$ is dynamical noise.

The definition of chaos used here is positive largest Lyapunov exponent of the underlying deterministic map which is one way to formulate the hallmark of chaos: sensitive dependence upon initial conditions (SDIC). This is a popular definition but not the only one (cf. Eckmann and Ruelle, 1985). We need the following.

DEFINITION. (*Largest Lyapunov exponent of map $F(x)$*). Let $F : \mathbb{R}^n \to \mathbb{R}^n$. The *largest Lyapunov exponent λ* is defined by

$$\lambda \equiv \lim_{t \to \infty} \ln\left[\|D_{x_0} F^t \cdot v\|\right] / t,\qquad\qquad\qquad (2.1.2)$$

where D_{x_0}, $\cdot v$, $\ln$, F^t, $\|\cdot\|$ denote derivative w.r.t initial condition x_0 at time zero, matrix product with direction vector v, natural logarithm, map F applied t times (the t-th iterate of F), and matrix norm respectively.

Consider the following scalar valued example, called the tent map,

$$F(x) = 1 - |2x - 1|.\qquad\qquad\qquad (2.1.3)$$

Here $F(x)$ maps $[0, 1]$ to itself, and for almost all initial conditions, $x_0 \in [0, 1]$, w.r.t. Lebesgue measure on $[0, 1]$, the trajectory $x_t(x_0)$ of the dynamics is second-order white noise, i.e., has flat spectrum and the autocorrelation function (ACF) is zero at all leads and lags. The largest Lyapunov exponent which can be computed using (2.1.2) is $\lambda = \ln(2) > 0$. Hence the tent map is chaotic on $[0, 1]$. We shall use Granger's term, 'white chaos', to denote a chaos which generates trajectories which are second-order white noise.

The key lesson to be learned from the study of white chaoses like the tent map is this. Linear time series methods will proclaim time series emitted by such dynamics as random and unpredictable. Yet it is obvious that such time series are short term predictable by nonlinear methods such as local linear approximation, nearest neighbors, neural networks, splines, and others (cf. Casdagli and Eubank, 1991). Note that $\lambda > 0$ implies that any small error in measurement of the initial state, x_0 will magnify in h-step-ahead forecasts at an exponential rate. Hence a chaotic process is not long term predictable even though it is short term predictable.

The reader is warned, however, it is possible to generate deterministic maps (indeed that is the purpose of good pseudo random number generator designs) that are impossible to short term predict by any nonlinear method using a machine of finite resolution. A simple example is to put $F(x) = T^q(x)$, where $T^q(x)$ denotes the tent map applied q times to x. By increasing q one can make the derivative of F oscillate more and more rapidly which makes the output appear 'more and more random'. We encourage the reader to try forecasting experiments using favorite nonlinear prediction algorithms on this example.

For the purposes of this article we do not wish to take a stand on the meaning of randomness hence the reader should feel free to interpret IID as a deterministic system with a sufficiently high dimension that prediction is prohibitively expensive and therefore, appears IID to all statistical tests when implemented on machines with finite resolution.

2.2. Some notations of stochastic linearity and nonlinearity

For ease of exposition we concentrate on scalar valued strictly stationary stochastic processes. The case of vector valued stochastic processes follows the same pattern as the development below by replacing the scalar innovation process $\{N_t\}$ with an $\mathbb{R}^n$-valued process, $\{N_t\}$, the scalars $\{a_j\}$ with the $n \times n$ matrices $\{A_j\}$, the summation condition $\Sigma_{j=0}^{\infty} a_j^2 < \infty$ with the condition $\Sigma_{j=0}^{\infty} \text{trace } A_j A_j' < \infty$, and so on. See Hansen and Sargent (1991, Chapters 2–4) for a development close to what we have in mind.

Consider the following purely nondeterministic (in the nonlinear sense, see Rosenblatt, 1971, p. 164) covariance stationary stochastic process:

$$Y_t - \mu = \sum_{j=0}^{\infty} a_j N_{t-j} = A(B)N_t , \tag{2.2.1}$$

where $A(B)$ is a polynomial in the back operator with $\Sigma_{j=0}^{\infty} a_j^2 < \infty$ and $a_0 = 1$. Here $\{N_t\}$ is a mean zero, finite variance denoted, $(0, \sigma^2)$, strictly stationary stochastic process with $E[N_s N_t] = 0$ for $s \neq t$. Except for the additional condition that $\{Y_t\}$ be purely nondeterministic in the nonlinear sense this is the Wold Representation.

In order to test the null hypothesis of stochastic linearity one first needs to decide what exactly it is. Clearly the existence of (2.2.1) requires one to consider more than the second moment properties of the process unless $\{N_t\}$ is a Gaussian stochastic process. One natural definition of linearity is that the best linear (i.e., based on the closed linear space of *linear* combinations of its history $\{Y_s, s < t\}$) predictor of Y_t is equal to the optimal mean square error predictor based on the past history of the process. The best linear predictor of $\{Y_t\}$ in (2.2.1) is given by $A(B)n_{t-1}$ (see Rosenblatt, 1985, p. 30). The optimal mean square predictor is the same as the conditional expectation of the process $\{Y_t\}$ given the sigma fields generated by $\{Y_s, s < t\}$.

In order to process we need to define the concept of a martingale difference sequence (MDS).

DEFINITION (*Martingale difference sequence*, Billingsley, 1986, pp. 480–481). Let $\{N_s\}$ be a sequence of random variables on a probability space $(\Omega, \mathcal{F}, P)$ and let $\{\mathcal{F}_s\}$ be a sequence of sigma fields in $\mathcal{F}$. The sequence $\{(N_t, \mathcal{F}_t):$ $t = \ldots, -2, -1, 0, 1, 2, \ldots\}$ is a *martingale difference* if
   (i) $\mathcal{F}_s \subset \mathcal{F}_{s+1}$,
   (ii) N_s is measurable $\mathcal{F}_s$,
   (iii) $E[N_s \mid \mathcal{F}_{s-1}] = 0$ a.s.

DEFINITION (*MDS linear*, Hall and Heyde, 1980, p. 183). The stochastic process $\{Y_t\}$ is *MDS linear* if it can be represented in the form (2.2.1) above where the 'innovations' $\{N_t\}$ are a martingale difference sequence (MDS) relative to the sigma fields $\mathcal{F}_t$ generated by $\{Y_s, s \leq t\}$.

There is an equivalence between the (completion) of sigma fields generated by $\{Y_s : s < t\}$ and those generated by the random variables $\{N_s : s < t\}$ defined by $N_t = Y_t - E[Y_t \mid \mathcal{F}_{t-1}^Y]$ (see Hall and Heyde, 1980, p. 183). Hence, $\{N_t\}$ is also a martingale difference sequence relative to the sigma fields generated by $\{N_s, s \leq t\}$.

The BDS test for chaos which is discussed below can be made into a specification test of the following stronger definition of stochastic linearity.

DEFINITION (*IID linear*, Priestley, 1988). We call the stochastic process $\{Y_t\}$ *IID linear* if it can be written in the form (2.2.1) where the innovations $\{N_t\}$ are IID $(0, \sigma^2)$.

It is well known in finance that measures of conditional variance or conditional volatility of asset returns are very persistent through time for an extremely wide range of assets. A popular class of models that display volatility persistence but yet are analytically tractable are the generalized auto regressive conditionally heteroscedastic (GARCH) class:

$$Y_t = h_t^{1/2} Z_t, \tag{2.2.2}$$

where $\{Z_t\}$ is IID with zero mean and variance one and

$$h_t = a_0 + a_1 Y_{t-1}^2 + \cdots + a_p Y_{t-p}^2 + b_1 h_{t-1} + \cdots + b_q h_{t-q}$$
$$\equiv a_0 + \theta X_t \,, \tag{2.2.3a}$$

$$X_t \equiv (Y_{t-1}^2, \ldots, Y_{t-p}^2, h_{t-1}, \ldots, h_{t-q}) \,. \tag{2.2.3b}$$

It is becoming popular to use model (2.2.2) to parameterize (and estimate) heteroscedasticity of the error structure of models of the conditional mean. See Bollerslev, Chou, and Kroner (1992) for an extensive survey of work related to this model of conditional volatility. Note that the process $\{Y_t^2\}$ has a conditional mean,

$$V_t \equiv \mathrm{E}[Y_t^2 \mid X_t] = h_t = a_0 + \theta X_t \,, \tag{2.2.4}$$

that is linear with respect to $\{X_t\}$. Hence $\{Y_t^2\}$ is linear in mean in a sense closely related to the definition of MDS linear:

$$Y_t^2 = V_t + N_t, \; N_t \equiv Y_t^2 - \mathrm{E}[Y_t^2 \mid X_t], \; \mathrm{E}[N_t \mid X_t] = 0 \,. \tag{2.2.5}$$

3. The BDS test

3.1. Applications of the correlation integral and other measures from nonlinear science to testing the IID hypothesis

It turns out that a method which is very effective at testing for chaos is also very effective and natural for testing for IID linearity. The basic strategy is to design a test of the null hypothesis of IID which has high power against chaos in general and white chaos in particular. At the same time we design the test so that it has the same first-order asymptotic distribution on the estimated residuals of a broad class of parametric models which includes 'most' linear models driven by IID innovations. In this way we also obtain a test of the null hypothesis of IID linearity. In order to explain this testing method we must exposit a measure of spatial correlation called the 'correlation integral'. This measure, in turn, is a member of a class of statistics called U-statistics. We first give a brief exposition of U- and V-statistics. Much of the material below is based upon Brock and Potter (1991). Distribution theory for general functions of the correlation integral is worked out and applied to testing problems in nonlinear science by Baek and Brock (1991).

Let $\{Y_t\}$ be an $\mathbb{R}^k$-valued stochastic process. V-statistics and their close relatives, *U*-statistics, are defined thus:

$$V(T) = \frac{1}{T^2} \sum_{1 \leq s, t \leq T} h(Y_t, Y_s),$$
(3.1.1a)

$$U(T) = \frac{2}{T(T-1)} \sum_{1 \leq s < t \leq T} h(Y_t, Y_s),$$
(3.1.1b)

where $h : \mathbb{R}^k \times \mathbb{R}^k \to \mathbb{R}$, $h(y, z) = h(z, y)$, is a symmetric function, called a 'kernel'.

Serfling (1980, p. 176) and Denker and Keller (1983) develop asymptotic theory, parallel to the more familiar case of single sum statistics, for *U*- and *V*-statistics. We concentrate on the *V*-statistic form in this paper. Denker and Keller (1983) show the expectation of $U(T)$ and $V(T)$ is the same as the expectation of h. We note that the first-order asymptotic distributions are the same for *U*- and *V*-statistics.

Denker and Keller (1983), under appropriate mixing conditions and some bounds on moments of the kernel function (the $2 + \delta$ absolute moment of h is finite for some $\delta > 0$), establish the following representation for the *V*-statistic (and also the *U*-statistic) in (3.1.1):

$$V(T) = \frac{2}{T} \sum_{s=1}^{T} h_1(Y_s) + R(T),$$
(3.1.2)

where $h_1(Y_s) = E[h(Y_t, Y_s)|Y_s]$, and $T^{1/2}R(T) \to 0$ in distribution. This technique is known as the 'projection method' because one is approximating a double sum statistic up to a term which converges to zero in distribution, when multiplied by $T^{1/2}$, with a single sum statistic by 'projection', i.e., taking the conditional expectation, h_1. Note that the mean of h_1 is the mean of h. Standard central limit theory and ergodic theory for single sum averages can now be applied.

We now develop the promised test of IID which is due to Brock, Dechert and Scheinkman (1987), hereafter 'BDS'. Write, for $\varepsilon > 0$, $m = 1, 2, \ldots, M$

$$C_m(\varepsilon, T) = \frac{1}{T^2} \sum_{1 \leq s, t \leq T} h(y_t^m, y_s^m),$$
(3.1.3)

$$D_m(\varepsilon, T) = C_m - C_1^m,$$
(3.1.4)

where $y_t^m = (n_{t-1}, \ldots, n_{t-m}) \in \mathbb{R}^m$ for C_m. Here $h(y, z)$ is a symmetric indicator function equal to one if the two *m* histories, y_s^m, y_t^m, are within ε of each other in the sup norm and equal to zero otherwise.[2] Hence, C_m, C_1 are

---

[2] A technical issue is how well the asymptotic behavior of the test statistic using the indicator function can be approximated by a symmetric 'kernel' function which is twice continuously differentiable. Simulation evidence as well as other arguments in Brock, Hsieh and LeBaron (1991) suggest that a workable approximation exists.

V-statistics, D is a smooth function of two *V*-statistics, $\{y_t^m\}$ is m-dependent, so the sufficient conditions to apply the theory of Denker and Keller (1983) hold. Denker and Keller's moment conditions on h are automatically satisfied when h is the indicator function.

Put $W(x, y) \equiv x - y^m$. We choose 'W' to remind us that the test is designed to reject IID when the 'width' between C_m and C_1^m is sufficiently large. Then

$$T^{1/2}D_m \equiv T^{1/2}W(C_m(\varepsilon, T), C_1(\varepsilon, T))$$
$$= T^{1/2}[W + W_1(C_m(\varepsilon, T) - C_m(\varepsilon)) + W_2(C_1(\varepsilon, T) - C_1(\varepsilon))]$$
$$+ o_p(1), \tag{3.1.5}$$

where W_1, W_2 denote the partial derivative of W w.r.t. the first argument, and the second argument respectively evaluated at the point $(C_m(\varepsilon), C_1(\varepsilon))$ and $o_p(1)$ denotes a term that converges to zero in probability as $T \to \infty$.

Under the null hypothesis, $\{N_t\}$ IID, BDS show $C_m(\varepsilon) = [C_1(\varepsilon)]^m$. Hence $W(C_m(\varepsilon), C_1(\varepsilon))$ is zero under the null. Now use the projection method and compute the partial derivatives W_i, $i = 1, 2$ to obtain, up to terms which converge to zero in probability as $T \to \infty$:

$$T^{1/2}D_m = [2/T^{1/2}]\left\{\sum [h_m(y_s^m) - C_m(\varepsilon)]\right.$$
$$\left. - mC_1(\varepsilon)^{m-1}[h_1(y_s^1) - C_1(\varepsilon)]\right\},$$
$$\equiv [2/T^{1/2}]\left\{\sum g_m(y_s^m)\right\}, \tag{3.1.6}$$

where the sum runs from $s = 1$ to T.

Under the null of $\{N_t\}$ IID this may be further simplified. Recall that $y_t^m \equiv (n_{t-1}, \ldots, n_{t-m})$, $m = 1, 2, \ldots$. Hence,

$$h_m(y_s^m) = \prod_{i=1}^{m} h_1(n_{t-i}). \tag{3.1.7}$$

Note that

$$h_1(x) = F(x + \varepsilon) - F(x - \varepsilon), \quad \text{where } F(x) \equiv \text{Prob}\{N_t \leq x\}. \tag{3.1.8}$$

It is now easy to work out the formulae for the limiting mean and variance under the null hypothesis, $\{N_t\}$ IID. The mean of g_m is zero. Using strict stationarity compute the variance of Σg_m and take T to infinity to obtain

$$V_m \equiv \lim \text{Var}(T^{1/2}D_m) = 4E\left\{g_m(y_1^m)^2 + 2\sum_{i>1} g_m(y_1^m)g_m(y_{1+i}^m)\right\}. \tag{3.1.9}$$

Now use the definition of g_m and $\{N_t\}$ IID to obtain the formula

$$(\tfrac{1}{4})V_m = m(m-2)C^{2m-2}(K-C^2) + K^m - C^{2m}$$
$$+ 2\sum_{j=1}^{m-1} [C^{2j}(K^{m-j} - C^{2m-2j}) - mC^{2m-2}(K-C^2)]$$
$$\equiv V(C, K, m) \equiv V_m , \tag{3.1.10}$$

where $C \equiv C_1(\varepsilon)$, $K \equiv E\{h(N_r, N_s)h(N_s, N_t)\}$. The formula (3.1.10) can be expressed in the possibly simpler alternative form

$$(\tfrac{1}{4})V_m = K^m + 2\sum_{j=1}^{m-1} K^{m-j}C^{2j} + (m-1)^2 C^{2m} - m^2 K C^{2m-2} . \tag{3.1.10'}$$

The BDS test statistic is given by

$$T^{1/2}D_m/V_m(T)^{1/2} \to N(0, 1) \quad \text{as } T \to \infty , \tag{3.1.11}$$

where $V_m(T)$ denotes a consistent estimator of the variance V_m, and the convergence takes place under the null hypothesis $\{N_t\}$ IID.

It is important to realize that the above argument crucially depends upon the variance V_m being positive which is true except for hairline cases. Theiler (1990) discusses a case (a uniform distribution on a circle) where the variance is zero. More elaborate limit theory can be developed for zero variance cases (cf. Serfling, 1980, Chapter 5).

A consistent estimator of the variance that is used in the IBM PC software of Dechert (1987) which computes BDS statistics is given by,

$$V_m(T) = V_m(C_1(\varepsilon, T), K(\varepsilon, T)) , \tag{3.1.12}$$

where $C_1(\varepsilon, T)$ is given by (3.1.3) above and

$$K(\varepsilon, T) \equiv \frac{1}{T^3} \sum h(N_r, N_s)h(N_s, N_t) , \tag{3.1.13}$$

where that sum run over $1 \leq r, s, t \leq T$.

REMARK. It is important to realize that the proof that the asymptotic distribution of (3.1.6) with the variance estimator (3.1.12) requires *no moment conditions* for the indicator kernel. This is so because Denker and Keller's (1983) sufficient condition is $E[|h|^{2+\delta}] < \infty$, for some $\delta > 0$, where h is the kernel function. But this is automatically satisfied for kernels which are zero off a compact set and bounded on a compact set like the indicator kernel. Note that Denker and Keller's conditions are easily satisfied for (3.1.13) as well. As we shall see in Section 4 being able to test for linearity with minimum moment conditions is very useful for financial time series. Different tests for nonlinearity are compared with respect to their moment requirements in De Lima (1991b) and briefly below in Section 4. The tentative conclusion of De Lima's work is that for high frequency financial data the possibility of nonexistence of

fourth or higher absolute moments means that many tests require robustifica-
tion (usually through some type of trimming) to be reliably applied to such
data series. The BDS test has the advantage of requiring minimal moment
requirements but it may require longer samples to be as effective as some of
the other tests we discuss below.

Baek and Brock (1992) generalize the BDS test by testing for both temporal
independence and cross sectional independence of a vector of time series. They
show that the distribution of their test statistic is the same on estimated vector
autoregression (VAR) residuals under the null of a VAR with known finite
number of lags driven by IID innovations provided that the residuals are
'standardized' by the estimated contemporaneous variance–covariance matrix.
The article shows how this procedure can be generalized to test adequacy of
general models of the form $Y_t = F(I_{t-1}, a) + u_t$ where $\{Y_t\}$ is an $\mathbb{R}^m$-valued
stochastic process, $\{I_t\}$ is an $\mathbb{R}^k$-valued stochastic process, a is a vector of
parameters which can be estimated root T consistently, $\{u_t\}$ is an IID $\mathbb{R}^m$-
valued stochastic process with mean $\mathbf{0}$ and finite positive definite variance
covariance matrix Σ and u_t is independent of I_{t-1} for each t.

The Savit and Green (1991) approach works as follows. Consider the
following sequence of conditional probability statements implied by IID,

$$P\{|x_t - x_s| < \varepsilon \text{ given } |x_{t-1} - x_{s-1}| < \varepsilon\} = P\{|x_t - x_s| < \varepsilon\}, \qquad (3.1.14)$$

$$P\{|x_t - x_s| < \varepsilon \text{ given } |x_{t-1} - x_{s-1}| < \varepsilon, |x_{t-2} - x_{s-2}| < \varepsilon\} \qquad (3.1.15)$$
$$= P\{|x_t - x_s| < \varepsilon \text{ given } |x_{t-1} - x_{s-1}| < \varepsilon\},$$

$$P\{|x_t - x_s| < \varepsilon \text{ given } |x_{t-1} - x_{s-1}| < \varepsilon, |x_{t-2} - x_{s-2}| < \varepsilon,$$
$$|x_{t-3} - x_{s-3}| < \varepsilon\}$$
$$= P\{|x_t - x_s| < \varepsilon \text{ given } |x_{t-1} - x_{s-1}| < \varepsilon, |x_{t-2} - x_{s-2}| < \varepsilon\}, \ldots$$
$$(3.1.16)$$

Use this stationarity, the definition of $C_m(\varepsilon)$ (cf. (3.1.13)), and the laws of
conditional probability to rewrite these statements thus,

$$C_2(\varepsilon)/C_1(\varepsilon) = C_1(\varepsilon), \qquad (3.1.14')$$

$$C_3(\varepsilon)/C_2(\varepsilon) = C_2(\varepsilon)/C_1(\varepsilon), \qquad (3.1.15')$$

$$C_4(\varepsilon)/C_3(\varepsilon) = C_3(\varepsilon)/C_2(\varepsilon), \qquad (3.1.16')$$

$$\vdots$$

$$C_{j+1}(\varepsilon)/C_j(\varepsilon) = C_j(\varepsilon)/C_{j-1}(\varepsilon). \qquad (3.1.17)$$

The Savit and Green (1991) methods of detecting at which lag temporal
dependence is strongest are based upon statistics based on (3.1.14')–(3.1.17).

The idea is to see at which j the equalities under an IID null tend to be most violated. For example, if the alternative is $x_t = F(x_{t-2})$ Savitt and Green's statistics would tend to find the largest violation at lag 2 (3.15'). Note that the direct dynamical dependence is at lag 2 in this example even though indirect dependence which is propagated by the dynamics occurs at all lags. Savit and Green (1991) demonstrate on a set of examples that their method works well at detecting the lag at which direct dynamical dependence occurs.

The Baek and Brock (1991) test for nonlinear Granger causality is based on a comparison of a string of conditional probabilities for vectors of series that is somewhat similar to the comparison of Savit and Green (1991) above, which was developed for the scalar case.

3.2. Estimation error

Many diagnostic tests of the adequacy of a parametric class of models are based upon the estimated residuals from the best fitting of a member of the class. Unfortunately, many of these diagnostic tests require a correction for estimation error to the asymptotic distribution of the test statistic under the null hypothesis. An example of a test that requires such a correction is the ACF calculated on estimated residuals to evaluate ARMA fits (cf. Brockwell and Davis, 1987 p. 298).

This part of our article is devoted to outlining the proof of the following property of the BDS test statistic (3.1.11): *The asymptotic distribution of the BDS statistic on estimated residuals is the same as on the true (IID) innovations.* Call this the *invariance property*.

We give an heuristic discussion, with an emphasis on locating minimal conditions needed on moments, of the proof of this property for an AR(1) case here. This is enough to illustrate the essential ideas behind the proof. Then we will indicate how the BDS test can be used to test IID linearity in general under minimal moment existence requirements.

Let us work on the numerator of the test statistic first. In order to take care of the denominator all one needs to do is to locate sufficient conditions for the variance estimator (3.1.13) to converge to the same limit whether evaluated at estimated or true residuals.

Consider the expression for $T^{1/2}D_m$ in (3.15) evaluated at estimated residuals. Assume enough consistency of the estimation process that the residuals are consistently estimated and the delta method as used in Pollard (1986, Appendix A) may be generalized to the case of estimated residuals. We are now reduced to examination of the asymptotic distribution of the estimators of C_m, C_1 but evaluated at estimated residuals.

In order to see the basic idea with a minimum of clutter consider the asymptotic distribution of,

$$T^{1/2}[\hat{C}_1^* - C_1],$$ (3.2.1)

where ^ over a symbol denotes its estimated counterpart at true residuals and
^* denotes estimated counterpart at estimated residuals.

In order to locate sufficient conditions for the limit distribution of (3.2.1) to
be independent of whether estimated residuals $\hat{n}_t$ or true residuals n_t, are used
let us examine the case of an AR(1) below,

$$X_s = bX_{s-1} + N_s , \quad |b| < 1 , \tag{3.2.2}$$

where we assume $\{N_s\}$ is IID with mean zero and finite variance.

Let b_T be an estimator of b from a sample of length T from (3.2.2) and let
$F(n, x) \equiv P\{(N_s, X_{s-1}) \leqslant (n, x)\}$ denote the joint cumulative distribution function of (N_s, X_{s-1}) generated by the stationary distribution of (3.2.2). Note that
N_s is independent of X_{s-1} for all s and the distribution is independent of s by
stationarity.

In order to focus on the basic ideas restrict attention to smooth kernels of
the form $h(x, y) = h(x - y)$ which are zero off of $[-\varepsilon - \delta, \varepsilon + \delta]$ and which are
one on $[-\varepsilon + \delta, \varepsilon - \delta]$. One should think of these kernels as smooth approximations to the indicator kernel as δ tends to zero (cf. Brock, Hsieh and
LeBaron (1991)). The properties we shall use are symmetry, zero off of a
compact set, and derivatives which are zero off of a compact set and bounded
on a compact set. Then (3.2.2) implies

$$\hat{N}_s = (b - b_T)X_{s-1} + N_s , \tag{3.2.3}$$

$$T^{1/2}[\hat{C}_1^* - C_1] = T^{1/2}[\hat{C}_1 - C_1] + A_T + B_T , \tag{3.2.4}$$

where

$$A_T \equiv \{(b - b_T)T^{1/2}/T^2\}\left\{\sum\sum h'(N_s - N_t)(X_{s-1} - X_{t-1})\right\}, \tag{3.2.5}$$

$$B_T \equiv \{(b - b_T)T^{1/2}/T^2\}\left\{\sum\sum \nabla h'_{st}(X_{s-1} - X_{t-1})\right\}, \tag{3.2.6}$$

$$\nabla h'_{st} \equiv h'[N_s - N_t + \eta_{st}(X_{s-1} - X_{t-1})(b - b_T)] - h'[N_s - N_t] . \tag{3.2.7}$$

Here (3.2.4) is obtained from an exact first-order Taylor expansion where the
point $N_s - N_t + \eta_{st}(X_{s-1} - X_{t-1})(b - b_T)$ lies between $N_s - N_t$ and $N_s - N_t +$
$(X_{s-1} - X_{t-1})(b - b_T)$. Note that since the points are random variables the
factor η_{st} produced by Taylor's theorem is also a random variable.

Look at term A_T given by (3.2.5). This one is the key to getting conditions
that are sufficient for the invariance property for the asymptotic distribution of
(3.2.1) We want to illustrate the trade off involved in locating conditions for
$A_T \to 0$ in probability. The trouble is in controlling the $T^{1/2}$. It can be 'soaked
up' in two ways:

  (i) Assume b is $T^{1/2}$ consistently estimated which is the case for OLS under
classical conditions.

  (ii) Recognize that the $(1/T^2)\sum\sum$ component is a V-statistic for the estimation of

$$EH(\mathbf{Z}_s, \mathbf{Z}_t), \quad \mathbf{Z}_r \equiv (N_r, X_{r-1}), \quad H(\mathbf{Z}_s, \mathbf{Z}_t) \equiv h'(N_s - N_t)(X_{s-1} - X_{t-1}).$$
(3.2.8)

Note that symmetry of h implies symmetry of H so H is a legitimate kernel. Under mixing conditions and $E\|H\|^{2+\upsilon} < \infty$ for some $\upsilon > 0$, Denker and Keller (1983, Theorem 1) prove

$$(T^{1/2}/T^2)\left\{\sum\sum h'(N_s - N_t)(X_{s-1} - X_{t-1}) - \mu\right\} \to N(0, \sigma^2), \quad T \to \infty,$$
(3.2.9)

where $\mu \equiv Eh'(N - N')(X - X')$, σ^2 is obtained as in Denker and Keller (1983, p. 507), the convergence is in distribution, and the notation E on the RHS means the integral against the distribution, $F(n, x)$, of (N, X) and (N', X') where the two vectors are treated as *independent* draws from F.

But the mean μ is zero in a leading case. Look at the first term, $Eh'(N - N')X$. Put $E[h(N - N')|N] \equiv h_1(N)$ and note that

$$E[Dh_1(N)] = 0,$$
(3.2.10)

where D denotes derivative, for the indicator kernel. This implies the first term is zero. Symmetry implies the second term is zero. Therefore μ is zero. Let us explain why (3.2.10) is true. Recall that in the case where the kernel $h(N - N')$ is the indicator function $I_\varepsilon(N - N')$, we have

$$Dh_1(N) \equiv E[I_\varepsilon(N - N')|N] = G(N + \varepsilon) - G(N - \varepsilon),$$
$$G(x) \equiv \text{Prob}\{N \leq x\}.$$
(3.2.11)

Computing (3.2.11), assuming G has a density g, we obtain

$$E[Dh_1(N)] = \int [g(n + \varepsilon) - g(n - \varepsilon)]g(n)\,dn = 0.$$
(3.2.12)

The last integral is easily seen to equal zero by noticing that

$$\int g(n + \varepsilon)g(n)\,dn = \int g(n - \varepsilon)g(n)\,dn$$
(3.2.13)

by a change of variable argument. We sum all this up into a proposition. All convergence is in distribution.

PROPOSITION. *Assume that the moment $\mu = 0$. Then if either*
  (i) *$T^{1/2}(b - b_T) \to N(0, \sigma^2)$, and $(1/T^2)\sum\sum H(\mathbf{Z}_s, \mathbf{Z}_t) \to EH \equiv \mu$, $T \to \infty$, or*
  (ii) *$b - b_T \to 0$, and $(T^{1/2}/T^2)\sum\sum\{H(\mathbf{Z}_s, \mathbf{Z}_t) - \mu\} \to N(0, \sigma^2)$, $T \to \infty$, then*

$$A_T \to 0.$$
(3.2.14)

PROOF. use the expression for A_T given in (3.2.5) above and Slutsky's theorem (cf. Serfling, 1980, p. 19). $\square$

Turn now to getting rid of term B_T. If one assumes a uniform Lipschitz condition on $h(\cdot)$ and $T^{1/2}(b - b_T) \to X$, $T \to \infty$ then it is easy to show that B_T converges to zero in probability. However, it appears that one should be able to get by with less since $b - b_T \to 0$ implies $\eta_{st} \to 0$, and $\nabla h \to 0$ fast as it goes to zero with the product $\eta_{st}(b - b_T)$. Location of minimal sufficient conditions for $B_T \to 0$, and the consistency of the variance estimator on estimated residuals is under investigation in De Lima (1991a,b).

REMARK. The proof technique for the invariance theorem that we outlined above does not apply to the indicator function I_ε because it is not differentiable. However, under modest regularity conditions one can find C^∞ symmetric approximations to I_ε such that (3.2.10) approximately holds and, hence our theory is valid for each of these approximations even though it is *not valid for the limit*. Although the approximation procedure has not been established for the limit it appears to work well in Monte Carlo evaluations of the equality of the approximation. See Brock and Dechert (1989), and Brock, Hsieh and LeBaron (1991). Furthermore, De Lima (1991b) has shown that theorems of Randles (1982) may be applied to obtain the invariance theorem for indicator kernels for a class of cases.

The same procedure outlined above easily generalizes to proof of the invariance theorem for $AR(p)$ models drive by IID innovations provided that p is finite and known by the investigator.[3] We have the following.

PROPOSITION. *The BDS test can be used to test IID Linearity provided the number of lags is finite and is known.*

PROOF. Follow the same outline above. $\square$

Turn now to more general models. Consider the general class of parametric models with additive IID errors:

$$Y_t = f(X_t, \alpha) + N_t , \quad \{N_t\} \text{IID} , \tag{3.2.15}$$

where X_t is an information set of 'regressor' variables which may include past Ys, α is a finite-dimensional vector of parameters which can be estimated root T consistently, i.e., $T^{1/2}(\hat{\alpha} - \alpha) \to N(0, \Sigma)$, where 0 is the zero vector and Σ is

---

[3] For some cases of general $ARMA(p, q)$ models without a finite autoregressive structure one would expect the true innovations to be well approximated by a truncation of the infinite autoregressive lag structure that grows with the sample size.

the variance–covariance matrix and $N(0, \Sigma)$ denotes the normal distribution with mean vector $\mathbf{0}$ and variance–covariance matrix Σ. It is easy to use the BDS test as a test of the adequacy of the class of models.

Estimate the parameter vector α by a consistent method. Many estimation methods are root T consistent under a fourth moment condition on $\{Y_t\}$ (see Gallant and White, 1988).[4] If $f(x, \cdot)$ can be estimated by linear least squares then only slightly more than second moments may be required (Lai and Wei, 1982 p. 164). Now one may repeat the same Taylor expansion argument we used above to show that the asymptotic distribution of the BDS statistic is the same on the estimated residuals $\{\hat{n}_s\}$ as on the true residuals. This specification testing procedure may be generalized to a class of cases where $\{N_s\}$ is not IID but is a MDS which can be parameterized and the parameter vector can be estimated consistently as in GARCH model.

Consider the following class of parametric models

$$Y_t = f(X_t, \alpha) + g(X_t, \beta)N_t , \quad \{N_t\}\text{IID} . \tag{3.2.16}$$

Note that this class is the same as the class (3.2.15) above except that the MDS errors are parameterized with β a finite-dimensional parameter vector to be estimated. One can transform the heteroscedastic error term of (3.2.16) into a form where the BDS test can be used to test the specifications of $g(x, \cdot)$ conditional on $f(x, \cdot)$ in (3.2.16) by writing

$$\hat{v}_t \equiv \ln[\hat{n}_t^2] = \ln[\{y_t - f(x_t, \hat{\alpha})]/g(x_t, \hat{\beta})\}^2] , \tag{3.2.17}$$

where $\{\hat{n}_t\}$ denotes estimated residuals. Using similar techniques to those above one can show that the asymptotic distribution of the BDS statistic under the null hypothesis $\{N_t\}$ IID and conditional on the estimate $\hat{\alpha}$ is the same for $\{\hat{v}_t(\hat{\alpha})\}$ as for $\{V_t(\hat{\alpha})\}$. Recall that by definition independence applies to all measurable functions hence it is valid to test for $\{N_t\}$ IID by using the transformation in (3.2.17) when α is known (e.g., when a GARCH model is applied directly to the data without a model for the conditional mean). In the general case when both α and β are estimated the BDS test will contain some bias term that requires Monte Carlo simulation for evaluation.[5]

Note that class (3.2.17) includes many (apparently all) of the GARCH models covered in the Bollerslev, Chou and Kroner (1992) survey. The ability to specification test such a large class of parametric models of conditional volatility by examining a simple transform of estimated standardized residuals

---

[4] Of course an assumption of weak dependence is also important. As mentioned in the introduction we are assuming that the investigator has already transformed the data into a stationary form. We now add the assumption that the dependence after this transformation is sufficiently weak to allow standard limit theorems to apply.

[5] For financial time series one might expect that the bias introduced from jointly estimating the conditional mean and variance and using the logarithmic transformation would not be great because of lack of predictability of the first moment compared to the second central moment.

is useful.[6] Another class of models which may be specification tested by the BDS procedure outlined above is nonparametric models estimated by procedures which are consistent but less than root T consistent. Consistency of nonparametric procedures typically depends upon the degree of smoothness of the regression function. Hence the type of proof of the invariance theorem outlined above may, possibly, be generalized to the nonparametric case (see De Lima, 1991b).

4. Tests for nonlinearity

4.1. Overview

Tests for nonlinearity in time series can be split into three broad categories: (1) nonparametric tests in the frequency domain; (2) nonparametric tests in the time domain; (3) parametric and semi-parametric tests in the time domain. As well as discussing tests for IID linearity and MDS linearity we also discuss the use of the various tests as diagnostics for estimated nonlinear models.

The spirit of nonlinearity testing that we shall stress fits naturally into the philosophy of time series analysis exposited by Priestley (1988, p. 14). In view of the prevalence of estimable heteroscedasticity in residuals of economic and finance models we state it thus: 'Estimate out' all 'structure' until the 'standardized' residuals are reduced to strict white noise, i.e., IID. To put it another way, our goal is to find the 'best' probability model for the data under scrutiny.

Much of the difficulty and controversy in time series analysis involves interpreting what is 'best'. We shall place a lot of weight on the goal of finding probability models that aid in improving 'genuine predictions' in the sense of Tong (1990 p. 419). Since large linear models can often produce good one-step ahead forecasts based on general multivariate information sets we are particularly interested in multi-step ahead prediction. In this case the large linear models can be very cumbersome predictive tools because of the need to predict the values of all the variables in the statistical model. It is important to realize that optimal multi-step prediction of nonlinear models requires one to locate at least an IID error (see Brock and Potter, 1991). In the case of linear models the MDS property of conditional mean zero is all one needs to know about the error distribution for optimal prediction. Two other important goals, of course are: (i) improved estimation of parameters of interest; (ii) improved use of the empirical data in hypothesis testing and resolving disputes in economics (see Potter, 1990).

In our review we also pay much attention to the moment requirements of the various tests. Our motivation is based on work in financial economics by

---

[6] Lumsdaine (1990) shows that a fourth moment assumption (which is frequently violated in applications) is not necessary for asymptotic normality in the GARCH(1,1) model.

Phillips and Loretan (1990) and the references they cite. They conclude that the existence of $2 + \delta$, $\delta > 0$, moments for δ small enough seems consistent with data but becomes highly suspect for δ approaching two for financial returns. Let us explain. Assume enough moment stationarity of $\{Y_t\}$ for (4.1.1) below to make sense. Phillips and Loretan estimate the maximal model exponent,

$$\alpha \equiv \sup_q \{E|Y_t|^q < \infty\} , \tag{4.1.1}$$

for monthly returns on a stock market index that ranges from 1935–1987 and for daily returns on the Standard and Poor's 500 index from 1962–1987. Point estimates of α range from 2.5 to 3.2 for the monthly series and 3.1 to 3.8 for the daily series. Since these estimates were more than two asymptotic standard deviations from 4, this evidence is consistent with *nonexistence of fourth moments*. Note, however, that their evidence does not support *nonexistence of the unconditional second moment*, i.e., *the variance*. Therefore, we shall interpret the evidence as providing some support for existence of the variance and nonexistence of all absolute moments greater than or equal to four.

4.2. Nonparametric tests in the frequency domain

Statisticians have known for a long time that properties of the higher order spectra could be used to test for IID linearity in an observed time series (see Brillinger and Rosenblatt, 1967) however, it was not until the work of Subba Rao and Gabr (1980) that a test based on the third-order spectrum or bispectrum was widely applied. Their approach to implementing the test was improved by Hinich (1982).

Following Priestley (1988), the intuition of the test is as follows. Let $\{Y_t\}$ be a third-order stationary stochastic process and define

$$c(m, n) = E[Y_{t+n} Y_{t+m} Y_t] , \tag{4.2.1}$$

$$B(\omega_1, \omega_2) = (1/2\pi)^2 \sum c(m, n) \exp[-i(\omega_1 m + \omega_2 n)] , \tag{4.2.2}$$

where the sum is over $-\infty < m, n < \infty$, and $(\omega_1, \omega_2) \in [-\pi, \pi]^2$.

It is easy to see the following:

(i) If $\{Y_t\}$ is Gaussian then all $c(m, n)$[7] are zero (see Brillinger, 1975 for the properties of higher order cumulants of Gaussian processes). Hence the bispectrum is zero for Gaussian processes.

(ii) Consider the generalized autoregressive conditionally heteroscedastic

---

[7] Ramsey and Rothman (1989) develop a time domain test based on third order moments of the special form $E[Y_t Y_{t+m}^2]$ by exploiting the time reversibility of Gaussian linear time series.

(GARCH) process (with finite absolute third moment)

$$X_t = h_t^{1/2} Z_t , \qquad \{Z_t\} \text{ IID } N(0, 1) , \qquad h_t = a_0 + a_1 h_{t-1} . \qquad (4.2.3)$$

A simple iterated expectations argument using (4.2.1) together with zero third moment of the normal shows that all $c(m, n)$ are zero. Hence $B(\omega_1, \omega_2)$ is zero for all frequency combinations. The same argument for more general GARCH processes driven by Gaussian innovations, such as those presented in Section 2, where h_t is a *linear* function of a finite number of lagged h as well as a finite number of lagged X_{t-j}^2 shows that all third-order cumulants, $c(m, n)$ are zero. We shall call such GARCH processes, *linear GARCH*. The point is this. No test based upon the bispectrum has asymptotic power against dependent Gaussian processes or dependent Gaussian driven linear GARCH processes. Depending upon the application this property, which follows from the result that all $c(m, n) = 0$, can be very useful.

For example suppose one wishes to test the hypothesis H_0 that a sample of stock returns, $\{x_t\}$ is a sample from a random walk $\{X_t\}$ driven by Gaussian linear GARCH innovations. Then the bispectrum will be zero. So this suggests a natural way to test H_0.

The bispectral test for IID linearity is based on a normalized version of the bispectrum which is constant in (ω_1, ω_2) if $\{Y_t\}$ is IID linear. Following Priestley (1988, p. 15, p. 43) the test of the IID linear null hypothesis in (2.2.1) is based upon the result

$$c(m, n) = E[N_t^3] \sum_{j=0}^{\infty} a_j a_{j+m} a_{j+n} , \qquad (4.2.5)$$

and the quantity

$$X(\omega_1, \omega_2) \equiv |B(\omega_1, \omega_2)|^2 / [h(\omega_1) h(\omega_2) h(\omega_1 + \omega_2)] , \qquad (4.2.6)$$

where $h(\omega)$ is the spectral density function of the process $\{Y_t\}$.

Under IID linearity, X is constant in (ω_1, ω_2), does not depend upon $A(B)$, and only depends upon the second and third moments of $\{N_t\}$. A very similar procedure applies to the 'noncausal' case where the sum in (4.5) ranges from $-\infty$ to ∞.

The Hinich (1982), Subba Rao and Gabr (1984), tests are implemented by constructing estimators of $B(\omega_i, \omega_j)$ and $h(\omega_k)$ over a grid of frequencies $(0 < \omega_i < \pi, \omega_i < \omega_j < \pi)$ with good properties. The sampling distribution of the resulting estimates of $\{X_{ij}\}$ are developed under the null of IID linearity, and used to construct a test of the constancy of X. Hinich's version of the test uses the asymptotic expression for the variance–covariance matrix of the bispectral and spectral estimates in constructing the test statistic. A choice of spectral window must be made to estimate the bispectrum and sometimes this makes the results hard to interpret when small changes in the window produce large changes in the test statistic (Tong, 1990, p. 223).

Linearity tests based on higher-order spectra can be applied directly to the data (after transformations to obtain stationarity). This is because of the invariance properties of cumulant spectra to linear filters (Brillinger, 1975 p. 34). The invariance of the bispectrum test statistic when the observed data is passed through a linear filter is a major advantage of this testing approach. All of the other tests require the investigator to commit to a particular linear filter before performing the nonlinearity test, thus introducing the possibility that rejection is due to misspecification within the class of linear models rather than nonlinearity.

Tong (1990, p. 224) points out that the bispectral based tests have poor power against processes of the form

$$Y_t = f(Y_{t-1}, \ldots, Y_{t-k}) + \varepsilon_t , \qquad (4.2.7)$$

where $\{\varepsilon_t\}$ is symmetrically distributed and $f(y_1, \ldots, y_k) = -f(-y_1, \ldots, -y_k)$.

In general the bispectral based test has not performed well in Monte Carlo evaluations of its finite sample performance unless the sample size has been over 500 (compare Ashley, Patterson and Hinich, 1986 with Chan and Tong, 1986).

Our reading of the bispectral test literature suggests that at absolute moments of least order 6 are required to ensure obtain consistent and asymptotically normal estimates of the bispectrum. The bispectral test statistics discussed are based on this asymptotic normality.

In interpreting evidence from the bispectral and other tests for nonlinearity discussed in this article it must be emphasized that the rejections may be due not only to failure of the moment conditions that the tests require but also the maintained hypothesis of stationarity may be false. Failure of the stationarity hypothesis may be serious for economic data which are known to be highly *nonstationary* due to, for example, regime changes.

4.3. Nonparametric tests in the time domain

Blum, Kiefer and Rosenblatt (1961), BDS (1987), and Robinson (1991), are examples of nonparametric tests of IID in the time domain. The BDS test was discussed in detail in Section 3. They are nonparametric in the sense that the investigator is not required to explicitly choose a function of the past history of the process against which the orthogonality of the current prediction error or residual is assessed. However, in any finite sample the tests require the choice of certain parameters that implicitly parameterize a certain class of alternatives (see Tong, 1990 p. 224 for similar comments). All three of the tests become tests for IID linearity when applied to the estimated residuals of linear models.

In general one can label tests that use estimated residuals to judge the adequacy of a class of fitted models without a specific alternative *diagnostic tests*. Standard examples of such tests are the Ljung–Box and McLeod–Li portmanteau tests which are discussed in Tong (1990, p. 324). These tests examine the estimated autocorrelations of residuals and of squared residuals. Under a null of IID the autocorrelations should be zero in population except at lag zero. Cox and Hinkley (1974 p. 66) call such diagnostic tests pure significance tests and argue that it is desirable for the distribution of the test under the null hypothesis to be known at least approximately in large samples and not to depend on the value of any nuisance parameters.

The BDS test which was discussed in Section 3 is an example of a nonparametric test for IID which can be machined into a diagnostic test of the adequacy of fitted models with additive errors that satisfies the desiderata of Cox and Hinkley. Apart from BDS there appears to be a gap in the literature for diagnostic tests for IID that have power against nonlinear alternatives and have been shown to have nuisance parameter free distributions (see the comments of Tong, 1990 p. 324).

The bispectral test has also been used as a diagnostic test of IID on estimated residuals by Ashley, Patterson and Hinich (1986) who do a Monte Carlo study of performance. However, neither the bispectral test nor the BDS test are consistent against all departures from IID. We mentioned departures from IID for which the bispectral test has no power above.[8] Work of Dechert (1988) (see also Brock and Dechert, 1991) has shown there exist departures from IID that the BDS test has no power to detect. In order to briefly explain Dechert's work, consider the case of testing '1-independence'. We will say that strictly stationary stochastic process $\{X_t\}$ is 1-*independent* if X_t is independent of X_s provided $|t - s| = 1$. Consider the equality

$$\text{Prob}\{|X_s - X_t| < \varepsilon_1, |X_{s-1} - X_{t-1}| < \varepsilon_2\}$$
$$= \text{Prob}\{|X_s - X_t| < \varepsilon_1\}\text{Prob}\{|X_{s-1} - X_{t-1}| < \varepsilon_2\},$$
$$\text{for all } \varepsilon_1 > 0, \, \varepsilon_2 > 0. \qquad (4.3.1)$$

One can see that the 1-dependent alternatives which satisfy (4.3.1) are the 1-dependent alternatives for which no generalization of a BDS type test could have power against. While (4.3.1) looks close to a characterization of 1-independence and, hence, a basis for a consistent test, Dechert has found a class of 1-dependent processes with satisfy (4.3.1). He proved existence of such processes by a Laplace transform type of argument. He has also shown that a correlation integral test based on (4.3.1) is consistent within the class of Gaussian processes. The point to carry away from this discussion is this. Neither BDS (1987) nor the bispectral tests are consistent tests of IID.[9]

Asymptotically consistent time domain tests of independence can be built by using the definition of independence (the joint distribution is the product of the

---

[8] Although the bispectral test is invariant to nuisance parameters from a linear model it is not clear whether this would be true if it was used as a diagnostic for nonlinear models.

[9] Tests based on cumulant spectra higher than the third-order would reduce the class of nonlinear processes against which 'bispectral' type tests were inconsistent.

marginals). Two candidates are (i) the classical test of independence due to Blum, Kiefer and Rosenblatt (1961); (ii) the entropy-based test of Robinson (1991). Robinson shows his test is consistent under what he admits (Robinson, 1991, p. 445) are 'extremely strong' assumptions. We do not know the extent to which the asymptotic distribution of Robinson's test or the Blum–Kiefer–Rosenblatt test would depend upon nuisance parameters from the estimation process. Hence, as far as we know, it is an open question how useful these tests would be as diagnostic tests on the estimated residuals of fitted models. The performance of the BDS test in this domain has been evaluated by rather extensive Monte Carlo work of Hsieh and LeBaron which appears in Brock, Hsieh and LeBaron (1991).

The safest conclusion is this. To a certain extent there is no substitute for performance evaluation via Monte Carlo work on useful experimental designs in order to assess the practical value of a testing procedure. Theoretical properties such as consistency, asymptotic efficiency, asymptotic normality may be of little use in practice unless Monte Carlo evaluation work is done for samples sizes and experimental designs likely to arise in practice.

4.4. Parametric and semi-parametric tests in the time domain

We are using semi-parametric and parametric to imply the choice of an explicit parametric form by the investigator for the function of the previous history used to assess the orthogonality of the prediction errors or residuals. Semi-parametric tests make no explicit statement of the distribution of the residuals or prediction errors.

For example consider the following standard model:

$$Y_t = f(X_t, \theta) + N_t , \quad \theta \in \Theta , \qquad E[N_t | X_t] = 0 , \tag{4.4.1}$$

where $\{X_t\}$ is a vector-valued process which may include past Ys,

The classical parametric approach to testing requires the investigator to specify a null hypothesis on a parameter lying in a finite-dimensional space (i.e., the joint distribution of $\{Y_t, X_t\}$ is assumed known up to a finite number of parameters). However, in order to test the assumption of a martingale difference sequence property for $\{N_t\}$ no distributional assumptions are required. We first outline methods for testing the MDS property in a semi-parametric manner. Then we consider some problems in implementing standard classical parametric tests to test for MDS and IID linearity.

Building on the work of Keenan (1985), Tsay (1986) and Lukkonen et al. (1988a,b) have constructed tests for linearity versus nonlinearity by considering orthogonality of estimated residuals to polynomial functions of the observed history of the time series. It is possible to give Lagrange multiplier interpretation of the tests as in Granger and Teräsvirta (1992) (see below). In the econometrics literature there is a separate testing literature known as conditional moment (CM) tests following Newey (1985) and Tauchen (1985). Many economic models have the implication that $E[N_t | I_{t-1}] = 0$, where I_{t-1} is the information available to the econometrician. Thus specification tests were built on the asymptotic behavior of moments of the following form:

$$\frac{1}{T} \sum_{t=1}^{T} \hat{n}_t f(I_{t-1}) , \quad \text{where } f(\cdot) \text{ is any measurable function .} \tag{4.4.2}$$

Under the martingale difference sequence null the sample moment in (4.4.2) goes to zero. Our interest will be in deciding upon good choices of $f(\cdot)$, known as the test function, for testing MDS linear and methods of constructing sampling distributions for (4.4.2). In doing so we will link the two literatures.

There are two conflicting approaches to choosing a good test function. One can seek to find a class of functions $\mathbb{T}$ such that

$$E[f(X_t)N_t] = 0 \text{ for all } t, \text{ all } f \in \mathbb{T} \Rightarrow E[N_t | X_t] = 0, \text{ for all } t . \tag{4.4.3}$$

Alternatively, one might concentrate in testing for nonlinearity in a certain direction by constructing $\mathbb{T}$ from specific nonlinear time series models.

Lee, White and Granger (1989) discuss a particularly interesting version of a CM-test based on neural network theory. They define a notion of linearity of stochastic process with respect to information set $\{X_t\}$ where $\{X_t\}$ is an $\mathbb{R}^k$-valued stochastic process as follows.

DEFINITION (*Linearity in mean*). $\{Y_t\}$ is *linear in mean* w.r.t $\mathbb{R}^k$-valued information process $\{X_t\}$ if there is a vector $\Theta \in \mathbb{R}^k$ such that

$$Y_t = \Theta' X_t + N_t , \qquad E[N_t | X_t] = 0 . \tag{4.4.4}$$

LWG test (4.4.4) by using a class $\mathbb{T}$ of test functions derived from neural network theory to approximate the 'consistency' property in (4.4.3).

In the regression context Bierens (1990 p. 1445 (8)) shows that one may base a consistent conditional moment test of null hypothesis (4.4.1) on a *single* sample moment which is the estimated errors $\hat{n}_t$ weighted by $\exp(s'\Phi(X_t))$ where $\Phi : \mathbb{R}^k \to \mathbb{R}^k$ is 1–1, $s \in \mathbb{R}^k$. Note, however, the performance of the test will depend upon the choice of s, and Φ. Since Bierens (1990, p. 1444) suggests that his methods will extend to the time series case this opens up the possibility of a consistent test of linearity in mean which uses a $\mathbb{T}$ containing only one element.

In the time series literature test functions have been generated by using Volterra series expansions starting with Keenan (1985). Other approaches to finding good test functions have been based on Lagrange multiplier type principles. If the investigator has some belief about the correct direction in which to test for nonlinearity this can be used in constructing the $f(\cdot)$ function. The standard example in the statistical literature is threshold nonlinearity of both the self-exciting and smooth type. For example, Lukkonen et al. (1988b) suggest using cubic as well as quadratic terms but note that if the investigator has a belief in a certain delay parameter then the higher-order terms should only involve products in the delay variable defining the nonlinearity.

A slightly different class of tests arises from considering recursive estimation of an autoregression when the ordering of the data is given by a delay variable. Tests along these lines have been developed by Petruccelli and Davies (1988) and Tsay (1989). Potter (1990) discusses the single index nature of the nonlinearity behind such tests and constructs a weighted least squares test based on a single index.

Given a choice of a test function the next question is how to form a sampling distribution for (4.4.2) that only utilizes the MDS condition. White (1991) gives a comprehensive discussion for the general case of (4.4.1), however, we concentrate on the case of a linear conditional mean from (4.4.4) using the techniques of Wooldridge (1990).

(i) Estimate Θ by $\hat{\Theta}_T$ such that $T^{1/2}(\hat{\Theta}_T - \Theta) = O_p(1)$ and choose a test function $f(x): \mathbb{R}^K \to \mathbb{R}^Q$. This gives $\{\hat{n}_t = y_t - \hat{\Theta}'_T x_t : t = 1, \ldots, T\}$.

(ii) Run the matrix regression of $f(x_t)$ on x_t and save the residuals $\{\Lambda_t : t = 1, \ldots, T\}$

(iii) Run the regression 1 on $\hat{n}'_t \Lambda_t$, $t = 1, \ldots, T$ and use $TR_u^2 = T - \text{SSR}$ (sum of squared residuals) as asymptotically χ_Q^2 under the martingale difference assumption. An intercept is not included in the regression unless already contained in the test function.

The second step allows one to ignore the fact that $\hat{\Theta}_T$ is estimated in forming the sampling distribution and the third step gives a sampling distribution that is asymptotically robust to the presence of higher-order dependence in $\{N_t\}$, for example, conditional heteroscedasticity. If one is interested in testing IID linearity then step (iii) can be replaced with

(iii)' Run the regression of $\hat{n}_t$ on Λ_t, $t = 1, \ldots, T$ and use the F-statistic.

The simplifications introduced by Wooldridge's methods in the case of testing MDS linearity are important because they allow the investigator to use standard regression software to conduct the nonlinearity tests.

The moment requirements of the CM type tests depend on two factors: the properties of the innovation sequence $\{N_t\}$ and the properties of the test function. In the form above one clearly requires at least second moments of the product $N'_t \Lambda_t$ in order for step (iii) to make sense. If (iii)' is used (i.e., IID linearity is tested) then weaker conditions are available. For example, in the Tsay (1986) test where second-order polynomials of the observed time series are used in the test function under $\{N_t\}$ IID one requires $E[N_t^4] < \infty$, whereas under the MDS condition alone one needs at least $E[N_t^6] < \infty$. If the test function was bounded as in the example used by LWG then one can appeal to the results of Lai and Wei (1982) under $\{N_t\}$ IID and hence only slightly more than second moments of $\{N_t\}$ are required.

CM tests have the advantage that the particular test function can be immediately used to construct a regression function that fits better in-sample than the linear model. When a large number of different test functions are used it is possible to concentrate on estimating nonlinear models suggested by the smallest probability values from the linearity test statistics. However, it is important to realize that the overall significance of the evidence against nonlinearity is harder to assess when more that one of the CM-tests is carried out.

Polynomial type tests tend to perform very well in Monte Carlo experiments for smaller sample size (i.e., less than 200). For example, Teräsvirta, Lin and Granger (1991) report results where cubic polynomials have power very close to Lagrange multiplier tests for the type of nonlinearity used in the experimental design. Petruccelli (1990) contains a comprehensive Monte Carlo evaluations of tests for threshold autoregressions. Of course until more nonlinear time series models are estimated on actual economic data one cannot be sure that the designs used in these Monte Carlo experiments are relevant.

In some circumstances an investigator might use theory to construct a specific nonlinear alternative to test against a *specific* linear alternative. Here the word specific means not only that the functional form of the nonlinear model and the density of the innovation sequence are assumed known but also the lag lengths of the two models. However, standard likelihood based testing theory is not likely to be applicable for three reasons as outlined by Hansen (1991a,b) building on the work of Davies (1977, 1987):

(1) There might be parameters of the nonlinear model unidentified under the null.

(2) The likelihood surface may have more than one local optimum and the null hypothesis may not lie on the same 'hill' as the global optimum.

(3) The score may be identically zero under the null hypothesis.

We concentrate on the first point which can be illustrated with a simple example,

$$Y_t = \phi_1 Y_{t-1} + \phi_2 F(\gamma, Y_{t-1}) + e_t , \quad e_t \sim \text{IID N}(0, \sigma^2) , \qquad (4.4.5)$$

$F(\cdot)$ is a nonaffine function from the line to the line and $\gamma \in \Gamma \subset \mathbb{R}$.

$H_0: \phi_2 = 0$ (IID linearity),
$H_A: \phi_2 \neq 0$.

Under the null hypothesis γ is not identified implying that the standard sampling theory for the likelihood ratio, Wald and Lagrange multiplier (score) statistics are not valid (see Davies, 1977). Such problems are pervasive in classical tests of a linear null model against a specific nonlinear alternative model. For example, Tong (1990, Chapter 5.3) and Chan (1990) construct special likelihood ratio tests to account for the problem in threshold autoregressions. But also see Granger and Teräsvirta (1992) and Godfrey (1988, pp. 88–89) for solutions based on normalizing the function $F(\cdot)$ so that $F(y, 0) = 0$.

The solution proposed by Davies is to view the test statistic as a function of the unidentified parameter and construct a test statistic based on the maximum or supremum of this function. There are two main problems: (i) it is computationally intensive to find the maximum in many cases, (ii) the asymptotic sampling distribution of the maximum is rarely free from nuisance parameter problems. One can construct bounds to deal with the second problem as in Davies (1987) or more generally use simulation methods to compute asymptotic critical values using the sample covariance function of the Gaussian empirical process produced by the maximization as in Hansen (1991, 1992). The advantage of Hansen's approach is its wider applicability but it can be computationally intensive.

Monte Carlo evidence in Teräsvirta, Lin and Granger (1991) suggests that alternatives to using the maximum of the test statistics such as randomly choosing a direction to test in (i.e., by random draws of the nuisance parameters) or fixing the nuisance parameters a priori can result in substantial loss of power. Both Davies's and Hansen's techniques are sufficiently general to allow their use in semi-parametric situations where investigators often maximize over test statistics.

We should note in passing that it is very difficult to derive specific nonlinear alternatives using economic theory. Hence most alternative specifications tend to be data-driven, thus producing a problem of pre-test bias (see Leamer, 1978). If the identification scheme can be transformed into a maximization problem over a suitable defined test statistic then once again the above techniques can be useful.

Another difficulty with classical testing approaches is the assumption that the underlying innovations to the two time series models are generated by the same distribution (i.e., in most cases Gaussian). Li and McLeod (1988) find evidence that non-Gaussian linear models can produce substantial improvements in in-sample fit over models estimated using a Gaussian likelihood. Thus, classical tests might be biased in favor of nonlinear models under the assumption of Gaussian innovations. One alternative that still maintains the fully parametric structure is to use Cox's nonnested approach (see Pesaran and Potter, 1991).

5. Evidence of nonlinearity and chaos

A lot of work has recently investigated the evidence of nonlinearity and chaos in economic data. Let us divide the discussion into: (i) macroeconomic and other economic data sets, (ii) financial data sets such as asset returns.

In describing the evidence we shall use the term 'low-dimensional chaos' to refer to a chaos (possibly noisy and possibly infected with measurement and observation error) whose dimension is low enough and whose derivative is 'regular' enough that short term forecasting with the algorithms in, for example, Casdagli and Eubank (1991), should give improvement over methods not designed to exploit properties of chaos, e.g., linear methods. The word 'regular' is used to exclude examples like a simple one-dimensional chaos, $x_{t+1} = F(x_t)$, where F is the q-th iterate of the tent map and q is large. For q large enough short term prediction is impossible with machines of finite resolution. Two recent conference volumes that contain much useful material on chaos are Barnett et al. (1988, 1989).

5.1. Macroeconomics

A rather large literature has emerged in economic theory on the possibility of chaos being consistent with rational expectations in intertemporal general equilibrium macroeconomic models. The Journal of Economic Theory, October 1986 conference volume was one of the early collections of papers. A recent survey in Boldrin and Woodford (1990). The conclusion is: Yes. Chaos is consistent with standard assumptions on preferences and technology in conventional equilibrium models used in dynamic economics. This raised interest in testing for the presence of chaos in data. The general (but not universal) conclusion is this: The evidence is weak for the presence of a chaos of a type that could be reliably predicted out of sample using nonlinear prediction algorithms that are tailor made to do well when chaos (even if it is noisy) is present. Linear prediction algorithms appear beatable but chaos has no special claim.

Brock and Sayers (1988) tested U.S. post WW II macroeconomic time series such as (i) quarterly U.S. employment; (ii) quarterly U.S. unemployment rate; (iii) monthly U.S. industrial production; and (iv) U.S. quarterly GNP and found some evidence consistent with nonlinearity (or possibly neglected nonstationarity) but found little evidence consistent with simple low-dimensional chaos even if infected with a moderate amount of noise. The testing methodology was to attempt to pre-filter out linear structure as well as 'pre-filter' out nonstationarity structure and apply the BDS test to the residuals using the methodology laid out in Section 3 above. Pre-filtering appears to be a useful operation when dealing with time series whose linear persistence is so strong that it overwhelms any other structure that may be present (economic time series exhibit strong linear persistence).

Brock (1986) and Frank and Stengos (1988) compared dimension estimates on detrended macroeconomic time series before and after prewhitening by low order autoregressions to explore, in a diagnostic way, the evidence for low-dimensional chaos. If the data was chaotic Brock (1986) proved the dimension of the AR(q) prewhitened data should not change. Note that the reverse procedure of applying an AR(q) to chaotic innovations will typically change the dimension of the output, however. The evidence for low-dimensional chaos was weak, but this procedure probably rejects chaos too often when it is true.

Scheinkman and LeBaron in Barnett et al. (1989) examined U.S. real per capita GNP over a much longer period and failed to reject an AR(2) on detrended data with correction for change of variance of the innovations over the periods 1872–1946 and 1947–1986 after dummies for the great depression (1930–1939) and WW II (1940–1945) were introduced. They applied the BDS test to the standardized residuals and bootstrapped the small sample distribution under the null.

LeBaron (1991) examined similar macroeconomic time series with a battery of nonlinearity tests, including BDS and Tsay, and found little evidence consistent with low-dimensional deterministic chaos but found evidence consistent with nonlinearity.

Ramsey, Sayers, and Rothman (1990) examined recent studies and found none that generated convincing evidence consistent with a low-dimensional chaos after correcting for robustness and linear persistence. They disputed earlier claims to have found chaos in economic and financial data.

Lee, White, and Granger (1989) examined: (i) US/Japan exchange rate 1973–1987 (little evidence of neglected nonlinearity); (ii) 3-month US treasury bill interest rate, monthly 1958–1987 (linearity rejected); (iii) US M2 money stock, monthly, 1958–1987, (neural network, McLeod–Li, bispectrum, BDS tests reject linearity; Keenan, Tsay, and information matrix tests do not reject); (iv) US personal income, monthly 1958–1987 (linearity is rejected except by the bispectral test); (v) US unemployment rate, monthly 1958–1987, (neural network, Tsay, McLeod–Li, bispectrum, BDS reject linearity, the others do not). All of the series were prewhitened by fitting AR models to first differences of logs, except for unemployment and treasury bill rates where first differences were directly applied to the data.

As well as testing macroeconomic time series for nonlinearities a number of parametric models have been estimated. In the nonlinear time series literature a number of parametric models have been suggested: bilinear, threshold autoregression (TAR), smooth transition autoregression (STAR) exponential autoregression (EXPAR) and doubly stochastic models. Tong (1990) contains descriptions of each type of model. Bilinear models were the first to enter the scene in economics with Granger and Anderson's 1978 book and have seen some limited applications (Maravall, 1983, for example). Threshold autoregressions have been more recently applied with work by Ham and Sayers (1990) on unemployment rates in the U.S., Cao and Tsay (1992) on volatility in financial data, Potter (1990) on U.S. GNP. STAR and EXPAR models are extensively analyzed in a book by Granger and Teräsvirta (1992) and applied to O.E.C.D. industrial production indices by Anderson and Teräsvirta (1991). Hamilton (1989) estimates a doubly stochastic time series model on U.S. GNP that has produced a number of other applications.

We concentrate on the threshold model for U.S. GNP from Potter (1991a) in order to illustrate how nonlinear time series models can bring fresh life to old debates in economics. The model is estimated on U.S. GNP from 1947 quarter 1 to 1990 quarter 4 and has the following restricted form:

$$Y_t = \begin{cases} -0.808 + 0.516Y_{t-1} - 0.946Y_{t-2} + 0.352Y_{t-5} + \varepsilon_{1t} & \text{if } Y_{t-2} \leqslant 0, \\ 0.517 + 0.299Y_{t-1} + 0.189Y_{t-2} - 0.143Y_{t-5} + \varepsilon_{2t} & \text{if } Y_{t-2} > 0, \end{cases}$$

$$(5.1)$$

where $\sigma_1^2 = 1.5$, $\sigma_2^2 = 0.763$ and $Y_t = 100 \times \log(\mathrm{GNP}_t / \mathrm{GNP}_{t-1})$.

Potter (1990, 1991a) contain an extensive analysis of the model's improved performance against traditional linear Gaussian models. In particular the recursive forecasting performance of the model in the 1980s is shown to be superior to a range of univariate linear models and multivariate linear models. The nonlinear model is also evaluated against some simple linear non-Gaussian models produced by exogenous regime changes such as switches in monetary policy, oil price changes and the political business cycle. The conclusion of this evaluation appears to be that the nonlinear model is picking up more than deterministic or nonpredictable regime changes. More recent work by Hansen (1991) provides statistically significant support for the specification using techniques that take into account the nuisance parameter problems.

The dynamics implied by the model are very different in an economically important way from standard linear models. Following the work of Romer (1986, for example) there has been a heated debate about the relative 'stability' of the post World War II U.S. economy compared to the pre World War II U.S. economy. Romer argued that previous studies finding increased stability in the post-war period were biased because of the methods used to construct pre-war data. The debate has centered on various estimates of the volatility of the U.S. economy, however, using the nonlinear model in (5.1) one can take a completely different approach.

From 1929 to 1933 the U.S. economy suffered a contraction in size of one third – the great depression. A decline unprecedented before or since. The threshold model of post-war U.S. GNP has an intrinsic stabilizer – the AR(2) coefficient in the first regime – that prevents such large declines from persisting. Potter (1991a) illustrates this property by taking residuals from models estimated on pre-1945 data and using them to propagate the post (1945) economy as represented by the threshold model. It is found that although the 'impulses' produce a severe recession it is not as deep or as long-lived as the actual great depression. However, if one performs the same experiment with standard linear models fitted to post-war U.S. GNP then the depth and longevity of the great depression is recreated almost exactly.[10]

The conclusion is that evidence consistent with nonlinearity in macroeconomics is strong but evidence for low-dimensional deterministic chaos is weak. An issue of burden of proof arises. Barnett and Hinich (1991) argue that the burden of proof should *not* be placed on low-dimensional chaos whereas

---

[10] Potter (1991b) discusses the use of impulse response functions for nonlinear time series and defines a measure of persistence for nonlinear time series.

we have taken the posture in this survey that *other plausible alternatives* must be discarded with reasonable probability. Whatever one's views are on this issue, it appears that the evidence for nonlinearity may have helped start a boom in the fitting of nonlinear parametric models to macroeconomic time series data.

5.2. Finance

Versions of the efficient markets hypothesis suggest that asset returns (especially high frequency) should approximate a martingale difference sequence with respect to publicly available information after correction for the opportunity costs of funds and transactions costs. This suggests that the conditional mean of asset returns should be near zero and difficult to forecast out of sample. This is consistent with evidence. For example, the latest evidence due to Diebold and Nason (1990) and Meese and Rose (1991) suggests that no nonlinear prediction algorithm can do any better at out-of-sample prediction of asset returns than the random walk. Therefore, the evidence consistent with chaos in studies such as Scheinkman and LeBaron (1989), Frank and Stengos (1988), Mayfield and Mizrach (1989), and others may be produced by nonpredictable nonstationarity or some other structure which is difficult to predict out of sample rather than chaos.

An interesting attempt to estimate the conditional probability distribution of returns is Gallant, Hsieh, and Tauchen's chapter in Barnett, Powell and Tauchen (1991) (using a set of techniques described in Gallant and Tauchen, 1990). They show that the daily British pound/dollar exchange rate, January 2, 1974 to December 30, 1983 is 'strongly conditionally heteroscedastic but cannot be fit using standard methods of the autoregressive conditional heteroscedasticity (ARCH) type'. They fit a 'conditional mixture model with an autocorrelated mixing process' which seems to do quite well.

It may be possible to improve nonlinear out-of-sample prediction by looking for periods when such prediction is possible by clever choice of conditioning information. To our knowledge LeBaron's paper in Casdagli and Eubank (1991) is the first to adduce evidence that such prediction may be possible by using past volatility as well as past returns. LeBaron finds that periods following relatively quiet episodes display more out-of-sample predictability evidence than periods following relatively noisy episodes. Weigend, Huberman and Rumelhart's paper in Casdagli and Eubank (1991) gives related results for returns on foreign exchange using neural net methods.

Brock, Lakonishok and LeBaron (1990) have shown using daily returns on the Dow Jones index that popular technical trading rules appears to be useful in locating periods of potential statistically significant out-of-sample predictability when measured against the standard of random walk models driven by innovations with parametric forms of heteroscedasticity such as GARCH models. We emphasize that none of this evidence of out-of-sample predictability implies market inefficiency because transactions costs of trading, adequate allowance for other sources of systematic risk, or correct adjustment for time dependence of the price and quantity of systematic risk has not been done.

However, it is well known that asset returns display structure in conditional variance that appears to be predictable out of sample, at least to some degree. The GARCH class of models and their off-shoots appear to do a quite good job of parameterizing structure in conditional heteroscedasticity. The paper of Bollerslev, Chou and Kroner (1992) gives an excellent guide to a huge literature. However, more recently some investigators have been examining whether the assumption of linearity in the conditional variance is appropriate (e.g., Cao and Tsay, 1992).

Hsieh (1991) attempted to test for the possibility that neglected nonstationarity was driving the findings consistent with nonlinearity by observing the pattern of rejections of linearity across frequencies. The pattern of rejections appeared similar across frequencies down to 15 minute periods. Unless one believes the probability structure of financial returns is changing every 15 minutes it seems safer to interpret the rejections as consistent with nonlinearity. Hsieh attempted to take out well-known nonstationarities before applying his tests.

The conclusion on chaos for financial returns appears similar as that for macro. The evidence for chaos is weak, evidence consistent with nonlinearity is strong. After GARCH effects are accounted for the evidence for 'remaining structure' is weakened. However, there still seems to be evidence consistent with neglected nonlinearity although, in some cases, it may well be evidence of neglected nonstationarity. Conditional forecasting work such as LeBaron's chapter in Casdagli and Eubank (1991) and the trading-rule-based specification tests of Brock, Lakonishok, and LeBaron (1990) suggest that not all the evidence consistent with nonlinearity is just a reflection of neglected nonstationarity.

6. Summary and conclusions

This article has selectively surveyed some recent work in the vast and rapidly growing area of nonlinear time series analysis. This survey concentrates on work that the authors themselves have been doing, and, especially, concentrates on statistical testing procedures that are designed to have high ability to detect chaos if it is present, but it also touches on related work. While the activity which we reported has already experienced a lot of development in over half a decade, we must warn the reader that many issues remain unsettled. For that reason we have discussed many very recent works which are on-going so the reader may contact the researchers that are cited for the latest results.

Acknowledgment

The first author would like to thank National Science Foundation, the Wisconsin Graduate School, the Wisconsin Alumni Research Foundation and the Vilas Trust for essential financial support. The second author gratefully acknowledges research support from the Academic Senate, UCLA. Pedro De Lima, Blake LeBaron, Hashem Pesaran and Philip Rothman provided many useful comments and suggestions for the paper.

References

Anderson, H. and T. Teräsvirta (1991). Modeling nonlinearities in business cycles using smooth transition autoregressive models. Department of Economics, The University of California, San Diego, CA.

Ashley, R., D. Patterson and M. Hinich (1986). A diagnostic test for nonlinearity and serial dependence in time series fitting errors. *J. Time Ser. Anal.* **7**, 165–178.

Baek, E. and W. Brock (1992). A nonparametric test for temporal dependence in a vector of time series. *Statist. Sinica* **2** (1), 137–156.

Baek, E. and W. Brock (1991). A general test for nonlinear Granger causality: Bivariate model. Department of Economics, Iowa State University and University of Wisconsin, Madison.

Barnett, W., E. Berndt and H. White, eds. (1988). *Dynamic Econometric Modeling, Proc. 3rd Internat. Sympos. in Economic Theory and Econometrics*. Cambridge Univ. Press, Cambridge.

Barnett, W., J. Geweke and K. Shell eds., (1989). *Economic Complexity, Chaos, Sunspots, Bubbles, and Nonlinearity, Proc. 4th Internat. Sympos. in Economic Theory and Econometrics*. Cambridge Univ. Press, Cambridge.

Barnett, W., J. Powell and G. Tauchen eds., (1991). *Nonparametric and Semiparametric Methods in Econometrics and Statistics, Proc. 5th Internat. Sympos. in Economic Theory and Econometrics*. Cambridge Univ. Press, Cambridge.

Barnett, W. and M. Hinich (1991). Empirical chaotic dynamics in economics. *Ann. Oper. Res.*, to appear.

Bierens, H. (1990). A consistent conditional moment test of functional form. *Econometrica* **58**, 1443–1458.

Billingsley, P. (1986). *Probability and Measure*. Wiley, New York.

Blum, J., J. Kiefer and M. Rosenblatt (1961). Distribution free tests of independence based on the sample distribution function. *Ann. Math. Statist.* **32**, 485–498.

Boldrin, M. and M. Woodford (1990). Equilibrium models displaying endogenous fluctuations and chaos. *J. Monetary Econ.* **25**, 189–222.

Bollerslev, T., R. Chou and K. Kroner (1992). ARCH Modeling in finance: A review of the theory and empirical evidence. *J. Econometrics* **52**, 5–50.

Brillinger, D. (1975). *Time Series Analysis: Data Analysis and Theory*. Holt, Reinehart and Winston, New York.

Brillinger, D. and M. Rosenblatt (1967). Asymptotic theory of k-th order spectra. In: B. Harris ed., *Spectral Analysis of Time Series*. Wiley, New York.

Brock, W. (1986). Distinguishing random and deterministic systems: Abridged version. *J. Econ. Theory*. **40**, 168–195.

Brock, W. and W. Dechert (1989). Statistical inference theory for measures of complexity in chaos theory and nonlinear science. In: N. Abraham, A. Albano, A. Passamente and P. Rapp, eds., *Measures of Complexity and Chaos*, Series B: Physics, Vol. 208, Plenum Press, New York.

Brock, W. and W. Dechert (1991). Nonlinear dynamical systems: Instability and chaos in economics. In: W. Hildenbrand and H. Sonnenschein, eds., *Handbook of Mathematical Economics, Vol. 4*. North-Holland, Amsterdam, Chapter 40.

Brock, W., W. Dechert and J. Scheinkman (1987). A test for independence based upon the correlation dimension. Department of Economics, University of Wisconsin, University of Houston, and the University of Chicago. [Revised Version (1991): W. Brock, W. Dechert, J. Scheinkman and B. LeBaron.]

Brock, W., J. Lakonishok and B. LeBaron (1990). Simple technical trading rules and the stochastic properties of stock returns. Social Systems Research Institute Working Paper #9022, University of Wisconsin, Madison, WI.

Brock, W., D. Hsieh and B. LeBaron (1991). *Nonlinear Dynamics, Chaos and Instability: Statistical Theory and Economic Evidence*. MIT Press, Cambridge, MA.

Brock, W. and S. Potter (1991). Diagnostic testing for nonlinearity, chaos, and general dependence in time series data: In: M. Casdagli and S. Eubank (1991).

Brock, W. and C. Sayers (1988). Is the business cycle characterized by deterministic chaos. *J. Monetary Econ.* **22**, 71–90.

Brockwell, P. and R. Davis (1987). *Time Series: Theory and Methods*. Springer, New York.

Cao, C. and R. Tsay (1992). Nonlinear time series analysis of stock volatilities. *J. Appl. Econ.* **7**, 165–185.

Casdagli, M. and S. Eubank, eds., (1991). *Proc. 1990 NATO Workshop on Nonlinear Modeling and Forecasting*. Santa Fe Institute Series, Addison-Wesley, Redwood City. CA.

Chan, K. (1990). Testing for threshold autoregression. *Ann. Statist.* **18**, 1886–1894.

Chan, W. and H. Tong (1986). On tests for non-linearity in time series analysis. *J. Forecast.* **5**, 217–228.

Cox, D. and D. Hinkley (1974). *Theoretical Statistics*. Chapman and Hall, London.

Davies, R. (1977). Hypothesis testing when a nuisance parameter is present only under the alternative. *Biometrika* **64**, 247–254.

Davies, R. (1987). Hypothesis testing when a nuisance parameter is present only under the alternative. *Biometrika* **74**, 33–43.

De Lima, P. (1991a). A test for IID time series based on the BDS statistic. Department of Economics, University of Wisconsin, Madison, WI.

De Lima, P. (1991b). Testing nonlinearities in economic time series under moment condition failure. Department of Economics, University of Wisconsin, Madison, WI.

Dechert, W. (1987). A program to calculate the BDS statistic for the IBM PC. Department of Economics, University of Houston, Houston, TX.

Dechert, W. (1988). A characterization of independence for a Gaussian process in terms of the correlation integral. Social Sciences Research Institute WP# 8812, Department of Economics, University of Wisconsin, Madison, WI.

Denker, M. and G. Keller (1983). On U-Statistics and Von Mises statistics for weakly dependent processes. *Z. Wahrsch. Verw. Geb.* **64**, 505–522.

Diebold, F. and Nason, J. (1990). Nonparametric exchange rate prediction, *J. Internat. Econ.* **28**, 315–332.

Eckmann, J. and D. Ruelle (1985). Ergodic theory of chaos and strange attractors. *Rev. Modern Phys.* **57**, 617–656.

Frank, M. and T. Stengos (1988). Some evidence concerning macroeconomic chaos. *J. Monetary Econ.* **22**, 423–438.

Frisch, R. (1933). Propagation problems and impulse problems in dynamic economics. In: *Economic Essays in Honor of Gustav Cassel*. Allen and Unwin, London.

Gallant, R. and C. Tauchen (1990). A nonparametric approach to nonlinear time series analysis: Estimation and simulation. Department of Statistics, North Carolina State University and Department of Economics, Duke University.

Gallant, R. and H. White (1988). *A Unified Theory of Estimation and Inference for Nonlinear Dynamics Models*. Blackwell, New York.

Godfrey, L. (1988). *Misspecification Tests in Econometrics*. Cambridge Univ. Press, Cambridge.

Granger, C. and T. Teräsvirta (1992). *Modeling Nonlinear Economic Relationships*. Oxford Univ. Press, Oxford, to appear.

Hall, P. and C. Heyde (1980). *Martingale Limit Theory and Its Application*. Academic Press, New York.

Ham, M. and C. Sayers (1990). Testing for nonlinearities in United States unemployment by sensor. Department of Economics, University of Virginia.

Hamilton, J. (1989). A new approach to the economic analysis of nonstationary time series and the business cycle. *Econometrica* **57**, 357–384.

Hansen, B. (1991). Inference when a nuisance parameter is not identified under the null hypothesis. Department of Economics, University of Rochester.

Hansen, B. (1992). The likelihood ratio test under non-standard conditions: Testing the Markov trend model of GNP. *J. Appl. Econ.* **7**, 61–82.

Hansen, L. and T. Sargent (1991). *Rational Expectations Econometrics*. Westview Press, Boulder, CO.

Hinich, M. (1982). Testing for Gaussianity and linearity of a stationary time series. *J. Time Ser. Anal.* **3**, 169–176.

Hsieh, D. (1991). Chaos and nonlinear dynamics: Applications to financial markets. *J. Finance* **46** (5), 1839–1877.

Jevons, W. S. (1984). *Investigations in Currency and Finance*. Macmillan, London.

Keenan, D. (1985). A Tukey nonadditivity-type test for time series nonlinearity. *Biometrika* **72**, 39–44.

Lai, T. and C. Wei (1982). Least squares estimates in stochastic regression models with applications to identification and control of dynamic systems. *Ann. Statist.* **10**, 154–166.

Leamer, E. E. (1978). *Specification Searches*. Wiley, New York.

LeBaron, B. (1991). Nonlinear econometrics of chaos: Empirical results. *Cuasdernos Economicos*, Bank of Spain, Madrid.

Lee, T., H. White and C. Granger (1989). Testing for neglected nonlinearity in time series models: A comparison of neural network methods and alternative tests. Department of Economics, University of California, San Diego, CA.

Li, W. and A. McLeod (1988). ARMA modeling with non-Gaussian innovations. *J. Time Ser. Anal.* **9**, 155–166.

Lukkonen, R., P. Saikkonen and T. Teräsvirta (1988a). Testing linearity against smooth transition autoregressions. *Biometrika* **74**, 491–499.

Lukkonen, R., P. Saikkonen and T. Teräsvirta (1988b). Testing linearity in univariate time series models. *Scand. J. Statist.* **15**, 161–175.

Lumsdaine, R. (1990). Asymptotic properties of the quasi-maximum likelihood estimator in GARCH(1,1) and IGARCH(1,1) models. Department of Economics, Harvard University.

Maravall, A. (1983). An application of nonlinear time series forecasting. *J. Econ. Business Statist.* **1**, 66–74.

Mayfield, E. and B. Mizrach (1989). On determining the dimension of real-time stock price data. Department of Economics, Boston College.

Meese, R. and A. Rose (1991). An empirical assessment of non-linearities in models of exchange rate determination. *Rev. Econ. Stud.* **58**, 603–619.

Newey, W. (1985). Maximum likelihood specification testing and conditional moment tests. *Econometrica* **53**, 1047–70.

Ozaki, T. (1985). Non-linear time series models and dynamical systems. In: *Handbook of Statistics*, Vol. 5. North-Holland, Amsterdam.

Pesaran, H. and S. Potter (1991). Applications of non-nested hypothesis testing in nonlinear time series. Depatment of Economics, University of California, Los Angeles, CA.

Petruccelli, J. (1990). A comparison of tests for SETAR-type non-linearity in time series. *J. Forecast.* **9**, 25–36.

Petruccelli, J. and N. Davies (1986). A Portmanteau test for self-exciting threshold type non-linearity in time series. *Biometrika* **73**, 687–694.

Phillips, P. and M. Loretan (1990). Testing covariance stationarity under moment condition failure with an application to common stock returns. Department of Economics, Yale University.

Pollard, D. (1986). *Covergence of Stochastic Processes*. Springer, Berlin.

Potter, S. (1990). Nonlinear time series and economic fluctuations. Unpublished Ph.D. Thesis, Department of Economics, University of Wisconsin, Madison, WI.

Potter, S. (1991a). A nonlinear approach to U.S. GNP. Department of Economics, University of California, Los Angeles, CA.

Potter, S. (1991b). Nonlinear impulse response functions. Department of Economics, University of California, Los Angeles, CA.

Priestley, M. (1988). *Non-linear and Non-stationary Time Series Analysis*. Academic Press, New York.

Ramsey, J. and P. Rothman (1989). Time irreversibility of stationary time series: Estimators and test statistics. Department of Economics, New York University.

Ramsey, J., C. Sayers and P. Rothman (1990). The statistical properties of dimension calculations using small data sets: Some economic applications. *Internat. Econ. Rev.* **31**, 991–1020.

Randles, R. (1982). On the asymptotic normality of statistics with estimated parameters. *Ann. Statist.* **10**, 462–474.

Robinson, P. (1991). Consistent nonparametric entropy-based testing. *Rev. Econ. Stud.* **58**, 437–453.

Romer, C. (1986). Is the statilization of the postwar economy a figment of the data? *Amer. Econ. Rev.* **76**, 314–334.

Rosenblatt, M. (1971). *Markov Processes, Structure and Asymptotic Behavior*. Springer, New York.

Rosenblatt, M. (1985). *Stationary Sequences and Random Fields*. Birkhäuser, Boston, MA.

Savit, R. and M. Green (1991). Time series and dependent variables, *Phys. D.* **50**, 521–544.

Scheinkman, J. and B. LeBaron (1989). Nonlinear dynamics and stock returns. *J. Business* **62**, 311–337.

Serfling, R. (1980). *Approximation Theories in Mathematical Statistics*. Wiley, New York.

Slutzky, E. E. (1927). The summation of random causes as the source of cyclical processes. In: *The Problems of Economic Conditions*, Conjecture Institute, Moscow.

Subba Rao, T. and M. Gabr (1984). *An Introduction to Bispectral Analysis and Bilinear Time Series Models*. Springer, New York.

Tauchen, G. (1985). Diagnostic testing and the evaluation of maximum likelihood models. *J. Econometrics* **30**, 415–443.

Teräsvirta, T., C. Lin and C. Granger (1991). Power of the neural network linearity test. Discussion Paper #91–01, Department of Economics, University of California, San Diego, CA.

Theiler, J. (1990). Statistical precision of dimension estimators. *Phys. Rev. A* **41**, 3038–3051.

Tong, H. (1990). *Non-linear Time Series: A Dynamical System Approach*. Clarendon Press, Oxford.

Tsay, R. (1986). Nonlinearity tests for time series. *Biometrika* **73**, 461–466.

Tsay, R. (1989). Testing and modeling threshold autoregression. *J. Amer. Statist. Assoc.* **84**, 231–240.

White, H. (1991). *Estimation, Inference and Specification Analysis*. Cambridge Univ. Press, New York, to appear.

Wooldridge, J. (1990). A unified approach to robust, regression-based specification tests. *Econometric Theory* **6**, 17–43.

Yule, G. U. (1927). On a method of investigating periodicities in disturbed series, with special reference to Wolfer's sunspot numbers. *Philos. Trans. Roy. Soc. London Ser. A* **226**, 267–98.

G. S. Maddala, C. R. Rao and H. D. Vinod, eds., *Handbook of Statistics, Vol. 11*

9

Estimation, Inference and Forecasting of Time Series Subject to Changes in Regime

James D. Hamilton

1. Introduction

Many economic and financial time series undergo episodes in which the behavior of the series changes quite dramatically. Figure 1, taken from Town (1990), displays the number of mergers of U.S. firms during 1895–1919. Merger activity seems to have been influenced by very different factors at the turn of the century than at other dates in the sample. Figure 2, taken from

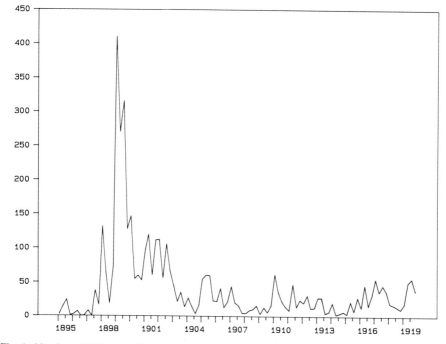

Fig. 1. Number of U.S. manufacturing and mining firms disappearing due to mergers, acquisition, or consolidation, quarterly 1895–1919. Source: Town (1990).

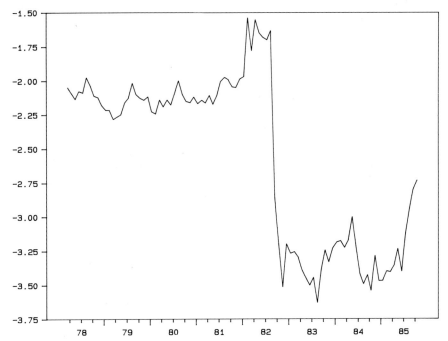

Fig. 2. Log of the ratio of (a) the peso value of dollar-denominated bank accounts in Mexico to (b) the peso value of peso-denominated bank accounts in Mexico, monthly 1978–1985. Source: Rogers (1992).

Rogers (1992), records the prevalence in Mexico of bank accounts denominated in U.S. dollars. The Mexican government took strong steps to curtail the use of such accounts in 1982, and this clearly has a significant effect on the behavior of this series. Figure 3, taken from Hetzel (1990), plots the ratio of total output to the money supply for the U.S. There was a persistent tendency each year from the end of World War II until 1980 for the public to hold less money relative to total spending; the trend of this series at other times seems very different. Figure 4, taken from Hamilton (1988), displays the nominal interest rate on U.S. treasury bills from 1962 to 1987. During 1979 to 1982, the Federal Reserve experimented with a policy of permitting more variability and a higher level of interest rates, and this policy experiment shows up clearly in this series.

Such changes in regime are the rule rather than the exception in economic and financial time series. Financial panics, wars, and major changes in policy dramatically change the behavior of many economic indicators.

It can be a serious error to fit a constant-parameter, linear time series representation across such episodes. Cecchetti, Lam and Mark (1990b) provided a compelling example of why. They fit a model allowing changes in regime to a hundred years of data on the dividends paid on U.S. stocks. The

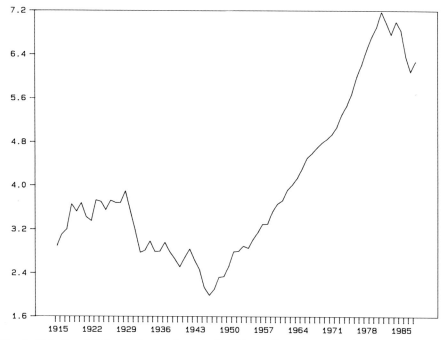

Fig. 3. Velocity of U.S. M1 (ratio of nominal GNP to M1 measure of money supply), annual 1915–1988. Source: Hetzel (1990).

results suggested that in a typical year dividends could be expected to grow a few percent faster than inflation. However, in several episodes over this century, the economy experienced such a serious shock that dividends started to fall by 35% per year. When they incorporated this feature of the data in a prominent model of the stock market, they concluded that least squares coefficient estimates and confidence intervals such as those in Fama and French (1988) and Poterba and Summers (1988) provide a very unreliable small-sample indication of the degree of serial correlation in stock returns. More-over, if purchasers of stock seek to avoid risk, the small probability of large changes will significantly affect the way stocks are valued. For these data, accurate modeling of the time series properties led to a reversal of earlier conclusions.

   How could we model a sudden, dramatic change in the behavior of a time series? Consider a Gaussian AR(1) process,

$$y_t - \mu = \phi(y_{t-1} - \mu) + \varepsilon_t, \tag{1.1}$$

with $\varepsilon_t \sim$ iid $N(0, \sigma^2)$ and $|\phi| < 1$. Suppose we believe that at some point in the sample, the mean value around which this series clusters (μ) changed from an initial value μ_1 to a new value μ_2.

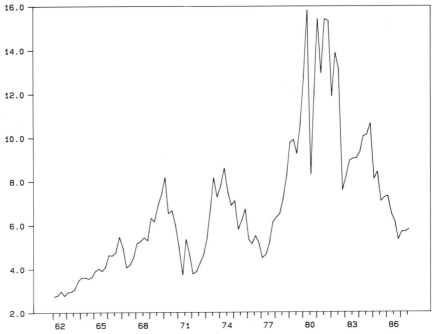

Fig. 4. Nominal interest rate on U.S. treasury bills, quarterly 1962–1987. Source: Hamilton (1988).

This by itself is not a useful description of the data. If we do not know what caused the change from μ_1 to μ_2, we cannot forecast this series; if the constant term has changed in the past, it is surely possible for it to change again in the future. If we are not sure how to forecast the series, we cannot use this description in any economic or financial model that tries to understand people's forward-looking behavior. And in the absence of an explicit probability law for what governed the change from μ_1 to μ_2, it is not clear what principle we should use to estimate parameters – what event are we conditioning on if we treat the change as deterministic, and how does this conditioning affect the validity of the statistical inference?

For these reasons, it is desirable to model the probability law for changes in regime. The threshold models in Tong (1983) describe the change as a deterministic function of past realizations of y_t; for example, if $y_{t-1} < 0$, then the constant term for observation t is taken to be μ_1, whereas when $y_{t-1} > 0$, the constant term is μ_2.

This chapter maintains the alternative view in Hamilton (1989) that changes in regime are the result of processes largely unrelated to past realizations of the series and are not themselves directly observable. Consider, for example, an unobserved state variable s_t that takes on the values 1 or 2 according to a

Markov chain:

$$p(s_t = 1 \mid s_{t-1} = 1) = p_{11}, \qquad (1.2a)$$

$$p(s_t = 2 \mid s_{t-1} = 1) = p_{12}, \qquad (1.2b)$$

$$p(s_t = 1 \mid s_{t-1} = 2) = p_{21}, \qquad (1.2c)$$

$$p(s_t = 2 \mid s_{t-1} = 2) = p_{22}, \qquad (1.2d)$$

with $p_{11} + p_{12} = p_{21} + p_{22} = 1$. We then model the data y_t as being governed by

$$(y_t - \mu_{s_t}) = \phi(y_{t-1} - \mu_{s_{t-1}}) + \varepsilon_t, \qquad (1.3)$$

where μ_{s_t} represents μ_1 when $s_t = 1$ and μ_2 when $s_t = 2$.
We can rewrite (1.3) as

$$(1 - \phi L)(y_t - \mu_{s_t}) = \varepsilon_t \qquad (1.4)$$

for $Lx_t \equiv x_{t-1}$. Applying $(1 - \phi L)^{-1}$ to both sides of (1.4) produces

$$y_t = \mu_{s_t} + z_t, \qquad (1.5)$$

where $z_t \equiv (1 - \phi L)^{-1} \varepsilon_t$ follows a Gaussian AR(1) process. The model (1.5) might thus be viewed as an extension of the standard mixture of normals distribution according to which

$$y_t = \mu_{s_t} + \varepsilon_t \qquad (1.6)$$

with s_t an iid Bernoulli sequence.[1] Expression (1.5) generalizes (1.6) by modeling s_t as a Markov chain as in Baum et al. (1970) and by replacing ε_t with an autocorrelated Gaussian process. The process (1.3) could alternatively be viewed as an application of the switching regression idea of Quandt (1958), Goldfeld and Quandt (1973), and Cosslett and Lee (1985) to an autoregression. Closely related models have been explored by Sclove (1983) and Tjøstheim (1986), though they did not discuss maximum likelihood estimation of parameters.

Some might object that a change in regime should be represented as a *permanent* change in the value of μ, rather than the cycling back and forth between states 1 and 2 that seems to be implicit in (1.2). However, the specification (1.2) allows the possibility of a permanent change as a special case if $p_{21} = 0$. Alternatively, we could have p_{21} quite close to zero, with the implication that in a sample of given size T we would likely see only a single shift, though at some point in the future we should see a return to regime 1. This second parameterization that some scientific appeal – if the stock market

---

[1] For a survey of mixture of normal distributions, see Titterington, Smith and Makov (1985).

can crash once, it is surely possible that it could crash again. Any atheoretical forecast is based on the assumption that the future will be like the past. The past has not been exclusively characterized by 'normal' behavior, so it seems unlikely that the future will be either.

Alternatively, by a change in regime we might have in mind an event such as World War II, that appears once in our sample of 100 years for a fixed five-year duration. The specification (1.2) could describe this episode by choosing p_{11} and p_{22} such that a typical sample of size 100 would likely include only one such episode. Again the implicit presumption is that given another 100 years of data we may well see another such event.

The advantage of (1.2) is that it allows these possibilities along with many others. By specifying the probability law rather than imposing particular dates a priori, we allow the data to tell us the nature and incidence of significant changes. Thus we view $\lambda \equiv (\phi, \sigma^2, \mu_1, \mu_2, p_{11}, p_{22})'$ as a vector of population parameters that characterize the probability density $p(y_1, y_2, \ldots, y_T; \lambda)$ of the observed data. Our tasks are then to find the value of the parameter λ that best describes the data, form an inference about when the changes occurred, and use these parameters and inference to forecast the series and test economic hypotheses.

Note that the process defined by (1.2) and (1.3) with $|\phi| < 1$ and $0 < p_{ii} < 1$ for $i = 1, 2$ is covariance-stationary, and admits a Wold representation of the form

$$y_t = k + \sum_{j=0}^{\infty} \psi_j e_{t-j} \tag{1.7}$$

for e_t a serially uncorrelated sequence. Although this representation exists, it does not yield optimal forecasts of y_t. While e_t is uncorrelated with e_{t-1} it is not independent of e_{t-1}, and indeed lagged values of e_{t-1} can help forecast e_t. The optimal forecasts of y_t are obtained by using the nonlinear formulas derived below for forming an inference about s_t.

Note also that we have modeled the shift in intercept as in equation (1.3) rather than

$$y_t - \mu_{s_t} = \phi(y_{t-1} - \mu_{s_t}) + \varepsilon_t . \tag{1.8}$$

The model (1.8) could of course be handled equally easily with the methods described in this chapter. Models (1.3) and (1.8), however, imply very different dynamic consequences of a shift in regime, and it is worth commenting on this difference. Suppose that the process shifts from state 1 to state 2 at date t and stays there for j periods. According to specification (1.8), the value of y_{t+j} will be $(1 + \phi + \phi^2 + \cdots + \phi^j)(\mu_2 - \mu_1)$ units higher as a consequence of the shift, whereas according to specification (1.3), the value of y_{t+j} will be $(\mu_2 - \mu_1)$ units higher for any j. Thus in (1.8), the consequences of the shift accumulate over time in the same way as for a permanent shift in ε. By contrast, the effect of a change in regime in (1.8) is immediate, is not tied down by the dynamic consequences of ε, and is the same for all observations from the new regime. Our anticipation is that the formulation (1.3) will provide a more promising description of many economic and financial time series.

We have so far confined the discussion of changes in regime to a simple AR(1) process with two possible values of μ. The general principles discussed below readily generalize to vector autoregressive specifications in which the intercepts, autoregressive coefficients, or variances may be functions of current or lagged values of an unobserved state, in which there may be K rather than two possible states, and where the probability law $p(s_t | s_{t-1}, y_{t-1}, \ldots, y_{t-r})$ can depend on lagged y and not just s_{t-1}. Such generalizations are in fact a fairly trivial extension of the basic approach. These extensions face a practical rather than theoretical restriction; if we only have a few observations on a regime, we cannot reliably estimate a large number of parameters for it. Thus most empirical applications have estimated scalar or small vector systems in which the change in regime is confined to a few parameters and in which only a few states for the Markov chain are allowed.

This chapter is organized as follows. Section 2 discusses statistical inference for systems subject to changes in regime. For ease of exposition we describe the example (1.2)–(1.3) in detail and then note how the approach readily generalizes. Section 3 discusses maximum likelihood estimation and specification testing, while Section 4 examines forecasting and rational-expectations analysis of such processes. Section 5 presents some empirical applications.

2. Inferences about the unobserved state

2.1. Filter inferences

We will shortly describe a procedure for estimating the population parameters λ from the data. Let us now put this question on hold, and assume that we already know the value of λ. Suppose we are further given observed values $(y_1, y_2, \ldots, y_t)$ generated from the process (1.2)–(1.3). What should we conclude about the state the process is in at date t?

Since the state s_t is not observed directly, our inference takes the form of a probability

$$p(s_t = 1 \mid y_t, y_{t-1}, \ldots, y_1; \lambda) . \tag{2.1}$$

Note that this denotes the probability that the process was in state 1 at date t, with the inference conditioned on data observed through that date $(y_t, y_{t-1}, \ldots, y_1)$ and on a fixed value for the population parameter vector λ. To simplify notation, we hereafter suppress the role of λ, though it is implicit in all the following expressions. We now show how to calculate (2.1) through a recursive filtering of the data.

We begin with the unconditional probability of the date $t = 1$ state, given by the well-known formula[2]

$$p(s_1 = 1) = \frac{1 - p_{22}}{(1 - p_{11}) + (1 - p_{22})} . \tag{2.2}$$

The joint unconditional probabilities for the $t = 1$ and $t = 2$ state are then found from (1.2) to be

$$p(s_2, s_1) = p(s_2 \mid s_1) \cdot p(s_1) . \tag{2.3}$$

The notation $p(s_2, s_1)$ denotes one of four numbers, one for each possible combination of s_2 and s_1. For example,

$$p(s_2 = 2, s_1 = 2) = p_{22} \cdot \frac{1 - p_{11}}{(1 - p_{11}) + (1 - p_{22})} . \tag{2.4}$$

The four numbers represented by (2.3) are each between zero and one and sum to one.

We further know the density of y_1 and y_2 conditional on s_1 and s_2,

$$p(y_2, y_1 \mid s_2, s_1)$$
$$= \frac{1}{2\pi} |\Omega|^{-1/2} \exp\left\{ -\tfrac{1}{2} [(y_2 - \mu_{s_2}) \quad (y_1 - \mu_{s_1})] \Omega^{-1} \begin{bmatrix} (y_2 - \mu_{s_2}) \\ (y_1 - \mu_{s_1}) \end{bmatrix} \right\}, \tag{2.5}$$

where Ω is the variance–covariance matrix of two successive draws from an AR(1) process:

$$\Omega = [\sigma^2 / (1 - \phi^2)] \begin{bmatrix} 1 & \phi \\ \phi & 1 \end{bmatrix} .$$

For given numerical values of y_2 and y_1, the expression $p(y_2, y_1 \mid s_2, s_1)$ denotes four distinct numbers, one for each possible value of (s_2, s_1).

We can then calculate the joint probability-density of states and observations by multiplying each element of (2.3) by the corresponding element of (2.5),

$$p(y_2, y_1, s_2, s_1) = p(y_2, y_1 \mid s_2, s_1) \cdot p(s_2, s_1) . \tag{2.6}$$

Again this expression denotes four distinct numbers. Note that the sum of these numbers has the interpretation as the unconditional density of (y_2, y_1),

$$p(y_2, y_1) = \sum_{s_1=1}^{2} \sum_{s_2=1}^{2} p(y_2, y_1, s_2, s_1) . \tag{2.7}$$

If we divide (2.6) by (2.7), we arrive at an inference about the first two

[2] See for example Hamilton (1989, p. 361).

states, conditional on the data,

$$p(s_2, s_1 \mid y_2, y_1) = \frac{p(y_2, y_1, s_2, s_1)}{p(y_2, y_1)}. \tag{2.8}$$

We can use this to obtain an inference just about the state for date 2, if we wish. For example,

$$
\begin{aligned}
p(s_2 = 1 \mid y_2, y_1) &= p(s_2 = 1, s_1 = 1 \mid y_2, y_1) \\
&\quad + p(s_2 = 1, s_1 = 2 \mid y_2, y_1).
\end{aligned} \tag{2.9}
$$

Let $\mathcal{Y}_t \equiv (y_t, y_{t-1}, \ldots, y_1)'$ denote observations obtained through date t. We have seen how to calculate $p(s_t \mid \mathcal{Y}_t)$ for $t = 2$. We can use the same ideas as above to calculate $p(s_{t+1} \mid \mathcal{Y}_{t+1})$ from $p(s_t \mid \mathcal{Y}_t)$ for any t. In particular,

$$
\begin{aligned}
p(s_{t+1}, s_t \mid \mathcal{Y}_t) &= p(s_{t+1} \mid s_t, \mathcal{Y}_t) \cdot p(s_t \mid \mathcal{Y}_t) \\
&= p(s_{t+1} \mid s_t) \cdot p(s_t \mid \mathcal{Y}_t),
\end{aligned} \tag{2.10}
$$

where the last equality follows from the assumed independent Markov law for s_t. Next we form

$$
\begin{aligned}
&p(y_{t+1} \mid s_{t+1}, s_t, \mathcal{Y}_t) \\
&= \frac{1}{\sqrt{2\pi}\sigma} \exp\{-[y_{t+1} - \mu_{s_{t+1}} - \phi(y_t - \mu_{s_t})]^2/(2\sigma^2)\},
\end{aligned} \tag{2.11}
$$

and multiply (2.10) by (2.11),

$$
\begin{aligned}
&p(y_{t+1}, s_{t+1}, s_t \mid \mathcal{Y}_t) \\
&= p(y_{t+1} \mid s_{t+1}, s_t, \mathcal{Y}_t) \cdot p(s_{t+1}, s_t \mid \mathcal{Y}_t).
\end{aligned} \tag{2.12}
$$

Summing these four numbers yields

$$p(y_{t+1} \mid \mathcal{Y}_t) = \sum_{s_{t+1}=1}^{2} \sum_{s_t=1}^{2} p(y_{t+1}, s_{t+1}, s_t \mid \mathcal{Y}_t), \tag{2.13}$$

while dividing (2.12) by (2.13) gives

$$p(s_{t+1}, s_t \mid \mathcal{Y}_{t+1}) = \frac{p(y_{t+1}, s_{t+1}, s_t \mid \mathcal{Y}_t)}{p(y_{t+1} \mid \mathcal{Y}_t)}. \tag{2.14}$$

Summing over s_t completes the date $t + 1$ inference,

$$p(s_{t+1} \mid \mathcal{Y}_{t+1}) = \sum_{s_t=1}^{2} p(s_{t+1}, s_t \mid \mathcal{Y}_{t+1}). \tag{2.15}$$

Proceeding recursively through the data in this fashion we can calculate (2.15) for any t. Note that the output of this recursion is a probability that the process was in regime 1 at any given date in the sample based on observations of y through that date. Again we emphasize that this recursion treated the population parameters in λ as known and fixed.

2.2. Smoothed inferences

Above we showed how to calculate $p(s_t | \mathcal{Y}_t)$, a filter inference about the current state based on currently available data. We now discuss how to calculate $p(s_t | \mathcal{Y}_T)$, a smoothed inference about the state at date t based on data available through some future date T.

Suppose we multiply (2.14) by $p(s_{t+2} | s_{t+1})$ and by $p(y_{t+2} | s_{t+2}, s_{t+1}, y_{t+1})$,

$$p(y_{t+2}, s_{t+2}, s_{t+1}, s_t | \mathcal{Y}_{t+1})$$
$$= p(s_{t+1}, s_t | \mathcal{Y}_{t+1}) \cdot p(s_{t+2} | s_{t+1}) \cdot p(y_{t+2} | s_{t+2}, s_{t+1}, y_{t+1}). \qquad (2.16)$$

Dividing this by the density from (2.13) calculated for date $t+2$ then yields

$$p(s_{t+2}, s_{t+1}, s_t | \mathcal{Y}_{t+2}) = \frac{p(y_{t+2}, s_{t+2}, s_{t+1}, s_t | \mathcal{Y}_{t+1})}{p(y_{t+2} | \mathcal{Y}_{t+1})}. \qquad (2.17)$$

Summing over s_{t+1} we could then find

$$p(s_{t+2}, s_t | \mathcal{Y}_{t+2}) = \sum_{s_{t+1}=1}^{2} p(s_{t+2}, s_{t+1}, s_t | \mathcal{Y}_{t+2}). \qquad (2.18)$$

Continuing recursively in this fashion, given $p(s_{t+j}, s_t | \mathcal{Y}_{t+j})$ we can calculate $p(s_{t+j+1}, s_t | \mathcal{Y}_{t+j+1})$ from

$$p(s_{t+j+1}, s_t | \mathcal{Y}_{t+j+1})$$
$$= \sum_{s_{t+j}=1}^{2} \{ p(s_{t+j}, s_t | \mathcal{Y}_{t+j}) \cdot p(s_{t+j+1} | s_{t+j})$$
$$\times p(y_{t+j+1} | s_{t+j+1}, s_{t+j}, y_{t+j}) \} / p(y_{t+j+1} | \mathcal{Y}_{t+j}). \qquad (2.19)$$

When we reach $p(s_T, s_t | \mathcal{Y}_T)$, we can calculate the full-sample smoothed inference from

$$p(s_t | \mathcal{Y}_T) = \sum_{s_T=1}^{2} p(s_T, s_t | \mathcal{Y}_T). \qquad (2.20)$$

2.3. Generalizations

The approach above is quite simple to generalize. For example, consider an *r*-th order autoregression with a changing intercept and variance,

$$(y_t - \mu_{s_t}) = \phi_1(y_{t-1} - \mu_{s_{t-1}}) + \phi_2(y_{t-2} - \mu_{s_{t-2}}) + \cdots$$
$$+ \phi_r(y_{t-r} - \mu_{s_{t-r}}) + \sigma_{s_t} \cdot \varepsilon_t \qquad (2.21)$$

with $\varepsilon_t \sim$ iid $N(0, 1)$ and with $s_t = 1, 2, \ldots, K$ according to a K-state Markov chain. To generalize the approach in Section 2.1 we need to calculate an inference about the r most recent realizations of the state variable,

$$p(s_t, s_{t-1}, \ldots, s_{t-r+1} | \mathcal{Y}_t) . \qquad (2.22)$$

Expression (2.22) denotes K^r separate values, one for each possible value of $(s_t, s_{t-1}, \ldots, s_{t-r+1})$, corresponding to the probability of that joint outcome conditional on the observed data. Again these numbers will sum to one by construction. To update this inference, we calculate

$$p(y_{t+1}, s_{t+1}, s_t, \ldots, s_{t-r+1} | \mathcal{Y}_t)$$
$$= p(y_{t+1} | s_{t+1}, s_t, \ldots, s_{t-r+1}, \mathcal{Y}_t) \cdot p(s_{t+1} | s_t)$$
$$\times p(s_t, s_{t-1}, \ldots, s_{t-r+1} | \mathcal{Y}_t) , \qquad (2.23)$$

where

$$p(y_{t+1} | s_{t+1}, s_t, \ldots, s_{t-r+1}, \mathcal{Y}_t)$$
$$= \frac{1}{\sqrt{2\pi}\sigma_{s_{t+1}}} \exp\left\{ \frac{-1}{(2\sigma_{s_{t+1}}^2)} \right.$$
$$\times [(y_{t+1} - \mu_{s_{t+1}}) - \phi_1(y_t - \mu_{s_t})$$
$$\left. - \phi_2(y_{t-1} - \mu_{s_{t-1}}) - \cdots - \phi_r(y_{t-r+1} - \mu_{s_{t-r+1}})]^2 \right\} . \qquad (2.24)$$

Then

$$p(y_{t+1} | \mathcal{Y}_t) = \sum_{s_{t+1}=1}^{K} \sum_{s_t=1}^{K} \cdots \sum_{s_{t-r+1}=1}^{K} p(y_{t+1}, s_{t+1}, s_t, \ldots, s_{t-r+1} | \mathcal{Y}_t)$$
$$\qquad (2.25)$$

and the updated inference is

$$p(s_{t+1}, s_t, \ldots, s_{t-r+2} | \mathcal{Y}_{t+1})$$
$$= \sum_{s_{t-r+1}=1}^{K} \frac{p(y_{t+1}, s_{t+1}, s_t, \ldots, s_{t-r+1} | \mathcal{Y}_t)}{p(y_{t+1} | \mathcal{Y}_t)} . \qquad (2.26)$$

To start this iteration on (2.22)–(2.26), we require an initial value for (2.22):

$$p(s_r, s_{r-1}, \ldots, s_1 | \mathcal{Y}_r) . \qquad (2.27)$$

Consider first the unconditional probabilities

$$\pi_j = p(s_t = j) . \tag{2.28}$$

Assuming that the Markov chain is ergodic, these probabilities can be found from the solutions to the following $K + 1$ equations:

$$\sum_{i=1}^{K} p_{ij}\pi_i = \pi_j \quad \text{for } j = 1, 2, \ldots, K , \tag{2.29}$$

$$\sum_{j=1}^{K} \pi_j = 1 . \tag{2.30}$$

We can then calculate

$$p(s_r, s_{r-1}, \ldots, s_1) = p(s_r \mid s_{r-1}) \cdot p(s_{r-1} \mid s_{r-2}) \cdots p(s_1) . \tag{2.31}$$

To generalize the procedure described in Section 2.1, we would next calculate

$$p(\mathcal{Y}_{r+1} \mid s_{r+1}, s_r, \ldots, s_1) \tag{2.32}$$

and from this evaluate (2.27). However, evaluation of (2.32) can be computationally involved, and a simpler strategy that promises to yield satisfactory inferences is simply to replace (2.27) with (2.31) and then iterate on (2.22)–(2.26).

From the value of (2.22) at step t of this filter recursion we can easily calculate an inference just about the state at date t,

$$p(s_t \mid \mathcal{Y}_t) = \sum_{s_{t-1}=1}^{K} \sum_{s_{t-2}=1}^{K} \cdots \sum_{s_{t-r+1}=1}^{K} p(s_t, s_{t-1}, \ldots, s_{t-r+1} \mid \mathcal{Y}_t) . \tag{2.33}$$

Alternatively, an $(r-1)$-lag smoothed estimate is also immediately available:

$$
\begin{aligned}
&p(s_{t-r+1} \mid \mathcal{Y}_t) \\
&= \sum_{s_t=1}^{K} \sum_{s_{t-1}=1}^{K} \cdots \sum_{s_{t-r+2}=1}^{K} p(s_t, s_{t-1}, \ldots, s_{t-r+1} \mid \mathcal{Y}_t) .
\end{aligned}
\tag{2.34}
$$

By carrying inferences about a larger number of lagged states through the recursion, we can increase the lag of the smoothed inference immediately available from the recursion without going to the full-sample smoother described above.

The strategy is exactly the same for an r-th-order vector autoregression in n variables y_t with any subset of the parameters changing. We simply replace

(2.24) with an expression such as

$$
p(\boldsymbol{y}_{t+1} \mid s_{t+1}, s_t, \ldots, s_{t-r+1}, \mathcal{Y}_t)
$$
$$
= (2\pi)^{-n/2} |\boldsymbol{\Omega}_{s_{t+1}}|^{-1/2}
$$
$$
\times \exp\left\{ -\tfrac{1}{2}\left[(\boldsymbol{y}_{t+1} - \boldsymbol{\mu}_{s_{t+1}}) - \sum_{j=1}^{r} \boldsymbol{A}_{j,s_t}(\boldsymbol{y}_{t+1-j} - \boldsymbol{\mu}_{s_{t+1-j}}) \right]' \right.
$$
$$
\left. \times \boldsymbol{\Omega}_{s_{t+1}}^{-1}\left[(\boldsymbol{y}_{t+1} - \boldsymbol{\mu}_{s_{t+1}}) - \sum_{j=1}^{r} \boldsymbol{A}_{j,s_t}(\boldsymbol{y}_{t+1-j} - \boldsymbol{\mu}_{s_{t+1-j}}) \right] \right\}.
$$

$$(2.35)$$

It is also possible to incorporate discrete-valued indicators in the recursion as in Cosslett and Lee (1985) and Kaminsky (1988). Suppose that we have observations on a variable I_t that is regarded as an imperfect indicator of the regime and otherwise uncorrelated with y_t,

$$
p(I_t = i \mid s_t = j, \mathcal{Y}_t) = q_{ji} \quad \text{for } i, j = 1, 2, \ldots, K .
$$

$$(2.36)$$

For a perfect indicator, $q_{ii} = 1$. Returning to the $r = 1$ example of Section 2.1, let $\mathcal{I}_t \equiv (I_t, I_{t-1}, \ldots, I_1)'$. Our recursion will then calculate $p(s_t \mid \mathcal{I}_t, \mathcal{Y}_t)$, which is updated as follows:

$$
p(I_{t+1}, y_{t+1}, s_{t+1}, s_t \mid \mathcal{I}_t, \mathcal{Y}_t)
$$
$$
= p(I_{t+1} \mid s_{t+1}) \cdot p(y_{t+1} \mid s_{t+1}, s_t, y_t) \cdot p(s_{t+1} \mid s_t) \cdot p(s_t \mid \mathcal{I}_t, \mathcal{Y}_t) ,
$$

$$(2.37)$$

$$
p(I_{t+1}, y_{t+1} \mid \mathcal{I}_t, \mathcal{Y}_t)
$$
$$
= \sum_{s_{t+1}=1}^{K} \sum_{s_t=1}^{K} p(I_{t+1}, y_{t+1}, s_{t+1}, s_t \mid \mathcal{I}_t, \mathcal{Y}_t) ,
$$

$$(2.38)$$

$$
p(s_{t+1} \mid \mathcal{I}_{t+1}, \mathcal{Y}_{t+1}) = \sum_{s_t=1}^{K} \frac{p(I_{t+1}, y_{t+1}, s_{t+1}, s_t \mid \mathcal{I}_t, \mathcal{Y}_t)}{p(I_{t+1}, y_{t+1} \mid \mathcal{I}_t, \mathcal{Y}_t)} .
$$

$$(2.39)$$

If we want to generalize the Markov chain assumption and allow the state transitions to be influenced by previous realizations of the series, we can replace $p(s_{t+1} = j \mid s_t = i) = p_{ij}$ in (2.10) with some more general parametric function $p(s_{t+1} \mid s_t, \mathcal{Y}_t)$ and the rest of the recursion would carry through unchanged.

3. Maximum likelihood estimation

3.1. Numerical maximization of the likelihood function

In the previous section we regarded the vector of population parameters $(\boldsymbol{\lambda} = (\phi, \sigma^2, \mu_1, \mu_2, p_{11}, p_{22})'$ for the AR(1) example) as known. Given observations on $\mathcal{Y}_t \equiv (y_t, y_{t-1}, \ldots, y_1)'$, we asked, where did the changes in regime seem to occur? Notice that in the course of answering this question we calculated the densities $p(y_2, y_1; \boldsymbol{\lambda})$ and $p(y_{t+1} | \mathcal{Y}_t; \boldsymbol{\lambda})$ as a natural byproduct in equations (2.7) and (2.13). Thus with exactly the same set of calculations used to form the inferences $p(s_t | \mathcal{Y}_t; \boldsymbol{\lambda})$ for $t = 1, 2, \ldots, T$ and given $\boldsymbol{\lambda}$, we will also know the value of the likelihood for that value of $\boldsymbol{\lambda}$:

$$p(\mathcal{Y}_T; \boldsymbol{\lambda}) = p(y_2, y_1; \boldsymbol{\lambda}) \prod_{t=2}^{T-1} p(y_{t+1} | \mathcal{Y}_t; \boldsymbol{\lambda}) . \tag{3.1}$$

We can thus find the maximum likelihood estimate of $\boldsymbol{\lambda}$ by maximizing (3.1) by numerical methods.[3] Where the procedure of Section 2.1 is followed, expression (3.1) gives the exact likelihood function. When (2.27) is replaced with (2.31) as recommended in Section 2.3, the result is an approximation to the conditional likelihood function $p(y_T, y_{T-1}, \ldots, y_{r+1} | y_r, y_{r-1}, \ldots, y_1; \boldsymbol{\lambda})$.

3.2. Analytic characterization of the score

Numerical optimization techniques typically make use of the gradient of (3.1). Usually we frame the problem as maximization of the log of (3.1), in which case the gradient is known as the score

$$\frac{\partial \log p(\mathcal{Y}_T; \boldsymbol{\lambda})}{\partial \boldsymbol{\lambda}} . \tag{3.2}$$

This can be calculated numerically, by examining what happens to the log of (3.1) under small perturbations in $\boldsymbol{\lambda}$. Alternatively, it can be characterized analytically, as we now discuss.

To do so, we introduce the notation $\mathcal{S}_T \equiv (s_T, s_{T-1}, \ldots, s_1)'$ to denote the full sample of realized states. This vector is not observed, and could take on K^T possible values. We reassure the reader that this vector never needs to be calculated nor these K^T probability assessed in order to implement the formulas in this section. Rather, the theoretical construction of this full vector is used solely to help facilitate the derivation of formulas that will subsequently emerge. In this spirit, let the operator $\int d\mathcal{S}_T$ denote summation over all the K^T

---

[3] See Judge et al. (1985) for an introduction to these techniques.

possible values of $\mathcal{S}_T$, for example,

$$\int p(\mathcal{S}_T \mid \mathcal{Y}_T)\, d\mathcal{S}_T = \sum_{s_T=1}^{K} \sum_{s_{T-1}=1}^{K} \cdots \sum_{s_1=1}^{K} p(s_T, s_{T-1}, \dots, s_1 \mid \mathcal{Y}_T) = 1 \;.$$

(3.3)

The sample likelihood could then be thought of as

$$p(\mathcal{Y}_T; \boldsymbol{\lambda}) = \int p(\mathcal{Y}_T \mid \mathcal{S}_T; \boldsymbol{\theta}) \cdot p(\mathcal{S}_T; \boldsymbol{\rho})\, d\mathcal{S}_T \;,$$

(3.4)

where we have decomposed the parameter vector $\boldsymbol{\lambda}' = (\boldsymbol{\theta}', \boldsymbol{\rho}')$ into those parameters that describe the density of y conditional on states ($\boldsymbol{\theta}$) and those that describe the transition probabilities of states ($\boldsymbol{\rho}$). For the AR(1) example, we would have

$$p(\mathcal{Y}_T \mid \mathcal{S}_T; \boldsymbol{\theta}) = p(y_2, y_1 \mid s_2, s_1; \boldsymbol{\theta}) \prod_{t=2}^{T-1} p(y_{t+1} \mid s_{t+1}, s_t, y_t; \boldsymbol{\theta})$$

(3.5)

for $p(y_2, y_1 \mid s_2, s_1; \boldsymbol{\theta})$ given by (2.5), $p(y_{t+1} \mid s_{t+1}, s_t, y_t; \boldsymbol{\theta})$ given by (2.11), and $\boldsymbol{\theta} = (\phi, \sigma^2, \mu_1, \mu_2)'$. Also,

$$p(\mathcal{S}_T; \boldsymbol{\rho}) = p(s_1; \boldsymbol{\rho}) \prod_{t=1}^{T-1} p(s_{t+1} \mid s_t; \boldsymbol{\rho}) \;,$$

(3.6)

where for K states we could parameterize

$$\boldsymbol{\rho} = (p_{11}, p_{12}, \dots, p_{1,K-1}, p_{21}, p_{22}, \dots, p_{2,K-1}, \dots, p_{K,K-1})' \quad (3.7)$$

with $p_{iK} = 1 - p_{i1} - p_{i2} - \cdots - p_{i,K-1}$. Again we emphasize that we would not want to try to calculate the likelihood from the formula (3.4); the number of calculations described in (3.4) grows with K^T whereas the number of calculations for the algorithm described in the previous section grows linearly with T.

From (3.4) the score with respect to $\boldsymbol{\theta}$ will take the form

$$\frac{\partial \log p(\mathcal{Y}_T; \boldsymbol{\lambda})}{\partial \boldsymbol{\theta}}$$

$$= \frac{1}{p(\mathcal{Y}_T; \boldsymbol{\lambda})} \int \frac{\partial p(\mathcal{Y}_T \mid \mathcal{S}_T; \boldsymbol{\theta})}{\partial \boldsymbol{\theta}}\, p(\mathcal{S}_T; \boldsymbol{\rho})\, d\mathcal{S}_T$$

$$= \int \frac{\partial \log p(\mathcal{Y}_T \mid \mathcal{S}_T; \boldsymbol{\theta})}{\partial \boldsymbol{\theta}} \frac{p(\mathcal{Y}_T \mid \mathcal{S}_T; \boldsymbol{\theta}) \cdot p(\mathcal{S}_T; \boldsymbol{\rho})}{p(\mathcal{Y}_T; \boldsymbol{\lambda})}\, d\mathcal{S}_T$$

$$= \int \frac{\partial \log p(\mathcal{Y}_T \mid \mathcal{S}_T; \boldsymbol{\theta})}{\partial \boldsymbol{\theta}}\, p(\mathcal{S}_T \mid \mathcal{Y}_T; \boldsymbol{\lambda})\, d\mathcal{S}_T \;.$$

(3.8)

Although in principle (3.8) involves summation over all the possible values of $\mathcal{S}_T$, in practice $\log p(\mathcal{Y}_T \mid \mathcal{S}_T; \boldsymbol{\theta})$ can be broken down into the sum of terms each of which just depends on a few elements of $\mathcal{S}_T$. For the AR(1) example we find on differentiating (3.5) that

$$
\frac{\partial \log p(\mathcal{Y}_T \mid \mathcal{S}_T; \boldsymbol{\theta})}{\partial \boldsymbol{\theta}}
$$

$$
= \frac{\partial \log p(y_2, y_1 \mid s_2, s_1; \boldsymbol{\theta})}{\partial \boldsymbol{\theta}} + \sum_{t=2}^{T-1} \frac{\partial \log p(y_{t+1} \mid s_{t+1}, s_t, y_t; \boldsymbol{\theta})}{\partial \boldsymbol{\theta}}
$$

$$(3.9)$$

in which case (3.8) becomes

$$
\frac{\partial \log p(\mathcal{Y}_T; \boldsymbol{\lambda})}{\partial \boldsymbol{\theta}}
$$

$$
= \sum_{s_2=1}^{K} \sum_{s_1=1}^{K} \frac{\partial \log p(y_2, y_1 \mid s_2, s_1; \boldsymbol{\theta})}{\partial \boldsymbol{\theta}} \, p(s_2, s_1 \mid \mathcal{Y}_T; \boldsymbol{\lambda})
$$

$$
+ \sum_{t=2}^{T-1} \sum_{s_{t+1}=1}^{K} \sum_{s_t=1}^{K} \frac{\partial \log p(y_{t+1} \mid s_{t+1}, s_t, y_t; \boldsymbol{\theta})}{\partial \boldsymbol{\theta}}
$$

$$
\times p(s_{t+1}, s_t \mid \mathcal{Y}_T; \boldsymbol{\lambda}) .
$$

$$(3.10)$$

Calculation of (3.10) requires only the smoothed probabilities $p(s_{t+1}, s_t \mid \mathcal{Y}_T; \boldsymbol{\lambda})$ for $t = 1, 2, \ldots, T-1$ and simple differentiation of (2.5) and (2.11).

Similarly, the score with respect to the transition probabilities in ρ is given by

$$
\frac{\partial \log p(\mathcal{Y}_T; \boldsymbol{\lambda})}{\partial \boldsymbol{\rho}} = \int \frac{\partial \log p(\mathcal{S}_T; \boldsymbol{\rho})}{\partial \boldsymbol{\rho}} \, p(\mathcal{S}_T \mid \mathcal{Y}_T; \boldsymbol{\lambda}) \, \mathrm{d}\mathcal{S}_T
$$

$$(3.11)$$

which from (3.6) becomes

$$
\frac{\partial \log p(\mathcal{Y}_T; \boldsymbol{\lambda})}{\partial \boldsymbol{\rho}}
$$

$$
= \sum_{s_1=1}^{K} \frac{\partial \log p(s_1; \boldsymbol{\rho})}{\partial \boldsymbol{\rho}} \, p(s_1 \mid \mathcal{Y}_T; \boldsymbol{\lambda})
$$

$$
+ \sum_{t=1}^{T-1} \sum_{s_{t+1}=1}^{K} \sum_{s_t=1}^{K} \frac{\partial \log p(s_{t+1} \mid s_t; \boldsymbol{\rho})}{\partial \boldsymbol{\rho}} \, p(s_{t+1}, s_t \mid \mathcal{Y}_T; \boldsymbol{\lambda}) .
$$

$$(3.12)$$

Thus recalling (3.7),

$$\frac{\partial \log p(\mathcal{Y}_T; \boldsymbol{\lambda})}{\partial p_{ij}} = \sum_{s_1=1}^{K} \frac{\partial \log p(s_1; \rho)}{\partial p_{ij}} \, p(s_1 \mid \mathcal{Y}_T; \boldsymbol{\lambda})$$

$$+ \sum_{t=1}^{T-1} p_{ij}^{-1} \cdot p(s_{t+1} = j, s_t = i \mid \mathcal{Y}_T; \boldsymbol{\lambda})$$

$$- \sum_{t=1}^{T-1} p_{iK}^{-1} \cdot p(s_{t+1} = K, s_t = i \mid \mathcal{Y}_T; \boldsymbol{\lambda}) \tag{3.13}$$

for $i = 1, 2, \ldots, K$, $j = 1, 2, \ldots, K - 1$.

3.3. Finding maximum likelihood estimates using the EM algorithm

The EM algorithm of Dempster, Laird and Rubin (1977) is very convenient for maximum likelihood estimation of parameters of these models.[4] This algorithm begins with an arbitrary initial guess of the parameter vector (denoted $\boldsymbol{\lambda}^{(0)}$) and then generates a sequence of improved guesses ($\boldsymbol{\lambda}^{(1)}, \boldsymbol{\lambda}^{(2)}, \ldots$) each one of which increases the value of the likelihood function, with the sequence converging to a local maximum of the likelihood function.

Given an initial estimate $\boldsymbol{\lambda}^{(l)}$, the EM improved estimate $\boldsymbol{\lambda}^{(l+1)}$ is the value that satisfies

$$\int \frac{\partial \log p(\mathcal{Y}_T, \mathcal{S}_T; \boldsymbol{\lambda}^{(l+1)})}{\partial \boldsymbol{\lambda}^{(l+1)}} \, p(\mathcal{S}_T \mid \mathcal{Y}_T; \boldsymbol{\lambda}^{(l)}) \, \mathrm{d}\mathcal{S}_T = \mathbf{0} \,. \tag{3.14}$$

For example, consider an autoregression or switching regression in which all of the parameters save the variance change with the state:

$$p(y_t \mid s_t, \mathcal{Y}_{t-1}; \boldsymbol{\theta}) = \frac{1}{\sqrt{2\pi}\sigma} \exp\{-(y_t - \boldsymbol{x}_t'\boldsymbol{\beta}_{s_t})^2/(2\sigma^2)\} \,, \tag{3.15}$$

where, say, $\boldsymbol{x}_t = (1, y_{t-1}, y_{t-2}, \ldots, y_{t-r})'$. Expression (3.14) is then particularly simple to implement if we use the likelihood conditional on the first r observations and treat the probability of the initial states as parameters to be estimated separately from $\boldsymbol{\rho}$. In this case we have

$$\log p(\mathcal{Y}_T, \mathcal{S}_T; \boldsymbol{\lambda})$$
$$= -[(T - r)/2] \log 2\pi - [(T - r)/2] \log \sigma^2$$
$$- \sum_{t=r+1}^{T} (y_t - \boldsymbol{x}_t'\boldsymbol{\beta}_{s_t})^2/(2\sigma^2) + \sum_{t=r+1}^{T} \log p(s_t \mid s_{t-1}; \boldsymbol{\rho}) \,. \tag{3.16}$$

[4] This discussion is based on Hamilton (1990).

In this case expression (3.14) produces

$$\sum_{t=r+1}^{T} [y_t - x_t' \boldsymbol{\beta}_i^{(l+1)}] x_t \cdot p(s_t = i \mid \mathcal{Y}_T; \boldsymbol{\lambda}^{(l)}) = 0 \quad \text{for } i = 1, 2, \ldots, K,$$

(3.17)

$$(T - r)[\sigma^{(l+1)}]^2 = \sum_{t=r+1}^{T} \sum_{i=1}^{K} (y_t - x_t' \boldsymbol{\beta}_i^{(l+1)})^2 \cdot p(s_t = i \mid \mathcal{Y}_T; \boldsymbol{\lambda}^{(l)}),$$

(3.18)

$$\sum_{t=r+1}^{T} [p_{ij}^{(l+1)}]^{-1} \cdot p(s_t = j, s_{t-1} = i \mid \mathcal{Y}_T; \boldsymbol{\lambda}^{(l)})$$

$$= \sum_{t=r+1}^{T} [p_{iK}^{(l+1)}]^{-1} \cdot p(s_t = K, s_{t-1} = i \mid \mathcal{Y}_T; \boldsymbol{\lambda}^{(l)})$$

(3.19)

for $i = 1, 2, \ldots, K$ and $j = 1, 2, \ldots, K - 1$. After some rearranging (3.19) becomes

$$[p_{ij}^{(l+1)}] = \frac{\sum_{t=r+1}^{T} p(s_t = j, s_{t-1} = i \mid \mathcal{Y}_T; \boldsymbol{\lambda}^{(l)})}{\sum_{t=r+1}^{T} p(s_{t-1} = i \mid \mathcal{Y}_T; \boldsymbol{\lambda}^{(l)})}$$

(3.20)

for $i, j = 1, 2, \ldots, K$.

Thus to implement a step of the EM algorithm for this example, we use the initial estimate $\boldsymbol{\lambda}^{(l)}$ to form the smoothed probabilities $p(s_t \mid \mathcal{Y}_T; \boldsymbol{\lambda}^{(l)})$. We then do an OLS regression of $\bar{y}_{t,i} \equiv y_t \cdot \sqrt{p(s_t = i \mid \mathcal{Y}_T; \boldsymbol{\lambda}^{(l)})}$ on $\bar{x}_{t,i} \equiv x_t \cdot \sqrt{p(s_t = i \mid \mathcal{Y}_T; \boldsymbol{\lambda}^{(l)})}$. The resulting OLS coefficient estimate $\boldsymbol{\beta}_i^{(l+1)}$ satisfies (3.17), and performing $i = 1, 2, \ldots, K$ such OLS regressions generates $\boldsymbol{\beta}_1^{(l+1)}, \boldsymbol{\beta}_2^{(l+1)}, \ldots, \boldsymbol{\beta}_K^{(l+1)}$. The average squared residual across these K regressions gives the estimate $[\sigma^{(l+1)}]^2$ satisfying (3.18). Our new estimate of the transition probability $p_{ij}^{(l+1)}$ is from (3.20) the imputed fraction of times that state i was followed by state j. Thus by zig-zagging back and forth between calculating smoothed probabilities and OLS regressions, we can find the maximum likelihood estimates of $\boldsymbol{\lambda}$. For other examples of using the EM algorithm, see Hamilton (1990).

EM estimation will produce the identical value $\hat{\boldsymbol{\lambda}}$ as numerical maximization of (3.1). Which algorithm we choose is simply a matter of convenience. The EM algorithm has the advantage of being robust with respect to poorly chosen starting values and convex portions of the likelihood surface. Phillips (1989) argued that the EM algorithm could be well-approximated by using m-lag smoothed probabilities $p(s_t \mid \mathcal{Y}_{t+m})$ in place of the full-sample smoothed inference $p(s_t \mid \mathcal{Y}_T)$.

3.4. Specification testing

Many useful tests of specification can be constructed from the conditional score of the *t*-th observation, defined as

$$h_t(\boldsymbol{\lambda}) \equiv \frac{\partial \log p(y_t \mid \mathcal{Y}_{t-1}; \boldsymbol{\lambda})}{\partial \boldsymbol{\lambda}} . \tag{3.21}$$

This is related to the full-sample score by

$$\frac{\partial \log p(\mathcal{Y}_T; \boldsymbol{\lambda})}{\partial \boldsymbol{\lambda}} = \sum_{t=1}^{T} h_t(\boldsymbol{\lambda}) . \tag{3.22}$$

For example, for the switching-regression specification (3.15) we have

$$\frac{\partial \log p(y_t \mid \mathcal{Y}_{t-1}; \boldsymbol{\lambda})}{\partial \beta_i}$$

$$= \frac{1}{\sigma^2} [y_t - x_t' \beta_i] x_t \cdot p(s_t = i \mid \mathcal{Y}_t; \boldsymbol{\lambda})$$

$$+ \frac{1}{\sigma^2} \sum_{\tau = r+1}^{t-1} [y_\tau - x_\tau' \beta_i] x_\tau \cdot [p(s_\tau = i \mid \mathcal{Y}_t; \boldsymbol{\lambda}) - p(s_\tau = i \mid \mathcal{Y}_{t-1}; \boldsymbol{\lambda})] . \tag{3.23}$$

The score for date *t* is a simple function of how the datum of date *t* causes us to change our inference about s_τ for $\tau \le t$.

One use of the conditional scores is to form an estimate of the information matrix as in Berndt et al. (1974),

$$\hat{\mathcal{I}}_1 = \frac{1}{T} \sum_{t=1}^{T} [h_t(\boldsymbol{\lambda})][h_t(\boldsymbol{\lambda})]' , \tag{3.24}$$

which could be compared with an estimate based on numerical second derivatives,

$$\hat{\mathcal{I}}_2 = \frac{-1}{T} \frac{\partial^2 \log p(\mathcal{Y}_T; \boldsymbol{\lambda})}{\partial \boldsymbol{\lambda} \, \partial \boldsymbol{\lambda}'} , \tag{3.25}$$

and used to infer the asymptotic variance–covariance matrix of the maximum likelihood estimate $\hat{\boldsymbol{\lambda}}$,

$$\hat{\boldsymbol{\lambda}} \approx N(\boldsymbol{\lambda}_0, (1/T) \cdot \mathcal{I}^{-1}) . \tag{3.26}$$

All of the asymptotic tests proposed in this subsection assume regularity conditions are satisfied, which to our knowledge have not yet been formally verified for this class of models. Certainly at corner solutions (e.g., $\hat{p}_{ij} = 0$ as may well occur in practice), the asymptotic distributions will not be correct, and the best recourse is probably to impose the values of the corner parameters a priori and calculate the score with respect to the remaining free parameters as in Hassett (1990).

The scores can also be used for Lagrange multiplier tests.[5] These are based on the principle that, when evaluated at the true value λ_0, the scores should have mean zero:

$$E(h_t(\lambda_0)) = 0. \tag{3.27}$$

If all of the elements of λ are estimated by maximum likelihood, the score evaluated at $\hat{\lambda}$ will have sample mean zero by construction,

$$\left. \frac{\partial \log p(\mathcal{Y}_T; \lambda)}{\partial \lambda} \right|_{\lambda = \hat{\lambda}} = \sum_{t=1}^{T} h_t(\hat{\lambda}) = 0. \tag{3.28}$$

If instead a subset of m elements of λ are imposed a priori and we find the maximum likelihood estimate $\tilde{\lambda}$ subject to this constraint, then

$$T \cdot \left[\frac{1}{T} \sum_{t=1}^{T} h_t(\tilde{\lambda}) \right]' \left[\frac{1}{T} \sum_{t=1}^{T} [h_t(\tilde{\lambda})][h_t(\tilde{\lambda})]' \right]^{-1} \left[\frac{1}{T} \sum_{t=1}^{T} h_t(\tilde{\lambda}) \right] \approx \chi^2(m). \tag{3.29}$$

The last m elements of λ might correspond to variables or complications that have been left out of the model, in which case $\tilde{\lambda}$ would consist of a vector of m zeros appended after the maximum likelihood estimate of the parameter vector for the simpler model. The score $h_t(\tilde{\lambda})$ is often easy to find. For example, suppose some variables z_t may have been omitted from the switching regression model (3.15),

$$p(y_t | s_t, \mathcal{Y}_{t-1}, z_t; \theta) = \frac{1}{\sqrt{2\pi}\sigma} \exp\{-(y_t - x_t'\beta_{s_t} - z_t'\delta)^2/(2\sigma^2)\}. \tag{3.30}$$

We can estimate the parameters under the null that $\delta = 0$ in the manner described earlier. The score with respect to δ (evaluated at $\delta = 0$) turns out to be

$$\frac{\partial \log p(\mathcal{Y}_T | \mathcal{Z}_T; \lambda)}{\partial \delta}$$

$$= \sum_{t=r+1}^{T} \sum_{i=1}^{K} [y_t - x_t'\beta_i^{(l+1)}]z_t \cdot p(s_t = i | \mathcal{Y}_T; \lambda^{(l)}). \tag{3.31}$$

Thus the score is found by taking the average product of the omitted variables z_t with the residual under regime i, $[y_t - x_t'\beta_i^{(l+1)}]$ and multiplying by the probability that date t's observation came from regime i. By comparing this average product with its square, we can test whether it is far enough from zero

---

[5] For an introduction to these tests see Breusch and Pagan (1980), Engle (1984), or Godfrey (1988).

to warrant rejection of the null hypothesis and cause us to conclude that the model is misspecified. Similar Lagrange multiplier tests for omitted autocorrelation or conditional heteroskedasticity are also easy to calculate from the smoothed probabilities of a model estimated without any of these features (see Hamilton, 1991b).

The conditional scores can also be used to implement a specification test suggested by White (1987). If the model is correctly specified, the scores should be serially uncorrelated. Tests based on this principle can be used to detect omitted autocorrelation, conditional heteroskedasticity, or departures from the assumed Markovian dynamics of state variable (again see Hamilton, 1991b).

One of the most basic hypotheses that we would like to test concerns the number of states; for example, we would like to test the null hypothesis of one state against the alternative that there are two states. We could represent this hypothesis in the AR(1) example (1.3) as the claim that $\mu_1 = \mu_2$. Unfortunately, under this null hypothesis the parameters p_{11} and p_{22} are unidentified, and the information matrix is singular under the null. The standard regularity conditions fail to apply. Davies (1977) and Hansen (1991) developed the appropriate principles for testing in such situations, though these techniques are computationally demanding. Cecchetti, Lam and Mark (1990b) used Monte Carlo methods to analyze the distribution of the likelihood ratio statistic for a regime-switching model. Alternatively, if the standard deviation of ε_t in (1.3) is also a function of the state σ_{s_t}, then the parameters p_{11} and p_{22} could still be identified under the null hypothesis that $\mu_1 = \mu_2$ through the time-dependent structure of the variance. For this view, we could test the null that $\mu_1 = \mu_2$ without running into this problem, as in Engel and Hamilton (1990). Other tests are discussed in Hamilton (1990) and Cecchetti, Lam and Mark (1990b).

3.5. Bayesian priors

There is no natural conjugate prior for this class of models. One very simple approach is to add the log of a prior distribution to the sample log likelihood (3.1). Maximizing the resulting function gives the posterior mode.

For example, consider univariate data drawn from one of K normal distributions,

$$y_t \,|\, s_t = k \sim N(\mu_k, \sigma_k^2) \quad \text{for } k = 1, 2, \ldots, K, \tag{3.32}$$

with s_t following a K-state Markov chain. Suppose we have independent normal-gamma priors for the parameters μ_k and σ_k^{-2},

$$\mu_k \,|\, \sigma_k^2 \sim N(m_k, \sigma_k^2/\nu) \tag{3.33}$$

$$\sigma_k^{-2} \sim \Gamma(\alpha_k, \beta_k). \tag{3.34}$$

Then we might choose μ_k and σ_k^2 so as to maximize

$$
\log p(\mathcal{Y}_T; \lambda) - \sum_{k=1}^{K} (a_k/2) \log \sigma_k^2 - \sum_{k=1}^{K} b_k/(2\sigma_k^2)
$$

$$
- \sum_{k=1}^{K} c_k (\mu_k - m_k)^2/(2\sigma_k^2) , \tag{3.35}
$$

where $a_k = 2\alpha_k - 1$, $b_k = 2\beta_k$, and $c_k = \nu_k$. The resulting Bayesian estimates satisfy

$$
\mu_k = \frac{c_k m_k + \sum_{t=1}^{T} p(s_t = k \mid \mathcal{Y}_T; \lambda) y_t}{c_k + \sum_{t=1}^{T} p(s_t = k \mid \mathcal{Y}_T; \lambda)} , \tag{3.36}
$$

$$
\sigma_k^2 = \frac{b_k + \sum_{t=1}^{T} p(s_t = k \mid \mathcal{Y}_T; \lambda)(y_t - \mu_k)^2 + c_k(m_k - \mu_k)^2}{a_k + \sum_{t=1}^{T} p(s_t = k \mid \mathcal{Y}_T; \lambda)} . \tag{3.37}
$$

These estimates can be found from the same EM algorithm described for equations (3.17)–(3.20). If $a_k = c_k$, we are basically treating the prior as if equivalent to a_k observations drawn from regime k with sample mean given by m_k and sample variance given by b_k/a_k. See Hamilton (1991a) for more details.

4. Forecasting and rational-expectations econometrics

4.1. Forecasting

An attractive feature of Markov chains is the simplicity of the forecasts they generate. Collect the transition probabilities in a $(K \times K)$ matrix:

$$
P \equiv \begin{bmatrix} p_{11} & p_{12} & \cdots & p_{1K} \\ p_{21} & p_{22} & \cdots & p_{2K} \\ \vdots & \vdots & & \vdots \\ p_{K1} & p_{K2} & \cdots & p_{KK} \end{bmatrix} . \tag{4.1}
$$

The row i, column j element of P gives the probability that the process will be in state j at date $t + 1$ given that it currently is in state i. The probability that the process will be in state j at date $t + m$ given that it is currently in state i is given by the row i, column j element of P^m.

If we summarize our current inference about the state with a $(1 \times K)$ vector a_t',

$$
a_t' \equiv [p(s_t = 1 \mid \mathcal{Y}_t) \quad p(s_t = 2 \mid \mathcal{Y}_t) \quad \cdots \quad p(s_t = K \mid \mathcal{Y}_t)] , \tag{4.2}
$$

then the forecast probabilities for the states at date $t + m$ are given by

$$[p(s_{t+m} = 1 \mid \mathcal{Y}_t) \quad p(s_{t+m} = 2 \mid \mathcal{Y}_t) \quad \cdots \quad p(s_{t+m} = K \mid \mathcal{Y}_t)] = a'_t P^m .$$

(4.3)

For a $K = 2$ state system, this has the particularly simple form

$$p(s_{t+m} = 1 \mid \mathcal{Y}_t) = \pi_1 + (-1 + p_{11} + p_{22})^m \cdot [p(s_t = 1 \mid \mathcal{Y}_t) - \pi_1] ,$$

(4.4)

where $\pi_1 = (1 - p_{22}) / [(1 - p_{11}) + (1 - p_{22})]$.

To forecast the value of y_{t+m}, we first calculate a forecast conditional on $\mathcal{S}_t \equiv (s_t, s_{t-1}, \ldots, s_1)'$, and then use the filter to form an optimal inference about $\mathcal{S}_t$,

$$\mathrm{E}(y_{t+m} \mid \mathcal{Y}_t) = \int \mathrm{E}(y_{t+m} \mid \mathcal{Y}_t, \mathcal{S}_t) p(\mathcal{S}_t \mid \mathcal{Y}_t) \, \mathrm{d}\mathcal{S}_t .$$

(4.5)

For example, for the AR(1) process written as in (1.5), we have

$$\mathrm{E}(y_{t+m} \mid \mathcal{Y}_t, \mathcal{S}_t) = \mathrm{E}(\mu_{s_{t+m}} \mid \mathcal{Y}_t, \mathcal{S}_t) + \mathrm{E}(z_{t+m} \mid \mathcal{Y}_t, \mathcal{S}_t) .$$

(4.6)

But from (4.3),

$$\mathrm{E}(\mu_{s_{t+m}} \mid \mathcal{Y}_t, \mathcal{S}_t) = [\delta_1(s_t) \quad \delta_2(s_t) \quad \cdots \quad \delta_K(s_t)]$$

$$\times \begin{bmatrix} p_{11} & p_{12} & \cdots & p_{1K} \\ p_{21} & p_{22} & \cdots & p_{2K} \\ \vdots & \vdots & & \vdots \\ p_{K1} & p_{K2} & \cdots & p_{KK} \end{bmatrix}^m \begin{bmatrix} \mu_1 \\ \mu_2 \\ \vdots \\ \mu_K \end{bmatrix} ,$$

(4.7)

where $\delta_i(s_t) = 1$ if $s_t = i$ and zero otherwise. Similarly, since $z_t = y_t - \mu_{s_t}$, we have for $\mathcal{Z}_t \equiv (z_t, z_{t-1}, \ldots, z_1)'$ that

$$\mathrm{E}(z_{t+m} \mid \mathcal{Y}_t, \mathcal{S}_t) = \mathrm{E}(z_{t+m} \mid \mathcal{Z}_t) = \phi^m z_t = \phi^m (y_t - \mu_{s_t}) .$$

(4.8)

Substituting (4.6)–(4.8) into (4.5) we find

$$\mathrm{E}(y_{t+m} \mid \mathcal{Y}_t) = a'_t P^m \mu + \phi^m (y_t - a'_t \mu) ,$$

(4.9)

where $\mu \equiv (\mu_1, \mu_2, \ldots, \mu_K)'$. The expected present value of the series is given by

$$\sum_{m=0}^{\infty} \beta^m \mathrm{E}(y_{t+m} \mid \mathcal{Y}_t) = a'_t [I - \beta P]^{-1} \mu + [1/(1 - \phi\beta)][y_t - a'_t \mu] .$$

(4.10)

For more details on forecasting see Tjøstheim (1986) and Hamilton (1988, 1989).

4.2. Rational-expectations analysis

Many theories in economics and finance assume that people's forecasts of one series have an effect on another series. It is often of interest to estimate such models under the hypothesis of rational expectations, which is the view that people use all the information available to them in the statistically optimal way.

Consider the following example, taken from Engel and Hamilton (1990). Let e_t denote the log of the number of dollars required to purchase a German mark. Let i_t denote the interest rate (in dollars) earned from a U.S. investment, and i_t^* denote the interest rate (in marks) available on a German investment. Then a popular model of the exchange rate holds that

$$i_t = i_t^* + \mathrm{E}[(e_{t+1} - e_t) \,|\, \Omega_t] + u_t \,. \tag{4.11}$$

Here Ω_t denotes information available to traders in the foreign exchange market at date t and $u_t \sim N(0, \sigma_u^2)$ is a disturbance term that reflects measurement and specification error. Equation (4.11) claims that if traders believe that the value of the mark is going to rise $(\mathrm{E}[(e_{t+1} - e_t) \,|\, \Omega_t] > 0)$, then they would be willing to invest in the German asset even if it offers a lower rate of return than the U.S. asset $(i_t^* < i_t)$. This is because by investing in the German asset, they will also enjoy a capital gain when the mark appreciates against the dollar.

The Markov-switching models are very convenient for such rational-expectations applications. We can make either of two assumptions about Ω_t, the information that people have available. One assumption is that the people in the economy, unlike the econometrician, know the true value of s_t at date t. The second assumption is that people in the economy must form an inference about s_t in the same manner as the econometrician. We discuss each of these specifications in turn.

4.3. The case when people know the true value of s_t

Suppose that the exchange rate itself follows a two-state regime-switching process,

$$e_t - e_{t-1} = \mu_{s_t} + \varepsilon_t \,, \tag{4.12}$$

with $\varepsilon_t \sim N(0, \sigma_\varepsilon^2)$. If foreign exchange speculators know the true value of s_t at date t, then from (4.7) they would forecast

$$\mathrm{E}[(e_{t+1} - e_t) \,|\, s_t = 1] = \mu_1 p_{11} + \mu_2 p_{12} \tag{4.13}$$

whenever the current state is 1, whereas they would forecast

$$\mathrm{E}[(e_{t+1} - e_t) \,|\, s_t = 2] = \mu_1 p_{21} + \mu_2 p_{22} \tag{4.14}$$

whenever the current state is 2. Substituting (4.13) and (4.14) into (4.11), we find

$$i_t - i_t^* = \alpha_{s_t} + u_t \,, \tag{4.15}$$

where

$$\alpha_1 = \mu_1 p_{11} + \mu_2 p_{12} , \tag{4.16}$$

$$\alpha_2 = \mu_1 p_{21} + \mu_2 p_{22} . \tag{4.17}$$

Equations (4.12) and (4.15) thus imply that the vector $[(e_t - e_{t-1})(i_t - i_t^*)]'$ obeys the following regime-switching process:

$$\begin{bmatrix} (e_t - e_{t-1}) \\ (i_t - i_t^*) \end{bmatrix} \sim N\left(\begin{bmatrix} \mu_1 \\ \alpha_1 \end{bmatrix}, \begin{bmatrix} \sigma_\varepsilon^2 & \sigma_{\varepsilon u} \\ \sigma_{\varepsilon u} & \sigma_u^2 \end{bmatrix} \right) \quad \text{when } s_t = 1 , \tag{4.18}$$

$$\begin{bmatrix} e_t - e_{t-1} \\ (i_t - i_t^*) \end{bmatrix} \sim N\left(\begin{bmatrix} \mu_2 \\ \alpha_2 \end{bmatrix}, \begin{bmatrix} \sigma_\varepsilon^2 & \sigma_{\varepsilon u} \\ \sigma_{\varepsilon u} & \sigma_u^2 \end{bmatrix} \right) \quad \text{when } s_t = 2 , \tag{4.19}$$

The likelihood for the vector $[(e_t - e_{t-1})(i_t - i_t^*)]'$ thus can be evaluated in the manner described in Section 3.1, and maximized while imposing the rational-expectations restrictions (4.16)–(4.17). For more on this approach, see Engel and Hamilton (1990).

4.4. *The case when people do not know the true value of s_t*

Alternatively, suppose that speculators' information consists only of observations on exchange rates:

$$\Omega_t = \{e_t - e_{t-1}, e_{t-1} - e_{t-2}, \dots\} = \mathcal{Y}_t . \tag{4.20}$$

In this case their forecast will be given by

$$E[(e_{t+1} - e_t) \mid \Omega_t] = \alpha_1 \cdot p(s_t = 1 \mid \mathcal{Y}_t) + \alpha_2 \cdot p(s_t = 2 \mid \mathcal{Y}_t) \tag{4.21}$$

for α_1 and α_2 given by (4.16) and (4.17) and $p(s_t \mid \mathcal{Y}_t)$ the outcome of the filter described in Section 2.1. If $\sigma_{u\varepsilon} = 0$ we then have from (4.11) that

$$p(i_t - i_t^* \mid \mathcal{Y}_t) = \frac{1}{\sqrt{2\pi}\sigma_u} \exp\{-[i_t - i_t^* - \alpha_1 \cdot p(s_t = 1 \mid \mathcal{Y}_t)$$

$$- \alpha_2 \cdot p(s_t = 2 \mid \mathcal{Y}_t)]^2 / (2\sigma_u^2)\} . \tag{4.22}$$

Note well the notation – $p(s_t = 1 \mid \mathcal{Y}_t)$ is not a function of the state, but rather is a function of current and lagged exchange rates. If we have gone through the recursion for forming inference described in Section 2.1, we have calculated this function. We also saw how to calculate $p(e_t - e_{t-1} \mid \mathcal{Y}_{t-1})$ through this same recursion. The product of $p(e_t - e_{t-1} \mid \mathcal{Y}_{t-1})$ with (4.22) then gives the joint likelihood $p[(i_t - i_t^*), (e_t - e_{t-1}) \mid \mathcal{Y}_{t-1}]$, the sum of whose logs for all t is then to be maximized with respect to p_{ij}, μ_i, σ_ε^2, and σ_u^2. For more details see Hamilton (1988).

Other rational-expectations applications of time-series switching models

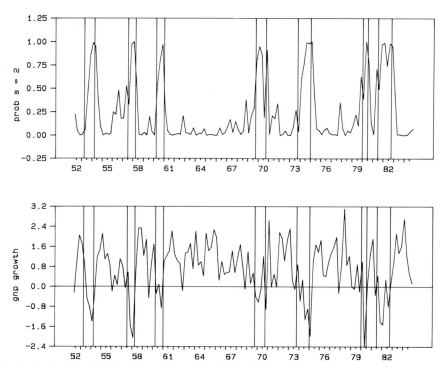

Fig. 5. Panel A: Probability that economy is in falling GNP state. Panel B: Rate of growth of U.S. real GNP, quarterly 1953–1984. Source: Hamilton (1989).

include Cecchetti, Lam and Mark (1990a,b), Kaminsky (1988), and Turner, Startz and Nelson (1989).

5. Applications

This section reviews some of the results obtained from fitting such regime-switching models to various economic and financial time series.

The bottom panel of Figure 5 plots the quarterly percent change in U.S. real GNP from 1953 to 1984. Hamilton (1989) fit a fourth-order autoregression with intercept switching between two states as in (2.21) but with constant variance to these data, resulting in the following maximum likelihood estimates:

$$(1 - 0.014L + 0.058L^2 + 0.247L^3 + 0.213L^4)(y_t - \mu_{s_t}) = \varepsilon_t \,,$$

$$\varepsilon_t \sim N(0, 0.591) \,,$$

$$\mu_1 = 1.164 \,, \qquad \mu_2 = -0.358 \,,$$

$$p_{11} = 0.905 \,, \qquad p_{22} = 0.755 \,. \tag{5.1}$$

Thus state 1 is typically characterized by rising GNP and state 2 by falling GNP, with state 1 expected to persist for $1/(1 - p_{11}) = 11$ quarters on average and state 2 for $1/(1 - p_{22}) = 4$ quarters.

The top panel of Figure 5 plots the inference $p(s_t = 2 \mid \mathcal{Y}_t; \hat{\lambda})$ associated with these maximum likelihood estimates. Evidently the falling GNP state was entered seven times over this sample period. Also plotted as vertical lines in Figure 5 are the starting and ending dates of economic recessions as determined by the National Bureau of Economic Research (NBER). These determinations are based on a good deal of evidence besides the behavior of GNP, and these values were not used in the econometric estimation. It is interesting that the atheoretical regime-switching approach comes up with essentially the same dating as NBER. This provides support for viewing economic recessions as episodes with clearly different dynamic behavior from expansions.

Other researchers have extended this characterization of output fluctuations. If we let $\bar{y}_t$ denote the log of the level of GNP, the growth rates in Figure 5

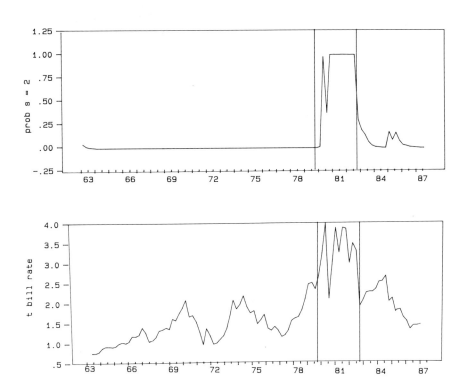

Fig. 6. Panel A: Probability that economy is in high interest rate, high volatility state. Panel B: Nominal interest rate on 3-month U.S. treasury bills, quarterly 1962–1987. Source: Hamilton (1988).

represent $y_t = (1 - L)\tilde{y}_t$. The specification (5.1) thus assumed that

$$\tilde{y}_t = y_0 + \sum_{\tau=1}^{t} \mu_{s_\tau} + \tilde{z}_t \tag{5.2}$$

with

$$\tilde{z}_t = \sum_{\tau=1}^{t} z_\tau \tag{5.3}$$

and z_t a stationary Gaussian AR(p) process; that is, $\tilde{z}_t$ is nonstationary with a unit root. Lam (1991) generalized this specification to allow $\tilde{z}_t$ to be stationary. Thus in Lam's model $\tilde{y}_t$ is stationary around an occasionally shifting trend. Lam's estimates again identify these shifts as occurring during severe recessions.

Phillips (1991) fit a bivariate switching model to growth rates in different countries, to see how recessions in one country interacted with those in another. Hassett (1990) studied real wages and output in a bivariate system to study the effects of the business cycle on wages. Cecchetti, Lam and Mark (1990b) found regime switches associated with severe economic downturns in century-long studies of consumption, output, and dividends.

In other samples, the switch in regime can be associated with one extreme episode. Figure 6 reports the results of estimating process (2.21) with $K = 2$ to the quarterly nominal interest rate on U.S. treasury bills. The bottom panel gives the raw data (quoted here at a quarterly rate), while the top panel plots $p(s_t = 2 \mid \mathcal{Y}_t)$. The second regime is characterized by much higher levels and volatility of interest rates. The vertical lines are drawn at the dates 1979:IV and 1982:IV, during which episode the U.S. Federal Reserve experimented with a policy of permitting higher interest rates and greater variability in an effort to curb the rate of monetary growth. Again, the institutional knowledge of these dates was not used in the estimation procedure, though it is very interesting that the atheoretical inference matches so closely with the known historical dates of the policy change. Garcia and Perron (1989) have explored a three-state description of interest rates adjusted for inflation.

Other applications of this approach include studies of financial panics (Pagan and Schwert, 1990; Schwert, 1989, 1990), corporate mergers (Town, 1990, and exchange rates (Engel and Hamilton, 1990; Kaminsky, 1988).

Acknowledgment

I am grateful to Gongpil Choi and Sang-Ho Nam for helpful comments, to Robert Hetzel, John Rogers, and Robert Town for graciously providing me with their data, and to the National Science Foundation for support through grant number SES-8920752.

References

Baum, L. E., T. Petrie, G. Soules and N. Weiss (1970). A maximization technique occurring in the statistical analysis of probabilistic functions of Markov chains. *Ann. Math. Statist.* **41**, 164–171.

Berndt, E. K., B. H. Hall, R. E. Hall and J. A. Hausman (1974). Estimation and inference in nonlinear structural models. *Ann. Econ. Social Measurement* **3/4**, 653–665.

Breusch, T. S. and A. R. Pagan (1980). The Lagrange multiplier test and its applications to model specification in econometrics. *Rev. Econ. Stud.* **47**, 239–254.

Cecchetti, S. G., P. Lam and N. C. Mark (1990a). Evaluating empirical tests of asset pricing models: Alternative interpretations. *Amer. Econ. Rev.* **80**, 48–51.

Cecchetti, S. G., P. Lam and N. C. Mark (1990b). Mean reversion in equilibrium asset prices. *Amer. Econ. Rev.* **80**, 398–418.

Cosslett, S. R. and L. Lee (1985). Serial correlation in discrete variable models. *J. Econometrics* **27**, 79–97.

Davies, R. B. (1977). Hypothesis testing when a nuisance parameter is present only under the alternative. *Biometrika* **64**, 247–254.

Dempster, A. P., N. M. Laird and D. B. Rubin (1977). Maximum likelihood estimation from incomplete data via the EM algorithm. *J. Roy. Statist. Soc. Ser. B* **39**, 1–38.

Engel, C. M. and J. D. Hamilton (1990). Long swings in the dollar: Are they in the data and do markets know it? *Amer. Econ. Rev.* **80**, 689–713.

Engle, R. F. (1984). Wald, likelihood ratio, and Lagrange multiplier tests in econometrics. In: Z. Griliches and M. D. Intriligator, eds. North-Holland, Amsterdam, 775–826.

Fama, E. F. and K. R. French (1988). Permanent and temporary components of stock prices. *J. Politic. Econ.* **96**, 246–273.

Garcia, R. and P. Perron (1989). An analysis of the real interest rate under regime shifts. Mimneographed, Princeton University.

Godfrey, L. G. (1988). *Misspecification Tests in Econometrics*. Econometric Society Monographs, Vol. 16. Cambridge Univ. Press, Cambridge, England.

Goldfeld, S. M. and R. M. Quandt (1973). A Markov model for switching regressions. *J. Econometrics* **1**, 3–16.

Hamilton, J. D. (1988). Rational-expectations econometric analysis of changes in regime: An investigation of the term structure of interest rates. *J. Econ. Dynamic Control* **12**, 385–423.

Hamilton, J. D. (1989). A new approach to the economic analysis of nonstationary time series and the business cycle. *Econometrica* **57**, 357–384.

Hamilton, J. D. (1990). Analysis of time series subject to changes in regime. *J. Econometrics* **45**, 39–70.

Hamilton, J. D. (1991a). A quasi-Bayesian approach to estimating parameters for mixtures of normal distributions. *J. Business Econ. Statistic.* **9**, 27–39.

Hamilton, J. D. (1991b). Specification testing in Markov-switching time series models. Mimeographed, University of Virginia.

Hansen, B. E. (1991). Inference when a nuisance parameter is not identified under the null hypothesis. Mimeographed, Rochester University.

Hassett, K. (1990). Markov switching and the changing cyclicality of the aggregate real wage. Mimeographed, Columbia University.

Hetzel, R. (1990). A critical appraisal of the empirical generalizations of Milton Friedman and Anna Schwartz on the behavior of the demand for money. Mimeographed, Federal Reserve Bank of Richmond.

Judge, G. G., W. E. Griffiths, R. C. Hill, H. Lutkepohl and T. Lee (1985). Numerical optimization methods. In: *The Theory and Practice of Econometrics*. 2nd ed., Wiley, New York, Appendix B, 951–969.

Kaminsky, G. (1988). The peso problem and the behavior of the exchange rate: The dollar/pound exchange rate, 1976–1987. Mimeographed, University of California, San Diego, CA.

Lam, P. (1990). The Hamilton model with a general autoregressive component: Estimation and comparison with other models of economic time series. *J. Monetary Econ.* **26**, 409–432.

Pagan, A. R. and G. W. Schwert (1990). Alternative models for conditional stock volatility. *J. Econometrics* **45**, 267–290.

Phillips, K. L. (1989). Full-sample versus long-lag inferences in markov-switching time-series models. Mimeographed, University of Rochester.

Phillips, K. L. (1991). A two-country model of stochastic output with changes in regime. *J. Internat. Econ.* **31**, 121–142.

Poterba, J. M. and L. H. Summers (1988). Mean reversion in stock prices: Evidence and implications. *J. Financ. Econ.* **22**, 27–59.

Quandt, R. E. (1958). The estimation of parameters of a linear regression system obeying two separate regimes. *J. Amer. Statist. Assoc.* **55**, 873–880.

Rogers, J. H. (1992). The currency substitution hypothesis and relative money demand in Mexico and Canada. *J. Money, Credit and Banking* **24**, 300–318.

Sclove, S. L. (1983). Time-series segmentation: A model and a method. *Inform. Sci.* **29**, 7–25.

Schwert, G. W. (1989). Business cycles, financial crises, and stock volatility. In: K. Brunner and A. H. Meltzer, eds., *IMF Policy Advice, Market Volatility, Commodity Price Rules, and Other Essays*, Carnegie–Rochester Conf. Ser. on Public Policy, Vol. 31. North-Holland, Amsterdam, 83–125.

Schwert, G. W. (1990). Stock volatility and the crash of '87. *Rev. Financ. Stud.* **3**, 77–102.

Titterington, D. M., A. F. M. Smith and U. E. Makov (1985). *Statistical Analysis of Finite Mixture Distributions*. Wiley, New York.

Tjøstheim, D. (1986). Some doubly stochastic time series models. *J. Time Ser. Anal.* **7**, 51–72.

Tong, H. (1983). *Threshold Models in Non-linear Time Series Analysis*. Springer, New York.

Town, R. J. (1990). Merger waves and the structure of merger and acquisition time series. Mimeographed, United States Justice Department.

Turner, C. M., R. Startz and C. R. Nelson (1989). A Markov model of heteroskedasticity, risk, and learning in the stock market. *J. Financ. Econ.* **25**, 3–22.

White, H. (1987). Specification testing in dynamic models. In: T. F. Bewley, ed., *Advances in Econometrics, 5th World Congress*, Vol. 2. Cambridge Univ. Press, Cambridge, England.

G. S. Maddala, C. R. Rao and H. D. Vinod, eds., *Handbook of Statistics, Vol. 11*
10

Structural Time Series Models

Andrew C. Harvey and Neil Shephard

1. Introduction

A structural time series model is one which is set up in terms of components which have a direct interpretation. Thus, for example, we may consider the classical decomposition in which a series is seen as the sum of trend, seasonal and irregular components. A model could be formulated as a regression with explanatory variables consisting of a time trend and a set of seasonal dummies. Typically, this would be inadequate. The necessary flexibility may be achieved by letting the regression coefficients change over time. A similar treatment may be accorded to other components such as cycles. *The principal univariate structural time series models are therefore nothing more than regression models in which the explanatory variables are functions of time and the parameters are time-varying.* Given this interpretation, the addition of observable explanatory variables is a natural extension as is the construction of multivariate models. Furthermore, the use of a regression framework opens the way to a unified model selection methodology for econometric and time series models.

The key to handling structural time series models is the *state space form* with the state of the system representing the various unobserved components such as trends and seasonals. The estimate of the unobservable state can be updated by means of a *filtering* procedure as new observations become available. Predictions are made by extrapolating these estimated components into the future, while *smoothing* algorithms give the best estimate of the state at any point within the sample. A structural model can therefore not only provide forecasts, but can also, through estimates of the components, present a set of stylised facts; see the discussion in Harvey and Jaeger (1991).

A thorough discussion of the methodological and technical ideas underlying structural time series models is contained in the monographs by Harvey (1989) and West and Harrison (1989), the latter adopting a Bayesian perspective. Since then there have been a number of technical developments and applications to new situations. One of the purposes of the present article is to describe these new results.

1.1. Statistical formulation

A structural time series model for quarterly observations might consist of trend, cycle, seasonal and irregular components. Thus

$$y_t = \mu_t + \psi_t + \gamma_t + \varepsilon_t, \quad t = 1, \ldots, T, \tag{1.1}$$

where μ_t is the trend, ψ_t is the cycle, γ_t is the seasonal and ε_t is the irregular. All four components are stochastic and the disturbances driving them are mutually uncorrelated. The trend, seasonal and cycle are all derived from deterministic functions of time, and reduce to these functions as limiting cases. The irregular is white noise.

The deterministic linear trend is

$$\mu_t = \alpha + \beta t. \tag{1.2}$$

Since μ_t may be obtained recursively from

$$\mu_t = \mu_{t-1} + \beta, \tag{1.3}$$

with $\mu_0 = \alpha$, continuity may be preserved by introducing stochastic terms as follows:

$$\mu_t = \mu_{t-1} + \beta_{t-1} + \eta_t, \tag{1.4a}$$

$$\beta_t = \beta_{t-1} + \zeta_t, \tag{1.4b}$$

where η_t and ζ_t are mutually uncorrelated white noise disturbances with zero means and variances, σ_η^2 and σ_ζ^2 respectively. The effect of η_t is to allow the level of the trend to shift up and down, while ζ_t allows the slope to change. The larger the variances, the greater the stochastic movements in the trend. If $\sigma_\eta^2 = \sigma_\zeta^2 = 0$, (1.4) collapses to (1.2) showing that the deterministic trend is a limiting case.

Let ψ_t be a cyclical function of time with frequency λ_c, which is measured in radians. The period of the cycle, which is the time taken to go through its complete sequence of values, is $2\pi / \lambda_c$. A cycle can be expressed as a mixture of sine and cosine waves, depending on two parameters, α and β. Thus

$$\psi_t = \alpha \cos \lambda_c t + \beta \sin \lambda_c t, \tag{1.5}$$

where $(\alpha^2 + \beta^2)^{1/2}$ is the amplitude and $\tan^{-1}(\beta / \alpha)$ is the phase. Like the linear trend, the cycle can be built up recursively, leading to the stochastic model

$$\begin{pmatrix} \psi_t \\ \psi_t^* \end{pmatrix} = \rho \begin{pmatrix} \cos \lambda_c & \sin \lambda_c \\ -\sin \lambda_c & \cos \lambda_c \end{pmatrix} \begin{pmatrix} \psi_{t-1} \\ \psi_{t-1}^* \end{pmatrix} + \begin{pmatrix} \kappa_t \\ \kappa_t^* \end{pmatrix}, \tag{1.6}$$

where κ_t and κ_t^* are mutually uncorrelated with a common variance, σ_κ^2, and ρ is a damping factor, such that $0 \le \rho \le 1$. The model is stationary if ρ is strictly less than one, and if λ_c is equal to 0 or π it reduces to a first-order autoregressive process.

A model of deterministic seasonality has the seasonal effects summing to zero over a year. The seasonal effects can be allowed to change over time by letting their sum over the previous year be equal to a random disturbance term ω_t, with mean zero and variance σ_ω^2. Thus, if s is the number of season in the year,

$$\sum_{j=0}^{s-1} \gamma_{t-j} = \omega_t \quad \text{or} \quad \gamma_t = -\sum_{j=1}^{s-1} \gamma_{t-j} + \omega_t . \tag{1.7}$$

An alternative way of allowing seasonal dummy variables to change over time is to suppose that each season evolves as a random walk but that, at any particular point in time, the seasonal components, and hence the disturbances, sum to zero. This model was introduced by Harrison and Stevens (1976, p. 217–218).

A seasonal pattern can also be modelled by a set of trigonometric terms at the seasonal frequencies, $\lambda_j = 2\pi j/s$, $j = 1, \ldots, [s/2]$, where $[s/2]$ is $s/2$ if s is even and $(s-1)/2$ if s is odd. The seasonal effect at time t is then

$$\gamma_t = \sum_{j=1}^{[s/2]} (\gamma_j \cos \lambda_j t + \gamma_j^* \sin \lambda_j t) . \tag{1.8}$$

When s is even, the sine term disappears for $j = s/2$ and so the number of trigonometric parameters, the γ_j and γ_j^*, is always $(s-1)/2$, which is the same as the number of coefficients in the seasonal dummy formulation. A seasonal pattern based on (1.8) is the sum of $[s/2]$ cyclical components, each with $\rho = 1$, and it may be allowed to evolve over time in exactly the same way as a cycle was allowed to move. The model is

$$\gamma_t = \sum_{j=1}^{[s/2]} \gamma_{j,t} , \tag{1.9}$$

where, following (1.6),

$$\begin{pmatrix} \gamma_{j,t} \\ \gamma_{j,t}^* \end{pmatrix} = \begin{pmatrix} \cos \lambda_j & \sin \lambda_j \\ -\sin \lambda_j & \cos \lambda_j \end{pmatrix} \begin{pmatrix} \gamma_{j,t-1} \\ \gamma_{j,t-1}^* \end{pmatrix} + \begin{pmatrix} \omega_{j,t} \\ \omega_{j,t}^* \end{pmatrix} , \tag{1.10}$$

where ω_{jt} and ω_{jt}^*, $j = 1, \ldots, [s/2]$, are zero mean white noise processes which are uncorrelated with each other with a common variance σ_ω^2. As in the cycles (1.6) $\gamma_{j,t}^*$ appears as a matter of construction, and its interpretation is not particularly important. Note that when s is even, the component at $j = s/2$ collapses to

$$\gamma_{j,t} = \gamma_{j,t-1} \cos \lambda_j + \omega_{jt} . \tag{1.11}$$

If the disturbances in the model are assumed to be normally distributed, the

Table 1
Principal structural time series components and models

Model	Component	Specification	Stationarity operator, $\Delta(L)$	Reduced form	Comments
(A) Local level / random walk plus noise model	(1a) Random walk	$\mu_t = \mu_{t-1} + \eta_t$	$\Delta = 1 - L$	—	—
	(1b) Random walk with drift	$\mu_t = \mu_{t-1} + \beta + \eta_t$	Δ	—	—
		$y_t = \mu_t + \varepsilon_t$, with μ_t as in (1a)	Δ	ARIMA(0, 1, 1)	Forecast function is EWMA
	(2) Stochastic trend	$\mu_t = \mu_{t-1} + \beta_{t-1} + \eta_t,$ $\beta_t = \beta_{t-1} + \zeta_t$	Δ^2	—	Random walk with drift if $\sigma_\zeta^2 = 0$. Doubly integrated random walk if $\sigma_\eta^2 = 0$.
(B) Local linear trend		$y_t = \mu_t + \varepsilon_t,$ with μ_t as in (2)	Δ^2	ARIMA(0, 2, 2)	Forecast function in nonseasonal Holt–Winters.
	(3) Stochastic cycle	$\begin{bmatrix} \psi_t \\ \psi_t^* \end{bmatrix} = \rho \begin{bmatrix} \cos\lambda_c & \sin\lambda_c \\ -\sin\lambda_c & \cos\lambda_c \end{bmatrix}\begin{bmatrix} \psi_{t-1} \\ \psi_{t-1}^* \end{bmatrix} + \begin{bmatrix} \kappa_t \\ \kappa_t^* \end{bmatrix},$ where ψ is cycle, $0 \leq \rho < 1$, and $0 \leq \lambda_c \leq \pi$	1	ARMA(2, 1)	Collapses to AR(1) if $\lambda_c = 0$ or π.
(C) Cycle plus noise model		$y_t = \mu + \psi_t + \varepsilon_t,$ where $0 \leq \rho < 1$	1	Constant + ARMA(2, 2)	—
(D) Trend plus cycle		$y_t = \mu_t + \psi_t + \varepsilon_t,$ with μ_t as in (2)	Δ^2	ARIMA(2, 2, 4)	—
(E) Cyclical trend		$y_t = \mu_t + \varepsilon_t,$ $\mu_t = \mu_{t-1} + \psi_{t-1} + \beta_{t-1} + \eta_t,$ with β_t as in (2)	Δ^2	ARIMA(2, 2, 4)	Gives the damped trend model if $\lambda_c = 0$ and β_t is removed.
	(4) Nonstationary cycle	As (3) but $\rho = 1$	$1 - 2\cos\lambda_c L + L^2$	$(1 - 2\cos\lambda_c L + L^2)\psi_t \sim$ MA(1)	—
	(5a) Dummy variable seasonality	$\gamma_t = -\sum_{j=1}^{s-1} \gamma_{t-j} + \omega_j$	$S(L) = 1 + L + L^2 + \cdots + L^{s-1}$	$S(L)\gamma_t \sim$ WN	—
	(5b) Trigonometric seasonality	$\gamma_t = \sum_{j=1}^{[s/2]} \gamma_{t,j},$ where $\gamma_{t,j}^\dagger$ is a nonstationary cycle, (4), with $\lambda_c = \lambda_j = 2\pi j/s,\ j = 1, 2, \ldots, [s/2]$	$S(L)$	$S(L)\gamma_t \sim$ MA($s-2$)	Evolves more smoothly than (5a).
(F) Basic structural model		$y_t = \mu_t + \gamma_t + \varepsilon_t,$ where μ_t is as in (2) and γ_t is as in (5a) or (5b)	$\Delta_s = (1 - L)(1 - L^s)$	$\Delta\Delta_s y_t \sim$ MA($s+1$)	(a) Forecasts from Holt–Winters are similar. (b) Close to 'airline model' for some series.

hyperparameters $(\sigma_\eta^2, \sigma_\zeta^2, \sigma_\omega^2, \sigma_\kappa^2, \rho, \lambda_c, \sigma_\varepsilon^2)$ may be estimated by maximum likelihood. This may be done in the time domain using the Kalman filter as described in Section 2, or in the frequency domain as described in Harvey (1989, Chapter 4). Harvey and Peters (1990) present simulation evidence on the performance of different estimators. Once the hyperparameters have been estimated, the state space form may be used to make predictions and construct estimators of the unobserved components.

EXAMPLE. A model of the form (1.1), but without the seasonal component, was fitted to quarterly, seasonally adjusted data on US GNP from 1947Q1 to 1988Q2. The estimated variances of η_t, ζ_t, κ_t, and ε_t were 0, 0.0015, 0.0664 and 0 respectively, while the estimate of ρ was 0.92. The estimate of λ_c was 0.30, corresponding to a period of 20.82 quarters. Thus the length of business cycles is roughly five years.

A summary of the main structural models and their properties may be found in Table 1. Structural time series models which are linear and time invariant, all have a corresponding *reduced form* autoregressive integrated moving average (ARIMA) representation which is equivalent in the sense that it will give identical forecasts to the structural form. For example in the local level model,

$$y_t = \mu_t + \varepsilon_t \,,$$
$$\mu_t = \mu_{t-1} + \eta_t \,, \tag{1.12}$$

where ε_t and η_t are mutually uncorrelated white noise disturbances, taking first differences yields

$$\Delta y_t = \eta_t + \varepsilon_t - \varepsilon_{t-1} \,, \tag{1.13}$$

which in view of its autocorrelation structure is equivalent to an MA(1) process with a nonpositive autocorrelation at lag one. Thus y_t is ARIMA(0, 1, 1). By equating autocorrelations at lag one it is possible to derive the relationship between the moving average parameter and q, the ratio of the variance of η_t to that of ε_t. In more complex models, there may not be a simple correspondence between the structural and reduced form parameters. For example in (1.1), $\Delta\Delta_s y_t$ is ARIMA(2, $s + 3$), where Δ_s is the seasonal difference operator. Note that the terminology of reduced and structural form is used in a parallel fashion to the way it is used in econometrics, except that in structural time series models the restrictions come not from economic theory, but from a desire to ensure that the forecasts reflect features such as cycles and seasonals which are felt to be present in the data.

In addition to the main structural models found in Table 1 many more structural models may be constructed. Additional components may be introduced and the components defined above may be modified. For example, quadratic trends may replace linear ones, and the irregular component may be formulated so as to reflect the sampling scheme used to collect the data. If observations are collected on a daily basis, a slowly changing day of the week effect may be incorporated in the model, while for hourly observations an intra-day pattern may be modelled in a similar way to seasonality. A more parsimonious way of modelling an intra-day pattern, based on time-varying splines, is proposed in Harvey and Koopman (1993).

1.2. Model selection

The most difficult aspect of working with time series data is model selection. The attraction of the structural framework is that it enables the researcher to formulate, at the outset, a model which is explicitly designed to pick up the salient characteristics of the data. Once the model has been estimated, it suitability can be assessed, not only by carrying out diagnostic tests, but also by checking whether the estimated components are consistent with any prior knowledge which might be available. Thus if a cyclical component is used to model the trade cycle, a knowledge of the economic history of the period should enable one to judge whether the estimated parameters are reasonable. This is in the same spirit as assessing the plausibility of a regression model by reference to the sign and magnitude of its estimated coefficients.

Classical time series analysis is based on the theory of stationary stochastic processes, and this is the starting point for conventional time series model building. Nonstationarity is handled by differencing, leading to the ARIMA class of models. The fact that the simpler structural time series models can be made stationary by differencing provides an important link with classical time series analysis. However, the analysis of series which are thought to be stationary does not play a fundamental role in structural modelling methodology. Few economic and social time series are stationary and there is no overwhelming reason to suppose that they can necessarily be made stationary by differencing, which is the assumption underling the ARIMA methodology of Box and Jenkins (1976). If a univariate structural model fails to give a good fit to a set of data, other univariate models may be considered, but there will be an increased willingness to look at more radical alternatives. For example, a search for outliers might be initiated or it may be necessary to concede that a structurally stable model can only be obtained by conditioning on an observed explanatory variable.

Introducing explanatory variables into a model requires access to a larger information set. Some prior knowledge of which variables should potentially enter into the model is necessary, and data on these variables is needed. In a structural time series model the explanatory variables enter into the model side by side with the unobserved components. In the absence of these unobserved components the model reverts to a regression, and this perhaps makes it clear as to why the model selection methodology which has been developed for dynamic regression is appropriate in the wider context with which we are concerned. Distributed lags can be fitted in much the same way as in econometric modelling, and even ideas such as the error-correction mechanism can be employed. The inclusion of the unobserved time series components does not affect the model selection methodology to be applied to the explanatory variables in any fundamental way. What it does is to add an extra dimension to the interpretation and specification of certain aspects of the dynamics. For example, it provides a key insight into the vexed question of whether to work with the variables in levels or first differences, and solves the problem by setting up a general framework within which the two formulations emerge as special cases.

The fact that structural time series models are set up in terms of components which have a direct interpretation means that it is possible to employ a model selection methodology which is similar to that proposed in the econometrics literature by writers such as Hendry and Richard (1983). Thus one can adopt the following criteria for a good model: parsimony, data coherence, consistency with prior knowledge, data admissibility, structural stability and encompassing.

2. Linear state space models and the Kalman filter

The linear state space form has been demonstrated to an extremely powerful tool in handling all linear and many classes of nonlinear time series models; see Harvey (1989, Chapters 3 and 4). In this section we introduce the state space form and the associated Kalman filter. We show how the filter can be used to deliver the likelihood. Recent work on smoothing is also discussed.

2.1. The linear state space form

Suppose a multivariate time series y_t possesses N elements. This series is related to a $p \times 1$ vector α_t, which labelled the state, via the measurement equation

$$y_t = Z_t \alpha_t + X_t \beta + \varepsilon_t, \quad t = 1, \ldots, T. \tag{2.1}$$

Here Z_t and X_t are nonstochastic matrices of dimensions $N \times p$ and $N \times k$ respectively, β is a fixed k-dimensional vector and ε_t is a zero mean, $N \times 1$ vector of white noise, with variance H_t.

The measurement equation is reminiscent of a classical regression model, with the state vector representing some of the regression coefficients. However, in the state space form, the state vector is allowed to evolve over time. This is achieved by introducing a transition equation, which is given by

$$\alpha_t = T_t \alpha_{t-1} + W_t \beta + R_t \eta_t, \quad t = 1, \ldots, T, \tag{2.2}$$

where T_t, W_t and R_t are fixed matrices of size $(p \times p)$, $(p \times k)$ and $(p \times g)$ respectively, η_t is a zero mean and g-dimensional vector of white noise, with variance Q_t. In the literature η_t and ε_s have always been assumed to be uncorrelated for all $s \neq t$. In this paper we will also assume that η_t and ε_t are uncorrelated, although Anderson and Moore (1979) and more recently De Jong (1991) and Koopman (1993) relax this assumption.

The inclusion of the R_t matrix is somewhat arbitrary, for the disturbance term can always be redefined to have a variance $R_t Q_t R_t'$. However, the transition equation above is often regarded as being more natural. The transition equation involves the state at time zero and so to complete the state space form we need to tie down its behaviour. We assume that α_0 has a mean a_0 and variance P_0. Further, α_0 is assumed to be uncorrelated with the noise in the transition and measurement equations. This completed state space form is said to be time invariant if Z_t, X_t, H_t, W_t, R_t and Q_t do not change over time.

To illustrate these general points we will put the univariate structural model (1.1) of trends, seasonals and cycles discussed in Section 1 into time invariant state space form by writing $\alpha_t = (\mu_t,\ \beta_t,\ \delta_t,\ \delta_{t-1}, \ldots, \delta_{t-s+2},\ \psi_t,\ \psi_t^*)'$, where

$$y_t = (1\quad 0\quad 1\quad 0\quad 0\quad \cdots\quad 0\quad 1\quad 0)\alpha_t + \varepsilon_t, \tag{2.3a}$$

$$\alpha_t = \begin{pmatrix} 1 & 1 & 0 & 0 & 0 & \cdots & 0 & 0 & 0 & 0 \\ 0 & 1 & 0 & 0 & 0 & \cdots & 0 & 0 & 0 & 0 \\ 0 & 0 & -1 & -1 & -1 & \cdots & -1 & -1 & 0 & 0 \\ 0 & 0 & 1 & 0 & 0 & \cdots & 0 & 0 & 0 & 0 \\ 0 & 0 & 0 & 1 & 0 & \cdots & 0 & 0 & 0 & 0 \\ \vdots & \vdots & \vdots & \vdots & \vdots & & \vdots & \vdots & \vdots & \vdots \\ 0 & 0 & 0 & 0 & 0 & \cdots & 1 & 0 & 0 & 0 \\ 0 & 0 & 0 & 0 & 0 & \cdots & 0 & 0 & \rho\cos\lambda_c & \rho\sin\lambda_c \\ 0 & 0 & 0 & 0 & 0 & \cdots & 0 & 0 & -\rho\sin\lambda_c & \rho\cos\lambda_c \end{pmatrix} \alpha_{t-1}$$

$$+ \begin{pmatrix} \eta_t \\ \zeta_t \\ \omega_t \\ 0 \\ 0 \\ \vdots \\ 0 \\ \kappa_t \\ \kappa_t^* \end{pmatrix}. \tag{2.3b}$$

2.2. The Kalman filter

In most structural time series models the individual elements of α_t are unobservable, either because of the presence of some masking irregular term ε_t or because of the way α_t is constructed. However, the observations do carry some information which can be harnessed to provide estimates of the unknowable α_t. This estimation can be carried out using a variety of information sets. We will write Y_s to denote this information, which will be composed of all the observations recorded up to time s and our initial knowledge of α_0. The two most common forms of estimation are smoothing, where we estimate α_t using Y_T, and filtering, where we estimate using only Y_t. We will focus on various aspects of smoothing in Section 2.4, but here we look at filtering.

Filtering allows the tracking of the state using contemporaneously available information. The optimal, that is minimum mean square error, filter is given by the mean of the conditional density of α_t, given Y_t, which is written as $\alpha_t | Y_t$. The Kalman filter delivers this quantity if the observations are Gaussian. If they are non-Gaussian the Kalman filter provides the optimal estimator amongst the class of linear estimators. Here we develop the filter under Gaussianity; see Duncan and Horn (1972) for an alternative derivation.

We start at time zero with the knowledge that $\alpha_0 \sim N(a_0, P_0)$. If we combine the transition and measurement equations with this prior and write Y_0 to express the information in it, then

$$\begin{pmatrix} \alpha_1 \\ y_1 \end{pmatrix} \Big| Y_0 \sim N\left(\begin{pmatrix} a_{1|0} \\ Z_1 a_{1|0} + X_1 \beta \end{pmatrix}, \begin{pmatrix} P_{1|0} & P_{1|0} Z_1' \\ Z_1 P_{1|0} & F_1 \end{pmatrix} \right), \tag{2.4}$$

where

$$P_{1|0} = T_1 P_0 T_1' + R_1 Q_1 R_1', \qquad F_1 = Z_1 P_{1|0} Z_1' + H_1,$$
$$a_{1|0} = T_1 a_0 + W_1 \beta. \tag{2.5}$$

Usually, we write $v_1 = y_1 - Z_1 a_{1|0} - X_1 \beta$ as the one-step ahead forecast error. It is constructed so that $v_1 | Y_0 \sim N(0, F_1)$. Consequently, using the usual conditioning result for multivariate normal distributions as given, for example, in Rao (1973)

$$\alpha_1 | Y_1 \sim N(a_1, P_1), \tag{2.6}$$

where

$$a_1 = a_{1|0} + P_{1|0} Z_1' F_1^{-1} v_1, \qquad P_1 = P_{1|0} - P_{1|0} Z_1' F_1^{-1} Z_1 P_{1|0}. \tag{2.7}$$

This result means that the filter is recursive. We will use the following notation throughout the paper to describe the general results: $\alpha_{t-1} | Y_{t-1} \sim N(a_{t-1}, P_{t-1})$, $\alpha_t | Y_{t-1} \sim N(a_{t|t-1}, P_{t|t-1})$ and $v_t | Y_{t-1} \sim N(0, F_t)$. The precise definition of these densities is given in the following three sets of equations. First the prediction equations

$$a_{t|t-1} = T_t a_{t-1} + W_t \beta, \qquad P_{t|t-1} = T_t P_{t-1} T_t' + R_t Q_t R_t', \tag{2.8}$$

then the one-step ahead forecast equations

$$v_t = y_t - Z_t a_{t|t-1} - X_t \beta, \qquad F_t = Z_t P_{t|t-1} Z_t' + H_t, \tag{2.9}$$

and finally the updating equations

$$a_t = a_{t|t-1} + P_{t|t-1} Z_t' F_t^{-1} v_t \quad \text{and} \quad P_t = P_{t|t-1} - P_{t|t-1} Z_t' F_t^{-1} Z_t P_{t|t-1} .$$

$$(2.10)$$

One immediate result which follows from the Kalman filter is that we can write the conditional joint density of the observations as

$$f(y_1, \ldots, y_T \mid Y_0) = \prod_{t=1}^{T} f(y_t \mid Y_{t-1}) = \prod_{t=1}^{T} f(v_t \mid Y_{t-1}) . \qquad (2.11)$$

This fracturing of the conditional joint density into the product of conditionals is called the prediction error decomposition. If α_t is stationary, an unconditional joint density can be constructed since the initial conditions, a_0 and P_0, are known. The case where we do not have stationarity has been the subject of some interesting research in recent years.

2.3. Initialization for non-stationary models[1]

We will derive the likelihood for a model in state space form using the argument in De Jong (1988a). A slightly different approach can be found in Ansley and Kohn (1985). We present a simplified derivation based partly on the results in Marshall (1992a). For ease of exposition β will be assumed to be zero and all the elements in α_0 can be taken to be nonstationary. We start by noting that if we write $y = (y_1', y_2', \ldots, y_T')'$, then

$$f(y) = \frac{f(\alpha_0 = 0) f(y \mid \alpha_0 = 0)}{f(\alpha_0 = 0 \mid y)} . \qquad (2.12)$$

The density $f(y \mid \alpha_0 = 0)$ can be evaluated by applying the Kalman filter and the prediction error decomposition if we initialize the filter at $a_0 = 0$ and $P_0 = 0$. We denote this filter by KF(0, 0), and the corresponding output as a_t^*, $a_{t|t-1}^*$ and v_t^*. The density $f(\alpha_0 = 0)$ has a simple form, which leaves us with the problem of $f(\alpha_0 = 0 \mid y)$. If we write $v^* = (v_1^{*\prime}, v_2^{*\prime}, \ldots, v_T^{*\prime})'$, then we can use the result that v^* is a linear combination of y in order to write $f(\alpha_0 = 0 \mid y) = f(\alpha_0 = 0 \mid v^*)$. To be able to evaluate $f(\alpha_0 = 0 \mid v^*)$ we will need to define F as a block diagonal matrix, with blocks being F_t and A as a matrix with row blocks $Z_t G_{t-1}$, where $G_t = T_{t+1}(I - K_t Z_t) G_{t-1}$, $G_0 = T_1$, and $K_t = P_{t|t-1} Z_t' F_t^{-1}$ (the so-called Kalman gain). In all cases the quantities are evaluated by the Kalman filter under the startup condition $P_0 = 0$. Then as

$$v_t(\alpha_0) = y_t - E(y_t \mid Y_{t-1}, \alpha_0) = y_t - Z_t a_{t|t-1}(\alpha_0) , \qquad (2.13)$$

---

[1] The rest of Section 2 is more technical and can be omitted on first reading without loss of continuity.

and

$$a_{t+1|t}(\alpha_0) = T_{t+1}a_{t|t-1}(\alpha_0) + T_{t+1}K_t v_t(\alpha_0)$$
$$= T_{t+1}(I - K_t Z_t)a_{t|t-1}(\alpha_0) + T_{t+1}K_t y_t$$
$$= G_t\alpha_0 + a_{t+1|t}^*, \qquad (2.14)$$

we have that

$$v_t(\alpha_0) = y_t - Z_t G_{t-1}\alpha_0 - Z_t a_{t|t-1}^*$$
$$= v_t^* - Z_t G_{t-1}\alpha_0, \qquad (2.15)$$

and so

$$v^* \mid \alpha_0 \sim N(A\alpha_0, F). \qquad (2.16)$$

Thus we can use Bayes' theorem to deliver the result that

$$\alpha_0 \mid y \sim N((P_0^{-1} + S_T)^{-1}(P_0^{-1}a_0 + s_T), (P_0^{-1} + S_T)^{-1}), \qquad (2.17)$$

where

$$S_T = A'F^{-1}A \quad \text{and} \quad s_T = A'F^{-1}v^*. \qquad (2.18)$$

S_T and s_T can be computed recursively, in parallel with KF(0, 0), by

$$S_t = S_{t-1} + G'_{t-1}Z'_t F_t^{-1}Z_t G_{t-1} \quad \text{and} \quad s_t = s_{t-1} + G'_{t-1}Z'_t F_t^{-1}v_t^*, \qquad (2.19)$$

with $s_0 = 0$ and $S_0 = 0$; see De Jong (1991). The log-likelihood is then constructed as

$$l(y) = -\tfrac{1}{2}\log|P_0| - \tfrac{1}{2}a_0'P_0^{-1}a_0 - \tfrac{1}{2}\sum_{t=1}^{T}\log|F_t| - \tfrac{1}{2}\sum_{t=1}^{T}v_t^{*\prime}F_t^{-1}v_t^*$$
$$- \tfrac{1}{2}\log|P_0^{-1} + S_T| + \tfrac{1}{2}(s_T + P_0^{-1}a_0)'(P_0^{-1} + S_T)^{-1}(s_T + P_0^{-1}a_0). \qquad (2.20)$$

Traditionally, nonstationary state space models have been initialised into two ways. The first is to use a diffuse prior on $\alpha_0 \mid Y_0$; this is to allow the diagonal elements of P_0 to go to infinity. We can see that in the limit the result from this is that

$$l(y) + \tfrac{1}{2}\log|P_0| \to -\tfrac{1}{2}\sum_{t=1}^{T}\log|F_t| - \tfrac{1}{2}\sum_{t=1}^{T}v_t^{*\prime}F_t^{-1}v_t^*$$
$$- \tfrac{1}{2}\log|S_T| - \tfrac{1}{2}s_T'S_T^{-1}s_T$$
$$= -\tfrac{1}{2}\log|S_T| - \tfrac{1}{2}\log|F|$$
$$- \tfrac{1}{2}v^{*\prime}(F^{-1} - F^{-1}A(A'F^{-1}A)^{-1}A'F^{-1})v^*. \qquad (2.21)$$

An approximation to (2.21) can be obtained for many models by running

$KF(a_0, P_0)$ with the diagonal elements of P_0 set equal to large, but finite, values. The likelihood is then constructed from the prediction errors once enough observations have been processed to give a finite variance. However, the likelihood obtained from (2.21) is preferable as it is exact and numerically stable.

The other main way nonstationary models are initialised is by taking α_0 to be an unknown constant; see Rosenberg (1973). Thus a_0 becomes a nuisance parameter and P_0 is set to zero. In this case, in the limit, the likelihood becomes

$$l(y) \to -\tfrac{1}{2} \sum_{t=1}^{T} \log |F_t| - \tfrac{1}{2} \sum_{t=1}^{T} v_t^{*\prime} F_t^{-1} v_t^* + a_0' s_T - \tfrac{1}{2} a_0' S_T a_0 , \qquad (2.22)$$

$$= -\tfrac{1}{2} \log |F| - \tfrac{1}{2} (v^* - A a_0)' F^{-1} (v^* - A a_0) , \qquad (2.23)$$

the term $a_0' S_T a_0$ in (2.22) appearing when $(P_0^{-1} + S_T)^{-1}$ is expanded out. We can concentrate a_0 out at its maximum likelihood value $\hat{a}_0 = (A'F^{-1}A)^{-1}A'F^{-1}v^*$, to deliver the profile or concentrated likelihood function

$$c(y) = -\tfrac{1}{2} \log |F| - \tfrac{1}{2} v^{*\prime} (F^{-1} - F^{-1}A(A'F^{-1}A)^{-1}A'F^{-1}) v^* . \qquad (2.24)$$

The difference between the profile likelihood and the likelihood given in (2.21) is simply the $\log |S_T|$ term. The latter is called a marginal or restricted likelihood in the statistics literature; cf. McCullagh and Nelder (1989, Chapter 7). It is based on a linear transformation of y making the data invariant to α_0.

The term $\log |S_T|$ can have a significant effect on small sample properties of maximum likelihood (ML) estimators in certain circumstances. This can be seen by looking at some results from the paper by Shephard and Harvey (1990) which analyses the sampling behaviour of the ML estimator of q, the ratio of the variances of η_t and ε_t, in the local level model (1.12). When q is zero the reduced form of the local level model is strictly noninvertible. Evaluating the probability that q is estimated to be exactly zero for various true values of q

Table 2
Probability that ML estimator of signal–noise ratio q is exactly equal to zero

Marginal likelihood $T-1$	$q = 0$	$q = 0.01$	$q = 0.1$	$q = 1$	$q = 10$
10	0.64	0.61	0.47	0.21	0.12
30	0.65	0.49	0.18	0.03	0.01
50	0.65	0.35	0.07	0.01	0.00

Profile likelihood $T-1$	$q = 0$	$q = 0.01$	$q = 0.1$	$q = 1$	$q = 10$
10	0.96	0.95	0.88	0.60	0.44
30	0.96	0.87	0.49	0.20	0.13
50	0.96	0.72	0.28	0.08	0.05

and sample sizes, gives the results summarised in Table 2. It can be seen that using a profile likelihood instead of a marginal results in a much higher probability of estimating q to be zero. Unless q is actually zero, this is undesirable from a forecasting point of view since there is no discounting of past observations. This provides a practical justification for the use of diffuse initial conditions and marginal likelihoods.

2.4. Smoothing

Estimating α_t using the full set of observations Y_T is called smoothing. The minimum mean square estimator of α_t using Y_T is $E\,\alpha_t | Y_T$. An extensive review of smoothing is given in Anderson and Moore (1979, Chapter 7).

Recently there have been some important developments in the way $E\,\alpha_t | Y_T$ is obtained; see, for example, De Jong (1988b, 1989), Kohn and Ansley (1989) and Koopman (1993). These breakthroughs have dramatically improved the speed of the smoothers. The new results will be introduced by using the framework of Whittle (1991). For ease of exposition, R_t will be assumed to be an identity matrix and β will be assumed to be zero.

Under Gaussianity, $E\,\alpha_t | Y_T$ is also the mode of the density of $\alpha_t | Y_T$. Thus we can use the general result that under weak regularity, if $f(\cdot)$ is a generic density function and m denotes the mode, then

$$\frac{\partial f(x \mid z)}{\partial x}\bigg|_{x=m} = 0 \quad \text{if and only if} \quad \frac{\partial f(x, z)}{\partial x}\bigg|_{x=m} = 0 \, . \tag{2.25}$$

The smoother can therefore be found by searching for turning points in the joint density of $\alpha_1', \alpha_2', \ldots, \alpha_T', y_1', \ldots, y_T'$, the logarithm of which is

$$D = \text{constant} - \tfrac{1}{2}(\alpha_0 - a_0)' P_0^{-1}(\alpha_0 - a_0)$$
$$- \tfrac{1}{2} \sum_{t=1}^{T} (y_t - Z_t\alpha_t)' H_t^{-1}(y_t - Z_t\alpha_t)$$
$$- \tfrac{1}{2} \sum_{t=1}^{T} (\alpha_t - T_t\alpha_{t-1})' Q_t^{-1}(\alpha_t - T_t\alpha_{t-1}) \, . \tag{2.26}$$

Thus

$$\frac{\partial D}{\partial \alpha_t} = Z_t' H_t^{-1}\varepsilon_t - Q_t^{-1}\eta_t + T_{t+1}' Q_{t+1}^{-1}\eta_{t+1} \quad \text{for } t = 1, \ldots, T \, . \tag{2.27}$$

Equating to zero, writing the solutions as $\hat{\alpha}_t$ and $\hat{\varepsilon}_t = y_t - Z_t\hat{\alpha}_t$ and $\hat{\eta}_t = \hat{\alpha}_t - T_t\hat{\alpha}_{t-1}$ results in the backward recursion

$$\hat{\alpha}_{t-1} = T_t^{-1}(\hat{\alpha}_t - Q_t(Z_t' H_t^{-1}\hat{\varepsilon}_t + T_{t+1}' Q_{t+1}^{-1}\hat{\eta}_{t+1}))$$
$$= T_t^{-1}(\hat{\alpha}_t - \hat{\eta}_t) \, , \quad t = 1, \ldots, T \, , \tag{2.28}$$

as

$$Z'_t H_t^{-1} \hat{\varepsilon}_t - Q_t^{-1} \hat{\eta}_t + T'_{t+1} Q_{t+1}^{-1} \hat{\eta}_{t+1} = 0 . \tag{2.29}$$

The starting point $\hat{\alpha}_T = a_T$ is given by the Kalman filter. Unfortunately, using

$$\hat{\eta}_t = Q_t (T'_{t+1} Q_{t+1}^{-1} \hat{\eta}_{t+1} + Z'_t H_t^{-1} \hat{\varepsilon}_t) , \tag{2.30}$$

will lead to a numerically unstable filter even though mathematically this result holds exactly. Koopman's (1993) shows that it can be stabilised by computing $\hat{\varepsilon}_t$ not by $y_t - Z_t \hat{\alpha}_t$, but by

$$\hat{\varepsilon}_t = H_t (F_t^{-1} v_t - K'_t T'_{t+1} Q_{t+1}^{-1} \hat{\eta}_{t+1}) , \tag{2.31}$$

where F_t and K_t are computed using KF(0, 0) and $v_t = v_t^* - Z_t G_{t-1} S_T^{-1} s_T$. Thus the efficient smoother uses (2.28), (2.30) and (2.31).

Recently, Harvey and Koopman (1992) have proposed using the smoothed estimates of ε_t and η_t to check for outliers and structural breaks, while Koopman (1993) uses them to implement a rapid EM algorithm and Koopman and Shephard (1992) show how to construct the exact score by smoothing.

3. Explanatory variables

Stochastic trend components are introduced into dynamic regression models when the underlying level of a nonstationary dependent variable cannot be completely explained by observable explanatory variables. The presence of a stochastic trend can often be rationalised by the fact that a variable has been excluded from the equation because it is difficult, or even impossible, to measure. Thus in Harvey et al. (1986) and Slade (1989), a stochastic trend is used as a proxy for technical progress, while in the demand equation for UK spirits estimated by Ansley and Kohn (1989) the stochastic trend can be thought of as picking up changes in tastes. Such rationalisation not only lends support to the specification of the model, but it also means that the estimated stochastic trend can be analysed and interpreted.

If stochastic trends are appropriate, but are not explicitly modelled, their effects will be picked up indirectly by time trends and lags on the variables. This can lead to a proliferation of lags which have no economic meaning, and which are subject to common factors and problems of inference associated with unit roots. An illustration of the type of problems which can arise with such an approach in a single equation context can be found in Harvey et al. (1986), where a stochastic trend is used to model productivity effects in an employment output equation and is compared with a more traditional autoregressive distributed lag (ADL) regression model with a time trend. Such problems may become even more acute in multivariate systems, such as vector autoregressions and simultaneous equation models; see Section 5.

Other stochastic components, such as time-varying seasonals or cycles, can also be included in a model with explanatory variables. Since this raises no new issues of principle, we will concentrate on stochastic trends.

3.1. Formulation and estimation

A regression model with a stochastic trend component may be written

$$y_t = \mu_t + x_t'\delta + \varepsilon_t , \quad t = 1, \ldots, T , \tag{3.1}$$

where μ_t is a stochastic trend (1.4), x_t is a $k \times 1$ vector of exogenous explanatory variables, δ is a corresponding vector of unknown parameters, ε_t is a normally distributed, white noise disturbance term with mean zero and variance σ_ε^2. A standard regression model with a deterministic time trend emerges as a special case, as does a model which could be estimated efficiently by OLS regression in first differences; in the latter case $\sigma_\varepsilon^2 = \sigma_\zeta^2 = 0$.

In the reduced form of (3.1), the stochastic part, $\mu_t + \varepsilon_t$, is replaced by an ARIMA(0, 2, 2) process. If the slope is deterministic, that is $\sigma_\zeta^2 = 0$ in (1.3), it is ARIMA(0, 1, 1). Box and Jenkins (1976, pp. 409–412) report a distributed lag model fitted to first differences with an MA(1) disturbance term. This model can perhaps be interpreted more usefully as a relationship in levels with a stochastic trend component of the form

$$\mu_t = \mu_{t-1} + \beta + \eta_t . \tag{3.2}$$

Maximum likelihood estimators of the parameters in (3.1) can be constructed in the time domain *via* the prediction error decomposition. This is done by putting the model in state space form and applying the Kalman filter. The parameters δ and β can be removed from the likelihood function either by concentrating them out of form of a profile likelihood function as in Kohn and Ansley (1985) or by forming a marginal likelihood function; see the discussion in Section 2.3. The marginal likelihood can be computed by extending the state so as to include β and δ, even though they are time-invariant, and then initializing with a diffuse prior.

The difference between the profile and marginal likelihood is in the determinantal term of the likelihood. There are a number of arguments which favour the use of marginal likelihoods for inference in small samples or when the process is close to nonstationarity or noninvertibility; see Tunnicliffe–Wilson (1989). In the present context, the difference in behaviour shows up most noticeably in the tendency of the trend to be estimated as being deterministic. To be more specific, suppose the trend is as in (3.2). The signal–noise ratio is $q = \sigma_\eta^2/\sigma_\varepsilon^2$ and if this is zero the trend is deterministic. The probability that q is estimated to be zero has been computed by Shephard (1993a). Using a profile likelihood by concentrating out β leads to this probability being relatively high when q is small but nonzero. The properties of the estimator obtained from the marginal likelihood are much better in this respect.

3.2. Intervention analysis

Intervention analysis is concerned with making inferences about the effects of known events. These effects are measured by including intervention, or dummy, variables in a dynamic regression model. In pure intervention analysis no other explanatory variables are present.

Model (3.1) may be generalized to yield the intervention model

$$y_t = \mu_t + x_t' \delta + \lambda w_t + \varepsilon_t, \quad t = 1, \ldots, T, \tag{3.3}$$

where w_t is the intervention variable and λ is its coefficient. The definition of w_t depends on the form which the intervention effect is assumed to take. If the intervention is transitory and has an effect only at time t, w_t is a pulse variable which takes the value one at the time of the intervention, $t = \tau$, and is zero otherwise. More generally the intervention may have a transitory effect which dies away gradually, for example, we may have $w_t = \varphi^{t-\tau}$, when $|\varphi| < 1$, for $t \geq \tau$. A permanent shift in the level of the series can be captured by a step variable which is zero up to the time of the intervention and unity thereafter. An effect of this kind can also be interpreted as a transitory shock to the level equation in the trend, in which case it appears as a pulse variable in (1.4a). Other types of intervention variable may be included, for example variables giving rise to changes in the slope of the trend or the seasonal pattern. The advantage of the structural time series model framework over the ARIMA framework proposed by Box and Tiao (1975) is that it is much easier to formulate intervention variables having the desired effect on the series.

Estimation of a model of the form (3.3) can be carried out in both the time and frequency domains by treating the intervention variable just like any other explanatory variable. In the time domain, various tests can be constructed to check on the specification of the intervention; see the study by Harvey and Durbin (1986) on the effect of the UK seat belt law.

4. Multivariate time series models

4.1. Seemingly unrelated time series equations (SUTSE)

The structural time series models introduced in Section 1 have straightforward multivariate generalisations. For instance, the local level with drift becomes, for an N-dimensional series $y_t = (y_{1t}, \ldots, y_{Nt})'$,

$$y_t = \mu_t + \varepsilon_t, \qquad \varepsilon_t \sim \text{NID}(0, \Sigma_\varepsilon),$$
$$\mu_t = \mu_{t-1} + \beta + \eta_t, \qquad \eta_t \sim \text{NID}(0, \Sigma_\eta), \tag{4.1}$$

where Σ_ε and Σ_η are nonnegative definite $N \times N$ matrices. Such models are called seemingly unrelated time series equations (SUTSE) reflecting the fact that the individual series are connected only via the correlated disturbances in the measurement and transition equations. Estimation is discussed in Fernández (1990).

The maximisation of the likelihood function for this model can be computationally demanding if N is large. The evaluation of the likelihood function requires $O(N^3)$ floating point operations and, although β can be concentrated, there are still $N \times (N + 1)$ parameters to be estimated by numerical optimisation. However, for many applications there are specific structures on Σ_ε and Σ_η that can be exploited to make the computations easier. One example is where Σ_ε and Σ_η are proportional, that is $\Sigma_\eta = q\Sigma_\varepsilon$. Such a system is said to be homogeneous. This structure allows each of the series in y_t to be handled by the same Kalman filter and so the likelihood can be evaluated in $O(N)$ operations. Further, Σ_ε can be concentrated out of the likelihood, leaving a single parameter q to be found by numerical maximisation. The validity of the homogeneity assumption can be assessed by using the Lagrange multiplier test of Fernández and Harvey (1990).

4.2. Error components models

Consider the classical error components model

$$y_{it} = \mu + \lambda_i + v_t + \omega_{it}, \quad i = 1, \ldots, N, \quad t = 1, \ldots, T, \quad (4.2)$$

where μ represents the overall mean and λ_i, v_t and ω_{it} are unit specific and time specific effects respectively, assumed to be serially and mutually independent, Gaussian and with expected values equal to zero. The dynamic versions of this model studied in the literature usually include lagged dependent variables and autoregressive processes for the components v_t and ω_{it}; see Anderson and Hsiao (1982).

A more natural approach to the specification of dynamic error components models, can be based on the ideas of structural time series models. This is suggested by Marshall (1992b), who allowed both time specific and time-unit specific effects to evolve over time according to random walk plus noise processes. The error components model becomes

$$y_{it} = \mu_{it} + \varepsilon_t + \varepsilon_{it}^*,$$
$$\mu_{it} = \mu_{i,t-1} + \eta_t + \eta_{it}^*, \quad (4.3)$$

where μ_{it} is the mean for unit i at time t and ε_t, ε_{it}^*, η_t and η_{it}^* are assumed to be independent, zero mean, Gaussian random variables, with variances σ_ε^2, $\sigma_{\varepsilon^*}^2$, σ_η^2 and $\sigma_{\eta^*}^2$ respectively. This model is a multivariate local level model, with the irregular and level random shocks decomposed as common effects, ε_t and η_t, and specific effects, ε_{it}^* and η_{it}^*. This means that

$$\Sigma_\varepsilon = \sigma_{\varepsilon^*}^2 I + \sigma_\varepsilon^2 u' \quad \text{and} \quad \Sigma_\eta = \sigma_{\eta^*}^2 I + \sigma_\eta^2 u', \quad (4.4)$$

where ι is the N-dimensional unit vector and I the identity matrix.

If σ_η^2 and $\sigma_{\eta^*}^2$ are equal to zero, the model reduces to the static error components model discussed in (4.2). On the other hand if σ_η^2 is greater than zero, but $\sigma_{\eta^*}^2$ is equal to zero, the N time series have, apart from a time invariant effect, the same time-dependent mean. In this situation, the time series are cointegrated in the sense of Engle and Granger (1987).

Optimal estimates of the components μ_{it} can be obtained by means of the Kalman filter. That requires the manipulation of $N \times N$ matrices and so it becomes cumbersome if N is large. However, the idea of homogeneity can be used to reduce these calculations dramatically. Take for each time t the average of the observations across units and the first $N-1$ deviations from this average. Thus, in an obvious notation, (4.3) becomes

$$\bar{y}_t = \bar{\mu}_t + \bar{\varepsilon}_t + \bar{\varepsilon}_t^* \,, \tag{4.5a}$$

$$\bar{\mu}_t = \bar{\mu}_{t-1} + \bar{\eta}_t + \bar{\eta}_t^* \,, \tag{4.5b}$$

$$t = 1, \ldots, T \,,$$

$$(y_{it} - \bar{y}_t) = (\mu_{it} - \bar{\mu}_t) + (\varepsilon_{it}^* - \bar{\varepsilon}_t^*) \,, \tag{4.6a}$$

$$(\mu_{it} - \bar{\mu}_t) = (\mu_{i,t-1} - \bar{\mu}_{t-1}) + (\eta_{it}^* - \bar{\eta}_t^*) \,, \tag{4.6b}$$

$$i = 1, \ldots, N-1 \,, \ t = 1, \ldots, T \,,$$

with the equations in (4.5) and (4.6) being statistically independent of one another. As the transformation to this model is nonsingular, the estimation of the trends μ_{it} can be obtained from this model instead of from the original error components model. The estimation of the average level can be carried out by running a univariate Kalman filter over the average values of the observations $\bar{y}_t$. The remaining $N-1$ equations can be dealt with straight-forwardly as they are a homogeneous system, with variances proportional to $(I - \iota\iota'/N)$, where I and ι are now $N-1$-dimensional unit matrices and vectors.

The Kalman filter which provides the estimator of $\bar{\mu}_t$ using the information available up to time t is

$$\bar{m}_t = \bar{m}_{t-1} + \frac{\bar{p}_{t-1} + \sigma_\eta^2 + \sigma_{\eta^*}^2/N}{\bar{p}_{t-1} + \sigma_\eta^2 + \sigma_{\eta^*}^2/N + \sigma_\varepsilon^2 + \sigma_{\varepsilon^*}^2/N} (\bar{y}_t - \bar{m}_{t-1}) \,, \tag{4.7}$$

where $\bar{p}_t$ is the MSE of $\bar{m}_t$, given by

$$\bar{p}_t = (\bar{p}_{t-1} + \sigma_\eta^2 + \sigma_{\eta^*}^2/N) - \frac{(\bar{p}_{t-1} + \sigma_\eta^2 + \sigma_{\eta^*}^2)^2}{(\bar{p}_{t-1} + \sigma_\eta^2 + \sigma_{\eta^*}^2/N + \sigma_\varepsilon^2 + \sigma_{\varepsilon^*}^2/N)} \,. \tag{4.8}$$

These recursions are run from $t = 2$ and with initial values $\bar{m}_1 = y_1$ and $\bar{p}_1 = (\sigma_\varepsilon^2 + \sigma_{\varepsilon^*}^2/N)$. With respect to the formulae to obtain the estimators of the components $(\mu_{it} - \bar{\mu}_t)$ using the information up to time t, m_{it}^* and their MSEs, p_{it}^*, these have exactly the same form as (4.7) and (4.8) but with $(\sigma_\eta^2 + \sigma_{\eta^*}^2/N)$ and $(\sigma_\eta^2 + \sigma_{\eta^*}^2/N)$ replaced by $((N-1)\sigma_{\eta^*}^2/N)$ and $((N-1)\sigma_{\varepsilon^*}^2/N)$ respectively and with initial values $m_{i1} = (y_{i1} - \bar{y}_1)$ for $i = 1, \ldots, N-1$. The estimators of each μ_{it}, m_{it}, and its MSE, p_{it}, are given by

$$m_{it} = \bar{m}_t + m_{it}^*, \quad i = 1, \ldots, N-1, \ t = 1, \ldots, T,$$
$$p_{it} = \bar{p}_t + p_{it}^*, \quad i = 1, \ldots, N-1, \ t = 1, \ldots, T, \tag{4.9}$$

while m_{Nt} is obtained by differencing.

EXAMPLE. In Marshall (1992b), a error components model of the form given above, but with a fixed slope as in (3.2), is estimated for the logarithm of the quarterly labour costs time series in Austria, Belgium, Luxembourg and The Netherlands. The sample period considered in 1970 to 1987 and so $N = 4$ and $T = 72$. The maximum likelihood estimates of the parameters were

$$\sigma_\varepsilon^2 = 0, \qquad \sigma_{\varepsilon^*}^2 = 0.115 \times 10^{-3},$$
$$\sigma_\eta^2 = 0.249 \times 10^{-3}, \qquad \sigma_{\eta^*}^2 = 0.159 \times 10^{-3}. \tag{4.10}$$

4.3. Explanatory variables in SUTSE models

The introduction of explanatory variables into the SUTSE model opens up the possibility of incorporating ideas from economic theory. This is well illustrated in the paper by Harvey and Marshall (1991) on the demand for energy in the UK. The assumption of a translog cost function leads to the static share equation system

$$s_i = \alpha_i + \sum_j \alpha_{ij} \log(p_j/\tau_j), \quad i = 1, \ldots, N, \tag{4.11}$$

where the α_i, $i = 1, \ldots, N$ and α_{ij}, $i, j = 1, \ldots, N$, are parameters, s_i is the share of the i-th input, p_j is the (exogenous) price of the j-th input and τ_j is an index of relative technical progress for the input j which takes the factor augmenting form; see Jorgenson (1986).

The model can be made dynamic by allowing the $\log \tau_{jt}$, relative technical progress at time t for input j, to follow a random walk plus drift

$$\log \tau_{jt} = \log \tau_{j,t-1} + \bar{\beta}_j + \bar{\eta}_{jt}, \quad i = 1, \ldots, N. \tag{4.12}$$

If the random disturbance term ε_{jt} is added to each share equation, this leads to a system of share equations which can be written in matrix form as

$$y_t = \mu_t + Ax_t + \varepsilon_t, \qquad \varepsilon_t \sim \text{NID}(0, \Sigma_\varepsilon),$$
$$\mu_t = \mu_{t-1} + \beta + \eta_t, \qquad \eta_t \sim \text{NID}(0, \Sigma_\eta), \tag{4.13}$$

where y_t is an $N \times 1$ vector of shares $(s_1, \ldots, s_N)'$. Here μ_t is an $N \times 1$ vector depending on the α_i', α_{ij}' and $\log \tau_{it}'$, so that the i-th element of μ_t is $\alpha_i + \Sigma \alpha_{ij} \log \tau_{jt}$, while A is an $N \times N$ matrix of α_{ij}' and x_t is the $N \times 1$ vector of the $\log p_{jt}$'s.

Harvey and Marshall (1991) estimated (4.13) under the assumption of statistical homogeneity, that is $\Sigma_\eta = q\Sigma_\varepsilon$ and found this to be a reasonable assumption using the LM test referred to in Section 4.1. One equation was dropped to ensure that the shares summed to one. Finally restrictions from economic theory, concerning cost exhaustion, homogeneity and symmetry, were incorporated into the A matrix.

4.4. Common trends

Many economic variables seem to move together, indicating common underlying dynamics. This feature of data has been crystalised in the econometric literature as the concept of cointegration; see, for example Engle and Granger (1987) and Johansen (1988). Within a structural time series framework this feature can be imposed by modifying (4.1) so as to construct a common trends model

$$
\begin{aligned}
y_t &= \Theta\mu_t^* + \varepsilon_t, & \varepsilon_t &\sim \text{NID}(0, \Sigma_\varepsilon), \\
\mu_t^* &= \mu_{t-1}^* + \beta^* + \eta_t^*, & \eta_t^* &\sim \text{NID}(0, \Sigma_{\eta^*}),
\end{aligned}
\tag{4.14}
$$

where Θ is a $N \times K$ fixed matrix of factor loadings. The $K \times K$ matrix Σ_{η^*} is constrained to be a diagonal matrix and $\Theta_{ij} = 0$ for $j > i$, while $\Theta_{ii} = 1$ in order to achieve identifiability; see Harvey (1989, pp. 450–451). As Σ_{η^*} is diagonal, the common trends, the elements of μ_t^*, are independent.

The common trends model has $K \leq N$, but if $K = N$, it is equivalent to the SUTSE model, (4.1), with $\beta = \Theta\beta^*$ and $\Sigma_\eta = \Theta\Sigma_{\eta^*}\Theta'$ where Θ and Σ_{η^*} are the Cholesky decomposition of Σ_η. This suggests first estimating a SUTSE model and carrying out a principal components analysis on the estimated Σ_η to see what value of K accounts for a suitably large proportion of the total variation. A formal test can be carried out along the lines suggested by Stock and Watson (1988), but its small sample properties have yet to be investigated in this context. Once K has been determined, the common trends model can be formulated and estimated.

EXAMPLE. Tiao and Tsay (1989) fitted various multivariate models to the logarithms of indices of monthly flour prices in three cities, Buffalo, Minneapolis and Kansas City, over the period from August 1972 to November 1980. In their comment on this paper, Harvey and Marshall fit (4.1) and

Table 3
Principal components analysis of estimated covariance matrix of trend disturbances

Eigenvalues	Cumulative proportion	Eigenvectors		
7.739	0.965	−0.55	−0.59	−0.59
0.262	0.998	0.35	0.48	−0.81
0.015	1.00	0.76	−0.65	−0.06

conduct a principal components analysis on the estimated Σ_n. The results, given in Table 3, indicate that the first principal component dominates the variation in the transition equation and represents the basic underlying price in the three cities. Setting K equal to one or two might be appropriate.

Models with common components have also been used in the construction of leading indicators; see Stock and Watson (1990).

4.5. Modelling and estimation for repeated surveys

Many economic variables are measured by using sample survey techniques. Examples include the labour force surveys which are conducted in each member state of the European Community. It is now quite common practice to analyse the results from repeated surveys using time series methods.

If sample surveys are nonoverlapping, then the survey errors are independent and a simple model for the vector of characteristics at time t, θ_t, might be

$$y_t = \theta_t + \varepsilon_t, \quad \varepsilon_t \sim N(0, H_t), \quad t = 1, \ldots, T, \tag{4.15}$$

where the sampling errors ε_t are independent over time and are independent of θ_t. A simple estimator of θ_t would then be y_t. However, by imposing a model on the evolution of θ_t, an improvement in the precision of the estimate is possible. This improvement will be very marked if θ_t moves very slowly and H_t is large.

Scott and Smith (1974) suggested fitting ARIMA models to θ_t; see also Smith (1978) and Jones (1980). A more natural approach is to use structural models. The analysis of repeated, nonoverlapping surveys is based on the same principles as standard time series model building except that constraints are imposed on the measurement error covariance matrix through sampling theory.

EXAMPLE. Consider the repeated sample survey of a set of proportions θ_{1t}, $\theta_{2t}, \ldots, \theta_{pt}$, using simple random sampling with sample size n_t for $t = 1, \ldots, T$. If $p = 2$, and y_t denotes the sample proportion in group one, the simple model

$$y_t = \theta_t + \varepsilon_t, \quad \varepsilon_t \sim N\left(0, \frac{\theta_t(1 - \theta_t)}{n_t}\right),$$

$$\theta_t = \frac{1}{1 + \exp(-\alpha_t)}, \tag{4.16}$$

$$\alpha_t = \alpha_{t-1} + \eta_t, \quad \eta_t \sim NID(0, \sigma_\eta^2),$$

will allow $\theta_{1t} = \theta_t$ and $\theta_{2t} = 1 - \theta_t$ to evolve over time in the range zero to one. If p is greater than two or the state α_t evolves in a more complicated way, perhaps with seasonals, the model can be modified appropriately. However, the modelling principle is unchanged, sampling theory dictates the measurement error and time series considerations the transition equation. A discussion of the way in which such models can be estimated may be found in Section 6.2.

When the repeated surveys are overlapping the model for the measurement equation can become very involved. A clear discussion of the principles involved is given in Scott and Smith (1974). More recent work in this area includes Hausman and Watson (1985), Binder and Dick (1989), Tam (1987), Pfeffermann and Burck (1990) and Pfeffermann (1991).

The work of Pfeffermann (1991) fits well within the framework of this discussion. He identifies three features of overlapping samples which may effect the way the measurement error is modelled. The first is the way the sample is rotated. For example a survey consisting of four panels which are interviewed quarterly, three of the panels will have been included in past surveys while one is wholly new. Thus each panel will remain in the panel for four quarters. This rotation will interact with the second feature of overlapping surveys, the correlation between individual observations. Pfeffermann, in common with most researchers in this area, relies on Henderson's behavioural model for the i-th individual of the survey made at time t. The model is

$$y_{it} - \theta_t = \rho(y_{i,t-1} - \theta_{t-1}) + \omega_{it} , \qquad \omega_{it} \sim \text{NID}(0, \sigma_\omega^2) , \qquad |\rho| < 1 .$$

$$(4.17)$$

The Pfeffermann model is completed by the third feature, which is that the design of the survey is ignorable, although this assumption can be relaxed at the loss of algebraic simplicity.

With these assumptions it is possible to derive the behaviour of the measurement error in a model. If we use y_{it}^{t-j} to denote the i individual at time t, from a panel established at time $t - j$, then we can write

$$\bar{y}_t^{t-j} = \frac{1}{M} \sum_{i=1}^{M} y_{it}^{t-j} , \qquad j = 0, 1, 2, 3 ,$$

$$(4.18)$$

as the aggregate survey estimate of θ_t from the panel established at time $t - j$, then

$$y_t = \begin{pmatrix} \bar{y}_t^t \\ \bar{y}_t^{t-1} \\ \bar{y}_t^{t-2} \\ \bar{y}_t^{t-3} \end{pmatrix} = \begin{pmatrix} 1 \\ 1 \\ 1 \\ 1 \end{pmatrix} \theta_t + \varepsilon_t , \qquad \varepsilon_t + \begin{pmatrix} \bar{\varepsilon}_t^t \\ \bar{\varepsilon}_t^{t-1} \\ \bar{\varepsilon}_t^{t-2} \\ \bar{\varepsilon}_t^{t-3} \end{pmatrix} ,$$

$$(4.19)$$

where

$$\varepsilon_t = \begin{pmatrix} 0 & 0 & 0 & 0 \\ \rho & 0 & 0 & 0 \\ 0 & \rho & 0 & 0 \\ 0 & 0 & \rho & 0 \end{pmatrix} \varepsilon_{t-1} + \begin{pmatrix} \bar{\varepsilon}_t^t \\ \bar{\omega}_t^{t-1} \\ \bar{\omega}_t^{t-2} \\ \bar{\omega}_t^{t-3} \end{pmatrix} = T\varepsilon_{t-1} + \eta_t .$$

$$(4.20)$$

The covariance of η_t will be

$$\frac{\sigma_\omega^2}{M} \begin{pmatrix} (1-\rho)^{-1} & 0 & 0 & 0 \\ 0 & 1 & 0 & 0 \\ 0 & 0 & 1 & 0 \\ 0 & 0 & 0 & 1 \end{pmatrix}. \tag{4.21}$$

The model can be routinely handled by using the Kalman filter to estimate θ_t, as well as the hyperparameters ρ, and σ_ω^2. In some cases the individual panel results will not be available, but instead only the aggregate will be recorded. Then the measurement equation becomes

$$\begin{aligned} y_t^* &= (\bar{y}_t^t + \bar{y}_t^{t-1} + \bar{y}_t^{t-2} + \bar{y}_t^{t-3}) \\ &= \theta_t + \tfrac{1}{4}(\bar{\varepsilon}_t^t + \bar{\varepsilon}_t^{t-1} + \bar{\varepsilon}_t^{t-2} + \bar{\varepsilon}_t^{t-3}) \,. \end{aligned} \tag{4.23}$$

5. Simultaneous equation system

This section considers how simultaneous equation models can be estimated when stochastic trend components of the kind described in Section 4 are specified in some or all of the structural equations. We draw on the paper by Streibel and Harvey (1993), which develops and compares a number of methods for the estimation of single equations using instrumental variable (IV) procedures or limited information maximum likelihood (LIML). The question of identifiability is dealt with in Harvey and Streibel (1991).

5.1. Model formulation

Consider a dynamical simultaneous model in which some or all of the structural equations contain stochastic trend components, which, to simplify matters, will be assumed to follow a multivariate random walk. Thus

$$\begin{aligned} \Gamma y_t &= \Phi_1 y_{t-1} + \cdots + \Phi_r y_{t-r} + B_0 x_t + \cdots + B_s x_{t-s} + S\mu_t + \varepsilon_t \,, \\ \mu_t &= \mu_{t-1} + \eta_t \,, \end{aligned} \tag{5.1}$$

where Γ is an $N \times N$ matrix of unknown parameters, $\Phi_1, \ldots, \Phi_r$ are $N \times N$ matrices of autoregressive parameters, $B_0, \ldots, B_s$ are $N \times K$ matrices of parameters associated with the $K \times 1$ vector of exogenous variables x_t and its lagged values, μ_t is an $n \times 1$ vector of stochastic trends, S is an $N \times n$ selection matrix of ones and zeros, such that each of the stochastic trends appears in a particular equation, and η_t and ε_t are mutually independent, normally distributed white noise disturbance vectors with positive definite covariance matrices Σ_η and Σ_ε respectively. Equations which do not contain a stochastic trend will usually have a constant term and if the exogenous variables are stochastic, it will be assumed that they are generated independently of μ_t and ε_t.

The model is subject to restrictions which usually take the form of certain variables being excluded from certain equations on the basis of prior economic knowledge. In a similar way, it will normally be the case that there is some rationale for the appearance of stochastic trend components in particular equations. Indeed many econometric models contain a time trend. For example the wage equation in the textbook Klein model has a time trend which is explained in terms of union pressure. Time trends also appear because of technical progress just as in single equations. The argument here is that such effects are more appropriately modelled by stochastic trends.

Pre-multiplying (5.1) by Γ^{-1} gives the econometric reduced form. Dropping the lags, this may be written as

$$y_t = \theta \mu_t + \Pi x_t + \varepsilon_t,\tag{5.2}$$

where $\Pi = \Gamma^{-1}B$, $\varepsilon_t^* = \Gamma^{-1}\varepsilon_t$ and $\theta = \Gamma^{-1}S$. If stochastic trends only appear in some of the equations, that is $1 \leq n < N$, then (5.2) contains common trends; see Section 4.4.

The presence of stochastic trend components in an econometric model has interesting implications for conventional dynamic simultaneous equation models, for the corresponding reduced form models, and for the associated vector autoregression (VAR) for $(y_t', x_t')'$. Some of the points can be illustrated with a simple demand and supply system. Let y_{1t} denote quantity, y_{2t} price and x_t an exogenous variable which is stationary after first differencing, that is integrated of order one, and write

$$\begin{aligned} D:\ &y_{1t} = \gamma_1 y_{2t} + \mu_t + \varepsilon_{1t}, \\ S:\ &y_{1t} = \gamma_2 y_{2t} + \beta x_t + \varepsilon_{2t}. \end{aligned}\tag{5.3}$$

The stochastic trend component μ_t may be a proxy for changes in tastes. The first equation could be approximated using lags of y_1 and y_2, but long lags may be needed and, unless μ_t is constant, a unit root is present; compare the employment-output equation of Harvey et al. (1986). The econometric reduced form is

$$\begin{aligned} y_{1t} &= \theta_1 \mu_t + \pi_1 x_t + \varepsilon_{1t}^*, \\ y_{2t} &= \theta_2 \mu_t + \pi_2 x_2 + \varepsilon_{2t}^*, \end{aligned}\tag{5.4}$$

where $\theta_1 = \gamma_2/(\gamma_2 - \gamma_1)$, $\theta_2 = 1/(\gamma_2 - \gamma_1)$, and so on. Thus there is a common trend. This can be regarded as a reflection of the fact that there is just a single co-integrating relationship, namely the supply curve; compare a similar, but simpler, example in Engle and Granger (1987, p. 263). Attempting to estimate a reduced form with lagged variables but without the stochastic trends runs into complications; if first differences are taken the stochastic part of the model is strictly noninvertible, so the approximation is not valid, while in levels any inference must take account of the unit root; see Sims, Stock and Watson (1990). The VAR representation of $(y_t', x_t')'$ is also subject to constraints because of the common trend, and although estimation can be carried out using the method of Johansen (1988), the point remains that long lags may be required for a satisfactory approximation and so the number of parameters may be very large for moderate size N and K.

In summary, models which approximate stochastic trends by lags may be highly unparsimonious and uninformative about dynamic relationships. If economic theory does suggest the presence of stochastic trend components, therefore, there are likely to be considerable gains from estimating the implied structural relationships directly. If the complete system of equations can be specified, a full information maximum likelihood (FIML) procedure may be employed. If only a subsystem is specified, but all the predetermined variables are named, a limited information maximum likelihood (LIML) procedure is appropriate. When the rest of the system has not been specified at all, ML methods cannot be applied, but a valid instrumental variable (IV) estimator can be obtained.

5.2. Instrumental variable estimation

Suppose the equation of interest is written in matrix notation as

$$y = Z\delta + u \tag{5.5}$$

where Z is a $T \times m$ matrix with observations on explanatory variables and u is a $T \times 1$ vector of disturbances with mean zero and covariance matrix, $\sigma_\varepsilon^2 V$. The explanatory variables may include variables which are not exogenous. However, the K exogenous variables in the system provide a set of instrumental variables contained in a $T \times K$ matrix, X.

Multiplying (5.5) through by a $T \times T$ matrix L with the property that $L'L = V^{-1}$ yields

$$Ly = LZ\delta + Lu , \tag{5.6}$$

where $\text{Var}(Lu) = \sigma_\varepsilon^2 I$. If the same transformation is applied to X, the matrix of optimal instruments is formed over a multivariate regression of LZ on LX. The resulting IV estimator is then

$$\hat{d} = (Z'L'P_v LZ)^{-1} Z'L'P_v Ly , \tag{5.7}$$

where P_v is the idempotent projection matrix $P_v = LX(X'V^{-1}X)^{-1}X'L'$. It is known as *generalized two stage least squares* (G2SLS). Under standard regularity conditions, as in Bowden and Turkington (1984, p. 26), $T^{1/2}\hat{d}$ has a limiting normal distribution. If V is unknown, but depends on a finite number of parameters which can be estimated consistently, the asymptotic distribution is unaffected. When there are no lagged endogenous variables in (5.5) it can be shown that the G2SLS estimator is at least as efficient as 2SLS in the sense that the determinant of its asymptotic covariance matrix cannot exceed the determinant of the corresponding expression for 2SLS. In a similar way, it can be shown that G2SLS is more efficient than an IV estimator in which instruments are formed from X without first transforming by L.

We now consider the estimation of a model which contains a random walk component as well as explanatory variables, that is

$$y_t = \mu_t + z_t'\delta + \varepsilon_t, \quad t = 1, \ldots, T. \tag{5.8}$$

If z_t were exogenous, the GLS estimator of δ could be computed by applying the Kalman filter appropriate for the stochastic part of the model, $\mu_t + \varepsilon_t$, to both y_t and z_t and regressing the innovations from y_t on those from z_t; see Kohn and Ansley (1985). The same approach may be used with IV estimation. In the notation of (5.5) the Kalman filter makes the transformations Ly, LZ and LX. However, the L matrix is now $(T-1) \times T$ because the diffuse prior for μ_t means that only $T-1$ innovations can be formed. The variables in (5.8) may be differenced so as to give a stationary disturbance term. Thus

$$\Delta y_t = \Delta z_t'\delta + u_t, \quad t = 2, \ldots, T, \tag{5.9}$$

where $u_t = \eta_t + \Delta\varepsilon_t$. This equation corresponds more directly to (5.5) than does (5.8) since a covariance matrix may be constructed for the disturbance vector and the associated L matrix is square. However, postmultiplying this matrix by the $(T-1) \times 1$ vector of differenced y_t's gives exactly the same result as postmultiplying the L matrix for (5.8) by the $T \times 1$ vector of y_t's.

A number of estimation procedures for (5.8) are considered in Streibel and Harvey (1993). In the preferred method, a consistent estimator of δ is first obtained by applying a suitable IV estimator to (5.9); if there are no lagged dependent variables, 2SLS will suffice. Consistent estimators of the hyperparameters are then obtained from the residuals, and these estimators are used to construct a feasible IV estimator of the form (5.7). There are a number of ways of estimating the hyperparameters. In simple cases, closed form expressions based on the residual autocorrelations are available but, even with δ known, such estimators are not efficient. However, what would be the ML estimator if δ were known can always be computed by an iterative optimisation procedure. Given values of the hyperparameters, an IV estimate is constructed for δ. The hyperparameters are then estimated by ML applied to the residuals. This procedure is then iterated to convergence. Although iterating will not change the asymptotic properties of the estimators of δ or the hyperparameters when there are no lagged dependent variables, it may yield estimators with better small sample properties. When this stepwise estimation procedure is used to estimate an equation in a simultaneous equation system it may be referred to as G2SLS/ML. All the above procedures can be implemented in the frequency domain as well as the time domain.

5.3. Maximum likelihood estimation

It is relatively easy to construct the likelihood function for a model of the form (5.1). Maximising this function then gives the FIML estimators. Of course this may not be straightforward computationally, and the estimators obtained for any one particular equation may be very sensitive to misspecification in other parts of the system.

If interest centres on a single equation, say the first, and there is not enough information to specify the remaining equations, a limited information estimation procedure is appropriate. In a model of the form (5.1) where u_t is NID$(0, \Omega)$, the LIML estimator of the parameters in the first equation can be obtained by applying FIML to a system consisting of the first (structural) equation and the reduced form for the endogenous variables appearing in that equation. Since the Jacobian of this system is unity, the estimator can be computed by iterating a feasible SURE estimator to convergence; see Pagan (1979).

Now consider the application of LIML in a Gaussian system with stochastic trends generated by a multivariate random walk. It will also be assumed that the system contains no lags, although the presence of lags in either the endogenous or exogenous variables does not alter the form of the estimator. Thus

$$\Gamma y_t = \mu_t + B x_t + \varepsilon_t , \quad \text{Var}(\varepsilon_t) = \Sigma_\varepsilon , \tag{5.10}$$

with Γ being positive definite and μ_t given by (5.1). Hence the reduced form is

$$y_t = \mu_t^* + \Pi x_t + \varepsilon_t^* , \quad \text{Var}(\varepsilon_t^*) = \Sigma_\varepsilon^* = \Gamma^{-1} \Sigma_\varepsilon (\Gamma^{-1})' , \tag{5.11a}$$

$$\mu_t^* = \mu_{t-1}^* + \eta_t^* , \quad \text{Var}(\eta_t^*) = \Sigma_\eta^* = \Gamma^{-1} \Sigma_\eta (\Gamma^{-1})' , \tag{5.11b}$$

where $\mu_t^* = \Gamma^{-1} \mu_t$. The equation of interest, the first in (5.10) corresponds to (5.8) and may be written as

$$y_{1t} = \mu_{1t} + \gamma' y_{2t} + \beta' x_{1t} + \varepsilon_{1t} , \tag{5.12a}$$

$$\mu_{1t} = \mu_{1,t-1} + \eta_{1t} , \tag{5.12b}$$

where y_{2t} is $g \times 1$, x_{1t} is $k \times 1$, and both ε_{1t} and η_{1t} may be correlated with the corresponding disturbances in the other structural equations. Prior knowledge suggests the presence of a stochastic trend in (5.10). There is no information on whether or not stochastic trends are present in the other structural equations in the system, and so they are included for generality. The reduced form for the endogenous variables included in (5.10) may be written as

$$y_{2t} = \mu_{2t}^* + \Pi_2 x_t + \varepsilon_{2t}^* , \tag{5.13a}$$

$$\mu_{2t}^* = \mu_{2,t-1}^* + \eta_{2t}^* . \tag{5.13b}$$

The LIML estimator is obtained by treating (5.12) and (5.13) as though they were the structural form of a system and applying FIML. The Jacobian is unity and estimation proceeds by making use of the multivariate version of the GLS algorithm described in Harvey (1989, p. 133).

Streibel and Harvey (1993) derive the asymptotic distribution of the LIML estimator and compare the asymptotic covariance matrix of the estimators of β and γ with the corresponding matrix from the G2SLS/ML estimation procedure for a model without lagged endogenous variables. If $\Sigma_\eta = q\Sigma_\varepsilon$ in (5.10), where q is a scalar, the multivariate part of the model is homogenous; see Section 4. In this case G2SLS/ML is as efficient as LIML. Indeed efficiency is achieved with G2SLS without iterating, provided an initial consistent estimator of q is used.

Although G2SLS/ML is not, in general, asymptotically efficient as compared with LIML, the Monte Carlo experiments reported in Streibel and Harvey suggest that in small samples its performance is usually better than that of LIML. Since it is much simpler than LIML, it is the recommended estimator.

6. Nonlinear and non-Gaussian models

Relaxing the requirement that time series models be linear and Gaussian opens up a vast range of possibilities. This section introduces the work in this field which exploits the structural time series framework. It starts with a discussion of conditionally Gaussian nonlinear state space models and then progresses to derive a filter for dynamic generalised linear models. Some recent work on exact filters for nonlinear, non-Gaussian state space models is outlined. Finally, some structural approaches to modelling changing variance is discussed.

6.1. Conditionally Gaussian state space models

The state space form and the Kalman filter provides such a strong foundation for the manipulation of linear models that it is very natural to try to extend their use to deal with nonlinear time series. Some progress can be made by defining a conditionally Gaussian state space model

$$
\begin{aligned}
y_t &= Z_t(Y_{t-1})\alpha_t + X_t\beta + \varepsilon_t\,, & \varepsilon_t &\sim N(0, H_t(Y_{t-1}))\,, \\
\alpha_t &= T_t(Y_{t-1})\alpha_{t-1} + W_t\beta + \eta_t\,, & \eta_t &\sim N(0, Q_t(Y_{t-1}))\,.
\end{aligned}
\tag{6.1}
$$

Here ε_t and η_s are assumed to be independent for all values of t and s. In this model the matrices in the state space model are allowed to depend on Y_{t-1}, the available information at time $t-1$. The Kalman filter still goes through in this case and so the likelihood for the model can be built up from the prediction error decomposition.

The theory behind this type of modelling framework has been studied at considerable length in Liptser and Shirayev (1978). The following examples illustrate its flexibility.

EXAMPLE. The coefficient of a first-order autoregression can be allowed to follow a random walk, as y_{t-1} is in Y_{t-1}. Thus

$$
y_t = y_{t-1}\alpha_{t-1} + \varepsilon_t, \qquad \varepsilon_t \sim \text{NID}(0, \sigma_\varepsilon^2),
$$
$$
\alpha_t = \alpha_{t-1} + \eta_t, \qquad \eta_t \sim \text{NID}(0, \sigma_\eta^2). \tag{6.2}
$$

EXAMPLE. Some macro-economic time series appear to exhibit cycles in which the downswing is shorter than the upswing. A simple way of capturing such a feature is to specify a cyclical component which switches from one frequency to another as it moves from downswing into upswing and vice versa. This could be achieved by setting

$$
\lambda_c = \begin{cases} \lambda_1, & \text{if } \hat{\psi}_{t|t-1} - \hat{\psi}_{t-1} > 0, \\ \lambda_2, & \text{if } \hat{\psi}_{t|t-1} - \hat{\psi}_{t-1} \leq 0, \end{cases} \qquad \lambda_1 \leq \lambda_2, \tag{6.3}
$$

where $\hat{\psi}_{t|t-1}$ and $\hat{\psi}_{t-1}$ are estimates of the state of the cycle at times t and $t-1$ respectively, made at time $t-1$. This model, which belongs within the class of threshold models described in Tong (1990), in effect fits two separate linear cycle models to the date, the division taking place and $\hat{\psi}_{t|t-1} - \hat{\psi}_{t-1}$ switches sign.

6.2. *Extended Kalman filter*

For ease of exposition suppose y_t and α_t are univariate and

$$
y_t = z_t(\alpha_t) + \varepsilon_t, \qquad \varepsilon_t \sim \text{NID}(0, \sigma_\varepsilon^2(\alpha_t)),
$$
$$
\alpha_t = T_t(\alpha_{t-1}) + \eta_t, \qquad \eta_t \sim \text{NID}(0, \sigma_\eta^2(\alpha_{t-1})). \tag{6.4}
$$

This model cannot be handled exactly by using the Kalman filter. However, for some functions it is possible to expand $z_t(\alpha_t)$ and $T_t(\alpha_{t-1})$ using a Taylor series to give

$$
z_t(\alpha_t) \cong z_t(a_{t|t-1}) + \frac{\partial z_t(a_{t|t-1})}{\partial \alpha_t}(\alpha_t - a_{t|t-1}),
$$
$$
\alpha_t \cong T_t(a_{t-1}) + \frac{\partial T_t(a_{t-1})}{\partial \alpha_{t-1}}(\alpha_{t-1} - a_{t-1}). \tag{6.5}
$$

If, in addition, the dependence of the variances on the states is dealt with by replacing them by estimates, made at time $t-1$, then the new approximate model becomes

$$
y_t = z_t(a_{t|t-1}) + \frac{\partial z_t(a_{t|t-1})}{\partial \alpha_t}(\alpha_t - a_{t|t-1}) + \varepsilon_t, \qquad \varepsilon_t \sim \text{N}(0, \sigma_\varepsilon^2(a_{t|t-1})),
$$
$$
\alpha_t = T_t(a_{t-1}) + \frac{\partial T_t(a_{t-1})}{\partial \alpha_{t-1}}(\alpha_{t-1} - a_{t-1}) + \eta_t, \qquad \eta_t \sim \text{N}(0, \sigma_\eta^2(a_{t-1})).
$$
$$
\tag{6.6}
$$

This model is then in the conditionally Gaussian framework and so the Kalman filter can be used to estimate the state. Since the model itself is an approximation, we call the conditionally Gaussian Kalman filter an extended Kalman filter for the original model (6.4); see Anderson and Moore (1979, Chapter 8).

EXAMPLE. Suppose the logistic transformation is being used to keep $z_t(\alpha_t)$ between zero and one as in (4.16). Then

$$z_t(\alpha_t) = \frac{1}{1 + \exp(-\alpha_t)} \,. \tag{6.7}$$

Then the expanded model becomes

$$y_t = \frac{1}{1 + \exp(-a_{t|t-1})} + \frac{\exp(-a_{t|t-1})}{(1 + \exp(-a_{t|t-1}))^2} (\alpha_t - a_{t|t-1}) + \varepsilon_t \,. \tag{6.8}$$

This idea can be used to construct a model of opinion polls. Suppose there are just two parties. If the level of support for one party is modelled as a logistic transformation of a Gaussian random walk and the measurement error originates from using a simple random sample size n_t, then

$$y_t = \mu_t + \varepsilon_t \,, \qquad \varepsilon_t \sim N(0, \sigma_t^2) \,, \qquad \sigma_t^2 = \frac{\mu_t(1 - \mu_t)}{n_t} \,, \tag{6.9a}$$

$$\mu_t = \frac{1}{1 + \exp(-\alpha_t)} \,, \tag{6.9b}$$

$$\alpha_t = \alpha_{t-1} + \eta_t \,, \qquad \eta_t \sim NID(0, \sigma_\eta^2) \,. \tag{6.9c}$$

As μ_t is unknown, this model cannot be analysed by using the Kalman filter. Instead, an estimate of α_t can be made at time $t-1$, written $a_{t|t-1}$, and it can be used to replace μ_t in the variance. One of the problems with this approach is that this model does not constrain the observations to lie between zero and one, as ε_t is assumed Gaussian. Although this could be a problem if μ_t were to be close to zero or one, this is unlikely to pose a difficulty for moderate sample sizes.

The Kalman filter can be applied in the standard way once the logistic transformation has been Taylor expanded. The resulting model is

$$y_t = m_{t-1} + \exp(-a_{t-1})m_{t-1}^2(\alpha_t - a_{t-1}) + \varepsilon_t \,,$$
$$\varepsilon_t \sim N\left(0, \frac{m_{t-1}(1 - m_{t-1})}{n_t}\right) \,, \tag{6.10a}$$

$$m_{t-1} = \frac{1}{1 + \exp(-a_{t-1})} \,. \tag{6.10b}$$

An approach similar to this, but using a multivariate continuous time model to allow for irregular observations, was followed by Shephard and Harvey (1989) in their analysis of opinion poll data from the British general election campaigns of October 1974, 1979, 1983 and 1987.

6.3. Non-Gaussian state space models

Although the Gaussian state space form provides the basis for the analysis of many time series, it is sometimes not possible to adequately model the data, or a transformation of it, in this way. Some series, such as count data, are intrinsically non-Gaussian and so using a Gaussian model could harm forecasting precision. In this section we outline the methods for directly modelling non-Gaussian series.

The key to modelling non-Gaussian time series is the non-Gaussian state space form. It will be built out of two assumptions. Firstly the measurement equation is such that we can write

$$f(y_1, \ldots, y_T \mid \alpha_1, \ldots, \alpha_T) = \prod_{t=1}^{T} f(y_t \mid \alpha_t) \,. \tag{6.11}$$

This assumes that given the state α_t, the observation y_t is independent of all the other states and observations. Thus α_t is *sufficient* for y_t. The second assumption is that the transition equation is such that

$$f(\alpha_1, \ldots, \alpha_T \mid Y_0) = f(\alpha_1 \mid Y_0) \prod_{t=2}^{T} f(\alpha_t \mid \alpha_{t-1}) \,, \tag{6.12}$$

that is the state follows a Markov process.

Filtering can be derived for a continuous state by the integrals

$$f(\alpha_t \mid Y_{t-1}) = \int f(\alpha_t \mid \alpha_{t-1}) f(\alpha_{t-1} \mid Y_{t-1}) \, \mathrm{d}\alpha_{t-1} \,, \tag{6.13a}$$

$$f(\alpha_t \mid Y_t) = f(y_t \mid \alpha_t) f(\alpha_t \mid Y_{t-1}) \Big/ \int f(y_t \mid \alpha_t) f(\alpha_t \mid Y_{t-1}) \, \mathrm{d}\alpha_t \,. \tag{6.13b}$$

Thus it is technically possible to carry out filtering, and indeed smoothing, for any state space model if the integrals can be computed. Kitagawa (1987) and Pole and West (1990) have suggested using particular sets of numerical integration rules to evaluate these densities. The main drawback with this general approach is the computational requirement, especially if parameter estimation is required. This is considerable if a reasonable degree of accuracy is to be achieved and the dimension of the state is larger; the dimension of the integral will equal the dimension of the state and so will be 13 for a basic structural model for monthly data. It is well known from the numerical analysis literature that the use of numerical integration rules to evaluate high-dimensional integrals is fraught with difficulty.

The computational explosion associated with the use of these numerical integration rules has prompted research into alternative methods for dealing with non-Gaussian state space models. Recent work by West and Harrison (1989) and West, Harrison and Migon (1985) has attempted to extend the use of the Kalman filter to cover cases where the measurement density is a member of the exponential family, which includes the binomial, Poisson and gamma densities, while maintaining the Gaussian transition density. As such this tries to extend the generalised linear model, described in McCullagh and Nelder (1989), to allow for dynamic behaviour.

For ease of exposition we will only look at the extension of the local level model to cover the exponential family measurement density. More specifically, we will assume that

$$f(y_t \mid \mu_t) = b(y_t, \sigma_{t\varepsilon}^2) \exp\left(\frac{y_t \mu_t - a(\mu_t)}{\sigma_{\varepsilon t}^2}\right),$$

$$f(\mu_t \mid \mu_{t-1}) = \frac{1}{\sqrt{2\pi\sigma_\eta^2}} \exp\left(-\frac{(\mu_t - \mu_{t-1})^2}{2\sigma_\eta^2}\right) \tag{6.14}$$

and follow the development given in West and Harrison (1989). Here $\sigma_{\varepsilon t}^2$ will be assumed to be known at time t. By selecting $a(\cdot)$ and $b(\cdot)$ appropriately, a large number of distributions can result. A simple example of this is the binomial distribution

$$f(y_t \mid \pi_t) = \frac{n_t!}{y_t!(n_t - y_t)!}\, \pi_t^{y_t}(1 - \pi_t)^{n_t - y_t}, \tag{6.15}$$

which is obtained by writing

$$\mu_t = \log\frac{\pi_t}{1 - \pi_t}, \qquad a(\mu_t) = \log(1 + \exp(\mu_t)),$$

$$b(y_t, \sigma_{\varepsilon t}^2) = \frac{n_t!}{y_t!(n_t - y_t)!}. \tag{6.16}$$

Although it is relatively straightforward to place densities into their exponential form, the difficulty comes from filtering the unobservable component μ_t as it progresses through time. Suppose we have a distribution for $\mu_{t-1} \mid Y_{t-1}$. The first two moments of this prior will be written as m_{t-1} and p_{t-1}. The random walk transition means that the first two moments of $\mu_t \mid Y_{t-1}$ will be

$$m_{t|t-1} = m_{t-1}, \qquad p_{t|t-1} = p_{t-1} + \sigma_\varepsilon^2. \tag{6.17}$$

As the measurement density is in the exponential family, it is always possible to find a conjugate density. Generically it takes the form

$$f(\mu_t \mid Y_{t-1}) = c(r_{t|t-1}, s_{t|t-1}) \exp(\mu_t r_{t|t-1} - s_{t|t-1} a(\mu_t)). \tag{6.18}$$

For a particular form of this density it is typically possible to select $r_{t|t-1}$ and $s_{t|t-1}$ so that the first two moments of this density match $m_{t|t-1}$ and $p_{t|t-1}$. Thus the actual prior density of $\mu_t \mid Y_{t-1}$ will be approximated by a density which has identical first two moments and is conjugate to the measurement density. Having determined r and s, this conjugate prior can be used to construct the one-step ahead density

$$f(y_t \mid Y_{t-1}) = \int f(y_t \mid \mu_t) f(\mu_t \mid Y_{t-1}) \, d\mu_t \tag{6.19a}$$

$$= \frac{c(r_{t|t-1}, s_{t|t-1}) b(y_t, \sigma^2_{\varepsilon t})}{c(r_{t|t-1} + y_t/\sigma^2_{\varepsilon t}, s_{t|t-1} + (1/\sigma^2_{\varepsilon t}))} . \tag{6.19b}$$

Further

$$f(\mu_t \mid Y_t) = c(r_t, s_t) \exp(r_t \mu_t - s_t a(\mu_t)) , \tag{6.20}$$

where

$$r_t = r_{t|t-1} + \frac{y_t}{\sigma^2_\varepsilon}, \qquad s_t = s_{t|t-1} + \frac{1}{\sigma^2_\varepsilon} . \tag{6.21}$$

By finding the first two moments of this density, implied values for m_t and p_t can be deduced, so starting the cycle off again. As the approximate density of $y_t \mid Y_{t-1}$ is known analytically, a maximum quasi-likelihood procedure can be used to estimate the unknown parameters of this model by using a predictive distribution decomposition of the joint density of the observations

$$f(y_1, \ldots, y_T \mid Y_0) = \prod_{t=1}^{T} f(y_t \mid Y_{t-1}) . \tag{6.22}$$

EXAMPLE. If the measurement equation is normal then

$$r_{t|t-1} = \frac{m_{t|t-1}}{p_{t|t-1}}, \qquad s_{t|t-1} = \frac{1}{p_{t|t-1}}, \tag{6.23}$$

so

$$r_t = \frac{m_{t|t-1}}{p_{t|t-1}} + \frac{y_t}{\sigma^2_\varepsilon}, \qquad s_t = \frac{1}{p_{t|t-1}} + \frac{1}{\sigma^2_\varepsilon} \tag{6.24}$$

implying

$$m_t = p_t r_t = \frac{p_t}{p_{t|t-1}} m_{t|t-1} + \frac{p_t}{\sigma^2_\varepsilon} y_t . \tag{6.25}$$

As

$$p_t = \frac{\sigma^2_\varepsilon p_{t|t-1}}{p_{t|t-1} + \sigma^2_\varepsilon}, \tag{6.26}$$

this is the usual Kalman filter.

EXAMPLE. If the measurement density is binomial then the conjugate prior is beta,

$$f(\pi_t \mid Y_{t-1}) = \frac{\Gamma(r_{t|t-1} + s_{t|t-1})}{\Gamma(r_{t|t-1})\Gamma(s_{t|t-1})} \pi_t^{r_{t|t-1}-1}(1 - \pi_t)^{s_{t|t-1}-1}. \tag{6.27}$$

But as $\mu_t = \log \pi_t / 1 - \pi_t$ it follows that using our prior knowledge of μ_t,

$$
\begin{aligned}
m_{t|t-1} &= E\mu_t \mid Y_{t-1} = \gamma(r_{t|t-1}) - \gamma(s_{t|t-1}), \\
p_{t|t-1} &= \text{Var } \mu_t \mid Y_{t-1} = \dot{\gamma}(r_{t|t-1}) + \dot{\gamma}(s_{t|t-1}),
\end{aligned}
\tag{6.28}
$$

where $\gamma(\cdot)$ is the digamma function and $\dot{\gamma}(\cdot)$ is its derivative, we can allow $r_{t|t-1}$ and $s_{t|t-1}$ to be selected numerically. When $r_{t|t-1}$ and $s_{t|t-1}$ are updated to give r_t and s_t, the corresponding m_t and p_t can be deduced from

$$
\begin{aligned}
m_t &= \gamma(r_t) - \gamma(s_t), \\
p_t &= \dot{\gamma}(r_t) + \dot{\gamma}(s_t).
\end{aligned}
\tag{6.29}
$$

This completes the cycle, since $m_{t+1|t} = m_t$ and $p_{t+1|t} = p_t + \sigma_\eta^2$.

The work on the dynamic generalised linear model and the extended Kalman filter share some important characteristics. The most important of these is that both are approximations, where the degree of approximation is difficult to determine. In neither case does the filtered estimate of the state possess the important property that it is the minimum mean square error estimate.

An alternative approach is to design transition equations which are conjugate to the measurement density so that there exists an exact analytic filter. In the last five years there has been some important work carried out on these exact non-Gaussian filters. Most of this work has been based on a gamma–beta transition equation; see the discussion in Lewis, McKenzie and Hugus (1989). A simple example is

$$
\begin{aligned}
\alpha_t &= \omega^{-1}\alpha_{t-1}\eta_t, \qquad \eta_t \sim \text{Beta}(\omega a_{t-1}, (1 - \omega)a_{t-1}), \\
\alpha_{t-1} \mid Y_{t-1} &\sim G(a_{t-1} b_{t-1}), \qquad \omega \in (0, 1].
\end{aligned}
\tag{6.30}
$$

The transition equation is multiplicative. The rather strange constraints on the form of the beta variable are required for conjugacy. They imply $\alpha_t \mid Y_{t-1} \sim G(a_{t|t-1}, b_{t|t-1})$, where

$$a_{t|t-1} = \omega a_{t-1}, \qquad b_{t|t-1} = \omega b_{t-1}. \tag{6.31}$$

This means that

$$
\begin{aligned}
E\alpha_t \mid Y_{t-1} &= \frac{a_{t|t-1}}{b_{t|t-1}} = \frac{a_t}{b_t} = E\alpha_{t-1} Y_{t-1}, \\
\text{Var } \alpha_t \mid Y_{t-1} &= \frac{a_{t|t-1}}{b_{t|t-1}^2} = \omega^{-1} \text{Var } \alpha_{t-1} \mid Y_{t-1}.
\end{aligned}
\tag{6.32}
$$

Thus the expectation of the level remains the same, but its variance increases just as it does in a Gaussian local model.

Gamma–beta transition equations have been used by Smith and Miller (1986) in their analysis of extreme value time series to enable them to forecast athletic world records. Harvey and Fernandes (1989a) exploited them to study the goals scored by the England football team, against Scotland in their matches at Hampden Park. A more interesting example from an economic viewpoint is the paper by Harvey and Fernandes (1989b) on insurance claims. Both papers use a Poisson measurement equation

$$f(y_t \mid \alpha_t) = \frac{e^{-\alpha_t} \alpha_t^{y_t}}{y_t!} . \tag{6.33}$$

As a gamma is the conjugate prior to a Poisson distribution, this model is closed by using a gamma–beta transition equation, for the use of Bayes' theorem shows that

$$\alpha_t \mid Y_t \sim G(a_t, b_t) , \quad a_t = a_{t\mid t-1} + y_t , \quad b_t = b_{t\mid t-1} + 1 . \tag{6.34}$$

This means that if $a_0 = b_0 = 0$, the filtered estimate of α_t is

$$E\alpha_t \mid Y_t = \frac{a_t}{b_t} = \frac{\displaystyle\sum_{j=0}^{t-1} \omega^j y_{t-j}}{\displaystyle\sum_{j=0}^{t-1} \omega^j} \tag{6.35}$$

which is an exponentially weighted moving average of the observations. The one-step ahead predictive distribution is

$$\begin{aligned} f(y_t \mid Y_{t-1}) &= \int f(y_t \mid \alpha_t) f(\alpha_t \mid Y_{t-1}) \, d\alpha_t \\ &= \frac{(a_t - 1)!}{y_t!(a_t - 1 - y_t)!} (b_{t\mid t-1})^{a_{t\mid t-1} - 1} b_t^{-a_t} , \end{aligned} \tag{6.36}$$

which is negative binomial and so the likelihood for this model can be computed using the predictive distribution decomposition, as in (6.22).

6.4. Stochastic variance models

One of the most important modelling techniques to emerge in the 1980s was autoregressive conditional heteroskedasticity (ARCH); see Engle (1982) and Bollerslev (1986). These authors suggested modelling the variability of a series by using weights of the squares of the past observations. The important

GARCH$(1, 1)$ model has

$$y_t \,|\, Y_{t-1} \sim N(0, h_t) \,,$$
$$h_t = \alpha_0 + \alpha_1 y_{t-1}^2 + \alpha_2 h_{t-1} \,, \tag{6.37}$$

that is the one step ahead predictive distribution depends on the variable h_t. Thus the conditional variance of the process is modelled directly, just like in ARMA models the conditional mean is modelled directly.

Although the development of these models has had a strong influence in the econometric literature, a rather different modelling approach has been suggested in the finance literature; see, for example, Hull and White (1987), Chesney and Scott (1989) and Melino and Turnbull (1990). These papers have been motivated by the desire to allow time varying volatility in opinion pricing models, so producing a more dynamic Black–Scholes type pricing equation. This requires that the volatility models be written down in terms of continuous time Brownian motion. In general ARCH models do not tie in with such a formulation, although as Nelson (1991) shows there are links with EGARCH.

The finance models, which are usually called stochastic volatility models, although we prefer to call them stochastic variance models, have some very appealing properties. They directly model the variability of the series, rather than the conditional variability. Thus they are analogous to the structural models discussed in the rest of this paper which are all direct models for the mean of the series at a particular point in time. A simple example is

$$y_t = \varepsilon_t \exp(h_t/2) \,, \qquad \varepsilon_t \sim NID(0, 1) \,,$$
$$h_t = \alpha_0 + \alpha_1 h_{t-1} + \eta_t \,, \qquad \eta_t \sim NID(0, \sigma_h^2) \,. \tag{6.38}$$

where, for simplicity, ε_t and η_s are assumed to be independent for all t and s. Here the logarithm of the standard deviation of the series follows an AR(1) process, which has an obvious continuous time generalisation. It is not observable, but it can be estimated from the linear state space form

$$\log y_t^2 = h_t + \log \varepsilon_t^2 = h_t + \varepsilon_t^* \,,$$
$$h_t = \alpha_0 + \alpha_1 h_{t-1} + \eta_t \,, \tag{6.39}$$

where ε_t^* is independent an identically distributed, but not Gaussian. In fact $E\varepsilon_t^* = -1.27$ and Var $\varepsilon_t^* = 4.93$; see Abramowitz and Stegun (1970, p. 943). The Kalman filter provides the minimum mean square linear estimator of h_t from the $\log y_t^2$ series. Further, the corresponding smoother inherits the same property of being the best linear estimator given the whole data set.

As y_t is the product of two strictly stationary processes, it must also be strictly stationary. Thus for any stochastic variance model, the restrictions needed to ensure the stationarity of y_t are just the standard restrictions to ensure the stationarity of the process generating h_t; compare the simplicity of this to the GARCH$(1, 1)$ model, as analysed by Nelson (1990). The properties of this particular autoregressive stochastic variance model can be worked out if $|\alpha_1| < 1$, for then h_t must be strictly stationary, with

$$\gamma_h = E h_t = \frac{\alpha_0}{1 - \alpha_1}, \qquad \sigma_h^2 = \text{Var } h_t = \frac{\sigma_\eta^2}{1 - \alpha_1^2}. \tag{6.40}$$

The fact that y_t is white noise follows almost immediately given the independence of ε_t and η_t. The mean is clearly zero, while

$$E y_t y_{t-\tau} = E \varepsilon_t \varepsilon_{t-\tau} E \left(\exp \left(\frac{h_t + h_{t-\tau}}{2} \right) \right) = 0 \tag{6.41}$$

as $E \varepsilon_t \varepsilon_{t-\tau} = 0$. The odd moments of y_t are all zero because ε_t is symmetric. The even moments can be obtained by making use of a standard result for the lognormal distribution, which in the present context tells us that since $\exp(h_t)$ is lognormal, its j-th moment about the origin is $\exp(j\gamma_h + j\sigma_h^2/2)$. Therefore

$$\text{Var } y_t = E\varepsilon_t^2 E \exp(h_t) = \exp(\gamma_h + \sigma_\eta^2/2). \tag{6.42}$$

The fourth moment is

$$E y_t^4 = E\varepsilon_t^4 E \exp(h_t)^2 = 3 \exp(2\gamma_h + 2\sigma_h^2) \tag{6.43}$$

and so the kurtosis is $3 \exp(\sigma_h^2)$, which is greater than 3 when σ_h^2 is positive. Thus the model exhibits excess kurtosis compared with the normal distribution. The dynamic properties of the model appear in $\log y_t^2$ rather than y_t^2. In (6.39) h_t is an AR(1) process and ε_t^* is white noise so $\log y_t^2$ is an ARMA(1, 1) process and its autocorrelation function is easy to derive.

The parameter estimation of stochastic variance models is also reasonably simple. Although the linear state space representation of $\log y_t^2$ allows the computation of the innovations and their associated variances, the innovations are not actually Gaussian. If this fact is ignored for a moment and the 'Gaussian' likelihood is constructed, then this objective function is called a quasi-likelihood. A valid asymptotic theory is available for the estimator which results from maximising this function; see Dunsmuir (1979, p. 502).

The model can be generalised so that h_t follows any stationary ARMA process, in which case y_t is also stationary and its properties can be deduced from the properties of h_t. Other components could also be brought into the model. For example, the variance could be related to a changing daily or intra daily pattern.

Multivariate generalisations of the stochastic volatility models have been suggested by Harvey, Ruiz and Shephard (1991). These models overcome many of the difficulties associated with multivariate ARCH based models; see Bollerslev, Chou and Kroner (1992) for a survey of these models. The basic idea is to let the ith element of the N-dimensional vector y_t be

$$y_{it} = \varepsilon_{it} \exp(h_{it}) ,$$
$$h_{it} = \alpha_{0i} + \alpha_{1i} h_{it-1} + \eta_{it} ,$$

(6.44)

where ε_t and η_t are N-dimensional multivariate Gaussian white noise processes with covariances Σ_ε and Σ_η. The matrix Σ_ε will be constrained to have ones down its leading diagonal and so can be thought of as being a correlation matrix.

The model can be put into state space form, as in (6.39), by writing

$$\log y_{it}^2 = h_{it} + \varepsilon_{it}^* , \quad i = 1, \ldots, N .$$

(6.45)

The covariance of $\varepsilon_t^* = (\varepsilon_{1t}^*, \ldots, \varepsilon_{Nt}^*)'$ can be analytically related to Σ_ε, so allowing straightforward estimation of Σ_ε and Σ_η by using a quasi-likelihood, although the signs of the elements of Σ_ε cannot be identified using this procedure. However, these signs can be estimated directly from the data, for $y_{it} y_{jt} > 0$ if and only if $\varepsilon_{it} \varepsilon_{jt} > 0$ implying the sign of the i,j-th element of Σ_ε should be estimated to be positive if the number of occurrences of $y_{it} y_{jt} > 0$ is greater than $T/2$.

Harvey, Ruiz and Shephard (1991) analyse four daily exchange rates for the US dollar using (6.38) and find that α_1 is approximately equal to unity for all the rates, suggesting that a random walk is appropriate for h_t. This model has very similar properties to IGARCH in which $\alpha_1 + \alpha_2 = 1$ in (6.37). The multivariate generalisation is straightforward and the transformed observations, as in (6.45), are a SUTSE model of the form (4.1). Further investigation of the model indicates that it can be made even more parsimonious by specifying just two common trends, thereby implying co-integration in volatility; compare (4.14). The first common trend affects all four exchange rates, while the second is associated primarily with the Yen.

Although stochastic variance models can be made to fit within the linear space framework and so can be handled by using the Kalman filter, this filter does not deliver the optimal (minimum mean square error) estimate. It is not possible to derive the optimal filter analytically and so it is tempting to change the transition equation in an attempt to allow the derivation of exact results for this problem. This approach has been followed by Shephard (1993b) using the techniques discussed in the previous subsection. He proposed a local scale model

$$y_t \mid \alpha_t \sim N(0, \alpha_t^{-1}) ,$$

(6.46)

where α_t, the precision of the series at time t, satisfies the gamma–beta transition equation of (6.30). Although α_t is unknown, it can be estimated because

$$\alpha_t \mid Y_t \sim G(a_t, b_t), \quad a_t = a_{t|t-1} + \tfrac{1}{2}, \quad b_t = b_{t|t-1} + \tfrac{1}{2} y_t^2$$

(6.47)

and also

$$
\mathrm{E}\alpha_t \mid Y_t = \frac{a_t}{b_t} = \frac{\displaystyle\sum_{j=0}^{t-1} \omega^j}{\displaystyle\sum_{j=0}^{t-1} \omega^j y_{t-j}^2} , \tag{6.48}
$$

this being the inverse of the EWMA of the squares of the observations.

When the focus shifts to the one-step ahead forecast density, then

$$
y_t \mid Y_{t-1} \sim t_{2a_{t|t-1}} \left(0, \frac{b_{t|t-1}}{a_{t|t-1}} \right) \tag{6.49}
$$

that is $y_t \mid Y_{t-1}$ is a scaled Student's t variable, with scale which is an exact EWMA of the squares of the past observations. If t is large then the degrees of freedom in the predictive density will approximately equal $\omega/(1-\omega)$. As $\omega \to 1$, the degrees of freedom increase and so the one-step ahead density becomes like a normal. The parameter ω has to be larger than 0.8 for the fourth moment to exist. Setting ω to 0.5 means that the density is a Cauchy random variable.

Many extensions of this model are possible, allowing, amongst other things, an exponential power measurement density instead of normal, irregularly spaced observations and multistep ahead forecasts. The difficulty with the model is that it is hard to significantly depart from the gamma–beta transition equation. As this is constrained to be a nonstationary process and is technically awkward to generalise to the multivariate case, it is of less practical use than the stochastic variance models. However, for dealing with this very special case it does provide a rather interesting alternative.

References

Abramowitz, M. and I. A. Stegun (1970). *Handbook of Mathematical Functions*. Dover, New York.

Anderson, B. D. O. and J. B. Moore (1979). *Optimal Filtering*. Prentice-Hall, Englewood Cliffs, NJ.

Anderson, T. W. and C. Hsiao (1982). Formulation and estimation of dynamic models using panel data. *J. Econometrics* 18, 47–82.

Ansley, C. F. and R. Kohn (1985). Estimation, filtering and smoothing in state space models with incompletely specified initial conditions. *Ann. Statist.* 13, 1286–1316.

Ansley, C. F. and R. Kohn (1989). Prediction mean square error for state space models with estimated parameters. *Biometrika* 73, 467–474.

Binder, D. A. and J. P. Dick (1989). Modelling and estimation for repeated surveys. *Survey Method.* 15, 29–45.

Bollerslev, T. (1986). Generalized autoregressive conditional heteroskedasticity. *J. Econometrics* 31, 307–327.

Bollerslev, T., R. Y. Chou and K. F. Kroner (1992). ARCH models in finance: A review of the theory and empirical evidence. *J. Econometrics* 52, 5–59.

Bowden, R. J. and D. A. Turkington (1984). *Instrumental Variables*. Cambridge Univ. Press, Cambridge.

Box, G. E. P. and G. M. Jenkins (1976). *Time Series Analysis: Forecasting and Control*. Revised edition, Holden-Day, San Francisco, CA.

Box, G. E. P. and G. C. Tiao (1975). Intervention analysis with applications to economic and environmental problems. *J. Amer. Statist. Assoc.* **70**, 70–79.

Chesney, M. and L. O. Scott (1989). Pricing European currency options: A comparison of the modified Black–Scholes model and a random variance model. *J. Financ. Quant. Anal.* **24**, 267–284.

De Jong, P. (1988a). The likelihood for a state space model. *Biometrika* **75**, 165–169.

De Jong, P. (1988b). A cross-validation filter for time series models. *Biometrika* **75**, 594–600.

De Jong, P. (1989). Smoothing and interpolation with the state space model. *J. Amer. Statist. Assoc.* **84**, 1085–1088.

De Jong, P. (1991). The diffuse Kalman filter. *Ann. Statist.* **19**, 1073–1083.

Duncan, D. B. and S. D. Horn (1972). Linear dynamic regression from the viewpoint of regression analysis, *J. Amer. Statist. Assoc.* **67**, 815–821.

Dunsmuir, W. (1979). A central limit theorem for parameter estimation in stationary vector time series and its applications to models for a signal observed with noise. *Ann. Statist.* **7**, 490–506.

Engle, R. F. (1982). Autoregressive conditional heteroscedasticity with estimates of the variance of UK inflation. *Econometrica* **50**, 987–1007.

Engle, R. F. and C. W. J. Granger (1987). Co-integration and error correction: Representation, estimation and testing. *Econometrica* **55**, 251–276.

Fernández, F. J. (1990). Estimation and testing of a multivariate exponential smoothing model. *J. Time Ser. Anal.* **11**, 89–105.

Fernández, F. J. and A. C. Harvey (1990). Seemingly unrelated time series equations and a test for homogeneity. *J. Business Econ. Statist.* **8**, 71–82.

Harrison, P. J. and C. F. Stevens (1976). Bayesian forecasting. *J. Roy. Statist. Soc. Ser. B* **38**, 205–247.

Harvey, A. C. (1989). *Forecasting, Structural Time Series Models and the Kalman Filter*. Cambridge Univ. Press, Cambridge.

Harvey, A. C. and A. Jaeger (1991). Detrending, stylized facts and the business cycle. Mimeo, Department of Statistics, London School of Economics.

Harvey, A. C. and C. Fernandes (1989a). Time series models for count or qualitative observations (with discussion). *J. Business Econ. Statist.* **7**, 407–422.

Harvey, A. C. and C. Fernandes (1989b). Time series models for insurance claims. *J. Inst. Actuar.* **116**, 513–528.

Harvey, A. C. and S. J. Koopman (1992). Diagnostic checking of unobserved components time series models. *J. Business Econ. Statist.* **10**, 377–389.

Harvey, A. C. and S. J. Koopman (1993). Short term forecasting of periodic time series using time-varying splines. *J. Amer. Statist. Assoc.*, to appear.

Harvey, A. C. and P. Marshall (1991). Inter-fuel substitution, technical change and the demand for energy in the UK economy. *Appl. Econ.* **23**, 1077–1086.

Harvey, A. C. and S. Peters (1990). Estimation procedures for structural time series models, *J. Forecast.* **9**, 89–108.

Harvey, A. C., E. Ruiz and N. G. Shephard (1991). Multivariate stochastic variance models. Mimeo, Department of Statistics, London School of Economics.

Harvey, A. C. and M. Streibel (1991). Stochastic trends in simultaneous equation systems. In: P. Hackl and A. Westlund, eds., *Economic Structural Change*, Springer, Berlin, 169–178.

Harvey, A. C., B. Henry, S. Peters and S. Wren-Lewis (1986). Stochastic trends in dynamic regression models: An application to the output-employment equation. *Econ. J.* **96**, 975–985.

Harvey, A. C. and J. Durbin (1986). The effects of seat belt legislation on British road casualties: A case study in structural time series modelling. *J. Roy. Statist. Soc. Ser. A* **149**, 187–227.

Hausman, J. A. and M. W. Watson (1985). Errors in variables and seasonal adjustment procedures. *J. Amer. Statist. Assoc.* **80**, 541–552.

Hendry, D. F. and J.-F. Richard (1983). The econometric analysis of economic time series. *Internat. Statist. Rev.* **51**, 111–164.

Hull, J. and A. White (1987). Hedging the risks from writing foreign currency options. *J. Internat. Money Finance* **6**, 131–152.

Johansen, S. (1988). Statistical analysis of cointegration vectors. *J. Econ. Dynamics Control* **12**, 231–254.

Jones, R. H. (1980). Best linear unbiased estimators for repeated survey. *J. Roy. Statist. Soc. Ser. B* **42**, 221–226.

Jorgenson, D. W. (1986). Econometric methods for modelling producer behaviour. In: Z. Giliches and M. D. Intriligator, eds. *Handbook of Econometrics*, Vol. 3, North-Holland, Amsterdam, 1841–1915.

Kitagawa, G. (1987). Non-Gaussian state-space modeling of nonstationary time series. *J. Amer. Statist. Assoc.* **82**, 1032–1041.

Kohn, R. and C. F. Ansley (1985). Efficient estimation and prediction in time series regression models. *Biometrika* **72**, 694–697.

Kohn, R. and C. F. Ansley (1989). A fast algorithm for signal extraction, influence and cross-validation in state space models. *Biometrika* **76**, 65–79.

Koopman, S. J. (1993). Disturbance smoother for state space models. *Biometrika* **80**, to appear.

Koopman, S. J. and N. Shephard (1992). Exact score for time series models in state space form. *Biometrika* **79**, 823–826.

Lewis, P. A. W., E. McKenzie and D. K. Hugus (1989). Gamma processes, *Comm. Statist. Stochast. Models* **5**, 1–30.

Liptser, R. S. and A. N. Shiryayev (1978). *Statistics of Random Processes II: Applications.* Springer, New York.

Marshall, P. (1992a). State space models with diffuse initial conditions. *J. Time Ser. Anal.* **13**, 411–414.

Marshall, P. (1992b). Estimating time-dependent means in dynamic models for cross-sections of time series. *Empirical Econ.* **17**, 25–33.

McCullagh, P. and J. A. Nelder (1989). *Generalized Linear Models.* 2nd ed., Chapman and Hall, London.

Melino, A. and S. M. Turnbull (1990). Pricing options with stochastic volatility. *J. Econometrics* **45**, 239–265.

Nelson, D. B. (1990). Stationarity and persistence in the GARCH(1, 1) model. *Econometric Theory* **6**, 318–334.

Nelson, D. B. (1991). ARCH models as diffusion approximations. *J. Econometrics* **45**, 7–38.

Pagan, A. R. (1979). Some consequences of viewing LIML as an iterated Aitken estimator. *Econ. Lett.* **3**, 369–372.

Pfeffermann, D. (1991). Estimation and seasonal adjustment of population means using data from repeated surveys (with discussion). *J. Business Econ. Statist.* **9**, 163–177.

Pfeffermann, D. and L. Burck (1990). Robust small area estimation combining time series and cross-sectional data. *Survey Method.* **16**, 217–338.

Pole, A. and M. West (1990). Efficient Bayesian learning in non-linear dynamic models. *J. Forecasting* **9**, 119–136.

Rao, C. R. (1973). *Linear Statistical Inference.* 2nd ed., Wiley, New York.

Rosenberg, B. (1973). Random coefficient models: The analysis of a cross section of time series by stochastically convergent parameter regression. *Ann. Econ. Social Measurement* **2**, 399–428.

Scott, A. J. and T. M. F. Smith (1974). Analysis of repeated surveys using time series models. *J. Amer. Statist. Assoc.* **69**, 674–678.

Shephard, N. (1993a). Maximum likelihood estimation of regression models with stochastic trend components. *J. Amer. Statist. Assoc.* **88**, 590–595.

Shephard, N. (1993b). Local scale model: State space alternatives to integrated GARCH processes. *J. Econometrics*, to appear.

Shephard, N. and A. C. Harvey (1989). Tracking to the level of party support during general election campaigns. Mimeo, Department of Statistics, London School of Economics.

Shephard, N. and A. C. Harvey (1990). On the probability of estimating a deterministic component in the local level model. *J. Time Ser. Anal.* **11**, 339–347.

Sims, C. A., J. H. Stock and M. W. Watson (1990). Inference in linear time series models with some unit roots. *Econometrica* **58**, 113–144.

Slade, M. E. (1989). Modelling stochastic and cyclical components of structural change: An application of the Kalman filter. *J. Econometrics* **41**, 363–383.

Smith, R. L. and J. E. Miller (1986). A non-Gaussian state space model and application to prediction of records. *J. Roy. Statist. Soc. Ser. B* **48**, 79–88.

Smith, T. M. F. (1978). Principles and problems in the analysis of repeated surveys. In: N. K. Nawboodivi, ed., *Survey Sampling and Measurement*, Academic Press, New York, 201–216.

Stock, J. H. and M. Watson (1988). Testing for common trends. *J. Amer. Statist. Assoc.* **83**, 1097–1107.

Stock, J. H. and M. Watson (1990). A probability model of the coincident economic indicators. In: K. Lahiri and G. H. Moore, eds., *Leading Economic Indicators*, Cambridge Univ. Press, Cambridge, 63–89.

Streibel, M. and A. C. Harvey (1993). Estimation of simultaneous equation models with stochastic trend components. *J. Econ. Dynamics Control* **17**, 263–288.

Tam, S. M. (1987). Analysis of repeated surveys using a dynamic linear model. *Internat. Statist. Rev.* **55**, 63–73.

Tiao, G. C. and R. S. Tsay (1989). Model specification in multivariate time series (with discussion). *J. Roy. Statist. Soc. Ser. B* **51**, 157–214.

Tong, H. (1990). *Non-Linear Time Series: A Dynamic System Approach.* Clarendon Press, Oxford.

Tunnicliffe-Wilson, G. (1989). On the use of marginal likelihood in time series estimation. *J. Roy. Statist. Soc. Ser. B* **51**, 15–27.

West, M., P. J. Harrison and H. S. Migon (1985). Dynamic generalized linear models and Bayesian forecasting (with discussion). *J. Amer. Statist. Assoc.* **80**, 73–97.

West, M. and P. J. Harrison (1989). *Bayesian Forecasting and Dynamic Models.* Springer, New York.

Whittle, P. (1991). Likelihood and cost as path integrals. *J. Roy. Statist. Soc. Ser. B* **53**, 505–538.

G. S. Maddala, C. R. Rao and H. D. Vinod, eds., *Handbook of Statistics, Vol. 11*

11

Bayesian Testing and Testing Bayesians

Jean-Pierre Florens and Michel Mouchart

1. Introduction

In general, a null hypothesis (H_0) and its alternative (H_1) may be considered as two regions (actually, a partition) of the parameter space of a unique sampling model or as two different models. These two interpretations cover a large class of problems and a wealth of different procedures have been suggested and analyzed in sampling theory. This survey focuses the attention on Bayesian methods and endeavours to illustrate both the intrinsic unity of Bayesian thinking and its basic flexibility to adjust to and to cope with a wide range of circumstances.

Broadly speaking two kinds of approaches seem to be fruitful. One approach starts by remarking that a test is a statistical procedure, i.e., a function defined on a sample space, with value in a two-points space, the elements of which may be, more or less arbitrarily, labelled 'accept' or 'reject' a given hypothesis. It seems therefore natural to approach a testing problem as a two-decision problem: this approach gives a rather straightforward logical background and leads to what we shall call a 'fully Bayesian approach'. Some colleagues among our Bayesian friends are tempted to assert 'that's all' and to consider testing exclusively as a two-decision problem. Another approach starts by remarking that testing may also be viewed as a way for the statistician to handle his own doubt about a statistical model: were the null hypothesis considered as certain, then he would go on with an inference restricted to the null hypothesis, i.e., with a statistical model whose parameters sweep the null hypothesis only. Thus the statistician implicitly considers two models,

$$\{P^\theta : \theta \in H_0\} \quad \text{and} \quad \{P^\theta : \theta \in H_1\}$$

and the mere fact of testing means that (s)he is uncertain about which model is the 'suitable' one. We shall see that this approach is, in a sense, more flexible. It is characterized by the fact that the two models share the same sample space and two parameter spaces characterizing different sets of sampling distributions but these parameters may possibly have an economic meaning which is quite different with the two models even if they appear in a similar analytical form.

As suggested by the title, this survey has two main sections: one on general principles, another one on procedures. Let us briefly review these sections.

Section 2, called 'Bayesian testing', surveys general principles and is divided into two main parts. The first one (Section 2.2) is rather traditional in the Bayesian literature and focuses attention directly on inference about the hypotheses under considation. Its main output is the posterior probability of hypotheses but may also take the form of Bayes factors or of posterior odds and is based, essentially, on the difference between the predictive distributions determined by each hypothesis. Side issues also consider comparison with the sampling theory analogue, in particular on possible conflict with p-values. A second part (Section 2.3), less traditional, focuses attention on inference on the parameter of interest under different models and is based on a Bayesian approach to the encompassing principle. This is a formalization of a simple idea: as far as inference is concerned, model M_0 encompasses model M_1 if any inference based on M_1, i.e., any of its posterior distributions, may be obtained by transforming a posterior distribution of model M_0 without retrieving the sample, in other words, if M_0 is a 'new' model it should be able, for being accepted, to explain the findings of the 'old' model M_1. A peculiarity of the encompassing approach is to base the binary choice among models, or hypotheses, on its relevance for the inference on the parameters of interest. These two parts are distinguished by writing (H_0, H_1) for the first one and (M_0, M_1) for the second one but it should be insisted that this notational distinction is contextual rather than substantial, i.e., it is aimed at drawing the attention to the question whether the interest lies in choosing among models, understood as hypotheses to 'explain the real world' or in choosing among models understood as learning rules to be used when analyzing data. We show in particular that this latter approach provides a Bayesian version of the Hausman (1978) test for model specification. Also Section 2 discusses the 'minimal amount' of prior specification required to make these approaches operational and some aspect of their asymptotic behaviour.

Section 3, called 'Testing Bayesians', surveys procedures derived from the general principles of Section 2 when facing specific problems of econometric interest. Section 3.1 considers the testing of a regression coefficient (with known variance). This problem is analytically the simplest one; it is used as an opportunity to survey most of the procedures suggested by the preceding section. In contrast, Section 3.2 considers an analytically more complex problem, namely testing for unit root(s); it surveys a literature that recently has been very active. It is therefore too early to claim any 'objectivity' in the appraisal of those recent achievements. We essentially endeavour to show how the general principles of Section 2 have generated useful and workable analysis of a problem, the solution of which has been judged of crucial importance in contemporary dynamic modelling.

It should be clear, from this presentation, that Sections 2 and 3 do not do full justice to the complete Bayesian activity in the domain of testing. The last section sketches some of the overlooked material and gives a rapid evaluation of the present state of the art.

2. Bayesian testing

2.1. Introduction

In sampling theory, a *statistical model* may be viewed as a family of probability measures on a sample space $(S, \mathscr{S})$ indexed by a parameter θ:

$$\{(S, \mathscr{S}), P^\theta : \theta \in \Theta\} . \tag{2.1}$$

In usual cases, these probability measures may be represented by densities on a random variable x representing the observations on the sample space:

$$\{p(x \mid \theta): \theta \in \Theta\} . \tag{2.2}$$

Most *econometric models* are of the conditional type, i.e., observation x is decomposed into y and z, thus $x = (y, z)$, and the statistical model is only partially specified, i.e., up to the conditional distribution of y given z only, thus,

$$\{p(y \mid z, \theta): \theta \in \Theta\} . \tag{2.3}$$

Bayesian models are obtained by endowing a sampling theory model with a (prior) probability measure P_θ on the parameter space $(\Theta, \mathscr{T})$ and interpreting the sampling model as a probability conditional on the parameter. This is allowed by defining a unique probability measure Π on the product space $\Theta \times S$, which is written as

$$\Pi = P_\theta \otimes P^\theta \tag{2.4}$$

and characterized by

$$\Pi(A \times B) = \int_{\theta \in A} P^\theta(B) \, \mathrm{d}P_\theta \quad A \in \mathscr{T}, \ B \in \mathscr{S} \tag{2.5}$$

or, in terms of density,

$$p(x, \theta) = p(\theta)p(x \mid \theta) . \tag{2.6}$$

Thus, in econometrics, a typical Bayesian model becomes a unique joint probability on y and θ conditional on z, i.e., in terms of densities,

$$p(y, \theta \mid z) = p(\theta \mid z)p(y \mid z, \theta) . \tag{2.7}$$

Bayesian methods aim at performing a dual decomposition of this joint distribution into a predictive distribution on $(y \mid z)$ and posterior distributions on $(\theta \mid y, z)$,

$$p(y, \theta \mid z) = p(y \mid z)p(\theta \mid y, z). \tag{2.8}$$

Inference problems are connected with the analysis of the transformation 'prior to posterior', i.e., the transformation of $p(\theta \mid z)$ into $p(\theta \mid y, z)$. Prediction problems may be considered either in prior terms, i.e., predicting y before it has been observed, or in posterior terms, i.e., decomposing y into a 'past' component y_p and a 'future' component y_f, $y = (y_f, y_p)$, and predicting y_f after observing y_p. In simple cases, predictions are considered conditionally on z and are handled by averaging the sampling distribution $p(y \mid z, \theta)$ – or $p(y_f \mid y_p, z, \theta)$ – weighted by the relevant distributions on the parameters $p(\theta \mid z)$ – or $p(\theta \mid y_p, z, \theta)$ – in order to obtain the predictive distributions

$$p(y \mid z) = \int p(y \mid z, \theta)p(z \mid \theta) \, \mathrm{d}\theta \,, \tag{2.9}$$

$$p(y_f \mid y_p, z) = \int p(y_f \mid y_p, z, \theta)p(\theta \mid y_p, z) \, \mathrm{d}\theta \,. \tag{2.10}$$

A rather precise exposition of the probabilistic foundation of Bayesian methods may be found in 'Elements of Bayesian Statistics' (Florens, Mouchart and Rolin, 1990), particularly Chapter 1, to be referred to as EBS. An exposition specifically oriented towards econometrics may be found in Zellner (1971) and with a more general orientation, in Berger (1985), De Groot (1970) Jeffreys (1967) or Lindley (1971).

REMARK 1. It will be seen later that both the posterior distributions *and* the predictive distributions are involved in Bayesian procedures of testing.

REMARK 2. Up to now we have not assumed the prior independence of θ and z, i.e., $\theta \perp\!\!\!\perp z$ or $p(\theta \mid z) = p(\theta)$. This is motivated by two types of considerations. First, at this level of generality, such an assumption does not substantially simplify the Bayesian model because even when θ and z are, a priori, independent, all other distributions involved in the Bayesian model, namely the sampling, the predictive and the posterior, still depend crucially on z; in particular, for the inference, i.e., the evaluation of the posterior distribution, y *and* z are taken as data. Furthermore, in sequential modeling, z would involve lagged values of y so that θ would not be independent of z. Second, the rationale of the hypothesis $\theta \perp\!\!\!\perp z$ is to ensure the admissibility of conditioning on z, i.e., of considering the joint distribution $p(y, \theta \mid z)$ rather than the joint distribution $p(y, z, \theta, \lambda)$ where λ would characterize the marginal sampling distribution of z, with the consequence that z becomes exogenous for the inference on θ. As the problem of exogeneity is not a basic issue in this survey, there is no real gain in assuming the exogeneity of z as a starting point (for a Bayesian treatment of exogeneity see EBS, Sections 3.4 and 6.3). As a consequence, most general ideas around testing may be presented in unconditional as well as in conditional models.

2.2. Posterior probability of hypotheses, posterior odds, Bayes factors

2.2.1. The traditional Bayesian approach: Comparison of predictive distributions

Two-decision problems. Consider a two-decision problem with the set of possible decisions $A = \{a_0, a_1\}$. The loss function may then be written as $l(a_j, \theta) = \bar{l}_j(\theta)$ for $j = 0, 1$ and H_0 and H_1 may be *defined* as $H_j = \bar{l}_j^{-1}(\{0\})$, i.e., the set of θ for which a_j is optimal (viz., has zero loss). A testing problem is characterized by the fact that H_0 and H_1 operate a partition of the parameter space constituting the maintained hypothesis. Thus a_j may be *interpreted* as 'decide *as if* H_j were true' and the loss function may be rewritten as

$$l(a_j, \theta) = \ell_j(\theta) \mathbb{1}_{H_{\bar{j}}}\theta) , \qquad (2.11)$$

where $\bar{j} = 0$ if $j = 1$ and $\bar{j} = 1$ if $j = 0$. A decision function $a : S \to A$ is an optimal one, a^*, when defined as

$$a^*(x) = \arg \inf_{a \in A} \mathrm{E}[l(a, \theta)\,|\,x] , \qquad (2.12)$$

in general, i.e., in the case of a two-decision problem

$$a^*(x) = a_1 \iff \mathrm{E}[l_1(\theta) \mathbb{1}_{H_0}(\theta)\,|\,x] \leq \mathrm{E}[l_0(\theta) \mathbb{1}_{H_1}(\theta)\,|\,x] . \qquad (2.13)$$

It has been argued that Neyman–Pearson theory may be interpreted in this decision theoretic approach by considering the particular case of a piece-wise constant loss function $l(a_j, \theta) = l_j \mathbb{1}_{H_{\bar{j}}}(\theta)$ so that

$$a^*(x) = a_1 \iff l_1 \mathrm{P}(H_0\,|\,x) \leq l_0 \mathrm{P}(H_1\,|\,x) , \qquad (2.14)$$

i.e., in terms of *posterior probability* of hypotheses

$$a^*(x) = a_1 \iff \mathrm{P}(H_0\,|\,x) \leq \frac{l_0}{l_0 + l_1} , \qquad (2.15)$$

or in terms of *posterior odds*,

$$a^*(x) = a_1 \iff \frac{\mathrm{P}(H_0\,|\,x)}{\mathrm{P}(H_1\,|\,x)} \leq \frac{l_0}{l_1} . \qquad (2.16)$$

Thus the rule $a^*(x) = a_1 \iff \mathrm{P}(H_0\,|\,x) \leq 5\%$ would be justified with the piece-wise constant loss function such that $l_1 = 19l_0$, a way of formalizing that type I-error is much more severe than type II-error. This analysis shows that Bayesian testing under piece-wise constant loss functions boils down to the evaluation of the posterior probability of the hypothesis in presence.

Posterior probabilities and posterior odds as foundations of Bayesian testing are as old as Bayesian statistics and are presented, e.g., in Jeffreys (1967). These definitions are given and discussed in many books and used in many papers: see, e.g., Berger (1985), Hodges (1990), Leamer (1978, 1983 and 1991), Zellner (1984). Asymptotic properties of posterior probabilities of the two hypotheses can be found in EBS, Section 7.5. Note that the posterior odds essentially mimic the likelihood ratio with however a crucial difference of interpretation: the posterior odds are based on the posterior distribution rather than on the sampling distribution and the critical value is defined by the loss structure rather that by an exogenously given level. Also the particular piece-wise constant structure of the underlying loss function should be stressed, an often disputable structure. For example, such a structure would be questionable when testing $H_0: \theta = 0$ for θ being a price elasticity in a brand demand equation but would be rather reasonable for testing $H_0: \theta \leq 0.5$ when θ is the percentage of favourable intention of votes in a forthcoming two-candidates election and when the underlying decision is a possible reorientation of the electoral campaign. The connection between testing and decision is discussed in particular in Savage (1954), Rubin (1971).

Prior specification and structure of the hypotheses. The literature on the posterior probability of hypotheses and on posterior odds has also paid some attention to the role of the prior specification, particularly for the case of a sharp null hypothesis and for improper prior distribution. (See, e.g., Klein and Brown, 1984; Leamer, 1978, 1983; Maddala, 1976).

Once it is recognized that the hypotheses H_0 and H_1 operate a partition of the parameter space Θ, the prior distribution (and also the posterior) may be decomposed conformably with that partition, namely

$$P_\theta = \pi_0 P_\theta^0 + (1 - \pi_0) P_\theta^1 , \qquad (2.17)$$

where $\pi_0 = P_\theta(H_0)$ and $P_\theta^j(A) = P(\theta \in A \mid H_j)$, or in terms of density,

$$p(\theta) = \pi_0 p^0(\theta) \mathbb{1}_{H_0}(\theta) + (1 - \pi_0) p^1(\theta) \mathbb{1}_{H_1}(\theta) , \qquad (2.18)$$

where $p^j(\theta) \mathbb{1}_{H_j}(\theta)$ are the respective conditional densities. One then obtains

$$P(H_0 \mid x) = \frac{\pi_0 p(x \mid H_0)}{\pi_0 p(x \mid H_0) + (1 - \pi_0) p(x \mid H_1)} \qquad (2.19)$$

or equivalently, in terms of posterior odds

$$\frac{P(H_0 \mid x)}{P(H_1 \mid x)} = \frac{\pi_0}{1 - \pi_0} \cdot \frac{p(x \mid H_0)}{p(x \mid H_1)}$$

$$= \frac{\pi_0}{1 - \pi_0} B_x(H_0; H_1) , \qquad (2.20)$$

where

$$p(x \mid H_j) = \int_{\theta \in H_j} p(x \mid (\theta) p^j(\theta) \mathbb{1}_{H_j}(\theta) \, d\theta \, , \quad j = 0, 1 \, , \tag{2.21}$$

are the predictive densities relative to each hypothesis and $B_x(H_0; H_1)$, called the *Bayes factor* of H_0 against H_1, is deemed to measure how far an observation x increases or decreases the prior odds $\pi_0(1 - \pi_0)^{-1}$ into the posterior odds, i.e., gives empirical evidence more or less in favour of H_0. Thus in case of piece-wise constant loss functions, the Bayes solution, in terms of posterior probability (2.15), posterior odds (2.16) or Bayes factor (2.20), essentially relies on the predictive densities (2.21) of each models. Let us now survey the impact of the prior specification on those predictive densities according to the structure of the hypotheses to be tested.

(i) If both hypotheses H_j are simple, i.e., $H_j = \{\theta_j\}$ so that $\Theta = \{\theta_0, \theta_1\}$, the Bayes factor is exactly equal to the likelihood ratio and is therefore independent of any prior specification. In this case, the Bayes factor and the likelihood ratio give the same empirical evidence in favour of H_0 but again the critical value for the likelihood ratio depends on the loss structure *and* on the prior weight π_0, viz.

$$a^*(x) = a_1 \quad \Leftrightarrow \quad B_x(H_0; H_1) \equiv \frac{p(x \mid \theta_0)}{p(x \mid \theta_1)} \leqslant \frac{l_0}{l_1} \cdot \frac{1 - \pi_0}{\pi_0} \, . \tag{2.22}$$

(ii) When one of the hypotheses (or both) is not simple, the corresponding predictive density (2.21) clearly depends on the prior specification. If P_θ^j is improper, i.e.,

$$\int p^j(\theta) \mathbb{1}_{H_j}(\theta) \, d\theta = \infty \, , \tag{2.23}$$

more precisely is a σ-finite measure, the decomposition (2.17) cannot anymore be interpreted as a marginal-conditional decomposition with respect to H_0 and H_1; and $p(x \mid H_j)$ is also improper. But once an improper prior distribution is justified by an invariance argument, its density is defined up to a multiplicative constant only; for instance when $\Theta = \mathbb{R}$, $p^j(\theta) = 1$ corresponds to Lebesgue measure and has the same (translation) invariance property as $p^j(\theta) = 2$ (or, $=1991$). Furthermore, two improper prior distributions with proportional densities are associated with identical posterior distributions and therefore a Bayesian cannot argue in favour of $p^j(\theta) = 2$ (or, $=1991$). This is actually reflected by writing $p^j(\theta) \propto 1$ instead of $p^j(\theta) = 1$. The difficulty is that the (2.21) suffers from the same indeterminacy and the Bayes factor is eventually indeterminate.

(iii) Consider now the case where H_0 is sharp but H_1 is not (heuristically the Lebesgue measure of H_0 is zero and that of H_1 is strictly positive; for instance: $\Theta = \mathbb{R}$ and $H_0 = \{\theta_0\}$). If P_θ is smooth (more precisely, dominated by Lebesgue measure) $\pi_0 = P(H_0) = 0$; this implies, with smooth sampling probabilities, that $P(H_0 | x) = 0$ and that the posterior odds and the Bayes factor are identically zero. Conversely, if $\pi_0 = P(H_0) > 0$, P_θ is not smooth but $\pi_0 > 0$ whereas P_θ^1 is smooth implies a discontinuity of P_θ which has been criticized in some contexts. Suppose, for instance, $\Theta = \mathbb{R}$, $H_0 = \{\theta_0\}$, $\pi_0 = 0.5$ and $(\theta | H_1) \sim N(m, v)$. The prior distribution function is smooth everywhere except at the point θ_0 where there is a jump of height equal to 0.5. This jump may be considered as undesirable if the sampling model is smooth, heuristically if the likelihood function is continuous at $\theta = \theta_0$. For instance, when equilibrium appears as a parametric restriction of the type $g(\theta) = 0$ in a model embodying structural disequilibrium, a prior distribution with a strictly positive mass on the (null measure) surface $g(\theta) = 0$ may be palatable whereas in a demand model where θ_i represents a price elasticity, a strictly positive prior probability on $\{\theta_i = -1\}$ may be much more questionable when the prior distribution is otherwise continuous. But it would seem unnatural to let the prior specification, and more particularly its points of discontinuity, depend on whether one intends to test for example $H_0 : \theta_i = 0$ against $H_0 : \theta_i \neq 0$ or to test $H_0 : \theta_i = 1$ against $H_0 : \theta_i \neq 1$.

Alternative approaches to testing. It has been suggested that testing a sharp hypothesis might be a workable approximation for testing a neighbourhood, i.e., $H_0 : g(\theta) = 0$ would be an approximation for $H_0 : |g(\theta)| < \varepsilon$ for some $\varepsilon > 0$ so that π_0 should be interpreted as $P[-\varepsilon < g(\theta) < \varepsilon] = \pi_0$ rather than $P(g(\theta) = 0) = \pi_0$. The difficulty is that the optimal decision rule $a^*(x)$, the posterior probability, posterior odds or Bayes factors all depend crucially on ε. Thus for the case of sharp hypothesis some statisticians have remarked that in a sampling theory approach a yes–no testing at a predefined critical level α may be less interesting than the evaluation of a confidence interval of given level. Similarly, in a Bayesian framework a yes–no decision problem may be less interesting, in practice, than the evaluation of a posterior probability interval, i.e., the evaluation of $c_1(x)$ and $c_2(x)$ (with $c_1(x) < c_2(x)$) such that $P[c_1(x) \leq g(\theta) \leq c_2(x) | x] = 1 - \alpha$ (see, e.g., Lindley, 1961). In this approach, the choice of level α is less crucial: it is introduced in the framework of a convenient summary of the complete posterior distribution.

Instead of confining the attention to the two-decision problem, attention has also been paid to the more general problem of the weight of the evidence provided by the data in favour of H_0 or of H_1. Comparing sampling theory and Bayesian approaches suggests comparing the p-value, considered as a measure of empirical evidence, and one of the Bayesian natural measures viz. posterior probability of H_0, posterior odds or Bayes factor. A vast literature has shown that an observation may look very favourable to the alternative hypothesis in a sampling theory framework but very favourable to the null hypothesis in a Bayesian framework; for given data a small p-value may be associated to a very high Bayes factor, so that a p-value cannot be viewed as an approximation of $P(H_0 | x)$, not even an indication of its order of magnitude. This situation has been known as Lindley's paradox, after Lindley (1957) and has received an impressive attention in the literature. Fundamentally, the problem is that any posterior distribution may be associated to a given likelihood function.

Relationships between Bayesian test and classical tests have been discussed in many papers see in particular Bernardo (1980), De Groot (1973), Gaver and Geisel (1974), Good (1985), Hill (1982, 1990), Poirier (1988), Raftery (1986); for the more particular problem of the relationship between p-value and Bayes factors, see Berger (1986), Berger and Berry (1988) Berger and Delampady (1987) (this paper also contains an important bibliography on this issue), Berger and Sellke (1987), Casella and Berger (1987) Dickey (1977), Shafter (1982). Moreno and Cano (1989) have however shown that the relationship between p-values and Bayes factors may be possibly reversed with respect to the undimensional case.

Another approach takes the point of view of estimating a binary valued function of the parameter $\beta = b(\theta)$ where $b : \Theta \rightarrow \{0, 1\}$ is such that $H_j = b^{-1}(j)$, $j = 0, 1$, i.e., $b(\theta) = \mathbb{1}_{H_0}(\theta)$. Thus some Bayesians have suggested to enlarge the two-point set of possible decisions into the unit interval $[0, 1]$ and to consider loss functions of the form $\ell(a, \mathbb{1}_{H_0}(\theta))$ with $a \in [0, 1]$. Thus for a quadratic loss function, $\ell(a, \mathbb{1}_{H_0}(\theta)) = [a - \mathbb{1}_{H_0}(\theta)]^2$, the Bayesian solution, is simply $a^*(x) = \mathrm{E}(\mathbb{1}_{H_0}(\theta) | x)$ and for

$$
\ell(a, \mathbb{1}_{H_0}(\theta)) = \begin{cases} \ell_0(a - \mathbb{1}_{H_0}(\theta)) & \text{for } a > \mathbb{1}_{H_0}(\theta) , \\ \ell_1(\mathbb{1}_{H_0}(\theta) - a) & \text{for } a < \mathbb{1}_{H_0}(\theta) , \end{cases}
$$

the Bayesian solution is a corner solution, namely

$$
a^*(x) = \begin{cases} 0 & \text{if } P(H_0 | x) \leqslant \dfrac{\ell_0}{\ell_0 + \ell_1} , \\ 1 & \text{otherwise} . \end{cases}
$$

This is exactly (2.15) with $a = 0$ (resp. $a = 1$) identified with a_1 (resp. a_0). For more details, see Hwang, Casella, Robert, Wells and Farrel (1992).

2.3. Inference on genuine parameters of interest: An encompassing approach

2.3.1. Model choice and hypothesis testing
A deep and recurrent theme of discussions in econometric modelling turns around the relationship between the economic meaning of a parameter and the model where it appears. These discussions suggest that parameters may possibly change their meaning under a null hypothesis. For instance we argue in Section 3.2.1. in the model $y = \beta z_1 + \gamma z_2 + \varepsilon$ the coefficient of z_1 may have a different meaning according to whether $\gamma = 0$ or $\gamma \neq 0$.

These considerations lead to the analysis of statistical models such that the 'parameter' θ has the form $(\lambda, \theta_0, \theta_1)$ where λ is a 'model label' ($\lambda \in \{0, 1\}$) and θ_j ($j = 0, 1$) are model-specific parameters. Thus the full Bayesian model would be specified through a joint distribution $p(\lambda, \theta_0, \theta_1, x)$, written as:

$$p(\lambda, \theta_0, \theta_1, x) = [\pi_0 p^0(\theta_0, \theta_1, x)]^{1-\lambda}[(1 - \pi_0)p^1(\theta_0, \theta_1, x)]^\lambda , \qquad (2.24)$$

where $\pi_0 = P(\lambda = 0)$ and $p^j(\theta_0, \theta_1, x) = p(\theta_0, \theta_1, x \mid \lambda = j)$, $j = 0, 1$, with the following characteristics:

$$p^j(\theta_0, \theta_1, x) = p^j(\theta_j)p^j(x \mid \theta_j)p^j(\theta_{\bar{j}} \mid \theta_j)$$
$$= p^j(x)p^j(\theta_j \mid x)p^j(\theta_{\bar{j}} \mid \theta_j) , \quad j = 0, 1 . \qquad (2.25)$$

This is, the sampling distribution of model j, $p^j(x \mid \theta)$, depends only on the corresponding θ_j with the consequence that the conditional distribution $p^j(\theta_{\bar{j}} \mid \theta_j)$ is not revised, in model j, by the observation x. Let us note the following points:

(i) In this formulation θ_0 may be a subvector of θ_1, or a function of θ_1 and represents the free parameters under H_0 in the usual hypothesis testing but this is not a necessity: θ_0 and θ_1 may also represent unrelated parameters characterizing different models.

(ii) When θ_0 is a subvector of θ_1 and when one is willing to specify that θ_0 keeps the same economic meaning whether $\lambda = 0$ or $\lambda = 1$, then the prior specification would be: $p^1(\theta_0 \mid \theta_1)$ is degenerate at θ_0 and $p^0(\theta_1 \mid \theta_0) = p^1(\theta_1 \mid \theta_0)$, the right-hand side being directly derived from $p^1(\theta_1)$.

These features are stressed by writing M_j (for model) instead of H_j (for hypothesis). Recall that this distinction is contextual rather than mathematical but we think the context of model choice is more general, in a sense to be made precise in the sequel. In particular, if the parameter of interest is λ, i.e., if the problem is actually deciding whether model M_0 or M_1 is preferred, the discussion of the preceding section applies. More specifically,

$$P(\lambda = 0 \mid x) = \frac{\pi_0 p^0(x)}{\pi_0 p^0(x) + (1 - \pi_0)p^1(x)} , \qquad (2.26)$$

where, again, $p^j(x)$ is the predictive density relative to model j,

$$p^j(x) = \int p^j(x \mid \theta_j)p^j(\theta_j) \, d\theta_j . \qquad (2.27)$$

Note that for the same reason as in Section 2.2 the evaluation of $p^j(x)$ requires $p^j(\theta_j)$ to be a proper (prior) distribution but also that, although formally present in the full Bayesian model, $p^j(\theta_{\bar{j}} \mid \theta_j)$ needs not be specified at all, it is only assumed to be implicitly an (arbitrary) proper distribution.

2.3.2. The encompassing approach: An overview
Let us pursue the approach of two models, M_0 and M_1, characterized by their parameters θ_0 and θ_1 but consider now that the parameter of interest is a function of θ_1, viz. $\varphi = f(\theta_1)$.

If model specification, prior elicitation, data handling and numerical computation were 'free' (or your research budget 'unlimited' in time and money) one could apply a 'full Bayesian approach', namely, start from the complete joint distribution $p(\lambda, \theta_0, \theta_1, x)$ sketched in the preceding section, marginalized into $p(\varphi, x)$ and therefrom evaluate $p(\varphi \mid x)$, which can also be decomposed as follows:

$$p(\varphi \mid x) = P(\lambda = 0 \mid x) p^0(\varphi \mid x) + P(\lambda = 1 \mid x) p^1(\varphi \mid x), \qquad (2.28)$$

where $p^j(\varphi \mid x)$ is the posterior distribution of φ obtained from each model separately, i.e., from each $p^j(\theta_0, \theta_1, x)$. Remember from the discussion of Section 2.2.1, that the evaluation of $P(\lambda \mid x)$, and therefore of $p(\varphi \mid x)$, is meaningful only under proper prior specification, i.e., when $p(\lambda, \theta_0, \theta_1)$ is a genuine probability measure. In practical cases, the formidable 'if' starting this paragraph makes this solution more often 'dully Bayesian' than 'fully Bayesian'!

Apart from the operationality requirement, there is another argument for thinking that the evaluation of $p(\varphi \mid x)$ as in (2.28) is not the end of the story. As far as M_0 and M_1 are two 'reasonable' models for explaining how data x has been generated or for helping in predicting a future realization of x, it is a standard practice in the history of science to look for 'parsimonious modelling' rather than keeping record of 'all reasonable models' and the use of the mixed model (2.28) reflects precisely the idea of keeping track of 'all reasonable models' as opposed to a search for as simple a model as possible (see also Dickey and Kadane, 1980; Hill, 1985).

If model 1 were as simple as model 0, inference on φ would then boil down to evaluating its posterior distribution $p^1(\varphi \mid x)$ from the sole model 1 viz. from $p^1(\theta_1 \mid x) \propto p^1(\theta_1) p^1(x \mid \theta_1)$; in such a case, neither model 0 nor $p^j(\theta_{\bar{j}} \mid \theta_j)$ would have any role. Suppose now that model 0 is 'definitively simpler'. A natural question is now: 'how far could we build an inference on φ relying on model 0 only?'. The very same question is also relevant when M_0 and M_1 are two intrinsically different models and the statistician is willing to consider M_0 as a 'true' (or 'valid') model with the idea that if M_0 were 'true' and M_1 were 'false', the inference on φ should be based on M_0 rather than on M_1, provided that φ can be interpreted under M_0.

Whereas the evaluation, in Section 2.3.1, of $P(\lambda \mid x)$, treats symmetrically M_0 and M_1, this last question introduces a basic asymmetry between M_0 and M_1: the parameter of interest is a function of θ_1 only and model 0 has *prima facie* an auxiliary role only. At this level of generality θ_0 may be a subvector of θ_1, or a function of θ_1 or a 'completely different' parameter and $f(\theta_1)$ might also be a function of θ_0 only: this will be examplified in Section 3. We consider the Bayesian extension of M_0, as in (2.25),

$$p^0(\theta_0, \theta_1, x) = p^0(\theta_0) p^0(x \mid \theta_0) p^0(\theta_1 \mid \theta_0), \qquad (2.29)$$

where the first two terms specify a standard Bayesian model on (x, θ_0) and the last term, designated as a 'Bayesian pseudo true value' (BPTV) calls for several remarks:

(i) Its name comes from the literature on the encompassing principle where a pseudo true value of a statistic means its expectation or its probabilistic limit under a model different from that where such a statistic 'naturally' appears. It is therefore a function of the parameters of that different model. This concept has known a wide diffusion in the classical literature since the seminal paper of Cox (1961). Its Bayesian version is in the form of a probability, conditional on the parameters of that different model, rather than a deterministic function of those parameters.

(ii) The role of a BPTV is to insert θ_1 into model 0 in order to make an inference on θ_1 possible from model M_0.

(iii) The role of a BPTV is also to 'interpret' θ_1 in the light of model M_0 whereas a classical pseudo true value is rather the interpretation of a statistic under M_0. This role gives full flexibility as far as adjusting the procedure to situation where θ_0 is a function of θ_1 or not, or where θ_1 keeps the same interpretation under M_0 and M_1 or not.

(iv) Finally the role of a BPTV is to make θ_0 a sufficient parameter in the Bayesian model extending M_0 (i.e., $x \perp\!\!\!\perp \theta_1 \mid \theta_0; p^0$ whereas $x \perp\!\!\!\perp \theta_1 \mid \theta_0; p$ and $x \perp\!\!\!\perp (\theta_1, \lambda); p$ are both false in general).

These ideas have been developed, from a Bayesian point of view in Florens (1990), Florens and Mouchart (1985, 1989), EBS (Chapter 3), Florens, Mouchart and Scotto (1983), and in various hitherto unpublished papers by Florens, Hendry, Richard and Scotto.

From (2.29) the posterior distribution of φ, $p^0(\varphi \mid x)$ can be evaluated as

$$p^0(\varphi \mid x) = E^0[p^0(\varphi \mid \theta_0) \mid x]$$

$$= \int p^0(\theta_0 \mid x) p^0(\varphi \mid \theta_0) \, d\theta_0 \,, \tag{2.30}$$

where $p^0(\varphi \mid \theta_0)$ is obtained by marginalizing on φ the BPTV $p^0(\theta_1 \mid \theta_0)$. Once we have built two posterior distributions on the parameter of interest, viz. $p^0(\varphi \mid x)$ and $p^1(\varphi \mid x)$, a natural question consists of asking how different they are.

If they are equal for $\varphi = \theta_1$, this means that any inference possible from model M_1 can be reproduced from model M_0 extended as in (2.29). This also means that model M_0 extracts from the observations all the information extracted by model M_1 along with the information on θ_0, the genuine parameter of M_0. In such a case we say that model M_0 *encompasses* model M_1. This concept may be viewed as a statistical translation of the idea that in order to be held as prevailing, a 'theory' M_0 should explain not only the observations generated by experiments naturally suggested by itself but also the observations generated by experiments suggested by a 'competing theory' M_1.

If $p^0(\varphi \mid x)$ and $p^1(\varphi \mid x)$ are not equal, one may measure how different they are by means of a discrepancy function $d(x)$ which may be a distance (D)

among distributions or among characteristics of distributions (typically, among expectations), or a divergence function (D),

$$d(x) = D(p^1(\varphi \mid x), p^0(\varphi \mid x)) . \tag{2.31}$$

The basic idea is the following: if $d(x)$ is 'small', the inference on φ, produced by model M_1, is 'almost' reproduced by model M_0. This suggests another way of testing model M_0 against model M_1, when the parameter of interest is φ and when the statistician is not willing to adopt a fully Bayesian attitude and let the model choice depend on prior probabilities of models.

The use of $d(x)$ for deciding to base the inference about φ on M_0 rather than on M_1 may be guided by the asymptotic behaviour of $d(x)$, and eventually of $p^0(\varphi \mid x)$ and of $p^1(\varphi \mid x)$. Instead of describing a general theory let us sketch the structure of a rather general situation. Let us denote $x_1^n = (x_1 \cdots x_n)$. Under M_0, i.e., under the joint distribution $p^0(\theta_0) p^0(x_1^n \mid \theta_0)$, $p^1(\varphi \mid x_1^n)$ typically (i.e., under 'good' conditions such as i.i.d. sampling with suitable smoothness of the likelihood) converges to a distribution degenerated at $f[g(\theta_0)]$ where $g(\theta_0)$ is the (classical) pseudo-true value of θ_1, i.e., the limit under $p^0(x_1^n \mid \theta_0)$ of the maximum likelihood estimator of θ_1 in $p^1(x_1^n \mid \theta_1)$ (see Berk, 1966). Under similar conditions $p^0(\theta_0 \mid x_1^n)$ also converges to a degenerate distribution, (see, e.g., EBS, Section 9.3 for cases more general than the i.i.d. one) but this is not sufficient to ensure the convergence of $p^0(\varphi \mid x_1^n)$ which crucially depends on the specification of the BPTV $p^0(\varphi \mid \theta_0)$ (derived from $p^0(\theta_1 \mid \theta_0)$). This analysis however shows that a 'natural' specification of the BPTV $p^0(\theta_1 \mid \theta_0)$ would be either a conditional distribution degenerated at the classical pseudo-true value $g(\theta_0)$ or a sample-size dependent specification $p_n^0(\theta_1 \mid \theta_0)$ such that $p_n^0(\theta_1 \mid x_n^n)$ converges to the same limit as $p^1(\theta^1 \mid x_1^1)$; some examples will be given later on. Under such a specification of the BPTV $p^0(\theta_1 \mid \theta_0)$ – or of $p_n^0(\theta_1 \mid \theta_0)$ – and with a suitable choice of the distance or of the divergence, $d(x_1^n)$ typically converges, under M_0, to a chi-square distribution and diverges to infinity under M_1. This situation is therefore formally similar to most testing problems in a sampling theory approach. It suggests either to evaluate a Bayesian p-value, i.e., $\mathrm{P}^0(d \geq d(x))$, or to build a critical partition of the sample space $S = S_0^{(k)} \cup S_1^{(k)}$ where

$$S_1^{(k)} = \{x \mid d(x) \geq k\} = d^{-1}([k, \infty)) , \tag{2.32}$$

where k is specified in such a way that $\mathrm{P}^0(S_1(k))$ obtains a prespecified level α, i.e., k in such that $\mathrm{P}^0(S_1(k)) = \alpha$.

Before illustrating those procedures by some examples, let us point out some remarks.

(i) Those procedures do not require the specification of π_0 because the problem is not any more to choose a model but rather to decide how to make inference on a specific parameter of interest. Even if φ is an injective transformation of θ_1, evaluating the predictive support of an observation x in favour of a model or of an hypothesis is different from evaluating the discrepancy between two inferences.

(ii) As far as the prior specification on (θ_0, θ_1) is concerned, $p^0(\theta_0)$ should be proper because $d(x)$ is to be calibrated against the predictive distribution $p^0(x)$ under M^0. However, $p^1(\theta_1)$ might be improper, provided that $p^1(\theta_1 | x)$ is well defined (i.e., that $p^1(x)$ is finite). As far as the BPTV is concerned, $p^1(\theta_0 | \theta_1)$ needs not be specified but $p^0(\theta_1 | \theta_0)$ is of crucial importance. Next subsection gives more comments on some issues related to the prior specification.

(iii) As mentioned earlier, a first motivation for model choice is parsimonious modelling. In a Bayesian framework, this leads to the idea of developing procedures based on partially specified Bayesian models. Remark (ii) gives, in this respect, a first rationale for the procedures just sketched. A second motivation for model choice is to introduce the statistician's own doubt about his own model. This is the idea that, in an exploratory study, as opposed to a completely specified decision problem, the statistician may like to entertain the idea of a 'small world', within which he is willing to be 'coherent' but, at the same time, to keep the idea of a 'grand world' where he is actually moving and the description of which is only partially specified in his small world. He is thus implicitly accepting the idea of receiving tomorrow information he would consider as unexpected today. Savage (1954, Sections 2.3 and 5.5) mentions the difficulty of delineating the border between the small world and the grand world. A possible interpretation of the critical partition $S = S_0(k) \cup S_1(k)$ is that a simple and operational approach of the small world is $S_0(k)$ under M_0 and that an observation in $S_0(k)$ leads to go on learning according to $p^0(\varphi | x)$ whereas an observation in $S_1(k)$ would lead to rethink the model without deciding today how it should be. In the same line, Pratt, Raiffa and Schalaiffer (1964) mention that the extensive-form analysis requires one more axiom than the normal-form analysis, namely their axiom 5 which says, heuristically, that present preferences among conditional lotteries are equivalent to conditional preferences among the corresponding unconditional lotteries. That supplementary axiom deals with the stability of the preferences with respect to the state of information. Again, the critical partition $S = S_0(k) \cup S_1(k)$ may be interpreted as describing the set $S_0(k)$ of observations x where one is willing to retain axiom 5 and eventually to use the learning rule specified by $p^0(\varphi | x)$ whereas an observations in $S_1(k)$ would lead to rethink the model without deciding today how it should be. Both interpretations make rather natural an a priori given level α defining k and its associated partition of the sample space S. The alternative to that specification would be a fully Bayesian approach sketched in the beginning of this subsection but also suggested as being of moderate interest in various actual situations.

2.3.3. Prior specification and Bayesian pseudo true-values

Comparing sampling theory procedures and Bayesian procedures, one may notice that in both types of procedures, M_0 and M_1 are not treated symmetrically. In particular the test statistics is calibrated against M_0 only. The main difference between those two types is the prior specification involved in the Bayesian procedure. The examples, in Section 3, illustrate how the prior specification is the main source of flexibility in the working of Bayesian procedures. Two types of prior elicitation are required, viz. the prior distributions for each model $p^j(\theta_j)$, $j = 0, 1$ and the Bayesian pseudo-true value $p^0(\theta_1 | \theta_0)$. We shall first discuss the specification of $p^0(\theta_1 | \theta_0)$. From a purely subjectivist point of view, $p^0(\theta_1 | \theta_0)$ represents, in probabilistic terms, the meaning of θ_1 under M_0, i.e., the interpretation of the parameter θ_1 if M_0 were considered as the 'true' model. It may nevertheless be helpful to suggest some devices for facilitating that specification. In broad terms, those devices are model-based and ensure reasonable asymptotic properties, viz. that $p^0(\varphi | x_1^n)$ and $p^1(\varphi | x_1^n)$ converge to a same limit. We sketch three such devices.

A first device is based on an idea close to Neyman–Pearson approach, namely that M_0 should be rejected only if there is kind of a compelling reason. Thus one may look for the BPTV which minimizes the expected discrepancy function $d(x)$,

$$p^0(\theta_1 | \theta_0) = \arg\inf \mathrm{E}^0[d(x)] \,, \tag{2.33}$$

where E^0 means the expectation under $p^0(x)$, and inf runs over the set of all conditional distribution of $(\theta_1 | \theta_0)$. This optimization raises, in general, difficult problems in the calculus of variation but an example in Section 3.3.1 will show how to obtain a restricted optimum in a specific case.

A second device is based on a Bayesian analogue of a sampling theory concept of pseudo-true value, i.e., the (sampling) expectation, under M_0, of the posterior distribution, in M_1, of θ_1 namely,

$$p_n^0(\theta_1 | \theta_0) = \int p^1(\theta_1 | x_1^n) p^0(x_1^n | \theta_0) \, \mathrm{d}x_1^n \,. \tag{2.34}$$

Section 3.1 gives an example of how operational such a device can be made. It may be mentioned that this construction typically leads to a BPTV depending on the sample size, and on the exogenous variables in case of conditional models, and in 'good' cases, produces a sequence of $p^0(\varphi | x_1^n)$ converging to a same degenerate limit as the sequence $p^1(\varphi | x_1^n)$.

A third class of devices consists of considering degenerate distributions, i.e.,

$$\mathrm{P}^0(\theta_1 \in F | \theta_0) = \mathbb{1}_{\{g(\theta_0) \in F\}} \,, \tag{2.35}$$

where $g : \Theta_0 \to \Theta_1$ (Θ_j in the parameter space for θ_j) is momentarily arbitrary. This implies

$$\mathrm{P}^0(\theta_1 \in F | x) = \mathrm{P}^0[g(\theta_0) \in F | x] \quad \text{and}$$
$$\mathrm{P}^0(\varphi \in Q | x) = \mathrm{P}^0[f[g(\theta_0)] \in Q | x] \,.$$

A natural specification for the function g is *a* sampling theory pseudo-true value. For instance, $g(\theta_0) = \mathrm{plim}^0 \, \hat{\theta}_{1,n}$ where $\hat{\theta}_{1,n}$ is a maximum likelihood (or another consistent) estimator of θ_1 in M_1 and plim^0 denotes plim under M_0 or, in a finite sample, $g_n(\theta_0) = \text{E}^0(\hat{\theta}_{1,n} \mid \theta_0)$ or $g_n(\theta_0) = \arg\inf_{\theta_1} D(p^0(x_1^n \mid \theta_0), p^1(x_1^n \mid \theta_1))$ for some divergence or distance function. In 'good' cases, all these specifications converge to a same limit and produce a sequence of $p^0(\varphi \mid x_1^n)$ converging to a same degenerate limit as the sequence $p^1(\varphi \mid x_1^n)$.

We like to stress that these three devices are offered as an eventual alternative to a purely subjectivist specification: whether a Bayesian statistician should or should not take care of the asymptotic properties of his procedure is not an issue to be discussed in this review. We simply suggest that different statisticians facing different real-life situations may be expected to adopt different positions on this issue.

Suppose now that the prior specification of $p^j(\theta_j)$ ($j = 0, 1$) and $p^0(\theta_1 \mid \theta_0)$ has been completed in some way. Experience with computer-assisted elicitation programs has shown the importance of cross-checking whether a prima facie elicitation correctly represents subjective opinions. In this context, it should be realized that the prior specification implies two distributions on θ_1, $p^1(\theta_1)$, directly specified, and $p^0(\theta_1) = \int p^0(\theta_0)p^0(\theta_1 \mid \theta_0)\,d\theta_0$. Thus, an important question is whether these distributions should or should not coincide (i.e., whether $\theta_1 \perp\!\!\!\perp \lambda$ or not). Similarly, when θ_0 is interpreted as a function of θ_1, one should ask whether $p^0(\theta_1 \mid \theta_0)$ and $p^1(\theta_1 \mid \theta_0)$, obtained from $p^1(\theta_1)$, should or should not coincide (i.e., whether $\theta_1 \perp\!\!\!\perp \lambda \mid \theta_0$ or not) and whether $p^1(\theta_0)$ and $p^0(\theta_0)$ should or should not coincide (i.e., whether $\theta_0 \perp\!\!\!\perp \lambda$ or not). These questions are the probabilistic translation of the question about the meaning of the parameters under alternative models. Finally, the prior specification also involves two predictive distributions, $p^0(x)$ and $p^1(x)$ but note that once they coincide, inference on λ looses any interests (i.e., once $\lambda \perp\!\!\!\perp x$, the prior and posterior probabilities of models coincide).

3. Testing Bayesians

3.1. Introduction

In this section we show, through some examples, how testing problems may be handled by statisticians open-minded towards Bayesian ideas. We call these statisticians 'Bayesians' and their activity we analyze 'testing'.

The first example starts form a rather standard problem: testing the significance of a regression coefficient in a multiple regression. Through this seemingly simple problem we try to illustrate the diversity, and propose a survey, of procedures suggested by the general approach sketched in Section 2. The next example handles a topic more genuinely relevant in econometrics, namely testing for a unit root.

3.2. Testing a regression coefficient: An overview of procedures

3.2.1. A simple problem of testing

Let us consider data $X = (y, Z)$ along with two conditional models,

$$M_0: y = bz_1 + u, \quad \text{i.e.,} \quad (y \mid Z, \theta_0, M_0) \sim \text{N}(bz_1, \sigma^2 I_n), \tag{3.1}$$

$$M_1: y = \beta z_1 + \gamma z_2 + u, \quad \text{i.e.,} \quad (y \mid Z, \theta_1, M_1) \sim \text{N}(\beta z_1 + \gamma z_2, \sigma^2 I_n), \tag{3.2}$$

where $Z = (z_1, z_2)$, $\theta_0 = b$, $\theta_1 = (\beta, \gamma)$ and with σ^2 known. Model M_0 *may* be interpreted as a restriction of model M_1 by means of '$\gamma = 0$' but this is not always suitable. For instance, an economist (M_1) could suggest that the quantity consumed (y) is explained by the price (z_2) and the income (z_1) and a sociologist could rather suggest that the quantity consumed is essentially a social-class issue and that income is a good proxy for his concept of social class; in such a case, the economist and the sociologist have different meanings in mind for the coefficient of z_1. A Bayesian statistician facing these two models may therefore want to recognize explicitly that these two models are deeply different and that b and β represent different concepts. From an operational point of view, this aspect will be modelled by means of the structure of the prior specification (including the specification of the BPTV). Note that the specification of known (and equal) variance is justified exclusively by an expository motivation: we want an example where all the analytical manipulations boil down to the exploitation of the multivariate normal distribution and nevertheless allow for rather subtle discussions. For the same reason, the prior distributions, in each model, are specified as follows:

$$(b \mid M_0) \sim \text{N}(b_p, \sigma^2 h_p^{-1}), \tag{3.3}$$

$$\begin{pmatrix} \beta \\ \gamma \end{pmatrix} \Big| M_1 \sim \text{N}\left(\begin{pmatrix} \beta_p \\ \gamma_p \end{pmatrix}, \sigma^2 H_p^{-1} \right). \tag{3.4}$$

If one wants to specify that the coefficient of z_1 has the same meaning under M_0 and under M_1, one may, although not formally necessary, write β instead of b but in any case, coherence in the prior specification implies that b is distributed under M_0 as $(\beta \mid \gamma = 0)$ under M_1, and consequently that $b_p = \beta_p + h_{12,p} h_{11,p}^{-1} \gamma_p$ and $h_p = h_{11,p}$ (here $h_{ij,p}$ is the element (i, j) of H_p). In such a case the specification $\gamma_p = 0$ may be recommended for symmetry reasons in which case, (3.3) and (3.4) become

$$(b \mid M_0) \sim \text{N}(\beta_p, \sigma^2 h_{11,p}^{-1}), \tag{3.5}$$

$$\begin{pmatrix} \beta \\ \gamma \end{pmatrix} \Big| M_1 \sim \text{N}\left[\begin{pmatrix} \beta_p \\ 0 \end{pmatrix}, \sigma^2 H_p^{-1} \right]. \tag{3.6}$$

Note also the following identity:

$$V(\gamma \mid M_1) = h_{11,p} |H_p|_p^{-1} . \tag{3.7}$$

In the following (3.5)–(3.6) are called, the 'coherent prior specification'.

3.2.2. Posterior probability of hypotheses

We first consider the traditional approach by means of posterior probability of hypotheses, posterior odds and Bayes factors. The literature is particularly abundant, see, in particular Dickey (1975), Geisser and Eddy (1979), Lempers (1971), Piccinato (1990), Poirier (1985), Spiegelhalter and Smith (1982), Zellner (1984), Zellner and Siow (1980). Thus we introduce a prior probability on models $\pi_0 = P(M_0)$. In order to evaluate the posterior probability we need the predictive distribution in each models.

$$(y \mid Z, M_0) \sim N[b_p z_1, \sigma^2 (I_n + h_p^{-1} z_1 z_1')] , \tag{3.8}$$

$$(y \mid Z, M_1) \sim N[\beta_p z_1 + \gamma_p z_2, \sigma^2 (I_n + Z H_p^{-1} Z')] . \tag{3.9}$$

This produces the Bayes factor

$$B_X(M_0; M_1) = \frac{|I_n + h_p^{-1} z_1 z_1'|^{-1/2} \exp[-(1/2\sigma^2) \| y - b_p z_1 \|_0^2]}{|I_n + Z H_p^{-1} Z'|^{-1/2} \exp[-(1/2\sigma^2) \| y - \beta_p z_1 - \gamma_p z_2 \|_1^2]} , \tag{3.10}$$

where

$$\| y - b_p z_1 \|_0^2 = (y - b_p z_1)'(I_n + h_p^{-1} z_1 z_1')^{-1}(y - b_p z_1) ,$$

$$\| y - \beta_p z_1 - \gamma_p z_2 \|_1^2 = (y - \beta_p z_1 - \gamma_p z_2)'(I_n + Z H_p Z')^{-1}$$
$$\times (y - \beta_p z_1 - \gamma_p z_2) .$$

The Bayes rule (2.13)–(2.16) may then then be written as

$$a^*(X) = a_1 \Leftrightarrow \frac{1}{\sigma^2} \{ \| y - b_p z_1 \|_0^2 - \| y - \beta_p z_1 - \gamma_p z_2 \|_1^2 \} \geqslant k_n(Z) , \tag{3.11}$$

where

$$k_n(Z) = -2 \ln \left[\frac{l_0}{l_1} \frac{1 - \pi_0}{\pi_0} |I_n + h_p^{-1} z_1 z_1'|^{1/2} |I_n + Z H_p^{-1} Z'|^{-1/2} \right] .$$

The LHS of (3.11) 'looks like' a sampling theory test statistics for testing the hypothesis '$\gamma = 0$' comparing the RSS under M_0 and M_1 with two important differences: (i) here the residuals are taken with respect to the predictive expectation in each model and the weighting matrix is given by the predictive precision matrix (ii) the critical values for the Bayesian decision problem, $k_n(Z)$, blends the utility values l_j, the prior specification π_0, h_p and H_p, and the exogenous variables Z. In particular, for any given data X, variations of π_0, h_p and H_p let $P(M_0 \mid X)$ sweep the whole interval $[0, 1]$.

Let us have a look at the asymptotic behaviour of (3.11). So we denote

$$V = \frac{1}{n} Z'Z = [v_{ij}], \quad i, j = 1, 2$$

$$v_{22.1} = \frac{|V|}{v_{11}} = v_{22} - v_{12}^2 v_{11}^{-1},$$

$$M_A = I_n - A(A'A)^{-1}A', \quad A : n \times k,$$

$$c = 2 \ln \frac{l_1}{l_0} \cdot \frac{\pi_0}{1 - \pi_0}.$$

For large n, the Bayesian critical region defined by (3.11) is approximately described as follows:

$$\frac{1}{\sigma^2} y'(M_{z_1} - M_Z)y \geq c + \ln h_p - \ln |H_p| + \ln v_{22.1} + \ln n. \tag{3.12}$$

Using (3.7), under the prior coherent specification (3.5)–(3.6), (3.12) simplifies as follows:

$$\frac{1}{\sigma^2} y'(M_{z_1} - M_Z)y \geq c + \ln V(\gamma \mid M_1) + \ln v_{22.1} + \ln n. \tag{3.13}$$

Both in (3.12) and (3.13), the LHS follows a chi-square distribution in sampling under M_0 so that the probability of rejecting (i.e., $a^*(X) = a_1$) tends to zero because of $\ln n$. Under M_1, the LHS increases as n whereas the RHS increases as $\ln n$ so that the testing procedure is consistent with a slowly increasing critical value. As mentioned before, a sharp hypothesis is often used in practice as an operational approximation for a 'small' interval. In such a case, a frequent criticism against a blind use of classical tests of sharp hypotheses is that for large samples, the null hypothesis is typically rejected, for any test the level of which is independent of the sample size. This is indeed the case for the rather general situation of a consistent test with continuous likelihood functions. Thus from a sampling point of view the Bayesian test may also be viewed as an operational way to make the level of the test a (decreasing) function of the sample size while keeping the test consistent. This also explains why, for large samples, a p-value may give a quite different message than a Bayesian test.

This example illustrates some difficulties raised by the use of noninformative prior distributions when evaluating Bayes factor or posterior probabilities of the hypothesis. Recall that, in general, the ratio of the predictive densities, under M_0 and M_1, is essentially undefined under noninformative prior specifications. Note also that (3.12) is undefined if $h_p = 0$ and/or $|H_p| = 0$, and that $\ln h_p / |H_p|$ may have an arbitrary limit if we let h_p and $|H_p|$ tend jointly to 0. In the case of coherent prior, the critical region, defined by (3.13) tends to become empty once $V(\gamma \mid M_1)$ tends to infinity.

It may be interesting to compare that two-sided test with a one-sided test. A simple case is the following. Let (3.2), (3.4) represent the sampling process and the prior specification respectively. This allows one to evaluate $P(\gamma \geq 0)$ and $P(\gamma \geq 0 \mid X)$ and to construct a Bayesian test with critical region characterized by $P(\gamma \geq 0 \mid X)/P(\gamma < 0 \mid X) < k$ where k is a constant defined as earlier. Note however, that, at variance from the two-sided test, this Bayesian test, is unambiguously defined even with improper priors (such as $P(\beta, \gamma) \propto 1$) and it is easily checked that the posterior probability of the null hypothesis and the sampling p-value are asymptotically equivalent, and that Lindley's paradox eventually vanishes.

3.2.3. Encompassing procedures

General procedures. Suppose first that the parameter of interest is the vector of regression coefficients. Thus in the notation of Section 2.4, we retain λ for the model labels, $\theta_0 = b$, and $\theta_1 = (\beta, \gamma) = \varphi$. Later on we shall also consider $\varphi = f(\theta_1) = \beta$ or $\varphi = \gamma$. We successively analyze several BPTVs, i.e., conditional distributions of $(\beta, \gamma \mid b, M_0)$ and always retain the same prior distributions as in (3.3) and (3.4). Consequently, for each model, the corresponding posterior distributions are

$$(b \mid X, M_0) \sim N(b_*, \sigma^2 h_*^{-1}) , \tag{3.14}$$

$$\left[\binom{\beta}{\gamma} \bigg| X, M_1 \right] \sim N\left[\binom{\beta_*}{\gamma_*}, \sigma^2 H_*^{-1} \right] , \tag{3.15}$$

where, as usual, see, e.g., Zellner (1971),

$$h_* = h_p + z_1' z_1 , \qquad b_* = h_*^{-1}(h_p b_p + z_1' y) , \qquad H_* = H_p + Z'Z ,$$

$$\binom{\beta_*}{\gamma_*} = H_*^{-1}\left[H_p \binom{\beta_p}{\gamma_p} + Z'y \right] .$$

Under the coherent prior specification (3.5)–(3.6), it may be shown, either through clumsy analytical manipulations or through a simple argument on conditioning on the parameter space (see EBS, Section 1.4.3.) that one also has that $(b \mid X, M_0) \sim (\beta \mid \gamma = 0, X, M_1)$, $b_* = E(\beta \mid \gamma = 0, X, M_1)$ and $\sigma^2 h_*^{-1} = V(\beta \mid \gamma = 0, X, M_1) = \sigma^2 h_{11,*}^{-1}$.

For illustrative purposes, let us concentrate the attention on the class of normal BPTVs, i.e.,

$$\left[\binom{\beta}{\gamma} \bigg| b, M_0 \right] \sim N[r_0 + r_1 b, \sigma^2 W] , \tag{3.16}$$

where $r_0, r_1 \in \mathbb{R}^2$ and W is a 2×2 SPDS matrix. This specification implies

$$\left[\binom{\beta}{\gamma} \Big| X, M_0 \right] \sim N[r_0 + r_1 b_*, \sigma^2 (h_*^{-1} r_1 r_1' + W)] . \qquad (3.17)$$

For the discrepancy function $d(X)$ let us consider the information theoretic divergence, i.e., $D(p, q) = \int \ln (p(x)/q(x)) p(x) \, dx$. The discrepancy between $p^0(\beta, \gamma \mid X)$ and $p^1(\beta, \gamma \mid X)$ is accordingly evaluated for the case of nonsingular variances as

$$
\begin{aligned}
d(X) &= D(p^0(\beta, \gamma \mid X), p^1(\beta, \gamma \mid X)) \\
&= \tfrac{1}{2} \Big[\ln |H_*|^{-1} - \ln |W + h_*^{-1} r_1 r_1'| + \operatorname{tr} H_* (W + h_*^{-1} r_1 r_1') \\
&\quad + \frac{1}{\sigma^2} \Big(r_0 + r_1 b_* - \binom{\beta_*}{\gamma_*} \Big)' H_* \Big(r_0 + r_1 b_* - \binom{\beta_*}{\gamma_*} \Big) - 2 \Big] .
\end{aligned}
$$
$$(3.18)$$

This statistic is to be calibrated against the predictive distribution under M_0. In this case, this is a normal distribution with parameters specified in (3.8) and $d(X)$ has the structure of a polynomial in y of degree 2, $u_0 + u_1' y + y' U_2 y$; the predictive distribution of $d(X)$ is therefore the distribution of the sum of a constant, a linear combination of normal variates and a linear combination of χ^2 variates; note that $u_1' y$ is not independent of $y' U_2 y$ but $u_1 = 0$ if r_0 is specified as

$$r_0 = H_*^{-1} H_p (\beta_p, \gamma_p)' - r_1 h_*^{-1} h_p b_p , \qquad (3.19)$$

a case to be met later on.

Bayesian pseudo-true value degenerate at the classical one. (i) Let us now consider some particular specifications of the BPTV in the class (3.16). A first case is a distribution degenerate at the classical pseudo-true value $(b \quad 0)'$. This corresponds to

$$r_0 = 0 , \qquad r_1 = (1 \quad 0)' , \qquad W = 0 \qquad (3.20)$$

in which case (3.17) becomes

$$\left[\binom{\beta}{\gamma} \Big| X, M_0 \right] \sim N\left[\binom{b_*}{0}, \sigma^2 \binom{h_*^{-1} \quad 0}{0 \quad \quad 0} \right] . \qquad (3.21)$$

Because (3.21) is a degenerate distribution, the information-theoretic discrepancy between the joint posterior distributions of $(\beta, \gamma)'$ does not anymore provide a suitable statistic for diverging to infinity for any data X. One may use another discrepancy function, such as a Prohorov distance or a Kolmogorov–Smirnov distance.

(ii) If γ is the only parameter of interest, i.e., in the notation of Section 2.4, $\varphi = f(\theta_1) = \gamma$, the comparison between $(\gamma \mid X, M_0) \sim \delta_{\{0\}}$ (the Dirac measure on 0) and $(\gamma \mid X, M_1) \sim N(\gamma_*, \sigma^2 \sigma_{22}^*)$ (where $\Sigma^* = [\sigma_{ij}^*] = H_*^{-1}$) can be done either in terms of some distance among probability measures, as above, or, more naturally, in terms of a distance among expected values. A natural such distance would be

$$d(X) = \frac{\gamma_*^2}{\sigma^2 \sigma_{22}^*} . \tag{3.22}$$

Again this statistic is easily calibrated against $p^0(y \mid Z)$ being, in this case, a general quadratic form in normal variates. When b and β are identified through the degenerate BPTV $\delta_{\{(b,0)'\}}$ and the prior specification satisfies $(b \mid M_0) \sim (\beta \mid \gamma = 0, M_1)$, one may also look at (3.22) as a function of two variables: the data X and the particular value of the parameter being tested (here $\gamma = 0$). Thus $d(X) = \rho(0, X)$ where

$$\rho(\gamma, X) = \frac{(\gamma_* - \gamma)^2}{\sigma^2 \sigma_{22}^*} . \tag{3.23}$$

Now $\rho(\gamma, X)$ is viewed as a measure of discrepancy between a particular hypothesis on γ and a particular data X. Florens and Mouchart (1989) have sketched a rather general approach based on that kind of function illustrated through this example. Identifying b and β means that $p^0(y \mid Z)$ may also be written as $p(y \mid Z, \gamma = 0)$ in the full Bayesian model characterized by a joint probability $p(\beta, \gamma, y \mid Z)$ and similarly $p^1(\gamma \mid X)$ becomes simply $p(\gamma \mid X)$. Now, $d(X) = \rho(0, X)$ may also be calibrated against that posterior distribution $p(\gamma \mid X)$. This is indeed in the spirit of Wald testing and also of evaluating a Bayesian p-value $\alpha_B(X)$ in the sense

$$\alpha_B(X) = P^1[\rho(\gamma, X) \geqslant \rho(0, X) \mid X] \tag{3.24}$$

or a posterior confidence interval in the sense of (see, e.g., Zellner, 1971)

$$P[|\gamma - \gamma_*| \leqslant |\gamma - 0| \mid X] . \tag{3.25}$$

But $d(X) = \rho(0, X)$ may also be calibrated against the marginal joint distribution $p(\gamma, y \mid Z)$. The general idea of this approach is to consider both the particular value γ_0 for an hypothesis on γ and a particular value X_0 of data $X = (y, Z)$ as two pieces of information (conditionally on Z), to measure their conformity with their distribution $p(\gamma, y \mid X)$ though a discrepancy function $\rho(\gamma, X)$ and to calibrate $\rho(\gamma_0, X_0)$ against $p(y \mid Z_0, \gamma_0)$, $p(\gamma \mid Z_0, y_0)$ or $p(\gamma, y \mid Z_0)$ according to whether the particular value γ_0, or y_0, or γ_0 and y_0 are deemed to be questionable.

(iii) Suppose now that β is the only parameter of interest. Under the normal prior specification in M_0 and in M_1 – see (3.3) and (3.4) – and a normal

BPTV – see (3.16) – the two posterior distributions of β are also normal, namely

$$(\beta \mid X, M_0) \sim (b \mid X, M_0) \sim N(b_*, \sigma^2 h_*^{-1}), \tag{3.26}$$

$$(\beta \mid X, M_1) \sim N(\beta_*, \sigma^2 h_*^{11}), \tag{3.27}$$

where h_*^{11} is the $(1,1)$ element of H_*^{-1}. Thus the discrepancy between $p^0(\beta \mid X)$ and $p^1(\beta \mid X)$ may be evaluated exactly as in (3.18), namely

$$\begin{aligned} d(X) &= D(p^0(\beta \mid \beta \mid X), p^1(\beta \mid X)) \\ &= \tfrac{1}{2}[\ln h_*^{11} - \ln h_*^{-1} + h_*^{-1}(h_*^{11})^{-1} + (\sigma^2 h_*^{11})^{-1}(b_* - \beta_*)^2 - 1]. \end{aligned} \tag{3.28}$$

Note that under the coherent prior specification (3.5)–(3.6), we also have that

$$(b_* - \beta_*)^2 = [h_*^{12}(h_*^{22})^{-1}\gamma_*]^2. \tag{3.29}$$

Putting together (3.28) and (3.29) one obtains a Bayesian version of Hausman's (1978) test, namely a test statistic based on a comparison of the inference on the parameter of interest β under the null ($p^0(\beta \mid X)$) and under the alternative hypothesis ($p^1(\beta \mid XZ)$) but the prior coherence implies that this is also a comparison of a marginal distribution on β ($p^1(\beta \mid X)$) and the conditional posterior distribution given the null hypothesis $p^0(\beta \mid X) = p^1(\beta \mid X, \gamma = 0)$. Analogously to the original Hausman test, $d(X) > 0$ even if $\gamma_* = E(\gamma \mid X, M_1) = 0$ and $d(X) = 0$ if and only if β and γ are a posteriori uncorrelated in Model 1, i.e., $h_*^{12} = 0$ and $h_*^{11} = h_*^{-1}$.

It should be noted that H_* and h_* involve both the prior specification and the value of the exogenous variable; a similar property has been noticed in a sampling theory framework by Hausman (1978). As in the previous case, $d(X)$ is distributed, under M_0, as a general quadratic form in normal variates. More details on the properties of that expression are given in Florens and Mouchart (1989).

Expected posterior distributions used as BPTV. A nondegenerate sample-based BPTV may be constructed by taking the sampling expectation, under M_0, of the posterior distribution of θ_1 under M_1,

$$p^0(\beta, \gamma \mid b, Z) = \int p^1(\beta, \gamma \mid X)p^0(y \mid Z, b)\, dy. \tag{3.30}$$

Embedding the two distributions of the RHS into a fictitious probability on $(\beta, \gamma, y \mid Z, b)$ with the condition of independence between (β, γ) and y given (Z, b), allows one to make use of standard manipulations on normal distributions, and to derive a normal distribution on $(\beta, \gamma \mid b, Z, M_0)$ with moments

$$E(\beta, \gamma \mid b, Z, M_0) = H_*^{-1}\left[H_p \begin{pmatrix} \beta_p \\ \gamma_p \end{pmatrix} + Z'z_1 b \right], \tag{3.31}$$

$$V(\beta, \gamma \mid b, Z, M_0) = \sigma^2 [H_*^{-1} + H_*^{-1} Z'ZH_*^{-1}]. \tag{3.32}$$

So one obtains a particular case of (3.16) with

$$r_0 = H_*^{-1} H_p \begin{pmatrix} \beta_p \\ \gamma_p \end{pmatrix},$$

$$r_1 = H_*^{-1} Z'z_1, \tag{3.33}$$

$$W = H_*^{-1} + H_*^{-1} Z'ZH_*^{-1} = H_*^{-1}(H_* + Z'Z)H_*^{-1}.$$

Note that for large n, and under rather general assumption on the behaviour of $Z_n'Z_n$ – such as $(Z_n'Z_n)^{-1} \to 0$ or $(1/n)Z_n'Z_n \to Q > 0 - (r_0, r_1, W_n)$ may be approximated by $(0, (1, 0)', 2(Z_n'Z_n)^{-1})$ and therefore $W_n \to 0$ as $n \to \infty$. Therefore this BPTV converges to a point mass on $(b, 0)'$. Thus, in finite samples, a discrepancy function $d(X)$ is evaluated as a particular case of (3.18) and is similarly calibrated against $p(y \mid Z, M_0)$. Note that a coherent prior specification does not affect (3.33) because (3.29) does not rely on the prior specification under M_0.

Optimal BPTV. Another strategy for specifying a BPTV is to look for a conditional distribution that minimizes the predictive expectation, under M_0, of a specified discrepancy function $d(X)$. Finding the general solution to this problem is a difficult question in the calculus of variations but restricted optima are often easily obtained. We now give an example of such a situation.

When the discrepancy function is the information theoretic divergence, the optimum BPTV is easily obtained in the class (3.16) of Gaussian BPTV when the prior specification is also normal as in (3.5)–(3.6). Indeed, in such a case, we have seen in (3.18) that $d(X)$ is a general quadratic form in y,

$$d(X) = u_0 + u_1'y + y'U_2 y, \tag{3.34}$$

where u_0, u_1 and U_2 are functions of the parameters of the BPTV, viz. r_0, r_1 and W, of the value of the exogenous variables Z and of the parameters of the prior distribution. As shown in Florens (1990), the solution of

$$\inf_{(r_0, r_1, W)} E^0[d(X)] \tag{3.35}$$

is given by

$$r_0^* = H_*^{-1}\left[H_p\binom{\beta_p}{\gamma_p} - h_p b_p \binom{1}{c} \right],$$

$$r_1^* = h_* H_*^{-1}\binom{1}{c}, \qquad (3.36)$$

$$W^* = H_*^{-1}\left[H_* - h_*\begin{pmatrix} 1 & c \\ c & c^2 \end{pmatrix} \right] H_*^{-1} = H_*^{-1} - h_*^{-1} r_1^*(r_1^*)',$$

where $c = (z_2' z_1)(z_1' z_1)^{-1}$ and provided that the term between brackets in W^* is SPDS, a condition to be commented upon later on. Note that the specification (3.36) satisfies condition (3.19) and therefore $u_1 = 0$ under an optimal BPTV. Asymptotically, under the usual conditions on $Z_n' Z_n$, we have

$$(r_{0,n}^*, r_{1,n}^*, W_n^*) \to (0, (1,0)', 0) \qquad (3.37)$$

and therefore the optimal BPTV also converges to a point mass on $(b, 0)'$. Under the optimal BPTV, the discrepancy function may be written as

$$d^*(X) = \frac{1}{2\sigma^2}(y' M_{z_1} Z H_*^{-1} Z' M_{z_1} y)$$

$$= \frac{1}{2\sigma^2} h_*^{22}(y' M_{z_1} z_2)^2, \qquad (3.38)$$

where h_*^{22} is the $(2,2)$-th element of H_*^{-1}. Note that under M_0, $\sigma^{-1} M_{z_1} y \sim N(0, I_{(n)})$ and therefore $d^*(X)$, under M_0, is distributed as a linear combination of independent $\chi^2_{(1)}$ variates. Note also that for large n, h_*^{22} may be approximated by $z_2' M_{z_1} z_2$ and $d^*(X)$ is approximately equal to a Wald test statistics.

Let us have a closer look on the term between brackets in W_* appearing in (3.36),

$$H_* - h_*\begin{pmatrix} 1 & c \\ c & c^2 \end{pmatrix} = H_p - h_p\begin{pmatrix} 1 & c \\ c & c^2 \end{pmatrix} + z_2' M_{z_1} z_2\begin{pmatrix} 0 & 0 \\ 0 & 1 \end{pmatrix}. \qquad (3.39)$$

Clearly this term is nonnegative only if the $(1,1)$ element of H_p is not smaller than h_p, i.e., $V(\beta \mid \gamma, M_1) \leq V(b \mid M_0)$ and this condition is also sufficient for large n because asymptotically $z_2' M_{z_1} z_2$ diverges to infinite whereas c tends to a limit. For a coherent prior specification, that condition is met through equality. Note also that when (3.39) is not SPDS, the optimum value of W is not given by (3.36) and should be obtained through a constrained optimization; such would be the case when the prior specification is noninformative under M_1 (i.e., $H_p = 0$) or for some values of z_2 in finite samples.

3.3. Testing for unit roots

Recent econometric literature has paid considerable attention to a proper treatment of nonstationary time-series. At the level of modelling, most effort is concerned with the extraction of a stationary component, either a conditional one, though the introduction of nonstationary regressors (trend and/or exogenous variables) or, a marginal one, through differencing up to a suitable order (or, more generally, looking for cointegrated components). Nelson and Plosser (1982) have been path breaking in this field by calling attention to the empirical relevance of the problem.

The discussion adopted a somewhat more controversial tone when it arrived at comparing Bayesian and sampling theory methods and became definitely hot when this comparison considered the problem of testing for unit root. A recent issue of the *Journal of Applied Econometrics* (Vol. 6, October–December 1991) offered a forum for exposing conflicting views, introduced by a 'critical' paper by Phillips (1991a,b) along with his response to eight comments viz. Koop and Steel (1991), Leamer (1991), Kim and Maddala (1991), Poirier (1991), Schotman and Van Dijk (1991b), Stock (1991), De Jong and Whiteman (1991) and Sims (1991). That issue provides an interesting and up-dated 'state of the art' reworking past arguments and supplying new ones, in particular in terms of new empirical evidence on both simulated and actual data. Other recent contributions also include Schotman and Van Dijk (1991a) and hitherto unpublished papers by Lubrano.

As often happened in such cases, the temperature of the discussion is raised by mixing several ingredients. Some of those ingredients are of general nature such as questions about the foundations and relevance of Bayesian and of sampling theory methods, the relevance of the problems raised by Bayesian inference under improper prior specification, the numerical problems such as the relative merits of the Laplace approximation of posterior distributions, the possibly striking difference between sampling characteristics, such as p-value, and the posterior characteristics, such as posterior odds or Bayes factors and, last but not least, the use of affectionate qualifications such as 'Sterile ideas', 'unreasonable', 'logically unsound' or 'wrong headed and unenlightening'. One ingredient, at least, is rather particular to the topic, and possibly explains the level of the temperature, namely that around the unit roots the likelihood is smooth in finite samples but asymptotically discontinuous: this issue has been raised in Dickey and Fuller (1979), see also Phillips (1987, 1991a,b). Thus Bayesian methods, being essentially of a small sample nature, may be expected to diverge from asymptotic sampling methods; also Bayesian inference based on improper prior specification, justifiable (when possible!) as providing asymptotic approximation, may also be expected to raise the controversies generally associated with the use of such prior specifications.

Clearly we cannot do justice to all arguments in the framework of this survey. The main ideas may nevertheless be sketched by discussing the simplest case, namely the univariate AR(1) case. Denoting $y_i^j = (y_i, y_{i+1}, \ldots, y_j)$ for any $i < j$, let us consider

$$(y_t \mid y_0^{t-1}) \sim N(\rho y_{t-1}, \sigma^2), \quad 1 \leq t \leq T. \tag{3.40}$$

In this dynamic context, observations are naturally indexed by t and T

becomes the sample size. In what follows, we only consider models conditional to y_0, which is therefore not modelled, without discussing under which circumstances is such a conditioning admissible. Thus the likelihood function is derived from

$$p(y_1^T \mid y_0, \rho, \sigma^2) = (2\pi)^{-(T/2)} \sigma^{-T} \exp - \frac{1}{2\sigma^2} \sum_{1 \leqslant t \leqslant T} (y_t - \rho y_{t-1})^2 \,.$$

$$(3.41)$$

From a sampling point of view, the asymptotic distribution associated with the sequence $p(\hat{\rho}_T \mid y_0, \rho, \sigma^2)$ – where $\hat{\rho}_T$ is the MLE of ρ based on y_0^T – is terribly different when $\rho < 1$, $\rho = 1$ or $\rho > 1$. This feature possibly produces disconnected (and therefore nonconvex) confidence regions. From a Bayesian point of view, a particular value of ρ is irrelevant as far as, once a prior distribution is assigned to (ρ, σ), the evaluation of the posterior distribution will run smoothly for any finite sample size, possibly calling for simple numerical integrations. However, for testing the hypothesis $\rho = 1$, the pathologies of the likelihood function implies a particular sensitivity to the prior specification (see Sims and Uhlig, 1991). We shall first discuss the prior specification and next the choice of a particular testing procedure.

Consider ing the decomposition (2.17)–(2.18) of the prior distribution, we first discuss the specification of $p(\rho, \sigma \mid \rho \neq 1)$. In general, one finds in the literature prior distributions of the form

$$p(\rho, \sigma \mid \rho \neq 1) \propto \frac{1}{\sigma} g_1(\rho)$$

$$(3.42)$$

with no discussion of the specification relative to σ. The alternative hypothesis is implicitly defined by the support of the second component. One finds at least three such specifications: (i) Sims (1988) employs $g_1(\rho) = \mathbb{1}_{\mathbb{R}}(\rho)$, i.e., the density of Lebesgue measure on the real line, therefore excluding no value of ρ and accepting eventually explosive models. Remember that Lebesgue measure favours extreme values in the sense that the measure of the interval $(-1, +1)$ relative to the measure of $(-a, +a)$ tends to zero as a tends to infinity. (ii) Schotman and Van Dijk (1991a) starts with a uniform proper distribution of ρ on the bounded interval $[a, 1]$, i.e., $g_1(\rho) = (1/(1-a))\mathbb{1}_{[a,1]}(\rho)$ (with $-1 < a < 1$) but leaves the component of σ improper. Thus their alternative hypothesis is $[a, 1]$, i.e., a stationary model (a priori a.e.). They show that the result of testing ρ crucially depends on the value of a and suggest an empirical procedure for specifying a and further develop their analysis in Schotman and Van Dijk (1991b). (iii) Phillips (1991a) criticizes the case of flat prior for favouring unduly the stationary use and argues instead for the case of Jeffrey's noninformative prior, i.e., $g_1(\rho) = (1 - \rho^2)^{-1/2} \{ T - (1 - \rho^{2T})[(1 - \rho^2)^{-1} - \sigma^{-2} y_0^2] \}^{1/2} \mathbb{1}_{\mathbb{R}}(\rho)$, taking again the real line as alternative hypothesis. He also uses the Laplace approximation for analyzing the posterior distribution and reinterprets the series analyzed by Nelson and Plosser (1982).

As far as the choice of a testing procedure is concerned, two approaches have been proposed. A first one, in line with Lindley (1961), starts with a smooth prior specification, i.e., $P(\rho = 1) = 0$ and evaluates the posterior probability either of regions around 1 with the idea of asking whether the unit root lies in a high enough posterior probability region as in Phillips (1991a), or of regions of nonstationarity such as $\{\rho > 1\}$ or $\{\rho < 1\}$ as in Phillips (1991a), Kim and Maddala (1991) or Schotman and Van Dijk (1991b). The advantage of that class of procedures is to make the economy of eliciting a prior probability for the null hypothesis and to be well defined even under improper prior specification. A second approach, maybe more traditional in the Bayesian establishment, evaluates Bayes factor, posterior odds or posterior probability of hypotheses. As mentioned in Section 2.2.1, this class of procedures requires a proper prior specification along with a strictly positive mass on the null hypothesis; Schotman and Van Dijk (1991a,b) report problems when this requirement is overlooked.

Extending model (3.40) to more complex structures raises new difficulties. For instance when $y_t = \mu + u_t$ with $u_t = \rho u_{t-1} + \varepsilon_t$ and $\varepsilon_t \sim \mathrm{IN}(0, \sigma^2)$, a local identification problem appears at the null hypothesis $\rho = 1$. This issue, similar to the rank condition in simultaneous equation model, see Maddala (1976) and Drèze and Mouchart (1990), is analyzed in the present context by Schotman and Van Dijk (1991b) under a partially noninformative prior specification. The same paper, along with Phillips (1991a), also considers an intercept term and a linear trend in order to analyze further on problems of transient dynamics or of testing trend stationarity against difference stationarity.

4. Other contributions

One of the first issues to be faced by the author(s) of a survey is to bound the field to be surveyed. In this survey we put much emphasis on two ideas. Firstly hypothesis testing and model choice have been dealt with as a single class of problems met with so strikingly varied motivations that no clear distinction among them seems to be operationally fruitful. Secondly Bayesian thinking is rich enough to accommodate to that variety of situations and is much more flexible that a mechanical prior-to-posterior transformation; in particular, the predictive distributions have been shown to play an important role for this class of problems.

Putting emphasis on general inference, on model label or on parameters of interest, has led to put less emphasis on solving specific decision problems. Thus strictly decision oriented procedures have at time been alluded to but not dealt with in any systematic way. This is, in particular, the case of model choice procedures based on specific criteria such as AIC or BIC with different degrees of involvement with the Bayesian idea. This literature is rather vast but somewhat disconnected from the main theme considered in this survey. The interested reader may consult Schwartz (1978) or Zellner (1978).

Section 3 has treated two exemplary fields of application but many more have been considered in the literature. A notable one is the testing for exogeneity considered by Florens and Mouchart (1989), Lubrano, Pierse and Richard (1986), Steel and Richard (1991). Many contributions have also dealt with the problem of specification testing in linear models, as in Bauwens and Lubrano (1991). A long list of applied works using Bayesian testing has been omitted. We just quote as an example a recent issue of the *Journal of Econometrics* (see, e.g., Connolly, 1991; Koop, 1991; McCulloch and Perossi, 1991; Moulton, 1991) and Shanken (1987).

Acknowledgment

The authors are particularly indebted to J. H. Drèze for discussions and comments on a preliminary version and to L. Bauwens, S. Larribeau-Nori, E. Moreno and J. Rodriguez-Poo for some very useful remarks. The authors are also deeply indebted to J. F. Richard with whom many ideas involving the encompassing principles have been elaborated. They are also thankful to J. Bouoiyour for bibliographical assistance. The authors retain however full responsibility, in particular for the kind of presentation they have finally adopted.

References

Bauwens, L. and M. Lubrano (1991). Bayesian diagnostics for heterogeneity. *Ann. Econ. Statis.* **20/21**, 17–40.
Berger, J. O. (1985). *Statistical Decision Theory and Bayesian Analysis.* 2nd ed., Springer, New York.
Berger, J. O. (1986). Are *p*-values reasonable measures of accuracy. In: I. S. Francis et al., eds., *Pacific Statistical Congress.* North-Holland, Amsterdam.
Berger, J. O. and D. Berry (1988). Statistical analysis and the illusion of objectivity. *Amer. Sci.* **76**, 159–165.
Berger, J. O. and M. Delampady (1987). Testing precise hypotheses. *Statist. Sci.* **2**, 317–352.
Berger, J. O. and T. Sellke (1987). Testing a point null hypothesis: The irreconcilability of *p*-values and evidence. *J. Amer. Statist. Assoc.* **82**, 112–122.
Berk, R. H. (1966). Limiting behavior of posterior distributions when the model is incorrect. *Ann. Math. Statist.* **37**, 51–58.
Bernardo, J. M. (1980). A Bayesian analysis of classical hypothesis testing. In: J. M. Bernardo, M. H. De Grout, D. V. Linley and A. F. M. Smith, eds., *Bayesian Statistics.* The University Press, Valencia, 605–618.
Casella, G. and R. L. Berger (1987). Reconciling Bayesian and frequentist evidence in the one-sided testing problem. *J. Amer. Statist. Assoc.* **82**, 106–111.
Connolly, R. A. (1991). Posterior odds analysis of the weekend effect. *J. Econometrics* **49**, 51–104.
Cox, D. R. (1961). Tests of separate families of hypotheses. In: *Proc. 4th Berkeley Sympos. on Mathematical Statistics and Probability,* Vol. 1. University of California Press, Berkeley, CA, 105–123.
De Groot, M. H. (1970). *Optimal Statistical Decisions.* McGraw-Hill, New York.

De Groot, M. H. (1973). Doing what comes naturally: Interpreting a tail area as a posterior probability or as a likelihood ratio. *J. Amer. Statist. Assoc.* **68**, 966–969.

De Jong, D. N. and C. H. Whiteman (1991). The case for trend-stationarity is stronger than we thought. *J. Appl. Econometrics* **6**, 413–422.

Dickey, D. A. and W. A. Fuller (1979). Distribution of the estimators for autoregressive time series with a unit root. *J. Amer. Statist. Assoc.* **74**, 427–451.

Dickey, J. M. (1975). Bayesian alternatives to the *F*-test and least-squares estimates in the normal linear model. In: S. E. Fienberg and A. Zellner, eds., *Studies in Bayesian Econometrics and Statistics in Honour of L. J. Savage.* North-Holland, Amsterdam.

Dickey, J. M. (1977). Is the tail area useful as an approximate Bayes factor? *J. Amer. Statis. Assoc.* **72**, 138–142.

Dickey, J. M. and J. Kadane (1980). Bayesian decision theory and the simplification of models. In: J. Kmenta and J. Ramsey, eds., *Evaluation of Econometric Models.* Academic Press, New York, 245–268.

Drèze, J. and M. Mouchart (1990). Tales of testing Bayesians. In: R. A. L. Carter, J. Dutta and A. Ullah, eds., *Contribution to Economic Theory.* Springer, New York, 345–366.

Florens, J. P. (1990). Parameter sufficiency and model encompassing. In: *Essays in Honor of Edmond Malinvaud*, Vol. 3. MIT Press, Cambridge, MA, 115–136.

Florens, J. P. and M. Mouchart (1985). Model selection: Some remarks from a Bayesian viewpoint. In: J. P. Florens, M. Mouchart, J. P. Raoult and L. Simar, eds., *Model Choice.* Publications des Facultés Universitaires Saint-Louis, Bruxelles, 27–44.

Florens, J. P. and M. Mouchart (1989). Bayesian specification test. In: B. Cornet and H. Tulkens, eds., *Contributions to Operations Research and Economics.* MIT Press, Cambridge, MA, 467–490.

Florens, J. P., M. Mouchart and J. M. Rolin (1990). *Elements of Bayesian Statistics.* Marcel Dekker, New-York.

Florens, J. P., M. Mouchart and S. Scotto (1983). Approximate sufficiency on the parameter space and model selection. In: *44th Session Internat. Statist. Inst.: Contributed Papers*, Vol. 2, 763–766.

Gaver, K. M. and M. S. Geisel (1974). Discriminating among alternative models: Bayesian and Non-Bayesian methods. In: P. Zarembka, ed., *Frontiers in Econometrics.* Academic Press, New York, 49–77.

Geisser, S. and W. F. Eddy (1979). A predictive sample approach to model selection. *J. Amer. Statist. Assoc.* **74**, 153–160.

Good, I. J. (1985). Weight of evidence: A brief survey. In: J. M. Bernado, M. H. De Groot, D. V. Lindley and A. F. M. Smith, eds., *Bayesian Statistics*, Vol. 2. North-Holland, Amsterdam.

Hausman, J. A. (1978). Specification tests in econometrics. *Econometrica* **46**, 1251–1272.

Hill, B. (1982). Comment on Lindley's paradox, by G. Shafer. *J. Amer. Statist. Assoc.* **77**, 344–347.

Hill, B. (1985). Some subjective Bayesian considerations in the selection of models. *Econometric Rev.* **4**, 191–282.

Hill, B. (1990). A theory of Bayesian data analysis. In: S. Geisser, J. S. Hodges, S. J. Press and A. Zellner, eds., *Bayesian and Likelihood Methods in Statistics and Econometrics.* Elsevier, Amsterdam, 49–73.

Hodges, J. S. (1990). Can/may Bayesian do pure tests of significance? In: S. Geisser, J. S. Hodges, S. J. Press and A. Zellner, eds., *Bayesian and Likelihood Methods in Statistics and Econometrics.* Elsevier, Amsterdam, 75–90.

Hwang, J. T., G. Casella, C. Robert, M. T. Wells and R. H. Farrel (1992). Estimation of accuracy in testing. *Ann. Statist.* **20**(1), 490–509.

Jeffreys, H. (1967). *Theory of Probability*. 3rd revised ed., Oxford Univ. Press, London.

Kim, I. M. and G. S. Maddala (1991). Flats priors vs. ignorance priors in the analysis of the AR(1) model. *J. Appl. Econometrics* **6**, 375–380.

Klein, R. W. and S. J. Brown (1984). Model selection when there is minimal prior information. *Econometrica* **52**, 1291–1312.

Koop, G. (1991). Cointegration tests in present value relationships: A Bayesian look at the bivariate properties of stock prices and dividends. *J. Econometrics* **49**, 105–140.

Koop, G. and M. F. J. Steel (1991). A comment on 'To criticize the critics: An objective Bayesian analysis of stochastic trends' by P. C. B. Phillips. *J. Appl. Econometrics* **6**, 365–370.

Leamer, E. E. (1978). *Specification Searches: Ad Hoc Inferences with Non-experimental Data*. Wiley, New York.

Leamer, E. E. (1983). Model choice and specification analysis. In: Z. Griliches and M. D. Intriligator, eds., *Handbook of Econometrics*, Vol. 1. North Holland, Amsterdam.

Leamer, E. E. (1991). Comment on 'To criticize the critics. *J. Appl. Econometrics* **6**, 371–374.

Lempers, F. B. (1971). *Posterior Probabilities of Alternative Linear Models*. Rotterdam Univ. Press, Rotterdam.

Lindley, D. V. (1957). A statistical paradox. *Biometrika* **44**, 187–192.

Lindley, D. V. (1961). The use of prior probability distributions in statistical inference and decisions. In: *Proc. 4th Berkeley Sympos. on Mathematical Statistics and Probability*, Vol. 1. Univ. of California Press, Berkeley, CA, 453–468.

Lindley, D. V. (1971). *Bayesian Statistics, A Review*. Regional Conf. Ser. in Appl. Math., SIAM, Philadelphia, PA.

Lubrano, M., R. G. Pierse and J. F. Richard (1986). Stability of a U.K. money demand: A Bayesian approach to testing exogeneity. *Rev. Econ. Stud.* **53**, 603–634.

Maddala, G. S. (1976). Weak priors and sharp posteriors in simultaneous equation models. *Econometrica* **44**, 345–351.

McCulloch, R. and P. E. Rossi (1991). A Bayesian approach to testing the arbitrage pricing theory. *J. Econometrics* **49**, 141–168.

Moreno, E. and J. A. Cano (1989). Testing a point null hypothesis: Asymptotic robust Bayesian analysis with respect to priors given on a subsigma field. *Internat. Statist. Rev.* **57**, 221–232.

Moulton, B. R. (1991). A Bayesian Approach to regression selection and estimation, with application to a price index for radio services. *J. Econometrics* **49**, 169–194.

Nelson, C. R. and C. Plosser (1982). Trends and random walks in macroeconomic time series: Some evidence and implications. *J. Monetary Econ.* **10**, 138–162.

Phillips, P. C. B. (1987). Time series regression with a unit root. *Econometrica* **55**, 277–301.

Phillips, P. C. B. (1991a). To criticize the critics: An objective Bayesian analysis of stochastic trends. *J. Appl. Econometrics* **6**, 333–364.

Phillips, P. C. B. (1991b). Bayesian routes and unit roots: De rebus prioribus semper est disputandum. *J. Appl. Econometrics* **6**, 435–474.

Piccinato, L. (1990). Sull'interpretazione del Livello di Significativita'Osservato. In: *Scritti in Omaggio a Luciano Daboni*. Edizioni Lint, Trieste, 199–213.

Poirier, D. J. (1985). Bayesian hypothesis testing in linear models with continuously induced conjugate priors across hypotheses In: J. M. Bernado, M. H. De Groot, D. V. Lindley and A. F. M. Smith, eds., *Bayesian Statistics*, Vol. 2. North-Holland, Amsterdam, 711–722.

Poirier, D. J. (1988). Frequentist and subjectivist perspectives on the problems of model building in economics. *J. Econ. Perspectives* **2**, 121–170.

Poirier, D. J. (1991). To criticize the critics: An objective Bayesian analysis of stochastic trends. *J. Appl. Econometrics* **6**, 381–386.

Pratt, J., H. Raiffa and R. Schlaifer (1964). Foundations of decisions under uncertainty: An elementary exposition. *J. Amer. Statist. Assoc.* **59**, 353–375.

Raftery, A. E. (1986). A note on Bayes factors for log-linear contingency table models with vague prior information. *J. Roy. Statist. Soc.* **48**, 249–250.

Rubin, H. (1971). A decision-theoretic approach to the problem of testing a null hypothesis. In: S. S. Gupta and J. Yackel, eds., *Statistical Decision Theory and Related Topics*. Academic Press, New York.

Savage, L. J. (1954). *The Foundations of Statistics*. Wiley, New York.

Schotman, P. and H. Van Dijk (1991a). A Bayesian analysis of the unit root in real exchange rates. *J. Econometrics* **49**, 195–238.

Schotman, P. and H. Van Dijk (1991b). On Bayesian routes to unit roots. *J. Appl. Econometrics* **6**, 387–402.

Schwarz, G. (1978). Estimating the dimension of a model. *Ann. Statist.* **6**, 461–464.

Shafter, G. (1982). Lindley's paradox (with discussion). *J. Amer. Statist. Assoc.* **77**, 325–351.

Shanken, H. (1987). A Bayesian approach to testing portfolio efficiency. *J. Financ. Econ.* **18**, 195–215.

Sims, C. A. (1988). Bayesian skepticism on unit root econometrics. *J. Econ. Dynamics Control* **12**, 463–474.

Sims, C. A. (1991). Comment on 'To criticize the critics' by P. C. B. Phillips. *J. Appl. Econometrics* **6**, 423–434.

Sims, C. A. and H. Uhlig (1991). Understanding unit rooters: A helicopter tour. *Econometrica* **59**, 1591–1600.

Spiegelhalter, D. J. and A. F. M. Smith (1982). Bayes factors for linear and log-linear models with vague prior information. *J. Roy. Statist. Soc. Ser.* B **44**, 377–387.

Steel, M. and J. F. Richard (1991). Bayesian multivariate exogeneity analysis: An application to UK demand equation. *J. Econometrics* **49**, 239–274.

Stock, J. H. (1991). Bayesian approaches to the 'unit root' Problem: A comment. *J. Appl. Econometrics* **6**, 403–412.

Zellner A. (1971). *An Introduction to Bayesian Inference in Econometrics*. Wiley, New York.

Zellner, A. (1978). Jeffreys Bayes posterior odds ratio and the Akaike information criterion for discriminating between models. *Econ. Lett.* **1**, 337–342.

Zellner, A. (1984). Posterior odds ratios for regression hypotheses: General considerations and some specific results. In: *Basic Issue in Econometrics*. Univ. of Chicago Press, Chicago, IL, 275–304.

Zellner, A. and A. Siow (1980). Posterior odds ratios for selected regression hypotheses. In: J. M. Bernado, M. H. De Groot, D. V. Lindley, and A. F. M. Smith, eds., *Bayesian Statistics*. University Press, Valencia, 585–603. Reply, 638–643.

G. S. Maddala, C. R. Rao and H. D. Vinod, eds., *Handbook of Statistics, Vol. 11*

12

Pseudo-Likelihood Methods

Christian Gourieroux and Alain Monfort

1. Introduction

The maximum likelihood methods of inference are certainly among the more important tools that can be used by statisticians. The success of these methods is due to their high degree of generality and to their nice asymptotic properties: consistency, asymptotic normality, efficiency . . . . However, it is clear that, a priori, these properties are valid only when the model is well-specified, i.e., if the true probability distribution of the observations belongs to the set of probability distributions which is used to define the likelihood function. This restriction is important since one can never be sure that the model is correctly specified and, therefore, it is worth considering the properties of the maximum likelihood methods when this assumption is not made; in this case the likelihood function is called a pseudo- (or quasi-) likelihood function. There are three kinds of situations in which a pseudo-likelihood approach can be advocated. In the first situation we are prepared to make assumptions about some conditional moments of the endogenous variables given the exogenous variables, but not on the whole conditional distribution. In this semiparametric context, the likelihood function is not defined, however it is possible to define pseudo-likelihood functions based on a family of density functions which does not necessarily contain the true density but which is compatible with the assumptions on the moments. The more familiar example of the previous situation is probably the nonlinear regression model with a constant variance, in which the maximization of the pseudo-likelihood function associated to the Gaussian family reduces to the nonlinear least squares and provides a consistent and asymptotically normal estimator (see Jennrich, 1969; Malinvaud, 1970; Gallant, 1987; Gallant and White, 1988; other well-known applications of Gaussian pseudo-likelihood method can be found in the simultaneous equation model (see, e.g., Hood and Koopmans, 1953, in dynamic models (see, e.g., Hannan, 1970, Chapters 6 and 7) or in serially correlated limited dependent variable models (Robinson, 1982, Gourieroux and Monfort, 1985). The second context in which the pseudo-likelihood approach is useful is the parametric situation where a likelihood function is available but numerically untractable. In this case we can think to use a simpler likelihood function which, as in the previous case, is adapted for some moments; moreover, since the moments are not likely to possess a closed form, simulated pseudo-likelihood techniques may be used (see Laroque and Salanié, 1989, 1990; Gourieroux and Monfort, 1991a, 1992). The third situation in which the pseudo-likelihood techniques are relevant is the nonnested hypotheses context. In this case there are two possible parametric models and an important point is the asymptotic behaviour of the pseudo-maximum likelihood estimator of the parameter of one model when the true probability distribution belongs to the other model (see Cox, 1961, 1962; Pesaran, 1974; Gourieroux, Monfort and Trognon, 1983b, Mizon and Richard, 1986); another important point is the asymptotic behaviour of the so-called pseudo-true value (Sawa, 1978) of the parameter of one model evaluated at the maximum likelihood estimator of the other model. These statistics are useful either for testing procedures or for model selection.

The aim of this chapter is to describe the properties of the inference methods based on pseudo-likelihood functions. In Section 2 we define more precisely the pseudo-likelihood methods. In Section 3 we describe the pseudo-maximum likelihood (PML) methods adapted for the mean (PML1) and we stress that they provided consistent estimators of the parameters appearing in the (conditional) mean if, and only if, the pseudo-likelihood function is based on a linear exponential family; moreover, the asymptotic normality is presented and a kind of Cramér–Rao bound is given. In Section 4, it is seen that this bound can be reached if the pseudo-likelihood function is based on a generalized linear exponential family and if a correct specification of the second-order moments is used; this method is called a quasi generalized PML method. In Section 5 we consider pseudo-likelihood methods which are adapted for the first two moments (PML2) and we show that they provide consistent estimators of the parameters of interest if and only if the pseudo-likelihood function is based on a quadratic exponential family. Section 6 considers the problem of hypothesis testing in the PML context. Section 7 studies the case where the moments do not have a closed form and must be replaced by approximations based on simulations. In Section 8, we describe the role of PML methods for testing nonnested hypotheses, and, in Section 9, we consider their role for model selection. Some remarks are gathered in a conclusion. The material presented in this chapter is mainly based on papers by Gourieroux, Monfort and Trognon (hereafter GMT) (1983a,b, 1984a,b) to which the reader is referred for the proofs.

2. General presentation of the pseudo-likelihood methods

Note that what we call a 'pseudo-likelihood' function is sometimes called a 'quasi-likelihood' function (see Hood and Koopmans, 1953; White, 1982), however, we prefer the prefix 'pseudo' for three reasons: first it is coherent with the notion of 'pseudo-true' value (see Sawa, 1978) which is widely accepted, secondly this choice avoids a confusion with 'quasi-generalized methods' (a notion also used in this paper) and, finally, the term 'quasi-likelihood' is also used in a different context where some relationship between the mean and the variance is assumed (see Wedderburn, 1974; McCullagh and Nelder, 1983; McCullagh, 1983).

2.1. Pseudo-likelihood methods based on conditional moments

Let us first present the basic notions introduced in GMT (1984a). Since we are interested in concepts and results and not in technicalities, we shall adopt very simple assumptions; more precisely, we assume that we observe iid vectors $(y_t', x_t')'$, $t = 1, \ldots, T$ where y_t is a G-dimensional vector and x_t is H-dimensional.

In the pseudo-likelihood approach based on conditional moments we are interested in the conditional mean $E(y_t/x_t)$ and, possibly, in the conditional variance–covariance matrix $V(y_t/x_t)$. The results presented hereafter may be generalized to the dynamic case where x_t is made of past values of y_t and of present and past values of a strongly exogenous variable z_t (see White, 1984, 1988). We assume that the true conditional expectation $F_0(y_t/x_t)$ belongs to some parametric family,

$$E_0(y_t/x_t) = m(x_t, \theta_0) , \quad \theta_0 \in \Theta \subset \mathbb{R}^P , \qquad (1)$$

where m is a known function. In other words we assume that the conditional mean is well specified. We may also assume that the true variance–covariance matrix belongs to some parametric family,

$$\Omega_0(x_t) = V_0(y_t/x_t) = v(x_t, \theta_0) , \quad \theta_0 \in \Theta \subset \mathbb{R}^P , \qquad (2)$$

where v is a known function.

The true conditional distribution of y_t given x_t will be denoted by $\lambda_0(x_t)$.

Let us first only make assumption (1); in other words nothing is assumed on $\Omega_0(x_t)$ and we are interested in θ_0 appearing in $m(x_t, \theta_0)$. Since no parametric assumption is made on $\lambda_0(x_t)$, the maximum likelihood method cannot be used; however, if we consider any family of probability density functions (pdf) indexed by their mean m, $f(u; m)$, $u \in \mathbb{R}^G$, it is possible to adapt this family for the mean, i.e., to replace m by $m(x_t, \theta)$, and to consider the pseudo-likelihood function,

$$l_{1T}(\theta) = \prod_{t=1}^{T} f[y_t; m(x_t, \theta)] . \qquad (3)$$

In general, the maximization of $l_{1T}(\theta)$, will not provide a consistent estimator of θ_0; however, in the next section we shall characterize the functions $f(u; m)$ giving this consistency result and the corresponding methods will be called pseudo-maximum likelihood (PML) methods of order 1 (PML1).

Now, if we also make assumption (2) and if we consider a family of pdfs indexed by their mean m and their variance–covariance matrix Σ, $f(u; m, \Sigma)$, we can adapt this family for the mean and for the covariance matrix and either consider the pseudo-likelihood function

$$l_{2T} = \sum_{t=1}^{T} f[y_t; m(x_t, \theta), v(x_t, \tilde{\theta}_T)] \tag{4}$$

when $\tilde{\theta}_T$ is some consistent estimator of (a subvector of) θ or consider the pseudo-likelihood function

$$l_{3T} = \prod_{t=1}^{T} f[y_t; m(x_t, \theta), v(x_t, \theta)] . \tag{5}$$

A pseudo-likelihood function like l_{2T} is called a quasi-generalized pseudo-likelihood function, since it has been fitted with a first step estimator of the $v(x_t, \theta)$ (considered as nuisance parameters) and the parameters of interest are those appearing in $m(x_t, \theta)$ (in general a subvector of θ). On the contrary, in l_{3T} the parameters of interest are those appearing in $m(x_t, \theta)$ and $v(x_t, \theta)$. Again, in general, the maximization of l_{2T} or l_{3T} does not provide a consistent estimator of θ. In Section 4 we give conditions on function f ensuring that the maximization of l_{2T} provides a consistent estimator of θ; the corresponding estimators are called quasi-generalized PML estimators. In Section 5 we give characterizations of function f giving the consistency result for l_{3T}; the corresponding estimators are called pseudo-maximum likelihood methods of order 2 (PML2).

The pseudo-likelihood methods presented above are adapted for the conditional mean and, possibly, for the conditional variance–covariance matrix. However, it is possible to use these methods for more general conditional moments restrictions, for instance conditional quantiles (see Gourieroux and Monfort, 1987, 1989a, Chapter 8).

2.2. Pseudo-likelihood methods based on nonnested parametric models

In this context we no longer start from assumptions on conditional moments. On the contrary we study the position of the true conditional density with respect to two families of conditional densities $H_f = \{f(y_t; x_t, \alpha), \alpha \in A \subset \mathbb{R}^H\}$ and $H_g = \{g(y_t; x_t, \beta), \beta \in B \subset \mathbb{R}^K\}$. More precisely we have to distinguish two approaches.

In the first approach we assume that the true density function belongs to either H_f or H_g and we want to test the null hypothesis H_f against H_g (or, symmetrically, H_g against H_f). This approach is a nonnested hypotheses testing approach and it is also called an encompassing approach (see Mizon, 1984; Mizon and Richard, 1986; Hendry and Richard, 1987) since it consists in examining if H_f can explain (or encompass) H_g in the sense that, if H_f is true, the pseudo-true value of β evaluated at the maximum likelihood estimator of α

is not significantly different from the pseudo-maximum likelihood estimator of β based on H_g. Methods based on this idea are developed in Section 8.

In the second approach we do not assume that the true density function belongs to H_f or H_g and we want to choose the model (H_f or H_g) which is the closest to the true density. This approach is called a model selection approach (see Hotelling, 1940; Amemiya, 1980; Chow, 1981, 1983, Chapter 9; Judge et al., 1985, Chapter 21); the procedure developed in Section 9 is based on the Kullback–Leibler information criterion (see Akaike, 1973; Sawa, 1978) and on pseudo-maximum likelihood estimators of the parameters α and β (see Vuong, 1989).

3. Pseudo-maximum likelihood methods of order one (PML1)

3.1. The problem

In this section we assume that the conditional expectation satisfies the condition

$$E_0(y_t/x_t) = m(x, \theta_0) , \quad \theta_0 \in \Theta \subset \mathbb{R}^K ,$$

and nothing is assumed on the conditional variance–covariance matrix $\Omega_0(x_t) = V_0(y_t/x_t)$. We want to estimate θ_0. For this purpose it is useful to introduce classes of probability distributions, the linear exponential families.

3.2. Linear exponential families

A family of probability measures on $\mathbb{R}^G$, indexed by a parameter $m \in \mathcal{M} \subset \mathbb{R}^G$ is called linear exponential if (i) every element of the family has a density function with respect to a given measure ν and if this density function can be written as

$$f(u, m) = \exp[A(m) + B(u) + C(m)u] , \tag{6}$$

where $u \in \mathbb{R}^G$, $A(m)$ and $B(u)$ are scalar and $C(m)$ is a row vector of size G; (ii) m is the mean of the distribution whose density is $f(u, m)$.

A linear exponential family has many important properties; some of them are given in the following proposition.

PROPOSITION 1. *If* $\{f(u, m), m \in \mathcal{M}\}$ *is a linear exponential family we have*

(a) $\quad \dfrac{\partial A(m)}{\partial m} + \dfrac{\partial C(m)}{\partial m} m = 0 ,$

(b) $\quad \dfrac{\partial^2 A}{\partial m\, \partial m'} + \sum_{g=1}^{G} \dfrac{\partial^2 C_g}{\partial m\, \partial m'} m_g + \dfrac{\partial C(m)}{\partial m} = 0 ,$

where C_g and m_g are respectively the g-th component of C and m,

(c) $\dfrac{\partial C}{\partial m} = \Sigma^{-1}$,

where Σ is the variance–covariance matrix associated with $f(u, m)$,

(d) $A(m) + C(m)m_0 \leqslant A(m_0) + C(m_0)m_0$,

and the equality holds if and only if $m = m_0$.

Many classical families of probability measures are linear exponential. Some examples are given in Table 1; the multivariate generalizations of Poisson, negative binomial distributions (see Johnson and Kotz, 1972, Chapter 11) are also linear exponential families.

3.3. Properties of the PML1 method based on linear exponential families

As mentioned above we assume that $E_0(y_t/x_t) = m(x_t, \theta_0)$, $\theta_0 \in \Theta \subset \mathbb{R}^K$ and we also make the identifiability assumption

$$m(x, \theta_1) = m(x, \theta_2), \forall x \Rightarrow \theta_1 = \theta_2 .$$

Table 1
Examples of linear exponential families

Family		Density function	$C(m)$
Binomial (n given)	$]0, n[$	$\dfrac{\Gamma(n+1)}{\Gamma(u+1)\Gamma(n-u+1)} \left(\dfrac{m}{n}\right)^u \left(1 - \dfrac{m}{n}\right)^{n-u}$	$\text{Log}\,\dfrac{m}{n-m}$
Poisson	$\mathbb{R}^+ - (0)$	$\dfrac{e^{-m}m^u}{u!}$	$\text{Log}\,m$
Negative binomial (a given)	$\mathbb{R}^+ - (0)$	$\dfrac{\Gamma(a+u)}{\Gamma(a)\Gamma(u+1)} \left(\dfrac{m}{a}\right)^u \left(1 + \dfrac{m}{a}\right)^{-(a+u)}$	$\text{Log}\,\dfrac{m}{a+m}$
Gamma (a given)	$\mathbb{R}^+ - (0)$	$\dfrac{u^{a-1}\,e^{-ua/m}}{\Gamma(a)\left(\dfrac{m}{a}\right)^a}$	$-\dfrac{a}{m}$
Normal (σ given)	$\mathbb{R}$	$\dfrac{1}{\sigma\sqrt{2\pi}} \exp\left[-\dfrac{1}{2}\dfrac{(u-m)^2}{\sigma^2}\right]$	$\dfrac{m}{\sigma^2}$
Multinomial (n given)	$\sum_g m_g = n$	$\dfrac{n!}{\prod_g (u_g)!} \prod_g \left(\dfrac{m_g}{n}\right)^{u_g}$	$\text{Log}\,\dfrac{m_1}{n}, \dots, \text{Log}\,\dfrac{m_g}{n}$
Normal multivariate (Σ given)	$\mathbb{R}^G$	$\dfrac{\exp - \frac{1}{2}(u-m)'\Sigma^{-1}(u-m)}{(2\pi)^{G/2}\sqrt{\det \Sigma}}$	$m'\Sigma^{-1}$

Let us consider any linear exponential family $f(u, m)$; we can adapt it for the mean and consider the pseudo-likelihood function $l_{1T}(\theta) = \Pi_{t=1}^{T} f[y_t, m(x_t, \theta)]$. It turns out that the PML1 estimator thus obtained has interesting properties.

PROPOSITION 2. *If $f(u, m)$ is a linear exponential family, the associated PML1 estimator $\hat{\theta}_T$ of θ_0 is strongly consistent and asymptotically normal, more precisely,*

$$\sqrt{T}(\hat{\theta}_T - \theta_0) \xrightarrow[T \to \infty]{d} N(0, J^{-1}IJ^{-1}),$$

where

$$J = E_x\left(\frac{\partial m'}{\partial \theta} \frac{\partial C}{\partial m} \frac{\partial m}{\partial \theta'}\right) = E_x\left(\frac{\partial m'}{\partial \theta} \Sigma_0^{-1} \frac{\partial m}{\partial \theta'}\right),$$

$$I = E_x\left(\frac{\partial m'}{\partial \theta} \frac{\partial C}{\partial m} \Omega_0 \frac{\partial C'}{\partial m'} \frac{\partial m}{\partial \theta'}\right) = E_x\left(\frac{\partial m'}{\partial \theta} \Sigma_0^{-1} \Omega_0 \Sigma_0^{-1} \frac{\partial m}{\partial \theta'}\right),$$

$\Sigma_0 = \Sigma(x_t, \theta_0)$ *[resp. $\Omega_0(x_t)$] is the variance–covariance matrix associated with the pdf $f[\cdot, m(x_t, \theta_0)]$ [resp. $\lambda_0(x_t)$] and all the functions are evaluated at θ_0.*

Note that it is equivalent to maximize

$$L_{1T} = \text{Log}\, l_{1T} = \sum_{t=1}^{T} \text{Log}\, f[y_t, m(x_t, \theta)]$$

and to maximize

$$\sum_{t=1}^{T} \{A[m(x_t, \theta)] + C[m(x_t, \theta)]y_t\}.$$

Therefore it is not necessary to impose on y_t the constraints which may be implied by the definition of B; for instance, the PML1 method associated with a Poisson family may be applied even if y_t is any real variable (however, in this case, $m(x_t, \theta)$ must be positive).

In Table 2 we give the objective functions of the PML1 method associated with some classical linear exponential families. Note that, for the gamma family and for the univariate normal family, the value of the nuisance parameters (a and σ) do not influence the maximization and these parameters could have been omitted; however, we kept them for reasons which will be clear in Section 4.

For the univariate and multivariate normal families the PML1 estimators are, respectively, the nonlinear least squares estimator and a minimum distance estimator (see Jennrich, 1969; Malinvaud, 1970). It is also worth noting that a reciprocal of Proposition 2 exists.

PROPOSITION 3. *A necessary condition for the PML1 estimator associated with a* *family $f(u, m)$, $m \in \mathcal{M}$ to be strongly consistent for any Θ, m, $\lambda_0(x)$, is that $f(u, m)$ be a linear exponential family.*

Table 2
Objective functions

Family	Objective functions
Binomial (n given, $n \in \mathbb{N}$)	$\displaystyle\sum_{t=1}^{T} \left\{ n \, \mathrm{Log}\left[1 - \frac{m(x_t, \theta)}{n} \right] + y_t \, \mathrm{Log}\left[\frac{m(x_t, \theta)}{n - m(x_t, \theta)} \right] \right\}$
Poisson	$\displaystyle\sum_{t=1}^{T} \{ -m(x_t, \theta) + y_t \, \mathrm{Log}\, m(x_t, \theta) \}$
Negative binomial (a given)	$\displaystyle\sum_{t=1}^{T} \left[-a \, \mathrm{Log}\left(1 + \frac{m(x_t, \theta)}{a} \right) + y_t \, \mathrm{Log}\left(\frac{m(x_t, \theta)}{a + m(x_t, \theta)} \right) \right]$
Gamma (a given)	$\displaystyle\sum_{t=1}^{T} \left(-a \, \mathrm{Log}\, m(x, \theta) - \frac{a y_t}{m(x_t, \theta)} \right)$
Normal (σ given)	$\displaystyle -\frac{1}{\sigma^2} \sum_{t=1}^{T} [y_t - m(x_t, \theta)]^2$
Multinomial (n given, $n \in \mathbb{N}$)	$\displaystyle\sum_{t=1}^{T} \sum_{g=1}^{G} y_{gt} \, \mathrm{Log}\, m_g(x_t, \theta), \quad \text{where } \sum_g m_g(x_t, \theta) = n$
Normal multivariate (Σ given)	$\displaystyle -\sum_{t=1}^{T} [y_t - m(x_t, \theta)]' \Sigma^{-1} [y_t - m(x_t, \theta)]$

In order to use the results of Proposition 2 for asymptotic tests or confidence regions, we need consistent estimators of I and J. A consistent estimator of J is obtained by replacing E_x by an empirical mean and θ_0 by $\hat{\theta}_T$. For I it is also necessary to replace Ω_0 by $[y_t - m(x_t, \hat{\theta}_T)][y_t - m(x_t, \hat{\theta}_T)]'$ within the empirical mean; moreover, it is clear that if the functional form of $\Omega_0(x_t) = v(x_t, \theta_0)$ is known, it is preferable to replace Ω_0 by $v(x_t, \hat{\theta}_T)$.

From Proposition 2 we now know that the adaptation for the mean of any linear exponential family provides a pseudo-likelihood function from which a consistent asymptotically normal estimator of θ_0 can be derived. However, in practice, the choice of the linear exponential family arises.

3.4. Choice of a PML1 estimator

In the problem of choosing a PML1 estimator an interesting information would be a lower bound of the asymptotic variance–covariance matrices of these estimators. It turns out that such a bound exists.

PROPOSITION 4. *The set of the asymptotic variance–covariance matrices of the PML1 estimators $\hat{\theta}_T$ based on a linear exponential family has a lower bound* *equal to*

$$\mathcal{B} = \left(\mathbb{E}_x \left[\frac{\partial m'}{\partial \theta} \, \Omega_0^{-1} \, \frac{\partial m}{\partial \theta'} \right] \right)^{-1}.$$

From Proposition 2, it is seen that $\mathcal{B}$ is reached if $\Omega_0(x_t) = \Sigma(x_t, \theta_0)$, that is if the true variance–covariance matrix $\Omega_0(x_t)$ can be reached by a linear exponential family (whose variance–covariance matrix is $\Sigma(x_t, \theta_0)$; a sufficient condition is obviously that $\lambda_0(x_t)$ belongs to the family of probability distributions whose PDF are $f[\cdot, m(x_t, \theta)]$ since, in this case, the PML1 method becomes a genuine maximum likelihood method. It is also worth noting that this lower bound is identical to the semi-parametric efficiency bound (see Stein, 1956; Begun et al., 1983; Chamberlain, 1987; Newey, 1989; Gourieroux and Monfort, 1989a, Chapter 23) based on conditional moment restrictions.

If nothing is known about $\Omega_0(x_t)$, it is possible to use the computational convenience as a choice criterion. For instance, for a given function $m(x, \theta)$ it may be useful to look for the pseudo-loglikelihood functions which are concave; such a discussion is made in GMT (1984b) for a count data model with $m(x, \theta) = \exp(x'\theta)$. More generally in the univariate case ($G = 1$), it may be possible to 'link' the pseudo-likelihood function with $m(x, \theta)$, in the same spirit as in the generalized linear model (see McCullagh and Nelder, 1983), if $m(x, \theta)$ can be written $C^{-1}(x'\theta)$ and if there exists a linear exponential family $f(u, m) = \exp\{A(m) + B(y) + C(m)y\}$. In this case the pseudo-loglikelihood function $\Sigma_{t=1}^T \{A[C^{-1}(x_t\theta)] + x_t\theta y_t\}$ can be shown to be strictly concave and, therefore, the PML1 estimator is unique and easily found (see GMT, 1983a). Mean functions $m(x, \theta)$ which are linked with some classical linear exponential families are given in Table 3.

Finally, it is also possible to compare PML1 estimators by simulation methods. Such a study is briefly made in Gourieroux, Monfort and Trognon (1984b) when the true model is a Poisson model with exogenous variables and unobservable heterogeneity factors; a more detailed study is also proposed in Bourlange and Doz (1988); both studies show that the PML1 method associated with the negative binomial family is particularly attractive in this case.

All these criteria do not guarantee that the lower bound of Proposition 4 is reached asymptotically but, in the next section, we shall see that when a

Table 3
Linked mean functions

Family	Linked mean function
Normal ($G = 1$)	$x_t'\theta$
Binomial ($n = 1$)	$1/[1 + \exp(-x_t'\theta)]$
Poisson	$\exp(x_t'\theta)$
Gamma ($a = 1$)	$-1/(x_t'\theta)$

parametric information on the second-order moments is available this bound can easily be reached.

4. Quasi-generalized PML methods

4.1. The problem

Let us now assume that not only

$$E_0(y_t/x_t) = m(x_t, \theta_0)$$

is true but also that

$$V_0(y_t/x_t) = v(x_t, \theta_0)$$

holds. For notational simplicity we denote by θ_0 the parameter appearing in m and v, but it is clear that, in practice, only subvectors of θ_0 will often appear in m and v. We are still interested in the parameter appearing in m; again this parameter may be in fact a subvector of θ which is assumed to be identifiable from m.

4.2. Generalized linear exponential families

As shown in Table 1, some linear exponential families (negative binomial, gamma, univariate or multivariate normal . . .) also depend on an additional parameter that will be denoted by η and this parameter is a function $\eta = \psi(m, \Sigma)$ of η and Σ (the mean and the variance–covariance matrix associated with the pdf) such that, for any given m there is a one to one relationship between η and Σ (denoted by σ^2 in the univariate case). For instance, in the negative binomial case we have $\eta = a = m^2/(\sigma^2 - m)$, in the gamma case $\eta = a = m^2/\sigma^2$, in the univariate normal case $\eta = \sigma^2$, and in the multivariate normal case $\eta = \Sigma$. Such a family will be called a generalized linear exponential family and denoted by

$$f^*(y, m, \eta) = \exp\{A(m, \eta) + B(\eta, y) + C(m, \eta)y\} . \tag{7}$$

4.3. Properties of the quasi-generalized PML estimators

Given any consistent estimator $\tilde{\theta}_T$ of θ, we can now define a QGPML estimator and give its main properties.

PROPOSITION 5. *Let $\tilde{\theta}_T$ be a strongly consistent estimator of θ, a QGPML* *estimator of θ, obtained by solving*

$$\max_{\theta} L_{2T} = \text{Log } l_{2T} = \sum_{t=1}^{T} \text{Log } f^*\{y_t, m(x_t, \theta), \psi[m(x_t, \tilde{\theta}_T), v(x_t, \tilde{\theta}_T)]\}$$

is strongly consistent, asymptotically normal and reaches the lower bound $\mathcal{B}$ given in Proposition 4.

So when a specification $v(x_t, \theta)$ is available, the previous proposition solves the problem of the optimal choice of a pseudo-likelihood function, since the bound is reached, and it shows that any QGPML estimator reaches the semi-parametric efficiency bound. Note that the asymptotic properties of a QGPML estimator is the same for all the generalized linear exponential families, so the choice among various possibilities can be based on computational considerations. Let us consider several examples.

Let us assume that $E_0(y_t/x_t) = m(x_t, \theta_{10})$ and $V_0(y_t/x_t) = \theta_{20}g^2(x_t, \theta_{10})$ (where θ_{10} and θ_{20} are subvectors of θ_0). It is possible, in a first step, to consistently estimate θ_{10} by any PML1 estimator $\tilde{\theta}_{1T}$ and to consistently estimate θ_{20} for instance by

$$\tilde{\theta}_{2T} = \frac{1}{T} \sum_{t=1}^{T} \frac{[y_t - m(x_t, \tilde{\theta}_{1T})]^2}{g^2(x_t, \tilde{\theta}_{1T})}.$$

In a second step a QGPML estimator of θ_1 can be based for instance on the normal or on the gamma family. In the first case the QGPML of θ_1 estimator is obtained by minimizing

$$\sum_{t=1}^{T} \frac{[y_t - m(x_t\theta_1)]^2}{g^2(x_t, \tilde{\theta}_{1T})\tilde{\theta}_{2T}}. \tag{8}$$

In the second case the QGPML estimator of θ_1 is obtained by minimizing

$$\sum_{t=1}^{T} \frac{m^2(x_t, \tilde{\theta}_{1T})}{g^2(x_t, \tilde{\theta}_{1T})\tilde{\theta}_{2T}} \left[\text{Log } m(x_t, \theta_1) + \frac{y_t}{m(x_t, \theta_1)} \right]. \tag{9}$$

Note that in both cases $\tilde{\theta}_{2T}$ can be omitted in the objective function; therefore $\tilde{\theta}_{2T}$ plays no role in the computation of the estimator but it appears in the estimator of the asymptotic variance–covariance matrix.

From the theory we know that these two estimators have the same asymptotic properties. In the particular case $g(x_t, \theta) = 1$ the QGPML estimator based on the normal family is simply the nonlinear least squares which, therefore, provides an optimal PML1 estimator in one step. In the particular case where $g(x_t, \theta) = m(x_t, \theta)$, the second QGPML is identical to the PML1 estimator based on the gamma family which, therefore, is an optimal PML1 estimator.

5. Pseudo-maximum likelihood estimators of order two (PML2)

As in Section 4 we make the assumptions

$$E_0(y_t/x_t) = m(x_t, \theta_0)$$

and

$$V_0(y_t/x_t) = v(x_t, \theta_0) .$$

However, contrary to the context of Section 4, we are interested in the whole parameter θ_0 and not only in the subvector appearing in m. So we want m and v to play symmetrical roles. For this purpose it is useful to introduce new families of probability density functions: the quadratic exponential families defined by

$$f(u, m, \Sigma) = \exp\{A(m, \Sigma) + B(u) + C(m, \Sigma)u + u'D(m, \Sigma)u\} ,$$

(10)

where

(a) $A(m, \Sigma)$, $B(u)$ are scalar, $C(m, \Sigma)$ is a row vector of size G and $D(m, \Sigma)$ is a square matrix (G, G),

(b) m is the mean and Σ the variance–covariance matrix associated with $f(u, m, \Sigma)$.

We can now define a pseudo-likelihood function adapted for the first two moments:

$$l_{3T} = \prod_{t=1}^{T} f[y_t, m(x_t, \theta), v(x_t, \theta)] .$$

(11)

The pseudo-maximum likelihood of order 2 (PML2) estimators thus obtained have the following properties.

PROPOSITION 6. *A PML2 estimator $\hat{\theta}_T$ of θ_0 based on a quadratic exponential family is strongly consistent and asymptotically normal; the asymptotic variance–covariance matrix of $\sqrt{T}(\hat{\theta}_T - \theta_0)$ is $J^{-1}IJ^{-1}$ with*

$$J = -E_x E_0 \frac{\partial^2 \text{Log } f}{\partial\theta \, \partial\theta'} [y, m(x, \theta_0), v(x, \theta_0)] ,$$

$$I = E E \frac{\partial \text{Log } f}{\partial\theta} [y, m(x, \theta_0), v(x, \theta_0)] \frac{\partial \text{Log } f}{\partial\theta'} [y, m(x, \theta_0), v(x, \theta_0)] .$$

More detailed expressions of I and J can be found (see GMT, 1984a, Appendix 5).

It is also remarkable to note that, as in the first-order case, there exists a reciprocal of the previous proposition.

PROPOSITION 7. *A necessary condition for a PML2 estimator based on a family*

$f(u, m, \Sigma)$ to be strongly consistent for any Θ, m, v and λ_0 is that $f(u, m, \Sigma)$ be a quadratic exponential family.

Thus we obtained results which directly generalize those obtained in the first-order case.

6. Hypothesis testing

6.1. General results

We make the assumption

$$E_0(y_t/x_t) = m(x_t, \theta_0)$$

and, possibly, the assumption

$$V_0(y_t/x_t) = v(x_t, \theta_0) .$$

We are interested in an hypothesis H_0 on θ_0. The more general form of such a null hypothesis is the mixed form (see Szroeter, 1983; Gourieroux and Monfort, 1989b) defined by

$$H_0: \{\theta/\exists a \subset \mathbb{R}^K: g(\theta, a) = 0\} , \tag{12}$$

where g is an L-dimensional function such that $\partial g/\partial \theta'$ is an $L \times p$ matrix of rank L and $\partial g/\partial a'$ is an $L \times K$ matrix of rank K (this implies $K \leqslant L \leqslant p$). This form contains as particular cases the explicit form $[\theta = h(a)]$ and the implicit form $[\phi(\theta) = 0]$. In Gourieroux and Monfort (1989b) we propose a general treatment of this kind of hypothesis when an unconstrained estimator $\hat{\theta}_T$ of θ_0 is obtained by maximizing a general objective function $L_T(\theta)$ and when the following assumptions are satisfied

$$\hat{\theta}_T \text{ is consistent} ,$$

$$\frac{1}{\sqrt{T}} \frac{\partial L_T}{\partial \theta} (\theta_0) \xrightarrow[T \to \infty]{D} N(0, I_0) , \tag{13}$$

$$-\frac{1}{T} \frac{\partial^2 L_T}{\partial \theta \, \partial \theta'} (\theta_0) \xrightarrow[T \to \infty]{P \cdot S} J_0 ,$$

where I_0 and J_0 are positive definite matrices.

The PML1, QGPML and PML2 methods (based on appropriate exponential families) fit in this general framework with $L_T = L_{1T} = \text{Log} \, l_{1T}$, $L_T = L_{2T} = \text{Log} \, l_{2T}$ or $L_T = L_{3T} = \text{Log} \, l_{3T}$; therefore all the results obtained in the general framework mentioned above can be used. In particular, we can define a pseudo-Wald, a pseudo-score and a pseudo-Lagrange multiplier test statistic for testing H_0. These statistics are asymptotically equivalent under H_0 and under a sequence of local alternatives and their asymptotic distribution under H_0 is $\chi^2(L - K)$. It is important to note that these statistics are not the same as the ones that we would have obtained in the classical maximum likelihood context, that is if we knew that the true pdf was in the family from which the pseudo-likelihood function was derived. The reason of this difference is that, contrary to the maximum likelihood context, matrices I_0 and J_0 are in general different in the PML1 and the PML2 contexts. However, these matrices are identical in the QGPML case; this property implies that the pseudo-Wald and pseudo-score statistics based on a QGPML method have the same form as in the maximum likelihood context and, moreover, that is is possible to base the pseudo-likelihood ratio test on the QGPML method; in other words, if $\hat{\theta}_T^0$ is the constrained estimator the statistic $2[L_{2T}(\hat{\theta}_T) - L_{2T}(\hat{\theta}_T^0)]$ is asymptotically equivalent to all the test statistics mentioned above.

6.2. Particular cases

Let us consider a PML1 method based on a linear exponential family (see Proposition 1); the unrestricted estimator of θ, denoted by $\hat{\theta}_T$, is obtained by maximizing

$$L_{1T} = \sum_{t=1}^{T} \mathrm{Log}\, f[y_t, m(x_t, \theta)] .$$

Let us assume that θ is partitioned into $\theta = (\alpha', \beta')'$, that H_0 is defined by $\beta = \beta_0$ and let us denote by p_β the size of β. The pseudo-Wald statistic can be shown to be (see Trognon, 1984, 1987)

$$\xi_T^W = T(\hat{\beta}_T - \beta_0)' \hat{F} \hat{W}^{-1} \hat{F}(\hat{\beta}_T - \beta_0) , \tag{14}$$

where

$$\hat{\theta}_T = (\hat{\alpha}_T', \hat{\beta}_T') ,$$

where $\hat{F}$ and $\hat{W}$ are consistent estimators of

$$F = J_{\beta\beta} - J_{\beta\alpha} J_{\alpha\alpha}^{-1} J_{\alpha\beta} , \quad \text{and}$$

$$W = I_{\beta\beta} - I_{\beta\alpha} J_{\alpha\alpha}^{-1} J_{\alpha\beta} - J_{\beta\alpha} J_{\alpha\alpha}^{-1} I_{\alpha\beta} + J_{\beta\alpha} J_{\alpha\alpha}^{-1} I_{\alpha\alpha} J_{\alpha\alpha}^{-1} J_{\alpha\beta} ,$$

and where the indexes α, β refer to submatrices of I and J defined in Proposition 2. Under H_0, ξ_T^W is asymptotically distributed as a chi-square with p_β degrees of freedom.

In the same context the pseudo-score or (pseudo-Lagrange multiplier) test statistic is

$$\xi_T^S = \frac{1}{T} \hat{\lambda}_t' \hat{W}^{-1} \hat{\lambda}_T , \tag{15}$$

where

$$\hat{\lambda}_T = \frac{\partial L_{1T}}{\partial \theta}(\hat{\alpha}_T^0, \beta_0),$$

$\hat{\alpha}_T^0$ being the constrained PML1 estimator of α.

It is also easy to give explicit formulae for the pseudo-Wald and the pseudo-score test statistics associated with the QPML method, when the null hypothesis is the same as above: $\beta = \beta_0$. Let us consider any generalized linear exponential family $f^*(u, m, \eta)$ (see formula (7)); the relevant objective function is

$$L_{2T} = \sum_{t=1}^{T} \mathrm{Log}\, f^* \{ y_t, m(x_t, \theta), \psi[m(x_t, \tilde{\theta}_T), v(x_t, \tilde{\theta}_T)] \},$$

where $\tilde{\theta}_T$ is a consistent estimator of θ.

Let us denote by $\theta_T^* = (\alpha_T^{*\prime}, \beta_T^{*\prime})'$ the estimator obtained from the maximization of L_{2T}. The pseudo-Wald test statistic is

$$\xi_T^{*W} = T(\beta_T^* - \beta_0)' \hat{W}^* (\beta_T^* - \beta_0), \tag{16}$$

where $\hat{W}^*$ is a consistent estimator of

$$W^* = I_{\beta\beta}^* - I_{\beta\alpha}^* (I_{\alpha\alpha}^*)^{-1} I_{\alpha\beta}^*$$

and where the indexes α, β refer to submatrices of

$$I^* = \mathrm{E}_x \left(\frac{\partial m'}{\partial \theta} v^{-1} \frac{\partial m}{\partial \theta'} \right).$$

The pseudo-score statistic is

$$\xi_T^{*S} = \frac{1}{T} \lambda_T^{*\prime} (\hat{W}^*)^{-1} \lambda_T^*, \tag{17}$$

with

$$\lambda_T^* = \frac{\partial L_{2T}}{\partial \theta}(\alpha_T^{*0}, \beta_0),$$

α_T^{*0} being the constrained QGPML estimator of α.

As mentioned above the pseudo-likelihood ratio test statistic

$$\xi_T^{*R} = 2[L_{2T}(\theta_T^*) - L_{2T}(\theta_T^{*0})]$$

is asymptotically equivalent to ξ_T^{*W} and ξ_T^{*S}; the asymptotic distribution of these statistics under H_0 is $\chi^2(p_\beta)$. It is also easily shown that the tests based on a QGPML method are asymptotically more powerful than those based on a PML method; this property is a consequence of the semi-parametric efficiency of the QGPML methods.

6.3. Pseudo-likelihood ratio tests

We have seen above that, in general, the pseudo-likelihood ratio tests based on a PML1 method are not asymptotically distributed as a chi-square; this distributions is, in fact, a mixture of chi-square distribution (Fourtz and Srivastava, 1977).

However, there are important cases where the pseudo-likelihood ratio tests based on a PML1 method are asymptotically equivalent to the pseudo-score and the pseudo-Wald tests. The more important case is probably the multivariate linear case,

$$y_t = Bx_t + u_t,\tag{18}$$

where y_t is a G-dimensional vector, B is a matrix of parameters, x_t a vector of exogenous variables, and u_t is a white noise process (independent of x_t), whose instantaneous variance–covariance matrix is denoted by Ω. The null hypothesis is any hypothesis on B (linear or nonlinear, in an explicit, implicit or mixed form). The pseudo-likelihood ratio test statistic based on the normal family is equal to $T \operatorname{Log} \det \hat{\Omega}_{0T}/\det \hat{\Omega}_T$, where $\hat{\Omega}_{0T}$ is the empirical variance–covariance matrix of the residuals obtained in the constrained PML2 estimation and $\hat{\Omega}_T$ is the similar matrix in the unconstrained case; note that in the unconstrained case the PML2 estimator of B is simply made of the OLS estimators of the rows of B. This statistic is asymptotically distributed as $\chi^2(K)$ (where K is the number of constraints), even if the true distribution of u_t is not normal, and is asymptotically equivalent to the pseudo-score statistic, which is equal to $T \operatorname{Trace}[\hat{\Omega}_{0T}^{-1}(\hat{\Omega}_{0T} - \hat{\Omega}_T)]$. Since the form is not necessarily implicit, it may not be possible to define a pseudo-Wald test statistic; however, for any form of the hypothesis, it is possible to consider a pseudo-generalized Wald test statistic, defined as

$$\operatorname*{Min}_{b \in H_0}(\hat{b}_T - b)'[\hat{\Omega}_T^{-1} \otimes X'X](\hat{b}_T - b),$$

where $b = \operatorname{vec}(B')$, and $\hat{b}_T$ is the unconstrained PML2 estimator of b, i.e., the ordinary least squares estimator equation by equation; it turns out that this statistic is equal to $T \operatorname{Trace}[\hat{\Omega}_T^{-1}(\tilde{\Omega}_{0T} - \hat{\Omega}_T)]$, where $\tilde{\Omega}_{0T}$ is the empirical variance–covariance matrix of the residuals when b is estimated by the generalized least squares estimator derived from the previous minimization. This statistic is asymptotically equivalent to the pseudo-score and to the pseudo-likelihood ratio test statistics.

7. Simulated PML methods

7.1. Motivations

As mentioned in the introduction the pseudo-likelihood methods may be useful for parametric models when the likelihood function does not have a closed form and cannot be maximized; it is the case, for example, in some multimarket disequilibrium models (see Laroque and Salanié, 1989). When the likelihood function does not have a closed form, the same is in general true for the moment functions and, therefore, the pseudo-likelihood methods do not directly apply. However, for a given value of the parameter, simulation techniques can be used in order to approximate these moments; if we replace these moments by their evaluations based on simulations we get a simulated pseudo-likelihood method.

More precisely, let us consider the following situation. We have a typical econometric model

$$y_t = r(x_t, e_t, \theta), \quad t = 1, \ldots, T, \tag{19}$$

where θ is a vector of parameters, x_t a vector of exogenous variables, e_t a vector of disturbances and y_t a vector of endogenous variables. θ is unobservable and deterministic, x_t is observable and stochastic with an unknown distribution, e_t is unobservable and stochastic with a known distribution; the function r is called the reduced form of the model. Note that the assumption of a known distribution for e_t is not very restrictive since a model with parametric assumptions on the distribution of the disturbance can be put in the previous form, for instance by writing this disturbance $e_t^* = G(e_t, \bar{\theta})$ where e_t has a known distribution and $\bar{\theta}$ is an unknown parameter which is incorporated into θ. As seen later it may be convenient to partition the disturbance vector into two subvectors, $e_t = (u_t', v_t')'$. For sake of simplicity we assume that the processes $\{x_t\}$, $\{u_t\}$, $\{v_t\}$ are independent and that each process is identically and independently distributed (but these assumptions can easily be weakened); the disturbances u_t and v_t are assumed to be zero-mean.

We are interested in θ and we consider the case where the conditional pdf $g(y_t; x_t, \theta)$ does not have a closed form. Since the maximum likelihood method cannot be used we can think of applying PML methods but, the problem is that the conditional moments of y_t given x_t do not have, in general, a closed form.

7.2. Description of the simulated PML methods

Let us first focus on the PML1 method. Since the functional form of the conditional mean $m(x_t, \theta) = E(y_t/x_t)$ is not known, we can try to approximate it by means of simulations. More precisely, we shall distinguish two cases. In the first case, the conditional mean of y_t, given x_t and a subvector u_t of e_t, has a known functional form

$$E_\theta(y_t/x_t, u_t) = m^*(x_t, u_t, \theta). \tag{20}$$

Such a situation occurs, for instance, in models with an individual heterogeneity factor; in this case the index t is an individual index and u_t is the heterogeneity factor (see Gourieroux and Monfort, 1991b).

In the second case such a conditioning does not exist (apart from the trivial conditioning $u_t = e_t$).

In the first case $m(x_t, \theta)$ can be replaced by $(1/H) \sum_{h=1}^{H} m^*(x_t, u_{ht}, \theta)$, where u_{ht}, $h = 1, \ldots, H$, $t = 1, \ldots, T$ are independent drawings in the distribution P^U of u_t. In the second case $m(x_t, \theta)$ can be replaced by $(1/H) \sum_{h=1}^{H} r(x_t, u_{ht}, \theta)$ (with $u_t = e_t$). A drawback of the latter approximation is that r may be nondifferentiable, or even discontinuous, with respect to θ; however, these technical problems can be overcome (see McFadden, 1989; Pakes and Pollard, 1989; Laroque and Salanié, 1989); moreover, it is possible to avoid these problems by using the importance sampling technique (see Gourieroux, 1992).

The simulated PML1 (SPML1) method consists in maximizing a PML1 objective function in which $m(x_t, \theta)$ is replaced by an approximation given above. For instance, when a relevant conditioning exists this objective function is

$$L_{1T}^S = \sum_{t=1}^{T} \mathrm{Log}\, f\left[y_t, \frac{1}{H} \sum_{h=1}^{H} m^*(x_t, u_{ht}, \theta) \right], \tag{21}$$

where $f(\cdot, m)$ is any linear exponential family, $f(y, m) = \exp[A(m) + B(y) + C(m)y]$.

This maximization is equivalent to the maximization of

$$\sum_{t=1}^{T} \left\{ A\left[\frac{1}{H} \sum_{h=1}^{H} m^*(x_t, u_{ht}, \theta) \right] + C\left[\frac{1}{H} \sum_{h=1}^{H} m^*(x_t, u_{ht}, \theta) \right] y_t \right\}. \tag{22}$$

A simulated method can also be associated with the QGPML method. Let $f^*(\cdot, m, \eta)$ be any generalized linear exponential family where $\eta = \phi(m, m_2)$, m_2 being the (noncentered) second moment and $\phi(m, \cdot)$ being one-to-one for any m. The simulated QGPML method consists in maximizing

$$\sum_{t=1}^{T} \mathrm{Log}\, f^*\Bigg\{ y_t, \frac{1}{H} \sum_{h=1}^{H} m^*(x_t, u_{ht}, \theta),$$
$$\phi\left[\frac{1}{H} \sum_{h=1}^{H} m^*(x_t, u_{ht}, \tilde{\theta}_T), \frac{1}{H} \sum_{h=1}^{H} m_2^*(x_t, u_{ht}, \tilde{\theta}_T) \right] \Bigg\}, \tag{23}$$

where $\tilde{\theta}_T$ is any consistent estimator of θ and m_2^* is the (noncentered) second order moment of y_t given x_t and u_t.

A simulated PML2 method can be defined in the same way.

7.3. Asymptotic properties of the simulated PML methods

It is important to note that the asymptotic properties given below are valid when the same drawings u_{ht}, $h = 1, \ldots, H$, $t = 1, \ldots, T$ are used in the computation of the objective functions for different values of θ.

The main asymptotic properties of the simulated PML estimators or of the simulated QGPML estimators are the following (see Gourieroux and Monfort, 1991) for the regularity conditions.

PROPOSITION 8. *If H and T go to infinity, the simulated PML or QGPML estimators $\hat{\theta}_T$ are consistent. If, moreover, $\sqrt{T}/H$ goes to zero, $\sqrt{T}(\hat{\theta}_T - \theta_0)$ has the same asymptotic distribution as the corresponding PML or QGPML estimator.*

So, in order to have the usual consistency and asymptotic normality properties, the number of drawings H per observation has to go to infinity at least as fast as the square root of the number observations; however, it seems that in practice the influence of the number of drawings H is quickly stabilized when H increases (see Laroque and Salanié, 1990). Moreover, by slightly modifying the procedures it is possible to obtain consistency and asymptotic normality when H is fixed and only T goes to infinity. Let us briefly discuss this point and consider, for sake of simplicity, the simulated nonlinear least squares (SNLS) method (which is a particular SPML method). When no relevant conditioning is available the SNLS estimator is a solution of the first-order equations

$$
\frac{1}{T} \sum_{t=1}^{T} \frac{1}{H} \sum_{h=1}^{H} \frac{\partial r}{\partial \theta} (x_t, u_{ht}, \theta) \left[y_t - \frac{1}{H} \sum_{h=1}^{H} r(x_t, u_{ht}, \theta) \right] = 0 . \tag{24}
$$

When H is fixed and T goes to infinity, equation (24) becomes

$$
E_x \frac{\partial m}{\partial \theta} (x, \theta)[m(x, \theta_0) - m(x, \theta)]
$$
$$
+ \frac{1}{H} E_x \, \mathrm{Cov}_u \left[\frac{\partial r}{\partial \theta} (x, u, \sigma), r(x, u, \theta) \right] = 0 . \tag{25}
$$

So, because of the correlation between $\partial r/\partial \theta(x, u, \theta)$ and $r(x, u, \theta)$ the solution in θ of (25) is, in general, different from θ_0 and, therefore, the SNLS estimator is not, in general, consistent. However, it is clear that this covariance term is eliminated if different drawings in P^U are used for r and $\partial r/\partial \theta$. Let us denote by u_{ht} (resp. u_{ht}^*) the drawings used in r (resp. $\partial r/\partial \theta$). Equation (24) becomes

$$
\frac{1}{T} \sum_{t=1}^{T} \frac{1}{H} \sum_{h=1}^{H} \frac{\partial r}{\partial \theta} (x_t, u_{ht}^*, \theta) \left[y_t - \frac{1}{H} \sum_{h=1}^{H} r(x_t, u_{ht}, \theta) \right] = 0 . \tag{26}
$$

PROPOSITION 9. *The SNLS estimator $\hat{\theta}_T$ based on (26) is consistent and asymptotically normal when H is fixed and T goes to infinity. The asymptotic* *variance–covariance matrix of* $\sqrt{T}(\hat{\theta}_T - \theta_0)$ *is*

$$
\left\{ E_x \frac{\partial m}{\partial \theta} \frac{\partial m}{\partial \theta'} \right\}^{-1} \left\{ E_x \sigma^2(x, \theta_0) \frac{\partial m}{\partial \theta} \frac{\partial m}{\partial \theta'} \right.
$$
$$
+ \frac{1}{H} E_x \sigma^2(x, \theta_0) \left[\left(1 + \frac{1}{H}\right) V_u \frac{\partial r}{\partial \theta} + \frac{\partial m}{\partial \theta} \frac{\partial m}{\partial \theta'} \right] \right\}
$$
$$
\times \left\{ E_x \frac{\partial m}{\partial \theta} \frac{\partial m}{\partial \theta'} \right\}^{-1},
$$

where $\sigma^2(x, \theta_0)$ *is the conditional variance of* y_t *given* x.

The previous approach can be generalized to any PML1 estimator based on a linear exponential family since, using the identity $(\partial A / \partial m) + (\partial C / \partial m)m = 0$, the first-order conditions can be written

$$
\sum_{t=1}^{T} \frac{\partial m}{\partial \theta}(x_t, \theta) \frac{\partial C[m(x_t, \theta)]}{\partial m} [y_t - m(x_t, \theta)] = 0 .
$$

The same is true for other PML methods. Also note that there exist other modifications making SPML methods consistent when H is fixed and T goes to infinity (see Laffont, Ossard and Vuong, 1991; Broze and Gourieroux, 1993).

8. Pseudo-likelihood methods and nonnested hypotheses

In this section and the following one we no longer consider the PML methods based on conditional moments but we focus on PML methods based on nonnested hypotheses.

8.1. Pseudo-true values

Let us consider a family of conditional densities of y_t given x_t, $t = 1, \ldots, T$,

$$
H_f = \{ f(y_t; x_t, \alpha), \alpha \in A \subset \mathbb{R}^H \} . \tag{27}
$$

For sake of simplicity $f(y_t; x_t, \alpha)$ will also be denoted by $f_t(\alpha)$. Let us denote by $f_0(y_t; x_t)$ for f_{0t} the true conditional density, which does not necessarily belong to H_f. The finite sample pseudo-true value of α, denoted by α_T^*, is the value of α minimizing the Kullback–Leibler information criterion (KLIC) (see Sawa, 1978):

$$
\sum_{t=1}^{T} E_0^t [\text{Log } f_{0t} - \text{Log } f_t(\alpha)] , \tag{28}
$$

where E_0^t is the expectation operator with respect to f_{0t}.

Equivalently α_T^* is obtained from

$$\underset{\alpha}{\text{Max}} \sum_{t=1}^{T} E_0^t \text{ Log } f_t(\alpha) . \tag{29}$$

Clearly $\Pi_{t=1}^{T} f_t(\alpha_T^*)$ can be interpreted as the pdf of the form $\Pi_{t=1}^{T} f_t(\alpha)$ which is the closest, in the KLIC sense, to the pdf $\Pi_{t=1}^{T} f_{0t}$.

As T goes to infinity the finite sample pseudo-true value α_T^* converges to the asymptotic pseudo-true value α^*, which is a solution of

$$\underset{\alpha}{\text{Max}} \, E_x E_0 \text{ Log } f(y; x, \alpha) . \tag{30}$$

Note that, in the iid case, i.e., when there is no exogenous variables, α_T^* is equal to α^*. α^* is also the limit of the PML estimator $\hat{\alpha}_T$ of α, obtained from

$$\underset{\alpha}{\text{Max}} \sum_{t=1}^{T} \text{Log } f_t(\alpha) . \tag{31}$$

Let us now consider another family of conditional densities,

$$H_g = \{ g(y_t; x_t, \beta), \beta \in B \subset \mathbb{R}^K \} . \tag{32}$$

$g(y_t; x_t, \beta)$ will also be denoted by $g_t(\beta)$.

For any β in B we can define the finite sample pseudo-true value $a_T(\beta)$ of α, as the solution of

$$\underset{\alpha}{\text{Max}} \sum_{t=1}^{T} E_\beta^t \text{ Log } f_t(\alpha) , \tag{33}$$

where E_β^t is the expectation operator with respect to $g_t(\beta)$.

Again, as T goes to infinity, $a_T(\beta)$ converges to the asymptotic pseudo-true value $a(\beta)$, solution of

$$\underset{\alpha}{\text{Max}} \, E_x E_\beta \text{ Log } f(y; x, \alpha) . \tag{34}$$

$a(\beta)$ is also the limit of the PML estimator $\hat{\alpha}_T$ of α, obtained from (31), when $g_t(\beta)$ is the true density.

Obviously, by reversing the roles of α and β, it is also possible to define the finite sample pseudo-true value of β for any α, denoted by $b_T(\alpha)$, and the asymptotic pseudo-true value, denoted by $b(\alpha)$.

8.2. Nonnested hypotheses

Let us now consider the problem of testing H_f against H_g. A natural idea is to compare the pseudo-maximum likelihood estimator $\hat{\beta}_T$ of β, obtained by maximizing $\Sigma_{t=1}^{T} \text{Log } g_t(\beta)$, with $b(\hat{\alpha}_T)$ or $b_T(\hat{\alpha}_T)$, which are respectively the estimation of the asymptotic and the finite sample pseudo-true value of β under H_f. Since $\hat{\beta}_T - b(\hat{\alpha}_T)$ and $\hat{\beta}_T - b_T(\hat{\alpha}_T)$ converge to zero under H_f, and since it is not the case in general under H_g, a significant departure from zero of $\hat{\beta}_T - b(\hat{\alpha}_T)$ or $\hat{\beta}_T - b_T(\hat{\alpha}_T)$ will be in favour of H_g. This idea is the basis of testing procedures which can be called Wald type procedures since, as easily seen, they both reduce to the classical Wald test in the case of nested hypotheses. The test based on $b(\hat{\alpha}_T)$ will be called the W1 test, and the test based on $b_T(\hat{\alpha}_T)$ will be called the W2 test. In fact the computation of the asymptotic pseudo-true values is, in general, difficult since it involves the distribution of the exogenous variables and, therefore, the W2 test based on the finite sample pseudo-true values is more useful in practice.

Let us now introduce the following notations:

$$C_{ff} = E_x E_{\alpha_0}\left(\frac{\partial \operatorname{Log} f}{\partial \alpha} \cdot \frac{\partial \operatorname{Log} f}{\partial \alpha'}\right) = -E_x E_{\alpha_0}\frac{\partial^2 \operatorname{Log} f}{\partial \alpha\, \partial \alpha'} = K_f\ ,$$

$$C_{fg} = E_x E_{\alpha_0}\left(\frac{\partial \operatorname{Log} f}{\partial \alpha} \cdot \frac{\partial \operatorname{Log} g}{\partial \beta'}\right) = C'_{gf}\ ,$$

$$C_{gg} = E_x E_{\alpha_0}\left(\frac{\partial \operatorname{Log} g}{\partial \beta} \cdot \frac{\partial \operatorname{Log} g}{\partial \beta'}\right),$$

$$K_g = -E_x E_{\alpha_0}\left(\frac{\partial^2 \operatorname{Log} g}{\partial \beta\, \partial \beta'}\right),$$

$$C^*_{gg} = E_x E_{\alpha_0}\left[\left(\frac{\partial \operatorname{Log} g}{\partial \beta} - E_{\alpha_0}\frac{\partial \operatorname{Log} g}{\partial \beta}\right)\left(\frac{\partial \operatorname{Log} g}{\partial \beta} - E_{\alpha_0}\frac{\partial \operatorname{Log} g}{\partial \beta}\right)'\right],$$

where α_0 is the true value of α and the derivatives of f (resp. g) are evaluated at α_0 (resp. $b(\alpha_0)$).

The definitions and the asymptotic properties of the W1 and W2 tests are given in the following proposition (see GMT, 1983b).

PROPOSITION 10. (a) *The W1 test is based on the test statistic*

$$\xi_{W1} = T[\hat{\beta} - b(\hat{\alpha})]'\, \hat{K}_g[\hat{C}_{gg} - \hat{C}_{gf}\hat{C}_{ff}^{-1}\hat{C}_{fg}]^-\hat{K}_g[\hat{\beta} - b(\hat{\alpha})]\ ,$$

where $\hat{K}_g$, $\hat{C}_{gg}$, $\hat{C}_{gf}$ and $\hat{C}_{ff}$ *are consistent estimators of* K_g, C_{gg}, C_{gf}, C_{ff}. *Under* H_f, ξ_{W1} *is asymptotically distributed as a chi-square whose number of degrees of freedom d is equal to the rank of* $C_{gg} - C_{gf}C_{ff}^{-1}C_{fg}$. *The critical region at the asymptotical level ε is* $\{\xi_{W1} \geqslant \chi^2_{1-\varepsilon}(d)\}$.

(b) *The W2 test is based on the test statistic*

$$\xi_{W2} = T[\hat{\beta} - b_T(\hat{\alpha})]'\, \hat{K}_g[\hat{C}^*_{gg} - \hat{C}_{gf}\hat{C}_{ff}^{-1}\hat{C}_{fg}]^-\hat{K}_g[\hat{\beta} - b_T(\hat{\alpha})]\ ,$$

where $\hat{C}^*_{gg}$ *is a consistent estimator of* C^*_{gg}. *Under* H_f, ξ_{W2} *is distributed as a chi-square whose number of degrees of freedom d^* is the rank of* $C^*_{gg} - C_{gf}C_{ff}^{-1}C_{fg}$. *The critical region at the asymptotic level ε is* $\{\xi_{W2} \geqslant \chi^2_{1-\varepsilon}(d)\}$.

It is easily seen that d^* cannot be greater than d. Moreover, since both $\hat{\beta}_T - b(\hat{\alpha}_T)$ and $\hat{\beta}_T - b_T(\hat{\alpha}_T)$ converge, under H_g, to $\beta_0 - b[a(\beta_0)]$, the Wald type tests proposed above are consistent except in the special case $\beta_0 = b[a(\beta_0)]$ (see GMT, 1983b, for a discussion of this case). It is also possible to propose two score-type tests. The first one, denoted by S1, is based on

$$\hat{\lambda}_1 = \frac{1}{T} \sum_{t=1}^{T} \frac{\partial \operatorname{Log} g}{\partial \beta} (y_t; x_t, b(\hat{\alpha}_T)) ;$$

the other one, S2, is based on

$$\hat{\lambda}_2 = \frac{1}{T} \sum_{t=1}^{T} \frac{\partial \operatorname{Log} g}{\partial \beta} (y_t; x_t, b_T(\hat{\alpha}_T)) .$$

PROPOSITION 11. *The statistics*

$$\xi_{S1} = T\hat{\lambda}_1'[\hat{C}_{gg} - \hat{C}_{gf}\hat{C}_{ff}^{-1}\hat{C}_{fg}]^{-}\hat{\lambda}_1$$

and

$$\xi_{S2} = T\hat{\lambda}_2'[\hat{C}_{gg}^* - \hat{C}_{gf}\hat{C}_{ff}^{-1}\hat{C}_{fg}]^{-}\hat{\lambda}_2$$

are respectively asymptotically equivalent under H_f *to* ξ_{W1} *and* ξ_{W2}.

8.3. Examples

Various cases can be found in GMT (1983b). Let us consider here the simple case of two families of pdf based on the same linear exponential family with the mean linked in the sense of Section 3.4 and with different exogenous variables.
   In this case the two families of pdf are defined by

$$\operatorname{Log} f(y_t; x_t, \alpha) = A[C^{-1}(x_t'\alpha)] + B(y_t) + y_t x_t'\alpha ,$$
$$\operatorname{Log} g(y_t; z_t, \beta) = A[C^{-1}(z_t'\alpha)] + B(y_t) + y_t z_t'\beta .$$

   For instance, in the case of a Bernoulli distribution with $C^{-1}(u) = e^u/(1 + e^u)$, it is the problem of the choice between two logit models with two sets of explanatory variables; in the case of a Poisson distribution with $C^{-1}(u) = \exp(u)$, it is the choice between two Poisson regression models.
   In this context, a simple computation shows that $b_T(\hat{\alpha})$ is the solution of

$$\sum_{t=1}^{T} z_t\{C^{-1}(x_t'\hat{\alpha}_T) - C^{-1}[z_t'b_T(\hat{\alpha}_T)]\} = 0 \quad \text{or}$$

$$\sum_{t=1}^{T} z_t\{\hat{y}_t^\alpha - C^{-1}[z_t'b_T(\hat{\alpha}_T)]\} = 0 , \tag{35}$$

where $\hat{y}_t^\alpha$ is the prediction of y_t under H_f, with $\alpha = \hat{\alpha}_T$; in other words $b_T(\hat{\alpha}_T)$ is the PML estimator of β under H_g based on the observations $\hat{y}_t^\alpha$. Moreover, it can be seen that, in the simple example considered here, the ξ_{S2} statistic is identical to the score statistic for testing $\gamma = 0$ in the model based on the same linear exponential family and the mean $m_t = C^{-1}(x_t'\alpha + z_t^{*\prime}\gamma)$ where z_t^{*} are the exogenous variables of H_g, linearly independent from the exogenous variables of H_f.

9. Model selection

Let us consider again the families of hypotheses H_f and H_g defined by (27) and (32). In a nonnested hypotheses testing method the idea is to examine the behaviour of some statistics when one of the hypotheses is assumed to be true. In a model selection procedure, none of the hypotheses is, a priori, assumed to be true and the idea is to evaluate a kind of distance between the true PDF and the models considered. Vuong (1989) has proposed a selection method based on PML estimators of α and β which also has the advantage to propose probabilistic statements, contrary to classical selection procedures (see also Rivers and Vuong, 1990).

Using the (asymptotic) KLIC as a proximity criterion we can define three hypotheses:

$$H_0: \mathrm{E}_x\mathrm{E}_0\left[\mathrm{Log}\,\frac{f(y;x,\alpha^*)}{g(y;x,\beta^*)}\right] = 0 , \tag{36}$$

$$H_F: \mathrm{E}_x\mathrm{E}_0\left[\mathrm{Log}\,\frac{f(y;x,\alpha^*)}{g(y;x,\beta^*)}\right] > 0 , \tag{37}$$

$$H_G: \mathrm{E}_x\mathrm{E}_0\left[\mathrm{Log}\,\frac{f(y;x,\alpha^*)}{g(y;x,\beta^*)}\right] < 0 , \tag{38}$$

where α^* and β^* are the asymptotic pseudo-true value of α and β.

Hypothesis H_0 means that the models are equivalent, whereas hypothesis H_F means that the family H_f is better than the family H_g and conversely for H_G.

Let us now assume that the models we are considering are strictly nonnested, i.e., that the two sets H_f and H_g have no element in common (the case of overlapping model is also treated in Vuong, 1989) and let us introduce the notations

$$\omega_*^2 = \mathrm{V}\left(\mathrm{Log}\,\frac{f(Y;X,\alpha^*)}{g(Y;X,\beta^*)}\right) , \tag{39}$$

where V is the variance taken with respect to the true joint distribution of

(Y, X), and

$$\hat{\omega}_T^2 = \frac{1}{T} \sum_{t=1}^{T} \left[\text{Log} \frac{f(y_t; x_t, \hat{\alpha}_T)}{g(y_t; x_t, \hat{\beta}_T)} \right]^2 - \left[\frac{1}{T} \sum_{t=1}^{T} \text{Log} \frac{f(y_t; x_t, \hat{\alpha}_T)}{g(y_t; x_t, \hat{\beta}_T)} \right]^2, \quad (40)$$

$$\hat{\omega}_T^2 = \frac{1}{T} \sum_{t=1}^{T} \left[\text{Log} \frac{f(y_t; x_t, \hat{\alpha}_T)}{g(y_t; x_t, \hat{\beta}_T)} \right]^2, \quad (41)$$

$$LR_T(\hat{\alpha}_T, \hat{\beta}_T) = \sum_{t=1}^{T} \text{Log} \frac{f(y_t; x_t, \hat{\alpha}_T)}{g(y_t; x_t, \hat{\beta}_T)}, \quad (42)$$

where $\hat{\alpha}_T$ and $\hat{\beta}_T$ are the PML estimators of α and β.
  The following proposition holds.

PROPOSITION 12. *If the families H_f and H_g are strictly nonnested,*
(a) *under H_0:*

$$\sqrt{T} LR_T(\hat{\alpha}_T, \hat{\beta}_T) / \hat{\omega}_T \xrightarrow[T \to \infty]{D} N(0, 1),$$

(b) *under H_F:*

$$\sqrt{T} LR_T(\hat{\alpha}_T, \hat{\beta}_T) / \hat{\omega}_T \xrightarrow[T \to \infty]{} + \infty, \text{ almost surely },$$

(c) *under H_G:*

$$\sqrt{T} LR_T(\hat{\alpha}_T, \hat{\beta}_T) / \hat{\omega}_T \xrightarrow[T \to \infty]{} - \infty, \text{ almost surely },$$

(d) *properties (a)–(c) holds if $\hat{\omega}_T$ is replaced by $\tilde{\omega}_T$.*

  So, the previous proposition provides a test procedure which can be easily implemented. At the asymptotic level ε, H_0 is accepted if

$$\left| \sqrt{T} LR_T(\hat{\alpha}_T, \hat{\beta}_T) / \hat{\omega}_T \right| \leq u_{1-\varepsilon/2}$$

(where $u_{1-\varepsilon/2}$ is the quantile of order $1 - \varepsilon/2$ of $N(0, 1)$); if $\sqrt{T} LR_T(\hat{\alpha}, \hat{\beta}_T) / \hat{\omega}_T > u_{1-\varepsilon/2}$, H_0 is rejected in favour of H_F and if $\sqrt{T} LR_T(\hat{\alpha}, \hat{\beta}) / \hat{\omega}_T < -u_{1-\varepsilon/2}$, H_0 is rejected in favour of H_G.

10. Concluding remarks

The methods described in the previous sections clearly have a wide applicability and they already have been used in various contexts. Cameron and Trivedi (1986) were interested in the number of consultations with a doctor or a specialist and they used various PML1 and QGPML methods. Boyer, Dionne and Vanasse (1990) applied the same kind of methods to explain the number of car accidents and to propose a bonus-malus system based on a Poisson model with individual effect. Laroque and Salanié (1990) used the simulated PML1, QGPML and PML2 methods in the context of a multimarket disequilibrium models, because the ML methods were untractable. Bollerslev and Wooldridge (1988) used the PML2 approach in the context of autoregressive conditionally heteroscedastic (ARCH) models, and Gourieroux and Monfort (1991b) used the same method for the qualitative threshold ARCH modelling of stock indexes. Arminger and Sobel (1990) used PML2 method in a model for education and occupational status with missing data (see also Arminger and Schoenberg, 1989). Wooldridge (1991) used PML1 methods in a model explaining the number of times an individual was arrested. Laffont, Ossard and Vuong (1991) used simulated PML1 methods, in particular simulated nonlinear least squares, for econometric models of descending auctions and they applied these methods to daily sales on an auction market of egg-plants. Extensions of the methods described here have also been proposed in order to estimate autocorrelation functions (Gourieroux, Monfort and Trognon, 1984c), spatial interactions (Strauss and Ikeda, 1990), possibly misspecified ARMA models (Tanaka and Satchell, 1989; Pötsher, 1991) or limited dependent variables models with serial correlation (Robinson, 1982; Gourieroux and Monfort, 1985). The simulated PML methods also seem promising; it is clear, for instance, that such methods could be applied in the many kinds of models where unobservable variables appear: factor models, index models, models with individual effects, model with heterogeneity, model with lagged endogenous variables (for instance dynamic disequilibrium models). Works in some of these fields are in progress and more and more experience will be accumulated.

References

Akaike, H. (1973). Information theory and an extension of the Maximum Likelihood Principle. In: Petron and Csaki, eds., *Proc. 2nd Int. Symp. Information Theory*, Budapest, 267–281.

Amemiya, T. (1980). Selection of regressors. *Internat. Econom. Rev.* **21**, 331–354.

Arminger, G. and R. Schoenberg (1989). Pseudo-maximum likelihood estimation and a test of misspecification in mean and covariance structure models. *Psychometrika* **4**, 409–426.

Arminger G. and M. E. Sobel (1990). Pseudo-maximum likelihood estimation of mean and covariance structures with missing data. *J. Amer. Statist. Assoc.* **85**, 195–203.

Begun, J., W. Hall, W. Huang and J. Wellner (1983). Information and asymptotic efficiency in parametric-nonparametric models. *Ann. Statist.* **11**, 432–452.

Bollerslev, T. and J. M. Wooldridge (1988). Quasi-maximum likelihood estimation of dynamic models with time-varying covariances. Mimeo, MIT, Cambridge, MA.

Bourlange, D. and C. Doz (1988). Pseudo-maximum de vraisemblance: Expériences de simulations dans le cadre d'un modèle de poisson. *Ann. Econom. Statist.* **10**, 139–176.

Boyer, M., G. Dionne and C. Vanasse (1990). Econometric models of accident distributions. Cahier du CRDE No. 9001, Université de Montréal.

Broze, L. and C. Gourieroux (1993). Covariance estimators and adjusted pseudo-maximum likelihood method. CORE DP.

Cameron, A. C. and P. K. Trivedi (1986). Econometric models based on count data: Comparisons and applications of some estimators and tests. *J. Appl. Econom.* 1, 29–53.

Chamberlain, G. (1987). Asymptotic efficiency in estimation with conditional moment restrictions. *J. Econometrics* **34**, 305–334.

Chow, G. (1981). Selection of econometric models by the information criterion. In: E. G. Charatsis, ed., *Proc. Econometric Soc. European Meeting*, North-Holland, Amsterdam.

Chow, G. (1983). *Econometrics*. North-Holland, Amsterdam.

Cox, D. R. (1961). Tests of separate families of hypotheses. In: *Proc. 4th Berkeley Sympos.*, Vol. 1, Univ. of California Press, Berkeley, CA, 105–123.

Cox, D. R. (1962). Further results on tests of separate families of hypotheses. *J. Roy. Statist. Soc. Ser. B.* **24**, 406–426.

Foutz, R. V. and R. C. Srivastava (1977). The performance of the likelihood ratio test when the model is incorrect. *Ann. Statist.* **5**, 1183–1194.

Gallant, A. R. (1987). *Nonlinear Statistical Models*. Wiley, New York.

Gallant, A. R. and H. White (1988). *Estimation and Inference in Dynamic Models*. Basil Blackwell, Oxford.

Gourieroux, C. and A. Monfort (1985). A general approach to serial correlation. *Econometric Theory* **1**, 315–340.

Gourieroux, C. and A. Monfort (1987). Consistent *M*-estimators in a semi-parametric model. ENSAE/INSEE, Discussion Paper No. 8706.

Gourieroux, C. and A. Monfort (1989a). *Statistique et Modèles Econométriques*, 2 Volumes. Economica, Paris.

Gourieroux, C. and A. Monfort (1989b). A general framework for testing a null hypothesis in a mixed form. *Econometric Theory* **5**, 63–82.

Gourieroux, C. and A. Monfort (1991a). Simulation based inference in models with heterogeneity. *Ann. Econom. Statist.* **20/21**, 69–107.

Gourieroux, C. and A. Monfort (1991b). Qualitative threshold ARCH models. *J. Econometrics*, to appear.

Gourieroux, C. and A. Monfort (1992). Simulation based inference: A survey with special reference to panel data models. *J. Econometrics*, to appear.

Gourieroux, C., A. Monfort and A. Trognon (1983a). Estimation par la méthode du pseudo-maximum de vraisemblance. *Cahier Séminaire Économétrie* **25**, 29–48.

Gourieroux, C., A. Monfort and A. Trognon (1983b). Testing nested or non-nested hypotheses. *J. Econometrics* **21**, 83–115.

Gourieroux, C., A. Monfort and A. Trognon (1984a). Pseudo maximum likelihood methods: Theory. *Econometrica* **52**, 681–700.

Gourieroux, C., A. Monfort and A. Trognon (1984b). Pseudo maximum likelihood methods: Applications to poisson models. *Econometrica* **52**, 701–720.

Gourieroux, C., A. Monfort and A. Trognon (1984c). Estimation and test in probit models with serial correlation. In: *Alternative Approaches to Time Series Analysis*, Publications des Facultés Universitaires Saint-Louis, Bruxelles.

Hannan, E. J. (1970). *Multiple Time Series*. Wiley, New York.

Hendry, D. F. and J. F. Richard (1987). Recent developments in the theory of encompassing. In: B. Cornet and H. Tulkens, eds., *Contributions to Operations Research and Econometrics*, The XXth Anniversary of CORE, MIT Press, Cambridge, MA.

Hood, W. and T. Koopmans (1953). The estimation of simultaneous linear economic relationships. In: *Studies in Econometric Method*, Yale Univ. Press, New Haven, CT.

Hotelling, H. (1940). The selection of variables for use in prediction with some comments on the problem of nuisance parameters. *Ann. Math. Statist.* **11**, 271–283.

Jennrich, R. I. (1969). Asymptotic properties of nonlinear least squares estimators. *Ann. Math. Statist.* **40**, 633–643.

Johnson, N. and S. Kotz (1972). *Discrete Distributions*. Wiley, New York.

Judge, G. G., W. E. Griffiths, R. C. Hill, H. Lutkepohl and T. Lee (1985). *The Theory and Practice of Econometrics*. 2nd ed, Wiley, New York.

Laffont, J. J., H. Ossard and Q. H. Vuong (1991). Econometrics of first price auctions. Mimeo, Université de Toulouse.

Laroque, G. and B. Salanié (1989). Estimation of multi-market fix-price models: An application of pseudo-maximum likelihood methods. *Econometrica* **57**, 831–860.

Laroque, G. and B. Salanié (1990). Estimating the canonical disequilibrium model: Asymptotic theory and finite sample properties. Document de travail, CREST, Département de la Recherche, INSEE No. 9005.

Malinvaud, E. (1970). The consistency of nonlinear regressions. *Ann. Math. Statist.* **41**, 956–969.

McCullagh, P. (1983). Quasi-likelihood functions. *Ann. Statist.* **11**(1), 59–67.

McCullagh, P. and J. A. Nelder (1983). *Generalized Linear Models*. Chapman and Hall, London.

McFadden, D. (1989). A method of simulated moments for estimation of discrete response models without numerical integration. *Econometrica* **57**, 995–1026.

Mizon, G. E. (1984). The encompassing approach in econometrics. In: D. F. Hendry and K. F. Wallis, eds., *Econometrics and Quantitative Economics*, Basil Blackwell, Oxford.

Mizon, G. E. and J. F. Richard (1986). The encompassing principle and its application to testing non-nested hypotheses. *Econometrica* **54**(3), 657–678.

Newey, W. (1989). Introduction à la théorie des bornes d'efficacité. *Ann. Econom. Statist.* **13**, 1–47.

Pakes, A. and D. Pollard (1989). Simulation and the asymptotics of optimization estimation. *Econometrica* **57**, 1027–1057.

Pesaran, M. H. (1974). On the general problem of model selection. *Rev. Econom. Stud.* **41**, 153–171.

Pötscher, B. M. (1991). Noninvertibility and pseudo maximum likelihood estimation of mis-specified ARMA models. *Econometric Theory* **7**, 435–449.

Rivers, D. and Q. H. Vuong (1990). Model selection tests for nonlinear dynamic models. Mimeo, Université de Toulouse.

Robinson, P. (1982). On the asymptotic properties of estimators of models containing limited dependent variables. *Econometrica* **50**, 27–41.

Sawa, T. (1978). Information criteria for discriminating among alternative regression models. *Econometrica* **46**, 1273–1292.

Stein, C. (1956). Efficient nonparametric testing and estimation. In: *Proc. 3rd Berkeley Sympos. on Mathematical Statistics and Probability*, Vol. 1, Univ. of California Press, Berkeley, CA.

Strauss, D. and M. Ikeda (1990). Pseudo-likelihood estimation for social networks. *J. Amer. Statist. Assoc.* **85**, 204–212.

Szroeter, J. (1983). Generalized Wald methods for testing nonlinear implicit and overidentifying restrictions. *Econometrica* **51**, 335–348.

Tanaka, K. and S. E. Satchell (1989). Asymptotic properties of the maximum likelihood and nonlinear least-squares estimator for noninvertible moving average models. *Econometric Theory* **5**, 333–353.

Trognon, A. (1984). Pseudo-asymptotic tests based on linear exponential families. *Cahier Sémin. Econométrie* **26**, 93–109.

Trognon, A. (1987). Les méthodes du pseudo-maximum de vrisemblance. *Ann. Econom. Statistique* **8**, 117–134.

Vuong, Q. H. (1989). Likelihood ratio tests for model selection and non-tested hypotheses. *Econometrica* **57**, 307–333.

Wedderburn, R. W. M. (1974). Quasi-likelihood functions, generalized models, and the Gauss–Newton method. *Biometrika* **61**, 439–447.

White, H. (1982). Maximum likelihood estimation of misspecified models. *Econometrica* **50**, 1–25.

White, H. (1984). Maximum likelihood estimation of misspecified dynamic models. In: T. K. Dijkstra, ed., *Misspecified Analysis*, Springer, Berlin.

White, H. (1988). Estimation, inference, and specification analysis. Mimeo.

Wooldridge, J. M. (1991). Specification testing and quasi-maximum likelihood estimation. *J. Econometrica* **48**, 29–55.

G. S. Maddala, C. R. Rao and H. D. Vinod, eds., *Handbook of Statistics, Vol. 11*
© 1993 Elsevier Science Publishers B.V. All rights reserved.

13

Rao's Score Test: Recent Asymptotic Results

*Rahul Mukerjee**

1. Historical introduction to Rao's score test

Let $L(x, \boldsymbol{\theta})$ be the (log-) likelihood function of a p-vector parameter $\boldsymbol{\theta} = (\theta_1, \ldots, \theta_p)'$ given a sample x. Then the p-vector function

$$l(x, \boldsymbol{\theta}) = \partial L(x, \boldsymbol{\theta})/\partial \boldsymbol{\theta} \tag{1.1}$$

is called the *score function*. For given $\boldsymbol{\theta}$ and random x, we have

$$\mathrm{E}_{\boldsymbol{\theta}}\{l(x, \boldsymbol{\theta})\} = 0, \quad \mathrm{cov}_{\boldsymbol{\theta}}\{l(x, \boldsymbol{\theta})\} = \mathscr{I}(\boldsymbol{\theta}) = ((\mathscr{I}_{\mathrm{rs}}(\boldsymbol{\theta}))),$$

where $\mathscr{I}(\boldsymbol{\theta})$ is the Fisher information matrix. Rao (1948) introduced two test criteria for testing simple and composite hypotheses and gave their large sample null distributions.

To test a simple hypothesis $H_0\colon \boldsymbol{\theta} = \boldsymbol{\theta}_0$, Rao's test statistic is

$$R_{\mathrm{s}} = \max_{m \neq 0} \frac{\{m'l(x, \boldsymbol{\theta}_0)\}^2}{m'\mathscr{I}(\boldsymbol{\theta}_0)m} = \{l(x, \boldsymbol{\theta}_0)\}'\{\mathscr{I}(\boldsymbol{\theta}_0)\}^{-1}\{l(x, \boldsymbol{\theta}_0)\}, \tag{1.2}$$

assuming the positive-definite (pd)-ness of $\mathscr{I}(\boldsymbol{\theta}_0)$. Under H_0, this is asymptotically distributed as a central chi-square with p degrees of freedom (df) under fairly general conditions. To test a composite hypothesis of the type that $\boldsymbol{\theta}$ lies on a surface defined by $\boldsymbol{\theta} = \boldsymbol{\psi}(\boldsymbol{\xi})$, where $\boldsymbol{\xi}$ is a q-vector parameter ($q < p$), Rao proposed the statistic

$$R_{\mathrm{c}} = \{l(x, \hat{\boldsymbol{\theta}}_{\mathrm{c}})\}'\{\mathscr{I}(\hat{\boldsymbol{\theta}}_{\mathrm{c}})\}^{-1}\{l(x, \hat{\boldsymbol{\theta}}_{\mathrm{c}})\}, \tag{1.3}$$

where $\hat{\boldsymbol{\theta}}_{\mathrm{c}}$ is the maximum likelihood estimator (MLE) of $\boldsymbol{\theta}$ under the condition $\boldsymbol{\theta} = \boldsymbol{\psi}(\boldsymbol{\xi})$. The asymptotic null distribution of R_{c} is, under some conditions, a central chi-square with $p - q$ df. About ten years later, Silvey (1959) proposed the same test (1.3) for a composite hypothesis and called it the Lagrangian

* On leave from Indian Institute of Management, Calcutta, India. This work was supported partially by a grant from the Center from Management and Development Studies, IIM, Calcutta, and partially by the Air Force Office of Scientific Research under Grant AFOSR-91-0242.

multiplier (LM) test which led to Rao's test (1.3) for composite hypotheses being referred to as the LM test. About that time, Neyman (1959) introduced what is called the $C(\alpha)$ test for testing composite hypotheses of the type

$$H_0: \theta_1 = \theta_{10}, \quad \theta_2, \ldots, \theta_p \text{ are arbitrary .}$$

The $C(\alpha)$ criterion is a signed root square of Rao's criterion (1.3) for one df with one difference. The estimators of the nuisance parameters $\theta_2, \ldots, \theta_p$ used in Neyman's statistic are any root n-consistent estimators whereas in Rao's formulation, they are MLEs given $\theta_1 = \theta_{10}$. Of course, up to the first order, the asymptotic distribution of (1.3) remains the same whether MLEs or any root n-consistent estimators are used for the nuisance parameters.

The $C(\alpha)$ test of Neyman is a test for one parameter in the presence of $p - 1$ nuisance parameters. This has been extended by Hall and Mathiason (1990) for testing more than one, say $p - q$, components of $\boldsymbol{\theta}$, in the presence of q nuisance parameters, in the form of Rao's statistic (1.3) with MLEs replaced by any root n-consistent estimators. They call such a modified version of (1.3) the Neyman–Rao test criterion.

While introducing the score test in 1948, Rao conjectured that it is likely to be locally more powerful than other tests like the likelihood ratio and Wald's tests (see also Rao, 1965, p. 350, in this context). Recent work, based on higher-order asymptotics, indicates the truth of Rao's conjecture. An objective of this article is to review the work done in recent years in this area. We shall also summarize some recent results on Bartlett-type adjustment for Rao's statistic, a problem posed by Cox (1988) and Rao, in a private communication. For a review of the developments in this field till the late eighties, we refer to Ghosh (1991); see also Bera and Ullah (1991) and the references therein for an informative general review on Rao's test as applied in econometrics.

In the sequel, we shall use the abbreviations LR, R and W to denote respectively the likelihood ratio, Rao's and Wald's statistics as well as the tests based on these statistics depending on the context. The symbol R will represent R_s or R_c (see (1.2), (1.3)) depending on whether a simple or a composite hypothesis is being considered.

2. Comparison of higher-order power

For the scalar parameter case, under a one-sided alternative, R is evidently locally most powerful (see, e.g., Ferguson, 1967, pp. 235). As a consequence, the comparison among LR, R and W is of more interest when (a) the parameter $\boldsymbol{\theta}$ is multi-dimensional or (b) the parameter is one-dimensional but the alternative is two-sided. Among the early authors, Peers (1971), Hayakawa (1975) and Harris and Peers (1980) studied these three tests, under the set-up of multi-dimensional $\boldsymbol{\theta}$ and contiguous (multi-sided) alternatives, and reported their noncomparability. In particular, they observed that, up to the second order of comparison, the local power function of none of these tests uniformly dominates those of the others. In consideration of this, subsequent authors treated the problem adopting the following two approaches:

(i) to compare slightly modified versions of the tests, the modification being done in a meaningful way;

(ii) to compare the tests in their original forms but using some reasonable criterion other than point-by-point power.

2.1. Comparison of locally unbiased versions

Chandra and Joshi (1983), following a suggestion of J. K. Ghosh, adopted the first approach and compared the locally unbiased, up to $o(n^{-1})$, versions of the tests. We refer to Ghosh (1991) for an illuminating discussion on the rationale behind this approach; see also Amari (1985, p. 172) in this context. With reference to a sequence of independent and identically distributed (iid) possibly vector-valued random variables $X_1, X_2, \ldots$, having a common density $f(\cdot, \theta)$, where θ is scalar-valued, Chandra and Joshi (1983) considered the problem of testing H_0: $\theta = \theta_0$ against a two-sided alternative, θ_0 being an interior point of the parameter space. They considered contiguous alternatives of the form $\theta(n) = \theta_0 + n^{-1/2}\delta$, where n is the sample size, and under the assumptions of Chandra and Ghosh (1980) (see also Bhattacharya and Ghosh, 1978), which are of quite general nature, compared the signed square-root versions of the tests as follows:

For $i = 1, 2, 3$, let

$$l_i^* = E_{\theta_0}\{d^i \log f(X_1; \theta_0)/d\theta^i\} \, ,$$

$$H_i = n^{-1/2} \sum_{j=1}^{n} [\{d^i \log f(X_j; \theta_0)/d\theta^i\} - l_i^*] \, .$$

Chandra and Joshi (1983) noted that for each of LR, R and W, there exists a set $\mathcal{A}_n$ with $P_{\theta(n)}$-probability $1 + o(n^{-1})$ uniformly over compact subsets of δ, such that over $\mathcal{A}_n$ the statistic admits an expansion of the form $T_n^2 + o(n^{-1})$, where

$$T_n = H_1 I^{-1/2} + n^{-1/2}(\vartheta_1 H_1 H_2 + \vartheta_2 H_1^2)$$
$$+ n^{-1}(y_1 H_1^2 H_2 + y_2 H_1 H_2^2 + y_3 H_1^3 + y_4 H_1^2 H_3) \, , \qquad (2.1)$$

$I \, (= -l_2^*$, under standard regularity conditions) is the per observation Fisher information at θ_0, and $\vartheta_1, \vartheta_2, y_1, y_2, y_3, y_4$ are constants, free from n. The constants $\vartheta_1, \vartheta_2, y_1, y_2, y_3, y_4$ depend on the particular test statistic under consideration. In particular, by (1.2), for R, $\vartheta_1 = \vartheta_2 = y_1 = y_2 = y_3 = y_4 = 0$.

Denoting the square-root versions of LR, R and W by T_{n1}, T_{n2} and T_{n3} respectively, Chandra and Joshi (1983) compared them on the basis of critical regions of the form

$$T_{ni} > z + n^{-1/2}a_{1i} + n^{-1}a_{2i} \quad \text{or}$$
$$T_{ni} < -z + n^{-1/2}a_{3i} + n^{-1}a_{4i} \quad (i = 1, 2, 3), \tag{2.2}$$

where z is the upper $\frac{1}{2}\alpha$-point of a standard normal variate, $a_{11} = a_{21} = a_{31} = a_{41} = 0$, and the constants $a_{1i}, a_{2i}, a_{3i}, a_{4i}$ $(i = 2, 3)$, free from n, are so chosen that

$$P_{\theta_0}(T_{ni} > z + n^{-1/2}a_{1i} + n^{-1}a_{2i})$$
$$= P_{\theta_0}(T_{n1} > z + n^{-1/2}a_{11} + n^{-1}a_{21}) + o(n^{-1}) \quad (i = 2, 3),$$
$$P_{\theta_0}(T_{ni} < -z + n^{-1/2}a_{3i} + n^{-1}a_{4i})$$
$$= P_{\theta_0}(T_{n1} < -z + n^{-1/2}a_{31} + n^{-1}a_{41}) + o(n^{-1}) \quad (i = 2, 3). \tag{2.3}$$

The conditions in (2.3) not only ensure that the three tests are of identical size up to $o(n^{-1})$ but also, as noted in Chandra and Joshi (1983), make them locally unbiased up to that order. Incidentally, with $a_{11} = a_{21} = a_{31} = a_{41} = 0$, LR is locally unbiased up to $o(n^{-1})$.

For $i = 1, 2, 3$, Chandra and Joshi (1983) considered an Edgeworth expansion for the distribution of T_{ni} under $\theta(n)$ $(=\theta_0 + n^{-1/2}\delta)$ and showed that the power function, $P^{(i)}(\delta)$, under continuous alternatives, of a test based on T_{ni} (see (2.2), (2.3)) can be expanded as

$$P^{(i)}(\delta) = P_0^{(i)}(\delta) + n^{-1/2}P_1^{(i)}(\delta) + n^{-1}P_2^{(i)}(\delta) + o(n^{-1}),$$

where $P_0^{(i)}(\delta)$, $P_1^{(i)}(\delta)$, $P_2^{(i)}(\delta)$ are free from n but involve δ and also z. As anticipated, it was seen that

$$P_0^{(1)}(\delta) \equiv P_0^{(2)}(\delta) \equiv P_0^{(3)}(\delta),$$

so that the three tests have identical power up to the first order. It was also observed by Chandra and Joshi (1983) that

$$P_1^{(1)}(\delta) \equiv P_1^{(2)}(\delta) \equiv P_1^{(3)}(\delta),$$

which implies that, for one-dimensional θ, identity of power up to the first order is accompanied by that up to the second order (cf. Bickel, Chibisov and Van Zwet, 1981) when tests are compared on the basis of their locally unbiased versions.

Therefore, in order to discriminate among the three tests, one has to compare third-order power, i.e., $P_2^{(i)}(\delta)$, $i = 1, 2, 3$. Since $P_2^{(i)}(\delta)$ involves not only δ but also z, one may write $P_2^{(i)}(\delta) \equiv P_2^{(i)}(\delta, z)$. By (2.3), the tests are of identical size up to $o(n^{-1})$ and are also locally unbiased up to that order.

Hence

$$P_2^{(1)}(0, z) \equiv P_2^{(2)}(0, z) \equiv P_2^{(3)}(0, z),$$

$$P_2^{(1)'}(0, z) \equiv P_2^{(2)'}(0, z) \equiv P_2^{(3)'}(0, z) \equiv 0,$$

identically in z, where primes denote differentiation with respect to δ. Considering explicit expressions for $P_2^{(i)}(\delta, z)$ ($i = 1, 2, 3$), Chandra and Joshi (1983) showed that

$$\lim_{\delta \to 0} \{P_2^{(2)}(\delta, z) - P_2^{(1)}(\delta, z)\}/\delta^2 > 0,$$

$$\lim_{\delta \to 0} \{P_2^{(2)}(\delta, z) - P_2^{(3)}(\delta, z)\}/\delta^2 > 0, \tag{2.4}$$

for large but reasonable z (i.e., for small but reasonable test size) provided the model has a nonzero statistical curvature at θ_0 (Efron, 1975).

The result (2.4), indicating the superiority of R over LR and W, in terms of third-order power under contiguous alternatives, was extended and strengthened in various directions by subsequent workers. Thus, Chandra and Mukerjee (1984, 1985) considered an entire family of test statistics with square root versions of the form (2.1), with ϑ_1, ϑ_2, y_1, y_2, y_3, y_4 free from n and z as happens with LR, R and W, and established the optimality of R in that family in the sense of (2.4). In the latter paper, they also presented more detailed expressions for the third-order power differences and investigated the implications thereof. Chandra and Samanta (1988) obtained similar results with reference to a larger family of test statistics. Mukerjee (1989a) proved the optimality of R, in an even wider class, in the sense of (2.4) and streamlined the algebraic computations to some extent. A discussion on Mukerjee (1989a), who gave a simple formula for the third-order power difference, is available in Ghosh (1991).

In consideration of the locally optimum property of R as noted above, it is natural to investigate its behaviour vis-a-vis the locally most powerful unbiased (LMPU) test under a two-sided alternative. Mukerjee and Chandra (1987), following a suggestion of J. K. Ghosh, considered this problem and observed that, under contiguous alternatives, R is as good as the LMPU test up to the second order of comparison and almost as good as the LMPU test at the third order for small but reasonable test size provided the statistical curvature of the model at θ_0 is not too large.

The results summarized in the last two paragraphs were all derived under the framework of one-dimensional θ, a two-sided alternative and iid observations and comparisons were made on the basis of the locally unbiased versions of the tests. Continuing with the iid case, Mukerjee (1990a,b) attempted to extend the findings of these authors to models with multi-dimensional $\boldsymbol{\theta}$. Compared to the scalar parameter case, this situation presents some novelties and, with reference to the final results, here we propose to highlight some details which were not discussed in Mukerjee (1990a,b). To that effect, we introduce some notation.

Let $X_1, X_2, \ldots$, be a sequence of iid possibly vector-valued random variables with a common density $f(\cdot; \boldsymbol{\theta})$, where $\boldsymbol{\theta} = (\theta_1, \ldots, \theta_p)' \in \mathbb{R}^p$ or some open subset thereof. Consider the problem of testing $H_0: \boldsymbol{\theta} = \boldsymbol{\theta}_0$ against $\boldsymbol{\theta} \neq \boldsymbol{\theta}_0$. Without loss of generality (by a reparametrization, if necessary), the per observation information matrix at $\boldsymbol{\theta}_0$ is supposed to equal the $p \times p$ identity matrix. Then the dispersion matrix of $\partial \log f(X_1; \boldsymbol{\theta}_0)/\partial \theta_i$ $(1 \leq i \leq p)$ and $\partial^2 \log f(X_1; \boldsymbol{\theta}_0)/\partial \theta_i \, \partial \theta_j$ $(1 \leq i, \, j \leq p)$, under $\boldsymbol{\theta}_0$, is of the form

$$\Sigma = \begin{pmatrix} I_p & A \\ A' & \Sigma* \end{pmatrix},$$

where I_p is the $p \times p$ identity matrix, and A and $\Sigma*$ are of orders $p \times p^2$ and $p^2 \times p^2$ respectively. The $p^2 \times p^2$ nonnegative definite (nnd) matrix

$$\Sigma_0 = \Sigma* - A'A$$

represents a generalized version of Efron's curvature at $\boldsymbol{\theta}_0$. For $1 \leq i, \, u \leq p$, define

$$H_{1i} = n^{-1/2} \sum_{j=1}^{n} \partial \log f(X_j; \boldsymbol{\theta}_0)/\partial \theta_i \, ,$$

$$H_{2iu} = n^{-1/2} \sum_{j=1}^{n} [\{\partial^2 \log f(X_j; \boldsymbol{\theta}_0)/\partial \theta_i \, \partial \theta_u\} - l_{iu}^{(0)}] \, ,$$

where $l_{iu}^{(0)} = E_{\boldsymbol{\theta}_0}\{\partial^2 \log f(X_1; \boldsymbol{\theta}_0)/\partial \theta_i \, \partial \theta_u\}$. Let H_1 be a $p \times 1$ vector with i-th element H_{1i} and H_2 be a $p \times p$ matrix with (i, u)-th element H_{2iu} $(1 \leq i, u \leq p)$.

For $1 \leq i, u, s \leq p$ let

$$\gamma_{i \cdot us}^{(1)} = E_{\boldsymbol{\theta}_0}[\{\partial \log f(X_1; \boldsymbol{\theta}_0)/\partial \theta_i\}\{\partial^2 \log f(X_1; \boldsymbol{\theta}_0)/\partial \theta_u \, \partial \theta_s\}] \, ,$$

$$\gamma_{ius}^{(2)} = E_{\boldsymbol{\theta}_0}\{\partial^3 \log f(X_1; \boldsymbol{\theta}_0)/\partial \theta_i \, \partial \theta_u \, \partial \theta_s\} \, ,$$

$$\gamma_{ius}^{(3)} = E_{\boldsymbol{\theta}_0}[\{\partial \log f(X_1; \boldsymbol{\theta}_0)/\partial \theta_i\}$$
$$\times \{\partial \log f(X_1; \boldsymbol{\theta}_0)/\partial \theta_u\}\{\partial \log f(X_1; \boldsymbol{\theta}_0)/\partial \theta_s\}] \, .$$

Define Γ as a $p \times p^2$ matrix with i-th row $(\gamma_{1 \cdot i1}^{(1)}, \ldots, \gamma_{1 \cdot ip}^{(1)}, \ldots, \gamma_{p \cdot i1}^{(1)}, \ldots, \gamma_{p \cdot ip}^{(1)})$, $1 \leq i \leq p$, and let $\boldsymbol{\tau}$ be a $p^2 \times 1$ vector with (i, i)-th element unity for each i $(1 \leq i \leq p)$ and all other elements zero (e.g., with $p = 3$, $\boldsymbol{\tau} = (1, 0, 0, 0, 1, 0, 0, 0, 1)'$).

In the following, for positive integral ν and nonnegative λ, $K_{\nu, \lambda}(\cdot)$ and $k_{\nu, \lambda}(\cdot)$ denote respectively the cumulative distribution function and the probability density function of a possibly noncentral chi-square variate with ν df and noncentrality parameter λ. Also, for a real valued function $\zeta(\cdot)$ defined over $\mathbb{R}^p$ and for $\lambda > 0$, we shall write

$$\bar{\zeta}(\lambda) = \int_{y'y=\lambda} \zeta(y) \, dy \Big/ \int_{y'y=\lambda} dy \qquad (2.5)$$

to denote the average of $\zeta(\cdot)$, along the sphere $\{y: y'y = \lambda\}$, provided (2.5) is well defined.

Mukerjee (1990a,b) considered a family $\mathcal{F}_0$ of test procedures as described below. For contiguous alternatives $\boldsymbol{\theta}(n) = \boldsymbol{\theta}_0 + n^{-1/2}\boldsymbol{\delta}$ and for every test in $\mathcal{F}_0$, a set $\mathcal{A}_n$, with $P_{\boldsymbol{\theta}(n)}$-probability $1 + o(n^{-1})$ uniformly over compact subsets of $\boldsymbol{\delta}$, can be obtained such that over $\mathcal{A}_n$ the test is given by a critical region of the form

$$T_n'T_n > z_p^2 + n^{-1/2}b_0 + n^{-1}c_0 + o(n^{-1}),\qquad(2.6a)$$

where

(i) z_p^2 is the upper α-point of a central chi-square variate with p df,

$$T_n = H_1 + n^{-1/2}(Q^{(1)} + b) + n^{-1}(Q^{(2)} + c),\qquad(2.6b)$$

$$Q^{(1)} = aH_2H_1 + B(H_1 \otimes H_1), \qquad Q^{(2)} = (Q_{p+1}, \ldots, Q_{2p})',$$

$$Q_i = g_i(Q_{i1}, \ldots, Q_{iu_i}) \quad (p+1 \leqslant i \leqslant 2p),$$

$$Q_{is} = n^{-1/2} \sum_{j=1}^{n} \{q_{is}(X_j) - \beta_{is}(\boldsymbol{\theta}_0)\} \quad (1 \leqslant s \leqslant u_i, \, p+1 \leqslant i \leqslant 2p),$$

$\otimes$ denotes Kronecker product, the $g_i(\cdot)$ are polynomials and the $q_{is}(\cdot)$ are such that

$$E_{\boldsymbol{\theta}}\{q_{is}(X_1)\} = \beta_{is}(\boldsymbol{\theta}) \quad \forall \boldsymbol{\theta} \quad (1 \leqslant s \leqslant u_i, \, p+1 \leqslant i \leqslant 2p),$$

which are assumed to exist,

(ii) the scalar a and the $p \times p^2$ matrix B in the expression for $Q^{(1)}$ are nonstochastic and free from n,

(iii) the scalars b_0, c_0 and the elements of the $p \times 1$ vectors b, c are constants, free from n, to be so determined that the test has size $\alpha + o(n^{-1})$ and is locally unbiased up to $o(n^{-1})$.

As noted in Ghosh (1991), if one thinks of the acceptance region as a sphere then introducing b_0, c_0 is equivalent to perturbing the radius and introducing b, c is equivalent to perturbing the centre with a view to attaining respectively the conditions of size and local unbiasedness up to $o(n^{-1})$. Note that a, B, the Q_i and the q_{is} may vary from one test in $\mathcal{F}_0$ to another. For any test in $\mathcal{F}_0$, we define

$$B^* = B + a\Gamma.$$

Let the i-th row of the $p \times p^2$ matrix B^* be $(b_{i11}^*, \ldots, b_{i1p}^*, \ldots, b_{ip1}^*, \ldots, b_{ipp}^*)$ $(1 \leqslant i \leqslant p)$, and

$$b(ius) = b_{ius}^* + b_{isu}^* + b_{siu}^* + b_{sui}^* + b_{uis}^* + b_{usi}^* \quad (1 \leqslant i, u, s \leqslant p).$$

The family $\mathcal{F}_0$ is very rich and includes, in particular, LR, R and W. It can be seen (cf. Mukerjee, 1993) that the expressions for a and $b(ius)$ for these three tests are respectively given by

$$a_{LR} = \tfrac{1}{2}, \qquad a_R = 0, \qquad a_W = 1, \tag{2.7a}$$

$$b_{LR}(ius) = -\gamma_{ius}^{(3)}, \qquad b_R(ius) = 0,$$
$$b_W(ius) = -(\gamma_{ius}^{(2)} + \gamma_{ius}^{(3)}) \quad (1 \leqslant i, u, s \leqslant p). \tag{2.7b}$$

Under standard assumptions and regularity conditions, it was shown by Mukerjee (1990a,b) that if b_0, c_0, b, c are chosen subject to the conditions of size and local unbiasedness, up to $o(n^{-1})$, then the power function of a test in $\mathcal{F}_0$, under contiguous alternatives $\boldsymbol{\theta}(n) = \boldsymbol{\theta}_0 + n^{-1/2}\boldsymbol{\delta}$, is given by

$$P(\boldsymbol{\delta}) = P_0(\boldsymbol{\delta}) + n^{-1/2}P_1(\boldsymbol{\delta}) + n^{-1}P_2(\boldsymbol{\delta}) + o(n^{-1}),$$

where
(i) $P_0(\boldsymbol{\delta}), P_1(\boldsymbol{\delta}), P_2(\boldsymbol{\delta})$ are free from n,
(ii) $P_0(\boldsymbol{\delta}) = 1 - K_{p,\lambda}(z_p^2)$, with $\lambda = \boldsymbol{\delta}'\boldsymbol{\delta}$, is the same for all tests in the family $\mathcal{F}_0$,
(iii) $P_1(\boldsymbol{\delta})$ is not necessarily identical for all tests in $\mathcal{F}_0$ but is such that for each $\lambda > 0$, $\bar{P}_1(\lambda)$, defined as in (2.5), is identical for all tests in $\mathcal{F}_0$,
(iv) $P_2(\boldsymbol{\delta})$ is such that for $\lambda > 0$,

$$\bar{P}_2(\lambda) = \bar{P}_{20}(\lambda) + \lambda U + O(\lambda^2),$$

with $\bar{P}_{20}(\lambda)$ identical for all tests in $\mathcal{F}_0$, $U = U_1 - U_2$,

$$U_1 = p^{-1}k_{p+2}[a\boldsymbol{\tau}'\Sigma_0\boldsymbol{\tau} - a^2 z_p^2(p+2)^{-1}\{\boldsymbol{\tau}'\Sigma_0\boldsymbol{\tau} + 2\mathrm{tr}(\Sigma_0)\}],$$

$$U_2 = (2p)^{-1}k_{p+6}\left[\tfrac{1}{3}\sum_{i,u,s=1}^{p}\{b(ius)\}^2 - (p+2)^{-1}\sum_{i=1}^{p}\left\{\sum_{u=1}^{p} b(iuu)\right\}^2\right],$$

and for positive integral v, $k_v = k_{v,0}(z_p^2)$.

The derivation of the above result required the use of a multivariate Edgeworth expansion for the distribution of $\boldsymbol{T}_n$ under $\boldsymbol{\theta}(n)$. The use of a new kind of polynomials, analogous to Hermite polynomials, was helpful in simplifying the algebra.

As a consequence of (ii) and (iii) above, if average power along spheres centered at $\boldsymbol{\theta}_0$ be the criterion, then up to the second order of comparison, all tests in $\mathcal{F}_0$ are equivalent and, as such, a third-order comparison on the basis of $\bar{P}_2(\lambda)$ is warranted. To that effect, we write Π for the set of triplets ius satisfying $1 \leqslant i, u, s \leqslant p$ such that i, u, s are all distinct and, recalling the permutation invariance of the $b(ius)$, note that for $p \geq 2$,

$$\frac{1}{3} \sum_{i,u,s=1}^{p} \{b(ius)\}^2 - (p+2)^{-1} \sum_{i=1}^{p} \left\{ \sum_{u=1}^{p} b(iuu) \right\}^2$$

$$= \frac{1}{3} \sum_{ius \in \Pi} \{b(ius)\}^2 + \sum_{i=1}^{p} \left[\frac{1}{3}\{b(iii)\}^2 + \sum_{\substack{u=1 \\ u \neq i}}^{p} \{b(iuu)\}^2 \right.$$

$$\left. - (p+2)^{-1} \left\{ \sum_{u=1}^{p} b(iuu) \right\}^2 \right]$$

$$\geq \frac{1}{3} \sum_{ius \in \Pi} \{b(ius)\}^2 + \sum_{i=1}^{p} \left[\frac{1}{3}\{b(iii)\}^2 + (p-1)^{-1} \left\{ \sum_{\substack{u=1 \\ u \neq i}}^{p} b(iuu) \right\}^2 \right.$$

$$\left. - (p+2)^{-1} \left\{ \sum_{u=1}^{p} b(iuu) \right\}^2 \right]$$

$$= \frac{1}{3} \sum_{ius \in \Pi} \{b(ius)\}^2$$

$$+ \frac{1}{3}(p-1)(p+2)^{-1} \sum_{i=1}^{p} \left[b(iii) - 3(p-1)^{-1} \left\{ \sum_{\substack{u=1 \\ u \neq i}}^{p} b(iuu) \right\} \right]^2 \geq 0,$$

the inequality being strict if and only if one of the following conditions holds:

(C1) Π is nonempty (i.e., $p \geq 3$) and $b(ius) \neq 0$ for some $ius \in \Pi$,

(C2) for some i $(1 \leq i \leq p)$, the quantities $b(iuu)$ $(1 \leq u \leq p, u \neq i)$ are not all equal,

(C3) for some i $(1 \leq i \leq p)$,

$$b(iii) - 3(p-1)^{-1} \left\{ \sum_{\substack{u=1 \\ u \neq i}}^{p} b(iuu) \right\} \neq 0 .$$

Thus for $p \geq 2$, $U_2 \geq 0$, with strict inequality provided one of (C1), (C2), (C3) holds. It may also be noted that if $p = 1$ then $U_2 = 0$ for each test in $\mathcal{F}_0$. In view of the nnd-ness of Σ_0, we next observe that for fixed a, $U_1 \leq 0$ whenever z_p^2 is sufficiently large, provided a does not depend on z_p^2. Thus if $\mathcal{F}_0^*$ be a subclass of $\mathcal{F}_0$ consisting of those tests in $\mathcal{F}_0$ for which a does not depend on the test size then for each test in $\mathcal{F}_0^*$ one obtains $U \leq 0$ whenever the test size α is sufficiently small. In fact, if Σ_0 is nonnull then for each test in $\mathcal{F}_0^*$ with $a \neq 0$, U is negative for sufficiently small α while if $\Sigma_0 = 0$ and $p \geq 2$ then for each test in $\mathcal{F}_0^*$ satisfying (C1), (C2) or (C3), U is negative for all α.

By (2.7a), LR, R and W belong to $\mathcal{F}_0^*$. For R one gets, $a = 0$, $B = 0$, so that $U = U_R$ (say) $= 0$. Hence, by the discussion in the last paragraph, for each test in $\mathcal{F}_0^*$, one obtains $U \leq U_R$ whenever α is sufficiently small, the inequality being strict in the situations indicated above. In this sense, R is optimal in $\mathcal{F}_0^*$ and hence superior to LR and W in particular.

It may be made explicit in this connection that, unlike in the scalar parameter case, with multi-dimensional $\boldsymbol{\theta}$, one may be able to discriminate among the tests in $\mathscr{F}_0^*$ in terms of third-order average power even under models having zero statistical curvature at $\boldsymbol{\theta}_0$, i.e., having $\Sigma_0 = 0$. This is because of the presence of U_2 in the expression for U. The following simple example serves as an illustration.

EXAMPLE 1. Consider the sequence $X_j = (X_{j1}, \ldots, X_{jp})'$, $j \geq 1$, of iid random variables with a common p-variate density over $\mathbb{R}^p$ given by

$$f(x; \boldsymbol{\theta}) = \prod_{i=1}^{p} \{(2\pi\theta_i)^{-1/2} \exp(-\tfrac{1}{2}\theta_i^{-1}x_i^2)\} \,,$$

where $\boldsymbol{\theta} = (\theta_1, \ldots, \theta_p)' > \mathbf{0}$. Suppose interest lies in testing $H_0: \boldsymbol{\theta} = \boldsymbol{\theta}_0$ against $\boldsymbol{\theta} \neq \boldsymbol{\theta}_0$, where $\boldsymbol{\theta}_0$ is a $p \times 1$ vector with each element $1/\sqrt{2}$. Then the per observation information matrix at $\boldsymbol{\theta}_0$ equals the $p \times p$ identity matrix. It can be seen that here $\Sigma_0 = 0$. Also, by (2.7b), $b_{LR}(ius) = b_W(ius) = 0$ unless $i = u = s$, and $b_{LR}(iii) = -2\sqrt{2}$, $b_W(iii) = -6\sqrt{2}$. Hence for each α, U is negative for LR and W, provided $p \geq 2$ (cf. (C3) above), showing the superiority of R over LR and W, with regard to third-order average power, in the context of this example.

It is interesting to note that, unlike in the scalar parameter case, with multi-dimensional $\boldsymbol{\theta}$, identity of point-by-point power up to the first order is not necessarily accompanied by that up to the second order even after adjustment for local unbiasedness. Considering in particular LR, R and W, Mukerjee (1990a) gave an example to demonstrate that none of these tests is uniformly superior to the other two in terms of second-order (point-by-point) power. In other words, with multi-dimensional $\boldsymbol{\theta}$, even after adjustment for local unbiasedness, the situation remains essentially similar to that observed in Peers (1971) in the sense that the tests remain noncomparable with regard to point-by-point power. This is why, in order to compare the tests in a meaningful manner, it becomes essential to invoke some other reasonable criterion and, as noted above, the criterion of average power is helpful in this regard. In this connection, reference is made to Ghosh (1991) who discussed how, even with multi-dimensional $\boldsymbol{\theta}$, identity of point-by-point power up to the second order can be achieved by introducing perturbations more general than those considered in (2.6a,b).

Earlier, Sengupta and Vermiere (1986) proposed a locally most mean power unbiased (LMMPU) test for the case of multi-dimensional $\boldsymbol{\theta}$. This test does not belong to $\mathscr{F}_0^*$ and, in consideration of the nice property of R with regard to average power as noted above, it is of interest to compare R with the LMMPU test. This problem was considered in Mukerjee and Sengupta (1993) and it was seen that although R is much simpler than the LMMPU test, being expressible only in terms of the first partial derivatives of the log-likelihood, it is almost as good as the latter with regard to third-order average power for small but reasonable test size provided the statistical curvature of the model is not too large. The findings in Mukerjee and Sengupta (1993) in a sense extended the results in Mukerjee and Chandra (1987) to the case of multi-dimensional $\boldsymbol{\theta}$. The method of derivation was, however, different and inversion of approximate characteristic functions under $\boldsymbol{\theta}(n)$ was required for obtaining the result.

Turning to the case of a composite null hypothesis, Mukerjee (1989b) continued with the iid set-up and, under an orthogonal parametrization (Cox and Reid, 1987), extended the results in Mukerjee (1989a) on the optimality of R to a setting where the interest parameter and the nuisance parameter are both one-dimensional. These results can, of course, be further extended in a routine manner to the case of a multi-dimensional nuisance parameter at the expense of heavier notation and algebra. The assumption that the interest parameter is one-dimensional is, however, nontrivial. In particular, if both the interest parameter and the nuisance parameter be multi-dimensional, then, as noted in Cox and Reid (1987), one may not in general be able to achieve an orthogonal parametrization. Anyway, it is strongly believed that the results discussed here should have their counterparts even in such a situation.

2.2. Comparison of tests in their original forms

As mentioned in the introduction of Ghosh (1991), comparison of tests on the basis of their locally unbiased versions 'has been the subject of some controversy'. There have been arguments in recent years in favour of comparing the tests on the basis of the forms in which they were originally proposed (cf. Madansky, 1989; Kallenberg, 1983). In the scalar parameter case, Madansky (1989) compared LR, R and W in their original forms and concluded that none of them dominates another even locally.

As noted in Ghosh (1991), the apparent conflict between the findings in Madansky (1989) and those discussed in the last subsection is easily resolved if one observes that in the former the tests are compared in their original forms while in the latter locally unbiased versions of the tests are compared. In fact, Mukerjee (1993) showed that even in the set-up of Madansky, a more detailed analysis can yield results similar to those discussed above.

Mukerjee (1993) dealt with the family of tests $\mathcal{F}_0$ considered in Mukerjee (1990a,b) with the change that the perturbations b, c employed in the earlier formulation to achieve local unbiasedness (see (2.6b)) were no longer used. He showed that if b_0, c_0 in (2.6a) are chosen subject to the size condition, up to $o(n^{-1})$, then the power function of a test in $\mathcal{F}_0$, under contiguous alternatives $\boldsymbol{\theta}(n) = \boldsymbol{\theta}_0 + n^{-1/2}\boldsymbol{\delta}$, is given by

$$P(\boldsymbol{\delta}) = P_0(\boldsymbol{\delta}) + n^{-1/2}P_1(\boldsymbol{\delta}) + n^{-1}P_2(\boldsymbol{\delta}) + o(n^{-1}),$$

where, as before, $P_0(\boldsymbol{\delta})$, $P_1(\boldsymbol{\delta})$, $P_2(\boldsymbol{\delta})$ are free from n, $P_0(\boldsymbol{\delta})$ and $\bar{P}_1(\lambda)$ are identical for all tests in $\mathscr{F}_0$, and $P_2(\boldsymbol{\delta})$ is such that for $\lambda > 0$,

$$\bar{P}_2(\lambda) = \bar{P}_{20}^*(\lambda) + \lambda U^* + \mathrm{O}(\lambda^2) ,$$

with $\bar{P}_{20}^*(\lambda)$ identical for all tests in $\mathscr{F}_0$, $U^* = U_1 + U_2^*$, U_1 as defined in the last subsection, and

$$U_2^* = \tfrac{1}{2} p^{-1} k_{p+4} \left[\sum_{i,u,s=1}^{p} b(iiu) \gamma_{u \cdot ss}^{(1)} \right.$$
$$\left. -z_p^2(p+4)^{-1} \left\{ \tfrac{1}{3} \sum_{i,u,s=1}^{p} (b(ius))^2 + \tfrac{1}{2} \sum_{i=1}^{p} \left(\sum_{u=1}^{p} b(iuu) \right)^2 \right\} \right]$$

the notational system being as introduced earlier.

Mukerjee (1993) considered a subclass $\mathscr{F}_0^{**}$ of $\mathscr{F}_0$ consisting of those members of $\mathscr{F}_0$ for which a and B do not depend on the test size. This subclass includes LR, R and W. Evidently, for R, $U^* = 0$ and for each test in $\mathscr{F}_0^{**}$, $U^* \leq 0$ for sufficiently small α. Furthermore, U^* is negative for sufficiently small α for any test in $\mathscr{F}_0^{**}$ with either $a \neq 0$ or $\Sigma \Sigma \Sigma_{i,u,s=1}^{p} \{b(ius)\}^2 > 0$ when $\Sigma_0 \neq 0$, and for any test in $\mathscr{F}_0^{**}$ with $\Sigma \Sigma \Sigma_{i,u,s=1}^{p} \{b(ius)\}^2 > 0$ when $\Sigma_0 = 0$.

Thus the optimality property of R, in terms of third-order average power under contiguous alternatives, continues to hold even when the tests are adjusted only for size but not corrected for local unbiasedness. It is interesting to note that for models with $\Sigma_0 = 0$, under this kind of comparison, it may be possible to discriminate among the members of $\mathscr{F}_0^{**}$ even in the case $p = 1$. As an illustration, one may consider the model in Example 1 and check that for each $p \geq 1$ and sufficiently small α, U^* is negative for LR and W. Mukerjee (1993) also reported some exact numerical results to demonstrate the validity of the asymptotic findings for moderate sample size. Further numerical results, in slightly different contexts, are available in Bera and McKenzie (1986), Patil, Taillie and Waterman (1991) and Sutradhar and Bartlett (1991).

Turning to the case of a composite null hypothesis, as part of a wider study in a different context, Mukerjee (1992a) presented results similar to those discussed above in a situation where the interest parameter is one-dimensional and parametric orthogonality holds. In this connection, he also considered a conditional version of R (see Liang, 1987, Godambe, 1991) based on the conditional profile likelihood of Cox and Reid (1987) and indicated its equivalence with the estimated scores statistic of Conniffe (1990) in terms of third-order power under contiguous alternatives.

It may be mentioned that if tests are compared in their original forms then a property of second-order local maximinity can be proved for LR in the case of a simple null hypothesis and for a conditional (Cox and Reid, 1987) or an adjusted (McCullagh and Tibshirani, 1990) version of LR in the case of a composite null hypothesis and orthogonal parametrization; see Mukerjee (1992a,b) and Ghosh and Mukerjee (1994) for details.

Most of the results discussed in this section were obtained considering 'square-root' versions of the test statistics. This technique is useful in other contexts as well – see, e.g., DiCiccio, Field and Fraser (1990), Bickel and Ghosh (1990) and Mukerjee (1992b) among others. It may also be remarked that the approach adopted here is different from the differential geometric one due to Kumon and Amari (1983, 1985) and Amari (1985) in the sense that no assumptions have been made here regarding curved exponentiality of the model or 'sphericity' of the power function.

It will be of interest to extend the present results on R to the non-iid case. A recent study, based on Taniguchi's (1991) work, indicates that this should be possible at least in Taniguchi's set-up. The details will be reported elsewhere.

3. Bartlett-type adjustments

That the usual technique of Bartlett-adjustment for LR will not work for R becomes evident if one considers a simple null hypothesis H_0 and notes from (1.2) that the expectation of R under H_0 is p; see also Bickel and Ghosh (1990) in this context. This makes the problem of developing a Bartlett-type adjustment for R, as posed by Rao, in a private communication, and Cox (1988), nontrivial. Recently, Chandra and Mukerjee (1991), Cordeiro and Ferrari (1991) and Taniguchi (1991) addressed this issue. The objective of this section is to review these developments briefly.

Chandra and Mukerjee (1991) started with the case of a scalar parameter and considered the null hypothesis H_0: $\theta = \theta_0$ with reference to a sequence $X_1, X_2, \ldots$, of iid, possibly vector-valued, random variables with a common density $f(\cdot; \theta)$, where $\theta \in \mathbb{R}^1$ or an open subset thereof. Without loss of generality, the per observation Fisher information at θ_0 was assumed to be unity. Under this set-up, they considered the square-root version of R which, by (1.2), is given by

$$H_1 = n^{-1/2} \sum_{j=1}^{n} \mathrm{d} \log f(X_j; \theta_0)/\mathrm{d}\theta .$$

They proposed a modified version of R, say $R_m = H_{1m}^2$, where

$$H_{1m} = H_1 + n^{-1/2} t_2 H_1^2 + n^{-1}(t_1 H_1 + t_3 H_1^3) , \tag{3.1}$$

the constants t_1, t_2, t_3, free from n, being so determined that the relation

$$P_{\theta_0}(R_m \leq \vartheta) = K_{1,0}(\vartheta) + o(n^{-1}) \quad \forall \vartheta \geq 0 \tag{3.2}$$

holds. As defined earlier, here $K_{1,0}(\cdot)$ is the cumulative distribution function of a central chi-square variate with 1 df. Under standard assumptions, on the basis of an Edgeworth expansion for the null distribution of H_{1m}, Chandra and Mukerjee (1991) showed that the unique choices of t_1, t_2, t_3 satisfying (3.2) are given by

$$t_1 = \tfrac{1}{8}(G_4 - 3) - \tfrac{5}{24}G_3^2, \qquad t_2 = -\tfrac{1}{6}G_3, \qquad t_3 = -\tfrac{1}{24}(G_4 - 3 - \tfrac{8}{3}G_3^2),$$

$$\tag{3.3}$$

where

$$G_i = \mathrm{E}_{\theta_0}[\{d \log f(X_1; \theta_0)/d\theta\}^i] \quad (i = 3, 4).$$

In particular, if $G_3 = 0$, as happens in many models of practical interest (e.g., while testing H_0: $\theta = 0$ under the bivariate normal model with zero means, unit variances and unknown correlation coefficient θ), then by (3.3),

$$R_m = R/\{1 - \tfrac{1}{4}n^{-1}(G_4 - 3)(1 - \tfrac{1}{3}R)\} + o(n^{-1}),\tag{3.4}$$

over a set with P_{θ_0}-probability $1 + o(n^{-1})$, and, to some extent, (3.4) resembles the usual Bartlett correlation for LR. Chandra and Mukerjee (1991) also proposed an extension of this approach to the case of multi-dimensional $\boldsymbol{\theta}$.

Taniguchi (1991) considered the scalar parameter case in a possibly non-iid set-up and, as a part of a wider study, suggested a Bartlett-type adjustment which, in its square-root version, is quite similar to but not identical with the one considered in (3.1). Mukerjee (1992c) extended the findings in Chandra and Mukerjee (1991) to a set-up where the null hypothesis is composite and the interest parameter is one-dimensional. In the same set-up, Mukerjee (1991) obtained a Bartlett-type adjustment for a conditional version of R.

Cordeiro and Ferrari (1991) considered a very general set-up involving a composite null hypothesis and allowing both the interest parameter and the nuisance parameter to be possibly multi-dimensional. On the basis of a null asymptotic expansion for the distribution of R (see (1.3)), given by Harris (1985), they proposed a modified statistic

$$R_m^* = R\{1 - (t_0^* + t_1^* R + t_2^* R^2)\},$$

where the multiplying correction factor in braces represents a Bartlett-type adjustment as a function of R itself. The coefficients t_0^*, t_1^*, t_2^*, of order n^{-1}, were so determined that, up to $o(n^{-1})$, the null distribution of R_m^* was given by a chi-square distribution with appropriate df. Explicit expressions for t_0^*, t_1^*, t_2^* were given and certain simplifications arising in the special case of orthogonal parametrization were highlighted.

It will be of interest to compare the three approaches for Bartlett-type adjustment as considered in Chandra and Mukerjee (1991), Taniguchi (1991) and Cordeiro and Ferrari (1991). The most obvious way of doing this is based on comparison of power properties of the adjusted versions. Work in this direction is currently in progress and will be reported elsewhere.

4. Concluding remarks

While concluding, we mention some open issues that deserve further attention. Three of these have already been noted in the concluding paragraphs of Sections 2.1, 2.2 and Section 3. Some more are presented below.

(a) For the scalar parameter case and under a one-sided alternative, R is locally most powerful. Is it possible to extend this result in a meaningful way to the vector parameter case under a restricted alternative? Preliminary studies indicate that this should be possible; see Mathiason (1982) in this context.

(b) What are the implications of the results discussed here in the discrete case?

(c) Can the calculation of power, under contiguous alternatives, be simplified and made more transparent via a Bayesian route (cf. Stein, 1985, Dawid, 1991; Ghosh and Mukerjee, 1991)?

References

Amari, S. (1985). *Differential Geometric Methods in Statistics*. Springer, New York.

Bera, A. K. and A. Ullah (1991). Rao's score test in econometrics. *J. Quant. Econom* **7**, 189–220.

Bera, A. K. and C. R. McKenzie (1986). Alternative forms and properties of the score test. *J. Appl. Statist.* **13**, 13–25.

Bhattacharya, R. N. and J. K. Ghosh (1978). On the validity of the formal Edgeworth expansions. *Ann. Statist.* **6**, 434–451. Correction ibid. **8**, 1399.

Bickel, P. J., D. M. Chibisov and W. R. Van Zwet (1981). On the efficiency of first and second order. *Internat. Statist. Rev.* **49**, 169–175.

Bickel, P. J. and J. K. Ghosh (1990). A decomposition for the likelihood ratio statistic and the Bartlett correction – A Bayesian argument. *Ann. Statist.* **18**, 1070–1090.

Chandra, T. K. and J. K. Ghosh (1980). Valid asymptotic expansions for the likelihood ratio and other statistics under contiguous alternatives. *Sankhyā Ser. A* **42**, 170–184.

Chandra, T. K. and S. N. Joshi (1983). Comparison of the likelihood ratio, Rao's and Wald's tests and a conjecture of C. R. Rao. *Sankhyā Ser. A* **45**, 226–246.

Chandra, T. K. and R. Mukerjee (1984). On the optimality of Rao's statistic. *Comm. Statist. Theory Methods* **13**, 1507–1515.

Chandra, T. K. and R. Mukerjee (1985). Comparison of the likelihood ratio, Wald's and Rao's tests. *Sankhyā Ser. A* **47**, 271–284.

Chandra, T. K. and R. Mukerjee (1991). Bartlett-type modification for Rao's efficient score statistic. *J. Multivariate Anal.* **36**, 103–112.

Chandra, T. K. and T. Samanta (1988). On the second-order local comparison between perturbed maximum likelihood estimators and Rao's statistic as test statistics. *J. Multivariate Anal.* **25**, 201–222.

Conniffe, D. (1990). Testing hypotheses with estimated scores. *Biometrika* **77**, 97–106.

Cordeiro, G. M. and S. L. P. Ferrari (1991). A modified score statistic having chi-squared distribution to order n^{-1}. *Biometrika* **78**, 573–582.

Cox, D. R. (1988). Some aspects of conditional and asymptotic inference: A review. *Sankhyā Ser. A* **50**, 314–337.

Cox, D. R. and N. Reid (1987). Parameter orthogonality and approximate conditional inference (with discussion). *J. Roy. Statist. Soc. Ser. B* **49**, 1–39.

Dawid, A. P. (1991). Fisherian inference in likelihood and prequential frames of reference (with discussion). *J. Roy. Statist. Soc. Ser. B* **53**, 79–109.

DiCiccio, T. J., C. A. Field and D. A. S. Fraser (1990). Approximations of marginal tail probabilities and inference for scalar parameters. *Biometrika* **77**, 77–95.

Efron, B. (1975). Defining the curvature of a statistical problem (with applications to second order efficiency). *Ann. Statist.* **3**, 1189–1242.

Ferguson, T. S. (1967). *Mathematical Statistics: A Decision Theoretic Approach*. Academic Press, New York.

Ghosh, J. K. (1991). Higher order asymptotics for the likelihood ratio, Rao's and Wald's tests. *Statist. Probab. Lett.* **12**, 505–509.

Ghosh, J. K. and R. Mukerjee (1991). Characterization of priors under which Bayesian and frequentist Bartlett corrections are equivalent in the multiparameter case. *J. Multivariate Anal.* **38**, 385–393.

Ghosh, J. K. and R. Mukerjee (1994). Adjusted versus conditional likelihood: Power properties and Bartlett-type adjustment. *J. Roy. Statist. Soc. Ser. B*, to appear.

Godambe, V. P. (1991). Orthogonality of estimating functions and nuisance parameters. *Biometrika* **78**, 143–151.

Hall, W. J. and D. J. Mathiason (1990). On large sample estimation and testing in parametric models. *Internat. Statist. Rev.* **58**, 77–97.

Harris, P. (1985). An asymptotic expansion for the null distribution of the efficient score statistic. *Biometrika* **72**, 635–639.

Harris, P. and H. W. Peers (1980). The local power of the efficient scores test statistic. *Biometrika* **67**, 525–529.

Hayakawa, T. (1975). The likelihood ratio criterion for a composite hypothesis under a local alternative. *Biometrika* **62**, 451–460.

Kallenberg, W. C. M. (1983). On likelihood ratio, Rao's and Wald's tests. Report No. 259, Department of Mathematics and Information Science, Vrije Universiteit, Amsterdam.

Kumon, M. and S. Amari (1983). Geometrical theory of higher order asymptotics of test, interval estimator and conditional inference. *Proc. Roy. Soc. Ser. A* **387**, 429–458.

Kumon, M. and S. Amari (1985). Differential geometry of testing hypothesis – A higher order asymptotic theory in multi-parameter curved exponential family. Preprint, Tokyo University.

Liang, K. Y. (1987). Estimating functions and approximate conditional likelihood. *Biometrika* **74**, 695–702.

Madansky, A. (1989). A comparison of the likelihood ratio, Wald and Rao Tests. In: L. J. Glesar et al., eds., *Contributions to Probability and Statistics: Essays in Honor of Ingram Olkin*, Springer, New York, 465–471.

Mathiason, D. (1982). Large sample test procedures in the presence of nuisance parameters. Ph.D. Thesis, University of Rochester, New York.

McCullagh, P. and R. Tibshirani (1990). A simple method for the adjustment of profile likelihoods. *J. Roy. Statist. Soc. Ser. B* **52**, 325–344.

Mukerjee, R. (1989a). Third-order comparison of unbiased tests: A simple formula for the power difference in the one-parameter case. *Sankhyā Ser. A* **51**, 212–232.

Mukerjee, R. (1989b). Comparison of tests in the presence of a nuisance parameter. In: Y. Dodge, ed., *Statistical Data Analysis and Inference*. North-Holland, Amsterdam, 131–139.

Mukerjee, R. (1990a). Comparison of tests in the multiparameter case I. Second order power. *J. Multivariate Anal.* **33**, 17–30.

Mukerjee, R. (1990b). Comparison of tests in the multiparameter case II. A third order optimality property of Rao's test. *J. Multivariate Anal.* **33**, 31–48.

Mukerjee, R. (1991). Existence of a Bartlett-type modification for a conditional version of Rao's statistic. *J. Quant. Econ.* **7**, 231–238.

Mukerjee, R. (1992a). Conditional likelihood and power: Higher order asymptotics. *Proc. Roy. Soc. Ser. A* **438**, 433–446.

Mukerjee, R. (1992b). Comparison between the conditional likelihood ratio and the usual likelihood ratio tests. *J. Roy. Statist. Soc. Ser. B* **54**, 189–194.

Mukerjee, R. (1992c). Parametric orthogonality and a Bartlett-type adjustment for Rao's statistic in the presence of a nuisance parameter. *Statist. Probab. Lett.* **13**, 397–400.

Mukerjee, R. (1993). Comparison of tests in their original forms. *Sankhyā Ser. A*, to appear.

Mukerjee, R. and T. K. Chandra (1987). Comparison between the locally most powerful unbiased and Rao's tests. *J. Multivariate Anal.* **22**, 94–105.

Mukerjee, R. and A. Sengupta (1993). Comparison between the locally most mean power unbiased and Rao's tests in the multiparameter case. *J. Multivariate Anal.*, to appear.

Neyman, J. (1959). Optimal asymptotic tests of composite statistical hypotheses. In: U. Grenander, ed., *Probability and Statistics* (H. Cramér Volume), Wiley, New York, 213–234.

Patil, G. P., C. Taillie and R. P. Waterman (1991). Small sample behaviour of Rao's efficient scores test for the two-sample gamma problem. *J. Quant. Econom.* **7**, 221–230.

Peers, H. W. (1971). Likelihood ratio and associated test criteria. *Biometrika* **58**, 477–487.

Rao, C. R. (1948). Large sample tests of statistical hypotheses concerning several parameters with applications to problems of estimation. *Proc. Cambridge Philos. Soc.* **44**, 50–57.

Rao, C. R. (1965). *Linear Statistical Inference and Its Applications*. Wiley, New York.

Sengupta, A. and L. Vermiere (1986). Locally optimal tests for multiparameter hypotheses. *J. Amer. Statist. Assoc.* **81**, 819–825.

Silvey, S. D. (1959). The Lagrange-multiplier test. *Ann. Math. Statist.* **30**, 389–407.

Stein, C. (1985). On coverage probability of confidence sets based on a prior distribution. In: *Sequential Methods in Statistics*, Banach Center Publications, Vol. 16, Polish Scientific Publishers, Warsaw, 485–514.

Sutradhar, B. C. and R. F. Bartlett (1991). A small and large sample comparison of Wald's, likelihood ratio and Rao's tests for testing linear regression with autocorrelated errors. Preprint.

Taniguchi, M. (1991). Third order asymptotic properties of a class of test statistics under a local alternative. *J. Multivariate Anal.* **37**, 223–238.

G. S. Maddala, C. R. Rao and H. D. Vinod, eds., *Handbook of Statistics, Vol. 11*
© 1993 Elsevier Science Publishers B.V. All rights reserved.

14

On the Strong Consistency of M-Estimates in Linear Models under a General Discrepancy Function

Z. D. Bai, Z. J. Liu and C. Radhakrishna Rao

1. Introduction

Consider the linear model

$$Y_i = X_i'\beta + e_i , \quad i = 1, 2, \ldots, n , \tag{1.1}$$

where Y_i are observations, X_i are $p \times 1$ known design matrices, β is a p-vector parameter to be estimated, and e_i are iid random errors. The M-estimate of β in the model (1.1) as defined by Huber (1964) is the value of β which minimizes

$$\sum_{i=1}^{n} \rho(Y_i - X_i'\beta) , \tag{1.2}$$

for a suitable choice of the function ρ, or a value of β satisfying the estimating equation

$$\sum_{i=1}^{n} \psi(Y_i, X_i, \beta) = 0 , \tag{1.3}$$

for a suitable choice of the function ψ. A natural method of setting up the equation (1.3) is by taking the derivative of (1.2) with respect to β when ρ is continuously differentiable. However, in general, ψ need not be the derivative of a function and the equation (1.3) can be set up directly by choosing a suitable ψ.

There is considerable literature devoted to the asymptotic theory of M-estimation under some assumptions on the functions ρ and ψ. Reference may be made to papers by Huber (1964, 1973, 1981, 1987), Jureckova (1971), Jackel (1972), Bickel (1975), Yohai and Maronna (1979), Basawa and Koul (1988), Heiler and Willers (1988) and others. The special case of $\rho(x) = |x|$ has been extensively studied; reference may be made to the paper by Rao (1988) for details. Most of the papers cited discuss particular choices of ρ and ψ, or general ρ and ψ under heavy restrictive conditions which do not cover some important special cases.

Recently, some authors have studied M-estimation using a convex function ρ with minimal restrictive conditions. Reference may be made to papers by Chen and Wu (1988) and Bai, Rao and Wu (1992), Rao and Zhao (1992), Zhao and Chen (1992), Zhao and Rao (1992) and Bai, Rao and Zhao (1993). Even though the results cited above are based on assumptions which are somewhat minimum, the assumption that ρ is a convex function is still too restrictive. For instance, the function

$$\rho(x) = \begin{cases} x^2 & \text{if } k_1 \leqslant x \leqslant k_2 \, 3, \\ k_1^2 & \text{if } x < k_1, \\ k_2^2 & \text{if } x > k_2 \end{cases} \tag{1.4}$$

is not a convex function, but for appropriate choices of k_1 and k_2, the M-estimate based on it is asymptotically equivalent to the well-known trimmed mean.

Instead of assuming ρ to be a convex function, we assume that $\rho(0) = 0$ and ρ is non-increasing in $(-\infty, 0]$ and non-decreasing in $[0, \infty)$, which widens the choice of the discrepancy functions. Our main results are cited in Section 2 and the proofs given in Section 3.

2. Main results

Consider the linear model (1.1), where, without loss of generality, we assume that the true value of β is 0. We rewrite the model (1.1) as

$$Y = X'_{n,i}\beta + e_i, \quad i = 1, 2, \ldots, n, \tag{2.1}$$

where $X_{n,i} = S_n^{-1/2} X_i$, $S_n = \Sigma_1^n X_i X_i'$. The M-estimate $\hat{\beta}$ of the model (1.1) and the M-estimate $\tilde{\beta}$ of the model (2.1) have the relationship, $\tilde{\beta} = S^{1/2}\hat{\beta}$. We need the following assumptions to establish our theory.

(A_1). $\rho(u) \geqslant 0$ is a function defined on R^1 such that it is continuous, non-increasing on $(-\infty, 0]$, non-decreasing on $[0, \infty)$ and is such that

$$\rho(\kappa u) \leqslant C(\kappa)\rho(u) \tag{2.2}$$

for any constant κ, where $C(\kappa)$ is a constant depending only on κ.

(A_2). The errors in the model (1.1) are iid random variables with $E\rho(e_1) < \infty$.

(A_3). $E\rho(e_1 - u)$ has a unique minimum at 0 and there exist $b_1 > 0$, $b_2 > 0$ such that

$$E[\rho(e_1 - u) - \rho(e_1)] > \min\{b_1 u^2, b_2\} \, . \tag{2.3}$$

(A_4). Denote by λ_n^2 the largest eigenvalue of S_n and

$$a_n = \max_{1 \leq i \leq n} \{\|X_{ni}\|\}, \qquad k_n = \min_{\beta} \#\{i : |X_{ni}'\beta| / \|\beta\| > h/\lambda_n, i = 1, \ldots, n\}.$$

(2.4)

Assume that

(i) $\lim_{n \to \infty} S_n/n = S$ exists with S positive definite , (2.5)

(ii) $\lim_{n \to \infty} k_n/n = \alpha > 0$ for some $h > 0$, (2.6)

(iii) $\rho(a_n \lambda_n) = O(n^\delta)$, $0 \leq \delta < \frac{1}{2}$, (2.7)

(A_5) $\lim_{u \to \infty} \alpha \min\{\rho(u), \rho(-u)\} > E\rho(e_1)$. (2.8)

NOTE 2.1. The condition A_1 is much weaker than those usually made on the discrepancy function ρ. We do not assume differentiability or convexity of $\rho(u)$. (2.2) includes almost every conventional discrepancy functions. The basic purpose of (2.2) is to exclude the possibility of ρ exponentially increasing.

NOTE 2.2. The condition A_2 is slightly stronger than those for the L_1-norm estimate and the least distance estimate where the assumption is $E|\rho(e_1 - u) - \rho(e_1)| < \infty$. (See Bai, Rao and Wu, 1992 for details.)

NOTE 2.3. Since we assume that $E\rho(e_1 - u)$ reaches its minimum at 0, (2.3) is reasonable. If $E\rho(e_1 - u)$ is second differentiable with positive second derivative at 0, then (2.3) is automatically satisfied. Note that even though $\rho(u)$ itself may not be differentiable, the assumption that $E\rho(e_1 - u)$ is differentiable is not restrictive.

NOTE 2.4. A_4 is a condition on the design matrix X. It is not difficult to verify that if for every $\varepsilon > 0$

$$\|S_n^2(M) - S_n^2\| \leq \varepsilon n$$

when M is large enough, where $S_n^2(M) = \Sigma X_i X_i' I(\|X_i\| < M)$, then (2.6) is true. In fact if the design is random having certain finite moments then both A_4 and the above condition are satisfied.

We have the following lemmas.

LEMMA 2.1. *Let the conditions A_1–A_5 be satisfied. Then*

$$\sup_{\|\beta\| \leq \lambda_n M} \left| \frac{1}{n} \sum_{i=1}^n \rho(e_i - X_{ni}'\beta) - \frac{1}{n} \sum_{i=1}^n E\rho(e_i - X_{ni}'\beta) \right| \to 0$$

a.s.   as $n \to \infty$ (2.9)

for any constant $M > 0$.

LEMMA 2.2. *Let the conditions* A_1–A_5 *be satisfied. Further, let* $\tilde{\beta}_n$ *be the M-estimate of* β *in the model* (2.1) *and* $B_n = \{\|\tilde{\beta}_n\| > \lambda_n M\}$. *Then*

$$P(B_n, \text{i.o.}) = 0 \quad \text{for some } M > 0, \tag{2.10}$$

where i.o. stands for infinitely often.

THEOREM 2.1. *Suppose the conditions* A_1–A_5 *are satisfied. Then the M-estimate* $\hat{\beta}_n$ *of the model* (1.1) *for the true parameter* β *(assumed to be 0 without loss of generality) is strongly consistent, i.e.,*

$$\lim_{n \to \infty} \hat{\beta}_n = 0 \quad \text{a.s.} \tag{2.11}$$

3. Proof of main results

We use C to denote a constant which may take different values in different equations and $I(\cdot)$ denote the indicator function.

PROOF OF LEMMA 2.1. We only prove this lemma when β is two-dimensional while other cases can be proved similarly. Let $d > 0$ be a constant which will be determined later. Denote

$$\gamma_{ni} = \rho(e_i - X'_{ni}\beta)I(\rho(e_i) > d), \qquad \gamma^*_{ni} = \rho(e_i - X'_{ni}\beta)I(\rho(e_i) \le d),$$

$$\varphi_n(\beta) = \frac{1}{n}\sum_{i=1}^{n}\gamma_{ni}, \qquad \varphi^*_n(\beta) = \frac{1}{n}\sum_{i=1}^{n}\gamma^*_{ni},$$

$$\psi_n(\beta) = \frac{1}{n}\sum_{i=1}^{n}E\gamma_{ni}, \qquad \psi^*_n(\beta) = \frac{1}{n}\sum_{i=1}^{n}E\gamma^*_{ni},$$

$$\varphi_{1n}(\beta) = \frac{1}{n}\sum_{i=1}^{n}\gamma^*_{ni}I(e_i \le X'_{ni}\beta), \qquad \psi_{1n}(\beta) = \frac{1}{n}\sum_{i=1}^{n}E[\gamma^*_{ni}I(e_i \le X'_{ni}\beta)],$$

$$\varphi_{2n}(\beta) = \frac{1}{n}\sum_{i=1}^{n}\gamma^*_{ni}I(e_i > X'_{ni}\beta), \qquad \psi_{2n}(\beta) = \frac{1}{n}\sum_{i=1}^{n}E[\gamma^*_{ni}I(e_i > X'_{ni}\beta)]. \tag{3.1}$$

We have

$$\sup_{\|\beta\| \le \lambda_n M} \left| \frac{1}{n}\sum_{i=1}^{n}\rho(e_i - X'_{ni}\beta) - \frac{1}{n}\sum_{i=1}^{n}E\rho(e_i - X'_{ni}\beta) \right|$$

$$= \sup_{\|\beta\| \le \lambda_n M} |\varphi_n(\beta) + \varphi^*_n(\beta) - \psi_n(\beta) - \psi^*_n(\beta)|$$

$$\le \sup_{\|\beta\| \le \lambda_n M} |\varphi^*_n(\beta) - \psi^*_n(\beta)| + \sup_{\|\beta\| \le \lambda_n M} |\varphi_n(\beta)| + \sup_{\|\beta\| \le \lambda_n M} |\psi_n(\beta)|. \tag{3.2}$$

Since $\|X'_{ni}\beta\| \leq \|X'_{ni}\| \|\beta\| \leq a_n\lambda_n M$, $i = 1, \ldots, n$, we have

$$\sup_{\|\beta\| \leq \lambda_n M} |\varphi_n(\beta)| \leq \frac{1}{n} \sum_{i=1}^n [\rho(e_i - a_n\lambda_n M) + \rho(e_i + a_n\lambda_n M)]I(\rho(e_i) > d),$$

$$\sup_{\|\beta\| \leq \lambda_n M} |\psi_n(\beta)\| \leq E[\rho(e_1 - a_n\lambda_n M) + \rho(e_1 + a_n\lambda_n M)]I(\rho(e_1) > d).$$

$$(3.3)$$

From A_1, we have

$$\rho(e_i - a_n\lambda_n M) + \rho(e_i + a_n\lambda_n M) \leq C[\rho(e_i) + \rho(a_n\lambda_n)].$$

We choose $d = d_n \geq c\rho(a_n\lambda_n)$ for some $c > 0$. Then by the condition A_2 we have

$$\lim_{n \to \infty} \sup_{\|\beta\| \leq \lambda_n M} |\psi_n(\beta)| = 0 \tag{3.4}$$

and

$$\lim_{n \to \infty} \sup_{\|\beta\| \leq \lambda_n M} |\varphi_n(\beta)| = 0 \quad \text{a.s.} \tag{3.5}$$

We now concentrate on estimating

$$\sup_{\|\beta\| \leq \lambda_n M} |\varphi_n^*(\beta) - \psi_n^*(\beta)|.$$

Note that

$$\sup_{\|\beta\| \leq \lambda_n M} |\varphi_n^*(\beta) - \psi_n^*(\beta)| \leq \sup_{\|\beta\| \leq \lambda_n M} |\varphi_{1n}(\beta) - \psi_{1n}(\beta)|$$

$$+ \sup_{\|\beta\| \leq \lambda_n M} |\varphi_{2n}(\beta) - \psi_{2n}(\beta)|.$$

We prove that the first term on the right in the above converges to 0 a.s.; the second term can be dealt with in the same way. Write

$$X_{ni} = \|X_{ni}\|(\cos\theta_{ni}, \sin\theta_{ni})', \qquad \beta = \|\beta\|(\cos\theta, \sin\theta)'. \tag{3.6}$$

Then $X'_{ni}\beta = \|X_{ni}\| \|\beta\| \cos(\theta - \theta_{ni})$ is a function of $(\|\beta\|, \theta)$ defined on $[0, \infty) \times [0, 2\pi)$. It is easy to see that there is a partition, denoted by $P_1, \ldots, P_q$, of $[0, 2\pi]$ such that $q \leq 3n$ and for each i, $X'_{ni}\beta$ is either increasing or decreasing with respect to θ in any subinterval P_k. We have

$$\sup_{\|\beta\| \leq \lambda_n M} |\varphi_{1n}(\beta) - \psi_{1n}(\beta)| \leq \max_{1 \leq k \leq q} \sup_{\|\beta\| \leq \lambda_n M, \theta \in P_k} |\varphi_{1n}(\beta) - \psi_{1n}(\beta)|. \tag{3.7}$$

For any fixed k, denote

$$\begin{align}
B_1 &= \{i: \cos(\theta - \theta_{ni}) \geq 0, \text{ and increasing in } P_k\}, \\
B_2 &= \{i: \cos(\theta - \theta_{ni}) \geq 0, \text{ and decreasing in } P_k\}, \\
B_3 &= \{i: \cos(\theta - \theta_{ni}) < 0, \text{ and increasing in } P_k\}, \\
B_4 &= \{i: \cos(\theta - \theta_{ni}) < 0, \text{ and decreasing in } P_k\}.
\end{align} \tag{3.8}$$

Then we have

$$\max_{1\leq k\leq q} \sup_{\|\beta\|\leq\lambda_n M,\theta\in P_k} |\varphi_{1n}(\beta) - \psi_{1n}(\beta)|$$

$$\leq \max_{1\leq k\leq q} \sup_{\|\beta\|\leq\lambda_n M,\theta\in P_k} \left| \frac{1}{n} \sum_{i\in B_1} \gamma_{ni}^* I(e_i \leq X_i'\beta) \right.$$

$$\left. - \frac{1}{n} \sum_{i\in B_1} E\gamma_{ni}^* I(e_1 \leq X_i'\beta) \right|$$

$$+ \max_{1\leq k\leq q} \sup_{\|\beta\|\leq\lambda_n M,\theta\in P_k} \left| \frac{1}{n} \sum_{i\in B_2} \gamma_{ni}^* I(e_i \leq X_i'\beta) \right.$$

$$\left. - \frac{1}{n} \sum_{i\in B_2} E\gamma_{ni}^* I(e_1 \leq X_i'\beta) \right|$$

$$+ \max_{1\leq k\leq q} \sup_{\|\beta\|\leq\lambda_n M,\theta\in P_k} \left| \frac{1}{n} \sum_{i\in B_3} \gamma_{ni}^* I(e_i \leq X_i'\beta) \right.$$

$$\left. - \frac{1}{n} \sum_{i\in B_3} E\gamma_{ni}^* I(e_1 \leq X_i'\beta) \right|$$

$$\leq \max_{1\leq k\leq q} \sup_{\|\beta\|\leq\lambda_n M,\theta\in P_k} \left| \frac{1}{n} \sum_{i\in B_4} \gamma_{ni}^* I(e_i \leq X_i'\beta) \right.$$

$$\left. - \frac{1}{n} \sum_{i\in B_4} E\gamma_{ni}^* I(e_1 \leq X_i'\beta) \right|$$

$$\stackrel{\Delta}{=} V_1 + V_2 + V_3 + V_4 . \tag{3.9}$$

Considering V_1, we have

$$U_1(\theta, \|\beta\|) = \frac{1}{n} \sum_{i\in B_1} \gamma_{ni}^* I(e_i \leq X_i'\beta, \theta \in P_k) ,$$

$$U_2(\theta, \|\beta\|) = \frac{1}{n} \sum_{i\in B_1} E[\gamma_{ni}^* I(e_i \leq X_i'\beta, \theta \in P_k)] . \tag{3.10}$$

Both $U_1(\theta, \|\beta\|)$ and $U_2(\theta, \|\beta\|)$ are decreasing with respect to θ for every fixed $\|\beta\|$ and they also are decreasing with respect to $\|\beta\|$ for every fixed $\theta \in P_k$. According to Lemma A.1 given in the Appendix, we have a partition $t_1 = 0 < t_2 < \cdots < t_r = \lambda_n M$ of $[0, \lambda_n M]$ and $0 \leq \eta_0 \leq \eta_2 < \cdots < \eta_t \leq 2\pi$ of P_k such that

$$r = O[\rho(a_n\lambda_n)] = O(n^\delta) , \qquad t = O[(\rho(a_n\lambda_n))^2] = O(n^{2\delta}) ;$$

$$\max_{i,j} \sup_{t_i\leq\|\beta\|\leq t_{i+1}} \sup_{\eta_j\leq\theta\leq\eta_{j+1},\theta\in P_k} |U_2(\theta, \|\beta\|) - U_2(\eta_j, \|t_i\|)| \leq \varepsilon .$$

Therefore, by the monotonicity of U_1 and U_2, we have

$$V_1 \leqslant \max_{k,i,j} \{ |U_1(\eta_j, \|t_i\|) - U_2(\eta_j, \|t_i\|)| + |U_1(\eta_{j+1}, \|t_i\|) - U_2(\eta_{j+1}, \|t_i\|)|$$

$$+ |U_1(\eta_j, \|t_{i+1}\|) - U_2(\eta_j, \|t_{i+1}\|)|$$

$$+ |U_1(\eta_{j+1}, \|t_{i+1}\|) - U_2(\eta_{j+1}, \|t_{i+1}\|)|\}$$

$$+ \max_{k,i,j} \sup_{t_i \leqslant \|\beta\| \leqslant t_{i+1}} \sup_{\eta_j \leqslant \theta \leqslant \eta_{j+1}, \theta \in P_k} |U_2(\theta, \|\beta\|) - U_2(\eta_j, \|t_i\|)|$$

$$\leqslant 4 \max_{1 \leqslant k \leqslant q} \max_{0 \leqslant i \leqslant r, 0 \leqslant j \leqslant t} |U_1(\eta_j, \|t_i\|) - U_2(\eta_j, \|t_i\|)| + \varepsilon. \tag{3.11}$$

Similar inequalities can be proved for V_2, V_3 and V_4. By using Lemma A.2 given in the Appendix and noting that the constant $C(\beta, n)$ here satisfies $C(\beta, n) \geqslant C[n^{-1}(\rho(a_n\lambda_n))^{-2}] \geqslant Cn^{-1-2\delta}$, we have

$$P(V_1 > 2\varepsilon) \leqslant P\{ \max_{1 \leqslant k \leqslant q} \max_{0 \leqslant i \leqslant r, 0 \leqslant j \leqslant t} |U_1(\eta_j, \|t_i\|) - U_2(\eta_j, \|t_i\|)| > \varepsilon/4 \}$$

$$\leqslant \sum_{k=1}^{q} \sum_{i=1}^{r} \sum_{j=1}^{t} P\{ |U_1(\eta_j, \|t_i\|) - U_2(\eta_j, \|t_i\|)| > \varepsilon/4 \}$$

$$\leqslant \sum_{k=1}^{q} \sum_{i=1}^{r} \sum_{j=1}^{t} \exp(-Cn^{1-2\delta}) \leqslant Cn^{3\delta+1} \exp(-Cn^{1-2\delta}). \tag{3.12}$$

Then $V_1 \to 0$, a.s. using the Borel–Cantelli lemma. Similarly we have $V_t \to 0$ a.s., $t = 2, 3, 4$, and further we have $\sup_{\|\beta\| \leqslant \lambda_n M} |\varphi_{2n}(\beta) - \psi_{2n}(\beta)| \to 0$ a.s. Thus the lemma is proved by combining (3.2) and (3.5). $\square$

PROOF OF LEMMA 2.2. Note that by the condition A_1 we have

$$\min_{\|\beta\| > \lambda_n M} \frac{1}{n} \sum_{i=1}^{n} \rho(e_i - X'_{ni}\beta)$$

$$\geqslant \min_{\|\beta\| > \lambda_n M} \frac{1}{n} \sum_{i=1}^{n} \min\{\rho(-|X'_{ni}\beta|/2), \rho(|X'_{ni}\beta|/2)\} I(|e_i| \leqslant |X'_{ni}\beta|/2). \tag{3.13}$$

By the condition A_4, we further get

$$\text{RHS of (3.13)} \geqslant \frac{1}{n} \sum_{i \in D} \min\{\rho(-hM/2), \rho(hM/2)\} I(|e_i| \leqslant hM/2), \tag{3.14}$$

where $D = \{i: |X'_{ni}\beta|/\|\beta\| > h/\lambda_n, i = 1, \ldots, n\}$.

Denote $k_n = \#D$. Then by condition $A_4(ii)$, we have for any fixed M,

$$\text{RHS of (314)} \to$$

$$\alpha P(|e_1| \leqslant hM/2) \min\{\rho(-hM/2), \rho(hM/2)\} \quad \text{a.s.} \tag{3.15}$$

By condition A_5, we may select M large enough such that

$$\text{limit of RHS of } (3.14) > E\rho(e_1) \quad \text{a.s.} \tag{3.16}$$

Note that

$$
\begin{aligned}
B_n &= \{\|\tilde{\beta}_n\| > \lambda_n M\} \\
&= \left\{ \min_{\|\beta\| > \lambda_n M} \frac{1}{n} \sum_{i=1}^n \rho(e_i - X'_{ni}\beta) \leqslant \min_{\|\beta\| \leqslant \lambda_n M} \frac{1}{n} \sum_{i=1}^n \rho(e_i - X'_{ni}\beta) \right\} \\
&\subseteq \left\{ \min_{\|\beta\| > \lambda_n M} \frac{1}{n} \sum_{i=1}^n \rho(e_i - X'_{ni}\beta) \leqslant \frac{1}{n} \sum_{i=1}^n \rho(e_i) \right\} \\
&\subseteq \left\{ \frac{1}{n} \sum_{i \in D} \min\{\rho(-hM/2), \rho(hM/2)\} \right. \\
&\qquad \left. \times I(|e_i| \leqslant hM/2) \leqslant \frac{1}{n} \sum_{i=1}^n \rho(e_i) \right\}. \tag{3.17}
\end{aligned}
$$

It is seen that $P(B_n, \text{i.o.}) = 0$ using (3.16) and the strong law of large numbers. $\square$

PROOF OF THEOREM 2.1. Using Lemmas 2.1 and 2.2, the strong law of large numbers and condition A_3, for every $\varepsilon > 0$, when n is large and $\|\beta_n\| \leqslant \lambda_n M$

$$
\begin{aligned}
0 &\geqslant \frac{1}{n} \sum_{i=1}^n [\rho(e_i - X'_{ni}\tilde{\beta}_n) - \rho(e_i)] \\
&> \frac{1}{n} \sum_{i=1}^n E[\rho(e_1 - X'_{ni}\beta)|_{\beta=\beta_n} - E\rho(e_1)] - \varepsilon \\
&> \frac{1}{n} \sum_{i=1}^n \min\{b_1 \|X'_{ni}\|^2 \|\tilde{\beta}_n\|^2, b_2\} - \varepsilon \\
&\geqslant \frac{k_n}{n} \min\{b_1(h\|\tilde{\beta}_n\|/\lambda_n)^2, b_2\} - \varepsilon.
\end{aligned} \tag{3.18}
$$

Therefore $\|\tilde{\beta}_n\|/\lambda_n \to 0$ a.s. for otherwise we can choose ε small enough such that with a positive probability the second expression in (3.18) is greater than 0, which contradicts the inequality in the first expression of (3.18). Using the relationship of $\tilde{\beta}_n$ with $\hat{\beta}_n$ of the model (1.1) and the condition (2.5) in A_4, we conclude that $\hat{\beta}_n \to 0$, a.s. as $n \to \infty$. $\square$

Appendix

LEMMA A.1. *Let $f(x, y) : [0, M] \times [0, N] \mapsto R$ be a continuous function. Suppose that for every x, $f(x, y)$ is an increasing (or decreasing) function of y, and for every y, $f(x, y)$ is an increasing (or decreasing) function of x. Then for any $\varepsilon > 0$, there are partitions of $[0, M]$, $a_0 = 0 < a_1 \cdots < a_m = M$, and $[0, N]$,*

$b_0 = 0 < b_1 \cdots b_n = N$ *with*

$$m \leqslant [\max\{f(x)\} - \min\{f(x)\}]/\varepsilon + 1 \quad and \quad n \leqslant \frac{m(m+2)}{2} \tag{A.1}$$

such that

$$\max_{|i_1 - i_2| \leqslant 1, |j_1 - j_2| \leqslant 1} |f(x_{i_1}, y_{j_1}) - f(x_{i_2}, y_{j_2})| \leqslant 2\varepsilon . \tag{A.2}$$

PROOF. Without loss of generality, we assume that $f(x, y)$ is increasing with respect to x, y respectively. We first prove the lemma when the function is strictly increasing. Note that we can find curves $(x_k(t), y_k(t))$ in the X, Y-plane such that $(x_k(0), y_k(0))$ and $(x_k(1), y_k(1))$ are of the boundary of $[0, M] \times [0, N]$ and

$$f(x_k(t), y_k(t)) = k\varepsilon + \min\{f(x, y)\} , \quad k = 1, \ldots, m . \tag{A.3}$$

These curves do not cross each other. And by the monotonicity of $f(x, y)$, for each k, there is a continuous curve satisfying (A.2). Let $a_0 = 0$ and denote by $a_k, k = 1, \ldots, m$ the x-coordinates of the crossing points of the k-th curve with $y = 0$. There are at most m such points. Using the monotonicity of $f(x, y)$ again, for each $k = 1, \ldots, m$, the curve $x = a_k$ only crosses each of the curves $(x_i(t), y_i(t))$, $i \geqslant k$ at most once. Therefore we can find at most a total of $n = m(m+2)/2$ such crossing points. Denote the y-coordinates of these crossing points by $b_1 < b_2 \cdots < b_n$ and $b_0 = 0$. Then by the structure of $\{a_i : i = 0, 1, \ldots, m\}$ and $\{b_j : j = 0, 1, \ldots, n\}$, (A.1) is proved in the case when $f(x, y)$ is strictly increasing.

We now assume that the function $f(x, y)$ is increasing with respect to x for fixed y and is increasing with respect to y for fixed x. Let $f_\delta(x, y) = f(x, y) + \delta(x + y)$, for some $\delta > 0$. $f_\delta(x, y)$ is strictly increasing. Therefore (A.1) is true for $f_\delta(x, y)$. (A.1) is also true for $f(x, y)$ which follows by letting $\delta \to 0$. □

NOTE A.1. It is easy to verify that Lemma A.1 is also true for a function defined on a closed compact set and satisfying the remaining conditions in the lemma.

LEMMA A.2. *Suppose that conditions* $(A_1)-(A_4)$ *in Section 2 are satisfied. For any* β *any* n *and subset* A *of* $\{1, \ldots, n\}$, *any* $d > 0$ *and any* $\varepsilon \geqslant 0$,

$$P\left\{ \left| \frac{1}{n} \sum_{i \in A} \xi_i - \frac{1}{n} \sum_{i \in A} E\xi_i \right| \geqslant \varepsilon \right\} \leqslant \exp[-cC(\beta, n)(\varepsilon n)^2] , \tag{A.4}$$

where $\xi_i = [\rho(e_i - X_i'\beta) - \rho(e_i)]I(\rho(e_i) \leqslant d)$, $c > 0$ *and*

$$[C(\beta, n)]^{-1} = n\varepsilon[\max\{\rho[-a_n\|\beta\| - u_1)], \rho[a_n\|\beta\| + u_2]\} + d]$$
$$+ \#\{A\}[\max\{\rho[-a_n\|\beta\| - u_1)], \rho[a_n\|\beta\| + u_2]\} + d]^2$$

$u_1 > 0$ *and* $u_2 > 0$ *satisfying* $\rho(-u_1) = \rho(u_2) = d$.

PROOF. Note that

$$|\xi_i| = |\rho(e_i - X_i'\beta) - \rho(e_i)|I(\rho(e_i) \leq d)$$
$$\leq \max\{\rho[-a_n\|\beta\| - u_1)], \rho[a_n\|\beta\| + u_2)]\} + d \qquad (A.5)$$

and

$$\mathrm{Var}(\xi_i) = \mathrm{Var}\{[\rho(e_i - X_i'\beta) - \rho(e_i)]I(\rho(e_i) \leq d)\}$$
$$\leq [\max\{\rho[-a_n\|\beta\| - u_1)], \rho[a_n\|\beta\| + u_2)]\} + d]^2 . \qquad (A.6)$$

By Bernstein's inequality, we have

$$P\left\{\left|\frac{1}{n}\sum_{i \in A}(\xi_i - E\xi_i)\right| \geq \varepsilon\right\} \leq \exp[-C(\beta, n)(\varepsilon n)^2] .$$

The lemma is proved. □

Acknowledgement

The research of this paper is supported by US Army Research Office under grant DAAL 03-89-K-0139.

References

Babu, G. J. and C. Radhakrishna Rao (1988). Joint asymptotic distribution of marginal quantile function in samples from a multivariate population. *J. Multivariate Anal.* **27**, 15–23.

Bai, Z. D., X. R. Chen, B. Q. Miao and C. R. Rao (1990). Asymptotic theory of least distance estimates in multivariate analysis. *Statistics* **21**, 503–519.

Bai, Z. D., X. R. Chen, Y. Wu and L. C. Zhao (1987). Asymptotic normality of minimum L_1-norm estimates in linear models. Technical Report No. 87–35, Center for Multivariate Analysis, University of Pittsburgh.

Bai, Z. D., C. R. Rao and Y. Wu (1992). M-estimation of multivariate linear regression parameters under a convex discrepancy function. *Statistica Sinica* **2**, 237–254.

Bai, Z. D., C. R. Rao and Y. Q. Yin (1990). Least absolute deviations analysis of variance. *Sankhyā* **52**, 166–177.

Bai, Z. D., C. R. Rao and L. C. Zhao (1993). MANOVA type tests under M-theory for the standard multivariate linear model. *J. Statist. Plann. Inference*, to appear.

Basawa, L. V. and H. L. Koul (1988). Large-sample statistics based on quadratic dispersion. *Internat. Statist. Rev.* **56**, 199–219.

Bickel, P. J. (1975). One-step Huber estimates in the linear model. *J. Amer. Statist. Assoc.* **70**, 428–433.

Chen, X. R. and Y. Wu (1988). Strong consistency of M-estimates in linear models. *J. Multivariate Anal.* **27**, 116–130.

Heiler, S. and R. Willers (1988). Asymptotic normality of R-estimates in the linear model. *Statistics* **19**, 173–184.

Huber, P. J. (1964). Robust estimation of a location parameter. *Ann. Math. Statist.* **35**, 73–101.

Huber, P. J. (1973). Robust regression: Asymptotics, conjectures, and Monte Carlo. *Ann. Statist.* **1**, 799–821.

Huber, P. J. (1981). *Robust Statistics*. Wiley, New York.

Huber, P. J. (1987). The place of the L_1-norm in robust estimation. In: Y. Dodge, ed., *Statistical Data Analysis Based on the L_1-Norm and Related Methods*, North-Holland, Amsterdam, 23–34.

Jackel, L. (1972). Estimating regression coefficients by minimizing the dispersion of the residuals. *Ann. Math. Statist.* **43**, 1449–1458.

Jureckova, J. (1971). Nonparametric estimate of regression coefficients. *Ann. Math. Statist.* **42**, 1328–1338.

Rao, C. R. (1988). Methodology based on the L_1-norm in statistical inference. *Sankhyā* **50**, 289–313.

Rao, C. R. and L. C. Zhao (1992). Linear representation of M-estimates in linear models. *Canad. J. Statist.* **20**, 359–368.

Yohai, V. J. and R. A. Maronna (1979). Asymptotic behavior of M-estimators for the linear model. *Ann. Statist.* **7**, 258–268.

Zhao, L. C. and X. R. Chen (1992). Asymptotic behavior of M-test statistics in linear models. *Statist. Probab. Lett.* **14**, 79–84.

Zhao, L. C. and C. R. Rao (1991). On the consistency of M-estimate in a linear model obtained through an estimating equation. Technical Report, No. 91-3, Center for Multivariate Analysis, Penn State.

G. S. Maddala, C. R. Rao and H. D. Vinod, eds., *Handbook of Statistics, Vol. 11*

15

Some Aspects of Generalized Method of Moments Estimation

Alastair Hall

1. Introduction

Since its introduction by Hansen (1982), generalized method of moments (GMM) estimation has had a considerable impact on econometrics. It provides a unifying framework for the analysis of many familiar estimators and includes least squares, instrumental variables and maximum likelihood as special cases. It also offers a convenient method of estimation in certain models which were computationally very burdensome to estimate by more traditional methods. GMM has been applied to a wide variety of models including the estimation of probit models with panel data (Avery, Hansen and Hotz, 1983) and nonlinear rational expectations models (e.g., Hansen and Singleton, 1982).

Due to the generality of the GMM estimation principle, many theoretical treatments of the estimator are at an advanced level. While this generality is very desirable for practical purposes, it can make it more difficult for the less technical reader to understand the intuition behind the estimation procedure. In this paper we provide an introduction to GMM which is designed to acquaint the applied researcher with the basic ideas behind GMM and its statistical properties. The emphasis is placed on intuition and not mathematical rigor. There are many other excellent sources which provide a rigorous treatment of GMM, e.g., see Hansen (1982); Gallant (1987); Gallant and White (1988).

Many researchers are aware that there is a close relationship between GMM and instrumental variables (IV) estimation, but are uncertain about the exact nature of the connection. This stems from the fact that GMM is most frequently applied to the estimation of nonlinear dynamic rational expectations models using a generalized IV procedure introduced by Hansen and Singleton (1982). In fact, as Hansen (1982) and Hansen and Singleton (1982) observe, IV is a special case of GMM. Although GMM can be applied to nonlinear dynamic models, many of the statistical issues which arise in this framework can be conveniently illustrated using the IV estimator of the familiar fixed regressor linear regression model. Sargan (1958, 1959) presents the first rigorous treatment of IV in linear systems, and although he concentrated on the linear model, his work was the first to address and solve many of these issues. In fact parts of Hansen's analysis can be viewed as direct extensions of Sargan's work to a more general class of models (see Hansen, 1982, for further discussion). Although, it should be noted that Hansen (1982) was the first paper to develop the complete framework we describe and our discussion of IV relies heavily on his work.

In this paper we use the IV estimator in the fixed linear regression model under the classical assumptions to introduce the general principle behind GMM. In many textbooks the IV estimator is derived in an ad hoc manner (e.g., see Johnston 1984, pp. 363–366). However, we consider an alternative derivation in which the estimator is obtained by minimizing a quadratic form in a vector of sample moments which are functions of the parameters β and the data (e.g., see White, 1984a, pp. 7–9). It becomes immediately apparent from this framework that IV has desirable asymptotic statistical properties provided the analogous population moments equal zero when evaluated at the true value of β, β_0. In this particular application the population moment condition is that the instrument vector is orthogonal to the errors, and so our analysis delivers the familiar condition that IV is consistent provided the instruments are valid. This is the essential structure of GMM. To estimate β all one needs are a set of population moments[1] whose expectation is zero when evaluated at β_0. The GMM estimate is obtained by minimizing a quadratic form in the analogous sample moments.

The linear model also provides a convenient framework for introducing various statistical issues which arise in the GMM inference framework. We examine (i) the consistency of the estimator; (ii) asymptotic normality of the estimator; (iii) the optimal choice of weighting matrix in the quadratic form; (iv) the overidentifying restrictions test. It is hoped that the ideas behind GMM are more readily accessible when first encountered within the context of the linear model because its algebra is familiar to most researchers.

We then show how these ideas are extended to nonlinear dynamic models to produce a very general principle of estimation. Our discussion inevitably relies heavily on Hansen (1982) but we place particular emphasis on showing that the structure of the arguments is identical to those employed for the analysis of IV in the linear model.

To illustrate the power of the GMM estimation principle, we consider its application to the estimation of Euler equation models. Hansen and Singleton (1982) showed how one can use the GMM estimation principle to construct generalized IV estimators of the parameters of these models. Following Hansen and Singleton (1982) we discuss this technique in the context of a consumption based asset pricing model. In comparison to maximum likelihood estimation of these models, GMM is seen to have considerable computational and statistical advantages.

---

[1] There must be at least as many moment conditions as parameters. This is discussed in detail below.

The original papers of Hansen (1982) and Hansen and Singleton (1982) have had such an impact on econometrics that they have prompted a number of studies both analyzing the properties of GMM and also extending GMM based inference. In this paper we offer a selective review of this recent research, and this discussion helps to illuminate both the strengths and weaknesses of the GMM framework.

An outline of the paper is as follows. In Section 2 we consider IV estimation in the classical linear regression model. In Section 3 we introduce Hansen's (1982) GMM estimator for nonlinear dynamic models. In Section 4 we discuss the application of this technique by Hansen and Singleton (1982) to the estimation of Euler equation models. In Section 5 we summarize recent research on GMM based estimation and inference. Finally in Section 6 we offer some concluding remarks.

2. Instrumental variables estimation in the linear model

Consider the classical linear regression model

$$y = X\beta_0 + u ,$$
(2.1)

where y is an $(n \times 1)$ vector of observations on the dependent variable, X is an $(n \times q)$ matrix of fixed in repeated sample regressors with $\text{rank}(X) = q$; u is an $(n \times 1)$ vector of observations on the error process with $\text{E}(u) = 0$, $\text{var}(u) = \sigma^2 I_n$; and β_0 is the true value of β, an $(q \times 1)$ vector of unknown parameters. Let Z be an $(n \times r)$ matrix of fixed in repeated sample instruments which satisfy $\text{E}(z_t u_t) = 0$ for any t, where z_t is the t-th row of Z. We define $Q_n(\beta)$ to be the following quadratic form:

$$Q_n(\beta) = [n^{-1}u(\beta)'Z]W_n[n^{-1}Z'u(\beta)] ,$$
(2.2)

where W_n is a positive definite symmetric matrix which converges in probability to a positive definite symmetric matrix W and $u(\beta) = y - X\beta$. For the present we assume $r = q$. Let $\tilde{\beta}$ be the value of β which minimizes $Q_n(\beta)$. If we substitute $u(\beta) = y - X\beta$ into (2.2), multiply out the quadratic form and differentiate with respect to β then the first-order conditions are

$$-2X'ZW_nZ'y + 2X'ZW_nZ'X\tilde{\beta} = 0$$

which in turn implies

$$X'ZW_nZ'y = X'ZW_nZ'X\tilde{\beta} .$$
(2.3)

Therefore if $Z'X$ is nonsingular the solution for $\tilde{\beta}$ is

$$\tilde{\beta} = (Z'X)^{-1}Z'y .$$

Within this framework it becomes immediately obvious why IV estimators are consistent. A heuristic explanation is as follows. The population moment condition $E[z_t u_t(\beta_0)] = 0$ (combined with the Weak Law of Large Numbers) implies $n^{-1}Z'u(\beta_0) \overset{p}{\to} 0$. Now W_n is positive definite for all n and so $Q_n(\beta) \geq 0$ with the equality only obtained for $n^{-1}Z'u(\beta) = 0$. Therefore if $\tilde{\beta}$ minimizes $Q_n(\beta)$ and $n^{-1}Z'u(\beta_0) \overset{p}{\to} 0$, it follows that $\tilde{\beta} \overset{p}{\to} \beta_0$.[2] Of course if $E[z_t u_t(\beta_0)] \neq 0$ then this argument breaks down and in general $\tilde{\beta}$ is not consistent. This corresponds to the case where at least some elements of z_t are invalid instruments. It is interesting to compare this derivation with the more familiar textbook treatment of IV. Note that because $X'Z$ and W_n are nonsingular, (2.3) implies $Z'u(\tilde{\beta}) = 0$, and these equations are the starting point for many textbook derivations of $\tilde{\beta}$ (e.g., see Johnston, 1984, p. 364).

It is important to emphasize the structure of our derivation of $\tilde{\beta}$. The estimator can be obtained by minimizing a quadratic loss function in a sample moment (i.e., $n^{-1}Z'u(\beta)$). The resulting estimators are consistent because the population moment equals zero when evaluated at β_0 (i.e., $E[z_t u_t(\beta_0)] = 0$). This is the basic principle that lies behind the generalized method of moments (GMM) estimator. However, before considering GMM in its full generality it is instructive to consider further the instrumental variables estimator in the basic linear model.

In our earlier discussion it was assumed that $r = q$ and so there were exactly the same number of moment conditions as parameters to be estimated. One can think of this as being the case where β is 'just identified' because we have just enough information (i.e., moment conditions) to estimate β. An immediate consequence of this was that $\tilde{\beta}$ does not depend on W_n and so the same estimator is obtained regardless of the choice of W_n. We now consider the statistical implications of $r \neq q$.

If $r < q$ then the number of parameters to be estimated exceeds the number of moment conditions. In this case β is 'underidentified' because there is insufficient information (i.e., moment conditions) from which to estimate β uniquely. The previous derivation of $\tilde{\beta}$ breaks down because if $r < q$ then the $(q \times q)$ matrix $X'ZW_nZ'X$ has rank less than or equal to r and so is singular. Consequently (2.3) cannot be uniquely solved for $\tilde{\beta}$.

If $r > q$ then the number of moment conditions exceeds the number of parameters to be estimated, and so β is 'overidentified' because there is more information (i.e., moment conditions) than is necessary to obtain an estimate of β. In this case the choice of W_n affects $\tilde{\beta}$. To see this we rewrite (2.3) as

$$X'ZW_nZ'u(\tilde{\beta}) = 0. \tag{2.4}$$

Now $X'ZW_n$ is $q \times r$ and so (2.4) does not imply $Z'u(\tilde{\beta}) = 0$. Rather $\tilde{\beta}$ is chosen to be the value which sets q linear combinations of the r moment conditions $Z'u(\beta)$ equal to zero, and the weights of these linear combinations

---

[2] We must also assume $E[z_t u_t(\tilde{\beta})] = \mu \neq 0$ for any $\tilde{\beta} \neq \beta_0$, to ensure $\tilde{\beta}$ is uniquely defined asymptotically.

are given by $X'ZW_n$. In this case the solution for $\tilde{\beta}$ is

$$\tilde{\beta} = (X'ZW_nZ'X)^{-1}X'ZW_nZ'y \tag{2.5}$$

which clearly depends on W_n. This naturally raises the question of which W_n leads to the most efficient choice of $\tilde{\beta}$. Recall that we have made no assumptions about the distribution of u_t and so the finite sample distribution of $\tilde{\beta}$ is unknown. Therefore our efficiency comparison is based on asymptotic behavior and so we must first characterize the asymptotic distribution of $\tilde{\beta}$.

In our discussion of the asymptotic distribution of $\tilde{\beta}$ we set $r \geq q$ and so include the 'just identified' case as well. Note that if $r = q$ then (2.5) reduces to $\tilde{\beta} = (Z'X)^{-1}Z'y$, and so (2.5) trivially holds for $r \geq q$. If we substitute for y from (2.1) into (2.5) and rearrange the equation we can obtain

$$n^{1/2}(\tilde{\beta} - \beta_0) = (n^{-1}X'ZW_n n^{-1}Z'X)^{-1}n^{-1}X'ZW_n n^{-1/2}Z'u . \tag{2.6}$$

We deduce the asymptotic distribution of $\tilde{\beta}$ by considering the behavior of the cross product matrices on the right-hand side of (2.6). Under suitable regularity conditions we can assume

(C1): $\lim_{n\to\infty} n^{-1}Z'Z = M_{zz}$, a finite nonsingular matrix of constants;
(C2): $\lim_{n\to\infty} n^{-1}X'Z = M_{xz}$, a finite matrix of constants with rank q;
(C3): $\lim_{n\to\infty} n^{-1/2}Z'u \overset{d}{\to} N(0, \sigma^2 M_{zz})$.

Each of these conditions places different restrictions on the asymptotic behavior of the instruments. (C1) requires that each instrument provides some unique information in the sense that no one instrument z_{ti} can be written as a linear combination of the others infinitely often as $n \to \infty$. Condition (C2) requires that there must be at least q of the r instruments which are correlated with x_t asymptotically, and so β is identified asymptotically. Finally (C3) requires that the sample moment vector evaluated at β_0 converges to a normal distribution when scaled by $n^{1/2}$. Note that the mean of this distribution is zero and so this condition restates the requirement that z_t be a valid instrument. Using (C1)–(C3) we can deduce from (2.6) that

$$n^{1/2}(\tilde{\beta} - \beta_0) \overset{d}{\to} N(0, \sigma^2 V) , \tag{2.7}$$

where $V = (M_{xz}WM_{zx})^{-1}M_{xz}WM_{zz}WM_{zx}(M_{xz}WM_{zx})^{-1'}$ and $M_{zx} = M'_{xz}$. Therefore we can perform asymptotic inference about β_0 based on (2.7) using either confidence intervals or using hypothesis tests (the latter will be discussed in more detail in Section 5). A consistent estimator of $\sigma^2 V$ is easily constructed from the data using W_n, the sample moment matrices such as $n^{-1}Z'X$ and $\hat{\sigma}^2 = (y - X\tilde{\beta})'(y - X\tilde{\beta})/n$. In the just identified case, V reduces to $M_{zx}^{-1}M_{zz}M_{xz}^{-1}$.

We now return to the issue of characterizing the optimal choice of W_n. This characterization is based on finding the choice of W, the probability limit of W_n, which yields the most efficient IV estimator asymptotically. From Hansen (1982) Theorem 3.2 it follows that for this model the optimal choice of W is

M_{zz}^{-1}, in which case V reduces to

$$V^* = [M_{zx}M_{zz}^{-1}M_{zx}]^{-1}. \tag{2.8}$$

Note that the optimal choice of W is proportional to the inverse of asymptotic covariance matrix of $n^{-1/2}Z'u$. One can gain some intuition into this choice of W by considering the role of the weighting matrix in $Q_n(\beta)$. The elements of W_n control the relative importance of each term of the form $(n^{-1}\Sigma z_{ti}u_t) \times (n^{-1}\Sigma z_{tj}u_t)$ in $Q_n(\beta)$. Due to the inherent variability in z_t each element of the moment condition contains different information about β and these elements (or pieces of information) are related to each other. This is reflected in the asymptotic covariance matrix $n^{-1/2}Z'u$ which from (C3) is $\sigma^2 M_{zz}$. The optimal weighting matrix is the one which takes account of this covariance structure in the construction of $Q_n(\beta)$. An obvious choice of W_n which converges in probability to M_{zz}^{-1} is $(n^{-1}Z'Z)^{-1}$, and from (2.5) the associated sequence of IV estimators is characterized by

$$\tilde{\beta}^* = [(X'Z(Z'Z)^{-1}Z'X)]^{-1}X'Z(Z'Z)^{-1}Z'y \tag{2.9}$$
$$= (\hat{X}'\hat{X})^{-1}\hat{X}'y,$$

where $\hat{X} = Z(Z'Z)^{-1}Z'X$ namely, the predicted value of X from regression on Z.

It was noted that the asymptotic normality of $\tilde{\beta}$ facilitates inference about β. However, such inference is based on the assumption that the model is correctly specified. Typically it is desired to test whether the data is consistent with the model before focusing on inference within the context of that model. For the regression model we have discussed above, many tests of model adequacy have been proposed, e.g., tests for serial correlation or heteroscedasticity in u_t. However, in the more general models examined below, we typically do not assume $E(uu') = \sigma^2 I_n$ and so these tests do not usefully extend. Instead we focus on a test principle which can be applied in nonlinear dynamic models. This test is often referred to as Hansen's (1982) overidentifying restrictions test. It is clear from our earlier discussion that the desirable statistical properties of $\tilde{\beta}$ rely crucially on the validity of the moment condition $E[z_t u_t(\beta_0)] = 0$. It is therefore important to test whether the data are consistent with this moment condition. Now in the 'just identified' case $Z'u(\tilde{\beta}) = 0$ by construction regardless of whether or not the population moment condition is true and so one cannot derive a useful test from the sample moment. However, if β is overidentified, then from (2.4) it is clear that only q linear combinations of $Z'u(\tilde{\beta})$ are set equal to zero and so $Z'u(\tilde{\beta}) \neq 0$ by construction. However, if the population moment condition is true then one would expect $Z'u(\tilde{\beta}) \approx 0$. This provides a basis for a test of the model specification, and we base this inference on the asymptotically efficient estimator $\tilde{\beta}^*$. From Hansen (1982) Lemma 4.2 it follows that in this model if $E[z_t u_t(\beta_0)] = 0$, then the statistic

$$\tau_n = n^{-1/2}u(\tilde{\beta}^*)'Z(n^{-1}Z'Z)^{-1}n^{-1/2}Z'u(\tilde{\beta}^*)/\tilde{\sigma}^2$$

converges in distribution to χ^2_{r-q} where $\tilde{\sigma}^2$ is a consistent estimator of σ^2. Note that the degrees of freedom are the number of moment conditions minus the number of parameters to be estimated. This is the case because only $r - q$ of the sample moment conditions $Z'u(\tilde{\beta}^*)$ are free on account of the q restrictions implied by the first-order conditions for $\tilde{\beta}^*$ in (2.4).[3] The statistic τ_n provides a simple test of the model and we will discuss its properties in greater detail in Section 5.

3. Generalized method of moments

In the previous section it was shown that the familiar instrumental variables estimator can be derived by minimizing a quadratic form in a sample moment which was a function of β. Within this framework it became apparent that the desirable properties of the IV estimator depended on three properties of this condition, namely: (i) the validity of the population moment condition $E[z_t u_t(\beta_0)] = 0$; (ii) there were at least as many moment conditions as parameters to be estimated; (iii) $n^{1/2}$ times the sample moment evaluated at β_0 converged to a normal distribution as $n \to \infty$, i.e., $n^{-1/2}Z'u(\beta_0) \overset{d}{\to} N(0, \sigma^2 M_{zz})$. It is important to realize that we could have performed a similar analysis with any moment conditions which satisfied (i)–(iii). For example we could have used a different set of instruments, r_t say, and although this estimator would be numerically different from $\tilde{\beta}$ in (2.5), it would have similar statistical properties. It would be consistent and asymptotically normal, the optimal choice of W_n would be $n^{-1}R'R$ and one can perform inference about the model using an analogous statistic to τ_n. Furthermore, the intuition behind our discussion was not specific to a static linear regression model. Rather to estimate the parameters of any model, we can proceed by finding moment conditions involving the parameter vector which satisfy (i)–(iii) and minimize a quadratic form in the analogous sample moment. This is the essence of generalized method of moments estimation.

In this section we discuss the extension of our analysis for IV estimators in static linear models to nonlinear dynamic models. We adopt the statistical framework in Hansen (1982) and delay discussion of its possible extensions until Section 5.

Consider the case where we wish to estimate the $(q \times 1)$ parameter vector β which indexes a statistical model. Suppose we have the following $(r \times 1)$

---

[3] Note that τ_n is not asymptotically equivalent to the well-known Hausman (1978) test for the endogeneity of regressors. Hausman's test compares $\tilde{\beta}$ with $\hat{\beta}$, the ordinary least squares estimator. Although Hausman's test can be set up using moment conditions (see White, 1982, 1984b) neither of these versions corresponds to τ_n. In particular the asymptotic properties of this Hausman test depend on $n^{-1/2}X'u$ which is irrelevant to τ_n. Newey (1985) discusses the connections between Hausman type and conditional moment tests.

moment conditions[4]

$$E[f(x_t, \beta_0)] = 0 , \tag{3.1}$$

where x_t is a $(p \times 1)$ stationary ergodic random vector $f(x, \beta)$ is a $(r \times 1)$ vector of continuous functions of β for every x, and β_0 is the true value of β. Before proceeding with our discussion we wish to address an issue of terminology. Hansen (1982) refers to the moment conditions in (3.1) as 'orthogonality conditions'. This term arises naturally in the IV framework because as we have seen the moment conditions are based on the orthogonality of two sets of variables, i.e., u_t and z_t in Section 2. Although one can use the two terms interchangeably, in this paper we refer to (3.1) as moment conditions.

If $r \geq q$ then these moment conditions provide sufficient information to estimate β. If we let $g_n(\beta)$ be the sample moments

$$g_n(\beta) = n^{-1} \sum_{t=1}^{n} f(x_t, \beta)$$

then the intuition from Section 2 leads us to consider the quadratic form

$$Q_n(\beta) = g_n(\beta)' W_n g_n(\beta) ,$$

where W_n is defined as before. The generalized method of moments estimator of β is $\tilde{\beta}$ the value which minimizes $Q_n(\beta)$ with respect to β. Given our earlier discussion one would anticipate that $\tilde{\beta}$ is consistent and asymptotically normally distributed just like the IV estimator in the linear model. In fact all our analysis of the IV estimator extends very naturally to the GMM estimator and in the remainder of this section we discuss the generalization of those arguments to this more general setting.

The first-order conditions for minimizing $Q_n(\beta)$ imply $\tilde{\beta}$ is the solution to

$$G_n(\tilde{\beta})' W_n g_n(\tilde{\beta}) = 0 , \tag{3.2}$$

where $G_n(\beta)$ is the $(r \times q)$ matrix with (i, j)-th element $[G_n(\beta)]_{ij} = \partial g_{ni}(\beta)/\partial \beta_j$ and, $g_{ni}(\beta)$ is the i-th element of $g_n(\beta)$. We assume $G_n(\tilde{\beta})$ is of full rank. Just as in the linear case[5] the first-order conditions set q linear combinations of the r sample moment conditions $g_n(\tilde{\beta})$ equal to zero. If β is just identified then

[4] In this section we follow Hansen's (1982) notation to expedite the readers progression from our discussion to the original work. However, this does create a slight notational conflict with Section 2. In this section x_t represents the vector of all variables appearing in the moment condition, which for the linear model are the regressors, the instruments and the dependent variable. With an obvious abuse of notation (3.1) reduces to the moment condition in Section 2 if we set $f(x_t, \beta_0) = z_t(y_t - x'\beta_0)$. Note that our assumptions in Section 2 did not include stationarity and so our linear model is not encompassed by Hansen's original framework. However, one can apply GMM under much weaker assumptions about x_t which would include the model of the previous section. These are discussed in Section 5.

[5] Note that in the linear model $G_n(\tilde{\beta}) = n^{-1}X'Z$, and $g_n(\tilde{\beta}) = n^{-1}Z'u(\tilde{\beta})$ and so (3.2) is identical to (2.4).

$G_n(\bar{\beta})$ and W_n are nonsingular, in which case $\bar{\beta}$ is the solution to $g_n(\bar{\beta}) = 0$ and so does not depend on W_n. However, if β is overidentified then $\bar{\beta}$ does depend on W_n in a similar fashion to the linear model. Notice that unlike the linear case, (3.2) does not imply an explicit solution and so one must use a numerical optimization routine to solve for $\bar{\beta}$ (e.g., see Gallant, 1987, pp. 26–46).

Most commonly used statistical packages do not include a convenient procedure for GMM estimation of nonlinear dynamic models. However, in the case where the moment condition arises from the orthogonality of some function $u_t(\beta)$ and an instrument vector, then one can use RATS (Doan, 1990, pp. 5-22, 5-23) and TSP (Hall and Cummins, 1991, pp. 67–68). One can also use matrix computer languages to perform GMM estimation. For example the Hansen/Heaton/Ogaki GMM GAUSS package (see Ogaki, 1992) contains suitable programs in GAUSS and Gallant (1987, pp. 448–449) presents a SAS PROC MATRIX (SAS, 1982) program which estimates the parameters of the Hansen and Singleton (1982) consumption-based asset pricing model and also calculates the other statistics described below. The latter provides a useful starting place for the structure of a numerical optimization procedure for more general GMM estimation or if it is desired to use an alternative matrix computer language.

Although we cannot obtain an explicit solution for $\bar{\beta}$ one can show that it is a consistent estimator. The heuristic argument presented for the IV estimator in the linear model extends to this more general setting. The population moment condition $E[f(x_t, \beta_0)] = 0$ combined with the Weak Law of Large Numbers implies $g_n(\beta_0) \xrightarrow{p} 0$. Now W_n is positive definite for all n and so $Q_n(\beta) \geq 0$ with the equality only obtained for $g_n(\beta) = 0$ for all n. Therefore if $\bar{\beta}$ minimizes $Q_n(\beta)$ and $g_n(\beta_0) \xrightarrow{p} 0$, it follows that $\bar{\beta} \xrightarrow{p} \beta_0$.[6]

We now derive the asymptotic distribution of $\bar{\beta}$. Due to the absence of an explicit solution for $\bar{\beta}$ from (3.2), it is necessary to develop an asymptotic approximation to $n^{1/2}(\bar{\beta} - \beta_0)$ using a mean value theorem expansion of the sample moment conditions. By the mean value theorem we have

$$g_n(\bar{\beta}) = g_n(\beta_0) + G_n(\bar{\beta})(\bar{\beta} - \beta_0), \tag{3.3}$$

where $\|\bar{\beta} - \bar{\beta}\| \leq \|\bar{\beta} - \beta_0\|$. If we premultiply both sides of (3.3) by $G_n(\bar{\beta})'W_n$ then from (3.2) the left-hand side of (3.3) is zero and so we obtain

$$(\bar{\beta} - \beta_0) = -[G_n(\bar{\beta})'W_n G_n(\bar{\beta})]^{-1} G_n(\bar{\beta})'W_n g_n(\beta_0). \tag{3.4}$$

Now $\bar{\beta} \xrightarrow{p} \beta_0$ implies $\bar{\beta} \xrightarrow{p} \beta_0$ and so by Slutsky's theorem we obtain

$$n^{1/2}(\bar{\beta} - \beta_0) = -[G_n(\beta_0)'W_n G_n(\beta_0)]^{-1} G_n(\beta_0)'W_n n^{1/2}g_n(\beta_0) + o_p(1), \tag{3.5}$$

---

[6] We must also assume that $E[f(x_t, \bar{\beta})] = \mu \neq 0$ for $\bar{\beta} \neq \beta_0$ to ensure that $\bar{\beta}$ is uniquely defined asymptotically.

Under certain regularity conditions (see Hansen, 1982),

$$n^{1/2}g_n(\beta_0) \xrightarrow{d} N(0, S_w),$$

where

$$S_w = \lim_{n\to\infty} E\left[n^{-1} \left(\sum_{t=1}^{n} f_t(\beta_0) \right) \left(\sum_{t=1}^{n} f_t(\beta_0) \right)' \right],$$

is a finite positive definite matrix. Therefore from (3.5)

$$n^{1/2}(\tilde{\beta} - \beta_0) \xrightarrow{d} N(0, V_G), \tag{3.6}$$

where $V_G = [G_0'WG_0]^{-1}G_0'WS_wWG_0[G_0'WG_0]^{-1}$, and $G_0 = E[\partial f(x_t, \beta_0)/\partial\beta]$. Notice that the structure of V_G is identical to V in (2.7).[7]

To perform inference about β_0 based on (3.6), it is necessary to construct a consistent estimator of V_G. This can be obtained by replacing the component matrices of V_G by their consistent estimators. It is easily verified that $G_n(\tilde{\beta}) \xrightarrow{p} G_0$ and by definition $W_n \xrightarrow{p} W$, but some care is needed in constructing a consistent estimator of S_w. There have recently been a number of studies proposing positive definite consistent estimators of covariance matrices like S_w (see inter alia Gallant, 1987, pp. 445 and 532–539; Newey and West, 1987a; Andrews, 1991). One such covariance matrix estimator originally proposed by Gallant (1987) is

$$\hat{S}_w = \sum_{m=-l(n)}^{l(n)} \omega_m \hat{S}_{nm}, \tag{3.7}$$

where

$$\omega_m = \begin{cases} 1 - 6m^2 + 6|m|^3, & 0 \leqslant m \leqslant 0.5l(n), \\ 2(1 - |m|)^3, & 0.5l(n) \leqslant m \leqslant 1, \end{cases}$$

$$\hat{S}_{nm} = n^{-1} \sum_{t=m+1}^{n} f(x_t, \tilde{\beta})f(x_{t-m}, \tilde{\beta})'$$

and $l(n) = O(n^{1/5})$. Therefore using $G_n(\tilde{\beta})$, W_n and $\hat{S}_w$ one can obtain a consistent estimator of V_G and so perform inference about β_0 using the asymptotic distribution of $\tilde{\beta}$.

In our discussion of IV in the linear model it was argued that the optimal choice of W_n is the sequence of matrices which yields the asymptotically most efficient estimator as $n \to \infty$. This criterion is still appropriate for GMM estimators in nonlinear dynamic models. It was noted above that the structure of V_G is identical to V in (2.7), and so we can use analogous arguments to characterize the optimal W. This time the analysis shows that the optimal W, is

---

[7] To see this put $G_0 = M_{zx}$, $S_w = \sigma^2 M_{zz}$.

S_w^{-1}, which implies the asymptotically efficient GMM estimator $\tilde{\beta}^*$ has covariance matrix $V_G^* = [G_0' S_w^{-1} G_0]^{-1}$. To construct $\tilde{\beta}^*$ we require a weighting matrix W which is both consistent for S_w^{-1} and is also positive definite. This presents a problem which we did not encounter in the linear model because in this more general setting such an estimator will inevitably depend on β because of the definition of S_w. The solution is to adopt a multi-step estimation procedure. For example one could estimate $\tilde{\beta}^*$ in two steps. In the first step we use a suboptimal choice of W_n (which does not depend on β) to obtain $\tilde{\beta}$. Although $\tilde{\beta}$ is inefficient it is still consistent and so we can use $\tilde{\beta}$ to construct $\hat{S}_w$ using (3.7). In the second step $\tilde{\beta}^*$ is obtained from (3.2) using $W_n = \hat{S}_w^{-1}$. While this two-step estimator is asymptotically efficient, one need not stop here. The second step estimator of β can be used to form a new estimator of S_w and the model reestimated to produce a new estimate of β which in turn yields a new estimator of S_w etc. This iterative procedure could be continued until convergence and the resulting estimator has the same asymptotic properties as the two-step estimator. However the finite sample properties may be different and we discuss this further in Section 5.

Finally we consider the extension of the overidentifying restrictions test to nonlinear dynamic models. It was observed above that if β is overidentified then $g_n(\tilde{\beta}) \neq 0$ in general. Following the intuition from the linear model, it would be anticipated that if the population moment condition $E[f(x_t, \beta_0)] = 0$ is correct then $g_n(\tilde{\beta}) \approx 0$. Therefore the sample moment provides a convenient test of the model specification. Consider the test statistic

$$\tau_n = n g_n(\tilde{\beta}^*)' \hat{S}_w^{-1} g_n(\tilde{\beta}^*) .$$

Under the null hypothesis that $E[f(x_t, \beta_0)] = 0$, τ_n converges in distribution to χ_{r-q}^2.

In this section it has been demonstrated that the GMM estimator can be used to perform inference about the parameters of a nonlinear dynamic econometric model. At this stage we wish to emphasize that we have actually assumed very little about the model. Apart from certain regularity conditions, we have only made two key assumptions. Firstly we assumed x_t is stationary and ergodic to facilitate the application of the Weak Law of Large Numbers and central limit theorem to various functions of x_t. This can be relaxed as we discuss in Section 5. Secondly and more importantly we assumed that there are sufficient moment conditions to identity β. However, it is important to realize that we did not make an explicit assumption about the parametric form of the data generation process for x_t. In some cases a model for x_t may be required to obtain the moment conditions. Our analysis of the IV estimator in the linear model was an example of this case. However, in many situations, one can deduce moment conditions without completely specifying a model for x_t. This makes GMM a very attractive estimation principle for two reasons. Firstly the data generation process for x_t may be a large (possibly nonlinear) system of equations and so GMM offers the potential to estimate β without the computational burden of estimating the complete system.[8] Secondly economic theory may imply a set of moment conditions but not a suitable model for x_t. This creates a problem for the implementation of a number of traditional estimation methods (e.g., maximum likelihood) which require an explicit model for x_t. In this case we could assume specification for x_t and estimate the complete system. However, if the model for x_t is misspecified, then this may bias our inference about β.[9] Both of these reasons are particularly relevant in the estimation of the parameters of discrete dynamic programming models and in the next section we describe how GMM can be applied to greatly simplify the estimation of these models.

4. GMM and Euler equation models

In his famous policy critique Lucas (1976) argued that econometric policy evaluations based on traditional dynamic simultaneous equation models are seriously flawed. Most of these analyses assume that the model's parameters are invariant across policy regimes. Lucas argued that rational agents take account of policy changes in their decision making and so one cannot expect the same marginal response to a change in a policy instrument in different policy regimes. Consequently it is more appropriate to view these parameters as functions of the economic environment and a set of underlying fundamental parameters which govern peoples preferences and the technology in the economy: 'taste and technology' parameters. This criticism has sparked a considerable research program formulating rational expectational models which are explicitly parameterized in terms of the 'taste and technology' parameters. These models are typically nonlinear and are computationally burdensome to estimate using standard methods such as maximum likelihood. However, Hansen and Singleton (1982) demonstrated that GMM can be applied in these models relatively easily and so facilitates inference about these parameters. In this section we summarize Hansen and Singleton's analysis and follow their approach of using a consumption based asset pricing model to illustrate the arguments. However, we consider a simplified version of their model to expedite the exposition.

Consider the case where a representative economic agent chooses consumption and investment to maximize his/her expected discounted utility

$$E_0 \left[\sum_{t=0}^{\infty} \delta^t U(C_t) \right], \tag{4.1}$$

---

[8] Note that we have made no assumption about the relationship between p, the dimension of x_t, and q the dimension of β.

[9] Gallant and Tauchen (1989) propose using maximum likelihood estimation using a semi-nonparametric approximation to the probability density function of x_t which is estimated from the data. This approach may avoid this bias and is discussed in the next section.

where C_t is consumption in period t, $U(\cdot)$ is a strictly concave utility function, δ is a constant discount factor and $E_t[\cdot]$ denotes conditional expectation given Ψ_t, the information set available to the agent at time t, for $t = 0, 1, \ldots$. In any period t the agent can choose to buy either consumption goods or purchase an asset which yields payoff R_{t+1} in the next period. Let P_t and Q_t be the price and quantity purchased of the asset in period t respectively. The agent is assumed to receive income from assets purchased in the previous period and labor income W_t. All prices are denominated in terms of the consumption good.[10] Therefore the agent's budget constraint is

$$C_t + P_t Q_t \leqslant R_t Q_{t-1} + W_t . \tag{4.2}$$

The maximization of (4.1) subject to (4.2) yields the first-order condition

$$P_t U'(C_t) = \beta E_t[R_{t+1} U'(C_{t+1})] , \tag{4.3}$$

where $U'(\cdot) = \partial U / \partial C$. It is convenient to rewrite (4.3) as

$$E_t \left[\delta \frac{R_{t+1}}{P_t} \frac{U'(C_{t+1})}{U'(C_t)} - 1 \right] = 0 \tag{4.4}$$

and we refer to (4.4) (or equivalently (4.3)) as the Euler equation of the system. To estimate this model it is necessary to specify the utility function. Following Hansen and Singleton (1982) we define

$$U(C_t) = C_t^\gamma / \gamma , \quad \gamma < 1 . \tag{4.5}$$

Therefore the Euler condition becomes

$$E_t \left[\delta \frac{R_{t+1}}{P_t} \left[\frac{C_{t+1}}{C_t} \right]^\alpha - 1 \right] = 0 , \tag{4.6}$$

where $\alpha = \gamma - 1$.

Now consider the problem of estimating (α, δ). Given the consumption and asset data customarily used in these models, it is reasonable to model R_{t+1}/P_t and C_{t+1}/C_t as stationary series. Therefore, to estimate this model by maximum likelihood it is necessary to specify the conditional distribution of $lw_{1t+1} = \log[R_{t+1}/P_t]$ and $lw_{2t+1} = \log[C_{t+1}/C_t]$ given Ψ_t.[11] The maximum likelihood estimates of the parameters of the model are obtained by maximizing the likelihood subject to the Euler equation constraint given in (4.6) for each t. In some cases the imposition of this constraint may reduce to restrictions on the parameters (e.g., see Hansen and Singleton, 1982, pp. 1279–1280). However, most often it is necessary to use a constrained optimization technique in which case the imposition of (4.6) requires numerical integration (see Gallant and Tauchen, 1989). Therefore the maximum likelihood method has both the

---

[10] In other words P_t is the price of the asset in dollars ÷ price of the consumption good in dollars.
[11] The log transformation is taken due to the nonnegativity of R_{t+1}/P_t and C_{t+1}/C_t.

problems discussed at the end of Section 3 namely: computational burden and potentially biased inference if the conditional distribution is misspecified. One can protect oneself from the second problem by adopting a flexible functional form for the joint conditional probability density function of (lw_{1t+1}, lw_{2t+1}). This is the strategy advocated by Gallant and Tauchen (1989) who estimate a semi-nonparametric approximation to the true density function. However, such methods are inevitably computationally more burdensome.

In contrast, now consider GMM estimation of (α, δ). To use GMM it is necessary to find at least two population moment conditions. The Euler condition yields one directly because by the law of iterated expectations

$$E\left\{\delta \frac{R_{t+1}}{P_t}\left[\frac{C_{t+1}}{C_t}\right]^\alpha - 1\right\} = E\left\{E_t\left\{\delta \frac{R_{t+1}}{P_t}\left[\frac{C_{t+1}}{C_t}\right]^\alpha - 1\right\}\right\} = 0$$

from (4.6). However, we can combine the Euler equation with the rational expectations hypothesis to obtain additional moment conditions. If agents are rational, then they use all available information at time t (i.e., Ψ_t) to form their expectations. It follows that if $y_{t+1} \notin \Psi_t$ but $z_t \in \Psi_t$ then

$$E_t[y_{t+1}z_t] = \{E_t[y_{t+1}]\}z_t .$$

Now if $E_t[y_{t+1}] = 0$ then by the law of iterated expectations

$$E[y_{t+1}z_t] = 0 .$$

Using the same argument in the consumption based asset pricing model, the Euler equation implies

$$E[u_{t+1}(\alpha, \delta)z_t] = 0 , \tag{4.7}$$

where $u_{t+1}(\alpha, \delta) = \delta(R_{t+1}/P_t)(C_{t+1}/C_t)^\alpha - 1$ and z_t is an $(r \times 1)$ vector of variables contained in Ψ_t. In practice there is no shortage of candidates for z_t. One can use $C_{t-i}, R_{t-i}, P_{t-i}, i \geq 0$, any function of these variables or any other macroeconomic variables, such as lagged money supply, which are known to the agent at time t. This abundance can create a problem because the parameter estimates will vary with the choice of z_t. This issue is discussed further in Section 5.

Notice that the structure of (4.7) is identical to that of the population moment condition for IV in the linear model. For this reason z_t is referred to as a vector of instruments. The key difference between the moment conditions in the two models is that in the linear model we had to explicitly specify the data generation process for y_t to construct $u_t(\beta)$, whereas in the Euler equation model $u_t(\alpha, \delta)$ is just a function of the data with conditional expectation zero. Due to this close relationship between the estimators,

Hansen and Singleton (1982) refer to the GMM estimator based on (4.7) as a generalized instrumental variables estimator.[12]

From this discussion it is clear that GMM has two advantages over ML estimation in these models.[13] Firstly it is computationally more convenient and secondly it avoids potential bias due to misspecification of the distribution of (lw_{1t+1}, lw_{2t+1}). However, GMM is not unambiguously better, because ML based on a correctly specified model yields the asymptotically most efficient estimators. The size of these efficiency gains depends on the model in question. This potential provides the incentive for the approach taken by Gallant and Tauchen (1989). However, to our knowledge no formal efficiency comparison has been made between GMM and MLE based on a semi-nonparametric likelihood function in the context of time series models.[14]

Due to its computational convenience Hansen and Singleton's approach has been used by many other researchers to estimate rational expectations models. In each case the Euler equation provides the basis for the moment conditions in the same way as we described above. Examples of these studies are (i) asset pricing: Mark (1985), Dunn and Singleton (1986), Epstein and Zin (1991); (ii) factor demand: Pindyck and Rotemberg (1983); (iii) labor supply: Mankiw, Rotemberg and Summers (1985), Eichenbaum, Hansen and Singleton (1988); (iv) inventory holdings: West (1986), Miron and Zeldes (1988), Fair (1989).

5. Further issues concerning GMM based inference

The discussion in Sections 3 and 4 was confined to the original articles about GMM by Hansen (1982) and Hansen and Singleton (1982). Subsequently there have been a number of studies both evaluating the performance of GMM and also further developing the GMM inference framework. In this section we provide a selective review of this literature.

So far the discussion has focussed on the asymptotic properties of GMM. For practical purposes, it is important to have evidence on its finite sample properties. Tauchen (1986) simulated data from a small artificial economy and examined the finite sample behavior of the GMM estimators of (α, δ) in the consumption based asset pricing model described in Section 4. He used the instrument vector $z_t = (1, w_{1t}, \ldots, w_{1t-L+1}, w_{2t}, \ldots, w_{2t-L+1})$ where $w_{1t} = C_t/C_{t-1}$, $w_{2t} = R_t/P_{t-1}$ for $L = 1, 2, 3, 4$. The sample sizes were set at 50 and 75.

---

[12] In this example we had only one asset and so there is only one Euler condition. If there are m assets then there will be m Euler equations each of which can be used to construct moment conditions in the way described above (see Hansen and Singleton, 1982).

[13] Hansen and Sargent (1982) provide a more detailed comparison of GMM and MLE for linear rational expectations models.

[14] However, in the case where the variables are iid, Chamberlain (1987) shows that GMM can be equally efficient asymptotically as maximum likelihood estimation in which the probability density function of x_t is estimated nonparametrically along with the parameters of interest (see Section 5 for further discussion).

He found that the estimator performed reasonably well but appeared sensitive to the choice of L. As L increased the estimators' variance decreased but there was an increase in bias. Tauchen concluded that it is advisable to choose L to be small. Finally he found that the finite sample distribution of τ_n was well approximated by its asymptotic distribution. Kocherlakota (1990) conducts a similar study to Tauchen (1986) but uses the iterated GMM estimator in which one reestimates with updated versions of $\hat{S}_w$ as the weighting matrix until the estimate converge (see Section 3). He considers exactly the same structure of artificial economy as Tauchen and also investigates the Hansen and Singleton (1982) consumption based asset pricing model. However, unlike Tauchen's study he also examines the model with multiple assets and different instrument sets all of which are indexed by t (i.e., $L = 0$ in Tauchen's notation). His simulations are for example size 90. In general he confirms many of Tauchen's findings although he reports evidence that τ_n tends to reject too frequently. Furthermore, he finds GMM performs worse when larger instrument sets are used. In particular some coefficients are biased and confidence intervals based on the asymptotic distribution are too narrow. His results suggest that Tauchen's finding about the sensitivity of GMM to L may in part occur because in Tauchen's framework an increase in L also increases the size of the instrument vector.

Both these studies concentrate on highly nonlinear but small systems of equations. Ferson and Foerster (1991) report evidence on the finite sample behavior of GMM in larger systems. Their simulation design is different from that of Tauchen (1986) and Kocherlakota (1990). Ferson and Foerster (1991) estimate a seemingly unrelated regression model with cross equation restrictions for asset returns using real financial data. The residuals from these equations are used to bootstrap artificial data on asset returns for the observed sequence of explanatory variables. They control the size of the system, the number of instruments and the sample size.[15] Unlike the other studies cited above they consider the behavior of both the two-step and the iterated GMM estimators. In their study GMM exhibits relatively small biases even in samples of size 60. However, the standard errors based on asymptotic theory understate the variability of the estimators and this bias increases as either the dimension of the system (e.g., number of assets) or the sample size decreases. They find that degrees of freedom adjustments to the asymptotic standard errors reduce but do not eliminate this bias. The behavior of the overidentifying restrictions test appears sensitive to the choice of estimator. When applied using the two-step estimator, the test rejects too often whereas with the iterated estimator the test is undersized but much closer to its nominal size.

All of these studies considered the generalized IV estimator proposed by Hansen and Singleton (1982) and described in the previous section. One

---

[15] The number of assets varies from 3 to 14, the number of instruments is 3 or 8 and the sample size varies from 60 to 720.

possible explanation for the small sample performance within these sampling designs may be the properties of the chosen instrument vector. In the context of a simple linear regression model, Nelson and Startz (1990) provide simulation evidence that the finite sample behavior of τ_n can be very sensitive to the quality of the instrument (i.e., the correlation between regressor and instrument). If the instrument is of very poor quality then τ_n tends to reject too frequently. They conjecture that a similar problem may be present in consumption based asset pricing models of the type described in Section 4 and may account for the frequent rejections of these models in practice. None of the other studies cited above explicitly control the correlation between $u_t(\beta_0)$ and z_t,[16] and so it is not clear to what extent instrument choice provides an explanation for the over rejections using τ_n reported in the simulation studies of Kocherlakota (1990) and Ferson and Foerster (1991). Further research is needed to explore the impact of instrument choice in nonlinear models. However this work is an important reminder that just as in linear models, the quality of instrument may be very important determinant of the finite sample properties of the 'generalized IV' estimator in nonlinear models.

Taken together these studies suggest that if the estimated model is correctly specified then the finite sample performance of GMM is sensitive to both the number of moment conditions and the sample size. In particular the asymptotic standard errors can understate the finite sample variances and the distribution of the overidentifying restriction test may not be well approximated by asymptotic theory in moderate size samples. Ferson and Foerster (1991) argue that the iterated GMM estimator exhibits better finite sample behavior than the two-step estimator and so should be used in practice.

Newey (1985) derived the asymptotic distribution of τ_n under local alternatives to the data generation process for x_t. Although in many cases this distribution is noncentral χ^2, he found that there was a class of local alternatives for which τ_n has power equal to size. This is an important reminder that τ_n should not be considered an 'omnibus' specification test. Clearly certain types of misspecification may not cause the moment condition to be violated and so cannot be detected using τ_n. More generally, Newey shows that there exist local alternatives for which both the assumed population moment condition is invalid and also $n^{1/2}(\bar{\beta}^* - \beta_0)$ is asymptotically biased but τ_n still converges to χ^2_{r-q}. This can happen because τ_n is a function of $n^{1/2}g_n(\bar{\beta}^*)$ and so depends on the behavior of both $n^{1/2}g_n(\beta_0)$ and $n^{1/2}(\bar{\beta}^* - \beta_0)$. Although both these vectors may not converge to mean zero distributions it is possible for their asymptotic biases to offset in such a way that $n^{1/2}g_n(\beta^*)$ converges to a mean zero normal distribution.[17] Ferson and Foerster (1991) also report evidence on the finite sample behavior of GMM when the model is mis-

---

[16] Tauchen (1986) found no evidence that τ_n was sensitive to the autocorrelation in lw_{1t} and lw_{2t} for his simulation design.

[17] An example is where the local alternative is characterized by structural instability of the moment condition (see Ghysels and Hall, 1990b) and is discussed further below.

specified. They consider the case where the data are generated from two different models for asset returns but the linear model described above is estimated. Their results suggests that the power of the τ_n to detect model misspecification depends crucially on the relationship between the true and estimated models. The test exhibits reasonable power against one of their alternatives but low power against the other.

In all our discussion of GMM we treated the moment condition as given. In many cases there are a large number of potential moment conditions which can be chosen, and so it is important to consider which set yield the most asymptotically efficient estimators. This question has been analyzed for the situation were $f(x_t, \beta) = u_t(\beta) \otimes z_t$.[18] In this case the problem is to find the choice of instrument, z_t, which yields the asymptotically most efficient estimator *given* $u_t(\beta)$. Hansen (1985) provides a very general characterization of the asymptotic efficiency bound of GMM estimators. Hansen, Heaton and Ogaki (1988) use Hansen's (1985) method to characterize the bound when the estimation is based on multiperiod conditional moment conditions.[19] While it is possible to characterize this bound, it has proved difficult in nonlinear dynamic models to calculate the instrument vector which attains this bound. However, if we place more structure on the model, then the situation is more favorable. In the case where $u_t(\beta)$ is serially uncorrelated, then Tauchen (1986) shows that Hansen's (1985) bound implies that GMM based on $E[u_t(\beta) \otimes z_t]$ with the optimal choice of instrument is asymptotically equivalent to GMM based on the population moment conditions

$$E[Z_t^* u_t(\beta)] = 0 , \tag{5.1}$$

where

$$Z_t^* = E_t[\partial u_t(\beta_0)/\partial \beta]' \{E_t[u_t(\beta_0)u_t(\beta_0)']\}^{-1} .$$

Typically these conditional expectations are not known and so Z_t^* is not a feasible instrument choice. Consequently interest has focused on the construction of feasible optimal GMM estimators which use an estimate of Z_t^* as instrument but are still asymptotically efficient. Most often these estimated instruments depend on β and so cannot be used in the first step estimation but can be calculated in subsequent estimations using $\tilde{\beta}$ from the previous step. Newey (1990) and Robinson (1991) demonstrate that under certain conditions on the dependence structure of x_t and $u_t(\beta)$, a feasible optimal GMM estimator can be constructed using certain nonparametric estimates of Z_t^*.[20]

---

[18] In this case $u_t(\beta)$ is $(m \times 1)$ and the Kronecker product notation denotes that the moment conditions are derived by interacting each element of $u_t(\beta)$ with each element of z_t.

[19] Also, see Heaton and Ogaki (1991) for an example of this bound in the context of a continuous time financial economics model.

[20] Newey (1990) restricts attention to the case where x_t, $u_t(\beta)$ are iid and Z_t^* is estimated by nonparametric regression using nearest neighbor or series approximation techniques. Robinson (1991) considers a bootstrap estimator of Z_t^* when (i) $u_t(\beta)$ is a function of contemporaneous and lagged values of the endogenous variables but $u_t(\beta)$ is itself uncorrelated; (ii) $u_t(\beta)$ is a function of only contemporaneous endogenous variables but may itself be serially correlated.

However, in more general models, the estimation of Z_t^* will probably require numerical integration and also the imposition of distributional assumptions about x_t. Furthermore, Tauchen (1986) found that a feasible optimal instrument GMM estimator often performed very poorly in finite samples for his simulation design. One case in which the optimal instrument is easily calculated is the linear regression model discussed in Section 2. For this model if we replace the fixed in repeated samples by the assumption by

$$x_{ti} = z_t' \gamma_i + v_{ti} \, ,$$

where x_{ti} is the i-th element of x_t, z_t is fixed in repeated samples, v_{ti} is an iid mean zero error and γ_i are unknown parameters, then the optimal instrument is $\hat{x}_t$. Therefore $\bar{\beta}^*$ in (2.9) is the minimum asymptotic variance GMM estimator.

Given that it is possible to characterize an optimal instrument GMM estimator, it is natural to consider its asymptotic efficiency relative to other estimators. In the case where x_t is iid Chamberlain (1987) shows that GMM based on (5.1) is asymptotically as efficient as maximum likelihood in which one estimates nonparametrically the probability distribution of the data along with the parameters of interest. Furthermore, in linear time series models with moving average errors, Hansen and Singleton (1988) present a method of calculating the optimal instrument and show the resulting GMM estimator is asymptotically as efficient as maximum likelihood under normality.[21]

There has been considerable interest in extending the inference framework for GMM. Gallant and White (1988, Chapter 7) and Newey and West (1987b), and Andrews and Fair (1988) propose Wald, likelihood ratio type and Lagrange multiplier tests for the null hypothesis that β satisfies a nonlinear set of restrictions. In general the likelihood ratio type statistic is only appropriate under more restrictive conditions which are not satisfied in many GMM applications. These authors show that all three tests have the same asymptotic power against local alternatives.[22] However, Monte Carlo evidence reported in Gallant (1987) suggests the likelihood ratio and Lagrange multiplier tests are more reliable in finite samples. In Section 3 we observed that τ_n can be used to test all of the overidentifying restrictions of the model. If this test is statistically significant one may wish to test whether only a subset of these restrictions are satisfied with the aim of identifying which moment conditions are violated. Eichenbaum, Hansen and Singleton (1988) propose a likelihood ratio type test which can be used to test this hypothesis.

It was observed in Section 4 that Euler equation models arose as part of the response to the Lucas (1976) policy critique. These models are formulated in terms of 'taste and technology' parameters which are believed to be constant over time. Therefore a natural test for these models is to examine whether the

---

[21] Also see Hansen and Singleton (1991).

[22] This only applies to the likelihood ratio test in the cases where it is appropriate.

parameter estimates exhibit the constancy predicted by the theory. Further-more, Ghysels and Hall (1990b) use Newey's (1985) analysis to show that τ_n has power equal to size against local alternatives characterized by structural instability. This suggests it may be wise to augment the test of overidentifying restrictions with structural stability tests. Andrews and Fair (1988) propose Wald, likelihood ratio type and Lagrange multiplier type tests for parameter constancy. The essential idea behind these tests is as follows. Suppose it is suspected that the parameters change their values after a particular point in the sample termed a breakpoint. Accordingly we split the sample into two subsamples which contain the observations from before and after the break-point. If the parameters remain constant over the sample, then estimates from either of the subsamples or the whole sample should be approximately the same. Ghysels and Hall (1990a) propose a predictive test for structural stability. In this approach parameter estimates from the first subsample are used to evaluate the moment conditions in the second subsample. If the model is structurally constant over the sample, then these predicted moment condi-tions should be statistically insignificantly different from zero. Ghysels and Hall (1990b) propose a test for parameter stability based on the likelihood ratio type procedure developed by Eichenbaum, Hansen and Singleton (1988). All of these tests have the twin drawbacks of requiring the breakpoint to be known[23] and also the subsamples must be asymptotically large. Andrews (1990) proposes a procedure for testing parameter stability when the breakpoint is not known. His strategy is to calculate the Wald statistic, say, for a set of possible breakpoints and to use the maximum as the test statistic. In other words we choose the test which maximizes the evidence against structural stability. Andrews derives the tabulates the distribution of this test. However, the subset of breakpoints must be restricted to ensure the subsamples are asymptotically large for each breakpoint chosen. Therefore like the other tests described above Andrews' test cannot be used to draw inference about parameter constancy at either end of the sample. Dufour, Ghysels and Hall (1991) propose a class of generalized predictive tests which permit inference at the ends of the sample. Within their framework, one must have an asymptotically large estimation sample from which to consistently estimate β. This estimate is used to evaluate $f(x_t, \beta)$ for every observation in the prediction sample, which can be of any size. Unlike the Ghysels and Hall (1990a) test which focussed on the average of the predicted moment conditions, the generalized predictive tests are based on the individual predictions $f(x_t, \tilde{\beta})$. Dufour, Ghysels and Hall discuss a number of methods for assessing whether these predictions residuals are statistically significantly different from zero.

All of these techniques permit inference within a given model. However, very often it is desired to discriminate between two economic models which imply nonnested Euler conditions for the same data. For example we may wish

---

[23] If the breakpoint is unknown a common strategy is to apply the above tests assuming the break occurs halfway through the sample. However, intuition suggests that in this case the tests will lose power as the distance between the true breakpoint and the middle of the sample increases.

to choose which of two different nonnested utility functions is more appropriate in a consumption based asset pricing model. Singleton (1985) proposes a simple test based on nesting the two Euler equations within a more general model whose Euler equation is a convex combination of the two. While computationally convenient, this approach may not always be appropriate because the convex combination of Euler equations may not be the Euler equation of an economically meaningful model (see Ghysels and Hall, 1990c). Ghysels and Hall (1990c) propose a test based on the encompassing principle (Mizon and Richard, 1986), which can be used to discriminate between two rational expectations models. However, to implement this test it is necessary to specify a model for x_t. This is undesirable because it requires much stronger assumptions that are necessary to estimate the individual Euler equation models by GMM.

Finally it should be noted that the stationarity and ergodicity assumption is not necessary for our analysis. Its role was to facilitate the application of laws of large numbers and central limit theorems to the data. As part of their development of a unified theory of dynamic models, Gallant and White (1988) generalize Hansen's (1982) results to the case where x_t is nonstationary but near epoch dependent on an α-mixing process (see Gallant and White, 1988, Chapter 2). This condition places sufficient restrictions on the memory of the process to allow the application of Laws of Large Numbers and Central Limit Theorems to functions of x_t. Many of the tests described above can be applied in this more general setting.

6. Concluding remarks

Generalized method of moments estimation has provided important contributions to both the theoretical and applied econometrics literature. In the theoretical literature it provides a unified framework for estimation theory. In the applied literature it provides a computationally convenient method of estimation in some models which were burdensome to estimate by other methods. We conclude our discussion of GMM by offering some final comments on both these contributions.

The first issue has not been explicitly addressed in this paper. In Section 2 we showed that IV is a special case of GMM and obviously the same result holds for OLS in this model because it is an IV estimator with $Z = X$. However, it may not be obvious how other familiar estimators can be nested within the GMM framework in more general models. To understand this connection we consider two estimators (i) $\hat{\beta}$ the value of β which optimizes $N_n(\beta)$; (ii) $\tilde{\beta}$ the GMM estimator obtained from minimizing $Q_n(\beta) = [\partial N(\beta)/\partial \beta]' W_n [\partial N(\beta)/\partial \beta]$. Now under certain regularity conditions $\hat{\beta}$ satisfies the first-order conditions $\partial N(\hat{\beta})/\partial \beta = 0.$[24] Similarly $\tilde{\beta}$ satisfies the first order conditions in (3.2)

---

[24] It is possible for $N(\beta)$ to have a unique optimum without the first-order conditions having a solution. Our discussion does not apply to these cases.

appropriate for this choice of $Q_n(\beta)$. Note that $\partial N(\beta)/\partial\beta$ is $(q \times 1)$ by construction and so β is just identified. In this case it follows from our earlier discussion that $\partial N(\tilde\beta)/\partial\beta = 0$. Therefore, provided there is a unique solution to these equations $\hat\beta = \tilde\beta$. The advantage to viewing any estimator from a GMM perspective is that it focuses attention explicitly on the moment condition being exploited in estimation. For example if $N_n(\beta) = \Sigma_{t=1}^{n} \text{LLF}_t(\beta)$ is the quasi log likelihood function (see White, 1982), then the condition for the consistency is that $\text{E}[\partial\text{LLF}_t(\beta_0)/\partial\beta)] = 0$, where $\text{LLF}_t(\beta_0)$ is the condition-al quasi log likelihood of the t-th observation. Therefore the GMM framework ties in very naturally with previous discussions of consistency in which this condition has received considerable attention, e.g., in the quasi maximum likelihood estimator literature (see White, 1982) and also in the context of nonlinear FIML estimation of simultaneous equation models (see Amemiya, 1977; Phillips 1982).

In this discussion we have implicitly concentrated on the situation in which all the elements of β are estimated simultaneously. Newey (1984) dem-onstrates that sequential estimators[25] also fit within the GMM framework. For example consider the following two-step estimation procedure. In the first step one estimates the just identified parameter vector β_1 from the sample moment conditions $n^{-1} \Sigma f_1(x_t, \beta_1)$. In the second step one estimates β_2 conditional on $\hat\beta_1$ from the sample moment conditions $n^{-1} \Sigma f_2(x_t, \hat\beta_1, \beta_2)$, which provides sufficient information so that β_2 is just identified given $\hat\beta_1$. Newey (1984) demonstrates that $\hat\beta = (\hat\beta_1', \hat\beta_2')'$ is identical to the GMM estimator obtained from the recursive sample moment $n^{-1} \Sigma f(x_t, \beta) = [n^{-1} \Sigma f_1(x_t, \beta_1)'$ $n^{-1} \Sigma f_2(x_t, \beta_1, \beta_2)']'$. An advantage of viewing sequential estimators from a GMM perspective is that one can use the results in equation (3.6) to facilitate calculation of the correct asymptotic covariance matrix of the estimators. One can also utilize the GMM framework to analyze the asymptotic behavior of certain simulation estimators. Lee and Ingram (1991) propose an estimation method for the time series models based on gathering artificial data. The idea is to estimate the parameters of the model by the values which yield sample moments for the artificial data that mimic the sample moments of the real data.[26] Lee and Ingram (1991) demonstrate that under certain regularity conditions their estimator is a special case of GMM and is therefore consistent and asymptotically normal.

The computational convenience of GMM has been illustrated using non-linear rational expectations models. This convenience is achieved because for GMM it is only necessary to specify the Euler equation in order to obtain sufficient moment conditions to identify the parameters. In other words we gain computationally by only specifying part of the statistical model for x_t.

---

[25] For example stage least squares (e.g., see Johnston, 1984, p. 442–443) or the residual adjusted Aitken estimator for partial adjustment models with serially correlated errors (see Hatanaka, 1974).

[26] Also see Duffie and Singleton (1990) and Gourieroux and Monfort (1993).

However, as we have seen in Section 5, there are limits to the inference one can perform using a partially specified model. For example τ_n is not an 'omnibus' specification test and one needs to specify a model for x_t to calculate either the optimal instrument in general nonlinear dynamic models or non-nested hypothesis tests based on the encompassing principle. In spite of these limitations GMM continues to be an important method of estimation in econometrics. Many interesting questions remain and future work will no doubt provide us with a clearer understanding of the properties of GMM based inference.

Acknowledgment

This paper was originally prepared for presentation in an invited lecture entitled 'An Introduction to Generalized Method of Moments Estimation' at the Division of Research and Statistics, the Board of Governors of the Federal Reserve System, Washington, DC 20551, November 12, 1991. I am very grateful to those who attended this lecture for valuable comments which have helped improve the exposition. I am particularly indebted to Glenn Rudebusch for suggesting this topic and providing detailed comments on the paper. This paper has also benefitted from the comments of Eric Ghysels, G. S. Maddala, Whitney Newey, Masao Ogaki, and John Seater.

References

Amemiya, T. (1977). The maximum likelihood and the nonsingular three-stage least squares estimator in the general nonlinear simultaneous equation model. *Econometrica* **45**, 955–968.

Andrews, D. (1990). Tests for parameter instability and structural change with unknown breakpoint. Cowles Foundation Discussion Paper #943, Cowles Foundation for Research in Economics, Yale University, New Haven, CT.

Andrews, D. (1991). Heteroscedasticity and autocorrelation consistent covariance matrix estimation. *Econometrica* **59**, 817–858.

Andrews, D. and R. Fair (1988). Inference in econometric models with structural change. *Rev. Econom. Stud.* **55**, 615–640.

Avery, R., L. Hansen and V. Hoitz (1983). Multiperiod probit models and orthogonality condition estimation. *Internat. Econom. Rev.* **24**, 21–36.

Chamberlain, G. (1987). Asymptotic efficiency in estimation with conditional moment restrictions. *J. Econometrics* **34**, 305–334.

Doan, T. (1990). *RATS, Version 3.10, Users Manual.* VAR Econometrics, Minneapolis, MN.

Duffie, D. and K. Singleton (1990). Simulated method of moments estimation of Markov models of asset prices. Discussion paper, Graduate School of Business, Stanford University, Stanford, CA.

Dufour, J.-M., E. Ghysels and A. Hall (1991). Generalized predictive tests and structural change analysis in econometrics. Unpublished mimeo, C.R.D.E., Université de Montréal, Quebec, Canada.

Dunn, K. and K. Singleton (1986). Modelling the term structure of interest rates under nonseparable utility and durable goods. *J. Financ. Econom.* **17**, 27–55.

Eichenbaum, M., L. Hansen and K. Singleton (1988). A time series analysis of representative agent models of consumption and leisure choice under certainty. *Quart. J. Econom.* **103**, 51–78.

Epstein, L. and S. Zin (1991). Substitution, risk aversion and the temporal behavior of asset returns. *J. Politic. Econom.* **99**, 263–286.

Fair, R. (1989). The production smoothing model is alive and well. *J. Monetary Econom.* **24**, 353–370.

Ferson, W. and E. Foerster (1991). Finite sample properties of the generalized method of moment in tests of conditional asset pricing models. Unpublished mimeo, Graduate School of Business, University of Chicago, Chicago, IL.

Gallant, A. R. (1987). *Nonlinear Statistical Models.* Wiley, New York.

Gallant, A. R. and G. Tauchen (1989). Seminonparametric estimation of conditionally constrained heterogeneous processes: Asset pricing applications. *Econometrica* **57**, 1091–1120.

Gallant, A. R. and H. White (1988). *A Unified Theory of Estimation and Inference for Nonlinear Dynamic Models.* Basil Blackwell, Oxford.

Ghysels, E. and A. Hall (1990a). A test for structural stability of Euler parameters estimated via the generalized method of moments estimator. *Internat. Econom. Rev.* **31**, 355–364.

Ghysels, E. and A. Hall (1990b). Are consumption-based intertemporal capital asset pricing models structural? *J. Econometrics* **45**, 121–139.

Ghysels, E. and A. Hall (1990c). Testing nonnested Euler conditions with quadrature-based methods of approximation. *J. Econometrics* **46**, 273–308.

Gourieroux, C. and A. Monfort (1993). Simulation based inference: A survey with special reference to panel data models. *J. Econometrics*, to appear.

Hall, B. and C. Cummins (1991). *TSP Users Guide Version 4.2.* TSP International, Palo Alto, CA.

Hansen, L. (1982). Large sample properties of generalized method of moments estimators. *Econometrica* **50**, 1029–1054.

Hansen, L. (1985). A method for calculating bounds on the asymptotic covariance matrices of generalized method of moments estimators. *J. Econometrics* **30**, 203–238.

Hansen, L., J. Heaton and M. Ogaki (1988). Efficiency bounds implied by multi-period conditional moment restrictions, *J. Amer. Stat. Assoc.* **83**, 863–871.

Hansen, K. and T. Sargent (1982). Instrumental variables procedures for estimating linear rational expectations models. *J. Monetary Econom.* **9**, 263–296.

Hansen, L. and K. Singleton (1982). Generalized instrumental variables estimation of nonlinear rational expectations models. *Econometrica* **50**, 1269–1286.

Hansen, L. and K. Singleton (1988). Efficient estimation of linear asset pricing models with moving average errors. Unpublished mimeo, Department of Economics, University of Chicago, Chicago, IL.

Hansen, L. and K. Singleton (1991). Computing semi-parametric efficiency bounds for linear time series models. In: W. A. Barnett, J. L. Powell and G. Tauchen, eds., *Proc. 5th Internat. Sympos. in Economic Theory and Econometrics.*

Hatanaka, M. (1974). An efficient two-step estimator for the dynamic adjustment model with autoregressive errors. *J. Econometrics* **2**, 199–220.

Hausman, J. (1978). Specification tests in econometrics. *Econometrica* **46**, 1251–1271.

Heaton, J. and M. Ogaki (1991). Efficiency bound calculations for a time series model with conditional heteroscedasticity. *Econom. Lett.* **35**, 167–171.

Johnston, J. (1984). *Econometric Methods.* McGraw-Hill, New York.

Kocherlakota, N. (1990). On tests of representative consumer asset pricing models. *J. Monetary Econom.* **26**, 285–304.

Lee, B.-S. and B. Ingram (1991). Simulation estimation of time series models. *J. Econometrics* **47**, 197–205.

Lucas, R. (1976). Econometric policy evaluation: A critique. In: K. Brunner, ed., *The Phillips Curve and Labor Markets*, Carnegie–Rochester Conference Series on Public Economics, Vol. 1. North-Holland, Amsterdam.

Mankiw, N. G., J. Rotemberg and L. Summers (1985). Intertemporal substitution in macroeconomics. *Quart. J. Econom.* **100**, 225–252.

Mark, N. (1985). On time varying risk premia in foreign exchange market. *J. Monetary Econom.* **16**, 3–18.

Miron, J. and S. Zeldes (1988). Seasonality, cost shocks and the production smoothing model of inventories. *Econometrica* **56**, 877–908.

Mizon, G. and J.-F. Richard (1986). The encompassing principle and its application to testing non-nested hypotheses. *Econometrica* **54**, 657–678.

Nelson, C. and R. Startz (1990). The distribution of the instrumental variables estimator and its *t*-ratio when the instrument is a poor one. *J. Business* **63**, 125–140.

Newey, W. (1984). A method of moments interpretation of sequential estimators. *Econom. Lett.* **14**, 201–206.

Newey, W. (1985). Generalized method of moments specification testing. *J. Econometrics* **29**, 229–256.

Newey, W. (1990). Efficient instrumental variables estimation of nonlinear models. *Econometrica* **58**, 809–837.

Newey, W. and K. West (1987a). A simple, positive definite, heteroscedasticity and autocorrelation covariance matrix. *Econometrica* **55**, 703–708.

Newey, W. and K. West (1987b). Hypothesis testing with efficient method of moments estimation. *Internat. Econom. Rev.* **28**, 777–787.

Ogaki, M. (1992). GMM: A user's guide. Unpublished mimeo, Department of Economics, University of Rochester, Rochester, NY.

Phillips, P. (1982). On the consistency of nonlinear FIML. *Econometrica* **50**, 1307–1324.

Pindyck, R. and J. Rotemberg (1983). Dynamic factor demands and the effects of energy price shocks. *Amer. Econom. Rev.* **73**, 1066–1079.

Robinson, P. (1991). Best nonlinear three stages least squares estimation of certain econometric models. *Econometrica* **59**, 755–786.

SAS (1982). *SAS User Guide: Statistics*. SAS Institute Inc., Cary, NC.

Sargan, J. (1958). The estimation of economic relationships using instrumental variables. *Econometrica* **26**, 393–415.

Sargan, J. (1959). The estimation of relationships with autocorrelated residuals by the use of instrumental variables. *J. Roy. Statist. Soc. Ser. B* **21**, 91–105.

Singleton, K. (1985). Testing specifications of economic agents' intertemporal optimum problems in the presence of alternative models. *J. Econometrics* **30**, 391–413.

Tauchen, G. (1986). Statistical properties of generalized method of moments estimators of structural parameters obtained from financial market data. *J. Business Econom. Statist.* **4**, 397–425.

West, K. (1986). A variance bounds test of the linear quadratic inventory model. *J. Politic. Econom.* **94**, 374–401.

White, H. (1982). Maximum likelihood estimation of misspecified models. *Econometrica* **50**, 1–26.

White, H. (1984a). *Asymptotic Theory for Econometricians*. Academic Press, New York.

White, H. (1984b). Comment on 'Tests of specification in econometrics' by P. Ruud. *Econometric Rev.* **3**, 261–267.

G. S. Maddala, C. R. Rao and H. D. Vinod, eds., *Handbook of Statistics, Vol. 11*
© 1993 Elsevier Science Publishers B.V. All rights reserved.

16

Efficient Estimation of Models with Conditional Moment Restrictions

Whitney K. Newey

1. Introduction

Often an economic data set is used to answer questions for which it was not designed, because it is too expensive to collect data to answer each new question. The lack of control of empirical workers over the form of the data suggests the need for models that impose few restrictions on the distribution of the data. Also, because economic data often embodies response of individual agents to market conditions and/or economic incentives, it is important to have models that control for these responses. The simultaneous equations models of econometrics, and corresponding instrumental variable methods, are designed to control for such phenomena: see Hausman (1984) for further motivation and discussion.

A useful type of model that imposes few restrictions and can allow for simultaneity is a conditional moment restriction model, where all that is specified is that a vector of *residuals*, consisting of known, prespecified functions of the data and parameters, has conditional mean zero given known variables. An example is regression with a disturbance that has conditional mean zero given the regressors, where the residual is the usual difference of the dependence variable and linear combination of the regressors. Other examples, to be discussed below, can allow for incorporation of information about the variance of the disturbance and for simultaneity. Estimators for the parameters of these models can be constructed by interacting functions of the residuals with functions of the conditioning variables and choosing the parameter estimates so that the sample moments of these interactions are zero. These estimators are conditional, implicit versions of the method of moments, that are typically referred to as *instrumental variables* (IV) estimators, where the *instruments* are the functions of conditioning variables that interacted with the residuals. These estimators have the usual advantage of method of moments over maximum likelihood, that their consistency only depends on correct specification of the residuals and conditioning variables, and not on the correctness of a likelihood function. Of course, maximum likelihood may be more efficient than IV if the distribution is correctly specified, so that the usual

419

bias/efficiency tradeoff is present for IV and maximum likelihood. Further description and motivation for IV estimators is given in Sections 2 and 3.

The precision of estimators for conditional moment models is a concern, because of the restrictions imposed are so weak. The purpose of this chapter is to discuss (asymptotically) efficient estimation of the parameters of conditional moment restriction models. Two notions of efficiency are of interest here. One is efficiency within the class of IV estimators and the other is efficiency in the semiparametric model sense of Stein (1956). It turns out that the two notions result in the same estimator, because the optimal estimator in the class of IV estimators is efficient for the semiparametric model. Thus, as far as efficient estimation is concerned, it suffices to restrict attention to the class of IV estimators.

Several approaches to efficient estimation are considered. Each is based on constructing an estimator of the optimal instruments, i.e., of those functions that are interacted with the residual to obtain the IV estimator with smallest asymptotic variance. These approaches will work because suitably regular estimation of the instruments has no effect on the distribution of estimators of the parameters of interest (a kind of information matrix block diagonality for the parameters of interest and parameters of the instruments). One approach is to specify the optimal instruments to be functions of auxiliary parameters, and replace the auxiliary parameters with consistent estimators. The resulting estimator of the parameters of interest will be efficient if the optimal instruments take the specific parametric form, and will be consistent even if they do not. Another approach is to use a nonparametric estimator of the optimal instruments. The resulting estimator of the parameter of interest will be efficient over all possible forms for the optimal instruments, subject to regularity conditions. Two types of nonparametric estimators are considered, one based on nearest neighbor estimation of conditional expectations that form the optimal instruments and the other on estimation of the optimal instruments by linear combinations of prespecified functions. Asymptotic efficiency of the corresponding estimators of parameters of interest is shown in this chapter, and a small Monte Carlo study of their properties in the heteroskedastic linear regression model is given. Also, some data based methods for choosing the number of nearest neighbors or the number of approximating functions in the nonparametric estimator are given.

The new results in this chapter are those on nonparametric estimation of the optimal instrumental variables. Other results have previously been given elsewhere. The form of the optimal instruments was derived by Amemiya (1974) and Berndt, Hall, Hall and Hausman (1974) for the homoskedastic residual case and Hansen (1985) for the general case. Chamberlain (1987) showed that the semiparametric efficiency bound for conditional moment restrictions models was attained by optimal instrumental variables estimators. Also, results on estimation when the optimal instruments are replaced by parametric estimators are given in Carroll and Ruppert (1988), nonparametric estimation of the optimal instruments has been considered by Carroll (1982),

Robinson (1987), and Newey (1988) for the linear regression model, and by Newey (1990) for the homoskedastic residual case.

Section 2 of the paper introduces the model, describes IV estimators, derives the form of the optimal instruments, and describes parametric estimation of the optimal instruments. Section 3 gives a number of examples, including estimation of regression models, models with second moment information, transformation models, and models with simultaneity. In each case a parametric estimator of the optimal instruments is discussed. Section 4 deals with nearest neighbor nonparametric estimation of the optimal instruments, Section 5 with estimation via linear combinations of functions, and Section 6 reports on a small Monte Carlo study.

2. Conditional moment restrictions and instrumental variables estimation

The general type of model that will be dealt with in this chapter can be described as follows. Let z denote a single $p \times 1$ observation on all the variables, and denote the data by $z_1, \ldots, z_n$. Let θ be a $q \times 1$ vector of parameters, $\rho(z, \theta)$ an $s \times 1$ *residual* vector of functions of a data observation and the parameter, and x a vector of conditioning variables. The conditional moment restriction model considered here is one where the true distribution of the data satisfies

$$E[\rho(z, \theta_0)|x] = 0, \tag{2.1}$$

where θ_0 denotes the true value of the parameters. An example of this type of model is the linear regression model

$$y = x'\beta_0 + \varepsilon, \qquad E[\varepsilon|x] = 0, \tag{2.2}$$

where $z = (y, x')$, $\theta = \beta$, $s = 1$, and the residual is $\rho(z, \theta) = y - x'\theta$.

The conditional moment restriction of equation (2.1) implies that $\rho(z, \theta_0)$ is uncorrelated with functions of x, an unconditional moment restriction. This restriction can be used to estimate θ_0 by setting the sample cross-product of $\rho(z, \theta)$ with functions of x close to zero. To describe this estimator, let $A(x)$ denote an $r \times s$ matrix of functions of x. Then $E[A(x)\rho(z, \theta_0)] = 0$ by equation (2.1) and iterated expectations, suggesting a method of moments estimator that sets the sample moment of $A(x)\rho(z, \theta)$ equal to its population value of zero. When $r > q$ it will generally not be possible to set the sample moments to be zero, but a similar method of moments estimator can be obtained by minimizing a quadratic form in the sample moments. Let $\hat{P}$ denote an $r \times r$ positive semi-definite matrix that may be random, and consider the estimator

$$\hat{\theta} = \mathrm{argmin}_{\theta \in \Theta} \hat{g}_n(\theta)' \hat{P} \hat{g}_n(\theta), \qquad \hat{g}_n(\theta) = \sum_{i=1}^{n} A(x_i)\rho(z_i, \theta)/n, \tag{2.3}$$

where Θ is some set of feasible values for θ.

This type of estimator was developed and analyzed in a number of econometrics papers, including Sargan (1959), Amemiya (1974), Jorgenson and Laffont (1974), Burguete, Gallant and Souza (1982), Hansen (1982), and Newey (1990). It is often referred to as a nonlinear IV estimator, and $A(x)$ as instruments. This type of estimator dates to Reiersol (1945), who suggested IV estimation as a method to treat measurement error in linear regression models. Also, IV estimators are very general, in that they include many familiar estimators as special cases. For example, in the linear model of equation (2.2), for a weight function $w(x)$ the weighted least squares estimator $\hat{\beta} = (\sum_{i=1}^{n} w(x_i) x_i x_i')^{-1} \sum_{i=1}^{n} w(x_i) x_i y_i$ solves equation (2.3) for instruments $A(x) = w(x)x$.

It is straightforward to derive the asymptotic variance of $\hat{\theta}$, as needed to discuss its (asymptotic) efficiency, by applying the usual mean-value expansion argument to the first-order conditions $\partial \hat{g}_n(\hat{\theta})/\partial\theta' \hat{P}\hat{g}_n(\hat{\theta}) = 0$ for $\hat{\theta}$. Suppose that there is a positive semi-definite matrix P such that $\hat{P} \overset{p}{\to} P$, that a uniform law of large numbers gives $\partial \hat{g}_n(\bar{\theta})/\partial\theta \overset{p}{\to} E[A(x)\,\partial\rho(z,\theta_0)/\partial\theta] = G$ for any $\bar{\theta} \overset{p}{\to} \theta_0$, and that $z_1, \ldots, z_n$ are iid so that a central limit theorem gives $\sqrt{n}\hat{g}_n(\theta_0) \overset{d}{\to} N(0, V)$, $V = E[A(x)\rho(z,\theta_0)\rho(z,\theta_0)'A(x)']$. The expanding $\hat{g}_n(\hat{\theta})$ around θ_0, solving for $\sqrt{n}(\hat{\theta} - \theta_0)$, replacing estimated averages by their probability limits, and applying the Slutzky theorem gives

$$n(\hat{\theta} - \theta_0) = -\left(\frac{\partial \hat{g}_n(\hat{\theta})}{\partial\theta'} \frac{\hat{P}}{} \frac{\partial \hat{g}_n(\bar{\theta})}{\partial\theta} \right)^{-1} \frac{\partial \hat{g}_n(\hat{\theta})}{\partial\theta'} \hat{P}\sqrt{n}\hat{g}_n(\theta_0)$$
$$= -(G'PG)^{-1}G'P\sqrt{n}\hat{g}_n(\theta_0) + o_p(1)$$
$$\overset{d}{\to} N(0, (G'PG)^{-1}G'PVPG(G'PG)^{-1}) . \qquad (2.4)$$

The asymptotic variance of $\hat{\theta}$ depends on the assumptions of independent observations through the form of V. With dependent observations, V might include covariances between $A(x)\rho(z,\theta_0)$ for different observations, rather than being just an expected outer product. Because of this complication the analysis of optimality is much more difficult with dependent observations, although Hansen (1985) and Hansen, Heaton and Ogaki (1988) have made progress on this problem. Here attention is restricted to the iid case to avoid further complications, and because the assumption of iid observations is sufficiently general to cover many cross-section and longitudinal data models of interest.

The asymptotic variance matrix $(G'PG)^{-1}PVPG(G'PG)^{-1}$ depends on both P and $A(x)$. As shown by Hansen (1982), the optimal choice of P, that minimizes the asymptotic variance, is $P = V^{-1}$. This optimal P can be implemented by using $\hat{P} = \hat{V}^{-1}$ for a consistent estimator $\hat{V}$ of V (because the asymptotic variance depends only on the probability limit of $\hat{P}$).

The main focus here is the optimal, asymptotic variance minimizing choice of instruments $A(x)$. It will turn out that the optimal $A(x)$ has q rows, so that the asymptotic variance of the corresponding estimator does not depend on P. To describe the optimal $A(x)$, let

$$D(x) \equiv \mathrm{E}[\partial\rho(z, \theta_0)/\partial\theta \,|\, x], \qquad \Omega(x) \equiv \mathrm{E}[\rho(z, \theta_0)\rho(z, \theta_0)' \,|\, x]. \qquad (2.5)$$

The optimal instruments are

$$B(x) = C \cdot D(x)'\Omega(x)^{-1}, \qquad (2.6)$$

where C is any nonsingular matrix. The asymptotic variance matrix for these instruments is

$$\Lambda = (\mathrm{E}[D(x)'\Omega(x)^{-1}D(x)])^{-1}. \qquad (2.7)$$

For example, in the linear model of equation (2.2), $D(x) = -x'$ and $\Omega(x) = \mathrm{E}[\varepsilon^2 \,|\, x]$, so that for $C = -I$, $B(x) = x/\sigma^2(x)$. The corresponding IV estimator is just a weighted least squares estimator with weight $1/\sigma^2(x)$, i.e., heteroskedasticity corrected generalized least squares.

The form of the optimal instruments has an intuitive explanation by way of an analogy with the linear model. The term $\Omega(x)^{-1}$ is a correction for heteroskedasticity (and correlation between different components of $\rho(z, \theta_0)$) similar to that for the linear model. The derivatives $\partial\rho(z, \theta_0)/\partial\theta$ correspond to the regressors, because as usual the model can be treated as approximately linear when calculating the asymptotic variance. These derivatives are not allowed as instruments in general, because they may not depend just on x, but the matrix $D(x)$ is the function of x that is most closely correlated with $\partial\rho(z, \theta_0)/\partial\theta$.

It is straightforward to show that $B(x)$ gives the optimal instruments. First, note that Λ does not depend on C, so that it suffices to show the result with $C = I$ in equation (2.6). Let $m_A = G'PA(x)\rho(z, \theta_0)$ and $m_B = B(x)\rho(z, \theta_0)$. Then by iterated expectations, $\mathrm{E}[m_A m_B'] = G'PE[A(x)\Omega(x)B(x)'] = G'PE[A(x)\Omega(x)B(x)'] = G'PE[A(x)D(x)] = G'PG$, $G'PVPG = \mathrm{E}[m_A m_A']$, and $\Lambda = (\mathrm{E}[m_B m_B'])^{-1}$. Therefore,

$$(G'PG)^{-1}G'PVPG(G'PG)^{-1} - \Lambda$$
$$= (\mathrm{E}[m_A m_B'])^{-1}\mathrm{E}[m_A m_A'](\mathrm{E}[m_B m_A'])^{-1} - (\mathrm{E}[m_B m_B'])^{-1}$$
$$= (\mathrm{E}[m_A m_B'])^{-1}\{\mathrm{E}[m_A m_A']$$
$$- \mathrm{E}[m_A m_B'](\mathrm{E}[m_B m_B'])^{-1}\mathrm{E}[m_B m_A'])\}\mathrm{E}[m_B m_A'] = \mathrm{E}[RR'],$$
$$R = (\mathrm{E}[m_A m_B'])^{-1}\{m_A - \mathrm{E}[m_A m_B'](\mathrm{E}[m_B m_B'])^{-1}m_B\}, \qquad (2.8)$$

and $\mathrm{E}[RR']$ is positive semi-definite, showing that Λ is a lower bound for the asymptotic variance of all IV estimators.

Chamberlain (1987) showed that Λ is a lower bound in an even stronger sense. In the semiparametric model where the only substantive restriction imposed on the distribution of the data is equation (2.1), Λ_B is an asymptotic minimax bound. Consequently, Λ_B is a lower bound for the asymptotic variance of any consistent, asymptotically normal (regular) estimator, and not just for IV estimators.

It is generally not feasible to use the optimal instruments $B(x)$ to form an efficient estimator, because they depend on unknown parameters and/or functions. Feasible approaches to efficient estimation can be based on an estimator of $\hat{B}(x)$ of $B(x)$. Such an estimated optimal instrument could be used in place of $A(x)$ in equation (2.3), with $\hat{P} = (\sum_{i=1}^{n} \hat{B}(x_i)\hat{B}(x_i)'/n)^{-1}$. The choice of $\hat{P}$ will not matter asymptotically, but this one has the virtue of making the objective function invariant to nonsingular linear transformations of the instruments and so may improve computation. The resulting estimator will be

$$\hat{\theta} = \operatorname*{argmin}_{\theta \in \Theta} \left\{ \sum_{i=1}^{n} \rho(z, \theta)' \hat{B}(x_i)' \left[\sum_{i=1}^{n} \hat{B}(x_i)\hat{B}(x_i)' \right]^{-1} \sum_{i=1}^{n} \hat{B}(x_i)\rho(z, \theta) \right\}.$$

(2.9)

This approach, based on using estimators of the optimal instruments, should work because estimation of optimal instruments should not affect the asymptotic distribution of the estimator. Intuitively, equation (2.1) implies that variation of $A(x)$ around $B(x)$ that is asymptotically small in an appropriate sense will not affect the asymptotic distribution of $\hat{\theta}$.

Linearized versions of feasible efficient estimators are convenient because an initial estimator is often needed anyway to form an estimator of the optimal instruments and the linearized estimator does not require iteration. Let $\hat{\theta}$ be an initial estimator, e.g., obtained form equation (2.3) with $A(x)$ and $\hat{P}$ known. One Newton–Raphson step toward the solution of (2.3) starting at $\hat{\theta}$, with $A(x) = \hat{B}(x)$ (i.e., one Newton–Raphson step toward the solution of $\sum_{i=1}^{n} \hat{B}(x_i)\rho(z_i, \theta) = 0$) gives

$$\tilde{\theta} = \hat{\theta} - \left[\sum_{i=1}^{n} \hat{B}(x_i) \, \partial\rho(z_i, \hat{\theta})/\partial\theta \right]^{-1} \sum_{i=1}^{n} \hat{B}(x_i)\rho(z_i, \hat{\theta}).$$

(2.10)

One approach to estimation of the optimal instruments is to assume that $D(x) = D(x, \eta_0)$ and $\Omega(x) = \Omega(x, \eta_0)$ for some known functions $D(x, \eta)$ and $\Omega(x, \gamma)$ and real vector η, to construct an estimator $\hat{\eta}$ of η_0, and form $\hat{B}(x) = D(x, \hat{\eta})'\Omega(x, \hat{\eta})^{-1}$. For example, since $D(x)$ and $\Omega(x)$ are conditional expectations, the parameters η could be estimated by, say, least squares regression with the elements of $\partial\rho(z_i, \hat{\theta})/\partial\theta$ and $\rho(z_i, \hat{\theta})\rho(z_i, \hat{\theta})'$ as dependent variables. This approach will lead to an efficient IV estimator if the specification of $D(x, \eta)$ and $\Omega(x, \eta)$ is correct. The IV estimator will not be efficient otherwise, although it will remain consistent. This approach will be discussed in the context of the examples of the next section.

Nonparametric estimates of the optimal instruments are also useful. Although the structure of the model may result in some elements of $D(x)$ and/or $\Omega(x)$ having known functional form, knowledge of the functional form of all these functions will generally require auxiliary distribution assumptions and/or difficult calculations. For example, in the linear model knowing the form of $\Omega(x) = E[\varepsilon^2 | x]$ amounts to knowing the form of heteroskedasticity, and in models where $D(x) = E[\partial\rho(z, \theta_0)/\partial\theta | x]$ it may be difficult to specify $D(x, \eta)$ so that it is consistent with the model, or to even calculate it when the conditional distribution of z given x is specified as an auxiliary assumption. Nonparametric estimation of the optimal instruments provides a means of constructing efficient estimators that do not rely on auxiliary assumptions or the outcome of difficult calculations.

3. Examples

This section describes a number of examples, in order to illustrate the broad applicability of conditional moment restriction models. These applications include standard ones, such as nonlinear regression, and some that are less familiar, but that are important in econometrics, such as models with endogenous dummy variables.

3.1. Nonlinear regression

To start on common ground, the first example is one that is very familiar. Suppose that $z = (y, x')$ where y is a dependent variable, that β is a vector of parameters with true value β_0, and that

$$y = f(x, \beta_0) + \varepsilon, \qquad E[\varepsilon | x] = 0. \tag{3.1.1}$$

This model is the standard nonlinear regression model, where the only restriction imposed on the disturbance distribution is that it has conditional mean zero. It is similar to the linear model example of equation (2.2), in that it is a special case of the general conditional moment restriction model of equation (2.1) with $\theta = \beta$ and $\rho(z, \theta) = y - f(x, \beta)$ being the regression residual.

In this example an optimal instrument $B(x) = D(x)'\Omega(x)^{-1}$ and its components $D(x)$ and $\Omega(x)$ have simple formulas,

$$D(x) = -\frac{\partial f(x, \beta_0)'}{\partial \beta}, \qquad \Omega(x) = E[\varepsilon^2 | x],$$

$$B(x) = (E[\varepsilon^2 | x])^{-1} \frac{\partial f(x, \beta_0)}{\partial \beta}. \tag{3.1.2}$$

Here the functional form of $D(x)$ is known, so that to construct an estimator $\hat{D}(x)$ it suffices to replace β_0 with an estimator $\hat{\beta}$. This feature of $D(x)$ having known functional form results from the derivative of the residual depending only on the conditioning variables. The more difficult components to deal with is the conditional variance $E[\varepsilon^2 | x]$. An estimator that is efficient over a parametric family of conditional variances can be constructed by specifying a functional form $\Omega(x, \eta)$ for the conditional variance, and using an estimator $\hat{\eta}$ of the true value η_0 to construct $\hat{\Omega}(x) = \Omega(x, \hat{\eta})$, and then form estimated optimal instruments as

$$\hat{B}(x) = -\frac{\partial f(x, \hat{\beta})}{\partial \beta} \cdot \Omega(x, \hat{\eta})^{-1}. \tag{3.1.3}$$

For example, $\hat{\eta}$ might be formed from a weighted nonlinear regression of squared least squares residuals on $\Omega(x, \eta)$, or might be the result of several iterations of such an estimator; an extensive discussion of specification of $\Omega(x, \eta)$ and construction of $\hat{\eta}$ is given in Carroll and Ruppert (1988). With estimator $\hat{B}(x)$ of an optimal instrument in hand one could construct a one-step efficient estimator as in equation (2.10). The resulting estimator will be efficient in the class of all estimators that use only the conditional moments restriction of equation (3.1.1), as long as $\Omega(x, \eta)$ and $\hat{\eta}$ are correctly specified, under appropriate regularity conditions. This efficiency will result from the instrument being optimal, and the well-known property that the estimation of the conditional variance will have no effect on the asymptotic distribution of $\hat{\beta}$.

The linearized estimator in equation (2.10) amounts to one iteration of the Gauss–Newton algorithm for minimizing the weighted nonlinear least squares criteria $\Sigma_{i=1}^{n} \Omega(x_i, \hat{\eta})^{-1}\{y_i - f(x_i, \beta)\}^2$. It is well-known that such weighted least squares criteria use only the moment restriction of equation (3.1.1), so that this estimator will be consistent and asymptoticially normal even if $\Omega(x, \eta)$ is misspecified. Other estimators have this property, in particular estimators that are quasi-maximum likelihood estimator for exponential families with conditional mean function $f(x, \beta)$, see McCullagh and Nelder (1983). As is well known, these estimators are asymptotically equivalent to weighted nonlinear least squares estimators, and so are contained in the class of instrumental variables estimators (with instruments equal to the product of $\partial f(x, \beta)/\partial \beta$ and the weight). For asymptotically efficient estimation there is no reason to prefer such estimators to weighted nonlinear least squares (or its linearized counterpart of equation (2.10)), because nonlinear weighted least squares is efficient if $\Omega(x, \eta)$ and η are correctly specified.

Nonparametric estimation of the conditional variance provides a way to guard against efficiency loss from misspecifying the form of the conditional variance, as suggested in Carroll (1982) and Robinson (1987). In the next two sections two different approaches to nonparmetric estimation of the optimal instruments will be discussed, and applied to the regression model as an example. Section 6 gives a Monte Carlo comparison of some of the different estimators.

3.2. Using second moment information

An example that illustrates how additional conditional moment restrictions may improve efficiency, at the cost of additional specification sensitivity, is the addition of a moment restriction based on knowing the form of the heteroskedasticity in regression models. Suppose that there is a known function $h(x, \beta, \pi)$ of β and some additional parameters π such that

$$y = f(x, \beta_0) + \varepsilon, \qquad E[\varepsilon \mid x] = 0, \qquad E[\varepsilon^2 \mid x] = h(x, \beta_0, \pi_0). \quad (3.2.1)$$

The specified functional form $h(x, \beta, \pi)$ of the heteroskedasticity could be used in construction of a weighted least squares estimator as discussed above. If one had great confidence in the heteroskedasticity specification, then one might want to incorporate this information in estimation. The way to do that in the context of equation (3.2.1), where only the conditional first and second moments are restricted, is to add the conditional variance residual as an additional conditional moment restriction, specifying

$$\rho(z, \theta) = (y - f(x, \beta), \{y - f(x, \beta)\}^2 - h(x, \beta, \pi))'. \quad (3.2.2)$$

The additional conditional moment restriction exploited by instrumental variables estimators using this residual will result in estimators that are at least as asymptotically efficient as the heteroskedasticity corrected least squares estimator, and more efficient in some cases. As usual, this efficiency gain comes at a price, that the resulting estimator may be inconsistent if the form of heteroskedasticity is not correctly specified.

The optimal instruments are straightforward to derive for the case, taking the form

$$D(x) = D(x, \theta_0), \qquad D(x, \theta) = \begin{bmatrix} \dfrac{\partial f(x, \beta)}{\partial \beta'} & 0 \\[2mm] \dfrac{\partial h(x, \beta, \pi)}{\partial \beta'} & \dfrac{\partial h(x, \beta, \pi)}{\partial \pi'} \end{bmatrix}, \quad (3.2.3)$$

$$\Omega(x) = \text{Var}((\varepsilon, \varepsilon^2)' \mid x), \qquad B(x) = D(x)'\Omega(x)^{-1}.$$

One question that can be addressed using this formula is whether the additional moment restriction can give more efficient estimators. This question can be answered by comparing the asymptotic variance $(E[\{E[\varepsilon^2 \mid x]\}^{-1}\{\partial f(x, \beta_0)/\partial \beta\}\{\partial f(x, \beta_0)/\partial \beta\}'])^{-1}$ of the heteroskedasticity corrected least squares estimator with the block of the bound $(E[D(x)'\Omega(x)^{-1}D(x)])^{-1}$ corresponding to β. It is easy to see that the two are equal if $E[\varepsilon^3 \mid x] = 0$ or β does not enter the variance function. If either $E[\varepsilon^3 \mid x] \neq 0$ or β does enter the variance function it will generally be true that the conditional moment bound is less than the asymptotic variance of optimally weighted least squares. Surprisingly, this potential efficiency gain is present even when $h(x, \pi, \beta)$ and $\Omega(x)$ do not depend on x or β, but $E[\varepsilon^3] \neq 0$, as previously noted by MaCurdy (1982).

An estimator that is efficient over a parametric family of conditional third and second moments could be obtained by specifying $\Omega(x, \eta)$. Since the conditional variance is already specified in the model, one only needs to specify the conditional third and fourth moments. If y is continuous then one reasonable, parsimonious specification is to assume that $E[\varepsilon^3 | x] = 0$ and that $\text{Var}(\varepsilon^2 | x) = \eta_0 h(x, \beta_0, \pi_0)^2$. This specification is more general than assuming normality, because it allows for a free parameter η_0, that essentially quantifies the degree of kurtosis. This parameter can be estimated by the sample variance of $\{y_i - f(x_i, \hat{\beta})\}^2 / h(x_i, \hat{\beta}, \hat{\pi})$, where $\hat{\beta}$ and $\hat{\pi}$ are some initial estimators. Then estimated optimal instruments can be constructed as

$$\hat{D}(x) = D(x, \hat{\theta}), \qquad \hat{\Omega}(x) = \begin{bmatrix} h(x, \hat{\beta}, \hat{\pi}) & 0 \\ 0 & \hat{\eta} \cdot h(x, \hat{\beta}, \hat{\pi})^2 \end{bmatrix}, \qquad (3.2.4)$$

$$\hat{B}(x) = \hat{D}(x)' \hat{\Omega}(x)^{-1}.$$

The resulting linearized estimator in equation (2.10) is similar to that of Jobson and Fuller (1980), except that it does not depend on normality for it to be efficient relative to weighted least squares. It will be efficient in the class of all estimators that use only the conditional moment restrictions of equation (3.2.1), and hence efficient relative to least squares, as long as $E[\varepsilon^3 | x] = 0$ and $\text{Var}(\varepsilon^2 | x) = \eta_0 h(x, \beta_0, \pi_0)^2$ for some η_0.

One could use the results to follow to construct an estimator that is asymptotically efficient over all (suitably regular) conditional third and fourth moments by replacing $\Omega(x, \hat{\eta})$ by a nonparametric estimator in equation (3.2.4). As a practical matter, though, it may be difficult to estimate higher-order conditional moments, so that large sample sizes may be needed for the asymptotic theory to provide a good approximation. Alternatively, depending on the context, it should be possible to specify other parametric families of conditional third and fourth moments that give good efficiency.

3.3. Box–Cox model

An interesting and important example is models where the dependent variable has been transformed. As pointed out in Amemiya and Powell (1981), it is possible to estimate these models when the disturbance term is only restricted to have conditional mean zero. The essential idea is that nonlinear functions of the regressors provide information that can be used to identify the transformation parameters. Surprisingly, as shown in Newey (1989b), the resulting estimators can have good efficiency relative to other procedures that use stronger restrictions on the disturbance distribution, such as independence or symmetry, and even do tolerably well relative to maximum likelihood estimators (that are inconsistent if the disturbance distribution is incorrectly specified).

The Box–Cox transformation model with conditional mean restriction is

$$T(y, \lambda_0) = x'\beta_0 + \varepsilon, \qquad E[\varepsilon | x] = 0, \qquad T(y, \lambda) = (y^\lambda - 1)/\lambda . \ (3.3.1)$$

The conditional moment restriction $E[\varepsilon | x] = 0$ will allow for β to be estimated by IV where $\rho(z, \theta) = T(y, \lambda) - x'\beta$, $\theta = (\beta', \lambda)'$, and the instruments consist of suitably chosen functions of x, e.g., including x and nonlinear functions of x. In this example, unlike the previous two, IV estimation rather than least squares is essential to finding a consistent estimator (the nonlinear least squares estimates are inconsistent).

The conditional moment restriction is not strong enough to allow interpretation of β and λ as parameters of the conditional distribution of y given x. One way to deal with this problem is to add the restriction that $\text{med}(\varepsilon \,|\, x) = 0$, in which case $\text{med}(y \,|\, y) = T^{-1}(x'\beta_0, \lambda_0)$. It also might be more natural to just impose $\text{med}(\varepsilon \,|\, x) = 0$ in estimation, as in Powell (1990), although the asymptotic theory for this case is more complicated, and so for estimation attention here is restricted to the conditional mean case in equation (3.3.1).

The optimal instruments for this model are, for $T_\lambda(y, \lambda) = \partial T(y, \lambda)/\partial\lambda$,

$$D(x) = (-x', \text{E}[T_\lambda(y, \lambda_0) \,|\, x]) , \qquad \Omega(x) = \text{E}[\varepsilon^2 \,|\, x] ,$$
$$B(x) = D(x)'\Omega(x)^{-1} . \tag{3.3.2}$$

Thus, in this example, unlike the previous two, the functional form of $D(x)$ is unknown, and difficult to specify a priori. One might try and specify a functional form for $D(x)$ by calculating $\text{E}[T_\lambda(y, \lambda_0) \,|\, x]$ for some distribution and/or values of λ, and then use this value in the instruments. For example, if $\text{E}[\varepsilon^2 \,|\, x]$ is constant so there is no heteroskedasticity, and x includes a constant, then as shown in Newey (1989b), at $\lambda_0 = 0$,

$$D(x) = C \cdot (x', (x'\beta_0)^2)$$

for a nonsingular matrix C. Thus, a specification of the optimal instruments that will be efficient at $\lambda_0 = 0$, corresponding to a log transformation, under homoskedasticity, is

$$\hat{B}(x) = (x', (x'\hat{\beta})^2)' , \tag{3.3.3}$$

where $\hat{\beta}$ is some initial estimator and $\hat{\Omega}(x)$ is not needed because it is assumed constant and ρ is a scalar. By continuity the resulting estimator should have good efficiency when λ is close to zero, as is often found in practice, and when there is little heteroskedasticity, as shown by Newey (1989b) for an example.

An estimator that is efficient over all true λ when there is heteroskedasticity could be formed by using as an instrument

$$\hat{B}(x) = (x', \hat{\text{E}}[T_\lambda(y, \hat{\lambda}) \,|\, x])(\hat{\text{E}}[\{T(y, \hat{\lambda}) - x'\hat{\beta}\}^2 \,|\, x])^{-1} , \tag{3.3.4}$$

where $\hat{\text{E}}[T_\lambda(y, \hat{\lambda}) \,|\, x]$ and $\hat{\text{E}}[\{T(y, \hat{\lambda}) - x'\hat{\beta}\}^2 \,|\, x]$ are nonparametric regression estimators based on the estimated derivative $T_\lambda(y, \hat{\lambda})$ and squared residual $\hat{\text{E}}[\{T(y, \hat{\lambda}) - x'\hat{\beta}\}^2 \,|\, x]$ respectively.

3.4. An endogenous dummy variable model

For an example of the form of the optimal instruments, consider the model

$$y = \lambda_0 s + f(x, \beta_0) + \varepsilon , \quad s \in \{0, 1\} , \qquad E[\varepsilon \,|\, x] = 0 . \tag{3.4.1}$$

This model has many important applications in economics to the effect of some event s on an economic variable, such as the effect of college education on income. In many of these applications it is important to allow s to be correlated with ε, because s represents a choice variable of the economic agent that may be affected by variables in ε that are observed by the empirical worker, such as 'ability'. Correlation between s and ε is allowed here, because $E[\varepsilon \,|\, x] = 0$ does not restrict the joint distribution of ε and s. See Heckman and Robb (1985) for further discussion and motivation.

Optimal instruments for this model take the form, for $\pi(x) = \mathrm{Prob}(s = 1 \,|\, x) = E[s \,|\, x]$,

$$D(x) = \left(\frac{\partial f(x, \beta_0)}{\partial \beta'}, \pi(x) \right) , \qquad \Omega(x) = E[\varepsilon^2 \,|\, x] ,$$
$$B(x) = D(x)'\Omega(x)^{-1} . \tag{3.4.2}$$

As in the last example, there is a component of $D(x)$ that does not have known functional form. Here this component is $\pi(x) = \mathrm{Prob}(d = 1 \,|\, x)$. An estimator that is efficient over a parametric family of possible $\pi(x)$ functions can be obtained by specifying a functional form for $\pi(x)$, estimating its parameters by binary choice maximum likelihood with s as the dependent variable, and then substituting the predicted probability for $\pi(x)$. For example, assuming that $\mathrm{Prob}(s = 1 \,|\, x) = \Phi(x'\eta_0)$ for some η_0 and the standard normal CDF $\Phi(\cdot)$, one could form an estimate $\hat{\eta}$ from probit with s as the dependent variable, and then construct $\hat{\pi}(x) = \Phi(x'\hat{\eta})$. Also one might assume homoskedasticity in constructing an instrument estimator. Then substituting into the formula gives

$$\hat{B}(x) = \left(\frac{\partial f(x, \beta_0)}{\partial \beta'}, \Phi(x'\hat{\eta}) \right)' , \tag{3.4.3}$$

where $\hat{\beta}$ is some initial estimator and $\hat{\Omega}(x)$ is not needed because it is assumed constant and ρ is a scalar. Estimators that are efficient over all (suitably regular) conditional probabilities for s, for unknown heteroskedasticity, could be constructed from nonparametric estimators of the optimal instruments.

4. Nearest neighbor estimation of the optimal instruments

The first approach to construction of nonparametric estimates of the optimal instruments is to nonparametrically estimate the conditional expectations that make up the optimal instruments and plug the estimates into the formula for the optimal instruments. Because of its technical convenience, the nearest neighbor estimation method is considered here.

A nearest neighbor estimator of a conditional expectation is formed by averaging over the values of the dependent variable for observations where the conditioning variable is closest to its evaluation value. To describe how this estimator is applied to estimation of the optimal instruments, let $\hat{\sigma}_{xl}$ be some estimate of the scale of the lth component x_i of x, satisfying the conditions given in Stone (1977), such as the sample standard deviation of x_{il}, and define $\|x_i - x_j\|_n = \{\sum_{l=1}^{r} (x_{il} - x_{jl})^2/(\hat{\sigma}_l^2)\}^{1/2}$, where r is the dimension of x, $(i, j = 1, \ldots, n)$. For a given integer $K \leq n$ consider constants $\omega_{kK'}$ satisfying

$$\omega_{kK} \geq 0, \quad 1 \leq k \leq K; \quad \omega_{kK} = 0, \quad k > K; \quad \sum_{k=1}^{K} \omega_{kK} = 1. \quad (4.1)$$

For given i let $W_{ii} = 0$, and rank the observations $j \neq i$ according to the distance $\|x_i - x_j\|_n$. If there are no ties among the distances assign to observation with j-th smallest value $\|x_i - x_j\|_n$ the weight $W_{ij} = \omega_{jK}$. If there are ties, follow the same procedure, but with equal weight given to observations with the same value of $\|x_i - x_j\|_n$. A nearest neighbor estimator of the conditional covariance $\Omega(x_i)$ at x_i can then be formed as

$$\hat{\Omega}(x_i) = \sum_{j=1}^{n} W_{ij}\rho(z_j, \hat{\theta})\rho(z_j, \hat{\theta})' . \quad (4.2)$$

This is a nearest neighbor estimator that excludes the own observation that is analogous to Robinson's (1987) conditional variance estimator. Examples of weights include uniform ones where $\omega_{kK} = 1/K$, $k \leq K$, and other smoother versions, e.g., as discussed in Robinson (1987). The theory here will utilize a uniform boundedness restriction on the weights, that there is a constant C such that

$$\omega_{kK} \leq \frac{C}{K}, \quad 1 \leq k \leq K . \quad (4.3)$$

This restriction is satisfied by the uniform weights, as well as the other weights discussed in Robinson (1987).

For many models at least some components of $D(x)$ will have known functional form, and depend only on x, and it seems wise to take advantage of this knowledge in construction of the estimator. One general formulation that allows for that knowledge is to specify an estimator that is a sum of parametric and nearest neighbor components. Let $D(x, \eta)$ be some prespecified function of x and nuisance parameters η with the same dimensions as $D(x)$, e.g., with components equal to those of $D(x)$ that are known and zero otherwise. For an estimator $\hat{\eta}$ of η_0, let

$$\hat{D}(x_i) = D(x_i, \hat{\eta}) + \sum_{j=1}^{n} W_{ij}\left[\frac{\partial\rho(z_j, \hat{\theta})}{\partial\theta} - D(x_j, \hat{\eta})\right]. \quad (4.4)$$

This estimator is fully nonparametric, in that it will be consistent for all $D(x, \eta)$ and (suitably regular) estimators $\hat{\eta}$, and components of the nearest neighbor term will be zero when the corresponding components of $D(x, \hat{\eta})$ and $\partial \rho(z, \theta)/\partial \theta$ are equal.

Another possible use of the $D(x, \eta)$ function is for 'detrending' in the sense of Stone (1977), where $D(x, \eta)$ is some simple function that is included to 'wash out' some of the dependence of $D(x)$ on x. For example, $D(x, \eta)$ might be linear in x, in which case the nearest neighbor term would be estimating the deviation from a linear function. This set-up does not allow for linearity, or other known functional form, to be imposed on the conditional expectation, e.g., as is often done in the linear simultaneous equations models (e.g., see Hausman, 1984). To get such an estimator one would have to make sure that the components of $D(x, \eta)$ had the right functional form and delete corresponding components from the nearest neighbor terms. Although this possibility is not explicitly allowed for in the paper, the conclusion of Theorem 1 below would still hold in this case.

With estimators of the conditional expectations in hand, one can combine them to form an estimator of the optimal instruments in the natural way, as $\hat{B}(x_i) = \hat{D}(x_i)' \hat{\Omega}(x_i)^{-1}$. An efficient estimator of θ_0 can then be constructed in the way described in Section 2. An important purpose for such an estimator is to make asymptotically efficient inferences about the population parameter value θ_0, such as to construct confidence intervals or tests statistics. For this purpose it is useful to have a consistent asymptotic variance estimator. One natural estimator can be obtained by replacing the conditional expectations in the variance bound by corresponding nearest neighbor estimates and the expectation by a sample average. The result is

$$\hat{\Lambda} = \left(\sum_{i=1}^{n} \hat{D}(x_i)' \hat{\Omega}(x_i) \hat{D}(x_i)/n \right)^{-1}. \tag{4.5}$$

Conditions for consistency of this estimator are given in Theorem 1 below.

An important problem of nearest neighbor estimation is the choice of number of nearest neighbors K. Because the focus here is on efficient estimation of θ, it seems desirable to base that choice on a criteria that focuses on the properties of $\hat{\theta}$. Although a theoretical investigation of how to formulate such a criteria is beyond the scope of this paper, some heuristic ideas can be used to suggest a choice of K that may lead to good properties for the estimator of $\hat{\theta}$. Suppose that one wants to choose K so as to minimize 'remainder terms' in the asymptotic theory that arise form estimation of the optimal instruments. From an expansion similar to that in equation (2.4) it is easy to see that there will be remainder terms of both the Jacobian matrix and the cross product of instruments with the residuals. Suppose that we can ignore the Jacobian term, which may be possible under some circumstances (e.g., if it is root-n consistently estimated and the size of the other remainder terms are greater than $1/\sqrt{n}$). This reasoning suggests a criteria based on an estimate of the magnitude of $\sum_{i=1}^{n} \{\hat{B}(x_i) - B(x_i)\}\rho(z_i, \theta_0)/\sqrt{n}$, a difference of estimated and true moment functions (or 'scores'). For the nearest neighbor estimator, there are two terms in this difference, one each for the estimation of $D(x)$ and $\Omega(x)$. Assuming higher-order terms can be ignored, this remainder can be linearized to give

$$\sum_{i=1}^{n} \hat{R}(x_i)\rho(z_i, \theta_0)/\sqrt{n},$$

$$\hat{R}(x_i) = \{\hat{D}(x_i) - D(x_i) + B(x_i)[\hat{\Omega}(x_i) - \Omega(x_i)]\}\Omega(x_i)^{-1}.$$

This is a vector remainder term, so to quantify its magnitude for minimization one has to choose a distance metric. Let Q be a positive definite matrix. Assuming that the 'hat' can be ignored in taking the conditional expectation over z_i, given the x_i observations (e.g., as would be the case if $\hat{R}(x)$ were constructed from another sample), leads to the criteria $\mathrm{tr}[Q \sum_{i=1}^{n} \hat{R}(x_i)\Omega(x_i)\hat{R}(x_i)']$. This criteria cannot be computed, but because $\hat{R}(x_i)$ depends on 'cross-validation' nearest neighbor estimates, where the i-th observation is not used in estimation of $\hat{D}(x_i)$ or $\hat{\Omega}(x_i)$, the usual crossvalidation reasoning suggests that one can estimate this criteria up to a term that does not depend on K by replacing the conditional expectations by their estimators and their estimators by the dependent variables, as in

$$C\hat{V}(K) = \mathrm{tr}\left[Q \sum_{i=1}^{n} \bar{R}(x_i)\hat{\Omega}(x_i)\bar{R}(x_i)' \right],$$

$$\bar{R}(x_i) = \left\{ \frac{\partial\rho(z_i, \hat{\theta})}{\partial\theta} - \hat{D}(x_i) + \hat{B}(x_i)[\rho(z_i, \hat{\theta})\rho(z_i, \hat{\theta})' - \hat{\Omega}(x_i)] \right\}\hat{\Omega}(x_i)^{-1}.$$

$$(4.6)$$

Thus, a cross-validation criteria for the choice of K, that takes some account for how the estimator of parameter of interest depends on K, is to choose k to minimize $C\hat{V}(K)$.

To illustrate the estimator and the cross-validation criteria it is helpful to consider an example. A simple, important example is the linear regression model. In this case $\hat{\Omega}(x_i) = \hat{\sigma}_i^2 = \sum_{j=1}^{n} W_{ij}\hat{\varepsilon}_j^2$, where $\hat{\varepsilon}_j = y_j - x_j'\hat{\beta}$ are residuals, and the linearized estimator of equation (2.10) and the asymptotic variance estimator of equation (4.5) are

$$\bar{\beta} = \left(\sum_{i=1}^{n} \hat{\sigma}(x_i)^{-2}x_ix_i' \right)^{-1} \sum_{i=1}^{n} \hat{\sigma}(x_i)^{-2}x_iy_i,$$

$$\hat{\Lambda} = \left(n^{-1} \sum_{i=1}^{n} \hat{\sigma}(x_i)^{-2}x_1x_1' \right)^{-1}.$$

$$(4.7)$$

These estimators were suggested and analyzed in Robinson (1987). The cross-validation criteria obtained by setting $\partial\rho(z_i, \hat{\theta})/\partial\theta - \hat{D}(x_i)$ to zero, as appropriate here where the form of $D(x)$ is known, and by choosing $Q = (\Sigma_{j=1}^{n} x_i x_i')^{-1}$, is

$$CV(K) = \sum_{i=1}^{n} (x_i' Q x_i)[(\hat{\varepsilon}_i / \hat{\sigma}_i)^2 - 1], \qquad Q = \left(\sum_{i=1}^{n} x_i x_i' \right)^{-1}. \qquad (4.8)$$

The choice of Q here makes this criteria invariant to nonsingular linear transformations of the regressors. In the Monte Carlo example of Section 6 this cross-validation criteria for choice of K, choosing K to minimize $CV(K)$ and then using this K to form the estimator in equation (4.7), leads to $\hat{\beta}$ with good properties.

To prove asymptotic efficiency it is helpful to impose some regularity conditions. The first condition is essentially a standard one involving compactness, existence of certain moments, and nonsingularity conditions.

ASSUMPTION 4.1. θ_0 is an element of the interior of Θ, which is compact, there is a neighborhood $\mathcal{N}$ of θ_0 and $d(z)$ such that with probability one $\rho(z, \theta)$ is continuous on Θ, continuously differentiable on $\mathcal{N}$, $\sup_{\theta \in \Theta} \| \rho(z, \theta) \| \leq d(z)$, $\sup_{\theta \in \mathcal{N}} \| \partial \rho(z, \theta) / \partial \theta \| \leq d(z)$, $E[d(z)^2] < \infty$. Also, $E[B(x)\Omega(x)B(x)']$ exists and is nonsingular.

The next Assumption is important for consistency of the fully iterated estimator given in equation (2.9).

ASSUMPTION 4.2. $E[B(x)B(x')']$ exists and is nonsingular, and there is a unique solution to $E[B(x)\rho(z, \theta)] = 0$ on Θ at $\theta = \theta_0$.

For the linearized estimator of equation (2.10) is important to have root-n consistency of the initial estimator. The following condition helps guarantee this.

ASSUMPTION 4.3. $\hat{\theta}$ satisfies equation (2.3) for $\hat{P} = (\Sigma_{i=1}^{n} A(x_i)A(x_i)')^{-1}$, there is a unique solution to $E[A(x)\rho(z, \theta)] = 0$ on Θ at $\theta = \theta_0$, $E[\|A(x)\|^2] < \infty$, $E[A(x)D(x)]$ and $E[A(x)A(x)']$ are nonsingular, and $E[A(x)\Omega(x)A(x)']$ is finite.

Finally, some additional smoothness and moment existence conditions are useful.

ASSUMPTION 4.4. There is a neighborhood $\mathcal{N}$ of θ_0 and $d(z)$ such that for all $\theta \in \mathcal{N}$,

$$\| \rho(z, \theta) \|^4 < d(z), \qquad \| \partial \rho(z, \theta) / \partial \theta \|^4 < d(z),$$
$$\| \partial^2 \rho(z, \theta) / \partial \theta \, \partial \theta \|^2 < d(z),$$

$$\|\partial^2\rho(z,\bar{\theta})/\partial\theta\,\partial\theta - \partial^2\rho(z,\theta)/\partial\theta\,\partial\theta\| \le d(z)\|\bar{\theta}-\theta\|,$$

and $\text{E}[d(z)^2] < \infty$.

For the special case of the heteroskedastic linear model, this condition is stronger than that imposed in Robinson (1987), in that it requires existence of eighth moments of the disturbance and of the regressors. This more restrictive condition allows for the presence of $\hat{D}(x)$ and leads to a simpler proof than given by Robinson (1987).

ASSUMPTION 4.5. $\text{E}[\|D(x,\eta_0)\|^8] < \infty$, and there is $d(z)$ and a neighborhood $\mathcal{N}$ of η_0 such that for all $\eta \in \mathcal{N}$,

$$\|\partial D(x,\eta)/\partial\eta\|^2 \le d(z),$$
$$\|\partial D(x,\eta)/\partial\eta - \partial D(x,\eta_0)/\partial\eta\| \le d(z)\|\eta-\eta_0\|,$$

$\text{E}[d(z)^2] < \infty$. Also $\sqrt{n}(\hat{\eta}-\eta_0) = \text{O}_\text{p}(1)$.

THEOREM 1. *If Assumptions 4.1–4.5 are satisfied and* $K = K(n)$ *such that* $K(n)/n \to 0$ *and* $K(n)^2/n \to \infty$, *then for* $\bar{\theta} = \hat{\theta}$ *or* $\bar{\theta} = \tilde{\theta}$,

$$\sqrt{n}(\bar{\theta}-\theta_0) \xrightarrow{d} \text{N}(0,\Lambda), \qquad \left[\sum_{i=1}^n \hat{D}(x_i)'\hat{\Omega}(x_i)^{-1}\hat{D}(x_i)/n\right]^{-1} \xrightarrow{p} \Lambda.$$

5. Series approximation of the optimal instruments

Another approach to estimation of the optimal instruments is by series approximation, where the estimator is formed as a linear combination of known functions. A potential advantage of this approach is that linear combinations of smooth functions can approximate a smooth function very well with only a few terms, while nearest neighbor estimators do not seem to exploit such smoothness.

As previously noted, it is useful to allow some components of the optimal instruments to have known functional form. A way to form a series approximation that allows for some known components is to let $D(x,\eta)'$ be a matrix with q rows, $\{a_{kK}(x)\}_{k=1}^K$ be matrices of approximating functions with number of rows equal to the number of columns of $D(x,\eta)'$, and estimate the optimal instruments by

$$\hat{B}(x) = D(x,\hat{\eta})'\left[\sum_{k=1}^K \hat{\gamma}_k a_{kK}(x)\right], \tag{5.1}$$

where $\hat{\gamma}_{kK}$ are estimated scalars described below, and $\hat{\eta}$ is an estimator of η. For example in the linear model $D(x,\hat{\eta})'$ could be specified as x, so that $[\sum_{k=1}^K \hat{\gamma}_k a_{kK}(x)]$ corresponds to an estimator of $1/\sigma^2(x)$.

The two keys to asymptotic efficiency are the choice of $a_{kK}(x)$ and of

$\hat{\gamma}_1, \ldots, \hat{\gamma}_K$. The functions $a_{kK}(x)$ should be specified in such a way that $D(x, \eta_0)'[\Sigma_{k=1}^K \gamma_k a_{kK}(x)]$ can approximate $B(x)$ for some choice of linear combination coefficient, $\gamma_1, \ldots, \gamma_K$. The form of this approximation will be specific to the form of $B(x)$. Given functions $a_{kK}(x)$ with the property, it is possible to form $\hat{\gamma}_1, \ldots, \hat{\gamma}_K$ as estimators of a minimum mean-square error approximation that leads to asymptotic efficiency. For any $\gamma = (\gamma_1, \ldots, \gamma_K)$ let $A_k(x) = D(x, \eta_0)'a_{kK}(x)$, $\rho = \rho(z, \theta_0)$, $u_k = A_k(x)\rho$, and $U = [A_1(x)\rho, \ldots, A_K(x)\rho]$. Also, let

$$M_k = E\left[A_k(x)\frac{\partial \rho(z, \theta_0)}{\partial \theta}\right] = E[A_k(x)D(x)] = E[A_k(x)\Omega(x)B(x)']$$
$$= E[u_k\rho'b(x)'], \tag{5.2}$$

where the second and fourth equalities follow by iterated expectations. For any positive definite matrix Q consider

$$\bar{\gamma} = \underset{\gamma \in \mathbb{R}^K}{\operatorname{argmin}} \operatorname{tr}\left(Q \cdot E\left[\left\{B(x) - \sum_{k=1}^K \gamma_k A_k(x)\right\}\Omega(x)\right.\right.$$
$$\left.\left. \times \left\{B(x) - \sum_{k=1}^K \gamma_k A_k(x)\right\}'\right]\right)$$
$$= \underset{\gamma \in \mathbb{R}^K}{\operatorname{argmin}} E[\{B(x)\rho - U\gamma\}'Q\{B(x)\rho - U\gamma\}]$$
$$= (E[U'QU])^{-1}E[U'QB(x)\rho]$$
$$= (E[U'QU])^{-1}[\operatorname{tr}(QE[B(x)\rho u_1']), \ldots, \operatorname{tr}(QE[B(x)\rho u_K'])]'$$
$$= (E[U'QU])^{-1}[\operatorname{tr}(QM_1), \ldots, \operatorname{tr}(QM_K)]', \tag{5.3}$$

where $\operatorname{tr}(\cdot)$ denotes the trace of a square matrix, the first equality holds by iterated expectations, and the last equality follows by equation (5.2).

From the first two equalities it is apparent that these coefficients have two interpretations as mean-square approximations, one as a weighted (by $\Omega(x)$) mean-square approximation of the optimal instruments by $\Sigma_{k=1}^K \gamma_k A_k(x)$ and the other as a mean-square approximation of $B(x)\rho$ by $\Sigma_{k=1}^K \gamma_k A_k(x)\rho$. The matrix Q is present to account for the fact that these approximations are scalar linear combinations rather than matrix linear combinations. For some choices of $a_{kK}(x)$ (where $\{a_{kK}(x)\}$ is zero except for one element), the approximation may actually be a matrix linear combination. In this case the coefficients γ can also be interpreted as minimizing the asymptotic variance; see Newey (1989a) for details.

It follows by equations (5.2) and (5.3) that if a linear combination of $A_k(x) = (D(x, \eta_0)'a_{kK}(x)$ can approximate $B(x)$ arbitrarily closely as K grows, in the weighted mean-square norm following the first equality of equation (5.3), then an IV estimator with $A(x) = \Sigma_{k=1}^K \bar{\gamma}_k A_k(x)$ will be approximately efficient for large K. Equation (5.2) implies equation (2.8), which in turn implies that the asymptotic variance of an IV estimator will be close to the bound if $A(x)\rho$

is close in mean-square to $B(x)\rho$. Then by the second inequality of equation (5.3) and Q positive definite, $A(x)\rho$ will be close in mean-square to $B(x)\rho$ when the weighted norm approximation error for the optimal instruments is small. Thus, under the spanning condition that linear combination of $D(x, \eta_0)'a_{kK}(x)$ can approximate $B(x)$ arbitrarily closely as k grows, the IV estimator with instruments $\Sigma_{k=1}^{K} \bar{\gamma}_k A_k(x)$ will be approximately efficient. This spanning condition is explicitly imposed in Assumptions 5.4 and 5.5 below.

The IV estimator based on $\bar{\gamma}_k$ is not feasible because $\bar{\gamma}_k$ are unknown, but the last equality in equation (5.3) can be used to construct an estimator. Let $\hat{Q}$ denote an estimator of Q, $\hat{u}_{ki} = D(x_i, \hat{\eta})'a_{kK}(x_i)\rho(z_i, \hat{\theta})$, $\hat{U}_i = [\hat{u}_{1i}, \dots, \hat{u}_{Ki}]$, and

$$\hat{M}_K = n^{-1} \sum_{i=1}^{n} D(x_i, \hat{\eta})'a_{kK}(x_i) \frac{\partial\rho(z_i, \hat{\theta})}{\partial\theta}.$$

Plugging in estimates and sample averages to the last equality gives

$$\hat{\gamma} = \left(\sum_{i=1}^{n} \hat{U}_i' Q \hat{U}_i / n \right)^{-1} [\text{tr}(\hat{Q}\hat{M}_1'), \dots, \text{tr}(\hat{Q}\hat{M}_K')]'. \tag{5.4}$$

A feasible IV estimator can then be constructed by using this $\hat{\gamma}$ in the instruments of equation (5.1). Under appropriate regularity conditions, $\hat{\gamma}$ will be consistent for $\bar{\gamma}$, so by estimation of instruments having no effect on the asymptotic variance of IV, the estimator will be approximately efficient for large K. The asymptotic efficiency result below is even stronger, giving a growth rate for K as a function of sample size to achieve asymptotic efficiency.

An efficient estimator can be constructed as in equation (2.10) using the estimator of the optimal instruments in equation (5.1). Also, an estimator of the asymptotic variance of $\bar{\theta}$ is

$$\hat{\Lambda} = \left(\sum_{k=1}^{K} \hat{\gamma}_k \hat{M}_k \right)^{-1} \left[\sum_{i=1}^{n} (\hat{U}_i'\hat{\gamma})(\hat{U}_i'\hat{\gamma})' \Big/ n \right] \left(\sum_{k=1}^{K} \hat{\gamma}_k \hat{M}_k \right)^{-1\prime}.$$

This estimator is a consistent estimator for the asymptotic variance of $\hat{\theta}$, even for K fixed. An alternative estimator that would be consistent as K goes to infinity is $[\Sigma_{i=1}^{n} (\hat{U}_i'\hat{\gamma})(\hat{U}_1'\hat{\gamma})'/n]^{-1}$.

An important problem for this estimator is the choice of K. One way to choose K, that is suggested a Newey (1989a), is to minimize a cross-validation estimator of the mean square error of product of the differences of the true and estimated instruments with the residual. This choice can be motivated by similar reasoning gives for the choice of nearest neighbors described in the last section. In particular, by the second equality of equation (5.3), this criterion is based on the difference of instruments multiplied by the residual vector, and so may be related to the magnitude of remainder terms. To describe this cross-validation method, let $\hat{\gamma}_{-i}$ be the estimator in equation (5.4) except that the i-th observation has been deleted when calculating the sample averages. For

$\hat{\rho}_i = \rho(z_i, \hat{\theta})$ and $\hat{A}_{ki} = D(x_i, \hat{\eta})'a_{kK}(x_i)$ consider

$$\sum_{i=1}^{n} [B(x_i)\hat{\rho}_i - \hat{U}_i'\hat{\gamma}_{-1}]'\hat{Q}[B(x_i)\hat{\rho}_i - \hat{U}_i'\hat{\gamma}_{-i}]$$

$$= \sum_{i=1}^{n} [\hat{\rho}_i'B(x_i)'\hat{Q}B(x_i)\hat{\rho}_i - 2\hat{\rho}_i'B(x_i)'\hat{Q}\hat{U}_i\hat{\gamma}_{-i} + \hat{\gamma}_{-i}'\hat{U}_i'\hat{Q}\hat{U}_i\hat{\gamma}_{-i}].$$

This criterion cannot be computed, because $B(x_i)$ is unknown. To obtain one that can be computed, the first term can be dropped because it does not depend on K and so is not needed to minimize over K. Also, equation (5.3) implies $E[\rho(z_i, \theta_0)'B(x_i)'QU_i] = [\mathrm{tr}(QM_1), \ldots, \mathrm{tr}(QM_K)]$ allowing replacement of the second term by $\mathrm{tr}(\hat{Q} \sum_{k=1}^{K} \hat{\gamma}_{-i,k}\hat{M}_{ki})$, for $\hat{M}_{ki} = D(x_i, \hat{\eta})'a_{kK}(x_i) \partial\rho(z_i, \hat{\theta})/\partial\theta$. These changes give

$$C\hat{V}(K) = -2\mathrm{tr}\left(\hat{Q} \sum_{i=1}^{n} \sum_{k=1}^{K} \hat{\gamma}_{-i,k}\hat{M}_{ki}\right) + \mathrm{tr}\left(\hat{Q} \sum_{i=1}^{n} \hat{U}_i\hat{\gamma}_{-i}(\hat{U}_i\hat{\gamma}_{-i})'\right). \quad (5.5)$$

To illustrate the estimator and the cross-validation criteria it is helpful to again consider the linear regression model as an example. In this case $B(x) = \sigma(x)^{-2}x$, and there are several ways that one might choose $D(x, \eta)$ and $a_{kK}(x)$ to approximate this function. One way is based on a multivariate approximation of the entire vector $\sigma(x)^{-2}x$. Let $D(x, \eta)$ be an identity matrix and each $a_{kK}(x)$ be a vector with the same dimension as x, such that there is an integer J and a vector $p_J(x)' = (p_{1J}(x), \ldots, p_{JJ}(x))'$ with

$$[a_{1K}(x), \ldots, a_{KK}(x)] = p_J(x)' \otimes I,$$

for an identity matrix I with the same row dimension as x. From example, $p_{JJ}(x)$ might be a power series. In this case the matrix $\hat{Q}$ factors out and the estimator of the optimal instruments is given by

$$\hat{B}(x) = \hat{\Gamma}p_J(x), \qquad \hat{\Gamma} = \left(\sum_{i=1}^{n} p_J(x_i)x_i'\right)\left(\sum_{i=1}^{n} p_J(x_i)p_J(x_i)'\hat{\varepsilon}_i^2\right)^{-1}. \quad (5.6)$$

The resulting IV estimator $\hat{\beta} = (\sum_{i=1}^{n} \hat{B}(x_i)x_i')^{-1} \sum_{i=1}^{n} \hat{B}(x_i)y_i$ is equal to the estimator of Cragg (1983). A cross-validation criterion for the choice of J for this estimator can be constructed as described above. Let $\hat{\Gamma}_{-i}$ be the co-efficients in equation (5.6) with the i-th observation deleted from the sums, and let $p_i = p_J(x_i)$. Then specializing the formula in equation (5.5) to this example gives

$$C\hat{V}(J) = -2\mathrm{tr}\left(\sum_{i=1}^{n} \hat{\Gamma}_{-i}p_ix_i'\right) + \mathrm{tr}\left[\sum_{i=1}^{n} \hat{\varepsilon}_i^2(\hat{\Gamma}_{-i}p_i)(\hat{\Gamma}_{-i}p_i)'\right]. \quad (5.7)$$

In the Monte Carlo example of Section 6 this cross-validation criteria for choice of J leads to $\hat{\beta}$ with good properties.

It is possible to construct alternative estimators that are more parsimonious, in that they use fewer functions to achieve the same degree of approximation. The idea here is that the optimal instruments consist of a product of a known vector with a single unknown function $1/\sigma^2(x)$, so that it should be possible to construct an estimator where the only function being approximated is $1/\sigma^2(x)$. The way to do this is to let $D(x, \eta)' = x$ and $a_{kK}(x)$ be scalars. In particular, consider letting $k = j$, $K = J$, and $a_{kK}(x) = p_{jJ}(x)$ for the $p_{jJ}(x)$ in the previous estimator. Also, let $\hat{Q} = (\sum_{i=1}^{n} x_i x_i'/n)^{-1}$, which will make the estimator equivariant with respect to nonsingular linear transformations of x. Then for $s_i = x_i' \hat{Q} x_i$, the estimator of the optimal instruments is

$$\hat{B}(x) = x \cdot (p_J(x)' \hat{\gamma}) , \qquad \hat{\gamma} = \left(\sum_{i=1}^{n} s_i p_i p_i' \hat{\varepsilon}_i^2 \right)^{-1} \sum_{i=1}^{n} s_i p_i . \qquad (5.8)$$

In this example, it follows form equation (5.3) that $\hat{\gamma}$ will be consistent for

$$\bar{\gamma} = \arg \min E[\sigma^2(x) x' Q x \{1/\sigma^2(x) - p_J(x)' \gamma\}^2] \quad \text{for } Q = (E[x_i x_i'])^{-1} ,$$

so that $p_J(x)' \hat{\gamma}$ can be interpreted as an estimator of $1/\sigma^2(x)$. In comparison with the previous estimator, the approximation is more parsimonious, because only a linear combination of J functions is required for a j-th order approximation, rather than the linear combination of $J \cdot \text{dimension}(x)$ functions. To choose J by cross-validation, let $\hat{\gamma}_{-i}$ be as given in equation (5.8), except that the i-th observation is deleted from the sum. The criterion of equation (5.5) is

$$C\hat{V}(J) = -2 \sum_{i=1}^{n} s_i(p_i' \hat{\gamma}_{-i}) + \sum_{i=1}^{n} s_i(p_i' \hat{\gamma}_{-i})^2 \hat{\varepsilon}_i^2 . \qquad (5.9)$$

The Monte Carlo example of Section 6 compares the performance of this estimator with the previous one.

To prove asymptotic efficiency of the estimators described in the section, it is useful to impose some regularity conditions. The first condition requires certain smoothness conditions and existence of certain moments.

ASSUMPTION 5.1. Q is positive definite, there is $\nu > 2$, $\delta > 0$, such that $E[\|\rho(z, \theta_0)\|^{\nu}] < \infty$, $E[\|D(x, \eta_0)\|^{[2\nu/(\nu-2)]+\delta}] < \infty$. $\sqrt{n}(\hat{Q} - Q) = O_p(1)$, $\sqrt{n}(\hat{\eta} - \eta_0) = O_p(1)$, $D(x, \eta)$ is continuously differentiable in η, there is $d_1(z), d_2(z), d_1'(z), d_2'(z)$ and neighborhoods of η_0 and θ_0 respectively such that

$$\|\partial \rho(z, \theta)/\partial \theta\| \leq d_1(z) ,$$

$$\|\partial \rho(z, \theta)/\partial \theta - \partial \rho(z, \theta_0)/\partial \theta\| \leq d_\rho(z)\|\theta - \theta_0\| ,$$

$$\sum_{j=1}^{J} \left\| \frac{\partial D(x, \eta)}{\partial \eta_j} \right\| \leq d_1'(z) ,$$

and

$$\sum_{j=1}^{J} \left\| \frac{\partial D(x,\eta)}{\partial \eta_j} - \frac{\partial D(x,\eta_0)}{\partial \eta_j} \right\| \le d_2'(z)\|\theta - \theta_0\| \,,$$

$$E[d_1(z)^{\nu}] < \infty \,, \qquad E[d_2(z)^{2\nu/(\nu+2)}] < \infty \,,$$

$$E[d_1'(z)^{2\nu/(\nu-2)}] < \infty \,, \qquad E[d_2'(z)^{\nu/(\nu-1)}] < \infty \,.$$

The moment conditions required here are weaker than in Section 4. Only slightly higher than two moments of the residual are required to exist, unlike the eight moments condition of Section 4. The next assumption imposes some conditions on the approximating functions.

ASSUMPTION 5.2. $a_{kK}(x)$ is bounded, uniformly in k, K, and the smallest eigenvalue of $E[U'QU]$ is bounded below by $\Delta^{-1}K^{-\Delta K^{1/r}}$ for some $\Delta > 0$.

The boundedness of the approximating functions is not restrictive, because the choice of functions is controlled, and boundedness can be relaxed without affecting any of the following results. The eigenvalue condition is not primitive, and is essential for the results to follow. Primitive conditions for this hypothesis can be obtained for power series. Let

$$p_j(x) = \prod_{l=1}^{r} \tau_l(x_l)^{\lambda_l(j)} \,, \qquad p^J(x) = (p_1(x), \ldots, p_J(x))' \,,$$

where $\lambda_l(j)$ are nonnegative integers.

ASSUMPTION 5.3. $a_{kK}(x) = p_{j(k)}(x)C_k$ for a constant matrix $C_k, \tau_j(x)$ are bounded, the distribution of $(\tau_1(x), \ldots, \tau_r(x))'$ has a continuously distributed component with density bounded away from zero on an open set $\mathcal{X}$, the smallest eigenvalue of $\{D(x,\eta_0)QD(x,\eta_0)'\} \otimes \Omega(x)$ is bounded away from zero on $\mathcal{X}$, $(\lambda_1(j), \ldots, \lambda_r(j))_{j=1}^{\infty}$ consists of all distinct vectors of nonnegative integers, $\Sigma_{l=1}^{r} \lambda_l(j)$ is increasing in j, for every K there is $J(K)$ and a constant matrix L_K such that

$$L_K[\{p^{J(K)}(x)p^{J(K)}(x)\} \otimes \{D(x,\eta_0)QD(x,\eta_0)'\}$$
$$\otimes \{\rho(z,\theta_0)\rho(z,\theta_0)\}]L_K' = U'QU \,,$$

the smallest eigenvalue of $L_K L_K'$ is bounded away from zero uniformly in K, and $J(K) \le CK$ for a constant C.

This condition, in particular the assumption that there is some continuity in the distribution of $\tau(x)$, will imply Assumption 5.2. It is also possible to allow for some discrete regressors with finite number of support points by including a full set of interactions of these variables with the power series, but for brevity this possibility is excluded here.

The next condition is the spanning condition.

ASSUMPTION 5.4. There exist $\tilde{\gamma}_{1K}, \ldots, \tilde{\gamma}_{KK}$ such that $E[\|D(x, \eta_0) \Sigma_{k=1}^{K}$ $\tilde{\gamma}_{kK} a_{kK}(x) - B(x)\|^2 \|\Omega(x)\|] \to 0$, and either $\hat{K} \in \mathcal{K}_n$ with probability approaching one and the number of elements of $\mathcal{K}_n$ is bounded, or

$$\sum_{K=1}^{\infty} \left\{ E\left[\left\| D(x, \eta_0) \sum_{k=1}^{K} \tilde{\gamma}_{kK} a_{kK}(x) - B(x) \right\|^2 \|\Omega(x)\| \right] \right\}^{1/2} < \infty .$$

This condition allows for an approximation rate that is useful in proving efficiency when k is data-based. Primitive conditions for this hypothesis with power series are given in the following condition.

ASSUMPTION 5.5. $\hat{K} \in \mathcal{K}_n$ with probability approaching one and the number of elements of $\mathcal{K}_n$ is bounded, $\tau(x)$ is one-to-one and there is a conformable matrix $R(x)$ such that $B(x) = D(x, \eta_0)'R(x)$, $E[\|D(x, \eta_0)\|^2 \|\Omega(x)\| \|R(x)\|^2] < \infty$. Also, $\text{vec}(R(x)) = (r_1(x), \ldots, r_v(x))'$ such that for any J and $\gamma_{11}, \ldots, \gamma_{1J}$, $\gamma_{21}, \ldots, \gamma_{vJ}$ there is K and $\gamma_1, \ldots, \gamma_K$ such that

$$\left\| R(x) - \sum_{k=1}^{K} \gamma_k a_k(x) \right\| \le \sum_{l=1}^{v} \left\| r_l(x) - \sum_{j=1}^{J} \gamma_{lj} p_j(x) \right\|$$

THEOREM 2. *If Assumptions* 4.1, 4.3, 5.1, *either* 5.2 *and* 5.4, *or* 5.3 *and* 5.5. *are satisfied, and* $K = \hat{K}$, $\hat{K} \xrightarrow{p} \infty$, *and there is* $\bar{K}(n)$ *such* $\hat{K} \le \bar{K}(n)$ *with probability approaching one and* $\bar{K}(n)^{1/r} \ln[\bar{K}(n)]/\ln(n) \to 0$, *then*

$$\sqrt{n}(\hat{\theta} - \theta_0) \xrightarrow{d} N(0, \Lambda) , \qquad \hat{\Lambda} \xrightarrow{p} \Lambda .$$

6. Sampling experiment for the heteroskedastic linear model

A small Monte Carlo study can suggest how the estimators might perform in practice. The model and design considered was the heteroskedastic linear model with normally distributed disturbance, lognormal regressor, and quadratic variance function considered by Cragg (1983), taking the form

$$y_i = \beta_{10} + \beta_{20} x_i + \varepsilon_i , \qquad \varepsilon_i/\sigma_i \sim N(0, 1) , \qquad \sigma_i^2 = 0.1 + 0.2x_i + 0.3x_i^2 ,$$
$$\ln(x_i) \sim N(0, 1) , \qquad x_i \text{ and } \varepsilon_i \text{ independent} . \tag{6.1}$$

The reported results are invariant to the values of β_0 and to multiplication of the disturbance by a fixed constant. Two sample sizes were considered, 50, and 200. Computations were carried out on a microcomputer using GAUSS, with 1000 replications of both the x_i and y_i samples.

Table 1 reports results for sample size 50 and Table 2 for sample size 200. Each table gives the ratios of standard deviation (STDEV), median absolute error (MAE), and coverage probabilities for the asymptotic 95% confidence

Table 1
Ratio of variance, median absolute error, and nominal 95 percent coverage probability to that of Aitken estimator, and distribution of cross-validated 'Bandwidth', $n = 50$

	STDEV	MAE	COV PROB	Distribution of K					
OLS	3.189	2.778	0.782						
	2.110	2.055	0.751						
FGLS	1.311	1.178	0.715						
	1.460	1.312	0.646						
				$k =$ 6	9	12	15	18	24
NN	1.515	1.344	0.878	1					
	1.436	1.294	0.733						
	1.523	1.333	0.875	0.32	0.28	0.18	0.10	0.05	0.07
	1.442	1.321	0.742						
				$J =$ 4	6	8	10	12	
MM-CRAGG	1.500	1.367	0.904			1			
	1.491	1.376	0.752						
	1.795	1.622	0.894	0.50	0.26	0.14	0.05	0.05	
	1.595	1.550	0.781						
				$J =$ 2	3	4	5	6	
MM-COMBINE	1.515	1.278	0.866			1			
	1.509	1.440	0.700						
	1.583	1.356	0.870	0.28	0.44	0.12	0.11	0.05	
	1.528	1.404	0.748						

interval (COV PROB) of several estimators to the corresponding results for the generalized least squares (Aitken) estimator. The estimators for which results are reported are ordinary least squares (OLS), feasible generalized least squares (FGLS), nearest neighbor estimators (NN), and two varieties of series estimators (MM). The FGLS estimator was calculated by taking the predicted values from a regression of the squared residual on linear and quadratic terms in x_i, dividing by the estimated variance of the disturbance, censoring the result below at 0.04, and then using the inverse of the resulting quantity as a weight in weighted least squares results. Different truncation points were tried, in results not reported here, but they did not seem to make much difference.

Several nearest neighbor estimators were calculated, one each for the grid of K values given in the table, and one where for each replication K was chosen to minimize the cross-validation criterion described in Section 4. The tables only report results for the K where the estimator has smallest variance and for the cross-validated K, with the distribution of K across replications reported on the right.

Two varieties of series estimators were considered. Both used approximating functions $p_j(x) = \tau(x)^j$, $\tau(x) = x/(1 + |x|)$, where x was normalized in each replication to have sample mean zero and variance one. The first type was the Cragg (1983) estimator that used these approximating functions (MM-CRAGG), and the second was the more parsimonious estimator of equation (5.8). For each type several estimators were calculated, one each for the grid

Table 2
Ratio of variance, median absolute error, and nominal 95 percent coverage probability to that of Aitken estimator, and distribution of cross-validated 'Bandwidth', $n = 200$

	VAR	MAE	COV PROB	Distribution of K					
OLS	4.892	3.933	0.856						
	2.949	2.731	0.836						
FGLS	1.369	1.156	0.717						
	1.321	1.231	0.733						
				$k =$	8	12	16	20	24	28
NN	1.462	1.200	0.871		1				
	1.449	1.346	0.809						
	1.462	1.178	0.904		0.28	0.27	0.18	0.13	0.08	0.06
	1.436	1.308	0.851						
				$J =$	6	8	10	12	14
MM-CRAGG	1.154	1.089	0.001		1				
	1.115	1.096	0.977						
	1.231	1.089	0.081		0.62	0.19	0.10	0.04	0.05
	1.205	1.173	0.938						
				$J =$	3	4	5	6	7
MM-COMBINE	1.154	1.067	0.974		1				
	1.192	1.250	0.948						
	1.246	1.089	0.953		0.64	0.18	0.10	0.04	0.05
	1.269	1.212	0.921						

of k values listed on the right of the table, and the one where for each replication K was chosen to minimize the cross-validation criterion. The tables report results for the estimator with fixed K that had the smallest variance and for the cross-validation estimator.

Before discussing the tables it is useful to note that all the estimators here are symmetrically distributed around the true parameter values, so that there is no need to be concerned about central tendency. Also, unlike Cragg (1983), the results are not conditional on a particular set of regressors, which here were simulated for each replication.

The results in the tables can be summarized by saying that for sample size 50, the FGLS estimator does somewhat better than the NN estimator (cross-validated), which in turn does slightly better than the MM estimators (cross-validated), but for sample size 200 the MM estimator does best, the FGLS estimator next best, and the NN estimator least best. Also, the estimators that use the cross-validation criteria suggested earlier do about as well as the ones with best choice of nearest neighbor or number of series terms, both in terms of dispersion and accuracy of asymptotic confidence intervals, particularly for the larger sample sizes. Indeed, in a number of cases the cross-validated estimators perform better in some respects than the fixed K versions. Also, the Cragg type series estimator does worse than the more parsimonious estimator for the smaller sample size, but better for the larger sample size. One would expect to find a bigger advantage for the more parsimonious estimator suggested here in more realistic cases where there are more regressors, and hence more linear combination coefficients in the Cragg estimator relative to the more parsimonious one.

Appendix

In order to state and prove some useful lemmas it is necessary to introduce some additional notation. Throughout C will denote a generic positive constant that can take on different values in different uses and $\Sigma_i = \Sigma_{i=1}^n$. The first lemma gives a general set of sufficient conditions for asymptotic efficiency of nonlinear instrumental variables estimators with estimated optimal instruments.

LEMMA A.1. *Suppose that Assumption 3.1 is satisfied,*

$$\sum_i \|\hat{B}(x_i) - B(x_i)\|^2/n \overset{p}{\to} 0,$$

and

$$\sum_i \{\hat{B}(x_i) - B(x_i)\}\rho(z_i, \theta_0)\sqrt{n} \overset{p}{\to} 0.$$

Then if Assumption 3.2 is satisfied, $\sqrt{n}(\hat{\theta} - \theta_0) \overset{d}{\to} N(0, \Lambda)$ for $\hat{\theta}$ from equation (2.9), and if Assumption 3.3 is satisfied, and $\sqrt{n}(\tilde{\theta} - \theta_0) \overset{d}{\to} N(0, \Lambda)$.

PROOF. Let $\hat{B}_i = \hat{B}(x_i)$, $B_i = B(x_i)$, $\hat{g}(\theta) = \sum_i \hat{B}_i\rho(z_i, \theta)/n$ and $\tilde{g}(\theta) = \Sigma_i B_i\rho(z_i, \theta)/n$. By CS and M,

$$\sup_{\theta \in \Theta} \|\hat{g}(\theta) - \tilde{g}(\theta)\| \le \left(\sum_i \|\hat{B}_i - B_i\|^2/n\right)^{1/2}\left(\sum_i d(z_i)^2/n\right)^{1/2}$$
$$= o_p(1)O_p(1) = o_p(1),$$

while by the usual uniform law of large numbers, $\sup_{\theta \in \Theta}\|\tilde{g}(\theta) - E[\tilde{g}(\theta)]\| \overset{p}{\to} 0$, so by T, $\sup_{\theta \in \Theta}\|\hat{g}(\theta) - E[\tilde{g}(\theta)]\| \overset{p}{\to} 0$. It follows similarly that for $\hat{g}_\theta(\theta) = \partial\hat{g}(\theta)/\partial\theta$ and $\tilde{g}_\theta(\theta) = \partial\tilde{g}(\theta)/\partial\theta$, $\sup_{\theta \in \mathcal{N}}\|\hat{g}_\theta(\theta) - E[\tilde{g}_\theta(\theta)]\| \overset{p}{\to} 0$. Also, by the Sluztky and Lindbergh–Levy theorems, for $\rho_i = \rho(z_i, \theta)$,

$$\sum_i \hat{B}_i\rho_i/\sqrt{n} = \sum_i (\hat{B}_i - B_i)\rho_i/\sqrt{n} + \sum_i B_i\rho_i/\sqrt{n}$$
$$= o_p(1) + \sum_i B_i\rho_i/\sqrt{n} \overset{d}{\to} N(0, \Lambda^{-1}).$$

The estimator of equation (2.9) is an IV estimator with $\hat{P} = (\Sigma_i \hat{B}_i \hat{B}_i' / n)^{-1} \xrightarrow{p} P = (E[B_i B_i'])^{-1}$ under Assumption 3.2, so $\hat{g}(\theta)' \hat{P} \hat{g}(\theta)$ converges uniformly in probability to $g(\theta)' P g(\theta)$, $g(\theta)' P g(\theta)$ is continuous, and has a unique minimum (of zero) at $\theta = \theta_0$, and hence is consistent by the standard Wald argument. The first conclusion then follows by a mean-value expansion like that of equation (2.4). For the second conclusion, asymptotic normality of the initial estimator follows by a similar argument to that just given. Then by a mean-value expansion

$$\sqrt{n}(\hat{\theta} - \theta_0) = \{I - [\hat{g}_\theta(\hat{\theta})]^{-1} \hat{g}_\theta(\bar{\theta})\} \sqrt{n}(\hat{\theta} - \theta_0) - [\hat{g}_\theta(\hat{\theta})]^{-1} \sqrt{n} \hat{g}(\theta_0)$$

$$= o_p(1) O_p(1) - [\hat{g}_\theta(\hat{\theta})]^{-1} \sqrt{n} \hat{g}(\theta_0) \xrightarrow{d} N(0, \Lambda). \qquad \square \ (A.1)$$

Some other Lemmas are useful for proving Theorem 1. Let $h(z, \theta)$ be a function of z and a parameter vector θ and let $\hat{\theta}$ be a consistent estimate of some value θ_0. Let

$$g_i = E[h(z_i, \theta_0) \,|\, x_i], \qquad \bar{g}_i = \sum_{j=1}^n W_{ij} E[h(z_j, \theta_0) \,|\, x_j],$$

$$\tilde{g}_i = \sum_{j=1}^n W_{ij} h(z_j, \theta_0), \qquad \hat{g}_i = \sum_{j=1}^n W_{ij} h(z_j, \hat{\theta}). \qquad (A.2)$$

The following assumption concerning $h(z, \theta)$ and θ will be maintained.

ASSUMPTION A.1. (i) $\hat{\theta} - \theta_0 = O_p(1 \sqrt{n})$. (ii) For $p > 2$, $E[|h(z_i, \theta_0)|^p]$ is finite. (iii) there is $M(z)$ with $E[M(z_i)^2]$ finite such that for θ close enough to θ_0, $|h(z_i, \theta) - h(z_i, \theta_0)| \leqslant M(z_i) \|\theta - \theta_0\|$. (iv) $k/\sqrt{n} \to$, $k/n \to 0$.

LEMMA A.2 (Stone, 1977, Proposition 1). $\lim_{n \to \infty} E[|\bar{g}_i - g_i|^p] = 0$.

The proofs of the following three lemmas are nearly identical to the proofs of Lemmas 8, 9, and 5, respectively, of Robinson (1987), and so will be omitted.

LEMMA A.3. $\{E[|\tilde{g}_i - \bar{g}_i|^p]\}^{1/p} = O(k^{-1/2})$.

LEMMA A.4. $\max_{i \leqslant n} |\tilde{g}_i - \bar{g}_i| = O_p(n^{1/p} k^{-1/2})$

LEMMA A.5. $\max_{i \leqslant n} |\hat{g}_i - \tilde{g}_i| = O_p(k^{-1/2})$.

Let $Z_n = (z_1, \ldots, z_n)$. The following two lemmas are proven in Newey (1990).

LEMMA A.6. *Suppose that* (i) $\rho_n(z, X_n)$ *is a function such that* $E[\rho_n(z_i, X_n) | x_i, Z_{-i}] = 0$ *and* $E[|\rho_n(z_i, X_n)|^{2p/(p-2)}] = O(1)$; (ii) $h(z_i, \theta)$ *is continuously differentiable with derivative* $h_\theta(z_i, \theta)$ *in a convex neighborhood N of* θ_0; (iii) *there are random variables* $M_\theta(z_i)$ *and* $M_{\theta\theta}(z_i)$ *satisfying* $\|h_\theta(z_i, \theta)\| \leq M_\theta(z_i) - h_\theta$ *and*

$$\|h_\theta(z_i, \theta) - h_\theta(z_i, \theta_0)\| \leq M_{\theta\theta}(z_i)\|\theta - \theta_0\| \quad \text{for } \theta \text{ in } N,$$

and $E[M_\theta(z_i)^p]$ *and* $E[M_{\theta\theta}(z_i)^{2p/(p+2)}]$ *finite. Then*

$$\sum_i (\hat{g}_i - g_i)\rho_n(z_i, X_n)/\sqrt{n} = o_p(1).$$ (A.3)

The following lemma is an 'asymptotic trimming' result, that allows us to ignore the 'denominator problem' associated with the nearest neighbor estimator $\hat{\Omega}(x_i)$. Let $\hat{\Omega}_i$, $\tilde{\Omega}_i$, $\bar{\Omega}_i$, Ω_i, $\hat{D}_i$, $\tilde{D}_i$, $\bar{D}_i$, D_i be the estimators corresponding to equation (A.1), where $h(z, \theta)$ is an element of $\rho(z, \theta)\rho(z, \theta)'$ and $\partial\rho(z, \theta)/\partial\theta$, respectively.

LEMMA A.7. *If the hypotheses of Theorem 3.1 are satisfied then there is a constant C such that* $\|\Omega_i^{-1}\| < C$, $\|\bar{\Omega}_i^{-1}\| < C$ *and the indicator* $\hat{1}_n = 1(\max_{i \leq n} \max\{\|\hat{\Omega}_i^{-1}\|, \|\tilde{\Omega}_i^{-1}\|\} < C)$ *is equal to one with probability approaching one. Furthermore, for any sequence of random variables* Y_n *and constants* b_n, *if* $Y_n\hat{1}_n = O_p(b_n)$ *then* $Y_n = O_p(b_n)$.

PROOF. Let $\lambda(A)$ denote the smallest eigenvalue of a symmetric matrix A. Then $\lambda(\Omega_i) > C$ for all i by $\lambda(\Omega(x))$ bounded away from zero. Also, by W_{ij} nonnegative and $\Sigma_{j=1}^n W_{ij} = 1$ the extremal characterization of $\lambda(\cdot)$ gives $\lambda(\bar{\Omega}_i) = \lambda(\Sigma_{j=1}^n W_{ij}\Omega_j) \geq \Sigma_{j=1}^n W_{ij}\lambda(\Omega_j) > C$, giving the first conclusion. As is well known, $|\lambda(\bar{A}) - \lambda(A)| \leq C\|\bar{A} - A\|$ where the constant C here depends only on the dimension of A. By Lemma A.4, with $h(z, \theta)$ and element of $\rho(z, \theta)\rho(z, \theta)'$ and $p = \nu/2 > 4$,

$$\max_{i \leq n} |\lambda(\tilde{\Omega}_i) - \lambda(\bar{\Omega}_i)| \leq C \max_{i \leq n} \|\tilde{\Omega}_i - \bar{\Omega}_i\| = O_p(n^{1/p}k^{-1/2})$$
$$= O_p(n^{1/4}k^{-1/2}) = o_p(1).$$

Similarly, by Lemma A.5, $\max_{i \leq n} |\lambda(\hat{\Omega}_i) - \lambda(\tilde{\Omega}_i)| \xrightarrow{p} 0$, so that $\text{Prob}(\hat{1}_n = 1) \to 1$ by T and specification of small enough C. The final conclusion follows by noting that $(\hat{1}_n - 1)Y_n$ is equal to zero with probability approaching one, and hence $(1 - \hat{1}_n)Y_n = O_p(b_n)$ for *any* b_n, giving $Y_n = \hat{1}_n Y_n + (1 - \hat{1}_n)Y_n = O_p(b_n)$. □

PROOF OF THEOREM 1. The result is first proved for the case where $D(x, \eta) = 0$, by verifying the hypotheses of Lemma A.6. For $\hat{1}_n$ in Lemma A.7, by CS,

$$\hat{1}_n \|\hat{\Omega}_i^{-1} - \bar{\Omega}_i^{-1}\| = \hat{1}_n \|\hat{\Omega}_i^{-1}(\bar{\Omega}_i - \hat{\Omega}_i)\bar{\Omega}_i^{-1}\|$$
$$\leq \hat{1}_n \|\hat{\Omega}_i^{-1}\| \, \|\hat{\Omega}_i - \bar{\Omega}_i\| \, \|\bar{\Omega}_i^{-1}\|$$
$$\leq C\hat{1}_n \|\hat{\Omega}_i - \bar{\Omega}_i\| \leq C \|\hat{\Omega}_i - \bar{\Omega}_i\| \,.$$

Therefore, by Lemmas A.4 and A.5,

$$\hat{1}_n \Big(\sum_i \|\hat{\Omega}_i^{-1} - \bar{\Omega}_i^{-1}\|^4/n \Big)^{1/4}$$
$$\leq C \Big(\sum_i \|\hat{\Omega}_i - \bar{\Omega}_i\|^4/n \Big)^{1/4}$$
$$\leq C \max_{i \leq n} \|\hat{\Omega}_i - \tilde{\Omega}_i\| + C \Big(\sum_i \|\tilde{\Omega}_i - \bar{\Omega}_i\|^4/n \Big)^{1/4}$$
$$= o_p(k^{-1/2}) + O_p(\{E[\|\tilde{\Omega}_i - \bar{\Omega}_i\|^{\nu/2}]\}^{2/\nu}) = o_p(k^{-1/2}) \,. \tag{A.4}$$

Similarly, $(\sum_i \|\hat{D}_i - \bar{D}_i\|^2/n)^{1/2} = o_p(k^{-1/2})$. Then by CS, H, T, and $\hat{1}_n = 1$ with probability approaching one,

$$\Big\| \sum_i (\hat{D}_i - \bar{D}_i)'(\hat{\Omega}_i^{-1} - \bar{\Omega}_i^{-1})\rho_i/\sqrt{n} \Big\|$$
$$= \hat{1}_n \Big\| \sum_i (\hat{D}_i - \bar{D}_i)'(\hat{\Omega}_i^{-1} - \bar{\Omega}_i^{-1})\rho_i/\sqrt{n} \Big\| + o_p(1)$$
$$\leq \sqrt{n} \Big(\sum_i \|\hat{D}_i - \bar{D}_i\|^2/n \Big)^{1/2} \cdot \hat{1}_n \Big(\sum_i \|\hat{\Omega}_i^{-1} - \bar{\Omega}_i^{-1}\|^4/n \Big)^{1/4}$$
$$\times \Big(\sum_i \|\rho_i\|^8/n \Big)^{1/8} + o_p(1) = O_p(\sqrt{n}/k) = o_p(1) \,. \tag{A.5}$$

Similarly, by $E[\|D_i\|^4] < \infty$, implying $E[\|\bar{D}_i\|^4] = o(1)$,

$$\Big\| \sum_i \bar{D}_i'(\hat{\Omega}_i^{-1} - \bar{\Omega}_i^{-1})\rho_i/\sqrt{n} - \sum_i \bar{D}_i'\bar{\Omega}_i^{-1}(\bar{\Omega}_i - \hat{\Omega}_i)\bar{\Omega}_i^{-1}\rho_i/\sqrt{n} \Big\|$$
$$\leq \hat{1}_n \sum_i \|\bar{D}_i\| \, \|\bar{\Omega}_i^{-1}\|^2 \|\hat{\Omega}_i - \bar{\Omega}_i\|^2 \|\hat{\Omega}_i\| \, \|\rho_i/\sqrt{n} + o_p(1)$$
$$\leq C \sum_i \|\bar{D}_i\| \, \|\hat{\Omega}_i - \bar{\Omega}_i\|^2 \|\rho_i\|/\sqrt{n}$$
$$\leq C \Big(\sum_i \|\bar{D}_i\|^4/n \Big)^{1/4} \Big(\sum_i \|\hat{\Omega}_i - \bar{\Omega}_i\|^4/n \Big)^{1/2} \Big(\sum_i \|\rho_i\|^8/n \Big)^{1/8}$$
$$= O_p(\sqrt{n}/k) = o_p(1) \,.$$

By Lemma A.6, with $\rho_n(z_i, X_n)$ equal to an element of $\text{vec}([\bar{D}_i'\bar{\Omega}_i^{-1}] \otimes [\bar{\Omega}_i^{-1}])$,

$p = 4$ and $h(z, \theta)$ equal to an element of $\rho(z, \theta)\rho(z, \theta)'$,

$$\sum_i \bar{D}_i' \bar{\Omega}_i^{-1}(\hat{\Omega}_i - \Omega_i)\bar{\Omega}_i^{-1}\rho_i/\sqrt{n} \overset{p}{\to} 0,$$

and for $h(z, \theta)$ equal to an element of $E[\rho(z, \theta)\rho(z, \theta)' \mid x]$,

$$\sum_i \bar{D}_i' \bar{\Omega}_i^{-1}(\bar{\Omega}_i - \Omega_i)\bar{\Omega}_i^{-1}\rho_i/\sqrt{n} \overset{p}{\to} 0.$$

Then by the triangle inequality,

$$\sum_i \bar{D}_i'(\hat{\Omega}_i^{-1} - \Omega_i^{-1})\rho_i/\sqrt{n} \overset{p}{\to} 0. \tag{A.6}$$

Also, by Lemma A.6 with $\rho_n(z_i, X_n)$ equal to an element of $\Omega_i^{-1}\rho_i$, $p = 4$ and $h(z, \theta)$ equal to an element of $\partial \rho(z, \theta)/\partial \theta$,

$$\sum_i (\hat{D}_i - D_i)' \bar{\Omega}_i^{-1}\rho_i/\sqrt{n} \overset{p}{\to} 0. \tag{A.7}$$

Also, by Lemma A.2 and $E[(\bar{D}_i - D_i)'(\bar{\Omega}_i^{-1} - \Omega_i^{-1})\rho_i] = 0$ and $E[\rho_i\rho_j \mid X_n] = 0$ for $i \neq j$,

$$E\left[\left\| \sum_i (\bar{D}_i - D_i)'(\bar{\Omega}_i^{-1} - \Omega_i^{-1})\rho/\sqrt{n} \right\|^2\right]$$
$$\leq E[\|\bar{D}_i - D_i\|^2\|(\bar{\Omega}_i^{-1} - \Omega_i^{-1})\Omega_i(\bar{\Omega}_i^{-1} - \Omega_i^{-1})\|] \leq C,$$
$$E[\|\bar{D}_i - D_i\|^2\|\bar{\Omega}_i - \Omega_i\|^2] \leq (E[\|\bar{D}_i - D_i\|^4])^{1/2}(E[\|\bar{\Omega}_i - \Omega_i\|^4])^{1/2} \to 0,$$
$$\sum_i (\bar{D}_i - D_i)'(\bar{\Omega}_i^{-1} - \Omega_i^{-1})\rho_i/\sqrt{n} \overset{p}{\to} 0. \tag{A.8}$$

It then follows by equations (A.5)–(A.8) and the triangle inequality that $\sum_{i=1}^n (\hat{B}_i - B_i)\rho_i\sqrt{n} \overset{p}{\to} 0$. Furthermore, by T, CS, and Lemma A.2, it follows similarly to equation (A.4) that

$$\sum_{i=1}^n \|\hat{B}_i - B_i\|^2/n \leq \left(\sum_i \|\hat{D}_i - D_i\|^4/n\right)^{1/4}\left(\sum_i \|\hat{\Omega}_i^{-1}\|^4/n\right)^{1/4}$$
$$+ \left(\sum_i \|D_i\|^4/n\right)^{1/4}\left(\sum_i \|\hat{\Omega}_i^{-1} - \Omega_i^{-1}\|^4/n\right)^{1/4} \overset{p}{\to} 0.$$

Similarly, $\sum_{i=1}^n \|\hat{B}_i\hat{D}_i - B_iD_i\|/n \overset{p}{\to} 0$, and by the law of large numbers, $\sum_{i=1}^n B_iD_i/n \overset{p}{\to} \Lambda^{-1}$, so the final conclusion follows by T.

For the case where $D(x, \eta)$ is not equal zero, by Assumption 4.5, the conclusions previously given hold with $\partial \rho(z, \theta)/\partial \theta - D(x, \eta)$ replacing $\partial \rho(z, \theta)/\partial \theta$ throughout. For simplicity, assume η is a scalar. Therefore, by

Assumption 4.5, a mean-value expansion, and H,

$$\left\|\sum_i \{D(x_i, \hat{\eta}) - D(x_i, \eta_0)\}(\hat{\Omega}_i^{-1} - \Omega_i^{-1})\rho_i/\sqrt{n}\right\|$$

$$\leqslant \sqrt{n}\|\hat{\eta} - \eta_0\| \sum_i \sup_{\eta \in \mathcal{N}} \left\|\frac{\partial D(x_i, \eta)}{\partial \eta}\right\| \|\hat{\Omega}_i^{-1} - \Omega_i^{-1}\| \|\rho_i\|/n$$

$$\leqslant O_p(1)\left(\sum_i d(z_i)^2/n\right)^{1/4}\left(\sum_i \|\hat{\Omega}_i^{-1} - \Omega_i^{-1}\|^4/n\right)^{1/4}\left(\sum_i \|\rho_i\|^8/n\right)^{1/8}$$

$$= O_p(1)o_p(1)O_p(1) = o_p(1) .$$

Also, it follows similarly to equation (A.6) that

$$\sum_i D(x_i, \eta_0)(\hat{\Omega}_i^{-1} - \Omega_i^{-1})\rho_i/\sqrt{n} \overset{p}{\to} 0 .$$

Also by the usual uniform law of large numbers,

$$\sum_i \left\{\frac{\partial D(x_i, \bar{\eta})}{\partial \eta}\right\}\rho_i/n \overset{p}{\to} E[\{\partial D(x_i, \eta_0)/\partial \eta\}\rho_i] = 0 ,$$

so that by a mean value expansion,

$$\left\|\sum_i \{D(x_i, \hat{\eta}) - D(x_i, \eta_0)\}\Omega_i^{-1}\rho_i/\sqrt{n}\right\|$$

$$\leqslant \sqrt{n}\|\hat{\eta} - \eta_0\| \left\|\sum_i \left\{\frac{\partial D(x_i, \bar{\eta})}{\partial \eta}\right\}\rho_i/n\right\| \overset{p}{\to} 0 .$$

Also, the previous proof gives

$$\sum_i \{(\hat{D}_i - D(x_i, \hat{\eta}))\hat{\Omega}_i^{-1} - (D_i - D(x_i, \eta_0))\Omega_i^{-1}\}\rho_i/\sqrt{n} \overset{p}{\to} 0 .$$

Therefore, by T,

$$\left\|\sum_i (\hat{B}_i - B_i)\rho_i/\sqrt{n}\right\| = \left\|\sum_i \{D(x_i, \hat{\eta})\hat{\Omega}_i^{-1} - D(x_i, \eta_0)\Omega_i^{-1}\}\rho_i/\sqrt{n}\right\| + o_p(1)$$

$$= o_p(1) . \tag{A.9}$$

Similar reasoning also gives $\Sigma_i \|\hat{B}_i - B_i\|^2/n \overset{p}{\to} 0$, so the first conclusion follows by Lemma A.1, and also gives, $\Sigma_i \|\hat{B}_i\hat{D}_i - D_iD_i\|/n \overset{p}{\to} 0$, so the second conclusion follows as above. $\square$

Two lemmas are useful for the proof of Theorem 2. Let $m_k(z, \theta, \eta) =$

$D(x, \eta)'a_{kK}(x)\rho(z, \theta)$, so that

$$U = [m_1(z, \theta_0, \eta_0), \ldots, m_K(z, \theta_0, \eta_0)] ,$$
$$\hat{U}_i = [m_1(z_i, \hat{\theta}, \hat{\eta}), \ldots, m_K(z_i, \hat{\theta}, \hat{\eta})] ,$$
$$\hat{M}_k = \sum_{i=1}^{n} \partial m_k(z_i, \hat{\theta}, \hat{\eta})/\partial\theta .$$

LEMMA A.8. *If Assumption 5.3 is satisfied then Assumption 5.2 is satisfied.*

PROOF. It follows by the extremal characterization of the smallest eigenvalue and Lemma A1 of Newey (1988) that

$$\lambda(E[U'QU])$$
$$\geq \lambda(L_K L_K')\lambda(E[\{p^{J(K)}(x)\rho^{J(K)}(x)\} \otimes \{D(x, \eta_0)QD(x, \eta_0)'\} \otimes \Omega(x)])$$
$$\geq CJ(K)^{-CJ(K)^{1/r}} \tag{A.10}$$

The conclusion then follows by $J(K) \leq CK$. □

LEMMA A.9. *If Assumptions 5.3 and 5.5 are satisfied then Assumption 5.4 is satisfied.*

PROOF. By Gallant (1980), for each l their exist $\gamma_{l1}^j, \ldots, \gamma_{lJ}^j$ such that

$$E\left[\|D(x, \eta_0)\|^2 \|\Omega(x)\| \left\{r_l(x) - \sum_{j=1}^{J} \gamma_{lj}^j p_j(x)\right\}^2\right] \to 0 ,$$

so the conclusion follows from Assumption 5.5. □

PROOF OF THEOREM 2. The proof proceeds by verifying the hypotheses of Lemma 5.1 of Newey (1989) (L5 henceforth). It follows by standard arguments that $\sqrt{n}\|\hat{\theta} - \theta_0\| = O_p(1)$ for the initial estimator $\hat{\theta}$. Consider nonrandom $K = K(n)$ such that $K \to \infty$, and let the $\nu(K)$ of L5 be $K^{1/r}$. By hypothesis Q is positive semidefinite. Also, by H and Assumption 5.1,

$$\|E[\partial m(z, \theta_0, \eta_0)/\partial\theta]\|$$
$$\leq K \sup_{k,x}\|a_{kK}(x)\|E\left[\|D(x, \eta_0)\| \left\|\frac{\partial\rho(z, \theta_0)}{\partial\theta}\right\|\right] \leq CK \leq C\nu(K)^{C\nu(K)}$$

and there is $\varepsilon > 0$ small enough that

$$E[\|\text{Vec}(U)\|^{2+\varepsilon}] \leq K^C E\left[\|D(x, \eta_0)\|^{2+\varepsilon} \left\|\frac{\partial\rho(z, \theta_0)}{\partial\theta}\right\|^{2+\varepsilon}\right] \leq C\nu(K)^{C\nu(K)} .$$

In addition, it follows by Assumption 5.2 or Assumption 5.3 and Lemma A.8 that $\lambda(E[U'QU]) \geq C\nu(K)^{-C\nu(K)}$, so that hypothesis (i) of L5 is satisfied.

Next, by Assumption 5.4, $\|\hat{Q} - Q\| = O_p(n^{-1/2})$. Also, by Assumption 5.1

$E[\|\partial m_k(z, \theta_0, \eta_0)/\partial\theta\|^{1+\varepsilon}] < C$ for some $\varepsilon > 0$, so by Newey (1988),

$$\left\| n^{-1} \sum_i \frac{\partial m(z_i, \theta_0, \eta_0)}{\partial\theta} - E\left[\frac{\partial m(z, \theta_0, \eta_0)}{\partial\theta}\right] \right\| = O_p(n^{-C}\nu(K)^{C\nu(K)}) .$$

(A.11)

By H, each of the following are finite:

$$E[d_2(z_i)d_1'(z_i)] , \qquad E[\|\rho_{\theta i}\|d_1'(z_i)] , \qquad E[\|d_2(z_i)\| \|D_{0i}\|] ,$$
$$E[d_1(z_i)^2 d_1'(z_i)^2] , \qquad E[\|\rho_i\|^2 d_1'(z_i)^2] , \qquad E[\|d_2(z_i)\|^2\|D_{0i}\|^2] .$$

Then, for $m(z, \theta, \eta) = (m_1(z, \theta, \eta)', \ldots, m_K(z, \theta, \eta)')'$, $\hat{D}_i = D(x_i, \hat{\eta})$, $D_{0i} = D(x_i, \eta_0)$, $\hat{\rho}_{\theta i} = \partial\rho(z_i, \hat{\theta})/\partial\theta$, $\rho_{\theta i} = \partial\rho(z_i, \theta_0)/\partial\theta$, $\Sigma_k = \Sigma_{k=1}^K$,

$$\left\| n^{-1} \sum_i \frac{\partial m(z_i, \hat{\theta}, \hat{\eta})}{\partial\theta} - E\left[\frac{\partial m(z, \theta_0, \eta_0)}{\partial\theta}\right] \right\|$$
$$\leq n^{-1}K \sum_i [\|\hat{\rho}_{\theta i} - \rho_{\theta i}\| \|\hat{D}_i - D_{0i}\| + \|\rho_{\theta i}\| \|\hat{D}_i - D_{0i}\|$$
$$+ \|\hat{\rho}_{\theta i} - \rho_{\theta i}\| \|D_{0i}\|] + \left\| n^{-1} \sum_i \frac{\partial m(z_i, \theta_0, \eta_0)}{\partial\theta} - E\left[\frac{\partial m(z, \theta_0, \eta_0)}{\partial\theta}\right] \right\|$$
$$\leq n^{-1}K \sum_i \{d_2(z_i)d_1'(z_i) + \|\rho_{\theta i}\|d_1'(z_i) + \|d_2(z_i)\| \|D_{0i}\|\}\{\|\hat{\theta} - \theta_0\|$$
$$+ \|\hat{\eta} - \eta_0\|\} + O_p(n^{-C}\nu(K)^{C\nu(K)}) = O_p(n^{-C}\nu(K)^{C\nu(K)}) . \quad (A.12)$$

$$n^{-1} \sum_i \|m(z_i, \hat{\theta}, \hat{\eta}) - m(z_i, \theta_0, \eta_0)\|^2$$
$$\leq n^{-1}K \sum_i \{d_1(z_i)^2 d_1'(z_i)^2 + \|\rho_i\|^2 d_1'(z_i)^2$$
$$+ \|d_2(z_i)\|^2 \|D_{0i}\|^2\}O_p(1/\sqrt{n}) \quad (A.13)$$
$$= O_p(n^{-C}\nu(K)^{C\nu(K)}) .$$

Furthermore, by a mean-value expansions and the same argument as for equation (A.12),

$$\sqrt{n}\left\| n^{-1} \sum_i m(z_i, \hat{\theta}, \hat{\eta}) - n^{-1} \sum_i m(z_i, \theta_0, \hat{\eta}) \right.$$
$$\left. - E\left[\frac{\partial m(z, \theta_0, \eta_0)}{\partial\theta}\right](\hat{\theta} - \theta_0) \right\|$$
$$\leq \left\| n^{-1} \sum_i \frac{\partial m(z_i, \bar{\theta}, \hat{\eta})}{\partial\theta} - E\left[\frac{\partial m(z, \theta_0, \eta_0)}{\partial\theta}\right] \right\| \sqrt{n}\|\hat{\theta} - \theta_0\|$$
$$= O_p(n^{-C}\nu(K)^{C\nu(K)}) . \quad (A.14)$$

where $\bar{\theta}$ denotes the mean value, satisfying $\sqrt{n}\|\bar{\theta} - \theta_0\| \leqslant \sqrt{n}\|\hat{\theta} - \theta_0\| = O_p(1)$. Also, $E[\partial m(z_i, \theta_0, \eta_0)/\partial \eta] = 0$ and for some $\varepsilon > 0$, by H,

$$E\left[\left\|\frac{\partial m_k(z_i, \theta_0, \eta_0)}{\partial \eta}\right\|^{1+\varepsilon}\right] \leqslant CE\left[\left\|\frac{\partial D(x, \eta_0)}{\partial \eta}\right\|^{1+\varepsilon}\|\rho_i\|^{1+\varepsilon}\right] < C,$$

where it is assumed that η is a scalar, for simplicity. Then by a lemma of Newey (1988),

$$\left\|n^{-1}\sum_i \frac{\partial m(z_i, \theta_0, \eta_0)}{\partial \eta}\right\| = O_p(n^{-C}v(K)^{Cv(K)}),$$

and expanding around η_0 gives,

$$\sqrt{n}\left\|n^{-1}\sum_i m(z_i, \theta_0, \hat{\eta}) - n^{-1}\sum_i m(z_i, \theta_0, \eta_0)\right\|$$

$$\leqslant \left\|n^{-1}\sum_i \frac{\partial m(z_i, \theta_0, \eta_0)}{\partial \eta}\right\|\|\sqrt{n}\|\hat{\eta} - \eta_0\|$$

$$+ K\left[\sum_{i=1}^n d_2'(z_i)\|\rho_i\|/n\right]\sqrt{n}\|\hat{\eta} - \eta_0\|^2$$

$$= O_p(n^{-C}v(K)^{cv(K)}). \tag{A.15}$$

It then follows by equations (A.12)–(A.15) that part (ii) of the hypotheses of L5 is satisfied, with $u = m(z, \beta_0, \eta_0)$. Part (iii) follows by equation (2.6). Also,

$$E\left[\left\|B_i\rho_i - \sum_{k=1}^K \gamma_k m_k(z_i, \theta_0, \eta_0)\right\|^2\right]$$

$$\leqslant E\left[\left\|B_i - D_{0i}\left\{\sum_{k=1}^K \gamma_k a_{kK}(x_i)\right\}\right\|^2\|\rho_i\|^2\right]$$

$$\leqslant E\left[\left\|B_i - D_{0i}\left\{\sum_{k=1}^K \gamma_k a_{kK}(x_i)\right\}\right\|^2\|\Omega_i\|^2\right],$$

so the remainder of the hypotheses of L5 follow by Assumption 5.4 or Assumption 5.5 and Lemma A.9. The conclusion then follows by the conclusion of L5. □

Acknowledgment

This research was partially supported by the NSF and the Sloan Foundation. An earlier version of this paper was presented at the 1986 European Meeting of the Econometric Society. Helpful comments were provided by L. Hansen and J. Robins.

References

Amemiya, T. (1974). The non-linear two-stage least-squares estimator. *J. Econometrics* **2**, 105–110.

Amemiya, T. and J. L. Powell (1981). A comparison of the Box–Cox maximum likelihood estimator and the non-linear two-stage least squares estimator. *J. Econometrics* **17**, 351–381.

Berndt, E. R., B. H. Hall, R. E. Hall and J. A. Hausman (1974). Estimation and inference in nonlinear structural models. *Ann. Econom. Social Measurement* **3**, 653–666.

Box, G. E. P. and D. R. Cox (1967). An analysis of transformations. *J. Roy. Statist. Soc. Ser. B* **26**, 211–252.

Burguete, J. F., A. R. Gallant and G. Souza (1982). On the unification of the asymptotic theory of nonlinear econometric models. *Econometric Rev.* **1**, 151–190.

Carroll, R. J. (1982). Adapting for heteroskedasticity in linear models. *Ann. Statist.* **10**, 1224–1233.

Carroll, R. J. and D. Ruppert (1988). *Transformation and Weighting in Regression*. Chapman and Hall, New York.

Chamberlain, G. (1987). Asymptotic efficiency in estimation with conditional moment restrictions. *J. Econometrics* **34**, 305–334.

Cragg, J. G. (1983). More efficient estimation in the presence of heteroskedasticity of unknown form. *Econometrica* **49**, 751–764.

Gallant, A. R. (1980). Explicit estimators of parametric functions in nonlinear regression. *J. Amer. Statist. Assoc.* **75**, 182–193.

Hansen, L. P. (1982). Large sample properties of generalized method of moments estimators. *Econometrica* **50**, 1029–1054.

Hansen, L. P. (1985). A method of calculating bounds on the asymptotic covariance matrices of generalized method of moments estimators. *J. Econometrics* **30**, 203–238.

Hansen, L. P., J. Heaton and M. Ogaki (1988). Efficiency bounds implied by multi-period conditional moment restrictions. *J. Amer. Statist. Assoc.* **83**, 863–871.

Hausman, J. A. (1983). Simultaneous equations models. In: Z. Griliches and M. D. Intriligator, eds., *Handbook of Econometrics*. North-Holland, Amsterdam, Chapter 7.

Jobson, J. D. and W. A. Fuller (1980). Least squares estimation when the covariance matrix and parameter vector are functionally related, *J. Amer. Statist. Assoc.* **75**, 176–181.

Jorgenson, D. W. and J. Laffont (1974). Efficient estimation of nonlinear simultaneous equations with additive disturbances. *Ann. Econom. Social Measurement* **3**, 615–640.

MaCurdy, T. E. (1982). Using information on the moments of the disturbance of increase the efficiency of estimation. Preprint, Stanford University.

McCullagh, P. and J. A. Nelder (1983). *Generalized Linear Models*. Chapman and Hall, New York.

Newey, W. K. (1988). Adaptive estimation of regression models via moment restrictions. *J. Econometrics* **38**, 301–339.

Newey, W. K. (1989a). Efficient estimation of semiparametric models via moment restrictions. MIT, Preprint.

Newey, W. K. (1989b). Locally efficient residual based estimation of nonlinear simultaneous equations models. MIT, Preprint.

Newey, W. K. (1990). Efficient instrumental variables estimation of nonlinear models. *Econometrica* **58**, 809–837.

Powell, J. L. (1991). Estimation of monotonic regression models under quantile restrictions. In: W. A. Barnett, J. L. Powell, G. E. Tauchen, eds., *Nonparametric and Semiparametric Methods in Econometrics and Statistics*, Cambridge Univ. Press, Cambridge.

Reiersol, O. (1945). Confluence analyses by means of instrumental sets of variables. *Ark. Math. Astronom. Fys.* **32**, 1–119.

Robinson, P. (1987). Asymptotically efficient estimation in the presence of heteroskedasticity of unknown form. *Econometrica* **55**, 875–891.

Sargan, J. D. (1959). The estimation of relationships with autocorrelated results by the use of instrumental variables. *J. Roy. Statist. Soc. Ser. B* **21**, 91–105.

Stein, C. (1956). Efficient nonparametaric testing and estimation. In: *Proc. 3rd Berkeley Sympos. on Mathematical Statistics and Probability*, Vol. 1. Univ. California Press, Berkeley, CA.

Stone, C. J. (1977). Consistent nonparametric regression (with discussion). *Ann. Statist.* **5**, 595–645.

Theil, H. (1971). *Principles of Econometrics*. Wiley, New York.

White, H. (1982). Instrumental variables regression with independent observations. *Econometrica* **50**, 483–499.

G. S. Maddala, C. R. Rao and H. D. Vinod, eds., *Handbook of Statistics, Vol. 11*
© 1993 Elsevier Science Publishers B.V. All rights reserved.

17

Generalized Method of Moments: Econometric Applications

Masao Ogaki

1. Introduction

The purpose of this paper is to explain Hansen's (1982) generalized method of moments (GMM) to applied researchers and to give practical guidance as to how GMM estimation should be implemented.[1] The statistical properties of GMM estimators and test statistics are discussed. This paper also presents some of the recent developments in the GMM procedure that have been used in applications. These include sequential (or two-step) estimation, GMM with deterministic trends, applications for cross sectional and panel data, and some statistics that are often used for hypothesis testing. In explaining empirical applications, the present paper emphasizes some of the pitfalls that researchers have encountered, and how they have dealt with them.[2]

The rest of this paper is organized as follows. Section 2 presents the basic GMM framework. Section 3 illustrates how ordinary least squares and linear and nonlinear instrumental variables estimation are embedded in the GMM framework as special cases. Section 4 presents some GMM related statistical procedures that extend the basic GMM framework. These include sequential (or two-step) estimation, GMM with deterministic trends, applications of GMM to cross sectional and panel data, and the minimum distance estimation. Section 5 discusses important assumptions for GMM that applied researchers should be aware of. In Section 6, methods for covariance matrix estimation are explained. These methods are necessary for calculating standard errors of GMM estimators and for using the optimal distance matrix for GMM estimation. Section 7 explains Wald, Lagrange multiplier and likelihood ratio type statistics for hypothesis testing and recently developed specification tests. In Section 8, empirical applications are discussed. Section 9 examines the optimal choice of instrumental variables, the relation between GMM and

---

[1] Hall (1993) provides a nontechnical introduction to GMM that offers the basic intuition behind GMM.

[2] In a companion paper, Ogaki (1993a), I describe the use of the Hansen/Heaton/Ogaki GAUSS GMM package for implementing GMM estimation and for forming test statistics.

semi-parametric estimation, and small sample properties of GMM estimators and test statistics. Section 10 concludes.

2. Generalized method of moments

This section explains the basic GMM framework.

2.1. Moment restrictions and GMM estimators

Let $\{X_t: t = 1, 2, \ldots\}$ be a collection of random vectors X_t, β_0 be a p-dimensional vector of the parameters to be estimated, and $f(X_t, \beta)$ a q-dimensional vector of functions. The time series context is maintained throughout this paper, except for Section 4.3, where applications of GMM to cross sectional data and panel data are discussed. Assume that X_t is (strictly) stationary.[3] We refer to $u_t = f(X_t, \beta_0)$ as the disturbance of GMM. Consider the (unconditional) moment restrictions

$$E(f(X_t, \beta_0)) = 0 . \tag{2.1}$$

Suppose that a law of large numbers can be applied to $f(X_t, \beta)$ for all admissible β, so that the sample mean of $f(X_t, \beta)$ converges to its population mean:

$$\lim_{T \to \infty} \frac{1}{T} \sum_{t=1}^{T} f(X_t, \beta) = E(f(X_t, \beta)) \tag{2.2}$$

with probability one (or in other words, almost surely). The basic idea of GMM estimation is to mimic the moment restrictions (2.1) by minimizing a quadratic form of the sample means

$$J_T(\beta) = \left\{ \frac{1}{T} \sum_{t=1}^{T} f(X_t, \beta) \right\}' W_T \left\{ \frac{1}{T} \sum_{t=1}^{T} f(X_t, \beta) \right\} \tag{2.3}$$

with respect to β; where W_T is a positive semidefinite matrix, which satisfies

$$\lim_{T \to \infty} W_T = W_0 , \tag{2.4}$$

with probability one for a positive definite matrix W_0. The matrices W_T and W_0 are both referred to as the distance or weighting matrix. The GMM estimator β_T is the solution of the minimization problem (2.3). Under fairly general regularity conditions, the GMM estimator β_T is a consistent estimator for arbitrary distance matrices.[4] The selection of the distance matrix which yields an (asymptotically) efficient GMM estimator is discussed below in Section 2.3.

---

[3] See Section 5 for a definition and a discussion of stationarity.
[4] Some regularity conditions that are important for applied researchers are discussed in Section 5.

2.2. Distributions of GMM estimators

Suppose that a central limit theorem applies to the disturbance of GMM, $u_t = f(X_t, \beta_0)$, so that $(1/\sqrt{T}) \sum_{t=1}^{T} u_t$ has an (asymptotic) normal distribution with mean zero and the covariance matrix Ω in large samples.[5] If u_t is serially uncorrelated, $\Omega = E(u_t u_t')$. If u_t is serially correlated,

$$\Omega = \lim_{j \to \infty} \sum_{-j}^{j} E(u_t u_{t-j}') . \tag{2.5}$$

Some authors refer to Ω as the long run covariance matrix of u_t. Let $\Gamma = E(\partial f(X_t, \beta)/\partial \beta')$ be the expectation of the $q \times p$ matrix of the derivatives of $f(X_t, \beta)$ with respect to β and assume that Γ has a full column rank. Under suitable regularity conditions, $\sqrt{T}(\beta_T - \beta_0)$ approximately has a normal distribution with mean zero and the covariance matrix

$$\text{Cov}(W_0) = \{\Gamma' W_0 \Gamma\}^{-1} \{\Gamma' W_0 \Omega W_0 \Gamma\} \{\Gamma' W_0 \Gamma\}'^{-1} \tag{2.6}$$

in large samples.

2.3. Optimal choice of the distance matrix

When the number of moment conditions (q) is equal to the number of parameters to be estimated (p), the system is just identified. In the case of a just identified system, the GMM estimator does not depend on the choice of distance matrix. When $q > p$, there exist overidentifying restrictions and different GMM estimators are obtained for different distance matrices. In this case, one may choose the distance matrix that results in (asymptotically) efficient GMM estimator. Hansen (1982) shows that the covariance matrix (6) is minimized when $W_0 = \Omega^{-1}$.[6] With this choice of the distance matrix, $\sqrt{T}(\beta_T - \beta_0)$ approximately has a normal distribution with mean zero and the covariance matrix

$$\text{Cov}(\Omega^{-1}) = \{\Gamma' \Omega^{-1} \Gamma\}^{-1} , \tag{2.7}$$

in large samples.

Let Ω_T be a consistent estimator of Ω. Then $W_T = \Omega_T^{-1}$ is used to obtain β_T. The resulting estimator is called the optimal or efficient GMM estimator. It should be noted, however, that it is optimal given $f(X_t, \beta)$. In the context of instrumental variable estimation, this means that instrumental variables are given. The optimal selection of instrumental variables is discussed in Section 9. Let Γ_T be a consistent estimator of Γ. Then the standard errors of the optimal GMM estimator β_T are calculated as square roots of the diagonal elements of

[5] An advantage of the GMM estimation is that a strong distributional assumption such that u_t is normally distributed is not necessary.

[6] The covariance matrix is minimized in the sense that $\text{Cov}(W_0) - \text{Cov}(\Omega^{-1})$ is a positive semidefinite matrix for any positive definite matrix W_0.

$T^{-1}\{\Gamma'_T \Omega_T^{-1} \Gamma_T\}^{-1}$. The appropriate method for estimating Ω depends on the model. This problem is discussed in Section 6. It is usually easier to estimate Γ by $\Gamma_T = (1/T) \sum_{t=1}^{T} (\partial f(X_t, \beta_T)/\partial \beta')$ than to estimate Ω. In linear models or in some simple nonlinear models, analytical derivatives are readily available. In nonlinear models, numerical derivatives are often used.

2.4. A chi-square test for the overidentifying restrictions

In the case where there are overidentifying restrictions ($q > p$), a chi-square statistic can be used to test the overidentifying restrictions. One application of this test is to test the validity of moment conditions implied by Euler equations for optimizing problems of economic agents. This application is discussed in Section 8. Hansen (1982) shows that T times the minimized value of the objective function $TJ_T(\beta_T)$, has an (asymptotic) chi-square distribution with $q - p$ degree of freedom if $W_0 = \Omega^{-1}$ in large samples. This test is sometimes called Hansen's J test.[7]

3. Special cases

This section shows how linear regressions and nonlinear instrumental variable estimation are embedded in the GMM framework above.

3.1. Ordinary least squares

Consider a linear model,

$$y_t = x'_t \beta_0 + e_t, \tag{3.1}$$

where y_t and e_t are scalar random variables, x_t is a p-dimensional random vector. OLS estimation can be embedded in the GMM framework by letting $X_t = (y_t, x'_t)'$, $f(X_t, \beta) = x_t(y_t - x'_t \beta)$, $u_t = x_t e_t$, and $p = q$. Thus the moment conditions (2.1) become the orthogonality conditions:

$$E(x_t e_t) = 0. \tag{3.2}$$

Since this is the case of a just identified system, the distance matrix W_0 does not matter. Note that the OLS estimator minimizes $\sum_{t=1}^{T} (y_t - x'_t \beta)^2$ while the GMM estimator minimizes $(\sum_{t=1}^{T} (x_t(y_t - x'_t \beta)))'(\sum_{t=1}^{T} (x_t(y_t - x'_t \beta)))$. It turns out that the GMM estimator coincides with the OLS estimator in this case. To see this, note that $(\sum_{t=1}^{T} (x_t(y_t - x'_t \beta)))'(\sum_{t=1}^{T} (x_t(y_t - x'_t \beta)))$ can be minimized by setting β_T so that $\sum_{t=1}^{T} f(X_t, \beta) = 0$ in the case of a just identified system. This implies that $\sum_{t=1}^{T} x_t y_t = \{\sum_{t=1}^{T} x_t x'_t\} \beta_T$. Thus as long as $\{\sum_{t=1}^{T} x_t x'_t\}$ is invertible, $\beta_T = \{\sum_{t=1}^{T} x_t x'_t\}^{-1} \{\sum_{t=1}^{T} x_t y_t\}$. Hence the GMM estimator β_T coincides with the OLS estimator.

---

[7] See Newey (1985) for an analysis of the asymptotic power properties of this chi-square test.

3.2. Linear instrumental variables regressions

Consider the linear model (3.1) and let z_t be a q-dimensional random vector of instrumental variables. Then instrumental variable regressions are embedded in the GMM framework by letting $X_t = (y_t, x'_t, z'_t)$, $f(X_t, \beta) = z_t(y_t - x'_t\beta)$, and $u_t = z_t e_t$. Thus the moment conditions become the orthogonality conditions

$$E(z_t e_t) = 0. \tag{3.3}$$

In the case of a just identified system ($q = p$), the instrumental variable regression estimator $\{\Sigma_{t=1}^{T} z_t x'_t\}^{-1}\{\Sigma_{t=1}^{T} z_t y_t\}$ coincides with the GMM estimator. For the case of an overidentifying system ($q > p$), that Sargan's (1958) generalized instrumental variables estimators, the two-stage least-squares estimators, and the three-stage least-squares estimators (for multiple regressions) can be interpreted as optimal GMM estimators when e_t is serially uncorrelated and conditionally homoskedastic.[8]

3.3. Nonlinear instrumental variables estimation

GMM is often used in the context of nonlinear instrumental variable estimation (NLIV). Section 8 presents some examples of applications based on the Euler equation approach. Let $g(x_t, \beta)$ be a k-dimensional vector of functions and $e_t = g(x_t, \beta_0)$. Suppose that there exist conditional moment restrictions, $E[e_t | I_t] = 0$, where $E[\cdot | I_t]$ signifies the mathematical expectation conditioned on the information set I_t. Here it is assumed that $I_t \subset I_{t+1}$ for any t. Let z_t be a $q \times k$ matrix of random variables that are in the information set I_t.[9] Then by the law of iterative expectations, we obtain unconditional moment restrictions:

$$E[z_t g(x_t, \beta_0)] = 0. \tag{3.4}$$

Thus we let $X_t = (x'_t, z'_t)'$ and $f(X_t, \beta) = z_t g(x_t, \beta)$ in this case. Hansen (1982) points out that the NLIV estimators discussed by Amemiya (1974), Jorgenson and Laffont (1974), and Gallant (1977) can be interpreted as optimal GMM estimators when e_t is serially uncorrelated and conditionally homoskedastic.

4. Extensions

This section explains econometric methods that are closely related to the basic GMM framework in Section 2.

---

[8] This interpretation can be seen by examining the first order condition for the minimization problem (2.3).

[9] In some applications, z_t is a function of β. This does not cause any problem as long as the resulting $f(X_t, \beta)$ can be written as a function of β and a stationary random vector X_t.

4.1. Sequential estimation

This subsection discusses sequential estimation (or two-step estimation). Consider a system

$$f(X_t, \beta) = \begin{bmatrix} f_1(X_t, \beta^1) \\ f_2(X_t, \beta^1, \beta^2) \end{bmatrix}, \tag{4.1}$$

where $\beta = (\beta^1, \beta^{2\prime})'$, β^i is a p_i-dimensional vector of parameters, and f_i is a q_i-dimensional vector of functions. Although it is possible to estimate β^1 and β^2 simultaneously, it may be computationally convenient to estimate β^1 from $f_1(X_t, \beta^1)$ first, and then estimate β^2 from $f_2(X_t, \beta^1, \beta^2)$ in a second step (see, e.g., Barro, 1977, and Atkeson and Ogaki, 1991, for examples of empirical applications). In general, the asymptotic distribution of the estimator of β^2 is affected by estimation of β^1 (see, e.g., Newey, 1984, and Pagan, 1984, 1986). A GMM computer program for a sequential estimation can be used to calculate the correct standard errors that take into account of these effects from estimating β^1. If there are overidentifying restrictions in the system, an econometrician may wish to choose the second step distance matrix in an efficient way. The choice of the second step distance matrix is analyzed by Hansen, Heaton and Ogaki (1992).

Suppose that the first step estimator β_T^1 minimizes

$$J_{1T}(\beta^1) = \left\{ \frac{1}{T} \sum_{t=1}^{T} f_1(X_t, \beta^1) \right\}' W_{1T} \left\{ \frac{1}{T} \sum_{t=1}^{T} f_1(X_t, \beta^1) \right\}, \tag{4.2}$$

and that the second step estimator minimizes

$$J_{2T}(\beta^2) = \left\{ \frac{1}{T} \sum_{t=1}^{T} f_2(X_t, \beta_T^1, \beta^2) \right\}' W_{2T} \left\{ \frac{1}{T} \sum_{t=1}^{T} f_2(X_t, \beta_T^1, \beta^2) \right\}, \tag{4.3}$$

where W_{iT} is a positive semidefinite matrix that converges to W_{i0} with probability one. Let Γ_{ij} be the $q_i \times p_j$ matrix $E(\partial f_i / \partial \beta_j')$ for $i = 1, 2$ and $j = 1, 2$.

Given an arbitrary W_{10}, the optimal choice of the second step distance matrix is $W_{20} = (\Omega^*)^{-1}$, where

$$\Omega^* = [-\Gamma_{21}(\Gamma_{11} W_{10} \Gamma_{11})^{-1} \Gamma_{11} W_{10}, I] \Omega \begin{bmatrix} -\Gamma_{21}(\Gamma_{11} W_{10} \Gamma_{11})^{-1} \Gamma_{11} W_{10} \\ I \end{bmatrix}. \tag{4.4}$$

With this choice of W_{20}, $(1/\sqrt{T}) \sum_{t=1}^{T} (\beta_T^2 - \beta_0^2)$ has an (asymptotic) normal distribution with mean zero and the covariance matrix

$$\{\Gamma_{22}'(\Omega^*)^{-1} \Gamma_{22}\}^{-1}, \tag{4.5}$$

and $T J_{2T}(\beta_T^2)$ has an (asymptotic) chi-square distribution with $q_2 - p_2$ degrees of freedom. It should be noted that if $\Gamma_{21} = 0$, then the effect of the first step estimation can be ignored because $\Omega^* = \Omega_{22} = E(f_2(X_t, \beta_0) f_2(X_t, \beta_0)')$.

4.2. GMM with deterministic trends

This subsection discusses how GMM can be applied to time series with deterministic trends (see Eichenbaum and Hansen, 1990, and Ogaki, 1988, 1989, for empirical examples). Suppose that X_t is trend stationary rather than stationary. In particular, let

$$X_t = d(t, \beta_0^1) + X_t^* , \tag{4.6}$$

where $d(t, \beta_1)$ is a function of deterministic trends such as time polynomials and X_t^* is detrended X_t. Assume that X_t^* is stationary with $E(X_t^*) = 0$ and that there are q_2 moment conditions

$$E(f_2(X_t^*, \beta_0^1, \beta_0^2)) = 0 . \tag{4.7}$$

Let $\beta = (\beta^{1\prime}, \beta^{2\prime})'$, $f_1(X_t, \beta^1) = X_t - d(t, \beta^1)$ and $f(X_t, \beta) = [f_1(X_t, \beta^1)', f_2(X_t^*, \beta^1, \beta^2)']'$. Then GMM can be applied to $f(X_t, \beta)$ to estimate β^1 and β^2 simultaneously as shown in Hansen, Heaton and Ogaki (1992).

4.3. Cross-sectional data and panel data

The GMM procedure has been applied to cross-sectional data and panel data. Empirical examples include the work of Holtz-Eakin, Newey and Rosen (1988), Hotz, Kydland and Sedlacek (1988), Hotz and Miller (1988), Shaw (1989), Altug and Miller (1990, 1991), Engen (1991) and Runkle (1991). These authors also discuss many of the econometrics issues. Avery, Hansen and Hotz (1983) develop a method to apply GMM to probit models in panel data. Chamberlain's (1992) comment on Keane and Runkle (1992) discusses applications of GMM to obtain efficient estimators in panel data. Arellano and Bond (1991) discuss a GMM estimation method in panel data and propose a test of serial correlation. The reader who is interested in econometric issues that are not treated in this subsection is referred to these papers and references therein. This section explains a simple method which allows for both a general form of serial correlation and different serial correlation structures for different groups in panel data (see, e.g., Atkeson and Ogaki, 1991, and Ogaki and Atkeson, 1991, for empirical examples).

Consider a panel data set in which there exist H groups, indexed by $h = 1, \ldots, H$ (for example, H villages). Suppose that group h consists of N_h individuals and that the data set contain T periods of observations. Let $N = \Sigma_{h=1}^H N_h$ be the total number of individuals. It is assumed that N is large relative to T, so that we drive N to infinity with T fixed in considering asymptotic distributions. Assume that individuals $i = 1, \ldots, N_1$ are in group 1 and $i = N_1 + 1, \ldots, N_1 + N_2$ are in group 2, etc. It is assumed that $\lim_{N \to \infty} N_h / N = \delta_h$ exists. Let x_{it} be a random vector of economic variables for an individual i at period t and $f_t(x_{it}, \beta)$ be a q_t-dimensional vector of functions. Let $q = \Sigma_{t=1}^T q_t$, $X_i = (x_{i1}', \ldots, x_{iT}')'$ and $f(X_i, \beta) = (f_1(x_{i1})', \ldots, f_T(x_{iT})')'$.

Thus a general form of serial correlation is allowed by stacking disturbance terms with different dates as different disturbance terms rather than treating them as different observations of one disturbance term. It is assumed that X_i is identically and independently distributed over the individuals. Assume that there exist q moment restrictions:

$$E_N(f(X_i, \beta_0)) = 0, \tag{4.8}$$

where E_N is the unconditional expectation operator over individuals. A subscript N is attached to emphasize that the expectation is taken over individuals.

It is assumed that a law of large number applies to f, so that

$$\lim_{N \to \infty} \frac{1}{N} \sum_{i=M_{h-1}+1}^{M_h} f(X_i, \beta) = \delta_h E_n(f(X_i, \beta)) \tag{4.9}$$

for each $h = 1, \ldots, H$, where $M_h = N_1 + \cdots + N_h$ and $M_0 = 0$. Let $g_N(X_i, \beta) = (\Sigma_{i=1}^{N_1} f(X_i, \beta)', \ldots, \Sigma_{i=M_{H-1}+1}^{M_H} f(X_i, \beta)')'$. Then the GMM estimator β_N minimizes a quadratic form

$$J_N(\beta) = \left\{ \frac{1}{N} g_N(X_i, \beta) \right\}' W_N \left\{ \frac{1}{N} g_N(X_i, \beta) \right\}, \tag{4.10}$$

where W_N is a positive definite matrix, which satisfies

$$\lim_{N \to \infty} W_N = W_0. \tag{4.11}$$

with probability one for a positive definite matrix W_0.

Suppose that a central limit theorem applies to the disturbance of GMM, $u_i = f(X_i, \beta_0)$, so that $(1/\sqrt{N}) \Sigma_{i=M_{h-1}+1}^{M_h} u_i$ has a (asymptotic) normal distribution with mean zero and the covariance matrix Ω_h for large N. Here $\Omega_h = \delta_h E_N(u_i u_i')$ for any individual i in group h. Let Ω be a matrix that has Ω_h in the h-th diagonal block for $h = 1, \ldots, H$ and the zeros elsewhere. With these modifications, the GMM framework explained in Section 2 can be applied to this problem with all limits taken as $N \to \infty$ instead of $T \to \infty$. For example, $W_0 = \Omega^{-1}$ leads to an efficient GMM estimator and $NJ(\beta_N)$ has an asymptotic chi-square distribution with this choice of the distance matrix.

In estimating rational expectations models with panel data, it is important to recognize that Euler equation of the form $E(u_{it} | I_t) = 0$ does not imply $(1/N) \Sigma_{i=1}^N u_{it}$ converges in probability to zero as N is increased. The sample counterpart of $E(u_{it} | I_t)$ converges to zero as the number of time periods increases, but not as the number of households increases (see, e.g., Chamberlain, 1984; Keane and Runkle, 1990; Runkle, 1991, and Hayashi, 1992). This problem is especially severe when idiosyncratic shocks are insured away and only aggregate shocks are present as implied by models with complete markets (see, e.g., Altug and Miller, 1990). One way to deal with this problem is to use a panel data set with relatively large number of time periods and to use asymptotic theories as $T\to\infty$. In this case, issues of nonstationarity must be addressed as in applications to time series data (see Section 5 below).

4.4. Minimum distance estimation

Minimum distance estimation (MDE) provides a convenient way of obtaining an efficient estimator that imposes nonlinear restrictions (see, e.g., Chiang, 1956; Ferguson, 1958, and Chamberlain, 1982, 1984) and a test statistic for these restrictions. See Altug and Miller (1991) and Atkeson and Ogaki (1991) for examples of empirical applications. The MDE is closely related to GMM and a GMM program can be used to implement the MDE (see, e.g., Ogaki, 1993a). Suppose that θ_T is an unrestricted estimator for a $p + s$ vector of parameters θ_0, and that $\sqrt{T}(\theta_T - \theta_0)$ converges in distribution to a normal random vector with the covariance matrix Ω. Consider nonlinear restrictions such that

$$\phi(\beta_0) = \theta_0 , \qquad (4.12)$$

where β_0 is a p-dimensional vector of parameters. The MFE estimator β_T minimizes a quadratic form

$$J_T(\beta) = \{\phi(\beta) - \theta_T\}'W_T\{\phi(\beta) - \theta_T\} , \qquad (4.13)$$

for a positive semidefinite matrix W_T that converges to a positive definite matrix W_0 with probability one. As with GMM estimation, $W_0 = \Omega^{-1}$ is the optimal choice of the distance matrix and $TJ_T(\beta_T)$ has an (asymptotic) chi-square distribution with s degrees of freedom. The null hypothesis (4.12) is rejected when this statistic is larger than critical values obtained from chi-square distributions.

5. Important assumptions

In this section, I discuss two assumptions under which large sample properties of GMM estimators are derived. These two assumptions are important in the sense that applied researchers have encountered cases where these assumptions are obviously violated unless special care is taken.

5.1. Stationarity

In Hansen (1982), X_t is assumed to be (strictly) stationary.[10] A time series $\{X_t: -\infty < t < \infty\}$ is stationary if the joint distribution of $\{X_t, \ldots, X_{t+\tau}\}$ are identical to those of $\{X_{t+s}, \ldots, X_{t+s+\tau}\}$ for any t, τ and s. Among other things,

[10] In the context of cross sectional data discussed in Section 4.3, this assumption corresponds with the assumption that X_t is identically distributed over individuals in cross sectional data.

this implies that when they exist, the unconditional moments $E(X_t)$ and $E(X_t X'_{t+\tau})$ cannot depend on t for any τ. Thus this assumption rules out deterministic trends, autoregressive unit roots, and unconditional heteroskedasticity.[11] On the other hand, conditional moments $E(X_{t+\tau} | I_t)$ and $E(X_{t+\tau} X'_{t+\tau+s} | I_t)$ can depend on I_t. Thus the stationarity assumption does *not* rule out the possibility that X_t has conditional heteroskedasticity. It should be noted that it is not enough for $u_t = f(X_t, \beta_0)$ to be stationary. It is required that X_t is stationary, so that $f(X_t, \beta)$ is stationary for all admissible β, not just for $\beta = \beta_0$ (see Section 8.1.4 for an example in which $f(X_t, \beta)$ is stationary but $f(X_t, \beta)$ is not for other values of β).

Since many macroeconomic variables exhibits nonstationarity, this assumption can be easily violated in applications unless a researcher is careful. As explained in Section 4.2, nonstationarity in the form of trend stationarity can be treated with ease. In order to treat another popular form of nonstationarity, unit-root nonstationarity, researchers have used transformations such as first differences or growth rates of variables (see Section 8 for examples).

5.2. Identification

Another important assumption of Hansen (1982) is related to identification. Let

$$J_0(\beta) = \{E[f(X_t, \beta)]\}' W_0 \{E[f(X_t, \beta)]\} . \tag{5.1}$$

The identification assumption is that β_0 is the unique minimizer of $J_0(\beta)$.[12] Since $J_0(\beta) \geq 0$ and $J_0(\beta_0) = 0$, β_0 is a minimizer. Hence this assumption requires $J_0(\beta)$ to be strictly positive for any other β. This assumption is obviously violated if $f(X_t, \beta) \equiv 0$ for some β which did not have any economic meaning (see Section 8 for examples).

6. Covariance matrix estimation

An estimate of Ω is necessary to calculate asymptotic standard errors for the GMM estimator from (2.6) and to utilize the optimal distance matrix Ω^{-1}.

---

[11] Gallant (1987) and Gallant and White (1988) show that the GMM strict stationarity assumption can be relaxed to allow for unconditional heteroskedasticity. This does *not* mean that X_t can exhibit nonstationarity by having deterministic trends or autoregressive unit roots. Some of their regularity conditions are violated by these popular forms of nonstationarity. It is still necessary to detrend X_t if it is trend stationary. For this reason, the strict stationarity assumption is emphasized in the context of time series applications rather than the fact that this assumption can be relaxed.

[12] Hansen, Heaton and Ogaki (1992) show that without the identification assumption, a sequence of sets of minimizers for (2.3) converges to the set of minimizers with probability one when all other regularity conditions hold.

This section discusses estimation methods for Ω. In the following, it is assumed that a consistent estimator β_T for β_0 is available to form an estimate of u_t by $f(X_t, \beta_T)$. In most applications, the first stage GMM estimator is obtained by setting $W_T = I$, and then Ω_T is estimated from the first stage GMM estimate β_T. The second stage GMM estimator is formed by setting $W_T = \Omega_T^{-1}$. This procedure can be iterated by using the second stage GMM estimate to form the distance matrix for the third stage GMM estimator, and so on. Kocherlakota's (1990) and Ferson and Foerster's (1991) Monte Carlo simulations suggest that the GMM estimator and test statistics have better small sample properties when this procedure is iterated. It is preferable to iterate this procedure until a convergence is obtained. In some nonlinear models, this may be costly in terms of time. In such cases, it is recommended that the third stage GMM be used because the gains from further iterations may be small.

6.1. Serially uncorrelated disturbance

This subsection treats the case where $E(u_t u_{t+\tau}) = 0$ for $\tau \neq 0$.[13] In this case, Ω can be estimated by $(1/T) \sum_{t=1}^{T} f(X_t, \beta_T) f(X_t, \beta_T)'$. In the models considered in Section 3, this is White's (1980) heteroskedasticity consistent estimator. For example, consider the NLIV model. In this model, $u_t = z_t g(X_t, \beta_0)$ and

$$\frac{1}{T} \sum_{t=1}^{T} f(X_t, \beta_T) f(X_t, \beta_T)' = \frac{1}{T} \sum_{t=1}^{T} z_t g(X_t, \beta_T) g(X_t, \beta_T)' z_t' .$$

Note that u_t is serially uncorrelated if $e_t = g(X_t, \beta_0)$ is in the information set I_{t+1} because

$$E(u_t u_{t+j}') = E(E(u_t u_{t+j}' \mid I_{t+1})) = E(u_t E(u_{t+j}') \mid I_{t+1})) = 0 \quad \text{for } j \geq 1 .$$

In some cases, conditional homoskedasticity is assumed and an econometrician may wish to impose this on his estimate for Ω. Then

$$\frac{1}{T} \sum_{t=1}^{T} z_t \left\{ \frac{1}{T} \sum_{t=1}^{T} g(X_t, \beta_T) g(X_t, \beta_T)' \right\} z_t'$$

is used to estimate Ω.

6.2. Serially correlated disturbance

This subsection treats the case where the disturbance is serially correlated in the context of time series analysis.

6.2.1. Unknown order of serial correlation
In many applications, the order of serial correlation is unknown. Let $\Phi(\tau) =$

---

[13] In the context of the cross sectional model of Section 4.3, this means that the disturbance is uncorrelated across households, even though it can be serially correlated.

$E(u_t u'_{t-\tau})$,

$$\Phi_T(\tau) = \frac{1}{T} \sum_{t=\tau+1}^{T} f(X_t, \beta_T) f(X_{t-\tau}, \beta_T)' \quad \text{for } \tau \geq 0, \tag{6.1}$$

and $\Phi_T(\tau) = \Phi_T(-\tau)'$ for $\tau < 0$. Many estimators for Ω in the literature have the form

$$\Omega_T = \frac{T}{T-p} \sum_{\tau=-T+1}^{T-1} k\left(\frac{\tau}{S_T}\right) \Phi_T(\tau), \tag{6.2}$$

where $k(\cdot)$ is a real-valued kernel, and S_T is a bandwidth parameter. The factor $T/(T-p)$ is a small sample degrees of freedom adjustment.[14] See Andrews (1991) for example of kernels. The estimators of Hansen (1982) and White (1984, p. 152) use the truncated kernel; the Newey and West (1987a) estimator uses the Bartlett kernel; and the estimator of Gallant (1987, p. 533) uses Parzen kernel. The estimators corresponding to these kernels place zero weights on $\Phi(\tau)$ for $\tau \geq S_T$, so that $S_T - 1$ is called the lag truncation number. Andrews (1991) advocates an estimator which uses the quadratic spectral (QS) kernel, which does not place zero weights on any $\Phi(\tau)$ for $|\tau| \leq T - 1$.[15]

One important problem is how to choose the bandwidth parameter S_T. Andrews (1991) provides formulas for optimal choice of the bandwidth parameter for a variety of kernels. These formulas include unknown parameters and Andrews proposes automatic bandwidth estimators in which these unknown parameters are estimated from the data. His method involves two steps. The first step is to parameterize to estimate the law of motion of the disturbance u_t. The second step is to calculate the parameters for the optimal bandwidth parameter from the estimated law of motion. In his Monte Carlo simulations, Andrew uses an AR(1) parameterization for each term of the disturbance. This seems to work well in the models he considers.

Another issue is the choice of the kernel. One serious problem with the truncated kernel is that the corresponding estimator is not guaranteed to be positive semidefinite. Andrews (1991) shows that the QS kernel is an optimal kernel in the sense that it minimizes asymptotic MSE among the estimators of the form (6.3) that are guaranteed to be positive semidefinite. His Monte Carlo simulations show that the QS kernel and the Parzen kernel work better than the Bartlett kernel in most of the models he considers. He also finds that even the estimators based on the QS kernel and the Parzen kernel are not satisfactory in the sense that the standard errors calculated from these estimators are not accurate in small samples when the amount of autocorrelation is large.

Because the estimators of the form (6.3) do not seem satisfactory, Andrews

---

[14] Some other forms of small sample adjustments have been used (see, e.g., Ferson and Foerster, 1991).

[15] Hansen (1992) relaxes an assumption made by these authors to show the consistency of the kernel estimators.

and Monahan (1992) propose an estimator based on a VAR prewhitening. The intuition behind this is that the estimators of the form (6.2) only take care of MA components of u_t and cannot handle the AR components well in small samples. The first step in the VAR prewhitening method is to run a VAR of the form

$$u_t = A_1 u_{t-1} + A_2 u_{t-2} + \cdots + A_n u_{t-n} + v_t . \tag{6.3}$$

Note that the model (6.3) need not be a true model in any sense. Then the estimated VAR is used to form an estimate of v_t and an estimator of the form (6.2) is applied to the estimated v_t to estimate the long-run variance of v_t, Ω^*. The estimator based on the QS kernel with the automatic bandwidth parameter can be applied to v_t for example. Then the sample counterpart of the formula

$$\Omega = \left[I - \sum_{\tau=1}^{n} A_\tau \right]^{-1} \Omega^* \left[I - \sum_{\tau=1}^{n} A'_\tau \right]^{-1} \tag{6.4}$$

is used to form an estimate of Ω. Andrews and Monahan use the VAR of order one in their Monte Carlo simulations. Their results suggest that the pre-whitened kernel estimator performs better than the nonprewhitened kernel estimators for the purpose of calculating standard errors of estimators.[16]

In sum, existing Monte Carlo evidence for estimation of Ω recommends VAR prewhitening and either the QS or Parzen kernel estimator together with Andrew's (1991) automatic bandwidth parameter. Though the QS kernel estimator may be preferred to the Parzen kernel estimator because of its asymptotic optimality, it takes more time to calculate the QS kernel estimators than the Parzen kernel estimators. This difference may be important when estimation is repeated many times.

6.2.2. Known order of serial correlation

In some applications, the order of serial correlation is known. Assume that the order of serial correlation is known to be s. For example, consider the NLIV model of Section 3. Suppose that e_t is in the information set I_{t+s+1}. In multi-period forecasting models, s is greater than one (see Hansen and Hodrick (1980, 1983) and Section 8 of the present paper for examples). Then $E(u_t u'_{t+\tau}) = E(E(u_t u'_{t+\tau} \mid I_{t+s+1})) = E(u_t E(u'_{t+\tau}) \mid I_{t+s+1})) = 0$ for $\tau \geq s+1$. Thus the order of serial correlation of u_t is s and u_t has an MA(s) structure in this case.

In this case, there exist the zero restrictions on the autocovariances that $\Phi(\tau) = 0$ for $|\tau| > s$. Imposing these zero restrictions on the estimator of Ω leads to a more efficient estimator.[17] Since $\Omega = \sum_{\tau=-s}^{s} \Phi(\tau)$ in this case, a

[16] Park and Ogaki's (1991b) Monte Carlo simulations suggest that the VAR prewhitening improves estimators of Ω in the context of cointegrating regressions.

[17] In some applications, the order of serial correlation may be different for different terms of u_t. The econometrician may wish to impose these restrictions.

natural estimator is

$$\Omega_T = \frac{T}{T-p} \sum_{\tau=-s}^{s} \Phi_T(\tau) , \qquad (6.5)$$

which is the truncated kernel estimator. Hansen and Hodrick (1980) study a multi-period forecasting model that leads to $s \geq 1$. They use (6.5) with conditional homoskedasticity imposed (as discussed at the end of Section 6.1). Their method of calculating the standard errors for linear regressions is known as Hansen–Hodrick correction.

A possible problem with the estimator (6.5) is that Ω_T is not guaranteed to be positive semidefinite if $s \geq 1$. In applications, researchers often encounter cases where Ω_T is invertible but is not positive semidefinite. If this happens, $W_T = \Omega_T^{-1}$ should not be used to form the optimal GMM estimator (e.g., Newey and West, 1987a). There exist at least two ways to handle this problem. One way is to use Eichenbaum, Hansen and Singleton's (1988) modified Durbin's method. The first step of this method is to estimate the VAR (6.3) for a large n by solving the Yule Walker equations. The second step is to estimate an MA(s) representation

$$u_t = B_1 v_{t-1} + \cdots + B_s v_{t-s} + e_t , \qquad (6.6)$$

by running estimated u_t on estimated lagged v_t. Then the sample counterpart of

$$\Omega = (I + B_1 + \cdots + B_s) \mathrm{E}(e_t e_t')(I + B_1 + \cdots + B_s)' \qquad (6.7)$$

is used to form an estimate of Ω that imposes the zero restrictions. One problem with this method is that this is not reliable when the number of elements in $u(t)$ is large compared with the sample size because too many parameters in (6.3) need to be estimated. The number of elements in $u(t)$ needs to be kept as small as possible when this method is to be used.

Another method is to use one of the kernel estimators of the form (6.2) (or VAR prewhitened kernel estimators if s is large) that are guaranteed to be positive semidefinite. When this method is used, the zero restrictions should *not* be imposed even though $\Phi(\tau)$ is known to be zero for $|\tau| > s$. In order to illustrate this in a simple example, consider the case where $s = 1$ and Newey–West's (1987a) Bartlett kernel estimator is used. Then

$$\Omega_T = \frac{T}{T-p} \sum_{\tau=-l}^{l} \frac{T-|\tau|}{T} \Phi_T(\tau) , \qquad (6.8)$$

where $l = S_T - 1$ is the lag truncation number. If $l = 1$ is used to impose the zero restrictions, then Ω_T converges to $\Phi(0) + \frac{1}{2}\Phi(1) + \frac{1}{2}\Phi(-1)$, which is not equal to Ω. Thus l needs to be increased as T is increased to obtain a consistent estimator. On the other hand, if $l > 1$ is used and the zero restrictions are imposed by setting $\Phi_T(\tau)$ in (6.8) to zero for $|\tau| > 1$, then the resulting estimator is no longer guaranteed to be positive semidefinite.

7. Hypothesis testing and specification tests

This section discusses specification tests and Wald, Lagrange multiplier (LM), and likelihood ratio type statistics for hypothesis testing. Gallant (1987), Newey and West (1987b), and Gallant and White (1988) have considered these three test statistics, and Eichenbaum, Hansen and Singleton (1988) considered the likelihood ratio type test for GMM (or a more general estimation method that includes GMM as a special case).

Consider s nonlinear restrictions

$$H_0: R(\beta_0) = r , \tag{7.1}$$

where R is an $s \times 1$ vector of functions. The null hypothesis H_0 is tested against the alternative that $R(\beta_0) \neq r$. Let $\Lambda = \partial R / \partial \beta'$ and Λ_T be a consistent estimator for Λ. It is assumed that Λ is of rank s. If the restrictions are linear, then $R(\beta_0) = \Lambda \beta_0$ and Λ is known. Let β_T^u be an unrestricted GMM estimator and β_T^r be a GMM estimator that is restricted by (9.1). It is assumed that $W_0 = \Omega^{-1}$ is used for both estimators.

The Wald test statistic is

$$T(R(\beta_T^u) - r)' [\Lambda_T (\Gamma_T' \Omega_T^{-1} \Gamma_T)^{-1} \Lambda_T']^{-1} (R(\beta_T^u) - r) , \tag{7.2}$$

where Ω_T, Γ_T, and Λ_T are estimated from β_T^u. The Lagrange multiplier test statistic is

$$\mathrm{LM}_T = \frac{1}{T} \sum_{t=1}^{T} f(X_t, \beta_T^r)' \Omega_T^{-1} \Gamma_T \Lambda_T' (\Lambda_T \Lambda_T')^{-1}$$

$$\times [\Lambda_T (\Gamma_T' \Omega_T^{-1} \Gamma_T)^{-1} \Lambda_T']^{-1} (\Lambda_T \Lambda_T')^{-1}$$

$$\times \Lambda_T \Gamma_T' \Omega_T^{-1} \sum_{t=1}^{T} f(X_t, \beta_T^r) , \tag{7.3}$$

where Ω_T, Γ_T, and Λ_T are estimated from β_T^r. Note that in linear models LM_T is equal to (7.2), where Ω_T, Γ_T, and Λ_T are estimated from β_T^r rather than β_T^u. The likelihood ratio type test statistic is

$$T(J_T(\beta_T^r) - J_T(\beta_T^u)) , \tag{7.4}$$

which is T times the difference between the minimized value of the objective function when the parameters are restricted and the minimized value of the objective function when the parameters are unrestricted. It is important that the same estimator for Ω is used for both unrestricted and restricted estimation for the likelihood ratio type test statistic. Under a set of regularity conditions, all three test statistics have asymptotic chi-square distributions with s degrees of freedom. The null hypothesis is rejected when these statistics are larger than critical values obtained from chi-square distributions.

Existing Monte Carlo evidence suggests that the small sample distributions of the Lagrange multiplier test and the likelihood ratio type test are better approximated by their asymptotic distributions than those of the Wald test (see Gallant, 1987). Another disadvantage of the Wald test is that in general, the test result for nonlinear restrictions depends on the parameterization (see, e.g., Gregory and Veall, 1985, and Phillips and Park, 1988).

Though the chi-square test for the overidentifying restrictions discussed in Section 2 has been frequently used as a specification test in applications of GMM, other specification tests applicable to GMM are available. These include tests developed by Singleton (1985), Andrews and Fair (1988), Hoffman and Pagan (1989), Ghysels and Hall (1990a,b,c), Hansen (1990), Dufour, Ghysels and Hall (1991), and Andrews (1993). Some of these tests are discussed by Hall (1993).

8. Empirical applications

The GMM estimation has been frequently applied to rational expectations models. This section discusses examples of these applications.[18] The main purpose is not to provide a survey of the literature but to illustrate applications.[19] Problems that researchers have encountered in applying GMM and procedures they have used to address these problems are discussed. In this section, the notations for the NLIV model of Section 3 will be used.

8.1. Euler equation approach to models of consumption

8.1.1. Hansen and Singleton's (1982) model
Hansen and Singleton (1982) show how to apply GMM to a consumption-based capital asset pricing model (C-CAPM). Consider an economy in which a representative agent maximizes

$$\sum_{t=1}^{\infty} \delta^t E(U(t) \mid I_0) \tag{8.1}$$

subject to a budget constraint. Hansen and Singleton (1982) use an isoelastic intraperiod utility function

$$U(t) = \frac{1}{1-\alpha} (C_t^{1-\alpha} - 1), \tag{8.2}$$

where C_t is real consumption at t and $\alpha > 0$ is the reciprocal of the intertemporal elasticity of substitution (α is also the relative risk aversion coefficient for consumption in this model). The standard Euler equation for the optimi-

---

[18] Some other empirical examples are mentioned in Section 4.
[19] See Cochrane and Hansen (1992) for a survey on asset pricing puzzles.

zation problem is

$$\frac{E[\delta C_{t+1}^{-\alpha} R_{t+1} \mid I_t]}{C_t^{-\alpha}} = 1 , \tag{8.3}$$

where R_{t+1} is the (gross) real return of any asset.[20] The observed C_t they use is obviously nonstationary, although the specific form of nonstationarity is not clear (difference stationary or trend stationary, for example). Hansen and Singleton use C_{t+1}/C_t in their econometric formulation, which is assumed to be stationary.[21] Then let $\beta = (\delta, \alpha)$, $X_t = (C_{t+1}/C_t, R_{t+1})'$, and $g(X_t, \beta) = \delta(C_{t+1}/C_t)^{-\alpha} R_{t+1} - 1$ in the notations for the NLIV model in Section 2.[22] Stationary variables in I_t, such as the lagged values of X_t, are used for instrumental variables z_t. In this case, u_t is in I_{t+1}, and hence u_t is serially uncorrelated. Hansen and Singleton (1984) find that the chi-square test for the overidentifying restrictions rejects their model especially when nominal risk free bond returns and stock returns are used simultaneously.[23] Their finding is consistent with Mehra and Prescott's (1985) equity premium puzzle. When the model is rejected, the chi-square test statistic does not provide much guidance as to what causes the rejection. Hansen and Jagannathan (1991) develop a diagnostic that could provide such guidance.[24]

8.1.2. Time aggregation

The use of consumption data for the C-CAPM is subject to a time aggregation problem (see, e.g., Hansen and Sargent, 1983a,b) because consumers can make decisions at intervals much finer than the observed frequency of the data and because the observed data consist of average consumption over a period of time.

In linear models, the time aggregation means that the disturbance has an MA(1) structure and the instrumental variables need to be lagged an additional period. See, e.g., Grossman, Melino and Shiller (1987), Hall (1988), and Hansen and Singleton (1988) for applications to C-CAPM and Heaton (1990)

---

[20] This asset pricing equation can be applied to any asset returns. For example, Mark (1985) applies the Hansen–Singleton model in asset returns in foreign exchange markets.

[21] In the following, assumptions about trend properties of equilibrium consumption are made. The simplest model in which these assumptions are satisfied is a pure exchange economy, with the trend assumptions imposed on endowments.

[22] When multiple asset returns are used, $g(X_t, \beta)$ becomes a vector of functions.

[23] Cochrane (1989) points out that the utility that the representative consumer loses by deviating from the optimal consumption path is very small in the Hansen–Eingleton model and in Hall's (1978) model. In this sense, the Hansen–Singleton test and Hall's test may be too sensitive to economically small deviations caused by small costs of information and transactions.

[24] Garber and King (1983) criticize Hansen and Singleton's methodology by pointing out that their estimators for nonlinear models are not consistent when unknown preference shocks are present. Nason (1991) applies GMM to his linear permanent income model with stochastic preference shocks.

and Christiano, Eichenbaum and Marshall (1991) for applications to Hall (1978) type permanent income models.

It is sometimes not possible for GMM to take into account the effect of time aggregation. For example, Heaton (1991) uses the method of simulated moments (MSM) for his nonlinear asset pricing model with time-nonseparable preferences in taking time aggregation into account. Bossaerts (1989), Duffie and Singleton (1989), MacFadden (1989), Pakes and Pollard (1989), Lee and Ingram (1991), and Pearson (1991), among others, have studied asymptotic properties of MSM.

8.1.3. Habit formation and durability

Many researchers have considered effects of time-nonseparability in preferences on asset pricing. Let us replace (8.2) by

$$U(t) = \frac{1}{1-\alpha} (S_t^{1-\alpha} - 1),$$ (8.4)

where S_t is service flow from consumption purchases. Purchases of consumption and service flows are related by

$$S_t = a_0 C_t + a_1 C_{t-1} + a_2 C_{t-2} + \cdots.$$ (8.5)

This type of specification for the time-nonseparability has been used by Mankiw (1982), Hayashi (1985), Dunn and Singleton (1986), Eichenbaum, Hansen and Singleton (1988), Ogaki (1988, 1989), Eichenbaum and Hansen (1990), Heaton (1991, 1993), Cooley and Ogaki (1991), Ferson and Constantinides (1991), Ferson and Harvey (1991) and Ogaki and Park (1993) among others.[25] Depending on the values of the a_τ, the model (8.4) leads to a model with habit formation and/or durability. Constantinides (1990) argues that habit formation could help solve the equity premium puzzle. He shows how the intertemporal elasticity of substitution and the relative risk aversion coefficient depend on the a_τ and α parameters in a habit formation model.

In this subsection, I will discuss applications by Ferson and Constantinides (1991), Cooley and Ogaki (1991) and Ogaki and Park (1993) to illustrate econometric formulations.[26] In their models, it is assumed that $a_\tau = 0$ for $\tau \geq 2$. Let us normalize a_0 to be one, so that $\beta = (\delta, \alpha, a_1)$. The asset pricing equation takes the form

$$\frac{E[\delta \{S_{t+1}^{-\alpha} + \delta a_1 S_{t+2}^{-\alpha}\} R_{t+1} \,|\, I_t]}{E[S_t^{-\alpha} + \delta a_1 S_{t+1}^{-\alpha} \,|\, I_t]} = 1.$$ (8.6)

Then let $e_t^0 = \delta(S_{t+1}^{-\alpha} + \delta a_1 S_{t+2}^{-\alpha}) R_{t+1} - (S_t^{-\alpha} + \delta a_1 S_{t+1}^{-\alpha})$. Though Euler equation

---

[25] Some of these authors allow for a possibility of a deterministic technological progress in the transformation technology (8.4).

[26] Eichenbaum, Hansen and Singleton (1988) and Eichenbaum and Hansen (1990) consider similar models with nonseparable preferences across goods.

(8.6) implies that $E(e_t^0 | I_t) = 0$, this cannot be used as the disturbance for GMM because both of the two regularity assumptions discussed in Section 5 of the present paper are violated. These violations are caused by the nonstationarity of C_t and by the three sets of trivial solutions, $\alpha = 0$ and $1 + \delta a_1 = 0$; $\delta = 0$ and $\alpha = \infty$; and $\delta = 0$ and $a_1 = \infty$ with α positive. Ferson and Constantinides (1991) solve both of these problems by defining $e_t = e_t^0 / \{S_t^{-\alpha}(1 + \delta a_1)\}$. Since $S_t^{-\alpha}$ is in I_t, $E(e_t | I_t) = 0$. The disturbance is a function of $S_{t+\tau}/S_t$ ($\tau = 1, 2$) and R_{t+1}. When C_{t+1}/C_t and R_t are assumed to be stationary, $S_{t+\tau}/S_t$ and the disturbance can be written as a function of stationary variables.

One problem that researchers have encountered in these applications is that $C_{t+1} + a_1 C_t$ may be negative when a_1 is close to minus one. In a nonlinear search for β_T or in calculating numerical derivatives, a GMM computer program will stall if it tries a value of a_1 that makes $C_{t+1} + a_1 C_t$ negative for any t. Atkeson and Ogaki (1991) have encountered similar problems in estimating fixed subsistence levels from panel data. One way to avoid this problem is to program the function $f(X_t, \beta)$, so that the program returns very large numbers as the values of $f(X_t, \beta)$ when nonadmissible parameter values are used. However, it is necessary to ignore these large values of $f(X_t, \beta)$ when calculating numerical derivatives. This can be done by suitably modifying programs that calculate numerical derivatives.[27]

8.1.4. Multiple-good models

Mankiw, Rotemberg and Summers (1985), Dunn and Singleton (1986), Eichenbaum, Hansen and Singleton (1988), Eichenbaum and Hansen (1990) and Osano and Inoue (1991), among others, have estimated versions of multiple-good C-CAPM. Basic economic formulations in these multiple-good models will be illustrated in the context of a simple model with one durable good and one nondurable good.

Let us replace (8.2) by Houthakker's (1960) addilog utility function that Miron (1986), Ogaki (1988, 1989), and Osano and Inoue (1991) among others have estimated:

$$U(t) = \frac{1}{1 - \alpha} (C_t^{1-\alpha} - 1) + \frac{\theta}{1 - \eta} (K_t^{1-\eta} - 1),\qquad(8.7)$$

where C_t is nondurable consumption and K_t is household capital stock from purchases of durable consumption good D_t.[28] The stock of durables is assumed to depreciate at a constant rate $1 - a$, where $0 \leqslant a < 1$:

$$K_t = aK_t + D_t .\qquad(8.8)$$

---

[27] Ogaki (1993a) explains these modifications for Hansen/Heaton/Ogaki GMM package.

[28] Since the addilog utility function is not quasi-homothetic in general, the distribution of initial wealth affects the utility function of the representative consumer. The existence of a representative consumer under complete markets is discussed by Ogaki (1990) for general concave utility functions and by Atkeson and Ogaki (1991) for extended addilog utility functions.

Alternatively, K_t can be considered as service flow in (8.5) with $a_\tau = a^\tau$. When $\alpha \neq \eta$, preferences are not quasi homothetic. In practice, the data for K_t is constructed from data for an initial stock K_0, and for D_t for $t = 1, \ldots, T$. Let P_t be the intratemporal relative price of durable and nondurable consumption. Then the intraperiod first order condition that equates the relative price with the marginal rate of substitution is

$$
P_t = \frac{\theta E\left(\sum_{\tau=1}^{\infty} \delta^\tau a^\tau K_{t+\tau}^{-\eta} \mid I_t \right)}{C_t^{-\alpha}}.
\tag{8.9}
$$

Assume that D_{t+1}/D_t is stationary. Then $K_{t+\tau}/D_t$ is stationary for any τ because $K_{t+\tau}/D_t = \sum_{\tau=0}^{\infty} a^\tau D_{t+\tau}/D_t$. From (8.9),

$$
\frac{P_t C_t^{-\alpha}}{D_t^{-\eta}} = \theta E\left[\sum_{\tau=1}^{\infty} \delta^\tau a^\tau \left(\frac{K_{t+\tau}}{D_t} \right)^{-\eta} \mid I_t \right].
\tag{8.10}
$$

Assume that the variables in I_t are stationary.[29] Then (8.10) implies that the $P_t C_t^{-\alpha}/D_t^{-\eta}$ is stationary because the right-hand side of (8.10) is stationary. Taking natural logs, we conclude that $\ln(P_t) - \alpha \ln(C_t) + \eta \ln(D_t)$ is stationary. This restriction is called the stationarity restriction.

From (8.9), define

$$
e_t^0 = P_t C_t^{-\alpha} - (1 - \delta a F)^{-1} \theta K_t^{-\eta},
\tag{8.11}
$$

where F is the forward operator. The first order condition (8.9) implies that $E(e_t^0 \mid I_t) = 0$. One problem is that e_t^0 involves $K_{t+\tau}$ for τ from 0 to infinity, so that e_t^0 cannot be used as the disturbance for GMM. To solve this problem, define $e_t = (1 - \delta a F) e_t^0$. Note that e_t involves only C_t, C_{t+1}, and K_t and that $E[e_t \mid I_t] = 0$. Hence e_t forms the basis of GMM. The only remaining problem is to attain stationarity. One might think it is enough to divide e_t^0 by $K_t^{-\eta}$, so that the resulting e_t is stationary as implied by the stationarity restriction. It should be noted that it is *not* enough for $e_t = g(X_t, \beta_0)$ to be stationary, rather it is also necessary for $g(X_t, \beta)$ to be stationary for $\beta \neq \beta_0$. Hence if α and η are unknown and C_t or D_t is difference stationary, GMM cannot be applied to the first order condition (8.9).[30] Ogaki (1988, 1989) assumes that C_t and D_t are trend stationary and applies the method of Section 4 above to utilize the detrended version of e_t. In these applications, the restrictions on the trend coefficients and the curvature parameters α and η implied by the stationarity restriction are imposed on the GMM estimators. Imposing the stationarity restrictions also leads to more reasonable point estimates for α and η.

Eichenbaum, Hansen and Singleton (1988) and Eichenbaum and Hansen

---

[29] If I_t includes nonstationary variables, assume that the right-hand side of (8.9) is the same as the expectation conditioned on the stationary variables in I_t.

[30] Cointegrating regressions can be used for this case as explained below.

(1990) use the Cobb–Douglas utility function, so that α and η are known to be one.[31] They allow preferences to be nonseparable across goods and time-nonseparable, but the stationarity restriction is shown to hold. In this case, the stationarity restriction implies that $P_t C_t^{-1}/K_t^{-1}$ is stationary. This transformation does not involve any unknown parameters. Hence this transformation is used to apply GMM to their intraperiod first order conditions.

8.1.5. The cointegration-Euler equation approach

When at least one of C_t and D_t is difference stationary, the stationarity restriction implies cointegration as defined by Engle and Granger (1987). Ogaki (1988) and Ogaki and Park (1993) propose to estimate the curvature parameters α and η of the addilog utility function, using a cointegrating regression.[32] Cooley and Ogaki (1991) combine this cointegration approach with the Euler equation approach based on GMM in a two-step procedure. In the first step, curvature parameters are estimated from a cointegrating regression. In the second step, we use this estimated value of α in the asset pricing equation (8.3) and estimate only δ.[33] This two-step procedure does not alter the asymptotic distributions of GMM estimators and test statistics because the cointegrating regression estimator for α is super consistent and converges at a faster rate than $T^{1/2}$.

Cooley and Ogaki (1991) propose a specification test like Hausman's (1978) based on the likelihood ratio type statistic (discussed in Section 7 of the present paper) that tests the cross equation restriction for the cointegrating regression and the GMM disturbance on α. This test has power against the factors that make the two estimates different, such as nonseparability in preferences across goods, measurement errors, and liquidity constraints.

8.1.6. Seasonality

Miron (1986) augments Hansen and Singleton's (1982) model by including deterministic seasonal taste shifters and argues that the empirical rejection of C-CAPM by Hansen and Singleton (1982) and others might be attributable to the use of seasonally adjusted data.[34] Although this is theoretically possible, English, Miron and Wilcox (1989) find that seasonally unadjusted quarterly

---

[31] Also see Ogaki (1992) for a discussion of the stationarity restriction implied by the Cobb–Douglas utility function.

[32] Ogaki and Park (1993) use Park's (1992) canonical cointegrating regressions and Park and Ogaki's (1991a) seemingly unrelated canonical regressions (also see Ogaki, 1993b,c).

[33] In the applications of Cooley and Ogaki (1991) and Ogaki and Park (1993), time-non-separability in preferences is allowed for nondurable consumption and the asset pricing equation (8.6) is used to estimate δ and a_1. In their applications, the first and second goods are assumed to be separable in preferences over time. See Ogaki (1992) for an application of the cointegration approach without this separability assumption.

[34] It should be noted that a deterministic seasonal dummy can be viewed as an artificial stationary and ergodic stochastic process (see, e.g., Ogaki, 1988, pp. 26–27). Hence GMM can be applied to models with deterministic seasonal taste shifts.

data reject asset pricing equations at least as strongly as seasonally adjusted data.[35] Ogaki (1988) also finds similar empirical results for seasonally un-adjusted and adjusted data in the system that involves both asset pricing equations and intraperiod first order conditions.

Singleton (1988) argues that the inclusion of taste shifters in C-CAPM is essentially equivalent to studying directly consumption data with deterministic seasonality removed. This is because we do not obtain much identifying information from seasonal fluctuations about preferences if most of seasonal fluctuations come from seasonal taste shifts.[36] On the other hand, seasonal fluctuations may contain useful identifying information about production functions if production functions are relatively stable over the seasonal cycle. Braun and Evans (1991b) utilize such identifying information.

Ferson and Harvey (1991) construct seasonally unadjusted monthly data and estimate a C-CAPM with time-nonseparable preferences. They find that seasonal habit persistence is empirically significant. Heaton (1993) also finds evidence for seasonal habit formation in Hall (1978) type permanent income models.[37]

8.1.7. State-nonseparable preferences

Epstein and Zin (1991) estimate a model with state-nonseparable preferences specification in which the life time utility level V_t at period t is defined recursively by

$$V_t = \{C_t^{1-\alpha} + \delta E[V_{t+1}^{1-\alpha} \mid I_t]\}^{(1-\rho)/(1-\alpha)} , \tag{8.12}$$

where $\alpha > 0$ and $\rho > 0$. The asset pricing equation for this model is

$$E[\delta^*(R_{t+1}^e)^\eta (C_{t+1}/C_t)^\theta R_{t+1}] = 1 , \tag{8.13}$$

for any asset return R_{t+1}, where $\delta^* = \delta^{(1-\alpha)/(1-\rho)}$, $\eta = (\rho - \alpha)/(1-\rho)$, $\theta = -\rho(1-\alpha)/(1-\rho)$, and R_{t+1}^e is the (gross) return of the optimal portfolio (R_{t+1}^e is the return from period t to $t+1$ of a security that pays C_t every period forever). Epstein and Zin use the value-weighted return of shares traded on the New York Stock Exchange as R_{t+1}^e. Thus Roll's (1977) critique of CAPM is relevant here as Epstein and Zin discuss.

Even though (8.13) holds for $R_{t+1} = R_{t+1}^e$, the identification assumption discussed in Section 5 is violated for this choice of R_{t+1} because there exists a trivial solution, $(\delta^*, \eta, \theta) = (1, 1, 0)$, for $g(X_t, \beta) = 0$. When multiple returns that include R_{t+1}^e are used simultaneously, then the whole system can satisfy the identification assumption but the GMM estimators for this partially

---

[35] Hoffman and Pagan (1989) obtain similar results.

[36] Beaulieu and Miron (1991) cast doubt on the view that negative output growth in the first quarter (see, e.g., Barskey and Miron, 1989) is caused by negative technology seasonal by observing negative output growth in the southern hemisphere.

[37] See Ghysels (1990, especially Section I.3) for a survey of the economic and econometric issues of seasonality.

unidentified system are likely to have bad small sample properties. A similar problem arises when R_{t+1} does not include R^e_{t+1} but includes multiple equity returns whose linear combination is close to R^e_{t+1}. It should be noted that Epstein and Zin avoid these problems by carefully choosing returns to be included as R_{t+1} in their system.

8.2. Monetary models

In some applications, monetary models are estimated by applying GMM to Euler equations and/or intratemporal first order conditions. Singleton (1985), Ogaki (1988), Finn, Hoffman and Schlagenhauf (1990), Bohn (1991) and Sill (1992) estimate cash-in-advance models, Poterba and Rotemberg (1987), Finn, Hoffman and Schlagenhauf (1990), Imrohoroglu (1991), and Eckstein and Leiderman (1992) estimate money-in-the-utility-function (MIUF) models, and Marshall (1992) estimates a transactions–cost monetary model.

It turns out that cash-in-advance models involve only minor variations on the asset pricing equation (8.3) as long as the cash-in-advance constraints are binding and C_t is a cash good (in the terminology of Lucas and Stokey (1987)). However, nominal prices of consumption, nominal consumption, nominal asset returns are aligned over time in a different way in monetary models than they are in Hansen and Singleton's (1982) model. Information available to agents at time t is also considered in a different way. As a result, instrumental variables are lagged one period more than in the Hansen–Singleton model, and u_t has an MA(1) structure (time aggregation has the same effects in linear models as discussed above). There is some tendency for chi-square test statistics for the overidentifying restrictions to be more favorable for the timing conventions suggested by cash-in-advance models (see Finn, Hoffman and Schlagenhauf, 1990, and Ogaki, 1988). Ogaki (1988) focuses on monetary distortions in relative prices for a cash good and a credit good and does not find monetary distortions in the U.S. data he examines.

8.3. Linear rational expectations models

There are two alternative methods to apply GMM to linear rational expectations models. The first method applies GMM directly to linear Euler equations implied by the optimization problems of economic agents. There are many empirical applications of this method, including those of Pindyck and Rotemberg (1983), Fair (1989), and Eichenbaum (1990). In linear models, two-stage least squares estimators and three-stage least squares estimators can be considered as special cases of GMM estimators when the disturbances of the regressions are serially uncorrelated and conditionally homoskedastic.

The second method is developed by Hansen and Sargent (1982), which applies GMM to Hansen and Sargent's (1980, 1981a) linear rational expectations models. This method imposes nonlinear restrictions implied by Wiener–Kolmogorov prediction formulas (see, e.g., Hansen and Sargent, 1981b) on a

VAR representation. Compared with the first method, this second method requires more assumptions about the stochastic law of motion of economic variables but utilizes more restrictions and is (asymptotically) more efficient when these assumptions are valid. West (1989) extends Hansen and Sargent's (1980) formulas to include deterministic terms, and Hansen and Sargent (1991, Chapters 7, 8, 9) provide the continuous time counterparts of these formulas. Maximum likelihood estimation has been used more frequently for the Hansen–Sargent type linear rational expectations model than GMM (see, e.g., Sargent, 1978, 1981a,b; Eichenbaum, 1984; Finn, 1989; and Giovannini and Rotemberg, 1989) even though Hansen and Sargent's (1982) method can be applied to these models. West (1987, 1988a) does not impose the nonlinear restrictions on his estimates but tests these restrictions. West (1987, 1988a) uses West's (1988b) results when difference stationary variables are involved.[38]

8.4. Calculating standard errors for estimates of standard deviation, correlation and autocorrelation

In many macroeconomic applications, researchers report estimates of standard deviations, correlations, and autocorrelations of economic variables. It is possible to use a GMM program to calculate standard errors for these estimates, in which the serial correlation of the economic variables is taken into account (see, e.g., Backus, Gregory and Zin, 1989, and Backus and Kehoe, 1992).

For example, let x_t and y_t be economic variables of interest which are assumed to be stationary and let $X_t = (x_t, y_t)$ and $f(X_t, \beta) = (x_t, x_t^2, y_t, y_t^2, x_t y_t, x_t x_{t-1})' - \beta$. Then the parameters to be estimated are the population moments: $\beta_0 = (E(x_t), E(x_t^2), E(y_t), E(y_t^2), E(x_t y_t), E(x_t x_{t-1}))$. Applying GMM to $f(X_t, \beta)$, one can obtain an estimate of β_0, β_T, and an estimate of the covariance matrix of $T^{1/2}(\beta_T - \beta_0)$, Σ_T. In most applications, the order of serial correlation of $(x_t, x_t^2, y_t, y_t^2, x_t y_t)'$ is unknown, and its long-run covariance matrix, Ω, can be estimated by any of the methods of Section 6 (such as Andrews and Monahan's prewhitened QS kernel estimation method).

Standard deviations, correlations, and autocorrelations are nonlinear functions of β_0. Hence one can use the delta method to calculate the standard errors of estimates of these statistics. Let $g(\beta_0)$ be the statistic of interest. For example, $g(\beta_0) = (\beta_{02} - \beta_{01}^2)^{1/2}$ for the standard deviation of x_t. Then $g(\beta_T)$ is a consistent estimator of $g(\beta_0)$. By the mean value theorem, $g(\beta_T) = g(\beta_0) + \Lambda_T(\beta_T - \beta_0)$, where Λ_T is the derivative of $g(\cdot)$ evaluated at an intermediate point between β_T and β_0. Since Λ_T converges in probability to $\Lambda_0 = \partial g(\beta_0)/\partial \beta'$, $(g(\beta_T) - g(\beta_0))$ has an approximate normal distribution with the variance $(1/T)\Lambda_T \Sigma_T \Lambda_T'$ in large samples.

---

[38] It should be noted that West (1986b) treats the special case of one difference stationary regressor with nonzero drift (which is relevant for his applications cited here). His results do not extend to multiple regressors (see, e.g., Park and Phillips, 1988).

8.5. Other empirical applications

Though I have focused on consumption-based pricing models that relate asset returns to the intertemporal decisions of consumers, GMM can be applied to production-based asset pricing models that relate asset returns to the intertemporal investment decisions (see, e.g., Braun, 1991, and Cochrane, 1991, 1992).

Singleton (1988) discusses the use of GMM in estimating real business cycle models. Christiano and Eichenbaum (1992) develop a method to estimate real business cycle models, using GMM. They apply their method to U.S. data. Braun (1990), Burnside, Eichenbaum and Rebelo (1993), Braun and Evans (1991a,b) have estimated real business cycle models, among others.

There has not been much work to apply GMM to models of asymmetric information. An exception is an application of GMM to a model of moral hazard by Margiotta and Miller (1991).

9. Further issues

9.1. Optimal choice of instrumental variables

In the NLIV model discussed in Section 3, there are infinitely many possible instrumental variables because any variable in I_t can be used as an instrument. Hansen (1985) characterizes an efficiency bound (that is, a greatest lower bound) for the asymptotic covariance matrices of the alternative GMM estimators and optimal instruments that attain the bound. Since it can be time consuming to obtain optimal instruments, an econometrician may wish to compute an estimate of the efficiency bound to assess efficiency losses from using ad hoc instruments. Hansen (1985) also provides a method for calculating this bound for models with conditionally homoskedastic disturbance terms with an invertible MA representation.[39] Hansen, Heaton and Ogaki (1988) extend this method to models with conditionally heteroskedastic disturbances and models with an MA representation that is not invertible.[40] Hansen and Singleton (1988) calculate these bounds and optimal instruments for a continuous time financial economic model.

9.2. GMM and semi-parametric estimation

In many empirical applications, the density of the random variables is unknown. Chamberlain (1987, 1992), Newey (1988), and Hansen (1988) among others have studied the relationship between GMM estimators and

---

[39] Hayashi and Sims' (1983) estimator is applicable to this example.

[40] Heaton and Ogaki (1991) provide an algorithm to calculate efficiency bounds for a continuous time financial economic model based on Hansen, Heaton and Ogaki's (1988) method.

efficient semi-parametric estimators in this environment. Chamberlain (1992) links optimal GMM estimators in panel data to recent semi-parametric work, such as that of Robinson (1987, 1991) and Newey (1990). Technically, Hansen (1988) shows that the GMM efficiency bound coincides with the semi-parametric efficiency bound for finite parameter maximum likelihood estimators for dependent processes. Chamberlain (1987) shows similar results for independently and identically distributed processes.

In order to give an intuitive explanation for the relationship between GMM and semi-parametric estimation, let us consider a simple model that is a special case of a model that Newey (1988) studies:[41]

$$y_t = x_t' \beta_0 + e_t, \tag{9.1}$$

where the disturbance e_t is a scalar iid random variable with unknown symmetric density $\phi(e_t)$, and x_t is p-dimensional vector of nonstochastic exogenous variables. The MLE of β, β_T, would maximize the log likelihood

$$L = \sum \log \phi(y_t - x_t' \beta), \tag{9.2}$$

and would solve

$$\sum d_t(\beta_T) = 0 \tag{9.3}$$

if ϕ were known, where $d = \partial \log \phi(y_t - x_t \beta)/\partial \beta$ is the score of β. An efficient semi-parametric estimator is formed by estimating the score by a nonparametric method and emulating the MLE.

On the other hand, GMM estimators can be formed from moment restrictions that are implied by the assumption that e_t is distributed symmetrically distributed: $E(x_t e_t) = 0$, $E(x_t e_t^3) = 0$, etc. Noting that the score is of the form $x_t \xi(e_t)$ for a function $\xi(\cdot)$, the GMM estimator with these moment restrictions approximates $\xi(e_t)$ with a polynomial in e_t. Because the density of e_t is assumed to be symmetric, $\xi(e_t)$ is an odd function of e_t and thus odd functions are used to approximate $\xi(e_t)$. With a sufficiently high order polynomial, the unknown score is well approximated and the GMM estimator is also efficient.

9.3. Small sample properties

Unfortunately, there has not been much work done on small sample properties of GMM estimators. Tauchen (1986) shows that GMM estimators and test statistics have reasonable small sample properties for data produced by simulations for a C-CAPM. Ferson and Foerster (1991) find similar results for a model of expected returns of assets as long as GMM is iterated for estimation of Ω. Kocherlakota (1990) uses preference parameter values of $\delta = 1.139$ and $\alpha = 13.7$ (in (8.1) and (8.2) above) in his simulations for a C-CAPM that is similar to Tauchen's model. While these parameter values do not violate any

---

[41] The material that follows in this subsection was suggested by Adrian Pagan.

theoretical restrictions for existence of an equilibrium, they are much larger than the estimates of these preference parameters by Hansen and Singleton (1982) and others. Kocherlakota shows that GMM estimators for these parameters are biased downward and the chi-square test for the overidentifying restrictions tend to reject the null too frequently compared with its asymptotic size. Mao (1990) reports that the chi-square test overrejects for more conventional values of these preference parameters in his Monte Carlo simulations.

Tauchen (1986) investigates small sample properties of Hansen's (1985) optimal instrumental variables GMM estimators. He finds that the optimal estimators do not perform well in small samples as compared to GMM estimators with ad hoc instruments. Tauchen (1986) and Kocherlakota (1990) recommend small number of instruments rather than large number of instruments when ad hoc instruments are used.

Nelson and Startz (1990) perform Monte Carlo simulations to investigate the properties of t-ratios and the chi-square test for the overidentifying restrictions in the context of linear instrumental variables regressions. Their work is concerned with small sample properties of these statistics when the instruments are poor (in the sense that it is weakly correlated with explanatory variables). They find that the chi-square test tends to reject the null too frequently compared with its asymptotic distribution and that t-ratios tend to be too large when the instrument is poor. Their results for t-ratios may seem counterintuitive because one might expect that the consequence of having a poor instrument would be a large standard error and a low t-ratio. Their results may be expected to carry over to NLIV estimation. Some of the findings by Kocherlakota (1990) and Mao (1990) that are apparently conflicting with those of Tauchen (1986) may be related to this problem of poor instruments (see Canova, Finn and Pagan, 1991, for a related discussion).

Arellano and Bond (1991) report Monte Carlo results on GMM estimators for dynamic panel data models. They report that the GMM estimators have substantially smaller variances than commonly used Anderson and Hsiao's (1981) estimators in their Monte Carlo experiments. They also report that the small sample distributions of the serial-correlation tests they study are well approximated by their asymptotic distributions.

10. Concluding remarks

Many researchers have used GMM to estimate nonlinear rational expectations models with aggregate time series data. There are many other possible applications of GMM and GMM programs. We will probably see more applications of GMM to panel data and to models with asymmetric information in the near future. Other uses of a GMM program discussed here include the implementation of minimum distance estimation, the calculation of standard errors that take into account serially correlated disturbances, and generating inferences that take into account the effects of the first estimation step in sequential (or two-step) estimation. Pagan and Pak (1993) present a method for using a GMM program to calculate tests for heteroskedasticity.

Acknowledgment

This is a revised version of 'An Introduction to the Generalized Method of Moments'. I thank R. Anton Braun, Mario Crucini, Mark Dwyer, Eric Ghysels, Lars Peter Hansen, Esfandiar Maasoumi, and Adrian Pagan for their suggestions and/or clarifications, and Changyong Rhee for a conversation that motivated this work. All remaining shortcomings are mine.

References

Amemiya, T. (1974). The nonlinear two-stage least-squares estimator. *J. Econometrics* **2**, 105–110.
Altug, S. and R. A. Miller (1990). Household choices in equilibrium. *Econometrica* **58**, 543–570.
Altug, S. and R. A. Miller (1991). Human capital, aggregate shocks and panel data estimation. Economic Research Center NORC Working Paper No. 91-1.
Anderson, T. W. and C. Hsiao (1981). Estimation of dynamic models with error components. *J. Amer. Statist. Assoc.* **76**, 598–606.
Andrews, D. W. K. (1991). Heteroskedasticity and autocorrelation consistent covariance matrix estimation. *Econometrica* **59**, 817–858.
Andrews, D. W. K. (1993). Tests for parameter instability and structural change with unknown change point. *Econometrica*, to appear.
Andrews, D. W. K. and R. Fair (1988). Inference in econometric models with structural change. *Rev. Econom. Stud.* **55**, 615–640.
Andrews, D. W. K. and J. C. Monahan (1992). An improved heteroskedasticity and autocorrelation consistent covariance matrix estimator. *Econometrica* **60**, 953–966.
Arellano, M. and S. Bond (1991). Some tests of specification for panel data: Monte Carlo evidence and an application to employment equations. *Rev. Econom. Stud.* **58**, 277–297.
Atkeson, A. and M. Ogaki (1991). Wealth-varying intertemporal elasticity of substitution: Evidence from panel and aggregate data. RCER Working Paper No. 303, University of Rochester.
Avery, R., L. Hansen and V. Hotz (1983). Multiperiod probit models and orthogonality condition estimation. *Internat. Econom. Rev.* **24**, 21–36.
Backus, D. K., A. W. Gregory and S. E. Zin (1989). Risk premiums in the term structure: Evidence from artificial economies. *J. Monetary Econom.* **24**, 371–399.
Backus, D. K. and P. J. Kehoe (1992). International evidence on the historical properties of business cycles. *Amer. Econom. Rev.* **82**, 864–888.
Barro, R. J. (1977). Unanticipated money growth and unemployment in the United States. *Amer. Econom. Rev.* **67**, 101–115.
Barksey, R. B. and J. A. Miron (1989). The seasonal cycle and the business cycle. *J. Politic. Econom.* **97**, 503–534.
Beaulieu, J. and J. A. Miron (1991). A cross country comparison of seasonal cycles and business cycles. *Econom. J.* **102**, 772–788.
Bohn, H. (1991). On cash-in advance models of money demand and asset pricing. *J. Money Credit Banking* **23**, 224–242.
Bossaerts, P. (1989). The asymptotic normality of method of simulated moments estimators of option pricing models. Manuscript.

Braun, P. A. (1991). Asset pricing and capital investment: Theory and evidence. Manuscript, Northwestern University.

Braun, R. A. (1990). The dynamic interaction of distortionary taxes and aggregate variables in postwar U.S. data. Manuscript, University of Virginia.

Braun, R. A. and C. L. Evans (1991a). Seasonality in equilibrium business cycle theories. Institute for Empirical Macroeconomics Discussion Paper No. 45.

Braun, R. A. and C. L. Evans (1991b). Seasonal Solow residuals and Christmas: A case for labor hoarding and increasing returns. Manuscript.

Burnside, C., M. Eichenbaum and S. Rebelo (1993). Labor hoarding and the business cycle. *J. Politic. Econom.*, to appear.

Canova, F., M. Finn and A. Pagan (1991). Econometric issues in the analysis of equilibrium models. Manuscript.

Chamberlain, G. (1982). Multivariate regression models for panel data. *J. Econometrics* **18**, 5–46.

Chamberlain, G. (1984). Panel data. In: Z. Griliches and M. D. Intriligator, eds., *Handbook of Econometrics*, Vol. 2. North-Holland, Amsterdam,

Chamberlain, G. (1987). Asymptotic efficiency in estimation with conditional moment restrictions. *J. Econometrics* **34**, 305–334.

Chamberlain, G. (1992). Comment: Sequential moment restrictions in panel data. *J. Business Econom. Statist.* **10**, 20–26.

Chiang, C. L. (1956). On regular best asymptotically normal estimates. *Ann. Math. Statist.* **27**, 336–351.

Christiano, L. J. and M. Eichenbaum (1992). Current real business cycle theories and aggregate labor market fluctuations. *Amer. Econom. Rev.* **82**, 430–450.

Christiano, L. J., M. Eichenbaum and D. Marshall (1991). The permanent income hypothesis revisited. *Econometrica* **59**, 397–423.

Cochrane, J. H. (1989). The sensitivity of tests of the intertemporal allocation of consumption to near-rational alternatives. *Amer. Econom. Rev.* **79**, 319–337.

Cochrane, J. H. (1991). Production-based asset pricing and the ling between stock returns and economic fluctuations. *J. Finance* **46**, 207–234.

Cochrane, J. H. (1992). A cross-sectional test of a production-based asset pricing model. Manuscript, University of Chicago.

Cochrane, J. H. and L. P. Hansen (1992). Asset pricing explorations for macroeconomics. In: V. J. Blanchard and S. Fischer, eds., *NBER Macroeconomics Ann. 1992*. MIT Press, Cambridge, MA, 115–165.

Constantinides, G. (1990). Habit formation: A resolution of the equity premium puzzle. *J. Politic. Econom.* **98**, 519–543.

Cooley, T. F. and M. Ogaki (1991). A time series analysis of real wages, consumption, and asset returns under optimal labor contracting: A cointegration–Euler approach. RCER Working Paper No. 285, University of Rochester.

Duffie, D. and K. J. Singleton (1989). Simulated moments estimation of Markov models of asset prices. Manuscript, Graduate School of Business, Stanford University.

Dufour, J.-M., E. Ghysels and A. Hall (1991). Generalized predictive tests and structural change analysis in econometrics. Manuscript, Université de Montréal.

Dunn, K. B. and K. J. Singleton (1986). Modeling the term structure of interest rates under non-separable utility and durability of goods. *J. Financ. Econom.* **17**, 27–55.

Eckstein, Z. and L. Leiderman (1992). Seigniorage and the welfare cost of inflation: Evidence from an intertemporal model of money and consumption. *J. Monetary Econom.* **29**, 389–410.

Eichenbaum, M. (1984). Rational expectations and the smoothing properties of inventories of finished goods. *J. Monetary Econom.* **14**, 71–96.

Eichenbaum, M. (1990). Some empirical evidence on the production level and production cost smoothing models of inventory investment. *Amer. Econom. Rev.* **79**, 853–864.

Eichenbaum, M. and L. P. Hansen (1990). Estimating models with intertemporal substitution using aggregate time series data. *J. Business Econom. Statist.* **8**, 53–69.

Eichenbaum, M., L. P. Hansen and K. J. Singleton (1988). A time series analysis of representative agent models of consumption and leisure choice under uncertainty. *Quart. J. Econom.* **103**, 51–78.

Engen, E. (1991). Stochastic life cycle model with mortality risk: Estimation with panel data. Manuscript, University of California, Los Angeles, CA.

Engle, R. F. and C. W. J. Granger (1987). Co-integration and error correction, representation, estimation, and testing. *Econometrica* **55**, 251–276.

English, W. B., J. A. Miron and D. W. Wilcox (1989). Seasonal fluctuations and the life cycle-permanent income model of consumption: A correction. *J. Politic. Econom.* **97**, 988–991.

Epstein, L. and S. Zin (1991). Substitution, risk aversion and the temporal behavior of asset returns. *J. Politic. Econom.* **99**, 263–286.

Fair, R. C. (1989). The production-smoothing model is alive and well. *J. Monetary Econom.* **24**, 353–370.

Ferguson, T. S. (1958). A method of generating best asymptotically normal estimates with application to the estimation of bacterial densities. *Ann. Math. Statist.* **29**, 336–351.

Ferson, W. E. and G. M. Constantinides (1991). Habit persistence and durability in aggregate consumption. *J. Financ. Econom.* **29**, 199–240.

Ferson, W. E. and S. R. Foerster (1991). Finite sample properties of the generalized method of moments in tests of conditional asset pricing models. Manuscript, University of Chicago and University of Western Ontario.

Ferson, W. E. and C. R. Harvey (1991). Seasonality and consumption-based asset pricing. *J. Finance* **417**, 511–552.

Finn, M. G. (1989). An econometric analysis of the intertemporal general equilibrium approach to exchange rate and current account determination. *J. Internat. Money Finance* **8**, 467–486.

Finn, M. G., D. L. Hoffman and D. E. Schlagenhauf (1990). Intertemporal asset-pricing relationships in barter and monetary economies, an example analysis. *J. Monetary Econom.* **25**, 431–451.

Gallant, A. R. (1977). Three-stage least-squares estimation for a system of simultaneous, nonlinear implicit equations. *J. Econometrics* **5**, 71–88.

Gallant, A. R. (1987). *Nonlinear Statistical Models.* Wiley, New York.

Gallant, A. R. and H. White (1988). *A Unified Theory of Estimation and Inference for Nonlinear Dynamic Models.* Basil Blackwell, New York.

Garber, P. M. and R. G. King (1983). Deep structural excavation? A critique of Euler equation methods. National Bureau of Economic Research Technical Paper No. 31, Cambridge, MA.

Ghysels, E. (1990). On the economics and econometrics of seasonality. Manuscript, University of Montreal.

Ghysels, E. and A. Hall (1990a). Are consumption-based intertemporal capital asset pricing models structural? *J. Econometrics* **45**, 121–139.

Ghysels, E. and A. Hall (1990b). A test for structural stability of Euler conditions parameters estimated via the generalized method of moments estimator. *Internat. Econom. Rev.* **31**, 355–364.

Ghysels, E. and A. Hall (1990c). Testing non-nested Euler conditions with quadrature-based methods of approximation. *J. Econometrics* **46**, 273–308.

Giovannini, A. and J. J. Rotemberg (1989). Exchange-rate dynamics with sticky prices: The Deutsche Mark 1974–1982, *J. Business Econom. Statist.* **7**, 169–178.

Gregory, A. and M. Veall (1985). On formulating Wald tests of nonlinear restrictions. *Econometrica* **53**, 1465–1468.

Grossman, S. J., A. Melino and R. Shiller (1987). Estimating the continuous time consumption based asset pricing model. *J. Business Econom. Statist.* **5**, 315–327.

Hall, A. (1993). Some aspects of generalized method of moments estimation. In: G. S. Maddala, C. R. Rao and H. D. Vinod, eds., *Handbook of Statistics*, Vol. 11. North-Holland, Amsterdam, Chapter 15.

Hall, R. (1978). Stochastic implications of the life cycle-permanent income hypothesis. *J. Politic. Econom.* **86**, 971–987.

Hall, R. (1988). Intertemporal substitution in consumption. *J. Politic. Econom.* **96**, 339–357.

Hansen, B. (1990). Lagrange multiplier tests for parameter instability in non-linear models. Manuscript, University of Rochester.

Hansen, B. (1992). Consistent covariance matrix estimation for dependent heterogeneous processes. *Econometrica* **60**, 967–972.

Hansen, L. P. (1982). Large sample properties of generalized method of moments estimators. *Econometrica* **50**, 1029–1054.

Hansen, L. P. (1985). A method for calculating bounds on the asymptotic covariance matrices of generalized method of moments estimators. *J. Econometrics* **30**, 203–238.

Hansen, L. P. (1988). Semi-parametric efficiency bounds for linear time series models. Manuscript.

Hansen, L. P., J. Heaton and M. Ogaki (1988). Efficiency bounds implied by multiperiod conditional moment restrictions. *J. Amer. Statist. Assoc.* **83**, 863–871.

Hansen, L. P., J. Heaton and M. Ogaki (1992). Lecture notes on generalized method of moments estimators. Manuscript in progress.

Hansen, L. P. and R. J. Hodrick (1980). Forward exchange rates as optimal predictors of future spot rates: An econometric analysis. *J. Politic. Economy.* **88**, 829–853.

Hansen, L. P. and R. J. Hodrick (1983). Risk averse speculation in the forward exchange market: An econometric analysis of linear models. In: J. A. Frenkel, ed., *Exchange Rates and International Macroeconomics*. Univ. of Chicago Press, Chicago, IL.

Hansen, L. P. and R. Jagannathan (1991). Implications of security market data for models of dynamic economies. *J. Politic. Economy* **99**, 225–262.

Hansen, L. P. and T. Sargent (1980). Formulating and estimating dynamic linear rational expectations models. *J. Econom. Dynamics Control* **2**, 7–46.

Hansen, L. P. and T. Sargent (1981a). Linear rational expectations models for dynamically interrelated variables. In: R. E. Lucas Jr and T. J. Sargent, eds., *Rational Expectations and Econometric Practice*. Univ. Minnesota Press, Minneapolis, MN, 127–156.

Hansen, L. P. and T. Sargent (1981b). A note on Wiener–Kolmogorov prediction formulas for rational expectations models. *Econom. Lett.* **8**, 255–260.

Hansen, L. P. and T. Sargent (1982). Instrumental variables procedures for estimating linear rational expectations models. *J. Monetary Econom.* **9**, 263–296.

Hansen, L. P. and T. Sargent (1983a). Aggregation over time and the inverse optimal predictor problem for adaptive expectations in continuous time. *Internat. Econom. Rev.* **24**, 1–20.

Hansen, L. P. and T. Sargent (1983b). The dimensionality of the aliasing problem in models with rational spectral densities. *Econometrica* **51**, 377–387.

Hansen, L. P. and T. Sargent (1991). *Rational Expectations Econometrics*. Westview Press, San Francisco, CA.

Hansen, L. P. and K. J. Singleton (1982). Generalized instrumental variables estimation of nonlinear rational expectations models. *Econometrica* **50**, 1269–1286.

Hansen, L. P. and K. J. Singleton (1984). Errata. *Econometrica* **52**, 267–268.

Hansen, L. P. and K. J. Singleton (1988). Efficient estimation of linear asset pricing models with moving average errors. Manuscript.

Hausman, J. A. (1978). Specification tests in econometrics. *Econometrica* **46**, 1251–1271.

Hayashi, F. (1985). The permanent income hypothesis and consumption durability: Analysis based on Japanese panel data. *Quart. J. Econom.* **100**, 1083–1113.

Hayashi, F. (1992). Comment. *J. Business Econom. Statist.* **10**, 15–19.

Hayashi, F. and C. A. Sims (1983). Nearly efficient estimation of time series models with predetermined, but not exogenous instruments. *Econometrica* **51**, 783–798.

Heaton, J. H. (1991). An empirical investigation of asset pricing with temporally dependent preference specifications. Sloan School of Management Working Paper No. 3245-91-EFA, Massachusetts Institute of Technology, Cambridge, MA.

Heaton, J. H. (1993). The interaction between time-nonseparable preferences and time aggregation. *Econometrica* **61**, 353–385.

Heaton, J. H. and M. Ogaki (1991). Efficiency bound calculations for a time series model with conditional heteroskedasticity. *Econom. Lett.* **35**, 167–171.

Hoffman, D. and A. Pagan (1989). Post-sample prediction tests for generalized method of moments. *Oxford Bull. Econom. Statist.* **51**, 333–344.

Holtz-Eakin, D., W. Newey and H. Rosen (1988). Estimating vector autoregressions with panel data. *Econometrica* **56**, 1371–1395.

Hotz, V. J., F. E. Kydland and G. L. Sedlacek (1988). Intertemporal preferences and labor supply. *Econometrica* **56**, 335–360.

Hotz, V. J. and R. A. Miller (1988). An emporical analysis of life cycle fertility and female labor supply. *Econometrica* **56**, 91–118.

Houthakker, H. S. (1960). Additive preferences. *Econometrica* **28**, 244–257.

Imrohoroglu, S. (1991). An empricial investigation of currency substitution. Manuscript, University of Southern California.

Jorgenson, D. W. and J. Laffont (1974). Efficient estimation of nonlinear simultaneous equations with additive disturbances. *Ann. Econom. Social Measurement* **3**, 615–640.

Keane, M. P. and D. E. Runkle (1990). Testing the rationality of price forecasts: New evidence from panel data. *Amer. Econom. Rev.* **80**, 714–735.

Keane, M. P. and D. E. Runkle (1992). On the estimation of panel-data models with serial correlation when instruments are not strictly exogenous. *J. Business Econom. Statist.* **10**, 1–9.

Kocherlakota, N. (1990). On tests of representative consumer asset pricing models. *J. Monetary Econom.* **26**, 285–304.

Lee, B. S. and B. F. Ingram (1991). Simulation estimation of time-series models. *J. Econometrics* **47**, 197–205.

Lucas, R. E. Jr and N. L. Stokey (1987). Money and interest in a cash-in-advance economy. *Econometrica* **55**, 5491–5513.

MacFadden, D. (1989). A method of simulated moments for estimation of discrete response models without numerical integration. *Econometrica* **57**, 995–1026.

Mankiw, N. G. (1982). Hall's consumption hypothesis and durable goods. *J. Monetary Econom.* **10**, 417–425.

Mankiw, N. G., J. Rotemberg and L. Summers (1985). Intertemporal substitution in macroeconomics. *Quart. J. Econ.* **100**, 225–252.

Mao, C. S. (1990). Hypothesis testing and finite sample properties of generalized method of moments estimators: A Monte Carlo study. Manuscript, Federal Reserve Bank of Richmond.

Margiotta, M. M. and R. A. Miller (1991). Managerial compensation and the cost of moral hazard. Manuscript.

Mark, N. C. (1985). On time varying risk premia in the foreign exchange market: An econometric analysis. *J. Monetary Econom.* **16**, 3–18.

Marshall, D. (1992). Inflation and asset returns in a monetary economy. *J. Finance* **47**, 1315–1342.

Mehra, R. and E. C. Prescott (1985). The equity premium: A puzzle. *J. Monetary Econom.* **15**, 145–161.

Miron, J. A. (1986). Seasonal fluctuations and the life cycle-permanent income model of consumption. *J. Politic. Econom.* **94**, 1258–1279.

Nason, J. M. (1991). The permanent income hypothesis when the bliss point is stochastic. Manuscript, University of British Columbia.

Nelson, C. and R. Startz (1990). The distribution of the instrumental variables estimator and its *t*-ratio when the instrument is a poor one. *J. Business* **63**, S125–S140.

Newey, W. K. (1984). A method of moments interpretation of sequential estimators. *Econom. Lett.* **14**, 201–206.

Newey, W. K. (1985). Generalized method of moments specification testing. *J. Econometrics* **29**, 229–256.

Newey, W. K. (1988). Adaptive estimation of regression models via moment restrictions. *J. Econometrics* **38**, 301–339.

Newey, W. K. (1990). Efficient instrumental variables estimation of nonlinear models. *Econometrica* **58**, 809–837.

Newey, W. K. and K. J. West (1987a). A simple, positive semi-definite, heteroskedasticity and autocorrelation consistent covariance matrix. *Econometrica* **55**, 703–708.

Newey, W. K. and K. J. West (1987b). Hypothesis testing with efficient method of moments estimation. *Internat. Econom. Rev.* **28**, 777–787.

Ogaki, M. (1988). Learning about preferences from time trends. Ph.D. dissertation, University of Chicago.

Ogaki, M. (1989). Information in deterministic trends about preferences. Manuscript, University of Rochester.

Ogaki, M. (1990). Aggregation of intratemporal preferences under complete markets. RCER Working Paper No. 249, University of Rochester.

Ogaki, M. (1992). Engel's law and cointegration. *J. Politic. Econom.* **100**, 1027–1046.

Ogaki, M. (1993a). GMM: A user's guide. RCER Working Paper No. 348, University of Rochester.

Ogaki, M. (1993b). Unit roots in macroeconometrics: A survey. *Monetary Econom. Studies*, to appear.

Ogaki, M. (1993c). CCR: A user's guide. RCER Working Paper No. 349, University of Rochester.

Ogaki, M. and A. Atkeson (1991). Estimating subsistence levels with Euler equations from panel data. Manuscript, University of Rochester and University of Chicago.

Ogaki, M. and J. Y. Park (1993). A cointegration approach to estimating preference parameters. RCER Working Paper No. 209R, University of Rochester.

Osano, H. and T. Inoue (1991). Testing between competitive models of real business cycles. *Internat. Econom. Rev.* **32**, 669–688.

Pakes, A. and D. Pollard (1989). Simulation and the asymptotics of optimization estimators. *Econometrica* **57**, 1027–1058.

Pagan, A. (1984). Econometric issues in the analysis of regressions with generated regressors. *Internat. Econom. Rev.* **25**, 221–247.

Pagan, A. (1986). Two stage and related estimators and their applications. *Rev. Econom. Stud.* **53**, 517–538.

Pagan, A. R. and Y. Pak (1993). Testing for heteroskedasticity. In: G. S. Maddala, C. R. Rao and H. D. Vinod, eds., *Handbook of Statistics*, Vol. 11. North-Holland, Amsterdam, Chapter 18.

Park, J. Y. (1990). Canonical cointegrating regressions. CAE Working Paper No. 88-29R, Cornell University. *Econometrica* **60**, 119–143.

Park, J. Y. and M. Ogaki (1991a). Seemingly unrelated canonical cointegrating regressions. RCER Working Paper No. 280, University of Rochester.

Park, J. Y. and M. Ogaki (1991b). Inference in cointegrated models using VAR prewhitening to estimate shortrun dynamics. RCER Working Paper No. 281, University of Rochester.

Park, J. Y. and P. C. B. Phillips (1988). Statistical inference in regressions with integrated processes: Part 1. *Econometric Theory* **4**, 468–497.

Pearson, N. (1991). A simulated moments estimator of discrete time asset pricing models. Manuscript, University of Rochester.

Phillips, P. C. B. and J. Y. Park (1988). On the formulation of Wald tests of nonlinear restrictions. *Econometrica* **56**, 1065–1083.

Poterba, J. and J. Rotemberg (1987). Money in the utility function: An empirical implementation. In: W. Barnett and K. Singleton, eds., *New Approaches to Monetary Economics*, Proc. 2nd *Internat. Sympos. in Economic Theory and Econometrics*. Cambridge Univ. Press, Cambridge, 219–240.

Pindick, R. S. and J. J. Rotemberg (1983). Dynamic factor demands and the effects of energy price shocks. *Amer. Econom. Rev.* **73**, 1066–1079.

Robinson, P. (1987). Asymptotic efficient estimation of nonlinear models. *Econometrica* **55**, 875–891.

Robinson, P. (1991). Best nonlinear three-stage least squares estimation of certain econometric models. *Econometrica* **59**, 755–786.

Roll, R. (1977). A critique of the asset pricing theory's tests. *J. Financ. Econom.* **4**, 129–176.

Sargan, J. D. (1958). The estimation of economic relationships using instrumental variables. *Econometrica* **26**, 393–415.

Sargent, T. J. (1978). Rational expectations, econometric exogeneity, and consumption. *J. Politic. Economy* **86**, 673–700.

Sargent, T. J. (1981a). The demand for money during hyperinflations under rational expectations. In: R. E. Lucas Jr and T. J. Sargent, eds., *Rotational Expectations and Economic Practice*. Univ. of Minnesota Press, Minneapolis, MN, 429–452.

Sargent, T. J. (1981b). Estimation of dynamic labor demand schedules under rational expectations. In: R. E. Lucas Jr and T. J. Sargent eds., *Rotational Expectations and Econometric Practice*. Univ. of Minnesota Press, Minneapolis, MN, 463–499.

Shaw, K. L. (1989). Life-cycle labor supply with human capital accumulation. *Internat. Econom. Rev.* **30**, 431–456.

Sill, K. (1992). Money and cash-in-advance models: An empirical implementation. Ph.D. dissertation, University of Virginia.

Singleton, K. J. (1985). Testing specifications of economic agents' intertemporal optimum problems in the presence of alternative models. *J. Econometrics* **30**, 391–413.

Singleton, K. J. (1988). Econometric issues in the analysis of equilibrium business cycle models. *J. Monetary Econom.* **21**, 361–386.

Tauchen, G. (1986). Statistical properties of generalized method of moments estimators of structural parameters obtained from financial market data. *J. Business Econom. Statist.* **4**, 397–425.

West, K. D. (1987). A specification test for speculative bubbles. *Quart. J. Econom.* **102**, 553–580.

West, K. D. (1988a). Dividend innovations and stock price volatility. *Econometrica* **56**, 37–61.

West, K. D. (1988b). Asymptotic normality, when regressors have a unit root. *Econometrica* **56**, 1397–1417.

West, K. D. (1989). Estimation of linear rational expectations models, in the presence of deterministic terms. *J. Monetary Econom.* **24**, 437–442.

White, H. (1980). A heteroskedasticity-consistent covariance matrix estimator and a direct test for heteroskedasticity. *Econometrica* **48**, 817–838.

White, H. (1984). *Asymptotic Theory for Econometricians*. Academic Press, New York.

G. S. Maddala, C. R. Rao and H. D. Vinod, eds., *Handbook of Statistics, Vol. 11*

18

Testing for Heteroskedasticity

A. R. Pagan and Y. Pak

1. Introduction

Although mathematical statistics has as its foundation the assumption that random variables are identically and independently distributed, it is generally recognized that the distribution functions may well not be identical. Despite the fact that a failure of this restriction could be due to any moments lacking constancy, it has been the second moment which has attracted the most attention, and which has led to interest in detecting whether an assumption of constancy across units of observation is reasonable. In econometrics a constant variance tends to be referred to as a random variable exhibiting 'homoskedasticity' whereas a non-constant one is said to be 'heteroskedastic'.[1] Sometimes one sees the equivalent term of heterogeneous; certainly the latter description is a more meaningful one for those unfamiliar with econometric rhetoric but the two terms will be used interchangeably in this paper.

Early interest in heteroskedasticity arose from the concerns of users of the linear regression model. It was demonstrated that the ordinary least-squares (OLS) estimator was not efficient if the errors in the regression model were heteroskedastic, and, more seriously, any inferences made with standard errors computed from standard formulae would be incorrect. To obviate the latter problem, methods were derived to make valid inferences in the presence of heteroskedasticity (Eicker, 1967; White, 1980). To address the former problem it was desirable to perform efficient estimation in the presence of heteroskedasticity. If the heteroskedasticity had a known parametric form the generalized least-squares (GLS) estimator could be invoked; if the form of the heteroskedasticity was unknown, generalized least squares based on a non-parametric estimation of the variance could be implemented along the lines of Carroll (1982) and Robinson (1987). One has the feeling that the development of these procedures has mitigated some of the concern about heteroskedasticity in the basic regression model.

---

[1] The argument given by McCulloch (1985) regarding the spelling of heteroskedasticity with a 'k' rather than a 'c' seems to have been almost universally accepted in econometrics in the last decade.

The basic regression model is now only one of the techniques used in econometric work, and the development of powerful packages for PCs such as LIMDEP, SHAZAM, GAUSS, and RATS has resulted in a much wider range of methods of examining data. Analyses of binary data, frequently called 'discrete choice models' in econometrics, censored data, 'count' data in which the random variable is discrete and takes only a limited number of values, and models in which 'volatility' affects the conditional mean of a variable to be explained, as in the ARCH-M model of Engle et al. (1987), have the characteristic that heterogeneity is an integral part of the model; or, in terms used later, the heteroskedasticity is *intrinsic* to the model. In these instances, what is of interest is whether the pattern of heteroskedasticity in the data differs from that in the model; if so, it is generally the case that the estimators of the specified model parameters would be inconsistent, and therefore, a re-specified model is called for, e.g., see Arabmazar and Schmidt (1981) for an analysis of this for a censored regression model. For such cases, the detection of the correct format for any such heteroskedasticity is of fundamental importance and should be a routine part of any empirical investigation.

This paper aims to provide a review of work done on testing for heteroskedasticity. The basic approach taken is that all existing tests can be regarded as 'conditional moment tests' (CM tests) in the sense of Newey (1985a), Tauchen (1985) and White (1987), with the differences between them revolving around the nature of the moments used, how nuisance parameters are dealt with, and the extent to which a full sample of observations is exploited. Given this view, it is natural to devote Section 2 of the paper to a general discussion of CM tests and complications in working with them. Section 3 proceeds to categorize existing tests for the regression model according to this framework. This section is lengthy, largely because most of the existing literature has concentrated upon the regression model. In fact, there are good reasons for working through the diversity of approaches in this area. Binary, count and censored regression models, dealt with in Section 4, can be regarded as specialized non-linear regression models, implying that approaches developed for the linear model will have extensions. What differentiates the models in Section 4 is that these exhibit intrinsic heteroskedasticity, and the prime question is whether there is any 'extra' heteroskedasticity that is not in the maintained model. Many terms to describe this situation are in use – for example over-dispersion – but it is useful to adopt the descriptor of 'extrinsic heteroskedasticity', as this is neutral towards the issue of whether there is 'too much' or 'too little' heteroskedasticity in the maintained model. Section 4 also contains a discussion of specification testing in volatility models; this material falls into the general framework advanced in this section, because it is likely that a simple model of volatility has already been fitted and the question posed is whether this simple model is an adequate explanation of the data. Section 5 reviews work done on the size and power of test statistics proposed in the literature, while Section 6 concludes the paper.

2. Conditional moment tests and their properties

When models are estimated, assumptions are made, either explicitly or implicitly about the behavior of particular combinations of random variables. Let such a combination be denoted as ϕ_i, $i = 1, \ldots, n$, and assume that the restriction is that $E(\phi_i \mid \mathcal{F}_i) = 0$, where $\mathcal{F}_i$ is some sigma field associated with the random variables.[2] This is a *conditional* moment restriction that is either implied by the model or is used in constructing an estimator to quantify it. It is useful to convert this to an *unconditional* moment restriction by denoting z_i as a $(q \times 1)$ vector of elements constructed from $\mathcal{F}_i$. By the law of iterated expectations it then follows that

$$E(z_i \phi_i) = E(m_i) = 0 . \tag{1}$$

Of course it is clear that (1) is not unique, as any non-singular transformation of it satisfies the restriction, i.e.,

$$E(A z_i \phi_i) = 0 , \tag{2}$$

where A is non-singular. A particularly useful choice of A is $(\Sigma z_i z_i')^{-1}$.

Given that (1) and (2) should hold in the population, it is natural to examine the sample moment(s) $\hat{\tau} = n^{-1} \Sigma z_i \phi_i$ or $\hat{\gamma} = \Sigma A z_i \phi_i$ as a test of this restriction. It is clear from this why choosing $A = (\Sigma z_i z_i')^{-1}$ is helpful, since then $\hat{\gamma}$ will be the regression coefficient of ϕ_i on z_i, whereas $\hat{\tau}$ is the regression coefficient of $z_i \phi_i$ against unity. As emphasized in Cameron and Trivedi (1991), the regression of ϕ_i on z_i allows one to think in traditional terms about 'null' and 'alternative' hypotheses simply by considering whether γ (the population counterpart to $\hat{\gamma}$) is zero or not. Selecting either $\hat{\tau}$ or $\hat{\gamma}$ it is logical to test if (1) holds by testing if either τ or γ is zero. If m_i does not depend upon any nuisance parameters that need to be estimated, one would expect that $\text{var}(\hat{\tau}) \simeq n^{-2} \text{var}(\Sigma m_i) = n^{-2} \Sigma \text{var}(m_i) = n^{-2} V$, if observations are independently distributed. Using a central limit theorem, $n^{1/2} \hat{\tau}$ should be $\mathcal{N}(0, \lim_{n \to \infty} n^{-1} V)$ and $S = n^2 \hat{\tau}' V^{-1} \hat{\tau} = (\Sigma m_i)' V^{-1} (\Sigma m_i)$ will be $\chi^2(q)$, where all these distributional statements are meant to hold under (1).[3] Hence a large value of this test statistic, relative to a $\chi^2(q)$ random variable, would be grounds for rejection of (1).

---

[2] Mostly ϕ_i will be a scalar in what follows, but there is no necessity for that.

[3] In what follows, m_i will either be $z_i \phi_i$ or $A z_i \phi_i$ as the argument does not depend on the specific format. No attempt is made to spell-out what conditions are needed for central limit theorems etc. to apply, but a recent detailed reference would be Whang and Andrews (1991).

Of course, V is an unknown and the issue of its estimation arises. One possibility is to evaluate $\text{var}(m_i) = E(m_i m_i')$ directly, but that may require some auxiliary assumptions about the density of m_i, or the random variables underlying it, which are not directly concerned with (1). This point has been made very forcibly by Wooldridge (1990) and Dastoor (1990); the latter emphasizes that large values of S might simply reflect a violation of the auxiliary assumptions rather than a failure of (1). Such arguments have led to proposals that the test statistics be made *robust*, i.e., dependent on as few auxiliary assumptions as possible, and to this end V is replaced by $\tilde{V} = \Sigma\, m_i m_i'$.[4] Unfortunately, there appears to be a tradeoff between the desire for robustness and the need to use asymptotic theory, as the test statistic $\tilde{S} = (\Sigma\, m_i)\tilde{V}^{-1}(\Sigma\, m_i)$ is likely to converge to a $\chi^2(q)$ slowly, because $\tilde{V}$ is a random variable itself. Much depends on how 'random' $\tilde{V}$ is, and that in turn depends on the nature of m_i. If the m_i are highly non-linear functions of the basic random variables, for example being quartic or higher polynomials, $\tilde{V}$ will exhibit a good deal of randomness, and this will result in large departures of $\tilde{S}$ from a $\chi^2(q)$. An example of this problem is in the component of White's (1980) information matrix test focusing on excess kurtosis, which involves the fourth power of a normally-distributed random variable – see Chesher and Spady (1991) and Kennan and Neumann (1988). For tests of heteroskedasticity in the basic regression model the m_i are not highly non-linear functions, and therefore no major difficulties have been reported; however, that situation may be modified when more complex models such as censored regression are thoroughly investigated.

It is worth drawing attention to a potential difference between tests of (1) based on $\hat{\gamma}$ and $\hat{\tau}$.[5] In theory, there should be no difference, but the fact that $\hat{\gamma}$ can be computed by regressing ϕ_i against z_i leads to the temptation to utilize the t-ratio from such a regression as a test of (1). But the correct t-ratio has to use $\text{var}(\hat{\gamma}) = A^2\,\text{var}(\Sigma\, z_i \phi_i)$, whereas the regression program takes it to be $\text{var}(\phi_i)A$. Unless it is known that the $\text{var}(\phi_i)$ is a constant, whereupon $\text{var}(\Sigma\, z_i \phi_i) = \text{var}(\phi_i)A^{-1}$, to obtain the correct test statistic it is necessary to use the option for finding 'heteroscedastic consistent standard errors' built into most econometric packages these days; failure to do so would create the potential for differing conclusions based on $\hat{\tau}$ and $\hat{\gamma}$.

In practice it will rarely be the case that m_i can be regarded as solely a function of random variables. Either ϕ_i or z_i will involve nuisance parameters θ that are replaced by estimates $\hat{\theta}$ when computing $\hat{\tau}$, i.e., $\hat{\tau} = n^{-1}\Sigma\, m_i(\hat{\theta})$. This feature may create difficulties in evaluating V. To see that, expand $\Sigma\, m_i(\hat{\theta})$ around the true value of θ, θ_0, retaining only the first terms

$$\sum m_i(\hat{\theta}) \approx \sum m_i(\theta_0) + M_\theta(\hat{\theta} - \theta_0)\,, \tag{3}$$

---

[4] When m_i is dependent this formula would need to be modified. A range of possibilities is set out in Andrews (1991).

[5] The discussion that follows takes γ and τ as scalars for simplicity.

where $M_\theta = \mathrm{E}[\Sigma\, \partial m_i / \partial \theta']'.$[6] Accordingly,

$$\mathrm{var}\left(\sum m_i(\hat\theta)\right) = V + \mathrm{cov}\left\{\sum m_i(\theta_0)(\hat\theta - \theta_0)'\right\} M_\theta'$$

$$+ M_\theta\, \mathrm{cov}\left\{(\hat\theta - \theta_0)\sum m_i'(\theta_0)\right\} + M_\theta\, \mathrm{var}(\hat\theta) M_\theta', \quad (4)$$

and the appropriate term to substitute for the variance of $\hat\tau$ will be $n^{-2}\mathrm{var}(\Sigma\, m_i(\hat\theta))$ rather than $n^{-2}V$. Inspection of (4) shows that the two are equal if $M_\theta = 0$ and, happily, for many tests of heteroskedasticity in the basic regression model, that restriction will hold. It is important to observe that M_θ is *to be evaluated under* (1), since it is the $\mathrm{var}(\Sigma\, m_i(\hat\theta))$ under that restriction which is desired. Some cases of heteroskedasticity feature $M_\theta \neq 0$, except 'under the null hypothesis'.

When $M_\theta \neq 0$ a separate computation of $\mathrm{var}(\Sigma\, m_i(\hat\theta))$ is needed and, although fairly easy with packages that have matrix manipulation capabilities, it is unlikely that a regression program can be utilized for the computations. Generally, there will be some set of first-order conditions defining $\hat\theta$, say $\Sigma\, h_i(\hat\theta) = 0$, and $(\hat\theta - \theta_0) \approx -H_\theta^{-1}\Sigma\, h_i(\theta_0)$, where $H_\theta = \mathrm{E}[\Sigma\, \partial h_i / \partial\theta],$[7] making the middle terms in (4) depend on the $\mathrm{cov}\{(\Sigma\, m_i(\theta_0))(\Sigma\, h_i(\theta_0))\}$. If this turns out to be zero, $\mathrm{var}(\Sigma\, m_i(\hat\theta)) \geqslant \mathrm{var}(\Sigma\, m_i(\theta_0))$, and any tests performed utilizing V would overstate the true value of the test statistic, i.e., result in over-rejection of the hypothesis (1). Unless $h(\cdot)$ is specified however, there is no way of knowing if such 'directional' statements might be made. By far the simplest procedure to effect an adjustment is to jointly specify the moment conditions to be used for estimation as $\mathrm{E}(m_i - \tau) = 0$ and $\mathrm{E}(h_i(\theta)) = 0$. By definition the method of moments solutions to this problem will be $\hat\tau$ and $\hat\theta$, and the $\mathrm{var}(\hat\tau)$ would be automatically computed by any program getting such estimates. Notice that with $\hat\theta$ and $\hat\tau$ as starting values iteration will terminate in one step, so there are no convergence problems.

The literature does contain one instance in which any dependence of $\mathrm{var}(\hat\tau)$ on $\hat\theta$ can be accounted for. This is when $\hat\theta$ is estimated by maximum likelihood. Then h_i are the scores for θ, and application of the generalized information equality – Tauchen (1985) – yields $\mathrm{E}(\partial m_i / \partial\theta) = -\mathrm{E}(h_i m_i')$, $\mathrm{E}(\partial h_i / \partial\theta) = -\mathrm{E}(h_i h_i')$. After substituting these into (4) it is possible to construct the test statistic as the joint test that the intercepts are all zero in the regression of $m_i(\hat\theta)$ against unity and $h_i(\hat\theta)$ (see Tauchen, 1985; Pagan and Vella 1989). A disadvantage of the proposal is that it introduces randomness into the 'denominator' of the test statistics owing to the move from M_θ to $\Sigma\, h_i m_i'$ etc. Some preliminary evidence in Skeels and Vella (1991) using simulated data

---

[6] The symbol $\approx$ is meant to indicate that terms have been neglected that will not affect the asymptotic properties of the left-hand side variable after it has been appropriately normalized.

[7] If h is not differentiable H_θ will be replaced by $\Sigma\, \partial \mathrm{E}(h_i)/\partial\theta$, see Whang and Andrews (1991).

from a censored regression model is that $\partial m_i / \partial \theta$ is poorly estimated by $n^{-1} \Sigma h_i m_i'$, and that the estimator deteriorates as the degree of censoring increases. However, provided the inaccuracy does not have too great an impact upon the properties of the test it may be a small price to pay for the convenience of the test.

(1) is a very general statement of what might be tested. Another viewpoint is to conceive of an alternative model to the one being investigated which has q extra parameters γ, with the alternative and basic models coinciding when γ takes values γ^*. By specifying a density or a set of moment conditions γ could be estimated and tested to see if it equals γ^*. However, if γ is not of interest per se, the most likely way to perform such a test is with something like the Lagrange multiplier (LM) test or score test. In this approach the score for γ, d_i, is evaluated at the MLE of θ and γ, given $\gamma = \gamma^*$, and this is tested for whether it is zero. Formally, this is a special case of (1), as the scores should have a zero expectation under the null hypothesis that $\gamma = \gamma^*$. Accordingly, setting $m_i = d_i$ makes the score test a special case of what has already been discussed. The main advantages of the score test are that it yields a very precise moment condition (1) and it also produces a test with optimal properties if the density it is based on is correct; its principal disadvantage is that it introduces an auxiliary assumption pertaining to densities that may be invalid, and such a circumstance would cause it to lose its optimality properties.[8] Nevertheless, the score test is very useful as a benchmark, in that it can suggest suitable moment conditions which may be modified to allow for unknown densities; a further discussion on this point is given in Section 3.

The presence of nuisance parameters in m_i may actually be converted into an advantage rather than a disadvantage. Suppose that there are two possible estimators of θ, $\hat{\theta}$ and $\bar{\theta}$, which are the solutions of $\Sigma h_i(\hat{\theta}) = 0$ and $\Sigma g_i(\bar{\theta}) = 0$ respectively, and that both $\hat{\theta}$, $\bar{\theta}$ are consistent if what is being tested is true, while they converge to different values for θ if it is false. A comparison of $\hat{\theta}$ with $\bar{\theta}$, i.e., forming $\psi = \hat{\theta} - \bar{\theta}$, as recommended in Hausman (1978), enables one to form a test statistic that the hypothesis being tested is true, since ψ will only be close to zero if this is so. Asymptotically, an exactly equivalent procedure is to test if $E(h_i(\theta)) = 0$ using $\Sigma h_i(\bar{\theta})$ (or $E(g_i(\theta)) = 0$ using $\Sigma g_i(\hat{\theta})$), since $\Sigma h_i(\bar{\theta}) \approx \Sigma h_i(\hat{\theta}) + H_\theta(\bar{\theta} - \hat{\theta}) = H_\theta(\bar{\theta} - \hat{\theta})$, and, if H_θ is non-singular, the tests must give the same outcome. Hence, one can define m_i as g_i and use $\hat{\theta}$ from $\Sigma h_i(\hat{\theta}) = 0$ to produce a moment test. As seen in later sections, such an idea has been a popular way to test for heteroskedasticity.

Ultimately, we are interested in testing for heteroskedasticity in various contexts. If data is ordered either chronologically or by some variable such as

---

[8] The LM test has been shown to possess a number of optimal properties. For local alternatives, it has maximal local power in the class of chi-square criteria, and in some situations, may be the locally best invariant test (see King and Hillier, 1985). The situations where this is true center largely on the regression model in which a single parameter entering the covariance matrix of u_i is tested for being zero against the alternative that it is positive. In fact it is not the LM test per se which has this property but the one-sided version of it.

(say) firm size, then it is natural to think of heteroskedasticity as involving structural change in whatever constitutes the scale parameter of the model.[9] Defining $E(m_i) = 0$ as the moment condition used to estimate this scale parameter, it is therefore reasonable to test for heteroskedasticity by examining the cumulative sums $\sum_{i=1}^{nk} m_i(\hat{\theta})$, where k is a fraction of the sample and θ includes both the scale parameter (θ_1) as well as any others (θ_2) which form part of the model. Since θ is being estimated from the same data as is being used for specification testing, some allowance has to be made for that fact in determining the $\text{var}(\sum_{i=1}^{nk} m_i(\hat{\theta}))$. It will be assumed that $E(\partial m_i / \partial \theta_2) = 0$, as this can be shown to be true for estimators of the scale parameter used later, and such a restriction therefore means that $(\hat{\theta}_1 - \theta_1)$ asymptotically behaves like

$$-\left(\sum_{i=1}^{n} \partial m_i / \partial \theta_1\right)^{-1} \left(\sum_{i=1}^{n} m_i\right).$$

Linearizing $\sum_{i=1}^{nk} m_i(\hat{\theta})$ around θ and applying the assumptions just made gives

$$\sum_{i=1}^{nk} m_i(\hat{\theta}) \approx \sum_{i=1}^{nk} m_i(\theta) + \left[\sum_{i=1}^{nk} (\partial m_i / \partial \theta_1)\right](\hat{\theta}_1 - \theta_1) \tag{5}$$

$$\approx \sum_{i=1}^{nk} m_i(\theta) + \left[\sum_{i=1}^{nk} (\partial m_i / \partial \theta_1)\right]\left(-\sum_{i=1}^{n} (\partial m_i / \partial \theta_1)\right)^{-1}\left(\sum_{i=1}^{n} m_i(\theta)\right) \tag{6}$$

$$= \sum_{i=1}^{nk} m_i(\theta) - (nk/n)\left[(nk)^{-1}\sum_{i=1}^{nk} (\partial m_i / \partial \theta_1)\right]$$
$$\times \left[n^{-1}\sum_{i=1}^{n} (\partial m_i / \partial \theta_1)\right]\left(\sum_{i=1}^{n} m_i(\theta)\right) \tag{7}$$

$$\approx \sum_{i=1}^{nk} m_i(\theta) - k\left(\sum_{i=1}^{n} m_i(\theta)\right), \tag{8}$$

as $(nk)^{-1}\sum_{i=1}^{nk}(\partial m_i / \partial \theta_1) - n^{-1}\sum_{i=1}^{n}(\partial m_i / \partial \theta_1)$ should be $o_p(1)$ for large enough n and for fixed k as they both estimate $E(\partial m_i / \partial \theta_1)$, which is constant under the null hypothesis. Consequently, the

$$\text{var}\left(\sum_{i=1}^{nk} m_i(\hat{\theta})\right) = \text{var}\left\{\sum_{i=1}^{nk} m_i(\theta) - k\sum_{i=1}^{n} m_i(\theta)\right\}.$$

To evaluate this variance assume that $m_i(\theta)$ is iid with variance v; the same results hold if it is dependent and Hansen (1990) has a formal proof of that

---

[9] To apply the theory that follows the heteroskedasticity cannot arise from the variable by which the data is ordered, since that variable now has a trend associated with it and the asymptotic theory being invoked explicitly rules out the possibility of trending variables.

fact. Then

$$\text{var}\left\{\sum_{i=1}^{nk} m_i(\theta) - k \sum_{i=1}^{n} m_i(\theta)\right\}$$

$$= \text{var}\left(\sum_{i=1}^{nk} m_i(\theta)\right) - 2k \,\text{cov}\left\{\left[\sum_{i=1}^{nk} m_i(\theta)\right]\left[\sum_{i=1}^{n} m_i(\theta)\right]\right\}$$

$$+ k^2 \,\text{var}\left(\sum_{i=1}^{n} m_i(\theta)\right) \tag{9}$$

$$= (nkv) - 2k(nkv) + k^2 nv \tag{10}$$

$$= (nkv) - k^2(nv). \tag{11}$$

Defining $V(k) = \text{var}(\Sigma_{i=1}^{nk} m_i(\theta)) = nkv$, (11) can be expressed as

$$V(k) - k^2 V(1) \tag{12}$$

$$= V(k) - V(k)V(1)^{-1}V(k) \tag{13}$$

using the fact that $k = V(k)/V(1)$. Consequently, $\text{var}(\Sigma m_i(\hat{\theta})) \approx V(k) - V(k)V(1)^{-1}V(k)$ and $V(k)$ can be estimated by $\hat{V}(k) = \Sigma_{i=1}^{nk} m_i^2(\hat{\theta})$. Using these pieces of information the following CUSUM test can be constructed:

$$C(k) = \left(\sum_{i=1}^{nk} m_i(\hat{\theta})\right)^2 / [\hat{V}(k) - \hat{V}(k)\hat{V}(1)^{-1}\hat{V}(k)]. \tag{14}$$

For any k this will be asymptotically a $\chi^2(1)$ if the model is correctly specified.

A number of different tests can be associated with this approach.

(a) Let $k = (1/n)$, $(2/n)$, etc. and define $\text{SC} = \sup_k C(k)$, i.e., look at the maximum of $C(k)$ for all values of k from $(1/n)$ to $(n-1)/n$ in increments of $(1/n)$. By definition of $\hat{\theta}_1$, $\Sigma_{i=1}^{n} m_i(\hat{\theta}_1) = 0$, forcing one to find the sup of $C(k)$ over a restricted range; Andrews (1990) suggests 0.15 to 0.85.

(b) $L_W = n^{-1} \Sigma_{j=1}^{n-1} C(j/n)$. This is an average test. The L comes from the fact that, if the scale parameter is estimated by ML and m_i are therefore the scores with respect to it, the statistic can be thought of as the LM test for the hypothesis that $\text{var}(v_i) = 0$ in the model $\theta_{1i} = \theta_{1i-1} + v_i$ (see Hansen, 1990). The distribution is non-standard and is tabulated in Hansen's paper.

(c) $L_C = n^{-1} V(1)^{-1} \Sigma_{j=1}^{n-1} [\Sigma_{i=1}^{j} \hat{m}_i]^2$. This is also an LM test like (b), differing in the covariance matrix assumed for v_i under the alternative. Hansen also tabulates the distribution of this test. On the basis of simulation studies (for testing constancy of location parameters) he finds it has better correspondence with asymptotic theory than (b) does. Probably this is because one is using less random elements in the denominator of the statistic. The more randomness one induces into denominators of test statistics the slower their convergence to limiting distributions tends to be. In some cases it can be very slow indeed, and leads to substantial over-rejections, e.g., Chesher and Spady (1991).

3. Testing heteroskedasticity in the regression model

3.1. Testing using general moment conditions

The basic regression model is

$$y_i = x_i'\beta + u_i , \tag{15}$$

where x_i is a $(p \times 1)$ vector and u_i will be assumed independently distributed $(0, \sigma_i^2)$, with σ_i^2 being a function of some variable summarized by the field $\mathcal{F}_i$. Initially, x_i will be taken to be weakly exogenous and y_i will be a scalar. If the errors are to be homoskedastic, $E(z_i(\sigma^{-2}u_i^2 - 1)) = E(z_i\phi_i)$ will be zero, where $\sigma_i^2 = \sigma^2$ under the assumption that there is no heteroskedasticity, while z_i is a $(q \times 1)$ vector drawn from $\mathcal{F}_i$ possessing the property $E(z_i) = 0$.[10] The set of moment conditions $E(z_i\phi_i) = E(m_i) = 0$ will therefore be used to test for heteroskedasticity, and this was the structure set out in (1).

There are obviously many tests for heteroskedasticity that may be generated by selection of z_i, and this was the theme of Pagan and Hall (1983). Examples would be $z_i = (x_i'\beta)^2$ used in MICROFIT (Pesaran and Pesaran, 1987); $z_i = (y_{i-1} - x_{i-1}'\beta)^2$, the test for first-order autoregressive conditional heteroskedasticity (ARCH) introduced in Engle (1982); $z_i = \text{vec}(x_i \otimes x_i')$ (excluding any redundant elements), used in White (1980); and $z_i = i$, which was suggested by Szroeter (1978), and applied by many others after him. All of these tests can be constructed by regressing ϕ_i upon z_i, and all the issues concerning robustness and dependence on nuisance parameters set out in Section 2 apply. Perhaps the issue that occupied most attention in Pagan and Hall was the latter one. As argued in Section 2, a necessary condition enabling one to ignore the fact that $\theta' = (\beta'\sigma^2)$ is estimated rather than known, would be $E(\partial m_i/\partial\theta) = 0$.[11] From the definition of m_i, $\partial m_i/\partial\theta = (\partial z_i/\partial\theta)\phi_i + z_i(\partial\phi_i/\partial\theta)$. Both of these two terms will have expectation of zero; the first because $E(\phi_i \mid \mathcal{F}_i) = 0$ and $\partial z_i/\partial\theta \in \mathcal{F}_i$; the second because it equals either $E(\sigma^{-2}u_ix_iz_i') = 0$ (for β) from $E(u_i \mid \mathcal{F}_i) = 0$, or $-E(z_i\sigma^{-4}u_i^2) = -E(z_i)\sigma^{-2} = 0$ (for σ^2), given the assumption $E(z_i) = 0$. Consequently, when testing for heteroskedasticity in the regular regression model, there will be no dependence of $\hat{\tau} = n^{-1}\sum \hat{m}_i$ upon $\hat{\beta}$ or $\hat{\sigma}^2$, and the variance is therefore simply found from $\text{var}(m_i)$.

When x_i is not weakly exogenous, i.e., some members of x_i are endogenous variables, it will no longer be true that $E(\partial m_i/\partial\theta) = 0$, since $E(\sigma^{-2}u_ix_iz_i') \neq 0$. In these circumstances, an allowance must be made for the estimation of β.

---

[10] Although, z_i will typically be a function of β, this dependence will be suppressed unless its recognition is important. The assumption that $E(z_i) = 0$ means that whatever is selected to represent z_i will need to be mean corrected.

[11] Because z_i has been assumed to have zero mean, there is implicitly another parameter, $E(z_i)$, that needs to be estimated. However, it is easily seen from the same argument as used later for β and σ^2 that it does not affect the distribution of $\hat{\tau} = n^{-1}\sum \hat{m}_i$.

The simplest procedure would be to jointly estimate τ and β and to then test if τ takes the value zero. An alternative is to use the variance given in (4), or to explicitly evaluate it in the simultaneous equation context as done in Pagan and Hall (1983, pp. 192–194). There are papers in the literature which claim that the distribution does not depend on $\hat{\beta}$ (Szroeter, 1978, and Tse and Phoon, 1985) but the assumptions made to get this result imply a degeneracy in the reduced form errors which has to be regarded as implausible; a fuller account of this point is contained in Pagan and Hall (1983, p. 195).

Another choice of moment condition that is slightly more complex leads to the Goldfeld–Quandt (1965) test. Essentially they compare the residual variance estimated over a sub-period $i = 1, \ldots, n_1$ with that over $i = n_1 + k, \ldots, n$, with k being the number of observations dropped.[12] One would effect such a comparison by making $m_i = z_i(y_i - x_i'\beta)^2$, with z_i being n_1^{-1} for $i = 1, \ldots, n_1$; $z_i = 0$ for $i = n_1 + 1, \ldots, n_1 + k$; and $z_i = n_2^{-1}$ for $i = n_1 + k + 1, \ldots, n$, where $n_2 = n - (n_1 + k)$. In fact, because Goldfeld and Quandt estimate β separately for both $i = 1, \ldots, n_1$ and $i = n_1 + k + 1, \ldots, n$, there are really two sets of parameters β_1 and β_2 in θ, with moment conditions for estimating these being

$$
E\left[\sum_{i=1}^{n_1} x_i(y_i - x_i'\beta_1)\right] = 0 , \qquad E\left[\sum_{i=n_1+k+1}^{n} x_i(y_i - x_i'\beta_2)\right] = 0 .
$$

However, Goldfeld and Quandt did not intend that β_1 and β_2 be different; they were simply trying to make the estimated residual variances independent of one another, and this could not be done if β is estimated utilizing the full sample. But this choice of method to estimate β should not be allowed to disguise the fact that, underlying Goldfeld and Quandt's test, is a very specific moment condition. It would be possible to generalize the Goldfeld–Quandt test to allow for more than one break. Doing so with three contiguous breaks would produce a test statistic emulating Bartlett's (1937) test for homogeneity, popularized by Ramsey (1969) as BAMSET after the OLS residuals are replaced by the BLUS residuals. It is not possible to express Bartlett's test exactly as a conditional moment test, but asymptotically it is equivalent to one in which the z_i are defined as for the Goldfeld–Quandt test over the three periods.

Some of the testing literature is concerned with robustness. Finding the variance of m_i could be done by writing $\text{var}(m_i) = \text{var}(z_i)\,\text{var}(\phi_i) = \text{var}(z_i)\sigma^{-4}\,\text{var}(u_i^2 - \sigma^2)$, after which a distributional assumption concerning u_i would allow $\text{var}(m_i)$ to be quantified exactly. However, a distributional assumption for u_i must be an auxiliary one, and it is not directly connected with a test for heteroskedasticity. Consequently, as discussed in Section 2, it may be desirable to estimate $\text{var}(m_i)$ without making distributional assump-

---

[12] In fact, they use the ratio of these variances and order the observations in ascending order; the difference in variances is used here so that $E(m_i) = 0$ when there is no heteroskedasticity.

tions, in particular, $n^{-1}\Sigma m_i m_i' = n^{-1}\Sigma z_i z_i' \phi_i^2$ could be adopted as the estimate. Alternatively, if $E(\phi_i^2)$ is a constant one might use $(n^{-1}\Sigma \phi_i^2)(n^{-1}\Sigma z_i z_i')$. This was Koenker's (1981) criticism of the test for heteroskedasticity introduced by Breusch and Pagan (1979) and Godfrey (1978), and his version using the second formulation above has become the standard way of implementing a test which stems from the moment condition $E(z_i \phi_i) = 0.$[13] It appears that there can be some major differences in tests constructed with different estimates of var(ϕ_i). In Monte Carlo experiments Kamstra (1990) finds that the Koenker variant which adjusts the size of the test using the outer product $n^{-1}\Sigma m_i m_i'$, leads to severe over-rejection.

3.2. Testing using the optimal score

Although the treatment of tests according to the selection of z_i and the extent to which robustness is addressed yields a satisfactory taxonomy, it does not address either the question of the optimal choice of z_i, or the possibility that the distribution of u_i might affect the nature of the moment condition itself. One resolution of this lacuna is to derive the Lagrange multiplier or score test. To this end, let the density of $\varepsilon_i = \sigma_i^{-1} u_i$ be $f(\varepsilon_i)$, where the ε_i are identically and independently distributed random variables. The log-likelihood of (15) will therefore be

$$L = -\tfrac{1}{2}\sum \log \sigma_i^2 + \sum \log f(\sigma_i^{-1}(y_i - x_i'\beta)). \tag{16}$$

If γ are parameters such that $\gamma = \gamma^*$ makes $\sigma_i^2 = \sigma^2$, the scores for γ are the basis of the LM test, and these will be

$$\partial L/\partial\gamma = -\tfrac{1}{2}\sum \sigma_i^{-2}\partial\sigma_i^2/\partial\gamma - \tfrac{1}{2}\sum f_i^{-1}(\partial f_i/\partial\varepsilon_i)\sigma_i^{-2}(\partial\sigma_i^2/\partial\gamma)\varepsilon_i. \tag{17}$$

After re-arrangement and simplification,

$$\partial L/\partial\gamma = \tfrac{1}{2}\sum (\partial\sigma_i^2/\partial\gamma)\sigma_i^{-2}[-\psi_i\varepsilon_i - 1], \tag{18}$$

where $\psi_i = f_i^{-1}(\partial f_i/\partial\varepsilon_i)$. Under the null hypothesis H_0: $\gamma = \gamma^*$,

$$\partial L/\partial\gamma|_{\gamma=\gamma^*} = \tfrac{1}{2}\sigma^{-2}\sum (\partial\sigma_i^2/\partial\gamma)_{\gamma=\gamma^*}[-f_i^{-1}(\partial f_i/\partial\varepsilon_i)\varepsilon_i - 1]. \tag{19}$$

---

[13] There can be some dangers to this strategy in that one is attempting to estimate $E(u_i^4)$ robustly. If $E(u_i^4)$ did not exist, Koenker's test might not even be consistent whereas the Breusch/Pagan/Godfrey test would be as it uses $2\sigma^4$ as the variance, i.e., only a second moment is used as a divisor. Phillips and Loretan (1990) make this observation in connection with recursive tests of the sorts to be discussed in Section 3.4. The problem is likely to be particularly acute when one is trying to make tests robust to ARCH errors as the conditions for the existence of a fourth moment in u_i are much more stringent than for a second moment. The problem will only affect the power of such robust tests as it is under the alternative that the moments may not exist. One of Kamstra's (1990) experiments had an ARCH(1) model for which the robust test had very poor power properties. When the density of $\sigma_i^{-1} u_i$ is $\mathcal{N}(0,1)$ the fourth moment fails to exist if the ARCH(1) parameter exceeds 0.57 and, although Kamstra sets the true parameter to 0.4, there may be some small sample impact of being near the boundary.

Studying (19) it is apparent that the 'optimal' choice of z_i should be $(\partial \sigma_i^2 / \partial \gamma)_{\gamma = \gamma^*}$, and that the nature of the distribution of ε_i impinges directly upon the 'optimal' test. For moment conditions having the structure $E(z_i \phi_i) = 0$, the best choice of ϕ_i is $-f_i^{-1}(\partial f_i / \partial \varepsilon_i)\varepsilon_i - 1$, constituting a non-linear function of $\varepsilon_i = \sigma^{-1} u_i$ that depends directly upon the density of ε_i. Interestingly enough, ϕ_i will only be $(\sigma^{-2} u_i^2 - 1)$ if $f(\cdot)$ is the standard normal density; in that instance $f_i^{-1}(\partial f_i / \partial \varepsilon_i) = -\varepsilon_i$, revealing that the moment conditions $E[z_i(\sigma^{-2} u_i^2 - 1)] = 0$ implicitly have the assumption of a Gaussian density for ε_i underlying their construction. Notice that $E[z_i(\sigma^{-2} u_i^2 - 1)] = 0$ regardless of the nature of the density; it will only be the *power* of the test statistic that is affected by not allowing ϕ_i to vary according to $f(\cdot)$.

Consideration of (19) points to the fact that there are two issues in devising an appropriate test for heteroskedasticity in the regression model. The first of these is how to approximate $(\partial \sigma_i^2 / \partial \gamma)_{\gamma = \gamma^*}$; the need to form a derivative of σ_i^2 emphasizes that the alternative has a major role to play in determining what z_i will be. If σ_i^2 has the 'single index' form $\sigma_i^2 = g(z_i' \gamma)$, where g is some function, then $(\partial \sigma_i^2 / \partial \gamma)|_{\gamma = \gamma^*}$ is $g_1 z_i$, with g_1 being the derivative of g. Setting $\gamma = \gamma^*$, $g(z_i' \gamma^*)$ must be a constant, σ^2, if there is to be no heteroskedasticity, and g_1 will therefore be constant under the null hypothesis. In these circumstances, $(\partial \sigma_i^2 / \partial \gamma)|_{\gamma = \gamma^*} = g_1^* z_i$, and the constancy of g_1^* enables it to be eliminated, leaving the appropriate moment condition as $E(z_i \phi_i) = 0$, i.e., the test statistic is invariant to g_1^* and is the same as if σ_i^2 was the linear function $z_i' \gamma$. This was the observation in Breusch and Pagan (1979). It is important to emphasize however, that the result depends critically on the single index format, and it is not true that the test statistic is invariant to general types of heteroskedasticity, an interpretation sometimes given to the result.

Another approach to estimating $\partial \sigma_i^2 / \partial \gamma$ is to use non-parametric ideas, i.e., since σ_i^2 is an unknown function of elements in $\mathscr{F}_i$, one might take z_i as known functions of these elements and then approximate σ_i^2 by the series expansion $z_i' \gamma$. Examples of z_i would be orthogonal polynomials or Fourier terms such as sines and cosines. Kamstra (1990) explores this idea through the theory of neural networks, which is a procedure for doing non-parametric regression by series methods. As z_i he selects a set of q principal components of $\zeta_{ij} = (1 + \exp(-x_i' \delta_j))$, where values of δ_j $(j = 1, \ldots, r)$ are found by randomly drawing from $[-R, R]$ and then used to construct ζ_{ij}. The parameters r and q are chosen as $4p$ and p if $n \leq 50$; for $n > 50$, r is increased according to $2 \log(n) n^{-1/6}$ and this rule is also applied to q after $n > 100$. R was always equal to unity in Monte Carlo experiments performed with the test. In his Monte Carlo work he finds that this 'nets' test works well in a wide variety of circumstances.

Although the score test is a useful benchmark for suggesting suitable choices for z_i, it is known that it is only 'locally' optimal in large samples, and if departures from the null are strong, one might do better using alternative information more directly. Considering the score in (18), $\sigma_i^{-2} \partial \sigma_i^2 / \partial \gamma = \partial \log \sigma_i^2 / \partial \gamma = -2 \partial \log \sigma_i^{-1} / \partial \gamma$. For small departures from the null, i.e., $\gamma = \bar{\gamma}$, a linear approximation to this quantity is likely to suffice and that can be regarded as being proportional to $\sigma_i^{-1}(\bar{\gamma}) - \sigma_i^{-1}(\gamma^*) = \sigma_i^{-1}(\bar{\gamma}) - \sigma^{-1}$. Hence, one interpretation of the LM test is that it takes as z_i, $\sigma_i^{-1}(\bar{\gamma})$ for a value of γ, $\bar{\gamma}$ close to γ^*. For larger departures this argument indicates that it would make sense to use $\sigma_i^{-1}(\bar{\gamma})$ as z_i, where $\bar{\gamma}$ is now some specified value of γ thought to reflect the alternative hypothesis. Thus a family of tests, $\hat{\tau}(\bar{\gamma})$, indexed upon $\bar{\gamma}$, could be formed. Evans and King (1985) make this proposal.[14] They find that choices of $\bar{\gamma}$ can be made that are superior to the LM test in small samples, even if $\bar{\gamma}$ lies away from the true value γ. In the event that $\gamma = \bar{\gamma}$ their test is a point optimal test, in the sense of the Neyman–Pearson lemma applied to testing the simple hypothesis of $\gamma = \gamma^*$ versus $\gamma = \bar{\gamma}$.

Even after a candidate for z_i has been determined, the optimal score in (19) depends upon the function ψ_i, and therefore requires some knowledge of or approximation to the density $f(\cdot)$. Because $f(\cdot)$ will be rarely known exactly, it is of interest to explore the possibility of allowing for general forms of ψ_i. Within the class of generalized exponential densities giving rise to generalized linear models (GLM), $\psi_i \varepsilon_i$ is known as the 'deviance' function, see McCullagh and Nelder (1983), and one could work within that framework in devising tests for heteroskedasticity, see Gurmu and Trivedi (1990). Alternatively, there is a large literature on estimating β efficiently in the face of unknown density for u_i, and it can be applied to the current situation, see Bickel (1978). Two interesting ways of approximating ψ_i are proposals by Potscher and Prucha (1986) and McDonald and Newey (1988) that the Student's t and the generalized t density be used for $f(\cdot)$, as that allows a diversity of shapes in ψ_i. For the generalized t density $\psi_i = (rs + 1)\text{sgn}(u)|u|^{r-1}/(q\sigma^r + |u|^r)$, with r, s being distributional parameters. McDonald and Newey propose that either r, s be estimated by maximizing $\Sigma \log f(r, s)$, where β is replaced by the OLS estimate, or by minimizing the $\text{var}(\tilde{\beta})$, where $\tilde{\beta}$ is the MLE, because the latter depends upon (r, s) solely through a scalar.

Within the literature there are examples of ϕ_i functions that can be regarded as performing the same task as ψ_i does, namely adapting the functional form of ϕ_i to the nature of the density. One that appears in many econometric packages is Glejser's (1969) test that sets $\phi_i = |u_i| - E(|u_i|)$. Glejser proposed regressing $|u_i|$ against a constant and z_i, and the intercept in such a regression essentially estimates $E|u_i|$ under the null hypothesis.[15] Since the optimal ϕ_i is $-\psi_i \varepsilon_i - 1$, Glejser's test will be optimal if $\psi_i = |u_i|/u_i = |\varepsilon_i|/\varepsilon_i = \text{sgn}(\varepsilon_i)$. The

---

[14] z_i has to be normalized such that γ could be interpreted as a coefficient of variation. In their test σ^2 is estimated as the OLS residual variance while the β appearing in $\phi_i = [\sigma^{-2}(y_i - x_i'\beta)^2 - 1]$ is estimated from the GLS moment condition $E[(1 + z_i'\bar{\gamma})^{-1/2}(y_i - x_i'\beta)] = 0$. Because the distribution of $\hat{\tau}$ does not depend on $\hat{\beta}$ or $\hat{\sigma}^2$, this switch is asymptotically of no consequence.

[15] In order that the distribution of Glejser's test be independent of $\hat{\beta}$ it will be necessary that $E(z_i x_i' \text{sgn}(u_i)) = 0$, and this requires conditional symmetry for the distribution of u_i. Thus in Kamstra's (1990) simulations one would expect that referring Glejser's test to a chi-square distribution would be in error if the underlying density was an exponential or a gamma, and this is apparent in his results. Conditional symmetry is also required for the optimal score test to be asymptotically independent of $\hat{\beta}$ as the derivative of (19) with respect to β will only be zero if $E(x_i \psi_i) = 0$. For independence from $\hat{\sigma}^2$, $E[(\partial \sigma_i^2/\partial \gamma)|_{\gamma = \gamma^*}] = 0$ is needed, the analogue of $E(z_i) = 0$ used earlier.

density with such an ψ_i is the double exponential $f(\varepsilon) = Ce^{-|\varepsilon|}$, showing that Glesjer's test is likely to be successful in the situation of fat tailed densities. This would constitute an argument for its use when ARCH is being tested for, as it has been observed that $f(\cdot)$ has fat tails even after an ARCH process has been allowed for, see Engle and Bollerslev (1986) and Nelson (1991).

Rather than approximating ψ_i it is tempting to estimate it non-parametrically. For example, one could estimate $f(\cdot)$ and its derivative by a kernel estimator at the points $\hat{\varepsilon}_i$, where $\hat{\varepsilon}_i$ are the standardized OLS residuals, and then proceed to form the test using this estimated quantity $\hat{\psi}_i$ in place of ψ_i. Whang and Andrews (1991) provide theorems regarding the distribution of conditional moment tests when a component of the test is estimated non-parametrically. A critical condition in their theorems needs to be verified in order to ensure that the distribution of $\hat{\tau}$ does not depend upon the non-parametric estimator of ψ_i asymptotically. Here that condition requires $n^{-1/2}\{E[z_i(-\zeta_i\varepsilon_i - 1)]\}|_{\zeta_i = \hat{\psi}_i}$ to be $o_p(1)$, where ζ_i is a function of data preserving whatever features $f(\cdot)$ is known to possess, such as symmetry, while the expectation is taken before the substitution of $\hat{\psi}_i$ for ζ_i. Writing the expectation in the condition to be tested as $n^{-1/2}E\{z_i[-(\zeta_i - \psi_i)\varepsilon_i - \psi_i\varepsilon_i - 1]\}$, independence of z_i and ε_i along with $E(z_i) = 0$ would ensure that $E(z_i\psi_i\varepsilon_i) = 0$, reducing the requirement to $n^{-1/2}z_i(\hat{\psi}_i - \psi_i)\varepsilon_i$ being $o_p(1)$, which necessitates $n^{1/4}$ consistency for whatever non-parametric estimator of ψ_i is used for $\hat{\psi}_i$.

3.3. Test statistics based on estimator comparison

As mentioned in Section 2, one possible test for a specification error is to compare estimators whose probability limit differs only if there is a misspecification. One way to effect such a comparison is to substitute the parameter estimates from a set of first-order conditions defining them into those for another estimator. When testing for heteroskedasticity there have been two proposals based on this line of thought.

Koenker and Bassett (1982) estimate β in (15) by a quantile estimator, i.e., $\hat{\beta}(\eta)$ was chosen to minimize $\Sigma \rho_\eta(y_i - x_i'\beta)$, where $\rho_\eta(\lambda) = |\eta - 1(\lambda < 0)| \, |\lambda|$, $1(\cdot)$ is the indicator function, and $0 < \eta < 1$ defines the η-th quantile. They show that the quantile estimators of the slope coefficients $\hat{\beta}_1$ are consistently estimated when there is no heteroskedasticity, but that plim $\hat{\beta}_1(\eta)$ differs according to η if there is heteroskedasticity. This feature leads to a test for heteroskedasticity based on a comparison of estimators of β_1 at two different quantiles η_1 and η_2, i.e., the test is based on $\hat{\beta}_1(\eta_1) - \hat{\beta}_1(\eta_2)$. Interpreted as a conditional moment test of the form $E(z_i\phi_i) = 0$, this would be $E[x_{1i}(\eta_1 - 1(y_i < x_i'\beta))u_i] = 0$, where x_{1i} are the mean corrected regressors corresponding to the slope coefficients β_1. Their computation of the asymptotic local power function of this test when $\sigma_i^2 = 1 + x_{1i}\delta n^{-1/2}$ revealed that power was larger for this 'comparison' test than for the LM test appropriate when $f(\cdot)$ is normal, i.e., one based on $\phi_i = \sigma^{-2}u_i^2 - 1$, whenever the true density $f(\cdot)$ was a contaminated normal. As Newey and Powell (1987) point out, these power computations made by Koenker and Bassett exaggerated the power gain due to an error in deriving the non-centrality parameters of the test statistics, but, even after correction, there was still an improvement.

A major disadvantage of working with quantile estimators is that the function $\rho_\eta(\cdot)$ is not differentiable. This feature led Newey and Powell to replace $\rho_\eta(\cdot)$ of the quantile estimators with $\rho_\nu(\lambda) = |\nu - 1(\lambda < 0)|\lambda^2$; the estimator of β found by minimizing this function is $\hat{\beta}(\nu)$, and was termed asymmetric least squares (ALS). Their recommended test is then based on $\hat{\beta}_1(\nu_1) - \hat{\beta}_1(\nu_2)$. After examining a numerical experiment they find that $\nu_1 = 0.46$, $\nu_2 = 0.54$ seems to give best power. With these values of ν their test performs in a very similar fashion to the Koenker–Bassett test when the density $f(\cdot)$ is contaminated normal, but has much better power if $f(\cdot)$ is normal, leading to their conclusion that the comparison be based on the ALS estimator. Now, the implicit moment condition used in the comparison is $E[x_{1i}(\nu_1 - 1(y_i < x_i'\beta))u_i] = 0$, and, when $\nu_1 = 0.5$, this becomes $E[x_{1i}(0.5 - 1(u_i < 0))u_i] = E[0.5x_{1i}\, \text{sgn}(u_i)u_i] = E(0.5x_{1i}|u_i|) = 0$, which is just the moment condition used in constructing Glejser's test, provided z_i is set to x_{1i}. Moreover, when the error density is symmetric, $\hat{\beta}_1(0.5)$ will be OLS. This argument points to the fact that the performance of the ALS comparison test $\hat{\beta}_1(0.46) - \hat{\beta}_2(0.54)$ should be very close to Glejser's test based on $\Sigma x_{1i}|\hat{u}_i|$. Indeed this is what Newey and Powell find, culminating in their conclusion that using Glejser's test would be a simple way of attaining the benefits of doing the ALS test.

3.4. Test statistics based on CUSUMS of moments

Under the null hypothesis the scale parameter σ^2 is estimated from some moment condition. If the errors ε_i are normally distributed, the moment defining an estimator of σ^2 would be $E(\Sigma \sigma^{-2}u_i^2 - 1) = 0$. For other densities, using the score for σ from (16), with σ_i^2 replaced by σ^2, might produce a more satisfactory estimate. Focusing upon the normal case, the general treatment of testing for structural change in the variance provided in Section 2 involved looking at the CUSUMS $\Sigma_{i=1}^{nk}(\hat{\sigma}^{-2}\hat{u}_i^2 - 1)$, or just $b(k) = \Sigma_{i=1}^{nk}\hat{\sigma}^{-2}\hat{u}_i^2$. Harrison and McCabe (1979) proposed b as a test for heteroskedasticity with fixed k, while Breusch and Pagan (1979) adopted the $C(k)$ test in (14). Because the $C(k)$ test is just a transformation of $\Sigma \hat{\sigma}^{-2}\hat{u}_i^2$, there will be no difference in conclusions based upon it or $b(k)$ provided they are referred to their appropriate critical values. An advantage of $C(k)$ is that it is centered and scaled so that asymptotically it is a χ^2 random variable. McCabe (1986) mentions the possibility of using $\max_k b(k)$. However, he did not find the distribution of this test. Instead he ordered $\hat{\sigma}^{-2}\hat{u}_i^2$ and computed a test based on the order statistics for this sequence. As Andrews (1990) has now tabulated the distribution of $\max_k C(k)$ it seems more satisfactory to perform a test in this way. The other two test statistics given earlier – L_W and L_C – do not seem to have been formally used in the literature.

4. Testing for heteroskedasticity in models featuring heteroskedasticity

Section 3 was devoted to procedures for detecting heteroskedasticity when the maintained hypothesis was that there was none. However, the last two decades have seen a proliferation of models incorporating heteroskedasticity as one of their characteristics. Such heteroskedasticity is *intrinsic* to the model and what needs to be tested is not the presence of heteroskedasticity per se but whether it departs from that featured in the maintained model, that is it is *extrinsic* heteroskedasticity which is important. Indeed, one might argue that it is rare to have a situation in which there is no intrinsic heteroskedasticity in linear models such as (15). If y_i was a member of the exponential family the density of u_i is rarely homoskedastic, with the normal density being the dominant exception. Moreover, the heteroskedasticity will generally have the characteristic of being a function of the conditional mean $\mu_i = E(y_i | x_i)$. Many examples of models with intrinsic heteroskedasticity might be given, but four representative 'types' are set out in this section. Each may be regarded as a regression model with heteroskedasticity, and it is desired to test if the predicted type of heteroskedasticity is sufficient to account for non-constancy in the variance of the errors. These models arise in situations where there is 'count', binary or censored data or in which there is interest in explaining volatility in a series. Our enumeration is scarcely exhaustive. Many extensions can be made to the basic models, for example, the type of censoring giving rise to selectivity bias or the possibility of multiple rather than binary responses, but the collection should illustrate the common themes regarding testing that will be found in all such models.

4.1. A general approach to testing for extrinsic heteroskedasticity

All the models considered in this section can be regarded as being characterized by an error term u_i that has variance $\tilde{\sigma}_i^2$ when the maintained model is correct. The variance $\tilde{\sigma}_i^2$ is a function of some parameters δ. Defining $e_i = \tilde{\sigma}_i^{-1} u_i$, it is e_i which is to be tested for heteroskedasticity, i.e., in terms of the analysis of Section 3, $\bar{\sigma}_i^2$ will now be the variance of u_i, becoming equal to $\tilde{\sigma}_i^2$ when there is none. Hence, under the null hypothesis, the variance of e_i, σ_i^2, is unity. With this change, the moment conditions used for tests of heteroskedasticity in Section 3 will simply be modified by replacing u_i by e_i and by setting σ^2 to unity. Thus the basic moment condition used below (15) becomes $E(z_i(e_i^2 - 1)) = 0$.

There are however some complications. A minor one arises because the parameters to be estimated will now include not only those like β in (15) but also δ, the parameters entering into the intrinsic form of heteroskedasticity. Except for a few instances, the distribution of tests for heteroskedasticity in the basic regression model did not depend upon any nuisance parameters such as β and σ^2, but this is unlikely for δ. When $m_i = z_i(e_i^2 - 1)$, and there is no overlap between δ and β,

$$\partial m_i / \partial \delta = (\partial z_i / \partial \delta)(e_i^2 - 1) - z_i u_i^2 \sigma_i^{-4}(\partial \sigma_i^2 / \partial \delta) ,$$

which has expectation of $-E[z_i \sigma_i^{-2}(\partial \sigma_i^2 / \partial \delta)]$, a quantity unlikely to be zero. Accordingly, the var($\hat{\tau}$) must be computed from (4), or τ and δ must be jointly estimated.

As pointed out in the introduction to this section, there are instances in which the variance of u_i, and hence σ_i^2, will always depend solely upon whatever parameters β enter the conditional mean (along with x_i), i.e., δ coincides with β. In these situations Cameron (1991) points to the possibility of modifying m_i, so as to asymptotically eliminate any distributional dependence. Defining $m_i' = m_i + [E(\partial m_i / \partial \mu_i) | \mu_i](y_i - \mu_i)$, it is clear that

$$E(\partial m_i' / \partial \delta) = E(\partial m_i / \partial \delta) + E\{(\partial E[(\partial m_i / \partial \mu_i) | \mu_i] / \partial \delta))(y_i - \mu_i)\}$$
$$- E\{E[(\partial m_i / \partial \mu_i) | \mu_i](\partial \mu_i / \partial \delta] .^{16}$$

In this expression the middle term is zero and the last is just $-E(\partial m_i / \partial \delta)$, making $E(\partial m_i' / \partial \delta) = 0$. Thereupon, adopting $E(m_i') = 0$ as the requisite moment condition would allow any distributional dependence upon δ to be eliminated. Cameron puts $m_i = z_i \{(y_i - \mu_i)^2 - \tilde{\sigma}_i^2\}$ so that m_i' would be $z_i \{(y_i - \mu_i)^2 - \tilde{\sigma}_i^2 - (\partial \tilde{\sigma}_i^2 / \partial \mu_i)(y_i - \mu_i)\}$. For the moment condition $m_i = z_i(e_i^2 - 1)$, and

$$e_i = \tilde{\sigma}_i^{-1}(y_i - x_i'\beta) ,$$
$$\mu_i = x_i'\beta , \qquad E[(\partial m_i / \partial \mu_i) | \mu_i] = -z_i E[(\partial \tilde{\sigma}_i^2 / \partial \mu_i) \tilde{\sigma}_i^{-2} | \mu_i]$$

making $m_i' = z_i(e_i^2 - E[(\partial \tilde{\sigma}_i^2 / \partial \mu_i) \tilde{\sigma}_i^{-1} | \mu_i]e_i - 1)$.

Inspection of the modified moment m_i' in Cameron's case highlights the fact that the new test involves a component $\zeta_i e_i$, where $\zeta_i = -z_i E[(\partial \tilde{\sigma}_i^2 / \partial \mu_i) \tilde{\sigma}_i^{-1} | \mu_i]$, that is testing for specification error in the conditional mean, which makes sense given that the variance $\tilde{\sigma}_i^2$ is a function solely of the conditional mean (due to the fact that there are no parameters in δ not appearing in μ_i). Although in the regression model with normally distributed errors it is possible to make a distinction between whether it is the conditional mean or the conditional variance which is misspecified, outside of that context it is frequently very difficult to conceive of an alternative model in which changes in μ_i do not impinge upon σ_i^2. Therefore, tests of extrinsic heteroskedasticity inevitably involve a test for the correct specification of the conditional mean. Many of the models analyzed in this section have such a

---

[16] The term $E[(\partial m_i / \partial \mu_i) | \mu_i]$ would actually be evaluated under the *null* hypothesis. It is also obvious that it could be replaced with the unconditional expectation $E(\partial m_i / \partial \mu_i)$ without changing the argument. In most instances it is probably easier to find the conditional moment, but not always.

property. Moreover, because tests for correct specification of the conditional mean generally involve lower order moments, i.e., involve a test of $E(\zeta_i e_i) = 0$, it is unclear that tests involving the square of e_i^2 would ever be preferred. Indeed, as will become apparent, score tests for some of the models of this section do in fact involve examining a moment condition like $E(\zeta_i e_i) = 0$ and do not involve the squares of e_i at all.

4.2. Testing for heteroskedasticity in discrete choice models

Discrete choice models are associated with observations on a binary random variable y_i taking values zero or one, and some causal variables x_i, with the two sets related in such a manner that $\Pr(y_i = 0 | x_i) = F(x_i, \theta) = F_i$, where $F(t)$ is a distribution function. A standard way to motivate this probability is to interpret it as arising from a latent variable model

$$y_i^* = x_i'\beta + u_i^* , \tag{20}$$

where $\operatorname{var}(u_i^*) = 1$ and $y_i = 1(y_i^* \geq 0)$. Then $F(\cdot)$ will be the cumulative distribution function of the errors u_i^* and, using the binary structure of y_i,

$$y_i = (1 - F_i) + u_i , \tag{21}$$

where $F_i = \operatorname{prob}(u_i^* \leq -x_i'\beta) = F(-x_i'\beta)$ and u_i is heteroskedastic with conditional variance $F_i(1 - F_i)$. Hence, the conditional variance is always related to the conditional mean.

One might introduce extrinsic heteroskedasticity into this model by setting $\operatorname{var}(u_i^*) = (1 + w_i'\gamma)$, thereby modifying F_i to $F(-x_i'\beta/(1 + w_i'\gamma)^{1/2})$, where $F(\cdot)$ is now the distribution function of the standardized errors, $(1 + w_i'\gamma)^{-1/2} u_i^*$. Intrinsic heteroskedasticity will be $\tilde{\sigma}_i^2 = F_{0i}(1 - F_{0i})$, where $F_{0i} = F(-x_i'\beta)$, and the task is to see if there is any extra heteroskedasticity, i.e., to test if $\gamma = 0$. Following the discussion in Section 4.1 one could form a test statistic based on $\Sigma z_i(e_i^2 - 1)$, where $e_i = \tilde{\sigma}_i^{-1}(y_i - F_{0i})$. Alternatively, following Davidson and Mackinnon (1984), the score test for γ being zero could be used. As the log likelihood of $(y_1, \ldots, y_n)$, conditional upon $\{x_i, z_i\}_{i=1}^n$, will be

$$L = \sum_{i=1}^n \{(1 - y_i) \log(F_i) + y_i \log(1 - F_i)\} , \tag{22}$$

under H_0: $\gamma = 0$, the scores become

$$d_\gamma = \sum_{i=1}^n [(\partial F_i / \partial \gamma)_{\gamma=0}](1 - F_{0i})^{-1} F_{0i}^{-1}(y_i - F_{0i}) \tag{23}$$

$$= \sum_{i=1}^n z_i e_i , \tag{24}$$

where $z_i = [(\partial F_i / \partial \gamma)_{\gamma=0}](1 - F_{0i})^{-1/2} F_{0i}^{-1/2} = 0.5 w_i(x_i'\beta) f(x_i'\beta)(1 - F_{0i})^{-1/2} \times F_{0i}^{-1/2}$. As foreshadowed earlier the optimal test therefore does not involve the squares of e_i, and is effectively testing for specification errors in the conditional mean function.

4.3. Testing for heteroskedasticity in censored data models

There are many types of censored data but the simplest would be the case of left censoring at zero of the latent variable y_i^* in (20) introduced by Tobin (1958). Observed data is then $y_i = 1(y_i^* > 0)y_i^*$. For a non-negative random variable it is known that

$$E(y_i | x_i) = \int_{-x_i'\beta}^{\infty} (1 - F_0(\lambda)) \, d\lambda ,$$

where $F_0(\cdot)$ is the distribution function of u_i^*, while the conditional variance of y_i would be

$$\tilde{\sigma}_i^2 = 2 \int_{-x_i'\beta}^{\infty} (1 - F_0(\lambda))\lambda \, d\lambda + 2x_i'\beta \int_{-x_i'\beta}^{\infty} (1 - F_0(\lambda)) \, d\lambda$$
$$- \left\{ \int_{-x_i'\beta}^{\infty} [1 - F_0(\lambda)] \, d\lambda \right\}^2 ,$$

and these could be used to define e_i for the purpose of constructing the moment $n^{-1} \Sigma z_i(e_i^2 - 1)$. A disadvantage of the approach is that $F_0(\lambda)$ must either be estimated or specified. One possibility is to estimate it by non-parametric methods, see Whang and Andrews (1991), but no applications in that vein are reported in the literature, and there would seem little benefit in so doing as a misspecification of either heteroskedasticity or the density for u_i^* essentially has the same impact, and it is going to be very difficult to distinguish between the two types of specification error. For that reason $F_0(\cdot)$ is likely to be specified, and therefore one might as well construct a score test for heteroskedasticity.

Assuming that $\bar{\sigma}_i^2 = \text{var}(u_i^*)$ is a function of some parameters γ such that $\gamma = \gamma^*$ produces a constant variance σ^2, $f(\cdot)$ is the density function of $u_i^*/\bar{\sigma}_i$, and $F(\lambda) = \int_{-\infty}^{\lambda} f(u) \, du$, the log likelihood of the data is

$$L = \sum_{i=1}^{n} (1 - y_i) \log F(-x_i'\beta/\bar{\sigma}_i)$$
$$+ \sum_{i=1}^{n} y_i \{-0.5 \log \bar{\sigma}_i^2 + \log f[(y_i - x_i'\beta)/\bar{\sigma}_i)]\} , \tag{25}$$

with scores evaluated at $\gamma = \gamma^*$

$$\tfrac{1}{2} \sum_{i=1}^{n} \sigma^{-1}(\partial \bar{\sigma}_i^2/\partial \gamma)|_{\gamma=\gamma^*} \{(1 - y_i)f_0(\xi_i)F_0^{-1}(\xi_i)\xi_i - y_i(\psi_i \varepsilon_i - 1)\} , \tag{26}$$

where $\xi_i = (x_i'\beta)/\sigma$, $e_i = \sigma^{-1}(y_i - x_i'\beta)$, $\varepsilon_i = \sigma_i^{-1}u_i^*$, and $\psi_i = f_{0i}^{-1}(\varepsilon_i)(\partial f_{0i}/\partial \varepsilon_i)$.

As expected, if there is no censoring ($y_i = 1$), the test would be identical to that for the uncensored case (see (19)). In general, it does not reduce to a test involving the squares of e_i. Jarque and Bera (1982) derived this test and Lee and Maddala (1985) interpret it as a conditional moment test. As with the regression case one might base a test on a comparison of the MLE of β and another estimator that is consistent when there is no heteroskedasticity. Powell's (1986) censored quantile estimator minimizing $\Sigma_{i=1}^{n} \rho[y_i - \max\{0, x_i'\beta\}]$, where $\rho(\lambda) = [\eta - 1(\lambda < 0)]\lambda$, could be used as the analogue of the Koenker–Bassett proposal for the linear regression model discussed in Section 3.3.

4.4. Testing for heteroskedasticity in count data models

The modelling of discrete count data, such as the number of patents granted or the number of visits to a medical facility, has become of greater interest to econometricians as large scale data sets containing such information have emerged. Naturally, the 'work horse' in the analysis of such data sets has been the Poisson regression model, but, owing to the fact that it forces a restriction, upon the data, that the conditional mean of y_i, μ_i, is equal to the conditional variance, there have been attempts to supplement it with models based on other densities not having such a restriction. An example would be the negative binomial density used by Hausman, Hall and Griliches (1984) and Collings and Margolin (1985). However, sometimes such alternatives are difficult to estimate, and it is not surprising that a literature developed to test for whether the type of heteroskedasticity seen in the data deviated from that intrinsic to the Poisson model, i.e., to test whether var(y_i) equaled the E(y_i).

Since the maintained model is generally the Poisson model the situation is one of a regression such as (15), albeit the conditional mean μ_i may no longer be linear in the x_i but rather may be a non-linear function such as $\exp(x_i'\beta)$. Given some specification for μ_i, the Poisson regression model has $\tilde{\sigma}_i^2 = \mu_i$ and the obvious moment condition to test is $E(z_i(e_i^2 - 1)) = 0$.

An alternative way to write this condition is as $E(z_i(e_i^2 - \mu_i^{-1}E(y_i))) = 0$ which, under the maintained hypothesis of a Poisson model, becomes $E\{z_i\mu_i^{-1}[(y_i - \mu_i)^2 - y_i]\} = E\{\bar{z}_i[(y_i - \mu_i)^2 - y_i]\} = 0$. Defining a class of regression models for count data that are indexed by a parameter γ, and which reduce to the Poisson model when $\gamma = 0$, Cameron and Trivedi (1990) point out that the last mentioned condition coincides with the score test based on γ if the wider class derives from the Katz system of densities set out in Lee (1986), or from the 'local to Poisson' case of Cox (1983). Differences in score tests therefore reside solely in the nature of $\bar{z}_i$.[17]

---

[17] Assuming that μ_i is a function of parameters β, when using the moment $m_i = \bar{z}_i[(y_i - \mu_i)^2 - y_i]$ it will be the case that $E[\partial m_i/\partial \beta] = 0$ and, consequently, there will be no nuisance parameter dependencies. In contrast, as Cameron and Trivedi observe, if m_i was replaced by $\bar{m}_i = \bar{z}_i[(y_i - \mu_i)^2 - \mu_i]$, now there would be nuisance parameter dependencies, even though $E(\bar{m}_i) = 0$ under the null hypothesis of a Poisson model.

Selecting $\bar{z}_i$ requires an alternative model for the variance of u_i, $\bar{\sigma}_i^2 = \bar{\sigma}_i^2 \sigma_i^2 = \mu_i \sigma_i^2$, and may be found as follows. From (18) z_i should be set to $(\partial \sigma_i^2 / \partial \gamma)|_{\gamma=0}$ and, if $\sigma_i^2 = 1 + \gamma g_1(\mu_i)$, this would make $z_i = g_1(\mu_i)$ under the Poisson specification. Converting to $\bar{z}_i$ gives $\bar{z}_i = \mu_i^{-1} g_1(\mu_i) = \mu_i^{-2} g(\mu_i)$, adopting Cameron and Trivedi's notation. For their test they employ $g(\mu_i)$ as either μ_i or μ_i^2, i.e., $g_1(\mu_i)$ is either unity or μ_i, leading to tests based on the moment conditions $E(e_i^2 - 1) = 0$ and $E(\mu_i(e_i^2 - 1)) = 0$. In simulation studies reported in their paper the variances of the test statistics are formed in a number of ways, either by explicitly evaluating $E(m_i m_i')$ under the maintained hypothesis of a Poisson model or by the adoption of a robust version, and it was the latter which had better performance.

4.5. Specification tests for additional ARCH effects

In recent years the ARCH model and its variants have become a very popular way of modelling heteroskedasticity in econometric models, particularly those concerned with financial time series – see Bollerslev et al. (1992) for a survey. In terms of the structure of Section 4.1, u_i is defined by (15) (perhaps with a non-linear rather than linear function of x_i) with variance $\bar{\sigma}_i^2$, becoming $\tilde{\sigma}_i^2$ with a particular maintained type of conditional heteroskedasticity. A number of alternative specifications for $\bar{\sigma}_i^2$ have emerged. A general expression would be $g(\alpha_0 + \Sigma_{j=1}^r \alpha_j h_{ij}(u_{i-j}))$, which is indexed by three characteristics, $g(\cdot)$, $h_{ij}(\cdot)$ and r. Table 1 provides a list of some of the most popular cases according to the values assigned to these functions and the parameter r. Others would be possible, e.g., one could make $\bar{\sigma}_i^2$ functions of a series expansion in u_{t-i} or e_{t-i}, e.g., using the flexible Fourier form as in Pagan and Schwert (1990) or the neural network approximation in Kamstra (1990).

One can distinguish two different situations in connection with the above formats. The first is when $\bar{\sigma}_i^2$ is nested within the alternative $\tilde{\sigma}_i^2$ so that $\bar{\sigma}_i^2 = \tilde{\sigma}_i^2$ when a set of parameters γ take the value γ^*, e.g., if the maintained model is ARCH and the alternative is GARCH or NARCH. Then, as detailed in Section 3.2, the optimal choice of z_i depends upon $(\partial \sigma_i^2 / \partial \gamma)_{\gamma=\gamma^*} = \bar{\sigma}_i^{-2}(\partial \bar{\sigma}_i^2 / \partial \gamma)|_{\gamma=\gamma^*}$, because $\sigma_i^2 = \bar{\sigma}_i^2 / \tilde{\sigma}_i^2$ and γ does not appear in the de-

Table 1
Autoregressive conditional heteroskedasticity formats

Name	r	$g(\psi)$	$h_{ij}(u_{i-j})$	Source
ARCH(p)	finite	identity	u_{ij}^2	Engle (1982)
GARCH	∞	identity	u_{ij}^2	Bollerslev (1986)
NARCH	finite	$\psi^{1/\gamma}$	$u_{i-j}^{2\gamma}$	Higgins and Bera (1989)
MARCH	∞	identity	$\sin(u_{i-j}^2)$ if $au_{i-j}^2 < \frac{1}{2}\pi$ unity if $au_{i-j}^2 \geq \frac{1}{2}\pi$	Friedman and Laibson (1989)
EGARCH	∞	$\exp(\psi)$	$\delta e_i + \{|e_i| - (2/\pi)^{1/2}\}$	Nelson (1991)

The basic model is $\bar{\sigma}_i^2 = g(\psi)$ where $\psi = \alpha_0 + \Sigma_{j=1}^r \alpha_j h_{ij}(\cdot)$, where $(\cdot)$ can be either u_{i-j} or e_{i-j}. When $r = \infty$ there are restrictions between the α_j.

nominator. Consequently, it is simply a matter of finding the derivatives of $\bar{\sigma}_i^2$ with respect to γ evaluated with $\gamma = \gamma^*$, i.e., $\bar{\sigma}_i^2 = \tilde{\sigma}_i^2$. For the NARCH model as alternative this becomes

$$z_i = \sum_{j=1}^{r} \hat{\alpha}_j \hat{e}_{t-j}^2 \log(\hat{e}_{t-j}^2) - \tilde{\sigma}_i \log(\tilde{\sigma}_i)$$

(Higgins and Bera, 1989). If, however, the two conditional variances are non-nested, as occurs with an EGARCH/GARCH comparison, this strategy will not work. Ideally one wants z_i to reflect the 'extra' information in $\bar{\sigma}_i^2$ not contained in $\tilde{\sigma}_i^2$. Because the term $\tilde{\sigma}_i^{-2}(\partial \bar{\sigma}_i^2/\partial \gamma)_{\gamma=\gamma^*}$ in the nested case essentially represents the difference between $\tilde{\sigma}_i^2$ and $\bar{\sigma}_i^2$, z_i is ideally very like $\bar{\sigma}_i^2$. However, to measure this we would need to estimate under both the null and alternative, which is not in the spirit of a diagnostic test. A simple solution is to think of $\bar{\sigma}_i^2$ as a function of $\tilde{\sigma}_i^2$ and to choose z_i in that way. If one has a precise alternative in mind, one could form $\hat{\bar{\sigma}}_i^2$ from $\hat{\tilde{\sigma}}_i^2$ using whatever transformation defines $\bar{\sigma}_i^2$, e.g., $\exp(\hat{\tilde{\sigma}}_i^2)$ might be used for z_i when EGARCH is thought of as the alternative. Pagan and Sabau (1992) used $\tilde{\sigma}_i^2$ itself, although, as Sabau (1988) found, the power of such a test is unlikely to be very strong in many instances. The reason is set out in Pagan and Sabau (1991); the power of their test derives from the extent of the inconsistency in the MLE estimator of β induced by misspecification of the conditional variance. In the basic regression model there will be no inconsistency, but, because β also enters into the determination of $\tilde{\sigma}_i^2$, the possibility of inconsistency arises in ARCH models. Pagan and Sabau determine that inconsistency only eventuates if the true conditional variance is an asymmetric function of u_i, which it would be if the alternative model to an ARCH was (say) EGARCH, but would not be if the alternative was GARCH. Apart from this research, the question of good choices for z_i does not seen to have been explored in the literature, and it is worthy of some further study.

Tests for different types of volatility specifications also encounter the same set of difficulties as arose when testing for whether there is any heteroskedasticity in the basic regression model viz. possible dependence upon estimated nuisance parameters and the fact that the optimal form of the test will depend upon the density of e_i. With regard to the first, $\tilde{\sigma}_i^2$ depends upon both β and other parameters δ (as seen in Table 1). Taking $m_i = z_i(e_i^2 - 1)$ it is necessary that $E(z_i(\partial e_i^2/\partial \theta)) = 0$ if there is to be no dependence upon estimates of θ. It is easily seen that this is unlikely to be true for $\theta = \delta$, and is even problematic for β. To appreciate the complications with the latter, differentiate $\tilde{\sigma}_i^{-2}(y_i - x_i'\beta)^2$ with respect to β, giving $-\tilde{\sigma}_i^{-2}x_i u_i - \tilde{\sigma}_i^{-4}u_i^2(\partial \tilde{\sigma}_i^2/\partial \beta)$. This will only have zero expectation if $\partial \tilde{\sigma}_i^2/\partial \beta$ is an odd function of u_i and u_i is in turn symmetrically distributed around zero (conditional upon $\mathcal{F}_i$). For the GARCH model, the errors u_i are generally taken to be conditionally normal, while $\partial \tilde{\sigma}_i^2/\partial \beta$ is an odd function, thereby satisfying both conditions, but that would not be true of the EGARCH model. It would also not be true of the GARCH model if the density of u_i was not symmetric. However, since the parameters are most likely to have been estimated by MLE, one could always regress $\hat{m}_i$ upon unity and the estimated scores to allow for the effects of prior estimation. Turning to the second question of the selection of ϕ_i in $m_i = z_i \phi_i$, there has been little research into using the alternative moment condition, mentioned in Section 3.2, in which ϕ_i is set to $(-\psi_i e_i - 1)$ rather than $(e_i^2 - 1)$, although Engle and Gonzalez-Rivera (1991) attempted estimation in this way.

Many applications of the ARCH technology are not to pure ARCH models but to ARCH-M (ARCH in mean) contexts, in which a function of $\bar{\sigma}_i^2$ appears among the regressors in (15). Thus a specification error in the conditional variance now affects the mean and the situation is reminiscent of the models discussed in Sections 4.2 and 4.3. Therefore, although a test might be based upon $\Sigma z_i(\hat{e}_i^2 - 1)$, it is likely to be better to directly test the mean using $n^{-1} \Sigma z_i \hat{e}_i$. Oddly enough, in Pagan and Sabau's (1992) application of these tests to the ARCH-M model estimated in Engle et al. (1987), the test based on the squares of $\hat{e}_i^2$ gave much stronger rejection than that based on $\hat{e}_i$.

5. The size and power of heteroskedasticity tests

5.1. The size of tests

The moment tests outlined in Section 2 are based on asymptotic theory, raising the possibility that the asymptotic results may fail to be a reliable indicator of test performance in small samples. Many simulation studies have shown that this is true for score tests of heteroskedasticity in the regression model, especially for those based upon normality in u_i, with a frequent finding being that the actual size of the tests is less than the nominal one available from asymptotic theory. When robust tests are utilized it is equally common to find that the nominal is less than the actual size, e.g., Skeels and Vella (1991) find that the true size for tests of heteroskedasticity in the censored regression model obtained by robustly estimating $E(\partial m_i / \partial \gamma)$ and $var(m_i)$ can be twice the nominal size. Only rarely can the exact distribution of any of these tests be analytically determined, an exception being the Goldfeld–Quandt test, creating an interest in approximating the finite sample distributions or modifying the test statistics to more closely approximate the asymptotic distribution. There are four broad approaches in the literature and these are summarized below.

(i) *Approximation by expansion.* When the m_i are the scores, the test statistic will be a score test and a general formula for the finite sample distribution of score tests (S) was provided by Harris (1985):

$$P[S \leq c] = P_q + (24n)^{-1}\{\alpha_3 P_{q+6} + (\alpha_2 - 3\alpha_3)P_{q+4}$$

$$+ (3\alpha_3 - 2\alpha_2 + \alpha_1)P_{q+2} + (\alpha_2 - \alpha_1 - \alpha_3)P_q\} + o(n^{-1}), \quad (27)$$

where $P_q = \text{Prob}(\chi_q^2 \leq c)$, q is the dimension of the extra parameters being tested by the score test, and α_1, α_2, α_3 are functions of cumulants of derivatives of the log likelihood. Computing α_1, α_2 and α_3 can be very complex and mostly needs to be done with a symbolic differentiation package. Honda (1988) specialized this general formula to the case where one was testing for heteroskedasticity in the linear regression model. A serious reservation with this approach is that the *exact* score test needs to be used; in particular, the information matrix needs to be employed as the var(m_i), thereby precluding the use of robust estimates. In practice the exact score test is rarely used, e.g., the modification in Koenker (1981) of the score test for heteroskedasticity in the linear regression model is what appears in most regression packages, and the distribution of that statistic would be different to what is presented in (27). Of course, if the robust statistic has the same asymptotic distribution as the score test we might hope that (27) would be a reliable guide to its distribution in finite samples. Recently, Smith (1990) has shown that the form of (27) remains valid even when var(Σm_i) is estimated by $\Sigma m_i m_i'$ except that the α need to be re-defined. To date his results have not been applied to heteroskedasticity tests.

(ii) *Approximation by distribution*. An alternative to an asymptotic expansion is to regard the small sample distribution as being well approximated by some density such as the beta, and to estimate the parameters of the latter by matching up the finite sample moments with those of the approximating distribution. The approximate Prob[$\hat{\tau} \leq c$] may then be found from the beta distribution. Harrison (1980) did this and found it worked quite well for tests of heteroskedasticity in the linear model.

(iii) *Numerical determination of p-values*. Rather than approximate the complete distribution of the statistic $\hat{\tau}$ it is only the *p*-value for a given estimate (c) which is sought. In the linear regression model with normally distributed errors and a single variable z_i, the statistic $\hat{\tau} = \Sigma z_i(\hat{\sigma}^{-2}\hat{u}_i^2 - 1)$ can be written as the ratio of quadratic forms in $\sigma^{-1}u_i$, allowing Imhof's (1961) method of computing *p*-values for such test statistics to be applied. With more than a single z_i this is no longer true, but the fact that the quadratic form is in $\sigma^{-1}u_i$, an $\mathcal{N}(0, 1)$ random variable, means that realizations of $\sigma^{-1}u_i$ can be drawn from an $\mathcal{N}(0, 1)$ random number generator. Counting the fraction of times for which $\hat{\tau}$, computed with these numbers, is greater than c constitutes an estimator of the *p*-value. Breusch and Pagan (1979) advocated this approach and regarded it as a simple and cheap way of finding *p*-values. The idea was originally mooted by Barnard (1963). In the context of testing for heteroskedasticity it has been adopted by Bewley and Theil (1987) when looking at this problem in systems of demand equations. Working with PCs the computation of *p*-values by simulation is very easy and quite cheap, although it does require re-estimation of the basic model, and, in the context of censored regression or discrete choice models, the cost may still be too high (although it should be remembered that one is only dealing with cases where the sample size is small and the iterative procedures to compute $\hat{\theta}$ can always be started with values from the previous replication).

The procedure also applies to tests modified to gain robustness or those designed to emulate the optimal score tests, since the latter are still functions of $\sigma^{-1}u_i$. However, if the density of u_i is unknown, one cannot simulate from it, and bootstrapping is now the obvious alternative numerical procedure, with the u_i (or m_i) being drawn from the empirical rather than the assumed density function. Technically, the conditions for the success of the bootstrap are not exactly satisfied here as the statistics are not 'pivotal', being dependent upon the estimated parameters θ. However, as this dependence disappears asymptotically one would expect that the method would work well.

(iv) *Modifying the test statistic*. Instead of finding an approximation to the small sample distribution of $\hat{\tau}$ it is sometimes more useful to modify the test statistic to make it correspond more closely to the asymptotic distribution. A simple adjustment in this vein is to form $\hat{\tau}' = \hat{\tau} - \bar{\tau}$, where $\bar{\tau}$ is the $E(\hat{\tau})$ in finite samples, and to refer $\hat{\tau}'$ to the asymptotic distribution of $\hat{\tau}$. Essentially this is an attempt to correct for the fact that $E(\hat{\tau}) = 0$ only in large samples, and therefore $\hat{\tau}$ will not be centered on zero in finite samples. Conniffe (1990) reports some success with this adjustment for score tests generally while Ara and King (1991) find that it works well for tests of heteroskedasticity in the linear regression model based on $\Sigma z_i(\hat{\sigma}^{-2}\hat{u}_i^2 - 1)$. The major difficulty in applying the idea is to determine $E(\hat{\tau})$, particularly if z_i is stochastic or the data is censored, although one might employ simulation methods to do this.

5.2. The power of tests

A number of studies have been developed to investigate the power of tests mentioned in the preceding sections at detecting heteroskedasticity. Most effort has been concentrated upon the linear regression model, although Skeels and Vella (1991), working with $n = 600$, found that score tests were good in the censored regression model but very poor in the Probit model. Ali and Giacotto (1984), Griffiths and Surekha (1986), Kamstra (1990) and Evans and King (1985, 1988) are perhaps the most comprehensive studies available of the linear regression case. Sometimes it is difficult to draw lessons from these reports as only overall results are provided, involving averaging across many experiments, and, unfortunately, some of these experiments fail to satisfy the assumptions needed to apply either asymptotic or finite sample theory when determining the distributions under the null hypothesis. Worst in this respect is Ali and Giacotto who have an extremely large number of different experiments, some of which feature moments of u_i that do not exist, while others are done with non-symmetric densities for u_i which would invalidate the reference of tests such as Glejser's to chi-square distributions. It is almost impossible therefore to draw any conclusions from their work, as one does not know which experiments are responsible for the poor performance of any test. In other instances, for example Kamstra's demonstration that the power of robust tests using $\Sigma m_i m_i'$ as an estimate of var(Σm_i) is very weak when testing for ARCH, no explanation for the phenomenon has emerged similar to those provided by

Chesher and Spady (1991) and Kennan and Neumann (1988) for kurtosis tests. Until one fully understands the causes of these results it is hard to know if one should recommend against the use of the associated tests.

Some experiments come up with clear cut results, but the experimental design seems to be too restricted or the conditions are not sufficiently qualified. For example, Griffiths and Surekha conclude that the use of $z_i = i$ is to be recommended over the Goldfeld–Quandt and Breusch/Pagan/Godfrey (B/P/ G) test if it is possible to order the observations by increasing variance, and that one should use BAMSET if it is not possible to do so.[18] Because the ability to order data by increasing variance means that the heteroskedasticity must be a monotonic function of i, it follows that setting $z_i = i$ rather than to dummy variables, as in Goldfeld–Quandt and BAMSET, should be advantageous. What is surprising is their conclusion concerning BAMSET, since the B/P/G test is invariant to ordering. In fact, the power of B/P/G can be directly compared to BAMSET in their Table 1, and it is clearly much larger. Hence, their conclusion is contradicted by their own results. It may be that the objective was to conclude that, within the class of tests that used no information about the variables forcing the conditional variance, BAMSET was best, and indeed the body of the text seems to read this way, but that is not the conclusion stated in the paper. Even adopting such an interpretation would be odd, since the ability to order the data by increasing variance means that one knows the variance is driven by a time trend.

A similar set of comments can be made about the studies by Evans and King (1985, 1988), and their conclusion that '. . . the emphasis on the B and P test in the recent econometric literature is probably misspecified'. Their preference is for the point optimal test described in Section 3.2 over the B/P/G or Goldfeld–Quandt tests. Again the data is generated so that the true heteroskedasticity is always a monotonic transformation of a trend term and the z_i used is also a monotonic transform of the variable. This feature produces a bias against the Goldfeld–Quandt test, but there are two further factors in the experiment that help the performance of the point optimal test. First, the true heteroskedasticity is generated with a single unknown parameter that is positive, and their test statistic takes account of the positivity of that parameter, whereas the B/P/G test does not. Second, as seen in Section 3.2, the point optimal test uses information about the alternative, rather than just local information as in the score test, so the fact that it has superior power when there is a high degree of heteroskedasticity is quite consistent with the nature of each of the tests. Even with these advantages the power differential is only moderate, of the order of 10%.

---

[18] It may be worth emphasizing that there is no such thing as a B/P/G test without specifying what z_i is. What one specifies the heteroskedasticity to be when devising the test, and what it actually is, are two different matters. For example, in Breusch and Pagan (1979) a test was given with z_i as a dummy variable, so one might even refer to it as the Goldfeld–Quandt test, showing how meaningless the appellation is.

6. Conclusion

This paper has surveyed methods of testing for heteroskedasticity in a variety of models. Some of these tests are routinely provided as the standard output of computer packages, whilst others still only have spasmodic use. Our strategy was to treat existing tests as focusing on the validity of certain conditional moment restrictions, since the general results from that literature can be brought to bear on this specific problem. Our inquiry also revealed that quite a deal of work remains to be done to understand the performance of tests. Some of the issues raised relate to finite sample performance, and others to the poor performance of tests designed to be robust to departures from the auxiliary assumptions made in constructing them. To date, simulation studies have not addressed these questions very effectively, even neglecting to exploit what existing theory gives as the expected outcomes. As mentioned at various points in Section 5, asymptotic theoretical analysis can predict whether certain tests would be expected to work well in a given experiment, yet such results have rarely been incorporated into the analysis. For example, the power of any conditional moment test against a sequence of local alternatives can be computed with formulae in Newey (1985). Combining together these different sources of information seems mandatory if we are to fully understand the sampling behavior of tests of heteroskedasticity.

Acknowledgment

We would like to thank Colin Cameron, Bruce Hansen and Pravin Trivedi for their comments on an earlier version of this paper.

References

Ali, M. M. and C. Giacotto (1984). A study of several new and existing tests for heteroscedasticity in the general linear model. *J. Econometrics* **26**, 355–373.

Arabmazar, A. and P. Schmidt (1981). Further evidence on the robustness of the tobit estimator to heteroscedasticity. *J. Econometrics* **17**, 253–258.

Ara, I. and M. L. King (1991). Marginal likelihood based tests of regression disturbances. Mimeo, Monash University.

Andrews, D. W. K. (1990). Tests for parameter instability and structural change with unknown change point. Cowles Foundation Discussion Paper No. 943, Yale University.

Andrews, D. W. K. (1991). Heteroskedasticity and autocorrelation consistent covariance matrix estimation . *Econometrica* **59**, 817–858.

Barnard, G. A. (1963). Comment. *J. Roy. Statist. Soc. Ser. B* **25**, 294.

Bartlett, M. S. (1937). Properties of sufficiency and statistical tests. *Proc. Roy. Soc. London Ser. A* **160**, 268–282.

Bewley, R. and H. Theil (1987). Monte Carlo testing for heteroscedasticity in equation systems. In: T. B. Fomby and G. F. Rhodes, eds., *Adv. in Econometrics*, Vol. 6. J.A.I. Press, Greenwich, CT, 1–15.

Bickel, P. (1978). Using residuals robustly: Tests for heteroscedasticity and nonlinearity. *Ann. Statist.* **6**, 266–291.

Breusch, T. S. and A. R. Pagan (1979). A simple test for heteroscedasticity and random coefficient variation. *Econometrica* **47**, 1287–1294.

Bollerslev, T. (1986). Generalized autoregressive conditional heteroskedasticity. *J. Econometrics* **31**, 307–327.

Bollerslev, T., Chou R. Y. and K. F. Kroner (1992). ARCH modeling in finance: A review of the theory and empirical evidence. *J. Econometrics* **52**, 5–60.

Cameron, C. (1991). Regression based tests of heteroscedasticity in models where the variance depends on the mean. Working Paper No. 379, University of California, Davis, CA.

Cameron, A. C. and P. K. Trivedi (1990). Regression based tests for overdispersion in the Poisson model. *J. Econometrics* **46**, 347–364.

Cameron, A. C. and P. K. Trivedi (1991). Conditional moment tests with explicit alternatives. Mimeo, University of Indiana.

Carroll, R. J. (1982). Adapting for heteroscedasticity in linear models. *Ann. Statist.* **10**, 1224–1233.

Chesher, A. and R. Spady (1991). Asymptotic expansions of the information matrix test statistic. *Econometrica* **59**, 787–815.

Collings, B. J. and B. H. Margolin (1985). Testing goodness of fit for the Poisson assumption when observations are not identically distributed. *J. Amer. Statist. Assoc.* **80**, 411–418.

Conniffe, D. (1990). Applying estimated score tests in econometrics. Paper presented to the 6th World Congress of the Econometric Society, Barcelona.

Cox. D. R. (1983). Some remarks on overdispersion. *Biometrika* **70**, 269–274.

Dastoor, N. K. (1990). The asymptotic behaviour of some tests for heteroskedasticity. Mimeo, University of Alberta.

Davidson, R. and J. G. Mackinnon (1984). Convenient specification tests for logit and probit models. *J. Econometrics* **25**, 241–262.

Eicker, F. (1967). Limit theorems for regressions with unequal and dependent errors. 5th Berkeley Sympos. on Mathematical Statistics and Probability, Vol. 1, Berkeley, University of California, 59–82.

Engle, R. F. (1982). Autoregressive conditional heteroscedasticity with estimates of the variance of United Kingdom inflation. *Econometrica* **50**, 987–1007.

Engle, R. F. and T. Bollerslev (1986). Modelling the persistence of conditional variances. *Econometric Rev.* **5**, 1–50.

Engle, R. F., L. M. Lillien and R. P. Robins (1987). Estimating time varying risk premia in the term structure. *Econometrica* **55**, 391–407.

Engle, R. F. and G. Gonzalez-Rivera (1991). Semiparametric ARCH models. *J. Business Econom. Statist.* **9**, 345–359.

Evans, M. A. and M. L. King (1985). A point optimal test for heteroscedastic disturbances. *J. Econometrics* **27**, 163–178.

Evans, M. A. and M. L. King (1988). A further class of tests for heteroscedasticity. *J. Econometrics* **37**, 265–276.

Friedman, B. M. and D. I. Laibson (1989). Economic implications of extraordinary movements in stock prices. *Brookings Papers Econom. Activity* **2**(89), 137–189.

Glejser, H. (1969). A new test for heteroscedasticity. *J. Amer. Statist. Assoc.* **64**, 316–323.

Godfrey, L. (1978). Testing for multiplicative heteroscedasticity. *J. Econometrics* **8**, 227–236.

Goldfeld, S. and R. Quandt (1965). Some tests for heteroscedasticity. *J. Amer. Statist. Assoc.* **60**, 539–547.

Gurmu, S. and P. K. Trivedi (1990). Variable augmentation specification tests in the exponential family. Mimeo, University of Indiana.

Griffiths, W. E. and K. Surekha (1986). A Monte Carlo evaluation of the power of some tests for heteroscedasticity. *J. Econometrics* **31**, 219–231.

Hansen, B. E. (1990). Lagrange multiplier tests for parameter instability in non-linear models. Mimeo, University of Rochester.

Harris, P. (1985). An asymptotic expansion for the null distribution of the efficient score statistic. *Biometrika* **72**, 653–659.

Harrison, M. J. (1980). The small sample performance of the Szroeter bounds test for heteroskedasticity and a simple test for use when Szroeter's test is inconclusive. *Bull. Econom. Social Res.* **42**, 235–250.

Harrison, M. J. and B. P. M. McCabe (1979). A test for heteroscedasticity based on ordinary least squares residuals. *J. Amer. Statist. Assoc.* **74**, 494–499.

Hausman, J. (1978). Specification tests in econometrics. *Econometrica* **46**, 1251–1271.

Hausman, J., B. H. Hall and Z. Griliches (1984). Econometric models for count data with an application to the patents-R&D relationship. *Econometrica* **52**, 909–938.

Higgins, M. L. and A. K. Bera (1989). A class of nonlinear ARCH models: Properties, testing and applications. Working paper 89-1554, Bureau of Economic and Business Research, University of Illinois, Urbana-Champaign, IL.

Honda, Y. (1988). A size correction to the Lagrange multiplier test for heteroskedasticity. *J. Econometrics* **38**, 375–386.

Imhof, J. P. (1961). Computing the distribution of quadratic forms in normal variables. *Biometrika* **48**, 419–426.

Jarque, C. M. and A. K. Bera (1982). Efficient specification tests for limited dependent variable models. *Econom. Lett.* **9**, 153–160.

Kamstra, M. (1990). A neural network test for heteroskedasticity. Discussion Paper No. 91-06 Simon Fraser University.

Kennan, J. and G. R. Neumann (1988). Why does the information matrix test reject so often? Working Paper in Economics E-88-10, Hoover Institution, Stanford University.

King, M. H. and G. H. Hillier (1985). Locally best invariant tests of the error covariance matrix of the linear regression model. *J. Roy. Statist. Soc. Ser. B* **47**, 98–102.

Koenker, R. (1981). A note on studentizing a test for heteroscedasticity. *J. Econometrics* **17**, 107–112.

Koenker, R. and G. S. Bassett (1982). Robust tests for heteroscedasticity based on regression quantiles. *Econometrica* **50**, 43–61.

Lee, L.-F. (1986). Specification tests for Poisson regression models. *Internat. Econom. Rev.* **27**, 689–706.

Lee, L.-F. and G. S. Maddala (1985). The common structure of tests for selectivity bias, serial correlation, heteroscedasticity and nonnormality in the tobit model. *Internat. Econom. Rev.* **26**, 1–20.

McCabe, B. P. M. (1986). Testing for heteroscedasticity occurring at unknown points. *Comm. Statist. Theory Methods* **15**, 1597–1613.

McCullagh, P. and J. A. Nelder (1983). *Generalized Linear Models*. Chapman and Hall, London.

McCulloch, J. H. (1985). On heteros*edasticity. *Econometrica* **53**, 483.

McDonald, J. B. and W. Newey (1988). Partially adaptive estimation of regression models via the generalized *t* distribution. *Econometric Theory* **4**, 428–457.

Nelson, D. B. (1991). Conditional heteroskedasticity in asset returns: A new approach. *Econometrica* **59**, 347–370.

Newey, W. K. (1985a). Maximum likelihood specification testing and conditional moment tests. *Econometrica* **53**, 1047–1070.

Newey, W. K. and J. L. Powell (1987). Asymmetric least squares estimation and testing. *Econometrica* **55**, 819–847.

Pagan, A. R. and A. D. Hall (1983). Diagnostic tests as residual analysis. *Econometric Rev.* **2**, 159–218.

Pagan, A. R. and H. Sabau (1991). On the inconsistency of the MLE in certain heteroskedastic regression models. *Estudios Economicos* **6**, 159–172.

Pagan, A. R. and H. Sabau (1992). Consistency tests for heteroskedasticity and risk models. *Estudios Economicos* **7**, 3–30.

Pagan, A. R. and G. W. Schwert (1990). Alternative models for conditional stock volatility. *J. Econometrics* **45**, 267–290.

Pagan, A. R. and F. X. Vella (1989). Diagnostic tests for models based on individual data. *J. Appl. Econometrics* **4**, S29–S52.

Pesaran, M. H. and B. Pesaran (1987). *MICROFIT: An Interactive Econometric Software Package*. Oxford University Press, Oxford.

Phillips, P. C. B. and M. Loretan (1990). Testing covariance stationarity under moment condition failure with an application to common stock returns. Cowles Foundation Discussion Paper No. 947, Yale University.

Potscher, B. M. and I. R. Prucha (1986). A class of partially adaptive one-step *M* estimators for the nonlinear regression model with dependent observations. *J. Econometrics* **25**, 219–251.

Powell, J. L. (1986). Censored regression quantiles. *J. Econometrics* **32**, 143–155.

Ramsey, J. (1969). Tests for specification error in the general linear model. *J. Roy. Statist. Soc. Ser. B* **31**, 250–271.

Robinson, P. M. (1987). Asymptotically efficient estimation in the presence of heteroskedasticity of unknown form. *Econometrica* **55**, 875–891.

Sabau, H. C. L. (1988). Some theoretical aspects of econometric inference with heteroskedastic models. Unpublished doctoral dissertation, Australian National University.

Skeels, C. L. and F. Vella (1991). A Monte Carlo investigation of the performance of conditional moment tests in tobit and probit models. Mimeo, Australian National University.

Smith, R. J. (1990). An Edgeworth approximation for the null distribution of the outer product form of the score or Lagrange multiplier statistic. Mimeo, University of Cambridge.

Szroeter, J. (1978). A class of parametric tests for heteroscedasticity in linear econometric models. *Econometrica* **46**, 1311–1328.

Tauchen, G. (1985). Diagnostic testing and evaluation of maximum likelihood models. *J. Econometrics* **30**, 415–443.

Tobin, J. (1958). Estimation of relationships for limited dependent variables. *Econometrica* **26**, 24–36.

Tse, Y. K. and C. T. Phoon (1985). Testing for heteroscedasticity in a dynamic simultaneous equation model. *Comm. Statist. Theory and Methods* **14**, 1283–1300.

Whang, Y. J. and D. W. K. Andrews (1991). Tests of specification for parametric and semiparametric models. Cowles Foundation Discussion Paper No. 968, Yale University.

White, H. (1980). A heteroskedasticity-consistent covariance matrix estimator and a direct test for heteroskedasticity. *Econometrica* **48**, 817–838.

White, H. (1987). Specification testing in dynamic models, In: T. Bewley, ed., *Adv. in Econometrics*, 5th World Congress, Vol. 1. Cambridge Univ. Press, New York, 1–58.

Wooldridge, J. M. (1990). A unified approach to robust, regression-based specification tests. *Econometric Theory* **6**, 17–43.

G. S. Maddala, C. R. Rao and H. D. Vinod, eds., *Handbook of Statistics, Vol. 11*
© 1993 Elsevier Science Publishers B.V. All rights reserved.

19

Simulation Estimation Methods for Limited Dependent Variable Models

V. A. Hajivassiliou

1. Introduction

This chapter discusses estimation methods for limited dependent variable (LDV) models that employ Monte Carlo simulation techniques to overcome numerical intractabilities of such models. These difficulties arise because high dimensional integral expressions need to be calculated repeatedly. In the past, investigators were forced to restrict attention to special classes of LDV models that are computationally tractable. The simulation estimation methods make it possible to estimate LDV models that are otherwise computationally intractable using classical estimation methods even on modern-day supercomputers.

Discussions of the estimation of various limited dependent variable models under restrictive parametric assumptions can be found in Maddala (1983), McFadden (1984), and Amemiya (1984). Typically, the estimation of many of these models involves the evaluation of multivariate integrals. This is generally the case with discrete choice models where the assumption is that each individual i evaluates all J available choices and selects the one that gives the maximum expected utility. Alternative j has observable attributes X_j and yields (random) utility $y_j^* = X_j\beta_j + \varepsilon_j$. McFadden (1973) solved the estimation problem by making the restrictive assumption that the error terms ε_j in the random utility model are iid with an extreme value distribution. Under this assumption, the multinomial discrete choice model has the convenient closed form expression:

$$\text{Prob}(y_i = k) = \exp(X_{ik}\beta_k)\Big/\sum_{j=1}^{J} \exp(X_{ij}\beta_j) . \tag{1.1}$$

Similar distributional assumptions enabled Dubin and McFadden (1984) to derive closed form expressions for a discrete/continuous model of choice of energy appliances and consumption of energy.

The drawback of the iid extreme-valued distributional assumption is that it severely restricts the pattern of discrete choices predicted by the model, which may be untenable in many realistic circumstances. This restriction, known as the independence of irrelevant alternatives (IIA), implies that the various alternatives are equally substitutable, neglecting, for example, that when selecting a mode of transportation between a car, a blue bus, and a red bus, the last two options are for all intents and purposes essentially perfect substitutes. See McFadden (1981). A restriction similar to the IIA is also exhibited by a multinomial independent probit model derived by Hausman and Wise (1978) by assuming that the errors ε_j are independent $N(0, \sigma_j^2)$.

Heckman (1981) attempted to trade off some of the computational simplicity of these models for a less restrictive structure on the unobservables, thus overcoming frequently undesirable restrictions like the IIA property. He achieved this by imposing a factor-analytic error structure on the error vector

$$\varepsilon = \Gamma \nu + S\zeta \,, \tag{1.2}$$

where ν is an $n \times 1$ vector of independent random 'factors', $(E\nu = 0, E\nu\nu' = \sigma_\nu^2 I_n)$, Γ is a $J \times n$ matrix of factor loadings, S is a $J \times J$ diagonal matrix, and ζ is a $J \times 1$ iid, random vector $(E\zeta = 0, E\zeta\zeta' = \sigma_\zeta^2 I_J)$. This implies that $E\varepsilon\varepsilon' = \sigma_\nu^2 \Gamma\Gamma' + \sigma_\zeta^2 SS$, which reduces the dimension of the integral necessary in calculating choice probabilities. Sometimes there exists a natural economic interpretation of such a factor analytic error structure, thus further increasing the appeal of this model. For example, ν can denote a small number of unmodelled factors affecting consumers' choice among airline carriers, like safety, comfort, on-time performance, etc. In a panel data context, ν can denote unobserved agent-specific and time-period-specific shocks, which make up the structure (1.2).

Another model that introduced some further computational complexity in exchange for avoiding the IIA property, is the nested multinomial model (NMNL) due to McFadden (1984). By introducing a hierarchical structure in the choice process, corresponding to blocks of 0s in the covariance matrix of ε, this model remains consistent with the random utility maximization hypothesis, exhibits the IIA property only for specific stages of the hierarchical decision making, and still avoids the need to calculate integrals of high dimension.

Avery et al. (1983), Chamberlain (1984), and Poirier and Ruud (1988) noted that in certain LDV models, notably multiperiod binary response and censored models with normally distributed disturbances, incorrect specification of the error covariance structure results in inefficient but still consistent and asymptotically normal estimators. Hence, these authors developed estimation techniques that rely on period-by-period orthogonality conditions, which are computational tractable. As already noted, however, these methods do not generalize to most LDV models, in which the covariance structure of the error terms determines crucially the joint as well as the marginal distributions of the observed limited dependent variables. Moreover, as Hajivassiliou (1986) points out, normality of the disturbances is a crucial requirement for these methods, since for general non-normal random variables, the joint, conditional, and marginal distributions all belong to different classes.

The other direction followed by researchers was to investigate numerical analysis techniques for approximating the *J*-dimensional integrals. Hausman and Wise (1978) showed that methods due to Divgi (1979) for the case $J = 3$ and Steck (1958) for $J = 4$ provided reasonably fast and accurate approximations. Clark (1961) and Daganzo et al. (1977) offered some approximations for multivariate normal integrals. Horowitz et al. (1981) investigated the accuracy of the Clark approximation and found that it can be quite poor.

The simulation methods discussed in this chapter offer a better solution than all of the alternative ways to address these computational problems. Section 2 discusses the key developments that led to simulation techniques suitable for the estimation of LDV models. Section 3 describes the leading methods analytically. Section 4 examines all known simulators for likelihood contributions and derivatives that are necessary for implementing the simulation estimation methods. Section 5 concludes with a summary and suggestions for future research.

2. Developments of simulation techniques for the estimation of LDV models

An important innovation occurred in 1981, in the form of the following idea due to Lerman and Manski (1981). These authors noted that Monte Carlo simulation methods are used in numerical analysis to approximate high dimensional integrals. (See, for example, Hammersley and Handscomb, 1964.) They used simulation to evaluate the choice probabilities for the multinomial discrete choice probit model. In this model, the utility derived from alternative j is assumed to be $y_j^* \sim \mathcal{N}(X_j \beta_j, \Omega_j)$. Lerman and Manski used the empirical frequency of observing $y_k^{*r} = \max\{y_1^{*r}, \ldots, y_J^{*r}\}$ to approximate $P_k \equiv \mathrm{Prob}(y = k; \beta, \Omega)$, where y^{*r} is a Monte Carlo draw of a latent vector $y^* \sim \mathcal{N}(X\beta, \Omega), r = 1, \ldots, R$. I will term this the *crude frequency simulation* (CFS) method. Their experience with this idea was disappointing; a huge number of simulations R was needed before the empirical frequency $\tilde{P}_k$, defined by $\tilde{P}_k \equiv (1/R) \Sigma_{r=1}^{R} \mathbf{1}(y_k^{*r} = \max\{y_1^{*r}, \ldots, y_J^{*r}\})$, provided a good approximation of P_k, particularly when P_k was close to 0 or 1.[1] This, of course, can be explained by the fact that since $\mathbf{1}(\cdot)$ is a Bernoulli random variable with probability of success P_k, the variance of the simulator $\tilde{P}_k$ is $P_k(1 - P_k)/R$, which falls only linearly with R. Moreover, the frequency simulator $\tilde{P}_k$ takes the value 0 with positive probability. Hence, attempts to estimate a discrete choice model by using the method of simulated maximum likelihood (SML) to maximize iteratively $\Sigma_i \log \tilde{P}_{ki}$ yielded very unsatisfactory estimates.

The breakthrough came with an idea by McFadden, first presented in 1986 and eventually published as McFadden (1989). McFadden's contribution was to recognize that using simulation to approximate choice probabilities in the

---

[1] The indicator function $\mathbf{1}(A)$ of event A takes the value 1 if the event is true and 0 if false.

context of estimation is a viable procedure even for a smaller number of simulations R, provided the following conditions are satisfied. (a) An unbiased simulator is used for the choice probabilities (which is satisfied by the crude frequency simulator of Lerman and Manski, 1981). (b) The functions to be simulated appear linearly in the conditions defining the estimator. (c) The same set of random draws is used to simulate the model at different trial parameter values in the process of iteratively searching for the estimator. Condition (b), violated by the SML procedure since the P_k appear inside the $\log(\cdot)$ function, is crucial in ensuring that the independent simulation errors made in approximating each P_{ik} average out over the N observations to $E(P_{ik} - \tilde{P}_{ik})$, which is 0 by requirement (a).[2] Conditions for simulation-based estimators to be consistent and asymptotically normal were also derived in another seminal paper by Pakes and Pollard (1989), which appeared at about the same time. The method that these three authors developed satisfies requirements (a), (b), and (c) above and became known as the method of simulated moments (MSM). The key point is that the choice probabilities appear linearly in the moment conditions, since the expected value of a Bernoulli dependent variable is the probability of its taking the value 1.

Based on a suggestion by Ruud (1986), Hajivassiliou and McFadden (1990) noted that another simulation estimation method can be devised by simulating directly the scores of likelihood function. This method of simulated scores (MSS) estimator is thus defined by

$$\hat{\theta}_{\mathrm{MSS}} = \arg \operatorname*{solves}_{\theta} \left\{ \frac{1}{N} \sum_i \tilde{s}_i(\theta; y_i) = 0 \right\}, \tag{2.1}$$

and it will be consistent, uniformly asymptotically normal (CUAN) provided unbiased simulators $\tilde{s}_i(\cdot)$ of the score vector $s_i(\cdot)$ are used. Van Praag and Hop (1987) were the first to propose the use of simulation to overcome the computational difficulties in the evaluation of likelihood scores of LDV models and also noted that this approach is applicable to all classical LDV models (and not just discrete choice problems), though they did not use the name 'method of simulated scores'. Their method relied on approximating the score expression by simulating both the linear derivative in the numerator and the likelihood in the denominator and taking the ratio as an approximation. It should be noted that, given the non-linearity of this expression, consistency and asymptotic normality of the resulting estimator require that the simulations of the denominator expression be based on an infinite number of draws. By contrast, the approach by Ruud, Hajivassiliou, and McFadden uses unbiased simulation to guarantee consistency and asymptotic normality for a finite number of simulations. Van Praag and Hop (1987) consider four examples as empirical applications. More empirical examples are given in Van Praag, Hop and Eggink (1989, 1991), Eggink, Hop and Van Praag (1992), and Niesing, Van Praag and Veenman (1991), where the authors deal with a cross-section

---

[2] The original SML procedure of Lerman and Manski also violated condition (c).

analysis of labor market data. It is pointed out in these studies that if one were able to draw from truncated multivariate normal distributions, the non-linearity problem of simulating the denominator would not arise. The authors find, however, that a computationally preferable alternative is to use the GHK algorithm, described in Section 4 below, to simulate the denominator expressions. Since this algorithm simulates probability expressions very accurately, the biases introduced by simulating the denominator expressions are negligible.

The next simulation-based estimation method, also to be discussed in greater detail later, is the method of simulated pseudo ML (SPML), developed by Laroque and Salanié (1989) for the estimation of disequilibrium models with correlation over time. This method is defined as follows: Suppose a model stipulates that a dependent variable y_i has conditional moments, given the values of the explanatory variables, $E(y_i | X_i) = g_1(X_i, \theta_1)$ and $V(y_i | X_i) = g_2(X_i, \theta_2)$. In the context of the LDV models we are discussing, the $g(\cdot)$ functions involve integrals of high dimensions, so that they are difficult to evaluate. The SPML method simulates R times the dependent variable y_i at the current trial parameter values θ_1 and θ_2, and then uses the empirical mean and variance of $\{y_i^{(r)}\}$ as simulating functions $\tilde{g}_1(\theta_1; R)$ and $\tilde{g}_2(\theta_2; R)$. By construction, these functions are consistent estimators for $g(\cdot)$ as $R \to \infty$. The SPML estimator, $\hat{\theta}_{\text{SPML}}$, is thus defined by

$$\hat{\theta}_{\text{SPML}} = \arg\max_{\theta_1, \theta_2} \left\{ -\sum_i \{[y_i - \tilde{g}_1(\theta_1; R)]^2 / \tilde{g}_2(\theta_2; R) + \log[\tilde{g}_2(\theta_2; R)]\} \right\}.$$

(2.2)

This amounts to a combination of simulation of integral expressions together with pseudo-maximum likelihood estimation. The method implicitly employs the assumption that the limited dependent variable y_i has a distribution in the linear exponential class. In this specific example (2.2) the distribution is assumed to be normal.[3] It should be noted that SPML is closer in spirit to the SML of Lerman and Manski (1981), in that consistency and asymptotic normality require $R \to \infty$.

Finally, a method that theoretically also requires $R \to \infty$ is the smooth simulated maximum likelihood (SSML) method due to Börsch-Supan and Hajivassiliou (1990). These authors showed that the linearity requirement that apparently caused the unsatisfactory performance of the SML estimator was not critical if extremely accurate simulators are used that are smooth functions of the underlying parameters. In particular, they showed that using the GHK/SRC simulator explained in Section 4 below makes the resulting SSML estimator perform well. Apart from smoothness, this simulator differs critically from the CFS used by Lerman and Manski in that it is bounded away from 0 and 1 and has extremely low variance, even when the true probability is very close to either 0 or 1.

---

[3] See Gourieroux et al. (1984a,b) for the PML method without simulation.

Evaluation of high dimensional integrals has also been considered by applied physicists and mathematicians. For example, Dutt (1973, 1976) discusses the special case of multivariate normal orthant probabilities. Deák (1980a,b) proposes Monte Carlo integration as a way of approximating such probabilities. Another field in which fast and accurate calculation of multivariate integrals is important is Bayesian statistics, where it is necessary to calculate posterior density expressions in the context of Bayesian inference. Selected work from this voluminous literature that has investigated Monte Carlo simulation of integrals is Bauwens (1984), Van Dijk (1987), Kloek and Van Dijk (1978), Geweke (1989a) and West (1990).

Finally, a third field that faces intractable integration problems is the estimation of econometric models of dynamic optimization. See Rust (1989) for an approach that circumvents some of the problems by using convenient distributional assumptions and an ingenious nested fixed point algorithm. Recently Hotz and Miller (1989), Hotz and Sanders (1990), and Hotz, Miller, Sanders and Smith (1991) have proposed introducing simulation techniques in the estimation of such problems.[4] These authors' preliminary work uses the simulated method of moments estimation framework to recover individual valuations of discrete alternatives by inverting observed conditional choice probabilities. They apply this methodology to the dynamic model of bus replacement considered by Rust (1989) to overcome some of the computational difficulties with the estimation of structural dynamic discrete choice models. In this work, however, no proofs of the asymptotic properties of the technique are yet available. Based on the Hotz et al. approach, Rust (1991) develops the *simulated value function* estimator, which is consistent and asymptotically normal, as well as computationally tractable.

3. Simulation estimation methods for LDV models

We shall discuss first the leading simulation estimation methods for the multinomial discrete choice model. This does not entail any loss of generality, because more general discrete/continuous LDV models can be decomposed into a continuous part and a discrete choice part, conditional on the continuous part. Specifically, suppose that for a given individual, the observed limited dependent variable vector y has some discrete elements, denoted by y_d, and some fully observed (continuous) ones, y_c. For example, consider the discrete/continuous model, where individual i chooses alternative j which provides the highest level of utility, and simultaneously takes a continuous decision y_{ij}^* which depends on the discrete choice. The observed limited dependent

---

[4] Two reviews that describe the state of the art in estimating dynamic optimization models are Rust (1991) and Pakes (1991).

variables (w_i, y_i) are then defined by

$$w_{ij}^* = Z_{ij}\gamma_j + \varepsilon_{ij},$$
$$y_{ij}^* = X_{ij}\beta_j + u_{ij},$$
$$w_i = \arg\max_j (w_{i1}^*, \ldots, w_{ij}^*, \ldots, w_{iJ}^*), \quad j = 1, \ldots, J, \qquad (3.1)$$
$$y_i = y_{iw_i}^*.$$

In this case, y_c corresponds to the J elements of the y_{ij}^* vector, while y_d to the J elements of w_{ij}^*.

Let $y = (y_d, y_c)'$ and let θ be the vector of unknown parameters in the model. Then

$$l(y; \theta, X) = l(y_d \mid y_c; \theta, X) \cdot l(y_c; \theta, X) \qquad (3.2)$$

and so

$$\ln l = \ln l_{d|c} + \ln l_c \qquad (3.3a)$$

and

$$\partial \ln l / \partial \theta = \partial \ln l_{d|c} / \partial \theta + \partial \ln l_c / \partial \theta. \qquad (3.3b)$$

The parts with only continuous components pose no difficulties, since they involve only (multivariate) continuous densities, which can be evaluated directly. The terms involving the probability $l_{d|c} \equiv \text{Prob}(y_d^* \in \{y_d^*: y_d = \arg\max_j(y_1^*, \ldots, y_J^*)\} \mid y_c^*)$ are integral expressions over a conditional density, of dimension equal to the number of discrete elements in y, which simulation estimation methods approximate.

In this discrete choice model, J mutually exclusive and exhaustive alternatives yield a vector of utilities or payoffs $y_i^* = X_i\beta + \varepsilon_i$. The disturbance vector ε_i is iid, mean-independent of X_i, with density function $f_\varepsilon(\varepsilon_i; \Omega_i(\sigma))$. Individual i chooses the alternative k which yields the highest payoff. The observed choice is characterized by the $J \times 1$ dummy variable vector y_i, with $y_{ij} = 1$ for $j = k$, and $y_{ij} = 0$ otherwise. In this case, the vector of unknown parameters is $\theta = (\beta', \sigma')'$. Given the non-linearity of this model, all estimation methods we consider will involve iterative search. Consider the trial parameter vector $\theta^{(n)}$ at iteration n. A maximum likelihood estimation algorithm requires the evaluation of $L(\theta^{(n)})$,

$$L(\theta^{(n)}) = \frac{1}{N} \cdot \sum_{i=1}^{N} \ln l_i(\theta^{(n)}; y_i). \qquad (3.4)$$

A method of scoring seeks to evaluate

$$S(\theta^{(n)}) = \frac{1}{N} \cdot \sum_{i=1}^{N} s_i(\theta^{(n)}; y_i) = \frac{1}{N} \cdot \sum_{i=1}^{N} \frac{l_{i\theta}(\theta^{(n)}; y_i)}{l_i(\theta^{(n)}; y_i)}. \qquad (3.5)$$

A method of moments algorithm calculates

$$M(\theta^{(n)}) = \frac{1}{N} \cdot \sum_{i=1}^{N} m_i(\theta^{(n)}; y_i) = \frac{1}{N} \cdot \sum_{i=1}^{N} w(\theta^{(n)}; X_i)'(y_i - g_{1i}(\theta^{(n)}; X_i)) ,$$

$$(3.6)$$

where $g_{1i}(\cdot) \equiv E(y_i; \theta^{(n)})$ and $w(\cdot)$ is an instrument function. Finally, a pseudo maximum likelihood (SPML) routine evaluates the quadratic form

$$Q(\theta^{(n)}) = \frac{1}{N} \cdot \sum_{i=1}^{N} \{[y_i - g_{1i}(\theta^{(n)}; X_i)]^2 / g_{2n}(\theta^{(n)}; X_i)$$

$$+ \log[g_{2n}(\theta^{(n)}; X_i)]\} ,$$

$$(3.7)$$

where $g_{1i}(\cdot) \equiv E(y_i; \theta^{(n)})$ and $g_{2i}(\cdot) \equiv V(y_i; \theta^{(n)})$.

If the expressions $l_i(\theta^{(n)}; y_i)$, $l_{i\theta}(\theta^{(n)}; y_i)$, $s_i(\theta^{(n)}; y_i)$, $g_{1i}(\theta^{(n)}; y_i)$, and $g_{2i}(\theta^{(n)}; y_i)$ are analytically or numerically tractable, computer routines can be written to evaluate these expressions as functions of any possible trial parameter vector $\theta^{(n)}$. Estimation by simulation relies on simulating routines we shall denote by $\tilde{l}_i(\theta^{(n)}; y_i, R)$, $\tilde{l}_{i\theta}(\theta^{(n)}; y_i, R)$, $\tilde{s}_i(\theta^{(n)}; y_i, R)$, $\tilde{g}_{1i}(\theta^{(n)}; y_i, R)$, and $\tilde{g}_{2i}(\theta^{(n)}; y_i, R)$ respectively. These routines are defined as follows: Draw a set of R uniform J-dimensional random vectors $\bar{u}_r^1, \dots, \bar{u}_r^r, \dots, \bar{u}_r^R$. By the assumptions of the model, the disturbance vector ε_i is iid with density function $f_\varepsilon(\varepsilon_i; \theta^0)$, with $E(\varepsilon_i | X_i) = 0$ and $E(\varepsilon_i \varepsilon_i' | X_i) = \Omega_i(\sigma)$.

Consider the trial parameter vector $\theta^{(n)} = (\beta^{(n)}, \sigma^{(n)})'$. Using the inverse of the cumulative distribution function of ε, $F_\varepsilon^{-1}(\cdot)$, the uniform draws u_i^r can be transformed into a set of R $\tilde{\varepsilon}_i$,

$$\tilde{\varepsilon}_i^r(\sigma^{(n)}) = F_\varepsilon^{-1}(\bar{u}_i^r; \Omega(\sigma^{(n)})) ,$$

$$(3.8)$$

which will imply a set of R simulated latent vectors $\tilde{y}_i^{*r}(\theta^{(n)})$, using the specification $y_{ij} = 1$ for $y_{ij}^* = \max(y_{1i}^*, \dots, y_{iJ}^*)$ and $y_{ij} = 0$ otherwise. From the R simulated $\tilde{y}_i^r$ vectors, we calculate the empirical counterparts of the $l_i(\cdot)$ etc. functions and thus define the simulators $\tilde{l}_i(\theta^{(n)}; y_i, R)$, $\tilde{l}_{i\theta}(\theta^{(n)}; y_i, R)$, $\tilde{s}_i(\theta^{(n)}; y_i, R)$, $\tilde{g}_{1i}(\theta^{(n)}; y_i, R)$, and $\tilde{g}_{2i}(\theta^{(n)}; y_i, R)$. For example, $\tilde{l}_i(\cdot)$ and $\tilde{g}_{1i}(\cdot)$ will correspond to the vectors of empirical frequencies with which alternative j yielded the highest simulated payoff. Keeping the same uniform random variates, $\bar{u}_i^r$, a new trial parameter vector $\theta^{(n+1)}$ will imply a new set of simulated $\tilde{\varepsilon}_i^r(\sigma^{(n+1)})$, leading to new $\tilde{y}_i^*$ and hence new values for $\tilde{l}_i$, etc. The iterative search algorithms will keep trying different parameter vectors θ, always using the same $\bar{u}_i^r$, to satisfy the relevant criterion, i.e., simulated ML will attempt to maximize $\tilde{L}(\theta)$, MSS will set $\tilde{S}(\theta)$ and MSM will set $\tilde{M}(\theta)$ as close to 0 as possible, while SPML will attempt to minimize $\tilde{Q}(\theta)$.

The main theoretical properties of such estimators can be summarized following arguments in Hajivassiliou and McFadden (1990). Suppose $\hat{\theta}$ is a simulation estimator that solves $0 = N^{1/2} E_N \tilde{q}(\hat{\theta}, \eta)$, where $\tilde{q}$ is an approximation (involving Monte Carlo elements η) to a function $\gamma(\theta)$ of l and its derivatives that has expectation zero at the true parameter θ^0. For example, for SML and MSS, $\gamma(\theta)$ is the logarithmic score of the likelihood function $S(\theta)$, whereas for MSM $\gamma(\theta)$ is the orthogonality condition $m(\theta)$. E_N denotes empirical expectation over an independent sample of size N. Then, one can write

$$
\begin{aligned}
0 = N^{1/2} E_N \tilde{q}(\hat{\theta}, \eta) &\equiv N^{1/2} E_N \gamma(\theta^0) + N^{1/2} E_N [\tilde{q}(\theta^0, \eta) - \gamma(\theta^0)] \\
&+ N^{1/2} E_N [\gamma(\hat{\theta}) - \gamma(\theta^0)] \\
&+ N^{1/2} E_N [\tilde{q}(\hat{\theta}, \eta) - \gamma(\hat{\theta}) - \tilde{q}(\theta^0, \eta) + \gamma(\theta^0)].
\end{aligned}
$$

$$(3.9)$$

Under standard regularity conditions, the first term is asymptotically normal, reflecting the noise in the observations, and the third term is proportional to $\sqrt{N}(\hat{\theta} - \theta^0)$.[5] The last term will be of order $o_p(1)$ for simulators that satisfy a 'stochastic equicontinuity condition'.[6]

Let $\tilde{q}_i(\theta, \eta)$ denote the simulated value of $q_i(\theta)$, for a sample of iid observations $i = 1, \ldots, N$. Define a *simulation bias*,

$$
B_N(\theta) = \frac{1}{\sqrt{N}} \sum_{i=1}^{N} [E_\eta \tilde{q}_i(\theta, \eta) - q_i(\theta)],
$$

$$(3.10)$$

where E_η denotes an expectation with respect to the simulation process, given the observation. Following the method of McFadden (1989) and Pakes and Pollard (1989), Hajivassiliou and McFadden (1990) show that assumptions on the simulation bias plus regularity assumptions, are sufficient for the simulation estimator $\hat{\theta}_N$ that solves $\sum_{i=1}^{N} \tilde{q}_i(\hat{\theta}_N, \eta) = 0$ to be consistent and asymptotically normal.[7]

THEOREM (Hajivassiliou and McFadden, 1990.) *Assume that the parameter θ is contained in a compact set Θ, and that the true value θ^0 is in the interior of Θ. Assume that the criterion $q_i(\theta)$ is continuously differentiable on Θ. Assume that*

---

[5] When q is a smooth function of crude frequency simulators of l, $\partial l / \partial \theta$, and $\partial \ln l / \partial \theta$ obtained using R Monte Carlo draws, Hajivassiliou and McFadden (1990) show that the second term will behave like $\sqrt{N/R}$ times an expression that is asymptotically normal, so that it will be comparable in magnitude to the first term when R and N are proportional. If, in addition, there is any averaging out of simulation noise across observations, the second term may be of order $o_p(1)$ when R and N are proportional, or comparable in magnitude to the first term for fixed R.

[6] The functions $\{\zeta_N(\cdot)\}$ are *stochastically equicontinuous* at $\Theta_1 \subseteq \Theta$ if for each $\varepsilon > 0$ and $\lambda > 0$, there exists $\delta > 0$ and N_0 such that for $N \geq N_0$, $\text{Prob}(\sup_{|\theta - \theta'| < \delta, \theta' \in \Theta, \theta \in \Theta_1} |\zeta_N(\theta) - \zeta_N(\theta')| > \varepsilon) < \lambda$.

[7] The proof of the following theorem can be found in Appendix 3 of Hajivassiliou and McFadden.

the criterion and its derivatives are dominated by a function independent of θ with finite first and second order moments. Assume that $E_i q_i(\theta) = 0$ if and only if $\theta = \theta^0$, and that $J = -E_i q_{i\theta}(\theta^0)$ is positive definite, where E_i denotes expectation with respect to the distribution of the observations. Assume that the observations and simulators are iid across observations. Assume that (i) the simulation bias converges to zero in probability, uniformly in θ, and (ii) the simulation residual process[8] is stochastically equicontinuous. Assume that a simulation estimator solving $0 = \Sigma_{i=1}^{N} \tilde{q}_i(\hat{\theta}_N, \eta)$ exists for each N.[9] Then, the estimator satisfies

$$\hat{\theta}_N \xrightarrow{P} \theta^0 \quad and \quad \sqrt{N}(\hat{\theta}_N - \theta^0) \xrightarrow{d} Z \sim \mathcal{N}(0, J^{-1} + J^{-1} \cdot V \cdot J^{-1}),$$

where $V = E[\tilde{q}_i(\theta^0, \eta) - E_\eta \tilde{q}_i(\theta^0, \eta)][\tilde{q}_i(\theta^0, \eta) - E_\eta \tilde{q}_i(\theta^0, \eta)]'$.

To avoid technical difficulties, Hajivassiliou and McFadden (1990) assume that the multivariate distribution y^* is truncated to a large compact rectangle.[10] The simulators $\tilde{l}_i(\theta)$, $\tilde{l}_{i\theta}(\theta)$, and $\tilde{s}_i(\theta)$ can be formed with several methods. These are discussed in the following section. Hajivassiliou and McFadden (1990) give general sufficient conditions for assumption (i) of asymptotic unbiasedness and assumption (ii) of stochastic equicontinuity in the theorem. Specifically, they show that if the simulation process is unbiased, as for example in MSM and MSS with unbiased simulators $\tilde{l}_i(\theta)$ and $\tilde{s}_i(\theta)$ respectively, or when the bias in an observation is dominated by a positive function independent of θ whose expectation is of order $o(1/\sqrt{N})$, then the simulation bias converges to 0. This results in consistent, asymptotically normal simulation estimators. McFadden and Ruud (1991) give further theoretical results along these lines. The suggestion to simulate the likelihood scores directly using the conditional distribution $Z_i \equiv \{y_i^* \mid y_i^* \in D(y_i)\}$, where $D(y) \equiv \{y^*: y = \arg\max_j(y_1^*, \ldots, y_J^*)\}$, is due to Ruud (1986).

It is important to note that the method of simulated scores differs in a very significant way from the method of simulated moments. MSS implicitly uses the *optimal* set of instruments, since as $R \to \infty$ it corresponds to MLE which is statistically efficient. On the other hand, the efficiency of MSM rests crucially on the choice of the instrument function $w(\theta; X_i)$. To highlight this issue, consider as a simple example the binary probit model for an independent cross-section of individuals, $i = 1, \ldots, N$, for which classical estimation is, of

---

[8] See Hajivassiliou and McFadden (1990) for precise definitions.

[9] It is sufficient to define $\hat{\theta}_N$ to be an approximate solution satisfying $\mathcal{O}(1) = \sum_{i=1}^{N} \tilde{q}_i(\hat{\theta}_N)$; such an estimator always exists.

[10] This does not entail any essential loss of empirical generality, since for distributions with unbounded support, like the multivariate normal, one can restrict attention to the same distribution truncated to the square defined by the limits of computing machine representation of floating-point numbers.

course, computationally very straightforward.

$$y_i^* = x_i'\beta + \varepsilon_i, \quad \varepsilon_i \sim N(0, 1),$$

$$y_i = \begin{cases} 1 \\ -1 \end{cases} \quad d_i = \begin{cases} 1 & \text{if } y_i^* > 0 \quad (y_i = 2d_i - 1), \\ 0 & \text{if } y_i^* \leq 0. \end{cases} \qquad (3.11)$$

Define

$$\ln l_i = \begin{cases} \ln \Phi(y_i \cdot x_i'\beta), & (3.12a) \\ d_i \cdot \ln \Phi(x_i'\beta) + (1 - d_i) \cdot \ln(1 - \Phi(x_i'\beta)), & (3.12b) \end{cases}$$

and

$$s_i = l_{i\theta}/l_i$$

$$= \begin{cases} x_i \cdot \dfrac{\phi(y_i \cdot x_i'\beta)}{\Phi(y_i \cdot x_i'\beta)} \cdot y_i \\ \quad = x_i \cdot E(\varepsilon_i \mid y_i^* \in D(y_i)), & (3.13a) \\ x_i \cdot \dfrac{\phi(x_i'\beta)}{\Phi(x_i'\beta)(1 - \Phi(x_i'\beta))} \cdot (d_i - \Phi(x_i'\beta)) & (3.13b) \\ \quad = w_i(\theta) \cdot (d_i - \Phi(x_i'\beta)). \end{cases}$$

In this case, $\theta = \beta$. Then the maximum likelihood estimator solves the first order conditions $L_{N\theta}(\hat{\theta}) = (1/N) \Sigma_i s_i(\hat{\theta}) = 0$.

Equation (3.13b) for the score of observation i highlights a method-of-moments interpretation of maximum likelihood estimation when the optimal instruments $w_i(\theta)$, defined in (3.13b), are used. Simulating the conditional expectation expressions in equation (3.13a) corresponds to the method of scoring. It should be noted that the basic consistency requirement that $E(s_i(y_i; \theta^*) \mid x_i) = 0$ is satisfied; in equation (3.13a) it is satisfied because $P(y_i \mid \theta^*, x_i) = \Phi(y_i \cdot x_i'\theta^*)$ and in equation (3.13b) because $E(d_i \mid \theta^*, x_i) = \Phi(x_i'\theta^*)$.

The original method of simulated moments (McFadden, 1989, and Pakes and Pollard, 1989) substitutes an unbiased simulator, $\tilde{\Phi}(x_i'\beta)$, for $\Phi(x_i'\beta)$ and exploits the linearity in $(d_i - \Phi(\cdot))$ of the score expression (3.13b). For high efficiency this method requires that consistent estimators for the optimal instruments, $w_i(\theta^*)$, be used. This is confirmed by the theoretical and Monte Carlo results of Hajivassiliou (1990), who reached the following conclusions. First, the optimal instrument function $w(\cdot)$ in (3.13b) (which, of course, in more realistic cases is intractable to calculate) yields considerable mean-square-error advantages over the simpler choice x_i, which choice also satisfies the theoretical requirements for consistency and asymptotic normality. Second, the SML method of Lerman and Manski (1981) that uses the crude frequency simulators for the choice probabilities (SML/CFS) offers satisfactory performance only when the number of simulations employed is very large. This number grows faster than linearly with the complexity of the LDV model under analysis.[11] The method that simulates separately the denominator of the scores by frequency methods performs unsatisfactorily, and it is easily dominated by all the other methods tried, primarily because frequency simulators are not bounded away from 0 and 1. Before barely satisfactory performance is achieved, a huge number of simulations for the denominator expressions in (3.13) must be employed. These problems are significantly alleviated once a smooth simulator, bounded away from 0, like the GHK/SRC simulator described in the next section, is used for the denominator expression. In all the cases investigated, the MSS based on the GSS, GHK/SRC, or PCF simulators, to be discussed in the next section, performs well. Moreover, the method is found to be numerically stable, which was to be expected given its continuity in the underlying parameters. Efficiency properties of various simulation estimation methods are also discussed in Lee (1990).

The method of simulated scores bypasses the issue of searching for the optimal instruments and simulates instead *directly* the expression $E(\varepsilon_i^* \mid y_i^* \in D(y_i))$, which implies that the optimal instruments are now available automatically in the form of x_i. In other words, MSS uses simulators for the expression $E(\varepsilon_i^* \mid y_i^* \in D(y_i))$, say $\tilde{E}(\varepsilon_i^* \mid y_i^* \in D(y_i))$. To see the relation of MSS to MLE, recall that

$$x_i \cdot E(\varepsilon_i^* \mid y_i^* \in D(y_i)) = x_i \cdot \frac{\phi(y_i \cdot x_i'\beta)}{\Phi(y_i \cdot x_i'\beta)} = s_i(y_i, \beta; x_i) \,.$$

The Lerman and Manski (1981) method uses unbiased and consistent frequency simulators of $\Phi(x_i'\beta)$ directly in the likelihood function (3.12a).

Gourieroux and Monfort (1990) discuss simulation estimation techniques for models with heterogeneity in terms of consistency, asymptotic normality, convergence rates, and asymptotic bias. A distinction is made between the case where simulations are the same across observations as opposed to different. Several studies have attempted to generalize the theoretical results outlined in this section about the properties of simulation estimators by relaxing the random sample assumption we have been employing. Duffie and Singleton (1989) use similar results to develop a simulation estimation method for models for financial data with temporal dependence. Laroque and Salanié (1989) propose simulation estimation methods for multi-market disequilibrium using SPML. Laroque and Salanié (1990) carry out an extensive Monte Carlo study to evaluate the relative performance of the various algorithms for disequilibrium models. This study finds that the SPML methods are less liable to spurious maxima. Moreover, the use of simulation does not seem to entail substantial efficiency losses compared to full ML, which is considerably less

---

[11] As theory suggests, the SML/CFS is improved significantly by maintaining the same set of underlying random variates while iterating the optimization algorithm to convergence.

tractable computationally. Finally, Lee and Ingram (1991) propose simulation to overcome estimation problems of dynamic optimization under uncertainty. The main differences from McFadden (1989) and Pakes and Pollard (1989) are that Lee and Ingram allow for disturbances to be correlated across units of observations, while they require the criterion functions defining the estimators be continuous functions of the underlying parameters.

As we shall see in the next section, some simulators like the crude frequency simulator (CFS) are not continuous functions of the unknown parameter vector or of the underlying Monte Carlo draws. Such a feature necessitates the use of derivative-free methods like the non-linear simplex algorithm of Nelder and Meade (1964), since standard derivative-based optimization methods like Gauss–Newton or Newton–Raphson[12], cannot be used. Ruud (1991) showed that the EM algorithm appears promising to overcome some of the speed problems of MSS. See also Van Praag et al. (1991). For certain types of LDV models, Berry and Pakes (1990) report satisfactory numerical stability of simulation estimators, even when based on non-smooth simulation algorithms.

The list of applications of simulation estimation techniques to estimate modern econometric models is growing rapidly. Hajivassiliou and McFadden (1990) apply the method of simulated scores to a model of external dept repayments problems using a panel data set of developing countries. Bolduc and Kaci (1991) use both SML and MSM to estimate a discrete choice model among five local residential telephone services. Keane (1990) independently developed the GHK/SRC simulator for the problem of estimating transition probabilities in his work on multi-period (panel data) probit models and used it to study temporal dependence in employment and wages. Berkovec and Stern (1991) use the method of simulated moments to investigate retirement decisions of older men and Stern (1991) also uses MSM to study the choice of transportation mode by elderly and disabled people. Hajivassiliou and Ioannides (1991) estimate by the method of simulated scores a generalized switching Euler equation model, to study consumption and labor supply behavior in the face of borrowing constraints using a large longitudinal data set of households. Bloemen and Kapteyn (1991) estimate a labour supply function jointly with a wage equation using smooth simulated maximum likelihood estimation following Börsch-Supan and Hajivassiliou (1990). Börsch-Supan et al. (1992) also apply SSML to investigate a multi-period, multinomial model of housing choices by the elderly.

4. Simulators for l, $\partial l/\partial\theta$, and $\partial\ln l/\partial\theta$

In the canonical LDV model analyzed here, the latent vector $y_i^* \in \mathbb{R}^M$ gives rise to the observed limited dependent variable vector $y_i \equiv \tau(y_i^*)$, such that $\tau(\cdot)$ partitions $\mathbb{R}^M$ into regions $d_i = 1, \ldots, M$. Let $D(X_i, \theta, d)$ denote the set of y_i^*

---

[12] See Quandt (1983).

that map into d_i. These regions typically correspond to a set of linear inequality constraints on the elements of y_i^* of the form

$$\{y_i^* \in D(X_i, \theta, d_i)\} \equiv \{a(X_i, \theta, d_i) \leqslant W(X_i, \theta, d_i) \cdot y^* \leqslant b(X_i, \theta, d_i)\},$$

(4.1)

where $W(\cdot)$ is a positive definite matrix and the boundary vectors $a(\cdot)$ and $b(\cdot)$ are allowed to have infinite elements. It is not difficult to set that the leading LDV models considered in the literature fit into this framework.

The estimation methods discussed in the previous section require fast and accurate simulation of the likelihood contribution, its derivatives, and the score, respectively:

$$l(D_i, \theta) = \int \mathbf{1}(y_i^* \in D_i) \cdot f(y_i^* - \mu_i; \Omega_i(\sigma)) \, dy_i^*,$$

(4.2a)

$$\nabla_\theta l(D_i, \theta) = \int \mathbf{1}(y_i^* \in D_i) \cdot \nabla_\theta f(y_i^* - \mu_i; \Omega_i(\sigma)) \, dy_i^*,$$

(4.2b)

$$\nabla_\theta \ln l(D_i, \theta) \equiv s(D_i, \theta)$$
$$= \int \mathbf{1}(y_i^* \in D_i) \cdot \nabla_\theta f(y_i^* - \mu_i; \Omega_i(\sigma)) \, dy_i^*$$
$$\times \left[\int \mathbf{1}(y_i^* \in D_i) \cdot f(y_i^* - \mu_i; \Omega_i(\sigma)) \, dy_i^* \right]^{-1},$$

(4.2c)

where $\mu_i \equiv X_i\beta$ and $f(\cdot)$ denotes the PDF of the latent vector y^*. In the remainder of this section, methods are discussed for simulating expressions (4.2).

It should be noted that if we assume further that the distribution of y^* is a member of the linear exponential family, such as the normal distribution, the score of observation i can be written

$$s_i(D_i, \theta) = E_{y^*}(h(y^*; \theta, X_i) \mid y^* \in D(X_i, \theta, d_i)),$$

(4.3)

where $h(y^*; \cdot)$ is a vector of polynomials in y^*. See Ruud (1986) for an illustration of this result. Hence, this argument shows that for the successful implementation of MSS it is useful to devise ways to generate draws from the truncated distribution $z \equiv \{y^* \mid y^* \in D\}$, since such draws $\tilde{z}^r$ could then be used to simulate the score unbiasedly by

$$\tilde{s}_i(D_i, \theta, \eta) \equiv \frac{1}{R} \sum_{r=1}^{R} h(\tilde{z}^r).$$

(4.4)

The simulation method that is perhaps the most intuitive to demonstrate is the following. Write the random vector y^* as

$$y^* = \mu + \Gamma\eta,$$

(4.5)

where η is an independent standard normal vector of dimension M and $\Gamma(\sigma)$ is a lower triangular Choleski factor of $\Omega(\sigma)$, that is, $\Omega(\sigma) = \Gamma(\sigma)\Gamma(\sigma)'$. A simple approach to approximating (4.2a) is to make repeated Monte Carlo draws for η, use (4.5) to calculate y^* for each parameter vector, and then form empirical analogs of the expectations in (4.2a) and (4.2b). This approach defines the *crude frequency simulator* (CFS) of $l(D;\theta)$ and its derivatives. Similarly, a crude frequency simulator for $\nabla_\theta \ln l$ can be formed by rejecting draws of y^* that do not satisfy the conditioning event $y^* \in D$, and then calculating an empirical analog of the *conditional* expectation in (4.2c) using the accepted draws.

The CFS are quick to compute and ideal for parallel processing. However, they are *not* continuous in parameters or in the underlying Monte Carlo draws, exhibiting jumps at different θ and η values. This complicates iterative parameter search. A second serious shortcoming of CFS is that they take the value 0 with a positive probability. This explains to a large extent the unsatisfactory performance of SML when CFS was used by Lerman and Manski (1981) to approximate l_i, since the SML criterion function is $\Sigma_i \ln \tilde{l}_i$.

Börsch-Supan and Hajivassiliou (1990) overcome these problems by developing the method of smooth SML (SSML), which uses instead a simulator for l_i that is (a) smooth in the unknown parameters and (b) is bounded away from 0. For the normal case $y^* \sim \mathcal{N}(\mu, \Omega)$, a simulation method that possesses both these properties and also is extremely fast to compute is the method termed *GHK* by Hajivassiliou et al. (1992).[13]

To discuss GHK and other simulation techniques, it is useful to introduce the following notation. For a vector of indices $(1, \ldots, n)$, we use '$<j$' to denote the subvector $(1, \ldots, j-1)$, and '$-j$' to denote the subvector that excludes component j. Thus, for a matrix Γ, $\Gamma_{j,<j}$ denotes a vector containing the first $j-1$ elements of row j, and $\Gamma_{-j,-j}$ denotes the subarray excluding row j and column j. For a vector η, $\eta_{<j}$ is the subvector of the first $j-1$ components, and η_{-j} is the subvector excluding component j.

Consider the triangularizing transformation $y^* = \mu + \Gamma\eta$, where Γ is the Choleski factor of Ω. The indicator $\mathbf{1}(y^* \in D)$ then becomes $\mathbf{1}(\mu + \Gamma\eta \in D)$, which can be written recursively as the product of indicators of the events

$$D_j(\eta_{<j}) = \{\eta_j \mid (a_j - \mu_j - \Gamma_{j,<j}\eta_{<j})/\Gamma_{jj} < \eta_j < (b_j - \mu_j - \Gamma_{j,<j}\eta_{<j})/\Gamma_{jj}\}$$

(4.6)

for $j = 1, \ldots, M$. Define $\phi(\eta_j \mid D_j(\eta_{<j})) = \phi(\eta_j)\mathbf{1}(\eta_j \in D_j(\eta_{<j}))/\Phi(D_j(\eta_{<j}))$, the conditional distribution of η_j given the event $D_j(\eta_{<j})$. A recursive scheme of this type was suggested by Van Praag and Hop (1987) and by Geweke (1989b). Define a weight

$$\omega(\eta) = \prod_{j=1}^{M} \Phi(D_j(\eta_{<j})) .$$

(4.7)

---

[13] This stands for Geweke, Hajivassiliou and Keane. I will use the same acronyms as in Hajivassiliou et al. (1992) to refer to the various simulators.

Then it follows that

$$l = \int f(\mu + \Gamma\eta)\omega(\eta) \prod_{j=1}^{M} \phi(\eta_j \,|\, D_j(\eta_{<j})) \,d\eta \tag{4.8a}$$

and

$$\nabla_\theta l = \int \nabla_\theta f(\mu + \Gamma\eta)\omega(\eta) \prod_{j=1}^{M} \phi(\eta_j \,|\, D_j(\eta_{<j})) \,d\eta \ . \tag{4.8b}$$

An unbiased simulator of l is an average of $f(\mu + \Gamma\eta)\omega(\eta)$ and an unbiased simulator of $\nabla_\theta l$ is an average of $\nabla_\theta f(\mu + \Gamma\eta)\omega(\eta)$, where $\omega(\eta)$ is the weighting function (4.7), over draws constructed recursively from the one-dimensional conditional densities $\phi(\eta_j \,|\, D_j(\eta_{<j}))$. Drawing η_j from this density can be achieved by the following method, which is continuous in the unknown parameters and the Monte Carlo draws:

$$\eta_j = \Phi^{-1}(\zeta_j \Phi((a_j - \mu_j - \Gamma_{j,<j}\eta_{<j})/\Gamma_{jj})$$
$$+ (1 - \zeta_j)\Phi((b_j - \mu_j - \Gamma_{j,<j}\eta_{<j})/\Gamma_{jj})) \ . \tag{4.9}$$

The ζ_j are drawn from the uniform $[0, 1]$ density.[14]

It should be noted that the GHK simulator defined by (4.6)–(4.9) is applicable also to some non-normal distributions, as long as the univariate draws form the conditional one-dimensional distributions correspond to the multivariate distribution of ε in the latent variable specification $y^* = X\beta + \varepsilon$. This useful property is not shared by many other simulators discussed here that rely on the very special additivity property of the normal distribution.

Another way to obtain a smooth simulator is to begin from CFS and introduce the *kernel smoothed frequency simulator* (KFS), suggested by McFadden (1989). KFS replaces the indicator function $\mathbf{1}(y^* \in D)$ in the crude frequency simulator with the function

$$\mathcal{H}_{D,\omega}(y^*) \equiv \mathcal{H}((y^* - b)/\omega) - \mathcal{H}((y^* - a)/\omega) \ , \tag{4.10}$$

where $\mathcal{H}(w)$ is a smooth kernel function from $\mathbb{R}^M$ onto $[0, 1]$ with $\mathcal{H}(-\infty) = 1$ and $\mathcal{H}(+\infty) = 0$, and ω is a window width parameter. This simulator is a biased estimate of l and $\nabla_\theta l$ for positive ω, but in statistical applications one can shrink ω as sample size increases.

Another important simulation principle is *acceptance/rejection sampling* (ARS). Methods based on this principle provide a mechanism for drawing from a conditional density when practical exact transformations from uniform or

---

[14] This is a simple application of the probability integral transform result (see Feller, 1971). Let X be distributed according to the univariate uniform distribution on $[0, 1]$. Then $Z \equiv G^{-1}(X) = \Phi^{-1}[(\Phi(b) - \Phi(a)) \cdot X + \Phi(a)]$ is distributed $N(0, 1)$ s.t. $a \le Z \le b$. The proof follows by recognizing that the corresponding CDF is $G(z) = (\Phi(z) - \Phi(a))/(\Phi(b) - \Phi(a))$, where Φ denotes the univariate normal cumulative distribution function. Note that Z is a continuous and differentiable function of the parameters a and b.

standard normal variates are not available. The crudest form of ARS is to sample from the unconditional distribution of y^* using (4.5), reject points not in D until R accepted points are found, and form an empirical average of $h(y^*)$ over the accepted points. The following refinement (see Devroye (1986) or Rubinstein (1981)) permits improvement in the 'yield' of the method by sampling from a comparison distribution that puts little or no weight outside D and has the property that the ratio of the comparison density to the target density is uniformly bounded above by a small number.[15]

Suppose $f(x)$ is an M-dimensional density, and one wishes to sample from the conditional density $f(\cdot \mid A)$ given the event $x \in A$. Suppose $g(x)$ is a density from which it is practical to sample, with the property that $\sup_A f(x)/g(x) \leqslant \alpha < +\infty$. Assume that either the support of g is A, or that it is practical to test if $x \in A$; that it is practical to calculate $f(x)$ and $g(x)$; and that it is practical to calculate a bound α. Draw x from g and ζ from a uniform density on $[0, 1]$, repeat this process until a pair satisfying $x \in A$ and $f(x) \geqslant \zeta \alpha g(x)$ is observed, and accept the associated x. Then, it follows, through a simple application of Bayes' theorem, that the accepted points have density $f(x \mid A) \equiv f(x)/f(A)$. The expected yield of this method is $1/\alpha$. In the specific example in Figure 1, the particular x drawn would be rejected. Possible comparison distributions for ARS are independent exponential or truncated normal distributions in y^* space, but greater yields can be obtained using the recursive truncated normal distribution (4.6) employed in the GHK simulator. Lemmas in McFadden (1989) and Hajivassiliou and McFadden (1990) give protocols for use of independent exponential or recursive truncated normal comparison distributions. To prevent lengthy computations, ARS may be modified to incorporate a *censoring rule*, such as if the first r trials do not yield an acceptance, then the last draw from $g(x)$ is accepted unconditionally. This method will be biased,

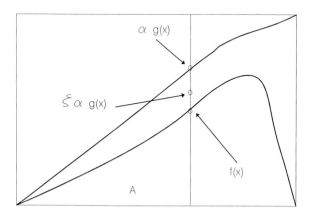

Fig. 1. Acceptance/rejection.

---

[15] The 'yield' of an ARS procedure is defined to be the proportion of random variates that are accepted out of all those drawn.

but Hajivassiliou et al. (1992) show that the bias is bounded at a geometric rate in r.

Note that ARS is not a continuous function of the unknown parameters. To see this, note that a point $y^* = \mu + \Gamma\eta$ may, for given η, move from the rejection to the acceptance region with small changes in the parameters. Hajivassiliou and McFadden (1990) show that the ARS nevertheless satisfies a stochastic equicontinuity condition that enables its use in simulation estimation applications.

An important case where bias may be a major issue is simulation of $1/l$ in the score expressions $\nabla_\theta l/l$. One technique for achieving an unbiased simulator is based on the observation made by Ruud that $1/l$ is the expectation of the number of independent draws R from (4.5) required to yield $y^* \in D$; this can be simulated by drawing sequentially from (4.5) until $y^* \in D$ is observed. See McFadden and Ruud (1991) for details. This method is termed the *sequentially unbiased simulator* (SUS).

Another general principle for devising simulators is *importance sampling*. See Hammersley and Handscomb (1964). Suppose the integrands in l and $\nabla_\theta l$ can, with multiplication and division by a factor if necessary, be written as the product of a density $\gamma(y^*)$, whose support coincides with or contains D, from which it is easy to sample, and the remainder. Then, l and $\nabla_\theta l$ can be written as

$$l = \int \{\mathbf{1}(v \in D)f(v - \mu, \Omega)/\gamma(v)\}\gamma(v)\,dv$$
$$\equiv E_\gamma \mathbf{1}(v \in D)f(v - \mu, \Omega)/\gamma(v)\,, \tag{4.11a}$$

and

$$\nabla_\theta l = \int \{\mathbf{1}(v \in D)\nabla_\theta f(v - \mu, \Omega)/\gamma(v)\}\gamma(v)\,dv$$
$$\equiv E_\gamma \mathbf{1}(v \in D)\nabla_\theta f(v - \mu, \Omega)/\gamma(v)\,, \tag{4.11b}$$

where $v \equiv y^*$, and $f(\cdot)$ denotes the PDF of y^*. An empirical expectation using draws from $\gamma(v)$ gives an unbiased simulator that is smooth is parameters. For the $y^* \sim \mathcal{N}(\mu, \Omega)$ case, this is termed *normal importance sampling* (NIS).

For fast computation, choose γ so that the components are independent, or are obtained as simple transformations of independent variates. Two possible choices of γ are considered in Hajivassiliou et al. (1992). First, the NISE method uses independent exponential densities,

$$\gamma(v) = \prod_{i=1}^{M} \exp((v_i - b_i)/c_i)c_i\,, \tag{4.12}$$

where c_i are parameters that can be set as part of the simulation. Draws from the density are easily computed using $v_i = b_i + c_i \cdot \log \zeta_i$, where ζ_i is a uniform $[0, 1]$ variate. An alternative that is more likely to concentrate probability for γ in the same region as the multivariate normal is the product of truncated normals,

$$\gamma(v) = \prod_{i=1}^{M} \phi((v_i - \alpha_i)/c_i)/[\Phi((b_i - \alpha_i)/c_i) - \Phi((a_i - \alpha_i)/c_i)], \quad v \in D,$$

(4.13)

with $\alpha_i = \mu_i$ and $c_i = \sqrt{\Omega_{ii}}$. This defines the NIST simulator. One can sample from this distribution using

$$v_i = \alpha_i + c_i \Phi^{-1}(\zeta_i \Phi((b_i - \alpha_i)/c_i) + (1 - \zeta_i)\Phi((a_i - \alpha_i)/c_i)), \quad (4.14)$$

with ζ_i a uniform $[0, 1]$ variate.[16]

A promising method, particularly well suited to be used in conjunction with the MSS estimator, is the *Gibbs sampler simulator* for $\nabla_\theta l$. This simulator is based on a Markov chain that utilizes computable univariate truncated normal densities to construct transitions, and has the desired truncated multivariate normal as its limiting distribution.[17] The simulator was developed by Hajivassiliou, starting from stochastic relaxation methods studied by Geman and Geman (1984). This simulator is defined by the following Markovian updating scheme.[18] Suppose D is finite. Start from any $v^{(0)} \in D$. Define a recursive procedure with steps $i = 1, \dots, M$ in rounds $j = 1, \dots, r$. Suppose at step i in round j, $v^{(j-1)}$ and $v_{<i}^{(j)}$ have been determined. Define

$$v_i^{(j)} = \kappa_{ij} + \sigma_i \Phi^{-1}[\zeta_{ij}\Phi((b_i - \kappa_{ij})/\sigma_i) + (1 - \zeta_{ij})\Phi((a_i - \kappa_{ij})/\sigma_i)], \quad (4.15)$$

where the ζ_{ij} are independent uniform $[0, 1]$ variates,

$$\kappa_{ij} = \mu_i + \Omega_{i,-i}\Omega_{-i,-i}^{-1}\begin{bmatrix} v_{<i}^{(j)} & -\mu_{<i}^{(j)} \\ v_{>i}^{(j-1)} & -\mu_{>i}^{(j-1)} \end{bmatrix}, \quad (4.16)$$

and

$$\sigma_i = [\Omega_{ii} - \Omega_{i,-1}\Omega_{-i,-i}^{-1}\Omega_{-i,i}]^{1/2}. \quad (4.17)$$

Note that $v \in D$ by construction. Repeat this process r 'Gibbs resampling rounds'. Then, as Hajivassiliou and McFadden (1990) prove, the random draws obtained by this simulator have a distribution which converges at a geometric rate to the true distribution $z \equiv \{y^* \mid y^* \in D\}$ as the number of Gibbs resampling rounds r grows to infinity. They also show that an MSS

---

[16] A third choice for $\gamma(\cdot)$ that in practice seems to be less successful than (4.13), is due to Moran (1984). West (1990) develops and investigates an adaptive Monte Carlo method, based on importance sampling and density estimation techniques using kernels. He finds that these methods possess the potential to develop automatic routines for Bayesian estimation methodology.

[17] GSS can in principle be generalized to non-normal distributions, provided the corresponding univariate distributions are easy to draw from.

[18] This description follows Hajivassiliou and McFadden (1990).

estimator based on GSS with a finite number of terminal draws R will be consistent and asymptotically normal provided r grows at the rate $\log N$, where N is the sample size. This is a very satisfactory rate. In contrast, consistency and asymptotic normality of a MSS estimator based on AUS or SUS require that R grows at rate $\sqrt{N}$.

Geweke (1991) implements the Gibbs sampler for efficient simulation from the truncated multivariate normal and Student-t distributions, by developing a speedy algorithm for generating univariate truncated normal variates, compared to the algorithm I will denote by RNDTRN that is given in footnote 14. Geweke denotes his algorithm by GGRNRM. I have performed simple Monte Carlo experiments which gave the following comparison. To draw $20\,000\,x \sim$ N(0, 1) truncated on $-1 < x < 1$, on a SUN4/80 workstation took 13.23 seconds using GGRNRM and 18.54 using RNDTRN. On the other hand, when the constraint was one-sided and far from the mean $(-10 < x < -5)$, then RNDTRN was slightly faster (22.2 vs. 20.0). This follows from the fact that Geweke's GGRNRM algorithm is a mixture of RNDTRN and a speedier method, which is only used in regions close to the unconditional mean.

Finally, mention must be made of three simulators for l, $\nabla_\theta l$, and $\nabla_\theta \ln l$ that were developed explicitly for the $y^* \sim \mathcal{N}(\mu, \Omega)$ case, and that may be difficult or impossible to generalize to non-normal y^*. First, consider the *Stern decomposition simulator* (SDS), suggested by Stern (1992). This method writes $y^* \sim \mathcal{N}(\cdot; \mu, \Omega)$ as a sum $y^* = Y + W$, with $Y \sim \mathcal{N}(\cdot; \mu, \lambda^2 I)$ and $W \sim \mathcal{N}(\cdot; 0, \Omega - \lambda^2 I)$. That is, y^* equals the sum of a 'small' independently distributed normal vector and a second normal vector that carries the information on the covariance matrix of y^*. Then, by the law of iterated expectations,

$$l = \int_w \left\{ \int_{y=a}^b \left[\prod_{i=1}^M \phi((y_i - w_i - \mu_i)/\lambda)/\lambda \right] dy \right\} \nabla_\theta n(w, \Omega - \lambda^2 I) \, dw \,,$$

(4.18)

where $n(\cdot)$ denotes the normal PDF. The term in braces can be integrated analytically; then the SDS averages this interior integral over r Monte Carlo draws $w = [\Omega - \lambda^2 I]^{1/2} \eta$, where η is a standard normal vector and $[\Omega - \lambda^2 I]^{1/2}$ is a Choleski factor of $\Omega - \lambda^2 I$. The SDS provides an unbiased smooth simulator. This simulator is fast to compute, but it can be computationally burdensome to determine λ such that $\Omega - \lambda^2 I$ is positive definite, and accuracy fails when M is large and the eigenvalues of Ω are uneven.

Another simulator, developed explicitly for the $y^* \sim \mathcal{N}(\mu, \Omega)$ case, can be interpreted as importance sampling with the uniform distribution on the unit sphere intersecting the negative orthant as the comparison density. This simulator was suggested by McFadden (1989). A related method is *Deák's chi-square simulator* (DCS). See Deák (1980a,b). The DCS simulator is obtained by drawing an antithetic random grid of points on the unit sphere and then using a spherical transformation about the mean of the multivariate normal distribution.[19] It is unbiased for l and $\nabla_\theta l$ and smooth in parameters.

Note that all the simulators for l, $\nabla_\theta l$, and $\nabla_\theta \ln l$ discussed in this section have been implemented in GAUSS and in FORTRAN computer code in Hajivassiliou et al. (1992). The code can be requested from these authors. It is also available via anonymous ftp at the Internet site 'econ.yale.edu'. The main conclusion of this study is that the GHK simulator is the best of all the 13 simulation algorithms considered. It consistently has the best (or among the best) mean and median bias, standard deviation, and RMSE characteristics. For details, readers can refer to Hajivassiliou et al. (1992). The main conclusion confirms other findings in the literature by Bolduc and Kaci (1989) and Mühleisen (1991), who considered GHK against a handful of alternative simulators. This result is found to hold in Hajivassiliou et al. (1992) against *all* other 12 simulators presented here.

5. Conclusion

This chapter discussed estimation methods for limited dependent variable (LDV) models that employ Monte Carlo simulation techniques to overcome numerical intractabilities of such models. These difficulties arise because high dimensional integral expressions need to be calculated repeatedly. In the past, investigators were forced to restrict attention to special classes of LDV models that are computationally tractable. The simulation estimation methods offer dramatic computational advantages over classical methods. In a typical example, computations that would require 3 months to estimate on a modern super-computer with classical methods can be carried out overnight on a high-end personal computer. Hence, simulation estimation methods now make it possible to estimate LDV models that are computationlly intractable using classical estimation methods even on state-of-the-art supercomputers.

The main simulation estimation methods for LDV models developed in the econometrics literature, namely SML, MSM, MSS, SPML, and SSML, have been discussed, and results have been presented about the asymptotic properties of such simulation-based estimators. Specific simulation algorithms to use

---

[19] The principle of *antithetic variates* is to introduce negative correlation between successive Monte Carlo draws in order to reduce the variance of simulation sample averages. See Hendry (1984) for a discussion. Hajivassiliou et al. (1992) generalize the principle to the multivariate case by selecting a regular grid of points whose location is random. This technique can be employed in simulators of l, ∇l, and $\nabla \ln l$ when the method has sufficient symmetry. Another way to reduce simulation variance in Monte Carlo methods is through the use of *control variates*. These are random variables with analytic expectations that are positively correlated with the random variable whose expectation is to be simulated. Then, simulation variance can be reduced by simulating only the difference between the expectations of the variate of interest and the control variate. See Hendry (1984) for details.

in conjunction with these five estimation methods were also described. The leading simulation estimation methods require the simulation of one or more of the following expressions: probabilities of the limited dependent variables, derivatives of such probabilities with respect to underlying parameters, and derivatives of the (natural) logarithm of the probabilities of the dependent variables.

There are two main areas in which future research in the field should prove particularly fruitful. The first is to design simulation algorithms that work satisfactorily for the case of non-normal distributions. The second is to introduce simulation methods into semi-parametric estimation approaches. This would be especially important in freeing the leading simulation estimation methods for LDV models discussed in this chapter from their restrictive fully parametric framework.

Acknowledgment

Research support through NSF grant No. SES 88-13630 is gratefully acknowledged. I am indebted to Yannis Ioannides, Guy Laroque, and Bernard Salanié for very useful comments. Yoosoon Chang and Carmela Quintos provided expert research assistance.

References

Amemiya, T. (1984). Tobit models. A survey. *J. Econometrics* **24**, 3–61.

Avery, R., L. Hansen and V. Hotz (1983). Multiperiod probit models and orthogonality condition estimation. *Internat. Econom. Rev.* **24**, 21–35.

Bauwens, L. (1984). *Bayesian Full Information Analysis of Simultaneous Equation Models Using Integration by Monte Carlo.* Springer, Berlin.

Berkovec, J. and S. Stern (1991). Job exit behavior of older men. *Econometrica* **59**, 189–210.

Berry, S. and A. Pakes (1990). The performance of alternative simulation estimators. Mimeo, Yale University.

Bloemen, H. and A. Kapteyn (1991). The joint estimation of a non-linear labour supply function and a wage equation using simulated response probabilities. Mimeo, Tilburg University.

Bolduc, D. and M. Kaci (1989). On the estimation of probabilities in multinomial probit models: An empirical comparative study of existing techniques. Mimeo, Université Laval.

Bolduc, D. and M. Kaci (1991). Multinomial probit models with factor-based autoregressive errors: A computationally efficient estimation approach. Mimeo, Université Laval.

Börsch-Supan, A. and V. Hajivassiliou (1990). Smooth unbiased multivariate probability simulators for maximum likelihood estimation of limited dependent variable models. Cowles Foundation Discussion Paper No. 960, Yale University; to appear in *J. Econometrics*.

Börsch-Supan, A., V. Hajivassiliou, L. Kotlikoff and J. Morris (1992). Health, children, and elderly living arrangements: A multi-period multinomial probit model with unobserved heterogeneity and autocorrelated errors. In: D. Wise, ed., *Topics in the Economics of Aging.* Univ. of Chicago Press, Chicago, IL, 79–107.

Chamberlain, G. (1984). Panel data. In: Z. Griliches and M. Intriligator, eds., North-Holland, Amsterdam, 1247–1318.

Clark, C. (1961). The greatest of a finite set of random variables. *Oper. Res.* **9**, 145–162.

Daganzo, C., F. Bouthelier and Y. Sheffi (1977). Multinomial probit and qualitative choice: A computationally efficient algorithm. *Transportation Sci.* **11**, 338–358.

Deák, I. (1980a). Three digit accurate multiple normal probabilities. *Numer. Math.* **35**, 369–380.

Deák, I. (1980b). Fast procedures for generating stationary normal vectors. *J. Statist. Comput. Simulation* **10**, 225–242.

Devroye, L. (1986). *Non-Uniform Random Variate Generation.* Springer, New York.

Divgi, D. (1979). Calculation of univariate and bivariate normal probability functions. *Ann. Statist.* **7**, 903–910.

Dubin, J. and D. McFadden (1984). An econometric analysis of residential electric appliance holdings and consumption. *Econometrica* **52**, 345–362.

Duffie, D. and K. Singleton (1989). Simulated moments estimation of Markov models of asset prices. Mimeo, Stanford University.

Dutt, J. (1973). A representation of multivariate normal probability integrals by integral transforms. *Biometrika* **60**, 637–645.

Dutt, J. (1976). Numerical aspects of multivariate normal probabilities in econometric models. *Ann. Econom. Social Measurement* **5**, 547–562.

Eggink, E., J. Hop and B. Van Praag (1992). A symmetric approach to the labor market with the household as unit of observation. Erasmus University, Working Paper, presented at the Rotterdam International Conference on Simulation and at the ESEM Brussels.

Feller, W. (1971). *An Introduction to Probability Theory and its Applications.* Wiley, New York.

Geman, S. and D. Geman (1984). Stochastic relaxation, Gibbs distributions, and the Bayesian restoration of images. *IEEE Trans. Patt. Anal. Mach. Intelligence* **6**, 721–741.

Geweke, J. (1989a). Bayesian inference in econometric models using Monte Carlo integration. *Econometrica* **57**, 1317–1339.

Geweke, J. (1989b). Efficient simulation from the multivariate normal distribution subject to linear inequality constraints and the evaluation of constraint probabilities. Mimeo, Duke University.

Geweke, J. (1991). Efficient simulation from the multivariate normal and student-t distributions subject to linear constraints. In: *Proc. 23rd Sympos. on the Interface: Computing Science and Statistics.* Amer. Statist. Assoc., Alexandria, VA, 571–578.

Gourieroux, C. and A. Monfort (1990). Simulation based inference in models with heterogeneity. Mimeo, INSEE.

Gourieroux, C., A. Monfort, E. Renault and A. Trognon (1984a). Pseudo maximum likelihood methods: Theory. *Econometrica* **52**, 681–700.

Gourieroux, C., A. Monfort, E. Renault and A. Trognon (1984b). Pseudo maximum likelihood methods: Applications to Poisson models. *Econometrica* **52**, 701–720.

Hajivassiliou, V. (1986). Serial correlation in limited dependent variable models: Theoretical and Monte Carlo results. Cowles Foundation Discussion Paper No. 803, Yale University.

Hajivassiliou, V. (1990). The method of simulated scores: A presentation and comparative evaluation. Mimeo, Cowles Foundation for Research in Economics, Yale University.

Hajivassiliou, V. and Y. Ioannides (1991). Switching regressions models of the Euler equation: Consumption, labor supply, and liquidity constraints. Mimeo, Cowles Foundation for Research in Economics, Yale University.

Hajivassiliou, V. and D. McFadden (1990). The method of simulated scores, with application to models of external debt crises. Cowles Foundation Discussion Paper No. 967, Yale University.

Hajivassiliou, V., D. McFadden and P. Ruud (1992). Simulation of multivariate normal orthant probabilities: Theoretical and Computational Results. Cowles Foundation Discussion Paper No. 1021, Yale University.

Hammersley, J. and D. Handscomb (1964). *Monte Carlo Methods.* Methuen, London.

Hausman, J. and D. Wise (1978). A conditional probit model for qualitative choice: Discrete decisions recognizing interdependence and heterogeneous preferences. *Econometrica* **46**, 403–426.

Heckman, J. (1981). Dynamic discrete models. In: C. Manski and D. McFadden, eds., *Structural Analysis of Discrete Data with Econometric Applications.* MIT Press, Cambridge, MA, 179–195.

Hendry, D. (1984). Monte Carlo experimentation in econometrics. In: Z. Griliches and M. Intriligator, eds., *Handbook of Econometrics*, Vol. 2. North-Holland, Amsterdam, 937–976.

Horowitz, J., J. Sparmonn and C. Daganzo (1981). An investigation of the accuracy of the Clark approximation for the multinomial probit model. *Transportation Sci.* **16**, 382–401.

Hotz, V. J. and R. Miller (1989). Conditional choice probabilities and the estimation of dynamic programming models. GSIA Working Paper 88–89–10.

Hotz, V. J., R. Miller, S. Sanders and J. Smith (1991). A simulation estimator for dynamic discrete choice models. Mimeo, NORC, University of Chicago.

Hotz, V. J. and S. Sanders (1990). The estimation of dynamic discrete choice models by the method of simulated moments. NORC, University of Chicago.

Keane, M. (1990). A computationally efficient practical simulation estimator for panel data, with applications to estimating temporal dependence in employment and wages. Mimeo, University of Minnesota.

Kloek, T. and H. Van Dijk (1978). Bayesian estimates of equation system parameters: An application of integration by Monte Carlo. *Econometrica* **46**, 1–20.

Laroque, G. and B. Salanié (1989). Estimation of multi-market disequilibrium fix-price models: An application of pseudo maximum likelihood methods. *Econometrica* **57**, 831–860.

Laroque, G. and B. Salanié (1990). The properties of simulated pseudo-maximum likelihood methods: The case of the canonical disequilibrium model. Working Paper No. 9005, CREST-Département de la Recherche, INSEE.

Lee, B.-S. and B. Ingram (1991). Simulation estimation of time-series models. *J. Econometrics* **47**, 197–205.

Lee, L.-F. (1990). On the efficiency of methods of simulated moments and maximum simulated likelihood estimation of discrete response models. Center for Economic Research, Discussion Paper No. 260, University of Minnesota.

Lerman, S. and C. Manski (1981). On the use of simulated frequencies to approximate choice probabilities. In: C. Manski and D. McFadden, eds., *Structural Analysis of Discrete Data with Econometric Applications*. MIT Press, Cambridge, MA, 305–319.

Maddala, G.S. (1983). *Limited Dependent and Qualitative Variables in Econometrics*. Cambridge Univ. Press, Cambridge.

McFadden, D. (1973). Conditional logit analysis of qualitative choice behavior. In: P. Zarembka, ed. *Frontiers in Econometrics*. Academic Press, New York, 105–142.

McFadden, D. (1981). Econometric models of probabilistic choice. In: C. Manski and D. McFadden, eds., *Structural Analysis of Discrete Data with Econometric Applications*. MIT Press, Cambridge, MA, 198–272.

McFadden, D. (1984). Econometric analysis of qualitative response models. In: Z. Griliches and M. Intriligator, eds., *Handbook of Econometrics*, Vol. 2. North-Holland, Amsterdam, 1395–1457.

McFadden, D. (1989). A method of simulated moments for estimation of discrete response models without numerical integration. *Econometrica* **57**, 995–1026.

McFadden, D. and P. Ruud (1991). Estimation by simulation. Mimeo, M.I.T.

Moran, P. (1984). The Monte Carlo evaluation of orthant probabilities for multivariate normal distributions. *Austral. J. Statist.* **26**, 39–44.

Mühleisen, M. (1991). On the use of simulated estimators for panel models with limited-dependent variables. Mimeo, University of Munich.

Nelder, J. and R. Meade (1964). A simplex method for function minimization. *Comput. J.* **7**, 308–313.

Niesing, W., B. Van Praag and J. Veenman (1991). The unemployment of ethnic minority groups in The Netherlands. Report no. 9175/A, Econometric Institute, Erasmus University, presented at ESEM, Cambridge, and at the International Workshop on The Economics of Labor Market Discrimination and Segregation at Bal Han University.

Pakes, A. (1991). Estimation of dynamic structural models: Problems and prospects Part II: Mixed continuous-discrete controls and market interactions. To appear in: J. J. Laffont and C. Sims, eds., *Advances in Econometrics*. Proc. 6th World Congress of the Economic Society.

Pakes, A. and D. Pollard (1989). Simulation and the asymptotics of optimization estimators. *Econometrica* **57**, 1027–1057.

Poirier, D. and P. Ruud (1988). Probit with dependent observations. *Rev. Econom. Stud.* **55**, 593–614.

Quandt, R. (1983). Computational problems in econometrics. In: Z. Griliches and M. Intriligator, eds., *Handbook of Econometrics*, Vol. 1. North-Holland, Amsterdam, 1395–1457.

Rubinstein, R. (1981). *Simulation and the Monte Carlo Method*. Wiley, New York.

Rust, J. (1989). Optimal replacement of GMC bus engines: An empirical model of Harold Zurcher. *Econometrica* **55**, 999–1033.

Rust, J. (1991). Estimation of dynamic structural models: Problems and prospects Part I: Discrete decision processes. To appear in: J. J. Laffont and C. Sims, eds., *Advances in Econometrics*. Proc. 6th World Congress of the Economic Society.

Ruud, P. (1986). On the method of simulated moments for the estimation of limited dependent variable models. Mimeo, University of California at Berkeley.

Ruud, P. (1991). Extensions of estimation methods using the EM algorithm. *J. Econometrics* **49**, 305–341.

Steck, G. P. (1958). A table for computing trivariate normal probabilities. *Ann. Math. Statist.* **29**, 780–800.

Stern, S. (1991). Discrete choice models with unobserved heterogeneity: Demand for transportation by elderly and disabled people. University of Virginia, Working Paper.

Stern, S. (1992). A method for smoothing simulated moments of discrete probabilities in multimomial probit models. *Econometrica* **60**, 943–952.

Van Dijk, H. K. (1987). Some advances in Bayesian estimation methods using Monte Carlo integration. In: T. B. Fomby and G. F. Rhodes, eds., *Advances in Econometrics*, Vol. 6. JAI Press, Greenwich, CT, 215–261.

Van Praag, B. and J. Hop (1987). Estimation of continuous models on the basis of set-valued observations. Erasmus University, Working Paper, presented at the ESEM Copenhagen.

Van Praag, B., J. Hop and E. Eggink (1989). A symmetric approach to the labor market by means of the simulated moments method with an application to married females. Erasmus University, Working Paper, presented at EEA Augsburg.

Van Praag, B., J. Hop and E. Eggink (1991). A symmetric approach to the labor market by means of the simulated EM-algorithm with an application to married females. Erasmus University, Working Paper, presented at the ESEM Cambridge.

West, M. (1990). Bayesian computations: Monte-Carlo density estimation. Discussion Paper #90-A10, Duke University.

G. S. Maddala, C. R. Rao and H. D. Vinod, eds., *Handbook of Statistics, Vol. 11*
© 1993 Elsevier Science Publishers B.V. All rights reserved.

20

Simulation Estimation for Panel Data Models with Limited Dependent Variables

*Michael P. Keane**

1. Introduction

Simulation estimation in the context of panel data, limited dependent-variable (LDV) models poses formidable problems that are not present in the cross-section case. Nevertheless, a number of practical simulation estimation methods have been proposed and implemented for panel data LDV models. This paper surveys those methods and presents two empirical applications that illustrate their usefulness.

The outline of the paper is as follows. Section 2 reviews methods for estimating panel data models with serial correlation in the linear case. Section 3 describes the special problems that arise when estimating panel data models with serial correlation in the LDV case. Section 4 presents the essential ideas of method of simulated moments (MSM) estimation, as developed by McFadden (1989) and Pakes and Pollard (1989), and explains why MSM is difficult to apply in the panel data case. Section 5 describes computationally practical simulation estimation methods for the panel data probit model. Section 5.1 describes an efficient algorithm for the recursive simulation of probabilities of sequences of events. This algorithm is at the heart of all the simulation estimators that have proven feasible for panel data LDV models. Section 5.2 describes the simulation estimators for panel data probit models that are based on such recursive simulation of probabilities. Section 5.3 describes some alternative estimators that are based on conditional simulation of the latent variables in the probit model via similar recursive methods. Section 6 discusses issues that arise in simulation estimation of models more complex than the probit model. In Section 7, I use the simulation estimation methods presented in Sections 5 to 6 to estimate probit employment equations and selection

* The Institute for Empirical Macroeconomics and the Alfred P. Sloan Foundation have supported this research. The views expressed herein are those of the author and not necessarily those of the Federal Reserve Bank of Minneapolis or the Federal Reserve System.

bias-adjusted wage equations on panel data from the national longitudinal survey of young men. Section 8 concludes.

Throughout the exposition in Sections 2–6, I assume strict exogeneity of the regressors. I do this in order to focus on the special problems that arise due to simulation itself. Thus, I ignore the important issues that arise when the regressors are endogenous or predetermined rather than strictly exogenous. For discussions of these issues, the reader is referred to the excellent surveys of Heckman (1981) and Chamberlain (1985).

I also ignore simulation estimation in the context of discrete dynamic programming models. This is despite the facts that the first important econometric application of simulation estimation was in this area (Pakes, 1986), the area continues to be a fertile one (see, e.g., Berkovec and Stern, 1991; Hotz and Miller, 1991; and Geweke, Slonim and Zarkin, 1992), and that much of my current research is in this area (Keane and Wolpin, 1992; Erdem and Keane, 1992). This omission stems from my desire to focus on the special problems that arise in the simulation of probabilities of sequences of events, excluding those additional problems that arise when the solution of a dynamic programming problem must also be simulated.

2. Methods for estimating panel data models with serial correlation in the linear case

Since the pioneering work of Balestra and Nerlove (1966), the importance of controlling for serial correlation in panel data models has been widely recognized. There are many situations where, if an agent is observed over several time periods, we would expect the errors for that agent to be serially correlated. For instance, in wage data, those workers who have wages that are high at a point in time (after conditioning on the usual human capital variables like education and experience) tend to have persistently high wages over time. As Balestra and Nerlove pointed out, failure to account for such serial correlation when estimating linear regressions on panel data leads to bias in estimates of the standard errors of the regressor coefficients. To deal with this problem, they proposed the random effects model, in which the existence of a time-invariant individual effect, uncorrelated with the regressors and distributed with zero mean in the population, is postulated.

The random effects model produces an error structure that is equicorrelated. That is, if the true model is

$$y_{it} = X_{it}\beta + \varepsilon_{it}, \tag{1}$$

for $t = 1, T$ and $I = 1, N$, where y_{it} is the dependent variable for person i at time t, X_{it} is a vector of strictly exogenous regressors, and ε_{it} is the error term, and if

$$\tag{2}$$

where μ_i is a time-invariant random effect and ω_{it} is iid, then the covariance structure of the ε_{it} is

$$\mathrm{E}\varepsilon_{it}\varepsilon_{i,t-j} = \begin{cases} \sigma_\varepsilon^2 & \text{for } j = 0\,, \\ \rho\sigma_\varepsilon^2 & \text{for } j \neq 0\,. \end{cases} \tag{3}$$

Here ρ is the fraction of the variance of ε due to the individual random effect. Thus, the correlation between the errors ε_{it} for any two different time periods is ρ regardless of how far apart the time periods are.

This equicorrelation assumption is obviously unrealistic in many situations. Its virtue lies in the fact that estimation of the random effects model is extremely convenient. The model (1)–(2) may be estimated using a simple two-step GLS procedure that produces consistent and asymptotically efficient estimates of the model parameters and their standard errors. If the equicorrelation assumption is incorrect, the estimates of β remain consistent but the estimated standard errors are biased.

In cases where equicorrelation does not hold, it is simple to replace (2) with a general covariance structure and apply the same two-step GLS procedure. In the first step, obtain a consistent estimate of β under the assumption that the ε are iid and use the residuals to estimate the covariance matrix $\Sigma = \mathrm{E}\varepsilon_i\varepsilon_i'$, where $\varepsilon_i = (\varepsilon_{i1}, \ldots, \varepsilon_{iT})'$ is a $T \times 1$ column vector. Then, letting $\hat{\Sigma}$ denote the estimate of Σ, take the Cholesky decomposition $\hat{\Sigma} = \hat{A}\hat{A}'$, where A is a lower-triangular matrix, and premultiply the y_i and X_i vectors by $\hat{A}'$. In a second step, estimate a regression of $\hat{A}'y_i$ on $\hat{A}'X_i$ to produce consistent and asymptotically efficient estimates of all model parameters and their standard errors. (See Amemiya and McCurdy, 1986 or Keane and Runkle, 1992.) Note that, with missing data, estimation of an unrestricted A matrix would be problematic. However, restricted structures where Σ is parameterized as, say, having random effects and ARMA error components pose no problem.

3. The problem of estimating LDV models with serial correlation

In sharp contrast to the linear case, estimation of LDV models with serial corelation poses difficult problems. As a leading case, consider the panel data probit model. This model is obtained if we do not observe y_{it} in equation (1), but only observe the indicator function d_{it}, where

$$d_{it} = \begin{cases} 1 & \text{if } y_{it} \geq 0\,, \\ 0 & \text{otherwise}\,, \end{cases} \tag{4}$$

and if we further assume that the error terms have a normal distribution, $\varepsilon_i \sim \mathrm{N}(0, \Sigma)$. Given this structure, we can write $\varepsilon_i = A\eta_i$, where $\eta_i = (\eta_{i1}, \ldots, \eta_{iT})'$ and $\eta_i \sim \mathrm{N}(0, I)$. Define θ as the vector consisting of elements of β and the parameters determining the error covariance structure Σ. Further, define $J_{it} = \{d_{i1}, \ldots, d_{it}\}$ as the set of choices made by person i through period

t, and $\text{Prob}(J_{it} \mid X_i, \theta)$ as the probability of this set, where $X_i = (X_{i1}, \ldots, X_{iT})'$. Then the log-likelihood function evaluated at a trial parameter estimate $\hat{\theta}$ is

$$\mathcal{L}(\hat{\theta}) = \sum_{i=1}^{N} \ln \text{Prob}(J_{iT} \mid X_i, \hat{\theta}) . \tag{5}$$

The difficulty inherent in evaluating this log-likelihood depends on the error structure. If the ε_{it} are iid, then

$$\text{Prob}(J_{it} \mid X_i, \hat{\theta}) = \prod_{l=1}^{t} \text{Prob}(d_{il} \mid X_{il}, \hat{\theta}) .$$

Thus, only univariate integration is necessary to form the log-likelihood. If there are random effects, as in (2), then

$$\text{Prob}(J_{it} \mid X_i, \hat{\theta}) = \int_{-\infty}^{\infty} \prod_{l=1}^{t} \text{Prob}(d_{il} \mid X_{il}, \hat{\theta}) f(\mu) \, \mathrm{d}\mu .$$

Here, bivariate integration is necessary. If $f(\cdot)$ is the normal density, such bivariate integrations can be evaluated simply using the Gaussian quadrature procedure described by Butler and Moffitt (1982). Unfortunately, for more general error structures, the order of integration necessary is T. This makes maximum-likelihood (ML) estimation infeasible for $T \geqslant 4$.

Results in Robinson (1982) indicate that, regardless of the correlation structure of the ε_{it}, if the ε_{it} are assumed iid, then the resultant misspecified model produces consistent estimates of β. Such an estimator is inefficient and produces biased estimates of the standard errors. However, a covariance matrix correction is available. Given these results, the value in having a capability to deal with complex serial correlation patterns in LDV models resides in four things. First, there is a potential for efficiency gain in estimating models with richer correlation structures. Second, no proof is available that misspecification of the correlation structure of ε_{it} results in a consistent estimator of β for cases other than that in which ε_{it} is specified to be iid. Third, in the presence of lagged dependent variables, consistent estimation requires that the serial correlation structure be properly specified. Fourth, and most importantly, allowing for more complex serial correlation patterns can potentially improve out-of-sample prediction of agents' future choice behavior.

4. MSM estimation for LDV models

A natural alternative to ML estimation for LDV models is simulation-based estimation, recently studied by McFadden (1989) and Pakes and Pollard (1989). McFadden developed the MSM estimator for the probit model. To motivate the MSM estimator, it is useful to first construct the method of moments (MOM) estimator for the panel data probit model.

To construct the MOM estimator, let $k = 1, K$ index all possible choice sequences J_{iT}. Let $D_{ik} = 1$ if agent i chooses sequence k and $D_{ik} = 0$ otherwise. Then, following McFadden (1989), the score of the log-likelihood can be written

$$\nabla_{\hat{\theta}} \mathscr{L}(\hat{\theta}) = \sum_{i=1}^{N} \sum_{k=1}^{K} W_{ik}[D_{ik} - \text{Prob}(D_{ik} = 1 \mid X_i, \hat{\theta})], \qquad (6a)$$

where $\hat{\theta}$ is a particular trial parameter estimate and

$$W_{ik} = \frac{\nabla_{\hat{\theta}} \text{Prob}(D_{ik} = 1 \mid X_i, \hat{\theta})}{\text{Prob}(D_{ik} = 1 \mid X_i, \hat{\theta})}. \qquad (6b)$$

Note that (6a) has the form of mean zero moments $[D_{ik} - \text{Prob}(D_{ik} = 1 \mid X_i, \hat{\theta})]$ times orthogonal weights W_{ik}. Thus, it can be used to form the first-order conditions (FOCs) of an MOM estimator for θ. The MOM estimator, $\hat{\theta}_{\text{MOM}}$, sets the FOC vector in (6a) equal to the zero vector. If the optimal weights W_{ik} are used, this MOM estimator is asymptotically as efficient as ML. Other choices of weights that are asymptotically correlated with the W_{ik} and orthogonal to the residuals produce consistent and asymptotically normal but inefficient MOM estimators. Of course, for general specifications of the error structure, this MOM estimator is not feasible because the choice probabilities are T-variate integrals.

The idea of the MSM estimator is to replace the intractable integrals $\text{Prob}(D_{ik} = 1 \mid X_i, \hat{\theta})$ in (6a) by unbiased Monte Carlo probability simulators. The most basic method for simulating the choice probabilities is to draw, for each individual i, a set of iid error vectors $(\eta_{i1}, \ldots, \eta_{iT})$ using a univariate normal random number generator and to count the percentage of these vectors that generate $D_{ik} = 1$. This is called the *frequency simulator*. More accurate probability simulators will be discussed below.

Because the simulation error enters linearly into the MSM FOCs, it will tend to cancel over observations. As a result, the MSM estimator based on an unbiased probability simulator is consistent and asymptotically normal in N for a fixed simulation size. If the frequency simulator is used, $\hat{\theta}_{\text{MSM}}$ has an asymptotic covariance matrix that is $(1 + S^{-1})$ times greater than that of $\hat{\theta}_{\text{MOM}}$, where S is the number of draws used in the simulation. Use of more accurate probability simulators improves relative efficiency. If consistent independent simulators of the optimal weights are used, then $\hat{\theta}_{\text{MSM}}$ is asymptotically (in N and S) as efficient as ML.

Unfortunately, the MSM estimator in (6a) is not practical to implement. The source of the problem is that K grows large quickly with T. In the binomial probit case, $K = 2^T$. Thus, for reasonably large T construction of (6a) requires a very large number of calculations. If a simple frequency simulator is used, such calculations can be done quickly. However, according to McFadden and Ruud (1987), frequency simulation does not appear to work well for this problem. One difficulty is that the FOCs based on frequency simulation are not smooth functions. This makes it impossible to use gradient-based optimization methods. This problem can, however, be dealt with by use of the simplex algorithm. A more serious problem is that the denominators of the optimal weights in (6b) are the probabilities of choice sequences. These probabilities will tend to become very small as T gets large, and frequency simulators based on reasonable numbers of draws will therefore tend to produce simulated probabilities of zero for many choice sequences. This makes it quite difficult to form good approximations to the optimal weights, so that the MSM estimator based on frequency simulation will tend to be very inefficient.

The natural solution to this problem is to use more efficient probability simulators that can accurately simulate small probabilities. Such simulators, based on importance sampling techniques, are considerably more expensive to construct than crude frequency simulators. Thus, it is not practical to use them in conjunction with (6a) to form the FOCs of an MSM estimator. In the next section, I describe a highly efficient algorithm for simulating probabilities of sequences of events and describe practical simulation estimators for panel data probit models based on this algorithm.

5. Practical simulation estimators for the panel data probit model

Recently, Keane (1990) and Hajivassiliou and McFadden (1990) have developed computational practical simulation estimators for panel data LDV models. Both methods rely on a highly accurate recursive algorithm for simulating probabilities of sequences of events that I describe in Section 5.1. In Section 5.2, I explain how these simulators can be used to construct practical simulation estimators for the panel data probit model. In Section 5.3, I describe some alternative estimators that are based on conditional simulation of the latent variables in the probit model via similar recursive methods.

5.1. Recursive simulation of probabilities of sequences of events

In Keane (1990), I developed a highly accurate algorithm for simulating the probabilities of choice sequences in panel data probit models. To see the motivation for this method, first observe that the choice $d_{it} = 1$ occurs if $\varepsilon_{it} \geq -X_{it}\beta$ while the choice $d_{it} = 0$ occurs if $-\varepsilon_{it} > X_{it}\beta$. Thus, the boundary of the ε_{it} distribution conditional on d_{it} is

$$(2d_{it} - 1)\varepsilon_{it} \geq (1 - 2d_{it})X_{it}\beta \ .$$

Since $\varepsilon_i = A\eta_i$, this constraint may be written

$$(2d_{it} - 1)\eta_{it} \geq \frac{(1 - 2d_{it})X_{it}\beta - (2d_{it} - 1)(A_{t1}\eta_{i1} + \cdots + A_{t,t-1}\eta_{i,t-1})}{A_{tt}} \ .$$

Recall that $J_{it} = \{d_{i1}, \ldots, d_{it}\}$ denotes the set of choices made by person i in periods 1 through t. Further define

$$\eta(J_{i1}) = \{\eta_{i1} \mid (2d_{i1} - 1)\eta_{i1} > (1 - 2d_{i1})X_{i1}\beta\},$$

$$\eta(J_{it}) = \left\{\eta_{i1}, \ldots, \eta_{it} \mid (2d_{is} - 1)\eta_{is}\right.$$

$$> \frac{(1 - 2d_{is})X_{is}\beta - (2d_{is} - 1)(A_{s1}\eta_{i1} + \cdots + A_{s,s-1}\eta_{i,s-1})}{A_{ss}}$$

$$\left. \text{for all } s \leq t \right\}. \tag{7}$$

These are the sets of η_i vectors that are consistent with the set of choices made by person i in periods 1 through t. The probability of a choice sequence $\text{Prob}(J_{it} \mid X_i, \hat{\theta})$ can be factored into a first-period unconditional choice probability times transition probabilities as follows:

$$\text{Prob}(J_{it} \mid X_i, \hat{\theta})$$
$$= \text{Prob}(\eta_{i1}, \ldots, \eta_{it} \in \eta(J_{it}))$$
$$= \text{Prob}(\eta_{i1} \in \eta(J_{i1})) \, \text{Prob}(\eta_{i1}, \eta_{i2} \in \eta(J_{i2}) \mid \eta_{i1} \in \eta(J_{i1}))$$
$$\times \cdots \times \text{Prob}(\eta_{i1}, \ldots, \eta_{it} \in \eta(J_{it}) \mid \eta_{i1}, \ldots, \eta_{i,t-1} \in \eta(J_{i,t-1})). \tag{8}$$

An unbiased simulator of this probability may be obtained by the following sequential procedure:

(1) Draw an η_{i1} from the truncated univariate normal distribution such that $\eta_{i1} \in \eta(J_{i1})$. Call the particular value that is drawn η_{i1}^*.

(2) Given η_{i1}^*, there is a range of η_{i2} values such that

$$(2d_{i2} - 1)\eta_{i2} > [(1 - 2d_{i2})X_{i2}\beta - (2d_{i2} - 1)A_{21}\eta_{i1}^*]/A_{22}.$$

Using the notation of (7), I denote this set of η_{i2} values by $\{\eta_{i2} \mid \eta_{i1}^*, \eta_{i2} \in \eta(J_{i2})\}$. Draw an η_{i2} from a truncated univariate normal distribution such that $(\eta_{i1}^*, \eta_{i2}) \in \eta(J_{i2})$. Call the particular value that is drawn η_{i2}^*.

(3) Continue in this way until a vector $(\eta_{i1}^*, \ldots, \eta_{i,T-1}^*) \in \eta(J_{i,t-1})$ is obtained.

(4) Form the simulator:

$$\widehat{\text{Prob}}(J_{it} \mid X_i, \hat{\theta}) = \text{Prob}(\eta_{i1} \in \eta(J_{i1})) \times \text{Prob}(\eta_{i2} \in \eta(J_{i2}) \mid \eta_{i1}^*)$$
$$\times \cdots \times \text{Prob}(\eta_{it} \in \eta(J_{it}) \mid \eta_{i1}^*, \ldots, \eta_{i,t-1}^*). \tag{9}$$

This probability simulator has been named the *Geweke–Hajivassiliou–Keane* or *GHK simulator* by Hajivassiliou, McFadden and Ruud (1992) because related independent work by Geweke (1991a) and Hajivassiliou led to the development of the same method. In an extensive study of alternative probability simulators, they find that the GHK simulator is the most accurate of all those considered.

Note that simulators of the transition probabilities in (8) can be obtained by the same method. In Keane (1990), I showed that, for $t \geq 3$, an unbiased simulator of the transition probabilities is given by

$$\widehat{\text{Prob}}(d_{it} \mid J_{i,t-1}, X_i, \hat{\theta})$$

$$= \text{Prob}(\eta_{it} \in \eta(J_{it}) \mid \eta_{i1}^*, \ldots, \eta_{i,t-1}^*) \omega(\eta_{i1}^*, \ldots, \eta_{it-1}^*) , \qquad (10a)$$

where

$$\omega(\eta_{i1}^*, \ldots, \eta_{i,t-1}^*)$$

$$= \frac{\omega(\eta_{i1}^*, \ldots, \eta_{i,t-2}^*) \text{Prob}(\eta_{i,t-1} \in \eta(J_{i,t-1}) \mid \eta_{i1}^*, \ldots, \eta_{i,t-2}^*)}{\text{Prob}(\eta_{i,t-1} \in \eta(J_{i,t-1}) \mid \eta_{i1}, \ldots, \eta_{i,t-2} \in \eta(J_{i,t-2}))}$$

$$= \frac{\text{Prob}(\eta_{i,t-1} \in \eta(J_{i,t-1}) \mid \eta_{i1}^*, \ldots, \eta_{i,t-2}^*) \cdots \text{Prob}(\eta_{i2} \in \eta(J_{i2}) \mid \eta_{i1}^*) \text{Prob}(\eta_{i1} \in \eta(J_{i1}))}{\text{Prob}(\eta_{i1}, \ldots, \eta_{i,t-1} \in \eta(J_{i,t-1}))}$$

$$(10b)$$

This procedure may be interpreted as importance sampling where the transition probability is simulated conditional on the draw $\eta_{i1}^*, \ldots, \eta_{i,t-1}^*$ from the importance sampling density defined by steps (1)–(3) and $\omega(\eta_{i1}^*, \ldots, \eta_{i,t-1}^*)$ is the importance sampling weight. The form of the weight is the ratio of (1) the probability of event sequence $d_{i1}, \ldots, d_{i,t-1}$ as simulated by the GHK method using the draw $\eta_{i1}^*, \ldots, \eta_{i,t-1}^*$ to (2) the actual probability of the event sequence $d_{i1}, \ldots, d_{i,t-1}$.

Unfortunately, for $t - 1 \geq 3$ it is not feasible to numerically evaluate the object $\text{Prob}(\eta_{i1}, \ldots, \eta_{i,t-1} \in \eta(J_{i,t-1}))$ that appears in the denominator of the importance sampling weights. However, this probability may itself be simulated by the GHK method. If this is done, a denominator bias is induced, and the resultant transition probability simulator will be asymptotically unbiased as the number of draws used to form the GHK simulator becomes large.

Let S be the number of draws used to simulate the choice sequence and transition probabilities by the GHK method. Letting $(\eta_{i1s}^*, \ldots, \eta_{i,T-1,s}^*)$ be the s-th sequence drawn in the GHK procedure, one obtains, for the simulated sequence probabilities,

$$\widehat{\text{Prob}}(J_{it} \mid X_i, \hat{\theta}) = \frac{1}{S} \sum_{s=1}^{S} \text{Prob}(\eta_{i1} \in \eta(J_{i1})) \text{Prob}(\eta_{i2} \in \eta(J_{i2}) \mid \eta_{i1s}^*)$$

$$\times \cdots \times \text{Prob}(\eta_{it} \in \eta(J_{it}) \mid \eta_{i1s}^*, \ldots, \eta_{i,t-1,s}^*)$$

$$(11)$$

and for the simulated transition probabilities,

$$\widehat{\text{Prob}}(d_{it} \mid J_{i,t-1}, X_i, \hat{\theta})$$

$$= \frac{1}{S} \sum_{s=1}^{S} \text{Prob}(\eta_{it} \in \eta(J_{it}) \mid \eta_{i1s}^*, \ldots, \eta_{i,t-1,s}^*) \hat{\omega}(\eta_{i1s}^*, \ldots, \eta_{i,t-1,s}^*) ,$$

(12a)

where

$$\hat{\omega}(\eta_{i1s}^*, \ldots, \eta_{i,t-1,s}^*)$$

$$= \frac{\text{Prob}(\eta_{i,t-1} \in \eta(J_{i,t-1}) \mid \eta_{i1s}^*, \ldots, \eta_{i,t-2,s}^*) \cdots \text{Prob}(\eta_{i2} \in \eta(J_{i2}) \mid \eta_{i1s}^*)}{S^{-1} \sum_{r=1}^{S} \text{Prob}(\eta_{i,t-1} \in \eta(J_{i,t-1}) \mid \eta_{i1r}^*, \ldots, \eta_{i,t-2,r}^*) \cdots \text{Prob}(\eta_{i2} \in \eta(J_{i2}) \mid \eta_{i1r}^*)}$$

(12b)

for $t \geqslant 3$ and

$$\widehat{\text{Prob}}(d_{i2} \mid J_{i1}, X_i, \hat{\theta}) = \frac{1}{S} \sum_{s=1}^{S} \text{Prob}(\eta_{i2} \in \eta(J_{i2}) \mid \eta_{i1s}^*)$$

for $t = 2$. Note that if the importance sampling weights are simulated as in (12b), they are constrained to sum to one by construction. Constraining importance sampling weights to sum to one is a standard variance reduction technique often recommended in the numerical analysis literature. In (12b), the simulation error in the numerator is positively correlated with that in the denominator, so in some cases a variance reduction in simulation of the ratio may be achieved by use of the simulated rather than the true denominator.

5.2. Practical simulation methods for panel data probit models based on recursive simulation of probabilities

Three classical methods of estimation for panel data probit models have been implemented in the literature, all based on the GHK method for simulation of sequence and transition probabilities. In Keane (1990), I expressed the log-likelihood function as a sum of transition probabilities

$$\mathcal{L}(\hat{\theta}) = \sum_{i=1}^{N} \ln \text{Prob}(J_{iT} \mid X_i, \hat{\theta}) = \sum_{i=1}^{N} \sum_{t=1}^{T} \ln \text{Prob}(d_{it} \mid J_{i,t-1}, X_i, \hat{\theta})$$

and proceed to express the score as

$$\nabla_{\hat{\theta}} \mathcal{L}(\hat{\theta}) = \sum_{i=1}^{N} \sum_{t=1}^{T} \{ W_{it}^1 [d_{it} - \text{Prob}(d_{it} = 1 \mid J_{i,t-1}, X_i, \hat{\theta})]$$

$$+ W_{it}^0 [(1 - d_{it}) - \text{Prob}(d_{it} = 0 \mid J_{i,t-1}, X_i, \hat{\theta})] \} ,$$

(13)

where the weights W_{it}^1 and W_{it}^0 have the form

$$W_{it}^1 = \frac{\nabla_{\hat{\theta}} \operatorname{Prob}(d_{it} = 1 \mid J_{i,t-1}, X_i, \hat{\theta})}{\operatorname{Prob}(d_{it} = 1 \mid J_{i,t-1}, X_i, \hat{\theta})},$$

$$W_{it}^0 = \frac{\nabla_{\hat{\theta}} \operatorname{Prob}(d_{it} = 0 \mid J_{i,t-1}, X_i, \hat{\theta})}{\operatorname{Prob}(d_{it} = 0 \mid J_{i,t-1}, X_i, \hat{\theta})}. \tag{14}$$

Note that (13) has the form of mean zero moments times orthogonal weights. Thus, it can be used to form the FOCs of an MOM estimator for θ, where $\hat{\theta}_{\text{MOM}}$ sets (13) to zero and the optimal weights are given by (14).

In Keane (1990), I formed an MSM estimator by substituting the simulated transition probabilities given by (12) into equation (13) and using independent simulations of the transition probabilities to simulate the optimal weights in (14). Using results in McFadden and Ruud (1991), I showed in Keane (1992) that the resultant MSM estimator is consistent and asymptotically normal if $S/\sqrt{N} \to \infty$ as $N \to \infty$. In a series of repeated sampling experiments on models with random effects plus AR(1) error components, setting $S = 10$, $N = 500$, and $T = 8$, I also showed that the bias in this MSM estimator is negligible, even when the degree of serial corelation is very strong.

The generalization of this method to more than two alternatives is straight-forward and is discussed in Keane (1990). Elrod and Keane (1992) successfully applied this MSM estimator to detergent choice models with eight alternatives and up to 30 time periods per household. By allowing for a complex pattern of serial correlation, Elrod and Keane were able to produce more accurate out-of-sample forecasts of agents' future choices than could be obtained with simpler models. This is a good illustration of why the ability to estimate LDV models with complex patterns of serial correlation is important.

Hajivassiliou and McFadden (1990) expressed the score of the log-likelihood as

$$\nabla_{\hat{\theta}} \mathcal{L}(\hat{\theta}) = \sum_{i=1}^N \frac{\nabla_{\hat{\theta}} \operatorname{Prob}(J_{iT} \mid X_i, \hat{\theta})}{\operatorname{Prob}(J_{iT} \mid X_i, \hat{\theta})}. \tag{15}$$

They implemented a method of simulated scores (MSS) estimator by using the GHK probability simulator in (11) to simulate the numerator and denominator of (15). $\hat{\theta}_{\text{MSS}}$ is obtained by setting the simulated score vector to zero. Hajivassiliou and McFadden showed that $\hat{\theta}_{\text{MSS}}$ is consistent and asymptotically normal if $S/\sqrt{N} \to \infty$ as $N \to \infty$.

A third alternative is simply to implement a simulated maximum likelihood (SML) estimator by using the GHK probability simulator to simulate the log-likelihood function (5) directly. $\hat{\theta}_{\text{SML}}$ maximizes the simulated log-likeli-hood function. By construction, $\hat{\theta}_{\text{SML}}$ is also a root of the simulated score expression (15), provided the same smooth probability simulators (with the same draws) are used in both. Thus the MSS estimator given by applying the

GHK simulator to (15) is identical to the SML estimator obtained by applying the GHK simulator to (4). $\hat{\theta}_{SML}$ is also consistent and asymptotically normal if $S/\sqrt{N} \to \infty$ as $N \to \infty$. See Gourieroux and Monfort (1991) for a proof.

Hajivassiliou and McFadden (1990) reported good results using the MSS procedure based on the GHK simulator with 20 draws to estimate panel data probit models in which the existence of repayment problems for less-developed countries is the dependent variable. Börsch-Supan, Hajivassiliou, Kotlikoff and Morris (1991) used the SML approach based on the GHK simulator to estimate panel data probit models where choice of living arrangements is the dependent variable.

In Keane (1992), I reported repeated sampling experiments for SML based on the GHK simulator, using the same experiment design I used to study the MSM estimator. In this experiment, SML based on GHK with $S = 10$ exhibits negligible bias when the degree of serial correlation is not extreme. However, in experiments on a model with AR(1) errors and an individual effect, with $\rho = 0.20$ and the AR(1) parameter set to 0.90, the SML estimator greatly overstates the fraction of variance due to the individual effect and understates the AR(1) parameter. The MSM estimator based on the GHK simulator does not exhibit this problem.

Finally, McFadden (1992) observed that the FOCs used in Keane (1990, 1992) can be rewritten in such a way that they have the form of weights times mean zero moments. The FOCs used in Keane (1990, 1992), obtained by substituting the simulators (12) into equation (13), have the form

$$\text{FOC}(\hat{\theta}) = \sum_{i=1}^{N} \sum_{t=1}^{T} \left\{ \hat{W}_{it}^{1} \left[d_{it} - \frac{1}{S} \sum_{s=1}^{S} \text{Prob}(d_{it} = 1 \mid \eta_{i1s}^{*}, \ldots, \eta_{i,t-1,s}^{*}) \right. \right.$$

$$\left. \times \omega(\eta_{i1s}^{*}, \ldots, \eta_{i,t-1,s}^{*}) \right]$$

$$+ \hat{W}_{it}^{0} \left[(1 - d_{it}) - \frac{1}{S} \sum_{s=1}^{S} \text{Prob}(d_{it} = 0 \mid \eta_{i1s}^{*}, \ldots, \eta_{1,t-1,s}^{*}) \right.$$

$$\left. \left. \times \omega(\eta_{i1s}^{*}, \ldots, \eta_{i,t-1,s}^{*}) \right] \right\},$$

where the importance sampling weights $\omega(\eta_{i1s}^{*}, \ldots, \eta_{i,t-1,s}^{*})$ are given in (12b) and the weights $\hat{W}_{it}^{1}$ and $\hat{W}_{it}^{0}$ are simulations by the GHK method of the optimal weights given in (14).

Define $\omega(\eta_{i1s}^{*}, \ldots, \eta_{i,t-1,s}^{*}) = \omega_{Ai,t-1,S}^{*} / \omega_{Bi,t-1,S}^{*}$, where $\omega_{Ai,t-1,S}^{*}$ is the numerator of (12b) and $\omega_{Bi,t-1,S}^{*}$ is the denominator. Then the FOCs can be rewritten as

$$\text{FOC}(\hat{\theta}) = \sum_{i=1}^{N} \sum_{t=1}^{T} \left\{ \frac{\hat{W}_{it}^{1}}{\omega_{Bi,t-1,S}^{*}} \left[d_{it} \omega_{Bi,t-1,S}^{*} \right. \right.$$

$$\left. \left. - \frac{1}{S} \sum_{s=1}^{S} \text{Prob}(d_{it} = 1 \mid \eta_{i1s}^{*}, \ldots, \eta_{i,t-1,s}^{*}) \omega_{Ai,t-1,S}^{*} \right] \right.$$

$$+ \frac{\hat{W}_{it}^0}{\omega_{Bi,t-1,S}^*} \left[(1 - d_{it}) \omega_{Bi,t-1,S}^* \right.$$

$$\left. - \frac{1}{S} \sum_{s=1}^{S} \mathrm{Prob}(d_{it} = 0 \mid \eta_{i1s}^*, \ldots, \eta_{i,t-1,s}^*) \omega_{Ai,t-1,s}^* \right] \right\} .$$

The terms in brackets are now mean zero residuals, so an MSM estimator based on these FOCs is consistent and asymptotically normal for fixed S. The potential drawback of this procedure is that, while the optimal weights W_{it}^1 and W_{it}^0 for the Keane (1990, 1992) estimator have transition probabilities in the denominator, the optimal weights $W_{it}^1/\omega_{Bi,t-1}^*$ and $W_{it}^0/\omega_{Bi,t-1}^*$ for this new estimator (where $\omega_{Bi,t-1}^* = \mathrm{E}(\omega_{Bi,t-1,S}^*)$) have sequence probabilities in the denominator. Since sequence probabilities will generally be very small relative to transition probabilities, the denominator bias in simulation of the optimal weights will tend to become more severe, and efficiency relative to ML may deteriorate. An important avenue for future research is to explore the small-sample properties of this estimator.

5.3. Alternative methods based on conditional simulation of the latent variables in the LDV model

Hajivassiliou and McFadden (1990) discussed a fourth classical method for estimating panel data probit models that has not yet been implemented in the literature. This is based on the idea, due to Van Praag and Hop (1987) and Ruud (1991), that the score can be written in terms of the underlying latent variables of the model as follows:

$$\nabla_{\hat{\beta}} \mathcal{L}(\hat{\theta}) = \sum_{i=1}^{N} X_i' \hat{E}^{-1} \mathrm{E}[y_i - X_i \hat{\beta} \mid J_{iT}],$$

$$\nabla_{\hat{A}} \mathcal{L}(\hat{\theta}) = \sum_{i=1}^{N} \{ -\hat{\Sigma}^{-1} \hat{A} + \hat{\Sigma} \mathrm{E}[(y_i - X\hat{\beta})(y_i - X\hat{\beta})' \mid J_{iT}] \hat{\Sigma}^{-1} \hat{A} \} . \quad (16)$$

Unbiased simulators of this score expression can be obtained if the error terms $\varepsilon_i = y_i - X_i \beta$ can be drawn from the conditional distribution determined by J_{iT}, X_i, and $\hat{\theta}$ as in equation (7). Given such draws, unbiased simulators of the conditional expectations in (16) may be formed. An MSS estimator that sets the resultant simulated score vector to zero is consistent and asymptotically normal for fixed S. The first application of this MSS procedure was by Van Praag and Hop (1987). They used MSS to estimate a cross section tobit model, for which it is feasible to draw error vectors from the correct conditional distribution.

Of course, it is difficult to draw the ε_i directly from complex conditional distributions such as that given by (7). One method, investigated by Albert and Chib (1993), Geweke (1991a,b) and McCulloch and Rossi (1992), is Gibbs sampling. The Gibbs sampling procedure is related to the GHK sampling scheme described earlier in that it requires recursive draws from univariate normals. Steps (1)–(3) of the GHK procedure generate a vector $\eta_{i1}^*, \ldots, \eta_{iT}^*$ that is drawn from an importance sampling distribution rather than from the true multivariate distribution of η_i conditional on J_{iT}, X_i, and $\hat{\theta}$. However, under mild conditions, the Gibbs sampling procedure produces, asymptotically, draws from the correct distribution. To implement the Gibbs procedure, first implement steps (1)–(3) of the GHK procedure to obtain a starting vector $(\eta_{i1}^*, \ldots, \eta_{iT}^*)$. Note that step (3) must be amended so the η^* vector is extended out completely to time T. Then perform the following steps:

(1) Starting with an initial vector $(\eta_{i1}^*, \ldots, \eta_{iT}^*)$, drop η_{i1}^* and draw a new η_{i1} from the truncated univariate normal distribution such that $(\eta_{i1}, \eta_{i2}^*, \ldots, \eta_{i3}^*) \in \eta(J_{iT})$. Replace the old value of η_{i1}^* with the new draw for η_{i1}.
(2) Starting with the vector $(\eta_{i1}^*, \ldots, \eta_{iT}^*)$ from step (1), drop η_{i2}^* and draw a new η_{i2} from the truncated univariate normal distribution such that $(\eta_{i1}^*, \eta_{i2}, \eta_{i3}^*, \ldots, \eta_{iT}^*) \in \eta(J_{iT})$. Replace the old value of η_{i2}^* with the new draw for η_{i2}.
(3) Continue in this way until a complete new vector $(\eta_{i1}^*, \ldots, \eta_{iT}^*) \in \eta(J_{iT})$ is obtained.
(4) Return to step (1) and, using the η_i^* vector from step (3) as the new initial η vector, obtain a new draw for η_{i1}, etc.

Steps (1)–(3) are called a *cycle* of the Gibbs sampler. Suppose that steps (1)–(3) are repeated C times, always beginning step (1) with the η_i^* vector that was obtained from the previous cycle. Gelfand and Smith (1990) showed that, under mild conditions, as $C \to \infty$ the distribution of $(\eta_{i1}^*, \ldots, \eta_{iT}^*)$ converges to the true conditional distribution at a geometric rate. Hajivassiliou and McFadden (1990) showed that using Gibbs sampling to simulate the score expression (16) results in an estimator that is consistent and asymptotically normal if $C/\log N \to \infty$ as $N \to \infty$.

The drawback of the Gibbs sampling approach to simulating the score expression (16) is that each time the trial parameter estimate $\hat{\theta}$ is updated in the search for $\hat{\theta}_{MSS}$ the Gibbs sampler must converge. I am not aware of applications in cross-section or panel data settings. (Recall that Hajivassiliou and McFadden, 1990 actually implemented $\hat{\theta}_{MSS}$ based on (15) in their work.)

An alternative GHK-like approach may also be used to simulate the conditional expectations in (16). As both Van Praag and Hop (1987) and Keane (1990) noted, weighted functions of the $(\eta_{i1}^*, \ldots, \eta_{iT}^*)$ vectors obtained by steps (1)–(3) of the GHK procedure, with importance sampling weights of the form (10b), give unbiased estimators of the conditional expectations in (16). That is, given a set of vectors $(\eta_{i1s}^*, \ldots, \eta_{iTs}^*)$ for $s = 1, S$ obtained by steps (1)–(3a) of the GHK procedure, one obtains unbiased simulators

$$\hat{E}[\varepsilon_{it} \mid J_{iT}] = \frac{1}{S} \sum_{s=1}^{S} \{A_{t1}\eta_{i1s}^* + \cdots + A_{tt}\eta_{its}^*\} \omega(\eta_{i1s}^*, \ldots, \eta_{i,T-1,s}^*),$$

$$\hat{E}[\varepsilon_{it}\varepsilon_{iu} \mid J_{iT}] = \frac{1}{S} \sum_{s=1}^{S} \{A_{t1}\eta_{i1s}^* + \cdots + A_{tt}\eta_{its}^*\}$$

$$\times \{A_{u1}\eta_{i1s}^* + \cdots + A_{uu}\eta_{its}^*\} \omega(\eta_{i1s}^*, \ldots, \eta_{i,T-1,s}^*). \quad (17)$$

Of course, as was discussed above, it is not feasible to construct the exact weights when $T - 1 \geqslant 3$. In that case the weights must be simulated as in (12b), and the resultant conditional expectation simulators will only be asymptotically unbiased in S. An estimator based on substituting the expectation simulators (17) into the score expression (16) has not been tried in the panel data case.

Albert and Chib (1993), Geweke (1991b) and McCulloch and Rossi (1992) have observed that Gibbs sampling may be used as a Bayesian inference procedure, rather than merely as a computational device for simulating the conditional expectations in (16). This procedure has the following steps.

(1) Given a starting parameter value $\hat{\theta} = (\hat{\beta}_0, \hat{A}_0)$ and an initial vector $\hat{\varepsilon}_0$, use steps (1)–(3) of the Gibbs sampler described above to obtain a draw $\hat{\varepsilon}_1$ from the distribution of ε conditional on J_T, X, $\hat{\beta}_0$, and $\hat{A}_0$.

(2) Construct $\hat{y}_1 = X\hat{\beta}_0 + \hat{\varepsilon}_1$. Regress $\hat{y}_1$ on X, using a seemingly unrelated regression framework to account for the cross-equation correlations determined by $\hat{A}_0$. The resultant point estimates and variance–covariance matrix for the β vector give the normal distribution of β conditional on J_T, X, $\hat{y}_1$, and $\hat{A}_0$. Draw $\hat{\beta}_1$ from this conditional distribution.

(3) Given $\hat{y}_1$ and $\hat{\beta}_1$, we may form the residuals from the regression. These residuals determine an inverse Wishart distribution of Σ conditional on J_T, X, $\hat{y}_1$, and $\hat{\beta}_1$. Draw $\hat{\Sigma}_1$ from this conditional distribution, and form $\hat{A}_1$.

(4) Return to step (1), using $\hat{\varepsilon}_1$ as the new initial ε vector, and obtain a new draw $\hat{\varepsilon}_2$ from the distribution of ε conditional on J_T, X, $\hat{\beta}_1$, and $\hat{A}_1$.

Steps (1)–(3) are a cycle of the Gibbs sampling inference procedure. Observe that ε, β, and A have a joint conditional distribution given by X and the observed choice sequences J_T. These can be decomposed into conditionals, and steps (1)–(3) represent sequential draws from these conditionals. Thus, the Gelfand and Smith (1990) result holds. Letting C index cycles, if steps (1)–(3) are repeated C times, then as $C \to \infty$, the distribution of $(\hat{\varepsilon}_C, \hat{\beta}_C, \hat{A}_C)$ for $C > C^*$ can be used to integrate the true joint distribution of ε, β, and A by Monte Carlo. Both Geweke (1991b) and McCulloch and Rossi (1992) show how priors for β and A may be incorporated into this framework by simple modifications of the normal and inverse Wishart distributions from which $\hat{\beta}$ and $\hat{A}$ are drawn on steps (2)–(3).

This Gibbs sampling inference procedure has been applied successfully to cross-section probit problems by McCulloch and Rossi (1992) and Geweke, Keane and Runkle (1992), and to cross-section tobit models by Chib (1993) and Geweke (1991b). McCulloch and Rossi (1992) have also successfully applied the method in a panel data setting. They estimate a probit model on margarine brand choice data, allowing for random effects in the brand intercepts and in the price coefficient.

The simulated EM algorithm, due to Van Praag and Hop (1987) and Ruud (1991), is a method for obtaining $\hat{\theta}_{\mathrm{MSS}}$ that is closely related to the Gibbs sampling inference procedure. The essential difference is that, on steps (2) and (3), which correspond to the M or 'maximization' step of the EM algorithm, the point estimates for β and A are used rather than taking draws for β and A from the estimated conditional distributions. With this amendment, repetition of steps (1)–(3) results in convergence of $(\hat{\beta}_C, \hat{A}_C)$ to a consistent and asymptotically normal point estimate as $C \to \infty$. Note that step (1) of the Gibbs inference procedure corresponds to the E or 'expectation' step of the EM algorithm. Here, any method for forming the conditional expectations in (16) may be substituted for the Gibbs sampler. Applications of the simulated EM algorithm to cross-section LDV models can be found in Van Praag and Hop (1987) and in Van Praag, Hop and Eggink (1991), who draw directly from conditional distributions in the E step. To my knowledge the simulated EM algorithm has not yet been applied in a panel data case.

6. Extensions to more general models

In deciding which simulation estimation method to use in a particular application, it is important to recognize that there are some models that are difficult to put in an MSM framework. This point was made by McFadden and Ruud (1991). Consider the case of the selection model:

$$
w_{it} = \begin{cases} X_{it}\gamma + v_{it} & \text{if } d_{it} = 1, \\ \text{unobserved} & \text{otherwise}, \end{cases} \tag{18}
$$

For $t = 1, T$, $i = 1, N$, where w_{it} is a continuous variable (1), that is observed only if $d_{it} = 1$, X_{it} is the same vector of exogenous regressors as in (1), γ is the corresponding coefficient vector, and v_{it} is the error term. Redefine J_{it} to include the w_{it}, giving $J_{it} = \{d_{i1}, w_{i1}, \ldots, d_{it}, w_{it}\}$. Let w_{it} have conditional density $f(w_{it} | J_{i,t-1}, X_i, \hat{\theta})$. Assume that ε_i and v_i are jointly normally distributed with covariance matrix Σ. Any exclusion restrictions in the model (i.e., variables in X that affect y but not w) are represented by restricting to zero the appropriate elements of γ.

As is discussed in Heckman (1979), OLS estimation of (18) using only observations where $d_{it} = 1$ produces biased estimates of β when ε_i and v_i are correlated. Thus, equations (1), (4), and (18) must be estimated jointly. The log-likelihood function for the selection model given by (1), (4), and (18) is

$$
\mathcal{L}(\hat{\theta}) = \sum_{i=1}^{N} \left\{ \sum_{t \in U_i} \ln \text{Prob}(d_{it} = 0 | J_{i,t-1}, X_i, \hat{\theta}) \right.
$$
$$
\left. + \sum_{t \in E_i} \ln \text{Prob}(d_{it} = 1 | J_{t,t-1}, w_{it}, X_i, \hat{\theta}) f(w_{it} | J_{i,t-1}, X_i, \hat{\theta}) \right\},
$$

where U_i is the set of time periods for which $d_{it} = 0$ and E_i is the set of time periods for which $d_{it} = 1$.

The score for this likelihood may be written as

$$
\nabla_{\hat{\theta}}\mathscr{L}(\hat{\theta}) = \sum_{i=1}^{N}\left\{\sum_{t\in U_i}\{W_{it}^0[(1-d_{it}) - \mathrm{Prob}(d_{it}=0\,|\,J_{i,t-1}, X_i, \hat{\theta})]\right.
$$

$$
+ W_{it}^1[d_{it} - \mathrm{Prob}(d_{it}=1\,|\,J_{i,t-1}, X_i, \hat{\theta})]\}
$$

$$
+ \sum_{t\in E_i}\{W_{it}^2[(1-d_{it}) - \mathrm{Prob}(d_{it}=0\,|\,J_{i,t-1}, w_{it}, X_i, \hat{\theta})]
$$

$$
+ W_{it}^3[d_{it} - \mathrm{Prob}(d_{it}=1\,|\,J_{i,t-1}, w_{it}, X_i, \hat{\theta})]
$$

$$
\left. + \nabla_{\hat{\theta}}\ln f(w_{it}\,|\,J_{i,t-1}, X_i, \hat{\theta})\}\right\}, \tag{19a}
$$

where

$$
W_{it}^0 = \nabla_{\hat{\theta}}\ln\mathrm{Prob}(d_{it}=0\,|\,J_{i,t-1}, X_i, \hat{\theta}),
$$

$$
W_{it}^1 = \nabla_{\hat{\theta}}\ln\mathrm{Prob}(d_{it}=1\,|\,J_{i,t-1}, X_i, \hat{\theta}),
$$

$$
W_{it}^2 = \nabla_{\hat{\theta}}\ln\mathrm{Prob}(d_{it}=0\,|\,J_{i,t-1}, w_{it}, X_i, \hat{\theta}),
$$

$$
W_{it}^3 = \nabla_{\hat{\theta}}\ln\mathrm{Prob}(d_{it}=1\,|\,J_{i,t-1}, w_{it}, X_i, \hat{\theta}). \tag{19b}
$$

Notice that (19a) is not interpretable as the FOCs for an MOM estimator because the objects $[(1-d_{it}) - \mathrm{Prob}(d_{it}=0\,|\,J_{i,t-1}, w_{it}, x_i, \hat{\theta})]$ and $[d_{it} - \mathrm{Prob}(d_{it}=1\,|\,J_{i,t-1}, w_{it}, X_i, \hat{\theta})]$ are not mean zero residuals in the population for which $t\in E_i$ due to the correlation between v_{it} and ε_{it}. Furthermore, the expression $\nabla_{\hat{\theta}}\ln f(w_{it}\,|\,J_{i,t-1}, X_i, \hat{\theta})$ can be written in terms of objects $[w_{it} - X_{it}\beta - E(v_{it}\,|\,J_{i,t-1}, X_i, \hat{\theta})]$ times weights, but these objects also have nonzero expectation in the population for which $t\in E_i$ because of the correlation between v_{it} and ε_{it}. Thus (19a)–(19b) cannot be used to construct an MSM estimator. If the score as given by (19a)–(19b) is simulated using unbiased simulators for the choice probabilities, including those in the numerator and denominator of the W_{it}^j for $j=0, 3$, then it is an MSS situation, where consistency and asymptotic normality are achieved only if $S/\sqrt{N}\to\infty$ as $N\to\infty$ because of the bias created by simulating the denominators of the W_{it}^j.

McFadden and Ruud (1991) discussed a bias correction technique that can be used to put a large class of models, including the selection model, into an MSM framework. The score contribution of person i at t is given by

$$
\nabla_{\hat{\theta}}\mathscr{L}_{it}(\hat{\theta}) = (1-d_{it})\nabla_{\hat{\theta}}\ln\mathrm{Prob}(d_{it}=0\,|\,J_{i,t-1}, X_i, \hat{\theta})
$$

$$
+ d_{it}\nabla_{\hat{\theta}}\ln\mathrm{Prob}(d_{it}=1\,|\,J_{i,t-1}, w_{it}, X_i, \hat{\theta})
$$

$$
\times f(w_{it}\,|\,J_{i,t-1}, X_i, \hat{\theta}). \tag{20}
$$

The expected value of this score contribution, conditional on X_i and $J_{i,t-1}$, is

$$E[\nabla_{\hat{\theta}}\mathscr{L}_{it}(\hat{\theta})\,|\,J_{i,t-1}, X_i]$$
$$= \text{Prob}(d_{it}=0\,|\,J_{i,t-1}, X_i, \hat{\theta})\nabla_{\hat{\theta}}\ln\text{Prob}(d_{it}=0\,|\,J_{i,t-1}, X_i, \hat{\theta})$$
$$+ E[d_{it}\nabla_{\hat{\theta}}\ln\text{Prob}(d_{it}=1\,|\,J_{i,t-1}, w_{it}, X_i, \hat{\theta})$$
$$\times f(w_{it}\,|\,J_{i,t-1}, X_i, \hat{\theta})\,|\,J_{i,t-1}, X_i]\,. \tag{21}$$

Although the expected value of the simulated score contribution at the true parameter vector is not zero due to denominator bias in the simulation, the difference between the simulated score contribution and the expected value of the simulated score contribution conditional on $J_{i,t-1}$ and X_i will have expectation zero at the true parameter vector. Thus, by subtracting (21) from (20), to obtain

$$\nabla_{\hat{\theta}}\mathscr{L}_{it} - E[\nabla_{\hat{\theta}}\mathscr{L}_{it}(\hat{\theta})\,|\,J_{i,t-1}, X_i]$$
$$= [(1-d_{it}) - \text{Prob}(d_{it}=0\,|\,J_{i,t-1}, X_i, \hat{\theta})]$$
$$\times \nabla_{\hat{\theta}}\ln\text{Prob}(d_{it}=0\,|\,J_{i,t-1}, X_i, \hat{\theta})$$
$$+ \{d_{it}\nabla_{\hat{\theta}}\ln\text{Prob}(d_{it}=1\,|\,J_{i,t-1}, w_{it}, X_i, \hat{\theta})f(w_{it}\,|\,J_{i,t-1}, X_i, \hat{\theta})$$
$$- E[d_{it}\nabla_{\hat{\theta}}\ln\text{Prob}(d_{it}=1\,|\,J_{i,t-1}, w_{it}, X_i, \hat{\theta})$$
$$\times f(w_{it}\,|\,J_{i,t-1}, X_i, \hat{\theta})\,|\,J_{it-1}, X_i]\}\,, \tag{22}$$

an expression is obtained that can be used to construct an MSM estimator. Both the term $[(1-d_{it}) - \text{Prob}(d_{it}=0\,|\,J_{i,t-1}, X_i, \hat{\theta})$ and the term in the braces $\{\cdot\}$ are mean zero residuals. The orthogonal weight on the former term is $\nabla_{\hat{\theta}}\ln\text{Prob}(d_{it}=0\,|\,J_{i,t-1}, X_i, \hat{\theta})$ while the weight on the latter term is simply one. Thus, substitution of unbiased simulators for all the probabilities in (22) gives an MSM estimator that is consistent and asymptotically normal for fixed simulation size. Of course, the transition probabilities in (22) are difficult objects to simulate. Using the GHK method described in Section 5.2 to simulate these probabilities would again produce an MSM estimator that is consistent and asymptotically normal if $S/\sqrt{N}\to\infty$ as $N\to\infty$.

Observe that in (22) the object $E[d_{it}\nabla_{\hat{\theta}}\ln\text{Prob}(d_{it}\,|\,J_{i,t-1}, w_{it}, X_i, \hat{\theta})f(w_{it}\,|\,J_{i,t-1}, X_i, \hat{\theta})\,|\,J_{it-1}, X_i]$ must be simulated. This situation is particularly difficult because, to take the outer expectation, w_{it} must be drawn from the $f(w_{it}\,|\,J_{i,t-1}, X_i, \hat{\theta})$ density, and then the term $\nabla_{\hat{\theta}}\ln\text{Prob}(d_{it}\,|\,J_{i,t-1}, w_{it}, X_i, \hat{\theta})$ must be simulated conditional on each w_{it} draw. If the first term in braces, the term $\nabla_{\hat{\theta}}\ln\text{Prob}(d_{it}\,|\,J_{i,t-1}, w_{it}, X_i, \hat{\theta})$ that involves the observed w_{it}, is simulated using S draws, then, in order for the difference in braces to have mean zero, the derivatives of the log-probabilities in the second term must also be simulated using S draws *per each* w_{it} draw.

Keane and Moffitt (1991) implemented the MSM estimator based on (22) in a cross-section choice problem – the choice by low-income single mothers of welfare program participation and work status – where it is feasible to construct unbiased probability simulators. Despite the fact that the MSM estimator is consistent and asymptotically normal for fixed S in this problem, Keane and Moffitt found that a very large number of draws is necessary for the estimator to produce reasonable results. This stems from the difficulty of simulating the expectation over wage draws described above. Thus, MSM estimation based on (22) may not be promising in the panel data case. Keane and Moffitt (1991) also reported results based on a direct simulation of the score as expressed in (19). This MSS estimator performed at least as well as the MSM estimator, and given that it is much easier to program, it may be the preferred course for panel data selection models. As discussed by McFadden and Ruud (1991), it is also rather difficult to put the tobit model in an MSM form. But Hajivassiliou and McFadden (1990) reported good results using MSS based on the GHK method to estimate panel data tobit models in which the dependent variable is the total external debt obligation of a country in arrears.

7. Estimating the serial correlation structure in employment and wage data

7.1. Results using NLS employment data

In this section, I use the MSM estimator obtained by substituting the transition probability simulator (12a)–(12b) into the MSM first-order condition (13)–(14) to estimate panel data probit models that relax the equicorrelation assumption, using employment data from the national longitudinal survey of young men (NLS). The goal is to determine whether the simple random effects model with equicorrelated errors can adequately capture the pattern of temporal dependence in these data. As I discussed in Section 3, the random effects model has been the most popular specification for panel data LDV models. Prior to the advent of simulation-based inference, it was not computationally feasible to relax the equicorrelation assumption. Thus, the results in this section provide the first test of the equicorrelation assumption for labor market data.

The NLS is a U.S. sample of 5225 males aged 14–24 selected in 1966 and interviewed in 12 of the 16 years from 1966 to 1981. Data were collected on employment status and other sociodemographic characteristics. The sample used here is exactly that employed by Keane, Moffitt and Runkle (1988). The data screens and overall properties of the data are discussed there. Following data screens, the analysis sample contains 2219 males with a total of 11 886 person-year observations. The regressors used in the employment equation are a constant (CONST), the national unemployment rate (U-RATE), a time trend (TREND), years of school completed (EDUC), years of labor force experience (EXPER), the square of experience (EXPER^2), a white dummy (WHITE), a dummy for wife present in the home (WIFE), and number of children (KIDS).

Estimation results are reported in Table 1. The first column gives constant cross-section estimates of the regressor coefficients obtained by ML. Columns (2)–(6) contain estimates when various patterns of serial correlation are assumed. These estimates are starred if they differ significantly from the

Table 1
Estimates of probit employment equations on NLS young men

Parameter	$\hat{\beta}$ ML	$\hat{\beta}$ ML-quadrature		$\hat{\beta}$ MSM		
		4 points	16 points	Random effects	RE + AR(1) error	RE + MA(1) error
	(1)	(2)	(3)	(4)	(5)	(6)
ρ	–	0.3792	0.3509	0.3577	0.3298	0.3377
		(0.0203)	(0.0192)	(0.0248)	(0.0294)	(0.0263)
AR(1)	–	–	–	–	0.1901	–
					(0.0437)	
MA(1)	–	–	–	–	–	0.1998
						(0.0685)
CONST	0.4644	0.5454	0.5713	0.4895	0.3934	0.5411
	(0.1161)	(0.1230)	(0.1283)	(0.1551)	(0.1576)	(0.1545)
U-RATE	−0.0740	−0.0678	−0.0697	−0.0647	−0.0590	−0.0664
	(0.0135)	(0.0122)	(0.0124)	(0.0157)	(0.0160)	(0.0162)
TREND	−0.0121	−0.0091	−0.0124	−0.0185	−0.0205	−0.0164
	(0.0059)	(0.0062)	(0.0063)	(0.0080)	(0.0082)	(0.0081)
EDUC	0.0664	0.0599	0.0593	0.0680	0.0720	0.0634
	(0.0061)	(0.0070)	(0.0078)	(0.0106)	(0.0107)	(0.0105)
EXPER	0.0176	0.0076	0.0113	0.0094	0.0107	0.0060
	(0.0098)	(0.0097)	(0.0099)	(0.0118)	(0.0123)	(0.0121)
EXPER^2	−0.1521	−0.1260	−0.1280	−0.1140	−0.1120	−0.1040
÷ 100	(0.0414)	(0.0400)	(0.0400)	(0.0470)	(0.0490)	(0.0490)
WHITE	0.2022	0.2355	0.2453	0.2205	0.2101	0.2230
	(0.0503)	(0.0639)	(0.0646)	(0.0637)	(0.0637)	(0.0627)
WIFE	0.4548	0.3271***	0.3394***	0.3218***	0.3316**	0.3332***
	(0.0352)	(0.0363)	(0.0365)	(0.0448)	(0.0457)	(0.0453)
KIDS	0.0716	0.0726	0.0712	0.0741	0.0713	0.0708
	(0.0138)	(0.0147)	(0.0150)	(0.0195)	(0.0196)	(0.0195)
$\gamma(1)$	0.0000	0.3792	0.3509	0.3577	0.4572	0.4520
$\gamma(2)$	0.0000	0.3792	0.3509	0.3577	0.3540	0.3377
$\gamma(3)$	0.0000	0.3792	0.3509	0.3577	0.3344	0.3377
Log-likelihood function	−3611	−3419	−3421	−3460	−3447	−3448
$\chi^2(9)$	–	24.68**	16.77*	15.16*	16.57*	15.83*
CPU minutes	1.76	2.87	5.19	11.55	12.67	12.59

Note: Standard errors of the parameter estimates are in parentheses. Three stars (***) indicate that a parameter differs from the ML no-effects estimate at the 1% significance level. Two stars (**) indicate the 5% level, and one star(*) indicates the 10% level. The $\chi^2(9)$ statistic is for the null hypothesis that the regressor coefficients equal the ML no-effects estimates (the 5% critical value is 16.92 and the 10% critical value is 14.68). The data set used is the NLS survey of young men. There are observations on 2219 individuals, with a total of 11 886 person–year observations. The MSM estimates were obtained using 10 draws for the GHK simulator. Log-likelihood function values for the MSM estimators are simulated.

consistent ML estimates in column (1). A $\chi^2(9)$ test for the null that all the regressor coefficients equal the column (1) values is also reported.

Random effects estimates using approximate-ML via 4- and 16-point quadrature are reported in columns (2) and (3). There is a non-negligible change in the parameter estimates in moving from 4- to 16-point quadrature, as indicated by the fact that, for 4-point quadrature, the null that the regressor coefficients equal the cross-section estimates is rejected at the 5 percent level, while with 16-point quadrature the null is only rejected at the 10 percent level. Thus, I will concentrate on the 16-point quadrature results. Random effects estimates obtained via MSM are reported in column (4). They were obtained using $S = 10$. The MSM estimates of both the parameters and their standard errors are quite close to the 16-point ML-quadrature estimates, and the null that the regressor coefficients equal the consistent cross-section estimates is again rejected at the 10 percent but not the 5 percent level.

If the random effects assumption is correct, then both the cross-section and random effects estimates are consistent, and we would expect no significant difference in the regressor coefficients obtained via random effects and no effects estimators. The effect of the random effects estimator should be simply to adjust standard errors to account for serial correlation. In going from column (1) to columns (2), (3), or (4) there is a general rise in the estimated standard errors. However, one of the estimated coefficients, that on the WIFE variable, changes substantially. The ML-quadrature and MSM estimates both show a drop of about three standard errors for this coefficient.

Since random effects estimates may be inconsistent in the equicorrelation assumption fails and because we are interested in discovering whether the actual pattern of temporal dependence in the data is more complex, I relax the equicorrelation assumption in columns (5) and (6). Here, estimates are obtained which allow for AR(1) and MA(1) error components in addition to the random effects. Since the individuals in the data are observed for up to 12 periods, these estimates require the evaluation of 12-variate integrals. Thus, the estimation is not feasible by ML and can only be performed using the MSM estimator.

Turning to the MSM results, first note that the time requirements for the MSM estimations are quite modest – the timings being about 12.6 cpu minutes on an IBM 3083 (compared to 5.2 for 16-point quadrature on the random effects model). Second, note that the equicorrelation assumption does fail. In column (5), the estimated AR(1) parameter is 0.1901 with a t-statistic of 4.4. In column (6), the estimated MA(1) parameter is 0.1998 with a t-statistic of 2.9. The $\gamma(j)$ reported in the table are the j-th lagged autocorrelations implied by the estimated covariance parameters. The first lagged autocorrelation is about 30 percent larger for the model with AR(1) components than it is for the models with random effects alone (0.46 vs. 0.35). Thus, the random effects model would overestimate the probability of a transition from employment to unemployment because it underestimates short-run persistence.

Although these results show a significant departure from equicorrelation, relaxing the equicorrelation assumption has little effect on the parameter estimates. Furthermore, the 10- to 11-point improvements in the simulated log-likelihood with inclusion of MA(1) or AR(1) components is not particularly great. Thus, it appears that false imposition of equicorrelation does not lead to substantial parameter bias or deterioration of fit in models of male employment patterns.

7.2. Temporal dependence in wages and the movement of real wages over the business cycle

In this section, I consider an application of the MSS estimator to nonrandom-sample selection models of the type described by Heckman (1979). In these models, a probit is estimated jointly with a continuous dependent-variable equation, where the dependent variable is only observed for the chosen state. Because of the truncation of the error term in the equation for the continuous dependent variable, OLS estimates of that equation are biased, and the residuals from the OLS regression produce biased estimates of the error structure for the continuous variable. Thus, joint estimation is necessary to obtain consistent estimates. As I described in Section 6, it is difficult to estimate such models by MSM. Instead, I implement an MSS estimator by simulating the score for the selection model as written in (19).

The particular application considered here is the estimation of selection bias-adjusted wage equations. Keane, Moffitt and Runkle (1988) used selection models with random effects in order to estimate the cyclical behavior of real wages in the NLS. Their estimates controlled for the cross-correlation of permanent and transitory error components in wage and employment equations. By controlling for these cross-correlations, they hoped to control for systematic movements of workers with high or low unobserved wage components in and out of the labor force over the business cycle. By so doing, they could obtain estimates of cyclical real wage movement holding labor force quality constant. Keane, Moffitt and Runkle found that real wage movements were procyclically biased by quality variation, with high-wage workers the most likely to become unemployed in a recession. It is possible that the Keane, Moffitt and Runkle results may be biased due to false imposition of the equicorrelation assumption. Thus, it is important to examine robustness of their results to the specification of the error structure.

The NLS data used in this analysis were already described in Section 7.1 and used in the employment equation estimates presented there. The only new variable is the wage, which is the hourly straight time real wage (deflated by the consumer price index) at the interview date. The log wage is the dependent variable.

Estimation results are reported in Table 2. The first column gives consistent cross-section estimates obtained by ML. Columns (2)–(6) contain estimates obtained assuming various patterns of serial correlation. These estimates are starred if they differ significantly from the consistent estimates in column (1).

Table 2
Estimates of selection model on NLS young men

| Parameter | $\hat{\beta}$ ML | $\hat{\beta}$ ML-quadrature | | $\hat{\beta}$ MSM | | |
		4 points	9 points	Random effects	RE + AR(1) error	RE + MA(1) error
	(1)	(2)	(3)	(4)	(5)	(6)
Wage equation						
U-RATE	−0.0039	−0.0063	−0.0055	−0.0057	−0.0095**	−0.0066
	0.0034	(0.0023)	(0.0023)	(0.0027)	(0.0026)	(0.0028)
TIME	0.0073	0.0125***	0.0105**	0.0119**	0.0124**	0.0119*
	(0.0015)	(0.0013)	(0.0015)	(0.0021)	(0.0021)	(0.0021)
EDUC	0.0606	0.0520***	0.0487***	0.0500***	0.0529**	0.0516***
	(0.0016)	(0.0018)	(0.0023)	(0.0032)	(0.0033)	(0.0032)
EXPER	0.0263	0.0242	0.0260	0.0242	0.0276	0.0256
	(0.0024)	(0.0015)	(0.0016)	(0.0027)	(0.0030)	(0.0028)
EXPER^2 ÷ 100	−0.0736	−0.0780	−0.0750	−0.0720	−0.0870	−0.0780
	(0.0108)	(0.0060)	(0.0050)	(0.0100)	(0.0130)	(0.0110)
WHITE	0.1923	0.1767	0.1829	0.1936	0.1934	0.1932
	(0.0134)	(0.0150)	(0.0236)	(0.0235)	(0.0234)	(0.0231)
CONSTANT	0.0494	0.0967*	0.1510***	0.1234*	0.0923	0.1054
	(0.0297)	(0.0284)	(0.0371)	(0.0450)	(0.0459)	(0.0450)
Employment equation:						
U-RATE	−0.0646	−0.0699	−0.0693	−0.0648	−0.0589	−0.0570
	(0.0133)	(0.0131)	(0.0126)	(0.0157)	(0.0160)	(0.0160)
TIME	−0.0126	−0.0118	−0.0169	−0.0200	−0.0208	−0.0226
	(0.0058)	(0.0058)	(0.0062)	(0.0081)	(0.0081)	(0.0082)
EDUC	0.0610	0.0578	0.0655	0.0664	0.0645	0.0707
	(0.0060)	(0.0058)	(0.0076)	(0.0106)	(0.0104)	(0.0104)
EXPER	0.0014	0.0067	0.0084	0.0017	−0.0020	0.0022
	(0.0095)	(0.0094)	(0.0099)	(0.0120)	(0.0122)	(0.0122)
EXPER^2 ÷ 100	−0.1034	−0.1020	−0.1130	−0.0920	−0.0740	−0.0860
	(0.0401)	(0.0390)	(0.0400)	(0.0480)	(0.0500)	(0.0490)
WHITE	0.1961	0.2148	0.2493	0.2345	0.2229	0.2223
	(0.0492)	(0.0500)	(0.0637)	(0.0635)	(0.0632)	(0.0635)
WIFE	0.4597	0.3393**	0.3770**	0.3550**	0.3664**	0.3498**
	(0.0323)	(0.0341)	(0.0359)	(0.0446)	(0.0449)	(0.0448)
KIDS	0.1151	0.0621***	0.0895*	0.0930	0.0869	0.0942
	(0.0127)	(0.0131)	(0.0142)	(0.0198)	(0.0199)	(0.0199)
CONSTANT	0.4922	0.6446	0.4936	0.5147	0.5083	0.4146
	(0.1142)	(0.1117)	(0.1274)	(0.1554)	(0.1551)	(0.1536)
Covariance parameters:						
ρ_{wage}	–	0.6073	0.5995	0.5449	0.4547	0.4807
		(0.0069)	(0.0075)	(0.0131)	(0.0162)	(0.0132)
$\rho_{employment}$	–	0.2364	0.3275	0.3548	0.3090	0.3285
		(0.0136)	(0.0182)	(0.0243)	(0.0266)	(0.0257)
$AR(1)_{wage}$	–	–	–	–	0.4803	–
					(0.0165)	
$AR(1)_{employment}$	–	–	–	–	0.2538	–
					(0.0442)	
$MA(1)_{wage}$	–	–	–	–	–	0.2426
						(0.0851)

Table 2 (*Continued*)

| Parameter | $\hat\beta$ ML | $\hat\beta$ ML-quadrature | | $\hat\beta$ MSM | | |
		4 points	9 points	Random effects	RE + AR(1) error	RE + MA(1) error
	(1)	(2)	(3)	(4)	(5)	(6)
MA(1)$_{\text{employment}}$	–	–	–	–	–	0.2003
						(0.0564)
Correlation of	–	0.4330	−0.2798	−0.2002	−0.1859	−0.2075
permanent parts		(0.0132)	(0.0213)	(0.0434)	(0.0508)	(0.0466)
Correlation of	−0.6947	−0.2651	−0.3339	−0.3491	−0.3861	−0.3944
transitory parts	(0.0228)	(0.0775)	(0.0654)	(0.0636)	(0.0566)	(0.0609)
σ_{wage}	0.4301	0.4162	0.4109	0.4055	0.4049	0.4052
	(0.0031)	(0.0027)	(0.0025)	(0.0030)	(0.0030)	(0.0031)
Log-likelihood function	−8984	−6312	−6216	−6321	−6004	−6244
$\chi^2(16)$	–	362**	164**	75**	78**	72**
CPU minutes	2.09	12.94	40.09	42.68	47.38	47.38

Note: Standard errors of the parameter estimates are in parentheses. Three stars (***) indicate that a parameter differs from the ML no-effects estimate at the 1% significance level. Two stars (**) indicate the 5% level, and one star (*) indicates the 10% level. The $\chi^2(16)$ statistic is for the null hypothesis that the regressor coefficients equal the ML no-effects estimates. The 5% critical value is 26.30. The data set used is the NLS survey of young men. There are observations on 2219 individuals, with a total of 11 886 person–year observations. The MSS estimates were obtained using 10 draws for the GHK simulator. Log-likelihood function values for the MSS estimators are simulated.

A χ^2 test for the null that all the regressor coefficients equal the column (1) values is also reported.

Random effects estimates via approximate ML with 4 and 9 quadrature points are reported in columns (2) and (3). Clearly, there is very strong persistence in the wage equation errors, as 60 percent of the wage error variance is accounted for by random effects. Observe that the ML-quadrature estimates are quite far from the cross-section estimates. Particularly noticeable is the coefficient on EDUC in the wage equation, which is from 4.8 to 5.2 standard errors below the cross-section estimate. The χ^2 tests overwhelmingly reject the null that the random effects estimates equal the consistent cross-section estimates.

Notice that 4- and 9-point quadratures produce very different estimates of the cross-correlation of random effects. With 4 points, this is estimated as 0.4330, and with 9 points, it is estimated as −0.2798, both estimates being highly significant. The 4-point results are what Keane, Moffitt and Runkle reported. Since use of roughly 4 quadrature points is typical in the literature, these results demonstrate the need to use larger numbers of quadrature points in applied work. Increasing the number of points to 12 did not produce much change in results (the likelihood changed only from −6216 to −6206). Use of 12 points is very expensive for this model, as it required 88 cpu minutes.

These random effects results overturn the Keane, Moffitt and Runkle finding that permanent wage and employment error components are positively correlated. However, it should be noted that Keane, Moffitt and Runkle considered their preferred specification to be a semiparametric random effects model estimated using the technique of Heckman and Singer (1982), and this technique did choose the likelihood peak which has a negative cross-correlation of the random effects. Such a negative correlation, indicating that those with permanently high wage errors supply less labor, is not surprising since it can be explained by income effects. More surprising is the negative correlation between the transitory error components, implying that those with the temporarily high wages supply less labor. As was noted by Keane, Moffitt and Runkle, this appears difficult to reconcile with intertemporal substitution theories of the business cycle.

The MSS estimates of the random effects model are reported in column (4). These were obtained using the GHK simulator with 10 draws to simulate the transition probabilities. The regressor coefficient estimates are all quite close to the 9-point ML-quadrature estimates. Larger standard errors for the MSS estimates account for the smaller (but still highly significant) χ^2 test for the null of equality with the no-effects estimates (75 vs. 164). Column (5) contains MSS estimates of a model that allows for random effects plus AR(1) error components. When the AR(1) components are included, the AR(1) parameter in the wage equation is a substantial 0.4803 (with standard error 0.0165) and the fraction of the wage error variance explained by the individual effects drops to 45 percent. In the employment equation, the AR(1) parameter is also highly significant (0.2538 with standard error 0.0442). Clearly, the equicorrelation assumption is overwhelmingly rejected by the data. The first four lagged autocorrelations of the wage equation error implied by the MSS estimates in column (5) are 0.72, 0.58, 0.52, 0.48 – as compared to the autocorrelation of 0.60 at all lags implied by the random effects model. The first four lagged autocorrelations of the employment equation error are 0.48, 0.35, 0.32, and 0.31 as compared to the 0.3275 at all lags implied by the random effects model. Note, also, that the computational cost of the MSM estimator that allows for this more complex error pattern (47.38 cpu minutes on an IBM 3083) is only slightly greater than the cost of ML-quadrature estimation of the random effects model (40.49 cpu minutes).

In the model with a moving-average error component (column (6)), the MA(1) parameter in the wage equation is 0.2426 (with standard error 0.0851) and that in the employment equation is 0.2003 (with standard error 0.0564). Based on the simulated log-likelihood values, this model does not seem to fit as well as the model with AR(1) error components.

Although the equicorrelation assumption is rejected by the data, the parameter estimates obtained via MSS change only slightly when AR(1) and MA(1) error components are included in the model. Thus, the divergence of random effects estimates from the consistent no-effects estimates does not appear to result from the false imposition of the equicorrelation assumption in this case. In particular, the most likely explanation for the substantial drop in the education coefficient in going from the model with no effects to the models with random effects is that the individual effect in the wage equation is correlated with the education variable. That is, the individual effect is actually a fixed effect.

I now turn to the issue of the cyclicality of the real wage. All three MSS models give estimates of the cross-correlations of the random effects in the range from -0.19 to -0.21, and estimates of the cross-correlations of the time varying error components in the range from -0.35 to -0.39. Since negative correlations imply that high-wage workers are most likely to leave work in a recession, these results imply a degree of procyclical bias in aggregate wage measures which is considerably stronger than that found by Keane, Moffitt and Runkle, who report a positive correlation of the permanent components and a -0.33 correlation for the transitory components (column (4)). Since Keane, Moffitt and Runkle's main conclusion was that aggregate wage measures are procyclically biased, this can be viewed as a strengthening of that result.

The estimated unemployment rate coefficients are -0.0039 for the no-effects model, -0.0055 for the random effects model estimated by 9-point quadrature, -0.0057 for the random effects model estimated by MSS, -0.0095 for the random effects plus AR(1) error model, and -0.0066 for the random effects plus MA(1) error model. These estimates imply that a one-percentage-point increase in the unemployment rate corresponds to a fall in the real wage of between 0.4 percent and 1 percent. Thus, Keane, Moffitt and Runkle's finding that movements in the real wage are weakly procyclical appears to be robust to relaxation for the equicorrelation assumption.

8. Conclusion

The application of simulation estimation techniques to panel data LDV models is clearly more difficult than the application of these methods to cross-section problems. Yet the recent development of highly accurate GHK simulators for transition and choice probabilities has made simulation estimation in the panel data LDV context feasible. Three classical methods, an MSM estimator based on using the GHK method to simulate transition probabilities, an MSS estimator based on using the GHK method to simulate the score and an SML estimator based on using GHK to simulate choice probabilities, have been successfully applied in the literature. As the empirical examples in Section 7 show, these methods allow one to estimate panel data LDV models with complex error structures involving random effects and ARMA errors in times similar to those necessary for estimation of simple random effects models by quadrature. A Bayesian method based on Gibbs sampling has also been successfully applied. An important avenue for future research is to further explore the performance of methods based on conditional simulation of the latent variables of the LDV model, such as the simulated EM and Gibbs sampling approaches, in the panel data setting, and to compare the performance of these methods to that of MSM, MSS and SML.

References

Albert, J. and S. Chib (1993). Bayesian analysis of binary and polychotomous choice data. *J. Amer. Statist. Assoc.*, to appear.

Amemiya, T. and T. E. McCurdy (1986). Instrumental-variables estimation of an error-components model. *Econometrica* **54**, 869–80.

Balestra, P. and M. Nerlove (1966). Pooling cross section and time series data in the estimation of a dynamic model: The demand for natural gas. *Econometrica* **34**, 585–612.

Berkovec, J. and S. Stern (1991). Job exit behavior of older men. *Econometrica* **59**(1), 189–210.

Börsch-Supan, A., V. Hajivassiliou, L. Kotlikoff and J. Morris (1991). Health, children, and elderly living arrangements: A multiperiod-multinomial probit model with unobserved heterogeneity and autocorrelated errors. In: D. Wise, ed., *Topics in the Economics of Aging*. Univ. of Chicago Press, Chicago, IL.

Butler, J. S. and R. Moffitt (1982). A computationally efficient quadrature procedure for the one-factor multinomial probit model. *Econometrica* **50**(3), 761–64.

Chamberlain, G. (1985). Panel data. In: Z. Griliches and M. D. Intriligator, eds., *Handbook of Econometrics*. North-Holland, Amsterdam.

Chib, S. (1993). Bayes inference in the tobit censored regression model. *J. Econometrics*, to appear.

Elrod, T. and M. Keane (1992). A factor-analytic probit model for estimating market structure in panel data. Manuscript, University of Alberta.

Erdem, T. and M. Keane (1992). A dynamic structural model of consumer choice under uncertainty. Manuscript, University of Alberta.

Gelfand, A. E. and A. F. M. Smith (1990). Sampling based approaches to calculating marginal densities. *J. Amer. Statist. Assoc.* **85**, 398–409.

Geweke, J. (1991a). Efficient simulation from the multivariate normal and student-*t* distributions subject to linear constraints. In: E. M. Keramidas, ed., *Computing Science and Statistics: Proc. 23rd Sympos. on the Interface*. Interface Foundation Inc., Fairfax, VA, 571–578.

Geweke, J. (1991b). Evaluating the accuracy of sampling-based approaches to the calculation of posterior moments. Research Department Staff Report 148, Federal Reserve Bank of Minneapolis.

Geweke, J., M. Keane and D. Runkle (1992). Alternative computational approaches to statistical inference in the multinomial probit model. Manuscript, University of Minnesota.

Geweke, J., R. Slonim and G. Zarkin (1992). Econometric solution methods for dynamic discrete choice problems. Manuscript, University of Minnesota.

Gourieroux, C. and A. Monfort (1993). Simulation based econometric methods. *J. Econometrics*, to appear.

Hajivassiliou, V. and D. McFadden (1990). The method for simulated scores for the estimation of LDV models with an application to external debt crises. Cowles Foundation Discussion Paper 967.

Hajivassiliou, V., D. McFadden and P. Ruud (1992). Simulation of multivariate normal orthant probabilities: Theoretical and computational results. Cowles Foundation Discussion Paper 1021.

Heckman, J. (1979). Sample selection bias as a specification error. *Econometrica* **47**, 153–61.

Heckman, J. (1981). Statistical models for discrete panel data. In: C. Manski and D. McFadden, eds., *Structural Analysis of Discrete Data with Econometric Applications*. MIT Press, Cambridge, MA.

Heckman, J. and B. Singer (1982). The identification problem in econometric models for duration data. In: W. Hildenbrand, ed., *Advances in Econometrics*. Cambridge Univ. Press, Cambridge.

Hotz, J. V. and R. Miller (1993). Conditional choice probabilities and the estimation of dynamic programming models. *Rev. Econom. Stud.*, to appear.

Keane, M. (1990). Four essays in empirical macro and labor economics. Unpublished Ph.D. Dissertation, Brown University.

Keane, M. (1992). A computationally practical simulation estimator for panel data. Institute for Empirical Macroeconomics Discussion Paper 16, Federal Reserve Bank of Minneapolis.

Keane, M. and R. Moffitt (1991). A structural model of multiple welfare program participation and labor supply. Working Paper, Brown University.

Keane, M., R. Moffitt and D. Runkle (1988). Real wages over the business cycle: Estimating the impact of heterogeneity with micro data. *J. Politic. Econom.* **96**(6), 1232–66.

Keane, M. and D. Runkle (1992). On the estimation of panel-data models with serial correlation when instruments are not strictly exogenous. *J. Business Econom. Statist.* **10**(1), 1–9.

Keane, M. and K. Wolpin (1992). Solution and estimation of discrete dynamic programming models by simulation: Monte Carlo evidence. Manuscript, University of Minnesota.

McCulloch, R. and P. E. Rossi (1992). An exact likelihood analysis of the multinomial probit model. Manuscript, Graduate School of Business, University of Chicago.

McFadden, D. (1989). A method of simulated moments for estimation of discrete response models without numerical integration. *Econometrica* **57**(5), 995–1026.

McFadden, D. (1992). Estimation by the method of simulated moments. Paper presented at Conference on Simulation Based Inference in Econometrics, Rotterdam, June 5–6.

McFadden, D. and P. Ruud (1987). Estimation of limited dependent variable models from the regular exponential family by the method of simulated moments. Working Paper, University of California, Berkeley.

McFadden, D. and P. Ruud (1991). Estimation by simulation. Working Paper, University of California, Berkeley.

Pakes, A. (1986). Patents as options: Some estimates of the value of holding European patent stocks. *Econometrica* **54**, 755–84.

Pakes, A. and D. Pollard (1989). Simulation and the asymptotics of optimization estimators. *Econometrica* **57**(5), 1027–58.

Robinson, P. (1982). On the asymptotic properties of models containing limited dependent variables. *Econometrica* **50**(1), 27–41.

Ruud, P. (1991). Extensions of estimation methods using the EM algorithm. *J. Econometrics* **49**(3), 305–41.

Van Praag, B. M. S. and J. P. Hop (1987). Estimation of continuous models on the basis of set-valued observations. Report 8705/A, Econometric Institute, Erasmus University.

Van Praag, B. M. S., J. P. Hop and E. Eggink (1991). A symmetric approach to the labor market by means of the simulated EM-algorithm with an application to married females. Report 9145/A, Econometric Institute, Erasmus University.

G. S. Maddala, C. R. Rao and H. D. Vinod, eds., *Handbook of Statistics, Vol. 11*

21

A Perspective on Application of Bootstrap Methods in Econometrics

Jinook Jeong and G. S. Maddala

'In a world in which the price of calculation continues to decrease rapidly, but the price of theorem proving continues to hold steady or increase, elementary economics indicates that we ought to spend a larger fraction of our time on calculation.'

J. W. Tukey, *American Statistician* (1986, p. 74).

1. Introduction

The bootstrap method, introduced by Efron (1979) is a resampling method whereby information in the sample data is 'recycled' for estimating variances, confidence interval, *p*-values and other properties of statistics. It is based on the idea that the sample we have is a good representation of the underlying population (which is all right if we have a large enough sample). As a result, the variances, confidence intervals and so on, of sample statistics are obtained by drawing samples from the sample.

Resampling methods are not new. Suppose we have a set of observations $\{x_1, x_2, \ldots, x_n\}$ and a test statistic $\hat{\theta}$. Resampling methods can be introduced for two purposes. First, resampling methods are often useful to examine the stability of $\hat{\theta}$. By comparing the $\hat{\theta}$ computed from different subsamples, one can detect outliers or structural changes in the original sample. Cross-validation tests, recursive residual tests,[1] or Goldfeld–Quant's test for heteroskedasticity are in this line of resampling methods. Furthermore, resampling can be used to compute alternative estimators for the standard error of $\hat{\theta}$, which are usually calculated from the deviations of $\hat{\theta}$ across the subsamples. In the cases that the distribution of $\hat{\theta}$ is unknown or that consistent estimators for the standard error of $\hat{\theta}$ are not available, the resampling methods are especially useful.

The Jackknife, introduced by Quenouille (1956), is one of the resampling

---

[1] Brown, Durbin and Evans (1975).

methods to reduce bias and provide more reliable standard errors. The procedure of the simplest delete-one-jackknife is:

(1) Compute $\hat{\theta}_{(i)}$ from $\{x_1, x_2, \ldots, x_{i-1}, x_{i+1}, \ldots, x_n\}$ for all i.
(2) Compute the 'pseudovalues' $p_i = n\hat{\theta} - (n-1)\hat{\theta}_{(i)}$.
(3) The jackknife point estimator is given by $\hat{\theta}_J = \Sigma \, p_i/n$.
(4) The jackknife variance estimator is given by $\hat{v}_J = \Sigma \, (p_i - \hat{\theta}_J)^2/n(n-1)$.

Hinkley (1977) shows that $\hat{\theta}_J$ is unbiased but generally inefficient and $\hat{v}_J$ is generally biased. The asymptotic properties of $\hat{\theta}_J$ and $\hat{v}_J$ can be found in Miller (1974) and Akahira (1983). More advanced jackknife methods such as the n-delete jackknife, the balanced jackknife, and the weighted jackknife are developed by Wu (1986) to overcome the above mentioned problems. Since much of econometric work is based on time-series data, these modifications do not solve all the problems. For time-series data, Cragg (1987) suggests a recursive jackknife method.

The bootstrap method is another resampling method for the same purpose as the jackknife: to reduce bias and provide more reliable standard errors.[2] Unlike the jackknife, the bootstrap resamples at random. In other words, while the jackknife systematically deletes a fixed number of observations in order (without replacements), the bootstrap randomly picks a fixed number of observations from the original sample with replacements. By repeating this random resampling procedure, the bootstrap can approximate the unknown true distribution of the estimator with the empirical 'bootstrap' distribution. Formally,

(1) Draw a 'bootstrap sample' $B_1 = \{x_1^*, x_2^*, \ldots, x_n^*\}$ from the original sample $\{x_1, x_2, \ldots, x_n\}$. Each x_i^* is a random pick from $\{x_1, x_2, \ldots, x_n\}$ with replacement.
(2) Compute $\hat{\theta}_1^B$ using B_1.
(3) Repeat steps (1) and (2) m times to obtain $\{\hat{\theta}_1^B, \hat{\theta}_2^B, \ldots, \hat{\theta}_m^B\}$.
(4) Approximate the distribution of $\hat{\theta}$ by the bootstrap distribution $\hat{F}$, putting mass $1/n$ at each point $\hat{\theta}_1^B, \hat{\theta}_2^B, \ldots, \hat{\theta}_m^B$.

The bootstrap estimators of bias and variance are easily derived from the empirical distribution $\hat{F}$.

Resampling does not add any information to the original sample. Thus, the advantage of resampling methods like the bootstrap must be the result of the way the sample information is processed. For instance, in the case of samples from a normal distribution, all the information about the distribution of the sample mean is summarized in the sample mean and variance, which are jointly sufficient statistics. Thus, other ways of processing sample information in this case does not yield any better results. It is in cases where there is no readily available finite sample distribution of the test statistics that one gets the most

---

[2] The method is called the 'bootstrap' because the data tighten their reliability by generating new data sets as if they pull themselves up by their own bootstraps.

mileage out of the bootstrap methods. In most econometric applications this is the case.

The bootstrap is computationally more demanding than the jackknife. Because of this, one might think that the bootstrap would be a more efficient procedure in estimating functionals of sampling distributions. On the other hand, it has been argued that the jackknife is more robust to departures from the standard assumptions. Liu and Singh (1992) suggest that we can divide all the commonly used re-sampling procedures for the linear regression models into two types: the E-type (the efficient ones like the bootstrap) and the R-type (the robust ones like the jackknife).

Recent developments on the bootstrap methods address the limitations of the simple bootstrap resampling methods. However, most of the work is for models with IID errors. Thus, these methods are not directly applicable to much of econometric work. If the observations in the original sample are not exchangeable, the bootstrap resampling does not provide the correct approximation of the true distribution. Thus, neither the simple bootstrap methods nor some recent modifications are appropriate for serially correlated or heteroskedastic data sets. Unfortunately, there are some misapplications of the bootstrap methods in econometrics that miss this point. Rather than criticize these studies, we shall outline the modifications of the bootstrap method that have been suggested. Obviously, much theoretical work needs to be done in these areas.

There are several bootstraps in the literature. The simple bootstrap, double bootstrap, weighted bootstrap, wild bootstrap, recursive bootstrap, sequential bootstrap, and so on. Many empirical applications in econometrics do not say which bootstrap is being used although one can infer that the simple bootstrap is being used. Hall (1988a, p. 927) makes a similar complaint regarding applications of bootstrap confidence intervals.

The present paper is addressed to the following questions:

  (i) What are the special problems encountered in econometric work?

  (ii) What modifications of the bootstrap method are needed?

  (iii) What are some fruitful applications and what new insights have been obtained by the use of the bootstrap method?

There appears to be a lot of confusion in the applied econometric literature about what the bootstrap is good for. Broadly speaking, there are two main uses of the bootstrap that have both sound theoretical justification and support from Monte Carlo and/or empirical work.

  (a) In some models (e.g., Manski's maximum score estimator) asymptotic theory is intractable. In such cases the bootstrap provides a tractable way to achieved confidence intervals, etc. Typically, these results are equivalent to those obtained through asymptotic theory. That is, they are accurate through the leading term of the asymptotic expansion of the distribution of interest.

  (b) In other models, asymptotic theory is tractable but not very accurate in samples of the sizes used in applications. In such cases the bootstrap often provides a way of improving on the approximations of asymptotic theory.

However, in many econometric applications, modifications of the simple bootstrap are needed to achieve this improvement. Some of these methods have been developed but others not as yet.

Much applied econometric work seems directed towards obtaining standard errors. But these are of interest only if the distribution is normal, and most finite sample distributions arising in applications are non-normal. If one wants to make confidence interval statements and to test hypotheses, one should use the bootstrap method directly and skip the standard errors, which are useless.

These points should be borne in mind while going through the following review. Many of the conflicting results on the usefulness of the bootstrap that we shall note can be explained by the differences in the approaches used (and wrong objectives).

The plan of the paper is as follows: We first review the bootstrap methods in regression models with IID errors and computational aspects of bootstraps. We then discuss the several econometric applications of the bootstrap methods.[3]

2. Bootstrap methods with IID errors

2.1. Bootstrap in regressions

Consider a regression model $y = X\beta + u$ where y is an $n \times 1$ vector of the dependent variable, X is an $n \times k$ matrix of k regressors, and u is an $n \times 1$ vector of independent identically distributed errors with mean 0 and variance σ^2 (not known). The true distribution of u is not known. The sampling distribution, or the mean and variance of an estimator $\hat{\beta}$ (for example, the OLS estimator) is of interest.

When the regressors are non-random, the fixed structure of the data should be preserved and the bootstrap estimation is done by resampling the estimated errors. The procedure is:

(1) Compute the predicted residuals $\hat{u} = y - x\hat{\beta}$.[4]
(2) Resample $\hat{u}$: obtain u^* by drawing n times at random with replacement from $\hat{u}$.
(3) Construct a 'fake data' y^* by the formula $y^* = X\hat{\beta} + u^*$.
(4) Reestimate β^* using X and y^*.
(5) Repeat (2)–(4) m times.
(6) Compute the bootstrap point estimator, $\hat{\beta}_B = \Sigma \beta_j^* / m$.
(7) Compute the bootstrap variance of $\hat{\beta}$, $\hat{V}_B = \Sigma (\beta_j^* - \hat{\beta}_B)(\beta_j^* - \hat{\beta}_B)' / (m-1)$.

---

[3] For an earlier survey of the econometric literature, see Veall (1989).
[4] If X does not include the constant vector so the residuals $\hat{u}$ are not centered, the bootstrap usually fails. Freedman (1981) recommends the use of the centered residuals, $\hat{u}_i - (\Sigma \hat{u}_i/n)$, to correct this problem.

It is worth noting that the bootstrap point estimator and bootstrap variance can be derived without any computer simulation when $\hat{\beta}$ is the OLS estimator. If the bootstrap size m is a sufficiently large number to ensure that the proportions of $\hat{u}_i$ is the bootstrap samples are equal to $1/n$ for all i, then

$$\hat{\beta}_B = E[(X'X)^{-1}X'y^*] = \hat{\beta} , \tag{2.1}$$

$$\hat{V}_B = \text{var}[(X'X)^{-1}X'y^*] = \hat{\sigma}^2(X'X)^{-1} = (1 - k/n)s^2(X'X)^{-1} , \tag{2.2}$$

where $\hat{\sigma}^2 \equiv \Sigma \, \hat{u}_i^2/n$ and $s^2 \equiv \Sigma \, \hat{u}_i^2/(n - k)$. The bootstrap variance estimator in (2.2) is identical to the MLE estimator with the normality assumption and is different from the classical estimator only by a scale factor.[5] So in this ideal situation, the bootstrap is not of much use.

Note that what we need to sample is the vector u. Since it is unobserved, we sample from $\hat{u}$. Even if $\text{Var}(u) = I\sigma^2$, the residuals $\hat{u}_i$ are correlated and heteroskedastic. Specifically we have

$$\text{Var}(\hat{u}) = \sigma^2(I - H) ,$$

where H is the 'hat matrix' defined by

$$H = X(X'X)^{-1}X' .$$

The bootstrap succeeds even in spite of the fact that we are sampling from correlated and heteroskedastic residuals. The bootstrap vector u^* consists of independent errors with constant variance regardless of the properties of $\hat{u}$.

Consider next the case where the regressors are random. In this case we sample the raw observations (y_i, X_i), not the residuals. As is well known, in the stochastic regressor case, only the asymptotic properties of least squares estimators are known. Thus, in this case the bootstrap gives different answers even when $\hat{\beta}$ is a simple linear estimator. The bootstrap method involves drawing a sample of size n with replacement from (y_i, X_i). We then calculate $\hat{\beta}$ for each bootstrap sample and then proceed as in the fixed regressor case to get $\hat{\beta}_B$ and $\hat{V}_B$. The only problem is that sometimes the matrix $(X'X)$ can be singular. In this case a new sample needs to be drawn.

The difference between the two resampling methods in the case of the linear regression model is more glaring in the presence of heteroskedasticity. Suppose that $V(u) = \sigma^2 D$ where D is a diagonal matrix of rank n. The variance of $\hat{\beta}_{OLS}$ is given by

$$V(\hat{\beta}_{OLS}) = (X'X)^{-1}X'DX(X'X)^{-1} .$$

If we use the bootstrap method for the fixed regressor case, that is resample the residuals $\hat{u}_i$, since the residuals are randomly scattered, the bootstrap data sets will show no signs of heteroskedasticity. On the other hand, random

---

[5] It is customary to 'fatten' the residuals, $\hat{u}_i$, by a factor of $(1 - k/n)^{1/2}$ to obtain an unbiased bootstrap variance estimator.

resampling from (y_i, X_i) does not change the heteroskedasticity and the bootstrap variance gives approximately the correct answer. Thus, in the presence of heteroskedasticity, even if X_i are fixed, it is better to use the bootstrap that is appropriate for X_i random.

In the case of heteroskedasticity of an unknown form, it is customary in econometric work to estimate, following the suggestion of White (1980), the covariance matrix of $\hat{\beta}_{OLS}$ by

$$\hat{V}(\hat{\beta}_{OLS}) = (X'X)^{-1}X'\hat{D}X(X'X)^{-1}$$

where

$$\hat{D} = \text{Diag}[\hat{u}_1^2, \hat{u}_2^2, \ldots, \hat{u}_n^2]$$

MacKinnon and White (1985) compare, by a Monte Carlo study, this estimator with

(i) a modification of the MINQUE estimator of Rao (1970) suggested by Horn, Horn and Duncan (1975), and

(ii) the 'delete-one' jackknife estimator.

They find the jackknife estimator the best. The Horn–Horn–Duncan estimator replaces D by D^* where $D^* = \text{Diag}[\sigma_1^{*2}, \sigma_2^{*2}, \ldots, \sigma_n^{*2}]$ with $\sigma_i^{*2} = \hat{u}_i^2/(1 - h_{ii})$ and h_{ii} is the i-th diagonal term of the 'hat-matrix' H. The jackknife estimator of $V(\hat{\beta}_{OLS})$ is

$$\frac{n-1}{n}(X'X)^{-1}[X'\bar{D}X - \frac{1}{n}(X'\bar{u}\bar{u}'X)](X'X)^{-1}$$

with $\bar{D} = \text{Diag}[\bar{u}_1^2, \bar{u}_2^2, \ldots, \bar{u}_n^2]$ and $\bar{u}_i = \hat{u}_i/(1 - h_{ii})$. MacKinnon and White, however, did not consider the weighted bootstrap.[6]

2.2. Asymptotic theory for bootstrap

The bootstrap estimators are known to be consistent under mild conditions. Bickel and Freedman (1981) and Singh (1981) show the asymptotic consistency of bootstrap estimators for sample mean and other statistics under mild regularity conditions. Freedman (1981, 1984) provides the asymptotic results for bootstrap in regression models. Navidi (1989) uses Edgeworth expansion to show that, asymptotically, the bootstrap is always at least as good as the classical normal approximation in linear regression models. Asymptotic properties of bootstrap estimation in more complicated situations, such as simultaneous equation systems or dynamic models, are presented in Freedman (1984). The following are some typical results. (We state the theorems without proof.)

Assume that X is non-random and $\lim(X'X/n) = V$ where V is a finite nonsingular matrix. Then the OLS estimator $\hat{\beta}(n)$ is consistent and the limiting

---

[6] For a comparison between the White correction, simple bootstrap and weighted bootstrap, see Jeong and Maddala (1992).

distribution of $\sqrt{n}[\hat{\beta}(n) - \beta]$ is normal with mean 0 and variance $\sigma^2 V^{-1}$. The bootstrap point estimator using r resampled errors from a simulation, $\hat{\beta}_B(r)$, has the following asymptotic properties.[7]

THEOREM 2.1. *Given y, as r and n tend to infinity, $\sqrt{m}[\hat{\beta}_B(r) - \hat{\beta}(n)]$ weakly converges in distribution to normal with mean 0 and variance $\sigma^2 V^{-1}$ (m is the number of bootstrap replications).*

THEOREM 2.2. *Given y, as r and n tend to infinity, the bootstrap estimator for the error variance, $\hat{\sigma}_B^2(r) \equiv \Sigma \, \hat{u}_i^2/r$ converges in distribution to point mass at σ^2.*

The proofs of the above theorems using the concept of the 'Mallows metric' are found in Bickel and Freedman (1981) and Freedman (1981). For surveys of asymptotic properties using Edgeworth expansions, see Babu (1989) and Hall (1992).

There are many papers that discuss sufficient conditions for consistency and give a number of examples where consistency does not hold. Some of these are Efron (1979), Singh (1981), Beran, Le Cam and Millar (1987), and Athreya (1983, 1987). If T_n is the statistic and n the sample size, the definition of consistency is

$$\rho(F_n, F_n^*) \to 0 \quad \text{a.s. or in prob. (weak)},$$

where ρ is some distance function between F_n, the actual DF of T_n and F_n^*, the bootstrap DF of T_n. Generally, ρ is chosen as the Kolmogorov or Mallows distance. These conditions for consistency are, however, difficult to check in the case of many of the estimators used in econometrics.

A more important question about the bootstrap methods in econometrics is how well they work in small samples. This is discussed in Section 4 with reference to a number of econometric applications. The dominating conclusion is that, under a variety of departures from the standard normal model, the bootstrap methods performed reasonably well in small samples, provided the modifications of the simple bootstrap are used.

2.3. Bootstrap confidence intervals

There is an enormous statistical literature on confidence intervals. Since surveys of this literature are available, for instance see the paper by Diciccio and Romano (1988), we shall not go through the intricate details here. Efron (1987) notes that bias and variance calculations require a small number of bootstrap replications (50 to 200), but the computation of sufficiently stable confidence intervals requires a large number of replications (at least 1000 to 2000). Even with today's fast machines this can be time consuming.

---

[7] In practice, as shown in the previous sections, $r = n$.

A major portion of the econometric work on bootstrap is concerned with the calculation of bias and standard errors.[8] This is not appropriate because even if the asymptotic and bootstrap standard errors agree, there can be large differences in the corresponding confidence intervals if the bootstrap distribution is sufficiently skewed (the asymptotic distribution is normal). For instance, Efron and Tibshirani (1986, p. 58) estimate the Cox proportional hazard model

$$h(t \mid x) = h_0(t) \, e^{\beta x}$$

and find $\hat{\beta} = 1.51$ with asymptotic SE 0.41. The bootstrap SE based on 1000 replications was 0.42. However, the bootstrap distribution was skewed to the right, thus, producing different confidence intervals.[9]

Again, for the autoregressive model

$$Z_t = \phi Z_{t-1} + \varepsilon_t$$

based on Wolfer's sunspot numbers for 1770–1889, they got $\hat{\phi} = 0.815$ with asymptotic SE of 0.053. The bootstrap standard error based on 1000 replications was 0.055, agreeing nicely with the asymptotic result. However, the bootstrap distribution was skewed to the left.

The earliest example in econometrics of using the bootstrap method for the construction of confidence intervals is that by Veall (1987a) which involves a complicated forecasting problem involving future electricity demand. He used the percentile method. He also did a Monte Carlo study (Veall, 1987b) for this specific example and found the method satisfactory. However, there is a large amount of statistical literature criticizing the simple percentile method. Eakin, McMillen and Buono (1990) use both percentile method and Efron's bias-corrected method but find no differences in the results. Using the bootstrap standard deviation makes the most difference but not the different bootstrap methods.[10]

The percentile method is the simplest method for the construction of confidence intervals. The $(1 - 2\alpha)$ confidence interval is the interval between the 100α and $100(1 - \alpha)$ percentiles of the bootstrap distribution of $\hat{\theta}^*$ ($\hat{\theta}^*$ is the bootstrap estimate of θ). Diciccio and Romano (1988) present unsatisfactory small-sample performance of the percentile method. Efron introduced a bias-corrected (BC) percentile method to improve the performance of the

---

[8] There are several examples. See for instance, Rosalsky, Finke and Theil (1984), Korajczyk (1985), Green, Hahn and Rocke (1987), Datt (1988), Selvanathan (1989), Prasada, Rao and Selvanathan (1992) and Wilson (1992).

[9] The Cox hazard model and its extensions are widely applied in econometric work. See for instance, Atkinson and Tschirhart (1986) and Butler et al. (1986). In all the applications, only asymptotic standard errors are reported. Bootstrap methods have not been used.

[10] Eakin et al. (1990) use also what they call the *basic bootstrap confidence interval*. This is the usual confidence interval obtained from the normal distribution with the bootstrap SE substituted for the asymptotic SE. This procedure is not generally recommended.

simple percentile method. Schenker (1985) shows that the coverage probabilities of the BC intervals are substantially below the nominal levels in small samples. To improve the BC intervals, Efron (1987) proposes the accelerated bias-corrected percentile (BC$_a$) method. Diciccio and Tibschirani (1987) show that the method is a combination of a variance-stabilizing transformation and a skewness-reducing transformation. They also present a computationally simpler procedure (BC$_a^0$ interval) which is asymptotically equivalent to the BC$_a$ interval.

The preceding methods are all *percentile methods*. In contrast, there is a second group of methods called *pivotal* methods. The methods that fall in this category are: the bootstrap-*t* (also known as the percentile-*t*) and Beran's *B* method (Beran, 1987, 1988). The idea behind the bootstrap-*t* method is that instead of using the bootstrap distribution of $\hat{\theta}$, we use the bootstrap distribution of the 'studentized' statistic (also called asymptotically pivotal statistic) $t = \sqrt{n}(\hat{\theta} - \theta)/s$ where s^2 is a $\sqrt{n}$ consistent estimate of the variance of $\sqrt{n}(\hat{\theta} - \theta)$. This method gives more reliable confidence intervals. Beran (1988) and Hall (1986a) have shown that the bootstrap distribution of an asymptotically pivotal test statistic based on a $\sqrt{n}$ consistent estimator coincides through order $\sqrt{n}$ with the Edgeworth expansion of the exact finite-sample distribution.

The bootstrap-*t* procedure is: (a) draw the bootstrap sample, (b) compute the *t*-statistic of interest $(\hat{\beta} - \beta)/\text{SE}(\hat{\beta})$ using the formulas of asymptotic theory, and (c) estimate the empirical distribution of the statistic by repeating (a) and (b). Beran (1988) shows that by using critical values from the resulting bootstrap distribution, one obtains tests whose finite sample sizes are closer to the nominal size than are tests with asymptotic critical values. These critical values can be used to form confidence intervals whose coverage probabilities are closer to the nominal values than are those based on first-order asymptotics (Hall, 1986a). Often the errors based on the bootstrap critical values are of $O(n^{-1})$, whereas with asymptotic distributions, they are of $O(n^{-1/2})$. By appropriately iterating the bootstrap, one can obtain further improvements in accuracy. For example, Beran (1987, 1988) shows that with pre-pivoting, one can obtain size errors of $O(n^{-3/2})$. Beran (1990) suggests further iteration and shows that this method, called the B^2 methods, performs better than the original *B* method. To conserve space, we shall not discuss Beran's method is detail here.

It is difficult to choose a single confidence interval as the best of all the above confidence intervals. However, the percentile-*t* method, Beran's *B* method and the BC$_a$ method are shown to be asymptotically superior to the other methods.[11] The small sample performance of these methods are known to be acceptable.[12] Hall (1986b) discusses the effect of the number of bootstrap simulations on the accuracy of confidence intervals.

---

[11] See Hall (1988a) and Martin (1990) among others.
[12] See Efron (1987), Beran (1988), and Diciccio and Tibshirani (1987) for examples.

Most econometric applications of confidence intervals have not incorporated these refinements. They are often based on the simple percentile method. Two notable exceptions are George, Oksanen and Veall (1988) who compare the results from asymptotic theory with those from the percentile method, the percentile-*t* method, and Efron's BC method, and Eakin et al. (1990), who use the percentile and Efron's BC method. The differences arising from the use of these methods were minor in these applications.

3. Computational advances in bootstrap methods

As Efron (1990) and many other authors point out, the computational burden of the bootstrap simulations for reliable bootstrap confidence intervals is a problem even with today's fast machines. Several methods to reduce the computational burden have been devised. One group of the methods tries to reduce the required number of bootstrap replications through more sophisticated resampling schemes such as balanced sampling, importance sampling, and antithetic sampling.[13] All these methods were originally developed for Monte Carlo analysis in the 1960s. In this section, we are interested in the bootstrap applications of these methods. The other line of research has focused on analytical approximations of bootstrap estimation. The saddle-point approximations by Davison and Hinkley (1988) and the BC_a^0 confidence intervals by Diciccio and Tibshirani (1987) are in this category.

3.1. Balanced sampling

Davison, Hinkley and Schechtman (1986) suggest the method of balanced bootstrap to reduce both the bias in bootstrap estimates and the number of simulations required in bootstrap estimations. To achieve the overall balance of bootstrap samples, the following sampling scheme is proposed: (1) copy the original sample $\{x_1, x_2, \ldots, x_n\}$ m times to make a string of length nm, (2) randomly permute this string and cut it off in m blocks to make m bootstrap samples of length n (this procedure is equivalent to selecting n observations from the nm pool *without* replacement).[14] It is easy to see that the first-order bias in bootstrap estimates disappear with the balanced sampling. Davison et al. (1986) provide the theoretical background and some numerical results.

In the regression context, the balanced resampling can be done with the estimated residuals. Flood (1985) introduces the *augmented bootstrap* which shares the basic idea with the balanced bootstrap: augment the estimated

---

[13] Weber (1984, 1986) suggests the *weighted resampling method* to improve the small sample performance of bootstrap methods, keeping the same asymptotic properties. However, it does not necessarily reduce the computational cost. Efron (1990) takes another route. He sticks to the usual way of generating bootstrap samples but seeks improvement in the final processing of the bootstrap data. For details, see Efron's paper.

[14] For the computing algorithms for the balanced sampling, see Gleason (1988).

residuals $\hat{u}_i = y_i - x_i\hat{\beta}$ $(i = 1, 2, \ldots, n)$ by their negatives to construct a balanced (and symmetric) vector of $\hat{u}_i$ of length $2n$, resample as usual from this new set of residuals. Rayner (1988) provides the asymptotic theory for the augmented bootstrap.

When a statistic has large higher-order components, the first-order balance does not significantly reduce the bias and computing time. Graham, Hinkley, John and Shi (1990) introduce the second-order balanced bootstrap method which principally reduces the bias in variance estimates.

3.2. Importance sampling

Since the primary purpose of balanced sampling is to reduce the bias, the required number of simulation for reliable bootstrap confidence intervals is not cut down significantly with balanced sampling. The importance resampling design by Davison (1988) and Johns (1988), however, is known to reduce the necessary replications by as much as 90%–95%. Intuitively, it is possible to keep higher accuracy by increasing the probabilities of samples that are of most 'importance' in the simulation process. The 'importance' can be determined using the likelihood ratio from a suitably chosen alternative distribution.

Hinkley and Shi (1989) applied the importance sampling technique to Beran's double bootstrap confidence limits (B^2) method. As expected, the importance sampling significantly (by 90%) reduces the computational burden involved in the computations. Do and Hall (1991), however, argue that antithetic re-sampling and balanced re-sampling produce significant improvements in efficiency for a wide range of problems whereas importance re-sampling cannot improve on uniform re-sampling for calculating bootstrap estimates of bias, variance and skewness.

3.3. Antithetic sampling

The antithetic sampling method was introduced by Hammersley and Morton (1956) and Hammersley and Mauldon (1956). Hall (1989) applies the antithetic resampling method to the bootstrap confidence intervals estimation. To explain the basic idea, let $\hat{\theta}_1$ and $\hat{\theta}_2$ be different estimates of θ, having the same (unknown) expectation and negative correlation. Then $\hat{\theta}_a \equiv (\hat{\theta}_1 + \hat{\theta}_2)/2$ has smaller variance than either $\hat{\theta}_1$ or $\hat{\theta}_2$ with no higher computational cost. In bootstrap estimations, the question is how to obtain the suitable second estimate $\hat{\theta}_2$. Hall (1989) proposes the 'antithetic permutation' which can be described as follows: (1) rearrange the original sample $\{x_1, x_2, \ldots, x_n\}$ so that $x_{(1)} < x_{(2)} < \cdots < x_{(n)}$, (2) select an ordinary bootstrap sample $B_1 = \{x_{(j)}, j$ is a RV uniformly distributed on $1, 2, \ldots, n\}$, (3) generate the corresponding antithetic-permuted sample $B_2 = \{x_{(k)}, k = n - j + 1\}$. Intuitively, to minimize $\Sigma\, p_i q_i$, the antithetic permutation takes the largest p_i with the smallest q_i, the second largest p_i with the second smallest q_i and so on. Hall (1989) shows that this type of permutation gives the greatest degree of negative correlation and so smallest variance of the antithetic variate.

To compute the confidence intervals, $\hat{\theta}_1$ and $\hat{\theta}_2$ are computed from the B_1 and B_2, respectively, and the anthithetic bootstrap empirical distribution $\hat{F}_a \equiv (\hat{F}_{B_1} + \hat{F}_{B_2})/2$ can be constructed after m replications. Because $\hat{F}_a$ is more stable (has less variance) than the usual bootstrap empirical distribution, reliable confidence limits can be constructed with less simulations. Hall (1989) also shows that the performance of antithetic resampling method is asymptotically better than the importance resampling.

The antithetic variates method can be seen as a generalized version of the *control variates method* by Fieller and Hartley (1954). Davidson and MacKinnon (1990) unify the two methods and suggest a regression procedure as an easier and better way to compute the control variates and antithetic variates in Monte Carlo analyses.

3.4. Efron's post hoc correction method

The resampling methods introduced so far are all a priori corrections in the sense that the sample-generating procedure is modified. Efron (1990) offers a different correction method which is applied to the final processing of the *usual* bootstrap samples and so is called the post hoc correction method. The primary goal of the method is to reduce the first-order bias in bootstrap estimates like the balanced sampling method by Davison et al. (1986).

Given the original sample $\{x_1, x_2, \ldots, x_n\}$, let P_i^j be the proportion of x_i in the j-th bootstrap sample. For example, if the first observation x_1 appears three times in the j-th bootstrap sample, $P_1^j = 3/n$. Define the 'resampling vector' P^j by $P^j \equiv [P_1^j \quad P_2^j \quad \cdots \quad P_n^j]'$ and the average of the resampling vector by $\bar{P} \equiv \Sigma \, P^j/m$. In this framework, the j-th bootstrap estimator $\hat{\theta}_j^B$ can be expressed as a function of the j-th resampling vector: $\hat{\theta}_j^B = \hat{\theta}(P^j)$. Similarly, the original estimator $\hat{\theta} = \hat{\theta}(P^0)$ where $P^0 \equiv [1/n \quad 1/n \quad \cdots \quad 1/n]'$, the resampling vector for the original sample.

Then the usual bootstrap bias estimate can be written as $\text{Bias}_B = \{\hat{\theta}_B - \hat{\theta}(P^0)\}$. Efron (1990) suggests a post hoc correction of the bias estimate: $\text{Bias}_B^* \equiv \{\hat{\theta}_B - \hat{\theta}(\bar{P})\}$. The intuition behind this is the following. The theoretical expectation of the resampling vector is P^0. However, the bootstrap average of P is $\bar{P}$, which is not equal to P^0. Thus, by using $\hat{\theta}(\bar{P})$ instead of $\hat{\theta}(P^0)$, we can correct the discrepancy. Efron (1990) shows the Bias_B^* is superior to Bias_B in magnitude and stability.

The idea can be extended to the estimation of variance and confidence limits. The estimation procedure involves the ANOVA decomposition and regression of $\hat{\theta}(P)$ on P. Details are found in Efron (1990). The balanced sampling method by Davison et al. (1986) and Graham et al. (1990) shares the same idea of bias correction with Efron's post hoc correction. What the balanced sampling does is choosing the resampling vectors P satisfying $P^0 = \bar{P}$. Numerical comparison by Efron (1990) shows that the post hoc corrected confidence intervals are more accurate than the balanced sampling confidence limits.

3.5. Saddlepoint approximation

Unlike all the above efforts trying to reduce the required number of simulations for bootstrap confidence limits, the saddlepoint approximation of the bootstrap distribution is an analytic approach which does not require any simulation. Davison and Hinkley (1988) propose the use of Daniels' (1954) saddlepoint approximation to approximate the distribution of bootstrap estimates which are usually sums of independent random variables. In their simulations, the saddlepoint approximation is surprisingly accurate. The drawback of the saddlepoint approximation is its limited applicability: the approximation is not found for all the cases so that the analytical validity of the approximation must be checked for each case. Young and Daniels (1990) apply the saddlepoint approximation to bootstrap bias estimation.

The re-sampling methods discussed in this section are all useful for reducing the number of bootstrap simulations required to achieve a given level of accuracy. Econometricians have been using these techniques in other areas such as Bayesian inference using Monte Carlo (see Kloek and Van Dijk, 1978, Van Dijk, 1987) and simulation based inference. However, in applications of bootstrap methods, they are not used that often.

4. Bootstrap methods with non-IID errors: Applications in econometrics

As shown in Sections 2 and 3, the standard bootstrap methods assume that the underlying (unknown) distributions are IID. In econometric applications, however, most of the data sets are not IID. Either in time series data or in cross-section data, the serial independence and homogeneity assumptions are not valid. Furthermore, distributions are obviously truncated in many economic applications, as in the logit, probit, tobit, and several limited dependent variable models. In all these complicated situations, bootstrap methods need to be modified to produce reliable estimates. In this section, advanced bootstrap methods which can be used in more complicated situations are reviewed. As we will see, the development of bootstrap methods in this direction is still in its early stages. Considering the frequent deviations of econometric data from standard assumptions, further research is expected. The discussion will be limited to the linear regression model with non-random regressors, given in Section 2.

4.1. Heteroskedasticity

Consider again the regression model $y = X\beta + u$, where y is an $n \times 1$ vector of the dependent variable, X is an $n \times k$ matrix of k regressors, and u is an $n \times 1$ vector of independent errors. If the errors are distributed with heteroskedastic variance, say $u_i \sim N(0, \sigma_i^2)$, then the standard bootstrap procedure introduced in Section 2 does not provide a consistent estimate of the variance of $\hat{\beta}$. The $\hat{V}_B$ is asymptotically equivalent to $(n^{-1} \Sigma \sigma_i^2)(X'X)^{-1}$, while the true variance of $\hat{\beta}$ is $(X'X)^{-1}(\Sigma \sigma_i^2 x_i' x_i)(X'X)^{-1}$.[15] Intuitively, the standard resampling scheme fails because the errors are not exchangeable.

Wu (1986) proposes a different bootstrap method for a consistent variance estimate: the *weighted bootstrap*. In his method, the i-th residual, instead of being resampled with replacement, goes with the i-th fitted value to keep the information contained in each observation. Instead, an additional artificial error vector is created and resampled. Formally, steps (2) and (3) of the standard bootstrap procedure given in Section 2 are modified to create the artificial data y^{**} as follows:

$$y_i^{**} = x_i \hat{\beta} + \{\hat{u}_i/(1-\omega_i)^{1/2}\}t_i \quad \forall i = 1, 2, \ldots, n, \tag{4.1}$$

where $\omega_i \equiv x_i(X'X)^{-1}x_i'$ and t_i is a random pick with replacement from a standard normal distribution. Thus, $E(t) = 0$ and $var(t) = I$ by construction. The remaining steps are exactly same as the standard bootstrap. It is easy to show that the bootstrap point estimate β_B^{**} using y^{**} is unbiased. The bootstrap variance estimate from Wu's weighted resampling is

$$V_B^{**} = (X'X)^{-1} \sum \{\hat{u}_i^2/(1-\omega_i)\}x_i' x_i(X'X)^{-1} \tag{4.2}$$

which is a very close form to the true variance of $\hat{\beta}$. Wu (1986) shows that V_B^{**} is consistent under mild conditions.[16] Wu's weighted bootstrap in the non-regression contexts is found in Liu (1988).

Härdle and Mammen (1990a) have generalized Wu's method by the *wild bootstrap*. In the wild bootstrap, an error vector u_w is resampled from a constructed distribution F_w satisfying:

$$E(u_w) = 0, \quad E(u_w^2) = \hat{u}^2, \quad \text{and} \quad E(u_w^3) = \hat{u}^3, \tag{4.3}$$

where the expectations are taken under F_w. It is called 'wild' because a single observation is used to estimate the true distribution of the residual. Wu's bootstrap simply sets $u_w = \hat{u}t$ where $t \sim N(0, I)$. It fulfills the conditions (4.3) and can be viewed as a special case of the wild bootstrap. The wild bootstrap estimates are computed using $y_w = X\beta + u_w$ as usual.

As noted earlier in Section 2, one other method of deriving the correct covariance matrix of the OLS estimator of β under heteroskedasticity is to bootstrap the data (y_i, X_i) instead of the residuals, as is done in the stochastic regressor case.

There are essentially two problems here. The first is to use the OLS method but get the correct covariance matrix and standard errors. This is what we have

---

[15] x_i is the i-th row of X.
[16] V_B^{**} is unbiased if $\omega_{ij} \equiv x_i(X'X)^{-1}x_j' = 0$ for any i, j with $\sigma_i \neq \sigma_j$.

discussed. It is essentially a non-parametric procedure. The second and more important problem is to get more efficient estimates (through GLS) of β and get the correct standard errors. For this we need a parametric specification. Carroll and Ruppert, in their discussion of the paper by Wu (1986), suggest that this is a better procedure. Cragg (1983) suggests a general parametric specification for handling heteroskedasticity. Most of these GLS procedures are iterative procedures. Although these procedures are iterated until convergence for most econometric models, a one step procedure starting with an initial consistent estimate is asymptotically efficient. The bootstrap procedure is then used to get estimates of the variances of the GLS estimates. As will be discussed in the next section, in the case of autocorrelated errors, a parametric specification of the error term is needed to use the bootstrap method. This is the case with heteroskedasticity as well.

4.2. *Autocorrelation and other dynamics*

In most time series data, the errors are serially correlated. When the errors are serially correlated, it is well known that OLS produces inconsistent standard errors and that GLS tends to over-reject the true null hypotheses in small samples.[17] While bootstrap estimation is a proper alternative for better small sample performance, the standard bootstrap resampling fails because the errors are not exchangeable. However, if the structure of serial correlation is known, a suitable bootstrap procedure can be designed utilizing the independent part of the error term. This group of bootstrap procedures can be called the *recursive* bootstraps because they resample error terms recursively to preserve the serial relationships in the error terms. Veall (1986) considers the following first-order autocorrelation model:

$$y = X\beta + u , \tag{4.4}$$

$$u_i = \rho u_{i-1} + e_i , \tag{4.5}$$

where $-1 < \rho < 1$ and e_i is IID with mean zero. The model is first estimated by feasible GLS or the Cochrane–Orcutt transformation to compute $\hat{\beta}$, $\hat{\rho}$, $\hat{u}$ and $\hat{e}$. Second, the independent residuals $\hat{e}_i$ are resampled with replacement, giving the bootstrapped residuals e^*. Third, one residual is randomly selected from e^* and divided by $(1 - \rho^2)^{1/2}$ to become $\hat{u}_1$.[18] Then u^* are recursively computed by (4.5), and y^* is constructed by substituting $\hat{\beta}$ and u^* for equation (4.4). The remaining procedure is the same as standard bootstrap. Veall (1986), however, finds that the finite sample performance of his bootstrap is no better than that of the asymptotic GLS. In a related study, Rayner (1990c) bootstraps the estimated *t*-values, $\hat{\beta}/\text{SE}(\hat{\beta})$, instead of the raw coefficient $\hat{\beta}$, and shows

---

[17] See Park and Mitchell (1980), King and Giles (1984), and Miyazaki and Griffiths (1984).
[18] Note that $\text{var}(u) = \text{var}(e)/(1 - \rho^2)$. This transformation is often called the Prais–Winsten transformation.

somewhat promising results on the small sample performance of the same bootstrap method. This method can be applied to any higher order autocorrelations if the structure is known.

The differences between the results of Veall and Rayner are presumably due to the fact that Rayner bootstrapped an asymptotically pivotal statistic and, therefore, obtained a higher-order approximation to the finite sample distribution of t. In contrast, Veall's results are no more accurate than those from asymptotic theory.[19] Morey and Wang (1985) bootstrap the Durbin–Watson statistic to eliminate the inconclusive regions. The performance of their recursive bootstrap is also moderate. One important thing to note in Rayner's study is that he considers samples of sizes 5 to 10. Bootstrap methods are based on the assumption that the observed sample is the same as true distribution. It is unrealistic to assume that this is true for samples as small as 5 or 10 observations.

The problem of recursive bootstrap is that it is not useful when the structure of serial correlation is not known or misspecified. Recently, a more general bootstrap procedure for time series data, 'moving block bootstrap' has been introduced by Künsch (1989) and Liu and Singh (1988). Suppose that a set of time series observations $\{\xi_1, \xi_2, \ldots, \xi_n\}$ is given. The moving block bootstrap first forms the blocks of length l, $L_k = \{\xi_k, \xi_{k+1}, \ldots, \xi_{k+l-1}\}$ for $k = 1, 2, \ldots, b$ where $b = n - l + 1$. Then resample $L_1, L_2, \ldots, L_b$ with replacement to create a bootstrap blocks $L_1^*, L_2^*, \ldots, L_{n/l}^*$. This procedure is repeated M times like the standard bootstrap. In our simple model (4.4), ξ_1 is replaced by $\hat{u}_1$.

Künsch (1989) and Lahiri (1991) show the validity of moving block bootstrap procedure in stationary, univariate case. Lahiri (1992) extends the proof to the nonstationary case. Shi and Shao (1988) and Moore and Rais (1990) propose different versions of bootstrap of m-dependence and for uniform mixing, respectively.

In time series analyses, stationary autoregressive models are often employed to capture the dynamics in economic variables. The simplest example would be the first-order autoregressive model

$$y_i = \alpha y_{i-1} + e_i , \tag{4.6}$$

where $|\alpha| < 1$ and e_i is assumed to be white noise. The hypothesis is $H_0: \alpha = \alpha_0$. It is well known that the Student's t-distribution is a very poor approximation for α in the finite samples.[20] Rayner (1990b) proposes a recursive bootstrap procedure for this AR(1) model. First, equation (4.6) is estimated by the least squares method, and $\hat{e}$ is resampled to create the bootstrap error

---

[19] This was pointed out to us by Joel Horowitz.
[20] See Tanaka (1983) and Nankervis and Savin (1988).

vector e^*. Second, y_0^* is computed by

$$y_0^* = \sum_{j=0}^{\infty} \alpha_0^j e_{-j}^* . \tag{4.7}$$

This transformation is plausible since the model (4.6) implies

$$y_0 = \sum_{j=0}^{\infty} \alpha^j e_{-j} . \tag{4.8}$$

Third, $y_1^*, y_2^*, \ldots, y_n^*$ are rescursively constructed by

$$y_i^* = \hat{a} y_{i-1}^* + e_i^* . \tag{4.9}$$

The remaining steps are the same as the standard bootstrap. Rayner (1990b) shows, through a Monte Carlo study, that his bootstrap method has better small sample properties than the usual t-approximation.

In fact, Rayner' recursive bootstrap is an extension of Freedman (1984) and Freedman and Peters (1984a). Their resampling procedure is: estimate the model and compute the estimated residuals, then with a given initial value of the dependent variable y_0 compute the dependent variable series $y_1^*, y_2^*, \ldots, y_n^*$ successively, keeping the dynamic relationship in y_i. Note that y_0 is assumed to be known to the researcher. In Rayner's study, it is computed from the equilibrium distribution.[21] Bose (1988) investigates the asymptotic properties of Freedman's bootstrap estimation and shows that the bootstrap improves the asymptotic accuracy of the least square estimates.[22] Rayner (1990a) shows that bootstrapping standardized statistics may give better small sample results than using the asymptotic results in the case of GLS estimation.

In contrast to these studies, there is the extensive Monte Carlo study by Kiviet (1984) of a model with lagged dependent variables which concludes that bootstrap methods do not outperform standard OLS. His Monte Carlo study was based on the model

$$y_t = \beta_0 + \beta_1 y_{t-1} + \beta_2 x_t + \beta_3 x_{t-1} + \varepsilon_t .$$

This simulations were performed where $\varepsilon_t \sim \mathrm{IN}(0, 1)$ and where $\varepsilon_t \sim \mathrm{IL}(0, 1)$. N indicates normal distribution, and L indicates the double-exponential or Laplace distribution. He argues that the deficiencies of ordinary least squares estimators in lagged dependent variable models are intensified when applied to bootstrap samples.

One other area of extensive research in econometrics is that of unit roots and cointegration. It is tempting to apply mechanically the usual bootstrap

---

[21] An earlier study by Chatterjee (1986) considers bootstrapping ARMA models but does not discuss the problem of initial values. De Wet and Van Wyk (1986) consider AR(1) and MA(1) models and stress the importance of the distribution of initial observations.

[22] Specifically, the accuracy is improved from $\mathrm{O}(n^{-1/2})$ to $\mathrm{o}(n^{-1/2})$.

methods, but there are many pitfalls. First, the asymptotic theory does not hold in the case of bootstrap for unit root autoregressive processes. Second, if both x and y are I(1) and cointegrated, then $y-\beta x$ is I(0), which is stationary. But stationarity does not mean the errors are IID. Thus, one cannot apply the bootstrap methods for IID distributions to cointegrating regressions, as done in Vinod and McCullough (1991). In this case one needs either a parametric specification for the errors or some extensions of the bootstrap method.

Basawa et al. (1991a), examine the case of unit roots, that is $|\alpha| = 1$ in equation (4.6). They find that the bootstrap estimate of α does not converge to the standard Wiener process but converges to a random distribution, even if e_i is normally distributed. They argue that bootstrap estimation is asymptotically invalid when $|\alpha| = 1$, and that one should be cautious in applying bootstrap procedures to autoregressive models when the root is suspected to be close to 1. Ferretti and Romo (1992) propose a bootstrap resampling scheme for this model and prove its asymptotic validity. This method is alternative to the invalid one studied by Basawa et al. (1991a). In a subsequent paper, Basawa et al. (1991b), suggest a *sequential bootstrap* procedure for the estimation of the parameter α in the explosive case. They establish the asymptotic validity of this procedure for all $|\alpha| \leqslant 1$. Basawa et al. (1989) analyze the case of explosive roots, that is $|\alpha| > 1$. They find that the bootstrap estimator has the same asymptotic distribution as the least square estimator.[23] It is not clear which estimator has better small sample performance.

There are a few other applications of the bootstrap in dynamic economic models. Runkle (1987) applies a recursive bootstrap procedure to the vector autoregressions (VAR).[24] He shows that his bootstrap does not perform any better than the normal approximations in computing confidence intervals for variance decompositions. Lamoureux and Lastrapes (1990) propose the use of recursive bootstrap in the generalized autoregressive conditional heteroskedasticity (GARCH) models. They consider the following GARCH(1, 1) model.

$$y_i = \alpha y_{i-1} + e_i , \tag{4.10}$$

$$h_i = \gamma + \theta e_{i-1}^2 + \lambda h_{i-1} , \tag{4.11}$$

where $e_i \sim f(0, h_i)$ with any distribution f. They first estimate the GARCH model (4.10) and (4.11) to retrieve $\hat{e}$ and $\hat{h}$. Second, $\hat{e}\hat{h}^{1/2}$ is resampled with replacement to create the bootstrap errors. The division by $\hat{h}^{1/2}$ is to adjust the heteroskedasticity in $\hat{e}$. Third, the bootstrap samples h^* and y^* are recursively computed with e_0 and y_0 specified to be 0 and h_0 to be the unconditional variance of e. These steps are repeated to compute the bootstrap estimates of the parameters. The purpose of their study was to get estimates of the bias and

---

[23] When the errors e_i are normally distributed, the estimators have a variation of the Cauchy distribution.

[24] Instead of computing y_0^* using (4.7), Runkle takes first m (the number of lags in the VAR) observations as given initial conditions. This might account for the disappointing results.

standard error of the bootstrap estimates. There is no comparison with asymptotic standard errors.

During recent years, there has been a lot of interest on testing for structural breaks in time-series models. The inference is complicated by the fact that the break point is unknown. Christiano (1992) derives small sample critical values using the bootstrap methods to test the hypothesis of no break in the trend in GNP. He argues that the standard critical values for testing the presence of a break are severely biased in favor of rejecting the no-break null hypothesis. He shows that in the case he studied, the conventional 5% critical value is 3.1, whereas the correct 5% critical value is closer to 5.0. If the break date is selected to maximize the *F*-statistic for a trend break, the 5% critical value is closer to 10.0.

4.3. Limited dependent variables

In many econometric applications, the dependent variable of the regression model is partially observed (binary, discrete, censored, truncated, etc.). For a discussion of the different types of models used in econometric work, see Maddala (1983). When the dependent variable is not fully observed, bootstrap methods can be a very useful tool because the small sample distributions are not known (even when the underlying distribution is known). However, the residual-resampling standard bootstrap introduced in Section 2 is not appropriate for limited dependent variable cases since the residuals have an incomplete distribution.

The first paper in this area is by Efron (1981a) who proposes a general bootstrap procedure for censored data. His method is as follows: (1) resample n pairs of (x_i^*, d_i) from the original sample $\{x_1, x_2, \ldots, x_n\}$ with replacement, where $d_i \equiv 1$ if x_i is not censored, and $d_i \equiv 0$ if x_i is censored, (2) apply a suitable estimation procedure to (x^*, d) to compute the parameter of interest, (3) repeat (1) and (2) m times to compute the bootstrap estimates. Efron (1981a) shows through simulation that the procedure performs reasonably well in finite samples. The estimation method that Efron uses is the non-parametric Kaplan–Meier estimation method. There were no covariates in his study. The data consisted of only observations on x_i (some of which were censored).

Teebagy and Chatterjee (1989) apply Efron's general procedure to logistic regressions. Thus, the estimation is parametric, and interest lies in testing the significance of the several covariates. They consider the model

$$I_i = \beta X_i + u_i, \tag{4.12}$$

where u_i is IID and has a logistic distribution, I_i takes 0 or 1. They first resample pairs of (I_i, X_i) with replacement from the original sample to create a bootstrap sample (I^*, X^*). Second, logit MLE is applied to (I^*, X^*). This procedure is repeated to compute the bootstrap estimator of β. The Monte Carlo study they conduct shows that (1) the bootstrap consistently overestimates the true value of the standard errors while the asymptotic estimate using Fisher information matrix consistently underestimates it in small samples, (2) the bootstrap standard errors are substantially closer to the true values than the asymptotic standard errors in small samples.

Adkins (1990b) estimates bootstrap standard errors in a probit model, $I_i = \beta X_i + u_i$, given that u_i has an IID normal distribution with mean zero. He considered bootstrap estimation because it was argued by Griffiths et al. (1987), that the small sample performance of probit MLE was unsatisfactory. His resampling plan is different from that of Teebagy–Chatterjee. The steps are:

(1) estimate $\hat{\beta}$ by probit MLE,
(2) generate a vector of uniform random numbers $u^* \sim [0, 1]$,
(3) generate I^* by

$$I_i^* = \begin{cases} 1 & \text{if } 0 \leqslant u_i^* \leqslant \Phi(x_i\hat{\beta}), \\ 0 & \text{if } \Phi(x_i\hat{\beta}) < u_i^* \leqslant 1, \end{cases} \qquad (4.13)$$

(4) compute a new $\hat{\beta}$ using I^*, and
(5) repeat (2)–(4) m times to compute the bootstrap standard errors.
Adkins (1990b) finds that his results contradict those of Griffiths et al., showing that the conventional MLE is satisfactory even in small samples. He also argues that his results are different from those of Teebagy–Chatterjee in that the bootstrap method is not superior to MLE. Of course, the procedures used to generate the bootstrap samples are different.[25]

Two points should be noted about the application of bootstrap methods to parametric binary response models, e.g., logit, probit, etc. First, the bootstrap methods are expected to be less effective in the parametric binary response models. The bootstrap methods for these models are based on a particular statistical distributions: logistic distribution for logit and normal distribution for probit. This voids the most important advantage of bootstrap, which is that it is distribution-free. Second, the benefit from bootstrap methods, in most cases of parametric binary response models, is only for small sample properties. In large samples, parametric bootstrap cannot be better than the ML estimation which gives asymptotically efficient estimators. Thus, bootstrap may not be useful unless the sample size is small, or some non-parametric approach is followed as in Efron (1981a). One interesting extension would be that of the Kaplan–Meier estimator with covariates. Another point worth mentioning is the one that is stated at the beginning, namely, the concentration of attention on standard errors (in both the Teebagy–Chatterjee study and the Adkins study). More attention needs to be developed to bootstrapping the t-statistics.

---

[25] Brownstone and Small (1989) investigate three estimators for the nested logit model: the sequential estimator, FIML, and LML (linearized ML). They compare the three estimators by a Monte Carlo study. They talk of the bootstrap method to get finite sample standard errors but do not describe how the bootstrap is to be implemented in the model.

Discriminant analysis is another technique often used in empirical work in economics and finance. The linear discriminant function is related to the linear probability model (see Maddala, 1983, Chapter 2) and the logistic discriminant function to the logit model. Often we not only need estimates of the misclassification probabilities but also the standard errors of these estimates. Chatterji and Chatterjee (1983) suggest the use of bootstrap methods in the analysis of the linear discriminant function. This method needs to be extended to the logit and probit models.

Manski and Thomson (1986) study the use of bootstrap in the maximum score estimation of binary response models. For this estimator the asymptotic distribution in intractable. Using the same bootstrap procedure as Teebagy and Chatterjee (1989), they find that the bootstrap standard errors are very close to the true ones. It may be worth noting that the asymptotic distribution of Manski's maximum score estimator is now known (although it was not at the time of the Manski–Thompson work). Roughly speaking, the normalized, centered estimator is distributed asymptotically as the maximum of Brownian motion with quadratic drift. The distribution is non-normal and highly intractable.[26] However, knowing the asymptotic standard error of the estimator is not helpful since the distribution is not normal. See Kim and Pollard (1990).

An illustration of the use of bootstrap in more complicated limited dependent variable models in the paper by Flood (1985). He applies the augmented bootstrap method to the simultaneous equation tobit model. He argues that whereas most of the other applications of bootstrap were concerned with getting small-sample standard errors (in contrast to asymptotic standard error that can be obtained from theory) his application of bootstrap to a model for which no asymptotic standard errors are available (which is, however, not true). He compares the bootstrap estimation and the two-stage estimation introduced by Nelson and Olson (1978). To clarify his method, let us consider the following simple tobit model rather than the system of tobit equations, he considers,

$$z_i = \beta X_i + u_i \,,$$
$$y_i = \begin{cases} z_i & \text{if } z_i > 0 \,, \\ 0 & \text{if } z_i \leq 0 \,, \end{cases} \tag{4.14}$$

where u_i is IID normal with mean zero. Flood's augmented bootstrap procedure is the following. First, estimate the model by tobit MLE and compute $\hat{u}^+$, where $\hat{u}_i^+$ are the residuals for the observations for which y_i is positive. Second, an augmented residual vector $\hat{u}$ is constructed where $\hat{u} = [\hat{u}^+ \ : \ -\hat{u}^+]$. If the total sample size is n and $z_i > 0$ for r observations, then this vector $\hat{u}$ will be of order $2r$. Third, $\hat{u}$ is resampled with replacement to create a bootstrap sample u^* of size n. Fourth, z^* is constructed using u^* and $\hat{\beta}$. Fifth, $y^*_i = \max(z^*_i, 0)$ and used to compute the first bootstrap estimator of β. The procedure is repeated to

---

[26] This was pointed out to us by Joel Horowitz.

estimate the bootstrap standard error of β. Flood (1985) finds, through simulation, that the augmented bootstrap gives standard errors that are close to the true values.

As shown thus far, the applications of bootstrap to models with limited dependent variables have used a variety of different (sometimes ad hoc) sampling schemes. The relative merits of these methods need to be studied. The key question is how to resample the bootstrap errors to preserve the information on both the underlying relationship and the censoring (or any other limited observability). There is considerable literature on 'generalized residuals' in these models. Resampling of generalized residuals appears to be an important alternative (results will be reported in another paper).

Quite a bit of work on limited dependent variable models is concerned with endogenously stratified samples and samples with self-selection (see Maddala, 1983, Section 6.10 and Chapter 9). Rao and Wu (1988) discuss extensions of the simple bootstrap to the case of complex survey data (stratified samples, cluster samples and so on). However, the stratification they consider is exogenous stratification whereas the econometric literature is concerned with endogenous stratification. Bootstrap methods need further modifications for these models.

Models with discrete data are widely used in econometric work. See Cameron and Trivedi (1986) for a survey. Rao (1973, Chapter 5) discusses in detail estimation of multinomial models. Many of the large sample procedures suggested can be studied further using the bootstrap.

4.4. Simultaneous equations models

When the econometric model has more than one endogenous variable, unbiased estimators of the coefficients are not available. This is a situation where bootstrap can be applied to improve the finite sample properties of estimators. Freedman (1984) discusses bootstrapping the two-stage least squares estimation (2SLS) in simultaneous equation models. Let us consider the following simple system of equations.

$$y_i = \alpha z_i + \beta X_i + u_i , \tag{4.15}$$

$$z_i = \gamma y_i + \delta X_i + v_i , \tag{4.16}$$

where y and z are endogenous and X is exogenous. The error terms u_i and v_i are assumed to be IID with zero means. Freedman (1984) suggests to resample the estimated residuals with the instrumental variables to preserve any possible relationship between them. Specifically, for the first equation (4.15), estimate the model by 2SLS and compute the estimated residual $\hat{u}$ and the instrument $\hat{z}$. Second, resample $(z^*, \hat{z}^*, \hat{u}^*)$. By resampling the data this way, any relationship between instruments and disturbances is preserved. Third, using z^* and $\hat{u}^*$, construct y^* according to (4.15). Fourth, compute the bootstrap $\hat{\alpha}$ and $\hat{\beta}$ using y^*, z^* and $\hat{z}^*$. Repeat this to complete bootstrap estimation. Similar procedure is applied for the second equation. Freedman (1984) shows that this procedure is asymptotically correct.

Freedman and Peters (1984b) apply a similar bootstrap procedure to the three-stage least square estimation (3SLS). Since the 3SLS estimate the whole system, the error terms $(\hat{u}^*, \hat{v}^*)$ are resampled simultaneously. The remaining procedure is identical. In this example, the bootstrap is not superior to the asymptotic formula in a small sample ($n = 24$). Park (1985) applies the bootstrap method to 2SLS estimation of Klein's model. He also finds that the bootstrap leads to little improvements in a small sample ($n = 21$).

Daggett and Freedman (1985) apply the bootstrap method to compute standard errors of two-stage least squares estimators in a simultaneous equations model of the tomato industry. They find that the conventional asymptotic standard errors are off by as much as 40 percent, *in either direction*. Thus, it is not true, in general, that the conventional asymptotic standard errors are always downward biased.[27] The computations in this example were done in response to a litigation that depended on the significance of the coefficient of the post harvest supply price. The conventional standard errors for the coefficient were biased downward by 39 percent, thus, reversing earlier conclusions.

4.5. Forecasting problems

One of the most important objectives of econometric models is to use them for forecasting. The usual procedure is to get a point forecast and its standard error. Consider first, the linear regression model. The standard textbook formulas are obtained using the normal distribution (or t-distribution) under the assumption that the forecast period explanatory variables are known. Stine (1985) suggests the bootstrap method as an alternative distribution-free method. Stine considers the model

$$y_i = \beta X_i + u_i ,\tag{4.20}$$

where u_i is IID with mean zero. The prediction is for y_{n+1} with a known X_{n+1}. The classical $(1 - 2\alpha)$ prediction interval with normality assumption is $[\hat{\beta} X_{n+1} - t(\alpha)s_f, \hat{\beta} X_{n+1} + t(\alpha)s_f]$, where s_f is the standard error of the forecast. The bootstrap procedure is as follows. First, regress (4.20) and compute $\hat{u}$. Resample $\hat{u}$ to construct a bootstrap sample $\{u_1^*, u_2^*, \ldots, u_n^*, u_{n+1}^*\}$. Use u_{n+1}^* to compute the bootstrap forecast y_{n+1}^* by $y_{n+1}^* = \hat{\beta} X_{n+1} + u_{n+1}^*$. Use $\{u_1^*, u_2^*, \ldots, u_n^*\}$ and $\{y_1^*, y_2^*, \ldots, y_n^*\}$ to compute the bootstrap estimator β^*. Construct the bootstrap forecast error $\text{FE} = y_{n+1}^* - \beta^* X_{n+1}$. Repeat this procedure enough times to construct the bootstrap empirical distribution $F^*(\text{FE})$ of the forecast errors. If we let $F^{*-1}(\alpha)$ denote the 100α percentile of this distribution, then the $(1 - 2\alpha)$ coverage bootstrap prediction interval for

---

[27] See McManus and Rosalsky (1985).

y_{n+1} is: $[\hat{\beta}X_{n+1} + F^{*-1}(\alpha), \hat{\beta}X_{n+1} + F^{*-1}(1-\alpha)]$. Stine (1985) shows through Monte Carlo experiments, that the coverage of bootstrap prediction intervals is very accurate in small samples ($n = 19, 40$). He also shows that the bootstrap intervals obtain the asymptotically correct coverage. Stine (1987) extends this method to forecasting from auto-regressive models. Masarotto (1990) also bootstraps the prediction intervals for autoregressive time series. He shows that the bootstrap prediction interval for autoregressions is asymptotically correct and performs very well in finite samples. Son et al. (1987) also present results from the use of bootstrap forecasting in a second-order autoregression model. They consider multi-period forecasts. The bootstrap standard errors in their study are *lower* than the conventional asymptotic standard errors, particularly for longer horizon forecasts. Peters and Freedman (1985) also use the bootstrap to attach standard errors to multi-period forecasts and to select between alternative model specifications in the context of a dynamic energy demand model fitted by generalized least squares. Using simulation experiments they show that the bootstrap SEs are more reliable than the asymptotic ones. Findley (1986), however, questions this conclusion. He argues that the estimates of mean square forecast error which result from the bootstrap procedure proposed by Freedman and Peters are not significantly more reliable than the large sample estimates which are ill-behaved in small samples. The same arguments apply to VAR models. This does not exclude the possibility that other methods of bootstrapping statistics could prove useful.

Of greater practical importance is the case where the forecast period explanatory variables are not known and they too need to be forecast. In this case the asymptotic standard errors, even with the normality assumption are very difficult to compute. Feldstein (1971) studied this problem with some restrictive assumptions. Here the bootstrap method would be very useful. This has been demonstrated by Bernard and Veall (1987) who apply the bootstrap method to estimate the probability distribution of future electricity demand for Hydro-Quebec. They follow the regression approach of Freedman and Peters (1984b) but allow for serially correlated disturbances and most importantly, the uncertainty in the explanatory variable. The standard econometric approach to this problem has been the use of stochastic simulation, which is somewhat similar in scope to the bootstrap method. For a discussion of the stochastic simulation approach, see Fair (1980).

4.6. Data mining

A common procedure often followed in econometric work is to try a model with several possible explanatory variables, delete the ones that are not significant (or have the 'wrong' signs) and present the final equation with the estimated coefficients and standard errors calculated as if that was the first equation estimated. Lovell (1983) criticized this 'data mining' and argued that even if y and $x, x_2, \ldots, x_k$ are all uncorrelated, by 'data mining' one can get a regression of y on some x_j with a significant coefficient provided k is large. It is well known that the distribution of the final estimates provided by this 'data mining' process is not known. Can bootstrap methods help in this case? If the data mining or regression strategy followed by the researcher is specified, then the bootstrap method can be used by treating the entire regression strategy as a single estimator. To simplify matters suppose we have the equation

$$y = \beta_1 x_1 + \beta_2 x_2 + \varepsilon$$

and we use the following regression strategy: we estimate this equation and if the t-value for $\beta_2 < 1$, we drop x_2 and reestimate the equation to get an estimate of β_1. Otherwise, we get an estimate of β_1 from the equation with both x_1 and x_2. What is the distribution of this conditional omitted variable estimator of β_1?

The way the bootstrap is used is as follows: we estimate the equation by OLS and resample the residuals $\hat{u}_i$ to generate the bootstrap samples. For each of the bootstrap samples (say 200 of them), we follow the same regression strategy (of omitting x_2 if its t-ratio is <1). This gives us the bootstrap distribution of β_1^*. We also get the proportion of samples in which x_2 was dropped.

Freedman, Navidi and Peters (1988) and Dijkstra and Veldkamp (1988) argue that the bootstrap does not work. The problem in the study by Freedman et al. is that the sample size n was 100, and the number of explanatory variables p was 75. This is an extreme case of data mining. In practice p/n is often not more than 0.25. Veall (1992) applies the bootstrap to the example of the deterrent effect of capital punishment to study the impact of data mining on the final results. (In his example, $n = 44$ and the constant and 5 variables are retained. Data mining is done over 7 other variables of which only two are finally retained). This example is further investigated by McAleer and Veall (1989) who use the bootstrap method to get estimates of the standard errors of the 'extreme bounds' advocated by Leamer and Leonard (1983). They argue that the standard errors are large enough to cast doubts on the usefulness of extreme bounds analysis.

Again, there appears, at first sight, a difference of opinion regarding the usefulness of bootstrap methods. However, in this case the negative conclusion is a consequence of a high p/n. Many pretesting problems and omitted variable problems (see Maddala, 1977, pp. 190–191) fall in the category of data mining, and hence, the bootstrap method can be used to analyze these problems, as well.

4.7. Panel data and frontier production models

Two areas of considerable interest to econometricians are panel data models (see Maddala, 1977, Chapter 14) and frontier production models (based on panel data) (see Schmidt and Sickles, 1984). In panel data models a commonly used model is the variance components model given by

$$y_{it} = \beta x_{it} + u_{it} , \qquad \alpha_i \sim \text{IID}(0, \sigma_\alpha^2) ,$$
$$u_{it} = \alpha_i + v_{it} , \qquad v_{it} \sim \text{IID}(0, \sigma_v^2) ,$$
$$\text{Cov}(\alpha_i, v_{it}) = 0 .$$

We then have

$$\text{Cov}(u_{it}, u_{js}) = \begin{cases} \sigma_\alpha^2 + \sigma_v^2 & \text{for } i = j, \ t = s , \\ \sigma_\alpha^2 & \text{for } i = j, \ t \neq s , \\ 0 & \text{for } i \neq j . \end{cases}$$

The standard bootstrap cannot be applied here because simple resampling of $\hat{u}_{it}$ ignores the covariance structure of u_{it}. The correct resampling procedure would be to resample $\hat{\alpha}_i$ and $\hat{v}_{it}$. This can be done only under a distributional assumption on the error components. This was what was done by Bellman et al. (1989). Complex covariance structures like this need modifications in the bootstrap. A multivariate example in which the obvious bootstrap fails is given in Beran and Srivastava (1985).

Simar (1991) presents an application of bootstrap to random effects frontier models with panel data. Hall, Härdle and Simar (1991a,b) use the iterated bootstrap in the estimation of frontier production models with fixed effects. In the problem considered by Hall et al. (1991b), the parameter of interest is the maximum of the intercepts in a fixed effects model. Statistics such as the maximum that lack a normal sampling distribution require more complicated bootstrap methods than the usual weighted average estimators commonly used in econometric work. Hall et al. suggest the use of the iterated bootstrap method for such cases. The iterated bootstrap is discussed in Sections 1.4 and 3.11 of Hall (1992). They illustrate the method with an analysis of the efficiency of railway companies in 19 countries over a period of 14 years (266 observations). The details of the iterated bootstrap procedures are complex and to conserve space, they will not be reproduced here.

4.8. Applications in finance

There are some applications of bootstrap methods in the finance area. All of them, however, use (sometimes incorrectly) the simplest bootstrap applicable to IID errors discussed in Section 2. We shall quote here only a few of these applications.

Marais (1984) is the earliest application. It is addressed to the problem of analyzing the prediction errors from the market model. Shea (1989a) uses bootstrap to study excess volatility in the stock market, and Shea (1989b) uses the bootstrap method to study the empirical reliability of the present-value relation. Hsieh and Miller (1990) use the bootstrap in a study of the relationship between margins and volatility. Chatterjee and Pari (1990) use bootstrap to study the question of how many factors need to be included in applications of the APT (arbitrage pricing theory). Levich and Thomas (1991) use the bootstrap to study the statistical significance of the profits generated by different trading rules in the foreign exchange market. The last study is an unusual application of the bootstrap since there are no statistical models. The data are resampled holding the initial and final observation fixed, and the profits from the different trading rules are generated. One possible problem with this is that the time-series structure is not preserved in the re-sampling, and the trading rules exploit this time-series structure. However, the results can be used to compare different trading rules if they all use the same bootstrap samples.

4.9. Specification tests

One of the areas of active research in econometrics is that of specification testing. Two of the most commonly used tests are the Hausman test and White's information matrix test (White, 1982). The latter test, which is an omnibus test, has been found to present some small-sample problems. In particular, the true size of the test often exceeds greatly the nominal size derived from asymptotic theory (the true size can exceed 0.50 when the nominal size is 0.05). Chesher and Spady (1991) propose dealing with this problem by obtaining the critical value for the IM test from the Edgeworth expansion through $O(n^{-1})$ of the finite sample distribution of the test statistic. However, this approach involves tedious algebra, and moreover, the approach may not be valid if consistent estimates are substituted for the unknown parameters in any but the highest order term. In the examples that Chesher and Spady consider, the IM test statistic is pivotal – that is under the null hypothesis, the finite sample distribution of the test statistic is independent of the parameters of the model being tested.

Horowitz (1991a) suggests a bootstrap method to obtain small-sample critical values for the IM test. This does not involve tedious algebra, nor the limitations of the Edgeworth expansions. He suggests a modification of the simple bootstrap that is applicable even if the IM test statistic is not pivotal since in practice, it is very difficult to determine whether the IM test statistic is pivotal. Horowitz also presents results from a Monte Carlo study for binary probit models and tobit models and shows that the bootstrap corrects the size bias of the IM test. Bootstrap methods have also been suggested for making Bartlett type corrections to the likelihood-ratio, Wald and Rao-'s score tests, as discussed in Rocke (1989) and Rayner (1990a). They have also been used for two-step GLS estimation methods, as discussed in Rayner (1990b). Horowitz and Savin (1992) use the bootstrap method to obtain finite-sample critical values for the Wald test and show that the Wald test can be superior to the LR test despite the lack of invariance.

4.10. Bayesian bootstraps

Since Bayesian methods are commonly used in econometrics, we shall discuss briefly the application of bootstrap methods in Bayesian inference. Resampling methods have been in use among Bayesians for a long time, since the paper by Geisser (1975). Computer intensive methods have also been popular since the paper by Kloek and Van Dijk (1978). The Gibbs sampling method advocated in Gelfand and Smith (1990) is similar in spirit to the bootstrap. Also, the term 'Bayesian bootstrap' occurs in Rubin (1981). But the direct application of the bootstrap in Bayesian inference is in Boos and Monohan (1986).

The usual approach to Bayesian inference is based on a specification of the likelihood function. The Bayesian posterior with given prior $\pi(\theta)$ is given by

$$\pi(\theta \mid \text{data}) \propto \pi(\theta)L(\text{data} \mid \theta) \, ,$$

where $L(\text{data} \mid \theta)$ is the likelihood function. Boos and Monohan suggest replacing this by an estimated posterior

$$\hat{\pi}(\theta \mid \text{data}) \propto \pi(\theta) \cdot \hat{L}_{\text{B}}(\text{data} \mid \theta)$$

where $\hat{L}_{\text{B}}(\text{data} \mid \theta)$ is based on bootstrap equation of the density of $(\hat{\theta} - \theta)$. A robust estimator $\hat{\theta}$ protects against heavy-tailed error distributions and the bootstrap makes this approach feasible in small samples.

An alternative approach to approximate Bayesian inference is suggested by Newton (1991) and Newton and Raftery (1991). They introduce the *weighted likelihood bootstrap* (WLB) method which they claim suggests natural bootstrap solutions to problem of inference in state–space models that may be non-Gaussian and non-linear and long memory time-series models.

4.11. Other econometric applications

There are several other areas where bootstrap methods have been used. Here we shall cite a few. Williams (1986) applies bootstrap to a seemingly unrelated regression model. His main result is that the parametrically estimated standard errors are biased downwards by a factor of two. This is important and changes the inference in an anti-trust case (as in the example considered earlier by Daggett and Freedman, 1985).

Rocke (1989) also studies bootstrap methods is seemingly unrelated regression models.[28] He suggests computing the Bartlett adjustment to the LR test statistic using bootstrap methods. He provides illustrations of his method, which performed very well, with detectable problems only in the presence of lagged dependent variables.

Though James–Stein type estimators have been demonstrated to be superior to least squares estimators under squared error loss, they have not been used

---

[28] A brief survey of seemingly unrelated regression models is in Srivastava and Dwivedi (1979).

much in empirical work since it is difficult to derive their sampling distributions. Brownstone (1990) and Adkins (1990a) show that bootstrap methods can be used to derive the sampling distributions of these estimators. For this line of research, see Adkins (1990c) and the references therein.

Srivastava and Singh (1989) use the bootstrap method to obtain confidence interval for the constant term in a multiplicative Cobb–Douglas model – a model often used in econometric work on production functions. In this model, the problem of estimating the constant term and finding a confidence interval for it had always presented some problems.

Dielman and Pfaffenberger (1986) consider bootstrapping the least absolute deviation (LAD) regression model (also known as L_1 model). This model can be estimated by an iterative weighted least squares method (see Maddala, 1977, pp. 310–311), but small sample standard errors are not available. The bootstrap method is useful in this case. Dielman and Pfaffenberger compare the bootstrap standard errors with the asymptotic standard errors and also compare hypothesis testing results using the bootstrap and the asymptotic results.

Another promising application of bootstrap methods is the bootstrap estimation of non-parametric regressions. Bootstrap estimation has been found useful in regression smoothing and kernel estimation. See Härdle and Bowman (1988), Moschini et al. (1988), Härdle and Mammen (1990a) and Härdle and Marron (1991). Härdle and Mammen (1990b) use bootstrap method for comparing parametric and non-parametric fits. A statistic often used is the integrated squared difference between these curves. They show that the standard way of bootstrapping this statistic fails. They suggest an alternative called the 'wild bootstrap'.

Stoffer and Wall (1991) apply bootstrap methods to investigate the properties of parameter estimates from state–space models estimated by the Kalman's filter. They find, on the basis of Monte Carlo simulation, the bootstrap to be of definitive value over conventional asymptotics. In particular the asymptotic distribution is normal whereas the bootstrap empirical distribution was often markedly skewed.

5. Conclusions

We have presented a review of the several applications of bootstrap in econometrics. It is clear that almost every type of model used in econometric work has been bootstrapped: regression models with heteroskedastic and autocorrelated errors, seemingly unrelated regression models, models with lagged dependent variables, state–space models and the Kalman filter, panel data models, simultaneous equation models, logit, probit, tobit, and other limited dependent variable models, GARCH models, robust estimators (LAD estimators), data mining, pretesting, James–Stein estimation, semi-parametric estimators, and so on. Estimation of standard errors of parameters, confidence intervals for parameters, as well as generating forecast intervals (for multiperiod forecasts), have been considered.

Most of the studies concentrate on comparison of asymptotic standard errors with bootstrap standard errors. This is not sufficient because the asymptotic distribution is normal, but the bootstrap distribution is often skewed. It is not true that one can use the t-values (with the bootstrap standard errors) for constructing confidence intervals or test statistics. The best procedure, as argued by Beran (1988) and Hall (1986a) and several others in the statistical literature, is to bootstrap an asymptotically pivotal statistic (e.g., a t-statistic) based on a $\sqrt{n}$ consistent estimator of the variance. This yields more accurate critical values for tests which can also be used to construct confidence intervals. Thus, the procedure of computing bootstrap standard errors should be skipped completely. There are a few illustrations of this in the econometric literature (see for instance Horowitz, 1991a,b), but by far, the econometric literature concentrates on standard errors.

In some models, the asymptotic theory of the estimator is intractable (Manski's maximum score estimator). In such cases bootstrap provides a tractable method of deriving confidence intervals and so on. There is the question of how valid this procedure is. It is difficult to answer this question, but one can check the validity of the bootstrap procedure by Monte Carlo results. For instance, Horowitz (1991b) bootstrapped a smoothed maximum score estimator, which is not $\sqrt{n}$ consistent. But Monte Carlo evidence suggests that critical values based on the bootstrap-t are much more accurate than those obtained from first order asymptotic theory. There are also some cases, as in Athreya (1987), for the heavy tailed distribution and Basawa et al. (1991a) for the unit root first order autoregressive process, where the asymptotic distribution and the limit of the bootstrap distribution are not the same. In such cases the naive bootstrap needs to be modified (Basawa et al., 1991b).

The computational advances (described in Section 3), like the use of balanced sampling, importance sampling, antithetic variates, and so on, do not seem to have been implemented in econometric work. These methods, if properly used, would substantially increase the efficiency of bootstrap computations, and it would be possible to use more bootstrap samples with no extra computational burden. Also, it would facilitate investigation of the several bootstrap procedures that have been suggested with Monte Carlo experiments.

There appears to be a conflict in the conclusions regarding the usefulness of bootstrap in several of the areas we have reviewed (as noted in the case of models with autocorrelated errors, lagged dependent variables, logit and probit models, data mining, and so on). As we noted, different investigators have used different bootstrap methods. Also, some have used the bootstrap to compute standard errors. Others have bootstrapped the t-statistics. The latter is the more desirable procedure.

The theoretical advances in bootstrap have mostly concentrated on models with IID errors. More theoretical work needs to be done for the models considered here. The case of dynamic econometric models needs further investigation because it has been demonstrated that the simple bootstrap fails in these models.

On important point to remember is that bootstrapping defective models is of no value. Bootstrap does not rescue bad models. A lot of recent econometric work is concerned with diagnostic checking and specification testing. Diagnostic checks should be applied to a model before it is bootstrapped. Bernard and Veall (1987), for instance, apply several diagnostic tests before computing bootstrap prediction intervals.

As the quote at the beginning of this paper states, the cost of computing relative to proving theorems has fallen, and economics suggests that we use more computing than theorizing. This does not mean that all theory should be dumped and all that students in econometrics need to learn is bootstrap. In fact, it is easy to jump on the computer and mechanically apply a bootstrap procedure when theory suggests that some other type of bootstrap ought to be used or that the bootstrap method does not work. Before one applies the bootstrap procedure, one should ask the following basic questions:

(i) When can I apply the bootstrap? What do I need to know about an estimator?

(ii) What is the appropriate bootstrap procedure for my problem?

(iii) Why does the bootstrap work in practice?

Acknowledgement

We would like to thank Martin Bailey, Matt Cushing, Stephen Donald, Joel Horowitz, In-Moo Kim and C. R. Rao for helpful comments. Responsibility for any errors is solely ours.

References

Adkins, L. C. (1990a). Small sample performance of jackknife confidence intervals for the James–Stein estimator. *J. Statist. Comput. Simulation* **19**, 401–418.

Adkins, L. (1990b). Small sample inference in the probit model. Oklahoma State University Working paper.

Adkins, L. C. (1990c). Finite sample moments of a bootstrap estimator of the James–Stein rule. Oklahoma State University Working paper.

Akahira, M. (1983). Asymptotic deficiency of the jackknife estimator. *Austral. J. Statist.* **25**, 123–129.

Athreya, K. (1983). Strong law for the bootstrap. *Statist. Probab. Lett.* **1**, 147–150.

Athreya, K. (1987). Bootstrap of the mean in the infinite variance case. *Ann. Statist.* **15**, 724–731.

Atkinson, S. E. and J. Tschirhart (1986). Flexible modelling of time to failure in risky careers. *Rev. Econom. Statist.* **68**, 558–566.

Babu, G. J. (1989). Applications of edgeworth expansions to bootstrap. A review. In: Y. Dodge, ed., *Statistical Data Analysis and Inference*. Elsevier Science, North-Holland, New York, 223–237.

Basawa, I. V., A. K. Mallik, W. P. McCormick and R. L. Taylor (1989). Bootstrapping explosive autoregressive processes. *Ann. Statist.* **17**, 1479–1486.

Basawa, I. V., A. K. Mallik, W. P. McCormick and R. L. Taylor (1990). Asymptotic bootstrap validity for finite Markov chains. *Comm. Statist. Theory Methods* **19**, 1493–1510.

Basawa, I. V., A. K. Malik, W. P. McCormick and R. L. Taylor (1991a). Bootstrapping unstable first order autoregressive processes. *Ann. Statist.* **19**, 1098–1101.

Basawa, I. V., A. K. Mallik, W. P. McCormick and R. L. Taylor (1991b). Bootstrap test of significance and sequential bootstrap estimation for unstable first order autoregressive processes. *Comm. Statist. Theory Methods* **20**, 1015–1026.

Bellmann, L., J. Breitung and J. Wagner (1989). Bias correction and bootstrapping of error component models for panel data: Theory and applications. *Empirical Econom.* **14**, 329–342.

Beran, R. (1987). Prepivoting to reduce level error of confidence sets. *Biometrika* **74**, 457–468.

Beran, R. (1988). Prepivoting test statistics: A bootstrap view of asymptotic refinements. *J. Amer. Statist. Assoc.* **83**, 687–697.

Beran, R. (1990). Refining bootstrap simultaneous confidence sets. *J. Amer. Statist. Assoc.* **85**, 417–426.

Beran, R. and M. Srivastava (1985). Bootstrap tests and confidence regions for functions of a covariance matrix. *Ann. Statist.* **13**, 95–115.

Beran, R. J., L. Le Cam and P. W. Millar (1987). Convergence of stochastic empirical measures. *J. Multivariate Anal.* **23**, 159–168.

Bernard, J.-T. and M. R. Veall (1987). The probability distribution of future demand. *J. Business Econom. Statist.* **5**, 417–424.

Bickel, P. J. and D. A. Freedman (1981). Some asymptotic theory for the bootstrap. *Ann. Statist.* **9**, 1196–1217.

Boos, D. D. and J. F. Monahan (1986). Bootstrap methods using prior information. *Biometrika* **73**, 77–83.

Bose, A. (1988). Edgeworth correction by bootstrap in autoregressions. *Ann. Statist.* **16**, 1709–1722.

Brown, R. L., J. Durbin and J. M. Evans (1975). Techniques for testing the constancy of regression relationships over time. *J. Roy. Statist. Soc. Ser. B* **37**, 149–192.

Brownstone, D. (1990). Bootstrapping improved estimators for linear regression models. *J. Econometrics* **44**, 171–187.

Brownstone, D. and K. A. Small (1989). Efficient estimation of nested logit model. *J. Business Econom. Statist.* **7**, 67–74.

Butler, J. S., K. H. Anderson and R. V. Burkhauser (1986). Testing the relationship between work and health: A bivariate hazard model. *Econom. Lett.* **20**, 383–386.

Cameron, A. C. and P. K. Trivedi (1986). Econometric models based on count data: Comparisons and applications of some estimators and tests. *J. Appl. Econometrics* **1**, 29–53.

Chatterjee, S. (1986). Bootstrapping ARMA models: Some simulations. *IEEE Trans. Software Man Cybernet.* **16**, 294–299.

Chatterjee, S. and R. A. Pari (1990). Bootstrapping the numbers of factors in the arbitrage pricing theory. *J. Financ. Res.* **13**, 15–21.

Chatterji, S. and S. Chatterjee (1983). Estimation of misclassification probabilities by bootstrap methods. *Comm. Statist. Simulation Comput.* **12**, 645–656.

Chesher, A. and R. Spady (1991). Asymptotic expansion of the information matrix test statistic. *Econometrica* **59**, 787–815.

Christiano, L. J. (1992). Searching for a break in GNP. *J. Business Econom. Statist.* **10**, 237–250.

Cragg, J. G. (1983). More efficient estimation in the presence of heteroskedasticity of unknown form. *Econometrica* **51**, 751–763.

Cragg, J. (1987). Adaptation of the jackknife to time-series models. The University of British Columbia Discussion Paper No. 87-24.

Daggett, R. S. and D. A. Freedman (1985). Econometrics and the law: A case study in the proof of antitrust damages. In: L. M. Le Cam and R. A. Olshen, eds., *Proc. Berkeley Conf. in Honor of Jerzy Neyman and Jack Kiefer*, Vol. 1. Wadsworth, Belmont, CA.

Daniels, H. E. (1954). Saddlepoint approximations in statistics. *Ann. Math. Statist.* **25**, 631–650.

Datt, G. (1988). Estimating Engel elasticities with bootstrap standard errors. *Oxford Bull. Econom. Statist.* **50**, 325–333.

Davidson, R. and J. G. Mackinnon (1990). Regression-based methods for using control and antithetic variates in monte carlo experiments. Queen's University Discussion Paper No. 781.

Davison, A. C. (1988). Discussion of paper by D. V. Hinkley. *J. Roy. Statist. Soc. Ser. B* **50**, 356–357.

Davison, A. C. and D. V. Hinkley (1988). Saddlepoint approximations in resampling methods. *Biometrika* **75**(3), 417–431.

Davison, A. C., D. V. Hinkley and E. Schechtman (1986). Efficient bootstrap simulation. *Biometrika* **73**(3), 555–566.

De Wet, T. and J. W. J. Van Wyk (1986). Bootstrap confidence intervals for regression coefficients when the residuals are dependent. *J. Statist. Comput. Simulation* **23**, 317–327.

Diciccio, T. J. and J. P. Romano (1988). A review of bootstrap confidence intervals. *J. Roy. Statist. Soc. Ser. B* **50**, 338–354.

Diciccio, T. and R. Tibshirani (1987). Bootstrap confidence intervals and bootstrap approximations. *J. Amer. Statist. Assoc.* **82**, 163–170.

Dielman, T. E. and R. C. Pfaffenberger (1986). Bootstrapping in least absolute value regression: An application to hypothesis testing. In: *ASA Proc. Business Econom. Statist.* 628–630.

Dijkstra, T. K. and J. H. Veldkamp (1988). Data-driven selection of regressors and the bootstrap. In: T. K. Dijkstra, ed., *On Model Uncertainty and its Statistical Implications*. Springer, Berlin, 17–38.

Do, K. and P. Hall (1991). On importance re-sampling for the bootstrap. *Biometrika* **78**, 161–167.

Eakin, K., D. P. McMillen and M. J. Buono (1990). Constructing confidence intervals using bootstrap: An application to a multiproduct cost function. *Rev. Econom. Statist.* **72**, 339–344.

Efron, B. (1979). Bootstrap methods: Another look at the jackknife. *Ann. Statist.* **7**, 1–26.

Efron, B. (1981a). Censored data and the bootstrap. *J. Amer. Statist. Assoc.* **76**, 312–319.

Efron, B. (1982). The jackknife, the bootstrap and other resampling plans. CBMS-NSF Regional Conference Series in Applied Mathematics, Monograph 38. Society for Industrial and Applied Mathematics, Philadelphia, PA.

Efron, B. (1987). Better bootstrap confidence intervals. *J. Amer. Stat. Assoc.* **82**, 171–200.

Efron, B. (1990). More efficient bootstrap computations. *J. Amer. Statist. Assoc.* **85**, 79–89.

Efron, B. and R. Tibshirani (1986). Bootstrap methods for standard errors, confidence intervals, and other measures of statistical accuracy. *Statist. Sci.* **1**, 54–77.

Fair, R. C. (1980). Estimating the expected predictive accuracy of econometric models. *Internat. Econom. Rev.* **21**, 355–378.

Feldstein, M. S. (1971). The error of forecast in econometric models when the forecast-period exogenous variables are stochastic. *Econometrica* **39**, 55–60.

Ferretti, N. and J. Romo (1992). Bootstrapping unit root AR(1) models. Working Paper #92-22. Division of Economics. Universidad Carlos III de Madrid.

Fieller, E. C. and H. O. Hartley (1954). Sampling with control variables. *Biometrika* **41**, 494–501.

Findley, D. F. (1986). On bootstrap estimate of forecast mean square errors for autoregressive processes. In: M. Allen, ed., *Proc. 17th Sympos. on the Interface*. North-Holland, Amsterdam, 11–17.

Flood, L. (1985). Using bootstrap to obtain standard errors of system tobit coefficients. *Econom. Lett.* **19**, 339–342.

Freedman, D. A. (1981). Bootstrapping regression models. *Ann. Statist.* **9**, 1218–1228.

Freedman, D. (1984). On bootstrapping two-stage least-squares estimates in stationary linear models. *Ann. Statist.* **12**, 827–842.

Freedman, D. A., W. Navidi and S. C. Peters (1988). On the impact of variable selection in fitting regression equations. In: T. K. Dijkstra, ed., *On Model Uncertainty and its Statistical Implications*. Springer, Berlin, 1–16.

Freedman, D. A. and S. C. Peters (1984a). Bootstrapping a regression equation: Some empirical results. *J. Amer. Statist. Assoc.* **79**(385), 97–106.

Freedman, D. A. and S. C. Peters (1984b). Bootstrapping an econometric model: Some empirical results. *J. Business Econom. Statist.* **2**(2), 150–158.

Geisser, S. (1975). The predictive sample re-use method with applications. *J. Amer. Statist. Assoc.* **70**, 320–328.

Gelfand, A. E. and A. F. M. Smith (1990). Sampling based approaches to calculating marginal densities. *J. Amer. Statist. Assoc.* **85**, 398–409.

George, P. J., E. H. Oksanen and M. R. Veall (1988). Analytic and bootstrap approaches to testing a market saturation hypothesis. Manuscript, McMaster University.

Gleason, J. R. (1988). Algorithms for balanced bootstrap simulations. *Amer. Statist.* **42**, 263–266.

Graham, R. L., D. V. Hinkley, P. W. John and S. Shi (1990). Balanced design of bootstrap simulations. *J. Roy. Statist. Soc. Ser. B* **52**, 185–202.

Green, R., W. Hahn and D. Rocke (1987). Standard errors for elasticities: A comparison of bootstrap and asymptotic standard errors. *J. Business Econom. Statist.* **5**, 145–149.

Griffiths, W. E., R. C. Hill and P. J. Pope (1987). Small sample properties of probit model estimators. *J. Amer. Statist. Assoc.* **399**, 929–937.

Hall, P. (1986a). On the bootstrap and confidence intervals. *Ann. Statist.* **14**, 1431–1452.

Hall, P. (1986b). On the number of bootstrap simulations required to construct a confidence intervals. *Ann. Statist.* **14**, 1453–1462.

Hall, P. (1988a). Theoretical comparison of bootstrap confidence intervals. *Ann. Statist.* **16**, 927–953.

Hall, P. (1988b). Unusual properties of bootstrap confidence intervals in regression problems. *Probab. Theory Related Fields* **81**, 247–273.

Hall, P. (1989). Antithetic resampling for the bootstrap. *Biometrika* **76**, 713–724.

Hall, P. (1992). *The Bootstrap and Edgeworth Expansions.* Springer, New York.

Hall, P., W. Härdle and L. Simar (1991a). On the inconsistency of bootstrap distribution estimators. CORE Discussion Paper No. 9120.

Hall, P., W. Härdle and L. Simar (1991b). Iterated bootstrap with applications to frontier models. CORE Discussion Paper No. 9121.

Hammersley, J. M. and K. W. Mauldin (1956). A new Monte Carlo technique: Antithetic variates. *Proc. Cambridge Philos. Soc.* **52**, 449–475.

Hammersley, J. M. and J. G. Morton (1956). General principles of antithetic variates. *Proc. Cambridge Philos. Soc.* **52**, 476–481.

Härdle, W. and A. Bowman (1988). Bootstrapping in nonparametric regression: Local adaptive smoothing and confidence bands. *J. Amer. Statist. Assoc.* **83**, 102–110.

Härdle, W. and E. Mammen (1990a). Bootstrap methods in nonparametric regression. CORE Discussion Paper No. 9049.

Härdle, W. and E. Mammen (1990b). Comparing non-parametric vs. parametric regression fits. CORE Discussion Paper No. 9065.

Härdle, W. and J. S. Marron (1991). Bootstrap simultaneous error bars for nonparametric regression. *Ann. Statist.* **19**, 778–796.

Hinkley, D. V. and S. Shi (1989). Importance sampling and the nested bootstrap. *Biometrika* **76**, 435–446.

Horn, S. D., R. A. Horn and D. B. Duncan (1975). Estimating heteroskedastic variances in linear models. *J. Amer. Statist. Assoc.* **70**, 380–385.

Horowitz, J. L. (1991a). Boot-strap based critical values for the information matrix test. Working paper #91-21, University of Iowa.

Horowitz, J. L. (1991b). Semiparametric estimation of a work-trip mode choice model. *J. Econometrics*, to appear.

Horowitz, J. L. and N. E. Savin (1992). Non-invariance of the Wald test: The boostrap to the rescue. Working paper 92-04, University of Iowa, Department of Economics.

Hsieh, D. A. and M. H. Miller (1990). Margin regulation and stock market volatility. *J. Finance* **45**, 3–29.

Jeong, J. and G. S. Maddala (1992). Heteroskedasticity and a nonparametric test for rationality of survey data using the weighted double bootstrap. Paper presented at the European Economic Society Meeting in Brussels.

Johns, M. V. (1988). Importance sampling for bootstrap confidence intervals. *J. Amer. Statist. Assoc.* **83**(403), 709–714.

Kim, J. and D. Pollard (1990). Cube root asymptotics. *Ann. Statist.* **18**, 191–219.

King, M. L. and D. E. A. Giles (1984). Autocorrelation pre-testing in the linear model. *J. Econometrics* **25**, 35–48.

Kiviet, J. F. (1984). Bootstrap inference in lagged-dependent variable models. University of Amsterdam, Working Paper.

Kloek, T. and H. K. Van Dijk (1978). Bayesian estimation of equation system parameters: an application of integration by Monte Carlo. *Econometrica* **46**, 1–19.

Knight, K. (1989). On the bootstrap on the sample mean in the infinite variance case. *Ann. Statist.* **17**, 1168–1175.

Korajczyk, R. (1985). The pricing of forward contracts for foreign exchange. *J. Politic. Econom.* **93**, 346–368.

Künsch, H. R. (1989). The jackknife and the bootstrap for general stationary observations. *Ann. Statist.* **17**, 1217–1241.

Lahiri, S. N. (1991). Second order optimality of stationary bootstrap. *Statist. Probab. Lett.* **11**, 335–341.

Lahiri, S. N. (1992). Edgeworth correction by 'moving block' bootstrap for stationary and nonstationary data. In: R. LePage and L. Billard, eds., *Exploring the Limits of Bootstrap*. Wiley, New York, 183–214.

Lamoureux, C. G. and W. D. Lastrapes (1990). Persistence in variance, structural change and the GARCH model. *J. Business Econom. Statist.* **8**, 225–234.

Leamer, E. E. and H. Leonard (1983). Reporting the fragility of regression estimates. *Rev. Econom. Statist.* **65**, 306–317.

Levich, R. M. and L. R. Thomas (1991). The significance of technical trading-rule profits in the foreign exchange market: A bootstrap approach. NBER Working paper series no. 3818.

Liu, R., (1988). Bootstrap procedures under some non i.i.d. models. *Ann. Statist.* **16**, 1696–1708.

Liu, R. Y. and K. Singh (1988). Moving blocks jackknife and bootstrap capture weak dependence. Preprint, Department of Statistics, Rutgers University.

Liu, R. Y. and K. Singh (1992). Efficiency and robustness in resampling. *Ann. Statist.* **20**, 370–384.

Lovell, M. C., (1983). Data mining. *Rev. Econom. Statist.* **65**, 1–12.

MacKinnon, J. G. and H. White (1985). Some heteroscedastic consistent covariance estimators with improved finite sample properties. *J. Econometrics* **29**, 305–325.

Maddala, G. S. (1977). *Econometrics*. McGraw-Hill, New York.

Maddala, G. S. (1983). *Limited Dependent and Qualitative Variances in Econometrics*. Cambridge Univ. Press, New York.

Manski, C. F. and T. S. Thomson (1986). Operational characteristics of maximum score estimation. *J. Econometrics* **32**, 85–108.

Marais, M. L. (1984). An application of the bootstrap method to the analysis of squared, standardized market model prediction errors. *J. Account. Res.* **22**, 34–54.

Martin, M. A. (1990). Bootstrap iteration for coverage correction in confidence intervals. *J. Amer. Statist. Assoc.* **85**, 1105–1118.

Masarotto, G. (1990). Bootstrap prediction intervals for autoregressions. *Internat. J. Forecasting* **6**, 229–239.

McAleer, M. and M. R. Veall (1989). How fragile are fragile inferences? A re-evaluation of the deterrent effect of capital punishment. *Rev. Econom. Statist.* **71**, 99–106.

McManus, W. S. and M. C. Rosalsky (1985). Are all asymptotic standard errors awful? *Econom. Lett.* **17**, 243–245.

Miller, R. G. (1974). An unbalanced jackknife. *Ann. Statist.* **2**, 880–891.

Miyazaki, S. and W. E. Griffiths (1984). The properties of some covariance matrix estimates in linear models with AR(1) errors. *Econom. Lett.* **14**, 351–356.

Moore, M. and N. Rais (1990). A bootstrap procedure for finite state stationary uniformly mixing discrete time series. Preprint, École Polytechnique de Montréal and Univesité de Montréal.

Morey, M. J. and L. M. Schenk (1984). Small sample behavior of bootstrapped and jackknifed estimators. In: *ASA Proc. Business Econom. Statist.*, 437–442.

Morey, M. J. and S. Wang (1985). Bootstrapping the Durbin–Watson statistic. In: *ASA Proc. Business Econom. Statist.*, 549–543.

Moschini, G., D. M. Prescott and T. Stengos (1988). Nonparametric kernel estimation applied to forecasting: An evaluation based on the bootstrap. *Empirical Econom.* **13**(3/4), 141–154.

Nankervis, J. C. and N. E. Savin (1988). The strudent's *t* approximation in a stationary first order autoregressive model. *Econometrica* **45**, 463–485.

Navidi, W. (1989). Edgeworth expansion for bootstrapping regression models. *Ann. Statist.* **17**, 1472–1478.

Nelson, F. and L. Olson (1978). Specification and estimation of a simultaneous-equation model with limited dependent variables. *Internat. Econom. Rev.* **19**, 695–710.

Newton, M. A. (1991). Results on bootstrapping and pre-pivoting. Ph.D. Dissertation, University of Washington.

Newton, M. A. and A. E. Raftery (1991). Approximate bayesian inference by the weighted likelihood bootstrap. Technical Report #199, Department of Statistics, University of Washington.

Park, S. (1985). Bootstrapping two-stage least squares estimates of a dynamic econometric model: Some empirical results. Carleton University Working Paper.

Park, R. E. and B. M. Mitchell (1980). Estimation the autocorrelated model with trended data. *J. Econometrics* **13**, 185–201.

Peters, S. C. and D. A. Freedman (1985). Using the bootstrap to evaluate forecasting equations. *J. Forecasting* **4**, 251–262.

Prasada Rao, D. S. and E. A. Selvanathan (1992). Computation of standard errors of Geary–Khamis parities and international prices: A stochastic approach. *J. Business Econom. Statist.* **10**, 109–115.

Quenouille, M. (1956). Notes on bias in estimation. *Biometrika* **43**, 353–360.

Rao, C. R. (1970). Estimation of heteroskedastic variances in linear models. *J. Amer. Statist. Assoc.* **65**, 161–172.

Rao, C. R. (1973). *Linear Statistical Inference and Its Applications*. Wiley, New York.

Rao, J. N. K. and C. F. J. Wu (1988). Resampling inference with complex survey data. *J. Amer. Statist. Assoc.* **83**, 231–241.

Rayner, R. K. (1988). Some asymptotic theory for the bootstrap in econometric models. *Econom. Lett.* **26**, 43–47.

Rayner, R. K. (1990a). Barlett's correction and the bootstrap in normal linear regression models. *Econom. Lett.* **33**, 255–258.

Rayner, R. K. (1990b). Bootstrap tests for generalized least squares regression models. *Econom. Lett.* **34**, 261–265.

Rayner, R. K. (1990c). Bootstrapping *p* values and power in the first-order autoregression: A Monte Carlo investigation. *J. Business Econom. Statist.* **8**, 251–263.

Rocke, D. M. (1989). Bootstrap bartlett adjustment in seemingly unrelated regression. *J. Amer. Statist. Assoc.* **84**, 598–601.

Rosalsky, M. C., R. Finke and H. Theil (1984). The downward bias of asymptotic standard errors of maximum likelihood estimates of non-linear systems. *Econom. Lett.* **14**, 207–211.

Rubin, D. B. (1981). The Bayesian bootstrap. *Ann. Statist.* **9**, 130–134.

Rubin, D. B. (1987). A noniterative sampling/importance resampling alternative to the data augmentation algorithm for creating a few imputations when fractions of missing information are modest: The SIR algorithm: Comment [the calculation of posterior distributions by data augmentation]. *J. Amer. Statist. Assoc.* **82**(398), 543–546.

Runkle, D. E. (1987). Vector auto-regression and reality. *J. Business Econom. Statist.* **5**, 437–454.

Schenker, N. (1985). Qualms about bootstrap confidence intervals. *J. Amer. Statist. Assoc.* **80**, 360–361.

Schmidt, P. and R. C. Sickles (1984). Production frontiers and panel data. *J. Business Econom. Statist.* **2**, 367–374.

Schucany, W. R. and L. A. Thombs (1990). Bootstrap prediction intervals for autoregression. *J. Amer. Statist. Assoc.* **85**, 486–492.

Selvanathan, E. A. (1989). A note on the stochastic approach to index numbers. *J. Business Econom. Statist.* **7**, 471–474.

Shea, G. S. (1989a). A re-examination of excess rational price approximations and excess volatility in the stock market. In: R. M. C. Guimaraes et al., eds., *A Reappraisal of the Efficiency of Financial Markets*. Springer, Berlin.

Shea, G. S. (1989b). Ex-post rational price approximations and the empirical reliability of the present-value relation. *J. Appl. Econometrics* **4**, 139–159.

Shi, X. and J. Shao (1988). Resampling estimation when observations are *M*-dependent. *Comm. Statist. A* **17**, 3923–3934.

Simar, L. (1991). Estimating efficiencies from frontier models with panel data: A comparison of parametric, nonparametric and semi-parametric methods with bootstrapping. CORE Discussion paper no. 9126.

Singh, K. (1981). On the asymptotic accuracy of Efron's bootstrap. *Ann. Statist.* **6**, 1187–1195.

Son, M. S., D. Holbert and H. Hamdy (1987). Bootstrap forecasts versus conventional forecasts: A comparison for a second order autoregressive models. In: *ASA Proc. Business & Econom. Statist.* 723–727.

Srivastava, V. K. and T. D. Dwivedi (1979). Estimation of seemingly unrelated regression equations: A brief survey. *J. Econometrics* **10**, 15–32.

Srivastava, M. S. and B. Singh (1989). Bootstrapping in multiplicative models. *J. Econometrics* **42**, 287–297.

Stine, R. A. (1985). Bootstrap prediction intervals for regression. *J. Amer. Statist. Assoc.* **80**(392), 1026–1031.

Stine, R. A. (1987). Estimating properties of autoregressive forecasts. *J. Amer. Statist. Assoc.* **82**, 1072–1078.

Stoffer, D. S. and K. D. Wall (1991). Bootstrapping state-space models: Gaussian maximum likelihood estimation and the Kalman filter. *J. Amer. Statist. Assoc.* **86**, 1024–1033.

Tanaka, K. (1983). Asymptotic expansions associated with the AR(1) model with unknown mean. *Econometrica* **51**, 1221–1232.

Teebagy, N. and S. Chatterjee (1989). Interference in a binary response model with applications to data analysis. *Decision Sci.* **20**, 393–403.

Van Dijk, H. K. (1987). Some advances in bayesian estimation methods using Monte Carlo integration. In: T. B. Fomby and G. F. Rhodes, eds. *Advances in Econometrics*, Vol. 6, Jai Press, Greenwich, CT, 100–120.

Veall, M. R. (1986). Bootstrapping regression estimators under first-order serial correlation. *Econom. Lett.* **21**, 41–44.

Veall, M. R. (1987a). Bootstrapping the probability distribution of peak electricity demand. *Internat. Econom. Rev.* **28**, 203–212.

Veall, M. R. (1987b). Bootstrapping forecast uncertainty: A Monte Carlo analysis. In: I. B. MacNeill and G. J. Umphrey, eds., *Time Series and Econometric Modelling*. Reidel, Dordrecht, 373–384.

Veall, M. R. (1989). Applications of computationally-intensive methods to econometrics. *Bull. Internat. Statist. Inst.* **47**(3), 75–83.

Veall, M. R. (1992). Bootstrapping the process of model selection: An econometric example. *J. Appl. Econometrics* **7**, 93–99.

Vinod, H. D. and B. D. McCullough (1991). Bootstrapping cointegrating regression. Paper presented at Statistics Canada Meetings, Montreal.

Weber, N. C. (1984). On resampling techniques for regression models. *Statist. Probab. Lett.* **2**, 275–278.

Weber, N. C. (1986). On the jackknife and bootstrap techniques for regressions models. In:

Francis, Manly, Lam, eds., *Pacific Statistical Congress*, Auckland 20–24 May 1985. North-Holland, Amsterdam, 51–55.

White, H. (1980). A heteroskedasticity–consistent covariance matrix and a direct test of heteroskedasticity. *Econometrica* **48**, 817–838.

White, H. (1982). Maximum likelihood estimation of misspecified models. *Econometrica* **50**, 1–26.

Williams, M. A. (1986). An economic application of bootstrap statistical methods: Addyston pipe revisited. *Amer. Econom.* **30**, 52–58.

Wilson, P. W. (1992). A bootstrap methodology for DEA-type efficiency models. Manuscript, Department of Economics, University of Texas at Austin, TX.

Wu, C. F. J. (1986). Jackknife, bootstrap and other resampling methods in regression analysis. *Ann. Statist.* **14**, 1261–1295.

Young, G. A. and H. E. Daniels (1990). Bootstrap bias. *Biometrika* **77**, 179–185.

G. S. Maddala, C. R. Rao and H. D. Vinod, eds., *Handbook of Statistics, Vol. 11*

22

Stochastic Simulations for Inference in Nonlinear Errors-in-Variables Models*

Roberto S. Mariano and Bryan W. Brown

1. Introduction and summary

Errors in variables are pervasive in econometric modelling work. For example, in the case of micro data sets, Griliches (1974, 1986) cites 'direct but fallible indicators of relevant . . . latent factors' and the use of proxy variables in the absence of direct measures as two main sources of errors. Test scores as measures of ability or achievement, reported income or estimated value of residence as proxies for permanent income, and schooling as a measure of 'true education' are some examples. Preliminary values in national income accounts data that are used in macromodelling provide yet another type of errors in variables which has been discussed in various references such as Conrad and Corrado (1979), Griliches (1986), Howrey (1978, 1984), Trivellato and Rettore (1986), and Mariano and Gallo (1988).

Although long recognized as a serious problem in statistical inference, only recently has there been a resurgence of econometric research on this topic. Fuller (1987) provides a comprehensive treatment of the linear regression model with measurement errors. Aigner et al. (1984), Chamberlain and Griliches (1975), Florens, Mouchart and Richard (1987), Geraci (1976, 1977, 1983), Goldberger (1972), Griliches (1974), Hausman (1977), Hsiao (1976, 1977, 1979), Hsiao and Robinson (1978), Joreskog and Goldberger (1975) and Zellner (1970) deal with the linear simultaneous-equations case.

While there has been relatively extensive coverage of the linear case, statistical inference in nonlinear errors-in-variables models has not been accorded the attention that it deserves. Nonlinearities with respect to structural disturbances or measurement errors comprise important features of many econometric models in current use. Immediate examples of models with nonlinearities in the structural errors are macroeconomic models and limited dependent variables in a simultaneous setting. A common example of non-

* Partial support from the National Science Foundation, grants SES 9011917 and SES 9011922, is gratefully acknowledged.

linearity with respect to measurement errors occurs in models where continuous independent variables are proxied by categorical measurements.

Most of what is available for nonlinear errors-in-variables models deals with the single-equation structural model with a linear relationship for measurement errors: Amemiya (1985), Fuller (1987), Hausman et al. (1986), Hausman, Newey and Powell – HNP – (1987, 1988), Hsiao (1988) and Wolter and Fuller (1982a,b). In a related set of literature, Newey (1985, 1986, 1987) developed semiparametric procedures for limited dependent variable models with endogenous explanatory variables. There is also an extensive set of papers dealing with measurement errors in single-equation qualitative response models; e.g., Burr (1988), Carroll et al. (1984), Clark (1982), Mouchart (1977), Schafer (1987), Schafer et al. (1988), Stefanski (1985, 1988), Stefanski and Carroll (1985) and Yatchew and Griliches (1985). Even in these cases, many important issues remain to be studied – especially the sensitivity of statistical tests to the presence of measurement errors. Surprisingly, measurement errors in simultaneous nonlinear models have received little treatment to date. Likewise, models with nonlinear measurement error processes have been virtually ignored in the econometric literature.

This paper addresses this vacuum and considers new econometric procedures for statistical inference in nonlinear econometric models in general and limited dependent variable models in particular, where explanatory variables are measured with (possibly) nonlinear errors. The approach utilizes the machinery that has been developed in earlier papers of ours dealing with forecasting and testing procedures for measurement-error-free nonlinear models. Results in these earlier papers – e.g., Brown and Mariano (1984, 1989a,b,c, 1991) and Mariano and Brown (1983a,b, 1985, 1988, 1989, 1991) – show that Monte Carlo and residual-based stochastic simulations, and variations of them, provide new statistical techniques for inference, prediction, and model validation. In the treatment of errors in variables, which we discuss in this paper, stochastic simulations of the model play a central role in providing numerical approximations to conditional moments of variables appropriate to the problem at hand – estimation or prediction or specification testing.

The potential uses of the stochastic simulators developed here are also indicated for generalizing McFadden's (1989) method of simulated moments to nonlinear errors-in-variables models and for the numerical evaluation of maximum likelihood estimates in nonlinear errors-in-variables models.

Before going into these general issues on stochastic simulations in nonlinear errors-in-variables models, we first consider in Section 2 the probit and tobit errors-in-variables models, focusing on the behavior of maximum likelihood estimators of basic parameters (quasi and appropriate) when measurement error parameters are estimated from the given sample. A reparameterization of the models establishes a direct correspondence between the MLEs when measurement errors are present and absent. This facilitates determination of the inconsistency in the quasi MLE which ignores measurement error. It shows further how this naive procedure can be modified in a fairly simple way to calculate the appropriate MLEs which take measurement errors into account. The discussion in this section serves to review the available results in the much covered area of probit models with measurement errors and to highlight future areas of research, especially the sensitivity of tests based on the quasi MLE to measurement errors and the statistical gains and perhaps losses in using the EIV MLE in terms of finite-sample behavior, skewness of distribution and performance of significance tests.

2. Probit errors-in-variables

First, we consider the case of a single-equation qualitative response model with additive measurement errors:

$$y_i^* = x_i'\beta + u_i ,$$ (2.1)

$$y_i = I(y_i^* > 0) ,$$ (2.2)

$$z_i = x_i + \varepsilon_i ,$$ (2.3)

where $I(A)$ is the indicator function which equals 1 if event A occurs and zero otherwise. We observe (z_i, y_i) for $i = 1, 2, 3, \ldots, n$ and assume

$$(u_i, \varepsilon_i, x_i) \sim \text{iid } N[(0, 0, \mu), \Sigma] ,$$ (2.4)

$$\Sigma = \begin{bmatrix} \sigma^2 & 0 & 0 \\ 0 & \Sigma_\varepsilon & 0 \\ 0 & 0 & \Sigma_x \end{bmatrix} .$$ (2.5)

We refer to the above as the probit errors-in-variables model. Take $\sigma = 1$ and suppress the subscript i. Then

$$\varepsilon \mid z \sim N[A(z - \mu), (I - A)\Sigma_\varepsilon] ,$$
$$A = \Sigma_\varepsilon (\Sigma_\varepsilon + \Sigma_x)^{-1} ,$$ (2.6)
$$y^* \mid z \sim N[z'\beta - (z - \mu)'A'\beta, 1 + \beta'(I - A)\Sigma_\varepsilon\beta] .$$

This implies that

$$\Pr(y = 1 \mid z) = \Pr(y^* > 0 \mid z)$$
$$= \Phi\{[z'\beta - (z - \mu)'A'\beta]/(1 + \beta'(I - A)\Sigma_\varepsilon\beta)^{1/2}\} ,$$ (2.7)

where $\Phi(\cdot)$ is the cdf of a standard unit normal. Take $\mu = 0$ and let

$$\beta_* = (I - A')\beta/(1 + \beta'(I - A)\Sigma_\varepsilon\beta)^{1/2}$$
$$= h(\beta, \Sigma_x, \Sigma_\varepsilon) .$$ (2.8)

Then

$$\Pr(y = 1 \,|\, z) = \Phi(z'\beta_*) \,. \tag{2.9}$$

If Σ_ε and Σ_x are known, the probit regression of y on z (the usual standard probit procedure) produces the MLE of β_*, not β. This estimator, say $\hat{\beta}_Q$ is also the quasi MLE of β, erroneously obtained under the assumption of no measurement errors on z. The appropriate MLE of β, say $\hat{\beta}_M$, is

$$\hat{\beta}_M = h^{-1}(\hat{\beta}_Q, \Sigma_x, \Sigma_\varepsilon) \,. \tag{2.10}$$

Thus, the inconsistency in the quasi MLE, which fails to take measurement errors into account, is $\beta_* - \beta$. Furthermore, from this quasi MLE, the appropriate MLE can be calculated by inverting the $h(\cdot)$ function, as indicated above. The following results also follow directly from this interpretation, under suitable regularity assumptions:

$$n^{1/2}(\hat{\beta}_Q - \beta_*) \xrightarrow{d} N(0, \mathscr{I}_*^{-1}) \,,$$

$$\mathscr{I}_* = -\mathrm{plim}(\partial^2 L(y\,|\,z)/\partial\beta_* \partial\beta_*')/n \,, \tag{2.11}$$

$$n^{1/2}(\hat{\beta}_M - \beta) \xrightarrow{d} N[0, (\partial h^{-1}/\partial\beta)\mathscr{I}_*^{-1}(\partial h^{-1}/\partial\beta')] \,.$$

In (2.11), $L(y\,|\,z)$ is the log likelihood of the observations $\{y_1, \ldots, y_n\}$ given the observations $\{z_1, \ldots, z_n\}$.

If the nuisance parameter $\psi = (\mu, \Sigma_\varepsilon, \Sigma_x)$ is not known, β will not be identifiable in the general case with more than one explanatory variable measured with error. With additional restrictions or additional information, such as replicated x observations, it may be possible to obtain consistent, asymptotically normal estimates of these nuisance parameters. In such cases, β will be identifiable through inversion of the $h(\cdot)$ function, e.g., (2.8). In fact the pseudo MLE of β would be

$$\hat{\beta} = h^{-1}(\hat{\beta}_Q, \hat{\mu}, \hat{\Sigma}_\varepsilon, \hat{\Sigma}_x) \,. \tag{2.12}$$

Suppose we have a consistent and asymptotically normal $\hat{\psi}$ based on the available sample of x observations, with the following limiting distribution:

$$n^{1/2}(\hat{\psi} - \psi) \to N(0, V_\psi) \,. \tag{2.13}$$

Since the log likelihood of (z, y) can be written as

$$L(y, z; \beta, \psi) = L(y\,|\,z; \beta, \psi) + L_z(z; \psi) \,, \tag{2.14}$$

the pseudo MLE of β, $\hat{\beta}$, which maximizes $L(y, z; \beta, \hat{\psi})$, with respect to β for a given estimate $\hat{\psi}$, equivalently maximizes the conditional likelihood of y

given z (assuming that $L_z(\cdot)$ does not depend on β):

$$\hat{\beta} = \arg\max_{\beta} L(y \mid z; \beta, \hat{\psi}) . \tag{2.15}$$

To obtain the asymptotic distribution of $\hat{\beta}$, we utilize the following lemma.

LEMMA. *Let* $S = (1/n)\, \partial L(y, z)/\partial\beta = (1/n)\, \partial L(y \mid z)/\partial\beta$. *Then*

$$E(S \cdot \hat{\psi}) = 0 . \tag{2.16}$$

PROOF. This follows directly from

$$E(S \cdot \hat{\psi}) = E_z E_{y\mid z}(S\hat{\psi} \mid z) = E_z\{\hat{\psi} E_{y\mid z}(S \mid z)\} = 0 . \quad \square$$

The following theorem now gives the limiting distribution and the asymptotic covariance of the pseudo MLE.

THEOREM. *Suppose regularity conditions hold so that* $n^{1/2}(S, \hat{\psi} - \psi)$ *is asymptotically normal with mean zero and covariance matrix*

$$\begin{pmatrix} \mathscr{I}_{\beta\beta} & 0 \\ 0 & V_{\psi} \end{pmatrix}, \tag{2.17}$$

where

$$\begin{aligned} \mathscr{I}_{\beta\beta} &= -\mathrm{plim}\{(1/n)\, \partial^2 L(y \mid z)/\partial\beta\, \partial\beta'\} , \\ V_{\psi} &= \text{asymptotic covariance matrix of } \hat{\psi} . \end{aligned} \tag{2.18}$$

Let $\hat{\beta}$ *be the pseudo MLE of* β *obtained by maximizing* $L(y \mid z; \beta, \psi)$. *Then*

$$n^{1/2}(\hat{\beta} - \beta) \to N(0, \mathscr{I}_{\beta\beta}^{-1} + \mathscr{I}_{\beta\beta}^{-1} \mathscr{I}_{\beta\psi} V_{\psi} \mathscr{I}_{\psi\beta} \mathscr{I}_{\beta\beta}^{-1}) , \tag{2.19}$$

where

$$\mathscr{I}_{\beta\psi} = \mathrm{plim}\{(1/n)\, \partial^2 L(y \mid z; \beta_0, \psi_0)/\partial\beta\, \partial\psi\} . \tag{2.20}$$

PROOF. Let $\eta = (\beta, \psi)$. Then

$$\begin{aligned} 0 = S(\hat{\beta}, \hat{\psi}) &= S(\eta_0) + H_{\beta\beta}(\eta_0)(\hat{\beta} - \beta_0) + H_{\beta\psi}(\eta_0)(\hat{\psi} - \psi_0) \\ &\quad + o_p(\|\hat{\eta} - \eta_0\|) . \end{aligned} \tag{2.21}$$

This implies that

$$n^{1/2}(\hat{\beta} - \beta_0) = -H_{\beta\beta}^{-1}(\eta_0)\{n^{1/2}S(\eta_0) - H_{\beta\psi}(\eta_0)[n^{1/2}(\hat{\psi} - \psi_0)]\} + o_p(1) . \tag{2.22}$$

The theorem now follows from the assumption on the limiting distribution of S

and $\hat{\psi}$ and the fact that

$$H_{\beta\beta}(\eta_0) = (1/n)\, \partial^2 L(y \mid z; \beta_0, \psi_0)/\partial\beta\,\partial\beta' ,$$
$$H_{\beta\psi}(\eta_0) = (1/n)\, \partial^2 L(y \mid z; \beta_0, \psi_0)/\partial\beta\,\partial\psi' . \qquad \square$$

(2.23)

Gong and Samaniego (1981) and Gourieroux, Monfort and Trognon (1984) discuss the asymptotic theory for pseudo maximum likelihood methods in a more general setting.

3. Tobit errors-in-variables

The tobit errors-in-variables model would have, instead of (2.2),

$$y_i = I(y_i^* > 0)y_i^* .$$

(3.1)

The conditional distribution of y given z (with subscript i suppressed) is

$$y \mid z \sim N\{z'\beta - (z - \mu)'A'\beta; \sigma_u^2 + \beta'(I - A)\Sigma\beta\}$$

(3.2)

and

$$\Pr(y = 0 \mid z) = \Pr(y \le 0 \mid z) = \Phi\{-z'(I - A')\beta/\sigma_*\} = \Phi(-z'\beta_{**}) ,$$

(3.3)

where

$$\sigma_*^2 = \sigma_u^2 + \beta'(I - A)\Sigma\beta ,$$
$$\beta_{**} = (I - A')\beta/\sigma_* = h(\beta, \sigma_*) .$$

(3.4)

The conditional likelihood of $\{y_1, y_2, \ldots, y_n\}$ given $(z_1, z_2, \ldots, z_n)$ is

$$\prod_{y_i=0} \Phi(z_i'\beta_{**}) \cdot \prod_{y_i=1} (1/\sigma_*)\phi((y_i - z_i'\beta_{**})/\sigma_*) ,$$

(3.5)

a standard tobit likelihood with parameters (β_{**}, σ_*).

Let $(\tilde{\beta}_Q, \tilde{\sigma}_Q^2)$ denote the quasi tobit MLE based on $\{(y_i, z_i): i = 1, \ldots, n\}$ and let $(\tilde{\beta}_M, \tilde{\sigma}_M^2)$ be the tobit MLE accounting for measurement errors. Then

$$\text{plim } \tilde{\beta}_Q = \beta_{**} ,$$
$$\text{plim } \tilde{\sigma}_Q^2 = \sigma_*^2 .$$

(3.6)

Furthermore, if we rewrite (3.3) and (3.4) as

$$(\beta, \sigma_u^2) = g(\beta_{**}, \sigma_*^2) ,$$

(3.7)

then

$$(\tilde{\beta}_M, \tilde{\sigma}_M^2) = g(\tilde{\beta}_Q, \tilde{\sigma}_Q^2) ,$$

(3.8)

assuming that Σ_ε and Σ_x are known. When these nuisance parameters are unknown, we utilize consistent estimates of them to obtain pseudo MLEs as in the previous section. The arguments in the preceding section also apply to the derivation of the asymptotic distributions of the modified MLEs in either case of known or unknown measurement error parameters.

The discussion here shows that apart from the scaling difference, where the disturbance variance is normalized to unity in the probit but not in the tobit model, the inconsistency effect of measurement error (of the type considered in this section) on probit and tobit coefficient estimates is basically the same.

To explain conflicts in the significance tests on β based on the probit and tobit alternatives in terms of measurement errors, one must go beyond the inconsistencies caused by measurement errors. The appropriateness of variance estimates used in the construction of the test statistics should be examined, and corrected if necessary. The probability distributions of the test statistics, their skewness in finite samples that show up in some limited experiments reported in the literature (e.g., Burr, 1988, and Carroll et al., 1984), and the true size and power of the tests should be examined more carefully. A Monte Carlo study along these lines is reported in Reyes (1991) and Mariano, Nerlove, Reyes and Lim (1990).

4. Inference in nonlinear systems with errors in variables

In this section, we consider a structural submodel in the form of a nonlinear simultaneous system of stochastic equations containing stochastic exogenous variables which are measured with error. The measurement error submodel, relating the observed to the true exogenous variables, is generalized from the standard formulation used in the two preceding sections to a nonlinear system of stochastic equations. We also assume, as before, that the disturbances in the two submodels and the unobservable exogenous variables are jointly independent. The two submodels combine to complete a system which explains the joint behavior of the endogenous variables and the observations on the exogenous variables.

The standard approach, which we have used in earlier sections, treats measurement errors as white noise. However, there are modeling situations – such as those involving preliminary values in national accounts data – where such standard treatment may be inappropriate. For instance, see Conrad and Corrado (1979), Denton and Kuiper (1965), Denton and Oksanen (1972, 1973), Griliches (1986), Howrey (1978, 1984), Trivellato and Rettore (1986) and Mariano and Gallo (1988). Nonlinearities with respect to measurement errors will also arise in cases where continuous explanatory variables are proxied by categorical measurements. In these cases, a wider class of measurement error submodels, such as the one adopted here, may prove useful. Further extensions of the submodel used here can be made (though not done here) through the introduction of dynamics and the inclusion of other variables which may be sources of systematic measurement errors.

Current literature on measurement error stresses the need for additional information to achieve identification of the whole system. (Here, identification is interpreted in the econometric sense of uniqueness of the data generating process.) Such information typically comes by way of replicated observations on the exogenous variables and/or further restrictions on coefficients or covariance parameters in the measurement error submodel. In the formulation of our model, another potential source of parameter identification is the nonlinearity of the measurement error submodel. Even if the true exogenous variables and the model disturbances are normally distributed, observations on the exogenous variables will not be normal. Consequently, third and higher order moments of the observed exogenous variables may provide information for parameter identification.

Given consistent estimates of the model parameters based on a sample of observations, the discussion here focuses on the problem of predicting the endogenous variables given the exogenous observations with measurement errors. Assuming squared error loss, the objective is to estimate the conditional expectation of the endogenous variables given the rest of the observations. The modified simulation methods developed here for this problem can be extended to higher moments and utilized in developing generalized method of moments estimators analogous to McFadden's (1989) method of simulated moments (MSM). They can also be used for numerical evaluation of the joint likelihood of the sample of observations on endogenous and erroneous exogenous variables, and, hence, lead to a numerical implementation of maximum likelihood estimation. Prediction-based specification tests, such as those developed for the measurement-error-free case in Mariano and Brown (1983b), Mariano and Tabunda (1987), and Brown (1988), can also be developed for the validation of errors-in-variables models. Such tests would be based on stochastic simulations of the estimated model over the sample period and their deviations from actual observations.

Consider a simultaneous system of n nonlinear stochastic equations

$$f(y_t, x_t; \alpha) = u_t,$$ (4.1)

where f, y_t, and u_t are $n \times 1$. The vector of functions f is completely known; α denotes the vector of unknown parameters; the u_t are unobservable disturbance terms. The components of y_t are the endogenous variables in the system. The vector x_t is exogenous.

Some or all of the components of x_t are measured with error. Thus, instead of x_t, what is observed is z_t, with the same dimension as x_t and related to x_t by the following measurement error model

$$m(z_t, x_t; \beta) = \varepsilon_t,$$ (4.2)

where $m(\cdot)$ has the same dimension as z_t. We assume that (4.1) and (4.2) define locally unique inverse relationships

$$y_t = g(u_t, x_t; \alpha) \, , \tag{4.3}$$

$$x_t = p(\varepsilon_t, z_t; \beta) \, , \tag{4.4}$$

$$z = q(\varepsilon_t, x_t; \beta) \, . \tag{4.5}$$

In general, $g(\cdot)$, $p(\cdot)$, and $q(\cdot)$ may not be available in closed form. In such cases, the values of y_t and x_t are calculated as numerical solutions to (4.1), and (4.2), respectively, corresponding to a set of input values. We further assume that, for any t, u_t, ε_t, and x_t are statistically independent of each other and that $(u_t, \varepsilon_t, x_t)$ are jointly iid with mean $(0, 0, \mu)$ and variance–covariance matrix

$$\Sigma = \begin{pmatrix} \Sigma_u & 0 & 0 \\ 0 & \Sigma_\varepsilon & 0 \\ 0 & 0 & \Sigma_x \end{pmatrix} . \tag{4.6}$$

Given consistent, asymptotically normal estimates of the model parameters $\theta = (\alpha, \beta, \mu, \Sigma)$ based on observations $\{(y_y, z_t): t = 1, 2, \ldots, T\}$, let us now consider the problem of predicting an unobserved value y_τ given the observations and the measurement z_τ. The objective is to estimate the conditional expectation of $E(y_\tau | z_\tau)$. From (4.1)–(4.5), we get

$$E(y_\tau | z_\tau) = \int_\varepsilon \int_u [g(u, p(\varepsilon, z_\tau; \beta); \alpha) \cdot f_{\tau|z}(u, \varepsilon)] \, du \, d\varepsilon \tag{4.7}$$

$$= \int_\varepsilon \int_u [g(u, p(\varepsilon, z_\tau; \beta); \alpha) \cdot f_u(u) \cdot f_{\varepsilon|z}(\varepsilon)] \, du \, d\varepsilon \, , \tag{4.8}$$

where $f_{\tau|z}(u, \varepsilon)$ is the conditional joint pdf of $(u_\tau, \varepsilon_\tau)$ given z_τ, $f_u(\cdot)$ is the unconditional pdf of u_τ, and $f_{\varepsilon|z}(\cdot)$ is the conditional pdf of ε_τ given z_τ. The expression simplifies to (4.8) since (4.1)–(4.6) imply that, for any t, the structural disturbances u_t are statistically independent of the variables $(\varepsilon_t, x_t, z_t)$ in the measurement error process.

In some special cases, the conditional distribution of ε_τ given z_τ can be determined explicitly from the assumed joint distribution of (ε_t, x_t). For example, in the standard measurement error model,

$$z_t = x_t + \varepsilon_t$$

with (ε_t, x_t) jointly normal, ε given z will be conditional normal with mean vector and covariance matrix easily determined as functions of μ and Σ_x, Σ_ε, $\Sigma_{\varepsilon x}$. In cases like these, one can apply a simulation technique, directly analogous to what we call Monte Carlo stochastic predictors in our earlier papers (e.g., Mariano and Brown, 1983a, Brown and Mariano, 1984):

$$\hat{y}_{mi} = \sum_{s=1}^{S} g(\bar{u}_s, p(\bar{\varepsilon}_s, z_\tau; \hat{\beta}); \hat{\alpha}) , \tag{4.9}$$

where, for $s = 1, 2, \ldots, S$, the u_s and ε_s are independent draws from the unconditional distribution of u_t and the conditional distribution (given z_τ) of ε_τ, respectively.

However, if we adopt the more complicated measurement-error model (4.2), generally, it would not be possible to draw directly from the conditional distribution of ε_τ given z_τ. In this case, further simplification of (4.8) leads to a modified stochastic simulation process. Note that for x_t stochastically independent of ε_τ,

$$f_{\varepsilon|z}(\varepsilon, z) = f_{\varepsilon,z}(\varepsilon, z)/f_z(z) , \tag{4.10}$$

$$f_{\varepsilon,z}(\varepsilon, z) = f_\varepsilon(\varepsilon) \cdot f_x(p(\varepsilon, z))|\partial p/\partial z'| \tag{4.11}$$

and

$$f_z(z) = \int_\varepsilon f_{\varepsilon,z}(\varepsilon, z)\, d\varepsilon = E_\varepsilon\{f_x(p(\varepsilon, z))|\partial p/\partial z'|\} = D , \tag{4.12}$$

where $f_{\varepsilon,z}(\cdot)$, $f_z(\cdot)$ and $f_x(\cdot)$ are unconditional pdfs of $(\varepsilon_\tau, z_\tau)$, z_τ, and x_τ, respectively.

Starting from (4.8), we get

$$E(y_\tau \mid z_\tau) = \left\{ \int_\varepsilon \int_u [g(u, p(\varepsilon, z_\tau)) \cdot f_u(u) \cdot f_\varepsilon(\varepsilon) \right.$$

$$\left. \cdot f_x(p(\varepsilon, z))|\partial p/\partial z'|]\, du\, d\varepsilon \right\} \Big/ D \tag{4.13}$$

$$= E_{u,\varepsilon}\{g(u, p(\varepsilon, z_\tau)) \cdot f_x(p(\varepsilon, z))|\partial p/\partial z'|\}/D , \tag{4.14}$$

where D is the expression in (4.12) and $E_{u,\varepsilon}(\cdot)$ and $E_\varepsilon(\cdot)$ represent expectations with respect to the unconditional distributions of $(u_\tau, \varepsilon_\tau)$ and (e_τ), respectively.

The simplification in (4.14) avoids the need to deal with the conditional distribution of ε_τ given z_τ and reduces the simulation requirements to draws from the unconditional distributions of u and ε. Explicitly, our Monte Carlo predictor of y_τ (given z_τ) is

$$\hat{y}_\tau = \sum_{s=1}^{S} \{g(\bar{u}_s, p(\bar{\varepsilon}_s, z_\tau; \hat{\beta}); \hat{\alpha}) \cdot f_x(p(\bar{\varepsilon}_s, z_\tau; \hat{\beta}))$$

$$\cdot |\partial p(\bar{\varepsilon}_s, z_\tau; \hat{\beta})/\partial z'|/(S \cdot \hat{D}_m)\} , \tag{4.15}$$

where, for $s = 1, 2, 3, \ldots, S$, $\bar{u}_s$ and $\bar{\varepsilon}_s$ are independent draws from the unconditional distributions of u_τ and ε_τ and $f_x(\cdot)$ is the unconditional pdf of x_τ, and

$$\hat{D}_m = \sum_{s=1}^{S} f_x(p(\bar{\varepsilon}_s, z_\tau; \hat{\beta}) \cdot |\partial p(\bar{\varepsilon}_s, z_\tau; \hat{\beta})/\partial z'|/S . \tag{4.16}$$

Note that our proposed stochastic predictors (4.15) are related to but differ from the naive approach, suggested by the ideal measurement-error-free case, of first using observed z_τ with the measurement error model to get an estimate $\hat{x}_\tau$ of $E(x_\tau | z_\tau)$ and then using the structural model alone (with $\hat{x}_\tau$ as an input) to forecast y_τ:

$$\hat{y}_{na} = E_u g(u, \hat{x}_\tau; \hat{\alpha}) . \tag{4.17}$$

To see the relationship between (4.8) and (4.17), expand $g(\cdot)$ around $x = \hat{x}_\tau$,

$$g(u, x_\tau; \alpha) \cong g(u, \hat{x}_\tau; \alpha) + g_x(u, \hat{x}_\tau; \alpha) \cdot (\hat{x}_\tau - x_\tau)$$
$$+ (\hat{x}_\tau - x_\tau)' g_{xx}(u, \hat{x}_\tau; \alpha) \cdot (\hat{x}_\tau - x_\tau)/2 \tag{4.18}$$

so that

$$E(y_\tau | z_\tau) \cong E_u g(u, \hat{x}_\tau; \alpha) + \mathrm{tr}\{E_u(g_{xx}(u, \hat{x}_\tau; \alpha))V\}/2 , \tag{4.19}$$

where V is the conditional covariance matrix of x_τ given z_τ.

To apply these results to limited dependent variable models, consider next a discrete choice model for c alternatives with vector attribute x_i corresponding to alternative i and let $X = (x_1, x_2, \ldots, x_c)$. The alternatives are mutually exclusive and exhaustive. A latent variable model (see McFadden, 1989) leads to the following representation of the choice probability for alternative i:

$$\pi(i) = \Pr[h(u, X; \alpha) \leqslant 0] , \tag{4.20}$$

where $h(\cdot)$ is a vector of smooth functions, α consists of unknown parameters, and u is a random vector.

Further assume that X is measured with error and, representing the measured attributes by Z, take the nonlinear measurement error submodel introduced in (4.2) and (4.4):

$$m(Z, X; \beta) = E , \qquad p(E, Z; \beta) = X , \tag{4.21}$$

with the same stochastic behavior for (u, E, X) as in the earlier part of this section.

A random sample of observations on N individuals consists of $\{(y_n, Z_n): n = 1, 2, 3, \ldots, N\}$, where

$$y_n = (y_{1n}, y_{2n}, \ldots, y_{cn}) ,$$
$$y_{in} = \begin{cases} 1, & \text{if the } n\text{-th individual chooses alternative } i ; \\ 0, & \text{otherwise} . \end{cases} \tag{4.22}$$

Here, y_{in} is the outcome of a multinomial trial with component probabilities $\{\pi(i): i = 1, 2, \ldots, c\}$ with expectation equal to these choice probabilities.

Prediction of an individual's choice, given the measured attributes for him, then corresponds to estimation of his choice probabilities. From (4.20), we get

$$\pi(i) = \Pr[h(u, p(E, Z; \beta); \alpha) \leqslant 0 \,|\, Z]$$

$$= \int_u \int_E \{I[h(u, p(E, Z; \beta); \alpha) \leqslant 0] \cdot f_u(u) \cdot f_{E|Z}(E; Z)\} \, du \, dE$$

$$= E_u E_E [I(h \leqslant 0) \cdot f_x(p) \cdot |\partial p / \partial Z|] / E_\varepsilon [f_x(p) \cdot |\partial p / \partial Z|] . \qquad (4.23)$$

The vector inequality $h \leqslant 0$ means satisfaction of the inequality component by component. The derivation of (4.23) follows from (4.8) and generalizes the case considered in McFadden (1989) of linear $m(\cdot)$ and jointly normal (X, Z, E).

Stochastic simulations can then be based on (4.23) with draws from the unconditional distribution of u and E for a numerical approximation of the choice probabilities conditional on Z. These can then be used not only for prediction but also to implement a generalized method of simulated moments or a numerical maximization of the appropriate likelihood of the sample observations.

In the error-free case, the log-likelihood of the observations on (y, X) is

$$L(\theta) = \sum_n \sum_i y_{in} \cdot \log[\pi_n(i \,|\, x_{in})] \qquad (4.24)$$

with first order conditions

$$\partial L / \partial \theta = \sum_n \sum_i [\partial \log(\pi_{in}) / \partial \theta \cdot (y_{in} - \pi_{in})] . \qquad (4.25)$$

The conventional method of moments leads to the minimization problem

$$\min_\theta \, (y - \pi(\theta))' W' W (y - \pi(\theta)) , \qquad (4.26)$$

where y and π are vectors of stacked y_{in} and π_{in} and W is a suitably chosen instrument matrix. Asymptotic efficiency obtains if we use $\partial \log(\pi_{in}) / \partial \theta$ as instruments – McFadden (1989). McFadden's method of simulated moments uses a simulator, instead of direct integration, to approximate $\pi(\theta)$ in the minimization process.

In the presence of measurement errors, the log-likelihood of the sample on (y, Z) is

$$L(\theta) = \sum_n \sum_i \{y_{in} \cdot \log[\pi_n(i \,|\, z_{in})] + \log[f_z(z_{in})]\} . \qquad (4.27)$$

Conditional MLE ignores the second term. Pseudo MLE uses estimates obtained elsewhere of the parameters in the distribution of Z. Unconditional MLE requires simultaneous treatment of both terms in (4.27). Stochastic simulations suggested in (4.23) can be used for a numerical implementation of unconditional MLE.

The method of moments, conventional or MSM, can proceed as in (4.26) with $\pi(\theta)$ replaced by the conditional probabilities given Z. This can be generalized further by considering alternative minimands and choice of appropriate instruments based on the score of the appropriate log-likelihood.

5. Concluding remarks

To estimate nonlinear models with measurement errors, we have considered in this paper iterative simulation-based procedures. For given values of the model parameters, the algorithm requires stochastic simulations for the numerical evaluation of the likelihood function or of first order conditions. For the limited-dependent-variable case, this entails numerical evaluation of choice probabilities, conditional on measured observations of exogenous variables. For the general case, the process revolves around evaluation of conditional expectations of endogenous variables.

Semiparametric approaches to the stochastic simulations considered in this paper can also be developed. They are linked closely to the related topic of semiparametric efficiency bounds which has received a great deal of attention recently in the econometric and statistical literature; e.g., Bickel and Ritov (1987), Bickel et al. (1989), Gourieroux and Monfort (1991), Klein and Spady (1991), Newey (1989a,b) and Robinson (1987, 1988, 1991). The potential uses of the stochastic simulators developed here are also indicated for generalizing McFadden's (1989) method of simulated moments and related procedures – e.g., Hajivassiliou and McFadden (1990) and Pakes and Pollard (1989) – to nonlinear errors-in-variables models and for the numerical evaluation of maximum likelihood estimates in nonlinear errors-in-variables models.

Some applications of the procedures discussed here may be found in Reyes (1991) and Lim (1990) concerning the adoption of modern technology in Philippine agriculture. The method has also been used to develop simulation-based alternatives to Kitagawa's (1987) approach (via numerical density approximations) to nonlinear filtering and applied to the prediction problem in the presence of preliminary data. For example, see Tanizaki (1991), Mariano and Tanizaki (1991), the Tanizaki and Mariano (1991, 1992).

References

Aigner, D. J., H. Cheng, A. Kapteyn and T. Wansbeek (1984). Latent variable models in econometrics. In: Z. Griliches and M. Intriligator, eds., *Handbook of Econometrics*, Vol. 2. North-Holland, Amsterdam, 1322–1393.

Amemiya, Y. (1985). Instrumental variable estimator for the nonlinear errors-in-variables model. *J. Econometrics* **28**, 273–290.

Bickel, P. J. and Y. Ritov (1987). Efficient estimation in the error in variables model. *Ann. Statist.* **15**, 513–540.

Bickel, P., C. A. J. Klaassen, Y. Ritov and J. A. Wellner (1989). *Efficient and Adaptive Inference in Semiparametric Models*. Johns Hopkins Univ. Press, Baltimore, MO.

Brown, B. W. (1988). Prediction-based tests of misspecification in dynamic nonlinear models. Rice University Discussion Paper.

Brown, B. and R. Mariano (1984). Residual-based stochastic prediction and estimation in a nonlinear simultaneous system. *Econometrica* **52**, 321–343.

Brown, B. W. and R. S. Mariano (1989a). Measures of deterministic prediction bias in nonlinear simultaneous systems. *Internat. Econom. Rev.* **30**, 667–684.

Brown, B. W. and R. S. Mariano (1989b). Predictors in dynamic nonlinear models: Large sample behavior. *Econometric Theory* **5**, 430–452.

Brown, B. W. and R. S. Mariano (1989c). Reduced variance prediction in nonlinear models. Rice University/University of Pennsylvania Discussion Paper.

Brown, B. W. and R. S. Mariano (1991). Prediction intervals and regions in nonlinear simultaneous systems. Econometrics discussion paper series, University of Pennsylvania/Rice University; February, 1991.

Burr, D. (1988). On errors-in-variables in binary regression – Berkson case. *J. Amer. Statist. Assoc.* **83**, 739–743.

Carroll, R. J. (1982). Adapting for heteroskedasticity in linear models. *Ann. Statist.* **10**, 1224–1233.

Carroll, R. J., C. H. Spiegelman, K. K. Gordon Lan, K. T. Bailey and R. D. Abbott (1984). On errors-in-variables for binary regression models. *Biometrika* **71**, 19–25.

Chamberlain, G. and Z. Griliches (1975). Unobservables with a variance-components structure: Ability, schooling and economic success in brothers. *Internat. Econom. Rev.* **16**, 422–450.

Clark, R. R. (1982). The errors-in-variables problem in the logistic regression model. Ph.D. Thesis, University of North Carolina at Chapel Hill, Department of Biostatistics.

Conrad, W. and C. Corrado (1979). Application of the Kalman filter to revisions in monthly retail sales data. *J. Econom. Dynamics Control* **1**, 177–198.

Denton, F. T. and J. Kuiper (1965). The effects of measurement error on parameter estimates and forecasts: A case study based on the Canadian preliminary national accounts. *Rev. Econom. Statist.* **47**, 198–206.

Denton, F. T. and E. H. Oksanen (1972). A multi-country analysis of the effects of data revisions on an econometric model, *J. Amer. Statist. Assoc.* **67**, 286–291.

Denton, F. T. and E. Oksanen (1973). Data revisions and forecasting accuracy: An econometric analysis based on preliminary and revised national accounting estimates. *Rev. Income Wealth* **19**, 437–452.

Florens, J.-P., M. Mouchart and J.-F. Richard (1987). Dynamic errors-in-variables models and limited information analysis, *Ann. Econom. Statist.* **6/7**, 289–310.

Fuller, W. A. (1987). *Measurement Error Models*. Wiley, New York.

Geraci, V. (1976). Identification of simultaneous equation models with measurement error. *J. Econometrics* **4**, 263–283.

Geraci, V. (1977). Estimation of simultaneous equation models with measurement error. *Econometrica* **45**, 217–236.

Geraci, V. (1983). Errors-in-variables and the individual structural equation. *Internat. Econom. Rev.* **24**, 217–236.

Gong, G. and F. J. Samaniego (1982). Pseudo maximum likelihood estimation: Theory and applications. *Ann. Statist.* **9**, 861–869.

Goldberger, A. (1972). Structural equation methods in the social sciences. *Econometrica* **40**, 979–1002.

Gourieroux, C. and A. Monfort (1991). Simulation based inference: A survey with special reference to panel data models. INSEE Discussion Paper No. 9106; March, 1991.

Gourieroux, C., A. Monfort and A. Trognon (1984). Pseudo maximum likelihood methods: Theory. *Econometrica* **52**, 681–700.

Griliches, Z. (1974). Errors in variables and other unobservables. *Econometrica* **30**, 491–500.

Griliches, Z. (1986). Economic data issues. In: Z. Griliches and M. Intriligator, eds., *Handbook of Econometrics*, Vol. 3. North-Holland, Amsterdam, 1465–1514.

Hajivassiliou, V. and D. McFadden (1990). The method of simulated scores for the estimation of limited dependent variable models, with an application to external debt crises. Cowles Foundation Discussion Paper #967.

Hausman, J. (1977). Errors in variables in simultaneous equation models. *J. Econometrics* **5**, 389–401.

Hausman, J., H. Ichimura, W. Newey and J. Powell (1986). Semiparametric identification and estimation of polynomial errors-in-variables models. SSRI Working Paper #8626, University of Wisconsin.

Hausman, J., W. Newey and J. Powell (1987). Consistent estimation of nonlinear error-in-variables models with few measurements. MIT Discussion Paper.

Hausman, J., W. Newey and J. Powell (1988). Nonlinear errors in variables: Estimation of some Engel curves. MIT Working Paper #504.

Howrey, P. (1978). The use of preliminary data in econometric forecasting. *Rev. Econom. Statist.* **60**, 193–200.

Howrey, P. (1984). Data revision, reconstruction, and prediction: An application to inventory investment. *Rev. Econom. Statist.* **66**, 386–393.

Hsiao, C. (1976). Identification and estimation of simultaneous equation models with measurement error. *Internat. Econom. Rev.* **17**, 319–339.

Hsiao, C. (1977). Identification for a linear dynamic simultaneous error-shock model. *Internat. Econom. Rev.* **18**, 181–194.

Hsiao, C. (1979). Measurement error in a dynamic simultaneous equation model with stationary disturbances. *Econometrica* **47**, 475–494.

Hsiao, C. (1988). Consistent estimation for some nonlinear errors-in-variables models. USC MRG Working Paper #M88-10.

Hsiao, C. and P. Robinson (1978). Efficient estimation of a dynamic error-shock model. *Internat. Econom. Rev.* **19**, 467–480.

Joreskog, K. G. and A. S. Goldberger (1975). Estimation of a model with multiple indicators and multiple causes of a single latent variable. *J. Amer. Statist. Assoc.* **70**, 631–639.

Kitagawa, G. (1987). Non-gaussian state–space modelling of nonstationary time series. *J. Amer. Statist. Assoc.* **82**, 1032–1063.

Klein, R. and R. Spady (1991). An efficient semiparametric estimator for binary response models. *Econometrica*, to appear.

Lim, P. (1990). *Measurement Error in Simultaneous Qualitative Response Models*. Ph.D. Dissertation, University of Pennsylvania, Department of Statistics.

Mariano, R. S. and B. W. Brown (1983a). Asymptotic behavior of predictors in a nonlinear system. *Internat. Econom. Rev.* **24**, 523–536.

Mariano, R. S. and B. W. Brown (1983b). Prediction-based tests for misspecification in nonlinear simultaneous systems. In: S. Karlin, T. Amemiya, and L. Goodman, eds., *Studies in Econometrics, Time Series, and Multivariate Statistics*. Academic Press, New York.

Mariano, R. S. and B. W. Brown (1985). Stochastic prediction in dynamic nonlinear systems. *Ann. INSEE* **59/60**.

Mariano, R. S. and B. W. Brown (1988). Predictors in dynamic nonlinear models: Finite-sample behavior. Econometrics Discussion Paper Series, University of Pennsylvania and Rice University.

Mariano, R. S. and B. W. Brown (1989). Stochastic simulation, prediction, and validation of nonlinear models. In: L. Klein and J. Marquez, eds., *Economics in Theory and Practice: An Eclectic Approach*. Kluwer Academic Publishers, Amsterdam.

Mariano, R. S. and B. W. Brown (1991). Stochastic-simulation tests of nonlinear econometric models. In: L. R. Klein, ed., *Comparative Performance of U.S. Econometric Models*. Oxford Univ. Press, New York, 250–259.

Mariano, R. S. and G. Gallo (1988). Predictors in nonlinear models with data uncertainty. Econometrics Discussion Paper Series, University of Pennsylvania.

Mariano, R. S. and A. Tabunda (1987). A test for misspecification in nonlinear simultaneous systems using the bootstrap predictor. Econometrics Discussion Paper Series, University of Pennsylvania.

Mariano, R. S., M. Nerlove, C. Reyes and P. Lim (1990). Measurement errors in limited dependent variable models. Econometrics Discussion Paper Series, University of Pennsylvania.

Mariano, R. S. and H. Tanizaki (1991). Nonlinear filtering: Simulation-based procedures and application to prediction with preliminary data. Econometrics Discussion Paper Series, University of Pennsylvania.

McFadden, D. (1989). Method of simulated moments for estimation of discrete response models without numerical integration. *Econometrica* **57**, 995–1026.

Mouchart, M. (1977). A regression model with an explanatory variable which is both binary and subject to errors. In: D. J. Aigner and A. Goldberger, eds., *Latent Variables in Socio-Economic Models*. North-Holland, Amsterdam, 48–66.

Newey, W. (1985). Semiparametric estimation of limited dependent variable models with endogenous explanatory variables. *Ann. INSEE* **59/60**, 219–235.

Newey, W. (1986). Linear instrumental variable estimation of limited dependent variable models with endogenous explanatory variables. *J. Econometrics* **32**, 127–141.

Newey, W. (1987). Efficient estimation of limited dependent variable models with endogenous explanatory variables. *J. Econometrics* **36**, 231–250.

Newey, W. (1989a). Semiparametric efficiency bounds. Princeton Discussion Paper.

Newey, W. (1989b). The asymptotic variance of semiparametric estimators. Princeton Discussion Paper.

Pakes, A. and D. Pollard (1989). Simulation and the asymptotics of optimization estimators. *Econometrica* **57**, 1027–1057.

Reyes, C. (1991). Adoption of modern technology in Philippine Agriculture: A simultaneous limited dependent variable approach. Ph.D. Dissertation, University of Pennsylvania, Department of Economics.

Robinson, P. (1987). Asymptotically efficient estimation in the presence of heteroskedasticity of unknown form. *Econometrica* **55**, 875–891.

Robinson, P. (1988). Root-*n*-consistent semiparametric regression. *Econometrica* **56**, 931–954.

Robinson, P. (1991). Best nonlinear three-stage least squares estimation of certain econometric models. *Econometrica* **59**, 755–786.

Schafer, D. (1987). Covariate measurement error in generalized linear models. *Biometrika* **74**, 385–391.

Schafer, D., L. A. Stefanski and T. D. Tosteson (1988). A measurement-error model for binary and ordinal regression. North Carolina State University Institute of Statistics, Mimeograph Series No. 1918R.

Stefanski, L. A. (1985). The effects of measurement error on parameter estimation. *Biometrika* **72**(3), 583–592.

Stefanski, L. A. (1988). Unbiased estimation of a nonlinear function of a normal mean with application to measurement error models. North Carolina State University, Institute of Statistics Mimeo Series #1930.

Stefanski, L. A. and R. J. Carroll (1985). Covariate measurement error in logistic regression. *Ann. Statist.* **13**, 1335–1351.

Tanizaki, H. (1991). Nonlinear Filters – Estimation and Applications. Ph.D. Dissertation, University of Pennsylvania, Department of Economics.

Tanizaki, H. and R. S. Mariano (1991). Prediction, filtering, and smoothing in nonlinear and nonnormal cases using Monte-Carlo integration. Econometrics Discussion Paper Series, University of Pennsylvania.

Tanizaki, H. and R. S. Mariano (1992). Nonlinear filters based on Taylor series expansions. Econometrics Discussion Paper Series, University of Pennsylvania.

Trivellato, U. and E. Rettore (1986). Preliminary data errors and their impact on the forecast error of simultaneous equation models. *J. Business Econom. Statist.* **4**, 445–453.

Wolter, K. M. and W. A. Fuller (1982a). Estimation of nonlinear errors-in-variables models. *Ann. Statist.* **10**, 539–548.

Wolter, K. M. and W. A. Fuller (1982b). Estimation of the quadratic errors-in-variables model. *Biometrika* **69**, 175–182.

Yatchew, A. and Z. Griliches (1985). Specification error in probit models. *Rev. Econom. Statist.* **67**, 134–139.

Zellner, A. (1970). Estimation of regression relationships containing unobservable independent variables. *Internat. Econom. Rev.* **11**, 441–454.

G. S. Maddala, C. R. Rao and H. D. Vinod, eds., *Handbook of Statistics, Vol. 11*
© 1993 Elsevier Science Publishers B.V. All rights reserved.

23

Bootstrap Methods: Applications in Econometrics

H. D. Vinod

1. Introduction and motivation for resampling methods in econometrics

Computer intensive methods are attractive in empirical research due to exponentially declining costs of computing. This chapter reviews Efron's method called the bootstrap, and briefly mentions its relation to the jackknife, with a particular emphasis on econometric applications. We review several theoretical results, especially those which appear to be practical to econometricians. Bootstrap literature has made tremendous progress in solving an old statistical problem: making reliable confidence statements in complicated small sample, multi-step, dependent, nonnormal cases. We mention examples which deal with important areas in both micro- and macroeconomics. For graduate students who do not enjoy theoretical statistics, bootstrap often substitutes raw computing power for intricate econometric theory, without sacrificing the quality of inference.

In social sciences, including econometrics, there are severe data limitations and yet realistic models tend to be highly complicated. Resampling methods provide radically new solutions to several modeling problems involving interdependence, simultaneity, nonlinearity, nonstationarity, instability, nonnormality, heteroscedasticity, small or missing data, Hawthorne effect, etc. The bootstrap handles these problems nonparametrically and intuitively, avoiding complicated power functions, Cramér–Rao lower bounds, bias corrections for Wald or Lagrange multiplier tests, etc.

Section 2 briefly reviews econometric applications. Many early applications of the bootstrap in econometrics, e.g., Freedman and Peters (1984a,b), attempt to provide an alternative to asymptotic standard error estimates. The jackknife is also used to find improved estimates of the standard errors. This survey hopes to be self-contained and accessible, showing that the bootstrap offers a potentially valuable insight into the sampling distributions, beyond simpler and improved estimation of standard errors. When two or more statistical tests are used, their power is often difficult to determine analytically. The bootstrap sampling distribution can eliminate the need for tedious computations of the power in some cases. Sections 3 and 4 concentrate on the regression context. Section 5 is the longest, discussing solutions to the pivot and bias problems, which generated criticisms of the early bootstrap methods. In Sections 7 through 10 we discuss recent results regarding estimation of confidence intervals with the help of the bootstrap. For example, we consider transformations to achieve stability of the variance and normality. Most users of confidence sets are painfully aware that the coverage probability of a 95% confidence set may not be 0.95 in practice. Our review shows tremendous promise in improving confidence statements, including the coverage correction algorithm by Beran (1987), a calibration adjustment by Loh (1987) and extensions by Martin (1990). In Sections 6 and 10 we review a post hoc technique for cleverly manipulating the bootstrap replications. These are appealing when computations are relatively expensive, perhaps due to the complexity of the inference problem. Section 9 discusses computational aspects, Section 11 discusses simultaneous equation and dynamic econometric models, which require a special setup different from the traditional bootstrap. Section 12 has our final remarks.

2. Econometric applications of the bootstrap

In this section we indicate a limited number of econometric and other applications of the bootstrap in model building, testing and forecasting. Economic theory often focuses on testing nonlinear functions $f(\beta)$ of parameters β estimated by $\hat{\beta}$. The expectation E of $f(\hat{\beta})$ is then more complicated than simply $f(E\hat{\beta})$ and matters get worse for estimating the corresponding standard errors, confidence intervals, etc., especially when simultaneous equations or nonnormal errors are present. Bootstrap applications below solve these and related problems rather simply. Lunneborg (1988) reports bootstrap software for applications in behavioral sciences. Resampling Stats is a software firm from Arlington, Virginia which offers an easy-to-use personal computer software language suited for learning elementary probability and statistics by naive resampling methods. I use the GAUSS and FORTRAN languages in my own work. The following classification of econometric applications is subject to some unavoidable overlap.

2.1. Least squares and least absolute value regression and model selection

Kundra (1985) evaluates linear regressions. Morey and Wang (1985) bootstrap the Durbin–Watson statistic. Dielman and Pfaffenberger (1986) test hypotheses in a least absolute value regression. Srivastava and Singh (1989) apply bootstrap in multiplicative models. Ghosh et al. (1984) discuss bootstrapping the median. Dijkstra and Veldkamp (1988) bootstrap data-driven model selection. Selvanathan (1989) estimates bootstrap standard errors of index numbers. Morey and Schenck (1984) study small sample behavior of the bootstrap. McAleer and Veall (1989) report an application to evaluation of the deterrent effect of capital punishment in terms of extreme bounds analysis which quantifies specification uncertainty.

2.2. Simultaneous equation models

Section 11 discusses this topic in greater detail. Freedman and Peters (1984a,b) study energy demand and input shares. Lagged dependent variables, cross equation restrictions, unknown covariance matrices and related complications are handled quite simply by the bootstrap. Green et al. (1987) apply bootstrap to estimate elasticities of a linear expenditure system in demand analysis, and find that the asymptotic standard errors were too large by a factor of two. Hu et al. (1986) show that both the jackknife and the bootstrap can reduce the bias of two stage least squares (2SLS). Korajczyk (1985) bootstraps three stage least squares (3SLS) applied to international currency markets.

2.3. Microeconomics

At the 1984 meeting of the Canadian Econometric Study group Vinod and Raj presented a microeconomic application of the bootstrap to ordinary and ridge regression, which is reported in Vinod and Raj (1988). They bootstrap inference problems associated with the 1984 breakup of Bell system telephone companies, and find that the Bell system enjoyed economies of scale, supporting Vinod (1976). They reject over-capitalization predicted by the static microeconomic (Averch and Johnson, 1962) theory for firms whose rate of return on total investment is regulated. Eakin et al. (1990) also bootstrap the statistics associated with profit maximization, scale elasticity, and scope economies. For large demand systems, Raj and Taylor (1989) evaluate tests for within-equation (homogeneity) restrictions showing high power and reliability of the bootstrap. Market demand will satisfy the law of demand when the mean of certain income effect matrices is positive definite. Hardle et al. (1991) bootstrap the distribution of the smallest eigenvalue to test the positive definiteness.

2.4. Forecasting and state space modeling

Peters and Freedman (1985) evaluate forecasting equations. Efron and Gong (1983) bootstrap a three-step prediction rule from a medical application which is 'hopelessly beyond' traditional theory. Veall (1987) reports a forecasting application where the bootstrap allows for the uncertainty associated with the need to project the regressors. Stoffer and Wall (1991) develop a bootstrap algorithm for state space and Kalman filter models.

2.5. Autoregressive models

In the first order autoregressions bootstrap can improve estimation of the *p*-values, power of tests, etc. The *p*-values are interpreted as Bayesian posterior tail probabilities by Sims and Uhlig (1991) to avoid complications of unit root asymptotics. Rayner (1990) advises against using the traditional *t* tests in favor of the bootstrap. Basawa et al. (1991) prove that for the zero mean unit root AR(1) models bootstrap will fail, which may not matter in econometric models having nonzero trends. Forecasting performance of second order autoregressive models is studied by Son et al. (1987). Generalized autoregressive conditional heteroscedasticity (GARCH) models are used for forecasting variances, studying volatility, persistence in variances and structural change. Lamoureux and Lastrapes (1990) simulate GARCH models with a bootstrap. Vector autoregressions or VAR models are common in applied macroeconomics, partly because they let the data speak for themselves. Runkle (1987) uses the bootstrap for confidence intervals around VAR estimates and finds them to be quite wide, similar to those of the asymptotic theory, concluding that the data are not 'talking very loudly'.

2.6. Shrinkage estimation

Delaney and Chatterjee (1986) bootstrap the biasing parameter of ridge regression and provide independent measures of prediction errors. Brownstone's (1990) simulation shows that bootstrap performs well when applied to the Stein rule, principal components and related shrinkage estimators. This should be contrasted with Sen's (1988, p. 417) careful asymptotic results showing that the bootstrap has no advantages over the jackknife for the Stein-rule estimators. Vinod (1991b) discusses applications of the double bootstrap to ridge regression.

2.7. Financial economics

Stock market data often need estimators of stable law parameters, whose sampling distribution can be studied with the help of the bootstrap, as in Akgiray and Lamoureux (1989). Schwartz and Torous (1989) estimate standard errors of maximum likelihood estimates in a study of prepayment and valuation of mortgage-backed securities. Affleck-Graves and McDonald (1990) report an application to multivariate testing of the capital asset pricing model (CAPM). Their tests include maximum entropy methods, designed to deal with the singularity when the number of assets included in the CAPM exceeds the number of time series data points. Bartow and Sun (1987) report confidence intervals for relative risk models.

2.8. Limited dependent variable models

Nested logit models are often used for qualitative choice situations including travel demand, energy conservation, auto ownership, scheduling, etc. A bootstrap comparison of various logit estimators is reported by Brownstone and Small (1989).

2.9. Income distributions

Elderton's kappa criterion is useful in characterizing various density functions used in the literature for income distributions including beta, Pareto, Gumbel, Weibull, etc. The bootstrap is used by Hirschberg et al. (1988) in studying the properties of estimated kappa. Distance type measures are used in econometrics, although they are not emphasized in econometrics textbooks. Vinod (1985) suggests a statistic for measuring the economic distance between blacks and whites. Romano (1988) provides six examples of distance type measures in applied statistics and shows the potential applicability of bootstrapping.

3. Definition and properties of the bootstrap in the regression context

This section may be skipped by those familiar with basic bootstrap methods. The bootstrap is primarily designed for obtaining sampling distributions in complicated situations where analytical results are difficult to obtain. To motivate the econometrician, let us consider the regression model

$$y = X\beta + u, \tag{1}$$

where y is a $T \times 1$ vector of the dependent variable, X is a $T \times p$ matrix of p regressors whose first column consists of all ones. The matrix X has rank p and u is a $T \times 1$ vector of independent and identically distributed (iid) errors with elements u_t and an unknown possibly nonnormal true distribution function F with mean zero and variance σ^2.

The ordinary least squares (OLS) estimator, $b = (X'X)^{-1}X'y$, leads to the residuals defined as $e = y - Xb$. The covariance matrix of b is

$$\mathrm{Cov}(b) = s^2(X'X)^{-1}, \quad s^2 = (e'e)/(T-p).$$

An empirical cumulative distribution function (CDF) of OLS residuals puts probability mass $1/T$ at each e_t, and is denoted here by F_e. Now the basic bootstrap idea is to use F_e with mean zero and variance σ_e^2 as a feasible, approximate, nonparametric estimate of the CDF of the true unknown errors denoted by F_u. Let J be a suitably large number ($=1000$, say). We draw J sets of bootstrap samples of size T, with elements denoted by e_{*jt} ($j = 1, 2, \ldots, J$ and $t = 1, 2, \ldots, T$) from F_e using random sampling *with replacement*. To understand this sampling, imagine T tickets marked with e_1 to e_T, the OLS residuals. Next, imagine drawing J random samples with replacement of size T from a box containing the T tickets. This generates J sets of $T \times 1$ vectors denoted by e_{*j} having elements e_{*jt} ($t = 1, 2, \ldots, T$). Hence the pseudo y data are obtained by

$$y_{*j} = Xb + e_{*j}, \quad j = 1, 2, \ldots, J \tag{2}$$

yielding a large number J of regression problems to be used for bootstrap inference described below.

Since repeated use of the same OLS residuals may intuitively seem to be peculiar, we will now discuss its motivation. Note that the bootstrap size J has been chosen to be a large number, which ensures that the probability $P(e_{*jt} = e_t) = 1/T$. Hence their variance is

$$\sigma_e^2 = \mathrm{E}(e_{*jt}^2) = \sum_{t=1}^{T} \frac{1}{T} \mathrm{var}(e_t) = \frac{1}{T} \sum_{t=1}^{T} e_t^2 = s^2(T-p)/T . \tag{3}$$

If each residual is 'scaled up' by multiplication by $\sqrt{[T/(T-p)]}$, the variance of the rescaled e_{*jt} should be equal to s^2. We will see that this property is crucial for the motivation we seek. Applying OLS to the pseudo y data leads to

$$b_{*j} = (X'X)^{-1}X'y_{*j} \quad \text{and} \quad \mathrm{Cov}(b_{*j}) = \sigma_e^2(X'X)^{-1} \tag{4}$$

for $j = 1, 2, \ldots, J$. This expression for the covariance matrix is the same as $\mathrm{Cov}(b)$ provided we use scaled up residuals $\sqrt{[T/(T-p)]}e_{*jt}$. For the familiar regression model satisfying standard assumptions the standard errors of OLS regression coefficients by the bootstrap and the conventional methods are almost identical. While this provides no benefit in the usual situation, it does show the desirability of the property when the bootstrap is applied to a messy situation.

Denote the i-th element of the $p \times 1$ vector b_{*j} by $b_{*j}[i]$. The bootstrap realizations of $b_{*j}[i]$ over the J resamples may be used for a preliminary estimate of its sampling distribution. Then, an estimate of the variance is

$$\mathrm{Var}(b_*[i]) = (J-1)^{-1} \sum_{j=1}^{J} (b_{*j}[i] - \bar{b}_*[i])^2 ,$$

$$\text{where } \bar{b}_*[i] = J^{-1} \sum_{j=1}^{J} b_{*j}[i] . \tag{5}$$

To achieve greater accuracy, bootstrap confidence intervals involve additional notation and complications. In the following discussion we omit the index $[i]$ when the reference to a single element is clear from the context. It is tempting to use the empirical sampling distribution of b_{*j} over J realizations for the construction of a confidence interval. Efron's (1982, p. 78) percentile method of constructing confidence intervals for β does precisely this. Let us denote the empirical CDF of the J estimates b_{*j} by $F_*(z) = \#(b_{*j} \leqslant z)/J$, where $\#(\ )$ denotes the number of times the condition in the parenthesis is observed. For given α between 0 and 0.5 (without loss of generality) we define the following limits of a confidence interval. Clearly, b_{*j} lies between the lower limit $b_{\mathrm{LO}}(\alpha) = F_*^{-1}(\alpha)$, and the upper limit $b_{\mathrm{UP}}(\alpha) = F_*^{-1}(1-\alpha)$, where $F_*^{-1}(z)$ denotes the inverse of $F_*(z)$. Assuming the approximate equality $b_{*j} \approx \beta$, we write the following probability from a bootstrap resample (distinguished by subscript ∗) intended for each element:

$$\text{Prob}_*[b_{\text{LO}}(\alpha) \leqslant b_{*j} \leqslant b_{\text{UP}}(\alpha)] = \text{Prob}_*[b_{\text{LO}}(\alpha) \leqslant \beta \leqslant b_{\text{UP}}(\alpha)]$$

$$= 1 - 2\alpha . \tag{6}$$

This may be called a naive percentile confidence interval based on the empirical CDF of bootstrap estimates. A useful property of these intervals is that they are invariant to any *monotonic* transformation. Hence, all it takes for them to be correct is that they are correct on some transformed scale. The naive interval may be unreliable when the estimator is biased and/or no such transformation exists. To remedy this, Efron also suggests relaxing $b_{*j} \approx \beta$ with a weaker assumption that $(b - \beta) \approx (b_{*j} - b)$. To visualize why this is plausible, note that

$$b - \beta = (X'X)^{-1}X'y - \beta = (X'X)^{-1}X'u = Wu , \tag{7}$$

where $W = (X'X)^{-1}X'$ is a known matrix and u are unobservable errors. Now,

$$b_{*j} - b = (X'X)^{-1}X'y_{*j} - b$$

$$= (X'X)^{-1}X'[Xb + e_{*j}] - b , \quad \text{from (2)}$$

$$= (X'X)^{-1}X'e_{*j} = We_{*j} . \tag{8}$$

Since e_{*j} and u have the same mean zero and same variance s^2, we have We_{*j} from the right-hand side of (8) approximately equal to Wu on the right-hand side of (7). To obtain the left-hand side of (8) into (6) we subtract b from each term of the first part of (6) and write

$$\text{Prob}_*[b_{\text{LO}}(\alpha) - b \leqslant b_{*j} - b \leqslant b_{\text{UP}}(\alpha) - b] = 1 - 2\alpha . \tag{9}$$

Now we replace $b_{*j} - b$ in the middle term of (9) by $b - \beta$ on the left-hand side of (7), which is appropriate because the right-hand side of (7) can be approximated by the right-hand side of (8). This manipulation is called a 'reflection' of the naive confidence interval (6) through b. Thus we write

$$\text{Prob}_*[2b - b_{\text{UP}}(\alpha) \leqslant \beta \leqslant 2b - b_{\text{LO}}(\alpha)] = 1 - 2\alpha \tag{10}$$

which is called bias-corrected (BC) confidence interval, and is almost as easy as the naive percentile interval of (6). If the sampling distribution of b_{*j} is nonnormal, the mean, median and mode of the empirical CDF will not coincide with that of b. The discrepancy between the sample and population medians called 'median bias' is present for asymmetric distributions. A correction for such a bias is discussed later (see (2) of Section 5 and (7) of Section 7), without restricting ourselves to the regression problem.

There is another direct method of bootstrapping regressions without using the special regression structure which gives rise to residuals. It provides information about the variability of b even if the regression specification is not correct. One simply uses the empirical multivariate distribution function of

(y, X) to draw the bootstrap samples with replacement. As before, imagine T tickets marked with $(y, X)_1$ to $(y, X)_T$, for the T original observations. Next, imagine drawing J random samples with replacement of size T from a box containing the T tickets leading to J sets of regression data sets. Efron (1981b) shows that this method gives exactly the same answer as the more complicated bootstrap for censored data. Vinod (1991a) applies the direct method for studying the cointegration between consumption and income and suggests a modification which makes it applicable for dependent time series data and for studying misspecifications. He uses Kunsch (1989) method for the dependent data bootstrap.

4. Definition and properties of the jackknife in the regression context

Since the bootstrap is a natural extension of the jackknife we shall briefly review the jackknife in the regression context, for an elementary comparison with the bootstrap. The jackknife is essentially leave-one-observation-out and iterate over the entire data set. Rarely, more than one observation may be left out. The algebra involved in leaving one observation out in a regression context is somewhat remarkable. We shall see that the so-called hat matrix $H = X(X'X)^{-1}X'$ plays an unexpectedly important role in this algebra. For the usual regression model $y_t = x_t\beta + u_t$, let x_t denote the t-th row vector from the matrix X of observations on the p regressors, with $t = 1, 2, \ldots, T$. Now, an omission of the t-th observation will result in only $T - 1$ observations and the corresponding ordinary least squares (OLS) estimate $b_{[t]}$ of β will change depending on the omission. It can be shown that

$$b_{[t]} = b - (X'X)^{-1}x_t u_t^0, \quad \text{where } u_t^0 = \hat{u}_t/(1 - H_{tt}), \tag{1}$$

where $\hat{u}_t$ is the t-th residual, $b = (X'X)^{-1}X'y$ from all T observations and H_{tt} denotes the t-th diagonal term of the hat matrix. Using the simple average $\bar{b} = (1/T) \sum_{t=1}^{T} b_{[t]}$ of the leave-one-out estimates one can define the $p \times p$ variance of $b_{[t]}$ as

$$\text{Var } b_{[t]} = (T - 1)T^{-1} \sum_{t=1}^{T} (b_{[t]} - \bar{b})(b_{[t]} - \bar{b})'. \tag{2}$$

Again, it is remarkable that one need not actually compute the variance by actually leaving one out and repeating. MacKinnon and White (1985) show that

$$\text{Var } b_{[t]} = (T - 1)T^{-1}(X'X)^{-1}[(X'\Lambda X) - T^{-1}X'u_t^0 u_t^{0\prime}X](X'X)^{-1}, \tag{3}$$

where Λ is a $T \times T$ diagonal matrix with t-th element $(u_t^0)^2$ which in turn involves the hat matrix. Liu and Singh (1987) show that the bootstrap estimate of variance or regression coefficients is inconsistent if the residuals are heteroscedastic, whereas the jackknife estimate is better. Many early applications of the bootstrap to regression use the variance estimate without making sure that the errors are not heteroscedastic. If the real interest is in the confidence intervals based on quantiles of the sampling distributions – rather than the standard errors themselves – Ghosh et al. (1984) show that the jackknife fails dramatically. The jackknife estimator of the variance of quantiles converges in law to a transform of a chi square *random* variable, not a constant. What would happen if we leave out two or more observations instead of one? Sen (1989) shows with asymptotic theory that there is no particular advantage to leaving out more observations.

Schechtman (1991) provides a readable account of application of infinitesimal jackknifing in asymptotic theory, and gives useful references to and examples of Hoeffding's U statistics and influence functions. Sen (1991) shows that for some problems having asymptotically degenerate distributions, bias reduction role of jackknifing may make it superior to the bootstrap. Since other surveys and explanations of the jackknife are available: Hinkley (1977), Miller (1974), Wu (1986), etc., we shall not discuss it any further.

5. The pivot and the bootstrap sampling distribution for a biased estimator

This section discusses making the bootstrap applicable in non-ideal situations. The complexity of some of the literature reviewed here should not distract from the basic simplicity in applications. Readers will benefit from a review of functional transformations to achieve normality and variance stabilization. See for example, Kendall et al. (1983, §6.27, §37.10) or Bickel and Doksum (1977, §1.5). Variance stabilization is achieved indirectly by the double bootstrap in Sections 5.4 and 5.5 and directly in Section 7 below. It may be helpful to review a simple proof of the asymptotic normality of the bootstrap arithmetic mean given in Yang (1988).

5.1. Pivot and normalization for the location scale family

Assume that there is a statistical model of the probability distribution of a statistic. The term *pivotal* was introduced by Sir R. A. Fisher in the 1930s to denote standardized quantities such as Student's $t = (\bar{x} - \mu)/\text{SE}$, where SE denotes the standard error. We have $\text{SE} = (s_x/\sqrt{n})$, where $\bar{x}$ and s_x denote the sample mean and standard deviation and μ denotes the population mean. Fisher named as *ancillary* any pivotal which is solely a function of the observables. See Kotz and Johnson (1988) for recent references and details. The pivotal quantities similar to Student's t above are commonly used in the construction of $100(1 - 2\alpha)$ percent confidence intervals for μ: $\Pr(\bar{x} + t_\alpha \text{SE} \leq \mu \leq \bar{x} = t_\alpha \text{SE}) = 1 - 2\alpha$, where the two observable limits are obtained by inverting the pivotal. The general location-scale (μ, σ) family is studied by writing the density $f(x; \mu, \sigma)$ of observations x_1 to x_n as $(1/\sigma)g(z)$, where

$z = (x_i - \mu)/\sigma$ is a pivotal quantity. Now we state some well-known results for the location-scale family of distributions without proof.

LEMMA 1. *The sampling distributions of the following three pivotal quantities do not depend on unknown parameters*: (i) *for* μ *if* σ *is known*, $\text{pivot}(\mu \mid \sigma) = \sqrt{n}(\hat\mu - \mu)/\sigma$, (ii) *for* μ *when* σ *is unknown*, $\text{pivot}(\mu) = \sqrt{n}(\hat\mu - \mu)/\hat\sigma$, (iii) *for* σ *when* μ *is unknown*, $\text{pivot}(\sigma) = \hat\sigma/\sigma$.

LEMMA 2. *The (cumulative) distribution function* $F(x; \hat\mu, \hat\sigma)$ *is a pivotal quantity.*

LEMMA 3. *The likelihood ratio for choosing between two models (subscripts 0 and 1) evaluated at the maximizing parameter values*, $\lambda_{01} = \Pi f(x_i; \hat\mu_0, \hat\sigma_0)/ \Pi f(x_i; \hat\mu_1, \hat\sigma_1)$ *is a pivotal quantity.*

In bootstrapping we have no assurance that the underlying distribution is from the location-scale family. Some criticisms on the bootstrap arise from the failure of the above lemmata for arbitrary distributions.

Efron's (1982, Chapter 10) normalized bias-corrected (NBC) method, after a standardization to $N(0, 1)$ – a unit normally distributed variable – makes the 'reflection' used in equation (10) of Section 3 above. The OLS estimator b is usually transformed to a pivotal quantity $\hat\theta = [(b - \beta_0)./\text{SE}]$, where the null hypothesis is assumed to state $H_0: \beta = \beta_0$ and where $./$ denotes element-wise division by corresponding standard errors (SE). It is convenient to use the same notation $\hat\theta$ for a scalar single element of the vector $\hat\theta$. From the empirical CDF of bootstrap replications evaluated at the pivotal quantity $\hat\theta$ compute $F_*(\hat\theta) = \text{Prob}_*(\hat\theta_* \leq \hat\theta)$, a scalar in the range $[0, 1]$. Now denote another scalar

$$z_0 = \Phi^{-1}(F_*(\hat\theta)) \tag{1}$$

using the inverse of the distribution function Φ of the standard normal variate. Now $\hat\theta - \theta \sim N(-z_0, 1)$. When $\hat\theta$ has a symmetric distribution, the median bias is zero and $z_0 = 0$. When the distribution is skewed to the right, its mean is larger than the median and the quantile $z_0 > 0$.

The normalized bias-corrected (NBC) percentile method leads to the following approximate $1 - 2\alpha$ confidence statement:

$$\text{Prob}_*[F_*^{-1}(\Phi[2z_0 - z_\alpha)] \leq \theta \leq F_*^{-1}(\Phi[2z_0 + z_\alpha])] = 1 - 2\alpha , \tag{2}$$

where F_*^{-1} denotes the inverse CDF, and z_α is the upper α point for the $N(0, 1)$ normal distribution function $\Phi(z_\alpha) = 1 - \alpha$. If the bootstrap distribution is (skewed) median biased, Efron (1982) shows that the bias correction by using (2) does help. If the distribution is median unbiased, $z_0 = 0$ and using (2) will not change the interval. For example, if $z_\alpha = 1.96$ and $z_0 = 0$, $2z_0 - z_\alpha = -1.96$, $\Phi(-1.96) = 0.025 = \alpha$ and the lower limit from (2) is simply the 0.025

quantile of the bootstrap CDF. While 'normalization' is accomplished by (2), direct 'variance stabilization' will be discussed in Section 7.

5.2. *Implications of Edgeworth expansion type asymptotics*

Starting with Singh (1981) much theoretical research was attempted to use asymptotic theory and advanced mathematical statistics including saddlepoint and Edgeworth expansions to study the bootstrap for estimation of the underlying sampling distribution. An insightful survey of various results related to Edgeworth expansions is made by Babu (1989), who also reviews empirical Edgeworth expansions, where population moments are replaced by corresponding sample moments. Babu also provides references to the Bayesian bootstrap and shows when the bootstrap does not work. For example, if one applies the bootstrap to obtain the sampling distribution of the square of the sample mean a chi square is appropriate. Babu indicates the modification needed to make the bootstrap work. Efron (1985) shows that in the parametric case one can use the Edgeworth approximation instead of the empirical CDF based on Monte Carlo replications.

Let us consider a univariate parameter μ with estimator $\hat{\mu}$ based on n observations, whose variance is σ^2/n. The underlying distribution is not assumed to be from the location-scale family and hence Lemma 1 above fails to hold. The basic idea is to use the asymptotic Edgeworth expansion of the underlying arbitrary distribution, whose leading term is Φ, the CDF of the unit normal. This expansion is used for approximating the distribution functions used in advanced econometrics as well, Amemiya (1985, p. 93). We use the usual notation μ_i for the i-th central moment, $O(\cdot)$ for order of magnitude and $O_p(\cdot)$ for order in probability. Now,

$$\Pr(\sqrt{n}(\hat{\mu} - \mu) \leq x)$$
$$= \Phi(x/\sigma) - n^{-1/2}(\mu_3/6\sigma^3)[(x/\sigma)^2 - 1]f(x/\sigma) + O(n^{-1}), \qquad (3)$$

where $(z^2 - 1)$ is the Hermite polynomial of degree 2 appears with $z = x/\sigma$ and where f is the density of the normal. For brevity, denote a polynomial in x and its moments appearing in (3) by $p_1(x)$, its estimate by $\hat{p}_1(x)$ and 'conditional on the sample' by $(\cdot | S)$. Recall from Section 3 equations (7) and (8) that the bootstrap insight in the present notation is to replace $\hat{\mu} - \mu$ from the left side of (3) by $\hat{\mu}_* - \hat{\mu}$, where the moments based on bootstrap replications are denoted by the subscript $*$. Hence,

$$\Pr(\sqrt{n}(\hat{\mu}_* - \hat{\mu}) \leq x \mid S) = \Phi(x/\hat{\sigma}) + \hat{p}_1(x)f(x/\hat{\sigma})/\sqrt{n} + O_p(n^{-1/2}). \quad (4)$$

Subtracting (4) from (3) and noting that $\hat{p}_1 - p_1$ and $\hat{\sigma} - \sigma$ are both of $O_p(n^{-1/2})$ we have

$$\Pr(\sqrt{n}(\hat{\mu} - \mu) \leq x) - \Pr(\sqrt{n}(\hat{\mu}_* - \hat{\mu}) \leq x \mid S)$$
$$= \Phi(x/\sigma) - \Phi(x/\hat{\sigma}) + O_p(n^{-1}) \qquad (5)$$

which is in error by $O_p(n^{-1/2})$, because $\hat\sigma - \sigma$ is $O_p(n^{-1/2})$. To reduce the error of $O_p(n^{-1})$ we use a studentized pivotal quantity with $\hat\sigma$ in the denominator, Babu and Singh (1983, 1984), Beran (1988), Fisher and Hall (1989) and Singh and Babu (1990). Then we have

$$\Pr(\sqrt{n}(\hat\mu - \mu)/\hat\sigma \leq x) = \Phi(x) + n^{-1/2}(\mu_3/6\sigma^3)(2x^2 + 1)f(x) + O(n^{-1}).$$

(6)

It can be shown that a bootstrap estimate similar to (4) leads to a cancellation of the $\Phi(x)$ term, when a subtraction similar to (5) is made. Thus, studentization reduces error and it is not surprising that the expression $\mu_3/6\sigma^3$ reappears in Section 7, equation (11) in the context of improving confidence intervals. The notion of error above is extended to an error in rejection probability (ERP) which permits formal comparison of tests in Beran (1988). These results have multivariate and multiparameter extensions by the same authors.

Babu and Singh (1983, 1984) show that the bootstrap can estimate the sampling distribution F up to a second order term. Their proofs require the technical assumption that the underlying distribution is strongly nonlattice defined as follows. Denote $\hat{F}(t) = \int e^{itx}\,dF$, the characteristic function. F is called strongly nonlattice if $|\hat{F}(t)| \neq 1$ for all $t \neq 0$. A practical implication of Babu and Singh's work is that *studentization is recommended*, even for non-location-scale families. For certain estimators like the ratios of means one can get around the problem of lattice distribution by a transformation (Babu, 1989, p. 227).

5.3. The definition of a root which may depend on unknown parameters

Beran (1987) has introduced a concept of a *root* which is important in the bootstrap literature. It has two properties. First, the root is motivated by a pivot, but is not necessarily a pivot, because the sampling distribution of a root may depend on the unknown parameters. Second, the form of a root should be such that its sampling distribution can be consistently estimated. Often, we have a root when an attempt to studentize or standardize by a monotonic transformation does not necessarily remove the dependence on unknown parameters.

5.4. Sampling distribution of a root is uniform only in the ideal situation

Since a CDF is always between 0 and 1, the estimated CDF of a root will also $\in [0, 1]$. If all values in $[0, 1]$ are equally likely, we have a uniform density over the $[0, 1]$ interval. Beran (1987) suggests a transformation of the scalar root R_n designed to improve the performance of the bootstrap. His subscript n reminds us about the presence of an underlying null hypothesis.

$$R_{n,1} = H_n(R_n),$$

(7)

where H_n is the estimated CDF of R_n and the subscript $n, 1$ will be replaced by n, L later in the multivariate context. Note that the original roots R_n are not restricted to the range $[0, 1]$, but the transformed roots are CDFs, and must be in the range $[0, 1]$. The *key result* here is that the sampling distribution of $R_{n,1}$ is uniform over $[0, 1]$ only in the ideal situation when the root is a pivot having a continuous distribution free from the problems of bias, lattice distribution, etc. When the situation is not ideal, often double bootstrap can be used to make a simple adjustment. The double bootstrap needs vast computations to estimate the CDF of $R_{n,1}$ denoted by $H_{n,1}$. From this, one finds the largest $1 - \alpha$ quantile called $c_{n,1}$. In other words, we solve for $c_{n,1}$ in

$$H_{n,1}(R_{n,1} = c_{n,1}) = 1 - \alpha \tag{8}$$

which must be in the range $[0, 1]$, because it is a quantile of a variable restricted to $[0, 1]$. However, $c_{n,1}$ itself need not be $1 - \alpha$, unless we have the ideal situation mentioned above. The difference between $c_{n,1}$ and $1 - \alpha$ suggests skewness, nonnormality, etc. The simple adjustment mentioned above is to use the $(c_{n,1})$-th quantile of the CDF of the original root denoted by H_n. A compact equivalent formula is to consider the confidence set defined by the inequality

$$R_n \leqslant H_n^{-1}\{H_{n,1}^{-1}(1 - \alpha)\} \tag{9}$$

which can be seen from (7) and (8).

5.5. Double bootstrap for regression: One parameter case

Now we explain the double bootstrap for the regression example of equations (1) and (2) of Section 3. Let us define a root $R_n = \tau(b)$ with a transformation τ (e.g., studentization). Recall that b_{*j} estimates from $j = 1, 2, \ldots, J$ bootstrap iterations are computed first; and then we store their residual vectors as e_{*j}. The CDF of $R_n = \tau(b_{*j})$ is called $H_n(w) = \Pr(R_n < w)$ for any w which is a function of b_{*j}. If we were to stop with the single bootstrap, the null hypothesis would have been rejected when $R_n \geqslant c_j = H_n^{-1}(1 - \alpha)$, where the critical value c_j is for a $100(1 - \alpha)$ percent test. The double bootstrap is designed to refine the critical values of the single bootstrap, whether studentizing was done at the first stage or not. For each j we compute a $T \times 1$ vector of pseudo y values defined by the equation: $y_{*k} = Xb_{*j} + e_{*jk}$, where e_{*jk} are found from the $T \times 1$ vector of e_{*j} values, by using sampling with replacement. This is repeated for $k = 1, 2, \ldots, K$ ($=1000$, say) second stage bootstrap iterations. Regressing these pseudo y values on X yields b_{*jk} and $R_{n,j} = \tau(b_{*jk})$ for each j. Let Z_j denote the fraction of $R_{n,j}$ values which are less than $R_n = \tau(b_{*j})$ in the second stage bootstrap over K iterations. Note that $Z_j \in [0, 1]$ is the key computation from the double bootstrap, used to adjust the quantile associated with R_n from the single bootstrap.

Vinod's (1991b) ridge regression example has $J = 1000$ and a 95% confidence interval is desired. Since 2.5% of 1000 is 25, the lower limit is based on R_n at the 25-th ranked value of the first stage bootstrap distribution. The corresponding Z_j from the second stage bootstrap with $K = 1000$ is 0.030. Why is 0.030 close to 0.025 for this example? A plot of the distribution of K times Z_j attached as Figure 1 is close to the uniform distribution over the range 0 to 1000, where the corresponding normal distribution is superimposed. Uniformity implies that there is no serious nonnormality, lack of a pivot, etc. According to above theory, 0.030 is a somewhat more believable location of the true quantile than 0.025, because the latter represents only one out of K realizations. For sufficiently large K and J, the CDF of Z_j over $j = 1, 2, \ldots, J$ approximates $H_{n,1}$ and its inverse evaluated at $1 - \alpha$ and (9) yield the confidence interval quite simply. In the above example, we just use the 30-th ranked value from the first stage sampling distribution as the lower limit of the desired confidence interval. Vinod (1991b) also reports the case where 1000 times the earlier ridge regression shrinkage factor is used, leading to a highly nonuniform sampling distribution in Figure 2, providing a warning that the ridge estimator is ill-behaved, with excess shrinkage suggested by the considerable probability mass in the left-most pillar. Figure 2 is similar to Figure 1 with the normal curve included for comparison.

5.6. Multiparameter regression case

Confidence intervals and significance testing in the multivariate case is discussed in detail in the readable work of Miller (1981, Section 2.1). In the

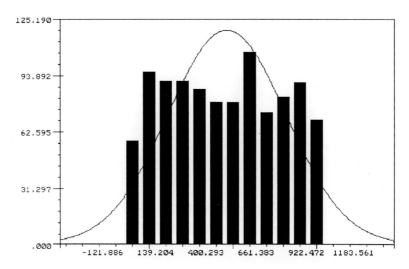

Fig. 1. Sampling distribution of 1000 times $Z_j = \#(\tau(b_{**jk}) \leq \tau(b_{*j}))$, the number of times transformed second stage bootstrap estimates are no greater than the first stage estimates.

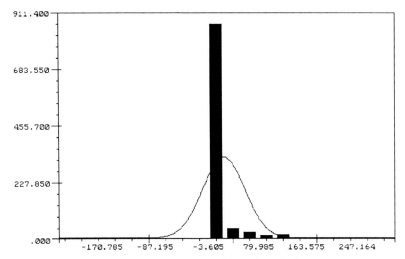

Fig. 2. Sampling distribution of 1000 times $Z_j = \#(\tau(b_{**jk}) \leq \tau(b_{*j}))$ for the case when excess shrinkage (1000 times that in Figure 1) is used, leading to highly nonuniform distribution.

normal regression framework where

$$b \sim N(\beta, \sigma^2(X'X)^{-1}),$$

$$s^2 = y'[I - X(X'X)^{-1}X']y/(n-p), \qquad (n-p)s^2\sigma^2 \sim \chi^2_{T-p} \qquad (10)$$

which is a chi square random variable with $T - p$ degrees of freedom (df). If we are interested in a fixed q-dimensional subspace of $\mathscr{L} = \{L = (L_1, L_2, \ldots, L_p)\}$ of the p-dimensional space, and let $L'\beta = \Sigma^p_{i=1} L_i\beta_i$ denote a linear combination defined in the q-dimensional subspace. For example, if $q = 2$ and $L_i = 1$ for all $i \leq 2$ and $L_i = 0$, otherwise, $L'\beta = \beta_1 + \beta_2$. The Scheffé technique gives simultaneous confidence intervals for $L'\beta$ implying that

$$\Pr\{L'\beta \in L'b \pm \sqrt{(qF^\alpha_{q,n-p})}s\sqrt{[L'(X'X)^{-1}L]}, \ \forall L \in \mathscr{L}\} = 1 - \alpha, \tag{11}$$

where $\forall$ denotes 'for all', $F^\alpha_{q,n-q}$ denotes the upper 100α percent point of the F distribution, with q degrees of freedom (df) in the numerator and $n - p$ df in the denominator. If only one linear combination is involved, the classical regression theory would lead to a similar interval except that $\sqrt{(qF^\alpha_{q,n-p})}$ is replaced by $t^{\alpha/2}_{n-p}$, the upper $100\alpha/2$ percent point of the t-distribution with $n - p$ degrees of freedom.

In Beran's (1990) terminology, the subscript n denotes the null hypothesis, subscript L refers to the matrix defining linear combinations and a root of the confidence set is defined by

$$R_{n,L} = |L'(b - \beta)|\mathrm{SE}^{-1}_{n,L}, \quad \text{where } \mathrm{SE}_{n,L} = s\sqrt{[L'(X'X)^{-1}L]} \tag{12}$$

which is studentized. In the nonparametric regression case the F distribution of (11) is replaced by q^{-1} times a chi square with q df in computing the standard error. In the nonnormal case the asymptotic distribution of the root depends upon both β and the linear combination L. The bootstrap method can generate the sampling distribution and CDF of $R_{n,L}$ and its supremum $\sup_L R_{n,L}$, over all possible linear combinations. Denote the above CDFs by $H_{n,L}$ and H_n (for the null) respectively, when the CDF is evaluated at the estimated values of the unknown parameters. In the regression case, we have the following analytical expressions for the CDFs, which can also be estimated from bootstraps.

$$H_{n,L} = \Psi(1/\sigma_L), \quad \text{where } \sigma_L = \sigma\sqrt{[L'(X'X)^{-1}L]}, \tag{13}$$

where Ψ denotes CDF of $|Z|$, where Z has a standard normal distribution. The reason for the absolute value is that the root in (12) is defined as an absolute value. For the regression case the null distribution is

$$H_n = \chi_q \cdot \Psi^{-1}(\cdot), \tag{14}$$

where χ_q is the CDF of the square root of chi square distribution with q df. The critical value of the underlying test is denoted by c_L. For a 100α percent test, the critical value is at $100(1-\alpha)$-th quantile of the CDF of the underlying null distribution. Denote by $H_{n,L}^{-1}(t)$ and $H_n^{-1}(t)$ the largest t-th quantiles of the corresponding CDFs. It can be verified that the critical value is

$$c_L = H_{n,L}^{-1}(H_n^{-1}(1-\alpha)) \tag{15}$$

by the method of bootstrapped roots, or the B method. In other words, when the value of the statistic $L'b$ is larger than c_L, the null hypothesis is rejected. This is similar to (9) above.

Beran (1990) renames double bootstrap as the B^2 method, which uses an induced root defined by

$$S_{n,L} = H_{n,L}^{-1}(H_n^{-1}(R_{n,L})) = \chi_q[|L'(b-\beta)|/\text{SE}_{n,L}], \tag{16}$$

where the standard error is from (12) above. This induced root becomes the root in the next iteration. The bootstrap CDF of $S_{n,L}$ is denoted by $K_{n,L}$. The bootstrap null CDF of $\sup_L S_{n,L}$ is denoted by K_n. The critical value of the B^2 method becomes

$$c_L = H_{n,L}^{-1}(H_n^{-1}\{K_{n,L}^{-1}(K_n^{-1}(1-\alpha))\}) \tag{17}$$

and generalizes the pre-pivoting transformation (7) of Beran (1988). It appears to be computationally burdensome, but achieves error reduction and increased balance compared to the B method. Beran (1990) shows that in the regression setting, B^2 method yields Scheffé's exact simultaneous confidence intervals, is balanced and has the correct asymptotic level at every sample size, whereas the B (single bootstrap) method may not. Vinod and Raj (1988) show that ridge regression leads to a lack of pivot and dependence on unknown regression parameters. Using the double bootstrap (B^2) method is a possible new solution to this and similar problems. Vinod (1991b) shows that the lack of a pivot for ridge regression problems need not be serious when the sample distribution (see Figure 1) of K times Z_j is close to being uniform. The computational pointers are given in Section 9. An econometric application to cointegrating regressions is found in Vinod and McCullough (1991). Although Veall (1986) finds that the bootstrap for regression under serially correlated errors does not help solve the bias problem, Rayner (1991) shows that it works with a simple modification.

6. Improved estimation of the bias in the regression context by the post hoc method

Bootstrap estimates of the bias in the regression context may be obtained directly from (4) of Section 3 as

$$\text{Bias}_d = J^{-1} \sum_{j=1}^{J} b_{*j} - b . \tag{1}$$

Efron (1990) has suggested an alternative estimator which retains the simple random sampling with replacement of the original bootstrap, but attempts to process the data differently. The aim is to reduce the number J of iterations and improve estimates of the bias, variance and quantiles of the sampling distribution. The new data processing keeps track of the number of times an individual value e_1 to e_T of the original vector of residuals $e = y - Xb$ occurs in the J bootstrap replications. For $t = 1, 2, \ldots, T$ let

$$p_t = (\text{total number of occurrences of } e_t \text{ over } J$$
$$\text{bootstrap replications})/J . \tag{2}$$

The following method is called a post hoc correction, because its data processing is made after the J bootstrap replications are chosen. It is obviously simpler than a balanced method of resampling suggested by Davison et al. (1986), where balancing is enforced before the bootstrap sample is chosen.

Consider a $T \times 1$ vector p^e whose t-th element is $p_t e_t$ and generate the pseudo y values by $y_{*a} = Xb + p^e$. Now, regressing y_{*a} on X yields the vector b_{*p} of post hoc corrected regression coefficients and an alternative post hoc estimate of the bias denoted by

$$\text{Bias}_p = J^{-1} \sum_{j=1}^{J} b_{*j} - b_{*p} . \tag{3}$$

With considerable ingenuity Efron proves that the post hoc Bias_p estimate is superior to the direct estimate Bias_d of (1). Efron also supplements his proofs with simulations. The post hoc method can also improve confidence interval estimation, and will be discussed later in Section 10, after we review newer confidence interval estimators.

7. Efron's bias-corrected accelerated BC_a interval

The progression from naive and bias-corrected (BC) confidence intervals (see (10) of Section 3) to normalized BC (see (2) of Section 5) involved normalization. In this section we consider the next step of 'variance stabilization', though it may be computationally burdensome. The accelerated bias correction BC_a method proposed by Efron (1987) stabilizes the variance and was motivated by Schenker's (1985) counterexample to the BC method. The expression 'acceleration' is used, because one computes the speed at which the standard deviation is changing. This section also reviews Diciccio and Tibshirani's (1987) extension of BC_a intervals designed to achieve second order correctness described by Efron (1987, p. 199) as follows. The coverage probability on each side of the confidence interval should be within $O(T^{-1})$ of the claimed correct value, and the endpoints should agree through order $O_p(T^{-1})$ with the endpoints of the correct interval.

For easy access to details in the original article, let us now use Efron's (1987) notation as much as possible. The starting point is the asymptotic result for an estimator $\hat{\theta}$ of θ

$$(\hat{\theta} - \theta)/\hat{\sigma} \sim N(0, 1) \text{ implying}$$
$$\Pr[\hat{\theta} + z^{(\alpha)}\hat{\sigma} \leq \theta \leq \hat{\theta} + z^{(1-\alpha)}\hat{\sigma}] = 1 - 2\alpha , \tag{1}$$

where $z^{(\alpha)}$ is 100α percentile of the unit normal. By defining a $100(1 - 2\alpha)$ percent confidence interval instead of the usual $100(1 - \alpha)$, Efron's notation avoids several expressions containing $\frac{1}{2}\alpha$. For example, when $\alpha = 0.025$, we have $z^{(\alpha)} = -1.96$ and $z^{(1-\alpha)} = 1.96$ giving the usual 95% interval. The interval (1) can be misleading if $E(\hat{\theta} - \theta) \neq 0$, that is if $\hat{\theta}$ is a biased estimator, or if $\hat{\sigma}$ is not a constant. The BC_a interval uses a monotone transformation which in turn involves a bias constant z_0 used above and an acceleration term denoted by a and derived in (11) below. For the transformed variable we seek the simple setup: $\hat{\phi} = \phi + (a$ transformation of $Z)$, where $Z \sim N(0, 1)$. Thus, we let

$$\hat{\phi} = g(\hat{\theta}) , \qquad \phi = g(\theta) , \qquad Z \sim N(0, 1) , \tag{2}$$

$$\sigma_\phi = 1 + a\phi \quad \text{subject to } \sigma_\phi > 0 , \tag{3}$$

which introduces flexibility in the true standard deviation by allowing it to vary with the true ϕ as a multiple of the acceleration constant a. Choosing

$\sigma_\phi(Z - z_0)$ as our transformation of Z,

$$\hat{\phi} = \phi + \sigma_\phi(Z - z_0) \quad \text{implying} \quad \text{E}(\hat{\phi} - \phi) = \sigma_\phi(-z_0) \tag{4}$$

providing an expression for the bias which depends on a, because σ_ϕ depends on a. From (2), (3) and (4) one can verify an algebraic identity:

$$(1 + a\hat{\phi}) = (1 + a\phi)[1 + a(Z - z_0)] . \tag{5}$$

Taking natural logs of both sides leads to the linear model:

$$\ln(1 + a\hat{\phi}) = \ln(1 + a\phi) + \ln[1 + a(Z - z_0)] , \quad \text{or briefly } \hat{\zeta} = \zeta + W . \tag{6}$$

The corresponding confidence interval is

$$\Pr[\hat{\zeta} - w^{(1-\alpha)} \leq \zeta \leq \hat{\zeta} - w^{(\alpha)}] = 1 - 2\alpha , \tag{7}$$

where $w^{(\alpha)}$ is 100α percentile for the error W in (6). Now, the transformation $g(\theta)$ is a sequence of two mappings $\theta \to \phi \to \zeta$ which stabilize the variance and normalize the original θ, as much as possible. Starting with (7) and using inverse transformation g^{-1} one improves the confidence interval (1). For example, the definition $\hat{\zeta} = \ln(1 + a\hat{\phi})$ implies that $\exp(\hat{\zeta}) = 1 + a\hat{\phi}$, or $\hat{\phi} = [\exp(\hat{\zeta}) - 1]/a$ is the inverse map $\hat{\zeta} \to \hat{\phi}$. Similarly, $Z - z_0 = (e^W - 1)/a$ can be derived from (6). Briefly, the BC$_a$ method assumes:

$$g(\theta) = (\hat{\phi} - \phi) \sim \text{N}(-z_0\sigma_\phi, \sigma_\phi^2) , \tag{8}$$

where σ_ϕ is affected by the acceleration constant a from (3). Hence, $z_0 + (\hat{\phi} - \phi)/\sigma_\phi \sim \text{N}(0, 1)$. Let $z^{(\alpha)}$ denote the α-level lower limit of the confidence interval from $\text{N}(0, 1)$. From (2), (4) and (8) after some algebra we have a *practical formula* for the lower limit of an α-level confidence interval for ϕ as

$$\phi_{\text{LO}}(\alpha) = \hat{\phi} + \sigma_\phi A/(1 - aA) , \quad \text{where } A = [z_0 + z^{(\alpha)}] \tag{9}$$

and the upper limit has a negative sign after $\hat{\phi}$. This formula can be used only after we develop expressions for z_0 and a. The expression for z_0 was derived earlier in (1) of Section 5 as

$$z_0 = \Phi^{-1}(F_*(\hat{\theta})) . \tag{10}$$

Efron's approximation for the acceleration constant a is

$$a = \tfrac{1}{6}\text{SKEW}(\text{SCORE}) , \quad \text{where SKEW}(u) = \mu_3/\mu_2^{3/2} = \mu_3/\sigma_u^3 . \tag{11}$$

SKEW(u) is related to the usual skewness coefficient, defined as a ratio of moments of u indicated by the subscripts of μ in (11). Note that u equals SCORE, or the score function of the density function $f(\hat{\theta})$ evaluated at $\theta = \hat{\theta}$. Thus, SCORE $= (d/d\theta) \ln f(\hat{\theta})$. In the nonparametric case, assuming iid observations $x_1, x_2, \ldots, x_T$ we have $\hat{\theta} = h(F)$, where $\hat{F}$ denotes the empirical CDF, and $h(F)$ is smoothly defined for choices of F near $\hat{F}$. Here, Efron (1987, p. 178) replaces the SCORE by the *empirical influence function* U_i, $i = 1, 2, \ldots, T$ defined by

$$U_i = \lim_{\Delta \to 0} (1/\Delta)[h((1 - \Delta)\hat{F} + \Delta\delta_i) - h(\hat{F})] ,$$

where δ_i is a point mass at x_i .

Observe that U_i measures the change in the estimate $\hat{\theta}$ with respect to the mass on point x_i and has a finite difference approximation and uses $\Delta = (1 + T)^{-1}$. In the robust statistics terminology, Hoaglin et al. (1983), U_i measures the empirical influence of the observation x_i on the estimate. The acceleration constant for the nonparametric case is given by

$$a = \frac{1}{6}\left\{\left(\sum_{i=1}^{T} U_i^3\right) \bigg/ \left(\sum_{i=1}^{T} U_i^2\right)^{3/2}\right\} \tag{11a}$$

if θ is the sample mean $U_i = (x_i - \bar{x})$ and both a and z_0 are sample skewness divided by $6\sqrt{T}$. Vinod and Ullah (1981, p. 44) give an elementary discussion of the definition of U_i and derive the particular case of the mean. The expression (11) with factor $\frac{1}{6}$ is justified on the basis of an asymptotic skewness-reducing transformation, DiCiccio (1984). Recall equation (6) of Section 5. The acceleration constant a measures the speed at which the standard deviation of $g(\hat{\theta})$ is changing with respect to $g(\theta)$. Martin (1990) provides further asymptotic results for the BC_a method and remarks that it suffers from two undesirable properties arising from the presence of inversion and the use of sample estimates of high order moments. Efron recommends using the BC_a method when $z_0 < 0.2$ and $|a| < 0.2$ on the basis of simulation experiments.

DiCiccio and Tibshirani (1987) have extended the BC_a method to what they call BC_a^0, where the superscript 0 reminds us that the starting point c of an integral in a variance-reducing transformation $g_1(t)$ of (13) below is chosen to make $g(\hat{\theta}) = 0$. Although explicit knowledge of g is not required for the BC_a method, DiCiccio and Tibshirani suggest that in one-parameter problems g can be explicitly written as

$$g(t) = g_A(g_1(t)) \quad \text{with } g_A(s) = (e^{As} - 1)/A , \tag{12}$$

where A is an acceleration constant. In particular, one may choose $A = a$ of (11) to achieve skewness reduction. Observe that the inverse of (12) leads to $s = \ln(1 + Ag_A)/A$, which is reminiscent of $\zeta = \ln(1 + a\phi)$ in (6) above, provided $A = a$ and $\phi = g_A \exp(1/A) + [\exp(1/A) - 1]/A$. Asymptotic theory suggests that a variance (related to the Fisher information) stabilizing transformation is given by

$$g_1(t) = \int_c^t \sqrt{[\kappa_2(u)]} \, du , \tag{13}$$

where c is an arbitrary constant chosen to make $g_1(\hat\theta) = 0$ and where $\kappa_2(\hat\theta) = E[d^2\ln \text{Lkhd}/d\theta^2]$ is the expected Fisher information evaluated at $\hat\theta$ for θ from the relevant log likelihood (denoted by ln Lkhd). Often, one can use asymptotic theory to obtain c and g_1 explicitly. Efron's (1987, p. 199) rejoinder states that if one uses g_A and g_1 the computational burden is reduced, but one is placing a greater reliance on asymptotic approximations. The BC_a method uses the bootstrap distribution $\hat F_*$ to compute z_0 whereas BC_a^0 computes $g = g_A(g_1)$ explicitly. It can be shown that BC_a and BC_a^0 are second order equivalent. Both methods generalize $(\hat\theta - \theta)/\hat\sigma \sim N(0, 1)$ to the assumption that

$$g(\hat\theta) - g(\theta) \sim N(-z_0(1 + ag(\theta)), [1 + ag(\theta)]^2) \tag{14}$$

designed to stabilize the variance and achieve normality by eliminating the skewness. The transformation g_1 stabilizes the variance and then g_A eliminates the skewness while changing the variance to $[1 + ag(\theta)]^2$. Although this destabilizes the variance somewhat, exact pivotal analysis is still possible because of the simplicity of the variance expression.

Using $g(\hat\theta) = 0$, DiCiccio and Tibshirani (1987) show that the explicit g from (12) and (13) leads to the following expression for the density

$$f(s) = f_N[z_0 + (\exp\{g_1(s)a\} - 1)/a] \exp\{g_1(s)a\}[\kappa_2(s)]^{1/2}, \tag{15}$$

where f_N is the $N(0, 1)$ unit normal density. The usual central limit theorem approximation leads to $N(\hat\theta, [\kappa_2(\hat\theta)]^{-1})$, which is correct to order $T^{-1/2}$. The BC_a^0 procedure refines it further. A practical use of (15) appears to be cumbersome, and further work is needed to mechanize the estimation of constants z_0, a and g functions. For example, estimation can involve empirical influence components, a matrix of second order influences and numerical integration, DiCiccio and Tibshirani (1987, p. 168). The method of importance sampling and exponential tilting described by Johns (1988) leaves the variance of the original statistic unchanged, uses a pivot and Huber's influence function and yields symmetric confidence intervals. However, symmetry may not be desirable in all situations. The BC_a method does not assume symmetry, whereas BC_a^0 may be effective even when a nonmonotonic transformation, similar to Fisher's classical $\tanh^{-1}$ transformation of the simple correlation coefficient, is needed.

8. Confidence interval: Coverage correction and adjustments

It was stated earlier that the practitioners are painfully aware that a 95% confidence set may not actually have a coverage probability of 0.95, and that the bootstrap can help. Consider a sample $\chi = \{X_1, X_2, \ldots, X_T\}$ aimed at estimating the parameter θ and a bootstrap resample $\chi^* = \{X_1^*, X_2^*, \ldots, X_T^*\}$ obtained by sampling with replacement. Let $CI_0(\alpha \mid \chi) = [\theta_{LO}, \theta_{UP}]$ denote a nominal $(1 - \alpha)$ level confidence interval for θ based on the sampling distribution of $\hat{\theta}$, where θ_{LO} and θ_{UP} denote the usual lower and upper $(\alpha/2)$-points. Let the coverage probability of CI_0 be denoted by

$$COVG_0(\alpha) = Prob\{\theta \in CI_0(\alpha \mid \chi) = [\theta_{LO}, \theta_{UP}]\} \,. \tag{1}$$

Thus the problem faced by the practitioner is that $COVG_0 \neq 1 - \alpha$. The idea behind the *coverage correction algorithm* is to try other values in the neighborhood of α and use the bootstrap resampling distribution to adjust the CI_0. One can then choose a value of α denoted by $\tilde{\alpha}$ which yields the correct coverage probability in the sense that $\tilde{\alpha}$ solves the following equation:

$$COVG_0(\tilde{\alpha}) = Prob\{\hat{\theta} \in CI_0(\tilde{\alpha} \mid \chi^*) = [\theta_{LO}^*, \theta_{UP}^*]\} = 1 - \alpha \,, \tag{2}$$

where it is understood that there may be nonuniqueness. That is, several values of $\tilde{\alpha}$ may satisfy (2). Martin (1990) calls this nonunique solution method the coverage correction algorithm and attributes it to Beran (1987), Hall and Martin (1988) and Loh (1987). Actually Loh calls this the method of calibration and considers a reflected confidence interval

$$RCI_0(\tilde{\alpha} \mid \chi^*) = [2\hat{\theta} - \theta_{UP}^*, 2\hat{\theta} - \theta_{LO}^*] \,. \tag{3}$$

Loh (1987) goes one step further and suggests choosing that $\tilde{\alpha}$ which minimizes the length $= (\theta_{UP}^* - \theta_{LO}^*)$ and ensures correct coverage of both the CI_0 and RCI_0. This obviously solves the nonuniqueness problem yielding a single $\tilde{\alpha}_{CSR}$ value. Loh calls the resulting interval the *calibrated shortest length reflection* (CSR) interval and reports its superiority in a simulation. Note that in finding the shortest interval CSR, there is no need to treat the tails symmetrically, providing further realism.

Considerable asymptotic theory is reported by Martin (1990) for the nonunique $\tilde{\alpha}$ case, providing a separate set of results for one-sided and two-sided confidence intervals. For example, he proves that the coverage correction algorithm reduces the error in coverage by a factor $1/\sqrt{T}$ for the one-sided and a factor $1/T$ for the two-sided intervals. The theory suggests superiority of RCI_0 intervals of (3) over Efron's accelerated bias-corrected BC_a method. Martin also considers χ^{**} as a resample drawn from χ^* which is similar to the double bootstrap.

9. Practical bootstrap computations from sorted resampling estimates

In this section we discuss some practical aspects in bootstrapping. As before, consider a sample $\chi = \{X_1, X_2, \ldots, X_T\}$ aimed at estimating the parameter θ and a bootstrap resample $\chi^* = \{X_1^*, X_2^*, \ldots, X_T^*\}$ obtained by sampling with replacement. Now χ^* yields a sampling distribution of $\hat{\theta}$ from the bootstrap replicates θ_j^* for $j = 1, 2, \ldots, J$ as follows. Simply sort the J values of θ_j^* from the smallest to the largest by a standard computer algorithm, and find the quantiles from the sorted values to represent the bootstrap distribution. Let us denote the integer part of a number x by $[x]$ and let $J = 101$. The median or the 50-th percentile with $\alpha = 0.5$ is the j-th sorted value with $j = [J\alpha] + 1 = [50.5] + 1$, which may be denoted by $\text{Sort}(\theta_j^*, 51)$. On the other hand, when $J = 100$ we have $J\alpha = 50$ is an integer, and the median is $0.5[\text{Sort}(\theta_j^*, 50) + \text{Sort}(\theta_j^*, 51)]$ the average of $[J\alpha] = 50$-th and $[J\alpha] + 1 = 51$-st sorted values. If the distribution of bootstrap replicates is median-unbiased, we expect the median to equal $\hat{\theta}$. It is convenient to write a separate computer procedure $\text{Qnt}(\theta_j^*, J\alpha)$ to compute a quantile from the sorted values for any α in the interval 0 to 1, which carefully deals with both cases, whether $J\alpha$ is an integer or not.

How do the sorted values help find the coverage probability COVG_0 of (1) above? Recall that we have $\text{CI}_0 = [\theta_{\text{LO}}, \theta_{\text{UP}}]$, where the limits may be from the normal (or asymptotic) theory. Since θ is unknown, we can never know the true coverage probability of (1). However, the bootstrap approximation of $\hat{\theta} - \theta$ by $\theta^* - \hat{\theta}$ may be used to find the number J' of the sorted θ_j^* values that belong to the $[\theta_{\text{LO}}, \theta_{\text{UP}}]$ interval. Now an estimate of COVG_0 is J'/J, which may not exactly equal $1 - \alpha$. The coverage correction algorithm suggests changing the α slightly, find the corresponding interval $[\theta_{\text{LO}}, \theta_{\text{UP}}]$, and a new J'/J, which may or may not equal $1 - \alpha$. The i-th change of α which yields the correct coverage probability, $J'/J = 1 - \alpha$, is denoted by $\tilde{\alpha}_i$, and their complete set is denoted by $\tilde{\alpha} = \{\tilde{\alpha}_i\}$. One can proceed to estimate the calibrated shortest length reflected (CSR) interval along the lines indicated above.

How do the $\text{Qnt}(\theta_j^*, J\alpha)$ from the sorted values yield a confidence interval? Consider a two-sided naive 95% interval which has 2.5% mass in each tail. We seek 2.5 percentile as the lower limit and 97.5 percentile as the upper limit. In standard textbook notation the confidence level is denoted by $1 - \alpha = 0.95$ with $\alpha = 0.05$ resulting in the interval $[\text{Qnt}(\theta_j^*, J\alpha/2), \text{Qnt}(\theta_j^*, J(1 - \alpha)/2)]$. However, this naive interval may be median-biased, or may not have the correct coverage probability. The BC, BC_a and BC_a^0 intervals are computed by using reflection, acceleration, etc. for appropriate quantiles.

The computation of the double bootstrap is costly. For each resample from the J sets of χ^* one further resamples K times. If $J = 1000$, and $K = 1000$ we are considering a million resample estimates. For each $j = 1, 2, \ldots, J$ there are $k = 1, 2, \ldots, K$ bootstrap estimates denoted by θ_{jk}^*. The corresponding confidence intervals are defined by $[\text{Qnt}(\theta_{jk}^*, K\alpha/2), \text{Qnt}(\theta_{jk}^*, K(1 - \alpha)/2)]$. Of course, one may use (9) of Section 7 and BC_a^0 methods here. The estimate of coverage probability in these cases is simply the proportion of J intervals of nominal level $1 - \alpha$ that covers $\hat{\theta}$. Clearly, by slightly changing α one obtains new intervals and new coverage probability estimates. We are interested in the set $\tilde{\alpha} = \{\alpha_i\}$ of α values yielding the correct coverage probability. The set $\tilde{\alpha}$ may be explored further for finding intervals with minimum length. The confidence intervals based on $\tilde{\alpha}$ are called coverage-corrected intervals. This is similar to the case above, where the initial interval, $\text{CI}_0 = [\theta_{\text{LO}}, \theta_{\text{UP}}]$ is from the normal theory, rather than from a first level bootstrap. In complex problems, it is recommended to start with the bootstrap, because they have stable variances and are invariant under monotone transformations.

In some applications one uses maximum likelihood estimates and the result that the likelihood is distributed as a chi square random variable. In the 1930s Bartlett suggested a correction to the chi square statistic with a linear transformation designed to equate the expected value to the theoretically correct expected value of the chi square. For the corresponding confidence intervals Martin (1990) shows that applying the bootstrap coverage correction algorithm reduces the coverage error of Bartlett-corrected confidence regions from $O(T^{-2})$ to $O(T^{-3})$.

10. Post hoc computational method for confidence intervals

The post hoc method of Efron (1990) cleverly manipulates the available bootstrap resample data, and was mentioned before. In this section we review it retaining a notation close to Efron's. From the observed data $x = (x_1, x_2, \ldots, x_n)$ it is assumed that one is interested in a statistic $S(x)$ which is unaffected by a reordering of x. Note that this means that the post hoc methods may not be reliable when they are applied to time series data where the ordering of observations is important. Each bootstrap sample $(x_1^*, x_2^*, \ldots, x_n^*)$ yields proportions $(P_1, P_2, \ldots, P_n)$ where $P_i = \#(X_j^* = x_i)/n$, where $\#(\cdot)$ denotes the number of times the condition in parenthesis is satisfied. Each j-th bootstrap $(j = 1, 2, \ldots, J)$ gives a new vector $P^j = \{P_i\}$, called *the resampling vector*. We expect J to be a large number, $J \geqslant 100$. The original observed value of the statistic uses all x_1 to x_n values exactly once. Hence, it is denoted by $S^0(P^0)$, where all components of the resampling vector are equal, or $P_i^0 = 1/n$ for all i. Bootstrap replications can be represented in the form of an analysis-of-variance decomposition from Efron and Stein (1981).

$$S(P) = \mu + P'\gamma + \varepsilon(P) \quad \text{subject to } P^{0\prime}\gamma = 0, \tag{1}$$

where $\mu = E(S(P))$ and γ is an $n \times 1$ vector. Now μ and γ are parameters to be estimated by minimizing the error sum of squares. From $j = 1, 2, \ldots, J$ bootstraps obtain pairs of the values of the statistic and resampling vector (S^j, P^j). Now regress S^j on P^j to obtain following estimates. Let p denote an $n \times J$ matrix of $(P^1, P^2, \ldots, P^J)$ comprising resampling vectors, define an $n \times 1$ vector of least squares slopes $A = (pp')^{-1}pS$, where S is a $J \times 1$ vector the values of the statistic. Now letting $1_n = (1, \ldots, 1)$ a column vector of n ones, μ is estimated as an average of n elements of A, or $\hat{\mu} = 1_n'A/n$. Also, $\hat{\gamma} = A - \hat{\mu}1_n$ estimates the γ vector. The familiar R^2 of regression analysis can be computed for (1) as the ratio of variances: $\text{var}(\hat{\gamma}(P))/\text{var}(S(P))$, measuring the proportion of $S(P)$ explained by the linear part. Hence it is intuitively apparent, that the post hoc methods described in this section are likely to be most helpful when the R^2 is large. In terms of the statistic, we write

$$S^j = \hat{L}^j + M^j, \quad \text{where } \hat{L}^j = P^{j\prime}\hat{\gamma} \text{ and } M^j = S^j - \hat{L}^j. \tag{2}$$

The residuals M^j will be added back in, after a transformation of $\hat{L}$ described below. With $\hat{\gamma}$ treated as fixed, compute the first four cumulants of $\hat{L} = P'\hat{\gamma}$ when P has the n-category multinomial distribution with the probability of each category fixed at $1/n$. When all elements of P are the same, the cumulants of $\hat{\gamma}$ and $\hat{L}$ are the same, except for the term $(1/n)$. The theoretical cumulants of $\hat{L}$ are as follows. The mean is zero. Denote $\sigma_\gamma^2 = \Sigma_{i=1}^n \hat{\gamma}_i^2/n$. The theoretical variance of $\hat{L}$ is σ_γ^2/n. The theoretical skewness is $(1/\sigma_\gamma^2\sqrt{n})\Sigma_{i=1}^n \hat{\gamma}_i^3/n$, and the theoretical kurtosis is $(1/n)[(1/\sigma_\gamma^4)\Sigma_{i=1}^n \hat{\gamma}_i^4/n - 3]$. The direct estimates of the mean, variance, skewness and kurtosis of the J estimates $\hat{L}^j$ are not expected to be exactly equal to the corresponding theoretical values given above for the multinomial. Improved estimates of quantiles are obtained by transforming $\hat{L}$ to $\bar{L}$ such that the first four cumulants match.

Consider a general cubic transformation given by Efron (1990, p. 86) to find the values of variable $x(\text{skw}_x, \text{krt}_x)$ from $y(\text{skw}_y, \text{krt}_y)$, where the skewness and kurtosis of x and y are denoted in an obvious notation, and where y is standardized to have zero mean and variance unity.

$$
\begin{aligned}
x = {}& (1 - \tfrac{1}{8}(\text{krt}_x - \text{krt}_y) + \tfrac{1}{36}(\text{skw}_x - \text{skw}_y)(5\text{skw}_x + 7\text{skw}_y))y \\
& + \tfrac{1}{6}(\text{skw}_x - \text{skw}_y)(y^2 - 1) \\
& + (\tfrac{1}{24}(\text{krt}_x - \text{krt}_y) - \tfrac{1}{9}(\text{skw}_x - \text{skw}_y)(\text{skw}_x/2 + \text{skw}_y))y^3 .
\end{aligned} \tag{3}
$$

In our application of (3), x represents the theoretical variable $\hat{L}$ whose cumulants use the n known values of $\hat{\gamma}$ and y represents the directly standardized J values of $\hat{L}$. It is more convenient to implement the mapping from $\hat{L}$ to $\bar{L}$ backwards, by first constructing J values of $\hat{L}^j$ from the standard normal, and simply mapping the sorted values of $\hat{L}$ to the sorted values of $\bar{L}$, as follows.

Step 1: Compute the skw_x and krt_x from the n estimates of $\hat{\gamma}$ using the formulas given above.

Step 2: Find direct estimates of skw_y and krt_y from J estimates of $\hat{L}$.

Step 3: Define J elements $y_j = \Phi^{-1}[(j - 0.5)/J]$ where Φ denotes the CDF of unit normal.

Step 4: Use equation (3) to map from y_j to x_j using the skewness and kurtosis values computed in the first two steps.

Step 5: Verify that the skewness and kurtosis of x_j are equal to the desired theoretical values. If they are not equal, repeat Steps 4 and 5 until the desired match is achieved. Of course, skw_x and krt_x remain fixed at the theoretical values, and skw_y and krt_y are sequentially improved.

Step 6: Transform x_j to $\bar{x}_j = (\sigma_\gamma/\sqrt{n})x_j$.

Step 7: Rank order $\bar{x}_j$ from the smallest to the largest and replace similarly sorted $\hat{L}^j$ values by the corresponding $\bar{x}_j$ values. This replacement is the mapping from $\hat{L}$ to $\bar{L}$. Note that the cumulants of $\bar{L}$ match with the theoretical cumulants.

Now we return to the statistic S of interest. Using (2) we obtain adjusted values of the statistic $\tilde{S}^j = \tilde{L}^j + M^j$. Care is needed here. We must add back the unsorted residual M^j in (2) to the correct (unsorted) $\tilde{L}$ values. Sorting the adjusted values of the statistic $\tilde{S}^j$ from the lowest to the largest, find the quantiles of the sampling distribution of the statistic S, which are more reliable than those based on S^j, the direct bootstrap estimates of the statistic. Efron (1990) also discusses properties of post hoc estimates of variance and bias, along with some examples.

11. Bootstrap for dynamic and simultaneous equation models in econometrics

Econometricians are often concerned with technical difficulties arising from simultaneity, heteroscedasticity, autocorrelated errors, temporal dependence, nonstationarity, etc. Among common methods for dealing with these problems are feasible generalized least squares (FGLS), maximum likelihood, instrumental variables, two- and three-stage least squares. For many of these techniques, the standard errors of estimates are estimated by asymptotic formulas. Freedman (1981, 1984), Freedman and Peters (1984a,b) suggested bootstrap methods for improving the asymptotic estimates of standard errors. The Berndt–Wood (1975) model seeks to explain the shares of capital, labor, energy and materials (KLEM) inputs in terms of their relative prices. The specific econometric model is the 'seemingly unrelated regression' equations model of Zellner (1962), Kmenta and Gilbert (1968). Freedman and Peters (1984b) apply the bootstrap to the Berndt–Wood model and find that the nominal standard errors may have been underestimated by about 10% if the traditional asymptotic methods are used instead of the bootstrap.

Freedman and Peters (1984a,b) suggested the preliminary steps needed to generate the pseudo data for bootstrapping in the presence of these technical difficulties, except for non-stationarity. In this section we review his suggestions with a notation close to his. A properly identified and well specified system for simultaneous equations is given by

$$Y_t = Y_t A + Y_{t-1} B + X_t C + \varepsilon_t ,\tag{1}$$

where the subscript t represents values at time t from a set of T observations, Y_t is a $1 \times g$ vector of endogenous variables, and X_t is a $1 \times k$ vector of exogenous variables. The parameter matrices are as follows: A is $g \times g$, B is $g \times g$, and C is $k \times g$. The error vector ε_t is $1 \times g$, assumed to be iid with mean zero and covariance matrix V. Rao and Wu (1988) show an extension of the bootstrap to non-iid sampling designs. It is well known that many higher order models can be reduced to the first order form (1). The initial values Y_0 are assumed to be known, and the bootstrap pseudo data for the initial time period is assumed to be Y_0 also. Various econometric estimation methods including two stage least squares (2SLS) yield estimates of the parameters denoted by $\hat{A}$,

$\hat{B}$, and $\hat{C}$. An important purpose of the bootstrap is to develop a deeper understanding of the sampling distribution of these parameter estimates. Pseudo data for Y_t^* in conjunction with the fixed data for X_t are used to generate $j = 1, 2, \ldots, J$, where $J \geq 100$ estimates of the parameter matrices by simply applying the 2SLS or similar estimation methods J times.

How to generate the Y_t^* from (1) retaining the basic properties of the data generating process? We assume that the process starts with Y_0 known values. Define a $1 \times g$ vector of residuals from (1) as

$$\hat{\varepsilon}_t = Y_t - [Y_t \hat{A} + Y_{t-1} \hat{B} + X_t \hat{C}] . \tag{2}$$

From the empirical distribution function of these residuals, which puts a mass $(1/T)$ at each of the computed residuals, one can generate a large number J of pseudo residuals $\varepsilon_{t,j}^*$ by sampling with replacement. Freedman and Peters (1984a,b) suggest rescaling the residuals of each equation by a factor $\sqrt{[T/(T - p)]}$, where p denotes the number of parameters in that equation. This removes an underestimation bias of regression residuals compared to the true errors.

Assuming that $I - A$ is an invertible matrix, we have from (1) the following

$$Y_t = (Y_{t-1} B + X_t C + \varepsilon_t)(I - A)^{-1} . \tag{3}$$

Hence,

$$Y_{t,j}^* = (Y_{t-1,j}^* \hat{B} + X_t \hat{C} + \varepsilon_{t,j}^*)(I - A)^{-1} \tag{4}$$

can be recursively used by using the same starting values Y_0 for all j. The consistency of a similar bootstrap procedure is proved by Freedman (1984). Each replicate $Y_{t,j}^*$ gives rise to a new estimation problem (1). There are J such estimates of each of the elements of the parameter matrices $\hat{A}_j$, $\hat{B}_j$ and $\hat{C}_j$. As before, we apply the basic bootstrap strategy of approximating the sampling distribution of $\hat{A} - A$ by the observable bootstrap difference $\hat{A}_j - \hat{A}$, and similarly for B and C.

Freedman and Peters (1984b) use $J = 400$ bootstrap replications to compute the variance of each of the elements of $\hat{A}$ and $\hat{C}$. In their application to the Berndt–Wood model the lag term is absent ($B \equiv 0$). Freedman and Peters (1984a) study the regional demand forecasting (RDFOR) model for energy with the bootstrap. They find that the traditional asymptotic standard errors may be too optimistic by a factor of nearly three. It is well known that econometric estimators for simultaneous equation models are biased in small samples, where the bias depends on unknown parameters. Vinod and Raj (1988) discuss a similar situation for ridge regression, where the pivot is missing. Recent bootstrap theory developed by Efron and Beran, among others, shows that double bootstrap with a heavy computational burden can provide reliable statistical inference in these situations.

Econometric estimators can be viewed as functionals, where the local properties (e.g., the derivatives at a point) of the underlying distribution are important. Then, results by Silverman and Young (1987) indicate advantages of using kernels to smooth the bootstrap. Hall, DiCiccio and Romano (1989) prove that smoothing with higher order kernels helps in estimating the variance of quantile estimators. Nonparametric regression analog of analysis of variance and tests for the differences between means are developed by Hall and Hart (1990). Hardle and Bowman (1988) show that the bootstrap can be better than the method of 'plugging' into asymptotic formulas for the mean squared error for choosing the smoothing parameter and to construct confidence interval around nonparametrically fitted regression curves. Hardle et al.'s (1991) application of the bootstrap (mentioned in Section 2.3) illustrates potential benefits of combining bootstrap with nonparametric regression for a sophisticated test of important economic propositions, such as the law of demand.

12. Final remarks

The bootstrap literature is increasing at an exponential rate, and it is difficult for any survey to be reasonably comprehensive. Both theoretical and applied statisticians have embraced the new tool, which would have been unthinkable before the era of modern computers with exponentially declining costs. Some highly mathematical papers of recent vintage may tend to discourage some applied econometricians by increasing the cost of entry. We hope that our review of the issues addressed by the mathematical papers helps reduce the cost. We find that applications-oriented researchers who have a comparative advantage in computer programming can continue to use the bootstrap. The computational pointers are given in Sections 9 and 10 above. Considerable theoretical research is shown to enhance the bootstrap by using basically simple transformations which normalize and stabilize the variance. Many econometric estimators are biased in small samples, where the bias and sampling distributions of estimators depend on the unknown parameters and the applicability of central limit theorems is unknown. For some of these problems double bootstrap with a million (if $J = K = 1000$) resamples can provide superior statistical inference. Some post hoc methods can reduce the computations by orders of magnitude. The bootstrap becomes attractive when: traditional variance approximations may be imprecise, especially for nonlinear functionals, nonnormality is suspected, dimensionality and the number of parameters of interest is large and the ratio of computing cost relative to the cost of researcher's own time is low. According to Efron and Tibshirani (1986, p. 55) the bootstrap provides a powerful arguement 'against unnecessary theory'. Graduate students will be grateful if the bootstrap lightens the burden of highly statistical econometrics.

Acknowledgment

I thank Jogesh Babu, Rudy Beran, Mike Veall and Bruce McCullough for helpful comments.

References

Abramovitch, L. and K. Singh (1985). Edgeworth corrected pivotal statistics and the bootstrap. *Ann. Statist.* **13**, 116–132.

Affleck-Graves, J. and B. McDonald (1990). Multivariate tests of asset pricing: The comparative power of alternative statistics. *J. Financ. Quant. Anal.* **25**, 163–185.

Akgiray, V. and C. G. Lamoureux (1989). Estimation of stable law parameters: A comparative study. *J. Business Econom. Statist.* **7**, 85–93.

Amemiya, T. (1985). *Advanced Econometrics.* Harvard Univ. Press, Cambridge MA.

Athreya, K. (1987). Bootstrap of the mean in the infinite variance case. *Ann. Statist.* **15**, 724–731.

Averch H. and L. L. Johnson (1962). Behavior of the firm under regulatory constraint. *Amer. Econom. Rev.* **52**, 1053–1069.

Babu, G. J. (1989). Applications of Edgeworth expansions to bootstrap – A review. In: Y. Dodge, ed., *Statistical Data Analysis and Inference.* Elsevier Science, North-Holland, New York, 223–237.

Babu, G. J. and K. Singh (1983). Inference on means using the bootstrap. *Ann. Statist.* **11**, 999–1003.

Babu, G. J. and K. Singh (1984). On one term Edgeworth correction by Efron's bootstrap. *Sankhyā* **46**, 219–232.

Bahadur, R. R. and L. J. Savage (1956). The nonexistence of certain statistical procedures in parametric problems. *Ann. Math. Statist.* **27**, 1115–1122.

Bartow, W. E. and W. H. Sun (1987). Bootstrapped confidence intervals for linear relative risk models. In: ASA Proc. Statist. Comput. Sections, 260–265.

Basawa, I. V., A. K. Mallik, W. P. McCormick, J. H. Reeves and R. L. Taylor (1991). Bootstrapping unstable first order autoregressive processes. *Ann. Statist.* **19**, 1098–1101.

Beran, R. (1982). Estimated sampling distributions: The bootstrap and competitors. *Ann. Statist.* **10**, 212–225.

Beran, R. (1984a). Bootstrap methods in statistics. *Jber. Deutsch. Math. Ver* **86**, 14–30.

Beran, R. (1984b). Jackknife approximations to bootstrap estimates. *Ann. Statist.* **12**, 101–118.

Beran, R. (1986a). Simulated power functions. *Ann. Statist.* **14**, 151–173.

Beran, R. (1986b). Confidence sets for a multivariate distribution. *Ann. Statist.* **14**, 431–443.

Beran, R. (1987). Prepivoting to reduce level error of confidence sets. *Biometrika* **74**, 457–468.

Beran, R. (1988). Prepivoting test statistics: A bootstrap view of asymptotic refinements. *J. Amer. Statist. Assoc.* **83**, 687–697.

Beran, R. (1990). Refining bootstrap simultaneous confidence sets. *J. Amer. Statist. Assoc.* **85**, 417–426.

Beran, R. and P. Millar (1985). Asymptotic theory of confidence sets. In: L. Le Cam and R. Olshen, eds., *Proc. Berkeley Conf. in Honor of Jerzy Neyman and Jack Kiefer*, Vol. 2. Wadsworth, Belmont, CA, 865–886.

Beran, R. and M. Srivastava (1985). Bootstrap tests and confidence regions for functions of a covariance matrix. *Ann. Statist.* **13**, 95–115.

Berndt, E. R. and D. O. Wood (1975). Technology, prices and derived demand for energy. *Rev. Econom. Statist.* **57**, 259–268.

Bickel, P. J. and D. A. Freedman (1981). Some asymptotic theory for the bootstrap. *Ann. Statist.* **9**, 1196–1217.

Bickel, P. J. and K. A. Doksum (1977). *Mathematical Statistics, Basic Ideas and Selected Topics.* Holden Day, New York.

Bickel. P. J. and D. A. Freedman (1983). Bootstrapping regression model with many parameters. In: P. Bickel, K. Doksum and J. L. Hodges, eds., *A Festschrift for Erich Lehmann.* Wadsworth, Belmont, CA, 28–48.

Brillinger, D. R. (1964). The asymptotic behaviour of Tukey's general method of setting approximate confidence limits (the jackknife) when applied to maximum livelihood estimates. *Rev. Inst. Internat. Statist.* **32**, 202–206.

Brownstone, D. (1990). Bootstrapping improved estimators for linear regression models. *J. Econometrics* **44**, 171–187.

Brownstone, D. and K. A. Small (1989). Efficient estimation of nested logit models. *J. Business Econom. Statist.* **7**, 67–74.

Cox, D. R. (1980). Local ancillarity. *Biometrika* **67**, 273–278.

Cox, D. R. and N. Reid (1987). Parameter othogonality and approximate conditional inference. *J. Roy. Statist. Soc. Ser. B* **49**, 1–39.

Davison, A. C., D. V. Hinkley and E. Schechtman (1986). Efficient bootstrap simulation. *Biometrika* **73**, 555–561.

Delaney, N. J. and S. Chatterjee (1986). Use of the bootstrap and cross validation in ridge regression. *J. Business Econom. Statist.* **4**, 255–262.

DiCiccio, T. and R. Tibshirani (1987). Bootstrap confidence intervals and bootstrap approximations. *J. Amer. Statist. Assoc.* **82**, 163–170.

DiCiccio, T. (1984). On parameter transformations and interval estimation. *Biometrika* **71**, 477–485.

DiCiccio, T. and J. P. Romano (1987). Accurate bootstrap confidence limits in parametric models. Technical Report No. 281, Department of Statistics, Stanford University.

Dielman, T. E. and R. C. Pfaffenberger (1986). Bootstrapping in least absolute value regression: An application to hypothesis testing. *ASA Proc. Business Econom. Statist.*, 628–630.

Dijkstra, T. K. and J. H. Veldkamp (1988). Data-driven selection of regressors and the bootstrap. In: T. K. Dijkstra, ed., *On Model Uncertainty and its Statistical Implications*. Springer, Berlin, 17–38.

Ducharme, G., M. Jhun, J. P. Romano and K. Truong (1985). Bootstrap confidence cones for directional data. *Biometrika* **72**, 637–645.

Eakin, K., D. P. McMillen and M. J. Buono (1990). Constructing confidence intervals using bootstrap: An application to a multiproduct cost function. *Rev. Econom. Statist.* **72**, 339–344.

Efron, B. (1979). Bootstrap methods: Another look at the Jackknife. *Ann. Statist.* **7**, 1–26.

Efron, B. (1981a). Non-parametric standard errors and confidence intervals. *Canad. J. Statist.* **9**, 139–172.

Efron, B. (1981b). Censored data and the bootstrap. *J. Amer. Statist. Assoc.* **76**, 312–319.

Efron, B. (1982). *The Jackknife, the Bootstrap and Other Resampling Plans*. CBMS-NSF Regional Conference Series in Applied Mathematics, Monograph 38, SIAM, Philadelphia, PA.

Efron, B. (1984). Comparing non-nested linear models. *J. Amer. Statist. Assoc.* **79**, 791–803.

Efron, B. (1985). Bootstrap confidence intervals for a class of parametric problems. *Biometrika* **72**, 45–58.

Efron, B. (1987). Better bootstrap confidence intervals (with discussion). *J. Amer. Statist. Assoc.* **82**, 171–200.

Efron, B. (1990). More efficient bootstrap computations. *J. Amer. Statist. Assoc.* **85**, 79–89.

Efron, B. and G. Gong (1983). A leisurely look at the bootstrap, the jackknife and cross-validation. *Amer. Statist.* **37**, 36–48.

Efron, B. and C. Stein (1981). The Jackknife estimate of variance. *Ann. Statist.* **9**, 586–596.

Efron, B. and R. Tibshirani (1986). Bootstrap methods for standard errors, confidence intervals, and other measures of statistical accuracy. *Statist. Sci.* **1**, 54–77.

Fisher, N. I. and P. Hall (1989). Bootstrap confidence regions for directional data. *J. Amer. Statist. Assoc.* **84**, 996–1002.

Freedman, D. A. (1981). Bootstrapping regression models. *Ann. Statist.* **9**, 1218–1228.

Freedman, D. A. (1984). On bootstrapping two-stage least-squares estimates in stationary linear models. *Ann. Statist.* **12**, 827–842.

Freedman, D. A. and S. C. Peters (1984a). Bootstrapping a regression equation: Some empirical results. *J. Amer. Statist. Assoc.* **79**, 97–106.

Freedman, D. A. and S. C. Peters (1984b). Bootstrapping an econometric model: Some empirical results. *J. Business Econom. Statist.* **2**, 150–158.

Ghosh, M., W. C. Parr, K. Singh and G. J. Babu (1984). A note on bootstrapping the sample median. *Ann. Statist.* **12**, 1130–1135.

Graham, R. L., D. V. Hinkley, P. W. M. John and S. Shi (1987). Balanced designs of bootstrap simulations. Technical Report 48, University of Texas at Austin, Mathematics Department.

Green, R., D. Rocke and W. Hahn (1987). Standard errors for elasticities: A comparison of bootstrap and asymptotic standard errors. *J. Business Econom. Statist.* **4**, 145–149.

Hall, P. (1983). Inverting an Edgeworth expansion. *Ann. Statist.* **11**, 569–576.

Hall, P. (1986a). On the bootstrap and confidence intervals. *Ann. Statist.* **14**, 1431–1452.

Hall, P. (1986b). On the number of bootstrap simulations required to consruct a confidence interval. *Ann. Statist.* **4**, 1453–1462.

Hall, P. (1987). On the bootstrapped and likelihood-based confidence regions. *Biometrika* **74**, 481–493.

Hall. P. (1988). Theoretical comparison of bootstrap confidence intervals (with discussion). *Ann. Statist.* **16**, 927–985.

Hall, P., T. J. DiCiccio and J. P. Romano (1989). On smoothing and the bootstrap. *Ann. Statist.* **17**, 692–704.

Hall. P. and M. A. Martin (1988). On bootstrap resampling and iteration. *Biometrika* **75**, 661–671.

Hall, P. and J. D. Hart (1990). Bootstrap test for difference between means in nonparametric regression. *J. Amer. Statist. Assoc.* **85**, 1039–1049.

Hardle, W. and A. W. Bowman (1988). bootstrapping on nonparametric regression: Local adaptive ᵻmoothing and confidence bands. *J. Amer. Statist. Assoc.* **83**, 102–110.

Hardle, W., W. Hildenbrand and M. Jerison (1991). Empirical evidence on the law of demand. *Econometrica* **59**, 1525–1549.

Hinkley, D. V. (1977). Jackknifing in unbalanced situations. *Technometrics* **19**, 285–292.

Hinkely, D. (1988). Bootstrap methods. *J. Roy. Statist. Soc. Ser. B* **50**, 321–337.

Hirschberg, J. G., D. J. Molina and D. J. Slottje (1988). A selection criterion for choosing between functional forms of income distribution. *Econometric Rev.* **7**, 183–197.

Hoaglin, D. C., F. Mosteller and J. W. Tukey (1983). *Understanding Robust and Exploratory Data Analysis.* Wiley, New York.

Hu. Y. S., K. N. Lau, H. G. Fung and E. F. Ulveling (1986). Monte Carlo studies on the effectiveness of the bootstrap bias reduction methods on 2SLS estimates. *Econom. Lett.* **20**, 233–239.

Johns, M. V. (1988). Importance of sampling for bootstrap confidence intervals. *J. Amer. Statist. Assoc.* **83**, 709–714.

Kendall, M. and A. Stuart (1977). *The Advanced Theory of Statistics*, Vol. 1. 4th ed., McMillan, New York.

Kendall, M., A. Stuart and J. K. Ord (1983). *The Advanced Theory of Statistics*, Vol. 3. 4th ed., McMillan, New York.

Kmenta, J. and R. F. Gilbert (1968). Small sample properties of alternative estimators of seemingly unrelated regressions. *J. Amer. Statist. Assoc.* **63**, 1180–1200.

Korajczyk, R. A. (1985). The pricing of forward contracts for foreign exchange. *J. Politic. Econom.* **93**, 346–368.

Kotz, S. and N. L. Johnson (1988). *Encyclopedia of Statistical Sciences.* Wiley, New York.

Kundra, I. (1985). Bootstrap evaluation of linear regression models. *ASA Proc. Business Econom. Statist.*, 240–244.

Kunsch, H. R. (1989). The jackknife and the bootstrap for general stationary observations. *Ann. Statist.* **17**, 1217–1241.

Lamoureux, C. G. and W. D. Lastrapes (1990). Persistence in variance, structural change and the GARCH model. *J. Business Econom. Statist.* **8**, 225–234.

Liu, R. Y. and K. Singh (1987). On partial correction by the bootstrap. *Ann. Statist.* **15**, 1713–1718.

Loh, W. (1987). Calibrating confidence coefficients. *J. Amer. Statist. Assoc.* **82**, 155–162.

Lunneborg, C. E. (1988). Bootstrap applications for the behavioral sciences. *Amer. Statist.* **42**, 86.

Martin, M. A. (1990). Bootstrap iteration for coverage correction in confidence intervals. *J. Amer. Statist. Assoc.* **85**, 1105–1118.

MacKinnon, J. G. and H. White (1985). Some heteroscedastic consistent covariance estimators with improved finite sample properties. *J. Econometrics* **29**, 305–325.

McAleer, M. and M. R. Veall (1989). How fragile are fragile inferences? A reevaluation of the deterrent effect of capital punishment. *Rev. Econom. Statist.* **71**(1), 99–106.

Miller, R. G. Jr (1981). *Simultaneous Statist. Inference.* 2nd ed., Springer, New York.

Miller, R. G. (1974). The jackknife: A review. *Biometrika* **61**, 1–17.

Morey, M. J. and L. M. Schenck (1984). Small sample behavior of bootstrapped and jackknifed estimators. *ASA Proc. Business Econom. Statist.* 437–442.

Morey, M. J. and S. Wang (1985). Bootstrapping the Durbin–Watson statistic. *ASA Proc. Business Econom. Statist.*, 549–553.

Peters, S. C. and D. A. Freedman (1984). Some notes on the bootstrap in regression problems. *J. Business Econom. Statist.* **2**(4), 406–409.

Peters, S. C. and D. A. Freedman (1985). Using the bootstrap to evaluate forecasting equations. *J. Forecasting* **4**, 251–262.

Raj, B. and T. G. Taylor (1989). Do bootstrap tests provide significance level equivalent to the exact test? *J. Quant. Econom.* **5**(1), 73–89.

Rao, J. N. K. and C. F. J. Wu (1988). Resampling inference with complex survey data. *J. Amer. Statist. Assoc.* **83**, 231–241.

Rayner, R. K. (1990). Bootstrapping *p* values and power in the first-order autoregression: A Monte Carlo investigation. *J. Business Econom. Statist.* **8**, 251–263.

Rayner, R. K. (1991). Resampling methods for tests in regression models with autocorrelated errors. *Econom. Lett.* **36**, 281–284.

Romano, J. P. (1988). Bootstrap revival of some nonparametric distance tests. *J. Amer. Statist. Assoc.* **83**, 698–708.

Runkle, D. E. (1987). Vector autoregressions and reality (with discussion). *J. Business Econom. Statist.* **5**, 437–454.

Schechtman, E. (1991). On estimating the asymptotic variance of a function of *U* statistics. *Amer. Statist.* **45**(2), 103–106.

Schenker, N. (1985). Qualms about bootstrap confidence intervals. *J. Amer. Statist. Assoc.* **80**, 360–361.

Schwartz, E. S. and W. N. Torous (1989). Prepayment and the valuation of mortgage-backed securities. *J. Finance* **45**, 375–392.

Selvanathan, E. A. (1989). A note on the stochastic approach to index numbers. *J. Business Econom. Statist.* **7**, 471–474.

Sen, P. K. (1988). Functional approaches in resampling plans: A review of some recent developments. *Sankhyā Ser. A* **50**, 394–435.

Sen, P. K. (1989). Whither delete-*k* jackknife for smooth statistical functionals. In: Y. Dodge, ed., *Statistical Data Analysis and Inference.* Elsevier, Amsterdam, 269–279.

Sen, P. K. (1991). Some informative aspects of jackknifing and bootstrapping. Mimeo No. 2050. University of North Carolina, Department of Statistics, Chapel Hill, North Carolina.

Silverman, B. W. and G. A. Young (1987). The bootstrap: To smooth or not to smooth. *Biometrika* **74**, 469–479.

Sims, C. A. and H. Uhlig (1991). Understanding unit rooters: A helicopter tour. *Econometrica* **59**, 1591–1599.

Singh, K. (1981). On the asymptotic accuracy of Efron's bootstrap. *Ann. Statist.* **9**, 1187–1195.

Singh, K. and G. J. Babu (1990). On asymptotic optimality of the bootstrap. *Scand. J. Statist.* **17**, 1–9.

Son, M. S., D. Holbert and H. Hamdy (1987). Bootstrap forecasts versus conventional forecasts: A comparison for a second order autoregressive model. *ASA Proc. Business Econom. Statist.*, 723–727.

Srivastava, M. S. and B. Singh (1989). Bootstrapping in multiplicative models. *J. Econometrics* **42**, 287–297.

Stoffer, D. S. and K. D. Wall (1991). Bootstrapping state space models: Gaussian maximum likelihood estimation and the Kalman filter. *J. Amer. Statist. Assoc.* **86**, 1024–1033.

Veall, M. R. (1986). Bootstrapping regression estimators under first order serial correlation. *Econom. Lett.* **21**, 41–44.

Veall, M. R. (1987). Bootstrapping the probability distribution of peak electricity demand. *Internat. Econom. Rev.* **28**(1), 203–211.

Vinod, H. D. (1976). Applications of new ridge regression methods to a study of Bell system scale economies. *J. Amer. Statist. Assoc.* **71**, 835–841.

Vinod, H. D. (1985). Measurement of economic distance between blacks and whites. *J. Business Econom. Statist.* **3**, 78–88.

Vinod, H. D. (1991a). Regression bootstrap without residuals for studying time series data. Economics Department Fordham University, Bronx, New York, Manuscript.

Vinod. H. D. (1991b). Double bootstrap for shrinkage estimators. Economics Department Fordham University, Bronx, New York, Manuscript.

Vinod, H. D. and B. D. McCullough (1991). Estimating cointegrating parameters. An application of the double bootstrap. Presented at Stats. 91 Canada meeting at Concordia University in Montreal. *J. Statist. Planning Inference*, to appear.

Vinod, H. D. and B. Raj (1988). Economic issues in Bell system divestiture: A bootstrap application. *Appl. Statist.* **37**, 251–261.

Vinod, H. D. and A. Ullah (1981). *Recent Advances in Regression Methods*. Dekker, New York.

Withers, C. (1983). Expansion for the distribution with applications to non-parametric confidence intervals. *Ann. Statist.* **11**, 577–587.

Wu. C. F. G. (1986). Jackknife, bootstrap and other resampling methods in regression analysis. *Ann. Statist.* **14**, 1261–1295.

Yang, S. S. (1988). A central limit theorem for the bootstrap mean. *Amer. Statist.* **42**, 202–203.

Zellner, A. (1962). An efficient method of estimating seemingly unrelated regressions and tests for aggregation bias. *J. Amer. Statist. Assoc.* **57**, 348–368.

G. S. Maddala, C. R. Rao and H. D. Vinod, eds., *Handbook of Statistics*, *Vol. 11*

24

Identifying Outliers and Influential Observations in Econometric Models

Stephen G. Donald and G. S. Maddala

Yesterday, ...
All my data seemed to fit okay,
Now it seems INFLUENCE is here to stay,
Oh I believe in yesterday.

From a poem by Michael Greenacre,
Journal of Applied Statistics **14** (1987) 185.

1. Introduction

The literature on the detection of outliers and influential observations is large. Most of it, however, is confined to the linear regression model and there is a plethora of diagnostics in the literature. Chatterjee and Hadi (1986, p. 387) list 14 diagnostics. Though many are minor variations of others, some standard diagnostics like hat value, studentized residual, DFFITS, Cook distance etc., are standard outputs in the popular regression programs like SAS, SPSS, MINITAB, SHAZAM and so on.

A useful distinction may be made between outliers and influential observations. Influential observations are data points that have a 'large' or influential impact on some aspect of the estimation of the model of interest. Outliers may be considered points that are (in some sense to be defined later) away from the rest of the data. It is often argued that the two terms are not synonymous; that is outliers may not be influential and influential observations may not be outliers.

The plan of the paper is as follows: In Section 2, we review the literature on the regression model. We also present a critique of the criteria commonly used to distinguish between outliers and influential observations. In Section 3, we relate the outlier and influence diagnostics to standard tests of the linear hypotheses and to commonly used specification tests in econometrics (such as the Hausman test). Section 4 discusses the issue of what to do with outliers. Section 5 presents a brief review of bayesian approaches. In Sections 6, 7 and 8 we present our extensions of influence diagnostics to nonlinear models and the probit, logit and tobit models commonly used in econometrics. A regression based method, using artificial regressions for computing the diagnostics is proposed. Section 9 contains some brief comments on outliers in time series models and panel data. The final section presents our conclusions.

2. Linear regression models

In this section we briefly review some of the methods that have been proposed in the context of the linear regression model for the detection of outliers and influential observations. A large literature exists[1] that addresses this problem, although most appears to be directed at the linear model. Since many of the ideas that arise in the context of the linear model are important when we consider the more complicated models it is useful to provide a short summary of some of the techniques developed for the detection of influential and outlying observations in the linear model.

2.1. Deletion methods

To check whether (y_i, x_i) is an outlying observation in multiple regression, the standard procedure is to begin by fitting the regression with this observation deleted. Let $\hat{\beta}(i)$ denote the estimator of β and $s(i)^2$ the estimator of σ^2 when the i-th observation is deleted. Let $X(i)$ be the submatrix of X with the i-th row, x_i' deleted. Define the residual

$$\bar{u}_i = y_i - x_i'\hat{\beta}(i)$$

which is the *predicted residual*. It is the residual from a prediction of the deleted observation y_i using the regression estimates $\hat{\beta}(i)$.

The sum of squares of the predicted residuals (PRESS) has long been considered as a criterion for model choice. Quan (1988) suggests using a statistic Q^2 (suggested by H. Wold in 1982) along with R^2 in the assessment of both model fit and data quality. Q^2 is defined as

$$Q^2 = 1 - \frac{\sum (y_i - \hat{y}(i))^2}{\sum (y_i - \bar{y}(i))^2}.$$

He argues that differences between R^2 and Q^2 suggest that some observations may have undue influence on the regression equation, and illustrates this with two examples. However, there is the issue of the significance of these differences and, moreover, since the predicted residuals are already available, one can use all the other criteria suggested in the literature without much computational effort.

---

[1] See for example, Barnett and Lewis (1978), Belsley, Kuh and Welsch (1980), Bollen and Jackman (1990), Cook and Weisberg (1982), Draper and John (1981), Hoaglin and Welsch (1978), Rousseeuw and Leroy (1987).

The OLS residual $\hat{u}_i$ divided by its standard error is called the *standardized residual*, and the predicted residual divided by its standard error is known as the *studentized residual*. We shall denote this by u_i^*. To derive the variances of these residuals, we shall define the hat matrix, $H = X(X'X)^{-1}X'$. It is discussed in Hoaglin and Welsch (1978) and plays an important part in the literature on outliers and influential observations. Hoaglin and Welsch define observations with high values of h_i, the i-th diagonal element of H, as being high leverage points. The H matrix is called the hat matrix because $\hat{y} = Hy$, and also $\hat{u} = (I - H)y$. It is easy to check that H and $I - H$ are idempotent matrices. Hence we have that if $E(uu') = \sigma^2 I$,

$$V(\hat{u}) = (I - H)\sigma^2 .$$

Then $V(\hat{u}_i) = (1 - h_i)\sigma^2$. Also provided $\hat{\beta}(i)$ is defined, $\bar{u}_i = \hat{u}_i/(1 - h_i)$ and hence, $V(\bar{u}_i) = \sigma^2/(1 - h_i)$. The standardized residual is $\hat{u}_i/(s(1 - h_i)^{1/2})$ and the studentized residual is

$$u_i^* = \frac{\bar{u}_i(1 - h_i)^{1/2}}{s(i)} = \frac{\hat{u}_i}{s(i)(1 - h_i)^{1/2}} .$$

Thus the two residuals differ only in the estimate of σ^2.

To compute $s(i)$ we do not need to estimate the regression equation with the i-th observation deleted. In Section 3, we shall see that

$$(n - k)s^2 - (n - k - 1)s(i)^2 = \frac{\hat{u}_i^2}{(1 - h_i)} .$$

Thus, using just the hat matrix, the OLS residuals and the estimate of σ^2 from the OLS regression, we can compute the predicted residuals and the studentized residuals (as well as $\hat{\beta}(i)$ as shown later). Thus, all the statistics for the row-deletion case can be calculated with the results from the OLS regression.

One way of modeling an outlier is through a mean shift model:

$$y_i = x_i'\beta + \gamma + u_i ,$$
$$y_j = x_j'\beta + u_j \quad \text{for } j \neq i .$$

Then $\hat{\gamma}$ is just the predicted residual $\bar{u}_i$ because the estimate of β is obtained from the $(n - 1)$ observations excluding the i-th and $\hat{\gamma} = y_i - x_i'\hat{\beta}(i)$. The significance of $\hat{\gamma}$ is given by a test involving the studentized residual (an alternative notation for this is t_i because this is in the form of a t-ratio). The distribution of the studentized residual is a t-distribution with df $n - k - 1$, where n is the number of observations and k is the dimension of β.

The studentized residuals, thus, determine the outliers. What about influential observations? To answer this questions, we have to ask: Influence on what? We can consider influence on
  (i) the prediction of y_i,

(ii) $\hat{\beta}$,
(iii) $\hat{\beta}_j$.

Consider first the influence on prediction. The change in the prediction of y_i from the whole sample and from the sample with the i-th observation deleted, is given by

$$x_i'(\hat{\beta} - \hat{\beta}(i)) = (y - x_i'\hat{\beta}(i)) - (y_i - x_i'\hat{\beta}) = \tilde{u}_i - \hat{u}_i = h_i\tilde{u}_i .$$

Since h_i is a given constant, the significance of this can be tested by testing the significance of $\tilde{u}_i$, that is by the studentized residual u_i^*. This reasoning leads us to the conclusion that an influential observation is an outlier and vice versa, contrary to what many have argued. However, there are exceptions to this, and we shall return to this point later.

Belsley, Kuh and Welsch (1980), hereafter referred to as BKW, suggest the use of DFFITS$_i$ to 'test' the change in prediction. They divide the change in prediction by what they call a scaling factor, which is the standard error of $\hat{y}_i = x_i'\hat{\beta}$. Note that $V(\hat{y}_i) = h_i\sigma^2$. They use $s(i)^2$ to estimate σ^2. Hence, they get

$$\text{DFFITS}_i = \frac{h_i\tilde{u}_i}{s(i)\sqrt{h_i}} = (h_i)^{1/2}\frac{\hat{u}_i}{s(i)(1 - h_i)} .$$

This gives

$$\text{DFFITS}_i^2 = \left(\frac{h_i}{(1 - h_i)^2}\right)\frac{\hat{u}_i^2}{s(i)^2} = \frac{h_i}{1 - h_i}u_i^{*2} .$$

Thus DFFITS$_i$ depends on both h_i and the studentized residual. Using this expression, it is also argued that an influential observation need not be an outlier (u_i^* not significant but DFFITS$_i$ is) or that an outlier need not be influential (u_i^* significant but DFFITS$_i$ is not). Note that this conclusion arises from an arbitrary deflation, that is dividing $x_i'(\hat{\beta} - \hat{\beta}(i))$ not by its correct standard error but by the standard error of $x_i'\beta$ with $s(i)^2$ used as an estimator for σ^2.

The Cook distance does the same but uses s^2 as an estimator for σ^2. It is given by

$$D_i = \left(\frac{1}{ks^2}\right)(\hat{\beta} - \hat{\beta}(i))'X'X(\hat{\beta} - \hat{\beta}(i)) .$$

The division by k allows an approximate F-distribution interpretation. Cook cautions against a strict test procedure or interpretation since, D_i does not actually have the $F(n, n - k)$ distribution. In large samples it may be more appropriate to 'compare' kD_i to a χ^2-distribution. Note that

$$\text{DFFITS}_i^2 = \frac{1}{s(i)^2}(\hat{\beta} - \hat{\beta}(i))'X'X(\hat{\beta} - \hat{\beta}(i)) = \frac{ks^2D_i}{s(i)^2} .$$

Cook (1987) argues that while D_i looks at $\hat{\beta} - \hat{\beta}(i)$ in a fixed scale, DFFITS$_i$ is based on a variable scale. Thus, D_i measures the influence on $\hat{\beta}$ whereas DFFITS$_i$ measures the influence on the estimates of β and σ^2 simultaneously.

Consider next the influence on $\hat{\beta}$. We have

$$\hat{\beta}(i) = (X(i)'X(i))^{-1}X(i)'y(i)$$

and a well-known result is that

$$\hat{\beta} - \hat{\beta}(i) = \frac{(X'X)^{-1}x_i\hat{u}_i}{1 - h_i} = (X'X)^{-1}x_i\tilde{u}_i .$$

Again since $(X'X)^{-1}x_i$ is a vector of constants, the significance of $\hat{\beta} - \hat{\beta}(i)$ is tested by the significance of $\tilde{u}_i$, that is by the studentized residual.

Finally, for the influence on individual β_j we have to consider $\hat{\beta}_j - \hat{\beta}_j(i)$. This is given by

$$\hat{\beta}_j - \hat{\beta}_j(i) = (X'X)_j^{-1}x_i\tilde{u}_i ,$$

where $(X'X)_j^{-1}$ is the j-th row of $(X'X)^{-1}$. Again the significance of this is tested by the studentized residual.

Thus as the saying goes: 'All roads lead to Rome'. Outlier tests and the three influence measures (when compared with their appropriate distributions) all lead to the studentized residual. We shall see later that this is because of concentration on influence on β alone rather than on σ^2 or both. BKW (1980) suggest the statistic DFBETAS$_{ij}$ to test the difference $\hat{\beta}_j - \hat{\beta}(i)_j$. It is defined by

$$\text{DFBETAS}_{ij} = \frac{(\hat{\beta}_j - \hat{\beta}(i)_j)}{s(i)\sqrt{(X'X)_{jj}^{-1}}} ,$$

where $(X'X)_{jj}^{-1}$ is the j-th diagonal element of $(X'X)^{-1}$. The expression is obtained by dividing $\hat{\beta}_j - \hat{\beta}(i)_j$, not by its correct standard error but by a 'scale factor' which is $\text{Var}(\hat{\beta}_j)^{1/2}$, with $s(i)$ substituted for σ. The expression BKW derive for DFBETA$_{ij}$ is complicated and we shall not present it here.

In summary, the differences between the different influence measures and the differences between outlier diagnostics and influence diagnostics that BKW (1980) and several others obtain is due to the arbitrary deflators of the relevant statistics. If the correct standard errors are used, then these differences vanish and everything leads to the studentized residual.

Turning next to the several 'cut-off' points used in practice we have the following 'rules of thumb'. (See Table 2, p. 387 of Chatterjee and Hadi, 1986 or Table 6.1, p. 268 of Bollen and Jackman, 1990). Since trace$(H) = k$, and the average of h_i is k/n (and in a balanced design $h_i = k/n$ for all i) the i-th observation is considered a *leverage point* if $h_i > 2k/n$. For DFFITS$_i$, BKW suggest the cutoff $2\sqrt{k/n}$ and for DFBETAS$_{ij}$ they suggest $2/\sqrt{n}$. As for the

Cook distance, Cook suggests comparing D_i^2/k to the F-distribution with k and $n-k$ degrees of freedom. Weisberg suggests using the 50 percent point of the F-distribution which translates roughly to an F-value of 1.

2.2. The conflict between outliers and influential observations

The preceding discussion suggests no conflict between outliers and influential observations. Where does this presumed conflict come from? Consider for instance DFFITS$_i$. It is defined as

$$\text{DFFITS}_i = \left(\frac{h_i}{1-h_i}\right)^{1/2} u_i^*$$

and if we consider DFFITS$_i > 2\sqrt{k/n}$ as 'significant', it can turn out that it is significant even if u_i^* is not (and vice versa). This is the argument, for instance, in Welsch (1980, p. 160). But this conflict is, as noted earlier a consequence of dividing the change in prediction, not by its standard error, but by an arbitrary scale factor. Implicit in this discussion is an assumption that large studentized residuals indicate outliers (as we shall see this is questionable) and that influence needs to be measured by something else, such as DFFITS, Cook's D and so on.

The argument that studentized residuals do not tell the whole story and one needs to consider h_i (the diagonals of the hat matrix) is a valid one. To illustrate this we generated data following Figure 2.1 (d) of BKW (1980, p. 8). The data consisted of nine observations around low values of x and y and the 10-th observation with a higher value x and y. By design the 10-th observation is an outlier. The question is: Does the studentized residual pick it? The answer is no. It is h_i that picks it. In all the simulations the h_i values ranged between 0.10 and 0.12 for the first nine observations but were greater than 0.99 for the 10-th. As for the studentized residuals, none were significant. Of course DFFITS$_i$ picked the 10-th observation but this is because of its dependence on h_i. We tentatively conclude that studentized residuals alone should not be used to detect outliers. It is h_i in conjunction with u_i^* that should be used. As for determining influential observations, the valid statistic is the studentized residual.

In the example we considered suppose that y denoted consumption and x family income for a group of families. The 10-th observation is an outlier (a high income family). But the studentized residual suggests that its behaviour is similar to that of the rest of the group. This implies that this outlier should not be thrown out.

There are two senses in which an observation can be considered an outlier. Observations consist of the pairs $\{x_i, y_i\}$. First, we may have that y_i is not 'close' to $E(y|x_i)$, i.e., it is in the tail of the distribution of y given $x=x_i$. Second, x_i may not be close to the other observations on x. Unfortunately, the presence of the second type of outlier may make it difficult to determine if one has an outlier of the first type. It is in this case that the studentized residual may fail to pick an outlier of the first type. Essentially, one does not have enough data on x near x_i to be able to get a very precise estimate of $E(y \mid x_i)$, which is obviously required if one wants to determine if the observed y_i is outlying or not.

The measures of 'influence' proposed by BKW are typically some combination of the studentized residual and the leverage measure. They construct cut off values based on the arguments that

(a) a value of 2 for the studentized residual is significant, based on formal tests of hypotheses,

(b) a value of $2k/n$ for the h_i measure is 'large' based on a largely subjective rule.

Clearly, one will not exceed the constructed cut off value unless one of the above are exceeded. Plus an element of subjectivity has been introduced.[2] The question is, however, whether these influence measures contain any information not already contained in the measures independently.

Mention must be made of the example of an 'influential observation' with a zero residual in Figure 2 of Chatterjee and Hadi (1986, p. 281). In this example $\hat{\beta}(i)$ is not defined. Thus there is no point in talking about influence on prediction of β. Examples like this are misleading and do not prove anything.

As an illustration of the conflicting results from h_i and u_i^*, consider the example from Reiss (1990) on the relationship between R and D and productivity. He had $n = 27$ and $k = 3$ (constant term included). The results were:

Industry	Stud. residual	Hat value	Cook distance
2. Missiles	−1.70	0.943*	14.78*
14. Engines	−2.13*	0.071	0.10
15. Farm machinery	2.57*	0.045	0.08
18. Computers	1.26	0.415*	0.37

What do we conclude? According to Hoaglin and Welsch (1978) the significant hat values for industries 2 and 18 indicate they have 'high leverage'. Reiss argues that the studentized residuals indicate that industries 14 and 15 are outliers. However, the significant studentized residuals for these observations, could be due to the fact that industry 2 has high leverage (and may also be an outlier), and so causes the regression line to move away from these points.

A major omission from the preceding discussion is that it considers influence on β only and it does not consider influence on σ^2. Although Cook argued that the Cook distance measures influence on β only whereas $DFFITS_i$ measures influence on both β and σ^2, in his comment on Chatterjee and Hadi (1986) he

---

[2] As has been noted by Chatterjee and Hadi (1988, p. 95) the notion of an influential observation (as distinct from an outlier) is 'subjective' so it is not surprising that determining cut off values for 'influence measures' is based on subjective criteria.

argues that $DFFITS_i$ is an unsatisfactory measure of the influence on β and σ^2 simultaneously. He suggests that the likelihood displacement $LD_i(\beta, \sigma^2)$ is a better measure. He notes that $LD_i(\beta)$ is related to the Cook distance. The Bayesian literature (reviewed in Section 5), also makes a distinction between influence on β only, on σ^2 only, and on β and σ^2 together. Before that we shall discuss the LD_i measures.

2.3. The likelihood displacement method

The likelihood displacement method discussed in Cook (1987) and Cook and Peña (1988) looks at the change in the value of the maximum of the likelihood function that results when observation i is omitted. In this case one is able to be more explicit about the parameters of interest. For example suppose that the value of the (normal) likelihood function at the MLE is $L(\beta, \sigma^2)$, then various measures of influence can be defined in terms of likelihood displacement – one may obtain different measures depending on the parameters of interest. In the case of the linear regression model it is fairly simple to concentrate the likelihood function so that it depends on either β or σ^2 alone. For example since

$$\hat{\sigma}^2 = (y - X\hat{\beta})'(y - X\hat{\beta})/n \,,$$

we may rewrite the concentrated likelihood function in terms of β alone as $L(\hat{\beta})$. If one were interested in a measure of the influence on β of deleting an observation, then a natural measure could be defined by

$$LD_i(\beta) = 2(L(\hat{\beta}, \hat{\sigma}^2) - L(\hat{\beta}(i)))$$

which is shown by Cook and Weisberg to be identical to

$$LD_i(\beta) = n \log(kD_i/(n - k + 1)) \,.$$

Alternatively one may be interested in a measure of influence on σ^2 alone or on β and σ^2 jointly. Thus depending on one's focus one may obtain displacement measures which can be written as $LD_i(\sigma^2)$, $LD_i(\beta)$ and $LD_i(\beta, \sigma^2)$, the latter being the difference between the unconcentrated likelihood functions evaluated at the different estimators, i.e., at $(\hat{\beta}, \sigma^2)$ and $(\hat{\beta}(i), \sigma^2(i))$. Note that the last measure provides an upper bound on the other two measures. Define

$$b_i = \frac{\hat{u}_i^2}{s^2(1 - h_i)(n - k)} \,.$$

Then,

$$LD_i(\sigma^2) = n \log\left(\frac{n}{n - 1}\right) + n \log(1 - b_i) + \frac{(n - 1)b_i}{b_i} - 1$$

and

$$\mathrm{LD}_i(\beta, \sigma^2) = \mathrm{LD}_i(\sigma^2) + \frac{(n-1)b_i h_i}{1 - b_i} .$$

The form of the LD_i diagnostics is suggestive of a likelihood ratio type test for influence since in large samples

$$2(L(\hat{\beta}, \hat{\sigma}^2) - L(\beta, \sigma^2)) \sim \chi^2(k+1)$$

however, Cook warns that this should be used more as a guide than as a formal testing procedure. This is because replacing the true parameters by the perturbed estimates (which gives rise to one of the LD_i measures) gives no reason to expect that the resulting limit distribution is appropriate. There are a plethora of other measures of influence in regression which are discussed more completely in references such as Cook and Weisberg (1982).

2.4. Local perturbation methods

Since there may be some apprehension on the part of the econometrician to actually delete an observation if it is 'outlying',[3] others have proposed methods that look at the effect of a small perturbation in the weight given to the i-th observation in the calculation of the estimator. Such methods are considered by Cook (1986, 1987). These methods are known as 'perturbation methods'. Instead of looking at the change in the estimate when an observation is dropped completely one looks at the effect of changing the weight infinitessimally evaluated at some point – a local perturbation. This is based on the idea that one may not really be interested in dropping outlying observations completely – rather one would just alter the weight given to the i-th observation.

The usual way one proceeds with this in the case of the linear model is to look at the derivative of

$$\hat{\beta}(w) = (X'WX)^{-1}X'Wy$$

with respect to the weight given to observation i

$$\frac{\partial}{\partial w_i} \hat{\beta}(w)$$

evaluated at some point. Points of interest would be where the set of weights is equal to one for all the observation – looking at the sensitivity of $\hat{\beta}$ to a small reduction in the weight given to observation i – or at the point where all observations have weight equal to 1 expect for the i-th which has value 0 – thus giving a measure of the change due to the inclusion of any information contained in observation i.

[3] See Leamer (1990) for example.

In the context of maximum likelihood estimation one may compute for each possible value of the $n \times 1$ weight vector w a likelihood displacement measure $LD(w)$. We can then study the curvature of $LD(w)$. To show how this is developed we follow Cook and write $L(\theta \mid w)$ for the likelihood function that has a $p \times 1$ vector of weights w attached and the MLE denoted $\hat{\theta}_w$ satisfies the usual normal equation

$$\frac{\partial(L(\hat{\theta}_w \mid w))}{\partial \theta} = 0 .$$

Then the curvature of the graph of $LD(w)$ in the direction l is given by Cook (1986) as

$$C_l = 2 \left| l' \frac{\partial^2 L(\hat{\theta} \mid w)'}{\partial \theta \, \partial w} \frac{\partial^2 L(\hat{\theta} \mid w)^{-1}}{\partial \theta \, \partial \theta} \frac{\partial^2 L(\hat{\theta} \mid w)}{\partial \theta \, \partial w} l \right| ,$$

where l is some directional $p \times 1$ vector with $l'l = 1$. One case that may be of interest, may be where one examines the effect of a perturbation in the weight being given to a particular observation – that is in the regression case having weights of 1 for all but the i-th observation and looking at the curvature when one changes the weight given to the i-th observation locally – Cook shows this is to be equal to

$$C = \frac{2\hat{u}_i^2 h_i}{\hat{\sigma}^2}$$

in the case of the regression model. This can be shown to be related to the statistic D_i by

$$C = k(1 - h_i)^2 D_i$$

and hence appears to be not as sensitive to extreme values in the design matrix. A measure analogous to this may be derived by appropriate standardization of the measure mentioned above

$$\frac{\partial}{\partial w_i} \hat{\beta}(w)$$

evaluated at the value where $w_i = 1$ and all other weights are 1. As shown by Pregibon (1981)

$$\frac{\partial}{\partial w_i} \hat{\beta}(1) = (X'X)^{-1} x_i \hat{u}_i$$

so that standardization by $\hat{\sigma}^2 (X'X)^{-1}$ would give a value equal to $\frac{1}{2}C$.

There may be other cases of interest. For example for a subset of weights one may be interested in the maximal curvature – i.e., the direction in which curvature is largest so the results may be most sensitive. This is related to eigen values of the matrix

$$\frac{\partial^2 L(\hat{\theta}\,|\,w)'}{\partial \theta \, \partial w} \frac{\partial^2 L(\hat{\theta}\,|\,w)^{-1}}{\partial \theta \, \partial \theta} \frac{\partial^2 L(\hat{\theta}\,|\,w)}{\partial \theta \, \partial w} \,.$$

See Cook (1986, 1987) for more discussion on the various uses of the C statistics.

In this paper we concentrate on measures related to the deletion diagnostics since they are relatively simple to compute. The measures mentioned in the previous section may also be developed for the models considered later, however, for ease of exposition and brevity we consider only deletion diagnostics for particular models.

3. Relationship between influence diagnostics, tests of linear hypotheses and specification tests

One question that deserves attention is what relationship, if any, do the diagnostics presented in the previous section have to standard tests of linear hypotheses and commonly used specification tests in econometrics (like the Hausman test). Consider the model with n observations and k regressors:

$$y = X\beta + u \,, \quad \text{where } u \sim \mathrm{N}(0, \sigma^2 I) \,.$$

Partition the data into two subsamples of sizes n_1 and n_2 respectively ($n_1 + n_2 = n$). We can then write

$$y_1 = X_1\beta_1 + u_1 \,,$$

$$y_2 = X_2\beta_2 + u_2 \,.$$

Let the residual sums of squares from the samples of size n_1, n_2 and n be denoted by RSS_1, RSS_2 and RSS respectively. Then we have the following two well-known results:

(i) $(\mathrm{RSS}_1 + \mathrm{RSS}_2)/\sigma^2$ and $(\mathrm{RSS} - \mathrm{RSS}_1 - \mathrm{RSS}_2)/\sigma^2$ are independently distributed as χ^2 with df $n - 2k$ and non-central χ^2 with df k respectively. If $\beta_1 = \beta_2$ then both have a central χ^2 distribution and

$$\frac{(\mathrm{RSS} - \mathrm{RSS}_1 - \mathrm{RSS}_2)/k}{(\mathrm{RSS}_1 + \mathrm{RSS}_2)/(n - 2k)}$$

has an F-distribution. (This is known as the second fundamental theorem of least squares, see Rao, 1973, p. 191.)

(ii) RSS_1/σ^2 and $(\mathrm{RSS} - \mathrm{RSS}_1)/\sigma^2$ are independently distributed as χ^2 with df $n_1 - k$ and non-central χ^2 with df n_2 respectively. If $\beta_1 = \beta_2$ then both have a central χ^2 distribution and

$$\frac{(\text{RSS} - \text{RSS}_1)/n_2}{\text{RSS}_1/(n-k)}$$

has an F-distribution. (This is known as the third fundamental theorem of least squares, see Rao, 1973, p. 193.)

Results (i) and (ii) are known in the econometric literature as Chow tests for stability. Result (i) was presented in a book by C. R. Rao in 1952, but result (ii) was published by Chow in 1960. If $n_2 < k$ it is not possible to use the first test and Chow suggests using test (ii). But as pointed out in Rea (1978), since β_2 cannot be estimated from the sample of size n_2, what is being tested is unbiasedness of predictions and not the hypothesis $\beta_1 = \beta_2$. Thus the second test is often called the predictive test for stability. In the case of deletion of a single observation, we have that $n_2 = 1$ and thus, test (i) can never be used.

3.1. Deletion of a single observation

In the case of, say, deletion of the i-th observation, it can be shown that

$$\text{RSS} - \text{RSS}_1 = \hat{u}_i^2/(1 - h_i) \,.$$

Thus the F-statistic in (ii) reduces to u_i^{*2}, the square of the studentized residual. This is not surprising since the test we derived earlier for influence on prediction is based on the studentized residual and the Chow test actually tests the unbiasedness of prediction.

Consider now, the relationship with Hausman's specification test. Define,

H_0: the i-th observation is not an influential observation,

H_1: the i-th observation is an influential observation.

Then $\hat{\beta}$ is efficient under H_0 but not unbiased under H_1, whereas $\hat{\beta}(i)$ is unbiased under both H_0 and H_1, but not efficient under H_0. Using the result (5a.2.2) in Rao (1973, p. 318) we get

$$V = \text{Var}(\hat{\beta}(i) - \hat{\beta}) = \text{Var}(\hat{\beta}(i)) - \text{Var}(\hat{\beta})$$
$$= \sigma^2(X(i)'X(i))^{-1} - \sigma^2(X'X)^{-1}$$

The Hausman test statistic is

$$H = (\hat{\beta}(i) - \hat{\beta})'V^-(\hat{\beta}(i) - \hat{\beta}) \,,$$

where V^- denotes the inverse of V if V^{-1} exists and the generalized inverse if V^{-1} does not exist. Now

$$\hat{\beta} - \hat{\beta}(i) = \frac{(X'X)^{-1}x_i\hat{u}_i}{1 - h_i}$$

and using the result that

$$(A + BDC')^{-1} = A^{-1} - A^{-1}B(D^{-1} + CA^{-1}B)^{-1}C'A^{-1}$$

we get that

$$(X(i)'X(i))^{-1} = (X'X - x_i x_i')^{-1} = (X'X)^{-1} + \frac{(X'X)^{-1}(x_i x_i')(X'X)^{-1}}{1 - h_i}.$$

Hence,

$$V^- = \frac{(1 - h_i)}{\sigma^2}(X'X)(x_i x_i')^-(X'X).$$

Substituting the expressions for $\hat{\beta} - \hat{\beta}(i)$ and V^- in H, and noting that (see Rao and Mitra, 1971)

$$x_i'(x_i x_i')^- x_i = I$$

we get that

$$H = \frac{\hat{u}_i^2}{(1 - h_i)\sigma^2}.$$

Using $s(i)^2$ for σ^2 we get $H = u^{*2}$, the square of the studentized residual. Thus the Hausman specification error test also gives the same result.

3.2. The case of multiple outliers

In Cook and Weisberg (1982, p. 136) expressions are given for the generalization of the Cook distance to the case of multiple outliers. However, the statistics do not have any known distributions though the F-distribution is suggested as an analogy. Following the paper by Reiss (1990) we shall show the relationship between outlier diagnostics, influence diagnostics, and the two F-tests (i) and (ii).

Consider the case of n_2 outliers. The mean shift model for detection of outliers would be to introduce a vector of parameters γ of dimension n_2 and estimate the model,

$$y_1 = X_1\beta + u_1,$$
$$y_2 = X_2\beta + \gamma + u_2.$$

A test of $\gamma = 0$ is given by

$$F = \frac{(RSS - RSS_1)/n_2}{RSS_1/(n_1 - k)}$$

which is distributed as $F(n_2, n_1 - k)$. This is the test given by (ii) or the Chow test for predictive stability.[4]

Consider next the Hausman test for testing the difference $\hat{\beta}_1 - \hat{\beta}_2$. The model now is $y_1 = X_1\beta + u_1$ and $y_2 = X_2\beta + u_2$. The Hausman test statistic is given above. For the case $n_2 \leq k$, Reiss (1990) shows, using the results for generalized inverses in Rao and Mitra (1971), that

$$H = \frac{RSS - RSS_1}{\sigma^2}$$

which has a χ^2 distribution with df n_2 under the null and for the case $n_2 > k$ (in this case V^{-1} is defined) he shows that

$$H = \frac{RSS - RSS_1 - RSS_2}{\sigma^2}$$

which has a χ^2 distribution with df k under the null. If we use $\hat{\sigma}^2 = RSS_1/(n_1 - k)$ in the case $n_2 \leq k$ and $\hat{\sigma}^2 = (RSS_1 + RSS_2)/(n - 2k)$ in the case $n > k$ we get the F-statistics in (ii) and (i) respectively. Thus the influence statistics to test $\hat{\beta}_1 - \hat{\beta}$ reduce to the familiar F-tests and it is interesting to note that the Hausman test also reduces to these tests.

If we use $\hat{\sigma}^2 = RSS/(n - k)$ as used in the Cook distance, we get a beta random variable instead of the F. (Note that Rao, 1973, p. 193, writes the test in the beta distribution form.)

In summary, when the test statistics for influence diagnostics are written with the appropriate covariance matrices, rather than with arbitrary scale factors, as in the Cook distance, we are back to the standard F-tests of linear hypotheses.

4. What do *we* do with outliers

> If among these errors are some which appear too large to be admissible, then those observations which produced these errors will be rejected, as coming from too faulty experiments, and the unknown will be determined by means of the other observations, which will then give much smaller errors.

Legendre, in 1805, in the first publication on least squares.

> The method of least squares is seen to be our best course when we have thrown a certain portion of our data – a sort of sacrifice

---

[4] Reiss (1990, p. 297) suggests that the test is a Chow test if and only if $n_2 \leq k$. However, the usual test for testing $\gamma = 0$ (third fundamental theorem in Rao, 1973, p. 191) is the test given here, and is the same for $n_2 \leq k$ or $n_2 \leq k$.

which has often to be made by those who sail upon the stormy seas of probability.

F. Y. Edgeworth, *Philosophical Magazine*, 1887, p. 269.

There are essentially three approaches to dealing with outliers and influential observations. These can be described as:
(1) Throw the rascals out.
(2) Leave the rascals in but keep them under control.
(3) Listen to what the rascals are saying and change the model.

4.1. Throwing out the observations

This approach goes back to Legendre and Edgeworth and is the one often followed in empirical work. It would be the correct approach if the outlier is due to a recording error, or there is some information why the observation does not belong to the sample. Solow (1957) in his famous paper found that some observations deviated from the rest. He called them 'mystery observations' and discarded them. Later it was found by Hogan that the mystery points resulted from computational errors, and these errors were corrected. However, in his original analysis, Solow was lucky that he threw away his mystery observations because, otherwise, he would have arrived at some strange results. This was a case where 'outliers' were initially thrown out but replaced by corrected values in subsequent analysis.

Fisher's (1962) study on the demand for aluminum ingot is an example of a case where prior information was brought in to discard some observations and to correct some others. First, he started with data for 1922–1940 and 1948–1955. He then discarded the data for 1948–1955 because of some structural changes in the aluminum market after the war. Next, the data for 1922–1924 and 1938 were discarded on the basis of some other information relating to the aluminum market. Finally, of the remaining 15 observations, the 10 observations for 1926–1935 were adjusted for stock piling. The final estimation gave 'satisfactory' results.

When outliers are caused by recording errors or there is some extraneous reason to discard them, the proper approach is to throw the 'rascals' out. In the case of time series data (discussed in Section 9) it is customary to distinguish between an 'additive outlier' and an 'innovation outlier'. The former is a bad piece of information and is thrown out. Things are different with cross section data. Consider an example where some high income families show up in a study of consumer behaviour. In this case it may not be appropriate to throw these observations out. The proper approach is to analyze the data within two groups (using some dummy variables or some pooling method) or use some robust estimation procedures that minimize the influence of these outlying observations on the estimated equation.

4.2. Controlling the influence of outliers

The second approach to the handling of outliers is to leave them in but use methods that minimize their influence. The robust estimators (M-estimators, L_p-norm estimators, R-estimators, bounded-influence estimators, etc.) are not as strongly affected by outliers as the OLS estimators. The earliest of these estimators is the LAD (least absolute deviation) estimator or the L_1 norm estimator. It is usually thought to have been suggested by Edgeworth in 1887 but Rao (1989) traces it back to Galilei in 1632, Boscovich in 1757, Laplace in 1793 and Gauss in 1809. Rao also provides a survey of recent developments in LAD estimation. In practice, the LAD estimation in the regression context is usually undertaken with iteratively weighted least squares (see Maddala, 1977, pp. 310–314). The LAD estimator minimizes,

$$Q = \sum |\hat{u}_i| = \sum w_i \hat{u}_i^2 \,,$$

where $w_i = 1/|\hat{u}_i|$. The iterative weighted least squares (WLS) procedure proceeds as follows: First we use OLS to get $\hat{u}_i$. Next we construct w_i and use WLS. The new residuals are used to get new weights and the WLS procedure is repeated. Fair (1974) found that this procedure converged after two or three iterations. As for small sample standard errors, it is not clear how to best calculate them and hence one could use the bootstrap methods.

There is an issue of when robust methods are to be used. One approach is to use the methods described in earlier sections to identify the outliers and influential observations and then to use robust methods if there are such observations and we have decided to retain them. This is a commonly used approach. An example of this is the simple bounded influence estimator suggested by Welsch (1980) which is a weighted least squares estimator that minimizes

$$\sum w_i (y_i - x_i'\beta)^2$$

which uses $c_i = |\mathrm{DFFITS}_i|$ and a cut off value $c_i = 0.34$ is chosen so that

$$w_i = \begin{cases} 1 & \text{if } c_i < 0.34 \,, \\ \dfrac{0.34}{c_i} & \text{if } c_i > 0.34 \,. \end{cases}$$

Welsch says that the cutoff value of 0.34 is chosen for approximately 95 percent asymptotic efficiency. In contrast to this two step procedure, the bounded influence estimation (BIE) method is an iterative weighted least squares method where the outliers are identified within the context of the BIE method.[5] Krasker (1981) uses this estimator for a forecasting problem faced by Korvette's department stores in 1975 which had to choose between two sites A

---

[5] For the sake of brevity, we are omitting the detailed expressions here. Furthermore, these expressions can be written in the score vector form which is useful when considering non-linear models and models more complicated than the linear regression model.

anc *B* for the location of a new store. Of the 25 existing stores, to develop a model, Krasker finds two to be outliers. But his bounded influence estimator and OLS with the outliers thrown out gave almost the same results. As far as prediction from the model goes, site *A* was similar to one of the outliers and hence the estimated model was useful only for predictions about site *B* but not for site *A*.

There is the question of what to do with the outliers identified by the BIE method. As far as estimation goes, the BIE method has already taken them into account. So, of what use is it to identify them as outliers? The answer is that it is useful when it comes to prediction, as in the example of Korvette's department stores. Since site *A* is similar to one of the outliers the model cannot be used to make any predictions for site *A*.

There are other examples where OLS with outliers thrown out and bounded influence estimation (BIE) gave almost the same results. The method of BIE has been extended to other models by Stefanski, Carrol and Rupert (1986) for logistic regression, by Peracchi (1990a,b, and 1991) to tobit models and seemingly unrelated regression models and by Kao and Dutkowsky (1989) to a switching regression model. One troublesome feature in all these models is the choice of the bounding constant for bounded influence which is arbitrary. Since there is no well defined theory for this, Powell (1990) suggests that semi-parametric and non-parametric methods with more well defined inference should be preferred to BIE. But these methods address a different problem – that of general distribution of errors, rather than the outlier problem that the robust procedures are concerned with. Often a byproduct of the BIE method is a vector of weights which some authors have suggested may be useful for the detection of influential observations. In this approach, thus, the influential observations are not determined first but are identified in the context of BIE estimation. If the data do not contain influential observations, however, the BIE estimation procedure is an unnecessary complication.

Rousseeuw and Leroy (1987) argue that robust procedures should not be used after detecting outliers from the OLS procedure. Rather, the robust procedures should be used first with all the data and then one should discover the outliers as those points that possess large residuals from the robust solution. A question again arises as to how large is large, and the distribution theory for robust residuals is very complicated. They suggest the LMS (least median squares) method, proposed earlier in Rousseeuw (1984) which minimizes med$\{y_i - x_i\beta\}^2$. In the LMS procedure the regression surface lies within the closest pair (in the direction of the dependent variable) of parallel hyperplanes that contain 50 percent of the data. It has a break down point[6] (fraction of contamination that can produce large changes in the regression surface) close to 50 percent in contrast to OLS, which can be broken down by a single observation.[7]

---

[6] The notion of breakdown point is discussed in Donoho and Huber (1983).

[7] Computer programs for LMS regression are discussed in *The American Statistician*, February, 1991, p. 74.

After computing the residuals u_i from the LMS regression, Rousseeuw and Leroy use (1987, p. 240) what they call 'resistant diagnostics' defined by

$$\text{RD}_i = \frac{u_i}{\text{med}\{u_j\}} \, ,$$

where the median is taken over the data set. 50 percent of the RD_i will be at most 1. They suggest using $\text{RD}_i > 2.5$ to detect outliers (this is arbitrary). They give two examples where the criteria based on least squares produced no outliers, but those based on their statistic RD_i produced some (pp. 243–245). This raises questions about the whole issue of what outliers are. In these illustrations, it appears that finding outliers is an end in itself.

The above discussion gives a rough summary of some robust procedures that have been used in empirical work relating to outliers and influential observations. Some have used the procedure of first identifying outliers and influential observations and then using methods that give less weight to these observations. Others have argued that we should use robust procedures first and then detect outliers and influential observations next. But then the problem arises as to what you do with outliers. In the BIE method, you do not throw them out. In the case of Rousseeuw and Leroy (1987) it is not clear.

4.3. Changing the model

Very often the outliers point out the deficiencies in the specification of the model. The outliers sometimes form a separate group in which case the data need to be analyzed in the framework of two groups (either separately or in a pooled sample with dummies). In fact, it is always best to investigate whether there are any special features about the outliers, before considering the options of throwing out the outliers or using robust estimation procedures. There are several illustrations for this but we shall discuss only one of them. Gray (1989) gives an example of how an outlier led to a change of a model. The example concerns a multiple regression of y on x_1, x_2, x_3 and x_4, based on data for the 48 contiguous states in the USA. The variables were:

y = state per capita fuel consumption,
x_1 = state gasoline tax,
x_2 = percent of licensed drivers in the state,
x_3 = state average per capita income,
x_4 = total length of federal aid primary roads in the state.

The multiple regression equation gave an R^2 of 0.68. Several regression diagnostics suggested that Wyoming was an outlier. The average fuel consumption per capita for that state was higher than that predicted by the model. One approach is to delete this observation. A better approach is to ask why it is an outlier. One possible reason one could suggest is the degree of isolation, the long distances that separate towns, cities, stores, facilities and so on, in Wyoming, thus requiring more driving. A proxy for this isolation is population density (ratio of state population to state area). Gray found, on plotting the variables, that the log of population density was a better explanatory variable. The simple r^2 between y and this variable was 0.73 (compared with the R^2 of 0.68 for the multiple regression of y on x_1, x_2, x_3 and x_4). Thus, Wyoming, the outlier, led to the reformulation of the model. However, Gray says, 'The irony is that Wyoming, which provided the clue to an important missing variable remains an outlier in a simple regression equation with log population density as the explanatory variable'!

Influential observations and outliers may contain important information and may suggest some important missing variables or other deficiencies in the formulation of the model. Mechanically throwing these observations out and staying with the original model, or using some estimation methods that minimize their influence, like M-estimators or BIE estimators (within the framework of the original model) might be the wrong thing to do.

5. Bayesian and decision theoretic approaches

There is a lot of work on bayesian approaches to the problem of outliers and influential observations. We shall present here only a brief review. As in the classical approach one can talk of outliers and influential observations and distinguish between influence on parameters and influence on prediction. In the case of a single outlier, we saw that in the classical approach, detecting outliers and observations with influence on parameters and on predictions, all are based on studentized residuals when the measures are deflated by their correct standard errors. The test statistics differ only in the case of multiple outliers when the number of outliers p is greater than the number of explanatory variables k (plus one if there is a constant term).

In the bayesian approaches, even with a single outlier, measures of influence on parameters and predictions differ, and also the expressions for multiple outliers do not depend on whether $p > k$ or $p < k$ as in the classical approach. This is because of incorporation of priors into the analysis, which essentially circumvents the indeterminacy problem outlined in Rea (1978).

The common point in several of these papers is the Kullback–Leibler divergence. In general, given two pdfs f_1 and f_2, the average information of proceeding from f_1 to f_2 is defined as

$$I(f_1, f_2) = \int \log(f_1/f_2)f_1 \, \mathrm{d}x \, .$$

This directed divergence is not symmetric. A more general measure of distance between f_1 and f_2 is the symmetric divergence

$$J(f_1, f_2) = I(f_1, f_2) + I(f_2, f_1) \, .$$

Using this measure of change with f_1 denoting the distribution based on the whole sample and f_2 denoting the corresponding distribution with some observations deleted, several measures of 'outlyingness' and influence have been developed. For instance, Pettit and Smith (1985) and Guttman and Peña (1988) study the change in the posterior distributions of the parameters: $p(\beta)$, $p(\sigma^2)$ and $p(\beta, \sigma^2)$ and Johnson and Geisser (1982, 1983, 1985) study the change in the predictive distributions.

The measures of influence, suggested in the several papers differ based on the differences in the priors and the approximations to the posteriors used. The measures have been derived for p outliers and the dichotomy $p > k$ and $p < k$ does not exist in the bayesian literature. Furthermore, influence on β as well as σ^2 is considered separately and jointly. Though the results are available for p outliers, we shall present the results for the case of a single outlier, so as to compare the results with those in our earlier discussion. In much of the bayesian literature p is the number of regressors and k is the number of outliers, but to maintain consistency with our earlier notation, we shall use k for the number of regressors and p for the number of outliers.

If f_1 and f_2 are k-variate normal distributions with means, μ_1 and μ_2 and covariance matrices Σ_1 and Σ_2 respectively, then the Kullback–Leibler divergence is,

$$J(f_1, f_2) = \tfrac{1}{2}(\mu_1 - \mu_2)'(\Sigma_1^{-1} + \Sigma_2^{-1})(\mu_1 - \mu_2) + \tfrac{1}{2}\mathrm{tr}(\Sigma_1 \Sigma_2^{-1} + \Sigma_2 \Sigma_1^{-1}) - k \ .$$

Consider the normal regression model,

$$y = X\beta + u$$

where $u \sim N(0, \sigma^2 I)$. Then Guttman (1991) assumes that the posteriors for β (with non-informative priors) from the whole sample and from the sample with p (equals 1) observations deleted are approximately given by

$$\beta \mid y \sim N(\hat{\beta}, s^2(X'X)^{-1}) \ ,$$

$$\beta \mid y(i) \sim N(\hat{\beta}(i), s(i)^2(X(i)'X(i))^{-1}) \ .$$

Then the Kullback–Leibler divergence, which they denote by $M(\beta)$ is given by (in the case of a single deleted variable),

$$M(\beta) = k(D_i^2 + D_{(i)}^2)/2 + \frac{s(i)^2}{2s^2}\left(k + \frac{h_i}{1 - h_i}\right) + \frac{s^2}{2s(i)^2}(k - h_i) - k \ ,$$

where D_i^2 is the Cook Distance, and

$$D_{(i)}^2 = \frac{1}{ks(i)^2}(\hat{\beta} - \hat{\beta}(i))'(X(i)'X(i))(\hat{\beta} - \hat{\beta}(i)) \ .$$

For σ^2 the corresponding measure is,

$$M(\sigma^2) = \tfrac{1}{2}\log\frac{s(i)^2}{s^2} + \tfrac{1}{2}(t_i^2 - r_i^2) \ ,$$

where $t_i = \hat{u}_i/((1 - h_i)^{1/2}s(i))$, the studentized residual and r_i is the standardized residual. The expression for $M(\beta, \sigma^2)$ is

$$M(\beta, \sigma^2) = M(\sigma^2) + \frac{1}{2} \frac{h^2}{1 - h_i^2} + \frac{k}{2} \left(\frac{s(i)^2}{s^2} D_{(i)}^2 + \frac{s^2}{s(i)^2} D_i^2 \right).$$

Instead of considering such 'estimative influence' measures Johnson and Geisser consider 'predictive influence'. They derive predictive density for future values, based on full data sets and subset deleted data sets and define Kullback–Leibler divergences between these predictive densities as predictive influence functions (PIFs). The expression for these PIFs are rather complex. For the case of a single deleted observation, Geisser (1987, p. 137) shows that the expression is only a function of n, h_i and u_i^*. [8]

Geisser has often argued (for instance, see his comment on Cook, 1986) that perturbations have much less effect on prediction, than they do on estimation. In the predictive approach suggested in Geisser (1987, 1990) and also discussed in Pettit and Smith (1985) one looks at the predictive distribution of y_i given $y(i)$. Geisser defines the conditional predictive ordinate (CPO), c_i as the predictive density of the i-th observation given $y(i)$ evaluated at the observed value y_i, that is $c_i = p(y_i \mid y(i))$. The values of c_i give a ranking of the observations, with the most discordant having the smallest value of c_i. The c_i work when the y_i are iid. For regression problems, Geisser suggests using the tail area of $P(y_i \mid y(i))$. This is defined by pd_i and Geisser calls this the 'predictive discordancy test'. This is the probability under $P(y_i \mid y(i))$ of an observation with a smaller c_i than the observed y_i. In the case of a linear model with non-informative priors, the predictive discordancy tests are closely related to studentized residuals. pd_i is the p-value from the outlier test based on comparing the studentized residual u_i^* to its t-distribution. Similarly, the value of c_i is the density of a t-distribution with $(n - k - 1)$ degrees of freedom multiplied by $(1 - h_i)^{1/2}/s(i)$. Thus these predictive discordancy tests are all related to the studentized residuals u_i^*.

The question of what to do with outliers still remains in the bayesian approaches. Kempthorne (1986) suggests using a decision theoretic approach, wherein the problems of detection of influential observations and what to do with them are handled simultaneously. He suggests measuring influence on posterior risk (which depends on the specification of the underlying loss function and prior distribution). For a detailed discussion see Kempthorne's paper.

6. Generalizing the results

The deletion measures have, in many cases, analogues in nonlinear econometric models. The main problem with computing them is that each time an

---

[8] One troublesome feature of the expression he derives in the term $\log(1 - u_i^{*2})$ which will be undefined if $u_i^* > 1$.

observation is dropped one must perform estimation of the model, and for more complicated models this will require iterative techniques.

Note that the actual perturbed estimator $\hat{\theta}(i)$ satisfies the pseudo normal equation

$$\sum_{t\neq i}^{n} \frac{\partial \log l_t(\hat{\theta}(i))}{\partial \theta} = 0 \,,$$

where $\log l_t$ denotes the contribution to the likelihood function for observation t. Instead of iterating to find the solution to this normal equation we will follow Pregibon (1981) and Cook and Weisberg (1982), for example, and approximate the perturbed estimator $\hat{\theta}(i)$ by taking one step away from the full sample MLE $\hat{\theta}$.

In particular taking one step using the method of scoring, using some estimate for the hessian (denoted $\hat{I}$) we get an equation of the form

$$\hat{\theta}(i) = \hat{\theta} + (\hat{I})^{-1} \sum_{t\neq i} \frac{\partial \log l_t(\hat{\theta})}{\partial \theta} \,.$$

There will be certain instances where particular $\hat{I}$ estimates are more convenient to use than others – examples below will show such cases.

We may interpret the value $\hat{\theta}(i)$, thus obtained, as an approximation to the perturbed estimate, and one would expect that the difference between the values $\hat{\theta}$ and $\hat{\theta}(i)$ would be small if the i-th observation were not influential. This will form the basis for diagnostics for influential observations in the class of models we have included. The use of the artificial regressions framework which has been developed and extensively used by Davidson and MacKinnon (1989) in various applications to testing specification, will provide a convenient means of computing diagnostics which are analogous to those for the linear regression model. The major advantage of the artificial regression framework is that one may compute many approximations to diagnostics for the linear model simply using the basic formulae for the linear model. Hence, any regression package that is able to compute diagnostics for the linear model may be used to compute such diagnostics for the models that fit into the likelihood type framework.

We will follow the setup in Gourieroux, Monfort, Renault and Trognon (1987a) (hereafter GMRT) which is flexible enough to include many econometric models and estimators, which can be put into the exponential family. Suppose that some latent variable y_t^* can be written as depending on a vector of explanatory variables x_t, a parameter vector θ which is a $p \times 1$ vector (where typically $p = k + 1$ when for example in the regression model $\theta = (\beta, \sigma^2)$, and a residual $u_t(\theta)$,

$$T(y_t^*) = f(x_t, \theta) + u_t(\theta) \,,$$

where T (which is a $q \times 1$ vector) is defined as the canonical, based on the assumption made by GMRT that y^* has density belonging to the exponential family. In many cases, for example the normal case with known variance, it is the identity mapping so that $q = 1$. Also it is assumed that

$$E(u_t(\theta)) = 0$$

and

$$\text{Var}(u_t(\theta) \mid x_t) = \Omega(x_t, \theta)$$

and Ω^{-1} can be decomposed as

$$\Omega^{-1}(x_t, \theta) = V'(x_t, \theta)V(x_t, \theta) \ .$$

We may also define the standardized error vector or S-error vector $v_t(\theta)$ (where standardized means it has covariance matrix equal to the identity matrix) by

$$v_t(\theta) = V(x_t, \theta)v_t(\theta) \ .$$

The variable y_t is actually observed through the relationship

$$y_t = g(y_t^*)$$

and we assume that the observations are independent. This framework is quite general and includes as special cases linear regression, nonlinear regression, limited dependent variable models and so on.

As GMRT show, the score vector can be written in a form that provides a pseudo normal equation interpretation. When the latent variable itself is observed (as would be the case in regression models) then we have the score vector

$$\sum_{t=1}^{n} \frac{\partial f(x_t, \theta)}{\partial \theta} V'(x_t, \theta)v_t(\theta) \ .$$

In limited dependent variable models where a transformation of the latent variable is observed the score vector can be written as,

$$\sum_{t=1}^{n} \frac{\partial f(x_t, \theta)}{\partial \theta} V'(x_t, \theta)\bar{v}_t(\theta) \ ,$$

where $\bar{v}$ is defined as the S-generalized residual, and is related to the respective latent S-error by the following expression

$$\bar{v}_t(\theta) = E(v_t(\theta \mid y_t)) \ ,$$

where the expectations are assuming the true model has parameter vector θ.[9] Note that although the S-error vector has covariance matrix equal to the identity matrix the same does not necessarily hold for the S-generalized residual – in fact it may be heteroskedastic and have non-zero off diagonals.

---

[9] Note that the generalized error, denoted $\bar{u}_t(\theta)$, may also be defined by $\bar{u}_t(\theta) = E(u_t(\theta \mid y_t))$.

Denote the covariance matrix of the S-generalized residual by

$$\Gamma(x_t, \theta) = Q'(x_t, \theta)Q(x_t, \theta).$$

In some instances Q will be simple to find – notably univariate models with known scale parameters. We will assume that the model is such that the information matrix inequality holds so that for the MLE of θ, $\hat{\theta}$ we have

$$\sqrt{n}(\hat{\theta} - \theta) \xrightarrow{d} N(0, nI(\theta)^{-1}),$$

where

$$I(\theta) = E\left(\sum_{t=1}^{n} \frac{\partial f(x_t, \theta)}{\partial \theta} V'(x_t, \theta)\Gamma(x_t, \theta)V(x_t, \theta) \frac{\partial f(x_t, \theta)}{\partial \theta'}\right).$$

In the case where the latent model and the observed model coincide (as occurs in nonlinear regression models) this simplifies to the expression,

$$I(\theta) = E\left(\sum_{t=1}^{n} \frac{\partial f(x_t, \theta)}{\partial \theta} V'(x_t, \theta)V(x_t, \theta) \frac{\partial f(x_t, \theta)}{\partial \theta'}\right).$$

There are a number of convenient estimators for the information matrix that will be consistent under reasonable conditions. These include, for example in the case where the latent and observed model are identical

$$\hat{I}_1 = \sum_{t=1}^{n} \frac{\partial f(x_t, \hat{\theta})}{\partial \theta} V'(x_t, \hat{\theta})V(x_t, \hat{\theta}) \frac{\partial f(x_t, \hat{\theta})}{\partial \theta'}$$

and when the observed and latent models do not coincide,

$$\hat{I}_2 = \sum_{t=1}^{n} \frac{\partial f(x_t, \hat{\theta})}{\partial \theta} V'(x_t, \hat{\theta})\bar{v}(\hat{\theta})\bar{v}'(\hat{\theta})V(x_t, \hat{\theta}) \frac{\partial f(x_t, \hat{\theta})}{\partial \theta'}$$

$$\hat{I}_3 = \sum_{t=1}^{n} \frac{\partial f(x_t, \hat{\theta})}{\partial \theta} V'(x_t, \hat{\theta})Q'(x_t, \hat{\theta})Q(x_t, \hat{\theta})V(x_t, \hat{\theta}) \frac{\partial f(x_t, \hat{\theta})}{\partial \theta'}.$$

6.1. Artificial regressions

We may define three different types of artificial regressions, that may be used to generate the approximations to the perturbed estimates for different circumstances. Suppose we define the following three matrices. Let

$$Z'_{1t} = V(x_t, \hat{\theta}) \frac{\partial f(x_t, \hat{\theta})}{\partial \theta},$$

$$Z'_{2t} = \bar{v}_t(\hat{\theta})V(x_t, \hat{\theta}) \frac{\partial f(x_t, \hat{\theta})}{\partial \theta},$$

and

$$Z'_{3t} = Q(x_t, \hat{\theta})V(x_t, \hat{\theta})\frac{\partial f(x_t, \hat{\theta})}{\partial \theta}$$

which are respectively $q \times p$, $1 \times p$ and $q \times p$ matrices and let

$$Z_l = (Z_{l1}, \ldots, Z_{ln})'$$

denote the matrix formed by stacking the respective matrices. Next, define

$$w_{1t} = Z'_{1t}\hat{\theta} + \bar{v}_t(\hat{\theta}),$$

$$w_{2t} = Z'_{2t}\hat{\theta} + 1,$$

$$w_{3t} = Z'_{3t}\hat{\theta} + Q^{-1}(x_t, \hat{\theta})\bar{v}_t(\hat{\theta})$$

and w_l denote the vectors (of dimension $qn \times 1$, $n \times 1$ and $qn \times 1$ respectively) formed by stacking these into a single vector. Denote the l-th artificial regression model

$$w_l = Z_l\theta + \text{errors}$$

by ARG_l. Given this set-up, the usual simple formulae for linear regression diagnostics may be used in the context of this artificial regression to generate diagnostics for the nonlinear models, that have an interpretation as being approximations to the exact analogues of those diagnostics. When all n observations are included, the OLS estimator will be the full MLE (which is obviously already known) and when the i-th observation is deleted[10] then the one step approximation to the estimate $\hat{\theta}(i)$ will be produced by OLS. Another nice feature is the fact that the OLS estimate of the variance covariance matrix of the OLS estimate,

$$\hat{\sigma}^2(Z'_l Z_l)^{-1}$$

will in general be a consistent estimate of the variance covariance matrix of the MLE – thus the analogy is practically complete with the only drawback being the fact that the perturbed estimates are really only approximations.

The artificial regressions ARG_1 and ARG_3 are quite similar and will be more convenient when $q = 1$.[11] The regression ARG_3 will be required when $q = 1$ and the latent and observed models do not coincide. The artificial regression ARG_2 will be needed when $q > 1$ (as in the regression model with unknown scale parameter and consequently also in the tobit model). In cases where the location and scale parameters are orthogonal, one may concentrate on either parameter separately and use the more convenient regression ARG_1.

---

[10] Note that for artificial regressions 1 and 3 one must omit the components of the w and Z matrices corresponding to the i-th observation. This will not be a single row unless $q = 1$, although in the examples that follow these artificial regressions are only convenient in cases where $q = 1$.

[11] In fact ARG_1 is a special case of ARG_3 corresponding to $Q(x, \theta) = 1$.

Generally, when $q > 1$ and the observed and latent models do not coincide, the orthogonality will not hold and the reduction of dimension (or concentration on a subset of parameters) will be problematic. The examples in the following sections will provide more guidance regarding the choice of artificial regression and interpretation of diagnostics.

One must be careful with ARG_2 since the residuals from the artificial regression will be identically equal to 1. Note however, that the orthogonality condition between the regressors and the residual holds since the regressors in this case are just the derivative of the log density for each observation. Thus the orthogonality condition is just that the average of the derivative of the likelihood function is zero. The analogue of the studentized residuals for this case can be shown to behave (in large samples) essentially like $1/(1 - h_i)$ where h_i formed using the regressor Z_2. Thus values that exceed 1 by 'a large amount' may be indicative of an observation with a large relative residual vector (or contribution to the derivative of the likelihood function). Of course the question of how large is 'large' remains.

For situations where this regression is most convenient it may be necessary, if one wishes to examine the residuals $\bar{v}_t(\theta)$, to plot them separately. In such situations the interpretation of the D_i and DFFITS measures is more clear in terms of an overall standardized measure of the difference in estimates of θ with and without the i-th observation included rather than being in terms of some aspect of the fit – such as the fitted value in a regression.

Below we will consider a number of popular non-linear models in most detail, and make suggestions regarding which of the artificial regression may be most appropriate and consider various aspects of the diagnostics. In discussing the different situations more closely we will focus on analogous measures to DFBETAS, D_i and DFFITS for the linear model – however, it is clear that the likelihood displacement measures and local perturbation measures could also be computed for each situation although these may not be as convenient as the aforementioned measures.

7. Nonlinear regression models

Suppose we have the nonlinear regression model given by

$$y_t = g(x_t; \beta) + u_t$$

and that there are n observations in total. It will be convenient to use the notation $g_t(\beta)$ for the term $g(x_t; \beta)$ and the notation $u_t(\beta)$ for $y_t - g_t(\beta)$. Also the notation $\hat{\beta}$ will be used for the least squares estimator and $\hat{g}_t$ will be used for h_t evaluated at the least squares estimator. Also let $G(\beta)$ denote the $n \times k$ matrix of first derivatives of the $n \times 1$ regression function vector $g(\beta)$ evaluated at β.

To set up the problem in a form that fits the framework of the previous section, suppose that $u_t \sim N(0, \sigma^2)$. This is not necessary, and in no way limits results since least squares and MLE under normality are equivalent. We may consider at least two cases – one where we are interested in looking at the sensitivity of the β estimates to observation deletion and the other where we are interested in looking at the sensitivity of the complete (β, σ^2) vector.

7.1. Case 1 – Influence on β

Since the covariance matrix of the MLE of (β, σ^2) is block diagonal, $\hat{\beta}$ and $\hat{\sigma}^2$ may be considered orthogonal, so it will be convenient to treat σ^2 as known to be equal to $\hat{\sigma}^2$ – this will simplify matters without altering the conclusions. This being the case the canonical statistic in this case is the identity map and is a scalar (see GMRT for details) and the normal distribution (with assumed known variance) belongs to the linear exponential family – in that case

$$T(y_t) = y_t = g(x_t, \beta) + u_t$$

so that $q = 1$, $V = 1/\hat{\sigma}$,

$$\frac{\partial f(x_t, \theta)}{\partial \theta} = \frac{\partial g(x_t, \beta)}{\partial \beta}$$

and

$$v_t(\hat{\beta}) = \frac{y_t - g_t(\hat{\beta})}{\hat{\sigma}} = \frac{1}{\hat{\sigma}} u_t(\hat{\beta}) .$$

It is most convenient in this case to use ARG_1, since V is known (and the artificial regression in this case will correspond to Gauss–Newton type iterations). Then $Z_1 = (1/\hat{\sigma})G(\hat{\beta})$ and

$$w_1 = \frac{1}{\hat{\sigma}} G(\hat{\beta})\hat{\beta} + v(\hat{\beta})$$

and the regression in this case will be

$$w_1 = Z_1\beta + \text{errors} .$$

It is easy to verity that OLS on the regression using all the observations will give $\hat{\beta}$ while omission of the i-th observation will give the one step approximation above for $\hat{\beta}(i)$. Then the result for the linear model approximation to the perturbation in the least squares estimator due to omitting the i-th observation can be written as[12]

$$\hat{\beta} - \hat{\beta}(i) = \frac{(G(\hat{\beta})'G(\hat{\beta}))^{-1}G_i(\hat{\beta})'u_i(\hat{\beta})}{1 - h_i(G(\hat{\beta}))} .$$

[12] This was also noted by Cook and Weisberg (1982) although they did not explicitly use the artificial regression formulation.

Which can be interpreted as an approximate DFBETA$_i$ vector. Analogues of DFFITS and D may be defined as in the linear model using this artificial regression, in terms of the elements of G and the residuals from the nonlinear regression.

In the context of the linear model the DFFITS measure had an interpretation in terms of the fit – in the case of the nonlinear model the perturbation in the fit is given by

$$g_i(\hat{\beta}) - g_i(\hat{\beta}(i)) .$$

The analogues of DFFITS using the artificial regression framework can be interpreted as an approximation to this since by a Taylor series approximation

$$g_i(\hat{\beta}) - g_i(\hat{\beta}(i)) = G_i(\hat{\beta})(\hat{\beta} - \hat{\beta}(i)) .$$

One could use a standardized version of the deviance in the fit itself,[13] however, this measure is not as convenient as the DFFITS type measure, which may be generated using a regression package that is able to compute such measures using the artificial regression.

7.2. Case 2 – Influence on (β, σ^2)

When σ^2 is treated as an unknown parameter and one is interested in measures of influence on (β, σ^2), things become more complicated. As shown by GMRT, the canonical in this type of situation is a vector

$$T(y_t) = (y_t, y_t^2)'$$

so that in terms of our notation $q = 2$. The corresponding error vector in this case is given by

$$u_t(\theta) = (y_t - g(x_t, \beta), y_t^2 - g(x_t, \beta)^2 - \sigma^2)'$$

and the S-error vector in this case is given by

$$v_t(\theta) = \frac{1}{\sigma} \left(u_t, \frac{(u_t^2 - \sigma^2)}{\sqrt{2}\sigma} \right)' .$$

For this case it is most convenient to use ARG$_2$. In doing so it is easy to see that

$$Z_{2t} = \frac{1}{\sigma^2} \left(\frac{\partial g(x_t, \hat{\beta})}{\partial \beta} \hat{u}_t, \frac{(\hat{u}_t^2 - \hat{\sigma}^2)}{\sqrt{2}\hat{\sigma}} \right)'$$

---

[13] Although as noted above the question of what the appropriate standardization is may be problematic.

and

$$w_{2t} = Z'_{2t}(\hat{\beta}, \hat{\sigma}^2)' + 1 ,$$

$$w_2 = Z_2(\beta, \sigma^2)' + \text{errors} .$$

Measures analogous to those for the linear model may be found for the individual components of the β vector or σ^2 and overall measures may also be found. As noted in the previous section the interpretation of the D_i and DFFITS type measures should be as an overall measure of the difference between the estimates with and without the i-th observation included.

8. Limited dependent variable models

It is relatively straightforward to show that the above analysis may be applied to a large class of limited dependent variable models. GMRT have shown how residuals may be defined for various LDVMs used in econometrics – probit, logit, Poisson regression, gompit, and tobit models plus others.[14]

These models may be separated into two categories. The first is where there is an index $x_t\beta$ appearing in the model and for the observed variable y_t,

$$E(y_t) = F(x'_t\beta)$$

and one only estimates the β vector. Models that satisfy this include all those mentioned above except for the tobit model – it may also include other so-called generalized linear models (see McCullagh and Nelder, 1989). The other case is where a scale parameter σ must be estimated along with the parameters of the index – usually one has

$$E(y_t) = G(x'_t\beta, \sigma) .$$

This includes, for example the tobit and sample selection models. Since in LDVMS, the scale parameter is not typically orthogonal to the β parameter, the analysis for the non-linear regression model with focus on β is not really appropriate. It will turn out to be move convenient and possibly more useful to look at the complete parameter vector (β, σ) in examining influence measures.

8.1. No scale parameters present

For models that fit into this category GMRT have shown that the score vector

[14] In Gourieroux, Monfort, Renault and Trognon (1987b) another form of residuals, termed simulated residuals were defined for LDVMs and an example given of how they may be used to detect outlying observations. It would appear that these residuals may be more useful for other specification tests, such as tests for heteroskedasticity, than in the detection of outliers.

may be written as

$$\sum_{t=1}^{n} x_t \bar{u}_t(\hat{\beta}) = 0,$$

where $\bar{u}$ is the generalized residual, which in some cases may be the same as the actual residual (e.g., Poisson). It is convenient to write this as

$$\sum_{t=1}^{n} x_t V(x_t, \hat{\beta}) Q(x_t, \hat{\beta}) Q^{-1}(x_t, \hat{\beta}) \bar{v}_t(\hat{\beta}) = 0.$$

Since the canonical statistic for these models is a scalar (i.e., $q = 1$) then it is relatively straightforward to find each of the components. This is because the S-generalized residual will be a scalar so that its variance and hence the $Q(x_t, \beta)$ will be easy to find. The use of ARG_3 is quite straightforward to derive for these models.

Two popular discrete choice models are the logit[15] and probit model and are motivated by the latent linear model

$$y_t^* = x_t'\beta + u_t,$$

where u_t is usually taken to be iid and without loss of generality can be assumed to have a variance of 1 so that for these models $V(x_t, \beta) = 1$. In actual fact the variance in the logit model is $\pi^2/3$, but it makes no difference to the actual diagnostics to be developed due to various cancellations. The Poisson model is usually motivated by letting the usual parameter λ in the Poisson density depend on the x_t variables through the relation

$$\lambda(x_t) = \exp(x_t'\beta).$$

The Poisson model then can be used as a latent model to motivate the gompit model, which is a form of discrete choice model. (See GMRT for more details on these models.) The Poission model may be written as a latent regression model with latent error

$$u_t(\beta) = y_t^* - \exp(x_t'\beta)$$

which has variance $\exp(x_t\beta)$, so using the results in Section 7 it can be seen that for these two models $V(x_t, \beta) = \exp(-\frac{1}{2}x_t'\beta)$. Each of these four models are covered in GMRT, so using their results it is easy to deduce that the components $Q(x_t, \beta)$ and $\bar{v}(\beta)$ are given by

---

[15] There is quite a large literature that has considered diagnostics for the logit model – sometimes referred to as the logistic regression model – see, Pregibon (1981), Johnson (1985), Bedrick and Hill (1990), Lesaffre and Albert (1989).

probit:

$$\bar{v}_t(\beta) = \frac{\phi(x_t'\beta)}{\Phi(x_t'\beta)(1 - \Phi(x_t'\beta))} (y_t - \Phi(x_t'\beta)),$$

$$Q(x_t, \beta) = \frac{\phi(x_t'\beta)}{(\Phi(x_t'\beta)(1 - \Phi(x_t'\beta)))^{1/2}},$$

logit:

$$\bar{v}_t(\beta) = y_t - \frac{1}{1 + \exp(-x_t'\beta)},$$

$$Q(x_t, \beta) = \frac{\exp(-\frac{1}{2}x_t'\beta)}{(1 - \exp(-x_t'\beta))},$$

Poisson:

$$\bar{v}_t(\beta) = \frac{(y_t - \exp(x_t'\beta))}{\exp(\frac{1}{2}x_t'\beta)},$$

$$Q(x_t, \beta) = 1,$$

gompit:

$$u_t(\beta) = \frac{-\exp(x_t'\beta)}{1 - \exp(-\exp(x_t'\beta))} (y_t - x_t'\beta),$$

$$Q(x_t, \beta) = \frac{\exp(x_t'\beta)\exp(-\frac{1}{2}\exp(x_t'\beta))}{(1 - \exp(-\exp(x_t'\beta)))^{1/2}}.$$

Using these results it is straightforward to set up the artificial regression ARG_3. One would let

$$Z_{3t} = Q(x_t, \hat{\beta})V(x_t, \hat{\beta})x_t,$$
$$w_{3t} = Z_{3t}'\hat{\beta} + Q^{-1}(x_t, \beta)\bar{v}_t(\hat{\beta})$$

and the regression would be

$$w_3 = Z_3\beta + \text{errors}.$$

Thus approximately valid diagnostics for these models can be provided by using the regression diagnostic formulae for the artificial regression model. Note that for the Poisson model ARG_3 is identical to performing ARG_1 since in that case $Q(x_t, \hat{\beta}) = 1$.

The interpretation of the measures should be noted. Although the DFBETAS, D_i and DFFITS measures have easy interpretations in terms of normalized differences between $\hat{\beta}$ and $\hat{\beta}(i)$ (using normalizations mentioned above) the interpretation of the latter two as measures of the change in the 'fit' due to the omission of the i-th observation must be looked at more closely.

There are at least two ways in which one could look at the effect on fit in the context of these models. The first is to look at the change in the fit of the latent index,

$$x_i'(\hat{\beta} - \hat{\beta}(i)) \, .$$

The second is to note that for these models,

$$E(y_i | x_i) = F(x_i'\beta)$$

so that one may be interested in the quantity

$$F(x_i'\hat{\beta}) - F(x_i'\hat{\beta}(i)) \, .$$

The DFFITS measure that would be generated using the artificial regression framework may be interpreted as linear approximations to either of these. Of course the problem of appropriate standardization remains with this type of measure.

8.2. Scale parameters present

In the case of more complicated models, for example the tobit or censored regression model we must also worry about the scale parameter. It is convenient to consider the complete (β, σ) vector when developing the sensitivity measures.[16] Unlike the regression model we can not really set up an artificial regression in such a way that we can look at changes in β alone – the variance covariance matrix does not have the block diagonal structure possessed by the latent model from which it is derived.

Note that since in this case we have an underlying latent model for which the canonical statistic is a vector ($q = 2$) (since σ is treated as unknown) it will prove to be convenient to use ARG_2 (as we did in the nonlinear regression model with focus on the complete (β, σ^2) vector which we write in shorthand as θ and denote the MLE by $\hat{\theta} = (\hat{\beta}, \hat{\sigma})$). It is easy to see that if the latent model is linear (which it usually is although need not be),

$$y_t^* = x_t'\beta + u_t \, ,$$

where $u_t \sim N(0, \sigma^2)$, then the components required to perform the artificial regression are

$$Z_{2t}' = \frac{1}{\hat{\sigma}} \, (x_t \bar{v}_{1t}(\hat{\theta}), \bar{v}_{2t}(\theta)) \, ,$$

$$w_{2t} = Z_{2t}'\hat{\theta} + 1$$

---

[16] Diagnostics for the censored model have been proposed by Weissfeld and Schneider (1990), based on one step approximations using the EM algorithm – the standardization in that case is not in terms of an approximation of the variance matrix of the estimator.

and the S-generalized residual vector $\tilde{v}$ in this case as given by GMRT has elements

$$\tilde{v}_{1t}(\theta) = I(y_t > 0)\frac{u_t}{\sigma} - I(y_t = 0)\frac{\phi(x_t'\beta/\sigma)}{\Phi(-x_t'\beta/\sigma)}$$

and

$$\tilde{v}_{2t}(\theta) = I(y_t > 0)\frac{(u_t^2 - \sigma^2)}{\sqrt{2}\sigma} + I(y_t = 0)\frac{1}{\sqrt{2}}\frac{x_t'\beta}{\sigma}\frac{\phi(x_t'\beta/\sigma)}{\Phi(-x_t'\beta/\sigma)},$$

where $u_t = y_t - x_t'\beta$. The artificial regression in this case is given by

$$w_2 = Z_2\theta + \text{errors}.$$

Again it should be stressed that the D_i and DFFITS type measures should be regarded as overall measure of the effect on the complete parameter vector of omitting the i-th observation since the measure does not correspond to any reasonable aspect of the fit of the model. Alternatively a measure of the change of fit in the latent index model, i.e., the change in $x_i\beta$, can be computed from the normalized change in $\hat{\beta}$ alone. This is more complicated due to the fact that the variance matrix of $(\hat{\beta}, \hat{\sigma})$ does not have a block diagonal structure so the VC($\hat{\beta}$) involves a partitioned inverse.

8.3. An example

It may be interesting to examine to what extent the diagnostics for different models agree. The tobit, probit and linear model can all be related to the same underlying latent variable. Let,

$$y_t^* = \beta_0 + x_t'\beta_1 + u_t$$

and then as is well known the observed dependent variables in the three models are $I(y^* > 0)y^*$, $I(y^* > 0)$ and y^*. Here we will generate the same series for y^* with an outlier or bad observation and then for each of the three models construct the various diagnostics to see if they agree on which observation is the culprit.

The example we use is similar in spirit to Gourieroux, Monfort, Renault and Trognon (1987b). We generate the 40 observations on x_t as being evenly spaced between -3 and 1, so that the mean is -1. In other words we let $x_t = -2.95 + (0.1)(t-1)$. The true values of both coefficients are 1 so that in the probit and tobit cases roughly half the observations on the observed dependent variable are zero. The u_t are generated as $N(0,1)$ random variables. There are many ways in which we can introduce outliers or influential observations. Here we will simply set the value of y_1^* equal to 10, which will generally result in the observed value in the probit model as being a 1 instead of the much more likely value of 0, and a positive value for the tobit model being observed. This may correspond to a situation where there is a coding error.

A second example is to put in an extreme value of x. In this case we let $x_{40} = 10$ and the data on y^* are generated as normal (with mean zero and variance one) random numbers (so in the notation of the above regression model $\beta_0 = 0$ and $\beta_1 = 0$). The y^* for the 40-th observation is generated as in the first example (that is with both coefficients equal to one). This is the classic case where the extreme observation will basically determine the regression line in the context of the linear regression model, so may have a small residual, but is quite influential.

In the first example, as expected h_i did not pick the outlier but the studentized residual, DFFITS$_i$ and the Cook distance did. There was no difference between the different methods of estimation. In the second example, again as expected, h_i picked the outlier but so did the other diagnostics. Also, there was not much difference between the different models.

We also tried the different diagnostics suggested in the section with the bankruptcy data analyzed by Johnson (1987). The data were on 46 firms, with $y = 1$ for 25 and $y = 0$ for 21 observations. The equation was estimated by the linear probability (LP), logit and probit models. The logit and probit models gave almost identical results. For both these models, the studentized residual, DFFITS$_i$ and Cook distance all picked observation 34 as an influential observation. As for the LP model, the Cook distance was larger than 1 for observations 16 and 46 but not for observation 34 which was identified as an influential observation by the other criteria.

Our aim was not to conduct an exhaustive study of the measures here but to check on how they perform with two simulated data sets and a real world data set. The computations were easy and straightforward (using the SHAZAM program) and the limited results suggested that this approach is worth pursuing.

9. Dynamic models and panel data

In dynamic models one must be careful about the interpretation of outliers. There may be two interpretations of outliers in dynamic models. The first, known as an *additive outlier* occurs when a particular observation is bad but subsequent observations are not affected by the badness. For example there is a misrecording of a particular observation in a time series, although the underlying model is unaffected. The second type of outlier in time series contexts is known as an *innovational outlier* and results when the effect of a large (or outlying innovation) is perpetuated through the dynamics of the model. An example will make the distinction more obvious. Suppose that w_t follows an AR(1) process so that

$$w_t = \rho w_{t-1} + \varepsilon_t .$$

An additive outlier at observation i would occur if we observed the time series y_t given by

$$y_t = w_t + I(t = i)z_t \, ,$$

where $I(t = i)$ is an indicator function for the event, and z_t represents perhaps a misrecording error. In the innovational outlier model we observe $y_t = w_t$ except that

$$w_t = \rho w_{t-1} + \varepsilon_t + I(t = i)z_t$$

so the z_t represents an 'unusually large' innovation occurring in period i.

The main complication that arises in the development of diagnostics is for an additive outlier. The case of an innovational outlier may be covered by the usual deletion diagnostics since the only place where the model fails is for the i-th observation i.e., in the example above ρw_{i-1} is not a very good predictor of w_i. The work in the previous sections is therefore applicable – and as GMRT suggest the generalized residuals may be easily adapted to deal with dynamic models. In the additive case the i-th observation is a bad piece of data so not only is it not well predicted by the previous observation i.e., $\rho \omega_{i-1}$, but it is also not very useful in predicting subsequent observations. Thus a useful diagnostic for this case would see how the model is affected by the omission of all data observed in period i – this raises a problem of dealing with a missing regressor.[17]

In dynamic models two issues need special attention. The first is that there are two sources of outliers: a shift in mean and an error term with increased variance. In dynamic models the distinction is important. The second issue is that of sensitivity of unit root tests to outliers. Most macroeconomic time series are judged to be unit root processes on the basis of unit root tests. However, these tests are sensitive to structural breaks and the presence of outliers. Liu and Praschnik (1991) compare the powers of four commonly used unit root tests, DF, ADF, Z_α and Z_t tests, through Monte Carlo and find the ADF test to be the only one robust to outliers.

The issues of outliers in panel data are complex. For the sake of simplicity, consider the case of N cross section units with T time series observations on each. We can analyze each cross section separately and determine the outliers. But very often the data from the different cross sections are not analyzed separately but are pooled. In this case each one of the outliers in the i-th cross section will have less effect on the individual $\hat{\beta}_i$ than without pooling, but the outliers will have some effect on $\hat{\beta}_j$ ($j \neq i$). In many of the pooling procedures,

---

[17] A number of papers have proposed methods of dealing with a missing regressor and diagnostics for an additive outlier, see Ledolter (1990), Peña (1990), Fiebig and Maasoumi (1990). Muirhead (1986), Abraham and Yatawara (1988) and Tsay (1988) discuss methods for determining the types of outliers. Balke and Fomby (1991) is an illustration of these methods to analyze GNP data.

the individual $\hat{\beta}_i$ are 'shrunk' towards a common estimator β^*, which is a weighted average of the $\hat{\beta}_i$. A common formula for β^* (see Lee and Griffiths, 1978, for example) is given by the equations

$$\beta_i^* = \left(\frac{1}{S_i^2}(X_i'X_i) + \Sigma^{*-1}\right)^{-1}\left(\frac{1}{S_i^2}X_i'X_i\hat{\beta}_i + \Sigma^{*-1}\mu^*\right),$$

$$\beta^* = \frac{1}{N}\sum \beta_i^*,$$

$$S_i^2 = \frac{1}{T}(y_i - X_i\beta_i^*)'(y_i - X_i\beta_i^*),$$

$$\Sigma^* = \frac{1}{N}\sum(\beta_i^* - \beta^*)(\beta_i^* - \beta^*)'.$$

Thus an outlier in the i-th cross section has an effect on β^* both through its effect on $\hat{\beta}_i$ and its effect on S_i^2.

10. Conclusion

We have presented a review of the literature on outliers and influential observations in the linear regression model and presented an extension of these methods to non-linear models and the logit, probit and tobit models. Though there are some earlier results on non-linear models in Cook and Weisberg (1982) and Pregibon (1981) and so on, we have presented here a unified and computationally simpler approach based on artificial regressions. This should be useful in further work on outliers and influential observations.

Though our critique of the literature on regression models suggests some problems with the commonly used diagnostics for outliers and influential observations, and that a likelihood based approach would be preferable, we have presented here an extension of the commonly used dignostics in the regression context. These are computationally much simpler and are adequate in many cases if carefully interpreted. Extensions based on the likelihood approach are under investigation.

Space limitations have prevented a more complete review of the literature on dynamic and time series models as well as models based on panel data. Also, we have presented only a cursory review of the bayesian approaches.

Acknowledgment

We would like to thank Professor C. R. Rao for his suggestions to relate the 'tests' for influential observations to tests of linear hypotheses and other helpful comments. We would also like to thank Stephen Cosslett for comments and suggestions on an earlier version of this paper. Responsibility for any errors is ours.

References

Abraham, B. and N. Yatawara (1988). A score test for detection of time-series outliers. *J. Time Ser. Anal.* **9**, 109–119.

Balke, N. S. and T. B. Fomby (1991). Shifting trends, segmented trends and infrequent permanent shocks. *J. Monetary Econom.* **28**, 61–85.

Barnett, V. and T. Lewis (1978). *Outliers in Statistical Data*. Wiley, New York.

Bedrick, E. J. and J. R. Hill (1990). Outlier tests for logistic regression: A conditional approach. *Biometrika* **77**, 815–827.

Belsley, D. A., E. Kuh and R. E. Welsch (1980). *Regression Diagnostics: Identifying Influential Data and Sources of Collinearity*. Wiley, New York.

Bollen, K. A. and R. W. Jackman (1990). Regression diagnostics: An expository treatment of outliers and influential cases. In: J. Fox and J. S. Long, ed., *Modern Methods of Data Analysis*. Sage, Beverly Hills, CA.

Chatterjee, S. and A. S. Hadi (1986). Influence, observations, high leverage points, and outliers in linear regression. *Statist. Sci.* **1**, 379–416.

Chatterjee, S. and A. S. Hadi (1988). *Sensitivity Analysis in Linear Regression*. Wiley, New York.

Cook, R. D. (1986). Assessment of local influence, with Discussion. *J. Roy. Statist. Soc. Ser. B* **48**, 134–169.

Cook, R. D. (1987). Influence assessment. *J. Appl. Statist.* **14**(2), 117–131.

Cook, D. R. and D. Peña (1988). The likelihood displacement: A unifying principle for influence measures. *Comm. Statist. Theory Methods* **17**(3), 623–640.

Cook, R. D. and S. Weisberg (1982). *Residuals and Influence in Regression*. Chapman and Hall, New York.

Davidson, R. and J. G. MacKinnon (1989). Testing for consistency using artificial regressions. *Econometric Theory* **5**, 363–384.

Donoho, D. L. and P. J. Huber (1983). The notation of breakdown point In: P. J. Bickel, K. A. Doksum and J. L. Hodges, eds., *A Festschrift for Eric Lehmann*. Wadsworth, Belmont, CA.

Draper, N. and J. A. John (1981). Influential observations and outliers in regression. *Technometrics* **23**, 21–26.

Fiebig, D. G. and E. Maasoumi (1990). Specification analysis in dynamic models. *J. Business Econom. Statist.* **8**(4), 443–451.

Fair, R. C. (1974). On the robust estimation of econometric models. *Ann. Econom. Social Measurement* **3**, 667–678.

Fisher, F. M. (1962). *A-Priori Information and Time-Series Analysis*. North-Holland, Amsterdam.

Geisser, S. (1987). Influential observations, diagnostics and discordancy tests. *J. Appl. Statist.* **14**, 133–142.

Geisser, S. (1990). Predictive approaches to discordancy testing. In: S. Geisser, J. S. Hodges, S. J. Press and A. Zellner, eds., *Bayesian and Likelihood Methods in Statistics and Econometrics*. North-Holland, Amsterdam, 321–335.

Gourieroux, C., A. Monfort, E. Renault and A. Trognon (1987a). Generalized residuals. *J. Econometrics* **34**, 5–32.

Gourieroux, C., A. Monfort, E. Renault and A. Trognon (1987b). Simulated residuals. *J. Econometrics* **34**, 201–252.

Gray, J. B. (1989). On the use of regression diagnostics. *Statistician* **38**, 97–105.

Guttman, I. (1991). A bayesian look at the question of diagnostics. University of Toronto, Technical Report No. 9104.

Guttman, I. and D. Peña (1988). Outliers and influence: Evaluation by posteriors of parameters in the linear model. In: J. M. Bernardo et al., eds., *Bayesian Statistics*, Vol. 3. Oxford Univ. Press, Oxford, 631–640.

Hausman, J. A. (1978). Specification tests in econometrics. *Econometrica* **46**, 1251–1271.

Hoaglin, D. C. and R. E. Welsch (1978). The hat matrix in regression and ANOVA. *Amer. Statist.* **32**, 17–22.

Johnson, W. (1985). Influence measures for logistic regression: Another point of view. *Biometrika* **72**(1), 59–65.

Johnson, W. (1987). The detection of influential observations for allocation, separation, and the determination of probabilities in a bayesian framework. *J. Business Econom. Statist.* **5**(3), 369–381.

Johnson, W. and S. Geisser (1982). Assessing the predictive influence of observations. In: G. Kallianpur, P. R. Krishniah and J. K. Ghosh, eds., *Essays in Honor of C. R. Rao*. North-Holland, Amsterdam, 343–358.

Johnson, W. and S. Geisser (1983). The detection and characterization of influential observations in regression analysis. *J. Amer. Statist. Assoc.* **8**, 137–144.

Johnson, W. and S. Geisser (1985). Estimative influence measures for the multivariate general linear model. *J. Statist. Planning Inference* **11**, 33–56.

Kao, C. and D. D. Dutkowsky (1989). An application of non-linear bounded influence estimation in aggregate bank borrowing from the federal reserve. *J. Amer. Statist. Assoc.* **84**, 700–709.

Kempthorne, P. J. (1986). Decision-theoretic measures of influence in regression. *J. Roy. Statist. Soc. Ser. B* **48**, 370–378.

Krasker, W. S. (1981). The role of bounded influence estimation in model selection. *J. Econometrics* **16**, 131–138.

Krasker, W. S. and R. E. Welsch (1982). Efficient bounded influence regression estimation. *J. Amer. Statist. Assoc.* **77**, 595–604.

Leamer, E. E. (1990). A heteroscedasticity diagnostic based on corrected standard errors. UCLA, Program in Applied Econometric Discussion Paper No. 27.

Ledolter, J. (1990). Outlier diagnostics in time series analysis. *J. Time Ser. Anal.* **11**, 317–324.

Lett, L. F. and W. E. Griffiths (1978). The prior likelihood and best linear unbiased prediction in stochastic coefficient linear models. Manuscript, University of Minnesota.

Lesaffre, E. and A. Albert (1989). Multiple-group logistic regression diagnostics. *Appl. Statist.* **38**(3), 425–440.

Liu, P. C. and J. Praschnik (1991). How sensitive are these non-stationarity tests to outliers? Manuscript, University of Florida.

Maddala, G. S. (1977). *Econometrics*. McGraw-Hill, New York.

McCullagh, P. and J. A. Nelder (1989). *Generalized Linear Models*. Chapman and Hall, New York.

Muirhead, C. R. (1986). Distinguishing outlier types in time series. *J. Roy. Statist. Soc. Ser. B* **48**, 39–47.

Peña, D. (1990). Influential observations in time series. *J. Business Econom. Statist.* **8**(2), 235–241.

Peracchi, F. (1990a). Bounded-influence estimators for the tobit model. *J. Econometrics* **44**, 107–126.

Peracchi, F. (1990b). Robust *m*-estimator. *Econometric Rev.* **9**(1), 1–30.

Peracchi, F. (1991). Bounded-influence estimators for the SURE model. *J. Econometrics* **47**, 119–134.

Pettit, L. I. and A. F. M. Smith (1985). Outliers and influential observations in linear models. In: J. M. Bernardo et al., eds., *Bayesian Statistics*, Vol. 2. Elsevier, North-Holland, Amsterdam, 473–494.

Powell, J. (1990). Comment on Peracchi's paper. *Econometric Rev.* **9**, 31–33.

Pregibon, D. (1981). Logistic regression diagnostics. *Ann. Statist.* **9**, 705–724.

Quan, N. T. (1988). The prediction sum of squares as a general measure of regression diagnostics. *J. Business Econom. Statist.* **6**, 501–504.

Rao, C. R. (1973). *Linear Statistical Inference and Its Applications*. Wiley, New York.

Rao, C. R. (1989). Methodology based on the L_1-norm in statistical inference. *Sankhyā* **50**, 289–313.

Rao, C. R. and S. K. Mitra (1971). *Generalized Inverse of Matrices and Its Applications*. Wiley, New York.

Rea, J. D. (1978). Indeterminacy of the Chow test when the number of observations is insufficient. *Econometrica* **46**, 229.

Reiss, P. C. (1990). Detecting multiple outliers with an application to R & D productivity, *J. Econometrics* **43**, 293–315.

Rousseeuw, P. J. (1984). Least median of squares regression. *J. Amer. Statist. Assoc.* **82**, 851–857.

Rousseeuw, P. J. and A. M. Leroy (1987). *Robust Regressions and Outlier Detection*. Wiley, New York.

Solow, R. M. (1957). Technical change and the aggregate production function. *Rev. Econom. Statist.* **39**, 312–320. See also comment by Hogan in **40**, 407–411, and reply by Solow, 411–413.

Stefanski, L. A., R. J. Caroll and D. Ruppert (1986). Optimally bounded score functions for generalized linear models with applications to logistic regression. *Biometrika* **73**(2), 413–424.

Tsay, R. S. (1988). Outliers, level shifts, and variance changes in time series. *J. Forecasting* **7**, 1–20.

Weissfeld, L. A. and H. Schneider (1990). Influence diagnostics for the normal linear model with censored data. *Austral. J. Statist.* **32**(1), 11–20.

Welsch, R. E. (1980). Regression sensitivity analysis and bounded-influence estimation. In: J. Kmenta and J. B. Ramsey, eds., *Evaluation of Econometric Models*. Academic Press, New York.

G. S. Maddala, C. R. Rao and H. D. Vinod, eds., *Handbook of Statistics, Vol. 11*
© 1993 Elsevier Science Publishers B.V. All rights reserved.

25

Statistical Aspects of Calibration in Macroeconomics

Allan W. Gregory and Gregor W. Smith

1. Introduction

Empirical questions in macroeconomics often are addressed with dynamic, equilibrium models. Studying such questions involves formulating a model, solving it, assigning parameter values (i.e., calibration), and then conducting experiments with the model and evaluating the results. This chapter reviews some methods for parameterization and evaluation. Researchers typically study models by conducting simulations and studying simulated data using statistics (such as moments) which also may be calculated with historical data. The aim may be deduce some of the model's properties or implications,[1] to compare its properties to those of data, or to test the model formally. In this chapter we study the statistical aspects of these calibration methods. We refer to illustrative applied studies, but do not provide a comprehensive bibliography.

Section 2 provides a background to calibration methods in macroeconomics. Section 3 describes a simple asset-pricing model, which serves as the setting for an outline of estimation and calibration. Section 4 discusses testing and evaluating calibrated models and demonstrates several tests using the asset-pricing model. Section 5 surveys some recently proposed, alternative tools for evaluation. A brief conclusion follows in Section 6.

2. Background

Calibration exercises begin with the assignment of parameter values. Just as in the calibration of applied general equilibrium models in the study of international trade or public finance (see for example Shoven and Whalley, 1984) parameter values are assigned on the basis of other studies or evidence.[2] For

---

[1] For example, Lucas (1987) and Îmrohoroğlu (1989) use calibrated models to measure the costs of business cycles.

[2] Lau (1984), MacKinnon (1984), and Pagan and Shannon (1985) suggest the use of formal estimation, testing, and sensitivity analysis in applied general equilibrium models.

example, dynamic, representative-agent models might be calibrated with reference to averages found in panel data. The rationale is not that identification and estimation are impossible; indeed Singleton (1988) notes that often standard econometric methods may be applied to estimate parameters. Rather the idea is to strengthen results and discipline modelling by avoiding free parameters. Usually model properties are studied with several different parameter vectors, as a check on sensitivity. Information drawn from other studies usually is informal and does not include standard errors. Canova (1991) and Hoover (1991) discuss this issue. Moreover, some method of aggregation is required in order to use parameters estimated from microeconomic panels in representative-agent models (i.e., to make sure one is measuring the same thing). If the relationships estimated from microeconomic studies do aggregate, then estimation also could be done in the aggregate data, at least as a check. If those relationships do not aggregate, then using the micro-based estimates may be misleading.

In some cases parameters are set so as to match exactly a statistic generated by the model with one in data. For example, Kydland and Prescott (1982) calibrated the coefficient of relative risk aversion in their business-cycle model by matching the variance of detrended output. This matching constitutes estimation, and is often done by simulation. In Section 3 we outline this aspect of these empirical methods.

Once a macroeconomic model is parameterized it can be evaluated using data and then perhaps used to answer quantitative questions. A second statistical method in macroeconomics involves more general comparison of a model's properties with those of data. A typical business-cycle study reports measures of variability and of covariance with output for actual data and for a business-cycle model, for such variables as consumption, investment, and hours; a good example is given in Tables 1.1 and 1.2 of McCallum (1989). This comparison can be viewed as an informal test, which guides reformulation or respecification of the model, particularly when the discrepancies appear to be large.

Obviously the inferences drawn from the comparison depend on the variables and moments used. The moments must exist for the comparison to be meaningful, so often data must be transformed to induce stationarity. Singleton (1988) and Cogley and Nason (1991) show that the detrending method (or spectral bandwidth) considered in calculating moments may itself have a large effect on conclusions. Typical comparisons involve variances, but one also could study dynamic properties, i.e., the shape of a spectrum rather than its integral.

Studies which use calibration methods in macroeconomics are now too numerous to list, and it is safe to say that the approach is beginning to predominate in the quantitative application of macroeconomic models. One influential example of calibration is the study of business cycles by Kydland and Precott (1982), in which fluctuations are driven by an unobservable productivity shock. They assigned most parameter values based on evidence from microeconomic studies and long-run averages and studied the model's business-cycle properties by simulation. Further study of equilibrium business-cycle models driven by technology shocks has led to several reformulations. For example, the variability of the labour input (hours worked) in the Kydland–Prescott economy was less than that in detrended historical data for the U.S. This discrepancy was largely resolved in versions of the business-cycle model which include labour supply variation caused by variation in the number of persons working as well as in hours per worker. Other versions have included labour contracts, government spending, and tax distortions to widen the range of questions studied and to improve the models' fit. Although reformulations like this are suggested partly by theory they also are impelled by comparisons of the models' predictions with data. Sections 4 and 5 discuss several ways to formalize such comparisons.

3. Estimation and calibration

To keep notation as simple as possible, we shall survey estimation and calibration methods entirely within an asset-pricing model, as outlined by Lucas (1978). This model is simple enough to allow clear and direct comparisons between calibration and standard econometric methods. Singleton (1990) provides a comprehensive outline of asset-pricing theory and evidence. In the example here a representative consumer has preferences represented by the utility functional

$$E\left[\sum_{s=0}^{\infty} \beta^s u(c_{t+s}) \mid \mathcal{F}_t\right], \tag{1}$$

in which E is the expectations operator, $\mathcal{F}_t$ is the consumer's information at time t, β is a discount factor, $u(c) = c^{1-\alpha}/(1-\alpha)$ (log c if $\alpha = 1$), and α is a positive, constant coefficient of relative risk aversion. Consumption c_t evolves according to $c_{t+1} = x_{t+1} \cdot c_t$, so that $\{x_t\}$ is the sequence of consumption growth rates.

Relative prices are calculated by equating them to intertemporal marginal rates of substitution. The price of a one-period, risk-free, discount bond which provides one unit of consumption at time $t + 1$ is given by

$$p_t^f = \beta E[u'(c_{t+1})/u'(c_t) \mid \mathcal{F}_t] = \beta E[(c_{t+1}/c_t)^{-\alpha} \mid \mathcal{F}_t]$$
$$= \beta E[x_{t+1}^{-\alpha} \mid \mathcal{F}_t], \tag{2a}$$

and the price of an equity claim to the consumption stream is given by

$$p_t^e = \beta E[(u'(c_{t+1})/u'(c_t)) \cdot (c_{t+1} + p_{t+1}^e) \mid \mathcal{F}_t]$$
$$= \beta E[x_{t+1}^{-\alpha} \cdot (c_{t+1} + p_{t+1}^e) \mid \mathcal{F}_t]. \tag{2b}$$

The structural parameters of this model are $\gamma = (\alpha, \beta)$. Denote the realized history $\{y_t = (p_t, x_t): t = 1, \ldots, T + 1\}$, where p_t is a vector of asset prices and x_t is the forcing variable, which here is a scalar for simplicity. We next consider estimation under various assumptions about the investigator's knowledge and aims. Estimation and inference usually are based on the sample moments of the observable variables:

$$W_T = T^{-1} \sum_{t=1}^{T} w(y_t), \tag{3}$$

where T is a sample size, w is a q-dimensional vector of observable continuous functions, and W_T is a vector of sample moments of the observable variables. For example, W_T could include the sample means and variances of bond and equity prices.

Next suppose that an economic theory predicts a vector $\tilde{w}(y_t, \gamma)$ where $\gamma \in \Gamma \subset \mathbb{R}^v$ is a v-vector of parameters, and the model determines the endogenous variables from the forcing variable and the parameters. Tildes label the predictions of theory. Denote the true parameter values γ_0 so that unconditionally $E[w(y_t)] = E[\tilde{w}(y_t, \gamma_0)]$ if the model is correct. We assume that these conditions are satisfied only at γ_0. The sample analogues to these population conditions may be used for estimation. The parameters of the economic model (such as α in the asset-pricing model above) may be consistently estimated if $q \geq v$ and some identification conditions are satisfied. For the most part we shall assume identification and sufficient regularity. We consider and contrast three different methods of obtaining parameter values: first the generalized method of moments (GMM), second the method of simulated moments (MSM), and third calibration.

First, if the econometrician can calculate the theoretical moments then estimation can be based on the generalized method of moments (i.e., generalized instrumental variables, surveyed by Ogaki, 1993):

$$\hat{\gamma}_{\mathrm{GMM}} = \arg \min_{\gamma \in \Gamma} \|W_T - \bar{W}_T(\gamma)\|, \tag{4}$$

where the asymptotic distribution of the estimator will depend on the norm $\|\cdot\|$. Hansen (1982) shows consistency and asymptotic normality (CAN) using the L^2 norm under regularity and stationarity conditions. For example if the minimization is

$$\hat{\gamma}_{\mathrm{GMM}} = \arg \min_{\gamma \in \Gamma} [(W_T - \bar{W}_T(\gamma))^{\mathrm{T}} S_T^{-1} (W_T - \bar{W}_T(\gamma))], \tag{4'}$$

where the superscript T denotes transposition and S_T equals the sample variance–covariance matrix of the moment condition $W_T - \bar{W}_T(\gamma)$, then $T^{1/2}(\hat{\gamma}_{\mathrm{GMM}} - \gamma_0) \overset{a}{\sim} N(0, (\nabla_{w0}^{\mathrm{T}} S_0^{-1} \nabla_{w0})^{-1})$, where ∇_{w0} is the expected Jacobian of the same condition and S_0 is the population variance–covariance matrix, both evaluated at γ_0. GMM describes the optimal weighting of moment conditions.

Efficiency may be increased if population moments $\mathrm{E}[\bar{w}(y_t, \gamma)]$ can be calculated for the model and used in place of $\bar{W}_T(\gamma)$.

An example of estimation is suggested by equation (2a). From the law of iterated expectations, $\mathrm{E}p_t^f = \mathrm{E}\beta x_{t+1}^{-\alpha}$. Thus one could estimate α by GMM with $q = v = 1$ (presetting β, say) based on the moments: $W_T = T^{-1} \sum_{t=1}^{T} p_t^f$ and $\bar{W}_T(\gamma) = T^{-1} \sum_{t=1}^{T} \beta \cdot x_{t+1}^{-\alpha}$. In this simple example a constant is the only instrument. Hansen and Singleton (1982) estimate α and β using this method with some additional moment conditions that provide overidentifying restrictions and hence a test of the model.

The advantage of this method is that one can estimate and test the model in (2a) and (2b) without specifying the law of motion for the forcing variable. Data on $\{x_t\}$ are used, and some weak restrictions on its properties are required for asymptotic distribution theory, but there is no parameterization of the $\{x_t\}$ process. The disadvantage of this method is that it cannot be used to predict asset prices since the expectations in (2a) and (2b) are unknown. Solving for asset prices requires further, testable assumptions on the data generation process (DGP). If the forcing process $\{x_t\}$ is parameterized then GMM or maximum likelihood methods can be used to estimate its parameters along with α and β. For example, Hansen and Singleton (1983) specify a joint, log-normal distribution for $\{y_t\}$ and hence solve for asset prices and estimate by maximum likelihood. Hansen and Sargent (1980) outline methods for testing cross-equation restrictions in the multivariate $\{y_t\}$ process for linear models.

Macroeconomic models frequently include unobservable or latent variables such as productivity shocks in growth models or, in the case of the asset-pricing example, measurement error in aggregate consumption. Computing the likelihood or even moments can be difficult with a latent variable. In these circumstances a heuristic device is to set the parameters and simulate the model. Then comparing statistics from the simulations to those in data, while varying the parameter settings to seek a good match, amounts to estimation. Formal simulation estimators in economics originated with McFadden (1989), and Pakes and Pollard (1989) (see the reviews by Hajivassiliou, 1993, and Gourieroux and Monfort, 1991). Simulation estimators sometimes can be constructed without the complete DGP (see McFadden and Ruud, 1990). In macroeconomics Kydland and Prescott (1982) estimated some of their parameters by grid search and simulation, while others were set on the basis of other evidence. Thus their method of parameterization was a hybrid of estimation by simulation and calibration. Several subsequent studies have simply calibrated related models with the Kydland–Prescott parameter settings.

Natural examples of moments which are difficult to calculate analytically in macroeconomics arise from measurement schemes. Typically data are collected by time-averaging, skip sampling, or other schemes the effects of which on moments may be difficult to work out analytically. Simulating the measurement or sampling model along with the underlying economic model provides a very simple estimation method. Other settings for estimation by simulation arise in financial modelling in continuous time. There the conditional likelihood (transition probability density function) often is the solution to a partial differential equation which, for interesting processes, is difficult to solve.

To illustrate a formal version of this second approach to estimation, suppose that the econometrician measures $\{x_t\}$ with error. In some cases α and β may still be estimatable by GMM but generally estimation (and certainly prediction) requires one to parameterize and simulate the unobserved process. Then the unknown expression for the theoretical moment can be replaced by a simulated moment $\bar{W}(y_n, \gamma)$, where n indexes simulated observations. For example, suppose that the researcher parameterizes the process for the consumption growth rate as Mehra and Prescott (1985) did. Let the growth rate x_n follow a Markov process on a finite, discrete state space $\Lambda = \{\lambda_1, \lambda_2, \ldots, \lambda_J\}$. This process is stationary and ergodic, with transition matrix ϕ,

$$\phi_{ij} = \text{Prob}[x_{n+1} = \lambda_j \,|\, x_n = \lambda_i], \quad i, j = 1, 2, \ldots, J. \tag{5}$$

The equilibrium or unconditional probabilities are given by

$$\phi_i = \text{Prob}[x_n = \lambda_i] \quad \forall n. \tag{6}$$

If the current state is (c_n, λ_i), then from equations (2a) and (2b) the prices (relative to one unit of the commodity at time t) of the two assets are

$$p^f(\lambda_i, c_n) = \beta E[(x_{n+1}^{-\alpha}) \,|\, \mathscr{F}_n] = \beta \sum_{j=1}^{J} \phi_{ij} \lambda_j^{-\alpha}, \tag{7a}$$

$$p^e(\lambda_i, c_n) = \beta E[(x_{n+1}^{-\alpha}) \cdot (c_{n+1} + p^e(\lambda_j, c_{n+1})) \,|\, \mathscr{F}_n]$$

$$= \beta \sum_{j=1}^{J} \phi_{ij} \lambda_j^{-\alpha} (\lambda_j c_n + p^e(\lambda_j, \lambda_j c_n)). \tag{7b}$$

The finite-state Markov process allows analytical expressions for the asset prices. In many cases realistic models will not have this feature and a recent and important development in macroeconomics is the use of numerical methods for *solving* models (see Taylor and Uhlig, 1990, and references therein). Burnside (1990) discusses estimation when moments are approximated analytically, rather than by Monte Carlo methods. So far there are few examples of estimation and testing in macroeconomics which take into account approximation error arising from solution methods. In this chapter we focus on estimation and testing and hence use an example in which deducing the predictions of the theory is straightforward, once $\{x_n\}$ is simulated, i.e., we assume that the true growth rate x_t (observable only by agents) also follows a J-state Markov chain.

Next simulations $\{x_n : n = 1, 2, 3, \ldots, N+1\}$ are drawn from this probability law and functions $\{\bar{w}(y_n, \gamma)\}$ are calculated using specific values of γ. Then estimation can be based on the method of simulated moments (MSM):

$$\hat{\gamma}_{\text{MSM}} = \arg\min_{\gamma \in \Gamma} \| W_T - \tilde{W}_N(\gamma) \|, \tag{8}$$

where $\tilde{W}_N(\gamma) = N^{-1} \sum_{n=1}^{N} \tilde{w}(y_n, \gamma)$ are the simulated moments. The vector γ now may include parameters of the forcing process. If the rationale for estimation by simulation is that $\{x_t\}$ is measured with error then W_T will include moments of asset prices only. Under ergodicity the two sample moments which are matched in (8) converge, as T and N approach infinity, to two population moments which are equal at γ_0; this equality forms the basis of estimation.

The argument in equation (8) can be rewritten as

$$W_T - \tilde{W}_N(\gamma) = [W_T - \tilde{W}_T(\gamma)] + [\tilde{W}_T(\gamma) - E\tilde{w}] + [E\tilde{w} - \tilde{W}_N(\gamma)]$$
$$= [W_T - \tilde{W}_T(\gamma)] + s_T + u_N. \tag{9}$$

In equation (9) the first term is the argument of the GMM estimator in (4). The second term s_T is a sampling error which arises if GMM or MSM is based on sample moments rather than population moments $E\tilde{w}$. The third term u_N is a simulation error. Thus the difference between GMM and MSM estimators depends on the properties of u_N. In many macroeconomic applications no simulation bias arises, but consistency and asymptotic normality results in MSM require some restrictions on the error u_N.

One possibility suggested by (9) is to prove a central limit theorem by applying empirical process methods (see Pollard 1984, 1985) to the simulation residual. Let ψ_N be the empirical process operator defined as $\psi_N \equiv N^{1/2}[E - N^{-1}\sum_{n=1}^{N}]$, where E is the population probability measure and $N^{-1}\sum_{n=1}^{N}$ is the empirical measure, with mass N^{-1} at each observation $\tilde{w}(y_N, \gamma)$. The standardized residual is $N^{1/2}u_N = \psi_N \tilde{w}(y_n, \gamma)$. An important necessary condition for CAN is that the empirical process $\psi_N \tilde{w}(y_n, \gamma)$ is stochastically equicontinuous in γ. This smoothness condition requires that Monte Carlo random numbers not be redrawn as γ is varied. It does allow some discontinuities. For example, in finance many applications (e.g., with kinked payoffs) involve functions w which are not pointwise differentiable with respect to γ. In these circumstances Taylor's theorem applied to $\tilde{w}(y_n, \gamma)$ cannot be used to establish asymptotic normality. Pakes and Pollard (1989) describe central limit theorems for such environments; as in (9) these theorems take limiting operations first, then rely on the differentiability of the expectation.

Duffie and Singleton (1990) note two reasons why standard proofs of CAN for MSM in iid environments may not apply to dynamic models. First, simulations begin from some initial values, yet the unconditional distribution of the forcing variables typically is not known as a function of the parameters. For example, one would simulate the asset-pricing model here by choosing an initial state (c_0, λ_i) then calculating prices as in (7a) and (7b) by drawing consumption growth rates from the conditional probability density function.

Geometric ergodicity in $\{x_n\}$ is sufficient for the effects of using arbitrary initial conditions in simulation to die out. Second, in a non-iid environment the simulated moment depends on the parameters directly through the moment condition (as in GMM) but also indirectly because values of parameters such as ϕ are used in generating the past history of the simulated variables. For example, the simulated mean price of the risk-free asset is

$$\bar{W}_N(\gamma) = N^{-1} \sum_{n=1}^{N} \beta \cdot x_{n+1}^{-\alpha}, \tag{10}$$

which is a function of β and α (just as in GMM) but also depends on the parameters through their use in simulating $\{x_n\}$. Duffie and Singleton provide CAN results for MSM under these conditions.

In fact, in this example one can calculate the unconditional mean of the risk-free price (given the form of the forcing process) as:

$$E[\bar{w}(y_t, \gamma)] = E(p_t^f) = \sum_{i=1}^{J} \sum_{j=1}^{J} \phi_i \phi_{ij} \lambda_j^{-\alpha}. \tag{11}$$

This population moment would provide more efficient estimates than would the simulated moment – both s_T and u_N can be avoided. In general, though, the simulation error u_N will make the MSM estimator less efficient than a comparable GMM estimator. For $E \bar{w}^2 < \infty$, $\psi_N \bar{w}$ is asymptotically distributed as $N(0, E \bar{w}^2 - (E \bar{w})^2)$, i.e., $N(0, \text{var}[\bar{w}])$. This result is a heuristic version of Lee and Ingram's (1991) finding that if $N = T$ then the asymptotic (as T and $N \rightarrow \infty$) variance is twice that of the GMM estimator. The idea is that simulations are independent of the observed data and hence their contribution to the variance is orthogonal to that of the usual GMM component.

Other simulation methods and variance-reduction techniques can reduce sampling variability. Duffie and Singleton (1990) note that averaging over R independent simulations with $N = T$ yields an asymptotic variance $(1 + R^{-1})$ times the GMM one. By ergodicity the same result holds if there is one long simulation with $N = RT$. Melino (1991) suggests other improvements: for example, if one is simulating an Itô process, then one need only simulate the predictable component, since the expectation (used in estimation) is unaffected by the martingale component. In many cases one can simply set N very large, calculate population moments, and then apply GMM; in such cases there is little efficiency loss from simulation, which is simply used as a calculation device.

Estimation sometimes may be based on matching properties other than moments. For example, macroeconomic evidence might be summarized in the coefficients of a vector autoregression or of a linear regression. Given identifiability, one could calculate the population coefficients in the same regressions in a theoretical model and match the two sets in order to estimate parameters. Smith (1989) shows that such matching yields consistent, asymptotically normal estimators provided it is based on regular functions of asymptotically normal variables.

In practice the choice among estimators often hinges on computation. Much remains to be learned about practical estimation in specific applications, particularly with non-differentiabilities. Bossaerts and Hillion (1991) outline applications of MSM in financial models. They describe methods for estimating option-pricing models in which prices are found by simulation (see also Boyle, 1977). In some economic models a further approximation arises because moments of a continuous-time process are approximated by moments from a simulated discrete-time process. Bossaerts and Hillion (1991) let the order of discretization grow with the sample size, and interpolate to reduce bias in finite samples. Duffie and Singleton (1990) discuss discretization schemes and asymptotic results.

So far we have noted that simulation methods may be useful in parameterizing macroeconomic models in which there are unobservable variables or simply analytical intractabilities. But there is a further, more conventional use for simulation methods even if GMM is feasible: repeated simulation can allow study of the sampling behaviour of estimators and tests. For example, Tauchen (1986) and Gregory and Smith (1990) find numerically that for this asset-pricing DGP and for realistic persistence in consumption growth rates $\hat{\alpha}_{GMM}$ is biased down if $\alpha_0 = 2.0$ or 4.0 (for $N = 100$ or 500). Setting $N = T$ and making R large traces out the finite-sample density of $\hat{\alpha}_{GMM}$ and hence can be used to make bias corrections. Canova, Finn and Pagan (1991) synthesize numerical and analytical evidence on instrument choice. Kocherlakota (1990) uses the same method to study properties of tests of this model.

A third method of parameterization, and an alternative to formal estimation methods such as GMM and MSM, is to assign parameter values with reference to other studies, i.e., to calibrate, as sketched in Section 2. One idea behind this method is simply to reduce uncertainty about a model's predictions, and hence strengthen tests, by assigning parameter values using point estimates from related studies. Gregory and Smith (1990) study mixed estimators in which some parameters are pre-set (calibrated) and others are estimated, as in Kydland and Prescott (1982). Obviously there is a trade-off between efficiency and robustness – generally estimators will be inconsistent if the pre-setting is incorrect but may have relatively low mean square error if the pre-setting error is not large. The importance of pre-setting a parameter, as opposed to estimating it consistently, can be gauged in sample size: How much larger an historical sample would be required with estimation, as opposed to calibration, to achieve as much precision in some measure? Moreover, in some cases moment conditions can be found which can consistently estimate some parameters even if others are set incorrectly. Gregory and Smith (1990) give an example.

Many models contain parameters which cannot be set with reference to other studies. In such cases calibration often proceeds by setting parameters to match a population moment from the model with a sample moment from the data.

One potential pitfall in informal moment-matching is that parameters may be selected even if they are not identifiable. Another is that parameters in business cycle models sometimes are assigned so that deterministic steady-state predictions of the model match sample averages of the data. An analogous method in the asset-pricing model discussed here would be to set β to equal the mean bill price, because that is its value in a deterministic steady state (by setting consumption growth equal to zero in equation (2a)) and then to find α by inserting this value for β in the equation for the equity price. As we have seen in this section, standard statistical methods (even in models with unobserved shocks) can avoid these pitfalls.

4. Model evaluation and testing

Once a model has been formulated, solved, and parameterized its properties can be studied and compared to those in data. Relatively informal comparisons of moments have become widespread in macroeconomics. These comparisons may illuminate respects in which the model seems inadequate. Of course, an exact match is unduly restrictive since historical moments have sampling variability and so can differ from a model's population moments even if the model is true. Therefore, some method for gauging the discrepancy between actual and predicted moments is necessary. Three sources of uncertainty may affect the comparison. First, uncertainty may arise from simulation or from approximation. Second, uncertainty arises if parameters are estimated. Third, there is sampling variability in the historical moments themselves.

This section illustrates and contrasts two standard techniques of model evaluation using a common data set. The data are annual returns used by Grossman and Shiller (1981) and Mehra and Prescott (1985) for 1889–1979. Consumption is measured as annual per capita real consumption on non-durables and services. The real return on equity is constructed from the corresponding consumption deflator, the annual average of the Standard and Poor composite stock price index, and annual dividends. The risk-free real return is based on prices of short-term securities (such as treasury bills).

Economic models typically restrict a wide range of properties, and hence one approach to formal testing is based on overidentification. Suppose that v parameters have been estimated using q moment conditions. Hansen (1982) shows that T times the minimized value of the criterion in (4′) is asymptotically $\chi^2(q - v)$ under H_0:

$$J = T[(W_T - \bar{W}(\hat{\gamma}_{\text{GMM}}))^\text{T} S_T^{-1} (W_T - \bar{W}(\bar{\gamma}_{\text{GMM}}))] \overset{a}{\sim} \chi^2(q - v), \qquad (12)$$

where S_T is defined in Section 3. This test of overidentifying restrictions allows for sampling variability in moments and for parameter uncertainty. A similar test can be applied if only v moments are first chosen for estimation, and then the remaining $q - v$ are used for testing.

To illustrate the test in equation (12) we first calculate GMM estimates of α and β by transforming equations (2a) and (2b) to give the following moment conditions:

$$E[(\beta x_{t+1}^{-\alpha} \cdot r_{t+1}^{f} - 1) \cdot z_t] = 0, \tag{13a}$$

$$E[(\beta x_{t+1}^{-\alpha} \cdot r_{t+1}^{e} - 1) \cdot z_t] = 0, \tag{13b}$$

where $r_{t+1}^{f} = 1/p_t^{f}$ and $r_{t+1}^{e} = (p_{t+1}^{e} + c_{t+1})/p_t^{e}$ are the real, annual, gross returns on bonds and equity and $z_t \subset \mathcal{F}_t$ is a vector of instruments in agents' information set. In this example $z_t = (1 \; x_t \; x_{t-1} \; r_t^{f} \; r_{t-1}^{f} \; r_t^{e} \; r_{t-1}^{e})$. With seven instruments and two equations $q = 14$ and $v = 2$. The parameter estimates are $\hat{\beta}_{\text{GMM}} = 1.030 \; (0.0681)$ and $\hat{\alpha}_{\text{GMM}} = 9.747 \; (2.383)$, with standard errors given in parentheses. Note that the estimate of β is outside the range to which it would usually be restricted in calibration. The value of the J-statistic is 29.689 and comparison to its asymptotic distribution $\chi^2(12)$ gives a prob-value of 0.0031 so that the model is rejected at the usual significance levels.

Many tests of calibrated models can be viewed as more detailed studies of the dimensions in which a model might fail empirically, because complete calibration of a model is not required to test it (as the J-test illustrates). The aim of calibrating a model economy is to conduct experiments in which its properties are derived and compared to those of an actual economy. A standard reporting style in business-cycle modelling involves listing unconditional moments of historical data alongside of population moments from a calibrated economic model.

For example, Mehra and Prescott (1985) calibrated a version of the asset-pricing model outlined above, by setting $\alpha = 1.5$, $\beta = 0.99$, $\lambda_1 = 0.982$, $\lambda_2 = 1.054$, and

$$\phi = \begin{bmatrix} 0.43 & 0.57 \\ 0.57 & 0.43 \end{bmatrix}.$$

The rationale for this calibration is that some of the population moments of this consumption growth-rate process (mean, variance, and autocovariance) match those of the U.S, annual sample for 1889–1979. Based on various applied studies which estimate α Mehra and Prescott concluded that α is probably between 1 and 2. This choice of α lies outside the 95% confidence interval around $\hat{\alpha}_{\text{GMM}}$ estimated from the annual returns data. In fact they examined the sensitivity of findings to values of α between 0 and 10 as well as values for β between 0 and 1; one also could study the moment comparison with these ranges.

Table 1 lists moments implied by the model and found in data, as is typically done in calibration studies. The first column presents the first two population moments of consumption growth, the risk-free return, and the equity premium for the model. The second column of the table gives the same moments for U.S. historical data. The population equity premium rate $(E r_t^{e} - E r_t^{f})$ is 0.20%.

Table 1
Population and sample moments (Mehra–Prescott model)

Moment	Model	1889–1979	95% confidence interval
$\mu(x_t)$	1.8	1.83	(1.2, 2.4)
$\text{std}(x_t)$	3.60	3.57	(3.6, 3.6)
$\mu(r_t^f - 1)$	3.51	0.80	(3.4, 3.6)
$\text{std}(r_t^f - 1)$	0.8	5.67	(0.8, 0.8)
$\mu(r_t^e - r_t^f)$	0.20	6.18	(−0.6, 1.0)
$\text{std}(r_t^e - r_t^f)$	3.9	16.67	(3.7, 4.0)

Note: Values are given in percent terms. μ denotes a mean, std denotes a standard deviation, r_t^f is the gross, real return on the risk-free asset (T-bill), r_t^e is the gross, real return on equity. Returns are measured as percentages. Confidence intervals are interquantile ranges from the empirical density function of the simulated moments, based on $R = 1000$ replications.

One way to describe the comparison between these two sets of moments is to use the language of classical statistical inference: if the actual properties could not have been generated by the economic model except with very low probability then the model is rejected and otherwise it is not. But nothing hinges on viewing the comparison as a classical test. For example, one could treat the comparison simply as a measurement exercise in which one gauges the proportion of some observed variance, say, which the theoretical model can reproduce. However, at some stage in an investigation one must test a model against data or against other models in order to have confidence in its economic implications.

In contrast to the J-test, most tests of calibrated models evaluate models while ignoring parameter uncertainty. However, one advantage in testing calibrated models is that exact procedures are available because the complete DGP is specified, including the density of the forcing variable x. Thus in a fully calibrated model an alternative to asymptotic tests is to use the sampling variability of the *simulated* moment to gauge the closeness of the historical moment to the model's population moment (see Gregory and Smith 1991, 1992). To conduct this test, one simulates repeatedly with the same sample size as is available in historical data and then forms the empirical density of the simulated moments $\{\bar{W}_N(\gamma)_r : r = 1, \ldots, R\}$. With this density one can calculate critical values, or treat the historical moment as a critical value. For example, the proportion of the sequence $\{\bar{W}_{Nr}\}$ that exceeds W_T gives the size of the one-sided test implicit in the comparison of the historical and population moments. Since $N = T$ the inference is exact as R becomes large. The same principle can underlie joint tests.

Mehra and Prescott tested the model by examining whether it could (with α and β in the restricted range) generate both a population value for the risk-free rate of return less than 4% and an equity premium of at least 6.2%, which is the value for the historical sample for the U.S. from 1889–1979. Formalizing this test using Monte Carlo methods requires no auxiliary assumptions, since the model is completely parameterized. The proportion of simulations (with

$N = T$) which satisfy the criterion given above is the size of the test. This proportion is zero, so that the model is very unlikely to have generated the data. Some other parameterizations lead to positive prob-values. The same method can be used to formalize comparisons using other moments shown in Table 1 and to construct confidence intervals. These prob-values and confidence regions are themselves estimates, but in this example increasing the number of replications or local smoothing of the empirical densities had no effect to several decimal places.

The two tests outlined – based on orthogonality restrictions and on matching the mean equity premium – both reject the model. In this case they yield similar results, although they use different information. For example, the first rejection does not require a parametric model of the consumption growth rate x_t and does not restrict the values of β and α. It thus suggests that reformulating the asset-pricing functional in (2a) and (2b) (as opposed to the forcing process in (5) and (6) only) is necessary. Numerous reformulations of this and other asset-pricing models have sought to generate features such as a larger mean equity premium than that generated by the DGP here.

5. Further topics in model evaluation

Models also may be evaluated according to their ability to reproduce features of standard 'windows' applied to historical data. For example, one could study a linear regression or vector autoregression which has been fitted to data, and calculate the population regression coefficients in the same statistical window implied by a fully calibrated model. Again sampling variability can be taken into account to gauge the distance between the two. Such comparisons can highlight particular directions towards which reformulations might aim. Backus, Gregory and Zin (1989) study the term structure of interest rates along these lines. Kwan (1990) matches impulse response functions in a business-cycle model. Cecchetti, Lam and Mark (1990) study negative autocorrelation in long-horizon stock returns, summarized in variance ratios or regression coefficients. They show that an equilibrium model of asset prices generates Monte Carlo samples of these statistics which include the values found in historical data.

One weakness of the simulation test outlined in Section 4 is that it ignores parameter uncertainty. Several proposals for model evaluation have been made which return to the issue of parameter uncertainty. One possibility is simply to examine the sensitivity of findings to parameter settings by reporting results for various sets of parameters. Cecchetti, Lam and Mark (1989) test a fully-parameterized version of the consumption-based asset-pricing model by comparing the unconditional moments of its predicted asset prices with those in historical data. Their asymptotic test allows for sampling variability in moments and in parameters of the $\{x_t\}$ process, and shows the effect of fixing α and β as is done in calibration. Canova, Finn and Pagan (1991) suggest local sensitivity analysis in calibrated models by differentiating statistics with respect to parameters, at the calibrated values.

An alternative suggested by Canova (1991) is to do exact tests again by constructing Monte Carlo densities of sample moments just as in Section 4, but to resample from a density of parameters γ as well as a density of underlying shocks x. This allows a global sensitivity analysis of results. In standard calibration methods the density of parameter values is sharp and has point mass at specific values. Canova suggests drawing from the frequency distribution of existing estimates to allow for observed, cross-study uncertainty about parameter values. He discusses other possible densities as well as the issue of efficient resampling when the parameter space is large. Kwan (1990) suggests a similar procedure, but based on formal Bayesian methods. He adopts subjective priors and evaluates models in relative terms according to posterior odds ratios rather than using an absolute comparison with historical data.

Investigators sometimes calibrate models which are not complete probability models and hence are not intended to mimic the complete random properties of the series under study. These models cannot be evaluated statistically, or fairly treated as null hypotheses, unless they are augmented by some random variables, perhaps interpreted as measurement error. For example, Hansen and Sargent (1980) observe that stochastic singularities often arise in dynamic economic models. An example can be given in the asset-pricing model. Recall that $p_t^f = E[\beta x_{t+1}^{-\alpha} \mid \mathcal{F}_t]$, and suppose that to test the model an investigator proposes that the expectation be modelled as $E[\beta x_{t+1}^{-\alpha} \mid x_t] = g(x_t)$. In that case the predicted asset price is a deterministic function of x_t. Since such deterministic relationships are not detected in data, this model would be rejected. It can be made testable if there is some component of the information set used in forecasts which is not observed by the investigator so that $p_t^f = g(x_t) + \varepsilon_t$, where $\varepsilon_t = E[\beta x_{t+1}^{-\alpha} \mid \mathcal{F}_t] - E[\beta x_{t+1}^{-\alpha} \mid x_t]$. A further example is given by Altuğ (1989) who begins with a one-shock business-cycle model and then augments variables with idiosyncratic error. Watson (1990) proposes identifying the error process by the requirement that its variance be as small as possible. He also proposes goodness-of-fit measures which evaluate the contribution of the original model to accounting for movements in the endogenous variables, by measuring the variance of error necessary to match theoretical and data properties.

6. Conclusion

Although we have attempted to give a formal statistical interpretation to some aspects of calibration in macroeconomics, it perhaps is best viewed as an informal guide to reformulating a theoretical model. Setting parameter values (i.e., calibrating), simulating a model, and comparing properties of simulations to those of data often suggests fruitful modifications of the model. Precisely this method has led to numerous modifications of the simple asset-pricing model used as an expository device in this chapter. Further statistical formalization and refinement of the methods used to evaluate calibrated models will help improve them.

Acknowledgment

We thank the Social Sciences and Humanities Research Council of Canada for support of this research, Tiff Macklem for providing data, Aly Jiwan for research assistance, and Fabio Canova, Narayana Kocherlakota, G. S. Maddala, Thomas McCurdy, Jeremy Rudin, A. A. Smith, Stanley Zin, and a referee for helpful comments.

References

Altuğ, S. (1989). Time-to-build and aggregate fluctuations: Some new evidence. *Internat. Econom. Rev.* **30**, 889–920.

Backus, D. K., A. W. Gregory and S. E. Zin (1989). Risk premiums in the term structure: Evidence from artificial economies. *J. Monetary Econom.* **24**, 371–399.

Bossaerts, P. and P. Hillion (1991). Arbitrage restrictions across financial markets: Theory, methodology, and tests. California Institute of Technology, Social Science Working Paper 751.

Boyle, P. P. (1977). Options: A Monte Carlo approach. *J. Financ. Econom.* **4**, 323–338.

Burnside, C. (1990). Asymptotic properties of method of moments estimators based on numerical solutions to an economic model. Mimeo, Department of Economics, Queen's University.

Canova, F. (1991). Sensitivity analysis and model evaluation in simulated dynamic general equilibrium economies. Mimeo, Department of Economics, Brown University.

Canova, F., M. Finn and A. R. Pagan (1991). Econometric issues in the analysis of equilibrium models. Mimeo, Department of Economics, University of Rochester.

Cecchetti, S. G., P.-S. Lam and N. C. Mark (1989). The equity premium and the risk free rate: Matching the moments. Mimeo, Ohio State University.

Cecchetti, S. G., P.-S. Lam and N. C. Mark (1990). Mean reversion in equilibrium asset prices. *Amer. Econom. Rev.* **80**, 398–418.

Cogley, T. and J. Nason (1991). Real business cycle models and the HP filter. Mimeo, Department of Economics, University of British Columbia.

Duffie, D. and K. J. Singleton (1990). Simulated moments estimation of Markov models of asset prices. Technical Working Paper No. 87, National Bureau of Economic Research.

Gourieroux, C. and A. Monfort (1991). Simulation-based inference: A survey with special reference to panel data models. Working paper 9106, INSEE.

Gregory, A. W. and G. W. Smith (1990). Calibration as estimation. *Econometric Rev.* **9**, 57–89.

Gregory, A. W. and G. W. Smith (1991). Calibration as testing: Inference in simulated macroeconomic models. *J. Business Econom. Statist.* **9**, 297–303.

Gregory, A. W. and G. W. Smith (1992). Sampling variability in Hansen–Jagannathan bounds. *Econom. Lett.* **38**, 263–267.

Grossman, S. J. and R. J. Shiller (1981). The determinants of the variability of stock market prices. *Amer. Econom. Rev.* **71**, 222–227.

Hajivassiliou, V. A. (1993). Simulation estimation methods for limited dependent variable models. Chapter 19 in this volume.

Hansen, L. P. (1982). Large sample properties of generalized method of moments estimators. *Econometrica* **50**, 1029–1054.

Hansen, L. P. and T. J. Sargent (1980). Formulating and estimating dynamic linear rational expectations models. *J. Econom. Dynamics Control* **2**, 7–46.

Hansen, L. P. and K. Singleton (1982). Generalized instrumental variables estimation of nonlinear rational expectations models. *Econometrica* **50**, 1269–1286.

Hansen, L. P. and K. Singleton (1983). Stochastic consumption, risk aversion, and the temporal behavior of asset returns. *J. Politic. Econom.* **91**, 249–265.

Hoover, K. D. (1991). Calibration versus estimation: Standards of empirical assessment in the new classical macroeconomics. Working Paper 72, University of California, Davis, CA.

Îmrohoroğlu, A. (1989). Cost of business cycles with indivisibilities and liquidity constraints. *J. Politic. Econom.* **97**, 1364–1383.

Kocherlakota, N. (1990). On tests of representative consumer asset pricing models. *J. Monetary Econom.* **26**, 285–304.

Kwan, Y.-K. (1990). Bayesian model calibration with an application to a non-linear rational expectations two-country model. Mimeo, Graduate School of Business, University of Chicago.

Kydland, F. E. and E. C. Prescott (1982). Time to build and aggregate fluctuations. *Econometrica* **50**, 1345–1370.

Lau, L. J. (1984). Comments. In: H. E. Scarf and J. B. Shoven, eds., *Applied General Equilibrium Analysis*. Cambridge Univ. Press, Cambridge.

Lee, B.-S. and B. F. Ingram (1991). Simulation estimation of time series models. *J. Econometrics* **47**, 197–205.

Lucas, R. E. Jr (1978). Asset prices in an exchange economy. *Econometrica* **46**, 1426–1445.

Lucas, R. E. Jr (1987). *Models of business cycles*. Yrjö Jahnsson Lectures. Basil Blackwell, Oxford.

MacKinnon, J. (1984). Comments. In: H. E. Scarf and J. B. Shoven, eds., *Applied General Equilibrium Analysis*. Cambridge Univ. Press, Cambridge.

McCallum, B. T. (1989). Real business cycle models. In: R. J. Barro, ed., *Modern Business Cycle Theory*. Harvard Univ. Press, Cambridge, MA, Chapter 1.

McFadden, D. (1989). A method of simulated moments for estimation of discrete response models without numerical integration. *Econometrica* **57**, 995–1026.

McFadden, D. and P. A. Ruud (1990). Estimation by simulation. Mimeo, Department of Economics, University of California, Berkeley, CA.

Mehra, R. and E. C. Prescott (1985). The equity premium: A puzzle. *J. Monetary Econom.* **15**, 145–161.

Melino, A. (1991). Estimation of continuous-time models in finance. Working Paper 9115, Department of Economics, University of Toronto.

Ogaki, M. (1993). Generalized method of moments: Econometric applications. Chapter 17 in this volume.

Pagan, A. and J. Shannon (1985). Sensitivity analysis for linearized computable general equilibrium models. In: J. Piggott and J. Whalley, eds., *New Developments in Applied General Equilibrium Analysis*. Cambridge Univ. Press, Cambridge.

Pakes, A. and D. Pollard (1989). Simulation and the asymptotics of optimization estimators. *Econometrica* **57**, 1027–1057.

Pollard, D. (1984). *Convergence of Stochastic Processes*. Springer, New York.

Pollard, D. (1985). New ways to prove central limit theorems. *Econometric Theory* **1**, 295–314.

Shoven, J. B. and J. Whalley (1984). Applied general-equilibrium models of taxation and international trade. *J. Econom. Literature* **22**, 1007–1051.

Singleton, K. (1988). Econometric issues in the analysis of equilibrium business cycle models. *J. Monetary Econom.* **21**, 361–386.

Singleton, K. (1990). Specification and estimation of intertemporal asset-pricing models. In: B. Friedman and F. Hahn, eds., *Handbook of Monetary Economics*. North-Holland, Amsterdam.

Smith, A. A. (1989). Estimation of dynamic economic models by simulation: A comparison of two approaches. Mimeo, Duke University.

Tauchen, G. (1986). Statistical properties of generalized method-of-moments estimators of structural parameters obtained from financial market data. *J. Business Econom. Statist.* **4**, 397–416.

Taylor, J. B. and H. Uhlig (1990). Solving nonlinear stochastic growth models: A comparison of alternative solution methods. *J. Business Econom. Statist.* **8**, 1–17.

Watson, M. W. (1990). Measures of fit for calibrated models, Mimeo, Department of Economics, Northwestern University.

G. S. Maddala, C. R. Rao and H. D. Vinod, eds., *Handbook of Statistics, Vol. 11*
© 1993 Elsevier Science Publishers B.V. All rights reserved.

26

Panel Data Models with Rational Expectations

Kajal Lahiri

1. Introduction

Econometric analysis based on panel data has many advantages over the ones which use only time-series or cross-section data. By tracking the behavior of a large number of economic agents over time, panel or longitudinal data sets allow researchers to estimate structural parameters after controlling for unobservable individual idiosyncracies and unforecastable aggregate shocks. Since economic theories are typically posited for a representative economic agent, such data can be used to test certain derivable implications of these theories without the aggregation problems associated with the use of either time-series or cross-section data only. Moreover, by pooling time-series data on a large cross-section of individuals, one can study the short-run dynamic behavior of economic agents in relation to their long-run equilibria in greater generality. The increased availability and the consequent use of panel data in recent years has led to a very rapid and impressive development in appropriate estimation and testing procedures.[1] Fortunately, there are now a number of excellent monographs and articles which have surveyed and summarized the literature; see, for instance, Chamberlain (1984), Dielman (1989), Heckman and Singer (1985), Hsiao (1986), and Maddala (1987a,b). Much of current research has considered models of the form $Y_{it} = X_{it}\beta + \eta_i + U_{it}$ where η_i is the individual (fixed or random) effect, where at least a subset of X_{it} is assumed to be strictly exogenous with respect to U_{it}; that is, $E(X_{it}U_{it}) = 0$ for all t and s. All right-hand side endogenous variables are taken to be correlated with both η_i and U_{it}. In the fixed-effect case, where η_i is assumed to be correlated with all the right-hand variables, the usual solution is to eliminate η_i by taking deviations from individual means (i.e. $Y_{it} - \bar{Y}_i$, where $\bar{Y}_i = (1/t) \Sigma Y_{it}$) and

---

[1] Three widely used U.S. panel data sets are the University of Michigan's Panel Study of Income Dynamics (PSID), National Longitudinal Surveys of Labor Market Experience (NLS) and the Survey of Income and Program Participation (SIPP). See Borus (1982) and Ashenfelter and Solon (1982) for an annotated inventory of such data sets for economists.

using instrumental variable estimation methods.[2] In the random-effects case, estimation is done with quasi-demean data of the form $Y_{it} - \lambda \bar{Y}_i$ where $\lambda = 1 - \sigma_u/(\sigma_u^2 + T\sigma_\eta^2)^{1/2}$, ($\sigma_\eta^2$ and σ_u^2 are the variances of η_i and U_{it} respectively) as suggested in Fuller and Battese (1973, 1974). The identifiability of the model depends on the availability of instruments which, in turn, is conditioned by the nature of correlation of η_i and U_{it} with X_{it}.[3] For instance, the demeaned exogenous variables are valid instruments whereas their means (i.e., $\bar{X}_i$) are not.

Much of the aforementioned developments took place under the assumption that potential instruments are strictly exogenous. In economics, there are important situations where regressors and other potential instruments are only predetermined or weakly exogenous in the sense that $E(X_{it}U_{is}) = 0$ for $t \leq s$, but the possibility that $E(X_{it}U_{is}) \neq 0$ for $t > s$ cannot be ruled out. Models with lagged dependent variables as in Balestra and Nerlove (1966) or with predetermined choice variables are two examples where similar one-sided moment conditions are present. In models with rational expectations U_{it}, which is the forecast error, can certainly affect future values of the instruments. The rational expectations hypothesis, however, rules out the possibility of any relationship between U_{it} and past values of the instruments. Unfortunately, the standard panel data estimation methods are no longer consistent when the instruments are only weakly exogenous. The problem of predetermined regressors in the context of time-series models was first analyzed by Hayashi and Sims (1983); Hansen and Hodrick (1980) and Brown and Maital (1981) analyzed the problem in models with rational expectations.[4] In a single equation model with autocorrelated errors, an otherwise consistent instrumental variable estimator becomes inconsistent when the autocorrelation is corrected for by the standard autoregressive transformation. In panel data models with predetermined instruments, the standard fixed-effects and random-effects procedures become inconsistent due to similar reasons. The presence of time-invariant individual effects creates certain structure of autocorrelation in the errors, and the conventional panel-data procedures are alternative ways of correcting for this.

It is thus clear that efficient estimation and testing strategies in the context of panel data models with rational expectations will be quite different from the conventional procedures. In what follows, we review this new literature in greater detail. In Section 2, we discuss efficient estimation of such models in a generalized method of moments (GMM) framework. Section 3 discusses certain specification tests whereas Section 4 extends the analysis to simultaneous equations. We present an empirical illustration in Section 5 where the

---

[2] See, for instance, Hausman and Taylor (1981), Atri and Lahiri (1984), Amemiya and MaCurdy (1986), Breusch, Mizon and Schmidt (1989), Bhargava and Sargan (1983), Arellano and Bover (1990), and Arellano and Bond (1991).

[3] Bhargava (1991) discusses the identifiability conditions in models of this type.

[4] See also Cumby, Huizinga and Obstfeld (1983) and Kinal and Lahiri (1988).

Euler equation for optimal consumption is estimated and analyzed using the Michigan Panel of Income Dynamics data over 1976–82. Finally, concluding remarks are given in Section 6.

2. Efficient estimation

2.1. Strictly exogenous instruments

Consider a structural equation

$$Y_{it} = X_{it}\beta + \varepsilon_{it} \quad (i = 1, 2, \ldots, N, \ t = 1, 2, \ldots, T), \tag{1}$$

where $\varepsilon_{it} = \eta_i + U_{it}$. η_i and U_{it} are unobserved individual effects and random error respectively with $\eta_i \sim \text{IID}(0, \sigma_\eta^2)$ and $U_{it} \sim \text{IID}(0, \sigma_u^2)$. X_{it} is a row vector of regressors. Since a part of X_{it} could be endogenous, we have data on k instrumental variables Z_{it} which include the subset of X_{it} which is exogenous. Rationally expected explanatory variables, when proxied by their ex-post counterparts, will have classical errors-in-variables problem, and can conveniently be handled as additional endogenous variables.[5] We can write the equation for individual i as

$$Y_i = X_i\beta + \eta_i + U_i \quad (i = 1, 2, \ldots, N), \tag{2}$$

where $Y_i = (Y_{i1}, \ldots, Y_{iT})$. X_i and U_i are similarly defined. Equation (1) for all NT observations can be written as

$$Y = X\beta + \eta + U, \tag{3}$$

where $Y' = (Y_1', \ldots, Y_n')$, $\eta' = (\eta_1, \ldots, \eta_N) \otimes l_T'$ where l_T is a $T \times 1$ vector of ones. X and U are defined similar to Y. All elements of η_i are assumed to be uncorrelated with all elements of U. Then the covariance matrix of ε is

$$\text{Cov}(\eta + U) = \Omega = \sigma_\eta^2 C + \sigma_u^2 I_{NT}, \tag{4}$$

where $C = I_N \otimes l_T l_T'$. Equation (3) can be transformed by $\Omega^{-1/2}$ to make the error term to have a scalar covariance matrix:

$$\Omega^{-1/2} Y = \Omega^{-1/2} X\beta + \Omega^{-1/2}(\eta + U). \tag{5}$$

However, equation (5) is equivalent to writing (1) in terms of quasi-demean variables:

$$Y_{it} - \lambda \bar{Y}_i = (X_{it} - \lambda \bar{X}_i)\beta + (\varepsilon_{it} - \lambda \bar{\varepsilon}_i), \tag{6}$$

where $\lambda = 1 - \sigma_u/(\sigma_u^2 + T\sigma_\eta^2)^{1/2}$. The error components instrumental variable estimator (EC-IV) uses instruments $A = [Q_v Z, P_v Z]$ where $P_v = (I_N \otimes l_T l_T'/T)$

---

[5] See McCallum (1976), Lahiri (1981) and Wickens (1982).

and $Q_v = I_{NT} - P_v$. Thus, $Q_v Z$ gives 'within' (or demean) and $P_v Z$ gives the 'between' version (i.e., individual means) of all instruments. Then, under the assumption that the Z_{it} are strictly exogenous, the EC-IV estimator of β becomes

$$\hat{\beta} = [X'\Omega^{-1/2}P_A\Omega^{-1/2}X]^{-1}X'\Omega^{-1/2}P_A\Omega^{-1/2}Y , \qquad (7)$$

where $P_A = A(A'A)^{-1}A'$, the projection onto the column space of A. The above estimator is also obtained by estimating (6) using instruments A. This is the so-called random-effects estimator.

However, if η_i is correlated with all the instruments Z_{it}, (7) is not consistent. In this case, so far as X_{it} is strictly exogenous, consistent estimation of β can be obtained from an instrumental variable estimation of (8) with $A = Q_v Z$,

$$Y_{it} - \bar{Y}_i = (X_{it} - \bar{Y}_i)\beta + (\varepsilon_{it} - \bar{\varepsilon}_i) . \qquad (8)$$

This is the so-called fixed effect estimator. Here the individual effects are first 'partialled out' by subtracting individual means from each variable and running an IV regression. Mundlak (1978) shows that when η_i is correlated with all instrumental variables, the 'within' estimator is, in fact, efficient.

Note that with $\sigma_\eta^2 = 0$ (i.e., no individual heterogeneity), a straightforward IV estimation of (1) will yield consistent estimates of β and its standard errors. Following Schmidt, Ahn and Wyhowski (1992) if we generalize U_i to have an unrestricted $T \times T$ covariance matrix (Σ) such that $\Omega = I_N \otimes \Sigma$ then the optimal IV estimator can be derived in Hansen's (1982) generalized method of moments (GMM) framework, (see Arellano and Bond, 1991). For $t = 1, 2, \ldots, T$, define $Z_{it}^0 = (Z_{il}, \ldots, Z_{it})$, a $1 \times kt$ row vector. Note that strong exogeneity assumption implies $E(Z_{is}U_{it}) = 0$ for all $t, s = 1, 2, \ldots, T$, which is a set of KT^2 moment conditions. These conditions can be expressed as $E(A'_{1i}U_i) = 0$, where $A_{1i} = I_T \otimes Z_{iT}^{0'}$. If A_1 is the full $NT \times KT^2$ matrix with i-th block A_{1i}, then the GMM estimator using the KT^2 moment conditions can be written as

$$\hat{\beta} = [X'A_1(A'_1\Omega A_1)^{-1}A'_1X]^{-1}X'A_1(A'_1\Omega A_1)^{-1}A'_1Y \qquad (9)$$

which is obtained by minimizing $g(\beta)'Wg(\beta)$ with respect to β, where $g(\beta)$ is the sample average orthogonality conditions specified above and W is the weighting matrix. Generally speaking, the optimal weighting matrix is the inverse of the covariance matrix of the orthogonality conditions. Note that GMM procedure estimates $A'_1\Omega A_1$ by $(1/N) \Sigma_i A'_{1i}\hat{\varepsilon}_i\hat{\varepsilon}'_iA_{1i}$ where $\hat{\varepsilon}_i$ is the residual from a consistent first-stage estimation. Also, the specific structure of $\Omega = I_N \otimes \Sigma$ can be relaxed to incorporate more general conditional heteroskedasticity and autocorrelation, cf. White and Domowitz (1984). Unlike time-series problems, estimation of Ω using panel data presents very little problem with $N \to \infty$.

Now if $\sigma_\eta^2 \neq 0$ such that $\varepsilon_{it} = \eta_i + U_{it}$, and η_i is correlated with Z_{it}, the strong exogeneity condition $E(U_{it}Z_{it}) = 0$ $(t, s = 1, \ldots, T)$ can be reformulated as the $T(T-1)K$ moment conditions that, for $s = 1, 2, \ldots, T$, $E(Z_{is}\varepsilon_{it}) = C$, the same value for all t. The fixed effect η_i can be removed either by first-differencing or by within transformation. In the case of first-differencing, these moment conditions become $E(Z_{is}\Delta\varepsilon_{it}) = 0$ $(s = 1, 2, \ldots, T; t = 2, \ldots, T)$. Define one $T \times (T-1)$ matrix D as follows:

$$
D = \begin{bmatrix}
-1 & 0 & 0 & \cdots & 0 \\
1 & -1 & 0 & \cdots & 0 \\
0 & 1 & -1 & \cdots & 0 \\
\vdots & \vdots & \vdots & \ddots & \vdots \\
0 & 0 & 0 & \cdots & -1 \\
0 & 0 & 0 & \cdots & 1
\end{bmatrix}.
\tag{10}
$$

We can first-difference equation (1) by premultiplying by D' and then using the instruments $B_{3i} = I_{T-1} \otimes Z_{iT}^{0'}$. This yields the moment conditions $E[B_{3i}'(D'\varepsilon_i)] = 0$. It is interesting to note that L has the same column space as the demeaning matrix $(I_T - l_T l_T'/T)$. This shows that the within and the first-difference transformation preserve the same amount of information in the data, see Ahn and Schmidt (1990).

2.2. Predetermined but not strictly exogenous instruments

With weakly exogenous instruments such that only

$$
E(Z_{is}\varepsilon_{it}) = 0 , \quad t = 1, 2, \ldots, T, \; s \leq t
\tag{11}
$$

the number of moment conditions dramatically falls. First, let us consider the case with no fixed effects, i.e., $\sigma_\eta^2 = 0$. The number of moment conditions available now is only $T(T+1)K/2$ rather than KT^2. These moment conditions can be written as $E(A_{2i}'\varepsilon_i) = 0$ where A_{2i} is the $T \times T(T+1)K/2$ matrix

$$
A_{2i} = \begin{bmatrix}
Z_{i1}^0 & 0 & \cdots & 0 \\
0 & Z_{i2}^0 & \cdots & 0 \\
\vdots & & \ddots & \vdots \\
0 & \cdots & & Z_{iT}^0
\end{bmatrix}.
\tag{12}
$$

Since econometric panel data sets are typically short, these models can conveniently be written as a set of simultaneous equations in which i is the observation index and t is the equation number. The main difference between conventional simultaneous equations models and the present model is that now the set of instruments $Z_{it}^0 = (Z_{i1}, \ldots, Z_{it})$ is different for different equations. Hayashi (1992) notes that with conditional homoskedasticity the above GMM estimator becomes equivalent to the full information instrumental variables estimator (FIVE) due to Brundy and Jorgenson (1971). Also, the asymptotic theory for such simultaneous equations models with $N \to \infty$ is fully developed, see White (1984). With $\sigma_\eta^2 = 0$, the $NT \times NT$ covariance matrix of U_{it} is $\sigma_u^2 I_{NT}$ and hence, GMM estimates can be readily obtained.

If we now allow $\sigma_\eta^2 \neq 0$ and η_i to be correlated with instruments, the number of moment conditions will be only $T(T-1)K/2$: for $s = 1, 2, \ldots, T$, $E(Z_{is}\varepsilon_{it}) = C$, the same for all $t \geq s$. The estimation then implies first-differencing (1) and then implementing GMM with instruments matrix:

$$
B_{4i} = \begin{bmatrix} Z_{i1}^0 & 0 & \cdots & 0 \\ 0 & Z_{i2}^0 & \cdots & 0 \\ \vdots & & \ddots & \vdots \\ 0 & \cdots & & Z_{iT-1}^0 \end{bmatrix}. \tag{13}
$$

Thus, the relevant moment conditions can be expressed as $E[B_{4i}'(D'\varepsilon_i)] = 0$. Looking at this as a system of $(T-1)$ first difference simultaneous equations, the $N(T-1) \times N(T-1)$ covariance matrix of errors takes the convenient form $\Sigma_d \otimes I_T$ where Σ_d is the $(T-1) \times (T-1)$ matrix

$$
\Sigma_d = \begin{bmatrix} -2\sigma_u^2 & -\sigma_u^2 & U & \cdots & 0 \\ -\sigma_u^2 & -2\sigma_u^2 & -\sigma_u^2 & \cdots & 0 \\ 0 & & & & \vdots \\ \vdots & & \ddots & & -\sigma_u^2 \\ 0 & & \cdots & & -2\sigma_u^2 \end{bmatrix}. \tag{14}
$$

Keane and Runkle (1992) have suggested an alternative way of estimating panel data models with predetermined instruments where $\Omega = I_N \otimes \Sigma$ and Σ is an unrestricted $T \times T$ matrix. They extend the idea of forward filtering (FF) due to Hayashi and Sims (1983) to panel data models. First obtain the upper-triangular Cholesky decomposition of Σ which they called P_{TS}. Then premultiplying (1) by $Q_{TS} = (I_N \otimes P_{TS})$ and estimating the transformed equation using the original instruments Z_{it}, they obtained the forward filter estimator:

$$
\hat{\beta}_{FF} = (X'Q_{TS}Z(Z'Z)^{-1}Z'Q_{TS}X)^{-1}X'Q_{TS}'Z(Z'Z)^{-1}Q_{TS}Y. \tag{15}
$$

As pointed out before, this estimator need not utilize the special structure of Ω as the random effects estimator does. The forward filter transformation removes autocorrelation while preserving weak exogeneity of the instruments. Hayashi and Sims (1983) have shown that as the number of instruments is increased, the GMM and FF estimators converge to the optimal estimator. Schmidt, Ahn and Wyhowski (1992) demonstrate the same result in the present context: forward filtering is irrelevant when the GMM optimal instruments set is used in estimation. However, Keane and Runkle (1992) have argued that in situations where the panel data has many missing values, the forward filter method may turn out to be more practical than the GMM method, which uses all predetermined instruments going back to the first observation in the panel.[6]

3. Specification tests

There are a number of specification tests which take special significance in this class of models. First, are the instruments only predetermined, or, can they be treated as strictly exogenous? Secondly, is there unmeasured individual heterogeneity affecting the dependent variable? If this is present, is there any evidence that the individual effects are correlated with the instruments? Third, can we identify a common component λ_t, called aggregate shock, as part of the time-varying forecast error U_{it}? These issues are important, because in short panels the interaction of aggregate shocks and random individual effects can make GMM estimators inconsistent. As Chamberlain (1984) has pointed out,

$$\mathrm{E}(U_{it}Z_{is}) = \mathop{\mathrm{plim}}_{T \to \infty} \frac{1}{T} \sum_{t=1}^{T} U_{it}Z_{is} \tag{16}$$

is indeed zero for $t \geq s$ under rational expectations. However,

$$\mathrm{E}(U_{it}Z_{is}) = \mathop{\mathrm{plim}}_{N \to \infty} \frac{1}{N} \sum_{i=1}^{N} U_{it}Z_{is} \tag{17}$$

is not necessarily zero for $t \geq s$. In short panels, it is the second one that needs to be zero for Z_{it} to be valid instruments. Hayashi (1992) presents a simple example where Z_{it} is predetermined in the time-series sense but not in the cross-section sense.

Suppose individual i's income ε_{it} is given by $\varepsilon_{it} = \alpha_i M_t$ where M_t is serially uncorrelated over time. M_t could be rainfall, common to all agents, whereas α_i is agent i's ability. Since M_t is assumed to uncorrelated, ε_{it} is also the farmer's

---

[6] It should, however, be noted that the problem of missing values can be handled very flexibly in the GMM framework, see for instance Blundell et al. (1992). Also, rational expectations models imply somewhat stronger conditions than $\mathrm{E}(\varepsilon_{it}Z_{is}) = 0$ for $s \leq t$, namely $\mathrm{E}(\varepsilon_{it}Z_{it}^0) = 0$ for $t = 1, 2, \ldots, T$. This implies that any measurable function of Z_{it}^0 like cross-products of elements of Z_{it}^0 will be valid instruments. See Chamberlain (1987, 1992), Robinson (1991), Newey (1985a, 1990) and Holtz-Eakin, Newey and Rosen (1988).

forecast error over period t. Define the instrument $Z_{it} = \varepsilon_{i\,t-1}$. Now

$$E(\varepsilon_{it}Z_{i.}) = \plim_{T \to \infty} \frac{1}{T} \sum_{t=1}^{T} \varepsilon_{it}Z_{is}$$

$$= \plim_{T \to \infty} \frac{1}{T} \sum_{t=1}^{T} (\alpha_i)^2 M_t M_{s-1}$$

$$= (\alpha_i)^2 \plim_{T \to \infty} \frac{1}{T} \sum_{t=1}^{T} M_t M_{s-1}$$

$$= 0 \quad \text{for } t \geq s, \tag{18}$$

$$E(\varepsilon_{it}Z_{is}) = \plim_{N \to \infty} \frac{1}{N} \sum_{t=1}^{N} \varepsilon_{it}Z_{is}$$

$$= \plim_{N \to \infty} \frac{1}{N} \sum_{t=1}^{N} (\alpha_i)^2 M_t M_{s-1}$$

$$= M_t M_{s-1} \plim_{N \to \infty} \frac{1}{N} \sum_{i=1}^{N} (\alpha_i)^2$$

$$\neq 0 \quad \text{even for } t \geq s. \tag{19}$$

Thus, the assumption of rational expectations does not guarantee that all the moment conditions based on information available at time t can be used for consistent estimation.

Following Newey (1985b) and Eichenbaum, Hansen and Singleton (1988), a simple specification test for the presence of aggregate shocks can be designed using the GMM framework. The presence of such shocks will invalidate time-dummies as valid instruments since these will be correlated with the aggregate shocks. Consider the model with weakly exogenous instruments without fixed effects. (The test with fixed effects is similar.) There are $T(T + 1)K/2$ valid moment conditions. Let the minimized value of the GMM criterion function using these instruments be J_α. If there are no aggregate shocks, the time dummies should be valid instruments. Re-estimate the equation adding $T - 1$ time dummies to the instruments set. Let the minimized value of GMM criterion function be J_β. In this case, $J_\beta - J_\alpha$ should be distributed asymptotically as a X^2_{T-1} variable. A large value of this test statistic will indicate that these $T - 1$ moment conditions are contaminated, implying the presence of aggregate shocks.

Let us now consider the test of the null hypothesis that instruments are strictly exogenous, maintaining the presence of fixed effects. One common feature of all these tests is that the set of moment conditions under the alternative is a subset of those under the null. Thus, the basic Hausman-principle can be directly applied. As we have discussed in Section 2, the instruments in B_{4i} is a subset of instruments in B_{3i}. There are $T(T-1)K$ instruments under the null, whereas $T(T-1)K/2$ under the alternative so that there are $T(T-1)K/2$ extra instruments under the former. If the dimension β is g then the Hausman test will be asymptotically χ^2 with g degrees of freedom, providing $g \leq T(T-1)K/2$.

Finally, using the same principle we can design a statistic to test for null hypothesis that effects and instruments are uncorrelated, maintaining only weak exogeneity of the instruments with respect to the time-varying U_{it}. The same test with strictly exogenous instruments is well known, cf. Hausman and Taylor (1981). Here the absence of fixed effects avoids the process of first-differencing, thereby generating additional TK (i.e., $T(T+1)K/2$ in A_{2i} minus $T(T-1)K/2$ in A_{4i}) moment conditions.

4. Simultaneous equations

The above ideas can be generalized to a system of simultaneous equations quite straightforwardly. Error component models in a conventional simultaneous equations framework have been analyzed by Baltagi (1981, 1984), Chamberlain (1982), Cornwell et al. (1992) and Kinal and Lahiri (1993). Let us write the g-th equation ($g = 1, 2, \ldots, G$) as

$$Y_{itg} = X_{itg}\beta_g + \varepsilon_{itg} , \tag{20}$$

where $\varepsilon_{itg} = \eta_{ig} + \nu_{itg}$. As before, let us assume that we have a set of instruments Z_{it} ($1 \times K$ vector) which is the same for all g, even though this assumption can be relaxed at no additional computational burden. If we rewrite (2) as the g-th structural equation

$$Y_g = X_g\beta_g + \varepsilon_g \tag{2'}$$

and stack the equations as in a SURE system:

$$\underline{Y} = \underline{X}\beta + \underline{\varepsilon} , \tag{21}$$

where $\underline{Y} = (Y_1', \ldots, Y_G')$, $\underline{\varepsilon} = (\varepsilon_1', \ldots, \varepsilon_g')$ and

$$\underline{X} = \begin{bmatrix} X_1 & 0 & \cdots & 0 \\ 0 & X_2 & \cdots & 0 \\ \vdots & \vdots & \ddots & \vdots \\ 0 & 0 & \cdots & X_G \end{bmatrix}$$

the assumption of weak exogeneity will imply

$$E(Z_{is}\varepsilon_{itg}) = 0 , \quad t = 1, 2, \ldots, T, \ s \leq t, \ g = 1, 2, \ldots, G \tag{22}$$

assuming that there are no individual-specific fixed effects. This gives $GT(T+1)K/2$ moment conditions. These moment conditions can be expressed as $E(\underline{A}_{2i}'\varepsilon_i) = 0$ where A_{2i} is the $GT \times GT(T+1)K/2$ block diagonal matrix with g-th block A_{2i} for all g. Defining $\underline{\Omega}$ as the $GNT \times GNT$ variance–covariance matrix of the stacked error $\underline{\varepsilon}$, this yields the three-stage least squares estimator (3SLS)

$$\hat{\beta} = [\underline{X}'\underline{\Delta}_2(\underline{\Delta}'_2\underline{\Omega}\underline{\Delta}_2)^{-1}\underline{\Delta}'_2\underline{X}]^{-1}\underline{X}'\underline{\Delta}_2(\underline{\Delta}'_2\underline{\Omega}\underline{\Delta}_2)^{-1}\underline{\Delta}'_2\underline{Y} \tag{23}$$

with predetermined instruments.[7]

5. Empirical illustration

In this section we apply the strategy for estimating and testing outlined so far to study the so-called Euler equation of the intertemporal consumption theory, which states that consumption growth should depend only on the real interest rate, cf. Hall (1988). In recent years many authors including Hall and Mishkin (1982), Zeldes (1989), Runkle (1991) and Keane and Runkle (1992) have used panel data from the Michigan panel on income dynamics (PSID) to test this basic prediction of the permanent income-life cycle hypothesis. Specifically, the equation is

$$\Delta C_{it+1} = a + b \cdot r_{it} + \varepsilon_{it+1}, \tag{24}$$

where $\Delta C_{it+1} = \ln C_{it+1} - \ln C_{it}$, r_{it} is the after-tax real interest rate from period t to $t + 1$. By the assumption of rational expectations, $E(\varepsilon_{it+1}I_{it}) = 0$ where I_{it} is the information available to individual i at time t. Note that b is an important structural parameter measuring a consumer's intertemporal elasticity of substitution. No other study before Runkle (1991) and Keane and Runkle (1992) found the coefficient of r_{it} in (24) to be statistically significant.[8]

If ε_{it+1} is conditionally homoskedastic and non-autocorrelated, $\text{var}(\varepsilon_{it+1}) = \sigma_e^2 I_{NT}$. Thus a simple instrumental variable estimator (2SLS) will give consistent estimates. We need 2SLS and not OLS as r_{it} and ε_{it+1} are expected to be correlated since they share the common forecast error over $(t, t + 1)$. There are a number of reasons why ε_{it+1} is expected to have a more complicated error-structure. First, there may be individual specific effects present in (24), viz. $\varepsilon_{it+1} = \eta_i + U_{it}$. If η_i is correlated with the instruments, the conventional solution (under the assumption of strict exogeneity) is to run IV regression on

$$\Delta C_{it+1} - \overline{\Delta C_i} = b(r_{it} - \bar{r}_i) + \varepsilon_{it+1} - \bar{\varepsilon}_i. \tag{25}$$

However, when the instruments are only weakly exogenous, $(\varepsilon_{it+1} - \bar{\varepsilon}_i)$ can be correlated with the instruments contemporaneously since we cannot rule out the possibility that $E(\varepsilon_{it}Z_{is}) \neq 0$ for $t < s$. The solution is to first-difference (24) and apply GMM estimation using instruments B_{4i} given in (13).

---

[7] The computational burden in implementing the 3SLS can be formidable. Kinal and Lahiri (1990, 1993) have suggested an alternative algorithm which can simplify the calculations under certain circumstances. See also Haque, Lahiri and Montiel (1990, 1993).

[8] For example, Hall (1988) and Zeldes (1989).

Following Kinal and Lahiri (1993), we found it convenient to implement the GMM estimation by stacking the data first by time and then by individual. Thus, we set (24) as a system of six equations (one for each $t = 1, 2, \ldots, 6$) and use different instruments in different equations.

One of the principal issues discussed by all authors using PSID consumption data is the problem of measurement errors. If $\ln C_{it+1}$ is observed with a random measurement error δ_{it+1} then even in the absence of individual effects, the error will be MA(1). That is

$$e_{it+1} = \delta_{it+1} - \delta_{it} + U_{it+1} . \tag{26}$$

Hence

$$\text{Cov}(\varepsilon_{it}\varepsilon_{js}) = \begin{cases} \sigma_u^2 + 2\sigma_g^2 & \text{if } i = j, \ t = s, \\ -\sigma_g^2 & \text{if } i = j, \ |t - s| = 1, \\ 0 & \text{otherwise} . \end{cases} \tag{27}$$

Note that with individual effects present, i.e.,

$$e_{it+1} = \delta_{it+1} - \delta_{it} + \eta_i + U_{it+1} , \tag{28}$$

η_i can be eliminated by first-differencing. The covariance structure of the resulting error $\varepsilon_{it+1} - \varepsilon_{it} = \Delta\varepsilon_{it+1} = \delta_{it+1} - 2\delta_{it} + U_{it+1} - U_{it}$ will be

$$\text{Cov}(\Delta\varepsilon_{it}, \Delta\varepsilon_{js}) = \begin{cases} 2\sigma_\varepsilon^2 + 6\sigma_g^2 & \text{if } i = j, \ t = s, \\ -\sigma_\varepsilon^2 - 4\sigma_g^2 & \text{if } i = j, \ |t - s| = 1, \\ \sigma_g^2 & \text{if } i = j, \ |t - s| = 2, \\ 0 & \text{otherwise} . \end{cases} \tag{29}$$

In other words, the $\Delta\varepsilon_{it}$ will have MA(2) errors. Note that since we are estimating (24) as a system of six SUR equations, the $NT \times NT$ covariance matrix $\Omega = \Sigma_{6\times6} \otimes I_N$ will be obtained very conveniently and the (ij) off-diagonal element of Σ will give an estimate of the $|i - j|$-th autocorrelation in the residuals.

We reported the estimated equations in Table 1. Following Keane and Runkle (1992) we have also included an age variable (Age_{it}) in (24) to control for demographic and other factors. Simple 2SLS and IV-within estimates are presented in first two columns. GMM1 estimates are based on a full set of instruments A_{1i} with assumed strong exogeneity, see equation (9). These estimates should be inconsistent. The last three columns of Table 1 are GMM estimates, assuming weakly exogenous instruments. GMM3 is fully efficient since it is based on A_{2i} in (12). GMM2 is consistent but not fully efficient since here we only use the latest instruments Z_{it}. GMM4 is obtained from the first-difference equation assuming the existence of η_i which are correlated with the instruments. GMM4 used B_{4i} as instruments, see equation (14). GMM1–3 were based on MA(1) whereas GMM4 assumed errors to be moving average of

Table 1
IV estimation of the Euler equation

	2SLS	Within	GMM1	GMM2	GMM3	GMM4
Const.	0.0854*	–	0.0713*	0.1470*	0.1467*	–
	(0.0271)		(0.0129)	(0.0358)	(0.0350)	
r_{it}	0.2537	0.4572*	0.2354	1.1997*	1.111*	1.029
	(0.1516)	(0.1653)	(0.1284)	(0.3530)	(0.2635)	(0.9901)
Age	−0.002*	−0.0145*	−0.0017*	−0.0024*	−0.0024*	0.0065
	(0.0006)	(0.0041)	(0.0002)	(0.0008)	(0.0008)	(0.0240)

Note: All GMM estimates are corrected for MA errors. GMM1 takes all instruments to be strictly exogenous. Rest of the GMM estimates are based on the assumption that instruments are predetermined. GMM2 uses only the latest set of instruments, whereas GMM3 uses the full optimal set. GMM4 is on first-difference Euler equation with full set of instruments. An estimate marked (*) means it is significant at the 5% level of significance. Standard errors are in parentheses. All estimates use the instrumental variables-hours worked in period $t-2$, log of disposable income in $t-2$, after-tax real interest rates in period t-2 based on passbook and T-bill rates, and a constant.

order 2. As expected, the gain in efficiency as we go from GMM2 to GMM3 is remarkable since the estimated standard error of the main parameter b is reduced from 0.35 to 0.26, whereas the parameter estimates remained very close to each other. The validity of the strong exogeneity assumption can be studied by testing the goodness of the additional instruments in GMM1 over those in GMM3. The difference between the minimized values of the GMM objective function times N gives the usual Hausman (1978) statistic which was calculated to be 194.25, thereby rejecting the strong exogeneity assumption quite resoundingly. The test for fixed effects can be similarly conducted by comparing the minimized values of the GMM criterion functions under GMM3 and GMM4. The statistic was calculated to be 1.916 which was not significant at the 5% level. Thus, like Keane and Runkle (1992) we find no evidence in favor of correlated fixed effects.

The existence of aggregate shocks can be very conveniently tested in our framework of SURE system. The presence of a common component in ΔC_{it+1} that was not explained by expected interest rates can lead to inconsistent parameter estimates in short panels. The composite error now becomes $\varepsilon_{it+1} = \lambda_t + U_{it}$ and as we have explained before, the sample version of the orthogonality condition $E(\varepsilon_{it+1} Z_{is})$ need not be zero for all $t \geqslant s$ even where the number of households is large (see equation (16)). We tested the importance of time dummies by allowing the intercepts in each of the six equations to vary without changing the optimal instruments set since each equation has already a constant in its list of instruments. The resultant Hausman test statistic computed in the same fashion as before was again very small and statistically insignificant.

The results of our specification tests are supported by the estimated variance–covariance matrices of residuals based on GMM3 and GMM4 estimations. GMM3 yielded

$$\hat{\Sigma} = \begin{pmatrix} 0.123 & & & & & \\ -0.047 & 0.119 & & & & \\ 0.008 & -0.063 & 0.137 & & & \\ 0.001 & -0.000 & -0.050 & 0.127 & & \\ -0.004 & -0.006 & -0.002 & -0.064 & 0.133 & \\ 0.001 & 0.002 & -0.001 & -0.007 & -0.038 & 0.126 \end{pmatrix} \qquad (27')$$

whereas GMM4 gave

$$\hat{\Sigma} = \begin{pmatrix} 0.338 & & & & \\ -0.239 & 0.383 & & & \\ 0.060 & -0.249 & 0.364 & & \\ 0.000 & 0.053 & -0.239 & 0.391 & \\ 0.004 & -0.006 & 0.056 & -0.228 & 0.337 \end{pmatrix}. \qquad (29')$$

The above two estimated matrices are consistent with the hypothesis that there are substantial measurement errors in consumption and that individual effects are not important. By comparing (27) with (27') we expect the diagonal terms to be $\sigma_u^2 + 2\sigma_\delta^2$, the MA(1) terms to be $-\sigma_\delta^2$ and all other entries to be zero. The results clearly support the hypothesis. On the average σ_u^2 and σ_δ^2 are estimated to be 0.022 and 0.053 respectively. By comparing (29) with (29') we again see the remarkable feature that, as expected, all autocorrelations in excess of order two are essentially zero, and the estimates are consistent with our previous $\sigma_\delta^2 = 0.053$ and $\sigma_u^2 = 0.022$. Since variance of $\ln(C_{it+1})$ over the sample was 0.233, we find that measurement errors constitute nearly 23% of measured consumption. The severity of measurement error problem in the consumption data from the PSID surveys has been of concern to all researchers who have used these surveys.[9] One advantage of the GMM framework is that these complications can be handled in a very convenient and effective manner.[10]

6. Conclusion

In panel data models with rational expectations the conventional fixed-effects or random-effects treatment of the error components will lead to inconsistency because instruments are only predetermined, and not strictly exogenous. Thus, the efficient instrumental variable procedures that have been developed in recent years by Hausman and Taylor (1981), Amemiya and MaCurdy (1986), Breusch, Mizon and Schmidt (1989) and others are no longer applicable. Panel data models with lagged dependent variables also pose similar problems. The

---

[9] See, for instance, Altonji and Siow (1987), Hall and Mishkin (1982), Hayashi (1987), Zeldes (1989), and Runkle (1991).

[10] We used TSP-PC (version 4.2) to obtain GMM estimates.

generalized method of moments framework seems to be the appropriate framework in which estimation and tests can be carried out efficiently. Fixed effects are handled by first-differencing rather than demeaning the variables. The appropriate GMM procedure can be interpreted as a 3SLS procedure with different instruments in different equations. Of course, as is well known, the GMM procedure will accommodate a very general error covariance matrix involving conditional heteroskedasticity and autocorrelation. The assumption of strong exogeneity is pitted against that of only predeterminatedness in terms of the use of certain contaminated instruments, whose validity can be tested using the Hausman principle. Tests for the existence of aggregate shocks, individual effects and measurement errors are considered in a unified framework. We illustrate the procedures by estimating the Euler equation of the intertemporal life-cycle consumption theory using PSID panel data. The empirical results clearly show that the extent of inconsistency and incorrect statistical inference can be substantial if one uses the instruments as strictly exogenous when they are only predetermined.

Data appendix

We followed Keane and Runkle (1992) to construct a balanced panel on 514 households over 1975–1982. This gave us a total of 3084 observations. For all regressions, the instrument list included a constant, the household's hours worked in period $t - 2$, the log of family's disposable income in period $t - 2$, the value of the after-tax real interest rate for passbook and 12-month treasury-bill interest rates in period $t - 2$. A household is included in the sample if actual data (not imputed) were available for all variables, no change occurred in the marital status of the head, or the household head is not a farmer or self-employed. Following Runkle (1991), we also excluded all households with head aged 65 years and older. This is the reason we ended up having 514 households rather than 627, as in Keane and Runkle (1992). Annual hours of work are directly available in the surveys; all other variables were constructed from data available in the survey. Real food consumption, disposable income and taxes were computed by following Keane and Runkle exactly. The after-tax interest rate was computed as $(1 - \Theta_{it})R_t$ where Θ_{it} is the marginal tax rate and R_t is the nominal interest rate. The average annual passbook savings rate was used as the interest rate. The after-tax real interest rate was computed by subtracting the actual inflation rate over the period $(t + 1, t)$ from R_t.

Acknowledgment

I thank Professor G. S. Maddala for many useful comments on an earlier version of the paper, and Anthony Davies and Ju Young Lim for their help with the empirical example of Section 5. However, for remaining errors and omissions the responsibility is solely mine.

References

Ahn, S. and P. Schmidt (1990). Efficient estimation of models for dynamic panel data. Unpublished Manuscript, Michigan State University, Department of Economics.

Altonji, J. G. and A. Siow (1987). Testing the response of consumption to income change with (noisy) panel data. *Quart. J. Econom.* **102**, 293–328.

Amemiya, T. and T. E. MaCurdy (1986). Instrumental-variables estimation of an error-components model. *Econometrica* **54**, 869–880.

Arellano, M. and O. Bover (1990). Another look at the instrumental-variable estimation of error-components models. Discussion Paper 7, London School of Economics, Center for Economic Performance.

Arellano, M. and S. Bond (1991). Some tests of specification for panel data: Monte Carlo evidence and an application to employment equations. *Rev. Econom. Stud.* **58**, 277–297.

Ashenfelter, D. and G. Solon (1982). Longitudinal labor market data-sources, use and limitations. In: *What's Happening to American Labor Force and Productivity Measurements?* Upjohn Institute for Employment Research, Kalamazoo, MI.

Atri, S. and K. Lahiri (1984). Estimated income and price elasticities of demand for hospital care free of quality bias. *Econom. Lett.* **17**, 387–392.

Balestra, P. and M. Nerlove (1966). Pooling cross section and time series data in the estimation of a dynamic model: The demand for natural gas. *Econometrica* **34**, 585–612.

Baltagi, B. H. (1981). Simultaneous equations with error components. *J. Econometrics* **17**, 189–200.

Baltagi, B. H. (1984). A monte carlo study for pooling time-series of cross-section data in the simultaneous equations model. *Internat. Econom. Rev.* **25**, 603–624.

Bhargava, A. (1991). Identification and panel data models with endogenous regressors. *Rev. Econom. Stud.* **58**, 129–140.

Bhargava, A. and J. D. Sargan (1983). Estimating dynamic random effects models from panel data covering short time periods. *Econometrica* **51**, 1635–1659.

Blundell, R., S. Bond, M. Devereux and F. Schiantarelli (1992). Investment and Tobin's Q: Evidence from company panel data. *J. Econometrics* **51**, 233–257.

Borus, M. E. (1982). An inventory of longitudinal data sets of interest to economists. *Rev. Public Data Use* **10**, 113–126.

Breusch, T., G. E. Mizon and P. Schmidt (1989). Efficient estimation using panel data. *Econometrica* **57**, 695–700.

Brown, B. W. and S. Maital (1981). What do economists know? An empirical study of experts expectations. *Econometrica* **49**, 491–504.

Brundy, J. and D. W. Jorgenson (1971). Efficient estimation of simultaneous equations systems using investments variables. *Rev. Econom. Statist.* **53**, 207–224.

Chamberlain, G. (1982). Multivariate regression models for panel data. *J. Econometrics* **18**, 5–46.

Chamberlain, G. (1984). Panel data. In: Z. Grilliches, M. Intrilligator, eds., *Handbook of Econometrics*, Vol. 2. North-Holland, Amsterdam, 1247–1313.

Chamberlain, G. (1987). Asymptotic efficiency in estimation with conditional moment restrictions. *J. Econometrics* **34**, 305–334.

Chamberlain, G. (1992). Comment: Sequential moment restructions in panel data. *J. Business Econom. Statist.* **10**, 20–26.

Cornwell, C., P. Schmidt and D. Wyhowski (1992). Simultaneous equations and panel data. *J. Econometrics* **51**, 151–181.

Cumby, R. E., J. Huizinga and M. Obstfeld (1983). Two-step two-stage least squares estimation in models with rational expectations. *J. Econometrics* **21**, 333–355.

Dielman, T. E. (1989). *Pooled Cross-sectional and Time Series Data Analysis*. Marcel Dekker, New York.

Eichenbaum, M. S., L. P. Hansen and K. J. Singleton (1988). A time series analysis of representative agent models of consumption and leisure choice under uncertainty. *Quart. Econom.* **102**, 51–78.

Fuller, W. A. and G. E. Battese (1973). Transformations for estimation of linear models with nested error structure. *J. Amer. Statist. Assoc.* **68**, 626–632.

Fuller, W. A. and G. E. Battese (1974). Estimation of linear models with cross-error structure. *J. Econometrics* **2**, 67–78.

Hall, R. E. (1988). Consumption and real interest rates. *J. Politic. Econom.* **96**, 339–357.

Hall, R. E. and F. S. Mishkin (1982). The sensitivity of consumption to transitory income: Estimates from panel data on households. *Econometrica* **50**, 1029–1054.

Hansen, L. P. (1982). Large sample properties of generalized method of moments estimators. *Econometrica* **50**, 1029–1054.

Hansen, L. P. and R. J. Hodrick (1980). Forward exchange rates as optimal preditors of future spot rates: An econometric analysis. *J. Politic. Econom.* **88**, 829–853.

Hausman, J. (1978). Specification tests in econometrics. *Econometrica* **46**, 1251–1271.

Hausman, J. and W. Taylor (1981). Panel data and unobservable individual effects. *Econometrica* **49**, 1377–1398.

Haque, N. U., K. Lahiri and P. Montiel (1990). A macroeconometric model for developing countries. *IMF Staff Papers* **37**, 537–559.

Haque, N. U., K. Lahiri and P. Montiel (1993). Estimation of a macroeconomic model with rational expectations and capital controls for developing countries. *J. Dev. Econom.*, to appear.

Hayashi, F. (1987). Tests for liquidity constraints: A critical survey. In: T. Bewley, ed., *Advances in Econometrics – Fifth World Congress*, Vol. II. Cambridge, Univ. Press, Cambridge, 91–120.

Hayashi, F. (1992). Comment. *J. Business Econom. Statist.* **10**, 15–17.

Hayashi, F. and C. Sims (1983). Nearly efficient estimation of time series models with pre-determined but not exogenous instruments. *Econometrica* **51**, 783–792.

Heckman, J. J. and B. Singer (1985). *Longitudinal Analysis of Labor Market Data*. Cambridge Univ. Press, Cambridge.

Holtz-Eakin, D., W. Newey and H. Rosen (1988). Estimating vector autoregressions with panel data. *Econometrica* **56**, 1371–1395.

Hsiao, C. (1986). *Analysis of Panel Data*. Cambridge Univ. Press, New York.

Keane, M. and D. Runkle (1992). On the estimation of panel data models with serial correlation when instruments are not strictly exogenous. *J. Business Econom. Statist.* **10**, 1–9.

Kinal, T. and K. Lahiri (1988). A model of ex ante real interest rates and derived inflation forecasts. *J. Amer. Statist. Assoc.* **83**, 665–673.

Kinal, T. and K. Lahiri (1990). A computational algorithm for multiple equation models with panel data. *Econom. Lett.* **34**, 143–146.

Kinal, T. and K. Lahiri (1993). On the estimation of simultaneous equations error components models with an application to a model of developing country foreign trade. *J. Appl. Econometrics* **8**, 81–92.

Lahiri, K. (1981). *Econometrics of Inflationary Expectations*. North-Holland, Amsterdam.

McCallum, B. T. (1976). Rational expectations and the natural rate hypothesis: Some consistent estimates. *Econometrica* **44**, 43–52.

Maddala, G. S. (1987a). Recent developments in the econometrics of panel data analysis. *Transportation Res.* **21**, 303–326.

Maddala, G. S. (1987b). Limited dependent variable models using panel data. *J. Human Resources* **22**, 307–338.

Mundlak, Y. (1978). On the pooling of time series and cross-section data. *Econometrica* **46**, 69–85.

Newey, W. K. (1985a). Maximum likelihood specification testing and conditional moments tests. *Econometrica* **53**, 1047–1070.

Newey, W. K. (1985b). Generalized method of moments specification testing. *J. Econometrics* **29**, 229–256.

Newey, W. K. (1990). Efficient instrumental variables estimation of non-linear models. *Econometrica* **58**, 809–837.

Robinson, P. (1991). Best nonlinear three-stage least squares estimating of certain econometric models. *Econometrica* **59**, 755–786.

Runkle, D. E. (1991). Liquidity constraints and the permanent income hypothesis: Evidence from panel data. *J. Monetary Econom.* **97**, 73–98.

Schmidt, P., S. C. Ahn and D. Wyhowski (1992). Comment. *J. Business Econom. Statist.* **10**, 10–14.

White, H. (1984). *Asymptotic Theory for Econometricians*. Academic Press, New York.

White, H. and I. Domowitz (1984). Nonlinear regression with dependent observations. *Econometrica* **52**, 143–161.

Wickens, M. R. (1982). The efficient estimation of econometric models with rational expectations. *Rev. Econom. Stud.* **49**, 55–67.

Zeldes, S. (1989). Consumption and liquidity constraints: An empirical investigation. *J. Politic. Econom.* **97**, 305–346.

G. S. Maddala, C. R. Rao and H. D. Vinod, eds., *Handbook of Statistics, Vol. 11*
© 1993 Elsevier Science Publishers B.V. All rights reserved.

27

Continuous Time Financial Models: Statistical Applications of Stochastic Processes

K. R. Sawyer

1. Introduction

If there were to be one characterization of the complexity, yet curiously the utility of modern finance, it would be in the use of continuous time models. The complexity of these models has distanced a significant number of practitioners except in rudimentary applications of the pricing of derivative assets. But the utility of these models is so powerful in pricing virtually any financial claim on a firm, that the number of applications in continuous time proliferates. Indeed Melino (1991) has documented this trend, illustrating that the proportion of articles using continuous time processes in four leading finance journals increased from 0.8% in 1970 to 17.1% in 1989.

Surveys of continuous time methods are also prolific; it is appropriate that some insightful surveys have been provided by Robert Merton who introduced Itô calculus to economics in his consideration of the problem of lifetime consumption and portfolio selection for an individual consumer under uncertainty (Merton 1971). The surveys to which I refer are Merton (1975) and Merton (1990), the latter a compilation of his writings over twenty years. From different perspectives, Malliaris (1983) and Melino (1991) have also reviewed continuous time methods in finance.

There are two principal justifications for the use of continuous time formulations in finance, the first theoretical and the second due to the richness of stochastic calculus. As Merton (1975) asserts, in multiperiod discrete time portfolio models, there are four time intervals relevant to the investor:

(1) The *trading interval*: the period between successive transactions.

(2) The *decision interval(h)*: the period between successive decisions.

(3) The *planning interval*: the length of time for which the investor gives non-zero weight to the utility of wealth function.

(4) The *observation interval*: the period between successive observations as sampled by the researcher.

The solution to the discrete time portfolio problem typically depends on the decision interval h. For if the solution were invariant to h, the portfolio decision for investors who hold portfolios for 20 years, and for those who revise daily, would be equivalent, a clearly implausible outcome. There are two possibilities; either specify a value for h or allow h to be stochastic. The continuous time solution ($h = 0$) has been shown to approximate a wide class of stochastic decision interval models with HARA utility functions (Magill and Constantinides, 1976) and a wide class of non-stochastic decision interval models for which h is small. This last approximation seems even more appropriate given the contemporary use of high frequency data (such as tick-by-tick and intra-daily data).

The convergence of discrete time asset models to a limiting form continuous time model involves the *convergence of the information* structure governing the evolution of asset prices and the *convergence of the stochastic process* describing asset prices. Willinger and Taqqu (1991) have shown that the limiting model can preserve characteristics hitherto only well defined in discrete markets, characteristics such as absence of arbitrage and completeness. Nelson (1990) has also shown that certain empirically rich discrete stochastic processes, such as the ARCH process, can be approximated by continuous time stochastic processes. These contributions strengthen the contention that continuous time financial models are indeed proper approximations to a wide class of discrete time formulations.

The processes generating latent financial variables are logically continuous time processes. For example, the processes describing the evolution of decisions, of information (Ross, 1989), of tastes and technology (Cox, Ingersoll and Ross, 1985) and of primitive asset prices (Black and Scholes, 1973) are best prescribed in a continuous time setting. Furthermore, theoretical restrictions are most easily imposed on the continuous time latent process rather than their discrete approximations, analogous to the arguments in continuous time econometric models (Bergstrom, 1988).

While the theoretical justifications for continuous time processes in finance are strong, there is arguably a more compelling reason for their use, due to the richness of Itô's stochastic calculus. Itô (1946, 1951) developed a consistent and operational calculus for analysing a set of continuous time random processes (Itô processes). The underpinnings of this calculus lie in the work of a British botanist Robert Brown who in 1827 sought to describe the perpetual irregular motions of particles immersed in a fluid. The Brownian motion identified in 1827 was later fully characterised by Einstein and Smoluchowski (see Doob, 1953) as a continuous time stochastic process with independent Gaussian increments, and by Wiener (1923) as having sample paths continuous with probability one. Wiener provided the mathematical antecedents for Itô who first established the conditions for the existence and uniqueness of solutions to stochastic differential equations (SDEs). The quintessential result of Itô was the definition of a stochastic integral when the integrator is a Brownian motion. Itô defined his integral as the limiting sum of terms composed of *non-anticipating* step functions, stochastic functions whose present increments are uncorrelated with future increments. The stochastic integral of Itô is one of many possible definitions of a stochastic integral; for example a well-known alternative is the Stratonovich (1966) integral. The use of non-anticipating functions in the Itô integral reflects the theoretical notion that agents cannot anticipate future price movements, and for this reason the Itô integral is often preferred in analysing intertemporal financial decisions.

Itô calculus confers two powerful results for the study of asset pricing in a complete market. First, a non-linear transformation of an Itô process is itself an Itô process under mild regularity conditions. This implies, for example, that the prices of contingent claims and indeed the wealth process itself will follow an Itô process given an Itô process for the underlying asset. Secondly, and more importantly, the precise dynamics of the transformed process may be deduced by using an additional result, Itô's lemma. It is this second result which permits the pricing of derivative assets as in the Black–Scholes option pricing formula. Indeed, the approach can be applied to the firm as a whole to price the entire capital structure. Huang (1985) has provided the conditions under which the complete price system may be represented by Itô processes; essentially these conditions are the absence of arbitrage opportunities in the economy and the existence of an information structure generated by a Brownian filtration.

The characterisation of the complete price system by Itô processes, while theoretically appealing, has often been found to be empirically inappropriate. In particular, Itô processes are typically misspecified in three important ways. First, financial innovations are often more realistically modelled as discrete jumps, rather than by the continuous sample paths of Itô processes. This contention has a long pedigree; Kendall in 1946 suggested such an innovation process and solutions to both the SDE generated by jump processes and to the prices of derivative assets based on jump processes are well established (see Kushner, 1984; Merton, 1976; Cox and Ross, 1976). Secondly, the assumption of a constant variance rate of diffusion in the simplest Itô processes is empirically questionable; such simple models have been replaced by heteroscedastic and stochastic volatility models, for which closed form solutions to the SDE or to the prices of derivative assets are not assured. Finally, Gaussian innovations have been replaced by innovations which better reflect the leptokurtosis in asset prices. The development of stochastic processes which exhibit greater empirical fidelity has not been costless; both the solutions to the SDE and to the pricing of derivative assets must usually be determined numerically. It is not surprising then that another literature more appealing to financial practitioners has emerged, whereby simple Itô processes are used to describe asset prices, and the consequent misspecification of the data generating process and the mispricing of derivative assets is assessed (see Davis, 1991 for an example).

While finance theory and the existence of a supportive stochastic calculus both provide strong justifications for the use of continuous time models, empirical considerations often dominate. There are two empirical issues in particular. First, the measurement of economic and financial data can take many forms; for example variables point sampled with fixed frequency or with random frequency, or variables observed as integrals (flows). By formalising the mapping from the *operational* time of the latent continuous time process to the *calendar* time of the observed process, an empirically rich stochastic process encompassing all types of economic variable can be formulated. In such a setting, continuous time models are clearly preferred. They are also preferred for accurately representing the dynamics of the latent continuous time process. For, as Sims (1971) has shown, the dynamics of some approximating discrete time process may be quite misleading. Unfortunately, continuous time processes lack the empirical acuity required for high frequency data, such as transactions and intra-daily data. High frequency data is replete with empirical anomalies, such as day of the week effects, heteroscedasticity and heterokurtosis. It is a paradox of modern finance that continuous time processes perform relatively better for low frequency sampling (e.g., monthly), where the decision interval is large, and rather poorly for high frequency data where the decision interval is small. In part, this is due to a higher incidence of theoretical anomalies in high frequency data, such as noise trading (Black, 1986).

It is important to distinguish the continuous time processes reviewed in the present paper from another class of continuous time models whose literature is well represented by Phillips (1974), Bergstrom (1976) and Harvey and Stock (1985). The processes that we consider satisfy non-linear first order stochastic differential equations while the Phillips and Bergstrom processes satisfy n-th order linear stochastic differential equations. The non-linear first order processes in finance are typically restricted to be generated by mixtures of Gaussian diffusion processes and Poisson jump processes. Lo (1988) and Melino (1991, p. 18) both discuss the difference between the non-linear first order and n-th order linear paradigms, and why the finance literature has tended to adopt the former. Essentially, non-linear first order processes tend to be preferred because of the non-linear structure of the conditional first moments of asset returns, but also because higher order processes may not be consistent with weak efficiency.

The structure of the present paper is as follows. In Section 2, the theoretical preliminaries and general theory of continuous time processes in finance is presented. In Section 3, the discussion centers on more specific issues in estimation and inference.

2. Theoretical issues

2.1. Preliminaries

There are now hierarchical surveys of stochastic processes in finance. Readers are referred to three collections of writings:

(1) The statistical literature inter alia Kopp (1984), Karlin and Taylor

(1981), Jacod and Shiryaev (1987), Karatzas and Shreve (1988) and Protter (1990).

(2) The stochastic differential equations literature; for example Schuss (1980) and Wu (1985).

(3) Stochastic processes in finance; Duffie (1988) and Melino (1991, Appendix).

Let $T = [0, \infty)$ be the set of all *trading dates* for an infinite time horizon. To describe an investor's information structure, let (Ω, F, P) be a probability space. Ω denotes the set of all states of nature ω, F is a σ-algebra of subsets of Ω called *events*, and P is a probability measure on F. The information available to an investor at time $t \in T$ is specified by the sub-σ-algebra $F_t \subseteq F$ so that at time t investors know which events in F_t have occurred and which have not. When investors learn without forgetting, the entire information structure is a non-decreasing family $F = \{F_0 \subseteq F_1 \subseteq \cdots F_\infty\}$ of sub-σ-algebra called a *filtration*.

An N-dimensional *stochastic process* $X = (X_t: t \in T)$ is a map $X : T \times \Omega \to R^N$ such that the maps $\omega \to X_t(\omega)$ are measurable $\forall t \in T$. The function $t \to X_t(\omega)$ mapping T into R^N is called the *sample path* (or trajectory) of the stochastic process. In financial data, it is common to assume the sample path to be right-continuous on $[0, \infty)$ with finite left-hand limits on $(0, \infty)$. These processes are labelled *RCLL*, alternatively cadlag, a French acronym for continu à droite, limites à gauche. RCLL processes include diffusions, for which the sample data is also left-continuous on $(0, \infty)$, and jump processes for which the sample path is left-discontinuous. The left limit of the process at time t is denoted by X_{t-} and the jump by $\Delta X_t = X_t - X_{t-}$.

A stochastic process is *measurable* if the mapping $(t, \omega) \to X_t(\omega)$ is jointly measurable. In particular, RCLL processes are measurable. A process is *adapted* to the filtration F if X_t if F_t-measurable $\forall t$. Clearly, every process is adapted to the so-termed *natural filtration* F_t^X generated by the process itself, i.e.,

$$F_t^X = \sigma(X_s; 0 \leqslant s \leqslant t) \tag{2.1.1}$$

the σ-field generated by the process up to time t.

The principal reason for defining RCLL and adapted processes is to introduce an important class of stochastic processes in finance, namely continuous time martingales. The filtration F is further assumed to be right-continuous, that is, $F_t = \bigcap_{s>t} F_s$. In this case the probability space is called a *filtered probability space* or *stochastic basis* and denoted (Ω, F, F, P). A real-valued, adapted process X on the stochastic basis (Ω, F, F, P), whose P-almost sure paths are RCLL, is called a *martingale* (resp. *submartingale*, resp. *supermartingale*) if for $s \leqslant t$:

(a) $E(|X_t^j|) < \infty$ for each component X_t^j; i.e., the process is integrable.

(b) $X_s = E(X_t \,|\, F_s)$ (resp. $X_s \leqslant E(X_t \,|\, F_s)$, resp. $X_s \geqslant E(X_t \,|\, F_s))$. $\tag{2.1.2}$

A martingale is *square-integrable* if $\sup_{t \geqslant 0} E(|X_t^j|^2) < \infty$ for each X_t^j.

The martingale property (2.1.2) is a sufficient condition for a price system not to admit any arbitrage opportunities. For this reason, it is common to characterize asset pricing using martingales. Furthermore, it is also common to assume square-integrability, due to a well-defined theory of stochastic integration for such processes developed by Kunita and Watanabe (1967). The purpose of the theory of *stochastic integration* discussed in Section 2.2 below, is to give meaning to the notion of a stochastic integral (and differential) for the widest possible class of stochastic processes. Square-integrable martingales are one such class; two other classes are Levy processes and semi-martingales.

An adapted process $X = (X_t)$ is a *Levy* process if

(a) X has *increments independent of the past*: that is, $X_t - X_s$ is independent of F_s.

(b) X has *stationary increments*: that is, $X_t - X_s$ has the same distribution as X_{t-s}, $0 \leqslant s < t < \infty$.

(c) X_t is *continuous in probability*: that is, $\lim_{t \to s} X_t = X_s$, where the limit is taken in probability.

Levy processes were the first stochastic processes to be studied in a modern way, and include Brownian motions and Poisson processes as special cases.

A *Brownian motion* is a Levy process for which $X_t - X_s$ is a Gaussian variable with mean zero and variance–covariance matrix $(t - s)C$, for a given non-random matrix C. When C is the identity matrix, we term the process a *standard Brownian* or *Wiener process*. The Brownian motion with $E(|X_0^j|) < \infty$ is a martingale. When the mean of the process is non-zero, $\mu(t - s)$, the process becomes a *Brownian motion with drift* or a *regular multivariate diffusion process*. There are a number of characterisations of diffusion processes, inter alia:

(1) If X is a stochastic process with stationary independent increments, and for which the sample paths are P-a.s. continuous, then X is a diffusion process.

(2) A sufficient condition for a RCLL process to be a diffusion is that

$$\frac{1}{h} P\{|X_{t+h}^j(\omega) - X_t^j(\omega)| > \varepsilon \mid X_t(\omega) = x\} \to 0 \quad \text{when } \varepsilon > 0, \ \forall j, \omega .$$

(2.1.3)

This condition is called the *Dynkin condition*.

The drift and variance parameters of multivariate diffusions can be extended to more general forms as in the generalised Itô processes discussed in Section 2.2.

A *Poisson process* is a Levy process which is also an adapted counting process. Specifically, the increment $X_t - X_s$ counts the number of times that a strictly increasing sequence of positive random variables T_n ($n \geqslant 0$) occurs between the fixed times s and t. The Poisson process follows a Poisson distribution with parameter λ, the intensity or arrival rate of the process.

The widest class of processes for which stochastic integrals can be defined is the vector space of semimartingales. A *semimartingale* is a process X of the form $X = X_0 + M + A$ where X_0 is finite-valued and F_0-measurable, M is a local martingale with $M_0 = 0$ and A is a process with $A_0 = 0$ and whose sample path $t \to A_t(\omega)$ has finite variation over finite intervals $[0, t]$. Most of the processes hitherto considered are semimartingales, including Levy processes and square integrable martingales with RCLL paths. In general, continuous time stochastic processes in finance can be represented as a stochastic integral of bounded predictable processes with respect to a semimartingale, where X is *predictable* if X_t is F_{t-1}-measurable for $t \geqslant 1$ and X_0 is F_0-measurable. This is the focus of the next section.

2.2. Stochastic integrals and differentials

The latent stochastic processes in finance are often assumed to be generated by a first order non-linear SDE

$$dX_t = a(t, X_{t-}, \theta) \, dt + b(t, X_{t-}, \theta) \, dM_t, \tag{2.2.1}$$

where X is an N-dimensional stochastic process adapted to a filtered probability space $(\Omega, F, \mathbf{F}, P)$ in operational time, $\theta \in R^K$ is a vector of parameters, dM_t is a G-vector of semimartingales, $a(t, X_{t-}, \theta)$ is an N-vector of bounded predictable processes, and $b(t, X_{t-}, \theta)$ is an $N \times G$ matrix with components $b^{ij}(t, X_{t-}, \theta)$ bounded predictable processes. There may be some additional restrictions, such as in stochastic volatility models that the components of the bivariate semimartingale process are uncorrelated, or that when modelling bond price dynamics that the price converges to the face value at maturity. An equivalent representation to (2.2.1) is the stochastic integral equation

$$X_t = X_0 + \int_0^t a(\tau, X_{\tau-}, \theta) \, d\tau + \int_0^t b(\tau, X_{\tau-}, \theta) \, dM_\tau, \tag{2.2.2}$$

where X_0 is F_0-measurable. The differential form is often used as a convenient abbreviation.

Stochastic processes of this form have been applied to variables as diverse as mortgage values, values of unlevered firms, inventories, portfolio values, information flows, bond, equity and derivative prices; some of these applications are reviewed in Section 4. The justification for these continuous-time specifications is principally that important state variables such as technology and information evolve continuously and stochastically; unfortunately there has been a tendency to overuse rather simple specifications such as geometric Brownian motions, making few concessions to observed empirical regularities or to finance theory. This is in contrast to the derivation of the original Brownian motion from the Langevin equation which followed well prescribed laws of physics (see Schuss, 1980, pp. 39–43).

In finance, the processes used are predominantly univariate. Melino (1991) finds that less than 15% of continuous time applications are multivariate, and most of these are bivariate stochastic volatility models. The most commonly used financial processes are summarised as:

Brownian motion with drift (regular diffusion).

$$dX_t = \mu_t \, dt + \sigma_t \, dW_t \, . \tag{2.2.3}$$

W_t is a standard Brownian motion. The drift μ_t and volatility σ_t^2 are independent of X. This is rarely used, but is a benchmark model to which other models can be transformed.

Geometric Brownian motion (lognormal diffusion).

$$dX_t = \mu X_t \, dt + \sigma X_t \, dW_t \, . \tag{2.2.4}$$

The most widely used model for equity prices. First proposed by Samuelson (1965), and the basis of Black–Scholes option pricing, this process has two main limitations – that equity returns tend to be leptokurtic and that volatilities are time-varying.

Ornstein–Uhlenbeck (arithmetic Brownian motion).

$$dX_t = (a_1 + a_2 X_t) \, dt + \sigma \, dW_t \quad \text{for } a_2 < 0 \, . \tag{2.2.5}$$

This process can be used to characterise *mean reversion* in asset prices, and is the basis of the Vasicek (1977) model of the term structure.

Reflected Brownian Motion. Let Y_t follow a Brownian motion with drift. Then

$$X_t = |Y_t| \tag{2.2.6}$$

is called a reflected Brownian motion with drift. When X_t reaches zero, it returns immediately to positive values. The model has been applied by Longstaff (1989).

Brownian bridge.

$$dX_t = -\frac{X_t}{(1-t)} + \sigma \, dW_t \quad \text{for } 0 \leq t \leq 1 \, , \ X_0 = X_1 = 0 \, . \tag{2.2.7}$$

The Brownian bridge process is subjected to a restoring force which drives it back to zero. The restoring force strengthens through time until at $t = 1$ the process is zero with probability one. This process has been used to price default-free discount bonds where the price of the bond equals the face value at maturity (Ball and Torous, 1983).

Square root process.

$$dX_t = (a_1 + a_2 X_t) \, dt + \sigma \sqrt{X_t} \, dW_t \, . \tag{2.2.8}$$

This process has been posited for interest rates (Cox, Ingersoll and Ross, 1985).

Constant elasticity of variance (CEV)

$$dX_t = \mu X_t \, dt + \sigma X_t^{\beta/2} \, dW_t \, . \tag{2.2.9}$$

The CEV model has been used for stocks (Beckers, 1980), interest rates (Marsh and Rosenfeld, 1983) and options (Emanuel and Macbeth, 1982). The elasticity of return variance with respect to price equals $\beta - 2$, and if $\beta < 2$ volatility and price are inversely related capturing leverage effects. When $\beta = 2$, prices follow a lognormal diffusion, and for $\beta > 2$, the process can also be analysed but it follows different boundary behaviour.

Generalised constant elasticity of variance.

$$dX_t = (a_1 X_t^{-(1-\beta)} + a_2 X_t)\, dt + \sigma X_t^{\beta/2}\, dW_t . \tag{2.2.10}$$

This process has been studied by Marsh and Rosenfeld (1983) and includes as special cases the lognormal diffusion ($\beta = 2$), square root process ($\beta = 1$), and when $\beta = 0$, the process behaves much like an Ornstein–Uhlenbeck process, but without mean reversion.

Double square root process.

$$dX_t = a_1(\mu - \sqrt{X_t})\, dt + \sigma \sqrt{X_t}\, dW_t \qquad \mu = \sigma^2/4a_1 , \quad a_1 > 0 . \tag{2.2.11}$$

Longstaff (1989) fitted a double square process to interest rates and noted the reflective properties of the process at $X_t = 0$.

Generalised diffusions.

$$dX_t = a(X_t, t, \theta)\, dt + \sigma(X_t, t, \theta)\, dW_t \tag{2.2.12}$$

for which there is greater flexibility, at the possible cost of tractability in determining the stationary and transitional densities discussed below.

Jump processes.

$$dX_t = c(X_t, t, \theta)\, dN_t(\lambda) , \tag{2.2.13}$$

where $N_t(\lambda)$ is a continuous time Poisson process, i.e., N_t records the number of price jumps during dt and is distributed as Poisson($\lambda\, dt$). λ is called the intensity of the process and c the jump amplitude.

Generalised Itô processes (jump-diffusion processes).

$$dX_t = a(X_t, t, \theta)\, dt + b(X_t, t, \theta)\, dW_t + c(X_t, t, \theta)\, dN_t(\lambda) . \tag{2.2.14}$$

This is a mixture of the generalised diffusion and jump processes defined before.

Leptokurtic process.

$$X_t = W(Y_t) , \tag{2.2.15}$$

where W is a standard Brownian motion, and Y_t is a process of independent gamma increments with mean dt and variance $\sigma^2\, dt$. This has been used by Madan and Seneta (1987) and Madan and Milne (1987).

Diffusion–white noise process.

$$dX_t = a(X_t, t) + \sigma_1\, dW_t + \sigma_2\, dZ_t , \tag{2.2.16}$$

where dZ_t is a drawing from an $N(0, 1)$ distribution. This is a generalisation of both Brownian motion and white noise. As dt increases, so does the variance at a rate σ_1^2. When dt becomes infinitely small, the variance of dX_t does not converge to zero, but rather to a residual noise related variance σ_2^2. This process is discussed in Hoel (1972, Chapter 4) and Merville and Pieptea (1989, p. 203).

Heteroscedastic process.

$$dX_t = a(X_t, t)\, dt + \sigma(X_t, Y_t, t)\, dW_t,\qquad (2.2.17)$$

where Y_t is some set of exogenous variables. For example, in the pricing of bond options Schaefer and Schwartz (1987) use a process where the standard deviation is proportional to the bond's duration.

Stochastic volatility processes.

$$dX_t = \mu X_t\, dt + \sigma_t X_t\, dW_t\qquad (2.2.18)$$

with a number of possible stochastic processes for σ_t:

$$d(\ln \sigma_t) = a_1(a_2 - \sigma_t)\, dt + a_3\, dW_{2t}, \quad \text{(Chesney and Scott, 1989)},$$
$$d\sigma_t = a_1(a_2 - \sigma_t)\, dt + a_3\, dW_{2t}, \quad \text{(Scott, 1987)},$$
$$d\sigma_t = a_1(a_2 - \sigma_t)\, dt + a_3\, dW_{2t}, \quad \text{(Hull and White, 1987)},$$
$$d\sigma_t = a_1\sigma_t\, dt + a_2\sigma_t\, dW_{2t}, \quad \text{(Johnson and Shanno, 1987)}.$$

These are well summarised by Taylor (1990). The process W_{2t} is another Wiener process, typically assumed independent of W_t.

The theory of stochastic integration which determines solutions to the SDE (2.2.1) began with Itô (1944) who defined an integral of a bounded measurable adapted process with respect to a Brownian motion. Briefly, we consider integrals of the form $\int b(\tau, X_{\tau-}, \theta)\, dM_\tau$ as in (2.2.2). For ease of exposition, we restrict the analysis to univariate processes (for the multivariate generalisation see Stroock and Varadhan, 1979). If the integrand b were a continuous process, and the differential dM a process of bounded variation on compact intervals $[t_k, t_{k+1}]$, the Riemann–Stieltjes integral would be defined in the usual sense as the limit of approximating sums. However, the Brownian motion process has paths of infinite variation on compact sets, so that the Riemann–Stieltjes integral is not defined. The idea of Itô was to restrict the integrands to those that could not see into the future increments. Formally, the Itô integral is defined to be

$$I_W(b) = \int b(\tau, X_{\tau-}, \theta)\, dW_t = \lim_{n\to\infty} \sum_{k=0}^{n-1} b(t_k, X_{t_k-}, \theta)[W(t_{k+1}) - W(t_k)]$$

$$\text{for max } |t_{k+1} - t_k| \to 0, \qquad (2.2.19)$$

where the integrand b_t is assumed to be non-anticipating, that is, independent of future increments in the Wiener process $W(t + s) - W(t)$. Non-anticipating is an older term for a process which is adapted to the filtration $\boldsymbol{F}$. The integral so defined has two fundamental properties of an integral, namely $I_W(b)$ is linear and satisfies a version of the bounded convergence theorem. However, the integral will differ markedly from the Riemann–Stieltjes integral; for example

$$\int_a^b W_\tau \, dW_\tau = \tfrac{1}{2}[W_b^2 - W_a^2] - \tfrac{1}{2}[b - a] \tag{2.2.20}$$

a result which can be proved quite simply by using the properties of telescoping sums and probability limits. Other types of stochastic integral have been defined for modelling physical phenomena, such as the backward integral and the Stratonovich (1965) integral. The Itô integral is particularly appropriate in finance since the non-anticipating process is consistent with market efficiency.

The Itô integral has been successively extended to more general differentials and to bounded predictable processes as in (2.2.2). An abridged bibliographic history would emphasise the following contributions for more general differentials and integrands:

(1) Doob (1953), *Martingales*.
(2) Kunita and Watanabe (1967), *Square-integrable martingales*.
(3) Meyer (1967), *Predictable integrands*.
(4) Meyer (1976), *Semimartingales*.

As a practical consideration, we are concerned primarily with the stochastic integrals associated with the processes defined in (2.2.3) to (2.2.18) and not with more general semimartingale processes, for which solutions to the SDE may be intractable, if they exist at all. The stochastic integral so defined determines the solution process of the SDE and its statistical properties. In the following sections, we discuss the existence and uniqueness of solutions to particular SDEs, and the statistical properties of those solutions, namely the conditional moments, the transitional density functions and the stationary distributions.

2.3. Existence and uniqueness of solutions

In presenting results on the existence and uniqueness of solutions to SDEs, there are many choices to be made. First, we may restrict ourselves to either generalised diffusions (2.2.12) or generalised Itô processes (2.2.14) for which existence theorems are well known and tractable solutions can often be obtained. Secondly, we may restrict ourselves to SDEs for which the coefficient processes $a(t, X_{t-}, \theta)$ and $b(t, X_{t-}, \theta)$ are linear in X. We discuss both of these restrictions. Typically, even if a solution exists, it cannot be represented in closed form. However, for most of the processes in (2.2.3)–(2.2.18), closed form solutions do exist.

For expositional purposes, we again consider univariate processes. The conditions required to ensure the existence and uniqueness of the solution to an SDE are now given, assuming as before bounded predictability for $a(t, X_{t-}, \theta)$ and $b(t, X_{t-}, \theta)$.

(1) *Generalised diffusion process* (2.2.12).

(a) *Growth condition.* There exists a constant C independent of $0 \leqslant \tau \leqslant t$ and of $-\infty < X < \infty$ s.t.

$$a^2(\tau, X, \theta) + b^2(\tau, X, \theta) \leqslant C^2(1 + X^2), \quad -\infty < X < \infty. \tag{2.3.1}$$

This restriction is crucial for otherwise the solution can reach infinity in finite time with positive probability.

(b) *Lipschitz condition.* There exists a constant L independent of $0 \leqslant \tau_1$, $\tau_2 \leqslant t$ and of $-\infty < X, Y < \infty$ s.t.

$$|a(\tau, X, \theta) - a(\tau, Y, \theta)| + |b(\tau, X, \theta) - b(\tau, Y, \theta)| \leqslant L|X - Y|, \tag{2.3.2}$$

$$|a(\tau_1, X, \theta) - a(\tau_2, X, \theta)| + |b(\tau_1, X, \theta) - b(\tau_2, X, \theta)| \leqslant L|\tau_1 - \tau_2|. \tag{2.3.3}$$

The Lipschitz condition is fundamental to the solution of SDEs.

(2) *Generalised Itô processes.* We can extend the above conditions to Itô processes, as given in Lo (1988).

There exists a constant L, independent of $0 \leqslant \tau_1, \tau_2 \leqslant t$ and of $-\infty < X, Y < \infty$ s.t.

(a) $\quad a^2(\tau, X, \theta) + b^2(\tau, X, \theta) + c^2(\tau, X, \theta) \leqslant L^2(1 + X^2),$ $\tag{2.3.4}$

(b) $\quad |a(\tau, X, \theta) - a(\tau, Y, \theta)| + |b(\tau, X, \theta) - b(\tau, Y, \theta)|$

$$+ |c(\tau, X, \theta) - c(\tau, Y, \theta)| \leqslant L|X - Y|, \tag{2.3.5}$$

$$|a(\tau_1, X, \theta) - a(\tau_2, X, \theta)| + |b(\tau_1, X, \theta) - b(\tau_2, X, \theta)|$$

$$+ |c(\tau_1, X, \theta) - c(\tau_2, X, \theta)| \leqslant L|\tau_1 - \tau_2|. \tag{2.3.6}$$

(3) *Semimartingales.* Conditions for the existence and uniqueness of the solution to the univariate form of (2.2.2) with $M_0 = 0$ are

(a) The processes $a(t, X_{t-}, \theta)$ and $b(t, X_{t-}, \theta)$ are left continuous with right limits (LCRL).

(b) There exists a constant L independent of $0 \leqslant \tau \leqslant t$ and of $-\infty < X < \infty$ s.t., for all $\tau_1, \tau_2, X, Y,$

$$|a(\tau, X, \theta) - a(\tau, Y, \theta)| + |b(\tau, X, \theta) - b(\tau, Y, \theta)| \leqslant L|X - Y| \tag{2.3.7}$$

and

$$|a(\tau_1, X, \theta) - a(\tau_2, X, \theta)| + |b(\tau_1, X, \theta) - b(\tau_2, X, \theta)| \leqslant L|\tau_1 - \tau_2|. \tag{2.3.8}$$

This result is shown in Protter (1990, Theorem 5.6).

The form of solution differs markedly for different types of processes. When the coefficient processes are linear in X, a quite general solution can be obtained. This is examined in detail by Melino (1991, pp. 14–20) and is quite generally considered by Protter (1990, Theorem 5.63). Formally, consider the SDE

$$\mathrm{d}X_t = [a_1(t, \theta) + a_2(t, \theta)X_{t-}]\,\mathrm{d}t + \sum_{i=1}^{G} [b_1^i(t, \theta) + b_2^i(t, \theta)X_{t-}]\,\mathrm{d}M_t^i.$$

(2.3.9)

Melino asserts that under certain regularity conditions on the discontinuities in the stochastic integral, the solution to (2.3.9) can be written as

$$X_t = U_t \left[X_0 + \int U_\tau^{-1} \left[\mathrm{d}H_\tau - \sum_{i=1}^{G} b_2^i(\tau, \theta) \right. \right.$$
$$\left. \left. \times \left\{ \mathrm{d}(H_\tau M_\tau^i) - \mathrm{d}\left(\int_0^\tau H_{s-}\,\mathrm{d}M_s^i \right) - \mathrm{d}\left(\int_0^\tau M_{s-}^i\,\mathrm{d}H_s \right) \right\} \right] \right]$$

where

$$H_t = X_0 + \int a_1(\tau)\,\mathrm{d}\tau + \sum_{i=1}^{G} \int b_1^i(\tau)\,\mathrm{d}M_\tau^i,$$

$$U_t = I + \int_0^t \mathrm{d}V_\tau U_{\tau-} \quad \text{for } V = \sum_{i=1}^{G} \int b_2^i(\tau)\,\mathrm{d}M_\tau^i.$$

(2.3.10)

This solution is too impractical for most purposes, except in the calculation of conditional first and second moments. However, it reduces in particular cases to tractable solutions. In particular, when the process is a linear generalised Itô process, conditional distributions of X_t given X_0 can be obtained. Other simplifications are possible. For example if $b_2^i = 0$ for all i, much simpler solutions obtain and the conditional moments may be readily determined.

Nonlinearities in the coefficient processes $a(t, X_{t-}, \theta)$ and $b(t, X_{t-}, \theta)$ obviously complicate matters, so that even restricting to generalised diffusions or generalised Itô processes does not guarantee tractable solutions. A general procedure is to establish directly the kinetic equation associated with a stochastic process. We denote by

(1) $f(X_t, t)$ the *probability density function*(pdf) of the process X at t,

(2) $f_k(X_k | X_{k-1})$ the *transitional or conditional density function* of X_k given X_{k-1} where $X_k = X_{t_k}$ for some discrete sampling process $t_0, \ldots, t_k, \ldots$,

(3) $\mathrm{E}(X_t^r)$ and $\mathrm{E}(X_k^r | X_{k-1})$ the r-th moment and r-th conditional moments,

(4) $\alpha_r(x, t) = \lim_{h \to 0} (1/h)\mathrm{E}([X_{t+h} - X_t]^r | X_t = x)$ as the r-th *derivate* moment.

The *kinetic equation* is derived by establishing the conditional characteristic equation and then applying an inverse Fourier transform to obtain

$$\frac{\partial f(x, t)}{\partial t} - \sum_{r=1}^{\infty} \frac{(-1)^r}{r!} \frac{\partial^r}{\partial x^r} [\alpha_r(x, t)f(x, t)] = 0.$$

(2.3.11)

This can be readily generalised to vector processes. The importance of this equation occurs when certain restrictions are imposed on the derivate moments α_r. In particular, it can be shown, using the Cauchy–Schwarz inequality, that if α_r exists for all r and is zero for some even r, then $\alpha_r = 0$ for all $r \geq 3$. Physically, this implies the stochastic process can only change by small amounts in small time intervals; the incremental moments approach zero faster than h as $h \to 0$. Processes which satisfy the condition that $\alpha_r = 0$ for all $r \geq 3$ include generalised diffusion processes. In the case of Markov processes, the transitional density function also satisfies the kinetic equation (2.3.11), and when the associated derivate moments are zero for higher than second order moments, the equation reduces to

$$\frac{\partial f_k}{\partial t}(X \mid X_{k-1}) = \frac{-\partial}{\partial X}[\alpha_1(X)f_k] + \tfrac{1}{2}\frac{\partial^2}{\partial X^2}[\alpha_2(X)f_k] \tag{2.3.12}$$

with the initial condition

$$f_k(X, t_{k-1} \mid X_{k-1}, t_{k-1}) = \delta(X - X_{k-1}), \tag{2.3.13}$$

where δ is the Dirac-delta generalised function centered at X_{k-1}.

Equation (2.3.12) is called the *Fokker–Planck equation*. It can be used to construct solutions for the transitional density function when the solution process is Markovian as in generalised diffusions. The Fokker–Planck equation has been extended to generalised Itô processes. Lo (1988) considers generalised Itô processes (2.2.14) satisfying the Lipschitz conditions (2.3.4)–(2.3.6), with the further requirement that the function $X + c(X, \theta)$ is bijective and $|\partial c/\partial X + 1| \neq 0$ and with true parameters in the interior of the parameter space. Under these conditions, he shows that

$$\frac{\partial}{\partial t}[f_k] = \frac{-\partial}{\partial X}[af_k] + \tfrac{1}{2}\frac{\partial^2}{\partial X^2}[b^2 f_k] - \lambda f_k + \lambda f_k(d^{-1}) \left| \frac{\partial}{\partial X}[d^{-1}] \right|,$$
$$\tag{2.3.14}$$

where $d = X + c(X)$, with the initial condition (2.3.13).

Solutions to the kinetic equation (2.3.11), or variants of the Fokker–Planck equation, (2.3.12) and (2.3.14), can often only be conjectured and then checked to satisfy the equations. The usual existence and uniqueness theorems for solutions to partial differential equations are not relevant in this case, except when the coefficient processes a, b, c are constant or when the equations can be transformed to constant coefficients. The solution for some relatively simple processes is given in the next section. Numerical solutions to either the kinetic equation or Fokker–Planck equations may be a feasible alternative, but have yet to be investigated.

2.4. Transitional density functions and moments

For general linear stochastic process of the form (2.3.9), the solution representation (2.3.10) can be used to calculate the conditional mean and variance of the process (Melino, 1991, p. 20). When the process is a generalised diffusion (2.2.12), the moments of the solution process can be shown to satisfy from the Fokker–Planck equation (2.3.12),

$$\frac{d}{dt} E(X_t^r) = r E[a(X_t)X_t^{r-1}] + r(r-1)E[b^2(X_t)X_t^{r-2}] . \tag{2.4.1}$$

This leads to a hierarchy of differential equations for the moments. When $a(X_t)$ is a polynomial of order 2 or more, the moment equation for $E(X_t^r)$ involves moments of order higher than r, so that an infinite hierarchy of differential equations for the moments is established. Unfortunately, this problem will be common to all non-linear generalised diffusions.

To construct the transitional density functions, solutions to either the kinetic equation (2.3.11) or the Fokker–Planck equations (2.3.12), (2.3.14) need to be found. If solutions exist, they may be found by a number of methods, either by Fourier transforms, by guessing possible solutions, or for generalised diffusions by reducing the Fokker–Planck equation to a constant coefficient PDE. This reduction involves the use of Itô's lemma.

Itô's lemma is one of the most powerful results in Itô calculus, it is used most widely in the pricing of derivative assets. In Section 2.6, we give a general statement of Itô's lemma for semimartingales, but for the moment we state the result for generalised diffusions (2.2.12).

Itô's Lemma. *Let $u(X, t) : R \times T \rightarrow R$ be a continuous non-random function with continuous partial derivatives $\partial u/\partial X$, $\partial^2 u/\partial X^2$ and $\partial u/\partial t$ of the diffusion process (2.2.12). Suppose $Y_t = u(X_t, t)$. Then the process Y satisfies the SDE*

$$dY_t = \left[\frac{\partial u}{\partial t} + \frac{\partial u}{\partial X} a(X) + \tfrac{1}{2} \frac{\partial^2 u}{\partial X^2} b^2(X) \right] dt + \frac{\partial u}{\partial X} b \, dW_t . \tag{2.4.2}$$

We can use Itô's lemma to transform a diffusion process with coefficients depending on X to a diffusion process with coefficients independent of X. Briefly, if X follows a generalised diffusion (2.2.12), Schuss (1980, Chapter 4) shows that provided the functions a and b satisfy the *reducibility condition*

$$\frac{\partial}{\partial X} \left[\frac{\partial b}{\partial t} \frac{1}{b} 2 - \frac{\partial}{\partial X} \left(\frac{a}{b} \right) + \tfrac{1}{2} \frac{\partial^2 b}{\partial X^2} \right] = 0 , \tag{2.4.3}$$

there exists a transformed process Y for which the transformed coefficients are independent of Y. The transitional density function can then be calculated. In Table 1, we present the transitional density functions for some of the important processes used in finance.

These represent the main transition density functions in finance, building on the work of Feller (1951) and others. Two notable omissions from the table are the double square root process and a Brownian motion with an absorbing barrier. The transitional densities of these processes are given in Longstaff (1989) and Schuss (1980, p. 117) respectively. Since all of the processes in the

Table 1.
Transitional density functions

Brownian motion with drift (2.2.3)

$$P(X_k \mid X_{k-1}) = \left\{ 2\pi \int \sigma^2(\tau)\, d\tau \right\}^{-1/2} \cdot \exp\left[\frac{-\left(X_k - X_{k-1} - \int \mu(\tau)\, d\tau \right)^2}{2 \int \sigma^2(\tau)\, d\tau} \right] \tag{2.4.4}$$

Geometric Brownian motion (2.2.4)

$$P(X_k \mid X_{k-1}) = \{ 2\pi\sigma^2\, \Delta t \}^{-1/2} \cdot \exp\left[\frac{-(\ln X_k - \ln X_{k-1} - \mu\, \Delta t)^2}{2\sigma^2\, \Delta t} \right] \tag{2.4.5}$$

for $\Delta t = t_k - t_{k-1}$.

Ornstein–Uhlenbeck (2.2.5)

$$P(X_k \mid X_{k-1}) = \{ 2\pi\sigma^2 t_a \}^{-1/2} \cdot \exp\left[\frac{-(X_k - X_a - a_1\, \Delta t)^2}{2\sigma^2 t_a} \right], \tag{2.4.6}$$

where $t_a = (-1/2a_2)[1 - \exp(2a_2\, \Delta t)]$ and $X_a = X_{k-1} \cdot \exp(a_2\, \Delta t)$

Brownian bridge (2.2.7)

$$P(X_k \mid X_{k-1}) = \{ 2\pi\sigma^2 t^b \}^{-1/2} \cdot \exp\left[\frac{-[x_k/(1 - t_k) - X_{k-1}/(1 - t_{k-1})]^2}{2\sigma^2 t_b} \right], \tag{2.4.7}$$

where $t_b = \Delta t/((1 - t_k)(1 - t_{k-1}))$

Generalised constant elasticity of variance (2.2.10)

$$P(X_k \mid X_{k-1}) = \frac{b}{a[\exp(b\, \Delta t) - 1]} \left\{ \exp \frac{-b[X_k + X_{k-1}\exp(b\, \Delta t)]}{a[\exp(b\, \Delta t) - 1]} \right\}$$
$$\times \left\{ 4b^2 \exp(-b\, \Delta t) \frac{X_k}{X_{k-1}} \right\}^c \times I_{-2c} \left\{ \frac{2b[\exp(-b\, \Delta t)X_k \cdot X_{k-1}]^{1/2}}{a[1 - \exp(-b\, \Delta t)]} \right\}, \tag{2.4.8}$$

where a, b, c are functions of a_1, a_2, σ, β and I_j is the modified Bessel function

Generalised Itô process (2.2.14) $(a = \mu \cdot X, \ b = \sigma \cdot X, \ c = c \cdot X)$

$$P(X_k \mid X_{k-1}) = \sum_{j=0}^{\infty} \exp(-\lambda\, \Delta t) \frac{(\lambda\, \Delta t)^j}{j!}$$
$$\times \{ 2\pi\sigma^2\, \Delta t \}^{-1/2} \exp\left[\frac{-(\ln X_k - \ln X_{k-1} - j\ln(1 + c) - a\, \Delta t)^2}{2\sigma^2\, \Delta t} \right] \tag{2.4.9}$$

---

table are Markovian, the transitional density will determine the likelihood function. This is considered in Section 3.2.

2.5. Stationary density function

Under conditions that the derivate moments $\alpha_r(x, t)$ used in defining the kinetic equation (2.3.11) are independent of t, the density function approaches a stationary solution $f_s(x)$ where $\partial f_s(x)/\partial t = 0$. From the kinetic equation, we have that

$$\sum_{r=1}^{\infty} \frac{(-1)^r}{r!} \frac{\mathrm{d}^r}{\mathrm{d}x^r} [\alpha_r(x) \cdot f_x(x)] = 0 \tag{2.5.1}$$

and if the derivate moments are zero for orders $r > 2$, we obtain the Fokker–Planck equation for the stationary solution

$$\frac{\mathrm{d}}{\mathrm{d}x} [\alpha_1(x) \cdot f_s(x)] - \tfrac{1}{2} \frac{\mathrm{d}^2}{\mathrm{d}x^2} [\alpha_2(x) \cdot f_s(x)] = 0 \tag{2.5.2}$$

which has a general solution

$$f_s(x) = \frac{c_2}{\alpha_2(x)} \exp\left[2 \int_0^x \frac{\alpha_1(s)}{\alpha_2(s)}\, \mathrm{d}s \right] - \frac{2c_1}{\alpha_2(x)} \int_0^x \exp\left[2 \int_r^x \frac{\alpha_1(s)}{\alpha_2(s)}\, \mathrm{d}s \right] \mathrm{d}r \, . \tag{2.5.3}$$

The tractability of stationary solutions has enhanced their use especially in term structure models (Cox, Ingersoll and Ross 1985; Longstaff, 1989). They have the advantage that quite flexible functional forms for the stochastic process may be adopted, provided the derivate moments are independent of t. Unfortunately, in most applications in finance, the first two derivate moments are likely to be time-dependent, attenuating this approach.

2.6. *Itô's lemma and the pricing of derivative assets*

We have already encountered Itô's lemma for diffusion processes in the derivation of the reducibility condition (2.4.3) Itô's lemma has a more pervasive role, however, in the pricing of derivative assets. Protter (1990, p. 71) gives a general representation of Itô's lemma.

ITÔ'S LEMMA. *Let X be a semimartingale and let f be a C^2 real function. Then $f(x)$ is a semimartingale, and the following formula holds*:

$$f(X_t) - f(X_0) = \int_0^t f'(X_{s-})\, \mathrm{d}X_s + \tfrac{1}{2} \int_0^t f''(X_{s-})\, \mathrm{d}[X, X]_s^c$$

$$+ \sum_{0 \leqslant s \leqslant t} \{ f(X_s) - f(X_{s-}) - f'(X_{s-}) \Delta X_s \} \, , \tag{2.6.1}$$

where $[X, X]_s^c = X^2 - 2 \int X_{s-}\, \mathrm{d}X_s - \sum_{0 \leqslant s \leqslant t} (\Delta X_s)^2$.

The use of Itô's lemma in the pricing of derivative assets originated with the work of Black and Scholes (1973). The Black–Scholes analysis is in three stages:

(a) *Stochastic process.* Assume a particular form of process for the underlying asset price. The most common assumptions are lognormal diffusions and constant elasticity of variance process.

(b) *Hedging.* Construct a hedged portfolio, that is, a riskless portfolio consisting of the stock and the derivative asset.

(c) *No arbitrage condition.* In the absence of arbitrage, the return on this hedged portfolio must equal the risk-free rate of return. The return on the hedged portfolio is derived using Itô's lemma. The equating of the return of the hedged portfolio with the risk-free rate generates a second order differential equation for the price of the derivative asset. This second order differential equation may admit closed form solutions, depending on the nature of the stochastic process governing the underlying asset price.

To make the Black–Scholes argument succinct, consider a lognormal diffusion process for an equity (2.2.4). Let the value of an option on the equity be given by $Y(X_t, t)$. By Itô's lemma, the stochastic dynamics governing the behavior of the option is given by

$$dY_t = \mu_Y Y_t \, dt + \sigma_Y Y_t \, dW_t \,,$$

where

$$\mu_Y = \mu \cdot X \cdot \frac{\partial Y}{\partial X} + \frac{\partial Y}{\partial t} + \frac{1}{2} \frac{\partial^2 Y}{\partial X^2} \cdot \sigma^2 X^2 \,, \tag{2.6.2}$$

$$\sigma_Y = \frac{\partial Y}{\partial X} \cdot \sigma X \,.$$

The no arbitrage condition reduces to

$$(\mu - r)/\sigma = (\mu_Y - r)/\sigma Y \,. \tag{2.6.3}$$

Inserting (2.6.2) into (2.6.3) gives the familiar Black–Scholes equation

$$\frac{1}{2} \sigma^2 X^2 \frac{\partial^2 Y}{\partial X^2} + rX \frac{\partial Y}{\partial X} + \frac{\partial Y}{\partial t} - rY = 0 \tag{2.6.4}$$

which admits a closed form solution.

There are several caveats to Black–Scholes approach. The no arbitrage condition can also be derived using the capital asset pricing model, and in some applications this is more convenient; for example in jump processes (Merton, 1976, p. 133) the hedging technique of Black–Scholes cannot be employed, but the CAPM approach generates a second order differential equation which can be solved computationally. Secondly, the Black–Scholes approach has been extended to a number of other applications where some problem-specific modifications need to be made.

One implication of the Black–Scholes approach is that it provides a second measure of the misspecification of the stochastic process generating the underlying asset price. For, mispricing of observed option prices using the generated option price from equation (2.6.4) will be attributable to misspecification of the SDE in addition to other biases, such as the European bias evident when pricing American options. There is considerable scope for tests of misspecification by using all the information in the asset markets, that is all prices of derivative assets. General misspecification tests should encompass this information.

3. Estimation and inference

3.1. *Measurement process*

In macroeconomics, especially business cycle theory, there is a wide class of models suggesting that latent economic processes evolve in *economic time* rather than *calendar time*. The relationship between economic and calendar time depends on the economic history of the latent process; for example, Flood and Garber (1980) contended that decisions concerning money balances will be made more often during periods of high inflation. Clark (1973) suggested that the operational or economic time scale for the evolution of commodity prices should be based on information flows. Models which explicitly characterise the transformation between economic time and calendar time are called time deformation models, and have been applied in papers by Stock (1985, 1988).

For illustrative purposes, consider a univariate stochastic process X defined on the economic time scale s. Let $g(t)$ be the transformation from calendar time t to economic time s. To be a valid transformation, Stock (1985) specifies the following requirements for g.

(1) For tractability, $\Delta g(t) = g(t) - g(t-1)$ must not depend on current or future values of X_t.

(2) Economic and calendar time proceed in the same direction, so that $0 < \Delta g(t) < \infty$.

(3) The unknown parameters of the time scale transformation must be identified. For example, linear transformations (such as from daily to weekly data) will not be identified.

(4) For simple estimation, the transformation should be continuous in its unknown parameters.

Stock (1985) posits an exponential transformation for g when estimating business cycle models. In financial data, a reasonable specification for g should include some non-anticipating measure of volatility, since increased volatility will usually correlate with enhanced information flows, and subsequent time deformation.

The process X is observed through some sampling procedure. It may be sampled in calendar time as:

(1) A point process sampled at fixed intervals,

$$X_k = X(g(t_k)) , \quad t_j - t_{j-1} = t_k - t_{k-1} \text{ for all } k, k .$$

(2) A point process sampled at random intervals,

$$X_k = X(g(t_k)) , \quad t_0 < t_1 < \cdots .$$

(3) An economic flow,

$$X_k = \int_{t_{k-1}}^{t_k} X(g(\tau))\, d\tau .$$

As an example, for a lognormal diffusion process in economic time, we observe that process in calendar time as

$$dX_{g(t)} = \mu X_{g(t)} + \sigma X_{g(t)}\, dW_{g(t)} . \tag{3.1.1}$$

An important question in the resolution of processes such as (3.1.1) is the dependence on the sampling procedure. For example, a plausible proposition is that time deformation properties are more likely to be stable for low frequency data (monthly) than high frequency data (transactions), so that the estimates recovered for μ and σ in (3.1.1) may well be more reliable in monthly data. The presence of significant empirical anomalies in high frequency data, including time varying second and higher order moments, may be induced by a time transformation that is appreciably sensitive to variables such as market volatility.

3.2. Discrete approximations

While continuity in time is assumed in building financial models, we are compelled to estimate their discrete time equivalents. The theoretical arguments given in the introduction of this paper suggest these approximations should be invoked using high frequency data. However, there are other theoretical considerations. First, the approximation by a discrete time model involves the convergence of the information structure (the filtration F) and of the stochastic process to their continuous time equivalents. A priori, while the filtration approximation has greater fidelity for high frequency data, the approximation of the stochastic process may be less accurate. Secondly, the degree of non-synchronous trading is likely to be greater in high frequency data; the proportionate error of approximation in daily and intra-daily will generally be greater. Finally, as noted by Marsh and Rosenfeld (1983) in many models it is necessary to impose additional theoretical assumptions, such as a zero term premium in some models of the term structure. These assumptions are less tenable as the length of approximating interval increases.

If the time process generating the data is in continuous time, inappropriate discretisations will produce biased and inconsistent estimates. This is a familiar proposition in higher order continuous time models, where the bias in approximating discrete time models has been shown to be $O(h^2)$ as h, the length of the observation period, tends to zero (see Bergstrom, 1988, pp. 371–373). The bias induced in approximating n-th order linear SDEs arises from truncating an infinite sum of matrices. The bias induced in approximating the non-linear SDEs of finance arises from using an incorrect transitional density and likelihood function. Lo (1988, pp. 240–242) discusses this point further for a lognormal diffusion process.

Suppose $t_k = kh$, for $k = 0, 1, \ldots, n = T/h$, denotes a partition of the trading time space. Then a discretisation of the lognormal diffusion model (2.2.4) is

$$X_{k+1} = X_k + \mu X_k h + \sigma X_k \Delta W_{k+1}$$

or

$$X_{k+1} - X_k = \mu X_k h + X_k \varepsilon_{k+1}, \tag{3.2.1}$$

where ε_{k+1} is iid $N(0, \sigma h)$.

The maximum likelihood estimators of μ and σ are given by

$$\hat{\mu}_h = \frac{1}{T} \sum_{k=1}^{n} \left[\frac{X_k}{X_{k-1}} - 1 \right] \qquad \hat{\sigma}_h^2 = \frac{1}{T} \sum_{h=1}^{n} \left[\frac{X_k}{X_{k-1}} - 1 - \hat{\mu} h \right]^2. \tag{3.2.2}$$

For fixed h, the estimates $\hat{\mu}_h$, $\hat{\sigma}_h^2$ are biased and inconsistent. If h approaches zero as n increases without bound so that T is constant, $\hat{\sigma}_h^2$ is consistent, but $\hat{\mu}_h$ remains inconsistent.

The inconsistency in the estimate of μ may not be economically important of course, because option pricing models are preference independent, i.e., do not depend on μ. Inconsistency in the volatility estimate is more important, but can be overcome by using the proper transitional density function (2.4.5), (i.e., the error process in (3.2.1) is lognormal not normal).

There is another type of discretisation bias which induces leptokurtosis in asset returns. This bias is due to asset prices being measured in discrete units, usually to the nearest eighth of a dollar of the major U.S. exchanges. Ball (1988) has formalised the estimation bias induced by discrete security prices when the underlying continuous time process is a continuous state process. He establishes the transition density function for a Brownian motion with zero drift, when prices are rounded to some discrete value. The transitional probabilities need to be calculated by numerical methods, but the volatility estimates are then essentially unbiased.

In assessing discretisation bias, it is important to regard the problem in a more general context as the approximation of one stochastic process to another. For example, the bias in the discretised form of the lognormal diffusion is due to the approximation of a Gaussian process by a lognormal, and the bias induced by discrete security prices is due to the approximation of a continuous state process to a discrete state process. There is now a quite extensive literature documenting stochastic process approximations. We cite just two rather important results. First, Cox and Ross (1976) show that the limiting form of the jump process

$$dX_t = \mu X_t \, dt + c X_t \, dN_t(\lambda) \tag{3.2.3}$$

as $\lambda \to \infty$ is the diffusion process

$$dX_t = \mu X_t \, dt + \sigma X_t \, dW_t \, , \tag{3.2.4}$$

where σ is determined as a function of c. This result extends to more general jump processes; that is, as the intensity increases, the process approaches a diffusion limit.

A second result connects the discrete time modelling of the second moment function (the ARCH and GARCH models) to diffusions. Nelson (1990) shows that by partitioning the trading space more and more finely, the GARCH (1, 1) mean process of Engle and Bollerslev (1986) for the log of cumulative excess returns Y_t on a portfolio:

$$X_t = X_{t-1} + C\sigma_t^2 + \sigma_t Z_t \, ,$$
$$\sigma_{t+1}^2 = \alpha_0[\alpha_1 + \alpha_2 Z_t^2] \tag{3.2.5}$$

approaches a limiting diffusion

$$dX_t = C\sigma_t^2 \, dt + \sigma_t \, dW_{1,t} \, ,$$
$$d\sigma_t^2 = (\alpha_0 - \theta\sigma_t^2) \, dt + \alpha_2 \sigma_t^2 \, dW_{2,t} \, , \tag{3.2.6}$$

where Z_t is $N(0, 1)$, $W_{1,t}$, $W_{2,t}$ are *independent* Wiener processes, and θ is a limiting parameter.

3.3. Estimation problems

The stochastic processes in Table 1 have all been estimated using maximum likelihood methods, but with mixed success. It is of course straightforward to estimate the discrete time equivalent of the lognormal diffusion model, simply by using logarithmic returns. In the only systematic study of the general constant elasticity of variance model, Marsh and Rosenfeld (1983) estimated the model for θ equal to 0, 1, and 2 for rates of return on T-bills with one-week and one-month to maturity. Marsh and Rosenfeld found it difficult to estimate the parameters A and B (both were found to have very large standard errors), yet the volatility estimate(σ) was strongly significant. Marsh and Rosenfeld did not maximise the likelihood across all feasible values of θ, but for the grid of values considered found the lognormal model ($\theta = 2$) to have marginally higher likelihood. This study represents the only formal attempt to embed a series of distributions within a family of distributions, and to test between them parametrically. There was no testing of whether the type of stochastic volatility embedded in this model is appropriate for this data.

Estimation of the jump-diffusion process presents rather more problems. Three methods have been used. Ball and Torous (1985) employed both method of cumulants and maximum likelihood estimation to estimate daily returns on NYSE listed common stocks. In the majority of returns, they found evidence of statistically significant jumps, but that these jumps did not induce significant differences in the pricing of call options. Indeed, this relative robustness of the Black–Scholes pricing model to extreme observations is confirmed in a study by Madan and Milne (1987), who find some robustness of the Black–Scholes values to leptokurtosis. One of the difficulties in estimating the jump-diffusion model by maximum likelihood methods is the requirement to replace an infinite sum in the density function by a finite approximation. This motivated the study of Stern (1989) who uses an empirical characteristic function in a Monte Carlo exercise on generated log returns. Stern's results indicate some superiority of the empirical characteristic function in terms of root mean squared errors particularly when the number of jumps is small.

The cumulative evidence from these results is that volatility and its associated stochastic dynamics is probably the most significant factor in the estimation of continuous time asset pricing models. While there is substantial evidence for the presence of jumps and for leptokurtosis in asset returns, these do not appear to significantly bias Black–Scholes pricing of derivative assets.

Stochastic volatility has at least three literatures, the *stylised fact* literature (see Black, 1976 and Trevor, 1990), stochastic volatility diffusions (see Wiggins, 1987 and Johnson and Shanno, 1987) and finally stochastic volatility in discrete time as encompassed by ARCH-GARCH models, It is apparent that some convergence in the literature is emerging following the seminal paper of Nelson (1990); for substantiation of this point, the paper of Taylor (1990) is useful.

Briefly, the stylised facts literature reflects certain empirical patterns concerning volatilities, inter alia leverage effects (volatility increases subsequent to large negative returns), financial leverage effects, trading day effects, autoregressive patterns, and macroeconomic volatilities. The challenge is to parameterise these effects, and some partial solutions have been posited by Nelson (1991) in the development of the EGARCH model.

In the stochastic volatility diffusion models, the volatility itself is modelled as an Itô process; a general formulation is

$$dX_t = \mu X_t \, dt + \sigma_t X_t \, dW_t \, ,$$
$$d\sigma_t = f(\sigma_t) \, dt + \theta \sigma_t \, dW_{2t} \, , \tag{3.3.1}$$

where dW and dW_2 are Wiener processes with correlation ρ, and θ is the variability of the stochastic volatility σ_t. Wiggins (1987) uses a form of Ornstein–Uhlenbeck process for the volatility as given in (2.2.18), but is unable to find a closed form solution for the transitional density. This is the typical case for stochastic volatility diffusion models. An additional concern is that the stochastic volatilities appear manufactured; it is difficult to envisage how some of the stylised facts would be assimilated into these models.

The importance of ARCH-GARCH models has been amplified by the work of Nelson (1990), who showed that properly chosen sequences of EGARCH and GARCH models will converge weakly to bivariate diffusion processes as the discrete time interval approaches 0. This may be relaxed to include

GARCH processes with symmetric non-normal distributions. These limiting theorems imply that we may replicate the behavior of bivariate stochastic diffusions through properly specified EGARCH and GARCH models. The limiting results do not extend to diffusions with random coefficients. However, as suggested by Nelson, such limiting theorems do apply to jump processes, so that a challenge in future work is the specification of discrete time approximations of bivariate jump-diffusions.

4. Concluding remarks

The discussion in this chapter has reviewed some of the critical applications of continuous time modelling in finance; in particular the estimation of Itô processes for asset pricing distributions and the use of Itô processes in pricing contingent claims.

References

Ball, C. (1988). Estimation bias induced by discrete security prices. *J. Finance* **43**, 841–865.

Ball, C. and W. Torous (1983). Bond price dynamics and options. *J. Financ. Quant. Anal.* **18**, 517–531.

Ball, C. and W. Torous (1985). On jumps in common stock prices and their impact on call option pricing. *J. Finance* **40**, 155–173.

Beckers, S. (1980). The constant elasticity of variance model and US implications for option pricing. *J. Finance* **35**, 661–673.

Bergstrom, A. R. (1976). *Statistical Inference in Continuous Time Economic Models*. North-Holland, Amsterdam.

Bergstrom, A. R. (1988). The history of continuous-time econometric models. *Econometric Theory* **4**, 365–383.

Black, F. (1976). Studies of Stock Price Volatility Price Changes. Proc. of the 1976 Meetings of the American Statistical Association, Business and Economics Division.

Black, F. and M. Scholes (1973). The pricing of options and corporate liabilities. *J. Politic. Econom.* **81**, 637–654.

Chesney, M. and L. Scott (1989). Pricing European currency options: A comparison of the modified Black–Scholes model and a random variance model. **24**, 267–284.

Clark, P. (1973). A subordinated stochastic process model with finite variance for speculative prices. *Econometrica* **41**, 135–155.

Cox, J. and S. Ross (1976). The valuation of options for alternative stochastic processes. *J. Financ. Econom.* **3**, 145–166.

Cox, J., J. Ingersoll and S. Ross (1985). A theory of the term structure of interest rates. *Econometrica* **53**, 363–384.

Davis, K. (1991). Pricing of Options on Bank Bill Futures. Paper presented to the 2nd Annual Asia–Pacific Futures Research Symposium, Singapore.

Doob, J. (1953). *Stochastic Processes*. Wiley, New York.

Duffie, D. (1988). *Security Markets: Stochastic Models*. Academic Press, San Diego, CA.

Emanuel, D. and J. Macbeth (1982). Further results on the constant elasticity of variance call option pricing model. *J. Financ. Quant. Anal.* **17**, 533–554.

Engle, R. and T. Bollerslev (1986). Modelling the persistence of conditional variances. *Econom. Rev.* **5**, 1–50.

Feller, W. (1951). Two singular diffusion problems. *Ann. Math.* **54**, 173–182.

Flood, R. and P. Garber (1980). Market fundamentals versus price-level bubbles: The first tests. *J. Politic. Econom.* **88**, 745–770.

Harvey, A. and J. Stock (1985). The estimation of higher-order continuous-time autoregressive models. *Econometric Theory* **1**, 97–112.

Hoel, P., Port, S. and C. Stone (1972). *Introduction to Stochastic Processes*. Houghton Mifflin, Boston.

Huang, C. (1985). Information structure and equilibrium asset prices. *J. Econom. Theory* **35**, 33–71.

Hull, J. and A. White (1987). The pricing of options on assets with stochastic volatilities. *J. Finance* **42**, 281–300.

Itô, K. (1944). Stochastic integral. *Proc. Japan Acad.* **20**, 519–524.

Itô, K. (1946). On stochastic integral equations. *Proc. Japan Acad.* **22**, 32–35.

Itô, K. (1951). Stochastic differential equations. *Mem. Amer. Math. Soc.* Amer. Mathematical Soc. Providence, RI.

Jacod, J. and A. Shiryaev (1987). *Limit Theorems for Stochastic Processes*. Springer, New York.

Johnson, H. and D. Shanno (1987). Option pricing when the variance is changing. *J. Financ. Quant. Anal.* **22**, 143–151.

Karatzas, I. and S. Shreve (1988). *Brownian Motion and Stochastic Calculus*. Springer, New York.

Karlin, S. and H. Taylor (1981). *A Second Course in Stochastic Processes*. Academic Press, New York.

Kopp, P. (1984). *Martingales and Stochastic Integrals*. Cambridge Univ. Press, Cambridge.

Kunita, H. and S. Watanabe (1967). On square integrable martingales. *Nagoya Math. J.* **30**, 209–245.

Kushner, H. (1984). *Approximation and Weak Convergence Methods for Random Processes, with Applications to Stochastic Systems Theory*. MIT Press, Cambridge.

Lo, A. (1988). Maximum likelihood estimation of generalized Itô processes with discretely sampled data. *Econometric Theory* **4**, 231–247.

Longstaff, F. (1989). A nonlinear general equilibrium model of the term structure of interest rates. *J. Financ. Econom.* **23**, 195–224.

Madan, D. and F. Milne (1987). Arrow debreu pricing for long-tailed return distributions. Working Paper presented at Analytic Economists Conference.

Madan, D. and E. Seneta (1987). Chebyshev polynomial approximations and characteristic function estimation. *J. Roy. Statist. Soc. B* **49**, 163–169.

Magill, M. and G. Constantinides (1976). Portfolio selection with transactions costs. *J. Econom. Theory* **13**, 245–263.

Malliaris, A. (1983). Itô's calculus in financial decision making. *SIAM Rev.* **25**, 481–496.

Marsh, T. and E. Rosenfeld (1983). Stochastic processes for interest rates and equilibrium bond prices. *J. Finance* **38**, 635–646.

Melino, A. (1990). Financial models in continuous time. Paper delivered at the Econometric Meetings, Barcelona.

Melino, A. (1991). Estimation of continuous time models in finance. University of Toronto, Department of Economics and Institute for Policy Analysis, Working Paper 9115.

Merton, R. (1971). Optimum consumption and portfolio rules in a continuous time model. *J. Econom. Theory* **3**, 373–413.

Merton, R. (1975). Theory of finance from the perspective of continuous time. *J. Financ. Quant. Anal.* **10**, 659–674.

Merton, R. (1976). Option pricing when underlying stock returns are discontinuous. *J. Financ. Econom.* **3**, 125–144.

Merton, R. (1990). *Continuous Time Models in Finance*. Basil Blackwell, Oxford.

Merville, L. and D. Pieptea (1989). Stock-price volatility, mean-reverting diffusion, and noise. *J. Financ. Econom.* **24**, 193–214.

Meyer, P. (1967). Integrales stochastiques I, II, III, and IV. *Lecture Notes in Mathematics* **39**. Springer, Berlin.

Meyer, P. (1976). Theorie des integrales stochastiques. In: seminaire de probabilites X. *Lecture Notes in Mathematics* **511**, 245–400.

Nelson, D. (1990). ARCH models are diffusion approximations. *J. Econometrics* **45**, 7–38.

Nelson, D. (1991). Conditional heteroskedasticity in asset returns: A new approach. *Econometrica* **59**, 347–370.

Phillips, P. C. B. (1974). The estimation of some continuous-time models. *Econometrica* **42**, 803–823.

Protter, P. (1990). *Stochastic Integration and Differential Equations: A New Approach*. Springer, Berlin.

Ross, S. (1989). Information and volatility: The no-arbitrage martingale approach to timing and resolution irrelevancy. *J. Finance* **44**, 1–17.

Samuelson, P. (1965). Proof that properly anticipated prices fluctuate randomly. *Ind. Manage. Rev.* **6**, 41–63.

Schaefer, S. and E. Schwartz (1987). Time-dependent variance and the pricing of bond options. *J. Finance* **42**, 1113–1128.

Schuss, Z. (1980). *Theory and Applications of Stochastic Differential Equations*. Wiley, New York.

Scott, L. (1987). Option pricing when the variance changes randomly: Theory, estimation, and an application. *J. Financ. Quant. Anal.* **22**, 419–438.

Sims, C. (1971). Discrete approximations to continuous time distributed lags in econometrics. *Econometrica* **39**, 545–563.

Stern, M. (1989). The Poisson jump-diffusion model for options on stocks: Small sample properties of maximum likelihood and characteristic function estimators. University of Virginia Working Paper.

Stock, J. (1987). Measuring business cycle time. *J. Politic. Econom.* **95**, 1240–1261.

Stock, J. (1988). Estimating continuous-time processes subject to time deformation. *J. Amer. Statist. Assoc.* **83**, 77–85.

Stratonovich, R. (1966). A new representation for stochastic integrals and equations. *SIAM J. Control* **4**, 362–371.

Stroock, S. and S. Varadhan (1979). *Multidimensional Diffusion Processes*. Springer, Berlin.

Taylor, S. (1990). Modelling stochastic volatility. Paper presented at the European Finance Meetings, Athens, Greece.

Trevor, R. (1990). Measuring changing financial risk. Paper presented for the 2nd Annual Melbourne Money and Finance Conference, *Risk Management in Financial Institutions*. Dallarat, Victoria.

Vasicek, O. (1977). An equilibrium characterization of the term structure. *J. Financ. Econom.* **5**, 177–188.

Wiener, N. (1923). Differential–space. *J. Math. Phys.* **2**, 131–174.

Wiggins, J. (1987). Option values under stochastic volatility: Theory and empirical estimates. *J. Financ. Econom.* **19**, 351–372.

Willinger, W. and M. Taqqu (1991). Toward a convergence theory for continuous stochastic securities market models. *Math. Finance* **1**, 55–99.

Wu, R. (1985). *Stochastic Differential Equations*. Pitman, Boston.

Subject Index

Handbook of Statistics
Contents of Previous Volumes

Volume 1. Analysis of Variance
Edited by P. R. Krishnaiah
1980 xviii + 1002 pp.

Volume 2. Classification, Pattern Recognition and Reduction of Dimensionality
Edited by P. R. Krishnaiah and L. N. Kanal
1982 xxii + 903 pp.

Volume 3. Time Series in the Frequency Domain
Edited by D. R. Brillinger and P. R. Krishnaiah
1983 xiv + 485 pp.

Volume 4. Nonparametric Methods
Edited by P. R. Krishnaiah and P. K. Sen
1984 xx + 968 pp.

Volume 5. Time Series in the Time Domain
Edited by E. J. Hannan, P. R. Krishnaiah and M. M. Rao
1985 xiv + 490 pp.

Volume 6. Sampling
Edited by P. R. Krishnaiah and C. R. Rao
1988 xvi + 594 pp.

Volume 7. Quality Control and Reliability
Edited by P. R. Krishnaiah and C. R. Rao
1988 xiv + 503 pp.

Volume 8. Statistical Methods in Biological and Medical Sciences
Edited by C. R. Rao and R. Chakraborty
1991 xvi + 554 pp.

Volume 9. Computational Statistics
Edited by C. R. Rao
1993 xix + 1045 pp.

Volume 10. Signal Processing and its Applications
Edited by N. K. Bose and C. R. Rao
1993 xvii + 992 pp.